EU COMPETITION LAW

VOLUME V

ABUSE OF DOMINANCE
UNDER ARTICLE 102 TFEU

EU COMPETITION LAW

VOLUME V

ABUSE OF DOMINANCE
UNDER ARTICLE 102 TFEU

EDITORS

Francisco Enrique González-Díaz
Robbert Snelders

CONTRIBUTORS

Matthew Bennett
Christopher Cook
Justin Coombs
Frédéric de Bure
Maurits Dolmans
Nicolas Gauss
Marcus Glader
Francisco Enrique González-Díaz
Thomas Graf
Ioannis Kokkoris
Anne Layne-Farrar
Andrew Leyden
David R. Little
Andrea Lofaro
Alison Oldale
Jorge Padilla
Ruchit Patel
Alice Setari
Robbert Snelders
Paul Stuart
Romano Subiotto QC
John Temple Lang

CLAEYS & CASTEELS
2013

All views expressed are strictly personal.

The opinions expressed in individual chapters are those of the authors in question

© 2013 by The authors

ISBN 978 90 7764 413 3

The paper and board used in the production of this book
is sourced exclusively from replanted forests.

Published in 2013 by
Claeys & Casteels Law Publishers bv
Deventer (Netherlands) – Leuven (Belgium)

P.O.Box 2013
7420 AA Deventer
Netherlands
www.claeys-casteels.com

CONTENTS – SUMMARY

TABLE OF CONTENTS

Chapter 1   Market Definition

Chapter 2   Dominance

Chapter 3   The Concept of Abuse

Chapter 4   Predatory Conduct

Chapter 5   Margin Squeeze

Chapter 6   Exclusive Dealing: Exclusive Obligations, Quasi-Exclusive Obligations and Rebates

Chapter 7   Refusal to Deal

Chapter 8   Tying and Bundling

Chapter 9   Abusive Discrimination

Chapter 10   Excessive Pricing

Chapter 11 Other Abuses

Chapter 12   Remedies

Table 1

Chronological List of Court Rulings

A. Rulings of the Court of Justice

Case 13/63 *Italian Republic v Commission* [1963] ECR 165.

Joined Cases 56 and 58/64 *Établissements Consten and Grundig-Verkaufs v Commission* (*"Consten and Grundig"*) [1966] ECR 299.

Case 24/67 *Parke, Davis v Probel and Others* (*"Parke Davis"*) [1968] ECR 55.

Case 41/69, ACF Chemiefarma NV v Commission [1970] ECR 661.

Case 40/70 *Sirena v Eda and Others* (*"Sirena"*) [1971] ECR 69.

Case 78/70 *Deutsche Grammophon v Metro-SB-Großmärkte* (*"Deutsche Grammophon"*) [1971] ECR 487.

Case 6/72 *Europemballage and Continental Can v Commission* (*"Continental Can"*) [1973] ECR 215.

Case 127/73 *Belgische Radio en Televisie and Société Belge des Auteurs, Compositeurs et éditeurs v SABAM and Fonior* (*"BRT-II"*) [1974] ECR 313.

Case C-6/73 *Istituto Chemioterapico Italiano and Commercial Solvents Corporation v Commission* [1974] ECR 223.

Joined Cases 6 and 7/73 *Istituto Chemioterapico Italiano and Commercial Solvents Corporation v Commission* (*"Commercial Solvents"*) [1974] ECR 223.

Joined Cases 40 to 48, 50, 54 to 56, 111, 113 and 114/73 *Coöperatieve Vereniging "Suiker Unie" and Others v Commission* (*"Suiker Unie"*) [1975] ECR 1663.

Case 15/74 *Centrafarm and Adriaan de Peijper v Sterling Drug* [1974] ECR 1147.

Case 16/74 *Centrafarm and Adriaan de Peijper v Winthrop* [1974] ECR 1183.

Case 3/75 R *Johnson & Firth Brown v Commission* [1975] ECR 7.

Case 26/75 *General Motors Continental v Commission ("General Motors")* [1975] ECR 1367.

Case 27/76 *United Brands and United Brands Continentaal v Commission ("United Brands")* [1978] ECR 207.

Case 85/76 *Hoffmann-La Roche v Commission ("Hoffmann-La Roche")* [1979] ECR 461.

Case 77/77 *Benzine en Petroleum Handelsmaatschappij and Others v Commission ("Benzine")* [1978] ECR 1513.

Case 102/77 *Hoffmann-La Roche v Centrafarm Vertriebsgesellschaft Pharmazeutischer Erzeugnisse* [1978] ECR 1139.

Case 3/78 *Centrafarm v American Home Products* [1978] ECR 1823.

Case 22/78 *Hugin Kassaregister and Hugin Cash Registers v Commission ("Hugin Judgment 1979")* [1979] ECR 1869.

Case 125/78 *GEMA, Gesellschaft für musikalische Aufführungs- und Mechanische Vervielfältigungsrechte v Commission* [1979] ECR 3173.

Case 258/78 *L.C. Nungesser and Kurt Eisele v Commission ("Nungesser")* [1982] ECR 2015.

Case 44/79 *Liselotte Hauer v Land Rheinland-Pfalz* [1979] ECR 3727.

Case 62/79 *Compagnie Générale Pour la Diffusion de la Télévision, Coditel, and Others v Ciné Vog Films and Others* [1980] ECR 881.

Case 792/79 R *Camera Care v Commission* [1980] ECR 119.

Case 169/80 *Administration des Douanes v Gondrand Frères and Garancini* [1981] ECR 1931.

Case 187/80 *Merck v Stephar and Petrus Stephanus Exler* [1981] ECR 2063.

Case 144/81 *Keurkoop v Nancy Kean Gifts* [1982] ECR 2853.

Case 232/81 R *Agricola Commerciale Olio and Others v Commission* [1981] ECR 2193.

Case 262/81 *Coditel, Compagnie Générale Pour la Diffusion de la Télévision, and Others v Ciné-Vog Films and Others* [1982] ECR 3381.

Case 322/81 *Nederlandsche Banden Industrie Michelin v Commission ("Michelin I")* [1983] ECR 3461.

Case 7/82 *Gesellschaft zur Verwertung von Leistungsschutzrechten (GVL) v Commission* [1983] ECR 483.

Joined Cases 96 to 102, 104, 105, 108 and 110/82 *IAZ International Belgium and Others v Commission* [1983] ECR 3369.

Cases 228 and 229/82 *Ford of Europe and Ford-Werke v Commission* [1984] ECR 1129.

Case 41/83 Italian Republic v Commission [1985] *ECR 873.*

Case 193/83 *Windsurfing v Commission* [1978] ECR 611.

Joined Cases 55 and 57/80 *Musik-Vertrieb Membran and K-tel International v GEMA* [1981] ECR 147.

Case 298/83 *CICCE v Commission ("CICCE")* [1985] ECR 1105.

Case 19/84 *Pharmon v Hoechst* [1985] ECR 2281.

Case 222/84 *Marguerite Johnston v Chief Constable of the Royal Ulster Constabulary* [1986] ECR 1651.

Case 226/84 *British Leyland v Commission ("British Leyland")* [1986] ECR 3263.

Case 311/84 *Centre Belge D'études de Marché – Télémarketing (CBEM) v Compagnie Luxembour-geoise de Télédiffusion (CLT) and Information Publicité Benelux (IPB) ("Télémarketing")* [1985] ECR 3261.

Joined Cases 142 and 156/84 *British-American Tobacco Company and R. J. Reynolds Industries v Commission ("Philip Morris")* [1987] ECR 4487.

Case 118/85 *Commission v Italian Republic* [1987] ECR 2599.

Case 434/85 *Allen and Hanburys v Generics (UK)* [1988] ECR 1245.

Case 66/86 *Ahmed Saeed Flugreisen and Silver Line Reisebüro v Zentrale zur Bekämpfung Unlauteren Wettbewerbs ("Ahmed Saeed")* [1989] ECR 803.

Case 136/86 *Bureau National Interprofessionnel du Cognac v Yves Aubert* [1987] ECR 4789.

Case C-62/86 *AKZO Chemie v Commission* ("*AKZO*") [1991] ECR I-3359.

Case 30/87 *Corinne Bodson v Pompes Funèbres des Régions Libérées* ("*Bodson*") [1988] ECR 2479.

Case 35/87 *Thetford and Others v Fiamma and Others* [1988] ECR 3585.

Case 53/87 *Consorzio Italiano della Componentistica di Ricambio per Autoveicoli (CICRA) and Maxicar v Régie Nationale des Usines Renault* ("*Renault*") [1988] ECR 6039.

Case 238/87 *Volvo v Erik Veng (UK)* ("*Volvo*") [1988] ECR 6211.

Case 395/87 *Ministère Public v Jean-Louis Tournier* ("*Tournier*") [1989] ECR 2521.

Joined Cases 92 and 93/87 *Commission v France and United Kingdom and Northern Ireland* [1989] ECR 405.

Joined Cases 110, 241 and 242/88 *François Lucazeau and Others v Société des Auteurs, Compositeurs et Editeurs de Musique and Others* ("*SACEM II*") [1989] ECR 2811.

Case C-18/88 *Régie des Télégraphes et des Téléphones v GB-Inno-BM* [1991] ECR I-5941.

Case C-18/88 *Régie des Télégraphes et des Téléphones v GB-Inno-BM* [1991] ECR I-5941.

Case C-10/89 *CNL-SUCAL v HAG GF* [1990] ECR I-3711.

Case C-234/89 *Stergios Delimitis v Henninger Bräu* [1991] ECR I-935.

Case C-235/89 *Commission v Italian Republic* [1992] ECR I-777.

Joined Cases T-1 to 4 and 6 to 15/89 *Rhône-Poulenc and Others v Commission* [1991] ECR II-867.

Case C-41/90 *Klaus Höfner and Fritz Elser v Macrotron* ("*Höfner*") [1991] ECR I-1979.

Case C-30/90 *Commission v United Kingdom of Great Britain and Northern Ireland* [1992] ECR I-829.

Case C-179/90 *Merci Convenzionali Porto di Genova v Siderurgica Gabrielli* ("*Merci Convenzionali*") [1991] ECR I-5889.

Case C-191/90 *Generics (UK) and Harris Pharmaceuticals v Smith Kline & French Laboratories* [1992] ECR I-5335.

Case C-320/91 *Procureur du Roi v Paul Corbeau* [1993] ECR I-2533.

Joined Cases C-241 and 242/91 P *Radio Telefís Eireann (RTE) and Independent Television Publications (ITP) v Commission ("Magill")* [1995] ECR I-743.

Case C-92/92 *Phil Collins v Imtrat Handelsgesellschaft* [1993] ECR I-5145.

Case C-53/92 P *Hilti v Commission ("Hilti Judgment 1994")* [1994] ECR I-667.

Case C-250/92 *Gøttrup-Klim Grovvareforening and Others v Dansk Landbrugs ("Gøttrup-Klim")* [1994] ECR I-5641.

Joined Cases C-92 and 326/92 *Phil Collins v IMTRAT and Others* [1993] ECR I-5145.

Case C-280/93 *Germany v Council* [1994] ECR I-4973.

Case C-441/93 *Panagis Pafitis and Others v Trapeza Kentrikis Ellados and Others* [1996] ECR I-1347.

Case C-9/93 *IHT Internationale Heiztechnik and Uwe Danzinger v Ideal-Standard and Wabco Standard* [1994] ECR I-2789.

Case C-18/93 *Corsica Ferries Italia v Corpo dei Piloti del Porto di Genova ("Corsica Ferries")* [1994] ECR I-1783.

Case C-33/94 *Tetrapak* [1996] ECR I-5951.

Case C-333/94 P *Tetra Pak International v Commission ("Tetra Pak II Judgment 1996")* [1996] ECR I-5951.

Joined Cases C-140 to 142/94 *DIP v Comune di Bassano del Grappa* [1995] ECR I-3257.

Case C-149/95 P(R) *Commission v Atlantic Container Line and Others* [1995] ECR I-2165.

Case C-349/95 *Frits Loendersloot v George Ballantine & Son and Others* [1997] ECR I-6227.

Joined Cases C-267 and 268/95 *Merck and Others v Primecrown and Others* [1996] ECR I-6285.

Joined Cases C-287 and 288/95 P *Commission v Solvay* [2000] ECR I-2391.

Joined Cases C-68/94 and 30/95 *France and Others v Commission* [1998] ECR I-1375.

Joined Cases T-133 and 204/95 *International Express Carriers Conference v Commission* [1998] ECR II-3645.

Case C-163/96 *Criminal Proceedings Against Silvano Raso and Others* [1998] ECR I-533.

Case C-55/96 *Job Centre* [1977] ECR I-7119.

Case C-367/96 *Alexandros Kefalas and Others v Elliniko Dimosio and Organismos Oikonomikis Anasygkrotisis Epicheiriseon* [1998] ECR I-2843.

Joined Cases C-395 and 396/96 P *Compagnie Maritime Belge Transports and Others v Commission* [2000] ECR I-1365.

Joined Cases C-147 and 148/97 *Deutsche Post v Gesellschaft für Zahlungssysteme and Citicorp Kartenservice* [2000] ECR I-825.

Case C-7/97 *Oscar Bronner v Mediaprint Zeitungs- und Zeitschriftenverlag and Others* ("*Oscar Bronner*") [1998] ECR I-7791.

Case C-61/97 *Foreningen af danske Videogramdistributører and Others v Laserdisken* [1998] ECR I-5171.

Case C-119/97 P *Union Française de L'express (Ufex), Formerly Syndicat Français de L'express International (SFEI), DHL International and Service CRIE v Commission and May Courier* [1999] ECR I-1341.

Case C-379/97 *Pharmacia & Upjohn v Paranova* [1999] ECR I-6927.

Case C-240/97 *Spain v Commission* [1999] ECR I-6571.

Case C-209/98 *Entreprenørforeningens Affalds/Miljøsektion (FFAD) v Københavns Kommune* [2000] ECR I-3743.

Case C-258/98 *Criminal proceedings Against Giovanni Carra and Others* [2000] ECR I-4217.

Case C-344/98 *Masterfoods v HB Ice Cream* [2000] ECR I-11369.

Case C-23/99 *Commission v French Republic* [2000] ECR I-7653.

Case C-453/99 *Courage v Bernard Crehan* [2001] ECR I-6297.

Case C-163/99 *Portuguese Republic v Commission* [2001] ECR I-2613.

Case C-497/99 P *Irish Sugar v Commission* ("*Irish Sugar Judgment 2001*") [2001] ECR I-5333.

Case C-143/00 *Boehringer Ingelheim and Others v Swingward and Dowelhurst* [2002] ECR I-3759.

Case C-241/00 P *Kish Glass v Commission* ("*Kish Glass Judgment 2001*") [2001] ECR I-7759.

Case C-280/00 *Altmark Trans GmbH and Regierungspräsidium Magdeburg v Nahverkehrsgesellschaft Altmark GmbH, and Oberbundesanwalt beim Bundesverwaltungsgericht* [2003] ECR I-7747.

Joined Cases C-83 and 93 to 94/01 *Chronopost SA, La Poste and French Republic v Union Française de L'express (Ufex), DHL International, Federal Express International (France) SNC and CRIE SA* [2003] ECR I-6993.

Case C-82/01 P *Aéroports de Paris v Commission* ("*Aéroports de Paris Judgment 2002*") [2002] ECR I-9297.

Case C-481/01 P (R) *NDC Health v Commission and IMS Health* [2002] ECR I-3401.

Case C-418/01 *IMS Health v NDC Health* ("*IMS Health*") [2004] ECR I-5039.

Case C-115/02 *Administration des Douanes et Droits Indirects (ADDI) v Rioglass and Transremar* [2003] ECR I-12705.

Joined Cases C-189/02 P, C-202/02 P, C-205/02 P to C-208/02 P and C 213/02 P *Dansk Rørindustri and Others v Commission* [2005] ECR I-5425.

Case C-12/03 P *Commission v Tetra Laval BV* [2005] ECR I-987.

Case C-53/03 *Synetairismos Farmakopoion Aitolias & Akarnanias and Others v GlaxoSmithKline* ("*Syfait*") [2005] ECR I-4609.

Case C-552/03 P *Unilever Bestfoods (Ireland) v Commission* [2006] ECR I-9091.

Case C-95/04 P *British Airways v Commission* ("*British Airways Judgment 2007*") [2007] ECR I-2331.

Case C-308/04 P *SGL Carbon AG v Commission* [2006] ECR I-5977.

Case C-313/04 *Franz Egenberger GmbH Molkerei und Trockenwek v Bundersanstalt für Landwirtschaft und Ernährung* [2006] ECR I-6331.

Case C-3/06 P *Groupe Danone v Commission* [2007] ECR I-1331.

C-275/06 *Productores de Música de España (Promusicae) v Telefónica de España SAU* [2008] ECR I-271.

Joined Cases C-468 to 478/06 *Sot. Lélos kai Sia and Others v GlaxoSmithKline ("GlaxoSmith-Kline Judgment 2006")* [2008] ECR I-7139.

Joined Cases C-501, 513, 515 and 519/06 P *GlaxoSmithKline Services and Others v Commission and Others* [2009] ECR I-9291.

Case C-52/07 *Kanal 5 and TV 4 v Föreningen Svenska Tonsättares Internationella Musikbyrå ("STIM")* [2008] ECR I-9275.

Case C-487/07 *L'Oréal and Others v Bellure and Others ("L'Oréal")* [2009] ECR I-5185.

Case C-202/07 P *France Télécom v Commission* [2009] ECR I-2369.

Case C-441/07 P *Commission v Alrosa* [2010] ECR I-5949.

Case C-280/08 P *Deutsche Telekom v Commission ("Deutsche Telekom Judgment 2010")* [2010] ECR I-9555.

Joined Cases C-236 to 238/08 *Google v Louis Vuitton Malletier and Others ("Google")* [2010] ECR I-2417.

Case C-52/09 *Konkurrensverket v TeliaSonera Sverige ("TeliaSonera Judgment 2011")* [2011] ECR I-527.

Case C-543/09 *Deutsche Telekom v Bundesrepublik Deutschland ("Deutsche Telekom Judgment 2011")* [2011] ECR I-3441.

Case C-549/10 P *Tomra and Others v Commission ("Tomra Judgment 2012")*, not yet reported.

Case C-109/10 P Solvay v Commission, not yet reported.

Case C-70/10 *Scarlet Extended v Société Belge des Auteurs, Compositeurs et Éditeurs SCRL (SABAM)*, not yet reported.

Case C-209/10 *Post Danmark v Konkurrencerådet*, not yet reported.

Case C-360/10 *Belgische Vereniging van Auteurs, Componisten en Uitgevers v Netlog ("SABAM")*, not yet reported.

Case C-457/10 P *AstraZeneca v Commission* ("*AstraZeneca Judgment 2012*"), not yet reported.

Case C-89/11 P *E.ON Energie AG v Commission*, not yet reported.

Case C-56/12 P *EFIM v Commission,* pending.

C-295/12 P *Telefónica de España v Commission*, pending.

B.   Rulings of the General Court

Case T-5/97 *Industrie des Poudres Sphériques v Commission* ("*IPS*") [2000] ECR II-3755.

Case T-30/89 *Hilti v Commission* ("*Hilti Judgment 1991*") [1991] ECR II-1439.

Case T-51/89 *Tetra Pak Rausing v Commission* ("*Tetra Pak I Judgment 1990*") [1990] ECR II-309.

Case T-65/89 *BPB Industries and British Gypsum v Commission* ("*BPB Industries*") [1993] ECR II-389.

Case T-69/89 *RTE v Commission* [1991] ECR II-485.

Case T-76/89 *ITP v Commission* [1991] ECR II-575.

Joined Cases T-68, 77 and 78/89 *Società Italiana Vetro and Others v Commission* ("*Società Italiana Vetro*") [1992] ECR II-1403.

Case T-23/90 *Peugeot v Commission* [1991] ECR II-653.

Case T-24/90 *Automec v Commission* [1992] ECR II-2223.

Case T-44/90 *La Cinq v Commission* [1992] ECR II-1.

Case T-32/91 *Solvay v Commission* [1995] ECR II-1825.

Case T-83/91 *Tetra Pak International v Commission* ("*Tetra Pak II Judgment 1994*") [1994] ECR II-755.

Case T-77/92 *Parker Pen v Commission* [1994] ECR II-549.

Joined Cases T-24 to 26 and 28/93 *Compagnie Maritime Belge Transports and Others v Commission* [1996] ECR II-1201.

Case T-504/93 *Tiercé Ladbroke v Commission ("Ladbroke")* [1997] ECR II-923.

Case T-229/94 *Deutsche Bahn v Commission* [1997] ECR II-1689.

Case T-374/94 *European Night Services and Others v Commission* [1998] ECR II-3141.

Joined Cases T-374, 375, 384 and 388/94 *European Night Services and Others v Commission ("European Night Services")* [1998] ECR II-3141.

Case T-395/94 *Atlantic Container Line and Others v Commission ("TACA Judgment 2002")* [2002] ECR II-00875.

Case T-86/95 *Compagnie Générale Maritime and Others v Commission* [2002] ECR II-1011.

Case T-221/95 *Endemol Entertainment Holding v Commission* [1999] ECR II-1299.

Case T-111/96 *ITT Promedia v Commission ("ITT Promedia Judgment 1998")* [1998] ECR II-2937.

Case T-102/96 *Gencor v Commission* [1999] ECR II-753.

Case T-41/96 *Bayer v Commission* [2000] ECR II-3383.

Case T-65/96 *Kish Glass v Commission ("Kish Glass Judgment 2000")* [2000] ECR II-1885.

Case T-228/97 *Irish Sugar v Commission ("Irish Sugar Judgment 1999")* [1999] ECR II-2969.

Case T-198/98 *Micro Leader Business v Commission ("Micro Leader")* [1999] ECR II-3989.

Case T-128/98 *Aéroports de Paris v Commission ("Aéroports de Paris Judgment 2000")* [2000] ECR II-3929.

Case T-139/98 *Amministrazione Autonoma dei Monopoli di Stato v Commission ("AAMS Judgment 2001")* [2001] ECR II-3413.

Case T-65/98 *Van den Bergh Foods v Commission ("Van den Bergh Foods")* [2003] ECR II-4653.

Joined Cases T-191 and 212 to 214/98 *Atlantic Container Line and Others v Commission ("TACA Judgment 2003")* [2003] ECR II-3275.

Case T-25/99 *Colin Arthur Roberts and Valérie Ann Roberts v Commission* [2001] ECR II-1881.

Case T-175/99 *UPS Europe v Commission* (*"UPS Europe"*) [2002] ECR II-1915.

Case T-219/99 *British Airways v Commission* (*"British Airways Judgment 2003"*) [2003] ECR II-5917.

Joined Cases T-67, 68, 71 and 78/00 *JFE Engineering and Others v Commission* [2004] ECR II-2501.

Case T-184/01 R *IMS Health v Commission* [2001] ECR II-3193.

Case T-310/01 *Schneider Electric v Commission* (*"Schneider Electric"*) [2002] ECR II-4071.

Case T-203/01 *Manufacture Française des Pneumatiques Michelin v Commission* (*"Michelin II"*) [2003] ECR II-4071.

Case T-210/01 *General Electric v Commission* [2005] ECR II-5575.

Case T-168/01 *GlaxoSmithKline Services v Commission* (*"GlaxoSmithKline Judgment 2006"*) [2006] ECR II-2969.

Case T-151/01 *Der Grüne Punkt – Duales System Deutschland v Commission* (*"DSD Judgment 2007"*) [2007] ECR II-1607.

Case T-57/01 *Solvay v Commission* (*"Solvay Judgment 2009"*) [2009] ECR II-4621.

Case T-5/02 *Tetra Laval v Commission* [2002] ECR II-4381.

Case T-38/02 *Groupe Danone v Commission* [2005] ECR II-4407.

Case T-279/03 *Galileo International Technology and Others v Commission* [2006] ECR II-1291.

Case T-340/03 *France Télécom v Commission* [2007] ECR II-107.

Case T-410/03 *Hoechst GmbH v Commission* [2008] ECR II-881.

Case T-271/03 *Deutsche Telekom v Commission* (*"Deutsche Telekom Judgment 2008"*) [2008] ECR II-477.

Case T-399/04 *Scandlines Sverige v Commission* (*"Scandlines 2005"*), OJ 2005 C 6/40 (Removed from the Register on 22/02/2005).

Case T-177/04 *EasyJet Airline v Commission* [2006] ECR II-1931.

Case T-201/04 *Microsoft v Commission ("Microsoft Judgment 2007")* [2007] ECR II-3601.

Case T-301/04 *Clearstream v Commission ("Clearstream Judgment 2009")* [2009] ECR II-3155.

Case T-321/05 *AstraZeneca v Commission ("AstraZeneca Judgment 2010")* [2010] ECR II-2805.

Case T-170/06 *Alrosa v Commission* [2007] ECR II-2601.

Case T-155/06 *Tomra Systems and Others v Commission ("Tomra Judgment 2010")* [2010] ECR II-4361.

Case T-411/07 *Aer Lingus Group v Commission* [2010] ECR II-3691.

Case T-336/07 *Telefónica v Commission*, not yet reported.

Case T-398/07 *Spain v Commission*, not yet reported.

Case T-167/08 *Microsoft v Commission, ("Microsoft Judgment 2012")* not yet reported.

Case T-427/08 *Confédération Européenne des Associations D'horlogers-réparateurs v Commission ("CEAHR")* [2010] ECR II-05865.

Case T-442/08 *CISAC v Commission*, OJ 2009 C 82/25.

Case T-296/09 *EFIM v Commission*, not yet reported.

C.   Advocate General Opinions

Advocate General Mischo in Case 238/87 *Volvo v Erik Veng (UK)* [1988] ECR 6211.

Advocate General Jacobs in Case C-10/89 *CNL-SUCAL v HAG GF* [1990] ECR I-3711.

Advocate General Kirschner in Case T-51/89 *Tetra Pak Rausing v Commission ("Tetra Pak I")* [1990] ECR II-309.

Advocate General Vesterdorf in Joined Cases T-1 to 4 and 6 to 15/89 *Rhône-Poulenc and Others v Commission* [1991] ECR II-867.

Advocate General Gulmann in Joined Cases C-241 and 242/91 P *Radio Telefis Eireann (RTE) and Independent Television Publications Ltd (ITP) v Commission ("Magill")* [1995] ECR I-743.

Advocate General Fenelly in Joined Cases C-395 and 396/96 P *Compagnie Maritime Belge Transports and Others v Commission* [2000] ECR I-1365.

Advocate General Jacobs in Case C-7/97 *Oscar Bronner v Mediaprint Zeitungs und Zeitschriftenverlag and Others* ("*Oscar Bronner*") [1998] ECR I-7791.

Advocate General Cosmas in Case C-344/98 *Masterfoods Ltd v HB Ice Cream Ltd* [2000] ECR I-11369.

Advocate General Tizzano in Case C-418/01 *IMS Health v NDC Health* ("*IMS Health*") [2004] ECR I-5039.

Advocate General Jacobs in Case C-53/03 *Synetairismos Farmakopoion Aitolias & Akarnanias and Others v GlaxoSmithKline* ("*Syfait*") [2005] ECR I-4609.

Advocate General Kokott in Case C-95/04 *British Airways v Commission* [2007] ECR I-2331.

Advocate General Ruiz-Jarabo Colomer in Joined Case C-468 to 478/06 *Sot. Lélos kai Sia and Others v GlaxoSmithKline* [2008] ECR I-07139.

Advocate General Kokott in Case C-441/07 P *Commission v Alrosa* [2010] ECR I-5949.

Advocate General Mazák in Case C-52/09 *Konkurrensverket v TeliaSonera Sverige* ("*TeliaSonera*"), [2011] ECR I-527.

Advocate General Mengozzi in Case C-209/10 *Post Danmark v Konkurrencerådet*, not yet reported.

Advocate General Mazák in Case C-549/10 P *Tomra Systems and Others v Commission* ("*Tomra Judgment 2012*"), not yet reported .

Advocate General Bot in Case C-89/11 P *E.ON Energie AG v Commission*, not yet reported.

D.   Reports of Hearing Officers

Case COMP/39.388 *German Electricity Wholesale Market* and Case COMP/39.389 *German Electricity Balancing Market*, Final Report of the Hearing Officer, 2009 OJ C 036/07.

Case COMP/39.401 *E.ON/GDF*, Final Report of the Hearing Officer, 2009 OJ C 248/04.

E.   Rulings of the European Court of Human Rights

Sunday Times v United Kingdom, ECtHR judgment of 26 April 1979, Series A. No. 30.

Silver and Others v United Kingdom, ECtHR judgment of 25 March 1983, Series A No. 61.

Table 2

Chronological List of European Commission Merger Decisions

Case 89/113/EEC *Decca Navigator* Systems, Commission Decision of 21 December 1988.

Case IV/M.053 *Aerospatiale-Alenia/de Havilland*, Commission Decision of 2 October 1991.

Case IV/M.149 *Lucas/Eaton*, Commission Decision of 9 December 1991.

Case IV/M.190 *Nestlé/Perrier*, Commission Decision of 22 July 1992.

Case IV/M.289 *PepsiCo/KAS*, Commission Decision of 21 December 1992.

Case IV/M.315 *Mannesmann/Valourec/Ilva*, Commission Decision of 31 January 1994.

Case IV/M.430 *Procter & Gamble/VP Schickedanz (II)*, Commission Decision of 21 June 1994.

Case IV/M.478 *Voith/Sulzer II*, Commission Decision of 29 July 1994.

Case IV/M.550 *Union Carbide/Enichem*, Commission Decision of 13 March 1995.

Case IV/M.612 *RWE-DEA/Augusta (II)*, Commission Decision of 27 July 1995.

Case IV/M.553 *RTL/Veronica/Endemol*, Commission Decision of 20 September 1995.

Case IV/M.619 *Gencor/Lonrho*, Commission Decision of 24 April 1996.

Case IV/M.784 *Kesko/Tuko*, Commission Decision of 20 November 1996.

Case IV/M.794 *Coca-Cola Enterprises/Amalgamated Beverages GB*, Commission Decision of 22 January 1997.

Case IV/M.878 *RTL 7*, Commission Decision of 14 February 1997.

Case IV/M.754 *Anglo American Corporation/Lonrho*, Commission Decision of 23 April 1997.

Case IV/M.984 *DuPont/ICI*, Commission Decision of 2 October 1997.

Case IV/M.950 *Hoffman La Roche/Boehringer Mannheim*, Commission Decision of 3 May 2011.

Case IV/M.1120 *Compaq/Digital*, Commission Decision of 23 March 1998.

Case COMP/M.1016 *Price Waterhouse/Coopers & Lybrand*, Commission Decision of 20 May 1998.

Case IV/M.1286 *Johnson & Johnson/DePuy*, Commission Decision of 28 October 1998.

Case IV/M.1225 *Enso/Stora*, Commission Decision of 25 November 1998.

Case IV/M.1221 *Rewe/Meinl*, Commission Decision of 3 February 1999.

Case IV/M.1313 *Danish Crown/Vestjyske Slagterier*, Commission Decision of 9 March 1999.

Case COMP/M.1672 *Volvo/Scania*, Commission Decision of 15 March 2000.

Case COMP/M.1671 *Dow Chemical/Union Carbide*, Commission Decision of 3 May 2000.

Case COMP/M.1684 *Carrefour/Promodes*, Commission Decision of 25 January 2000.

Case COMP/M.1795 *Vodafone Airtouch/Mannesmann*, Commission Decision of 12 April 2000.

Case COMP/M.1693 *Alcoa/Reynolds*, Commission Decision of 3 May 2000.

Case COMP/M.1882 *Pirelli/BICC*, Commission Decision of 19 July 2000.

Case COMP/M.1806 *AstraZeneca/Novartis*, Commission Decision of 26 July 2000.

Case COMP/M.1879 *Boeing/Hughes*, Commission Decision of 27 September 2000.

Case COMP/M.2220 *General Electric/Honeywell*, Commission Decision of 1 March 2001.

Case COMP/M.2277 *Degussa/Laporte*, Commission Decision of 12 March 2001.

Case COMP/M.2139 *Bombardier/Adtranz*, Commission Decision of 3 April 2001.

Case COMP/M.2345 *Deutsche BP/Erdölchemie*, Commission Decision of 26 April 2001.

Case COMP/M.2268 *Pernod Ricard/Diageo/Seagram Spirits*, Commission Decision of 8 May 2001.

Case COMP/M.2283 *Schneider/Legrand*, Commission Decision of 10 October 2001.

Case COMP/M.2187 *CVC/Lenzing*, Commission Decision of 17 October 2001.

Case COMP/M.2544 *Masterfoods/Royal Canin*, Commission Decision of 15 February 2002.

Case COMP/M.2706 *Carnival Corporation/P&O Princess*, Commission Decision of 24 July 2002.

Case COMP/M.2416 *Tetra Laval/Sidel*, Commission Decision of 13 January 2003.

Case COMP/M.3060 *UCB/Solutia*, Commission Decision of 31 January 2003.

Case COMP/M.2861 *Siemens/Drägewerk/JV*, Commission Decision of 30 April 2003.

COMP/M.3130 *Arla Foods/Express Dairies*, Commission Decision of 10 June 2003.

Case COMP/M.2947 *Verbund/Energie Allianz*, Commission Decision of 11 June 2003.

Case COMP/M.3056 *Celanese/Degussa/European Oxo Chemicals*, Commission Decision of 11 June 2003.

Case COMP/M.3184 *Wolseley/Pinault Bois & Matériaux*, Commission Decision of 3 July 2003.

Case COMP/M.2978 *Lagardère/Natexis/VUP*, Commission Decision of 7 January 2004.

Case COMP/M.3304 *GE/Amersham*, Commission Decision of 21 January 2004.

Case COMP/M.3280 *Air France/KLM*, Commission Decision of 11 February 2004.

Case COMP/M.3397 *Owens-Illinois/BSN Glasspack*, Commission Decision of 9 June 2004.

Case COMP/M.3099 *Areva/Urenco/ETC JV*, Commission Decision of 6 October 2004.

Case COMP/M.3431 *Sonoco/Ahlstrom/JV*, Commission Decision of 6 October 2004.

Case COMP/M.3216 *Oracle/Peoplesoft*, Commission Decision of 26 October 2004.

Case COMP/M.3688 *UTC/Kidde*, Commission Decision of 18 March 2005.

Case COMP/M.3178 *Bertelsmann/Springer/JV*, Commission Decision of 3 May 2005.

Case COMP/M.3625 *Blackstone/Acetex*, Commission Decision of 13 July 2005.

Case COMP/M.3687 *Johnson & Johnson/Guidant*, Commission Decision of 25 August 2005.

Case COMP/M.3868 *DONG/Elsam/Energi E2*, Commission Decision of 14 March 2006.

Case COMP/M.4108 *T-Systems/Gedas*, Commission Decision of 27 February 2006.

Case COMP/M.4094 *Ineos/BP Dormagen*, Commission Decision of 10 August 2006.

Case COMP/M.3796 *Omya/J.M. Huber PCC*, Commission Decision of 19 July 2006.

Case COMP/M.4187 *Metso/Aker Kvaerner*, Commission Decision of 12 December 2006.

Case COMP/M.4215 *Glatfelter/Crompton Assets*, Commission Decision of 20 December 2006.

Case COMP/M.4524 *Nemak/Hydro Castings*, Commission Decision of 23 February 2007.

Case COMP/M.4561 *GE/Smiths Aerospace*, Commission Decision of 23 April 2007.

Case COMP/M.4439 *Ryanair/Aer Lingus*, Commission Decision of 27 June 2007.

Case COMP/M.4540 *Nestlé/Novartis* ("*Medical Nutrition Business*"), Commission Decision of 29 June 2007.

Case COMP/M.4523 *Travelport/Worldspan*, Commission Decision of 21 August 2007.

Case COMP/M.4533 *SCA/P&G (European Tissue Business)*, Commission Decision of 5 September 2007.

Case COMP/M.4439 *Ryanair/Aer Lingus*, Commission Decision of 11 October 2007.

Case COMP/M.4824 *Kraft/Danone Biscuits*, Commission Decision of 9 November 2007.

Case COMP/M.4513 *Arjowiggins/M-Real Zanders Reflex*, Commission Decision of 4 June 2008.

Case COMP/M.4734 *Ineos/Kerling*, Commission Decision of 30 January 2008.

Case COMP/M.4747 *IBM/Telelogic*, Commission Decision of 5 March 2008.

Case COMP/M.4731 *Google/Doubleclick*, Commission Decision of 11 March 2008.

Case COMP/M.5125 *Marel/SFS*, Commission Decision of 21 April 2008.

Case COMP/M.4956 *STX/Aker Yards*, Commission Decision of 5 May 2008.

Case COMP/M.5047 *REWE/ADEG*, Commission Decision of 23 June 2008.

Case COMP/M.4980 *ABF/GBI Business*, Commission Decision of 23 September 2008.

Case COMP/M.5264 *Invitrogen/Applied Biosystems*, Commission Decision of 11 November 2008.

Case COMP/M.5152 *Posten AB/Post Danmark A/S*, Commission Decision of 21 April 2009.

Case COMP/M.5532 *Carphone Warehouse/Tiscali UK*, Commission Decision of 29 June 2009.

Case COMP/M.5547 *Koninklijke Philips Electronics/Saeco International Group*, Commission Decision of 17 July 2009.

Case COMP/M.5529 *Oracle/Sun Microsystems*, Commission Decision of 21 January 2010.

Case COMP/M.5732 *Hewlett-Packard/3COM*, Commission Decision of 12 February 2010.

Case COMP/M.5771 *CSN/Cimpor*, Commission Decision of 15 February 2010.

Case COMP/M.5932 *News Corp/BskyB*, Commission Decision of 21 December 2010.

Case COMP/M.6025 *Ardagh/Impress*, Commission Decision of 29 November 2010.

Case COMP/M.5999 *Sanofi-Aventis/Genzyme*, Commission Decision of 12 January 2011.

Case COMP/M.5984 *Intel/McAfee*, Commission Decision of 26 January 2011.

Case COMP/M.6117 *Assa Abloy/Cardo*, Commission Decision of 9 March 2011.

Case COMP/M.6128 *Blackstone/Mivisa*, Commission Decision of 25 March 2011.

Case COMP/M.6126 *Thermo Fisher/Dionex Corporation*, Commission Decision of 13 May 2011.

Case COMP/M.6189 *Imerys/Rio Tinto Talc Business*, Commission Decision of 7 July 2011.

Case COMP/M.6292 *Securitas/Niscayah Group*, Commission Decision of 2 August 2011.

Case COMP/M.6267 *Volkswagen/MAN*, Commission Decision of 26 September 2011.

Case COMP/M.6281 *Microsoft/Skype*, Commission Decision of 7 October 2011.

Case COMP/M.6388 *Ecolab/Nalco Holding Company*, Commission Decision of 8 November 2011.

Case COMP/M.6393 *Astrium Holding/Vizada Group*, Commission Decision of 30 November 2011.

Case COMP/M.6380 *Bridgepoint/Infront Sports and Media*, Commission Decision of 20 December 2011.

Case COMP/M.6490 *EADS/Israel Aerospace Industries/JV*, Commission Decision of 16 July 2012.

Table 3

Chronological List of European Commission Antitrust Decisions

Case IV/26.760 *GEMA I*, Commission Decision of 2 June 1971, OJ 1971 L 134/15.

Case IV/26.811 *Continental Can Company*, Commission Decision of 9 December 1971, OJ 1972 L 7/25.

Case IV/26.918 *European Sugar Industry*, Commission Decision of 2 January 1973, OJ L 140/17.

Case IV/28.851 *General Motors Continental*, Commission Decision of 19 December 1974, OJ 1975 L 29/14.

Case *National Carbonizing*, Commission Decision 76/185/ECSC of 29 October 1975, OJ 1976 L 35/6.

Case IV/26.699 *Chiquita*, Commission Decision of 17 December 1975, OJ 1976 L 95/1.

Case IV/29.020 *Vitamins*, Commission Decision of 9 June 1976, OJ 1976 L223/27.

Case IV/28.841 *ABG/Oil Companies*, Commission Decision of 19 April 1977, OJ 1977 L 117/1.

Case IV/29.132 *Hugin/Liptons* ("*Hugin Decision 1977*"), Commission Decision of 8 December 1977, OJ 1978 L 22/23.

Case *Bayer/Tanabe Agreement*, in Eighth Report on Competition Policy (1978), paras 125–7.

Case IV/29.021 *BP Kemi/DDSF*, Commission Decision of 5 September 1979, OJ 1979 L 286/32.

Case *Pilkington/BSN-Gervais-Danone*, in Tenth Report on Competition Policy (1980), paras 152–5.

Case *Sterling Airway*, in Tenth Report on Competition Policy (1980), paras 136–8.

Case IV/29.491 *Bandengroothandel Frieschebrug BV/NV Nederlandsche Banden-Industrie Michelin*, Commission Decision of 7 October 1981, OJ 1982 L11/28.

Case IV/29.491 *Bandengroothandel Frieschebrug/Nederlandsche Banden-Industrie Michelin*, Commission Decision of 7 October 1981, OJ 1981 L 353/33.

Case IV/29.839 *GVL*, Commission Decision of 29 October 1981, OJ 1981 L 370/49.

Case *Osram/Airam* ("*Osram/Airam*"), in Eleventh Report on Competition Policy (1981), p. 66.

Case *Salora-IGR Stereo Television*, in Eleventh Competition Policy Report (1981), para. 94.

Case *Amicon/Fortia/Wright Scientific* ("*Amicon Corp./Fortia AB/Wright Scientific Ltd*"), in Eleventh Report on Competition Policy (1981), para. 112.

Case IV/30.696, *Distribution System of Ford Werke AG: Interim Measures*, Commission Decision of 18 August 1982, OJ 1982 L 256/20.

Case IV/29.877 *British Telecommunications*, Commission Decision of 10 December 1982, OJ 1982 L 360/36.

Case IV/30.698 *ECS/AKZO*, Commission Decision of 29 July 1983, OJ 1983 L 252/13.

Case *IBM*, Fourteenth Report on Competition Policy (1984), pp. 96–103.

Case IV/30.615 *British Leyland*, Commission Decision of 2 July 1984, OJ 1984 L 207/11.

Case IV/30.849 *IBM Personal Computer*, Commission Decision of 18 April 1984, OJ 1984 L 118/24.

Case IV/30.698 *ECS/AKZO*, Commission Decision of 14 December 1985, OJ 1985 L 374/1.

Case *Oliofiat*, Seventeenth Report on Competition Policy (1987), pp. 77–8.

Cases IV/30.787 and 31.488 *Eurofix-Bauco/Hilti* ("*Hilti Decision 1987*"), Commission Decision of 22 December 1987, OJ 1988 L 65/19.

Case IV/32.279 *BBI/Boosey and Hawkes*, Commission Decision of 29 July 1987, OJ 1987 L 286/36.

Case *British Airways/British Caledonian* (*"British Airways/British Caledonian"*), in Eighteenth Report on Competition Policy (1988), para. 81.

Case IV/30.178 *Napier Brown/British Sugar* (*"Napier Brown"*), Commission Decision of 18 July 1988, OJ 1988 L 284/41.

Case IV/31.043 *Tetra Pak I (BTG Licence)* (*"Tetra Pak I Decision 1988"*), Commission Decision of 26 July 1988, OJ 1988 L 272/27.

Case IV/32.318 *London European/Sabena*, Commission Decision of 4 November 1988, OJ 1988 L 317/47.

Case IV/31.851 *Magill TV Guide/ITP, BBC and RTE*, Commission Decision of 21 December 1988, OJ 1989 L 78/43.

Case *Consolidated Goldfields/Minorco* (*"Consolidated Goldfields/Minorco"*), in Nineteenth Report on Competition Policy (1989), para. 68.

Case *Coca-Cola Italia Undertaking*, Nineteenth Report on Competition Policy (1989), para. 50.

Case IV/31.900 *BPB Industries*, Commission Decision of 5 December 1988, OJ 1989 L 10/50.

Case IV/31.906 *Flat Glass (Italy)*, Commission Decision of 7 December 1988, OJ 1989 L 33/44.

Case *Iberian Trading UK Ltd v BPB Industries Plc and British Gypsum Ltd* [1990] 4 CMLR 464.

Case IV/33.133 *Soda-ash – Solvay, ICI*, Commission Decision of 19 December 1990, OJ 1991 L 152/21.

Case IV/31.043 *Tetra Pak II* (*"Tetra Pak II Decision 1991"*), Commission Decision of 24 July 1991, OJ 1992 L 72/1.

Case IV/33.157 *Ecosystem/Peugeot: Provisional Measures*, Commission Decision of 4 December 1991, OJ 1992 L 66/1.

Case IV/33.242 *Yves Saint Laurent Parfums*, Commission Decision of 16 December 1991, OJ 1992 L 12/24.

Case IV/33.544 *British Midland/Aer Lingus*, Commission Decision of 26 February 1992, OJ 1992 L 96/34.

Case IV/32.450 *French-West African Shipowners' Committees*, Commission Decision of 1 April 1992, OJ 1992 L 134/1.

Case IV/34.174 *B&I Line v Sealink Harbours and Stena Sealink*, Commission Decision of 11 June 1992 [1992] 5 C.M.L.R. 255.

Cases IV/33.440 *Warner-Lambert/Gillette and Others* and IV/33.486 *BIC/Gillette and Others* ("*Gillette*"), Commission Decision of 10 November 1992, OJ 1993 L 116/21.

Cases IV/32.448 and 32.450 *Cewal*, Commission Decision of 23 December 1992, OJ 1993 L 34/20.

Case IV/32.745 *Astra*, Commission Decision of 23 December 1992, OJ 1993 L 20/23.

Case 94/119/EC *Port of Rødby*, Commission Decision of 21 December 1993, OJ 1994 L 55/52.

Case IV/34.689 *Sea Containers/Stena Sealink – Interim Measures*, Commission Decision of 21 December 1993, OJ 1994 L 15/8.

Case IV/33.941 *HOV SVZ/MCN*, Commission Decision of 29 March 1994, OJ 1994 L 104/34.

Case IV/34.600 *Night Services*, Commission Decision of 21 September 1994, OJ 1994 L 259/20.

Case 95/364/EC *Brussels National Airport*, Commission Decision of 28 June 1995, OJ 1995 L 216/8.

Case *Pelikan/Kyocera*, in Twenty-fifth Report on Competition Policy (1995), pp. 41–2.

Case *Novo Nordisk*, Twenty-first Report on Competition Policy (1996), pp. 142–3.

Case *Digital Undertaking*, Twenty-seventh Report on Competition Policy (1997), para. 69.

Case IV/35.268 *ITT Promedia/Belgacom* ("*ITT Promedia Decision 1997*"), in Twenty-seventh Report on Competition Policy (1997), para. 67.

Cases IV/34.621 and 35.059 *Irish Sugar* ("*Irish Sugar Decision 1997*"), Commission Decision of 14 May 1997, OJ 1997 L 258/1.

Case IV/36.120 *La Poste/SWIFT + GUF*, Commission Decision of 6 November 1997, OJ 1997 C 335/3.

Case *Flughafen Frankfurt v Main*, Commission Decision 98/387/EC of 14 January 1998, OJ 1998 L 173/32.

Case IV/34.801 *FAG – Flughafen Frankfurt/Main* (*"Frankfurt Airport"*), Commission Decision of 14 January 1998, OJ 1998 L 72/30.

Cases IV/34.073, 34.395 and 35.436 *Van den Bergh Foods*, Commission Decision of 11 March 1998, OJ 1998 L 246/1.

Case IV/35.613 *Alpha Flight Services/Aéroports de Paris* (*"Aéroports de Paris Decision 1998"*), Commission Decision of 11 June 1998, OJ 1998 L 230/10.

Case IV/36.010 *Amministrazione Autonoma dei Monopoli di Stato* (*"AAMS Decision 1998"*), Commission Decision of 17 June 1998, OJ 1998 L 252/47.

Case IV/35.134 *Trans-Atlantic Conference Agreement* (*"TACA Decision 1998"*), Commission Decision of 16 September 1998, OJ 1999 L 95/1.

Case IV/37.770 *Electricity Transmission Tariffs in the Netherlands*, Twenty-ninth Report on Competition Policy (1999), p. 165.

Case IV/35.703 *Portuguese Airports*, Commission Decision of 10 February 1999, OJ 1999 L 69/31.

Case IV/35.767 *Ilmailulaitos/Luftfartsverket* (*"Finnish Airports"*), Commission Decision of 10 February 1999, OJ 1999 L 69/24.

Cases IV/30.373 *P&I Clubs, IGA* and IV/37.143 *P&I Clubs, Pooling Agreement* (*"P&I Clubs"*), Commission Decision of 12 April 1999, OJ 1999 L 125/12.

Case COMP/36.081 *Bass*, Commission Decision of 16 June 1999, OJ 1999 L 186/1.

Case 2000/521/EC *Spanish Airports*, Commission Decision of 26 July 2000, OJ 2000 L 208/36.

Case IV/34.780 *Virgin/British Airways*, Commission Decision of 14 July 1999, OJ 2000 L 30/1.

Case IV/36.888 *1998 Football World Cup*, Commission Decision of 20 July 1999, OJ 2000 L 5/55.

Case IV/36.539 *British Interactive Broadcasting/Open*, Commission Decision of 15 September 1999, OJ 1999 L 312/1.

Case COMP/38.074 *Vodafone + 10* ("*Vodafone*"), Commission Decision of 8 February 2001, OJ 2001 C 42/13.

Case COMP/35.141 *Deutsche Post*, Commission Decision of 20 March 2001, OJ 2001 L 125/27.

Case COMP/34.493 *DSD* ("*DSD Decision 2001*"), Commission Decision of 20 April 2001, OJ 2001 L 166/1.

Cases IV/36.957 *Glaxo Wellcome*, IV/36.997 *Aseprofar and Fedifar*, IV/37.121/F3 *Spain Pharma*, IV/37.138 *BAI*, IV/37.380 *EAEPC*, Commission Decision of 8 May 2001, OJ 2001 L 302/1.

Case COMP/36.041 *Michelin*, Commission Decision of 20 June 2001, OJ 2002 L 143/1.

Case COMP/36.915 *Deutsche Post AG – Interception of Cross-border Mail* ("*Deutsche Post*"), Commission Decision of 25 July 2001, OJ 2001 L 331/40.

Case IV/37.614 *Interbrew and Alken-Maes* ("*Belgian Beer Market*"), Commission Decision of 5 December 2001, OJ 2003 L 200/1.

Case COMP/37.859 *De Post-La Poste*, Commission Decision of 5 December 2001, OJ 2002 L 61/32.

Case COMP/37.904 *Interbrew*, Commission Notice of 20 November 2002, OJ 2002 C 283/14.

Case 2005/145/EC Commission Decision of 16 December 2003 on the State Aid Granted by France to EDF and the Electricity and Gas Industries, OJ 2005 L 49/9.

Cases COMP/37.451, 37.578, 37.579 *Deutsche Telekom* ("*Deutsche Telekom Decision 2003*"), Commission Decision of 21 May 2003, OJ 2003 L 263/9.

Case COMP/38.233 *Wanadoo*, Commission Decision of 16 July 2003, not yet published.

Case COMP/38.369 *T-Mobile Deutschland/O2 Germany – Network Sharing Rahmenvertrag* ("*O2*"), Commission Decision of 16 July 2003, OJ 2004 L 75/32.

Case COMP/37.685 *GVG/FS*, Commission Decision of 27 August 2003, OJ 2004 L 11/17.

Case COMP/38.044 *NDC Health/IMS Health: Interim Measures*, Commission Decision of 13 August 2003, OJ 2003 L 268/69.

Case COMP/37.761 *Euromax/Imax*, Commission Decision of 25 March 2004, not yet published.

Case COMP/37.792 *Microsoft* (*"Microsoft Decision 2004"*), Commission Decision of 24 March 2004, not yet published.

Case COMP/38.096 *Clearstream* (*"Clearstream Decision 2004"*), Commission Decision of 2 June 2004, not yet published.

Case COMP/36.568 *Scandlines Sverige v Port of Helsingborg* (*"Scandlines Decision 2004"*), Commission Decision of 23 July 2004, not yet published.

Case COMP 36.570 *Sundbusserne v Port of Helsingborg*, Commission Decision of 23 July 2004, not yet published.

Case COMP/38.745 *BdKEP/Deutsche Post AG and Bundesrepublik Deutschland* (*"BdKEP"*), Commission Decision of 20 October 2004, not yet published.

Case COMP/37.507 *Generics/AstraZeneca* (*"AstraZeneca Decision 2005"*), Commission Decision of 15 June 2005, not yet published.

Case COMP/39.116 *Coca-Cola*, Commission Decision of 22 June 2005, not yet published.

Case COMP/38.307 *PO/Territorial Restrictions Germany* (*"Gazprom"*), not yet published.

Case COMP/38.381 *De Beers*, Commission Decision of 22 February 2006, OJ 2006 L 205/24.

Case COMP/38.113 *Prokent/Tomra*, Commission Decision of 29 March 2006, not yet published.

Case COMP/37.792 *Microsoft* (*"Microsoft Decision 2006"*), Commission Decision of 12 July 2006, not yet published.

Case COMP/38.784 *Telefónica (Broadband)* (*"Telefónica"*), Commission Decision of 4 July 2007, not yet published.

Case COMP/37.860 *Morgan Stanley Dean Witter/Visa*, Commission Decision of 3 October 2007, not yet published.

Case COMP/37.966 *Distrigaz*, Commission Decision of 11 October 2007, not yet published.

Cases COMP/34.579 *MasterCard*, COMP/36.518 *EuroCommerce*, COMP/38.580 *Commercial Cards*, Commission Decision of 19 December 2007, not yet reported.

Case COMP/37.792 *Microsoft* (*"Microsoft Decision 2008"*), Commission Decision of 27 February 2008, not yet published.

Case COMP/38.700 *Greek Lignite and Electricity Markets*, Commission Decision of 5 March 2008, not yet published.

Case COMP/38.698 *CISAC Agreement* (*"CISAC"*), Commission Decision of 16 July 2008, not yet published.

Case COMP/39.097 *Independent Watch Repairers*, Commission Decision of 10 July 2008, not yet published.

Cases COMP/39.388 *German Electricity Wholesale Market* and COMP/39.389 *German Electricity Balancing Market*, Commission Decision of 26 November 2008, not yet published.

Case COMP/37.990 *Intel*, Commission Decision of 13 May 2009, not yet published.

Case COMP/39.391 *Printers (EFIM Complaint)* (*"EFIM"*), Commission Decision of 20 May 2009, not yet published.

Case COMP/39.402 *RWE Gas Foreclosure*, Commission Decision of 18 March 2009, OJ 2009/C 133/06.

Case COMP/37.990 *Intel*, Commission Summary Decision of 22 September 2009, OJ 2009 C 227/13.

Case COMP/38.636 *Rambus*, Commission Decision of 9 December 2009, not yet published.

Case COMP/39.316 *GDF Foreclosure*, Commission Decision of 3 December 2009, not yet published.

Case COMP/39.530 *Microsoft (Tying)* (*"Browser Commitment Decision"*) Commission Decision of 16 December 2009, not yet published.

Case COMP/39.386 *Long Term Electricity Contracts France*, Commission Decision of 17 March 2010, not yet published.

Case COMP/39.351 *Swedish Interconnectors*, Commission Decision of 14 April 2010, not yet published.

Case COMP/39.317 *E.ON Gas Foreclosure,* Commission Decision of 4 May 2010, not yet published.

Case COMP/39.315 *ENI,* Commission Decision of 29 September 2010, not yet published.

Case COMP/39.525 *Telekomunikacja Polska* (*"Telekomunikacja Polska"*), Commission Decision of 22 June 2011, not yet published.

Case COMP/39.592 *Standard & Poor's,* Commission Decision of 15 November 2011, not yet published.

Case COMP/39.692 *IBM Maintenance Services,* Commission Decision of 13 December 2011, not yet published.

Case COMP/39.654 *Reuters Instrument Codes* (*"RICs"*), Proposed Commitments of 12 July 2012, not yet published.

Case COMP/39.230 *Rio Tinto Alcan,* Commission Decision of 20 December 2012.

Case COMP/39.523 *Slovak Telekom,* Commission Decision of 3 September 2009.

Table 4

Cases and Decisions of Other Jurisdictions

A. Belgium

Case 99-RPR-1 *Importers of Motorcycles*, Belgian Competition Council Decision of 21 January 1999.

Case 2004-VM-30 *Source Belgium v Febelco*, Belgian Competition Council Decision of 25 March 2004.

Case 2006-I/O-12 *FNUCM and Unizo v Banksys*, Belgian Competition Council Decision of 31 August 2006.

Cases 2005/MR/3 and 2005/MR/4 *Importers of Motorcycles*, Brussels' Court of Appeal Decision of 2 February 2009.

B. Cyprus

Areeba/Cyprus Telecommunications Authority, Cyprus Competition Authority Decision of 20 May 2006.

C. Denmark

MetroXpress Danmark v Berlingske Gratisaviser, Danish Competition Authority Decision of 29 May 2002.

Case 3/1120-0100-0557/MHA/SEK *Song Networks/TDC- SONOFON*, Danish Competition Council Decision of 28 April 2004.

Elsam, Danish Competition Council Decision of 30 November 2005.

Elsam, Danish Competition Appeal Tribunal Decision of 14 November 2006.

Elsam, Danish Competition Authority Decision of 20 June 2007.

D. Estonia

Case 3-3-1-66-02 *AS Eesti Telefon*, Estonian Supreme Court Judgment of December 2002.

Case Vj-93/2003 *Excessive Price Increase in the Cable TV Sector*, Estonian Competition Council Decision of 9 December 2003.

E. Finland

Lännen Puhelin, Finnish Competition Authority Decision of 25 October 2004.

F. France

Case No 59928 *Gaz de Bordeaux*, French Conseil d'Etat Judgment of 30 March 1916.

Decision No 07-D-43 *EDF/Direct Energie*, French Competition Council Decision of 10 December 2007.

Decision 04-D-48 *SFR–France Telecom*, French Court of Cassation Judgment of 3 March 2009.

Case No 10-MC-01 *Relative à la Demande de Mesures Conservatoires Présentée par la Société Navx*, French Autorité de la Concurrence Decision of 30 June 2010.

Bottin Cartographes v Google Inc. & Google France, Paris Commercial Court Judgment of 31 January 2012.

G. Germany

Case 2-03 O 629/00 *IMS Health v Insight Health*, Frankfurt am Main's Regional Court Judgment of 12 July 2001.

Case B8-113/03-1 *E.ON Ruhrgas AG*, Bundeskartellamt Decision of 13 January 2006.

Case 11 U 48/08 *IMS Health v Insight Health*, Brandenburg's Higher Regional Court Judgment of 5 December 2006.

Case 4b O 104/12 Decision of Landgericht Duesseldorf, 21 March 2013.

H. Greece

Decision No 512/63 *Organismós Tilepikoinonión tis Elládos*, Greek Competition Authority Decision 23 February 2009.

I. Hungary

Case Vj-100/2002/72 *Magyar Távközlési*, Hungarian Competition Authority Decision of 22 January 2004.

Case Vj-116/2005/84 *TIGÁZ Tiszántúli Gázszolgáltató*, Hungarian Competition Council Decision of 20 June 2006.

Case Vj-156/2005/42 *E.ON Észak-dunántúli Áramszolgáltató*, Hungarian Competition Council Decision of 26 April 2007.

J. Italy

Case No. 10115 A306 *Veraldi/Alitalia*, Italian Competition Authority Decision of 14 November 2001.

Case No. 13752 A351 *Telecom Italia*, Italian Antitrust Authority Decision of 16 November 2004.

Case No.19020 A376 *Aeroporti di Roma/Tariffe Aeroportuali*, Italian Competition Authority Decision of 23 October 2008.

K. Latvia

Case No.765/03/05/12k *Olaines Kudra*, Latvian Competition Council Decision of 7 June 2004.

L. Poland

Case DDI-63/2002 *OPCC President v Polskie Koleje Państwowe Intercity* ("*PKP Intercity*"), Polish Office for Protection of Competition and Consumers ("OPCC") Decision of 7 August 2002.

M.   Spain

Case MTZ 2003/1000 *Telefónica de España*, Spanish Telecommunications Regulator (CMT) Decision of 31 March 2004.

Case S/0207/09 *Transporte Televisión*, Spanish Competition Authority Decision of 8 February 2012.

N.   Sweden

DNR 1135/2004 *TeliaSonera*, Swedish Competition Authority Decision of 21 December 2004.

Cases FT 2875-06 and FT 27829-06 *Administration av Litterära Rättigheter i Sverige* ("*ALIS*"), Stockholm City Court Judgments of 26 August 2008.

O.   The Netherlands

Case 2910/700 *Interpay*, Dutch Competition Authority Decision of 28 April 2004.

Case 3528/199 *Kabeltarieven UPC*, Dutch Competition Authority Decision of 27 September 2005.

Case 3588/201 *Kabeltarieven Casema*, Dutch Competition Authority Decision of 27 September 2005.

P.   United Kingdom

Taylor v Caldwell [1863] EWHC QB J1 122 ER 309; 3 B. & S. 826.

Case 1001/1/1/01 *Napp Pharmaceutical Holdings*, UK Competition Appeal Tribunal Decision of 15 January 2002.

Case 1005/1/1/01 *Aberdeen Journals v Director General of Fair Trading*, UK Competition Appeal Tribunal Decision of 19 March 2002.

Case CA98/20/2002 *BSkyB Investigation: Alleged Infringement of the Chapter II Prohibition*, Decision of the Director General of Fair Trading of 17 December 2002.

Cases A3/2002/1380; A3/2002/1381 *Intel Corporation v Via Technologies and Elitegroup Computer Systems (UK)*, UK Competition Appeal Tribunal Decision of 20 December 2002.

Arkin v Borchard Lines & Others [2003] EWHC 687 (Comm).

Case 1009/1/1/02 *Aberdeen Journals Limited and The Office of Fair Trading*, UK Competition Appeal Tribunal Decision of 23 June 2003.

Case CW/00613/04/03 *Freeserve.com – BTOpenworld's Broadband Pricing*, Decision of the Office of Communications (OFCOM) of 20 November 2003.

Case 1016/1/1/03 *Genzyme v Office of Fair Trading*, UK Competition Appeal Tribunal Decision of 11 March 2004.

Case CW/00760/03/04 *Own-initiative* Investigation *Against BT About Potential Anticompetitive Exclusionary Behaviour*, Decision of the Office of Communications (OFCOM) of 12 July 2004.

Attheraces v British Horseracing Board [2005] EWHC 1553 (ch).

Attheraces v British Horseracing Board [2005] EWHC 3015 (ch).

Case 1046/2/4/04 *Albion Water v Water Services Regulation Authority*, UK Competition Appeal Tribunal Decision of 18 December 2006.

Attheraces v British Horseracing Board [2007] EWCA Civ 38.

Dwr Cymru Cyfyngedig v Albion Water Ltd & Anor [2008] EWCA Civ 536.

Q.   United States

1900–2000

Standard Oil of New Jersey v United States, 221 US 1 (1911).

United States v Colgate, 250 US 300 (1919).

Falls City Industries v Vanco Beverage, 460 US 428 (1923).

Carbice Corp. of America v America Patents Development Corp., 283 US 27, 32 (1931).

United States v Aluminum of America, 148 F.2d 416 (2nd Cir. 1945).

International Salt Co. v United States, 332 U.S. 392 (1947).

Federal Trade Commission v Morton Salt, 334 US 37 (1948).

United States v E.I Du Pont De Nemours, 351 US 377 (1956).

Northern Pacific R. v United States, 356 US 1 (1958).

Jacobellis v Ohio, 378 US 184 (1964).

K-91 v Gershwin Publishing, 389 US 1045 (1968).

Brief for the United States as Amicus Curiae, BMI, *K-91 v Gershwin Publishing*, 389 US 1045 (1968).

Memorandum for the United States as Amicus Curiae, *K-91 v Gershwin Publishing* (filed Dec. 1967), Included as Appendix to Brief for the United States as Amicus Curiae, BMI, *K-91 v Gershwin Publishing*, 389 US 1045 (1968).

Belliston v Texaco, 455 F.2d 175, 184 (10th Cir.) cert denied, 408 U.S 928 (1972).

Ungar v Dunkin Donuts, 531 F.2d 1211, 1219, (3rd cir), cert. denied, 429 U.S 823 (1976).

Broadcast Music v Columbia Broadcasting System, 441 US 1 (1979).

Bob Maxfield v American Motors, 637 F.2d 1033, 1037 (5th Cir.), cert. denied, 454 U.S. 860 (1981).

Unijax v Champion Intl., 683 F.2d 678, 685 (2nd Cir. 1982).

Barry Wright v ITT Grinnel, 724 F.2d 227 (1st Cir. 1983).

Montvale Management Group v The Snowshoe, 1984-1 Trade Cas. ¶ 65,990 at 68, 375 (N.D.W.V. 1984).

Matsushita Electric Industrial v Zenith Radio, 475 US 574 (1986).

Stephen Jay Photography v Olan Mills, 903 F. 2d 988,991 (4th Cir. 1990).

Suburban Propane v Proctor Gas, 953 F.2d 780,788 (2d Cir. 1992).

Professional Real Estate Investors v Columbia Pictures Industries ("*Professional Real Estate*"), 508 US 49 (1993).

Brooke Group v Brown & Williamson Tobacco, 509 US 209 (1993).

United States v Microsoft, 84 F. Supp. 2d 9 (D.D.Cir. 1999) (Findings of Fact).

United States v Microsoft, 87 F. Supp. 2d 30 (D.D.Cir. 2000) (Conclusions of Law).

Concord Boat v Brunswick, 207 F. 3d 1039 (8th Cir. 2000).

2000–2013

Virgin Atlantic Airways v British Airways, 257 F.3d 256 (2nd Cir. 2001).

Sony Electronics v Soundview Technologies, 157 F. Supp. 2d 180 (D. Conn. 2001).

United States v Microsoft, 253 F.3d 34 (D.C. Cir. 2001).

US v AMR., American Airlines and American Eagle, 140 F. Supp. 2d 1141 (2001).

Biovail ("*Biovail*"), 134 F.T.C. 407 (2002).

Bristol-Myers Squibb ("*Bristol-Myers Squibb*"), 135 F.T.C. 444 (2003).

US v AMR and American Airlines, 335 F.3d 1109 (10th Cir. 2003).

Verizon Communications v Law Offices of Curtis v Trinko ("*Trinko*"), 540 US 398 (2004).

Massachusetts v Microsoft, 373 F. 3d 1199 (DC Cir. 2004).

Novell v Microsoft, No. JFM-05-1087, 2005 US Dist. LEXIS 11520 (D. Md. June 10, 2005).

Volvo Trucks North America v Reeder-Simco GMC, 126 S. Ct. 860 (2006).

Abbott Laboratories v Teva Pharmaceuticals USA, 432 F. Supp. 2d 408 (D. Del. 2006).

Broadcom v Qualcomm, 501 F.3d 297 (3rd Cir. 2007).

Cascade Health Solutions v PeaceHealth, 502 F.3d 895 (9th Cir. 2007).

FTC Final Order of February 5, 2007 in the Matter of Rambus Inc., FTC Docket No. 9302.

Opinion of the Commission on Remedy of February 5, 2007 in the Matter of Rambus Inc., FTC Docket No. 9302.

Opinion of Commissioner Pamela Jones Harbour of February 5, 2007 in the Matter of Rambus, Inc., FTC Docket No. 9302.

Opinion of Commissioner J. Thomas Rosch of Feburary 5, 2007 in the matter of Rambus, Inc. FTC Docket No. 9302.

Rambus v F.T.C., 522 F.3d 456, 469 (DC Cir. 2008).

Pacific Bell Telephone v Linkline Communications ("*Linkline*"), 555 US 438 (2009).

Microsoft v Motorola, 696 F.3d 872, 876 (9th Cir. 2012).

J. Posner in *Apple v Motorola*, No. 1:11-cv-08540, slip op. (N.D. Ill. Jun. 22, 2012), https://www.eff.org/sites/default/files/Posner_Apple_v_Motorola_0.pdf.

B. Crabb in *Apple v Motorola*, No. 11-cv-178-bbc, slip op. (W.D. Wis. Nov. 2, 2012).

FTC Decision and Order of January 3, 2013 in the Matter of *Motorola Mobility and Google*, FTC File No. 121 0120.

Table 5

Primary and Secondary Legislation of the European Union

A. Treaties & Charters

Charter of Fundamental Rights of the European Union, OJ 2000 C 364/1.

Consolidated Versions of the Treaty on European Union and the Treaty on the Functioning of the European Union, OJ 2008 C 115/1.

Consolidated Version of the Treaty on the Functioning of the European Union, OJ 2010 C 83/49.

B. Regulations

Council Regulation (EEC) 17 of 6 February 1962 First Regulation Implementing Articles 85 and 86 of the Treaty (*"Regulation 17/62"*), OJ 1962 13/204.

Commission Regulation 67/67/EEC of 22 March 1967 on the Application of Article 85(3) of the Treaty to Certain Categories of Exclusive Dealing Agreements (*"Regulation 67/67"*), OJ 1967 57/849.

Commission Regulation (EEC) 1983/83 of 22 June 1983 on the Application of Article 85(3) of the Treaty to Categories of Exclusive Distribution Agreements, OJ 1983 L 173/1.

Council Regulation (EEC) 4064/89 of 21 December 1989 on the Control of Concentrations Between Undertakings (*"Merger Regulation"*), OJ 1989 L 395/1.

Council Regulation (EEC)1768/92 of 18 June 1992 Concerning the Creation of a Supplementary Protection Certificate for Medicinal Products (*"Regulation 1768/92"*), OJ 1992 L 182/1.

Council Regulation (EEC) 2309/93 of 22 July 1993 Laying Down Community Procedures for the Authorization and Supervision of Medicinal Products for Human and Veterinary

Use and Establishing a European Agency for the Evaluation of Medicinal Products, OJ 1993 L 214/1.

Council Regulation (EC) 1/2003 of 16 December 2002 on the Implementation of the Rules on Competition Laid Down in Articles 81 and 82 of the Treaty ("*Regulation 1/2003*"), OJ 2003 L 1/1.

Council Regulation (EC) 139/2004 of 20 January 2004 on the Control of Concentrations Between Undertakings ("*EC Merger Regulation*"), OJ 2004 L 24/1.

Parliament and Council Regulation (EC) 726/2004 of 31 March 2004 Laying Down Community Procedures for the Authorisation and Supervision of Medicinal Products for Human and Veterinary Use and Establishing a European Medicines Agency, OJ 2004 L 136/1.

Commission Regulation (EC) No 773/2004 Relating to the Conduct of Proceedings by the Commission Pursuant to Articles 81 and 82 of the EC Treaty ("*Regulation 773/2004*") OJ L 123/18.

Commission Regulation (EC) 772/2004 of 27 April 2004 on the Application of Article 81(3) of the Treaty to Categories of Technology Transfer Agreements ("*Technology Transfer Block Exemption Regulation*"), OJ 2004 L 123/11.

Commission Regulation (EU) 330/2010 of 20 April 2010 on the Application of Article 101(3) of the Treaty on the Functioning of the European Union to Categories of Vertical Agreements and Concerted Practices, OJ 2010 L 102/1.

C. Directives

Council Directive 65/65/EEC of 26 January 1965 on the Approximation of Provisions Laid Down by Law.

Regulation or Administrative Action Relating to Proprietary Medicinal Products, OJ 1965 22/369.

Council Directive 87/601/EEC of 14 December 1987 on Fares for Scheduled Air Services Between Member States ("*Directive 87/601*"), OJ 1987 L 374/12.

Council Directive 93/13/EEC of 5 April 1993 on Unfair Terms in Consumer Contracts, OJ 1993 L 95/29.

Parliament and Council Directive 2001/83/EC of 6 November 2001 on the Community Code Relating to Medicinal Products for Human Use, OJ 2001 L 311/67.

Parliament and Council Directive 2002/19/EC of 7 November 2002 on Access to and Interconnection of Electronic Communications Networks and Associated Facilities ("*Access Directive*"), OJ 2002 L 108/7.

Parliament and Council Directive 2002/21/EC of 7 March 2002 on a Common Regulatory Framework for Electronic Communications Networks and Services ("*Framework Directive*"), OJ 2002 L 108/33.

Parliament and Council Directive 2006/116/EC of 12 December 2006 on the Term of Protection of Copyright and Certain Related Rights, OJ 2006 L 372/12.

Parliament and Council Directive 2009/73/EC of 13 July 2009 Concerning Common Rules for the Internal Market In Natural Gas and Repealing Directive 2003/55/EC, OJ 2009 L 211/94.

Parliament and Council Directive 2009/24/EC of 23.04.2009 on the Legal Protection of Computer Programs, OJ 2009 L 111/16.

D.   Notices and Guidelines of the European Commission

Proposal for a Council Directive on the Legal Protection of Computer Programs ("*Draft Software Directive*"), COM/88/816 final – SYN 183, OJ 1989 C 91/4.

Commission Conclusions Decided on the Occasion of the Adoption of the Commission's Proposal for a Council Directive on the Legal Protection of Computer Programs, OJ 1989 C 91/16.

Guidelines on the Application of EEC Competition Rules in the Telecommunications Sector, OJ 1991 C 233/2.

Commission Notice on the Definition of Relevant Market for the Purposes of Community Competition Law ("*Market Definition Notice*"), OJ 1997 C 372/5.

Commission Notice on the Application of the Competition Rules to Access Agreements in the Telecommunications Sector – Framework, Relevant Markets and Principles ("*Telecom Access Notice*"), OJ 1998 C 265/2.

Notice from the Commission on the Application of the Competition Rules to the Postal Sector and on the Assessment of Certain State Measures Relating to Postal Services, OJ 1998 C 39/2.

Commission Notice – Guidelines on Vertical Restraints, OJ 2000 C 291/1.

Commission Notice – Guidelines on the Applicability of Article 81 of the EC Treaty to Horizontal Cooperation Agreements (*"2001 Horizontal Guidelines"*), OJ 2001 C 3/2.

Notice Pursuant to Article 16(3) of Council Regulation (EEC) No 3975/87 of 14 December 1987 Concerning Case IV/37.730 – Austrian Airlines Österreichische Luftverkehrs AG/Deutsche Lufthansa AG, OJ 2001 C 356/5.

Commission Notice on Remedies Acceptable Under Council Regulation (EEC) 4064/89 and Under Commission Regulation (EC) 447/98, 2001 OJ C 68/3.

Commission Notice – Guidelines on the Application of Article 81(3) of the Treaty, OJ 2004 C 101/ 97.

Guidelines on the Assessment of Horizontal Mergers Under the Council Regulation on the Control of Concentrations Between Undertakings (*"Horizontal Merger Guidelines"*), OJ 2004 C 31/5.

Commission Notice – Guidelines on the Application of Article 81 of the EC Treaty to Technology Transfer Agreements (*"2004 Technology Transfer Guidelines"*), OJ 2004 C 101/2.

Commission Notice – Guidelines on the Application of Article 81(3) of the Treaty (*"Notice on Article 101(3) TFEU"*), OJ 2004 C 101/97.

DG Competition Discussion Paper on the Application of Article 82 of the Treaty to Exclusionary Abuses (*"Discussion Paper"*), December 2005.

Guidelines on the Method of Setting Fines Imposed Pursuant to Article 23(2)(a) of Regulation No 1/2003, OJ 2006 C 210/2.

Guidelines on the Method of Setting Fines Imposed Pursuant to Article 23(2)(a) of Regulation No 1/2003, 2006 OJ C 210/02.

Explanations Relating to the Charter of Fundamental Rights, OJ 2007 C 303/17.

Proposal for a Directive of the European Parliament and of the Council on Consumer Rights, October 8, 2008.

Guidance on the Commission's Enforcement Priorities in Applying Article 82 of the EC Treaty to Abusive Exclusionary Conduct by Dominant Undertakings (*"Guidance Paper"*), OJ 2009 C 45/7.

Communication from the Commission to the European Parliament and the Council, Report on the Functioning of Regulation 1/2003 (2009).

Guidelines on Vertical Restraints, OJ 2010 C 130/1.

Commission Notice – Guidelines on the Applicability of Article 101 of the Treaty on the Functioning of the European Union to Horizontal Co-operation Agreements (*"2011 Horizontal Guidelines"*), OJ 2011 C 11/1.

Commission Notice on Best Practices for the Conduct of Proceedings Concerning Articles 101 and 102 TFEU, 2011 OJ C 308/06.

Antitrust Manual of Procedures, Internal DG Competition Working Documents on Procedures for the Application of Articles 101 and 102 TFEU (*"Manual of Procedures"*), March 2012.

E. Reports, Newsletters & Press Releases of the European Commission

DG COMP Competition Policy Newsletter (1998), No. 1.

DG COMP Competition Policy Newsletter (1998), No. 2.

DG COMP Competition Policy Newsletter (1998), No. 3, pp. 7–11.

DG COMP Competition Policy Newsletter (1999), No. 1.

DG COMP Competition Policy Newsletter (2005), No. 3.

DG COMP Competition Policy Newsletter (2007), No. 1, pp. 23–34.

DG COMP Competition Policy Newsletter (2010), No. 3, pp. 17–22.

DG COMP Competition Policy Newsletter (2011), No. 1, pp. 18–23.

Fifth Report on Competition Policy (1975).

Thirteenth Report on Competition Policy (1983).

Twenty-fourth Report on Competition Policy (1994).

Twenty-fifth Report on Competition Policy (1995).

Twenty-sixth Report on Competition Policy (1996).

Twenty-seventh Report on Competition Policy (1997).

Thirty-first Report on Competition Policy (2001).

European Commission Report on Competition Policy (2005).

Economic Advisory Group on Competition Policy (EAGCP), "*An Economic Approach to Article 82*" (July 2005) DG COMP.

Pharmaceutical Sector Inquiry – Final Report, Commission Staff Working Document of 08.07.09.

Press Release IP/88/814 of 15 December 1988.

Press Release IP/97/868 of 10 October 1997.

Press Release IP/98/141 of 10 February 1998.

Press Release IP/01/1832 of 14 December 2001.

Press Release IP/02/1008 of 5 July 2002.

Press Release MEMO/04/217 of 17 September 2004.

Press Release IP/05/710 of 10 June 2005.

Press Release SPEECH/05/537 of 23 September 2005.

Press Release IP/06/857 of 28 June 2006.

Press Release MEMO/06/256 of 28 June 2006.

Press Release MEMO/07/330 of 23 August 2007.

Press Release MEMO/07/389 of 1 October 2007.

Press Release SPEECH/08/317 of 10 June 2008.

Press Release IP/08/1877 of 3 December 2008.

Press Release MEMO/09/143 of 1 April, 2009.

Press Release MEMO/09/235 of 13 May 2009.

Press Release IP/09/745 of 13 May 2009.

Press Release MEMO/09/516 of 24 November 2009.

Press Release MEMO/09/544 of 9 December 2009.

Press Release IP/09/1897 of 9 December 2009.

Press Release IP/11/842 of 6 July 2011.

Press Release IP/11/952 of 5 August 2011.

Press Release IP/11/1044 of 20 September 2011.

Press Release IP/12/89 of 31 January 2012.

Press Release IP/20/89 of 31 January 2012.

Press Release IP/12/208 of 1 March 2012.

Press Release IP/12/345 of 3 April 2012.

Press Release SPEECH/12/428 of 8 June 2012.

Press Release SPEECH/12/453 of 15 June 2012.

Press Release IP/12/777 of 12 July 2012.

Press Release IP/12/835 of 30 July 2012.

Press Release SPEECH/12/760 of 24 October 2012.

IP/12/1448 of 21 December 21 2012.

Press Release SPEECH/13/192 of March 6, 2013.

Table 6

Primary and Secondary Legislation
of Other Jurisdictions

Primary Legislation

Code de Commerce.

Code de la Consommation.

European Convention on Human Rights – as Amended by Protocols Nos. 11 and 14, *Council of Europe Treaty Series*, No. 5.

Protocol No. 1 to the Convention for the Protection of Human Rights and Fundamental, 20 March 1952, *Council of Europe Treaty Series*, No. 9.

Gesetz gegen Wettbewerbsbeschränlungen.

Robinson-Patman Act of 1936, 15 U.S.C. § 13.

The Sherman Antitrust Act of 1890, 15 U.S.C. §§ 1–7.

Secondary Legislation

U.S. Department of Justice & Fed. Trade Commission, *Horizontal Merger Guidelines*, April 2, 1992 (Revised April 8, 1997).

Office of Fair Trading, *Assessment of Individual Agreements and Conduct*, OFT 414, September 1999.

Office of Fair Trading, *Competition Act 1998: The Application in the Telecommunications Sector*, OFT 417, February 2000.

Danish Competition Council, *2 Promotion of Competition*, Annual Report 2002.

Office of Fair Trading, *Assessment of Market Power*, OFT 415, December 2004.

Office of Fair Trading, *Competition Act 1998: The Application in the Telecommunications Sector*, OFT 417, February 2004.

Office of Fair Trading, *Assessment of Conduct: Draft Competition Law Guideline for Consultation*, OFT 414a, April 2004.

Office of Fair Trading, *Assessment of Conduct: Draft Competition Law Guideline for Consultation*, OFT 414a, April 2004.

Office of Fair Trading, *Abuse of a Dominant Position*, OFT 402, December 2004.

Office of Fair Trading, *Market Definition – Understanding Competition Law*", Competition Law Guideline – OFT 403, December 2004, ss. 5.1–5.3.

Antitrust Modernization Commission, *Report and Recommendations*, April 2007.

Authorité de la Concurrence, *Pratiques de Ciseau Tarifaire*, Rapport Annuel 2008.

U.S. Dep't of Justice, *Competition and Monopoly: Single-Firm Conduct Under Section 2 of the Sherman Act* (2008).

Ofcom, "Pay TV Statement", 31 March 2010.

UK Competition Commission, "Guidelines for Market Investigations – Their Role, Assessment, Remedies and Procedures", June 2012.

List of Tables and Figures

TABLES

FIGURES

List of Abbreviations

LEGISLATION

Abbreviation	Definition
2004 Technology Transfer Guidelines	Commission Notice – Guidelines on the application of Article 81 of the EC Treaty to technology transfer agreements, OJ 2004 C 101/2
2006 Fining Guidelines	Guidelines on the method of setting fines imposed pursuant to Article 23(2)(a) of Regulation No 1/2003, OJ 2006 C 210/2
Access Directive	Directive 2002/19/EC of 7 November 2002 on access to, and interconnection of, electronic communications networks and associated facilities, OJ 2002 L 108/7
Discussion Paper	DG Competition discussion paper on the application of Article 82 of the Treaty to exclusionary abuses, December 2005
ECHR	Convention for the Protection of Human Rights and Fundamental Freedoms
Framework Directive	Parliament and Council Directive 2002/21/EC of 07 March 2002 on a common regulatory framework for electronic communications networks and services, OJ 2002 L 108/33
Guidance Paper	Guidance on the Commission's enforcement priorities in applying Article 82 of the EC Treaty to abusive exclusionary conduct by dominant undertakings, OJ 2009 C 45/7
Manual of Procedures	Antitrust Manual of Procedures, Internal DG Competition working documents on procedures for the application of Articles 101 and 102 TFEU, March 2012
Market Definition Notice	Commission Notice on the definition of relevant market for the purposes of Community competition law, OJ 1997 C 372/5
Merger Regulation	Council Regulation (EEC) 4064/89 of 21 December 1989 on the control of concentrations between undertakings, OJ 1989 L 395/1
Notice on Article 101(3) TFEU	Commission Notice – Guidelines on the application of Article 81(3) of the Treaty, OJ 2004 C 101/97

Abbreviation	Definition
Regulation 1/2003	Council Regulation (EC) 1/2003 of 16 December 2002 on the implementation of the rules on competition laid down in Articles 81 and 82 of the Treaty, OJ 2003 L 1/1
Regulation 17/62	Council Regulation (EEC) 17 of 6 February 1962 first regulation implementing Articles 85 and 86 of the Treaty, OJ 1962 13/204
Regulation 1768/92	Council Regulation (EEC)1768/92 of 18.06.1992 concerning the creation of a supplementary protection certificate for medicinal products, OJ 1992 L 182/1
Telecom Access Notice	Commission Notice on the application of the competition rules to access agreements in the telecommunications sector – framework, relevant markets and principles, OJ 1998 C 265/2
TEU	Treaty on European Union
TFEU	Treaty on the Functioning of the European Union

CASES

Abbreviation	Definition
Aéroports de Paris Decision 1998	Case IV/35.613 *Alpha Flight Services/Aéroports de Paris*, Commission Decision of 11 June 1998, OJ 1998 L 230/10
Aéroports de Paris Judgment 2000	Cases T-128/98 *Aéroports de Paris v Commission* [2000] ECR II-3929
Ahmed Saeed	Case 66/86 *Ahmed Saeed Flugreisen and Silver Line Reisebüro v Zentrale zur Bekämpfung unlauteren Wettbewerbs* [1989] ECR 803
AKZO	Case 62/86 *AKZO Chemie v Commission* [1991] ECR I-3359
BdKEP	Case COMP/38.745 *BdKEP/Deutsche Post AG and Bundesrepublik Deutschland*, Commission Decision of 20 October 2004, not yet published
BMS	*Bristol-Myers Squibb*, 135 F.T.C. 444 (2003)
Bodson	Case 30/87 *Corinne Bodson v Pompes funèbres des régions libérées* [1988] ECR 2479
BPB Industries	Case T-65/89 *BPB Industries and British Gypsum v Commission* [1993] ECR II-389

Abbreviation	Definition
British Airways Judgment 2003	Case T-219/99 *British Airways v Commission* [2003] ECR II-5917
British Airways Judgment 2007	Case C-95/04 P *British Airways v Commission* [2007] ECR I-2331
British Leyland	Case 226/84 *British Leyland v Commission* [1986] ECR 3263
Browser Commitment Decision	Case COMP/39.530 *Microsoft (Tying)* Commission Decision of 16 December 2009, not yet published
BRT-II	Case 127/73 *Belgische Radio en Televisie and société belge des auteurs, compositeurs et éditeurs v SABAM and Fonior* [1974] ECR 313
CEAHR	Case T-427/08 *Confédération européenne des associations d'horlogers-réparateurs v Commission*, not yet reported
CISAC	Case COMP/38.698 *CISAC Agreement*, Commission Decision of 16 July 2008, not yet published
Clearstream Decision 2004	Case COMP/38.096 *Clearstream*, Commission Decision of 2 June 2004, not yet published
Clearstream Judgment 2009	Case T-301/04 *Clearstream v Commission* [2009] ECR II-3155
Commercial Solvents	Joined Cases 6 and 7/73 *Istituto Chemioterapico Italiano and Commercial Solvents Corporation v Commission* [1974] ECR 223
Continental Can	Case 6/72 *Europemballage and Continental Can v Commission* [1973] ECR 215
Corsica Ferries	Case C-18/93 *Corsica Ferries Italia v Corpo dei Piloti del Porto di Genova* [1994] ECR I-1783
Deutsche Grammophon	Case 78/70 *Deutsche Grammophon v Metro-SB-Großmärkte* [1971] ECR 487
Deutsche Post	Case COMP/36.915 *Deutsche Post AG – Interception of cross-border mail*, Commission Decision of 25 July 2001, OJ 2001 L 331/40
Deutsche Telekom Decision 2003	Cases COMP/37.451, 37.578, 37.579 *Deutsche Telekom*, Commission Decision of 21 May 2003, OJ 2003 L 263/9
Deutsche Telekom Judgment 2008	Case T-271/03 *Deutsche Telekom v Commission* [2008] ECR II-477
Deutsche Telekom Judgment 2010	Case C-280/08 P *Deutsche Telekom v Commission* [2010] ECR I-9555
DSD Decision 2001	Case COMP/34.493 *DSD*, Commission Decision of 20 April 2001, OJ 2001 L 166/1

Abbreviation	Definition
EFIM	Case COMP/39.391 *Printers (EFIM Complaint)*, Commission Decision of 20 May 2009, not yet published
European Night Services	Joined Cases T-374, 375, 384 and 388/94 *European Night Services and others v Commission* [1998] ECR II-3141
Finnish Airports	Case IV/35.767 *Ilmailulaitos/Luftfartsverket*, Commission Decision of 10 February 1999, OJ 1999 L 69/24
General Motors	Case 26/75 *General Motors Continental v Commission* [1975] ECR 1367
Google	Cases C-236 to 238/08 *Google v Louis Vuitton Malletier and others* [2010] ECR I-2417
Gøttrup-Klim	Case C-250/92 *Gøttrup-Klim Grovvareforening and Others v Dansk Landbrugs* [1994] ECR I-5641
Hilti	Case T-30/89 *Hilti v Commission* [1991] ECR II-1439
Hilti Decision 1987	Cases IV/30.787 and IV/31.488 *Eurofix-Bauco/Hilti*, Commission Decision of 22 December 1987, OJ 1988 L 65/19
Hilti Judgment 1991	Case T-30/89 *Hilti v Commission* [1991] ECR II-1439
Hoffmann-La Roche	Case 85/76 *Hoffmann-La Roche v Commission* [1979] ECR 461
Hugin	Case 22/78 *Hugin Kassaregister and Hugin Cash Registers v Commission* [1979] ECR 1869
Hugin Decision 1977	Case IV/29.132 *Hugin/Liptons*, Commission Decision of 8 December 1977, OJ 1978 L 22/23
IMS Health	Case C-418/01 *IMS Health v NDC Health* [2004] ECR I-5039
IPS	Case T-5/97 *Industrie des poudres sphériques v Commission* [2000] ECR II-3755
Irish Sugar Judgment 1999	Case T-228/97 *Irish Sugar v Commission* [1999] ECR II-2969
ITT Promedia	Case T-111/96 *ITT Promedia v Commission* ("*ITT Promedia*") [1998] ECR II-2937
Kish Glass Judgment 2000	Case T-65/96 *Kish Glass v Commission* [2000] ECR II-1885
L'Oréal	Case C-487/07 *L'Oréal and others v Bellure and others* [2009] ECR I-5185
Ladbroke	Case T-504/93 *Tiercé Ladbroke v Commission* [1997] ECR II-923
Linkline	*Pacific Bell Telephone v Linkline Communications*, 555 US 438 (2009)

Abbreviation	Definition
Magill	Joined Cases C-241 and 242/91 P *Radio Telefís Eireann (RTE) and Independent Television Publications (ITP) v Commission* [1995] ECR I-743
Merci Convenzionali	Case C-179/90 *Merci convenzionali porto di Genova v Siderurgica Gabrielli* [1991] ECR I-5889
Michelin I	Case 322/81 *Nederlandsche Banden Industrie Michelin v Commission* [1983] ECR 3461
Michelin II	Case T-203/01 *Manufacture française des pneumatiques Michelin v Commission* [2003] ECR II-4071
Micro Leader	Case T-198/98 *Micro Leader Business v Commission* [1999] ECR II-3989
Microsoft Decision 2004	Case COMP/37.792 *Microsoft*, Commission Decision of 24 March 2004, not yet published
Microsoft Decision 2008	Case COMP/37.792 *Microsoft*, Commission Decision of 27 February 2008, not yet published
Microsoft Judgment 2007	Case T-201/04 *Microsoft v Commission* [2007] ECR II-3601
Microsoft Judgment 2012	Case T-167/08 *Microsoft v Commission*, not yet reported
Napier Brown	Case IV/30.178 *Napier Brown/British Sugar*, Commission Decision of 18 July 1988, OJ 1988 L 284/41
Oscar Bronner	Case C-7/97 *Oscar Bronner v Mediaprint Zeitungs – und Zeitschriftenverlag and others* [1998] ECR I-7791
SACEM II	Joined Cases 110, 241 and 242/88 *François Lucazeau and others v SACEM and others* [1989] ECR 2811
Scandlines Decision 2004	Case COMP/36.568 *Scandlines Sverige v Port of Helsingborg*, Commission Decision of 23 July 2004, not yet published
Schneider Electric	Case T-310/01 *Schneider Electric v Commission* [2002] ECR II-4071
Sirena	Case 40/70 *Sirena v Eda and others* [1971] ECR 69
Solvay Judgment 2009	Case T-57/01 *Solvay v Commission* [2009] ECR II-4621
STIM	Case C-52/07 *Kanal 5 and TV 4 v Föreningen Svenska Tonsättares Internationella Musikbyrå* [2008] ECR I-9275
Suiker Unie	Joined Cases 40 to 48, 50, 54 to 56, 111, 113 and 114/73 *Coöperatieve Vereniging "Suiker Unie" and others v Commission* [1975] ECR 1663
Syfait	Advocate General Jacobs in Case C-53/03 *Synetairismos Farmakopoion Aitolias & Akarnanias and others v GlaxoSmithKline* [2005] ECR I-4609

Abbreviation	Definition
TACA Decision 1998	Case IV/35.134 *Trans-Atlantic Conference Agreement*, Commission Decision of 16 September 1998, OJ 1999 L 95/1
TACA Judgment 2003	Joined Cases T-191 and 212 to 214/98 *Atlantic Container Line and others v Commission* [2003] ECR II-3275
Telefónica	Case COMP/38.784 *Telefónica (broadband)*, Commission Decision of 4 July 2007, not yet published
Telefónica Judgment 2012	Case T-336/07 *Telefónica v Commission*, not yet reported
Telekomunikacja Polska	Case COMP/39.525 *Telekomunikacja Polska*, Commission Decision of 22 June 2011, not yet published
Télémarketing	Case 311/84 *Centre belge d'études de marché – Télémarketing (CBEM) v Compagnie luxembourgeoise de télédiffusion (CLT) and Information publicité Benelux (IPB)* [1985] ECR 3261
TeliaSonera	Advocate General Mazák in Case C-52/09 *Konkurrensverket v TeliaSonera Sverige*, [2011] ECR I-527
TeliaSonera Judgment 2011	Case C-52/09 *Konkurrensverket v TeliaSonera Sverige* [2011] ECR I-527
Tetra Pak I Decision 1988	Case IV/31.043 *Tetra Pak I (BTG Licence)*, Commission Decision of 26 July 1988, OJ 1988 L 272/27
Tetra Pak I Judgment 1990	Case T-51/89 *Tetra Pak Rausing v Commission* ("*Tetra Pak I Judgment 1990*") [1990] ECR II-309
Tetra Pak II Decision 1991	Case IV/31.043 *Tetra Pak II*, Commission Decision of 24 July 1991, OJ 1992 L 72/1
Tetra Pak II Judgment 1994	Case T-83/91 *Tetra Pak International v Commission* [1994] ECR II-755
Tetra Pak II Judgment 1996	Case C-333/94 P *Tetra Pak International v Commission* [1996] ECR I-5951
Tomra Decision 2006	Case COMP/38.113 *Prokent/Tomra*, Commission Decision of 29 March 2006, not yet published
Tomra Judgment 2010	Case T-155/06 *Tomra Systems and others v Commission* [2010] ECR II-4361
Tomra Judgment 2012	Case C-549/10 P *Tomra Systems and others v Commission*, not yet reported
Tournier	Case 395/87 *Ministère Public v Jean-Louis Tournier* [1989] ECR 2521
Trinko	*Verizon Communications v Law Office of Curtis v Trinko*, 540 US 398 (2004)

Abbreviation	Definition
United Brands	Case 27/76 *United Brands and United Brands Continentaal v Commission* [1978] ECR 207
Van den Bergh Foods	Case T-65/98 *Van den Bergh Foods v Commission* [2003] ECR II-4653
Volvo	Case 238/87 *Volvo v Erik Veng (UK)* [1988] ECR 6211

PUBLICATIONS

Abbreviation	Definition
AJIL	American Journal of International Law
Bl Comm	Blackstone, Commentaries on the Law of England
Bracton	Bracton, On the Laws and Customs of England
Brooke Abr	Brooke, La Graunde Abridgement
BTR	British Tax Review
CLJ	Cambridge Law Journal
CLP	Current Legal Problems
CML Rev	Common Market Law Review
Co Inst	Coke, Institutes of the Laws of England
Co Litt	Coke, Commentary upon Littleton
Comp Law	Competition Law Journal
Crim LR	Criminal Law Review
EAGCP Report	P. Rey and others, "An Economic Approach to Article 82", Report by the Economic Advisory Group on Competition Policy, July 2005
EBOR	European Business Organization Law Review
EC Bull	EC Bulletin
ECC	European Commercial Cases
ECLR	European Competition Law Review
EG	Estates Gazette
EIPR	European Intellectual Property Review
EIRR	European Industrial Relations Review
ELJ	European Law Journal
Fitz Abr	Fitzherbert, La Graunde Abridgement
Fitz NB	Fitzherbert, La Novel Natura Brevium
Glanvill	Glanvill, Treatise on the Laws and Customs of England

Abbreviation	Definition
Hale PC	Hale, The History of the Pleas of the Crown
Hawk PC	Hawkins, A Treatise on the Pleas of the Crown
ICLQ	International & Comparative Law Quarterly
ILJ	Industrial Law Journal
Intl Rev IP & Comp L	International Review of Intellectual Property and Competition Law
JBL	Journal of Business Law
J Comp L & Econ	Journal of Competition Law and Economics
JL Econ & Org	Journal of Law, Economics and Organization
JPEL	Journal of Planning and Environmental Law
LIEI	Legal Issues of Economic Integration
LMCLQ	Lloyd's Maritime & Commercial Law Quarterly
LQR	Law Quarterly Review
LS Gaz	Law Society Gazette
OJLS	Oxford Journal of Legal Studies
MLR	Modern Law Review
NLJ	New Law Journal
OJ	Official Journal of the European Communities
OJLS	Oxford Journal of Legal Studies
OUCLJ	Oxford University Commonwealth Law Journal
Rev Econ Stud	Review of Economic Studies
Rev Econ & Stat	Review of Economics and Statistics
SJ	Solicitor's Journal
Stan L Rev	Stanford Law Review
U Chi L Rev	University of Chicago Law Review
YEL	Yearbook of European Law

GENERAL

Abbreviation	Definition
AAC	Average Avoidable Cost
AAMS	Amministrazione Autonoma dei Monopoli di Stato
Abertis	Abertis Telecom S.A.

Abbreviation	Definition
AC	Average Cost
AFC	Average Fixed Cost
affd	Affirmed
AG	Attorney General
Anon	Anonymous
App.	Appendix
Apps	Appendices
AR	Average Revenue
Art.	Article
Arts	Articles
ASCAP	American Society of Composers, Authors and Publishers
ATC	Average Total Cost
AVC	Average Variable Costs
BA	British Airways
BTG	British Technology Group
BMI	Broadcast Music, Inc.
Bros	Brothers
CAT	UK Competition Appeal Tribunal
Ch.	Chapter
Chs	Chapters
CNC	Spanish National Competition Commission
Co	Company
CoGS	Cost of Goods Sold
Comr/Comrs	Commissioner/Commissioners
Conv	Conveyancer
Co-op	Co-operative
Corp	Corporation
CPS	Crown Prosecution Service
CPUs	Central Processing Units
Crim	Criminal
CUP	Cambridge University Press
DC	District Council
DCF	Discounted Cash Flow

Abbreviation	Definition
decd	Deceased
Dept	Department
DoJ	US Department of Justice
DPP	Director of Public Prosecutions
DRAM	Dynamic Random Access Memory
DSD	Duales System Deutschland
DTT	Digital Terrestrial Television
e.g.	For example
EC	European Communities
ECR	European Court Reports
Ed.	Edition
Eds	Editors
Eur	European
Exor	Executor
Exrx	Executrix
FDA	Federal Drug Administration
Fig.	Figure
Fn/Fns	Footnote/Footnotes (external to the work)
FRAND	Fair, Reasonable and Non-Discriminatory
FTC	US Federal Trade Commission
GB	Great Britain
GSK	GlaxoSmithKline
HA	Health Authority
ICN	International Competition Network
Inc	Incorporated
Intl	International
IP	Intellectual Property
IPR	Intellectual Property Rights
IRC	Inland Revenue Commissioners
J	Journal
L	Law or Legal
liq	Liquid
LRAIC	Long-Run Average Incremental Cost

Abbreviation	Definition
LRATC	Long-Run Average Total Cost
LS	Legal Studies
Ltd	Limited
MC	Marginal Cost
MR	Marginal Revenue
n.	Footnote
nn.	Footnotes
No.	Number
Nos	Numbers
NPV	Net Present Value
NRA	National Regulatory Authority
NZ	New Zealand
OCoS	Other Costs of Sales
OFT	UK Office of Fair Trading
ors	Others
P&I Clubs	Protection & Indemnity Clubs
p.	Page
para.	Paragraph
paras	Paragraphs
PCoS	Product Cost of Sales
PEM	Péchiney Électrométallurgie
PL	Public Law
plc	Public Limited Company
pp.	Pages
Pt.	Part
Pts	Parts
Q	Quarterly
R&D	Research and Development
RAND	Reasonable and Non-Discriminatory
Rep	Report(s)
Rev	Review
s.	Section
Sch.	Schedule

Abbreviation	Definition
Schs	Schedules
SMEs	Small and Medium-sized Enterprises
SO	Statement of Objections
SPC	Supplementary Protection Certificate
ss.	Sections
SSO	Standard Setting Organisation
TeliaSonera	TeliaSonera Sverige AB
U	University
UK	United Kingdom
US	United States
USA	United States of America
Vol.	Volume
Vols	Volumes
YB	Yearbook

Foreword

The purpose of this book is to carry out a comprehensive review of the principles that underpin the application of Article 102 TFEU, which prohibits the abuse of a dominant position as incompatible with the internal market. This book combines both legal and economic analysis with the aim of providing readers with an intellectual framework to facilitate the normative analysis and constructive criticism of the law.

In particular, chapters one to three focus on market definition, dominance and the concept of abuse. In turn, chapters four to eleven discuss the individual forms of abuse, including predatory conduct, margin squeeze, exclusive dealing, refusal to deal, tying and bundling, abusive discrimination, excessive pricing and other abuses. Chapter twelve deals with remedies in the context of Article 102 enforcement.

The application of Article 102 by the Commission and the European Courts has often been controversial and raises complex questions as to how dominance should be defined and what conduct should be deemed abusive.

Article 102 was first laid out in the Treaty of Rome in 1957. This provision did not prohibit the acquisition or the mere holding of a dominant position, but only its abuse. Since what was then Article 86 did not contain a definition of what an "abuse" actually is, the notion of "abuse" had to be inferred from the four examples set out therein.

The first key issue which the Commission and the EU Courts had to tackle in the early years of application of Article 102 was the question of the potential applicability of this provision to the control of concentrations. In the *Continental Can* judgment in 1973, the Court of Justice established that the acquisition by a dominant company of a significant competitor could indeed infringe Article 102 in as much as it led to the strengthening of a dominant position.

In the 1974 *Commercial Solvents* judgment, the Court of Justice confirmed that the four examples of anticompetitive conduct explicitly set out in Article 102 are not exhaustive. Indeed, this provision was understood as a *numerus apertus* list and it was accepted that there would be types of conduct that would be illegal under Article 102 even if they were not expressly described nor derived from the four examples of abuse set out therein.

By 1979, the different types of "abuses" had been classified as either "exclusionary" (foreclosure), "exploitative" (imposition of unduly onerous terms or excessive prices on consumers), "discriminatory" (set out in Article 102(c) TFEU) or "reprisal" abuses (warning or punishing an operator for competing strongly or for complaining to a competition authority). Today, the first two categories are commonly used when analysing individual cases of potential abuse.

For many years, the Commission focused chiefly on Article 101 cases and on seeking the adoption of a EU system of merger control. Several cases were however brought under Article 102 against collection societies, essentially for the application of unduly onerous terms and for discrimination on grounds of nationality. Consequently, the case law developed slowly, *United Brands* (1978), *Hoffmann-LaRoche* (1979) and *Michelin I* (1983) being the key Article 102 judgments for a long time.

The Commission focused on exclusionary abuses rather than on the other types of abuse, such as exploitative abuses. In 1991 the Court set out a structured test based on costs to identify predatory conduct, in its *AKZO* judgment. In its 1996 *Tetra Pak II* judgment, the Court handed down a key judgment on contractual tying and aftermarkets. In 1998, in *Oscar Bronner*, the Court clarified the strict conditions under which access to a facility may be ordered. In 2000, the Court delivered its *Compagnie Maritime Belge* judgment, confirming the applicability of Article 102 to collective dominance abuses. In 2003, the General Court followed an effects-based approach to exclusive purchasing under Article 102, in *Van den Bergh Foods*. In its *British Airways* judgment in 2007, the Court developed its approach for the assessment of the anti-competitive effects of discounts or rebates, in light of its previous findings in *Hoffmann-LaRoche* and *Michelin I*. In the same year, the General Court's judgment in *Microsoft* built on the previous case law concerning refusal to supply with regard to intellectual property rights, such as the *Magill* and *IMS Health* judgments of 1995 and 2004. In 2008, in *Deutsche Telekom*, the General Court established margin squeeze as an independent abuse and spell out its views, later confirmed by the Court in its 2011 *TeliaSonera* judgment, on the interplay between competition and regulation.

Despite the progressive definition of the constituent elements of Article 102 and of the specificities of the individual forms of abuse during the nineties and over the last decade, several key issues concerning the enforcement of Article 102 remain open. These issues, have been treated throughout this book.

This is the case for instance of the intensity of judicial review. Traditionally, the Court has granted the Commission a "margin of appreciation" in its assessment of complex economic matters, declining to substitute its own assessment for that of the Commission. This means that in these cases, the Court confines itself to verifying whether the rules on procedure and on the statement of reasons have been complied with, as well as whether the facts have been accurately stated and whether there has been a manifest error of appraisal or a misuse of powers.

There is considerable uncertainty as to when an economic matter may be deemed sufficiently complex to justify such judicial deference, and as to what the precise scope and intensity of the judicial review which must be exercised in these cases actually is. This has given rise to serious concerns as to the compatibility of the administrative procedure before the Commission with Article 6 of the European Convention on Human Rights and Article 47 of the European Charter of Fundamental Rights.

Another open issue addressed in this book is that of the modernization of Article 102 enforcement and of the Commission and the European Courts' shift towards a more effects-based and economic approach.

One of the milestones of this trend was the adoption of the *Guidance on the Commission's Enforcement Policies in Applying Article 82 EC Treaty to Exclusionary Conduct by Dominant Undertakings* in February 2009, where the Commission established its Article 102 enforcement priorities with the declared aim of setting out an economic and effects-based approach to exclusionary conduct under EU antitrust law. At the same time, the Court of Justice also welcomed a more effects-based approach in recent judgments such as *Deutsche Telekom* (2010), *TeliaSonera* (2011) or *Danish Post* (2012).

Despite these developments, the fact that the Commission's Guidance Paper maintained a *per se* approach as regards certain types of abuse and that in certain judgments the EU Courts seem to have set a very low standard of proof on the Commission to establish actual or probable anticompetitive effects, confirms that this shift towards a more effects-based approach remains unsettled.

Finally, there remains considerable uncertainty as to what test must be applied to distinguish between competition on the merits and anticompetitive foreclosure.

In its Guidance Paper, the Commission stated, for example, that it would normally only intervene in order to prevent anticompetitive foreclosure resulting from price-based exclusionary conduct when such conduct was capable of hampering competition from competitors who are as efficient as the dominant undertaking. However, the Commission also referred to certain cases in which constraints exerted by less efficient competitors should be taken into account. In reality, the Commission seemed to concentrate on situations in which it is said that foreclosure may occur, without clearly differentiating between legitimate foreclosure due to normal competition and anticompetitive foreclosure resulting from exclusionary conduct. The Commission's reference to the need for consumer harm to be shown for a finding of abuse may be insufficient, since this standard does not appear to have been applied as a test.

The authors have ample experience in this area of the law and have relied on their exposure both to the public and the private sector. They wish to thank all those who have provided their input and assistance in the preparation of this book. These include: Jose Baño, Laurence Bary, Pierantonio D'Elia, Sofie de Nil, Andrea de Vos, Ben Holles, Shin-Shin Hua, Stephen Lewis, Farrell Malone, Stanislas de Margerie, Jorge Piernas, Flora Pitti-Ferrandi, Cristina Sjodin, Jon Zimmerman and Lea Zuber.

The editors further wish to thank the Brussels legal support team of Cleary Gottlieb, Steen & Hamilton, as well as the administrative team in Brussels and New York for their assistance. In particular they wish to thank Pia Caruana, Laurent Cenatiempo, Montana Sarisky and Franziska Kötten for their valuable contribution.

Finally, the authors wish to make clear that the opinions expressed in this book are exclusively personal and that none of them represent the opinions of their firms or clients.

Francisco Enrique González-Díaz and Robbert Snelders

1. – Market Definition
Nicolas Gauss and Alison Oldale

Market Definition

*Nicolas Gauss and Alison Oldale**

I. Introduction

Market definition is the starting point for every Article 102 TFEU analysis. **1.1**
Its main purpose is to systematically identify the immediate competitive constraints faced by an undertaking that supposedly engages in abusive behaviour.
As the *Market Definition Notice* states, the objective of product and geographic
market definition is to identify the actual competitors of the undertakings
concerned that are capable of constraining the undertakings' behaviour and
of preventing them from behaving independently.[1] This is done in order to
determine if an undertaking can behave freely of effective competitive pressure, *i.e.*, if it is dominant.[2]

The question whether a company holds a dominant position depends to a large **1.2**
extent on how broadly the market is defined. Market definition determines
market shares, and market shares are important when determining whether a
company is dominant. A finding of low market shares is usually considered
as evidence of the absence of substantial market power[3] and thus can put an
end to an Article 102 TFEU analysis, while very high market shares can be

---

* Nicolas Gauss is a corporate counsel at Amazon EU and a former associate of Cleary Gottlieb Steen &
Hamilton, Brussels. He wishes to thank Stanislas de Margerie for his very valuable help and contribution to
the chapter. Alison Oldale is an Executive Vice President at Compass Lexecon in Washington, DC. The views
expressed in this chapter are those of the authors and do not reflect in any way those of Amazon EU or
Compass Lexecon.

[1] Commission Notice on the definition of relevant market for the purposes of Community competition law
("*Market Definition Notice*"), OJ 1997 C 372/5, para. 2. The *Market Definition Notice* covers market definition under
Article 101, Article 102 and merger control.
[2] Case 6/72 *Europemballage and Continental Can v Commission* ("*Continental Can*") [1973] ECR 215, para. 32;
Case 27/76 *United Brands and United Brands Continentaal v Commission* ("*United Brands*") [1978] ECR 207, para. 10;
Case T-219/99 *British Airways v Commission* ("*British Airways Judgment 2003*") [2003] ECR II-5917, para. 91.
[3] The Commission states in the Guidance on the Commission's enforcement priorities in applying Article 82 of the
EC Treaty to abusive exclusionary conduct by dominant undertakings ("*Guidance Paper*"), para. 14, that low market
shares are generally a good proxy for the absence of substantial market power (see OJ 2009 C 45/7, para. 14.).

1. – Market Definition
Nicolas Gauss and Alison Oldale

sufficient to establish dominance.[4] This often makes market definition under Article 102 TFEU a highly controversial issue. Strong market players subject to an allegation of abuse of dominance will tend to claim that the market on which they operate should be defined more broadly. Conversely, the competition authorities choose to delineate the market more narrowly, making it more likely that a company will be found dominant and hence subject to Article 102 TFEU. The Commission and the European courts have been criticised for applying a result-oriented approach to market definition – defining markets so narrowly that the company under scrutiny is found to be dominant.[5]

1.3 From a lawyer's perspective, market definition is a prerequisite to the analysis of dominance, since assessing whether an undertaking can behave independently of effective competitive pressure requires identifying its competitors, which in turn depends on the scope of the market defined. It is only thereafter that the actual abuse can be examined. From the perspective of some economists, the preliminary and separate assessment of dominance and hence market definition is not required if there is a verifiable and consistent anticompetitive effect. According to this reasoning, the existence of an anticompetitive effect is proof of dominance[6] and hence renders market definition redundant.[7] This approach sees the assessment of dominance as a part of the analysis of likely effects, rather than as a test of Article 102 TFEU's applicability. However, this approach has not managed to prevail, above all, because of the clear wording of Article 102 TFEU, which requires a "dominant position" and hence a preliminary market definition.

1.4 Apart from being a pre-stage to assessing dominance, market definition under Article 102 TFEU serves the purpose of determining if an allegedly dominant company has engaged in abusive multi-market strategies like leveraging its market power from one market to the other. As established by case law, the

---

[4] Case T-340/03 *France Télécom v Commission* [2007] ECR II-107, para. 100; Case 85/76 *Hoffmann-La Roche v Commission* ("*Hoffmann-La Roche*") [1979] ECR 461, para. 41. *See also* chapter 2 on dominance on the importance of market shares.

[5] National Economic Research Associates, *The Role of Market Definition in Monopoly and Dominance Inquiries*, Office of Fair Trading Economic Discussion Paper 2, OFT 342, July 2001, p. 35; R. O'Donoghue and A. J. Padilla, *The Law and Economics of Article 82 EC* (Oxford, Hart Publishing, 2006), pp. 67–8; V. Korah, *An Introductory Guide to EC Competition Law and Practice* (9th Ed., Oxford, Hart Publishing, 2007), p. 109.

[6] P. Rey and others, "An Economic Approach to Article 82", Report by the Economic Advisory Group on Competition Policy ("*EAGCP Report*"), July 2005, p. 4.

[7] Even under this approach, it is necessary to distinguish between abusive behaviours within one market, abusive behaviour in adjacent markets, and abusive behaviour in vertically related markets (*EAGCP Report supra* note 6, p. 18).

1. – Market Definition
Nicolas Gauss and Alison Oldale

relevant competitive harm may also arise on a different market from the one which is dominated.[8]

The *Market Definition Notice*,[9] which dates back to 1997, is still the authoritative **1.5** Commission interpretation on market definition. While the *Discussion Paper*[10] from 2005 contained a section on market definition, the *Guidance Paper* from 2009 remained silent on the topic. However, it should be noted that the *Discussion Paper* does not bind the Commission: its statements on market definition serve only as an indication of how the law should be applied.[11] The comments on market definition in the *Discussion Paper* mainly concern an interpretation of dominance, according to which the price charged by the allegedly dominant undertaking "*will almost inevitably have been raised above the competitive level*".[12] As the *Discussion Paper* noted, but the *Guidance Paper* did not, this kind of dominance creates a practical problem when defining the market. If current prices are higher than competitive ones then techniques to define the market based on looking at substitution at current prices may not be very useful: customers may only be willing to switch to an alternative because the price of the product in question is so high, and they may have been much less willing to switch if the product's price had been competitive. Failure to acknowledge this point is known as the "cellophane fallacy".[13] This point, that market definition in Article 102 TFEU cases should be done at competitive prices, is not new; it can be found in the *Market Definition Notice*[14] and is repeated in the *Discussion Paper*.[15] However, it is fair to say that neither the Commission[16] nor

---

[8] This principle was established in Case T-83/91 *Tetra Pak International v Commission* ("*Tetra Pak II Judgment 1994*") [1994] ECR II-755, paras 116, 122; upheld on appeal in Case C-333/94 P *Tetra Pak International v Commission* ("*Tetra Pak II Judgment 1996*") [1996] ECR I-5951, paras 25–32. In Case COMP/37.792 *Microsoft*, Commission Decision of 24 March 2004 ("*Microsoft Decision 2004*"), not yet published, the Commission defined a streaming media player market (paras 402–25) not to assess dominance on that market, but to delineate the market on which the abusive behaviour took place, *i.e.*, the bundling of Windows and Windows media player, which allowed Microsoft to leverage its PC operating system dominance into the market for media players (paras 792 *et seq.*, notably 968 *et seq.*). *See also* Case C-52/09 *Konkurrensverket v TeliaSonera Sverige* ("*TeliaSonera Judgment 2011*"), not yet reported, paras 85 *et seq.*

[9] *Market Definition Notice supra* note 1.

[10] DG Competition discussion paper on the application of Article 82 of the Treaty to exclusionary abuses ("*Discussion Paper*"), December 2005, paras 11–9.

[11] F. W. Bulst, in E. Langen and H.-J. Bunte (Eds.), *Kommentar zum deutschen und europäischen Kartellrecht* (11th Ed., Luchterhand), Art. 82 EG, para. 30.

[12] *Discussion Paper supra* note 10, para. 13.

[13] *Ibid.*, paras 13 and 15.

[14] *Market Definition Notice supra* note 1, para. 19.

[15] *Discussion Paper supra* note 10, paras 15–16.

[16] *Ibid.*, para. 16.

1. – Market Definition
Nicolas Gauss and Alison Oldale

commentators have managed to devise robust methods for dealing with this issue in practice. The lack of comment in the *Guidance Paper* on market definition more likely reflects uncertainty on the part of the Commission about how to deal with the cellophane fallacy, rather than a change in its view that avoiding the fallacy is important.

1.6 Given that the *Market Definition Notice* is somewhat dated,[17] and not all of its methods have been applied in practice, reliance on case law is of major importance in relation to market definition.[18] However, some of the seminal cases on Article 102 TFEU date back to the 1970s (*Continental Can, United Brands, Hoffmann-La Roche*)[19] and 1980s (*Michelin I*).[20] While their principles remain authoritative for the application of Article 102 TFEU, the methods applied in these decisions to define the market are also dated to some extent. In particular, the older case law on market definition does not reflect the current trend towards greater reliance on economic analysis. Given the significantly higher number of merger control decisions in which market definition issues arise, it is therefore helpful to draw on the rich case law from merger control, notably on cases that apply a quantitative analysis to market definition.

1.7 Despite its more objective approach, the SSNIP test is not without flaws. The major shortcoming of the test in the context of abuse cases is the risk of the "cellophane fallacy" (*see* above), which is caused if the reference for the SSNIP, the current price, is above the competitive level.

---

[17] There are currently no clear indications that the Commission will soon publish a revised version of the *Market Definition Notice* – be it again an all-encompassing notice, or separate notices on market definition for Articles 101, 102 and merger control, *see supra* note 1.

[18] The courts have noted that, insofar as the definition of the market involves complex economic assessments on the part of the Commission, it should only be subject to limited review by the Community judicature. However, the courts have also emphasised that they are required *"to decide whether the Commission based its assessment on accurate, reliable and coherent evidence which contains all the relevant data that must be taken into consideration in appraising a complex situation and whether it is capable of substantiating the conclusions drawn from it"* (*see* Case T-201/04 *Microsoft v Commission* (*"Microsoft Judgment 2007"*) [2007] ECR II-3601, para. 482 and Case T-301/04 *Clearstream v Commission* [2009] ECR II-3155, para. 47). As a result, both Commission precedents and court case law represent a valuable source for identifying the principles of market definition.

[19] Case IV/26.811 *Continental Can Company*, Commission Decision of 9 December 1971, OJ 1972 L 7/25; *Continental Can supra* note 2; Case IV/26.699 *Chiquita*, Commission Decision of 17 December 1975, OJ 1976 L 95/1; *United Brands supra* note 2; Case IV/29.020 *Vitamins*, Commission Decision of 9 June 1976, OJ 1976 L 223/27; *Hoffmann-La Roche supra* note 4.

[20] Case IV/29.491 *Bandengroothandel Frieschebrug/Nederlandsche Banden-Industrie Michelin*, Commission Decision of 7 October 1981, OJ 1981 L 353/33; Case 322/81 *Nederlandsche Banden Industrie Michelin v Commission* (*"Michelin I"*) [1983] ECR 3461.

1. – Market Definition
Nicolas Gauss and Alison Oldale

Notwithstanding the difficulty of defining the market at current, rather than **1.8**
competitive prices, the market definition exercise remains worthwhile for two
principle reasons:

- First, the exercise does provide information about the market at competitive prices; products which are excluded from the market at current
  prices will also be excluded from the market at competitive ones.[21]
- Secondly, the market definition exercise at current prices can provide
  valuable information about the rationality and/or likely effects of the
  alleged conduct. Take the example of alleged anticompetitive bundling.
  The theory of harm would be based on the idea that a firm is refusing
  to supply a product for which there are few good substitutes unless
  customers also buy another of its products which is competitively supplied. In order to assess the likely effects of this conduct, what matters
  are the alternatives that customers have at prevailing prices, not the
  alternatives they would have had at competitive ones. The economic
  methods that are commonly used to define the market in merger proceedings are well designed to identify the extent of these alternatives.

In other words, while the legal purpose of market definition is clearly related **1.9**
to establishing dominance, the economic methods for defining the market
that have become established in merger control could in some cases also be
used to assess the likely effects of any conduct by the dominant company.

In order to determine the market position of companies, it is necessary to **1.10**
determine where, when, and in relation to which products/services companies compete. To answer these questions, it is necessary to define the
market according to the relevant product (service) in question (Section II),
geographically (Section III) and, if necessary, temporally (Section IV).

II. Defining the Relevant Product Market

The definition of the relevant market usually starts with selecting a fairly **1.11**
homogenous product or service group and continues with determining if
there are products (or services) that are substitutable with this product or service group, and therefore belong to the same product market. According to

---

[21] *Discussion Paper supra* note 10, para. 16.

1. – Market Definition
Nicolas Gauss and Alison Oldale

the Commission's *Market Definition Notice*, the relevant product market comprises all those products and services *"which are regarded as interchangeable or substitutable by the consumer, by reason of the products' characteristics, their prices and their intended use."*[22] The courts traditionally define the market as comprising those products whose characteristics make them particularly apt to satisfy a constant need, and which are only to a limited extent interchangeable with other products.[23] Both these definitions focus on identifying substitutable products, *i.e.*, products that impose a competitive constraint on the company whose behaviour is being analysed.[24] While substitutability is often reciprocal, it can also be one-way: product A may be a substitute for product B without product B being a substitute for product A. In this situation, product A and B belong to different markets.[25] To assess substitutability and thus the scope of the relevant product market, the Commission relies on two types of competitive constraints: "demand-side substitutability" and "supply-side substitutability".[26] Demand-side substitutability will be examined first since it is the primary tool to define the relevant product market (Section II.1), subsequently, supply-side substitutability will be assessed (Section II.2).

1. Demand-side Substitutability

1.1. Introduction

1.12   Demand-side substitutability refers to the ability of a sufficient number of consumers to switch their consumption to alternative products[27] in case of a small change in relative prices.[28] In practice, demand-side substitutability

---

[22] *Market Definition Notice supra* note 1, para. 7.

[23] *Continental Can supra* note 2, para. 32; *Michelin I supra* note 20, para. 37; Case T-30/89 *Hilti v Commission* ("*Hilti*") [1991] ECR II-1439, para. 64; Case T-301/04 *supra* note 18, para. 48.

[24] R. O'Donoghue and A. J. Padilla, *supra* note 5, p. 69.

[25] This was illustrated in two Article 102 TFEU decisions. In *Microsoft Decision 2004 supra* note 8, para. 415, the Commission concluded that while media players with a streaming function were substitutes for media players without this functionality, substitution the other way around was not readily available. In *Wanadoo*, the Commission noted that although some form of substitutability existed between high-speed and low-speed Internet access, it was extremely asymmetrical, given the value attached by users to the features of high-speed access *see* Case COMP/38.233 *Wanadoo*, Commission Decision of 16 July 2003, not yet published, para. 194 (confirmed in Case T-340/03 *supra* note 4, paras 88–91).

[26] *Market Definition Notice supra* note 1, paras 13–14.

[27] In the following, references to "products" also comprise references to services.

[28] *See* P. Roth and V. Rose (Eds.), *Bellamy & Child: European Community Law of Competition* (6th Ed., Oxford, Oxford University Press, 2008), p. 259.

1. – Market Definition
Nicolas Gauss and Alison Oldale

is the most effective competitive constraint and hence the most important criterion to define markets. The *Market Definition Notice* states – and the Community courts have confirmed this – that "[from] *an economic point of view, for the definition of the relevant market, demand substitution constitutes the <u>most immediate and effective disciplinary force</u> on the suppliers of a given product, in particular in relation to their pricing decisions"*.[29] The reason is that a company cannot freely influence its product's price if consumers are able to switch to the substitutes of another supplier. Demand-side substitutability is measured using quantitative tests (Section II.1.2) that rely on numerical analyses of variables such as price and demand, and qualitative tests (Section II.1.3) that focus on product attributes. In addition, further types of evidence are used to support or complement these two approaches (Section II.1.4).

1.2. *Quantitative Evidence*

The search for products that are close enough to the product or group of products examined to exercise a competitive constraint on them cannot, without risk of error, solely rely on an intuitive assessment of how "similar" they appear to be. This is why several quantitative tests have been developed to provide a numerically substantiated and more objective approach to market definition. The *Market Definition Notice* formalises the "Small but Significant and Non-transitory Increase in Price" (SSNIP) test,[30] which analyses customers' reactions to changes in the price of the product. Other quantitative tests analyse the reaction of the product's price in response to changes in prices of products outside the candidate market; they include price correlation analysis and stationarity and co-integration analysis (Section II.1.2.2). **1.13**

1.2.1. The SSNIP Test

1.2.1.1. Introduction

The SSNIP test, also known as the hypothetical monopolist test,[31] defines the relevant product market as comprising the products whose price a hypothetical sole seller of these products could durably and profitably increase by a small but **1.14**

---

[29] *Market Definition Notice supra* note 1, para. 13; *see, for instance,* Case T-177/04 *easyJet Airline v Commission* [2006] ECR II-1931, para. 99.

[30] *Market Definition Notice supra* note 1, paras 15 *et seq.*

[31] The hypothetical monopolist test was first formally adopted in the 1992 US Horizontal Merger Guidelines, *see* U.S. Department of Justice & Federal Trade Commission, *Horizontal Merger Guidelines,* August 19, 2010, available at http://www.justice.gov/atr/public/guidelines/hmg-2010.pdf, *see also* A. ten Kate and G. Niels, "The

1. – Market Definition
Nicolas Gauss and Alison Oldale

significant amount, assuming prices outside the market remain constant. In other words, it addresses the question whether the market is "worth monopolising". In practice, the Commission will examine the effect of a 5–10 per cent[32] price increase over the market price[33] of the product or the group of products assessed. The *Market Definition Notice* describes the SSNIP test as "one way" among others to assess demand-side substitution.[34] However, it is debatable whether there actually exists equally satisfying alternatives.[35] In any event, the SSNIP test has conceptually helped to clarify the meaning of substitutability.

1.2.1.2.   SSNIP Methodology

1.15   Market assessment under the hypothetical monopolist test is an iterative process. If a hypothetical sole seller of the product being examined could profitably apply a SSNIP, the relevant product market only comprises this product. If this is not the case – as it usually is not – some substitutes exercise a sufficient competitive constraint on the product. Consequently, other products will have to be added to the candidate market of the seller. This operation is repeated until a candidate market has been found for which a hypothetical sole seller could profitably apply a SSNIP. The question will usually involve selecting a few alternative candidate markets.[36] The group of products satisfying a profitable SSNIP constitutes a market worth monopolising,[37] *i.e.*, the relevant product market in the sense of EU competition law.

1.2.1.3.   Types of data needed

1.16   To apply the SSNIP, three types of data are necessary. First, the seller's margins on each sale. Secondly, the extent to which demand for the product would decrease as a result of a price increase (the product's "own-price elasticity", which measures the effect on demand for a product of a change in

---

Relevant Market: A Concept Still in Search of a Definition" (2008) 5(2) *Journal of Competition Law & Economics*, p. 304.

[32] *Market Definition Notice supra* note 1, para. 17; Case T-340/03 *supra* note 4, para. 87.

[33] *Market Definition Notice supra* note 1, para. 19.

[34] *Ibid.*, para. 15.

[35] *See* S. Bishop and M. Walker, *The Economics of EC Competition Law: Concepts, Application and Measurement* (3rd Ed., London, Sweet & Maxwell, 2010), p. 132, where the authors argue that, not only does the *Market Definition Notice* "[provide] *no indication as to what the alternative to the Hypothetical Monopolist Test might be*", but additionally, "*any statement to the effect that the Hypothetical Monopolist Test is just one example of how to define a relevant market … runs the risk of a return to a process of market definition by ad hoc reference to product characteristics*" (see *supra* note 1).

[36] *Market Definition Notice supra* note 1, para. 25.

[37] *Discussion Paper supra* note 10, para. 14.

1. – Market Definition
Nicolas Gauss and Alison Oldale

that product's price). Thirdly, the extent to which sales lost when the price is increased are recaptured by the other products in the candidate market. In practice, this analysis is often carried out by comparing two figures: the "critical loss" and the "actual loss". The critical loss represents the percentage of lost sales above which a given price increase becomes unprofitable. On the other hand, the actual loss is the actual percentage of lost sales that the hypothetical monopolist would incur as a result of this price increase. If the hypothetical price increase leads to actual losses above the critical loss, the candidate market does not constitute a relevant market and will need to be broadened to include the products that consumers switched to in a reaction to the price increase.[38]

The Commission obtains the necessary data for assessing the seller's margin **1.17** and carrying out a critical loss analysis by asking the seller. Information about the own-price elasticity and the diversion ratio (the diversion ratio from product A to product B measures the proportion of the sales of product A lost due to a price increase of A that are taken over by product B)[39] can come from a number of qualitative and quantitative sources. These include (1) internal documents indicating the products a firm considers to be its closest competitors, (2) customer surveys asking about their likely response to a SSNIP,[40] (3) econometric analyses of price and sales data examining the past response of customers to changes in prices, and (4) consideration of the functional substitutability of different products.

1.2.1.4. Substitutability and marginal customers

It is important to highlight that the question is not whether *all* customers **1.18** would switch, but whether a *sufficient* number of them would do so, so that the loss in sales resulting from the price increase would offset the increased margin for each unit sold. The SSNIP test therefore exclusively focuses

---

[38] For a full description of the critical loss analysis, *see* R. O'Donoghue and A. J. Padilla, *supra* note 5, pp. 79 *et seq.*
[39] J. Faull and A. Nikpay (Eds.), *The EC Law of Competition* (2nd Ed., Oxford, Oxford University Press, 2007), p. 46, para. 1.153.
[40] *See, for instance*, Case COMP/37.860 *Morgan Stanley Dean Witter/Visa*, Commission Decision of 3 October 2007, not yet published, para. 53; Case COMP/38.233 *supra* note 25, para. 199. Markku Stenborg points out that because these interviews tend to focus on the largest customers, they might give too much weight to infra-marginal customers (*see* 1.2.1.4.), thereby falsifying the SSNIP analysis, in M. Stenborg, "Are there biases in the market definition procedure?", ETLA, *Keskusteluaiheita – Discussion Papers*, Paper No. 903, March 2004, p. 12.

1. – Market Definition
Nicolas Gauss and Alison Oldale

on this group of "marginal" customers[41] who might react to a small price increase and, in so doing, constrain the hypothetical monopolist's behaviour. The fact that the remaining, "inframarginal" customers are willing to accept the increase in price is irrelevant.[42] When assessing whether a product serves as a demand or supply-side substitute, what matters is not the inframarginal customers' behaviour, but the reaction of the possibly smaller group of customers whose willingness to pay does not extend to a small but significant and non-transitory increase above the current market price. These marginal customers are the ones who will be able to defeat a SSNIP in case the hypothetical monopolist loses more from switching to substitutes than it would gain by increasing its margins.

1.19   The focus on marginal customers is fundamental and should, in principle, guide the whole market definition process. The purpose of defining the market is to identify the products that exercise the most immediate competitive constraint on the product under examination, since marginal customers could easily switch to them. This highlights the main problem of the traditional approach to market definition that focuses on product characteristics rather than customers' reactions to a small increase in price. Substitutability analyses based on an estimation of whether two products are "similar enough" are not only subject to criticism because they rely on intuition rather than on analysis. More importantly, they are problematic because they focus on "average" customers rather than marginal ones. The question they answer is whether the "average" customer would consider these products interchangeable, whereas what matters is whether there are enough marginal customers to defeat any temptation to increase prices.[43]

1.20   Moreover, this flaw is hardly solved by paying lip service to the SSNIP test instead of identifying the proportion of marginal vs. inframarginal customers, as the Commission has done in several Decisions.[44] In *1998 Football World*

---

[41] Marginal customers are those who generally value the product at the price paid and not much more; *see supra* note 39, para. 1.140.

[42] This was recognised in the *Discussion Paper supra* note 10, para. 18; *see also* T. Klein, "SSNIP-Test oder Bedarfsmarktkonzept?" (2010) 2 *Wirtschaft und Wettbewerb*, pp. 169 and 173.

[43] Some competition authorities, like the German Bundeskartellamt, still mainly focus on the "average" customer's reaction. The Bundeskartellamt mainly relies on the *Bedarfsmarktkonzept*, according to which it is not the substitutability by the marginal customer that matters, but substitutability by the average reasonable customers ("*vernünftiger durchschnittlicher Abnehmer*"). *See* T. Klein, *supra* 42, p. 169.

[44] *See, for instance*, Case IV/31.043 *Tetra Pak I (BTG Licence)* ("*Tetra Pak I Decision 1998*"), Commission Decision of 26 July 1988, OJ 1988 L 272/27, para. 31; *Tetra Pak II Judgment 1994 supra* note 8, para. 68; Cases IV/30.787

1. – Market Definition
Nicolas Gauss and Alison Oldale

Cup, for instance, taking note of the exceptional popularity of football, it concluded that "[members] *of the general public seeking to attend World Cup finals matches are ... unlikely to have considered attendance at international events involving sports other than football as adequate substitutes, whether or not the price of tickets for World Cup football matches was increased by (at least) 10 per cent*".[45] This reasoning does not reflect the hypothetical monopolist test. What it does is to assess the reaction of the "average" customer to a SSNIP – a question which is irrelevant for the SSNIP analysis. To avoid this, a qualitative analysis of substitutability should not address the question whether two products are too different to be interchangeable. Rather, the question should be asked as to whether two products are so different that there would not be enough customers to defeat a SSNIP. While the latter approach can often not be applied in a fully quantitative manner due to a lack of data for a SSNIP, it is possible to apply it conceptually. For example, some information on customers' past reactions to price changes and on average profit margins in the industry might be available, which at least indicates whether a switch of customers is likely.

While looking at the average customer will, in many cases, lead to a narrower **1.21**
market definition, an increased focus on marginal customers will tend to broaden the relevant market. In the event of a SSNIP, the number of marginal customers ready to switch to a given substitute might be high enough to make the price increase unprofitable, even though average customers would not have considered both products to be interchangeable. Only in rare circumstances could this lead to further narrowing of the market.[46]

---

and 31.488 *Eurofix-Bauco/Hilti*, Commission Decision of 22 December 1987, OJ 1988 L 65/19, para. 63; Case IV/36.888 *1998 Football World Cup*, Commission Decision of 20 July 1999, OJ 2000 L 5/55, para. 68.a.

[45] *See* Case IV/36.888 *supra* note 44, para. 68.a.

[46] Take, for instance, two types of raw material (A and B) that are similarly priced and considered interchangeable by 80 per cent of users, while 20 per cent of users need a characteristic that is specific to type A. The result of a qualitative analysis, focusing on the needs of the average user, would be to include types A and B in the same market. Let's imagine now that a hypothetical sole producer of type A decides to increase the price of type A by 10 per cent. As a result, 80 per cent of users will surely switch to type B, but 20 per cent will have no choice but to stick to type A and accept the price increase. If the initial number of users of type A is N, the initial margin per unit of type A is m and the initial price of a unit of type A is p, the producer will lose 80 per cent * N * m and gain 20 per cent * N *10 per cent * p. A quick calculation shows that if m<0.025*p (margin below 2.5 per cent, which is very low), the producer would actually gain by applying a SSNIP, indicating that the relevant market should only comprise type A.

1. – Market Definition
Nicolas Gauss and Alison Oldale

1.2.1.5. Limits of the SSNIP test

1.22 Despite its more objective approach, the SSNIP test is not without flaws. The major shortcoming of the test in the context of abuse cases is the risk of the "cellophane fallacy" (*see* introduction), which is caused if the reference for the SSNIP – the current price – is above the competitive level. This problem regularly arises in cases of dominance, and is susceptible to affect all quantitative and qualitative evidence examined in that context. It is important to point out that choosing the current price as the reference price for the SSNIP has very different implications depending on whether the market is being defined in the context of merger control or of Article 102 TFEU.

1.23 In merger cases, the objective of the competitive analysis is to determine whether the concentration might significantly impede competition on the market (Article 2 of the Merger Regulation).[47] To answer this, the Commission assesses whether the companies under examination will, as a result of their merger, be able to eliminate some of the constraints that currently discipline their behaviour. The analysis is forward-looking; it compares the competitive constraints that exist at the current, pre-merger price, with the likely post-merger conditions. It is therefore appropriate to identify these competitive constraints within a market comprising the demand-side substitutes at the *current* price.[48] Contrary to that, in Article 102 TFEU cases, the main purpose of market definition is to assess whether a firm is dominant, *i.e.,* is able to exercise market power. However, this assessment can be distorted if the reference used for the SSNIP test is the *prevailing* price of the product, which a dominant firm is likely to set above the competitive level.[49] This is because the elasticity of demand, *i.e.,* customers' sensitivity to the price, increases with the product's price. Customers who would have tolerated a small price increase might indeed start switching to other products if the price continues to rise. The SSNIP method applied to a supra-competitive price might thus result in the identification of an artificially broad product market, which comprises demand-side substitutes that would not have been included had the reference price been set at a competitive level. As a result, a firm under examination might wrongly be found not to be dominant. This is the so-called "cellophane

---

[47] Council Regulation (EC) 139/2004 of 20 January 2004 on the control of concentrations between undertakings ("*EC Merger Regulation*"), OJ 2004 L 24/1.

[48] Based on National Economic Research Associates, *The Role of Market Definition in Monopoly and Dominance Inquiries, supra* note 5, para. 2.26.

[49] This problem is recognised in the *Market Definition Notice supra* note 1 para. 19.

1. – Market Definition
Nicolas Gauss and Alison Oldale

fallacy", named after a US Supreme Court decision on the then-dominant supplier of cellophane, where the Court overlooked the issue.[50]

The cellophane fallacy cannot be easily avoided, since reconstructing the non-existent competitive price usually evokes considerable difficulties. In addition, the SSNIP test requires information on the demand curve at the competitive price, which is equally difficult to obtain. This is why the Commission's *Discussion Paper* recognised that the SSNIP test *"is rather difficult to apply in practice"* in Article 102 TFEU cases.[51] In its *AstraZeneca* Decision, the Commission rejected the defendant's SSNIP study in part because it failed to take due account of the cellophane fallacy.[52] As a consequence, applying the SSNIP test is likely to be insufficient to properly define an antitrust market in Article 102 TFEU cases.[53] This is reflected in the Commission's practice.[54] While the SSNIP test constitutes a central part of the Commission's approach to market definition in merger cases,[55] it is much less frequently applied in abuse of dominance cases. **1.24**

Another flaw of the SSNIP test – relevant to both merger control and abuse of dominance – is its fallacy in all instances where the product's characteristics are more important to consumers than the price.[56] The functionality of **1.25**

---

[50] *See United States v E.I Du Pont De Nemours*, 351 US 377 (1956), where the Supreme Court wrongly considered that cellophane was part of a wider packaging market without taking account of the fact that the price set by DuPont was largely above the competitive level.

[51] *Discussion Paper supra* note 10, para. 16. However, when a market is defined for assessing whether there has been an abuse on a separate market (*e.g.*, in the case of leveraging) and that second market is not dominated, then the SSNIP test may be more readily applicable (*Discussion Paper supra* note 10, para. 17).

[52] Case COMP/37.507 *Generics/Astra Zeneca*, Commission Decision of 15 June 2005, not yet published, para. 466; *see also* Cases COMP/34.579 *MasterCard*, COMP/36.518 *EuroCommerce*, COMP/38.580 *Commercial Cards*, Commission Decision of 19 December 2007, not yet reported, paras 286–7.

[53] *Discussion Paper supra* note 10, para. 13.

[54] *See, for instance*, Case COMP/38.233 *supra* note 25, paras 175, 199–201, where the Commission based the market definition on quantitative and qualitative evidence.

[55] *Discussion Paper supra* note 10, para. 16.

[56] *See, for instance*, Case T-25/99 *Colin Arthur Roberts and Valérie Ann Roberts v Commission* [2001] ECR II-1881, para. 40, where the Court of First Instance confirmed the Commission's finding that the choice between consuming beer in a pub or in a club was more dependent on the "environment and atmosphere" of these establishments than on the price charged for the beer. For examples of product characteristics taken into account in defining markets in merger cases, *see* Case IV/M.430 *Procter & Gamble/VP Schickedanz (II)*, Commission Decision of 21 June 1994, where the Commission identified distinct markets for two kinds of feminine protection products, tampons and sanitary towels (pads), thus rejecting the contention of Procter & Gamble that these products together constituted a single market; Case COMP/M.2187 *CVC/Lenzing*, Commission Decision of 17 October 2001, where the Commission found that viscose staple fibres constituted a separate product market because of its very specific characteristics, distinguishing it from any other fibre (para. 33); Case COMP/M.2706 *Carnival*

1. – Market Definition
Nicolas Gauss and Alison Oldale

a product, its design or its image can be of higher importance to consumers than a small price difference with a comparable product.[57] While product characteristics are indirectly taken into account in the SSNIP test – they influence the customers' readiness to switch to substitutes in case of price increases – the sole variable the SSNIP test measures is the constraining character of the price. This is particularly problematic in the case of dynamic markets (*see* Section V.4).

1.26 Finally, it must be noted that the SSNIP test ignores the reaction of competitors to a SSNIP on the products concerned. On the contrary, it relies on the (unrealistic) assumption that the prices of the substitutes would remain constant. This neglects that competitive success, such as implementing a profitable SSNIP, depends on strategic interaction, in which an individual's success in making choices depends on the choices of others.

1.2.1.6.   Practical relevance of the SSNIP test

1.27 The SSNIP test provides a coherent analytical tool to assess the size of the market, and has therefore gained widespread acceptance among competition authorities throughout the world and in the European Union. Its applicability, however, appears to be restrained by the considerable amount of data required and by its tendency to produce misleading results in case of the cellophane fallacy under Article 102 TFEU. Nevertheless, this should not be a reason for discarding the test. Its most important contribution is arguably more conceptual than quantitative,[58] as it tends to encourage a less judgmental and more evidence-based approach to market definition. Even when it cannot be applied in its "pure" quantitative form, it remains possible to assess the likely effect of a SSNIP by relying on other evidence. For instance, the

---

Corporation/P&O Princess, Commission Decision of 24 July 2002, where the Commission determined that oceanic cruises constituted a separate market distinct from other (land-based) holidays; Case COMP/M.2978 *Lagardère/Natexis/VUP*, Commission Decision of 7 January 2004, where the Commission identified distinct markets for different types and genres of books and different types of resellers.

[57] For example, in merger proceedings in the commercial beverage sector, the Commission identified a market limited to cola-flavoured beverages, *inter alia* because of the allegedly distinctive image, taste, and brand perception of these beverages (Case IV/M.794 *Coca-Cola Enterprises/Amalgamated Beverages GB*, Commission Decision of 22 January 1997, paras 26 *et seq*; Case IV/M.190 *Nestlé/Perrier*, Commission Decision of 22 July 1992, paras 11–12, where the Commission distinguished between soft drinks and bottled mineral water; Case IV/M.289 *PepsiCo/KAS*, Commission Decision of 21 December 1992, where the Commission examined different soft drink flavours; Case COMP/M.3130 *Arla Foods/Express Dairies*, Commission Decision of 10 June 2003, para. 19, where the Commission distinguished fresh and long-life flavoured milks, *inter alia*, due to their different flavours.

[58] *See supra* note 39, p. 44, para. 1.147.

1. – Market Definition
Nicolas Gauss and Alison Oldale

fact that the product examined only represents a small part of the cost of the overall product being purchased makes it unlikely that a small increase in its price will have a material impact on demand.[59] Similarly, if a product has particularly unique characteristics, substitution is unlikely to occur in response to a small price increase. In its *1998 Football World Cup* Decision, the Commission thus concluded that it was unlikely that tickets to other tournaments would be considered as substitutes for World Cup final tickets in the event of a SSNIP.[60] The Commission applied the SSNIP test in the *Wanadoo* Decision, where it undertook an analysis of demand elasticity (as measured by customer surveys) and seller's margins to support its finding that low-speed Internet access was not a substitute for high-speed access.[61]

1.2.2. Other Quantitative Tests

1.2.2.1. Own- and cross-price elasticity

"Own-price elasticity" measures the impact of changes in a given product's **1.28** price on demand for this product. While it can be used within the framework of a SSNIP analysis, it can also be used autonomously. Whereas high own-price elasticity tends to indicate that a product is subject to competitive constraints from other products, low own-price elasticity supports a finding that the product, or group of products, constitutes a single relevant market.[62] "Cross-price elasticity", on the other hand, measures the impact of changes in the price of a product on demand for *another* product. Unlike own-price elasticity, it does not provide direct input into a SSNIP analysis. However, it remains a useful indicator of the existence and extent of the competitive relationship between products.[63] In the *Chiquita* (later *United Brands*) case, the Commission partly based its conclusion that bananas formed a single relevant market on the lack of cross-price elasticity between them and other fruit.[64] More recently, in the *AstraZeneca* Decision, the Commission closely examined

---

[59] *Tetra Pak I Decision 1998 supra* note 44, paras 31–32, later confirmed in *Tetra Pak II Judgment* 1994 *supra* note 8, para. 68; *see also* Cases IV/30.787 and 31.488 *supra* note 44, para. 63.

[60] Case IV/36.888 *supra* note 44, paras 66 *et seq.*

[61] Case COMP/38.233 *supra* note 25, paras 199–201, confirmed in Case T-340/03 *supra* note 4, paras 86–91.

[62] Case IV/M.619 *Gencor/Lonrho*, Commission Decision of 24 April 1996, paras 42–43, confirmed in Case T-102/96 *Gencor v Commission* [1999] ECR II-753.

[63] As such, it can be used to determine which products to include in the candidate markets iteratively examined in the context of a SSNIP analysis.

[64] Case IV/26.699 *supra* note 19, under II.A.2, confirmed in *United Brands supra* note 2, para. 32.

1. – Market Definition
Nicolas Gauss and Alison Oldale

the cross-price elasticity analyses submitted by the parties to support its conclusion that two medicines did not belong to the same product market.[65]

1.2.2.2.   Analysis of price correlations, stationarity and co-integration

1.29   Measures of price correlation, stationarity and co-integration all concern the extent to which the prices of two different products are related to each other.

- The basic idea underlying correlation analysis[66] is that the prices of substitute products will move together. If the price of one of them falls (for example, because the cost of making it falls), then the price of the other one will fall as well, since otherwise the supplier of the second product will lose substantial business. The correlation between two prices measures the extent of this co-movement.

- Stationarity analysis of two price series usually considers whether the ratio of the two prices reverts towards a constant value over time. The idea here is that, if two products are in the same market, their relative prices cannot diverge for long, and if one of them is subject to a shock for some reason, the effects on relative prices will dissipate over time.

- Co-integration analysis is very similar to stationarity analysis. It examines whether the linear relationship between two prices reverts to a constant value over time, so that any departures are only temporary.

1.30   Correlation analysis has two well-known limitations. First, the correlation between two prices can be high because both are affected by a common factor such as the exchange rate (if both are made using imported inputs), inflation, or because both use a common raw material, rather than because their demands are linked. This is known as the problem of spurious correlation.[67] The second limitation is that there are often no clear benchmarks for deciding whether a particular level of correlation is high enough that the two products should be included in the same market. In some cases this second problem

---

[65] Case COMP/37.507 *supra* note 52, paras 366, 406, 465, 475.
[66] *See Market Definition Notice supra* note 1, para. 39.
[67] *See, for instance*, Case COMP/M.4734 *Ineos/Kerling*, Commission Decision of 30 January 2008, where a price correlation study submitted by the parties was rejected by the Commission because it failed to control for common cost factors (raw material costs, energy costs etc.).

1. – Market Definition
Nicolas Gauss and Alison Oldale

can be addressed using as a benchmark the correlation between two other products that are *known* to belong to the same market. However this is not always conclusive, and there may be no products for which there is agreement that they belong in the market. Moreover, a high correlation between prices could also simply be a consequence of the fact that competitors tend to follow the prices set by one firm, rather than an indicator that they exercise competitive constraints between themselves.[68]

1.31 Stationarity and co-integration analyses are less prone to spurious results as both control for common costs to some extent. In *Anglo American Corporation/Lonrho*, a co-integration analysis of the prices of platinum, gold, silver, rhodium and palladium revealed a lack of long-run relationships between the prices of these various metals, and showed that a price correlation which had been identified was in fact spurious. Each metal was thus found to constitute a separate market.[69]

1.32 The Commission has also noted that stationarity and co-integration analysis can be used as a robustness check on each other. In *Arjowiggins/M-Real Zanders Reflex*, the Commission noted that, particularly for geographic market definition, stationarity analysis should be supplemented by co-integration if relative prices were found to be stationary in relation to a particular country, suggesting a wide geographic market.[70]

1.33 However stationarity and co-integration analyses still suffer from the lack of a benchmark for deciding whether the relationship between two prices is so high that they indicate the products are in the same market. For all these reasons, the Commission is quite cautious with the results of such analyses, and has stated that they should rather be used as a supplement to traditional market definition tools.[71] While correlation and stationary analysis do not appear to have been used to this date in the context of Article 102 TFEU decisions, the Commission has relied on them in several merger cases.[72]

---

[68] A. Amelio and D. Donath, "Market Definition in Recent EC Merger Investigations: The Role of Empirical Analysis" (2009) *Concurrences,* No. 3-2009, p. 4, n. 17.

[69] *See* Case IV/M.754 *Anglo American Corporation/Lonrho*, Commission Decision of 23 April 1997; *see also* Case COMP/M.2187 *supra* note 56, para. 109, n. 83.

[70] Case COMP/M.4513 *Arjowiggins/M-Real Zanders Reflex*, Commission Decision of 4 June 2008, Annex I, para. 16.

[71] Case COMP/M.2187 *supra* note 56, para. 113.

[72] *See, among others, supra* note 70, paras 54–55, 68–72; Case COMP/M.3687 *Johnson & Johnson/Guidant*, Commission Decision of 25 August 2005, para. 17; Case IV/M.190 *supra* note 57, para. 16.

1. – Market Definition
Nicolas Gauss and Alison Oldale

1.3. Qualitative Evidence

1.3.1. Definition

1.34   According to the *Market Definition Notice*, "*all* [products] *which are regarded as interchangeable or substitutable by the consumer, by reason of the*[ir] *characteristics, their prices and their intended use*" belong to the same product market.[73] The analysis of product characteristics and intended use has played a crucial role in most of the major Article 102 TFEU decisions and judgments. For instance, in the seminal *United Brands* case, both the Commission and the Court of Justice concluded that bananas were in a relevant market separate from other fruit because, among other factors, their seedlessness, softness and ease of handling made them particularly appealing to the very young, the sick and the elderly.[74] As the Community judges put it in a more recent Decision, "[it] *is apparent from the case law that, in order to be considered a sufficiently distinct market, it must be possible to distinguish the service or the goods in question by virtue of particular characteristics that so differentiate them from other services or other goods that it is only to a small degree interchangeable with those alternatives and affected by competition from them*".[75]

1.3.2.   Practical Relevance of Qualitative Evidence

1.35   The Commission acknowledges that although the analysis of product characteristics, price, and intended use may allow it, as a first step, to limit the field of possible substitutes, it should not suffice to show whether two products are demand substitutes.[76] Despite the above-described introduction of quantitative techniques, qualitative analysis remains essential for market definition in recent Article 102 TFEU decisions. A qualitative analysis was, for instance, carried out in the *Microsoft* Decision, when streaming media players where distinguished from media players without a streaming function based on the fact that streaming media players offered the consumer more functionalities such as news broadcast.[77] In the *Wanadoo* Decision, the Commission concluded that high-speed and low-speed Internet access constituted two different markets, relying, among other factors, on the inconvenience of using

---

[73] *Market Definition Notice supra* note 1 para. 7.

[74] *United Brands supra* note 2, para. 31 and Case IV/26.699 *supra* note 19, under II.A.2.

[75] Case T-86/95 *Compagnie générale maritime and others v Commission* [2002] ECR II-1011, para. 48.

[76] *Market Definition Notice supra* note 1, para. 36.

[77] *Microsoft Decision 2004 supra* note 8, paras 414 *et seq.*, partially confirmed and partially annulled (on other grounds) in *Microsoft Judgment 2007 supra* note 18.

1. – Market Definition
Nicolas Gauss and Alison Oldale

certain functions such as network gaming and video downloading with a low-speed Internet access.[78] In *Michelin II*, the Commission similarly relied on the different specific characteristics and use of new tyres and retreads to conclude that they were not really substitutable, and thus, belonged to different markets.[79]

1.3.3. Price Differences

Likewise, absolute price differences between the prices of products can be an indication that consumers do not regard them as substitutes. In *Wanadoo*, the Commission noted that the price ratio of at least one-to-two between low-speed and high-speed Internet access could be taken as a basis for defining two separate product markets.[80] In the *Intel* Decision, the significantly different prices of central processing units for desktop computers, laptops, and servers supported the conclusion that they could not be regarded as demand-side substitutes.[81] However, the Commission has also held that the analysis of absolute price differences was not sufficient for market definition purposes, insofar as only the effect of changes in relative prices (for instance, of a SSNIP) can provide a correct measure of substitutability.[82]

1.36

1.3.4. Competitive Conditions and Structure of Supply and Demand

The Community courts have repeatedly emphasised that "*an examination limited to the objective characteristics only of the relevant products cannot be sufficient: the competitive conditions and the structure of supply and demand on the market must also be taken into consideration*" (emphasis added).[83] The "competitive conditions of the market" have been found to include a wide range of factors, ranging from consumer habits and preferences to switching costs and differences in quality (they are described below in section (III.2.2)).[84] This led the Court of Justice to hold in *Michelin I* that, regardless of their shared characteristics,

1.37

---

[78] Case COMP/38.233 *supra* note 25, para. 175, confirmed in Case T-340/03 *supra* note 4, para. 82.

[79] Case COMP/36.041 *Michelin*, Commission Decision of 20 June 2001, OJ 2002 L 143/1, paras 116–118, upheld in Case T-203/01 *Manufacture française des pneumatiques Michelin v Commission* ("*Michelin II*") [2003] ECR II-4071.

[80] Case COMP/38.233 *supra* note 25, not yet published, paras 188–92, confirmed in Case T-340/03 *supra* note 4, para. 85.

[81] Case COMP/37.990 *Intel*, Commission Decision of 13 May 2009, not yet published, para. 799.

[82] Case COMP/37.507 *supra* note 52, para. 344.

[83] *Michelin I supra* note 20, para. 37; *see also Tetra Pak II Judgment* 1994 *supra* note 8, para. 63; *supra* note 75, para. 48; *British Airways Judgment* 2003 *supra* note 2, para. 91; Case T-340/03 *supra* note 4, para. 78.

[84] *See, for instance, Tetra Pak II Judgment 1996 supra* note 8, para. 19, and Case COMP/37.507 *supra* note 52, para. 370.

1. – Market Definition
Nicolas Gauss and Alison Oldale

tyres for new vehicles and replacement tyres belonged to different markets, because tyres for new vehicles were directly ordered by vehicle manufacturers and thus subject to very different competitive factors.[85] Interestingly, this reasoning may also lead to a finding that products that are not technically interchangeable, but are nevertheless subject to similar conditions of competition, belong to the same market. For instance, the Commission frequently noted that there is a separate market comprising all retailers selling the range of food and non-food products that customers expect to find in a supermarket environment. Although the different products in this "basket of daily consumer goods" are not interchangeable, supermarkets offer customers a global "one-stop shopping" service that should be the relevant unit for a competitive analysis.[86]

1.4. *Additional Types of Evidence*

1.38 Numerous forms of evidence can be used to either support the described quantitative and qualitative tests or serve as independent indicators of what the relevant market might be. Market definition is not an abstract process; the type of evidence that can be relied on depends on the specificities of the industry examined.[87] For this reason, the list below does not purport to be exhaustive, but to indicate some types of evidence that are frequently used.

1.4.1. Revealed Preferences

1.39 Past shocks or events can provide direct evidence of what products consumers consider interchangeable. A change in the relative prices of two products, due for example to an increase in the price of a component of one of the products, may translate into material switching to a substitute. Similarly,

---

[85] *Michelin I supra* note 20, para. 38; *see also Tetra Pak II Judgment 1996 supra* note 8, para. 13, where the Court of Justice upheld the Commission's conclusion that, because the majority of packaging cartons were used for milk, it was not necessary to carry out a separate substitutability analysis for other beverages.

[86] *See* Case IV/M.784 *Kesko/Tuko*, Commission Decision of 20 November 1996, paras 18–20; Case IV/M.1221 *Rewe/Meinl*, Commission Decision of 3 February 1999, paras 10, 76; for similar reasoning in the case of distributors of building materials, *see* Case COMP/M.3184 *Wolseley/Pinault Bois & Matériaux*, Commission Decision of 3 July 2003, para. 10. It is useful to note, however, that while a range of products may belong to the same relevant market at the downstream level, the same may no longer be the case when the upstream (*i.e.*, "demand" or "procurement") market is examined. Indeed, the producers' frequent lack of ability to switch to other channels of distribution or to the production of another output suggest that market definition at the upstream level should be broken down by product category; *see, for instance,* COMP/M.3184 *Wolseley/Pinault Bois & Matériaux*, paras 76–81.

[87] *Market Definition Notice supra* note 1, para. 25.

1. – Market Definition
Nicolas Gauss and Alison Oldale

a sudden important decrease in the supply of a product may cause custom-ers to switch to other products. The launch of a new product or brand can also provide useful information when it is possible to identify the products from which it won shares of sales. Such objective evidence, if of sufficient quality, can be fundamental for market definition.[88] However, evidence of past switching events is only relevant if it reflects current market conditions. Many factors may have changed in the meantime, for instance, in terms of consumer preferences or competitive landscape; this is why the *Market Definition Notice* focuses on "recent" events or shocks.[89]

1.4.2. Consumer Preferences and Perceptions

Depending on consumer perceptions, products, which might be functional **1.40** substitutes, may nevertheless belong to different relevant markets. In the *Nestlé/Perrier* Decision, the Commission first noted that bottled source water and soft drinks could be seen as substitutes due to their common function of quenching thirst, but then went on to a detailed review of additional fac-tors, including the reasons why some consumers valued bottled water above tap water, and eventually concluded that they belonged to different product markets.[90] A similar conclusion was reached in the *Yves Saint Laurent* Decision, where it was held that the mainstream equivalents of luxury products, despite being functionally comparable, did not enjoy the same *"aura of exclusivity and prestige"* for consumers.[91]

1.4.3. Barriers and Costs Associated with Switching

Two products that, upon first examination, look like they are close enough **1.41** substitutes to belong to the same relevant market, might belong to separate markets if the costs of switching, or other barriers to switching, are too high for a sufficient number of customers.[92] These barriers can be of many dif-ferent types, whether external (such as regulatory constraints) or internal (learning costs, sunk costs etc.). The Commission heavily relied on switch-ing costs to delineate markets for broadband Internet access in its *Telefónica*

---

[88] *Market Definition Notice supra* note 1, para. 38.
[89] *Ibid.*
[90] Case IV/M.190 *supra* note 57, para. 19.
[91] Case IV/33.242 *Yves Saint Laurent Parfums*, Commission Decision of 16 December 1991, OJ 1992 L 12/24, under II.A.5.
[92] *Market Definition Notice supra* note 1, para. 42.

1. – Market Definition
Nicolas Gauss and Alison Oldale

Decision.[93] The Commission noted that Internet providers were unlikely to start deploying local networks for the sole purpose of avoiding an increase in regional wholesale prices, as this would entail extremely high investments. As a result, local and regional wholesale offers were found to belong to different markets.[94]

1.4.4.   Price Discrimination

1.42   When a distinct group of customers for a product can be subject to price discrimination (*i.e.*, it is possible to charge the customers belonging to this group a different price than that charged to other customers buying the same product), this may be an indication that a narrow relevant market exists for this customer group.[95] Price discrimination occurs in a multitude of markets. The *Market Definition Notice* identifies the two cumulative factors that usually point to the existence of a distinct market: it must be possible to identify clearly which group an individual customer belongs to, and trade among customers or arbitrage by third parties ought not to be feasible. In *Microsoft*, it was held that Microsoft's discrimination between different customer demands by charging significantly different prices for its different versions of the Windows server operating system confirmed the absence of demand-side substitutability and the existence of a separate market for work group server operating systems.[96]

1.4.5.   Patterns of Demand

1.43   A stable demand for a product over a long period of time can serve as a good indication that this product belongs to a distinct market. In the *Tetra Pak II* case, for instance, the Court of Justice upheld the Opinion of the Court of First Instance that the stability of the market share for carton UHT-milk packaging was a valid criterion to assess whether it was really interchangeable with non-carton packaging.[97] Evidence that very few customers currently switch between two products may similarly suggest that they belong to different markets.[98] Finally, order and bidding patterns may help to identify which

---

[93] Case COMP/38.784 *Telefónica S.S. (broadband)* ("*Telefónica*"), Commission Decision of 4 July 2007, not yet published, paras 163, 172–4, 185, 200.

[94] *Ibid.*, paras 163–66.

[95] *Market Definition Notice supra* note 1, para. 43.

[96] *Microsoft Judgment 2007 supra* note 18, paras 516–23 and *Microsoft Decision 2004 supra* note 8, paras 369–82.

[97] *Tetra Pak II Judgment 1996 supra* note 8, para. 15; *see also* Joined Cases T-191 and 212 to 214/98 *Atlantic Container Line and others v Commission* ("*TACA Judgment 2003*") [2003] ECR II-3275, para. 799.

[98] *TACA Judgment 2003 supra* note 97, paras 800 *et seq.*

1. – Market Definition
Nicolas Gauss and Alison Oldale

products are considered as substitutes by the customers placing the orders or sending the invitations to tender.[99]

1.4.6. Surveys and Internal Documents

The Commission often consults the main customers and competitors of the companies examined to gather information that is needed for its analysis of the scope of the market.[100] Internal documents from the companies under examination, such as evidence of what products they consider as exercising a competitive constraint or how they analyse consumer demand, may also provide useful information. These documents can be of many types (marketing studies, business plans, contracts).[101] The Commission will be more cautious when dealing with documents that were produced by the undertakings whose behaviour is scrutinised or by their competitors for the purpose of the case being examined, rather than in the normal course of business.[102]

1.44

2. Supply-side Substitutability

2.1. Definition

Unlike demand-side substitutability, which examines whether *customers* consider two products as close enough substitutes, supply-side substitutability examines the competitive constraints exercised by other *suppliers*. It measures the latter's ability to switch production to the products under consideration and market them in the short term without incurring significant additional costs or risks, in response to small and permanent changes in relative prices,[103] *i.e.*, a SSNIP[104] test.

1.45

---

[99] Case COMP/M.3178 *Bertelsmann/Springer/JV*, Commission Decision of 3 May 2005, paras 40–44; Case COMP/M.3216 *Oracle/Peoplesoft*, Commission Decision of 26 October 2004, paras 22–26.

[100] *Market Definition Notice supra* note 1, para. 40; *see also* Case COMP/37.860 *supra* note 40; Case COMP/38.233 *supra* note 25; Case COMP/M.4824 *Kraft/Danone Biscuits*, Commission Decision of 9 November 2007, paras 21–22; and Case COMP/M.4187 *Metso/Aker Kvaerner*, Commission Decision of 12 December 2006, paras 57–58.

[101] Case COMP/37.859 *De Post-La Poste*, Commission Decision of 5 December 2001, OJ 2002 L 61/32, paras 41–42; Case IV/32.279 *BBI/Boosey and Hawkes*, Commission Decision of 29 July 1987, OJ 1987 L 286/36, para. 17; Case C-62/86 *AKZO Chemie v Commission* ("*AKZO*") [1991] ECR I-3359, para. 53.

[102] *Market Definition Notice supra* note 1, para. 41.

[103] *Market Definition Notice supra* note 1, para. 20; *Microsoft Judgment 2007 supra* note 18, para. 484.

[104] On the SSNIP test, *see* section II.1.2.1.

1. – Market Definition
Nicolas Gauss and Alison Oldale

1.46   Two products that are supply-side substitutes may thus belong to the same relevant product market without being demand-side substitutes. Supply-side substitutability will typically be relevant when companies market a wide range of different qualities or grades of a product. Although these products might not be perceived as substitutes by the consumer, they are produced on similar equipment and most of the suppliers are able to start selling all qualities at short notice.[105] The *Market Definition Notice* provides a practical example regarding the production of paper: although different qualities of paper may not be substitutes from the perspective of demand, paper plants can easily switch their production from one quality to another, meaning that all qualities would be included in the same relevant product market.[106] In similar fashion, the Court of First Instance in *Kish Glass* upheld the Commission's finding that, due to the ease of switching from the production of glass of a certain thickness to glass of another thickness, the relevant market was the sale of glass of all thicknesses.[107]

2.2. Conditions for Testing Supply-side Substitutability

1.47   The assessment of the competitive constraints posed by supply-side substitutability is subject to strict conditions. The *Market Definition Notice* restrains its use to those situations *"in which its effects are equivalent to those of demand substitution in terms of demand or immediacy"*.[108] This is only ensured if the following conditions are met.

2.2.1. Absence of Sunk Costs and Major Barriers to Switching

1.48   The assets needed for the production and marketing of the product in question have to be accessible without incurring sunk costs[109] or facing major barriers to switching. There are numerous potential costs incurred when switching production to a different product, *e.g.*, changes of manufacturing equipment, training of staff, launching marketing campaigns or finding

---

[105] *Market Definition Notice supra* note 1, paras 20–21 and the practical example given in para. 23 in the field of paper production.

[106] *Market Definition Notice supra* note 1, para. 22.

[107] Case T-65/96 *Kish Glass v Commission* ("*Kish Glass Judgment 2000*") [2000] ECR II-1885, paras 68–69; appeal dismissed on other grounds in Case C-241/00 P *Kish Glass v Commission* ("*Kish Glass Judgment 2001*") [2001] ECR I-7759.

[108] *Market Definition Notice supra* note 1, para. 20, quoted in Case T-301/04 *supra* note 18, para. 50.

[109] Sunk costs are the fixed costs (*i.e.*, costs that are incurred independent of the activities of the business) that will not be recovered in the case that a company stops its activities.

1. – Market Definition
Nicolas Gauss and Alison Oldale

appropriate distribution channels. Other barriers can also consist in regulatory or technological constraints.[110]

2.2.2. Immediate Substitutability

1.49 For supply-side substitution to act as a competitive constraint, switching production must be possible quickly. Otherwise, the competitive constraint will just amount to potential competition (*see* Section II.2.4 below). The *Market Definition Notice* does not provide a benchmark for "how quickly" the switch would have to occur;[111] and while case law and literature often speak of a one-year period, there are no indications that this is a set rule.[112]

2.2.3. Economic Incentives to Switch Production

1.50 The fact that switching production is possible at low costs and immediately is not sufficient for supply-side substitution. It is necessary that the opportunity costs[113] associated with giving up production and supply of other products – if the producer does not have spare capacity – are not so large that they render the switch unprofitable.[114]

2.2.4. Demand-side Substitutability

1.51 In order to determine whether supply-side substitutability suffices to discipline a company's behaviour, it is also necessary to verify whether a sufficient number of consumers would turn to the products that competitors will start supplying in response to a SSNIP. This is not problematic if competitors can start to produce and sell cheaper versions of the same product. The issue is

---

[110] *Microsoft Decision 2004 supra* note 8, paras 418–22; *see also Michelin I supra* note 20, para. 41.

[111] It restricts itself to noting that such a period should not entail a significant adjustment of existing tangible and intangible assets (*Market Definition Notice supra* note 1, para. 20, fn. 3).

[112] R. O'Donoghue and A. J. Padilla, *supra* note 5, p. 73 and *supra* note 39, p. 47, n. 97; Case IV/M.149 *Lucas/Eaton*, Commission Decision of 9 December 1991, para. 339; and *Microsoft Decision 2004 supra* note 8, para. 339 and fn. 425.

[113] Opportunity costs are the benefits associated with choosing the next-best option instead of the option that has effectively been chosen.

[114] As explained by the Commission in Case COMP/M.3796 *Omya/J.M. Huber PCC*, Commission Decision of 19 July 2006, para. 143; *see also* Case COMP/M.1693 *Alcoa/Reynolds*, Commission Decision of 3 May 2000, para. 94, where the Commission found that although the conversion costs from production of one grade of high-purity aluminium to another were low, the additional returns of the switch would be more than offset by the extra operating costs, meaning that there was no economic incentive for producers to switch in the case of a SSNIP.

1. – Market Definition
Nicolas Gauss and Alison Oldale

more complex if competitors are only able to produce similar products that customers might or might not regard as valid substitutes. In other words, it is necessary to determine whether supply-side competitors will be able to produce effective demand-side substitutes.[115]

1.52   Only if these criteria are met will supply-side substitutability be taken into account when defining the market.

2.3.   Practical Relevance of Supply-side Substitutability

1.53   Supply-side substitutability's relevance to competition law is long-established, beginning with the *Continental Can* case, in which the Court of Justice criticised the Commission's market definition because the Commission had not given thought to supply-side substitution when assessing the scope of the market of food containers.[116] It is broadly used in Article 102 TFEU cases, although seldom with the effect of broadening the relevant market that was identified on the basis of demand substitution.[117]

1.54   As mentioned, the *Market Definition Notice* envisages the analysis of supply-side substitutability in the context of *"small and permanent changes in relative prices"*,[118] *e.g.*, a SSNIP. However, the supply-side substitutability analysis in the decisional practice of the Commission tends to rely on factors such as the costs, times, and risks associated with switching rather than the hypothetical monopolist test. In *Intel*, the Commission restricted itself to point out the substantial costs and delays involved in switching from one production platform to another (billions of dollars of sunk costs and more than one year switching time) in order to conclude that central processing units (CPUs) for non-computer devices and for computers were not supply-side substitutes.[119] As in the case of demand-side substitutability, analysis of past events may also provide useful information. In its *Michelin I* judgment, the Court of Justice upheld the Commission's view that Michelin's failure to respond to a shortage in supply of tyres for heavy vehicles in 1977 by using its surplus production

---

[115] R. O'Donoghue and A. J. Padilla, *supra* note 5, p. 90.

[116] *Continental Can supra* note 2, para. 33.

[117] R. O'Donoghue and A. J. Padilla, *supra* note 5, p. 74, and recent cases: Case COMP/38.096 *Clearstream*, Commission Decision of 2 June 2004, not yet published, para. 200; *Microsoft Decision 2004 supra* note 8, paras 334–1; Case COMP/38.113 *Prokent/Tomra*, Commission Decision of 29 March 2006, not yet published, paras 41–5; *supra* note 81, paras 831–2.

[118] *Market Definition Notice supra* note 1, para. 20.

[119] *See supra* note 81, paras 825–30.

1. – Market Definition
Nicolas Gauss and Alison Oldale

capacity for car tyres was a good indication that these products were not supply-side substitutes.[120]

2.4. *Distinction from Potential Competition*

It is also important to distinguish supply-side substitution from potential **1.55** competition, as the latter may not be taken into account to delineate the relevant product market, but will be dealt with when assessing dominance. The difference between supply-side substitution and potential competition lies in two alternative factors. First, length of the reaction time – supply-side substitution occurs quickly, whereas potential competitors may need more time (*e.g.*, more than one year) to enter the market. Secondly, costs of entry differ. While potential competitors will incur heavy sunk costs if they start supplying the market, supply-side substitution is reversible, representing a form of "*uncommitted entry*".[121]

The long-term entry of potential competitors poses a different kind of com- **1.56** petitive constraint than supply-side substitution. While supply-side substitution represents an immediate restraint, the ability of potential competitors to discipline a given company's behaviour is more remote and will depend on how easy it is for them to enter the relevant market.[122]

For this reason, the analysis of potential competition is only made when **1.57** assessing dominance.[123] Despite the differences between supply-side substitutability and potential competition, the Court of First Instance has acknowledged in the *Atlantic Container Line* judgment that "[a]*lthough potential competition and supply-side substitution are conceptually different issues, ... , those issues overlap in part*",[124] since the main distinction rests in the immediacy of the competitive constraints. It added that most of the evidence in the Commission Decision at issue was "*capable of justifying both the absence of significant potential competition and the absence of supply-side substitution*".[125] This shows that the distinction between market definition and the assessment of market power can be difficult to

---

[120] *Michelin I supra* note 20, para. 41.
[121] R. O'Donoghue and A. J. Padilla, *supra* note 5, p. 73.
[122] *Market Definition Notice supra* note 1, para. 24.
[123] *Ibid.*
[124] *TACA Judgment 2003 supra* note 97, para. 834.
[125] *Ibid.*, para. 834.

1. – Market Definition
Nicolas Gauss and Alison Oldale

draw and can be contentious.[126] Where the evidence of supply-side substitutability is insufficient to justify placing two products in the same relevant product market, the Commission may nonetheless consider the competitive constraints resulting from a certain degree of supply-side substitutability in the context of its overall competition analysis.[127]

2.5. *Assessing Supply-side Substitutability*

1.58 Given the strict conditions for a finding of supply-side substitutability, it is generally only of subsidiary importance for market definition.[128] The Commission has been criticised for placing too little emphasis on it, and for only examining supply-side competition at the later stage of assessing dominance.[129] While this is a valid criticism in some cases, the difference between supply-side substitutability and potential competition is often of rather gradual nature. Overall, examining supply-side substitution serves as a control on markets defined according to demand-side substitutability, since the assessment of demand-side substitutability can lead to too narrow a market definition.

1.59 Supply-side substitutability has to be assessed with caution, though, since it carries the risk that the scope of the market is falsely delineated. Due to the fact that supply-side substitutability is based on information obtained from competitors of the company under examination, the information might not be objective. Competitors may be interested in either narrowing the scope of the relevant market to increase the odds of the company being fined or, on the contrary, broadening it in order to reduce their market share and thus decrease their chance of becoming subject to future Commission scrutiny.[130] Moreover, it remains unclear if it can be reliably measured to what extent unused capacities will be used for supply-substitution in the case of a fictitious

---

[126] *See, for instance*, Case COMP/M.4215 *Glatfelter/Crompton Assets*, Commission Decision of 20 December 2006, paras 35–48, where the Commission found that, contrary to the parties' contention, there was no supply-side substitutability between wet laid fibre material used in tea and coffee filtration and wet laid fibre material used for other applications, as switches in production between these two categories would entail considerable costs and require a long time. It accepted to take into account the limited competitive pressure from the supply side when assessing market power.

[127] *Market Definition Notice supra* note 1, para. 14. *See, for example*, Case IV/M.984 *DuPont/ICI*, Commission decision of 2 October 1997.

[128] *See supra* note 28.

[129] A. Jones and B. Sufrin, *EC Competition Law* (3rd Ed., Oxford, Oxford University Press, 2008), p. 81.

[130] N. Gauss, *Die Anwendung des kartellrechtlichen Missbrauchsverbots nach Art. 82 EG (Art. 102 AEUV) in innovativen Märkten* (Baden-Baden, Nomos, 2010), p. 78.

1. – Market Definition
Nicolas Gauss and Alison Oldale

price increase or to what extent companies not yet active on the market will enter it.[131]

III. Defining the Relevant Geographic Market

1. The Concept of a Geographic Market

The identification of the product market is only one aspect of market **1.60** definition, the other being geographic market definition. Determining the geographic market means assessing the area in which the conditions of competition are sufficiently homogeneous so that the relevant products and services within it exercise a competitive constraint on each other. Geographic market definition has two aims. First, it is carried out to determine the geographic area in which the company concerned exercises its economic power,[132] as an initial step for assessing dominance. Companies that produce or offer their services outside this zone are not considered to offer an effective alternative supply for the customers of the company under scrutiny. Secondly, it serves to assess whether a given company's dominant position is affecting the internal market or a substantial part thereof, so that Article 102 TFEU becomes applicable.[133]

In the following, the emphasis will be on the first aspect of geographic mar- **1.61** ket definition, since the question of the geographic area in which a company exercises its economic power is much more relevant in practice. The European courts have recognised the importance of defining the geographic market since *United Brands*, when the Court of Justice noted that *"the conditions for the application of Article 86 [now 102 TFEU] to an undertaking in a dominant position presuppose the clear delimitation of the substantial part of the common market in which it may be able to engage in abuses which hinder effective competition"*.[134] The *Market Definition Notice* effectively summarised the then-existing case law by defining the relevant geographic market as comprising *"the area in which the undertakings concerned are involved in the supply and demand of products or services,*

---

[131] Critical: E.-J. Mestmäcker and H. Schweitzer, *Europäisches Wettbewerbsrecht* (2nd Ed., Munich, C. H. Beck, 2004), paras 23 and 25.
[132] *United Brands supra* note 2, para. 81.
[133] Case C-7/97 *Oscar Bronner v Mediaprint Zeitungs- und Zeitschriftenverlag and others* ("*Oscar Bronner*") [1998] ECR I-7791, para. 32.
[134] *United Brands supra* note 2, para. 44.

1. – Market Definition
Nicolas Gauss and Alison Oldale

in which the conditions of competition are sufficiently homogeneous and which can be distinguished from neighbouring areas because the conditions of competition are appreciably different in those areas".[135] The term *conditions of competition* is understood very broadly, to comprise factors such as consumer preferences, stability of demand and price, structure of distribution networks, transport costs and volume of exports.[136] The Commission and the courts have identified a wide range of geographic markets, from worldwide[137] to EU-wide,[138] and from national[139] to local.[140]

2. The Delineation of the Geographic Market

2.1. *Approach under the Market Definition Notice*

1.62 The Commission sets out its analytical approach to geographic market definition in the *Market Definition Notice*, describing a three-stage process.[141]

- The first step consists in devising an initial "working hypothesis" as to the geographic scope of the market, based on broad indications as to the distribution of market shares between the parties and their competitors, as well as a preliminary analysis of pricing and price differences at national and Community level. This working hypothesis is then checked against an analysis of demand characteristics (such as the importance of national preferences or the local patterns of purchases) in order to establish whether companies in other areas do indeed constitute a real alternative source of supply for customers. The conceptual framework to be applied is, once again, that of the SSNIP test: Will customers in the case of a change in relative prices

---

[135] *Market Definition Notice supra* note 1, para. 8. This definition has been cited by the Court, *see* Case T-310/01 *Schneider Electric v Commission* ("*Schneider Electric*") [2002] ECR II-4071, para. 153. For more case law, *see United Brands supra* note 2, para. 11; *Tetra Pak II Judgment 1994 supra* note 8, para. 91; Joined Cases C-68/94 and 30/95 *France and others v Commission* [1998] ECR I-1375, para. 143; Case T-139/98 *Amministrazione Autonoma dei Monopoli di Stato v Commission* ("*AAMS Judgment 2001*") [2001] ECR II-3413, para. 39.

[136] *See, for instance, Tetra Pak II Judgment 1994 supra* note 8, paras 92–98; *Schneider Electric supra* note 135, para. 159; *Kish Glass Judgment 2000 supra* note 107, paras 81–82.

[137] *See Microsoft Decision 2004 supra* note 8, para. 427; *supra* note 81, para. 836.

[138] *See Tetra Pak I Decision 1998 supra* note 44, paras 40–1; Cases IV/30.787 and 31.488 *supra* note 44, para. 56.

[139] *See* Case COMP/38.096 *supra* note 117, paras 196–8; Case COMP/38.233 *supra* note 25, paras 205–6.

[140] *See* Case IV/34.689 *Sea Containers/Stena Sealink – Interim measures*, Commission Decision of 21 December 1993, OJ 1994 L 15/8, paras 62–65.

[141] *Market Definition Notice supra* note 1, paras 28–32.

1. – Market Definition
Nicolas Gauss and Alison Oldale

switch their orders to companies located elsewhere in the short term and at negligible costs?

- Secondly, the Commission focuses on supply-side considerations. It seeks to identify possible obstacles and barriers that could isolate companies in a given area from the competitive pressure of companies located outside that area. Such barriers can take many forms, ranging from the requirement of a local presence to the existence of local regulatory constraints.

- Finally, the Commission will examine the continuing process of market integration in the context of the internal market. This applies in particular to concentrations and joint ventures. In situations where legislative barriers formerly isolating national markets have been removed, a cautious assessment of past evidence regarding prices, market shares and trade patterns is required, possibly leading to a broader definition of the geographic market.

2.2. *Delineating the Geographic Market in Practice*

Although it is not explicitly mentioned in the *Market Definition Notice*, geo- **1.63**
graphic market definition in practice is often affected by the presence of price discrimination. As with price discrimination in product markets, this can lead to separate geographic markets being defined if (1) customers in one area can be distinguished from those in another area by their different pattern of demand, or different alternative supply options; and, (2) there is no arbitrage between the different areas, either by customers in one area selling to customers in another area, or through independent traders buying in one area and shipping to the other. In practice, therefore, the Commission only relies to a minimal extent on concepts such as the SSNIP or demand and supply-side substitutability in Article 102 TFEU cases.[142] Consistent with the principles

---

[142] A study of merger cases between 1991 and 2001 (Copenhagen Economics, *The Internal Market and the Relevant Geographical Market: The Impact of the Completion of the Single Market Programme on the Definition of the Relevant Geographic Market*, Enterprise Directorate-General, Enterprise Papers No. 15, 2004, pp. 31–2, already reached a similar conclusion: the Commission directly or indirectly referred to the SSNIP test in 3.8 per cent of the cases and to demand/supply substitution in 5.3/6.3 per cent of the cases. For a notable exception to this trend, *see* the recent decision in Case COMP/M.4734 *supra* note 67, paras 84–105, 123–39, where the Commission undertook a detailed analysis of demand- and supply-side substitutability for commodity S-PVC, complete with an assessment of customer switching patterns, critical and actual loss in the case of a SSNIP, although this finally turned out to be inconclusive.

1. – Market Definition
Nicolas Gauss and Alison Oldale

of market definition in the presence of price discrimination, and with the definition of geographic markets in the case law of the courts, the focus is rather on identifying areas in which the <u>conditions of competition are "<i>sufficiently homogeneous</i>"</u>.[143]

2.2.1. Customers Purchasing Patterns and Trade Flows

1.64   The analysis of customer purchasing patterns provides a good indication of which products customers consider to be demand-side substitutes and are frequently relied upon by the Commission and the courts. In the *Michelin II* case, the parties had argued that the market had become worldwide, insofar as tyre suppliers were now competing internationally. The Commission found, however, that French dealers obtained their supplies almost exclusively from national subsidiaries of the manufacturers, for reasons that were economical (no rebates in case the tyres were purchased abroad), historical (lack of wholesalers which would have fostered parallel imports) and technical (need of local contacts with the manufacturers).[144] Moreover, the fact that international suppliers competed in many different countries was "*perfectly compatible with the existence of conditions of competition that are different in each of the relevant countries*".[145] Consistent with the previous Court finding in *Michelin I*,[146] the Commission thus concluded that the geographic market was limited to the French territory.[147] Similarly, in *Prokent-Tomra*, the Commission noted that customers of beverage container collectors and their procurement processes were predominantly organised at national level, and that these collectors were delivered and installed by national subsidiaries of the manufacturer. These findings pointed toward a national geographic market.[148]

---

[143] *See, for instance, Telefónica supra* note 93, para. 210; Case COMP/37.860 *supra* note 40, para. 60; Case COMP/36.041 *supra* note 79, para. 119.

[144] Case COMP/36.041 *supra* note 79, paras 121, 125–130.

[145] *Ibid.*, para. 123.

[146] *Michelin I supra* note 20, para. 26.

[147] Case COMP/36.041 *supra* note 79, para. 152; *see also British Airways Judgment 2003 supra* note 2, where the fact that an overwhelming majority of travellers reserved airline tickets in their country of residence pointed to a national market for air travel agency services.

[148] *See* Case COMP/38.113 *supra* note 117, para. 53. *See also* Case COMP/M.1672 *Volvo/Scania*, Commission Decision of 15 March 2000, paras 58–60, 66–70, where the Commission noted that the majority of heavy truck purchasers in the Nordic countries bought nationally because of the need for after-sales support, the reduced second-hand value of imported trucks and the country-specific technical requirements for heavy trucks.

1. – Market Definition
Nicolas Gauss and Alison Oldale

The *Market Definition Notice* further specifies that when the number of cus-   **1.65**
tomers is so large that it is not possible to obtain a clear picture of their geographic purchasing patterns, information on trade flows and, above all, the
rationale underlying these trade flows may be useful, though not conclusive.[149]
In general, trade flows between countries or regions representing less than 10
per cent of local production or consumption are not regarded by the Commission as sufficient to constitute the same geographic market, absent powerful evidence to the contrary. Where trade flows amount to 10–20 per cent of
local production or consumption, the Commission may be inclined to accept
the existence of a single geographic market, depending on the circumstances.
Where trade flows between countries or regions exceed 20 per cent of local
production or consumption, the Commission is likely to qualify those countries or regions as a geographic market.[150] In *Blackstone/Acetex*, for instance,
the Commission based its conclusion that the market for acetic acid was global
on the facts that imports satisfied 20 per cent of European demand, unex-
pected outages in the EEA had caused a surge in imports from other regions,
and that the transaction costs for the trade of acetic acid (*i.e.*, transport costs,
storage costs and duties) did not present significant material barriers to trade
flows among the world regions.[151]

2.2.2.   Variations in Prices

The existence of non-transitory material price differences between two areas   **1.66**
suggests that they do not belong to the same geographic market, as effective
competition between these areas should lead to the homogenisation of prices.
The Commission stated in its *Volvo/Scania* Decision that "*the ability of manufacturers to price discriminate between different geographic areas is a central element of defining
the relevant market.*"[152] The Commission concluded that the markets could not
be wider than national in scope. This was based on the fact that Volvo had
been able to maintain substantial price differences and apply different margins between neighbouring countries. Therefore, buyers or arbitrageurs would
have taken advantage of these price differences had the markets not been
national in scope.[153] In *Schneider/Legrand*, the Commission found that the fact

---

[149] *Market Definition Notice supra* note 1, para. 49.
[150] *See* N. Levy, *European Merger Control Law – A Guide to the Merger Regulation* (8th Ed., Lexis Nexis, 2011),
para. 8.07[4].
[151] Case COMP/M.3625 *Blackstone/Acetex*, Commission Decision of 13 July 2005, paras 26–49; *see also* Case
COMP/M.4734 *supra* note 67, paras 107–12.
[152] Case COMP/M.1672 *supra* note 148, para. 233.
[153] *Ibid.*, para. 49.

1. – Market Definition
Nicolas Gauss and Alison Oldale

that identical products, manufactured in the same plant, distributed through the same logistical network, and for which the transport cost was minimal were priced at materially different levels in different Member States was a criterion "*sufficient on its own*" to reject the notion that the relevant market was European.[154] In certain sectors, such as the pharmaceutical sector, differentiated state-regulated prices lead to the identification of geographic markets which are national in scope.[155]

1.67   The fact that the correlation between prices in two areas is high or low is not in itself conclusive evidence. In *Pirelli/BICC*, the Commission found that price differences between Member States were not meaningful because, in this case, prices depended heavily on the quantities purchased in each transaction and the specifications of each individual tender rather than heterogeneous conditions of competition.[156] Conversely, it noted in *Mannesmann/ Vallourec/Ilva* that "*the existence of price correlations does not necessarily indicate a single market in the absence of other elements such as mutual interpenetration or similar structures of supply and demand in the different areas.*"[157] Generally, where price differences between countries or regions are low (*i.e.*, less than five per cent) or converging, the Commission is likely to accept that those countries or regions constitute one relevant geographic market. However, price differences between countries or regions exceeding 5–10 per cent may lead the Commission to determine that those countries or regions do not form part of the same relevant geographic market, depending on the magnitude of and reasons for those differences.[158]

---

[154] Case COMP/M.2283 *Schneider/Legrand*, Commission Decision of 10 October 2001, para. 238. In *Schneider Electric supra* note 135, paras 171 *et seq.*, 176, 178 *et seq.*, 243, the Court of First Instance annulled the Commission Decision based, *inter alia*, on the finding that the Commission cited the national dimension of the geographical markets to demonstrate the strengthening or the creation of a dominant position for the merged entity, but based its assessment of the impact of the concentration's operation on transnational, global considerations without demonstrating its relevance at the national level.

[155] For instance, in Cases IV/36.957 *Glaxo Wellcome*, IV/36.997 *Aseprofar and Fedifar*, IV/37.121/F3 *Spain Pharma*, IV/37.138 *BAI*, IV/37.380 *EAEPC*, Commission Decision of 8 May 2001, OJ 2001 L 302/1, para. 114, the Commission noted: "*In all Commission decisions adopted hitherto,* [the scope of the geographic market] *has been defined as national. In the present case, the Commission does not divert from this because of a number of factors. These include different price and reimbursement regulations, different brand and packing strategies and different distribution systems as well as different prescribing habits of physicians (reflected by the different market shares for the same product in different Member States)*".

[156] Case COMP/M.1882 *Pirelli/BICC*, Commission Decision of 19 July 2000, para. 42.

[157] Case IV/M.315 *Mannesmann/Valourec/Ilva*, Commission Decision of 31 January 1994, para. 32.

[158] *See supra* note 150, para. 8.07[2].

1. – Market Definition
Nicolas Gauss and Alison Oldale

2.2.3. Market Shares

If the market shares of producers vary materially between different areas, **1.68**
these areas should probably be treated as different geographic markets, as
this suggests that the conditions of competition differ in each of them.[159]
Similarly, if suppliers are able to maintain high and stable market shares in a
particular area, this may indicate that they do not face substantial competitive
pressure from forces outside that area.[160] The Commission will usually further
explore the reasons behind the allocation of market shares, notably, to verify
that they do not only relate to the *"weight of the past"*.[161] In *Siemens/Drägewerk*,
after noticing that European suppliers of medical equipment enjoyed different market shares in different Member States, the Commission proceeded
to verify that real barriers to market integration explained this situation.[162]
The extent to which information on market shares can be used to define a
geographic market is unclear. While such information may be useful to identify areas where competitive conditions are "sufficiently homogeneous", it is
unclear how it relates to the fundamental criteria of demand and supply-side
substitutability.[163]

2.2.4. Barriers to Trade

Barriers to trade give rise to separate geographic markets if they increase **1.69**
the ability of hypothetical monopolists to increase their prices without facing competitive constraints from the outside. The analysis of such barriers is
an important step in defining markets; it serves as an autonomous indication
of the scope of the market, and also helps to verify the rationale underlying
other empirical findings. In *Danish Crown/Vestjyske Slagterier*, the parties had
submitted evidence showing a high price correlation between the prices of
live pigs in several Member States. The Commission decided that despite this
fact, trade flows between Denmark and other countries remained very low as
a result of Danish farmers' contractual obligation to deliver their pigs to local
slaughterhouses. Accordingly, this justified the Commission's conclusion that
the market was national, rather than regional in scope.[164]

---

[159] *See, for instance*, Case COMP/36.041 *supra* note 79, para. 133.
[160] Case COMP/M.3099 *Areva/Urenco/ETC JV*, Commission Decision of 6 October 2004, para. 76.
[161] *Market Definition Notice supra* note 1, paras 28–29.
[162] Case COMP/M.2861 *Siemens/Drägewerk/JV*, Commission Decision of 30 April 2003, paras 36–40.
[163] On this issue, *see* S. Bishop and M. Walker, *supra* note 35, pp. 141–2.
[164] Case IV/M.1313 *Danish Crown/Vestjyske Slagterier*, Commission Decision of 9 March 1999, paras 63–65.

1. – Market Definition
Nicolas Gauss and Alison Oldale

1.70 Barriers to trade can be extremely diverse; the barriers most frequently identified in the Commission's decisions are the following:

2.2.4.1. Transport costs

1.71 Transport costs represent one of the most significant barriers to trade, and may successfully isolate certain areas from outside competitive constraints; as such, they play a pre-eminent role in the Commission's assessment of geographic markets. In *Napier Brown/British Sugar*, the Commission found that the relevant market was national since the natural barrier of the English Channel gave rise to additional transport costs, which allowed UK producers of sugar to charge a premium on the price of sugar compared with continental European prices.[165] Furthermore, import tariffs and duties have to be taken into account, since they can increase the costs of transport.[166] If transport costs only represent a small proportion of the price of the product, different areas are likely to be found to belong to the same product market. In *Hilti*, the Court of First Instance concluded that despite important price differences between the company's products in each Member State, the low transport costs made parallel trading highly likely and therefore justified the Commission's decision to define the market as European-wide.[167] As a rule, the relevance of transport costs for market definition decreases with the increasing complexity and price value of the related product.

2.2.4.2. Consumer preferences

1.72 Factors such as national preferences, language, and culture, have a strong potential to limit the geographic scope of competition.[168] Customers might be reluctant to switch to products that do not meet their local preferences, thereby reducing the ability of non-local competitors to discipline the behaviour of local suppliers. In *Bass*, for instance, the preference of British consumers for draught beer was found to distinguish them from the rest of the Community, which was an argument in favour of treating

---

[165] Case IV/30.178 *Napier Brown/British Sugar* ("*Napier Brown*"), Commission Decision of 18 July 1988, OJ 1988 L 284/41, para. 44; *see also* Cases IV/34.621 and 35.059 *Irish Sugar*, Commission Decision of 14 May 1997, OJ 1997 L 258/1, para. 95; *supra* note 81, para. 836.

[166] *See, for instance*, Case COMP/M.2345 *Deutsche BP/Erdölchemie*, Commission Decision of 26 April 2001, para. 28, where import duties of 8.5 per cent into the EEA supported a market definition limited to Western Europe.

[167] *Hilti supra* note 23, para. 81; *see Kish Glass Judgment 2000 supra* note 107, paras 81–82; *United Brands supra* note 2, paras 55–56.

[168] *Market Definition Notice supra* note 1, para. 46.

1. – Market Definition
Nicolas Gauss and Alison Oldale

the United Kingdom as a separate market.[169] In *RTL/Veronica/Endemol*, the Commission considered the Flanders region of Belgium and the Netherlands, despite the common Dutch language, as separate geographic markets, because of differences in verbal expressions, national taste, and preference for certain television personalities.[170]

2.2.4.3.   Import tariffs or duties

Import tariffs or duties may present direct barriers to entry. As a general guide-   **1.73**
line, import tariffs that represent less than 5 per cent of a product's total costs may be too small to limit trade,[171] whereas tariffs in excess of 10 per cent may be sufficiently high to potentially limit competitively significant imports.[172]

2.2.4.4.   Local presence

When customers value the benefits of dealing with suppliers present at the   **1.74**
local level (such as regularity of supply or access to after-sale services), out-side companies are placed at a disadvantage. In *MasterCard*, the Commission found that markets were national due to the need to open local branches or cooperate with local banks in order to enter the business of issuing "payment cards" in individual Member States.[173] The geographic organisation of com-panies' distribution networks is a useful indicator of what companies consider as the relevant geographic market. In *Michelin II*, it was held that the fact that large tyre manufacturers organised their distribution and sale along national lines evidenced that conditions of competition were not homogeneous at

---

[169] *See* Case COMP/36.081 *Bass*, Commission Decision of 16 June 1999, OJ 1999 L 186/1, paras 21, 116; *see also* Case COMP/M.4533 *SCA/P&G (European Tissue Business)*, Commission Decision of 5 September 2007, para. 56, where the preference of Austrian and German consumers for thick and strong, rather than soft and flexible, toilet paper helped conclude that both countries should be considered as a cluster separated from the rest of the EEA.

[170] Case IV/M.553 *RTL/Veronica/Endemol*, Commission Decision of 20 September 1995, para. 26.

[171] *See, e.g.*, Case IV/M.478 *Voith/Sulzer II*, Commission Decision of 29 July 1994, para. 25, and Case IV/M.612 *RWE-DEA/Augusta (II)*, Commission Decision of 27 July 1995, para. 19. *See,* however, Case IV/M.1225 *Enso/Stora*, Commission Decision of 25 November 1998, para. 56, in which the Commission considered duties of around 4–6.6 per cent on imports from the United States as one of the elements insulating the European market for liquid packaging board.

[172] *See,* Case IV/M.550 *Union Carbide/Enichem*, Commission Decision of 13 March 1995, para. 49; Case COMP/M.1671 *Dow Chemical/Union Carbide*, Commission Decision of 3 May 2000, para. 47.

[173] Cases COMP/34.579, COMP/36.518 and COMP/38.580 *supra* note 52, para. 318; *see also* Case IV/31.906 *Flat Glass (Italy)*, Commission Decision of 7 December 1988, OJ 1989 L 33/44, para. 77; Case COMP/36.041 *supra* note 79, para. 128; Case IV/M.1286 *Johnson & Johnson/DePuy*, Commission Decision of 28 October 1998, para. 18.

1. – Market Definition
Nicolas Gauss and Alison Oldale

European level.[174] On the other hand, in *Tetra Pak II*, the Court of First Instance found that the company's presence in each Member State by way of subsidiaries was no proof of national markets, since the subsidiaries' commercial policy was determined EU-wide at the group level.[175]

2.2.4.5. Regulatory factors

1.75   Regulatory regimes for certain products may create barriers to trade (typically nation-wide) and restrain the scope of the geographic market. In *GVG/FS*, the Commission found that due to national technical standards for locomotives and national qualification requirements for drivers, neither the locomotive nor the crew of another Member State could be used to provide traction in Italy.[176] Similarly, in *Prokrent/Tomra*, State-specific waste management regimes were found to delineate the markets for beverage container collectors.[177] Parties often advocate an EU-wide market based on EU legislation, which seeks to harmonise competitive conditions across Member States. The *Market Definition Notice* supports considering market integration processes.[178] In such cases, the Commission closely examines the facts at hand and has reached different conclusions depending on the markets examined. In *DONG/Elsam/ Energi E2*, it found that despite the ongoing creation of an internal market for gas, this process was not currently at the stage where very significant market share differences were of mere historic relevance, which is why it declined to include Germany in the Danish wholesale market for gas.[179] Conversely, in the *UTC/Kidde* Decision, the Commission found that, due to the harmonisation of the EU, the market was EEA-wide, even though the import of fire

---

[174] Case COMP/36.041 *supra* note 79, para. 125.

[175] *Tetra Pak II Judgment 1994 supra* note 8, para. 92, upheld in *Tetra Pak II Judgment 1996 supra* note 8.

[176] Case COMP/37.685 *GVG/FS*, Commission Decision of 27 August 2003, OJ 2004 L 11/17, para. 57.

[177] Case COMP/38.113 *supra* note 117, para. 48. *See also* Case COMP/M.4540 *Nestlé/Novartis* ("*Medical Nutrition Business*"), Commission Decision of 29 June 2007, para. 49, where state-specific reimbursement systems for healthcare nutrition products pointed toward national markets.

[178] *Market Definition Notice supra* note 1, para. 32. The *Market Definition Notice* specifies, however, that this mostly applies to merger control (where the assessment focuses on the future effects on competition, hence the need to examine the long-term transformations of the market).

[179] Case COMP/M.3868 *DONG/Elsam/Energi E2*, Commission Decision of 14 March 2006, para. 160; *see also* Case COMP/M.2947 *Verbund/Energie Allianz*, Commission Decision of 11 June 2003, para. 59, where the market for the supply of electricity was found to be domestic, *inter alia*, because of the differences between national implementation measures of the Electricity Market Directive; Case COMP/39.386 *Long Term Electricity Contracts France*, Commission Decision of 17 March 2010, not yet published, para. 24, where the Commission found that the French electricity market was geographically distinct, in particular because of its specific regulatory framework. *See also* Case COMP/38.113 *supra* note 117, para. 48.

1. – Market Definition
Nicolas Gauss and Alison Oldale

extinguishers was still subject to approval in most Member States.[180] Thus, over time, European Union harmonisation of regulatory standards aimed at market integration may create an EU-(EEA-) wide geographic market.

IV. Temporal Markets

Although the *Market Definition Notice* does not refer to temporal markets, **1.76** another dimension of markets is that of time, particularly when demand and supply for a given product are highly dependent on, say, the time of day or the season of the year.[181] Rush hour passengers, for instance, will likely not be willing to switch to other travel times in the event of an increase in rush hour prices. Holidaymakers might similarly be constrained in their ability to respond to price increases in hotels during the peak season by choosing other travel dates. As a result, it could be argued that in addition to the relevant product and geographic markets, the relevant temporal market should be identified. The Commission has had few occasions to deal with this question. In *United Brands*, it found that there existed some level of seasonal competition between bananas and certain fruits, but eventually identified a single year-round market rather than several seasonal markets.[182] Similarly, in *Prokent/Tomra*, it identified a temporal dimension to the market for beverage container collectors, namely "key years" during which demand for such collectors increased considerably in anticipation of new legislation. While it did not restrict its market definition and competitive analysis to these periods, it noted that the effects of exclusionary practices were particularly harmful during the key years.[183] Finally, in *European Night Services*, the Commission argued on appeal that market shares for the air transport of travellers should be calculated in relation to early morning flights and evening flights rather than by reference to all flights available round the clock.[184] The Commission's reluctance to define relevant temporal markets can be explained by the

---

[180] Case COMP/M.3688 *UTC/Kidde*, Commission Decision of 18 March 2005, para. 29.

[181] Other competition authorities rely on temporal market definition: *see* Office of Fair Trading, *Market Definition – Understanding Competition Law*, Competition Law Guideline – OFT 403, December 2004, paras 5.1–5.3.

[182] Case IV/26.699 *supra* note 19, under II.A.2, confirmed by the Court of Justice on appeal in *United Brands supra* note 2, paras 32–34.

[183] Case COMP/38.113 *supra* note 117, paras 56, 287, 343.

[184] Joined Cases T-374, 375, 384 and 388/94 *European Night Services and others v Commission* ("*European Night Services*") [1998] ECR II-3141, paras 83–105.

1. – Market Definition
Nicolas Gauss and Alison Oldale

possibility of directly integrating the temporal dimension into the definition of the relevant product market.[185]

V. Specific Issues in Defining Markets

1. Aftermarkets

1.1. *Introduction*

1.77 The complex question of how to analyse aftermarkets or "secondary markets" under EU competition law occurs whenever durable goods generate after sales in the form of consumables (toners for photocopiers, bags for vacuum cleaners, etc.), spare parts, or services. In other words, aftermarkets appear when the purchaser of a primary product will also need to purchase secondary products or services related to the primary product.

1.78 Because secondary products and services may constitute a critical source of income for the producers of the primary product, producers will typically be tempted to remain or become the dominant players in these secondary product markets. This may be all the more easy as many secondary products are compatible with only *one* type of primary product (*e.g.*, spare parts for a specific car manufacturer, games for a specific game console, etc.), causing consumers to be locked-in.[186] As a consequence, infringements of Article 102 TFEU are likely to occur regarding secondary markets. As in the case of all Article 102 TFEU market definitions, a too narrow analysis of aftermarkets can result in an overly broad application of Article 102 TFEU. Narrowly defining aftermarkets may also not be in the interest of consumer welfare, since the incentive of generating margins in an aftermarket may drive manufacturers to lower prices for their primary products as long as the primary market is competitive. This is illustrated by game consoles that are sold below costs because of the prospect of generating margins from the sale of computer games. Conversely, if margins in aftermarkets decrease, either prices in

---

[185] For example, instead of distinguishing a product market for "hotel bookings" and a temporal market for "peak season", the product market can be defined as "peak season hotel bookings".

[186] However, it is not sufficient for a definition of a distinct aftermarket that existing customers might face switching costs or may be locked in (T. Graf, "The General Court of the European Union addresses the competitive analysis of aftermarkets in the luxury watches and spare parts markets (*CEAHR*)" (December 2010) *e-Competitions*, No. 35223, p. 2).

the primary market will have to increase or the service in the aftermarket may have to decline.[187] On the other hand, problems of finding compatible secondary products together with the existence of high prices and a long life-time of the primary products may render relative price increases of secondary products profitable.[188] Although the Commission and the European courts have had occasions to deal with aftermarkets cases, aftermarkets remain a complex and sometimes unclear area of competition law.[189]

1.2. Commission and Courts Precedents

In its first case dealing with aftermarkets, *Hugin/Liptons*,[190] the Commission **1.79** was confronted with a complaint arising from the refusal by Hugin, a Swedish manufacturer of cash registers, to supply independent companies active in the maintenance, repair, reconditioning and renting of its machines with the spare parts necessary for their operations. Hugin's main defence was that there was no separate market for spare parts and maintenance services; the latter were simply a "parameter of competition" for the market of cash registers, where Hugin only enjoyed relatively small market shares and therefore could not be found to be dominant. The Court of Justice did not follow this reasoning; instead, it narrowly defined the relevant market as that constituted by Hugin spare parts required by independent companies. Since Hugin was the only supplier of such spare parts, it could determine its conduct without taking account of competing sources of supply, and was thus found to occupy a dominant position.[191]

Hugin stands for the proposition that the relevant market may be that of sec- **1.80** ondary products adapted to one specific primary product. This narrow market definition was used again for nails designed for a specific brand of nail guns (*Hilti*),[192] replacement parts for cars of a particular brand (*Renault* and

---

[187] *See supra* note 186.

[188] *Market Definition Notice supra* note 1, para. 56.

[189] *See,* for further reference, J. Temple Lang, "Practical Aspects of Aftermarkets in European Competition Law", (2011) 7(1) *Competition Policy International Journal*.

[190] Case IV/29.132 *Hugin/Liptons* ("*Hugin Decision 1977*"), Commission Decision of 8 December 1977, OJ 1978 L 22/23.

[191] Case 22/78 *Hugin Kassaregister and Hugin Cash Registers v Commission* ("*Hugin Judgment 1979*") [1979] ECR 1869, paras 3–10.

[192] Cases IV/30.787 and 31.488 *supra* note 44, para. 57, confirmed in *Hilti supra* note 23, paras 65–68, upheld on appeal in Case C-53/92 P *Hilti v Commission* [1994] ECR I-667.

1. – Market Definition
Nicolas Gauss and Alison Oldale

Volvo),[193] and toner cartridges for printers and copiers (*Info-Lab/Rycoh* and *Pelikan/Kyocera*).[194]

1.81   The General Court in *CEAHR v Commission* ("*CEAHR*") clarified the conditions of aftermarket analysis and required the Commission to carry out an in-depth analysis to reach a conclusion on market definition.[195] The case was triggered by a complaint of the Confédération Européenne des Associations d'Horlogers-Réparateurs (European Confederation of Watch & Clock Repairers' Associations – "*CEAHR*") about refusals by luxury watch makers to supply independent watch repairers with spare parts, which *CEAHR* claimed violated Articles 101 and 102 TFEU. The Commission examined the primary market for luxury and prestige watches as well as two aftermarkets; the market for spare parts and the market for repair and maintenance services in connection with luxury and prestige watches. The Commission reached the *prima facie* conclusion that the two aftermarkets did not constitute separate relevant markets, but should instead be viewed together with the primary market. According to the Commission, the aftermarket of spare parts of one brand of primary products could not be a distinct relevant market in two instances. First, if it is possible for a consumer to switch to the secondary products of another producer, and secondly, if a consumer can switch to another primary product to avoid a price increase of the secondary product. With regard to the first possibility, the Commission found that the complainants had not managed to provide a full, clear-cut and consistent explanation of the extent of and limitation on substitutability of spare parts for luxury/prestige watches. With regard to the second situation, the Commission found that consumers were not locked in, as they could shift to another primary product in case of price increases of the relevant spare parts. Therefore, existing customers could switch to a different primary product to avoid higher repair prices by selling their watch on a second-hand market and switching to a different watch.[196] Furthermore, the Commission added that even if the markets were regarded

---

[193] Indirectly confirmed in Case 238/87 *Volvo v Erik Veng (UK)* ("*Volvo*") [1988] ECR 6211; Case 53/87 *Consorzio italiano della componentistica di ricambio per autoveicoli (CICRA) and Maxicar v Régie nationale des usines Renault* ("*Renault*") [1988] ECR 6039.

[194] *Info-Lab/Rycoh* complaint rejected (*see* DG COMP Competition Policy Newsletter (1999), No. 1, p. 35); *Pelikan/Kyocera* complaint rejected (*see* Twenty-fifth Report on Competition Policy (1995), para. 87).

[195] Case T-427/08 *Confédération européenne des associations d'horlogers-réparateurs v Commission* ("*CEAHR*"), not yet reported. *See also* the Twenty-fifth Report on Competition Policy (1995), para. 86, where the Commission noted that "*an in-depth fact-finding exercise and analysis on a case-by-case basis was required*".

[196] Case COMP/39.097 *Independent Watch Repairers*, Commission Decision of 10 July 2008, not yet published, paras 24–26.

1. – Market Definition
Nicolas Gauss and Alison Oldale

as separate, the primary market appeared to be competitive, which made possible anticompetitive effects in the aftermarkets very unlikely as consumers would have reacted to price increases in the secondary market of repairs by switching to other secondary products or by purchasing a different primary product.[197] On appeal, the General Court agreed with the legal and analytical framework applied by the Commission, but stated that an aftermarket may not be a separate relevant market if *"it is shown that, in the event of a moderate and permanent increase in the price of secondary products, a sufficient number of consumers would switch to other primary or secondary products, in order to render such an increase unprofitable."*[198] The Court thus examined whether it had been proven that it was possible for a customer to react to a price increase of the spare parts by switching to a different luxury watch. The Court noted that the total cost of repair and maintenance of luxury watches over a ten-year period is, for most models, less than five per cent of the price of a new watch and that the price of spare parts is normally included in the cost of repair and maintenance. Thus, a moderate increase in the price of spare parts would be negligible in comparison with the price of a new luxury watch.[199] According to the Court, given the high prices of luxury watches, the Commission had not shown that consumers who already own a luxury watch may reasonably switch to another primary product to avoid a price increase for repair and maintenance services resulting from a moderate price increase for spare parts.[200] The mere possibility for potential consumers to choose between several brands on the primary market was not considered sufficient *"to treat the primary market and the aftermarkets as a single market, unless it is established that that choice is made, among others, on the basis of the competitive conditions on the secondary market"*.[201] On a more general note, the Court repeated there is a strong indication of the existence of a specific market *"if certain economic operators are specialised and are active solely on the market linked to the primary market or on the after market"*.[202] The General Court annulled the Commission's decision principally on the ground that it did not provide sufficient reasoning. The Commission therefore reopened its investigation of the *CEAHR* complaint.[203]

---

[197] *See supra* note 196, para. 18.
[198] *CEAHR supra* note 195, para. 80.
[199] *Ibid.*, para. 95.
[200] *Ibid.*, paras 96, 102 and 107.
[201] *Ibid.*, para. 105.
[202] *Ibid.*, paras 108 and 112.
[203] *See* Press Release IP/11/952 of 5 August 2011.

1.82   In the *IBM Maintenance Services* case, the Commission identified a primary market for large corporate servers on which IBM sold its mainframes, and two possible aftermarkets which were adjacent to the primary market.[204] According to the Commission, a first possible adjacent product market was the market for the inputs required for the maintenance of IBM mainframes, which only IBM could supply. Spare parts and operating system software updates from other brands were incompatible or not substitutable with IBM's. Consequently, the first aftermarket consisted of the secondary IBM products (or services) for the IBM primary product. A second possible adjacent product market was that for the provision of IBM mainframe hardware and operating system software maintenance services, on which IBM was allegedly carrying out an abuse. The Commission preliminarily concluded that there were separate markets. It argued that customers could not switch to the secondary products of other producers and that there were high switching costs in the market for the primary product. Consequently, a moderate increase in the aftermarket prices would not affect customers' choices in the primary market.[205] Although this assessment is in line with the established approach for defining aftermarkets, there were indications pointing to a finding of a system market: IBM argued that its customers were not "locked in" to its primary products, as they could and did switch to other primary mainframe products and, given that there were sellers of IBM second-hand parts on which customers could rely, it was possible to switch to other secondary products. Finally, IBM's mainframe customers were also customers of other IBM products, therefore they could exercise constraints on IBM's aftermarkets in case of a price increase. However, given that the case was closed by a commitment decision, the Commission's preliminary findings on market definition were not challenged.

1.3.   Possible Market Definitions

1.83   There are three possible ways to define the relevant market regarding primary and secondary products:

- The market might be that of secondary products adapted to one specific primary product. This is the narrowest market definition conceivable; it was applied by the Commission in the above-mentioned case law.

---

[204] Case COMP/39.692 *IBM Maintenance Services*, Commission Decision of 13 December 2011, not yet published, para. 20.
[205] *Ibid.*, paras 20–4.

1. – Market Definition
Nicolas Gauss and Alison Oldale

- The market could be defined as a "system market" if for each primary product secondary products or services have been exclusively developed.

- Finally, the market could be defined as comprising secondary products generally, without reference to a specific product or brand, this will only occur, if secondary products are compatible with multiple primary products (*i.e.*, no customer lock-in).

Determining which of the three market definitions above is appropriate often raises difficulties. According to the *Market Definition Notice*, the proper way to define markets in this context is to rely on the hypothetical monopolist test while taking into account the interactions between the primary and the secondary market.[206] This raises the question under which conditions a SSNIP on secondary products will be profitable. This is normally only relevant when there is limited or no compatibility between secondary products either designed for one primary product or other primary products. Different scenarios may arise: **1.84**

- If it is difficult for purchasers of secondary products to react to a SSNIP on a secondary market by switching to a competing primary or secondary product. Therefore, the price increase may be profitable and, accordingly, the aftermarket will be defined narrowly as only comprising the secondary products. A switch to another primary product will be difficult when switching costs between products on the primary market are high (*i.e.*, when the price of the primary product is high) or when a switch would entail other substantial investments like the training of personnel).[207]

- On the contrary, if "*it is shown that, in the event of a moderate and permanent increase in the price of secondary products, a sufficient number of consumers would switch to other primary or secondary products, in order to render such an increase unprofitable*",[208] it would be more appropriate to assume that the relevant market is a system market comprising both the primary and secondary product.[209]

---

[206] *Market Definition Notice supra* note 1, para. 56. *Discussion Paper supra* note 10, para. 247, further develops these points.

[207] Compare *CEAHR supra* note 195, paras 79 *et seq.* and 96. *See Discussion Paper supra* note 10, paras 248 *et seq.*

[208] *CEAHR supra* note 195, para. 80.

[209] *See* the *Market Definition Notice supra* note 1, para. 56, and *Discussion Paper supra* note 10, para. 249.

1. – Market Definition
Nicolas Gauss and Alison Oldale

1.85   Until *CEAHR*, market definition in the context of aftermarkets relied on remarkably traditional tools. For instance, in the *Eurofix-Bauco/Hilti* Decision, the Commission defined a separate market for nails adapted to Hilti nail guns by exclusively relying on the structure of supply and demand. Several factors militated in favour of a separate market for Hilti-compatible nails, such as the presence of independent nail producers who did not produce nail guns, nail guns and nails were not purchased together and the products constituted different types of expenditure (long term investments v. current expenditures).[210] This was confirmed by the Court of First Instance, which noted that the existence of independent producers of nails was "*in itself sound evidence that there* [was] *a specific market for Hilti-compatible nails*".[211] The different structure of supply and demand on the markets for primary and secondary products were again invoked by the Commission in the *Digital* and *Pelikan/ Kyocera* Decisions to justify identifying two separate markets instead of one system market.[212]

1.4.   Assessing Competitive Interactions between Markets

1.86   It is well-accepted that a market definition analysis of aftermarkets cannot be carried out in isolation without regard to the interaction with the relevant primary market.[213] However, the closely related question to know whether the primary markets may exercise a competitive constraint on the secondary markets is not examined by the Commission at the market definition level, but instead when assessing dominance. The Twenty-fifth Report on Competition Policy, for instance, stated that "*in order to assess dominance, the Commission will take into account all important factors such as the price and life-time of the primary product, transparency of prices of secondary products, prices of secondary products as a proportion of the primary products value, information costs* [etc.]."[214] This approach was applied to examine the abuses of dominance in the *Digital*[215] and *Kyocera*[216] cases, where the Commission examined infringements of Article 102 TFEU in the markets of maintenance services for computers and software by Digital and of toner cartridges for Kyocera printers, respectively. In line

---

[210] Cases IV/30.787 and 31.488 *supra* note 44, para. 57.
[211] *Hilti supra* note 23, para. 67, confirmed on appeal in Case C-53/92 P *Hilti v Commission* [1994] ECR I-667.
[212] DG COMP Competition Policy Newsletter (1998), No. 1, p. 29.
[213] *Market Definition Notice supra* note 1, para. 56. *CEAHR supra* note 195, paras 80 *et seq.*
[214] Twenty-fifth Report on Competition Policy (1995), para. 86.
[215] The European Commission accepted an undertaking from Digital concerning its supply and pricing practices in the field of computer maintenance services (*see* Press Release IP/97/868 of 10 October 1997).
[216] *Supra* note 214, para. 87.

1. – Market Definition
Nicolas Gauss and Alison Oldale

with the approach described above, the Commission initially concluded that the aftermarkets were autonomous product markets. It then assessed whether Digital and Kyocera exercised dominance on these markets, *i.e.*, whether they had the power to behave to an appreciable extent independently of their competitors and customers. It found that (1) Digital had a large base of locked-in customers for whom it would be difficult to switch to other computer systems, (2) purchasers of its products seldom took consideration of the subsequent costs of maintenance, and (3) the costs were in any case relatively low compared to the initial price of the equipment. As a result, Digital could act independently of its competitors. On the contrary, Kyocera was found to be unable to act independently of its competitors in the aftermarket for toner cartridges due to, among others, the ease of switching to printers of other brands and to the importance of the cost-per-page price for the initial purchase decision for a printer.[217] The reasoning in *Kyocera* was followed by the Commission in the *EFIM* case,[218] where the Commission held that, "[e]*ven if the various markets for cartridges compatible with a certain printer brand may constitute separate relevant aftermarkets, but dominance on the aftermarket can be excluded if competition on the printer market results in effective discipline in the secondary market. Even if each of the various markets for cartridges constitute separate relevant markets, … it is unlikely that the primary market and the aftermarkets are not closely linked in view of the above-mentioned criteria* [the *Kyocera* criteria]".[219]

2. Captive Production and Merchant Markets

Intermediary goods can either be sold to third parties on a so-called "merchant" market or they can be used internally by vertically integrated manufacturers that produce both the intermediary and the downstream product. Therefore, should the captive production by the vertically integrated manufacturers be considered part of the relevant product market? Following the principles of market definition, one should examine to what extent in-house producers would respond to a SSNIP on the merchant market by diverting **1.87**

---

[217] These cases are well described in DG COMP Competition Policy Newsletter (1998), No. 1, pp. 26–31. Note that, if the abuses examined related to multi-market strategies like tying, it would have been sufficient to show that these companies were dominant on the primary market.

[218] Case COMP/39.391 *Printers (EFIM Complaint)* ("*EFIM*"), Commission Decision of 20 May 2009, not yet published, paras 15 and 21. The decision has been confirmed by the General Court (Case T-296/09 *EFIM v Commission*, not yet reported) but has been appealed to the Court of Justice (Case C-56/12 P *EFIM v Commission*, pending).

[219] *EFIM supra* note 218, para. 25.

1. – Market Definition
Nicolas Gauss and Alison Oldale

some of their captive production to the sale to third parties (*i.e.*, by engaging in supply-side substitution).

1.88   Normally, in-house producers would not divert their production in the case of a SSNIP as they need their entire production of intermediary goods for their downstream production. In addition, they risk facing increased competition in the downstream market if they increase the supply of intermediary goods on the merchant market, which explains the Commission's traditional exclusion of captive production from the market.[220] On the other hand, it was necessary to avoid a so-called "merchant market rule" that would have led to a systematic exclusion of captive production at the cost of a detailed examination of the individual markets examined.[221] The Commission's approach can be criticised given that, in many markets, merchant suppliers are constrained by captive producers that are able to divert production to serving the merchant market in response to increased prices.

1.89   The Court of First Instance dealt with this issue in its judgment in *Schneider Electric*, where it found that vertically integrated manufacturers of certain intermediary goods (components for the electrical switchboards placed inside buildings) competed with non-integrated manufacturers in the context of bids for large construction projects, subjecting the latter's pricing to direct competitive pressure. For this reason, it overruled the Commission, which excluded the captive production of these components from the calculation of market shares.[222] As a result, the Commission adjusted its approach in later decisions, where it took into account the fact that in-house producers could either start serving merchant markets or increase their presence thereon in the case of a price increase.[223] Even when such a diversion is not likely to happen, a hypothetical monopolist on the merchant market might still be wary of

---

[220] At the stage of market definition: *see, for instance*, Case COMP/M.1693 *supra* note 114, para. 13 and Case COMP/M.4094 *Ineos/BP Dormagen*, Commission Decision of 10 August 2006, para. 32; or at the dominance stage (market share calculation and potential competition): Case COMP/M.2277 *Degussa/Laporte*, Commission Decision of 12 March 2001, paras 39, 43.

[221] *See, for instance*, S. Baker, "The Treatment of Captive Sales in Market Definition: Rules or Reason?" (2003) 4 *European Competition Law Review*, p. 161; N. Levy, *European Merger Control Law: A Guide to the Merger Regulation* (LexisNexis Matthew Bender, 2003), pp. 12–13; *supra* note 39, p. 52.

[222] *Schneider Electric supra* note 135, paras 281–97.

[223] *See, for instance*, Case COMP/M.3056 *Celanese/Degussa/European Oxo Chemicals*, Commission Decision of 11 June 2003, paras 55, 72, where the Commission noted that some vertically integrated producers of n-butyric aldehyde had enough spare capacities to start supplying the entire merchant market in response to an increase in prices.

1. – Market Definition
Nicolas Gauss and Alison Oldale

implementing a SSNIP on the intermediary goods. Although non-integrated downstream producers are unable to switch to another source of supply in the case of a SSNIP, they become less competitive than vertically integrated downstream producers, thereby losing market shares to the latter. In the long run, this would decrease the demand for intermediary goods on the merchant market. The SSNIP might therefore be unprofitable unless the hypothetical monopolist controls both captive and merchant production, indicating that a broad market definition is required.[224]

Since no single rule can encompass all possible situations, the decision whether to include captive production in the merchant market should therefore be taken on a case-by-case basis. At present, it remains unclear from the Commission's practice at which stage this decision should be made, whether at the market definition stage,[225] or as is more frequently the case, at the stage of examining market power, in particular through market share calculation.[226] The stage at which captive production is considered matters; if it is done under market definition, the strict criteria of supply-side substitutability must be fulfilled (most producers have to be able to immediately switch in case of a SSNIP). On the contrary, an examination of captive production under dominance allows competition authorities to rely on less rigorous requirements. **1.90**

3. Chains of Substitution

All products within a relevant product market are not necessarily direct substitutes for each other, for instance, product B may be a substitute for product A and product C may be a substitute for product B but not for product A. Nonetheless, C might exercise an indirect competitive constraint on A via a ripple effect. The same applies to geographic markets; if transport costs limit the delivery area from a plant to a certain catchment area around the plant, but this area partially overlaps with another plant's catchment area, each **1.91**

---

[224] For similar thoughts on the notion of indirect substitution in input markets, *see* P. Hofer, M. Williams and L. Wu, "The Economics of Market Definition Analysis in Theory and in Practice" (2007) *Asia-Pacific Antitrust Review*, pp. 10–13. The competitive constraint exercised by the downstream market can also be taken into account at the next stage of the competitive assessment, as illustrated in Case COMP/M.3060 *UCB/Solutia*, Commission Decision of 31 January 2003, paras 31–33.

[225] *See, for instance, supra* note 170, paras 24, 88–89, confirmed in Case T-221/95 *Endemol Entertainment Holding v Commission* [1999] ECR II-1299, paras 107–112.

[226] *See, for instance,* Case COMP/M.4524 *Nemak/Hydro Castings*, Commission Decision of 23 February 2007, para. 23; Case COMP/M.4108 *T-Systems/Gedas*, Commission Decision of 27 February 2006, paras 15–18.

1. – Market Definition
Nicolas Gauss and Alison Oldale

area may end up constraining the pricing conditions in the neighbouring area. This phenomenon is described under the term "chains of substitution"; it is described in the *Market Definition Notice*[227] and is frequently invoked by parties in competition cases to broaden the scope of the relevant market.

1.92　The concept of chains of substitution has so far mostly been used in merger cases, where the Commission has relied on the chain of substitution existing between local telecommunications exchanges to conclude that the geographic retail market for Internet access in the United Kingdom was national in scope.[228] Herbicides used for broadleaf were similarly held to exercise a competitive pressure on herbicides used for grass because while they were not direct substitutes, they both competed with broad-spectrum herbicides that served both purposes.[229] Based on the same reasoning, the fact that prices followed a continuum along different qualities of the same product, has led the Commission to define product markets comprising all these different qualities.[230]

1.93　The idea that markets can be widened by a chain of substitution should not be pushed too far. There are three important caveats. First, to some extent the concept is a result of the way the SSNIP test is defined in the Market Definition Notice. The SSNIP test is dependent on whether a hypothetical monopolist could profitably apply a 5–10 per cent permanent price increase affecting all products in the candidate market.[231] In the U.S., by contrast, the SSNIP test considers a price increase of just one of the products of the firm in question, assuming the hypothetical monopolist is free to vary other prices in the candidate market in a way that maximises the profitability of the increase in the price of the starting product.[232] Under the U.S.' definition, no chain of substitution arises, because the hypothetical monopolist can always choose not to raise the price of direct substitutes, thereby preventing indirect substitutes from affecting the profitability of the price increase.

1.94　Secondly, even if the SSNIP test is implemented using a uniform price increase, there are limits to the extent to which chains of substitution will widen the market. Adding a new product or area makes the candidate market

---

[227] *Market Definition Notice supra* note 1, para. 27.

[228] Case COMP/M.5532 *Carphone Warehouse/Tiscali UK*, Commission Decision of 29 June 2009, paras 40–47.

[229] Case COMP/M.1806 *AstraZeneca/Novartis*, Commission Decision of 26 July 2000, para. 60.

[230] Case COMP/M.2268 *Pernod Ricard/Diageo/Seagram Spirits*, Commission Decision of 8 May 2001, paras 13–17; *see also*, for pet food, Case COMP/M.2544 *Masterfoods/Royal Canin*, Commission Decision of 15 February 2002, paras 15–17.

[231] *Market Definition Notice supra* note 1, para. 17.

[232] *See* U.S. Horizontal Merger Guidelines *supra* note 31, para. 4.1.1.

1. – Market Definition
Nicolas Gauss and Alison Oldale

bigger, and therefore, the relative size of the overlap between it and indirect substitutes smaller. Thus, this overlap will have an increasingly smaller effect on the profitability of a price rise as the market widens, and eventually its effect will be too small to justify widening the market further.

Thirdly, if there are breaks in the chain of substitution, for instance, a sparsely populated area with a few shops that breaks a chain of overlapping retail catchment areas, then these will put a stop to further widening the market.   **1.95**

Given these limitations, the *Market Definition Notice* rightly states that *"the con-   **1.96**
cept of chains of substitution has to be corroborated by actual evidence, for instance related to price interdependence at the extremes of the chains of substitution, in order to lead to the extension of the relevant market in an individual case. Price levels at the extremes of the chains would have to be of the same magnitude as well."*[233]

Such corroborating evidence was, for instance, lacking in the *Sonoco/Ahlstrom*   **1.97**
merger case, where the Commission found that despite overlapping areas of distribution for the product concerned, the evidence showed a weak level of market share interpenetration.[234] Likewise, breaks in a potential chain of substitution should prevent the chain from being used to broaden the market definition.[235] In the *Owens-Illinois/BSN Glasspack* Decision, the Commission also rejected an argument relating to a continuous geographic chain of substitution, based on the finding that suppliers of glass packaging could price discriminate between customers within their own catchment area.[236]

4. Dynamic Markets

4.1. Introduction

The Court of Justice in *TeliaSonera* held that the application of competition   **1.98**
rules *"cannot depend on whether the market concerned has already reached a certain level*

---

[233] *Market Definition Notice supra* note 1, para. 58.

[234] Case COMP/M.3431 *Sonoco/Ahlstrom/JV*, Commission Decision of 6 October 2004, paras 50–54, 75.

[235] The Commission recently described a break in the chain of substitution ranging from smaller to larger cruise vessels, although it ultimately declined to define the scope of the product market: Case COMP/M.4956 *STX/Aker Yards*, Commission Decision of 5 May 2008, para. 24.

[236] It reasoned as follows: *"a* [BSN-owned] *plant in the south of France may find that customer A located toward the west of its catchment area has only* [competitor 1] *as a potential alternative.... However, customer B located east of the* [BSN-owned] *plant, has the additional option of purchasing its glass bottles from* [competitor 2] *plants in Asti or Milan. BSN, therefore, must take the additional competitor into account in its pricing to customer B, but not to A."* Case COMP/M.3397 *Owens-Illinois/BSN Glasspack*, Commission Decision of 9 June 2004, para. 25 and n. 6.

1. – Market Definition
Nicolas Gauss and Alison Oldale

of maturity. Particularly in a rapidly growing market, Article 102 TFEU requires action as quickly as possible, to prevent the formation and consolidation in that market of a competitive structure distorted by the abusive strategy of an undertaking which has a dominant position on that market or on a closely linked neighbouring market, in other words it requires action before the anti-competitive effects of that strategy are realised".[237]

1.99 It is often criticised that the application of competition rules to markets with a high rate of innovation (dynamic markets) is too focused on restrictions of short-term price competition, and not focused enough on the long-term effects on innovation and technological progress.[238] Dynamic markets include, for instance, markets for computer hardware and software, Internet applications, communication technologies and pharmaceutical markets. There is a danger that the reliance of traditional market definition on demand-side substitutability may lead to incorrect market definitions in dynamic markets where competition does not come from readily available demand substitutes, but from new products and services (dynamic competition), which are not yet commercialised.[239]

1.100 Dynamic competition is not only characterised by the creation and commercialisation of new products and processes, but also by significant product differentiation and rapid response to change.[240] Contrary to that, competition in traditional industries, like steel and food manufacturing, is characterised by price and output competition of products already on the market and by incremental innovation.[241]

1.101 In some dynamic markets, competition does not take place *in* the market, but *for* the market. This means companies are not trying to win market shares by lowering prices in a market, in which they are already active (competition in the market), but are trying to win a market by introducing new products and

---

[237] *TeliaSonera Judgment 2011 supra* note 8, para. 108.

[238] H. Hovenkamp, "Signposts of Anticompetitive Exclusion: Restraints on Innovation and Economies of Scale", in B. E. Hawk (Ed.), *Fordham Competition Law Institute: International Antitrust Law and Policy 2006* (New York, Juris Publishing, 2007), pp. 409 and 415.

[239] C. Ahlborn and others, "*DG Comp's Discussion Paper on Article 82: Implications of the Proposed Framework and Antitrust Rules for Dynamically Competitive Industries*", March 2006, p. 22.

[240] J. G. Sidak and D. J. Teece, "Dynamic Competition in Antitrust Law" (2009) 5(4) *Journal of Competition Law & Economics*, pp. 602 *et seq.*

[241] D. S. Evans and R. Schmalensee, "Some Economic Aspects of Antitrust Analysis in Dynamically Competitive Industries", *NBER Working Paper Series*, Working Paper No. 8268, May 2001, available at http://ssrn.com/abstract=268877, pp. 2 *et seq.*

1. – Market Definition
Nicolas Gauss and Alison Oldale

services (competition for the market).[242] However, dynamic competition does not necessarily imply competition for the market; the latter has to be proven on a case-by-case basis.[243]

Should markets that are characterised by dynamic competition be defined dif- **1.102** ferently? While this does not seem generally necessary, the following special considerations apply.

4.2.   *Demand-side Substitutability*

The SSNIP test only takes customers' reactions to short-term price increases **1.103** into account. However, in dynamic markets, products are usually differenti- ated in terms of quality, and price is not the main competitive constraint.[244] Features and functionalities are more important than price. For instance, it would be wrong to conclude from the fact that most Blackberry users would not switch to iPhones in the case of a SSNIP that these two products belong to different markets. The competitive constraint, which different types of smartphones exert on each other, is, to a large extent, independent of small changes in relative price, and focuses more on factors such as functionality of the products, data security, design, and product image. Furthermore, dynamic markets often feature a high degree of product differentiation, which fur- ther reduces the extent to which products constrain each other as a result of price. This is why the SSNIP test might be uninformative or unworkable – at least before a dominant technology prevails in the market.[245] Finally, applying the SSNIP test in innovative markets is also problematic because the test is based on the static hypothesis that the current competitive structure does not change, *e.g.*, that the pricing of substitutes remains constant and that technol- ogy does not advance.[246] This is an unrealistic assumption for an innovation- driven market.

More generally, the important role of product differentiation in dynamic mar- **1.104** kets renders price-related tests less important. But qualitative approaches to

---

[242] *Ibid.*, p. 16 and *supra* note 237, p. 12.

[243] *See supra* note 130, p. 38.

[244] *See supra* note 238, p. 613.

[245] *Ibid.*, pp. 613 *et seq.*

[246] Charles River Associates, *Innovation and Competition Policy: Part 1 – Conceptual Issues*, Office of Fair Trading Economic Discussion Paper 3, OFT 377, March 2002, available at http://www.oft.gov.uk/shared_oft/reports/comp_policy/oft377part1.pdf, para. 4.53.

1. – Market Definition
Nicolas Gauss and Alison Oldale

market definition based on product characteristics can also lead to fallacious results, since subdividing the relevant market based on the different product characteristics can lead to overly narrow markets.[247]

1.105 Overall, demand-side substitutability is not an adequate criterion to measure the competitive constraints in dynamic markets, since it only considers products that are currently available.

4.3. Supply-side Substitutability

1.106 Supply-side substitutability only takes account of products that competitors could start producing in the short-term and without significant additional costs. Technological development in dynamic markets is much more rapid than in commodity goods markets, but it usually takes longer than one year for an innovative product to be commercialised. For instance, in *Microsoft*, it was found that there was no supply-side substitutability from other operating systems to client PC operating systems, since developing a new operating system was too time-consuming and costly.[248] In addition, the Commission held that the timeframe of 29 months between announcing the first Beta version and launching the final version of a new work group server operating system was too long for assuming that this constituted supply-side substitutability of work group server operating systems.[249]

1.107 Making a finding of supply-side substitutability even more unlikely, market entry in dynamic markets often entails research and development, which necessitates high sunk costs. While the commercialisation of an innovative product or service is often costly and not possible in the short term, such a product or service regularly exercises competitive constraints on market players long before it is commercialised. It is necessary to take this short-term effect into account. Thus, the scope of the traditional interpretation of supply-side substitutability in dynamic markets has to be broadened to product entries that are not possible within one year or that result in sunk costs.[250] Otherwise, a finding of supply-side substitutability will almost be impossible in dynamic markets.

---

[247] *See supra* note 237, p. 22.
[248] *Microsoft Decision 2004 supra* note 8, paras 335–41.
[249] *Ibid.*, para. 398.
[250] *See* M. Dreher, "Die Kontrolle des Wettbewerbs in Innovationsmärkten – Marktabgrenzung und Marktbeherrschung in dynamischen Märkten" (2009) *Zeitschrift für Wettbewerbsrecht*, pp. 149, 164 *et seq.* and 168.

1. – Market Definition
Nicolas Gauss and Alison Oldale

4.4. *Potential Competition*

It has been suggested to consider potential competition at the market defini-   **1.108**
tion stage to reflect the fact that the main competitive constraint in dynamic
markets comes from new, superior products. According to this viewpoint, the
consequence of ignoring potential competition in dynamic markets is that
markets will be defined too narrowly, which will lead to frequent, though
mostly unjustified findings of dominance in innovative industries.[251] While
this approach is appealing at first glance, it is impractical and unnecessary
if supply-side substitutability is applied more flexibly, as suggested above.
Admittedly, the difference between supply-side substitutability and potential
competition is a matter of degree. However, potential competition also takes
account of products that are not yet under development and therefore clearly
do not exercise an immediate competitive constraint. Taking potential competition into account at the first stage of the assessment would therefore not
only be contrary to the *Market Definition Notice*;[252] it would also be problematic
insofar as, in order to assess dominance, hypothetical market shares would
have to be assigned to potential competitors, even though only some of them
would eventually become actual competitors.[253] The concern that a market
definition devoid of potential competition could too easily lead to an incorrect finding of dominance,[254] and therefore to the scrutiny of a company's
behaviour under Article 102 TFEU,[255] is usually unjustified. A narrow market
definition, which leads to high market shares, is not tantamount to a finding
of dominance in a dynamic market, especially since the Commission inter-
prets market shares in the light of the dynamics of the market.[256]

5. Two-sided Markets

Companies operating in two-sided markets (also called "two-sided platforms")   **1.109**
offer goods or services to two distinct groups of customers that are dependent on each other, but that cannot get together easily without an intermediary. In such a setting, each group of customers benefits when the number

---

[251] *See supra* note 238, p. 614 and *supra* note 237, p. 25.

[252] *Market Definition Notice supra* note 1, para. 24.

[253] L. Peeperkorn and V. Verouden, in J. Faull and A. Nikpay (Eds.), *The EC Law of Competition, supra* note 39,
para. 1.156, Fn. 98.

[254] *See supra* note 237, p. 25.

[255] *See supra* note 248, pp. 149 and 167.

[256] *Guidance Paper supra* note 3, para. 13.

1. – Market Definition
Nicolas Gauss and Alison Oldale

of customers in the other set increases. Two-sided platforms usually lower transaction costs and thereby facilitate value-creating exchanges.[257]

1.110 A typical example is that of producers of video game consoles, which provide game developers with software tools on which they can design games and consumers with a device on which they can play these games. The more consumers that own a particular game console, the more attractive it becomes for game developers to design games for this console; conversely, the more games that have been developed for a particular console, the more attractive this console becomes to consumers. Examples of two-sided platforms include: online search engines (which provide search services and advertisement to users, and clicks of users to advertisers), online auction websites such as eBay (which provide sellers of goods a platform to sell, and buyers an intermediary, where they can purchase goods they are interested in), but also traditional shopping malls (which provide businesses with store space and clients with shopping opportunities), and can extend to multi-sided platforms that bring together multiple sets of customers. The Commission has dealt with two-sided markets in merger cases involving intermediation in travel distribution systems and intermediation in online advertising.[258]

1.111 Market definition can be particularly complex regarding two-sided platforms, as the traditional tools can lead to an erroneous assessment of competitive constraints. For instance, when applying the hypothetical monopolist test to one side of a platform (A) that comprises two sides (A and B), it is necessary to take into account the following: a small price increase for customers on side A might be profitable in the very short-term, but will also reduce demand on side A, which will likely reduce demand on side B, which further decreases demand on side A, and so on. Because of this negative feedback loop, an

---

[257] D. S. Evans, "Antitrust Issues Raised by the Emerging Global Internet Economy" (2008) 102(4) *Northwestern University Law Review*, p. 293.

[258] Case COMP/M.4523 *Travelport/Worldspan*, Commission Decision of 21 August 2007. Travelport and Worldspan were both active on the market for electronic travel distribution services through a GDS. A GDS is a two-sided platform through which travel service providers (TSPs) distribute their travel content to travel agents (TAs) and ultimately to end-consumers, while TAs can access and book travel content through GDSs. The Commission noticed that GDS providers act as intermediaries in a market of a two-sided nature, connecting two separate customer categories (para. 10). In Case COMP/M.4731 *Google/Doubleclick*, Commission Decision of 11 March 2008, the Commission analysed intermediation in online advertising. It held that an ad network is a two-sided platform serving (1) publishers (websites) that want to host advertisements, and (2) advertisers that want to run ads on those sites, which is a two-sided market in which ad networks match publishers and advertisers (para. 20).

1. – Market Definition
Nicolas Gauss and Alison Oldale

apparently profitable SSNIP on one side of the platform might in fact turn out to be unprofitable, suggesting that a narrow market definition that comprises solely one side of the platform would be wrong.

This challenges the traditional understanding of relevant markets as comprising substitutes of the products or services observed. For market definition in two and multi-sided markets, it may be necessary to take account of the competitive constraints exercised by the *complementary* products or services sold on the other side of the market.[259]   **1.112**

VI.   Conclusions

Market definition serves as a starting point of the competitive analysis under Article 102 TFEU – it is a first "filter". It should, as far as possible, make use of quantitative techniques, thereby guaranteeing objectivity and ensuring a common approach is taken to market definition under both merger control and Article 102 TFEU. Most importantly, market definition should not just be used in a result-orientated way to prove or rebut a finding of dominance or of multi-market abuse; it should be applied in an open-ended manner.   **1.113**

1.   Market Definition as a Foundation for the Competitive Assessment

Market definition is an intermediate, but indispensable step in structuring the competitive analysis.[260] It serves as a first "filter"[261] by allowing competition authorities to exclude cases where the company under examination is unlikely to be dominant (in particular, because its market shares are too low). In addition, defining the relevant market provides a framework for the whole analysis of market power and abuse. It is not possible to analyse the position of the   **1.114**

---

[259] D. S. Evans, "*Two-Sided Market Definition*", in ABA Section of Antitrust Law, Market Definition in Antitrust: Theory and case studies, November 11, 2009, Chapter XII, available at http://ssrn.com/abstract=1396751, p. 10, note 30. Different methods have been proposed in order to provide a better understanding of the competitive constraints in multi-sided markets (*see ibid.*, pp. 12 *et seq.*).

[260] L. Peeperkorn and V. Verouden, in J. Faull and A. Nikpay (Eds.), *The EC Law of Competition*, *supra* note 39, para. 1.184; H. W. Friederiszick, in J. Schwarze (Ed.), *Recht und Ökonomie im Europäischen Wettbewerbsrecht* (Baden-Baden, Nomos, 2006), pp. 29 *et seq.* and 38; R. J. van den Bergh and P. D. Camesasca, *European Competition Law and Economics: A Comparative Perspective* (2nd Ed., London, Sweet & Maxwell, 2006), p. 119.

[261] Compare Friederiszick, who speaks of a "screening function", *see* H. W. Friederiszick, in J. Schwarze (Ed.), *Recht und Ökonomie im Europäischen Wettbewerbsrecht* (Baden-Baden, Nomos, 2006), pp. 29 *et seq.* and 38.

1. – Market Definition
Nicolas Gauss and Alison Oldale

dominant undertaking, the conditions on the relevant market (*e.g.*, barriers to entry), the position of the dominant undertaking's competitors,[262] or the markets on which a multi-market leveraging strategy is conducted, without a prior definition of the market. Market definition, however, should be applied in an open-ended and flexible manner, taking into account the particularities of the industry in question. This means that the methods applied to market definition do not just depend on the available information, but also on the character of the market examined.

1.115 Market definition is of limited importance if the competitive assessment would be the same under all conceivable market definitions. In these cases, the market definition can be left open.[263]

1.116 Market definition should not anticipate the next steps of the competitive analysis, for instance, by already examining potential competition, which is part of the dominance analysis. This also applies to defining dynamic markets. Considering potential competition on the market definition level would unnecessarily burden the assessment of market definition, the first level of the analysis.[264] Moreover, it would not correspond to the purpose of market definition, *i.e.*, to identify immediate competitive constraints.

2. Quantitative v Qualitative Analysis

1.117 The Commission has made it clear it relies on different methods for defining a market, and is making use of all available relevant information without rigidly prioritising one form of evidence over another.[265] In general, quantitative methods provide a more objective approach to market definition than a market definition based on the analysis of a product's characteristics. Quantitative

---

[262] These are some of the factors that the Commission takes into account when assessing if there is anticompetitive foreclosure that requires an intervention under Article 102 TFEU; *see Guidance Paper supra* note 3, para. 20.

[263] *See Market Definition Notice supra* note 1, para. 27 and *Microsoft Decision 2004 supra* note 8, para. 326, where the distinction between Intel and non-Intel compatible client PC operating systems was found to be unnecessary as it would not alter the assessment of Microsoft's market power; *see also* Case COMP/38.113 *supra* note 117, para. 9. In Case COMP/M.4731, the Commission saw no need to define two separate markets for the provision of search and non-search online advertising space as (*supra* note 256, para. 56) and it saw no need to further subdivide the market for intermediation in online advertising (para. 73), since in both cases, under any of these market definitions, the transaction would not have given rise to any competition concerns.

[264] *See supra* note 130, p. 82.

[265] *Market Definition Notice supra* note 1, para. 25; *Discussion Paper supra* note 10, para. 13.

1. – Market Definition
Nicolas Gauss and Alison Oldale

tests also allow for a more evidence-based and less judgmental approach to market definition than qualitative approaches.

However, qualitative evidence remains a fundamental element of the Commis- **1.118**
sion's market definition analysis. In light of the difficulties involved in implementing the SSNIP or other quantitative tests for market definition under Article 102 TFEU – such as the cellophane fallacy or lack of relevant data – it is unlikely that qualitative analysis will become confined to a purely preliminary phase of market definition.[266] Moreover, qualitative analysis will remain indispensable in product-differentiated markets such as dynamic markets.

Even if a fully quantitative approach can be applied without difficulty, a **1.119**
qualitative approach will be needed to provide corroborating evidence. If the SSNIP test can be fully applied, the focus should not be on average (or infra-marginal) customers' reaction, but on whether there are enough customers whose willingness to pay does not extend to a SSNIP (*i.e.*, marginal customers). When a qualitative test is applied, it is useful to give thought to the question as to whether products are so different that not enough customers will defect in case of a price increase of 5–10 per cent, so as to make the increase unprofitable. The answer depends on customers' willingness to switch and on the profit margin made before the SSNIP was implemented. If the profit margin is very low, then a lot of customers must defect in order to make a price increase unprofitable.[267] While this method can often not be applied in a fully quantitative manner due to a lack of necessary data, it is possible to apply it conceptually.

3. Market Definition under Article 102 TFEU and under Merger Control

Under Article 102 TFEU market definition has not reached the same level of **1.120**
economic sophistication[268] as under merger control, where it is common to apply quantitative techniques to test possible substitution among products or services. One reason for this might be that under merger control, the future situation after the structural change caused by the merger is assessed, whereas

---

[266] Some authors suggest that its importance might be on the wane, *see* R. O'Donoghue and A. J. Padilla, *supra* note 5, pp. 87–88.

[267] T. Klein, *supra* note 42, pp. 169, 175.

[268] *See, for instance*, Case COMP/35.141 *Deutsche Post*, Commission Decision of 20 March 2001, OJ 2001 L 125/27, paras 26–29; *supra* note 176, paras 59–67; Case COMP/36.041 *supra* note 79, paras 109–118.

1. – Market Definition
Nicolas Gauss and Alison Oldale

under Article 102 TFEU, a certain behaviour and its effects on consumers are examined. The analysis under Article 102 TFEU is thus generally more related to the behaviour of one or several companies and less focused on the market situation than under merger control. Another reason for the higher level of economic sophistication under merger control is the mere fact that there is a significantly higher number of merger cases than Article 102 TFEU cases, which has given the Commission and the courts many more opportunities to comment on complex questions of market definition under merger control than under Article 102 TFEU.

1.121 However, a very important reason for continued scepticism on the part of the Commission about the usefulness of very precise approaches to defining the market in Article 102 TFEU cases is the cellophane fallacy. The constraints that are relevant to assessing whether a firm is able to price at above competitive levels are those that would operate if prices were competitive, rather than those that do operate at current prices (if the two differ). The techniques that have been developed for defining the market in merger cases rely on information about substitution patterns at current prices, raising concerns that these techniques are not applicable. This scepticism may be overstated as there are important benefits from using economic techniques from merger control, including: (1) products that can be excluded from the market at current prices would also be excluded at competitive ones, so that the exercise of defining the market at current prices provides important information about the boundaries of the market at competitive ones; and (2) the likely effects of the alleged conduct can depend on the options that customers have at prevailing market conditions, and defining the market using standard merger control techniques is a good way to learn about these constraints.

Dominance

Christopher Cook and Ruchit Patel

I. Introduction

Article 102 TFEU prohibits the abuse of a dominant position. In accordance **2.1** with case law, an infringement consists of two elements: showing that the firm in question holds a dominant position and showing that the conduct in question is abusive. The dominance finding is thus an essential element of any determination of infringement, and every Article 102 infringement decision includes a finding that the firm holds a dominant position.

This chapter summarises how the Commission and courts have applied the **2.2** concept of dominance since the modern era of Article 102 enforcement began in the 1970s. Developments in the analysis of dominance over the last four decades have been evolutionary rather than transformational, and given the wealth of Commission and court precedent, the main parameters are by now well established.[1] The language of the Commission's *Guidance Paper*, which outlines a new effects-based approach to Article 102, adheres relatively closely to the familiar definition of dominance fashioned by the courts. However, the *Guidance Paper* signals a shift in emphasis that could have important consequences both for whether or not certain firms would be found dominant and for the significance of such a finding in the Article 102 analysis. This

---

[1] This chapter focuses on the analysis of single-firm dominance, where the dominant firm is the seller in a market. Buyer-side dominance is also possible, and is discussed briefly in Section III.3 below. A separate concept is "collective dominance", whereby a number of firms in an oligopolistic market together hold a dominant position, and the abuse would consist in one or more of the firms taking part in a tacitly agreed collective exclusionary or exploitative strategy. While such situations can in principle arise, cases based on a theory of abuse of collective dominance have been rare (the principal example is Joined Cases C-395 and 396/96 P *Compagnie Maritime Belge Transports and others v Commission* [2000] ECR I-1365) and in practice such fact patterns seem more likely to be addressed as unlawful concerted practices under Article 101 TFEU. The European Commission's 2009 *Guidance Paper* setting forth its Article 102 enforcement priorities also does not address collective dominance, and the concept is not addressed further in this Chapter. *See* Guidance on the Commission's enforcement priorities in applying Article 82 of the EC Treaty to abusive exclusionary conduct by dominant undertakings ("*Guidance Paper*"), OJ 2009 C 45/7.

2. – Dominance
Christopher Cook and Ruchit Patel

shift could subtly but significantly change the way future cases are argued and decided.

2.3 This chapter is organised as follows. By way of introduction, Section II explains the European definition of "dominant position" and how the focus has shifted from the firm's commercial power (*i.e.*, the ability to behave independently of competitors and customers) to a more economically grounded approach that equates dominance with sustained market power (*i.e.*, the ability to charge supra competitive prices or depress output). Section III analyses each of the principal factors that are considered in the Article 102 dominance assessment: the firm's market position, barriers to entry or expansion by rivals, constraints imposed by the firm's customers (buyer power), and other factors. Section IV discusses the implications of the evolution to an effects-based approach to Article 102 TFEU for the dominance analysis and explains how this shift implicitly relegates the dominance finding to a role of far lesser significance in the determination of when an infringement of Article 102 TFEU has occurred.

II.   The Concept of Dominance under Article 102 TFEU

2.4 The Treaty on the Functioning of the European Union and its predecessors provide no definition of a dominant position. However, one of the most familiar statements in EU competition law is the Court of Justice's 1978 definition of dominance in *United Brands* as: "*a position of economic strength enjoyed by an undertaking which enables it to prevent effective competition being maintained on the relevant market by affording it the power to behave to an appreciable extent independently of its competitors, its customers and ultimately of its consumers.*"[2]

2.5 The Court of Justice repeated and thereby cemented this language the following year in *Hoffmann-La Roche*, adding that "[s]*uch a position does not preclude some competition, … but enables the undertaking which profits by it, if not to determine, at least to have an appreciable influence on the conditions under which that competition will develop, and in any case to act largely in disregard of it so long as such conduct does not relate to its detriment.*"[3]

---

[2] Case 27/76 *United Brands and United Brands Continentaal v Commission* ("*United Brands*") [1978] ECR 207, para. 65.
[3] Case 85/76 *Hoffmann-La Roche v Commission* ("*Hoffmann-La Roche*") [1979] ECR 461, para. 39.

2. – Dominance
Christopher Cook and Ruchit Patel

This basic definition of dominance has survived unchanged for more than **2.6** 30 years, reappearing in virtually every Article 102 decision and judgment since and cited with approval in the Commission's *Guidance Paper*.[4]

1.   The Classical Definition of Dominance under Article 102 TFEU

Since the early Court of Justice judgments, it has been recognised that a domi-   **2.7** nant position typically derives from a combination of factors, none of which may individually be determinative. Assessing dominance therefore requires a thorough examination of the relevant market's structure (*i.e.*, the market shares of the firm in question and its competitors) and the conditions of competition that exist on it.[5] The Commission and courts have never applied the classical formulation's "independence" criterion literally, no doubt in implicit recognition that no firm can act entirely independently: even a pure monopolist is constrained by the demand curve for its product, which is affected by both its competitors (who will have products that compete, even if they are not in the same relevant market) and its customers (who will typically reduce their demand as price increases).[6] Rather, as the concept has traditionally been applied, the dominant firm is one that has sufficient commercial power to control or influence the conditions of competition and thereby distort the competitive process to its benefit in ways that its rivals cannot. Professor Whish refers to this as "*freedom from competitive constraint*".[7]

Thus, for example, in *United Brands* the Court of Justice acknowledged that   **2.8** United Brands' market share of 40–45 per cent did not in itself show that the firm was dominant; the Court's dominance assessment focused more on United Brands' high degree of vertical integration, which "*guarantees it commercial stability and well being*" as compared to its smaller rivals.[8] United Brands owned extensive, geographically diverse banana plantations (reducing its exposure to natural disasters), controlled its own shipping and distribution (ensuring reliable supply), was a leader in technical knowledge (improving productivity in its plantations), and owned the market's premier brand (making it an unavoidable trading partner for distributors). As a result of the "cumulative effect" of

---

[4] *Guidance Paper supra* note 1, para. 10.
[5] *See, e.g., United Brands supra* note 2, paras 66–7 and *Hoffmann-La Roche supra* note 3, para. 39.
[6] *See, e.g.*, J.P. de Azevedo and M. Walker, "Dominance: Meaning and Measurement" (2002) *European Competition Law Review*, p. 364.
[7] R. Whish, *Competition Law* (6th Ed., Oxford, Oxford University Press, 2008), p. 175.
[8] *United Brands supra* note 2, para 81.

2. – Dominance
Christopher Cook and Ruchit Patel

all these "advantages", even on occasions when United Brands encountered "lively" and "fierce" competitive struggles as rivals offered discounts and made promotions, United Brands was able to defend its market position by adopting "*a flexible overall strategy directed against new competitors establishing themselves on the whole of the relevant market.*"[9] The Court of Justice found that these factors outweighed evidence that the banana market was competitive and that United Brands had been lossmaking over the previous five years.

2.9 The *Hoffman-La Roche* judgment also highlights the essential relationship between dominance and the competitive process as applied in the early cases. As discussed in Section III below, in its dominance assessment the Court of Justice in *Hoffman-La Roche* appears to place greater emphasis on the market share of the firm and its competitors. The Court clearly conceives of dominance not in terms of market outcomes (prices and output), but in terms of the distorting effect of the firm's presence on the competitive process. Roche's high market share is problematic because it means that Roche "*is entirely free to decide what attitude to adopt when confronted by competition.*"[10] This "*freedom of action ... is the special feature of a dominant position.*"[11]

2.10 This basic view of dominance as the power to resist the constraints normally posed by the competitive process is also apparent in *Michelin I*. In its dominance assessment, the Court of Justice highlights Michelin's large network of commercial representatives whose "*efficiency and quality of service are unquestioned*", which enables Michelin "*to maintain and strengthen its position on the market and to protect itself more effectively against competition.*"[12] The Court expressly recognises that Michelin has been unprofitable and even that Michelin's prices are competitive ("*the prices charged by Michelin NV do not constitute an abuse and are not even particularly high*"),[13] but this market outcome does not override the fact that Michelin's high level of service and strong reputation render it "*largely immune to competition*"[14] and thus dominant.

---

[9] *United Brands supra* note 2, para. 121.
[10] *Hoffmann-La Roche supra* note 3, para. 51.
[11] *Ibid.*, para. 41.
[12] Case 322/81 *Nederlandsche Banden Industrie Michelin v Commission* ("*Michelin I*") [1983] ECR 3461, para. 58.
[13] *Ibid.*, para. 59.
[14] *Ibid.*, para. 56.

2. – Dominance
Christopher Cook and Ruchit Patel

Under this approach, dominance is conceived as "commercial power",[15] **2.11**
assessed by reference to the firm's influence over, or independence from, the
competitive process itself rather than by reference to the desired outcomes of
a properly functioning market (*i.e.*, competitive prices and consumer welfare).
This view is not limited to a few anachronistic early judgments but has in fact
prevailed throughout most of the history of Article 102 application. More
recently, in her 2006 opinion in *British Airways*, Advocate General Kokott
referred with approval to the 1970s judgments, explaining that,

> *"Article [102 TFEU], like the other competition rules of the Treaty, is not
> designed only or primarily to protect the immediate interests of individual competi-
> tors or consumers, but to protect the <u>structure of the market</u> and thus <u>competition
> as such (as an institution)</u>, which has already been weakened by the presence of
> the dominant undertaking on the market. In this way, consumers are also indi-
> rectly protected. Because where competition as such is damaged, disadvantages for
> consumers are also to be feared."*[16]

Thus, the dominant firm is one that is able to hinder the maintenance or **2.12**
growth of the limited degree of competition that still remains in the market.[17]
Rivals may nibble away at the fringes and a degree of competition may remain,
but the dominant firm's size or other advantages enable it to prevent the
emergence of competition that would threaten its pre-eminence. The dominant firm will be able to counter competitive initiatives by smaller rivals, and
because competitors know this, the dominant firm's mere presence increases
risk and creates *"almost insuperable practical and financial obstacles"*[18] to entry and
expansion, deterring investment and entrenching the dominant firm's position. Under the classical approach, dominance is commercial power, interpreted as the dominant firm's ability to contain competition and resist the
constraints that healthy competitive markets impose.

---

[15] *See, e.g.*, G. Monti, "The Concept of Dominance in Article 82" (2006) 31 *European Competition Journal*, pp. 38–9.
[16] Advocate General Kokott in Case C-95/04 *British Airways v Commission* ("*British Airways*") [2007] ECR I-2331, para. 68 (emphasis in original).
[17] *See Hoffmann-La Roche supra* note 3, para. 91.
[18] *United Brands supra* note 2, para. 123.

2. – Dominance

Christopher Cook and Ruchit Patel

2. The Definition of Dominance in the 2009 *Guidance Paper*

2.13 The *Guidance Paper* repeats and endorses the classical definition of dominance from *United Brands* and *Hoffman-La Roche*. At the same time, however, the *Guidance Paper* introduces the concept of dominance as "substantial market power", representing a shift in focus away from the competitive process (*i.e.*, how the firm can avoid competitive constraints) and toward market outcomes (*i.e.*, the firm's ability to increase prices or reduce output).

2.14 The *Guidance Paper* signals this shift by placing the section covering the definition of and test for dominance in a section entitled "Market Power". In defining dominance, the *Guidance Paper* first presents the Court of Justice's classical formula ("*the power to behave to an appreciable extent independently of its competitors, its customers and ultimately of consumers*"),[19] but then immediately equates this concept with substantial market power: "*The notion of independence is related to the degree of competitive constraint exerted on the undertaking in question. Dominance entails that these competitive constraints are not sufficiently effective and hence that the undertaking in question enjoys substantial market power over a period of time.*"[20]

2.15 The standard economic definition of market power is the power to raise prices profitably above the competitive level.[21] The *Guidance Paper* brings together the concepts of substantial market power, dominance, and competitive constraints by expressly making the lack of competitive constraints equivalent to the standard economic definition of market power: "*The Commission considers that an undertaking which is capable of profitably increasing prices above the competitive level for a significant period of time does not face sufficiently effective competitive constraints and can thus generally be regarded as dominant.*"[22]

---

[19] *Guidance Paper supra* note 1, para. 10.

[20] *Ibid.*

[21] *See, e.g.*, Office of Fair Trading, *Assessment of Market Power*, OFT 415, December 2004, para. 1.4: "*Market power can be thought of as the ability profitably to sustain prices above competitive levels or restrict output or quality below competitive levels. An undertaking with market power might also have the ability and incentive to harm the process of competition in other ways; for example, by weakening existing competition, raising entry barriers or slowing innovation. However, although market power is not solely concerned with the ability of a supplier to raise prices, this guideline often for convenience refers to market power as the ability profitably to sustain prices above competitive levels.*"

[22] *Guidance Paper supra* note 1, para. 11. The *Guidance Paper* also makes clear that in its terminology, "*the expression 'increase prices' includes the power to maintain prices above the competitive level and is used as short-hand for the various ways in which the parameters of competition – such as prices, output, innovation, the variety or quality of goods or services – can be influenced to the advantage of the dominant undertaking and to the detriment of consumers.*" This Chapter generally follows the same convention.

2. – Dominance
Christopher Cook and Ruchit Patel

The equation of dominance and substantial market power had previously been **2.16** suggested in some EU publications,[23] but the link had not previously been made express in the context of Article 102 TFEU. The *Guidance Paper* thus subtly shifts the definition of dominance from the classical formula of dominance as commercial power and the ability to resist competitive constraints (*i.e.*, a concept based on the working of the competitive process), to dominance as the ability to price above the competitive level (*i.e.*, a concept based on market outcomes). This shift is entirely in line with the *Guidance Paper*'s announced effects-based approach and focus on consumer welfare.

Recent Commission decisions have sought to reconcile the wording of the **2.17** courts and the language of the *Guidance Paper*. For example, in *Telekomunikacja Polska*, the Commission held that:

> "*The notion of independence, which is a special feature of dominance, is related to the level of competitive constraints facing the undertaking in question. It is not required for a finding of dominance that the undertaking in question has eliminated all opportunity for competition on the market. However, for dominance to exist, the <u>undertaking concerned must have substantial market power so as to have an appreciable influence on the conditions under which competition will develop</u>.*" (Emphasis added).[24]

In considering the *Guidance Paper*'s equation of dominance with the power to **2.18** price above the competitive level, it is important to distinguish between the *definition* of dominance and the *test* for determining when dominance exists. Although the text is ambiguous, the *Guidance Paper* should not be read as suggesting that in order to identify dominance (*i.e.*, substantial market power), the Commission intends to identify the competitive price level and compare

---

[23] *See, e.g.*, Commission Notice – Guidelines on Vertical Restraints, OJ 2000 C 291/1, para. 119 ("*Conceptually, market power is the power to raise price above the competitive level and, at least in the short term, to obtain supra-normal profits. Companies may have market power below the level of market dominance, which is the threshold for the application of Article* [102].*"). The parallel statement in the 2010 Vertical Restraints Guidelines more closely tracks the effects-based approach in the *Guidance Paper* (*supra* note 1), removing the reference to "supra-normal profits", adding other market outcomes indicative of dominance besides pricing above competitive levels: Commission Notice – Guidelines on Vertical Restraints, para. 97 ("*Market power is the ability to maintain prices above competitive levels or to maintain output in terms of product quantities, product quality and variety or innovation below competitive levels for a not insignificant period of time. The degree of market power normally required for a finding of an infringement under Article 101(1) is less than the degree of market power required for a finding of dominance under Article 102.*").

[24] Case COMP/39.525 *Telekomunikacja Polska* ("*Telekomunikacja Polska*"), Commission Decision of 22 June 2011, not yet published, para. 641.

2. – Dominance
Christopher Cook and Ruchit Patel

this to the dominant firm's price. As economists have recognised, identifying the competitive price level in a market is virtually impossible,[25] so such a test would not be administrable. And this is not what the *Guidance Paper* proposes. In fact, as discussed in Section III below, the *Guidance Paper* sets forth a methodology for detecting substantial market power that is in line with current economic thinking, based on the examination of competitive constraints imposed by existing competitors, the threat of new entry or expansion, and customer bargaining power.

2.19 It should be noted, as the *Guidance Paper* emphasises, that the *Guidance Paper* is intended merely to provide guidance on the Commission's Article 102 enforcement priorities: it is not intended to constitute a statement of the law and is without prejudice to the interpretation of Article 102 TFEU by the courts.[26] In particular, the Commission lacks legal authority to change the definition of dominance under Article 102 TFEU and does not pretend to have done so. Yet, as discussed in Section IV below, the subtle difference between the case law's classical formulation of dominance as commercial power and the definition of dominance as substantial market power presented in the *Guidance Paper* could have important practical effects for how future cases are argued and decided.

III. The Principal Factors in the Article 102 Dominance Assessment

2.20 After defining dominance as substantial market power, the *Guidance Paper* presents the methodology that the Commission will apply in assessing when a dominant position exists.

2.21 *"The assessment of dominance will take into account the competitive structure of the market, and in particular the following factors:*

- *constraints imposed by the existing supplies from, and the position on the market of, actual competitors (the market position of the undertaking and its competitors),*

---

[25] *See, e.g.,* D. S. Evans and A. J. Padilla, "Excessive Prices: Using Economics to Define Administrable Legal Rules" (2005) 1(1) *Journal of Competition Law and Economics*, p. 99 (*"There is no pricing rule or benchmark that can be used to distinguish effectively (i.e., without error) between competitive and excessive prices in practice."*).

[26] *Guidance Paper supra* note 1, para. 2.

2. – Dominance
Christopher Cook and Ruchit Patel

- *constraints imposed by the credible threat of future expansion by actual competitors or entry by potential competitors (expansion and entry),*
- *constraints imposed by the bargaining strength of the undertaking's customers (countervailing buyer power)."*[27]

This section considers each of these potential constraints on the putatively **2.22** dominant firm's competitive behaviour and the role that they play in the dominance assessment.

1. Market Structure and Market Shares

The *Guidance Paper*'s methodology for assessing dominance considers market **2.23** shares as a first indicator of possible dominance, but eschews any bright-line rule and cautions that share data must be interpreted in light of particular market characteristics:

> *"Market shares provide a useful first indication of the market structure and of the relative importance of the various undertakings active on the market. However, the Commission will interpret market shares in the light of the relevant market conditions, and in particular the dynamics of the market and of the extent to which products are differentiated."*[28]

As this section explains, this approach is in line with most current economic **2.24** thinking and is reconcilable with precedent from the courts, but it has not always been followed rigorously.

1.1. *Market Share-based Presumptions of Dominance*

The *Guidance Paper* states that in the Commission's experience, *"the higher the* **2.25** *market share and the longer the period of time over which it is held, the more likely it is that it constitutes an important preliminary indication of the existence of a dominant position."*[29] This stops well short of suggesting that high market shares held over a period of time give rise to a "presumption" of dominance, representing a retreat from certain Commission and court precedent indicating the

---

[27] *Guidance Paper supra* note 1, para. 12.
[28] *Ibid.*, para. 13.
[29] *Ibid.*, para. 15.

2. – Dominance
Christopher Cook and Ruchit Patel

appropriateness of such a presumption. Most notably, in the 1991 *AKZO* judgment, the Court of Justice cited *Hoffman-La Roche* as support for creating a rebuttable market share-based presumption of dominance: *"With regard to market shares the Court has held that very large shares are in themselves, and save in exceptional circumstances, evidence of the existence of a dominant position. That is the situation where there is a market share of 50% such as that found to exist in this case."*[30]

2.26   A few months later, in *Hilti*, the General Court cited *AKZO* and applied its approach: *"In this case it is established that Hilti holds a share of between 70% and 80% in the relevant market. Such a share is, in itself, a clear indication of the existence of a dominant position in the relevant market (see the judgment of the Court of Justice in* [AKZO])."*[31]

2.27   These judgments were by and large understood to establish that, absent exceptional circumstances, dominance could be presumed where the undertaking's share exceeded 50 per cent.[32] The General Court's summary of precedent in *Irish Sugar* is illustrative of the typical approach to the use of market share data in the dominance assessment as applied by the Commission and the courts during the 1990s:

> *'The applicant has … nowhere denied that throughout the period in question (1985 to 1995) it held a market share of industrial sugar in Ireland of over 90%. As the Commission has emphasised in the decision, a dominant position relates to a position of economic strength enjoyed by an undertaking which enables it to prevent effective competition being maintained on the relevant market by affording it the power to behave to an appreciable extent independently of its competitors, its customers and ultimately consumers (Hoffmann-La Roche, paragraph 38). The existence of a dominant position may derive from several factors which, taken separately, are not necessarily decisive. Amongst these factors, however, extremely large market shares are in themselves, save in exceptional circumstances, evidence of the existence of a dominant position (Hoffmann-La Roche, paragraph 41; Case C-62/86 AKZO v Commission [1991] ECR I-3359, paragraph 60; Case T-30/89 Hilti v Commission [1991] ECR II-1439, paragraph 91; Case T-83/91 Tetra Pak v Commission [1994] ECR II-755, paragraph 109; Compagnie Maritime*

---

[30] Case C-62/86 *AKZO Chemie v Commission* ("*AKZO*") [1991] ECR I-3359, para. 60, citing as support *Hoffmann-La Roche supra* note 3, para. 41, discussed *infra*.

[31] Case T-30/89 *Hilti v Commission* ("*Hilti*") [1991] ECR II-1439, para. 92.

[32] *See, e.g., supra* note 7, p. 177; B. E. Hawk, "Article 82 and Section 2: Abuse and Monopolizing Conduct" (2008) 2 *Issues of Competition Law and Policy*, p. 872.

2. – Dominance
Christopher Cook and Ruchit Patel

Belge Transports, paragraph 76). The case-law thus demonstrates that a market share of over 50% in itself constitutes evidence of the existence of a dominant position on the market in question (AKZO, paragraph 60)."[33]

The use of market share-based presumptions of dominance by the EU institutions is by no means unique. Most directly, in Germany, the Act against Restraints of Competition specifies market share thresholds that establish a rebuttable presumption of dominance.[34] In the United States, Judge Hand's oft-cited dictum from *Alcoa* has also been interpreted as seeking to create bright-line market share thresholds for the presumption of monopoly power: "*The percentages we have already mentioned – over ninety – results only if we both include all Alcoa's production and exclude secondary. That percentage is enough to constitute a monopoly; it is doubtful whether sixty or sixty-four percent would be enough; and certainly 33 per cent is not.*"[35] **2.28**

However, the presumption of dominance based on market shares alone has increasingly been criticised, as commentators have come to understand better the particular difficulties associated with defining markets and calculating shares in Article 102 cases (*e.g.,* the "cellophane fallacy")[36] and to regard market shares as, at best, only a rough guide to market power.[37] **2.29**

It is submitted that the market share-based presumption of dominance established in *AKZO* and cited approvingly in many cases since was in fact not compelled, nor even clearly supported, by the judgment of the Court of Justice in *Hoffmann-La Roche*, which was cited as precedent. In fact, in the cited paragraph from *Hoffmann-La Roche*, the Court clearly emphasises that high market shares are only indicative of dominance in markets where smaller competitors face barriers to expansion: **2.30**

> *"An undertaking which has a very large market share and holds it for some time, by means of the volume of production and the scale of the supply which it stands for – <u>without those having much smaller market shares being able to meet rapidly</u>*

---

[33] Case T-228/97 *Irish Sugar v Commission* ("*Irish Sugar*") [1999] ECR II-2969, para. 70.

[34] Gesetz gegen Wettbewerbsbeschränkungen, §19(3) (an undertaking is presumed to be dominant if it has a market share above 33.3 per cent; three or fewer undertakings are presumed dominant if they have together a market share above 50 per cent; and five or fewer undertakings are deemed to be dominant if they have a cumulated market share of at least 66.6 per cent).

[35] *United States v Aluminum of America*, 148 F.2d 416 (2nd Cir. 1945).

[36] *See* Chapter 2 above and Chapter 1.

[37] *See, e.g.,* F. M. Fisher, "Detecting Market Power" (2008) 1 *Issues in Competition Law and Policy*, pp. 353–72; R. O'Donoghue and A. J. Padilla, *The Law and Economics of Article 82 EC* (Oxford, Hart Publishing, 2006), pp. 111–2.

2. – Dominance
Christopher Cook and Ruchit Patel

the demand from those who would like to break away from the undertaking which has the largest market share – is by virtue of that share in a position of strength which makes it an unavoidable trading partner and which, already because of this, secures for it, at the very least during relatively long periods, that freedom of action which is the special feature of a dominant position." (Emphasis added).[38]

2.31 In other words, this passage says that no market share-based dominance presumption applies if competitors could meet the demand from customers who want to switch away from the largest firm in response to an attempt to raise prices – *i.e.*, if there are no material barriers to entry or expansion. Other passages in the *Hoffmann-La Roche* judgment similarly emphasise the Court's view that an analysis of market conditions will always be required to establish dominance: *"The existence of a dominant position may derive from several factors which, taken separately, are not necessarily determinative but among these factors a highly important one is the existence of very large market shares. [However], substantial market share as evidence of the existence of a dominant position is not a constant factor and its importance varies from market to market*[.]"[39]

2.32 Independent of this language, the approach followed by the Court in *Hoffmann-La Roche* supports the conclusion that, at most, sustained very high market shares will count as evidence of dominance. In its analyses of various vitamin markets, the Court states that shares in the range of 75–87 per cent (Vitamin B) are *"so large that they are in themselves evidence of a dominant position"*;[40] that shares of 84–90 per cent (Vitamin B6) are *"so large that they prove the existence of a dominant position"*;[41] and that shares of 93–100 per cent (Vitamin H) mean that the firm *"in fact has a monopoly"*.[42] Shares in the range of 63–66 per cent (Vitamin C) supported a dominance finding in view of the fact that the shares of the next-largest competitors were much lower (15 per cent and 6 per cent).[43] When Roche's market shares were still lower (47 per cent in respect of Vitamin A and 54 per cent in respect of Vitamin E), the Court endorsed the Commission's dominance findings only upon consideration of additional factors.[44] And in the Vitamin B3 market where Roche's share was up to

---

[38] *Hoffmann-La Roche supra* note 3, para. 41.
[39] *Ibid.*, paras 39–40.
[40] *Ibid.*, para. 56.
[41] *Ibid.*, para. 60.
[42] *Ibid.*, para. 67.
[43] *Ibid.*, paras 61–3.
[44] *Ibid.*, paras 50–2 and 64–6.

2. – Dominance
Christopher Cook and Ruchit Patel

51 per cent, the Court overturned the Commission's finding that Roche was dominant because, unlike the other markets, the Commission had not indicated what "additional factors" besides market share would support this conclusion.[45] Thus, the *AKZO* Court's reading of *Hoffmann-La Roche* as supporting a dominance presumption when the firm's market share exceeds 50 per cent clearly lowered the bar.[46]

Over the past two decades, and including in major recent decisions, the Commission and courts have often cited the wording of *AKZO* to support a finding of dominance.[47] In practice, however, their conclusions have not tended to rely exclusively on market shares. It seems reasonable to regard the Commission's decision not to refer to *AKZO* in the *Guidance Paper* as a conscious effort to distance itself from what could be seen as an unduly formalistic and/or overly strict approach,[48] but because the *AKZO* market share-based presumption of dominance has rarely been applied strictly, the *Guidance Paper*'s approach does not represent a major departure from past practice in calling for the interpretation of market shares in light of actual market conditions. **2.33**

1.2.   Low Market Shares

While the *Guidance Paper* retreats from any suggestion that high market shares on their own create a presumption of dominance, it suggests that a presumption **2.34**

---

[45] *Hoffmann-La Roche supra* note 3, para. 58.

[46] The Court later made clear that there were limits to how low a market share would justify a presumption of dominance, holding in *Gøttrup-Klim* that a share of 32–36 per cent could not, on its own, constitute conclusive evidence of a dominant position. Case C-250/92 *Gøttrup-Klim Grovvareforening and Others v Dansk Landbrugs ("Gøttrup-Klim")* [1994] ECR I-5641, para. 48.

[47] *See, e.g.,* Case COMP/37.990 *Intel,* Commission Decision of 13 May 2009, not yet published, para. 852 ("*It follows from the market share data in subsections 3.2.1 to 3.2.4 that Intel consistently held very high market shares in excess of or around 80% in an overall x86 CPU market and in excess or around 70% in any of the sub-markets mentioned in these subsections throughout the six year observation period. In this regard, it should be recalled that very large market shares, of over 50%, are considered in themselves, and but for exceptional circumstances, evidence of the existence of a dominant position. Market shares between 70% and 80% have, according to the case law, been held to be in themselves a clear indication of the existence of a dominant position.*") and Case COMP/37.792 *Microsoft ("Microsoft Decision 2004"),* Commission Decision of 24 March 2004, not yet published, in which the Commission cited *AKZO* to support its finding that Microsoft was dominant in client PC operating systems at para. 435.

[48] Interestingly, the *Discussion Paper,* which preceded the *Guidance Paper,* expressly referred to the presumption of dominance test set in *AKZO,* para. 31: "*It is very likely that very high market shares, which have been held for some time, indicate a dominant position. This would be the case where an undertaking holds 50% or more of the market, provided that rivals hold a much smaller share of the market (Case C-62/86 AKZO Chemie BV v Commission [1991] ECR I-3359, paragraph 60)*". *See* DG Competition Discussion paper on the application of Article 82 of the treaty to exclusionary abuses ("*Discussion Paper*"), December 2005, and Commission's *Guidance Paper supra* note 1.

2. – Dominance
Christopher Cook and Ruchit Patel

may be more valid with respect to the other end of the scale: *"The Commission considers that low market shares are generally a good proxy for the absence of substantial market power. The Commission's experience suggests that dominance is not likely if the undertaking's market share is below 40 per cent in the relevant market."*[49]

2.35 The *Guidance Paper* does not exclude that dominance can arise where the share is below 40 per cent, noting that dominance may still arise where competitors are not in a position to constrain effectively the conduct of a dominant undertaking, for example where they face serious capacity limitations. But this paragraph effectively establishes a "soft safe harbour": absent unusual circumstances, firms with market shares below 40 per cent are unlikely to face scrutiny under Article 102 TFEU.

2.36 This largely reflects existing case law, according to which market shares below 40 per cent have not typically led to dominance findings. Under such circumstances, competitors normally make up a sufficient percentage of the market that customers and ultimately consumers will have adequate access to competing sources of input.[50]

2.37 There have, however, been exceptions. In *British Airways*, British Airways had a share of 39.7 per cent on the relevant market, and this figure had fallen for the five consecutive years prior to the Commission's decision. However, the gap between British Airways and its competitors was significant: British Airways' market share was almost four times larger than the combined shares of its four biggest competitors. Moreover, British Airways held rights to substantially more slots at Heathrow and Gatwick Airports than any other carrier, and offered the largest range of flights in and out the United Kingdom. The Commission found that the combination of these factors supported a finding of dominance.[51] This was later confirmed by the Court of First Instance.[52]

2.38 In *United Brands*, the Court of Justice held that United Brands' share of 40–45 per cent was indicative of dominance, *inter alia* because its share was considerably higher than those of its principal competitors:

---

[49] *Guidance Paper supra* note 1, para. 14.

[50] *See* P. Roth and V. Rose (Eds.), *Bellamy & Child: European Community Law of Competition* (6th Ed., Oxford, Oxford University Press, 2008).

[51] Case IV/34.780 *Virgin/British Airways*, Commission Decision of 14 July 1999, OJ 2000 L 30/1, para. 88.

[52] Case T-219/99 *British Airways v Commission* ("*British Airways*") [2003] ECR II-5917, paras 175–226.

2. – Dominance
Christopher Cook and Ruchit Patel

"Without going into a discussion about percentages, which when fixed are bound to be to some extent approximations, it can be considered to be an established fact that UBC's share of the relevant market is always more than 40 per cent and nearly 45 per cent. This percentage does not however permit the conclusion that UBC automatically controls the market. It must be determined having regard to the strength and number of the competitors. It is necessary first of all to establish that on the whole of the relevant market the said percentage represents grosso modo a share several times greater than that of its competitor Castle and Cooke which is best placed of all the competitors. The others come far behind. This fact together with the others to which attention has been drawn may be regarded as a factor which affords evidence of UBC's preponderant strength."[53]

In each of these judgments, the main factor supporting the dominance find- **2.39**
ing in markets where the firm's share was around 40 per cent seems to have been the fragmentation of the remainder of the market. As discussed above, this was also a central consideration in the Court of Justice's analysis of the Vitamin A and Vitamin E markets in *Hoffman-La Roche*. In view of this body of clear precedent, it is interesting that the *Guidance Paper* only refers to the situation where competitors face serious capacity limitations as an exception to its 40 per cent "safe harbour" below which dominance concerns are unlikely to arise, particularly when the previous *Discussion Paper* on Article 82 had mentioned market fragmentation as a relevant factor.[54]

Although the *Guidance Paper* does not introduce a formal "block exemption" **2.40**
for firms with market shares below 40 per cent, the inclusion of a soft "safe harbour" is a useful confirmation of existing case law. Market shares clearly are relevant and instructive in the assessment of dominance, particularly in quickly identifying and screening out unproblematic cases. Some commentators have objected that the 40 per cent threshold is both too soft (using market shares as a jurisdictional criterion, below which Article 102 TFEU would not apply, would be better) and too low (70 per cent might be a more appropriate level).[55] It is submitted, however, that one logical consequence of applying an economics-based approach to Article 102 TFEU that examines all the conditions of competition and bases infringement decisions on the market effects of the conduct in question is that market shares alone can neither conclusively establish dominance nor exclude the possibility of actions having anticompetitive effects. If one is

---

[53] *United Brands supra* note 2, paras 108–12.
[54] *See Discussion Paper supra* note 48.
[55] *See, e.g., supra* note 15, pp. 31–52, pp. 46–8.

2. – Dominance
Christopher Cook and Ruchit Patel

happy to eliminate market share-based presumptions of dominance at the high end of the scale, one should also be prepared to acknowledge the possibility of dominance being found at the lower end.

1.3. *Differentiated Product Markets*

2.41   The *Guidance Paper* notes that product differentiation is a factor that may affect the probative value of market shares in assessing dominance.[56] Two products may be "differentiated" but still in the same relevant market, particularly if the products are differentiated in respect of non-use-based factors (*e.g.*, brand). In markets that contain differentiated products, firms with relatively lower market shares might have a degree of market power because other products in the market are not very close substitutes.[57] Product differentiation can also directly affect the extent to which rivals represent competitive constraints. As DG Competition's *Discussion Paper* explains:

> *"The importance of market shares may be qualified by an analysis of the degree of product differentiation in the market. Products are differentiated when they differ in the eyes of consumers for instance due to brand image, product features, product quality, level of service or the location of the seller. The level of advertising in a market may be an indicator of the firms' efforts to differentiate their products. When products are differentiated the competitive constraint that they impose on each other is likely to differ even where they form part of the same relevant market. Substitutability is a question of degree. In assessing the competitive constraint imposed by rivals, it must therefore be taken into account what is the degree of substitutability of their products with those offered by the allegedly dominant undertaking. It may be that a rival with 10 per cent market share imposes a greater competitive constraint on an undertaking with 50 per cent market share than another rival supplying 20 per cent of the market. This may for instance be the case where the undertaking with the lower market share and the allegedly dominant undertaking both sell premium branded products whereas the rival with the larger market share sells a bargain brand."*[58]

2.42   Product differentiation is thus a factor to be weighed in assessing the constraints that rivals impose on the putatively dominant firm, and may be particularly relevant when considering the significance of market fragmentation.

---

[56] *Guidance Paper supra* note 1, para. 13.
[57] *See supra* note 21, p. 11.
[58] *See Discussion Paper supra* note 48, para. 33.

2. – Dominance
Christopher Cook and Ruchit Patel

In assessing competitive constraints, the Commission will examine how competition on a market works, and will not simply assume that the firm with the next highest share is the closest competitor.

1.4. Bidding Markets

2.43 As another factor that may affect the probative value of market share data, the *Guidance Paper* states that the "*trend or development of market shares over time may also be taken into account in volatile or bidding markets.*"[59] In markets where customers choose their suppliers through organised tenders, competition might be intense even if there are only a few suppliers. This is particularly likely where tenders are large and infrequent ("lumpy" demand), which creates strong incentives for all suppliers to bid aggressively. Market shares in such markets are also more likely to fluctuate significantly over time. DG Competition's *Discussion Paper* explains the Commission's basic approach:

> "*Normally, the Commission uses current market shares in its competitive analysis. However, historic market shares may be used if market shares have been volatile, for instance when the market is characterised by large, lumpy orders. Changes in historic market shares may also provide useful information about the competitive process and the likely future importance of the various competitors, for instance, by indicating whether firms have been gaining or losing market shares. In any event, the Commission interprets market shares in the light of likely market conditions, for instance, whether the market is highly dynamic in character and whether the market structure is unstable due to innovation or growth.*"[60]

2.44 The Commission has previously considered the relevance of market share figures in bidding markets primarily in the context of mergers and horizontal agreements, rather than under Article 102 TFEU. The Commission has recognised that market share figures in bidding markets "*only take into account the activity of the winners of a given contract but do not show how many credible competitors actually participated as bidders and thus created competitive constraints.*"[61] In bidding

---

[59] *Guidance Paper supra* note 1, para. 13.

[60] *See Discussion Paper supra* note 48.

[61] Case COMP/M.2139 *Bombardier/Adtranz,* Commission Decision of 3 April 2001, para. 39. *See also* Case COMP/M.1016 *Price Waterhouse/Coopers & Lybrand,* Commission Decision of 20 May 1998, in which the Commission favoured data showing the numbers of tendered contracts won over four years as opposed to annualised market share data, and Case COMP/M.1879 *Boeing/Hughes,* Commission Decision of 27 September 2000, in which merging parties were found to have a combined share of 40–60 per cent, but the Commission examined the number of credible competitors and emphasised that "*satellite markets are bidding markets, where the conditions of competition are determined by the existence of credible alternatives to* [the merging entity's] *products*".

2. – Dominance
Christopher Cook and Ruchit Patel

markets characterised by "lumpy," "winner takes all" demand, market shares provide only a snapshot of the market at a particular time and are not a good indicator of the degree of competition involved in the bidding process.[62] Market shares in bidding markets are therefore generally not good indicators of market power; the number of firms capable of bidding for supply opportunities may better reflect the degree of competition in the market.[63]

1.5. "New" Markets

2.45 Firms that contribute to the development of or become active early in the emergence of "new" markets (*e.g.*, technology markets) may benefit from a "first mover" advantage that allows them to acquire substantial market share in a short period of time.[64] High shares in such markets may not be sustainable and are thus not necessarily indicative of market power, in particular where competitors have recently entered or are expected to enter. Even a persistently high share may not indicate a lack of effective competition if the market is characterised by rapid innovation, as the market leader might be forced to continuously improve its products and processes to stay ahead of rivals.[65]

2.46 The *Guidance Paper* is silent on the need for special consideration of market shares in "new" markets, but the Commission has previously recognised these principles in the context of Horizontal Agreements: "*The first companies to reach the market with a new product/technology will often enjoy very high initial market shares and successful R&D is also often rewarded by intellectual property protection. A strong market position due to this 'first mover advantage' cannot normally be interpreted as elimination of competition.*"[66]

---

[62] Case COMP/M.1882 *Pirelli/BICC*, Commission Decision of 19 July 2000, paras 79 and 82. *See also* D. Patterson and C. Shapiro, "Transatlantic Divergence in GE/Honeywell: Causes and Lessons" (2001) 16(1) *Antitrust Magazine*, pp. 18–26; and P. Klemperer, *Bidding Markets*, UK Competition Commission Occasional Paper No. 1, June 2005.

[63] Case COMP/M.1882, *ibid.*, para. 88.

[64] *See also* N. Gauss, *Die Anwendung des kartellrechtlichen Missbrauchsverbots nach Art. 82 EG (Art. 102 AEUV) in innovativen Märkten* (Baden-Baden, Nomos, 2010).

[65] *See supra* note 21, p. 11.

[66] Commission Notice – Guidelines on the applicability of Article 81 of the EC Treaty to horizontal cooperation agreements ("*2001 Horizontal Guidelines*"), OJ 2001 C 3/2, para. 73.

2. – Dominance
Christopher Cook and Ruchit Patel

The Commission's approach in the context of merger control has largely been **2.47** similar.[67] By analogy, in the Article 102 context, the Commission should be receptive to evidence linking high market shares to first mover advantages or successful ongoing innovation in deflating any preliminary indications of dominance that might otherwise be associated with such shares. The firm's possible ability to use its first mover advantage to limit the prospects for increased future competition will, however, likely also be considered.

2. Barriers to Entry and Expansion by Competitors

As the preceding section explains, the market shares of the firm in question **2.48** and its competitors can provide a useful first indication of the likely presence or absence of substantial market power. But the exercise of calculating market shares and assessing their weight in the specific market under investigation contains pitfalls, imprecision, and exceptions, so market shares should be used only as a screening guide in the assessment of dominance. As the *Guidance Paper* explains, "[c]*ompetition is a dynamic process and an assessment of the competitive constraints on an undertaking cannot be based solely on the existing market situation. The potential impact of expansion by actual competitors or entry by potential competitors, including the threat of such expansion or entry, is also relevant.*"[68]

When dominance is equated with substantial market power, the central ques- **2.49** tion becomes whether the undertaking is able profitably to sustain supracompetitive prices. In a market with low entry and expansion barriers, even a firm with a large market share is unlikely to have market power. As the Court of Justice in *Hoffman-La Roche* expressly recognised, any presumption of market strength that might accompany a high market share is inapplicable in markets where competitors are able to meet rapidly the demand from customers who

---

[67] *See, e.g.,* the Commission's thirty-first Report on Competition Policy (2001), p. 71 ("*high market shares were not held against the parties because they resulted from the so-called 'first mover' advantage*"). Compare with Case COMP/M.1795 *Vodafone Airtouch/Mannesmann*, Commission Decision of 12 April 2000, in which the Commission found that the merged firm would become the first supplier capable of offering "*seamless pan-European mobile telephony services*" with a market share of 100 per cent. The Commission recognised that this share did not reflect an elimination of competition but was the consequence of the creation of a new market unto itself. But the Commission was concerned that the firm would be able to use its 'first mover' advantage to limit competition and consolidate a dominant position on the market, and required among other remedies that the merged entity provide non-discriminatory access to its integrated pan-European network).

[68] *Guidance Paper supra* note 1, para. 16.

2. – Dominance
Christopher Cook and Ruchit Patel

want to switch away from the firm with the largest share.[69] This suggests that a central factor in the assessment of dominance should be the presence or absence of barriers to entry and expansion by competitors. If such barriers are low, there will be strong reason to doubt the existence of dominance, because if actual or potential competitors are easily able to expand or enter then even a firm with a very high market share would be unable to sustain prices above the competitive level. In other words, if entry or expansion is easy, the largest firm will normally be constrained to keep prices at competitive levels in order to avoid attracting rivals into the market. As Frank Fisher has put it, *"what matters is not what the defendant's … market share is, but rather what would become of that share in the event of an attempt to exercise* [market] *power."*[70]

2.50 The *Guidance Paper* states that *"an undertaking can be deterred from increasing prices if expansion or entry is likely, timely and sufficient."*[71] This determination of whether entry will prevent the exercise of market power principally involves an examination of barriers to entry in the relevant market. Entry barriers may make entry on a sufficient scale less likely or less rapid by affecting the expected sunk costs of entry and/or the expected profits for new entrants once they are in the market, or by establishing physical or legal obstacles to entry.[72] Thus, according to the *Guidance Paper*, in assessing the likelihood of entry, the Commission will consider the entry barriers themselves, the likely reactions of the allegedly dominant undertaking and other competitors, and the risk and cost of failure by the new entrant.[73] Expansion or entry must also be *"sufficiently swift to deter or defeat the exercise of substantial market power."*[74] Precisely what this means is not spelled out in the *Guidance Paper*, and very likely depends upon the characteristics and dynamics of the market and of potential competitors.[75] Finally, according to the *Guidance Paper*, for *"expansion or entry to be considered sufficient, it cannot be simply small-scale entry, for example into some market niche, but must be of such a magnitude so as to deter any attempt to increase prices by the putatively dominant undertaking."*[76]

---

[69] *Hoffmann-La Roche supra* note 3, para. 41.

[70] F. M. Fisher, *supra* note 37, p. 358.

[71] *Guidance Paper supra* note 1, para. 16. (This formulation is drawn from the Commission's merger control practice and appears in the Commission's 2004 Horizontal Merger Guidelines, though it has not previously been applied expressly under Article 102 TFEU).

[72] *See supra* note 21.

[73] *Guidance Paper supra* note 1, para. 16.

[74] *Ibid.*, para. 16.

[75] *See, e.g.,* Case COMP/M.1693 *Alcoa/Reynolds*, Commission Decision of 3 May 2000, paras 31–32 and 38.

[76] *Guidance Paper supra* note 1, para. 16.

2. – Dominance
Christopher Cook and Ruchit Patel

The *Guidance Paper* does not expressly define barriers to entry, but the Com- **2.51**
mission's *Discussion Paper* states that "*barriers to expansion and entry are factors
that make entry impossible or unprofitable while permitting established undertakings to
charge prices above the competitive level.*"[77] Whether expansion or entry is profitable
depends on the cost of efficient expansion or entry and the likely market price
post expansion or entry. Prices post expansion or entry will depend on both
the market impact of the new entrant's additional output and on the reaction
of incumbent suppliers, particularly the alleged dominant one. In this framework, assessing barriers to entry will take into account any factor that might
make entry or expansion by rivals unprofitable and therefore unlikely, including the characteristics of the market and the characteristics and behaviour of
the allegedly dominant firm.

Entry barriers can be studied directly by examining how the business in ques- **2.52**
tion works and considering whether and, if so, why competitors of the firm
under investigation would have difficulty entering the market or expanding
their output sufficiently to defeat an attempt by the largest firm to raise prices
or reduce output. In the *Guidance Paper*'s methodology for assessing dominance, such considerations should represent the heart of the analysis. The
specific entry barriers identified in the *Guidance Paper* are each discussed below.

2.1. *Analysis of Specific Barriers to Entry and Expansion*

The *Guidance Paper* does not discuss barriers to entry or expansion in detail. **2.53**
However, it does list the forms and characteristics that barriers to entry and
expansion may take:

> "*Barriers to expansion or entry can take various forms. They may be legal barriers,
> such as tariffs or quotas, or they may take the form of advantages specifically enjoyed
> by the dominant undertaking, such as economies of scale and scope, privileged access
> to essential inputs or natural resources, important technologies or an established dis-
> tribution and sales network. They may also include costs and other impediments,
> for instance resulting from network effects, faced by customers in switching to a new
> supplier. The dominant undertaking's own conduct may also create barriers to entry,
> for example where it has made significant investments which entrants or competitors
> would have to match, or where it has concluded long-term contracts with its customers*

---

[77] *Discussion Paper supra* note 48, para. 38.

2. – Dominance
Christopher Cook and Ruchit Patel

that have appreciable foreclosing effects. Persistently high market shares may be indicative of the existence of barriers to entry and expansion."[78]

2.54   Each of the potential entry barriers identified in the *Guidance Paper* is considered in turn below.

2.1.1.   Legal Barriers

2.55   Legal rules may constitute barriers to entry or expansion. The *Guidance Paper* mentions regulations such as tariffs and quotas as examples, but as explained below, statutory monopolies and intellectual property rights are likely to be the legal barriers that are more relevant to modern-day enforcement of Article 102.

2.1.1.1.   Tariffs and Quotas

2.56   Notwithstanding the explicit mention in the *Guidance Paper*, tariffs and quotas have rarely formed part of the analysis of a dominance finding in the Commission's decisional practice. The relevance of tariffs and quotas to the Commission's assessment of dominance will depend on the specific dynamics and characteristics of the market in question, but the range of circumstances where these factors might apply seems to be narrow, in part because discriminatory quotas or tariffs, which were once prevalent among and between EU countries,[79] have progressively been eliminated in the common market. Licensing requirements that limit the number of firms that can operate in a market or jurisdiction are arguably a form of quota, but so long as there is no discrimination between undertakings, the mere fact that the market size is limited (perhaps efficiently by reference to prevailing demand) will not necessarily be regarded as a barrier to entry.[80] Protectionist tariffs that have the

---

[78] *Guidance Paper supra* note 1, para. 17.

[79] *Cf., e.g.,* Joined Cases 40 to 48, 50, 54 to 56, 111, 113 and 114/73 *Coöperatieve Vereniging "Suiker Unie" and others v Commission* (*"Suiker Unie"*) [1975] ECR 1663, paras 12–24, 71 (national sugar quotas led to the partitioning of national markets, reduced the level of sugar imports, and left only "a residual field for the operation of competition").

[80] *See, e.g.,* Joined Cases C-140 to 142/94 *DIP v Comune di Bassano del Grappa* [1995] ECR I-3257, para. 27 (*"National rules which require a licence to be obtained before a new shop can be opened and limit the number of shops in the municipality in order to achieve a balance between supply and demand cannot be considered to put individual traders in dominant positions or all the traders established in a municipality in a collective dominant position, a salient feature of which would be that traders did not compete against one another."*). *See also* Case C-313/04 *Franz Egenberger GmbH Molkerei und Trockenwerk v Bundesanstalt für Landwirtschaft und Ernährung* [2006] ECR I-6331, para. 57 (Regulation 2535/2001 on import arrangements for milk and milk products and opening tariff quotas did not prevent the New Zealand government from allocating the entire New Zealand quota for reduced duty imported butter to an undertaking from New Zealand with a subsidiary established in the UK, thereby discriminating between EU undertakings and granting the recipient of the quota an effective monopoly; since the relevant articles of the regulation were held to be invalid, the questions relating to the abuse of this import monopoly under Article 102 were not addressed).

2. – Dominance
Christopher Cook and Ruchit Patel

impact of (directly or indirectly) shielding EU businesses from entry by foreign corporations are relatively rare but may be relevant to the assessment of dominance in certain markets.

2.1.1.2.   Statutory Monopolies

2.57 Article 106 TFEU requires a statutory monopolist (*i.e.*, an undertaking granted special or exclusive rights by a Member State) to be subject to competition law insofar as the application of the competition rules do not hinder the performance of the particular tasks assigned to the undertaking. Legislation conferring a statutory monopoly can in practice represent an insurmountable barrier to entry or expansion by competitors, especially where the grant confers exclusive access to a finite resource.[81] Accordingly, existing statutory monopolists are especially susceptible to a finding of dominance[82] (regardless of whether the statutory monopoly was conferred directly or indirectly).[83]

2.58 Reflecting the advantages conferred by statutory monopolies, which may persist even after the industries have been liberalised, a significant proportion of Commission enforcement actions under Article 102 TFEU has been directed toward former state monopolies. For example, the Commission has brought cases in many industries that were previously statutory monopolies (*e.g.*, airlines,[84]

---

[81] *See, e.g.*, Case 89/113/EEC *Decca Navigator* Systems, Commission Decision of 21 December 1988 (exclusive access to radio frequencies).

[82] *See, e.g.*, Case 30/87 *Corinne Bodson v Pompes funèbres des régions libérées* ("*Bodson*") [1988] ECR 2479 (exclusive concession for the provision of undertaking services considered undeniable evidence of a dominant position); Case C-179/90 *Merci convenzionali porto di Genova v Siderurgica Gabrielli* ("*Merci Convenzionali*") [1991] ECR I-5889 (monopoly for the running of port operations in a given port); Case C-320/91 *Procureur du Roi v Paul Corbeau* [1993] ECR I-2533 (monopoly for the collection, transportation, and distribution of mail); Case C-209/98 *Entreprenørforeningens Affalds/Miljøsektion (FFAD) v Københavns Kommune* [2000] ECR I-3743 (exclusive rights to collect recycling waste shared between three entities), Case COMP/39.351 *Swedish Interconnectors*, Commission Decision of 14 April 2010, not yet published, para. 25.

[83] *See, e.g.*, Joined Cases C-241 and 242/91 P *Radio Telefis Eireann (RTE) and Independent Television Publications (ITP) v Commission* ("*Magill*") [1995] ECR I-743 (RTE benefited from a statutory monopoly over television broadcasting, and Irish IP law operated so as to also grant it exclusive rights over TV listings); Case IV/30.615 *British Leyland*, Commission Decision of 2 July 1984, OJ 1984 L 207/11 (under British law an imported car had to obtain a "certificate of conformity" from the manufacturer in the UK and, as a result, British Leyland enjoyed an administrative or legal monopoly over this particular service when providing dealers with such certificates.).

[84] *See, e.g.*, *supra* note 51; and Case IV/33.544 *British Midland/Aer Lingus*, Commission Decision of 26 February 1992, OJ 1992 L 96/34. *See also* O. Blanco and B. van Houtte, *EC Competition Law in the Transport Sector* (Oxford, Oxford University Press, 1996), p. 194 ("*Control of abuses of dominant positions is of high importance in the air transport sector. On the one hand, many of the major Community airlines inherited dominant positions from the earlier regulatory regimes: most Member States conducted their air transport policy with a view to putting their 'flag carriers' in the strongest possible position on their home market. On the other hand, these dominant airlines often have the power, by means of control of essential facilities and by their own overwhelming weight in their local market, to hinder the development of competition*").

2. – Dominance
Christopher Cook and Ruchit Patel

railways,[85] electricity[86] and telecommunications service[87] providers, and postal operators[88]), principally because the former statutory monopolist was deemed to continue to benefit post-liberalisation from large and economically non-replicable past investments by the State (such as privileged access to essential, non-replicable installations and networks). In such industries, the Commission and courts have used competition law as a means to promote and foster the emergence of a competitive dynamic.[89]

2.1.1.3.   Intellectual Property

2.59   Intellectual property rights (or rights conferred by standard-setting bodies[90]) may represent a legal barrier to entry or expansion, in particular where the right in question blocks entry or expansion entirely.[91] Where it is possible for competitors to "invent around" the intellectual property right (*i.e.*, compete in the relevant market without infringing the right holder's protections), a finding of dominance is more difficult to sustain.[92]

---

[85] *See, e.g.*, Case IV/33.941 *HOV SVZ/MCN*, Commission Decision of 29 March 1994, OJ 1994 L 104/34; Case COMP/37.685 *GVG/FS*, Commission Decision of 27 August 2003, OJ 2004 L 11/17.

[86] *See, e.g.*, Cases COMP/39.388 *German Electricity Wholesale Market* and COMP/39.389 *German Electricity Balancing Market*, Commission Decision of 26 November 2008, not yet published.

[87] In February 1998, the Commission launched fourteen separate investigations into incumbent telephone and/or mobile operators, *see* Press Release IP/98/141 of 10 February 1998. *See also* Case COMP/38.233 *Wanadoo*, Commission Decision of 16 July 2003, not yet published; Case COMP/38.784 *Telefónica (broadband)* ("*Telefónica*"), Commission Decision of 4 July 2007, not yet published, and *Telekomunikacja Polska supra* note 24.

[88] *See, e.g.*, Case COMP/35.141 *Deutsche Post*, Commission Decision of 20 March 2001, OJ 2001 L 125/27; and Case COMP/37.859 *De Post-La Poste*, Commission Decision of 5 December 2001, OJ 2002 L 61/32.

[89] Case COMP/39.315 *ENI*, Commission Decision of 29 September 2010, not yet published, at para. 33. *See also*, Case COMP/39.317 *E.ON Gas Foreclosure*, Commission Decision of 4 May 2010, not yet published, para. 30.

[90] *See* Case COMP/39.592 *Standard & Poor's*, Commission Decision of 15 November 2011, not yet published, paras 24 and 25 (the finding of dominance was based on the fact that Standard and Poor's was designated as the national numbering agency for ISO standard 6166, which meant that it was the only designated issuer of International Securities Identification Numbers for US securities).

[91] *See, e.g.*, Case C-333/94 P *Tetra Pak International v Commission* ("*Tetra Pak II Judgment 1996*") [1996] ECR I-5951 (acquisition of an exclusive patent license prevented access to the technology); *see also Hilti* (patents and copyright protected the firm's cartridge strip products); Case 22/78 *Hugin Kassaregister and Hugin Cash Registers v Commission* ("*Hugin*") [1979] ECR 1869 (IP right prevented other suppliers from competing in the market for spare parts for Hugin cash registers); Case COMP/37.507 *Generics/AstraZeneca*, Commission Decision of 15 June 2005, not yet published, paras 517–35 (strength of AstraZeneca's patent protection and corollary threat of infringement proceedings constituted barriers to entry on the market for proton pump inhibitors).

[92] Case 40/70 *Sirena v Eda and others* ("*Sirena*") [1971] ECR 69, at para. 16 (the mere ownership of a trademark right does not confer a dominant position so long as actual or potential competitors are able to invent or supply similar goods or goods that may be substituted).

2. – Dominance
Christopher Cook and Ruchit Patel

2.1.2. Economies of Scale and Scope

Economies of scale arise where the average cost of producing and/or distrib- **2.60** uting a product falls as output rises. Economies of scope arise where it costs less to produce two types of products together than to produce each of them separately. In a market characterised by large economies of scale, a potential entrant may need to enter the market on a large scale relative to overall market demand in order to achieve a cost position that would allow it to compete effectively against a large incumbent (minimum efficient scale).[93] Similarly, in a market characterised by large economies of scope, a potential entrant into one product market may need also to produce additional products in order to be cost-competitive. In either case, the large-scale entry required to be competitive might require the new entrant to incur relatively large sunk costs (*i.e.*, costs that must be incurred to compete in the market but that are not recoverable upon exiting the market), and the output produced will constitute a significant increase in output, which may itself significantly reduce prices post-entry. The larger the minimum efficient scale on the relevant market, the more costly and risky entry or expansion is likely to be. In this way, economies of scale and scope can represent barriers to entry or expansion.

In several cases, the Commission and courts have regarded economies of **2.61** scale and scope as barriers to entry and expansion. For example, in *United Brands* the Court of Justice identified the extensive investments that a new entrant to the banana market would need to make (including large and diversified plantations and logistical systems) as "*particular barriers to competitors entering the market*" since they generate "*economies of scale from which newcomers to the market cannot derive any immediate benefit and … the costs of which are irrecoverable if the* [entry] *attempt fails.*"[94] More recently, in *Intel* the Commission found that barriers to entering the market for x86 CPUs were substantial because entry would require significant sunk costs in plant production and R&D, and the significant economies of scale in the industry mean that the minimum efficient scale is high relative to overall market demand.[95] The question of whether it

---

[93] *See Discussion Paper supra* note 48, para. 40 "[if] *expansion or entry occurs at an inefficient scale, the competitive constraint imposed on the incumbents will be less effective. In assessing barriers to expansion and entry it is therefore useful to consider the minimum efficient scale in the market concerned.*"

[94] *United Brands supra* note 2, para. 122. *See also* Case IV/31.900 *BPB Industries*, Commission Decision of 5 December 1988, OJ 1989 L 10/50, at para. 116 (BPB enjoyed substantial economies of scale and scope by producing on a large scale in integrated industrial complexes).

[95] Case COMP/37.990, *supra* note 47 para. 866. *See also* Case IV/31.900, *ibid.*, at para. 116 (BPB enjoyed substantial economies of scale and scope by producing on a large scale in integrated industrial complexes);

2. – Dominance
Christopher Cook and Ruchit Patel

is appropriate to treat economies of scale as entry and expansion barriers has been the subject of some economic debate. Traditional critics have challenged the basic idea that scale economies can create a meaningful entry barrier on the basis that once an entrant has invested in an efficient plant, there is no difference (under the usual assumptions) between its position and that of established firms: without post-entry difference, so the argument runs, there is no real barrier to entry.[96] Some more recent thinking, however, suggests that established firms may still be able profitably to deter entry if they can commit to a level of capacity before potential entrants appear (assuming that potential entrants expect the post-entry market equilibrium to be a *Cournot* duopoly).[97]

2.1.3. Privileged Access to Essential Inputs or Natural Resources

2.62 Privileged access to an essential input or natural resources may favour an incumbent undertaking and create high barriers to entry. Several cases have identified privileged access to raw materials as a barrier to entry. For example, in *Napier Brown/British Sugar*, the Commission considered British Sugar's position as exclusive recipient of the UK's entire production of beet-origin sugar relevant to the analysis of dominance.[98] Privileged access to physical infrastructure has been treated similarly. In *Sea Containers/Stena Sealink*,[99] the

---

Cases IV/33.440 *Warner-Lambert/Gillette and others* and IV/33.486 *BIC/Gillette and others* ("*Gillette*"), Commission Decision of 10 November 1992, OJ 1993 L 116/21, para. 9 (The decision highlights the importance of economies of scale in production. According to the parties and the Commission decision, new entrants would need to manufacture 500–600 razor blades per annum in order to achieve those economies of scale, at a cost of between $75 million and $150 million). *See also Telekomunikacja Polska supra* note 24, para. 656, in which the Commission held that the economies of scale enjoyed by the incumbent Polish telecommunications operator in local loop unbundling were such that a competitor would *"need high penetration to be viable … market entry is therefore much more difficult in the presence of an already established, ubiquitous operator"*.

[96] *See* R. Schmalensee, "Economies of Scale and Barriers to Entry" (1981), 89(6) *The Journal of Political Economy*, pp. 1228–38, citing G. J. Stigler, "Barriers to Entry, Economies of Scale, and Firm Size" in G. J. Stigler (Ed.), *The Organization of Industry* (Homewood, Ill., Irwin, 1968), pp. 67–70.

[97] *See* A. Dixit, "A Model of Duopoly Suggesting a Theory of Entry Barriers" (1979), 399 *Antitrust Law & Economics*, pp. 20–32; and A. Dixit, "The Role of Investment in Entry-Deterrence" (1980), 90 *The Economic Journal*, pp. 95–106. *See also* R. Schmalensee, *ibid*.

[98] Case IV/30.178 *Napier Brown/British Sugar* ("*Napier Brown*"), Commission Decision of 18 July 1988, OJ 1988 L 284/41, paras 56–7 (note that although the UK Government was entitled to reallocate sugar quantities to other producers, the Commission considered that it was unlikely to do so since British Sugar had capacity to process the entire production).

[99] Case IV/34.689 *Sea Containers/Stena Sealink – Interim measures*, Commission Decision of 21 December 1993, OJ 1994 L 15/8; *See also Merci Convenzionali* (a monopoly for the running port operations in a given port) *supra* note 82; Case COMP/38.700 *Greek Lignite and Electricity Markets*, Commission decision of 5 March 2008, not yet published (The Commission stressed that PPC enjoyed a privileged access to lignite, the most attractive and cheapest input for the generation of electricity in Greece. The Greek State, which controls PPC, granted it a privileged access

2. – Dominance
Christopher Cook and Ruchit Patel

Commission considered that Stena's position as owner of the Holyhead port and operator of the Dublin to Holyhead ferry service gave rise to barriers to entry because Sea Containers *"could not, if they wished to introduce a ferry service on the central corridor route, do so without substantially increasing the length of the crossing or building a new port themselves. The latter course of action would not be economically or physically realistic."*[100] In *Aer Lingus*, the Commission regarded the lack of available take-off and landing slots at London Heathrow airport and Aer Lingus' access to such slots as creating barriers to new entry on the London-Dublin route.[101]

2.63 In many instances, privileged access to essential inputs or natural resources may emanate or originate from a state grant; the analysis of privileged access to essential inputs as barriers to entry may thus overlap significantly with the analysis of statutory monopolies.

2.1.4.   Technological Advantage

2.64 The Commission and courts have regarded technological advantages by the incumbent company over its competitors and potential entrants as barriers to entry contributing to a finding of dominance. For example, in *United Brands*, the Court of Justice emphasised that the finding of dominance was based *inter alia* on United Brands' productivity, which was a function of its superior technical ability to develop bananas that had strong resistance to disease (which could not be easily matched by competitors):

> *"In the field of technical knowledge and as a result of continual research* [United Brands] *keeps on improving the productivity and yield of its plantations by improving the draining system, making good soil deficiencies and combating effectively plant disease. It has perfected new ripening methods in which its technicians instruct the distributor/ripeners of the Chiquita banana. That is another factor to be borne in mind when considering* [United Brands'] *position since competing firms cannot develop research at a comparable level and are in this respect at a disadvantage compared with the applicant."*[102]

---

to lignite. This lead to dominant and quasi-monopolistic position of PPC according to the Commission) and Case IV/28.841 *ABG/Oil Companies*, Commission Decision of 19 April 1977, OJ 1977 L 117/1 (Commission decided that each of the oil companies active in the Netherlands was dominant towards its customers during the 1973 oil crisis because the shortage of motor spirit rendered customers dependent on the suppliers).

[100] Case IV/34.689, *ibid.*, para. 64.
[101] Case IV/33.544, *supra* note 84, at para. 19.
[102] *United Brands supra* note 2, paras 82–84.

2. – Dominance
Christopher Cook and Ruchit Patel

2.65 In a number of other cases, the courts and Commission have identified the dominant firm's "technological lead" over its competitors as evidence of its dominant position.[103]

2.1.5. Established Distribution and Sales Network

2.66 Many Commission decisions and court judgments have identified the existence of an established distribution and sales network as an entry barrier and an important indicator of dominance. This factor is likely to carry greater weight in industries where developing an efficient route to market is difficult (*e.g.*, because trained sales personnel are required or where sales and distribution facilities are not quickly replicable through recourse to third-party outsourcing companies). Thus, for example, in *United Brands* the Court of Justice held that United Brands enjoyed a dominant position in part because it was present at all levels of the banana supply chain: plantation, packaging, transport, ripening and distribution.[104] It emphasised that "*UBC even extends its control to ripener/distributors and wholesalers by setting up a complete network of agents.*"[105] Similarly, in *Hoffmann-La Roche*, the Court of Justice held that the existence of a "*highly developed sales network*" was, in itself, a technical and commercial advantage representing a barrier to competitors.[106] The same logic has been applied in several cases under related circumstances. For example, in *Soda-Ash*,[107] Solvay's "*excellent market coverage*" was considered to be a material indicator of dominance, and the Commission regarded EDF's competitors lack of "*access to information on customers*" as a barrier to entry to the electricity market.[108] In *Michelin II*, the Commission identified Michelin's representation in local commercial and technical centres in France and its strong distribution channel[109] as barriers to entry.

---

[103] *See, e.g., Hoffmann-La Roche supra* note 3, para. 48; Case COMP/36.041 *Michelin*, Commission Decision of 20 June 2001, OJ 2002 L 143/1, paras 182–3.

[104] *United Brands supra* note 2, paras 69–93.

[105] *Ibid.*, para. 71.

[106] *Hoffmann-La Roche supra* note 3, para. 48.

[107] Case IV/33.133 *Soda-ash – Solvay, ICI*, Commission Decision of 19 December 1990, OJ 1991 L 152/21, recital 32.

[108] Case COMP/39.386 *Long Term Electricity Contracts France*, Commission Decision of 17 March 2010, not yet published, para. 26.

[109] Case COMP/36.041, *supra* note 103, paras 191–196.

2. – Dominance
Christopher Cook and Ruchit Patel

2.1.6. Network Effects

"Network effects" refers to the phenomenon whereby a product or service **2.67** becomes more valuable to each user when more people use it – the telephone, the internet, and social networks are commonly cited examples of businesses that have significant network effects.[110]

Network effects can act as barriers to entry or expansion if they function to **2.68** reduce the value of a competitive offering. Where network effects are present, competitors may be unable to enter or expand effectively, as efforts to offer even cheaper or technologically more advanced products will usually be unsuccessful (in particular where the market has "tipped" in favour of the incumbent). Network effects are especially strong entry barriers where they are self-reinforcing (*i.e.*, a function of the installed base of customers that grows reliant on one another) and not linked to the intrinsic qualities of the product in question.[111]

The main Article 102 case where network effects were an important factor in **2.69** the dominance analysis is *Microsoft*, where the Commission found that network effects contributed to Microsoft's dominance in PC operating systems (since an operating system's utility depends upon the amount and quality of programs that will run on it, and software developers are more likely to invest in developing products for operating systems with many users) and also affected the market for media players: "*The network effects characterising the media software markets ... translate into entry barriers for new entrants. A streaming media player would not meet with significant consumer demand if there was no or no significant amount of corresponding digital content which this player could play back.*"[112]

---

[110] *See Microsoft Decision 2004, supra* note 47, at para. 419 ("*A product market is said to exhibit network effects when the overall utility derived by consumers who use the product in question is dependent not only on their private use of the product, but also on the number of other consumers who use the product. Such network effect is a direct network effect. An indirect network effect occurs when the value of a good to a user increases as the number and variety of complementary products increase.*").

[111] Case COMP/39.530 *Microsoft (Tying)* ("*Browser Commitment Decision*") Commission Decision of 16 December 2009, not yet published, at paras 25–8 (The utility of a pc depends on the number of applications that the user can use on it or will be able to use. The independent software vendors write their applications by preference for pc operating systems being the most popular. Given the high market penetration of the Microsoft pc operating system, nearly all of the applications are compatible with Windows and making it more attractive to the user. Many applications are even only available to Windows users. This advantage helps Microsoft to increase its market presence.).

[112] *Microsoft Decision 2004, supra* note 47, at para. 420.

2. – Dominance
Christopher Cook and Ruchit Patel

2.1.7.   Undertaking's Own Conduct

2.70   The *Guidance Paper* states that an undertaking's *"own conduct may also create barriers to entry, for example where it has made significant investments which entrants or competitors would have to match, or where it has concluded long-term contracts with its customers that have appreciable foreclosing effects."*[113]

2.1.7.1.   Significant Investment

2.71   Where the dominant undertaking has made investments in its business that competitors would have to match to be able to compete effectively, this may create barriers to entry or expansion. Some such investments would relate directly to developing extensive distribution and sales networks or new technologies, which are specifically identified elsewhere in the *Guidance Paper* (and discussed above). The supporting footnote to this section of the *Guidance Paper* refers to the advertising and promotional campaigns used by United Brands to make its products distinctive to consumers.[114] Brand loyalty has been cited in support of a dominance finding in several other court judgments and Commission decisions.[115] While customer loyalty to the leading supplier's brand may often be perceived as a real hurdle for competitors to get over, it is submitted that actual market conditions should be considered before brand loyalty is treated as a significant barrier to entry.[116] Many decisions under Article 102 involve fast-moving technology markets where brand awareness and loyalty can be built – and can erode – quickly. In such circumstances the investments in advertising and promotion needed to create a viable competitor to a strong incumbent may be relatively low.

---

[113] *Guidance Paper supra* note 1, para. 17.

[114] *Ibid.*, para. 18, footnote 4, and *United Brands supra* note 2, para. 91 (*"UBC has made this product distinctive by large-scale repeated advertising and promotion campaigns which have induced the consumer to show a preference for it in spite of the difference between the price of labelled and unlabelled bananas (in the region of 30 to 40%) and also of chiquita bananas and those which have been labelled with another brand name (in the region of 7 to 10%)."*).

[115] *See, e.g.*, Case COMP/37.990, *supra* note 47, paras 867–74 (The Commission considered Intel's strong brand as a barrier to entry and expansion. First, the OEMs specifically ask for Intel CPUs to be included in their orders. Secondly, the Commission refers to the important value of the brand "Intel". Thirdly, Intel's past marketing expenses have been much higher than the expenses of its main competitor AMD.); Case COMP/36.041, *supra* note 103, paras 184–5; Case COMP/39.116 *Coca-Cola*, Commission Decision of 22 June 2005, not yet published, para. 25 (in this settlement decision, the Commission identified the strong brand recognition of *Coca-Cola* as a barrier to entry and expansion).

[116] *See* Case C-234/89 *Stergios Delimitis v Henninger Bräu* [1991] ECR I-935 (*"[A]ccount must be taken of the conditions under which competitive forces operate on the relevant market. In that connection it is necessary to know not only the number and the size of producers present on the market, but also the degree of saturation of that market and customer fidelity to existing brands, for it is generally more difficult to penetrate a saturated market in which customers are loyal to a small number of large producers than a market in full expansion in which a large number of small producers are operating without any strong brand names."*).

2. – Dominance
Christopher Cook and Ruchit Patel

2.1.7.2. Long-term Contracts with Appreciable Foreclosure Effects

The *Guidance Paper* considers that the existence of *"long-term contracts with appre-* **2.72** *ciable foreclosure effects"* may be a barrier to entry or expansion, but does not cite any supporting case law for the proposition. It is clear that new entrants would find it difficult to sell their products in a market where the incumbent supplier(s) had tied up most or all customer demand through long-term exclusive supply contracts; such contracts would constitute a barrier to entry or expansion.[117] Traditionally, however, in Article 102 cases long-term contracts with exclusionary effects have been analysed directly, in the context of "abuse," rather than indirectly, as entry barriers in connection with "dominance."[118] There are at least two possible explanations for the *Guidance Paper's* inclusion of this item as a potential barrier to expansion or entry: (1) the Commission may have in mind a situation where long-term exclusive supply agreements entered into by a single large incumbent are not abusive (*e.g.*, because the market was competitive when the contracts were entered into) but still make entry difficult; and (2) the Commission may intend to capture situations of collective dominance, where no individual supplier's contracts could be considered abusive but the prevalent use by multiple suppliers of long-term exclusive supply agreements makes it very difficult for new entrants to find demand for their products.

2.1.8. Persistently High Market Shares

The *Guidance Paper* states that *"persistently high market shares may be indicative of* **2.73** *the existence of barriers to entry and expansion."*[119] The key word is "persistently." High market shares themselves are not a barrier to entry – even a weak first mover may capture a large share of a new market – but if a large incumbent supplier maintains a high market share over an extended period of time, the Commission is likely to look for reasons why this is so. One possible explanation is that the market is characterised by barriers to entry or expansion by competitors, which would be analysed as discussed above.

---

[117] *See Discussion Paper supra* note 48, para. 40 (*"Finally, the incumbent firms may through the use of long-term contracts with customers have made it difficult for rivals at a particular point in time to find a sufficient number of customers able to switch supplier that expansion or entry would be profitable."*).

[118] *See, e.g., supra* note 50, para. 10.098, pp. 979 *et seq.*

[119] *Guidance Paper supra* note 1, para. 18.

2. – Dominance
Christopher Cook and Ruchit Patel

2.1.9. Switching Costs for Consumers

2.74 Although not recognised expressly in the *Guidance Paper*, high switching costs can also represent barriers to entry and expansion. These costs could be financial (*e.g.*, contractual termination clauses) or non-financial (*e.g.*, the loss of advantages offered by the existing supplier or as regards network effects – *see* above).[120] In *Microsoft*, the Commission concluded that barriers to entry arose as a result of the high direct and indirect switching costs that customers would have incurred for changing suppliers of operating systems. The switching costs, so the Commission argued, allowed Microsoft to act independently of customer wishes and exercise market power.[121]

3. Countervailing Buyer Power

3.1. *Theory and Basic Approach*

2.75 The exercise of market power, and thus the possible existence of a dominant firm, may be rendered impossible if customers exercise sufficient countervailing buyer power. John Kenneth Galbraith coined the term "countervailing power" in 1952[122] to describe the ability of large buyers to extract price concessions from their suppliers. One of Galbraith's examples of countervailing power involves a large grocery chain extracting wholesale price discounts from food producers – a fact-pattern that has been examined in several of the leading EU merger decisions on countervailing buyer power.[123]

2.76 In the Article 102 context, the Commission and courts have accepted that undertakings may not be able to exercise market power in circumstances where they are constrained by the existence of powerful customers. In *Gottrup-Klim*, the Court of Justice stated: "*In a market where product prices vary according to the*

---

[120] *Microsoft Decision 2004 Tetra Pak I (BTG Licence)*, Commission Decision of 26 July 1988, OJ 1988 L 272/27, para. 44; Case COMP/38.044 *NDC Health/IMS Health: Interim measures*, Commission Decision of 13 August 2003, OJ 2003 L 268/69, paras 87 and 103 (Commission highlighted costs for pharmaceutical companies to switch between IMS's "1860" brick structure map and a different structure).

[121] *Microsoft Decision 2004*, *supra* note 47, para. 463 (Commission cited as evidence an internal communication of Microsoft's, declaring "[it] *is this switching cost that has given customers the patience to stick with Windows through all our mistakes, our buggy drivers, our high TCO, our lack of a sexy vision at times, and many other difficulties.*").

[122] J. K. Galbraith, *American capitalism: The concept of countervailing power* (Boston, Houghton Mifflin, 1952).

[123] *See*, *e.g.*, Case IV/M.1221 *Rewe/Meinl*, Commission Decision of 3 February 1999, para. 101; Case COMP/M.1684 *Carrefour/Promodes*, Commission Decision of 25 January 2000; and Case COMP/M.5047 *REWE/ADEG*, Commission Decision of 23 June 2008, para. 93.

2. – Dominance
Christopher Cook and Ruchit Patel

volume of orders, the activities of cooperative purchasing associations may, depending on the size of their membership, constitute a significant counterweight to the contractual power of large producers and make way for more effective competition."[124]

The Commission has at times been criticised for failing adequately to consider **2.77** the constraints exercised by powerful buyers. For example, in *Italian Flat Glass*, the Court of First Instance criticised the Commission for failing properly to consider the impact of Fiat as the monopoly purchaser of glass for motor vehicles.[125] However, large customers will not always be found to exercise buyer power sufficient to constrain an otherwise dominant firm, and in most cases defendants' buyer power arguments have not been sufficient to overcome dominance findings. For example, in *United Brands*, the Court rejected the threat of countervailing buyer power on the basis that United Brands' reliance on a few large retailers and ripeners was due to company policy seeking to streamline supply and not an indication of true countervailing power.[126]

The *Guidance Paper* summarises the conditions under which the exercise of **2.78** market power may be constrained by countervailing buyer power as follows:

> "*competitive constraints may be exerted not only by actual or potential competitors but also by customers. Even an undertaking with a high market share may not be able to act to an appreciable extent independently of customers with sufficient bargaining strength. Such countervailing buying power may result from the customers' size or their commercial significance for the dominant undertaking, and their ability to switch quickly to competing suppliers, to promote new entry or to vertically integrate, and to credibly threaten to do so.*"[127]

In other words, the key in assessing the relative bargaining power of suppliers **2.79** and customers is to weigh the alternatives each party has to dealing with the other (in economic terms, their "outside options"); a customer will have significant bargaining power if its outside option is better than the seller's. The

---

[124] *Gøttrup-Klim*, para. 32. *See also supra* note 50, para. 10.042.

[125] Joined Cases T-68, 77 and 78/89 *Società Italiana Vetro and others v Commission* ("*Società Italiana Vetro*") [1992] ECR II-1403, para. 366 ("*It follows that, even supposing that the circumstances of the present case lend themselves to application of the concept of "collective dominant position" … the Commission has not adduced the necessary proof. The Commission has not even attempted to gather the information necessary to weigh up the economic power of the three [glass] producers against that of Fiat, which could cancel each other out.*").

[126] *United Brands supra* note 2, para. 95.

[127] *Guidance Paper supra* note 1, para. 18.

2. – Dominance
Christopher Cook and Ruchit Patel

value of the buyer's outside option depends on its ability and willingness to substitute to alternative suppliers, and the value of the seller's outside option depends on its ability and willingness to substitute to alternative buyers.[128] If the buyer can easily switch to alternative suppliers, sponsor new entry, or self-supply without incurring substantial sunk costs – or credibly threaten to do so – it will have significant buying power.

2.80   Finally, the existence of one or more customers with significant buyer power is not sufficient to defeat a finding of dominance in the upstream market. The *Guidance Paper* states that, "[i]*f countervailing power is of a sufficient magnitude, it may deter or defeat an attempt by the undertaking to profitably increase prices. Buyer power may not, however, be considered a sufficiently effective constraint if it only ensures that a particular or limited segment of customers is shielded from the market power of the dominant undertaking.*"[129]

2.81   In other words, if a dominance finding is to be avoided, the strong buyer(s) should not only protect themselves, but effectively protect the entire market. The logic behind this position is that even if the dominant firm is constrained by one or more strong buyers it may still be able to exercise market power against other customers whose outside option is less attractive. Thus, the presence of strong buyers will only counter a dominance finding if it is likely that in response to prices being increased above the competitive level, the buyers in question will pave the way for effective new entry or lead existing suppliers in the market to significantly expand their output so as to defeat the price increase, thereby protecting all the allegedly dominant firm's customers in the downstream market. If strong buyers are likely to simply extract more favourable conditions from the dominant supplier than their weaker competitors, the Commission may define separate relevant markets for strong and weak buyers.[130]

3.2.   Unavoidable Trading Partners

2.82   Although not mentioned in the *Guidance Paper*, the Commission has, in a number of leading Article 102 cases, concluded that buying power – even in the presence of large, aggressive customers that were in position to extract favourable terms – was not sufficient to avoid a dominance finding because even the

---

[128] *See* OECD Competition Committee, "*Policy Roundtables: Monopsony and Buyer Power, 2008*" OECD roundtable discussion, Section 1.1.3.
[129] *Guidance Paper supra* note 1, para. 18.
[130] *See Discussion Paper supra* note 48, para. 42.

2. – Dominance
Christopher Cook and Ruchit Patel

largest customers had no choice but to deal with the dominant firm.[131] In *Intel*, the Commission rejected arguments that the Original Equipment Manufacturers (*i.e.*, laptop and desktop computer hardware manufacturers) exercised significant countervailing buyer power on the basis that Intel had become an unavoidable trading partner:

> *"throughout its argumentation on buyer power, Intel ignores the fundamental element in its relationship with OEMs, namely the fact that it is an unavoidable trading partner for them: OEMs depend on Intel for what is the most important single hardware component in their computers. As such, Intel is a must-stock brand."*[132]

> *"It is of course natural that OEMs will attempt to exert leverage vis-à-vis Intel by using the possibility that they could switch some of their supplies to AMD, in particular when AMD is an increasing competitive threat. But this does not change the fundamentals of their relationship with Intel – Intel remains an unavoidable trading partner on which the OEMs depend. Given this, it is not plausible to argue that OEMs hold buyer power over Intel (at least not to the extent that Intel would not possess substantial market power). Therefore, in this case, buyer power may not be considered a sufficiently effective constraint because it only ensures that a limited segment of OEMs' purchases from Intel could at any time be shielded from the market power of Intel."*[133]

In support of this conclusion on buyer power, the Commission initially cites **2.83** the same factors cited earlier in the dominance assessment: Intel's high historical market share and its formidable brand presence, supported by its large marketing budget.[134] Neither point is persuasive: these factors may reflect customers' historical preference for Intel processors over those of AMD (Intel's principal competitor), but they do not explain the attractiveness of customers' outside option (*i.e.*, switching significant purchases away from Intel). In assessing buyer power, what matters is not whether OEMs have preferred Intel in the past, but the extent to which they could do without Intel in the future. However, the Commission goes on to reference its analysis of barriers to entry and expansion in the processor market, including high sunk

---

[131] Case IV/34.780, *supra* note 51, para. 92; Case COMP/37.990, *supra* note 47, para. 894; Case COMP/38.096 *Clearstream*, Commission decision of 2 June 2004, not yet published (Commission press release identifies Clearstream as an "unavoidable trading partner").

[132] Case COMP/37.990 *Intel*, *ibid.*, para. 886.

[133] *Ibid.*, para. 894.

[134] *Ibid.*, paras 887–89.

2. – Dominance
Christopher Cook and Ruchit Patel

costs related to R&D and manufacturing and economies of scale, which are more pertinent to the issue of buyer power. If entry barriers in the processor market were low (*e.g.*, if AMD had significant spare capacity or could expand quickly, or if OEMs could realistically self-supply or sponsor new processor manufacturers), OEMs would be able to shift significant purchases away from Intel, *i.e.*, they would have a viable outside option that might be sufficient to constrain the exercise of market power in the upstream market.

2.84   It does not follow that because a supplier is an unavoidable trading partner, it is immune to countervailing buyer power. Buyer power is a matter of degree, and the *Guidance Paper* is silent on the amount of it that is necessary to constrain an otherwise dominant supplier. It might be that a supplier is an unavoidable trading partner, in the sense that customers are in practice obliged to deal *to some extent* with it (*e.g.*, because the supplier has a strong brand or there are capacity constraints in the upstream market), but even if customers cannot entirely walk away, they may be able to discipline unavoidable trading partners by reducing orders, switching part of their demand to other suppliers, sponsoring entry, or vertically integrating. Whether such behaviour would be sufficient to prevent the exercise of market power in the upstream market will require case-by-case analysis considering issues such as: how much of the allegedly dominant supplier's sales could be switched to others (which will depend on factors such as spare capacity in the upstream market and the importance of brand preferences), how quickly such switching could take place, and how much such switching would cost both the supplier (in terms of lost sales) and the buyer (in terms of sunk costs of sponsoring entry or vertical integration, or lost sales due to lack of the dominant brand).

3.3.   Observations on Significance of Buyer Power Analysis

2.85   The *United Brands* definition of dominance as "*the power to behave to an appreciable extent independently of its competitors, its customers, and ultimately of consumers*"[135] compels consideration of the extent to which a supplier's customers may constrain its ability to exercise market power before concluding that it is dominant. To that extent, assessing countervailing buyer power can be considered as an integral part of the dominance analysis.

2.86   It is submitted, however, that the principal factors on which an analysis of buyer power ought to be based are by and large identical to those considered

---

[135] *United Brands supra* note 2, para. 65.

2. – Dominance
Christopher Cook and Ruchit Patel

in the assessment of barriers to entry and expansion. A customer has countervailing power over a large supplier to the extent that it has a viable outside option – *i.e.*, to the extent that it can plausibly threaten to switch a substantial amount of demand to an alternative source of supply, for a cost that is less than the resulting loss to the original supplier. There will only be viable alternative sources of supply in markets where barriers to entry or expansion are relatively low: for example, where competitors of the allegedly dominant supplier have idle spare capacity or can quickly ramp up production, where there are limited technological or IP hurdles for new entrants, where sunk costs of new entry are low relative to the expected gains, and where switching suppliers is unlikely itself to impose major costs on the customer (*e.g.*, as a result of consumer brand preferences).

Put differently, it is hard to imagine a situation in which countervailing **2.87** buyer power would be sufficient to negate a dominance finding in an industry where entry and expansion barriers were very high and/or where the support of a customer would not assist in overcoming those barriers. And, as explained in Section II above, the assessment of barriers to entry and expansion represents the heart of the dominance analysis under the *Guidance Paper*'s methodology – so the relevant factors will be considered in the dominance analysis of whether or not countervailing buyer power is treated as a separate prong. This is not to say that the concept of buyer power is irrelevant to assessing dominance: it can be useful to think about same issues from different angles. For example, new entry or expansion in a particular market may be unlikely without major customer sponsorship, so the existence of a strategy that would prevent the exercise of market power by a large supplier might be more evident when considering likely customer responses (*i.e.*, buyer power) than direct competitor responses. Ultimately, however, the intuitions behind – and the factors taken into account in assessing – countervailing buyer power and barriers to entry in the dominance analysis are largely the same, making separate treatment of buyer power somewhat redundant.

4. Other Indicators of Dominance

4.1. *Economic Performance*

The *Guidance Paper* does not recommend that the economic performance of **2.88** an undertaking should be taken into account in the assessment of market

2. – Dominance
Christopher Cook and Ruchit Patel

power (but seems to reserve that assessment to the analysis of effects).[136] The decisional practice of the courts supports such an interpretation at least as regards the relevance of economic performance to the assessment of dominance. For example, in *United Brands*, the Court of Justice held: "*An undertaking's economic strength is not measured by its profitability; a reduced profit margin or even losses for a time are not incompatible with a dominant position, just as large profits may be compatible with a situation where there is effective competition, the fact that an undertaking's profitability is for a time moderate or non-existent must be considered in light of the whole of that undertaking's operations.*"[137]

2.89 Similarly, in *Hoffmann-La Roche* the Court of Justice held that reductions in prices are not inconsistent with a dominance finding where such price reductions are determined not by competitive pressure but by a price policy intentionally and freely adopted.[138] In *Michelin I*, the Court of Justice went further, holding that:

> "*As regards the additional criteria and evidence to which Michelin NV refers in order to disprove the existence of a dominant position, it must be observed that temporary unprofitability or even losses are not inconsistent with the existence of a dominant position. By the same token, the fact that the prices charged by Michelin NV do not constitute an abuse and are not even particularly high does not justify the conclusion that a dominant position does not exist.*"[139]

2.90 These judgments effectively establish that an allegedly dominant undertaking will not be able to use its own poor financial performance to negate a dominance finding. At the same time, however, the Commission's decisional practice suggests that the reverse is not necessarily the case – some decisions have invoked financial success as an indicator of dominance. For example, in *Microsoft*, the Commission held that:

> "*Microsoft's financial performance is consistent with its near-monopoly position in the client PC operating system market. ... According to the most recent available figures, ... for its Windows PC client operating system range of products ... Microsoft incurred costs of USD 1,994 million and received revenues of USD*

---

[136] *Guidance Paper supra* note 1, para. 20 ("*if the conduct has been in place for a sufficient period of time, the market performance of the dominant undertaking and its competitors may provide direct evidence of anti-competitive foreclosure.*").
[137] *United Brands supra* note 2, para. 4.
[138] *Hoffmann-La Roche supra* note 3, para. 74.
[139] *Michelin I*, paras 11 and 59.

2. – Dominance
Christopher Cook and Ruchit Patel

10,394 million, resulting in an operating income of USD 8,400 million. This means that for its client PC operating system product, Microsoft operated on a profit margin of approximately 81 per cent. This is high by any measure."[140]

These asymmetric positions of the courts and Commission (high profits indi- **2.91**
cate dominance; low profits do not indicate an absence of dominance) are consistent with a result-driven approach having been applied. It appears from the cases that often, having already decided that the firm under investigation was dominant, evidence of financial performance was either invoked in further support (if strong) or disregarded as irrelevant (if poor). This is unsatisfactory: financial performance should either be treated as an indicator of dominance – or its absence – or not. If financial performance is to be taken into account in the dominance assessment, a balanced approach along the lines advocated by the UK Office of Fair Trading would be appropriate:

"An undertaking's conduct in a market or its financial performance may provide evidence that it possesses market power. Depending on other available evidence, it might, for example, be reasonable to infer that an undertaking possesses market power from evidence that it has:

- *set prices consistently above an appropriate measure of costs, or*
- *persistently earned an excessive rate of profit.*

High prices or profits alone are not sufficient proof that an undertaking has market power: high profits may represent a return on previous innovation, or result from changing demand conditions. As such, they may be consistent with a competitive market, where undertakings are able to take advantage of profitable opportunities when they exist. However, persistent significantly high returns, relative to those which would prevail in a competitive market of similar risk and rate of innovation, may suggest that market power does exist. This would be especially so if those high returns did not stimulate new entry or innovation."[141]

However, as the OFT guidance suggests, there are great difficulties in iden- **2.92**
tifying the real "competitive" price level of any product or service, and therefore pitfalls in basing any inferences regarding dominance on perceived

---

[140] *Microsoft Decision 2004, supra* note 47, para. 464.
[141] Office of Fair Trading, *Assessment of Market Power*, OFT 415, December 2004, paras 1.7, 3.5, 6.5 and 6.6.

2. – Dominance
Christopher Cook and Ruchit Patel

"supra competitive" pricing or profitability.[142] The better course, as the *Guidance Paper* implicitly recognises, is not to take a firm's economic performance into account in assessing dominance.

4.2. *Abuse*

2.93 The *Guidance Paper* does not propose that an ability to carry out abusive conduct (*e.g.*, the ability to exclude or foreclose) or an abuse *per se* is evidence of market power. Accordingly, the Commission sensibly refrains from suggesting that market power is itself a function of the effects of specific conduct, perhaps because this could lead to circular reasoning and distil significantly the importance of a dominance finding in exclusionary cases (the logic is perhaps more relevant to exploitative cases). Interestingly, however, the courts have previously indicated that it "*may be advisable to take into account … facts put forward as acts amounting to abuses without necessarily having to acknowledge that they are abuses.*"[143] The Commission's decisional practice also shows signs of succumbing to this tendency. In *Michelin*, for example, the Commission held: "*The business practice of granting a wide range of loyalty rebates that are paid very late is also a clear indication of Michelin's dominant position. The fact that dealers until at least 1997 were prepared to sell Michelin tyres at a loss in the expectation of rebates that were finally paid in February of the following year is evidence of the manufacturer's market power.*"[144]

4.3. *Related Markets*

2.94 The *Guidance Paper* does not suggest that dominance in a neighbouring or related market should be taken into account when assessing dominance in the market at issue. However, the courts have previously held that the Commission is entitled to take into account dominance in neighbouring or related markets where such dominance reinforces the putatively dominant undertaking's market power. For example, in *Tetra Pak*, the Court of Justice held:

> "*In relation, next, to the alleged associative links between the relevant markets, it is common ground that they are due to the fact that the key products packaged in aseptic and non-aseptic cartons are the same and to the conduct of manufacturers*

---

[142] *See* S. Park, "Market Power in Competition for the Market" (2009) 5(3) *Journal of Competition Law & Economics*, pp. 571–9; and F. Russo and others, *European Commission Decisions on Competition, Economic Perspectives on Landmark Antitrust and Merger Cases* (Cambridge, Cambridge University Press, 2010), p. 115, Section 3.1(A).

[143] *United Brands supra* note 2, para. 68. *See also Hilti*, para. 93.

[144] Case COMP/36.041, *supra* note 103, para. 198.

2. – Dominance
Christopher Cook and Ruchit Patel

and users. Both the aseptic and the non-aseptic machines and cartons at issue in this case are used for packaging the same liquid products intended for human consumption, principally dairy products and fruit juice. Moreover, a substantial proportion of Tetra Pak's customers operate both in the aseptic and the non-aseptic sectors. In its written observations submitted in reply to the statement of objections, confirmed in its written observations before the Court, the applicant thus stated that in 1987 approximately 35% of its customers had purchased both aseptic and non-aseptic systems. Furthermore, the Commission correctly noted that the conduct of the principal manufacturers of carton-packaging systems confirmed the link between the aseptic and the non-aseptic markets, since two of them, Tetra Pak and PKL, already operate on all four markets and the third, Elopak, which is well-established in the non-aseptic sector, has for some considerable time been trying to gain access to the aseptic markets.

It follows that the Commission was entitled to find that the abovementioned links between the two aseptic markets and the two non-aseptic markets reinforced Tetra Pak's economic power over the latter markets. The fact that Tetra Pak held nearly 90% of the markets in the aseptic sector meant that, for undertakings producing both fresh and long-life liquid food products, it was not only an inevitable supplier of aseptic systems but also a favoured supplier of non-aseptic systems. Moreover, by virtue of its technological lead and its quasi-monopoly in the aseptic sector, Tetra Pak was able to focus its competitive efforts on the neighbouring non-aseptic markets, where it was already well-established, without fear of retaliation in the aseptic sector, which meant that it also enjoyed freedom of conduct compared with the other economic operators on the non-aseptic markets as well.

It follows from all the above considerations that, in the circumstances of this case, Tetra Pak's practices on the non-aseptic markets are liable to be caught by Article 86 of the Treaty without its being necessary to establish the existence of a dominant position on those markets taken in isolation, since that undertaking's leading position on the non-aseptic markets, combined with the close associative links between those markets and the aseptic markets, gave Tetra Pak freedom of conduct compared with the other economic operators on the non-aseptic markets, such as to impose on it a special responsibility under Article 86 to maintain genuine undistorted competition on those markets."[145]

---

[145] Case T-51/89 *Tetra Pak Rausing v Commission* ("*Tetra Pak I Judgment 1990*") [1990] ECR II-309, paras 120–2.

2. – Dominance
Christopher Cook and Ruchit Patel

2.95   The Commission has also taken a similar approach. For example, in *Michelin*, the Commission held that Michelin's strong presence on the market for original equipment truck tyres (*i.e.*, for new tyres) "*act*[ed] *to its advantage*" on the replacement and retread markets, in part because users intended to remain loyal.[146]

2.96   The judgment in *Tetra Pak* and decision in *Michelin* give strong indications that the Commission is entitled, in the right circumstances, to consider an undertaking's market power in a related market when assessing dominance in a market that is distinct for antitrust purposes. However, for the Commission to sustain such an allegation the links between the two markets must be strong and the position of the allegedly dominant undertaking in the related market must be quasi-monopolistic: in practice, there are likely to be few such industries.[147]

IV.   Implications of the Shift to Effects-Based Analysis under Article 102

2.97   As noted at the outset of this Chapter, changes in how the concept of dominance has been defined and applied in Article 102 cases over the past four decades have been evolutionary rather than transformational. As the preceding sections indicate, the changes in the approach to dominance that are introduced in the *Guidance Paper* can at least largely be reconciled with existing precedent and will likely be of less practical impact in future cases than the Commission's new thinking on the notion of abuse. Yet several likely implications of the new approach to dominance can be identified.

1.   "Substantial Market Power": A Higher Standard For Dominance?

2.98   The shift from the case law's classical formulation of dominance as commercial power to the *Guidance Paper*'s definition of dominance as substantial market power implies that there should be changes in how the Commission treats certain types of evidence in its dominance assessment. In some cases, these changes could be outcome-determinative, as firms that were found dominant under court precedent would not be found so today, so the shift arguably represents a raising of the legal standard for identifying dominance. At a minimum,

---

[146] Case COMP/36.041, *supra* note 103, paras 186–90.
[147] *See Discussion Paper supra* note 48, footnote 69, which characterises the *Tetra Pak* case as "exceptional".

2. – Dominance
Christopher Cook and Ruchit Patel

the new definition of dominance as substantial market power will affect how dominance issues in future Article 102 cases are argued and analysed.

First, in future cases it will be more difficult for the Commission to cite as evidence of dominance advantages that the firm in question holds over its competitors merely as a result of its organisational structure or efficiency. The *Guidance Paper* expressly recognises that protecting competitors is not the objective of Article 102 enforcement and that less efficient competitors may well be driven out of the market by legitimate behaviour.[148] Thus, disadvantages faced by smaller competitors deriving merely from their being less efficient than the firm under investigation should not, in themselves, be regarded as evidence that the firm is dominant. Applying this approach in connection with the assessment of dominance is consistent with, if not compelled by, the *Guidance Paper*'s focus on the "equally efficient competitor" test for assessing pricing abuses.[149] **2.99**

In this context, for example, it is at least arguable that several of the factors cited by the Court of Justice as important indicators of dominance in *United Brands* (*e.g.*, the firm's geographical diversification and leading technical knowledge as compared to its rivals) would not today be recognised as such by the Commission. The Commission's analysis of barriers to entry and expansion will need to be conducted with particular care, as several of the market features cited in the *Guidance Paper* as potential barriers to entry or expansion by competitors – *e.g.*, investments by the incumbent supplier in technology, distribution, or brand-building – look like things that equally efficient rivals should normally be able to replicate. Large firms should no longer risk being accused of a supposed "efficiency offense." **2.100**

Secondly, the Commission should be more receptive to direct evidence that the market in question is functioning competitively. As explained in Section I above, the definition of dominance implies that when a dominant firm is present on the market, competition is already functioning imperfectly. Therefore, evidence that the market is creating competitive outcomes should be viewed as directly contradictory to the hypothesis of dominance and therefore impossible to ignore. In fact, this point has been recognised since the time of *Hoffman-La Roche*, as the Court of Justice expressly confirmed: "*[T]he fact that an undertaking is compelled by the pressure of its competitors' price* **2.101**

---

[148] *Guidance Paper supra* note 1, para. 6.
[149] *Ibid.*, paras 23–7.

2. – Dominance
Christopher Cook and Ruchit Patel

reductions to lower its own prices is in general incompatible with that independent conduct which is the hallmark of a dominant position."[150]

2.102 The principle that evidence of effective competition in the market should undermine a finding of dominance sounds uncontroversial but has by no means been applied consistently. For example, as noted in Section I above and notwithstanding the clear principle expressed in *Hoffman-La Roche*, in assessing dominance in *United Brands* and *Michelin I*, the Court of Justice pointedly held that factors indicating supposed deficiencies in the competitive process outweighed evidence – including evidence of price competition – indicating that the markets were in fact competitive.[151] In the merger context, the Courts have also made statements tending to follow the *United Brands* approach. For example, in its judgment in *GE/Honeywell*, the Court of First Instance expressly acknowledged the principle from *Hoffman-La Roche* that price competition is generally incompatible with dominance, but held that "*even the existence of lively competition on a particular market does not rule out the possibility that there is a dominant position on that market. [T]he fact that there may be competition on the market is indeed among the relevant factors for the purposes of ascertaining whether a dominant position exists, but it is not itself a decisive factor.*"[152]

2.103 It will of course always be necessary to weigh apparently contradictory evidence, but it seems clear that in these judgments the Court was more concerned about the dominant firm's perceived ability to influence and control the competitive process than about market outcomes. Going forward, the Commission should be more receptive to evidence that the market under investigation is competitive. Such evidence could take several forms, including data demonstrating the existence of strong price competition[153] or showing market share gains by rivals or internal business planning documents reflecting competitive pressures faced by the "dominant" firm.[154]

---

[150] *Hoffmann-La Roche supra* note 3, para. 71.

[151] *Michelin I*, para. 59; *United Brands supra* note 2, paras 114–29.

[152] Case T-210/01 *General Electric v Commission* [2005] ECR II-5575.

[153] *See Hoffmann-La Roche supra* note 3, para. 78, in which the Court rejected the defendant's argument that observed price declines demonstrated the existence of strong competition in the market, concluding that the price declines were attributable to factors other than competition.

[154] *Ibid.*, paras 74–5, in which the Court cited internal Roche documents in concluding that falls in market prices were not attributable to the pressure of competition but to Roche's freely adopted pricing policy.

2. – Dominance
Christopher Cook and Ruchit Patel

2. The Death of "Super-Dominance"

Paragraph 1 of the *Guidance Paper* restates the long-standing principle from **2.104**
Michelin I that dominant firms have a "special responsibility" not to allow their
conduct to impair genuine undistorted competition on the common market.[155]
Article 102 TFEU prescribes no specific requirements as to what this special
responsibility requires; according to the Court of Justice in *Tetra Pak II*, the
scope of the special responsibility must be considered in light of the specific
circumstances of each case.[156] It follows that the special responsibility must not
consist of a single set of rules prescribed *ex ante* to which all dominant firms
are equally subject; rather, it must be possible for certain types of behaviour
to be abusive when carried out by some dominant firms but not when carried
out by other dominant firms. Some commentators have observed that the idea
that the obligations on dominant firms can become more onerous depending
on the special circumstances of the case implies the existence of a concept,
over and above that of dominance, for companies that have particularly strong
market power. This has often been referred to as "super-dominance."[157]

Neither the courts nor the Commission have employed the term "super- **2.105**
dominance" in an infringement decision. The term was first employed by
Advocate General Fennelly in his opinion in *Compagnie Maritime Belge*, where
he equates the term with "dominance verging on monopoly" and argues that
Article 102 TFEU imposes a "particularly onerous special obligation" on
firms in such a position not to impair the emergence of a new competitor:

> *"To my mind, Article [102 TFEU] cannot be interpreted as permitting monop-
> olists or quasi-monopolists to exploit the very significant market power which
> their superdominance confers so as to preclude the emergence either of a new or
> additional competitor. Where an undertaking ... enjoys a position of such over-
> whelming dominance verging on monopoly ... it would not be consonant with the
> particularly onerous special obligation affecting such a dominant undertaking not
> to impair further the structure of the feeble existing competition for [it] to react,
> even to aggressive price competition from a new entrant, with a policy of targeted,
> selective price cuts designed to eliminate that competitor."*[158]

---

[155] *See Michelin I*, para. 57.

[156] *Tetra Pak II Judgment 1996*, para. 24.

[157] *See, e.g., supra* note 7, p. 185.

[158] Joined Cases C-395 and 396/96 P, *supra* note 1, Opinion of AG Fennelly, para. 137.

2. – Dominance
Christopher Cook and Ruchit Patel

2.106 In its judgment, the Court of Justice cited *Tetra Pak II* in support of the principle that *"the actual scope of the special responsibility imposed on a dominant undertaking must be considered in the light of the specific circumstances of each case"*[159] and suggested that because the defendant had a market share of over 90 per cent and only one competitor, the pricing conduct in question could be found abusive without the need precisely to delineate the boundary between permissible and impermissible behaviour.[160] Neither in this judgment nor elsewhere, however, has the Court of Justice adopted the term "super-dominance" or expressly endorsed the concept that quasi-monopolists are subject to stricter duties under Article 102 TFEU. The concept of "super-dominance" has thus not clearly taken hold as part of Article 102 analysis.

2.107 However, the Commission has on several occasions argued that this principle exists, relying on the Court's statement from *Tetra Pak II* as authority. For example, in *Deutsche Post AG*, the Commission stated expressly that *"[t]he actual scope of the dominant firm's special responsibility must be considered in relation to the degree of dominance held by that firm and to the special characteristics of the market which may affect the competitive situation."*[161] Similarly, in *1998 Football World Cup*, the Commission again relied on *Tetra Pak II* as implying that *"[t]he scope of the parties' responsibility must therefore be considered in relation to the degree of dominance held by the parties and to any special characteristics of the market which might affect the competitive situation."*[162]

2.108 At the national level, in its *Napp Pharmaceutical* decision, the UK Competition Appeal Tribunal (CAT) expressly endorsed and adopted Advocate General Fennelly's proposed approach:

> *"We for our part accept and follow the opinion of Mr Advocate General Fennelly in Compagnie Maritime Belge ... that the special responsibility of a dominant undertaking is particularly onerous where it is a case of a quasi-monopolist enjoying 'dominance approaching monopoly', 'superdominance' or 'overwhelming dominance verging on monopoly.' In our view, Napp's high and persistent market*

---

[159] *Tetra Pak II Judgment 1996*, para. 24.

[160] Joined Cases C-395 and 396/96 P, *supra* note 1, para. 119 (*"It is sufficient to recall that the conduct at issue here is that of a conference having a share of over 90% of the market in question and only one competitor. The appellants have, moreover, never seriously disputed, and indeed admitted at the hearing, that the purpose of the conduct complained of was to eliminate G & C from the market."*).

[161] Case COMP/36.915 *Deutsche Post AG – Interception of cross-border mail* (*"Deutsche Post"*), Commission Decision of 25 July 2001, OJ 2001 L 331/40, para. 103.

[162] Case IV/36.888 *1998 Football World Cup*, Commission Decision of 20 July 1999, OJ 2000 L 5/55, para. 86.

2. – Dominance
Christopher Cook and Ruchit Patel

shares put Napp into the category of 'dominance approaching monopoly' – i.e. superdominance – and the issue of abuse in this case has to be addressed in that specific context."[163]

In this judgment, the CAT was applying Chapter II of the UK Competition **2.109** Act 1998, but this statute closely follows Article 102 TFEU and under EU law must be interpreted in a manner consistent with Article 102 TFEU. The judgment is thus not binding on the Commission or courts, but could still be regarded as persuasive precedent.

Whether or not the concept of super-dominance now plays an identifiable **2.110** role in Article 102 analysis, in economic terms, the concept is comprehensible: market power is not an either/or proposition, but a matter of degree,[164] so if dominance is equated with market power, then it follows that there are different degrees of dominance. Yet the legal implications of having a concept of super-dominance are not self-evident, and commentators have differed in their proposed approaches to the issue. Some observers regard the concept as a useful one and seek clarification as to exactly what "super-dominance" means. For example, Whish notes that the idea that super-dominant firms may be subject to particularly onerous special responsibilities is consistent with the requirement that owners of "essential facilities" must in certain circumstances provide access to them, since the market power associated with essential facilities is particularly strong, and suggests that "*a dominance/superdominance calibration may be a helpful one in understanding why certain types of behaviour, such as selective price cutting and refusal to supply, are treated more seriously in some cases than in others.*"[165]

Others find the concept of super-dominance more problematic. For example, **2.111** O'Donoghue & Padilla question the appropriateness of the basic intuition

---

[163] Case 1001/1/1/01 *Napp Pharmaceutical Holdings v DG Fair Trading*, UK Competition Commission Appeal Tribunal Decision of 15 January 2002, para. 219.

[164] Economists have traditionally measured market power by reference to the index devised by Abba Lerner in 1934 (*see* A. Lerner, "The Concept of Monopoly and the Measurement of Monopoly Power" (1934) 1(3) *Review of Economic Studies*, pp. 157–75). Among other things, the Lerner Index demonstrated that even for a pure monopolist, the more elastic the demand, the less monopoly power the firm possesses (*see* R. D. Blair, J. E. Lopatka and J. B. Herndon, "Evaluating Market Power" (1997) 27 *Journal of Reprints for Antitrust Law & Economics*, pp. 457–70).

[165] *See supra* note 7, pp. 185–6. *See also* D. Geradin, P. Hofer, F. Louis, N. Petit and M. Walker, "The Concept of Dominance" (2005), *Global Competition Law Centre*, p. 8 ("absent any clear statement by the Court and the Commission on the concept of super dominance, it would indeed be helpful if the Commission could clarify this issue").

2. – Dominance
Christopher Cook and Ruchit Patel

behind super-dominance, arguing that there is no reason why companies with especially high market shares should be subject to duties not applicable to other dominant companies. They also point out that there is no economic test for determining when a position of "super-dominance" short of monopoly exists and that, should such a concept nonetheless be introduced into law, the notions of abuse applicable to super-dominant companies under Article 102 TFEU would need to be redefined. The concept thus suffers from both theoretical and practical difficulties.[166] Faull & Nikpay similarly note that the idea of subjecting "super-dominant" firms to stricter rules under a "sliding scale" approach would have drawbacks in terms of legal certainty.[167]

2.112 It is submitted that the *Guidance Paper*'s move to an effects-based analysis resolves these issues, eliminating any need for a concept of super-dominance in Article 102 TFEU. Under an effects-based approach to exclusionary conduct there are no rules prescribed *ex ante* for dominant firms: the task is to assess whether the conduct in question is likely to lead to anticompetitive foreclosure. It is natural that as a dominant firm's position approaches monopoly, certain types of potentially exclusionary conduct become more likely to result in the foreclosure of competitors, so the *Guidance Paper*'s effects-based approach implicitly imposes stricter standards of conduct on firms with stronger market positions, without subjecting them to any different rules.

2.113 An example will illustrate. In the context of a retroactive conditional growth rebate,[168] as the market power of the dominant firm increases, customers' willingness and ability to shift a portion of their demand to competing suppliers very likely decreases. This means that in assessing the legality of any retroactive rebate they offer, more strongly dominant firms will have to apply the full value of the conditional rebate to a smaller "relevant range" of contestable demand. This implies in turn that the effective price of the relevant range will more quickly drop below the dominant firm's long-run average incremental cost, and thereby potentially run afoul of the *Guidance Paper*'s test. In crude terms, a five per cent retroactive growth rebate is much more likely to fail the *Guidance Paper*'s test and be found abusive if the dominant firm holds a 90 per cent market share than if it holds a 50 per cent market share.

---

[166] R. O'Donoghue and A. J. Padilla, *supra* note 37, pp. 167–68.

[167] J. Faull and A. Nikpay (Eds.), *The EC Law of Competition* (2nd Ed., Oxford, Oxford University Press, 2007), para. 4.104.

[168] *See Guidance Paper supra* note 1, paras 37–45.

2. – Dominance
Christopher Cook and Ruchit Patel

The *Guidance Paper* thus implicitly sets stricter standards of conduct for firms **2.114** as their market power increases, capturing the Court's pronouncements that duties imposed by the dominant firm's special responsibility depend on the particular circumstances of each case, and that firms whose position approaches monopoly are subject to particularly onerous duties under Article 102 TFEU. But this is a straightforward consequence of the *Guidance Paper's* approach to identifying abusive conduct; it does not require either (1) defining "super-dominance" and establishing a test for identifying such firms or (2) prescribing different rules for "super-dominant" firms. The *Guidance Paper* framework eliminates any need for the concept of super-dominance under Article 102 TFEU.

3. Role of the Dominance Finding in Article 102 Infringement Decisions

As explained in Section I above, four decades of case law have put in place **2.115** an analytical approach whereby establishing an infringement of Article 102 TFEU consists of two elements: (1) showing that the undertaking in question holds a dominant position in a properly defined market; and (2) showing that the conduct in question is abusive. The dominance finding is an essential element of any determination of infringement, and non-dominant firms are not subject to the restrictions imposed by Article 102 TFEU. The Commission's *Guidance Paper* gives no indication that it intends to adopt a different approach but, as explained below, the shift to a more economically grounded effects-based approach to Article 102 TFEU fundamentally diminishes the significance of the dominance finding in establishing an infringement.

The two-step analysis was developed as the courts and Commission were **2.116** applying what may be described as primarily a "form-based" (as opposed to "effects-based") approach to Article 102 TFEU. In broad terms, under a form-based approach, the assessment focuses on the form that the particular business practice in question takes (*e.g.*, exclusive supply arrangements, target rebates, predatory pricing, tying). In principle at least, Article 102 TFEU prescribes a set of rules (or a "black list" of prohibited types of conduct), established in advance, that the "special responsibility" of dominant firms requires them to obey – in effect, certain practices become *per se* illegal for dominant firms. The rationale underlying this approach is that such practices, when applied by dominant firms (but not non-dominant ones), are either

2. – Dominance
Christopher Cook and Ruchit Patel

intended or tend to bring about anticompetitive effects and should therefore be prohibited.[169]

2.117 The form-based approach may, at least in principle, bring benefits in terms of legal certainty since the rules are known in advance, and the basic approach is consistent with the language and structure of Article 102 TFEU. On the other hand, the approach has inherent shortcomings. First, it risks establishing rules that are too strict, penalising and deterring procompetitive behaviour (false positives).[170] Secondly, it may be too permissive, failing to identify all possible forms of anticompetitive conduct and inviting dominant companies to circumvent the policy objective by devising alternative exclusionary strategies that are not included on the "black list" (false negatives).

2.118 Under an idealised model of the form-based approach, the rules applying to dominant firms are established precisely in advance and it is the "special responsibility" of dominant firms to follow them. In practice, things have never been quite so simple. Articles 102(a)–(d) TFEU set forth only the outlines of such rules, and the specifics that have been developed through case law have by no means always been clear. In part for these reasons, perhaps the paradigm EU law example of a form-based approach to regulating unilateral conduct is found not in an infringement decision under Article 102 TFEU but in a commitment decision under Article 9 of Regulation 1/2003. The Commission's decision in *Coca-Cola*[171] is based on an undertaking that consists of highly detailed rules governing a range of commercial practices including exclusive supply arrangements, target rebates, tying, and mixed bundling. The undertaking's rules apply when the company's share in the relevant market (as defined in the undertaking) exceeds 40 per cent and is more than twice that of its largest rival. Thus, the undertaking provides an *ex ante* list of specific rules and prohibitions (analogous to "abuses") and an objective test for whether these rules, as a whole, apply or

---

[169] *See, e.g., Hoffmann-La Roche supra* note 3, para. 90 (exclusive purchasing obligations offered by dominant firms are illegal because they are "designed to deprive the purchaser of or restrict his possible choices of sources of supply and to deny other producers access to the market" and because they "tend to consolidate" the firm's dominant position through "distorted" means of competition).

[170] P. Rey and others, "An Economic Approach to Article 82", Report by the Economic Advisory Group on Competition Policy ("*EAGCP Report*"), July 2005. "[M]*any business practices may have different effects in different circumstances: distorting competition in some cases and promoting efficiencies and innovation in others. A competition policy approach that directly confronts this duality will ensure that consumers are protected (through the prevention of behaviour that harms them) while promoting overall increased productivity and growth (since firms will not be discouraged in their search for efficiency).*"

[171] Case COMP/39.116 *supra* note 115.

2. – Dominance
Christopher Cook and Ruchit Patel

not (analogous to the dominance test) – representing something close to an ideal form-based approach to Article 102 application.[172]

Case law under Article 102 TFEU does not so clearly reflect the form-based analytical paradigm, but the basic approach was established in the seminal Court of Justice judgments of the late 1970s. For example, in its assessment of the refusal to supply issue in *United Brands*, at the outset of the discussion, the Court of Justice announces as a premise that *"an undertaking in a dominant position ... cannot stop supplying a long standing customer who abides by regular commercial practice, if the orders placed by that customer are in no way out of the ordinary"*;[173] the Court then finds that United Brands violated this rule after dismissing its argument that the conduct at issue was justified.[174] Similarly, the assessment of exclusive supply agreements in *Hoffman-La Roche* begins with the Court of Justice's announcement of a clear prohibition on dominant firms applying exclusive purchasing obligations (and rebates of similar effect),[175] which are unlawful because they are *"not based on an economic transaction"* but *"designed to deprive the purchaser of or restrict his possible choices of sources of supply and to deny other producers access to the market."*[176] **2.119**

In each of these cases, the Court of Justice is clearly applying a rule that, if not amounting to a *per se* prohibition, at a minimum carries a <u>strong presumption of illegality</u>.[177] The Court's analyses of whether the conduct in question **2.120**

---

[172] In drawing this comparison, it is imperative to recall that Article 9 decisions are negotiated settlements: they do not involve a finding that the firm has violated Article 102 TFEU; they do not establish legal rules that apply directly to third parties; and there can be no legitimate presumption that the rules they contain define the boundary between lawful and unlawful conduct. *See* C. Cook, "Commitment Decisions: The Law and Practice Under Article 9" (2006) 29(2) *World Competition*, pp. 227–28.

[173] *United Brands supra* note 2, para. 182.

[174] The Court's discussion suggests that a justification based on showing that the conduct resulted in (or at least did not inhibit) competitive market outcomes would not have been accepted. The Court rejects United Brands' argument that a 40 per cent market price drop shows that the refusal to supply a distributor did not affect competition, on the puzzling ground that *"this fall in prices was only due to the very lively competition – called at the time 'The Banana War' in which* [United Brands and its main competitor] *engaged"* (para. 196).

[175] *Hoffmann-La Roche supra* note 3, para. 89: *"An undertaking which is in a dominant position on a market and ties purchasers – even if it does so at their request – by an obligation or promise on their part to obtain all or most of their requirements exclusively from the said undertaking abuses its dominant position within the meaning of Article [102], whether the obligation in question is stipulated without further qualification or whether it is undertaken in consideration of the grant of a rebate." See also Suiker Unie supra* note 79.

[176] *Hoffmann-La Roche supra* note 3, para. 90.

[177] The Courts have since relaxed the *quasi-per se* prohibitions set out in *United Brands* (*supra* note 2) and *Hoffmann-La Roche* (*supra* note 3), departing to some extent from the form-based approach in favour of an analysis that more seriously considers the conduct's harmful and beneficial effects. Regarding exclusive dealing, *see* Case T-65/98 *Van den Bergh Foods v Commission* ("*Van den Bergh Foods*") [2003] ECR II-4653. Regarding refusals to supply, *see* Joined Cases C-468 to 478/06 *Sot. Lélos kai Sia and others v GlaxoSmithKline* ("*GlaxoSmithKline*") [2008] ECR I-7139.

2. – Dominance
Christopher Cook and Ruchit Patel

is abusive primarily concern whether as a factual matter the conduct falls into the prohibited category.[178] These are for the most part inquiries into the conduct's form, not its effect; the Court of Justice generally pays little attention to the actual harmful or beneficial market effects of the specific conduct at issue, and normally considers effects (if at all) only at a general level insofar as they tend to follow from the type of conduct when practiced by a dominant firm. Thus, for example, the Court of Justice in *Hoffman-La Roche* explains its *quasi-per se* rule against exclusive supply agreements by reference to the effects this form of behaviour tends to have on market structure. Competitive harm in the individual case need not be established. *"These practices by an undertaking in a dominant position and especially on an expanding market tend to consolidate this position by means of a form of competition which is not based on the transactions effected and is therefore distorted."*[179]

2.121 In sum, under a form-based approach to Article 102, the abuse prong of the two-step analysis consists in verifying whether the firm has practiced a certain form of behaviour. This is a factual question. As a legal matter, the most important issue in individual cases becomes whether or not the firm is subject to that set of rules that defines the boundary between permissible and unlawful conduct. In other words, under a form-based approach the dominance finding, not the assessment of abuse, is the most important legal element in the "abuse of dominance" analysis.

2.122 The effects-based analysis embodied in the *Guidance Paper* turns this approach on its head. Under an effects-based approach, the concern is with the effects of the conduct in question in the marketplace. The specific nature of the conduct (*i.e.*, its form) is immaterial, since all practices having the same anticompetitive effect will be treated equally. Moreover, analytically, even the market position of the firm in question is not strictly relevant, since all conduct that has anticompetitive effect should be condemned. In other words, from the economic perspective, under an effects-based approach to Article 102 TFEU, there is no need to look separately at dominance. As the *EAGCP Report* explains: *"In terms of procedure, the economic [effects-based] approach implies that there is no need to establish a preliminary and separate assessment of dominance. Rather, the emphasis is on the establishment of a verifiable and consistent account of significant competitive harm."*[180]

---

[178] *See, e.g., Hoffmann-La Roche supra* note 3, paras 92–96, and *United Brands supra* note 2, paras 184–94.
[179] *Hoffmann-La Roche supra* note 3, para. 90.
[180] *EAGCP Report*, p. 4.

2. – Dominance
Christopher Cook and Ruchit Patel

As noted above, the *Guidance Paper* does not purport to modify or depart from **2.123** the established two-step "dominance and abuse" procedure for identifying infringements of Article 102 TFEU. Each Article 102 infringement decision will still include a separate finding that the firm in question is dominant. The logical consequence of the move to an effects-based approach, however, is that in future cases the Commission's primary focus will be on identifying competitive harm.

This new approach will not reduce to irrelevance the factors weighed in the **2.124** dominance analysis. First, information on market structure can provide a useful initial indication as to whether the hypothesis of anticompetitive effects (likely as embodied in a complaint) is plausible, and market shares might be used as a *de minimis* criterion to weed out clearly unproblematic cases. In fact, as explained in Section II above, the *Guidance Paper* proposes just such an approach, noting at the outset that market shares *"provide a useful first indication"* of the market structure and creating a "soft" safe harbour for firms with market shares below 40 per cent.[181] Secondly, the consideration of barriers to entry and expansion will remain central to the analysis of competitive effects. The *Guidance Paper* states that the aim of enforcement activity in the area of exclusionary conduct is to prevent dominant firms from engaging in "anticompetitive foreclosure," which is defined as *"a situation where effective access of actual or potential competitors to supplies or markets is hampered or eliminated as a result of the conduct of the dominant undertaking."*[182] The close link between the concepts of anticompetitive foreclosure and entry barriers is clear, so it is unsurprising when the *Guidance Paper* states that assessing the conditions of entry and expansion is central to determining whether anticompetitive foreclosure is likely.[183] In effect, this means that the most important *indicia* of dominance are integrated into the procedure for establishing competitive harm.

---

[181] *Guidance Paper supra* note 1, paras 13–14.
[182] *Ibid.*, para. 19.
[183] *Ibid.*, para. 20.

3. – The Concept of Abuse
Francisco Enrique González-Díaz and John Temple Lang

The Concept of Abuse

Francisco Enrique González-Díaz and John Temple Lang*

I.   Introduction

Article 102 TFEU prohibits "[a]*ny abuse by one or more undertakings of a dominant* **3.1** *position within the internal market or in a substantial part of it* […] *in so far as it may affect trade between Member States*". It does not provide, however, a general definition of "abuse" but merely a series of examples of potentially abusive conduct. Similarly, the Commission decisional practice and the case law of the EU Courts have provided relatively little guidance on the notion of abuse. Against this background, several legal and economic theories have been developed to provide a meaningful definition of abuse that allows to distinguish unlawful conduct from competition on the merits. None of these theories has, however, formally been endorsed by the Commission and/or the EU Courts at least so far. This chapter summarises the different approaches to the definition of abuse (and, in particular, of "exclusionary abuse") and, drawing upon the Commission decisional practice, the EU Courts' case law, and the ongoing debate in the legal and economic community, attempts to propose a legally and economically sound test to identify abusive conduct that the Commission and the EU Courts could rely upon in future cases.

II.   The Notion of Abuse in Article 102 TFEU

Article 102 TFEU, which was already included in the EEC Treaty in 1957,[1] **3.2** does not prohibit a company holding or attaining a dominant position, but

---

* The authors wish to thank Ben Holles and Pierantonio D'Elia for their valuable contribution to this chapter.

[1] A comprehensive reconstruction of the historical steps leading to the current formulation of Article 102 TFEU is provided by H. Schweitzer, "The History, Interpretation and Underlying Principles of Section 2 Sherman Act and Article 82 EC", in C.-D. Ehlermann and M. Marquis (Eds.), *A Reformed Approach to Article 82 EC* (Oxford, Hart Publishing, 2008), pp. 119–64.

3. – The Concept of Abuse
Francisco Enrique González-Díaz and John Temple Lang

only its *abuse*.[2] However, neither Article 102 TFEU nor any other provision of the TFEU contains any definition of what an abuse is. The only leads to the definition of "abuse" are to be found in the four examples set out in the Article 102 TFEU itself, namely:

- Article 102.2 (a): "*directly or indirectly imposing unfair purchase or selling prices or other unfair trading conditions*";
- Article 102.2 (b): "*limiting production, markets or technical development to the prejudice of consumers*";
- Article 102.2 (c): "*applying dissimilar conditions to equivalent transactions with other trading parties, thereby placing them at a competitive disadvantage*"; and
- Article 102.2 (d): "*making the conclusion of contracts subject to acceptance by the other parties of supplementary obligations which, by their nature or according to commercial usage, have no connection with the subject of such contracts.*"

3.3 Even though these examples of possible abusive conduct provide a useful starting point to develop a cogent definition of abuse, it is now clear that "*the list of abusive practices set out in the second paragraph of Article [102] of the Treaty is not exhaustive*".[3] The Commission and the EU Courts have indeed applied Article 102 TFEU to conduct not specifically falling within one of the categories of abusive conduct listed in Article 102 TFEU. However, when so doing, they have not identified the underlying principle and/or the rationale for the inclusion of the relevant conduct under the general notion of abuse. As a result, a widespread debate about the definition of abusive conduct has developed with the aim of providing some guiding principles as to what conduct should be considered as abusive within the meaning of Article 102 TFEU.

III. Classification of Abuses

3.4 When analysing Article 102 TFEU, the Commission's decisional practice and the case-law of the European Courts, two general categories of abuses have been identified: "exclusionary" abuses (*i.e.*, conduct which is aimed at or has the effect of foreclosing competitors, preventing them from entering

---

[2] Case 322/81 NV *Nederlandsche Banden Industrie Michelin v Commission* ("*Michelin I*"), [1983] ECR 3461, para. 57: "*A finding that an undertaking has a dominant position is not in itself a recrimination but simply means that, irrespective of the reasons for which it has such a dominant position, the undertaking concerned has a special responsibility not to allow its conduct to impair genuine undistorted competition on the Common Market*".

[3] Case C-333/94 P *Tetra Pak International v Commission* ("*Tetra Pak II Judgment 1996*") [1996] ECR I-5957, para. 37.

3. – The Concept of Abuse
Francisco Enrique González-Díaz and John Temple Lang

the market and/or from expanding) and "exploitative" abuses (*i.e.*, conduct which is aimed at taking advantage of the dominant company's market power to impose unduly onerous terms or conditions on customers or suppliers).[4] It is worth noting, however, that the two categories are not mutually exclusive. It is perfectly possible for a given type of conduct to fall into both categories.

This classification may be useful when analysing individual cases of potential **3.5** abuse, particularly when the allegations against the dominant company are vague or unspecified and the conduct does not fall into any of the well-established categories of potential abuses. The conduct of the dominant company may be unwelcome to other companies without constituting a breach of competition law, *e.g.*, a major advertising campaign or a promotional campaign. It may also be in breach of some other legal rule, or it may not be illegal at all. Distinguishing abusive conduct from competition on the merits is thus of crucial importance, since if legitimate competitive conduct is incorrectly treated as abusive, this will lead to an anticompetitive result, not only in the specific case in which the mistake is made, but in all other situations that will be regarded as similar, and for which the original case will be considered as a precedent.

1. Exploitative Abuses

Article 102 TFEU applies to "exploitative abuses" as it prohibits dominant **3.6** undertakings from imposing excessive prices and unfair trading conditions. In fact, exploitative abuses are probably the most obvious examples of conduct directly affecting customers and/or consumers. There have been, however, only a limited number of exploitative abuse cases at EU level.[5]

The EU Courts have held that it may be a violation of Article 102 TFEU for an **3.7** undertaking in a dominant position to charge a price which is excessive in relation to the economic value of the service provided or the good supplied,[6] but that the excessive nature of the price in question must be objectively determined.

---

[4] J. Temple Lang, "Abuse of Dominant Positions in European Community Law, Present and Future: Some Aspects", in B. E. Hawk (Ed.), *Fifth Annual Fordham Corporate Law Institute, Law & Business* (1979), pp. 25–83.

[5] For an exhaustive discussion of exploitative abuse cases, *see* chapter 9.

[6] Case 26/75 *General Motors v Commission* ("*General Motors*") [1975] ECR 1367 and Case 27/76 United Brands and *United Brands Continentaal v Commission* ("*United Brands*") [1978] ECR 207. The Court indicated in the latter case that "*it is for the Commission to prove that the applicants charged unfair prices*". The Commission normally passes the burden of prima facie proof on to the complainant. *See also* M. Siragusa, "The Application of Article 86 to the Pricing Policy of Dominant Companies: Discriminatory and Unfair Prices" (1976) 16 *Common Market Law Review*, pp. 179–94.

3. – The Concept of Abuse
Francisco Enrique González-Díaz and John Temple Lang

3.8 The EU judicature has not provided, so far, a comprehensive definition of exploitative abuse which is not limited to "unfair" prices, but that also encompasses unduly onerous contractual terms. Yet, in *United Brands*, the Court of Justice seemed to suggest that a conduct is exploitative where *"the dominant undertaking has made use of the opportunities arising out of its dominant position in such a way as to reap trading benefits which it would not have reaped if there had been normal and sufficiently effective competition".*[7]

3.9 Articulating a comprehensive definition of exploitation faces several obstacles. For example, one of the forms of exploitation that have been considered abusive, *i.e.* geographical price discrimination and related behaviour, has been more linked to the "single market imperative" than to economic analysis of the conditions under which such type of behaviour is likely to lead to consumer welfare harm. Accordingly, in *United Brands* it was held that *"these discriminatory prices, which varied according to the circumstances of the Member States, were just so many obstacles to the free movement of goods…".*[8] Similarly, the Commission has defined exploitative abuses as, *e.g.*, *"charging excessively high prices or certain behaviour that undermines the efforts to achieve an integrated internal market".*[9]

3.10 Secondly, the subject matter of this form of abuse contributes to the absence of a comprehensive definition. Exploitative abuses require a case-by-case judgment upon the undertaking's commercial policy, prices, and output, which may not lend itself to abstract definition. In fact, it has been submitted that the very assessment of exploitation might be inappropriate for the courts and competition agencies as it comes very close to regulatory supervision.[10] Section 2 of the Sherman Act does not sanction exploitative abuses.[11]

3.11 Thirdly, exploitative behaviour frequently seems *prima facie* economically rational. "Excessive" prices may be argued to be a legitimate and desired outcome of market success and in fact provide the incentives for entry and competitive

---

[7] *See United Brands supra* note 6, para. 250.

[8] *Ibid.*, para. 232.

[9] Guidance on the Commission's enforcement priorities in applying Article 82 of the EC Treaty to abusive exclusionary conduct by dominant undertakings ("*Guidance Paper*"), OJ 2009 C 45/7, para. 7.

[10] *See supra* note 1, p. 143.

[11] *Ibid.*, p. 144.

3. – The Concept of Abuse
Francisco Enrique González-Díaz and John Temple Lang

innovation. An analogous rationale applies to price discrimination, which also may enhance consumer welfare.[12]

In any event, both the *Discussion Paper* and the *Guidance Paper* appear to con- **3.12** firm that exploitative abuses do not constitute an enforcement priority for the Commission, which will focus its efforts on exclusionary abuses.[13]

2. Exclusionary Abuses

2.1. *Uncertainty Surrounding its Definition and Alternative Tests*

As Article 102 TFEU appears to expressly address only exploitative abuses, **3.13** early commentators[14] were split on the issue whether Article 102 TFEU also embodied a prohibition of "exclusionary" behaviour, namely conduct which excludes competitors. The decisional practice of the Commission and the case law of the EU Courts confirmed that Article 102 TFEU also prohibits "exclusionary" abuse as it "*is not only aimed at practices which may cause damages to consumers directly, but also at those which are detrimental to them through their impact on an effective competition structure*".[15]

With regards to the definition of such practices, in *Hoffmann-La Roche* the **3.14** Court held that an abuse is:

> "*an objective concept relating to the behaviour of an undertaking in a dominant position which is such as to influence the structure of the market where, as a result of the very presence of the undertaking in question, the degree of competition is weakened and which, through recourse to methods of competition different from those which condition normal competition in products or services on the basis of the transactions*

---

[12] W.J. Kolasky, "What is competition? A comparison of U.S. and European perspectives" (2004) *The Antitrust Bulletin*, p. 2953. *See also* D. Geradin and N. Petit "Price Discrimination under EC Competition Law: The Need for a Case-by-Case Approach" Global Competition Law Centre Working Paper Series, *GCLC Working Paper Series*, Working Paper 07/05, 2007, p. 2 stating that "[I]*t is hard to say* a priori *whether a given form of price discrimination increases or decreases welfare*".

[13] DG Competition Discussion paper on the application of Article 82 of the treaty to exclusionary abuses ("*Discussion Paper*") December 2005, para. 3; *See also Guidance Paper supra* note 9, para. 7.

[14] R. Joliet, *Monopolization and Abuse of Dominant Position: A Comparative Study of American and European Approaches to the Control of Economic Power* (Liège, Faculté de Droit, 1970); *See also* M. Siragusa, *Application of Art. 86: Tying Arrangements, Refusal to Deal, Discrimination and Other Cases of Abuse* (Bruges, 1974).

[15] Case 6/72 *Europemballage Corporation and Continental Can v Commission* ("*Continental Can*") [1975] ECR 215, para. 26.

3. – The Concept of Abuse
Francisco Enrique González-Díaz and John Temple Lang

> *of commercial operators, has the effect of hindering the maintenance of the degree of competition still existing in the market or the growth of that competition."* [16]

3.15   As is apparent from its wording, this designation is only applicable to exclusionary abuses, and not to exploitative abuses or to discrimination. In addition:

- The notion of abuse is an <u>objective concept</u>, meaning that intention or negligence are, in principle, irrelevant.

- The Court refers to "the structure of the market" without defining it. In some cases, such as the earlier case of *Commercial Solvents*,[17] in which a refusal to supply an input was considered likely to force the only competitor of a vertically integrated company out of the market, it was relatively easy to ascertain what the Court meant. In a case in which the abuse in question consisted of giving rebates on condition that the buyer buys all or a large proportion of its total requirements from the dominant company, this reference is less self-explanatory and does not provide a clear-cut guiding principle to distinguish competition on the merits from exclusionary behaviour.

- The reference to "*methods of competition different from those which condition normal competition in products or services*"[18] is not explained and does not provide a clear guiding principle to distinguish competition on the merits from exclusionary behaviour. It is not difficult to identify kinds of conduct which are obviously "normal", such as offering lower prices or better quality. It is also certainly possible to imagine extreme cases of kinds of conduct that are not "normal." However, the "normal methods of competition test" leaves a very large range of commercial practices undefined. Insofar as "normal competition" means competition in price, quality, or services to the customer, the position is relatively clear. It is much more difficult to apply this test to, *e.g.*, low prices that benefit the consumer but may harm inefficient competitors, or obtaining patents that strengthen the position of the dominant company in its competition with actual or potential rivals. This is understandable, as this definition was written in 1979, at a time when there had been very few judgments of the Court of Justice, and little of the extensive economic

---

[16] Case 85/76 *Hoffmann-La Roche v Commission* ("*Hoffmann-La Roche*") [1979] ECR 461, para. 91.

[17] *See* Joined Cases 6 and 7/73 *Istituto Chemioterapico Italiano and Commercial Solvents Corporation v Commission* ("*Commercial Solvents*") [1974] ECR 223.

[18] *Hoffmann-La Roche supra* note 16, para. 91.

3. – The Concept of Abuse
Francisco Enrique González-Díaz and John Temple Lang

literature on exclusionary abuse (or the near-equivalent under Section 2 of the US Sherman Act) which has emerged since.

- The conduct must have the effect of *hindering* existing competition or hindering the growth of that competition. Although this part of the test appears to be more precise it does not provide guidance as to how material this "hindering" effect should be or whether it should be directly related to a real harm to consumer welfare.

3.16 This definition of exclusionary abuse has been repeated frequently by the Commission and the EU Courts since it was first stated in 1979. However, it fails to provide an operational test to assess whether a conduct should be considered an exclusionary abuse falling under Article 102 TFEU. For years the Commission concentrated on what are now Article 101 TFEU cases (in light of the notification system previously in place under Regulation 17/62) and on trying to promote the approval of a regulation on the control of concentrations, which was ultimately adopted in 1989. The Commission did bring several cases under Article 102 TFEU against copyright collection societies, but primarily for unduly onerous terms and for discrimination on grounds of nationality.[19]

3.17 Apart from those cases, the Commission did not proactively open *ex officio* Article 102 cases, but rather responded to complaints, mostly from competitors, without setting any specific priorities or long term strategy or policy.

3.18 As a result, the case law developed slowly. *United Brands* (1978),[20] *Hoffmann-La Roche* (1979),[21] and the first *Michelin* judgment (1983)[22] remained the most important points of reference. Some of the key Article 102 issues of interpretation arose before national courts and were referred to the Court of Justice under what is now Article 267 TFEU. In practice, most abuse cases involved exclusionary abuses. In 1991, the European Courts decided the first *AKZO* case,[23] on predatory pricing. *Tetra Pak II* was decided in 1996[24] and

---

[19] Case 395/87 *Ministère Public v Tournier* ("*Tournier*") [1989] ECR 2521 and Joined Cases 110, 241 and 242/88 *François Lucazeau and others v Société des Auteurs, Compositeurs et Editeurs de Musique and others* ("*SACEM II*") [1989] ECR 2811.

[20] *See United Brands supra* note 6.

[21] *See Hoffmann-La Roche supra* note 16.

[22] *See Michelin I supra* note 2.

[23] Case C-62/86 *AKZO Chemie v Commission* ("*AKZO*") [1991] ECR I-3359.

[24] *See Tetra Pak II Judgment 1996 supra* note 3, para. 37, confirmed that the list of abuses in Article 102 TFEU is not exhaustive.

3. – The Concept of Abuse
Francisco Enrique González-Díaz and John Temple Lang

Microsoft in 2007[25.] More recently, the Court of Justice has confirmed that a margin squeeze is a category of abuse separate from unfairly high or unfairly low prices.[26]

3.19 Against the background of uncertainty surrounding the notion of "abuse", many commentators criticised the development of the law under Article 102 TFEU for being too "formalistic" and focusing excessively on the "nature" of the conduct of the dominant company.[27] An "effects-based" approach was therefore advocated, focusing more on anticompetitive effects that harm consumers, and closely examining the merits of each specific case.

3.20 Identifying an underlying criterion distinguishing legitimate from exclusionary market conduct by a dominant company is of paramount importance since erroneously considering a conduct as exclusionary can *"chill the very conduct the antitrust laws are designed to protect"*.[28] Thus, the *"challenge [...] lies in stating a general rule for distinguishing between exclusionary acts, which reduce social welfare, from competitive acts, which increase it"*.[29] The following section will review and discuss a number of tests developed primarily in the US to guide the enforcement of Section 2 of the Sherman Act.[30]

---

[25] *See also* Case T-201/04 *Microsoft v Commission ("Microsoft Judgment 2007")* [2007] ECR II-3601, para. 861.

[26] Case C-280/08 P *Deutsche Telekom v Commission ("Deutsche Telekom Judgment 2010")* [2010] ECR I-9555 and Case C-52/09 *Konkurrensverket v TeliaSonera Sverige ("TeliaSonera Judgment 2011")*, not yet reported.

[27] J. Vickers, "Abuse of Market Power" (2005) 115 (6) *The Economic Journal*, pp. 244–61; *See also* D. Ridyard, "Exclusionary Pricing and Price Discrimination Abuses under Article 82 – An Economic Analysis" (2002) 23(6) *European Competition Law Review*, pp. 286–303.

[28] *Verizon Communications v Law Office of Curtis v Trinko ("Trinko")* 540 US 398 (2004), p. 414.

[29] *United States v Microsoft*, 253 F.3d 34, 58 (D.C. Cir. 2001) (*en banc*) (*per curiam*).

[30] L. Borlini, "Methodological issues of the *'more economic approach'* to unilateral exclusionary conduct. Proposal of analysis starting from the treatment of retroactive rebates" (2009) 5 *European Competition Journal*, pp. 409–50, which discusses the EAGCP paper (at pp. 417–20). Borlini defines a *"more economic approach"* as *"a method orientated towards a careful assessment of how competition works in a specific market and how a certain business conduct of the dominant firm may affect the competitive process and thereby consumer welfare"* (p. 440). *See also* E. Elhauge, "Defining better monopolization standards" (2003) 56(2) *Stanford Law Review*, pp. 253–344 who strongly criticises the sacrifice tests suggested. The present analysis concerns only the principal and more economic-oriented tests to assess unilateral conducts. Yet, other tests had been developed such as, for instance, the "specific intent" test, *see* A. E. Kahn, "Standards for Antitrust Policy" (1953) 67(1) *Harvard Law Review*, pp. 28–54; R. A. Cass and K. N. Hylton, "Antitrust Intent" (2001) 74(3) *Southern California Law Review*, pp. 657–745. The authors propose the use of intent in order to minimise the total costs arising from legal errors. Similarly, it has been argued that no single test satisfactorily meets error costs. Thus, different tests should apply to different unilateral behaviours, in order to minimise such error costs. *See* K. H. Hylton "The Law and Economics of Monopolization Standards" in K. H. Hylton (Eds.) *Antitrust Law And Economics* (Cheltenham, Edward Elgar Publishing, 2009), pp. 82–115.

3. – The Concept of Abuse
Francisco Enrique González-Díaz and John Temple Lang

2.2. *Economic Tests of Foreclosure*

2.2.1. Impairment of Opportunities of Rivals, with Consumer Harm

This test proposes that unilateral exclusionary conduct should be illegal if **3.21**
it were reasonably capable of creating, enlarging or prolonging monopoly
power by impairing the opportunities of rivals, and either it does not benefit
consumers, or it is unnecessary for the benefits provided to consumers, or it
causes harm that is disproportionate to the benefits.[31]

This *impairment test* is very similar to the "limiting rivals' possibilities" test under **3.22**
Article 102(b) TFEU. It is a comprehensive and all-encompassing test covering
all kinds of exclusionary conduct.

This test has several advantages: **3.23**

- It provides a test for cases of conduct restricting innovation because
  it prohibits conduct preventing competitors from becoming more
  efficient. Given the importance of innovation, it is an essential advantage of any suggested test that it deal with restrictions on innovation
  as well as with restrictions on price or output. The impairment test
  and the limiting rivals' possibilities test seem to deal satisfactorily with
  dynamic markets or conduct interfering with innovation. Likewise,
  the test is especially appropriate in markets characterised by network
  effects, in scenarios where the dominant company impairs rivals'
  opportunities to gain access to the necessary base of customers.[32]

- It does not prevent the dominant company from taking full advantage
  of any lawfully acquired economies of scale or scope, or make the dominant company into *"a trustee for the scale economies of its rivals"*.[33]

---

[31] P. Areeda and H. Hovenkamp, *Antitrust Law* (2nd Ed., Vol. 3, New York, Aspen Publishers, 2002), p. 651.
The earlier definition excluded "competition on the merits". *See also* J. F. Brodley, "The Economic Goals of
Antitrust: Efficiency, Consumer Welfare and Technological Progress" (1987) 62 *New York University Law Review*,
p. 1020, and H. Hovenkamp, "Signposts of Anticompetitive Exclusion: Restraints on Innovation and Economies
of Scale", in B. E. Hawk (Ed.), *Fordham Competition Law Institute: International Antitrust Law and Policy 2006* (New
York, Juris Publishing, 2007), pp. 412–13. *See also* M. Lao, "Defining Exclusionary Conduct under Section 2:
The Case for Non-Universal Standards", in B. E. Hawk (Ed.), *Fordham Competition Law Institute: International
Antitrust Law and Policy 2006* (New York, Juris Publishing, 2007), pp. 434 and 437–9.
[32] *See* E. Elhauge *supra* note 30, p. 322.
[33] *See* H. Hovenkamp *supra* note 31, p. 425. Compare with the Commission's *Discussion Paper*, which would require
the dominant company to adjust its price to allow a new entrant to obtain a "required share" of the market
(*supra* note 13).

3. – The Concept of Abuse
Francisco Enrique González-Díaz and John Temple Lang

- It appears to provide a test for protection of the <u>competitive process</u>, which is presumed in the long term to <u>promote efficiency</u> and <u>consumer welfare</u>, without introducing a criterion that would lead to protection of competitors. The competitive process, on this view, is competition without handicaps, obstacles or difficulties caused by the conduct of dominant companies.

- It has a simple rationale: if the monopolist impairs rival efficiency (*e.g.,* by unduly depriving them of economies of scale or scope), rivals will be obliged to raise the prices imposed on consumers. This would lead to a twofold harm: first, it would worsen the options available in the market; secondly it would lower the competitive pressure exercised on the monopolist.[34]

- Thus, it is the more "European" of the US monopolisation tests, as it combines the focus on competitors with the need to prevent consumer harm. However, there is no presumption that hindering competitors leads to the reduction of long-term welfare,[35] as consumer harm must be established.

3.24 This test is, however, more difficult to administer if the alleged abusive conduct is price-based. In these instances, tests that are more cost-oriented, such as the "no economic sense" or the "profit sacrifice" test, may be more appropriate. Moreover, the application of the test requires a twofold assessment: first the conduct must impair rivals' opportunities; secondly, it must not provide any benefit to consumers, be unnecessary, or cause a disproportionate harm. Thus, the test requires assessing the exclusionary effect and the actual or potential consumer harm.

3.25 A variant of the test assesses whether the conduct impairs rival efficiency by increasing the monopolist's power, regardless of whether it enhances its efficiency (or entails a sacrifice).[36] On the one hand, this variant has the advantage of not assessing the intention of the undertaking (*i.e.,* whether the company sought to take advantage of its own efficiency or whether it rather wanted to impair rivals). On the other hand, it depends on whether the increase of

---

[34] *See* E. Elhauge *supra* note 30, p. 321.

[35] On the link between protection of rivalry and long-term welfare *see* C. Ahlborn and A.J. Padilla, "From Fairness to Welfare: Implications for the Assessment of Unilateral Conduct under EC Competition Law", in C.-D. Ehlermann and M. Marquis (Eds.), *A Reformed Approach to Article 82 EC* (Oxford, Hart Publishing, 2008), pp. 55–101.

[36] *See* E. Elhauge *supra* note 30, p. 323.

3. – The Concept of Abuse
Francisco Enrique González-Díaz and John Temple Lang

the aggregated social welfare due to the enhanced efficiency of the dominant company counterbalances the loss arising from the exclusion of competitors.[37] Conduct which has an overall positive effect on total welfare can be prohibited because it impairs one or more specific competitors. In this scenario, the variant tends to protect competitors more than competition and consumer welfare.

2.2.2. Equally Efficient Competitor

Under this test, unilateral exclusionary conduct is illegal only if it is likely, in the circumstances, to exclude from the market a competitor that is as efficient as the dominant company.[38] This test is recommended by the Commission in the *Guidance Paper*.[39]   **3.26**

This test was devised for predatory pricing cases, and has more recently applied in margin squeeze cases.[40] The test does not ask whether the conduct has a legitimate purpose.   **3.27**

According to Judge Richard A. Posner: **3.28**

> "*in every case in which* [exclusionary conduct] *is alleged, the plaintiff must prove first that the defendant has monopoly power and second that the challenged practice is likely in the circumstances to exclude from the defendant's market an equally or more efficient competitor. The defendant can rebut by proving that although it is a monopolist and the challenged practice is exclusionary, the practice is, on balance, efficient.*" [41]

The main advantage of this test is that it avoids most false positives. Thus, if conduct meets this test, it should normally be regarded as illegal. However, if this were the only test used, some exclusionary conduct would be permitted. Indeed, so the argument runs, in some cases, even the exclusion of a less efficient competitor may sometimes be detrimental to consumer welfare, for   **3.29**

---

[37] Practices such as (selective) above costs price cuts represent a scenario where this problem may arise.

[38] R. Posner, *Antitrust Law* (2nd Ed., Chicago, University of Chicago Press, 2001), pp. 194–95; *See also* J. Vickers *supra* note 27, pp. 256–58.

[39] *See Guidance Paper supra* note 9.

[40] *See* Chapters 4 and 5 for a detailed discussion.

[41] *See* R. Posner, *supra* note 38.

3. – The Concept of Abuse
Francisco Enrique González-Díaz and John Temple Lang

instance, if the less efficient undertaking triggers price competition.[42] In other words, one of the main limits of the "equally efficient" test is the absence of any direct link with consumer welfare, as it assumes that (only) the foreclosure of an "equally efficient" competitor harms consumers. This test may, for instance, condemn as illegal conduct that has no detrimental effect on consumer welfare as, depending on how the test is performed, it may prohibit behaviour that would not harm competitors and hence consumers, if, for instance, competitors are actually more efficient than the dominant firm.

3.30   This test has several weaknesses, and gives rise to several questions:

- The test has little or no relevance or usefulness in cases of conduct restricting innovation.

- Except perhaps in predatory price and margin squeeze cases, it is too difficult for a competition authority to compare the efficiency of different companies and more so for the dominant firm. Even if the efficiency benchmark were to be based on the costs of the dominant firm,[43] the test would fail to identify conduct that, while "exclusionary", based on these costs would not actually exclude more efficient competitors and/ or competitors involved in bundling against bundle competition.

- The test does not take account of the fact that the entry of a less efficient competitor may stimulate competition if its lack of efficiency is short-lived and due only to the need to achieve economies of scale.[44] A less efficient competitor may also enhance consumer welfare in the short term, provided that it is perceived as a potential entrant. Facing the threat of its potential entry, a rational monopolist may lower its monopolist price in order to deter entry. In particular, the monopolist may set its price at a level equal or slightly below the variable costs of the inefficient competitor. This behaviour would lead to a reduction in price and an increase of output, and thus increase consumer welfare.[45] Despite this possible deficiency, it seems difficult to devise an operational test to determine when a less efficient competitor should be protected from competition because in the long term it is thought

---

[42] K. Fjell and L. Søgard, "How to test for abuse of dominance" (2006) 2 (Special issue) *European Competition Journal*, pp. 69–83.

[43] *See Deutsche Telekom Judgment 2010 supra* note 26, paras 202–3.

[44] *See* M. Lao *supra* note 31, p. 446.

[45] S. C. Salop, "Exclusionary conduct, effect on consumers, and the flawed profit-sacrifice standard" (2006) 73(2) *Antitrust Law Journal*, p. 328.

3. – The Concept of Abuse
Francisco Enrique González-Díaz and John Temple Lang

that it may have a welfare-enhancing effect. Indeed, a dominant company may have economies of scale or scope that are not available to its rivals,[46] which are as a result less efficient. In this type of case it would not be appropriate to prevent dominant companies from passing on to consumers all the benefits of their economies of scale or scope.

- In many cases, efficiencies such as network effects or economies of scale can be obtained only by denying them *pro tanto* to competitors.

- This test may not be applied to many kinds of potentially exclusionary abuses involving non-price or non-market conduct which might be exclusionary irrespective of the rival's efficiency, such as false declarations to regulatory authorities, concealment of essential patents from standards bodies, or refusal to licence standard essential patents. It would also not easily be applied to, *e.g.*, acquisition by a dominant company of the only alternative technology.[47]

2.2.3. Profit Sacrifice and no Economic Sense

Under the "profit sacrifice" test, the unilateral conduct is illegal if an undertaking deliberately "sacrifices" profits to foreclose its competitors. **3.31**

This test arose from, and is certainly useful in, predatory pricing cases, and has **3.32** been considered to be the "*most direct effort to extend the predatory pricing approach to all exclusionary conduct*".[48] However, despite having a significant number of supporters,[49] the "profit sacrifice" test has been met with substantial criticism:

- Whether short-term profits are sacrificed has no necessary connection with whether the conduct is anticompetitive or undesirable. Failing to maximise profits is not the same as selling at a loss. In the short term, consumers may benefit directly if profits are sacrificed,

---

[46] *See, however Discussion Paper supra* note 13, para. 67 : "*Fourthly, it may sometimes be necessary in the consumers' interest to also protect competitors that are not (yet) as efficient as the dominant company. Here too the assessment does not (only) compare cost and price of the dominant company but will apply the as efficient competitor test in its specific market context, for instance taking account of economies of scale and scope, learning curve effect or first mover advantages that later entrants cannot be expected to match even if they were able to achieve the same production volumes as the dominant company*".

[47] Case T-51/89 *Tetra Pak Rausing v Commission* ("*Tetra Pak I Judgment 1990*") [1990] ECR II-309.

[48] A. Gavil, "Exclusionary Distribution Strategies by Dominant Firms: Striking a Better Balance" (2004) 72(1) *Antitrust Law Journal*, pp. 3–82.

[49] M. Patterson, "The Sacrifice of Profits in Non-Price Predation" *Antitrust* (2003) 18, p. 37.

3. – The Concept of Abuse
Francisco Enrique González-Díaz and John Temple Lang

for example, if the dominant firm decides to launch a promotion or to invest in the creation of a new market.

- These tests do not appear to deal with conduct that has <u>both</u> anti-competitive effects and other benefits to the dominant company, and which would thus require some kind of balancing test.[50]

- Many kinds of exclusionary conduct involve no sacrifice because they cost nothing. Providing false information, or providing no information, to a governmental body or a standard setting organisation or to the market may not cost more than providing accurate information. Raising rivals' costs may not involve any profit sacrifice and some procompetitive conduct may involve a profit sacrifice – all price reductions do.

- The test may also be of little use in cases of conduct restricting innovation, or other conduct increasing the dominant company's market power. Profit sacrificed in one year to buy an asset or develop a patent that may drive rivals out of the market later is "profit sacrifice" in the short term, but is procompetitive in itself: if there are anticompetitive consequences, they are due to denying possibilities to rivals, and not to the profits sacrificed. The "profit sacrifice" test may prohibit some conduct that promotes efficiency, such as procompetitive price reductions to launch a new product or enter a new market.

- The test appears to be based on the intention and incentives of the dominant company and not on the effects of the conduct.[51]

- The "profit sacrifice" test may be difficult to apply in a meaningful way: the "sacrifice" would have to be assessed in comparison to a proper benchmark of "profit", which may involve a complicated economic determination. It may be impossible to measure what profits would have been made if there had been no suspect conduct. A rule that made profit maximising legally obligatory, either in the short term or in the longer term, would be unworkable.

- In the European context the "profit sacrifice" test may not be applicable because it appears to be premised on the assumption that dominant firms may charge monopoly prices.

---

[50] This is particularly the case where there is not a single and well-defined "but for" scenario, *see* G. J. Werden, "Competition Policy on Exclusionary Conduct: Towards an Effect-Based Analysis?" (2006) 2 (Special issue) *European Competition Journal* 53–67.

[51] *See* G. J. Werden *supra* note 50; R. C. Romaine and S. C. Salop, "Preserving Monopoly: Economic Analysis, Legal Standards and Microsoft" (1999) 7 *George Mason Law Review*, pp. 617–671. *Contra*, A. E. Kahn *supra* note 30. *See also* R. A. Cass and K. N. Hylton *supra* note 30.

3. – The Concept of Abuse
Francisco Enrique González-Díaz and John Temple Lang

- The "profit sacrifice" test may leave the door open to several inter-pretations, for instance, on whether recoupment of the loss is a *conditio sine qua non*.[52]

Under the related "no economic sense" test, unilateral conduct would be illegal only if it would "make no economic sense" for the dominant company except for its tendency to eliminate or lessen competition.[53] Thus, the "no economic sense" is a variant of the "profit sacrifice" test developed to address the latter's perceived flaws.[54] First, the "no economic sense" test is more inclusive: it is not limited to the existence of a sacrifice of profits,[55] but it addresses other economically irrational behaviour. Secondly, it responds to the consideration that *"profit sacrifice is neither necessary nor sufficient"*[56] for a conduct to be exclusionary. In a short-term scenario, it allows the identification of conduct that is exclusionary, although it does not entail a sacrifice: for instance, if there is no temporal gap between the sacrifice and the recoupment (*i.e.,* the recoupment is immediate). In a long-term scenario, the "no economic sense" allows assessing whether the sacrifice of short-term profits is reasonable in light of the long-term profits the investment will bring.[57]   **3.33**

However, the "no economic sense" or "no rational explanation" test risks   **3.34** being circular, because it postulates that a conduct is illegal if the only explanation for it is that it is intended to foreclose, and this necessitates a definition of foreclosure, which is what the test needs to define. This is important, because a rival can be "foreclosed", in the sense of being excluded from the market, if the dominant company legitimately offers better bargains. The suggested test does not appear to deal with the situation in which the dominant

---

[52] C. S. Hemphill, "The Role of recoupment in Predatory Pricing Analysis" (2001) 53 *Stanford Law Review*, pp. 1581–1612.

[53] *See* G. J. Werden, "The '*No Economic Sense*' test for Exclusionary Conduct" (2006) 31 *Journal of Corporation Law*, pp. 293–306; A. D. Melamed, "Exclusive Dealing Agreements and other Exclusionary Conduct – Are there Unifying Principles" (2006) 73(2) *Antitrust Law Journal*, pp. 375–412; A. D. Melamed, "Exclusionary Conduct Under the Antitrust Laws: Balancing, Sacrifice, and Refusals to Deal" (2005) 20 *Berkeley Technology Law Journal*, pp. 1247–67; *see* M. Lao *supra* note 31, pp. 433–68, 440–46 and G. J. Werden, "Identifying Single Firm Exclusionary Conduct: From Vague Concepts to Administrable Rules" (2007) *International Antitrust Law & Policy: Fordham Competition Law 2006*, pp. 509–40; *See also* J. Vickers *supra* note 27, pp. F253–F258, who affirms that the sacrifice test *"does not naturally yield a substantive standard of what behaviour is exclusionary"*. He concludes that *"the sacrifice test seems incapable of providing, by itself, a sufficient condition for a finding of unlawfully exclusionary behaviour"*, and that *"sacrifice is by no means necessary for abuse"*; *See* S. C. Salop *supra* note 45, p. 311.

[54] R. O'Donoghue and A. J. Padilla, *The Law and Economics of Article 82 EC* (Oxford, Hart Publishing, 2006), p. 191.

[55] A. Jones and B. Sufrin, *EC Competition Law* (3rd Ed., Oxford, Oxford University Press, 2008), p. 329.

[56] *See* G.J. Werden *supra* note 53.

[57] *Ibid.*

3. – The Concept of Abuse
Francisco Enrique González-Díaz and John Temple Lang

company knowingly sells at a price that is barely above its marginal cost ("limit pricing").

3.35   Both these tests also raise problems of timing, in terms of establishing when the dominant company will ultimately get its lost profit back for reasons other than having foreclosed competitors.

3.36   It has thus been concluded that all efforts to modify or re-state these two tests necessarily require distinguishing between desirable ways of making profits (which may legitimately exclude rivals) and undesirable ways of making profits (which exclude rivals in undesirable ways)[58] and that they could be "*a good rule of inclusion, but not necessarily a good rule of exclusion*".[59]

2.2.4.   Raising Rivals' Costs

3.37   Under the "raising rivals' costs" test, unilateral conduct is illegal if the dominant undertaking raises competitors' costs with the effect of reducing their output or raising their prices, therefore allowing the dominant undertaking to charge supra competitive prices to consumers.[60] For example, monopolising the most efficient methods of production or distribution may raise rivals' costs.[61] Rivals' costs may also be raised directly by, *e.g.*, charging them high prices for a necessary input, or indirectly by discriminating in favour of buyers who do not buy from rivals. This test also deals with conduct restricting innovation, if it affects rivals' costs.

3.38   Compared to other tests, the "raising rivals' costs" test has two main advantages:[62]

- First, a finding of abuse does not require the comparison between the costs of the dominant undertaking and the costs of its competitors.

- Secondly, and unlike the "equally efficient" and the "profit sacrifice" tests, the "raising rivals' costs" test encompasses many types of non-price or

---

[58] *See* E. Elhauge *supra* note 30, p. 293.

[59] *See* A. Gavil *supra* note 48.

[60] *See* S. C. Salop *supra* note 45, p. 315.

[61] S. C. Salop, "The Controversy over the Proper Antitrust Standard for Anticompetitive Exclusionary Conduct", in B. E. Hawk (Ed.), *Fordham Competition Law Institute: International Antitrust Law and Policy 2006* (New York, Juris Publishing, 2007), pp. 479–480. *See also Tetra Pak I Judgment 1990 supra* note 47.

[62] *See* A. Jones and B. Sufrin *supra* note 55, p. 585 and the reference made therein to R. Rapp, "Predatory Pricing and Entry Deterring Strategies: the Economics of AKZO" (1986) 7 *European Competition Law Review*, pp. 233–40.

3. – The Concept of Abuse
Francisco Enrique González-Díaz and John Temple Lang

non-market abuses, such as vexatious litigation or false declarations to regulatory authorities. At the same time, it also addresses classical forms of abuses, *e.g.,* refusal to deal, exclusive dealing, or tying, which all have the effect of raising the costs incurred by competitors.[63]

3.39 This test, however, appears to share some of the deficiencies of the "as efficient competitor test":

- Every sale made by the dominant company instead of a rival is likely to reduce *pro tanto* the economies of scale obtained by the rival, and thus raise the rival's unit costs to that extent.

- If the dominant company produces more than is necessary to achieve its own economies of scale to lower its costs, the excess benefits consumers but will reduce the economies of scale available to rivals. Such "overproduction" may not be necessarily deliberate, as, for example, a company producing a new product may not know for some time at what level of production it will reach its lowest production costs. The same uncertainty can be caused <u>every</u> time a company makes any significant change in its production or distribution systems.

- Denying competitors access to a network controlled by the dominant company might be unjustified and exclusionary, but it would be illegal because it reduced the value of the competitors' products, not (or not primarily) because it raised the competitors' costs.

3.40 Raising rivals' costs, of course, may limit their market opportunities, contrary to Article 102(b) TFEU. Lowering the value of rivals' products, *e.g.,* by depriving them of network effects, may just be as exclusionary as raising their costs.

2.2.5.   The Consumer Welfare Test

3.41 Under this test, conduct which reduces consumer welfare should be considered exclusionary.[64] While the "aggregate" economic welfare standard[65] would permit any conduct that increases overall welfare regardless of how wealth is

---

[63] *See* A. Jones and B. Sufrin *supra* note 55, p. 585.

[64] Among the promoters of a consumer welfare standard, *see* S. C. Salop *supra* note 45, p. 311.

[65] On the debate of the proper welfare standard, *see* K. J. Cseres, "The Controversies of the Consumer Welfare Standard" (2007) 3(2) *Competition Law Review*, pp. 121–73. As explained by G. J. Werden, "Essays on Consumer Welfare and Competition Policy" (2009), although based on economic principles, the term consumer welfare is a legal term, introduced by Bork in 1966 (*See* R. H. Bork, "Legislative Intent and the Policy of the Sherman Act" (1966) 9 *Journal of Law & Economics*, pp. 7–48. The term used in economics is "social welfare".

3. – The Concept of Abuse
Francisco Enrique González-Díaz and John Temple Lang

distributed, the "pure" consumer welfare standard concentrates on the impact on consumers.[66] A "pure" test based on whether the unilateral conduct in question, on balance, promotes or harms consumer welfare would appear consistent with the objectives of EU competition law,[67] at least in theory.[68] The evaluation under this test is said to be *"really about whether consumers are harmed from (sic) higher prices, reduced quality or (in some cases) reduced innovation"*.[69] Harm to consumers should be regarded as an essential element in all kinds of abuse under Article 102 TFEU.

3.42 However, this test would need to be combined with a set of satisfactory criteria that indicate what kinds of conduct are inherently likely to cause exclusionary effects and harm consumer welfare.

3.43 This "pure" consumer welfare test would necessitate an analysis of the relative efficiency, in the future, of the course of action proposed, and of whatever different courses of action might be available at the relevant time. However, it may be impossible for a dominant company to rely on such a test with confidence when it launches a new product or a new distribution practice. A test that is difficult to apply even with hindsight would give so little predictability that it may be unacceptable and likely contrary to the principle of legal certainty.[70] It would also make the law difficult to administer as courts are generally not well equipped to measure even short-term effects on prices, production volumes or product quality.

3.44 In addition, a pure consumer welfare effects test[71] would necessarily involve balancing <u>future</u> harms and benefits, and would do this <u>without</u> the requirement that the conduct must "impair the opportunities" of rivals. If such a prior

---

[66] Moreover, the notion of "consumer welfare" differs according to the static or dynamic view endorsed. According to the "static view", consumer welfare is expressed by allocative efficiency, while in a "dynamic view", also the emergence of new products or technical development has an impact on consumer welfare. *See* C. Ahlborn and A.J. Padilla, *supra* note 35, where the Authors argue that the view endorsed by the European Commission is static.

[67] *See* S. C. Salop *supra* note 61, pp. 477–508.

[68] *Ibid.*, p. 483.

[69] *Ibid.*

[70] *See Deutsche Telekom Judgment 2010 supra* note 26, paras 202–03. This is one of the objections to the approach advocated by the EAGCP group of economists in their 2005 paper for the Commission.

[71] *See* M. Lao *supra* note 31, pp. 448–51; *see also* G. J. Werden, *supra* note 50. As described by E. Paulis, in "The Burden of Proof in Article 82 Cases", in B. E. Hawk (Ed.), *Fordham Competition Law Institute: International Antitrust Law and Policy 2006* (New York, Juris Publishing, 2007), pp. 472–74, it would be difficult if not impossible for the dominant company to decide whether a new pricing policy would be considered legal or not. Paulis did not mention, and does not seem to consider, any prior "impairment" or "limiting rivals' possibilities" requirement.

3. – The Concept of Abuse
Francisco Enrique González-Díaz and John Temple Lang

requirement were to be added, then the ensuing reformulation would lead, essentially, to the "impairment" or "limiting" tests. In fact, a consumer welfare effects test, without an "impairment" requirement, may be especially difficult (indeed, often impossible) to apply to innovation cases.[72] In any event, Article 102(b) TFEU requires harm to consumers for a finding of abuse, and requires a definition of exclusionary or anticompetitive conduct as well.

Consumer harm is an essential element in any satisfactory definition of exclu-   **3.45**
sionary abuse because it prevents or should prevent protection of competitors, but it cannot be the only element in a test of exclusionary abuse.[73]

2.2.6.   Article 102(b) – The Treaty Test

EU law provides a legal basis for the use of a standard that includes both   **3.46**
a test based on "limiting" rivals' possibilities and causing consumer harm. Article 102(b) TFEU indeed prohibits "*the limitation of production, markets or technical development to the prejudice of consumers.*"

The case law of the European Courts confirms that this provision limits   **3.47**
the ability of the dominant enterprise to restrict the production, marketing or technical development *of its competitors.*[74] Harm to consumers is explicitly

---

[72] *See* H. Hovenkamp *supra* note 31, p. 413.

[73] *See* J. Vickers *supra* note 27, pp. F258–59.

[74] Joined Cases 40 to 48, 50, 54 to 56, 111, 113 and 114/73 *Coöperatieve Vereniging "Suiker Unie" and others v Commission* ("*Suiker Unie*") [1975] ECR 1663, paras 399, 482–83, and 523–27 (para.526: "*the system complained of was likely to limit markets to the prejudice of consumers within the measure of Article [102](b) because it gave other producers [...] no chance or restricted their opportunities of competing with sugar sold by SZV*"); Case 41/83 *Italian Republic v Commission* [1985] ECR 873; Case 311/84 *Centre belge d'études de marché – Télémarketing (CBEM) v Compagnie luxembourgeoise de télédiffusion (CLT) and Information publicité Benelux (IPB)* ("*Télémarketing*") [1985] ECR 3261, para. 26; Case 53/87 *Consorzio italiano della componentistica di ricambio per autoveicoli (CICRA) and Maxicar v Régie nationale des usines Renault* ("*Renault*") [1988] ECR 6039; Case 238/87 *Volvo v Erik Veng* ("*Volvo*") [1988] ECR 6211; Joined Cases C-241 and 242/91 P *Radio Telefis Eireann (RTE) and Independent Television Publications (ITP) v Commission* ("*Magill*") [1995] ECR I-743, para. 54 ("*The applicants' refusal to provide basic information by relying on national copyright provisions thus prevented the appearance of a new product, a comprehensive weekly guide to television programmes, which the applicants did not offer and for which there was a potential consumer demand. Such refusal constitutes an abuse under heading (b) of the second paragraph of Article [102] of the Treaty*"); Case C-41/90 *Klaus Höfner and Fritz Elser v Macrotron* ("*Höfner*") [1991] ECR I-1979, para. 30 ("*Pursuant to Article [102](b), such an abuse may in particular consist in limiting the provision of a service, to the prejudice of those seeking to avail themselves of it*"); Case C-55/96 *Job Centre* [1977] ECR I-7119; Case C-258/98 *Criminal proceedings against Giovanni Carra and others* [2000] ECR I-4217; and *Microsoft Judgment 2007 supra* note 25, paras 643–8 (para. 647: "*The circumstance relating to the appearance of a new product, as envisaged in Magill and IMS Health [...] cannot be the only parameter which determines whether a refusal to licence an intellectual property right is capable of causing prejudice to consumers within the meaning of Article 82(b) EC. As that provision states, such prejudice may also arise where there is a limitation not only of production or markets, but also of technical development*"). *See also* P. Roth and V. Rose (Eds.),

3. – The Concept of Abuse
Francisco Enrique González-Díaz and John Temple Lang

required by Article 102(b) TFEU which prohibits foreclosure and exclusionary abuse. There is thus a solid basis, based on the need for a consistent interpretation of the whole of Article 102 TFEU, for concluding that harm to consumers should be an essential element in *any* definition of foreclosure or exclusionary abuse.[75]

3.48 However, as well as harm to consumers, there must be a clear basis for harm to competition to be established if conduct is to be prohibited. So even an economics-based or effects-based approach must include a definition of exclusionary abuse, foreclosure, or harm to competition. Without a concept of exclusionary abuse, dominant firms may not be able to tell whether, *e.g.*, a price so low that rivals go out of business is beneficial or harmful to consumers.[76]

3. The Position of the Commission and the EU Courts

3.49 In this section we review the position of the Commission and the EU Courts on the "special responsibility" of dominant undertakings and on its evolution towards a more effects-based approach to Article 102 TFEU.

3.1. The Notion of "Special Responsibility"

3.1.1. "Special Responsibility" in the Case Law

3.50 The notion of "special responsibility" is rooted in the ordoliberal tradition, developed in the 1930s in Germany. This tradition advocates an "economic

---

Bellamy & Child, European Community Law of Competition (5th Ed., Oxford, Oxford University Press, 2001), pp. 754–55 and Cases IV/30.373 *P&I Clubs, IGA* and IV/37.143 *P&I Clubs, Pooling Agreement* ("*P&I Clubs*"), Commission Decision of 12 April 1999, OJ 1999 L 125/12, paras 128–33.

[75] J. Temple Lang, "Anticompetitive Abuses under Article 82 Involving Intellectual Property Rights", in C.-D. Ehlermann and I. Atanasiu (Eds.), *European Competition Law Annual 2003: What Is Abuse of Dominant Position?* (Oxford, Hart Publishing, 2006), pp. 589–658; *See also* E. Elhauge *supra* note 30, who proposes a test of "impairing rivals' efficiency"; *See also* J. Faull and A. Nikpay (Eds.), *The EC Law of Competition* (2nd Ed., Oxford, Oxford University Press, 2007), p. 351, says that conduct is an abuse if it "*is able to alter the structure of the market, by weakening or eliminating competitors*".

[76] The limitation of competitors' possibilities test based on Article 102(b) TFEU, including the requirement of harm to consumers, is similar to the impairment tests suggested by various economists, and by the *Discussion Paper. See* J. Vickers, *supra* note 27, p. 254: "*There is no escape from the fundamental question of what is harm to, or distortion of, competition*" and as stated in the OECD report on "Competition Law and Policy in the EU" (2005): "*A thorough-going economic approach to dominant firm conduct requires some methodologically clear means of identifying claims about exclusionary conduct that presents threats to sound competition and distinguishing them from demands from competitors for help in keeping prices up.*"

3. – The Concept of Abuse
Francisco Enrique González-Díaz and John Temple Lang

constitution" in which competition is perceived as a value in itself.[77] This notion of special responsibility was first introduced by the Court of Justice in the *Michelin I* case:

> "*A finding that an undertaking has a dominant position is not in itself a recrimination but simply means that, irrespective of the reasons for which it has such a dominant position, the undertaking concerned has a special responsibility not to allow its conduct to impair genuine undistorted competition on the common market.*"[78]

What the "special responsibility" criterion essentially means in practice is that ordinary business behaviour may constitute an abuse of a dominant position within the meaning of Article 102 TFEU, even if such conduct would not be prohibited if engaged in by a non-dominant undertaking. Although being in a dominant position is not prohibited as such, this legal doctrine would impose a rather imprecise obligation on dominant firms, obliging them to act in a way proportionate to their economic strength.[79]   **3.51**

Since *Michelin I*, this notion has appeared repeatedly in the Article 102 TFEU case law.[80] The concept of special responsibility might be understood as a sliding scale. Thus, in *Compagnie Maritime Belge*, the Court took account the fact that the dominant firm had a market share of over 90 per cent, and held that "*the actual scope of the special responsibility imposed on a dominant undertaking must be considered in the light of the specific circumstances of each case which show that competition has been weakened*".[81] This idea was reiterated by the Commission in *Deutsche Post*:   **3.52**

---

[77] *See, e.g.,* E. Osterud, *Identifying Exclusionary Abuses by Dominant Undertakings under EU Competition Law: the Spectrum of Tests* (Kluwer Law International, 2010) pp. 33–4, and E. Rousseva, "Modernizing by Eradicating: How the Commission's New Approach to Article 81 EC Dispenses with the Need to Apply Article 82 EC to Vertical Restraints" (2005) 42(3) *Common Market Law Review*, p. 592, and L. Lovdahl Gormsen, "Article 82 EC: Where are we coming from and where are we going to?" (2006) 2(2) *Competition Law Review*, p. 10.

[78] *See Michelin I supra* note 2, para. 57 (emphasis added).

[79] K. McMahon, "A Reformed Approach to Article 82 and the Special Responsibility not to Distort Competition", in A. Ezrachi, *Article 82 EC: Reflections on its Recent Evolution* (Oxford, Hart Publishing, 2009), p. 123.

[80] *See, e.g.,* Case T-65/89, *BPB Industries and British Gypsum v Commission* ("*BPB Industries*") [1993] ECR II-389, paras 65–66; Case T-228/97, *Irish Sugar v Commission* ("*Irish Sugar Judgment 1999*") [1999] ECR II-2969, para. 112; Case T-65/98 *Van den Bergh Foods v Commission* ("*Van den Bergh Foods*") [2003] ECR II-4653, para. 158; *Microsoft Judgment 2007 supra* note 25, para. 229; and Case C-202/07 P, *France Télécom v Commission* [2009] ECR I-2369.

[81] Joined cases C-395 P and C-396/96 P, *Compagnie Maritime Belge Transports and others v Commission* ("*Compagnie Maritime Belge*") [2000] ECR I-1365, para. 114.

3. – The Concept of Abuse
Francisco Enrique González-Díaz and John Temple Lang

> "*An undertaking in a dominant position has a special responsibility not to allow its conduct to* *impair undistorted* *competition in the common market. The actual* *scope of the dominant firm's special responsibility must be considered* *in relation* *to the degree of dominance held by that firm* *and to the special characteristics of the market which may affect the competitive situation.*"[82]

3.53   In *Tetra Pak* the Court made it clear that an undertaking's special responsibility is not limited to the dominated market, but also applies to other markets which are vertically or horizontally related to it. When assessing a conduct with exclusionary effects on markets adjacent to the dominated one (Tetra Pak was dominant on the aseptic markets but the Court of First Instance found that it was unnecessary to prove dominance on the non-aseptic markets as a condition for concluding that Tetra Pak had a special responsibility to maintain genuine competition on these markets), the Court held that the Court of First Instance had been correct in asserting the applicability of Article 102 TFEU, in view of the "*specific circumstances*" of the case.[83]

3.54   The notion of "special responsibility" is also referred to by the Commission in its *Guidance Paper*.[84]

3.1.2.   The Notion of "Special Responsibility" and the Economic Tests of Foreclosure

3.55   The notion of "special responsibility" has been subject to much criticism. First, it has been maintained that such a notion forms part of an obsolete approach to Article 82, and is incompatible with the current modernisation efforts as well as with the more recent emphasis on consumer welfare.[85] Secondly, it has been submitted that it is a broad and far-reaching concept, and that by referring to such a notion "[w]*hat was gained in flexibility in the application of Article 86 was lost in legal certainty*".[86] Indeed, it has been argued that it is difficult to determine what

---

[82] Case COMP/36.915, *Deutsche Post AG – Interception of cross-border mail* ("*Deutsche Post*"), Commission Decision of 25 July 2001, OJ 2001 L 331/40, para. 103.

[83] *See Tetra Pak II Judgment 1996 supra* note 3, para. 24.

[84] *See Guidance Paper supra* note 9, para. 1 and 9.

[85] R. Allendesalazar, "Can We Finally Say Farewell to the "Special Responsibility" of Dominant Companies?", in C.D. Ehlermann and M. Marquis (eds.), *European Competition Law Annual 2007: A Reformed Approach to Article 82 EC* (Oxford, Hart Publishing, 2008), p. 319.

[86] R. Subiotto, "The Special Responsibility of Dominant Undertakings Not to Impair Genuine Undistorted Competition" (1995) 18(3) *World Competition*, p. 6.

3. – The Concept of Abuse
Francisco Enrique González-Díaz and John Temple Lang

the precise duties and responsibilities attached to such responsibility would be and how these would manifest themselves in relation to the different forms of abuse.[87] Thirdly, and specifically concerning the *Tetra Pak* extension of the "special responsibility" to markets in which an undertaking has not been proven dominant, this risks undermining the essential principle that the mere existence of dominance may not give rise to Article 102 TFEU liability.[88]

Some authors have highlighted the apparently profound differences between the EU "special responsibility" approach and the US approach.[89]   **3.56**

However, it has also been argued that Article 102 TFEU simply spells out   **3.57** what the prohibition of engaging in conduct which may be deemed abusive under this legal provision means for dominant firms.[90] From this perspective, this notion would not impose any specific behavioural obligations on undertakings and may not define any legal rule or doctrine.[91] Thus, the "special responsibility" would simply serve the purpose of providing a general description of Article 102 TFEU, whilst specific duties and liabilities may only be imposed by resorting to one of the specific economic tests of foreclosure summarised above.[92] This indeed seems to be the position adopted by the EU Courts.[93] For this reason, it remains of crucial importance to determine what test/s of foreclosure is/are applied by the Commission and the EU Courts and hence what the precise boundaries of dominant undertakings' "special responsibility" are. In Tomra[94] the Court seems to have put an end to the difficulties caused by the notion of "special responsibility". The Court held: *"the degree of market strength is, as a general rule, significant in relation to the extent of the effects of the conduct of the undertaking concerned rather than in relation to the question of whether the abuse as such exists"*.

---

[87] *See* K. McMahon *supra* note 79, p. 125.

[88] *See* R. Subiotto *supra* note 86, p. 30.

[89] *See* K. McMahon *supra* note 79, p. 125.

[90] *See* R. Nazzini, *"The Foundations of European Union Competition Law* The Objective and Principles of Article 102" (Oxford, Oxford University Press, 2011), p. 175.

[91] *Ibid.*

[92] *Ibid.*

[93] Joined Cases T-191 and 212 to 214/98 *Atlantic Container Line and others v Commission* ("*TACA Judgment 2003*") [2003] ECR II-3275, para. 1460.

[94] Case C-549/10 P *Tomra and Others v Commission* ("*Tomra Judgment 2012*"), not yet reported, para. 39. This confirms the statement of the Court in Joined Cases T-191 and 212 to 214/98 *Atlantic Container Line and others v Commission* ("*TACA Judgment 2003*") [2003] ECR II-3275 at para. 1460 *"That special responsibility means only that a dominant undertaking may be prohibited from conduct which is legitimate where it is carried out by un-dominant undertakings"*.

3. – The Concept of Abuse
Francisco Enrique González-Díaz and John Temple Lang

3.2. *Economic Tests of Foreclosure and Effects-Based Approach in the Commission Practice and EU Case Law*

3.2.1. Consumer Welfare and Effects-based Approach

3.58   As explained above, the so-called "special responsibility" of dominant undertakings does not provide a clear-cut criterion for the allocation of duties and responsibilities on these companies. Indeed, such allocation may only be carried out on the basis of a specific test.

3.59   Neither the Commission nor the EU Courts have adopted a coherent and unified test which could be consistently applied to determine whether the conduct of a dominant undertaking is abusive or not.[95] As a result, in 2003, the Commission engaged in an internal review of its policy concerning Article 102 TFEU, with the aim of introducing the consumer welfare standard as the key criterion to assess whether a conduct constitutes anticompetitive foreclosure, and of re-orienting the application of Article 102 TFEU towards an effects-based analysis.[96]

3.60   Certain authors have argued that the consumer welfare test constitutes the best standard to govern exclusionary conduct.[97] According to this line of reasoning, the essential reason why the consumer welfare standard would lead to more satisfactory results than *e.g.,* the profit sacrifice, the no economic sense, or the equally efficient competitor standards, is that the former "*focuses on the effect of the conduct on the market, that is, consumers and the competitive process*".[98] Moreover, in this view, and contrary to what critics of the consumer welfare standard contend, the fact that the consumer welfare analysis is of an essentially *ex ante* nature (*i.e.,* conduct is only condemned if, *ex ante*, the magnitude and the likelihood of potential consumer harm outweighs that of potential consumer benefit) would render such a test compatible with the principle of legal certainty, as it would enable undertakings to escape Article 102 TFEU liability when they could not reasonably foresee the harmful consequences of their conduct on consumer welfare.[99]

---

[95] P. Akman, "Consumer Welfare and Article 82 EC: Practice and Rhetoric" (2009) 32(1) *World Competition*, p. 88.
[96] *See* A. Jones and B. Sufrin *supra* note 55, pp. 273–4.
[97] *See* S. C. Salop *supra* note 45, p. 313.
[98] *Ibid.,* p. 331.
[99] *Ibid.,* pp. 341–3.

3. – The Concept of Abuse
Francisco Enrique González-Díaz and John Temple Lang

However, as noted in Section III.2.1, there is still significant uncertainty **3.61** and controversy as to which test must be used under EU law to determine whether a conduct is exclusionary or not.[100] Indeed, whilst the Commission *Guidance Paper* has clearly advocated the need to protect consumer welfare in the enforcement of Article 102 TFEU (albeit arguably without applying this standard, as an economic test of foreclosure), the EU Courts have not adopted this test.[101] For example, in some of its most recent judgments, the Court referred to the as-efficient competitor test in determining whether certain conduct is in breach of Article 102 TFEU.[102] In addition, the Commission's position in this respect is not completely clear as its *Guidance Paper* is claimed to be only aimed at establishing "enforcement priorities".

The announced aim of moving towards a more effects-based approach **3.62** constituted a reaction against the wide-spread criticism that the case law of the EU Courts and the Commission's decisional practice on exclusionary abuses was too formalistic and too divorced from the actual or likely impact of the conduct in question on consumer welfare and/or on competitors. Although the need to take account of effects in Article 102 TFEU proceedings was never excluded, the essential idea advocated by scholars and practitioners was that such analysis ought to apply effectively, consistently and systematically,[103] leaving no room for *per se* rules or subjective considerations.[104]

Although after some years of implementation of the newly announced **3.63** approach there is still significant ambiguity and uncertainty as to the nature and scope of the announced shift in the approach towards anticompetitive foreclosure, some change is progressively emerging in the interpretation and application of Article 102 TFEU.[105] The following section focuses on the changes in the Commission and the EU Courts' approach to Article 102 TFEU and on the gradual evolution towards an effects-based analysis and

---

[100] *See* R. Nazzini *supra* note 90, p. 155.

[101] For a detailed account of the application of the different tests of economic foreclosure by the EU Courts, *see* R. Nazzini *supra* note 90 and chapters 5 to 8.

[102] *See* section III.3.4.2 discussing the recent shift towards a more effects-based approach.

[103] *See* A. Jones and B. Sufrin *supra* note 55, p. 274.

[104] *See e.g.,* D. Waelbroeck, "Tough Competition – What is the relevance of intention in article 82 cases?" (2006) 5(6) *Competition Law Insight.*

[105] G. Monti, "Article 82 EC: What Future for the Effects-Based Approach?" (2010) 1(1) *Journal of European Competition Law & Practice*, pp. 2–11.

3. – The Concept of Abuse
Francisco Enrique González-Díaz and John Temple Lang

towards an increased focus on the potential impact of the alleged anticompetitive conduct on consumer welfare.

3.3.   The Position of the European Commission

3.3.1.   The Commission Discussion Paper

3.64   In July 2005, the Commission published a *Report on an Economic Approach to Article 82 EC* by the Economic Advisory Group for Competition Policy ("EAGCP"), which questioned the traditional "form-based" approach under Article 102 TFEU. The "effects-based" approach advocated in the Report focuses "*on the presence of anti-competitive effects that harm consumers, and is based on the examination of each specific case, based on sound economics and grounded on facts*".[106]

3.65   The Report by the EAGCP was followed by the publication of the Commission's *Discussion Paper on the Application of Article 82 of the Treaty to exclusionary abuses* (the "*Discussion Paper*").[107] The *Discussion Paper* had the aim of setting out a general framework for the analysis of abusive exclusionary conduct. For price-based conduct, such as rebates, the Commission considered that only conduct which would exclude a hypothetical as efficient competitor should be considered as abusive.[108]

3.66   In the *Discussion Paper*, the Commission referred to the definition of abuse given in *Hoffmann-La Roche*.[109] However, it then went on to use the term "foreclosure", which had not been used by the Court in this judgment:

> "*This definition implies that the conduct in question must in the first place have the capability, by its nature, to foreclose competitors from the market. To establish such capability it is in general sufficient to investigate the form and nature of the conduct in question. It secondly implies that, in the specific market context, a likely market distorting foreclosure effect must be established. By foreclosure is meant that actual or potential competitors are completely or partially denied profitable access to a market. Foreclosure may discourage entry or expansion of rivals or*

---

[106] Economic Advisory Group on Competition Policy (EAGCP), "*An economic approach to Article 82*" (July 2005) DG COMP, p. 2.
[107] *Discussion Paper supra* note 13.
[108] *Ibid.*, para. 63.
[109] *Ibid.*, para. 57.

3. – The Concept of Abuse
Francisco Enrique González-Díaz and John Temple Lang

encourage their exit. Foreclosure thus can be found even if the foreclosed rivals are not forced to exit the market: it is sufficient that the rivals are disadvantaged and consequently led to compete less aggressively. Rivals may be disadvantaged where the dominant company is able to directly raise rivals' costs or reduce demand for the rivals' products. Foreclosure is said to be market distorting if it likely hinders the maintenance of the degree of competition still existing in the market or the growth of competition and thus have as a likely effect that prices will increase or remain at a supra-competitive level." [110]

The Commission's definition in the *Discussion Paper* prompts the following comments: **3.67**

- "Foreclosure" of competitors can occur legitimately, if the dominant company offers lower prices or better products or services than its competitors. The Commission has therefore tried to distinguish between "foreclosure", which can result from lawful and desirable competition, and "anticompetitive foreclosure", which is what needs to be defined.

- The idea that competitors are "completely or partially denied profitable access to a market" is, however, ambiguous. Indeed, competitors may be "denied profitable access" to a market if the dominant company is so efficient that it can offer prices that are so much lower than its competitors that nobody will buy their products. This part of the test does not provide a precise enough criterion to distinguish between legitimate competition and anticompetitive conduct.

- The concept of a "disadvantaged" competitor or the reference to the fact that the rivals are *"disadvantaged where the dominant company is able directly to [...] reduce demand for the rivals' products"* raises similar concerns, as a dominant company's low prices will certainly *"reduce demand for the rivals' products"*.

In the same section of the *Discussion Paper* and as regards the underlying objectives of Article 102 TFEU, the Commission stated: **3.68**

"The essential objective of Article 82 when analyzing exclusionary conduct is the protection of competition on the market as a means of enhancing consumer

---

[110] *See Discussion Paper supra* note 13, para. 58.

3. – The Concept of Abuse
Francisco Enrique González-Diaz and John Temple Lang

welfare and of ensuring an efficient allocation of resources. The concern is to prevent exclusionary conduct of the dominant firm which is likely to <u>limit</u> the remaining competitive constraints on the dominant company, including entry of newcomers, so as to avoid that consumers are harmed. This means that it is competition, and not competitors as such, that is to be protected. Furthermore, the purpose of Article 82 is not to protect competitors from dominant firms' genuine competition based on factors such as higher quality, novel products, opportune innovation or otherwise better performance, but to ensure that these competitors are also able to expand in or enter the market and compete therein on the merits, without facing competition conditions which are <u>distorted or impaired</u> by the dominant firm.

Article 82 prohibits exclusionary conduct which produces actual or likely anticompetitive effects in the market and which can harm consumers in a direct or indirect way. The longer the conduct has already been going on, the more weight will in general be given to actual effects. Harm to intermediate buyers is generally presumed to create harm to final consumers. Furthermore, not only short term harm, but also medium and long term harm arising from foreclosure is taken into account.

The central concern of Article 82 with regard to exclusionary abuses is thus foreclosure that hinders competition and thereby harms consumers." [111]

3.69   The Commission went on to say that more detailed tests may be needed in order to determine whether a conduct constitutes anticompetitive foreclosure:

"To establish such a market distorting foreclosure effect it is in general necessary not only to consider the nature or form of the conduct, but also its incidence, i.e. the extent to which the dominant company is applying it in the market, including the market coverage of the conduct or the selective foreclosure of customers to newcomers or residual competitors. Other market characteristics including the existence of network effects and economies of scale and scope may also be relevant to establish a foreclosure effect. In addition the degree of dominance will be a relevant factor. In general, the higher the capability of conduct to foreclose and the wider its application and the stronger the dominant position, the higher the likelihood that an anticompetitive foreclosure effect results. In view of these sliding scales, where [...]

---

[111] *See Discussion Paper supra* note 13, paras 54–6 (emphasis added).

3. – The Concept of Abuse
Francisco Enrique González-Díaz and John Temple Lang

various factors are used to indicate circumstances under which a likely foreclosure effect is considered to occur with high(er) or low(er) likelihood, it needs to be kept in mind that these descriptions cannot be applied mechanically.

Where a certain exclusionary conduct is clearly not competition on the merits, in particular conduct which clearly creates no efficiencies and which only raises obstacles to residual competition, such conduct is presumed to be an abuse." [112]

The Commission used the words "exclusionary conduct" and the references to "genuine competition" and "competition on the merits" in order to differentiate between lawful and unlawful behaviour. These notions seem to imply an approach similar to that of the Court when it used the phrase "methods different from those which condition normal competition" and thus raise the same theoretical and practical difficulties. **3.70**

In principle, the *Discussion Paper* advocated a shift away from the formalistic theories associated with a number of judgments from the EU Courts and Commission decisions towards a more economic "effects-based" approach to the analysis of the potentially abusive conduct of dominant companies. **3.71**

In particular, the Commission underlined that its main concern when applying Article 102 TFEU is the promotion of consumer welfare and not the protection of competitors: **3.72**

"... the objective of Article 82 is the protection of competition on the market as a means of enhancing consumer welfare and of ensuring an efficient allocation of resources". [113]

Such emphasis on consumer welfare was similarly stressed by Commissioner Kroes when stating that the enforcement of Article 102 TFEU should focus on conduct that affects consumer welfare. [114] **3.73**

---

[112] *See Discussion Paper supra* note 13, paras 59–60.

[113] *Ibid.*, para. 2.

[114] *See* Press Release SPEECH/05/537 of 23 September 2005.

3. – The Concept of Abuse
Francisco Enrique González-Díaz and John Temple Lang

3.74 However, the definition of "abuse" in the *Discussion Paper* relied on the *Hoffmann-La Roche* judgment, which made no mention of harm to consumers.[115]

3.3.2.   The Commission Guidance Paper

3.75 The publication of the EAGCP Report and the *Discussion Paper* gave rise to an extensive debate on the scope and characteristics of exclusionary conduct analysis in dominance cases. After receiving a significant number of comments, in December 2008 the Commission published a Guidance on the Commission's Enforcement Policies in Applying Article 82 EC Treaty to Exclusionary Conduct by Dominant Undertakings (the "*Guidance Paper*").[116] The *Guidance Paper* aims at setting out "*an economic and effects-based approach to exclusionary conduct under EC antitrust law*",[117] and outlines the analytical framework that the Commission wishes to employ when assessing the potentially exclusionary conduct of dominant companies.

3.76 As a preliminary point, the *Guidance Paper* states that:

> "*The aim of the Commission's enforcement activity in relation to exclusionary conduct is to ensure that dominant undertakings do not impair effective competition by foreclosing their competitors in an anti-competitive way, thus having an adverse impact on consumer welfare, whether in the form of higher price levels than would have otherwise prevailed or in some other form such as limiting quality or reducing consumer choice.*"[118]

3.77 The *Guidance Paper* describes the Commission's general approach to exclusionary conduct, including how the Commission will determine whether a company accused of violating Article 102 TFEU has a dominant position and how the Commission will seek to determine whether the conduct in question has or is likely to result in anticompetitive foreclosure. The *Guidance Paper* discusses the application of this analysis to four categories of conduct: exclusive dealing; tying and bundling; predation; and refusals to supply and margin squeezes.

---

[115] *See Discussion Paper supra* note 13, para. 57.
[116] *See Guidance Paper supra* note 9.
[117] *See* Press Release IP/08/1877 of 3 December 2008.
[118] *See Guidance Paper supra* note 9, para. 19 (emphasis added).

3. – The Concept of Abuse
Francisco Enrique González-Díaz and John Temple Lang

In its analysis of Article 102 TFEU cases, the Commission begins by dis- **3.78** cussing the criteria to establish dominance. The *Guidance Paper* clarifies the Commission's multi-factor analysis of whether a company holds a dominant position. As a first indication, the Commission will look at the allegedly dominant company's market shares, taking into account market conditions, in particular market dynamics, product differentiation and market share trends over time. The *Guidance Paper* sets out a market share safe harbour of 40 per cent, below which a company is unlikely to be considered dominant. Other factors which are taken into account include barriers to entry or expansion in the relevant market and countervailing buyer power.[119]

The Commission then examines whether the conduct in question has resulted **3.79** or is likely to result in "anticompetitive foreclosure", i.e. in a situation in which actual or potential competitors' access to suppliers or markets is hampered or eliminated and the dominant company is likely to be in a position enabling it to profitably increase prices to the detriment of consumers.

As stated above, the Commission's Article 102 TFEU enforcement policy **3.80** is intended to protect consumers by ensuring that dominant companies do not foreclose competitors in an anticompetitive way. The Commission will normally only intervene under Article 102 TFEU where, based on "cogent and convincing evidence", the allegedly abusive conduct is likely to lead to anticompetitive foreclosure. The Commission will consider the following factors in its assessment:[120]

- <u>Strength of dominant position.</u> The stronger the dominant position, the higher the likelihood of anticompetitive foreclosure.
- <u>Market conditions</u>. These include barriers to entry and expansion, the existence of economies of scale or scope, and network effects, which might allow a dominant undertaking to "tip" a market or to further entrench its position.
- <u>Position of competitors</u>. A competitor with even a small market share can play a significant competitive role, for example, if it is the closest competitor, if it is particularly innovative, or if it has the reputation of systematically cutting prices.

---

[119] *See* Chapter 2.
[120] *See Guidance Paper supra* note 9, para. 20.

3. – The Concept of Abuse
Francisco Enrique González-Díaz and John Temple Lang

- <u>Position of customers and suppliers</u>. The likelihood of anticompetitive foreclosure will be greater where the dominant company is able to apply the practice in question selectively. Conduct directed at customers may have a greater foreclosure effect if it targets customers who are most likely to respond to offers from alternative suppliers, who represent a means of distributing products that would be suitable for a new entrant, who may be situated in a geographic area well suited to new entry, or who may be likely to influence the behaviour of other customers. Exclusive supply arrangements may have a greater foreclosure effect if targeted at suppliers who might be most likely to respond to requests by competitors of the dominant firm or who would otherwise be particularly suitable suppliers for a new entrant competing with the dominant company (*e.g.*, based on location or the characteristics of the supplier's products).

- <u>Extent of abusive conduct</u>. The higher the proportion of total sales affected by the challenged conduct, the longer the duration, and the greater the regularity with which it is applied, the greater is the likely foreclosure effect.

- <u>Evidence.</u> The anticompetitive foreclosure effect of the challenged conduct may be evidenced by the market performance of the dominant firm, if the conduct has been in place for a sufficient period of time. Otherwise, direct evidence of the dominant firm's strategy may help to interpret the conduct in question.

3.81 These factors are however primarily structural, not behavioural and, except for the last two, seem more relevant to dominance than to abuse. They therefore do not distinguish between anticompetitive conduct and legitimate competition.

3.82 The Commission supplements this section of the *Guidance Paper* in two ways. First, it proposes the "as-efficient competitor" test, which was originally suggested in below-cost pricing cases. Secondly, as previously noted, the Commission emphasises that the key standard is whether consumers are harmed: conduct that harms competitors but benefits consumers would be procompetitive.

3.83 As to the former, the Commission states that it will normally only intervene in order to prevent anticompetitive foreclosure resulting from price-based exclusionary conduct when such conduct is capable of hampering competition

3. – The Concept of Abuse
Francisco Enrique González-Díaz and John Temple Lang

from competitors who are as efficient as the dominant undertaking.[121] This approach is consistent with EU case law, which has endorsed it in the context of predatory pricing[122] and margin squeeze.[123] The *Guidance Paper* also suggests this test in assessing the potential anticompetitive impact of conditional rebates.[124]

In these cases, the Commission will seek to determine whether the dominant company's effective prices are above or below an appropriate cost measure, average avoidable cost ("AAC") or long-run average incremental cost ("LRAIC"). The *Guidance Paper*'s discussion of this analysis is more concise than that in the *Discussion Paper*, and it also recognises that the data for such an analysis may not always be available. **3.84**

The Commission will not normally challenge conduct that would not hamper competition from a hypothetical competitor whose costs – measured by AAC or LRAIC – would be equal to those of the dominant company. **3.85**

The *Guidance Paper* notes, however, that constraints exerted by less efficient competitors may also be taken into account, in particular where the dominant company's efficiency benefits from demand-related advantages such as network and learning effects.[125] **3.86**

The application of the equally efficient competitor test depends on the data on cost and sales prices of the dominant undertaking. If no such data are available, the Commission may use cost data of competitors or other comparable reliable data. **3.87**

The consumer welfare standard, plays a more general role in the *Guidance Paper*, as it applies to all conduct for the purposes of setting the Commission's enforcement priorities. It has been argued that although "[w]*hen the as efficient competitor test applies, the case law is clear that consumer harm is not a necessary element of* **3.88**

---

[121] *Guidance Paper supra* note 9, para. 23.

[122] *See, e.g., AKZO supra* note 23, and Case T-83/91, *Tetra Pak International v Commission* ("*Tetra Pak II Judgment 1994*") [1994] ECR II-755.

[123] *See, e.g.,* case T-271/03, *Deutsche Telekom v Commission* ("*Deutsche Telekom Judgment 2008*") [2008] ECR II-477, and *also TeliaSonera Judgment 2011 supra* note 26.

[124] *See Guidance Paper supra* note 9, paras 23–27 in combination with paras 37–45.

[125] *Ibid.*, para. 24.

3. – The Concept of Abuse
Francisco Enrique González-Díaz and John Temple Lang

the test", the *Guidance Paper*, "*would appear always to require proof of consumer harm, albeit only for the purpose of prioritization of cases*".[126]

3.89 The Commission's *Guidance Paper* has been considered unsatisfactory in several respects:

- Overall, it concentrates on situations in which it is said that foreclosure of competitors may occur, without clearly distinguishing between legitimate foreclosure due to normal competition, and anticompetitive foreclosure due to exclusionary conduct. The Commission's references to the need for harm to consumers to be shown for a finding of abuse to be established may not be sufficient, because it is not applied as a test. For example, in the discussion of rebates the Commission appears to be more concerned about possible difficulties for competitors than about the benefits of rebates to consumers.

- The *Guidance Paper* does not suggest any comprehensive concept of "*foreclosure*" or "*exclusionary abuse*". In places it refers to "*foreclosure*" without making it clear whether it refers to foreclosure due to illegal conduct, and without recognising that a less efficient competitor may be lawfully and legitimately "*foreclosed*" and pushed out of the market by normal competition, that is, as a result of the dominant company offering better products at lower prices.

- Despite the announced evolution towards an effects-based approach, the *Guidance Paper* identifies categories of behaviour that are virtually *per se* abuses, because to find a violation the Commission will not conduct a detailed assessment of the conduct's effect before concluding that the conduct is likely to result in consumer harm (*e.g.,* a dominant company preventing its customers from testing a competitor's products or paying a distributor or customer to delay introduction of such products) or for which no defence is likely to be accepted (*e.g.,* predatory conduct). This approach, combined with the fact that the *Guidance Paper* only sets out enforcement priorities and the way in which the Commission has applied Article 102 TFEU in certain

---

[126] *See* R. Nazzini *supra* note 90, p. 221.

3. – The Concept of Abuse
Francisco Enrique González-Díaz and John Temple Lang

cases,[127] reveals that the genuine shift towards a coherent effects-based analysis is still in the making.[128]

3.4. The Position of the EU Courts

3.4.1. Evolution of the Article 102 TFEU Case Law and the Traditional Approach

Since *Hoffmann-La Roche*, two lines of cases on exclusionary abuses appeared **3.90** to develop. In a first line of cases, which includes most of the better-known judgments, the Commission and the EU Courts did not refer to any one of the four clauses of Article 102 TFEU, but to the Article as a whole when proceeding to the legal qualification of a given conduct as an abuse of dominant position. For example, in determining that fidelity discounts had an exclusionary effect, in *Hoffmann-La Roche*[129] and *Michelin*,[130] the Court based its argument on Article 86 of the EEC Treaty (subsequently Article 82 EC, now Article 102 TFEU) in its entirety, and not just on subparagraph (b) of its second paragraph. Similarly in *BPB*, with reference to exclusive dealing, the Court observed that *"an undertaking which is in a dominant position in a market and ties purchasers - even if it does so at their request - by an obligation or promise on their part to obtain all or most of their requirements exclusively from the said undertaking abuses its dominant position within the meaning of Article 86 of the EEC Treaty"*, whether or not the obligation is undertaken in consideration of the grant of a rebate.[131]

There was, however, a second line of cases in which the Court did refer specifically to clause (b) of Article 102 TFEU, on limiting production, markets **3.91** or technical development. These cases show that it is an abuse, contrary to Article 102(b) TFEU, for a dominant company to limit the production, markets, or technical development of its competitors, as well as its own, if harm is caused to consumers.[132]

---

[127] *See* Case T-336/07 *Telefónica v Commission*, not yet reported.

[128] *See* P. Akman *supra* note 95, p. 77.

[129] *See* *Hoffmann-La Roche supra* note 16, para. 89.

[130] *See* *Michelin I supra* note 2, p. 3461, para. 86: *"by binding dealers in the Netherlands to itself by means of the discount system described above Michelin NV committed an abuse within the meaning of Article 86 of the Treaty of its dominant position in the market for new replacement tyres for heavy vehicles"*.

[131] *See* *BPB Industries supra* note 80, para. 68.

[132] The case law has made it clear that Art. 102(b) applies to limiting the production, marketing or technical development of competitors, and not merely to limiting the dominant company's own activities. *See* all cases *supra* note 74. *See also* P. Roth and V. Rose (Eds.), *Bellamy & Child: European Community Law of Competition* (6th Ed., Oxford, Oxford University Press, 2008), pp. 1025–6.

3. – The Concept of Abuse
Francisco Enrique González-Díaz and John Temple Lang

3.92 In another series of cases, the Court stated that over reaction by a dominant company to a competitive initiative or threat could be an abuse. Although this rule was not expressed as being based on any one of the four examples listed in Article 102, these references should perhaps be regarded as a sub-set of situations under Article 102(b) TFEU.[133] In addition, in other judgments reference was made to discrimination as an element contributing to the abuse, and in those cases, Article 102(c) was referred to specifically.

3.93 The significance of the line of cases based on Article 102(b) TFEU is however not clear since *British Airways*.[134] In that case the company argued that clause (b) provides a comprehensive definition of exclusionary abuses, and that all abuses had to fall under one of the four clauses. On this view, there would be the four kinds of well-recognised abuses, but no fifth rule or principle. The Court rejected the argument, saying that the four clauses are merely examples, and that a number of "underlying factors" may justify a finding of abuse even

---

J. Temple Lang, "Anticompetitive Non-Pricing Abuses Under European and National Antitrust Law", in B. E. Hawk (Ed.), *Fordham Competition Law Institute: International Antitrust Law and Policy 2003* (New York, Juris Publishing, 2004), pp. 235–340; J.Temple Lang, "The Requirements for a Commission Notice on the Concept of Abuse under Article 82 EC", in *Finnish Competition Law Yearbook 2007*, pp. 271–306, and in *CEPS Special Reports* of December 10, 2008; R. O'Donoghue and A. J. Padilla, *supra* note 54, Ch. 4; R. O'Donoghue, "Verbalizing a general test for exclusionary conduct under Article 82 EC", in Ehlermann & Marquis (Eds.), *European Competition Law Annual 2007: A Reformed Approach to Article 82* (Oxford, Hart Publishing, 2008); *See* J. Vickers *supra* note 27, who discusses three tests, on sacrifice, as-efficient-competitors, and consumer welfare. Other tests suggested have included no-economic-sense test, and the consumer surplus test. *See also* E. Elhauge *supra* note 30, who concludes that "*the proper monopolization standard should* [...] *focus on whether the alleged exclusionary conduct succeeds in furthering monopoly power (i) only if the monopolist has improved its own efficiency or (ii) by impairing rival efficiency whether or not it enhances monopolist efficiency* [...] *This standard would permit the former conduct and prohibit the latter*".

[133] *See, inter alia*: United Brands *supra* note 6, paras 189–91; BPB Industries *supra* note 80; Joined Cases T-24 to 26 and 28/93 *Compagnie Maritime Belge Transports and others v Commission* [1996] ECR II-1201; Joined Cases T-133 and 204/95 *International Express Carriers Conference v Commission* [1998] ECR II-3645; Case T-111/96 *ITT Promedia v Commission* ("*ITT Promedia Judgment 1998*") [1998] ECR II-2937, para. 60; Case T-5/97 *Industrie des poudres sphériques v Commission* ("*IPS*") [2000] ECR II-3755, paras 211–18; *see also* Irish Sugar Judgment 1999 *supra* note 80; Case T-210/01 *General Electric v Commission* [2005] ECR II-5575, para. 306; Case C-52/07 *Kanal 5 and TV 4 v Föreningen Svenska Tonsättares Internationella Musikbyrå* ("*STIM*") [2008] ECR I-9275; Joined Cases C-468 to 478/06 *Sot. Lélos kai Sia and others v GlaxoSmithKline* ("*GlaxoSmithKline Judgment 2008*") [2008] ECR I-7139, paras 50, 69–71 and 76. The Commission's *Discussion Paper*, referred to this case law, but says that it is "best viewed" as concerning refusals to supply as an instrument to achieve, *e.g.*, exclusive dealing (*supra* note 13, para. 208), which is too narrow an understanding of the cases, and disregards the fact that the principle has been repeatedly stated in cases not concerned with exclusive dealing. The *Guidance Paper* (*supra* note 9, para. 77) also says that refusals to supply to punish customers for dealing with competitors will be examined on the basis of the principles on exclusive dealing, tying and bundling. *See* J. Temple Lang, "How can the Problems of Exclusionary Abuses under Article 102 TFEU be resolved?" (2012) 37 *European Law Review* pp. 136–55.

[134] Case T-219/99 *British Airways v Commission* [2003] ECR II-5917.

3. – The Concept of Abuse
Francisco Enrique González-Díaz and John Temple Lang

if it did not seem to fall under any of the four clauses. This suggested that the concept of (exclusionary) abuse is open-ended.

The General Court based its reasoning on earlier case law, the validity of which was not put into question, without endorsing a more "effects-based" approach. Indeed, the General Court noted that the Commission could not be blamed for **3.94**

> "*failing to demonstrate that its practices produced an exclusionary effect. In the first place, for the purposes of establishing an infringement of Article 82 EC, it is not necessary to demonstrate that the abuse in question had a concrete effect on the markets concerned. It is sufficient in that respect to demonstrate that the abusive conduct of the undertaking in a dominant position tends to restrict competition, or, in other words, that the conduct is capable of having, or likely to have, such an effect*".[135]

Similarly, in the *Michelin II* case,[136] in reply to the applicant's argument that the case law supported the view that the abusive conduct should have **3.95**

> "*the effect of hindering the maintenance of the degree of competition still existing in the market or the growth of that competition*", the General Court observed that "[t]*he 'effect' referred to in the case-law cited in the preceding paragraph does not necessarily relate to the actual effect of the abusive conduct complained of. For the purposes of establishing an infringement of Article 82 EC, it is sufficient to show that the abusive conduct of the undertaking in a dominant position tends to restrict competition or, in other words, that the conduct is capable of having that effect*".[137]

Likewise, in the *Microsoft* case[138] the General Court followed, at least formally, the traditional approach of "exceptional circumstances" in its analysis of the refusal to license intellectual property rights and held that no direct effects on consumers were required for the finding of an abuse. It said that **3.96**

---

[135] *See supra* note 134, para. 293.
[136] Case T-203/01 Manufacture Française des Pneumatiques Michelin v Commission ("*Michelin II*") [2003] ECR II-4071, para. 239.
[137] *Ibid.*, para. 238-9.
[138] *Microsoft Judgment 2007 supra* note 25.

3. – The Concept of Abuse
Francisco Enrique González-Díaz and John Temple Lang

> " *it is settled case-law that Article 82 EC covers not only practices which may prejudice consumers directly but also those which indirectly prejudice them by impairing an effective competitive structure* [...]. *In this case, Microsoft impaired the effective competitive structure on the work group server operating systems market by acquiring a significant market share on that market.*" [139]

3.97   This is consistent with the position of the Court according to which Article 102 TFEU applies not only to conduct directly damaging consumers, but also to practices which are detrimental to them by negatively affecting the effective competition "structure". The preservation of an effective competitive process is therefore considered to ensure that consumers' interests are safeguarded.

3.98   In *France Telecom v Commission*,[140] the General Court considered Wanadoo Interactive's alleged predatory practices. Once again, the General Court endorsed the traditional view that there is no need to prove the actual effects of the conduct in question. In particular, it stated that

> " *showing an anti-competitive object and an anti-competitive effect may, in some cases, be one and the same thing. If it is shown that the object pursued by the conduct of an undertaking in a dominant position is to restrict competition, that conduct will also be liable to have such an effect.* [...] *Furthermore, it should be added that, where an undertaking in a dominant position actually implements a practice whose object is to oust a competitor, the fact that the result hoped for is not achieved is not sufficient to prevent that being an abuse of a dominant position within the meaning of Article 82 EC (Compagnie maritime belge transports and Others v Commission, paragraph 104 above, paragraph 149, and Case T-228/97 Irish Sugar v Commission [1999] ECR II-2969, paragraph 191)*".[141]

3.99   Advocate General Ruiz-Jarabo Colomer seemed to endorse a more effects-based approach in his Opinion in the *GlaxoSmithKline* case[142] noting that "[a]*llowing preconceived and formalistic ideas on abuse of a dominant position to prevail would mask the fact that sometimes dominance can benefit consumers*" and that "*a defence of the dominant company based on economic results obtained might be advocated*".[143]

---

[139] *Microsoft Judgment 2007 supra* note 25, para. 664.

[140] Case T-340/03 *France Télécom v Commission* [2007] ECR II-107.

[141] *Ibid.*, para. 195–6.

[142] Advocate General Ruiz-Jarabo Colomer in Joined Case C-468 to 478/06 *Sot. Lélos kai Sia and others v GlaxoSmithKline* [2008] ECR I-07139.

[143] *Ibid.*, paras 73–4.

3. – The Concept of Abuse
Francisco Enrique González-Díaz and John Temple Lang

Moreover, in his conclusions the Advocate General proposed to move away from a formalistic *per se* rule in abuse cases, even when the circumstances of the case show that the dominant company's conduct had some anticompetitive effect. The Court of Justice did not follow the Advocate General's plea to endorse a more "effects-based" approach and analysed the conduct following the traditional scheme.

In a number of relatively recent judgments the European Courts seem to have followed this traditional approach, and did not follow the effects-based approach suggested in the *Guidance Paper*. **3.100**

In *AstraZeneca*, the General Court was faced with two new types of abuse arising from an alleged abusive misuse of regulatory provisions and procedures. According to the Commission's findings, AstraZeneca had abused its dominant position by illegitimately taking advantage of the patent system and marketing procedures for pharmaceutical products with the aim of excluding generic drugs producers from the market and avoiding parallel imports. The Court stated that an abuse may be identified where the relevant conduct is liable to restrict competition, and that **3.101**

> "[i]*n a situation such as that of the present case, where the practices in question – if they are established – cannot, in any way, be regarded as being covered by normal competition between products on the basis of an undertaking's performance, it is sufficient for it to be established that, in view of the economic or regulatory context of which those practices form part, they are capable of restricting competition. Thus, the ability of the practice in question to restrict competition may be indirect, provided that it is shown to the requisite legal standard that it is actually liable to restrict competition*".[144]

In the *Tomra* judgment the General Court repeated the same reasoning, stressing that **3.102**

> "*for the purposes of establishing an infringement of Article 82 EC, it is not necessary to show that the abuse under consideration had an actual impact on the relevant markets. It is sufficient in that respect to show that the abusive conduct*

---

[144] Case T-321/05 *AstraZeneca v. Commission* [2010] ECR II-2805, para. 376.

3. – The Concept of Abuse
Francisco Enrique González-Díaz and John Temple Lang

of the undertaking in a dominant position tends to restrict competition or, in other words, that the conduct is capable of having that effect".[145]

3.103 Tomra was held to have put in place an exclusionary strategy to prevent the entry or expansion of other market players, including supply agreements providing for exclusivity and individualised, retroactive rebates. Tomra argued that since the relevant agreements only covered 39 per cent of total demand, there was still a contestable part of the market sufficient to allow the entry or expansion of a number of competitors. The Court rejected this argument by affirming that "*the customers on the foreclosed part of the market should have the opportunity to benefit from whatever degree of competition is possible on the market and competitors should be able to compete on the merits for the entire market and not just for a part of it*".[146]

3.4.2.   The Recent Shift towards a More Effects-Based Approach

3.104 In some recent judgments, the European courts appear to have shown a willingness to advance in the direction of a more effects-based approach.

3.105 This can be traced back to the judgment rendered by the Court of Justice in the *Deutsche Telekom* case,[147] in relation to a margin squeeze. In its judgment the Court stated that, when a dominant undertaking squeezes the margins of its equally efficient competitors having a clearly exclusionary aim, the fact that the result is not achieved does not alter its categorisation as an abuse within the meaning of Article 102 TFEU.

3.106 However, the Court also held that "*in the absence of any effect on the competitive situation of competitors, a pricing practice such as that at issue cannot be classified as exclusionary if it does not make their market penetration any more difficult*".[148]

3.107 The Court noted that: "*a pricing practice* [...] *constitutes an abuse within the meaning of Article 82 EC if it has an exclusionary effect on competitors who are at least* <u>*as efficient as the*</u> *dominant undertaking itself by squeezing their margins and is capable of making market entry more difficult or impossible for those competitors, and thus of strengthening its dominant position on that market to the detriment of consumers' interests*".[149]

---

[145] Case T-155/06 Tomra Systems and others v. Commission ("*Tomra Judgment 2010*") [2010] ECR II-4361, para. 289.

[146] *Ibid.*, para. 241.

[147] *See Deutsche Telekom Judgment 2010 supra* note 26.

[148] *Ibid.*, para. 254.

[149] *Deutsche Telekom Judgment 2010 supra* note 26, para. 253.

3. – The Concept of Abuse
Francisco Enrique González-Díaz and John Temple Lang

Similarly, in *TeliaSonera*,[150] another margin squeeze case, the Court noted, refer- **3.108**
ring to its judgment in *Deutsche Telekom* that "*the Court has ruled out the possibility that the very existence of a pricing practice of a dominant undertaking which leads to the margin squeeze of its equally efficient competitors can constitute an abuse within the meaning of Article 102 TFEU without it being necessary to demonstrate an anti-competitive effect*".[151]

The Court held that although for an abuse to constitute a breach of Article 102 **3.109**
TFEU the conduct must give rise to anticompetitive effects, "*the effect does not necessarily have to be concrete, and it is sufficient to demonstrate that there is an anti-competitive effect which may potentially exclude competitors who are at least as efficient as the dominant undertaking*".[152] The Court seemed to hold that although proving actual/potential anticompetitive effects is essential to consider that conduct is abusive in certain situations (*i.e.,* when the wholesale product is indispensable and when the margin is negative) there may be a rebuttable presumption of anticompetitive effects from a margin squeeze.[153]

Furthermore in *TeliaSonera*, the Court referred to the "as-efficient competitor" **3.110**
test.[154] The potential effect of the conduct on consumer welfare was only considered when referring to the possibility of justifying such conduct on efficiency grounds.[155]

Danish Post[156] involved a preliminary reference concerning the compatibility **3.111**
of selective price reductions with Article 102 TFEU. The Court again referred to the "as-efficient competitor" test[157] and stated that selective price reductions are not exclusionary merely because the price charged to some customers is lower than the average total cost. Rather, the Court emphasised that "*in order to assess the existence of anti-competitive effects* […] *it is necessary to consider whether that pricing policy, without objective justification, produces an actual or likely exclusionary effect, to the detriment of competition and, thereby, of consumers' interests*".[158]

---

[150] *See TeliaSonera Judgment 2011 supra* note 26.
[151] *Ibid.,* para. 61.
[152] *Ibid.,* para. 64.
[153] *Ibid.,* para. 70 *et seq.*
[154] *Ibid.,* paras 63, 64 and 67.
[155] *Ibid.,* para. 76.
[156] Case C-209/10 *Post Danmark A/S v Konkurrenceradet* ("*Danish Post*"), not yet reported.
[157] *Ibid.,* para. 25.
[158] *Ibid.,* para. 44.

3. – The Concept of Abuse
Francisco Enrique González-Díaz and John Temple Lang

3.112 However, in *Telefónica* the General Court, while confirming the need to establish actual or potential/probable effects,[159] seemed to set a very low standard of proof on the Commission to show probable effects and conversely, a very high standard of proof on the applicant to refute.[160]

3.113 The General Court considered that the Commission had correctly *inferred* from the existence of the margin squeeze and its likely consequences that it was probable that Telefónica's conduct limited the ability of DSL operators to grow sustainably in the downstream market and that its conduct probably harmed consumers.[161]

3.114 When Telefónica argued that these conclusions were not corroborated by any concrete showing of effects, the Court merely stated that *"the Commission did not incur in a manifest error of assessment when concluding that it was probable that Telefónica's conduct strengthened the barriers to entry and expansion in the market and if the resulting distortions had not existed, competition would have been more intense in the downstream market, which would have benefit consumers in terms of price, choice and innovation"*.[162]

3.115 Despite what may be seen as a shift in focus towards a more effects-based approach,[163] recent General Court cases confirm that the Commission can still rely on probable effects even in cases where the conduct has continued for a long time and where a test of concrete effects could have been used to validate the often questioned methodologies used by the Commission in pricing cases.

IV. Objective Justification and Efficiencies

3.116 According to well-established case law, *"it is open to a dominant undertaking to provide justification for behaviour that is liable to be caught by the prohibition under*

---

[159] *See supra* note 127, para. 268.

[160] In this judgment the General Court upheld the Commission's decision finding that the Spanish incumbent telecommunications provider had engaged in abusive margin squeeze. *See Ibid.*

[161] *Ibid.*, paras 274 *et seq.*

[162] *Ibid.*, para. 276.

[163] A. Ezrachi, "The Commission's Guidance on Article 82", in A. Ezrachi (Ed.) *Article 82, Reflection on its Recent Evolution* (Oxford, Hart Publishing, 2009), p. 59.

3. – The Concept of Abuse
Francisco Enrique González-Díaz and John Temple Lang

Article 82 EC".[164] Such justification may be based either on legitimate public interest objectives,[165] or on efficiency claims.[166]

The Commission has also acknowledged this possibility in section III.D of **3.117** the *Guidance Paper*, entitled *"Objective necessity and efficiencies".*[167] The Commission states that in the enforcement of Article 102, it will also examine claims put forward by a dominant undertaking that its conduct is justified. A dominant undertaking may do so either by demonstrating that its conduct is objectively necessary or by demonstrating that it produces substantial efficiencies which outweigh any anti-competitive effects on consumers. In this context, the Commission will assess whether the conduct in question is indispensable and proportionate to the goal allegedly pursued by the dominant undertaking.

The question whether conduct is objectively necessary and proportionate **3.118** must, according to the Commission, be determined on the basis of factors external to the dominant undertaking. Exclusionary conduct may, for example, be considered objectively necessary for health or safety reasons related to the nature of the product in question. However, the Commission is of the view that proof of whether conduct of this kind is objectively necessary must take into account that it is normally the task of public authorities to set and enforce public health and safety standards. Indeed, it is not the task of a dominant undertaking to take steps on its own initiative to exclude products which it regards, rightly or wrongly, as dangerous or inferior to its own product.[168]

The Commission considers that a dominant undertaking may also justify con- **3.119** duct leading to foreclosure of competitors on the ground of efficiencies that are sufficient to guarantee that no net harm to consumers is likely to arise. In this context, the dominant undertaking is expected to demonstrate, with a

---

[164] *See supra* note 156, para 40; *See also* Case 27/76 *supra* note 6, para 184; Case 311/84 *supra* note 74, para 27; Case T-30/89 *Hilti* v *Commission* [1991] ECR II-1439, paras 102–19; Case T-83/91 *supra* note 122, paras 136 and 207; Joined Cases C-241 and 242/91 *supra* note 74, paras 54 and 55; Case C-95/04 P *British Airways v Commission* [2007] ECR I-2331, para 69; Case C-202/07 P *supra* note 80, para. 111; Case C-52/09 *supra* note 26, paras 31 and 75.

[165] *See* Case C-52/07 *supra* note 133, para. 47 (*"Such* [objective] *justification may arise, in particular, from the task and method of financing of public service undertakings"*).

[166] *See* Case C-52/09 *supra* note 26, para 76 (*"it has to be determined whether the exclusionary effect arising from such a practice, which is disadvantageous for competition, may be counterbalanced, or outweighed, by advantages in terms of efficiency which also benefit the consumer"*).

[167] *See Guidance Paper*, Section III.D (paras 28–31).

[168] *See, for instance*, Case T-30/89 *supra* note 164, paras 118–9; Case T-83/91 *supra* note 122, paras 83, 84 and 138.

3. – The Concept of Abuse
Francisco Enrique González-Díaz and John Temple Lang

sufficient degree of probability, and on the basis of verifiable evidence, that the following cumulative conditions are fulfilled:[169]

- The efficiencies have been, or are likely to be, realised as a result of the conduct. They may, for example, include technical improvements in the quality of goods, or a reduction in the cost of production or distribution,
- The conduct is indispensable to the realisation of those efficiencies: there must be no less anti-competitive alternatives to the conduct that are capable of producing the same efficiencies,
- The likely efficiencies brought about by the conduct outweigh any likely negative effects on competition and consumer welfare in the affected markets,
- The conduct does not eliminate effective competition, by removing all or most existing sources of actual or potential competition.

3.120   The Commission considers that rivalry between undertakings is an essential driver of economic efficiency, including dynamic efficiencies in the form of innovation. In its absence the dominant undertaking would lack adequate incentives to continue to create and pass on efficiency gains. Where there is no residual competition and no foreseeable threat of entry the Commission is of the view that the protection of rivalry and the competitive process outweighs possible efficiency gains. The Commission also takes the view that exclusionary conduct which maintains, creates or strengthens a market position approaching that of a monopoly can normally not be justified on the grounds that it also creates efficiency gains.

3.121   As to the allocation of the burden of proof, the Commission considers that it is incumbent upon the dominant undertaking to provide all the evidence necessary to demonstrate that the conduct concerned is objectively justified. It then falls to the Commission to make the ultimate assessment of whether the conduct concerned is not objectively necessary and, based on a weighing-up of any apparent anti-competitive effects against any advanced and substantiated efficiencies, is likely to result in consumer harm."

3.122   The concrete application of these justifications shall be discussed in the following chapters, by reference to the specific forms of abuse.

---

[169] *See also*, in the context of Article 81, Commission Notice – Guidelines on the application of Article 81(3) of the Treaty, OJ 2004 C 101/97.

4. – Predatory Conduct
Robbert Snelders, Andrew Leyden and Andrea Lofaro

Predatory Conduct

*Robbert Snelders, Andrew Leyden and Andrea Lofaro**

I.   Introduction

Price competition is the *"central nervous system of the economy"*.[1] The basic goal **4.1**
of antitrust law is to encourage vigorous price competition, creating incentives for firms to maximise output and to set prices as close as possible to
their marginal cost of production. This goal applies with equal (if not greater)
force to dominant firms.[2] Despite this strong policy in favour of low prices,
some forms of price competition are deemed to be abusive under Article 102
TFEU. This chapter concerns the abuse of predatory pricing, whereby a dominant firm offers low prices in the short-term in order to foreclose rivals from
the market, with a view to gaining the ability to charge higher prices in the
long term.

1.   The Notion of Predation

Predation is typically understood as a two-step process. In the first phase (the **4.2**
"sacrifice" phase) the dominant firm reduces its prices below an appropriate
measure of costs, to a level that does not allow its rivals to remain profitably

* The authors wish to thank Stephen Lewis (RBB Economics) for his substantial contribution to this chapter.

[1] *Broadcast Music v Columbia Broadcasting System*, 441 US 1 (1979), para. 23.
[2] *See* Advocate General Fennelly in Joined Cases C-395 and 396/96 P *Compagnie maritime belge transports and others v Commission* [2000] ECR I-1365, paras 117 and 132. *See also*, Cases IV/30.787 and IV/31.488 *Eurofix-Bauco/Hilti*, Commission Decision of 22 December 1987, OJ 1988 L 65/19, where the Commission emphasised that *"aggres-sive price rivalry is an essential competitive instrument"*. Similarly, the Commission stated in *AKZO* that *"a dominant firm is entitled to compete on the merits"* and rejected the notion that *"larger producers should be under an obligation to refrain from competing vigorously with smaller competitors or new entrants"*. *See* Case IV/30.698 *ECS/AKZO*, Commission Decision of 14 December 1985, OJ 1985 L 374/1. *See also* Cases IV/32.448 and IV/32.450 *Cewal*, Commission Decision of 23 December 1992, OJ 1993 L 34/20, upheld on appeal in Joined Cases T-24 to 26 and 28/93 *Compagnie Maritime Belge Transports and others v Commission* [1996] ECR II-1201.

4. – Predatory Conduct
Robbert Snelders, Andrew Leyden and Andrea Lofaro

in the market.[3] In the second phase (the "foreclosure" phase) the dominant firm benefits from its sacrifice.[4] So the theory goes, the dominant firm might benefit from predatory pricing by preventing new entry, causing existing competitors to exit the market, or deterring them from expanding their capacity, leaving the dominant firm free to charge higher prices than it would otherwise be able to. Even if the dominant firm cannot recoup its sacrifice through post-predation price increases, it might nevertheless benefit in the long term, notably by creating a "predatory reputation", insulating itself from the threat of future entry in markets in which it is active.

4.3   Most commentators agree that predatory pricing is rare in practice.[5] The challenge is to identify those unusual situations in which low prices and higher output are damaging to consumer welfare. As the US Supreme Court observed, *"mistaken inferences in [predatory pricing cases] are especially costly, because they chill the very conduct the antitrust laws are designed to protect"*.[6] The legal response to predation must therefore balance the need to deter predatory behaviour against the risk of deterring legitimate price competition.

4.4   True predatory conduct is notoriously difficult to identify. Given this uncertainty, most commentators agree that where there is doubt, the law ought to err on the side of caution.[7] Even if some cases of predatory pricing are not caught by a permissive rule, low prices at least produce tangible consumer benefit in the short term. An overly stringent rule, on the other hand, could have a significant chilling effect on legitimate pricing behaviour in exchange for uncertain future benefits. As Justice Breyer held in *Barry Wright*, *"the antitrust laws very rarely reject such beneficial 'birds in hand' for the sake of more speculative*

---

[3] *"Sacrifice"* and *"foreclosure"* are the terms used by the Commission in its *Guidance Paper*. *See* Guidance on the Commission's enforcement priorities in applying Article 82 of the EC Treaty to abusive exclusionary conduct by dominant undertakings (*"Guidance Paper"*), OJ 2009 C 45/7, para. 63. *See also* discussion of the *Guidance Paper* in Section III.6.1 below.

[4] Note, however, that proof of recoupment of losses incurred during the sacrifice phase is not a legal requirement for a finding of predatory pricing under Article 102 TFEU. *See* discussion of recoupment in Section IV.4, below.

[5] *See, e.g.*, D. Crane, "The Paradox of Predatory Pricing" (2005) 91(1) *Cornell Law Review*, pp. 1–66; F. H. Easterbrook, "Predatory Strategies and Counterstrategies" (1981) 48 *University of Chicago Law* Review, p. 264. The Commission has also recognised that predation is *"to a certain extent self-deterring"*. *See* DG Competition discussion paper on the application of Article 82 of the Treaty to exclusionary abuses (*"Discussion Paper"*), December 2005, para. 97.

[6] *Matsushita Electric Industrial v Zenith Radio*, 475 US 574 (1986).

[7] *See* D. Crane, *supra* note 5, pp. 7–8.

4. – Predatory Conduct
Robbert Snelders, Andrew Leyden and Andrea Lofaro

'birds in the bush'".[8] Moreover, the rules chosen must be sufficiently clear to allow dominant firms to assess the legality of their conduct. Even if a given rule is the best in theory, it might not be workable in practice, due to its complexity or the lack of perfect information.

2. Cost Rules and Objective Justifications

The law in the European Union (and most major jurisdictions) uses cost **4.5** benchmarks to determine whether given pricing conduct is predatory.[9] Such rules are premised on the basic assumption that firms are rational and seek to maximise their profits. If revenues do not exceed an appropriate measure of costs, then the firm is making losses that *prima facie* can only be explained as part of a predatory strategy.[10] There is broad consensus as to the usefulness of such rules (although the correct measure of costs will depend greatly on the specificities of the industry at hand). More controversially, however, the EU law concept of predation has in the past been stretched to include above-cost price cuts designed to exclude rivals.[11] Prohibiting such conduct runs the risk that the law will facilitate the entry of less-efficient rivals, to the ultimate detriment of productive efficiency and consumer welfare.

There is also broad recognition that in some circumstances a firm might **4.6** decide to price below cost based on legitimate considerations, such as the need to get rid of excess stock, build up a viable user base for a new technology, promote a new product, or to match an offer made by a rival. The application of strict cost-based rules would condemn such rational commercial behaviour as predatory, placing dominant undertakings at a competitive disadvantage. A safety valve in the form of "objective justifications" should therefore be allowed, provided that the company's below-cost prices are proportionate to legitimate ends.[12]

---

[8] *Barry Wright v ITT Grinnel*, 724 F.2d 227 (1st Cir. 1983).

[9] Case C-62/86 *AKZO Chemie v Commission* ("*AKZO*") [1991] ECR I-3359. *See* discussion of the basic rules of predatory pricing in Section IV below.

[10] P. Areeda and D.F. Turner, "Predatory Pricing and Related Practices Under Section 2 of the Sherman Act" 88(4) *The Harvard Law Review Association*, pp. 697–733. *See* discussion of the basic rules on predatory pricing in Section IV below.

[11] *See* discussion on above-cost predation in Section IV.6 below.

[12] *See* discussion of objective justifications in Section V below.

4. – Predatory Conduct
Robbert Snelders, Andrew Leyden and Andrea Lofaro

3. Predatory Pricing and Other Abuses

4.7 Predatory pricing analysis, and in particular the use of cost benchmarks to assess a dominant company's conduct, cuts across other exclusionary practices, notably margin squeeze, exclusive dealing, mixed bundling, and price discrimination.

3.1. Margin Squeeze

4.8 A margin squeeze occurs where a vertically integrated firm (1) increases the upstream price it charges to a downstream competitor, and/or (2) reduces its own downstream price, such that the downstream competitor cannot achieve a profitable margin and is forced to exit the market.[13] Although margin squeeze is a distinct abuse under Article 102 TFEU, the relevant legal test (whether the dominant firm's downstream business would be profitable if it faced the same input prices as it sets for third parties) amounts to a test of downstream predatory pricing in the context of a vertically integrated firm. On the other hand, it should be noted that in a margin squeeze case the dominant company is not necessarily losing money overall. It might simply be transferring its profit upstream throughout the period of the abuse.

3.2. Exclusive Dealing

4.9 In its *Guidance Paper*,[14] the Commission proposes to use predatory pricing cost benchmarks in its approach to conditional rebate schemes. The Commission is of the view that where the "effective price" offered by a dominant firm (*i.e.*, the non-discounted price less the rebate a customer will lose by switching suppliers) is below a relevant measure of costs, as a general rule the rebate scheme is capable of foreclosing equally efficient competitors.[15]

3.3. Mixed Bundling

4.10 There is also broad recognition that in some circumstances a firm might decide to price below cost based on legitimate considerations, such as the need to get rid of excess stock, build up a viable user base for a new technology, promote a new product, or to match an offer made by a rival. The

---

[13] *See Guidance Paper supra* note 3, para. 80. *See also* discussion of the relevant test for margin squeeze at Chapter 5, Section II.

[14] *Ibid.*

[15] *Ibid.*, paras 37–45. *See also* discussion of mixed bundling at Chapter 8 Section III.

4. – Predatory Conduct
Robbert Snelders, Andrew Leyden and Andrea Lofaro

application of strict cost-based rules would condemn such rational commercial behaviour as predatory, placing dominant undertakings at a competitive disadvantage. A safety valve in the form of "objective justifications" should therefore be allowed, provided that the company's below-cost prices are proportionate to legitimate ends.[16]

Mixed bundling occurs where a customer can acquire two products separately, but the dominant firm sets a lower price where the two are purchased together. This runs the risk of excluding competitors who only sell one of the products in question.[17] Many authors argue that the appropriate test for exclusionary mixed bundling is whether the price charged for the allegedly tied component is predatory, *i.e.*, is below an appropriate measure of costs.[18]   **4.11**

3.4. *Price Discrimination*

Many instances of alleged "predatory" conduct involve selective price cuts by a dominant company for customers targeted by competitors. Such strategies are often designed to foreclose new entrants by preventing them from gaining traction in the market. Strategies of this type could therefore be analysed either as a form of predation or a form of primary-line price discrimination.   **4.12**

Although these are distinct abuses, the principles of predatory pricing arguably underpin them all. The use of predatory pricing benchmarks has at least two advantages: (1) there is a relatively rich body of precedent interpreting predatory pricing rules, and (2) cost benchmarks provide useful safe harbours for firms wishing to engage in, *e.g.*, exclusive dealing or mixed bundling for legitimate business reasons.   **4.13**

II.   The Economic Theory of Predation

The concept of predation has existed in antitrust law for over a century. Despite its vintage, the theoretical underpinnings of predatory pricing have   **4.14**

---

[16] *See* discussion of objective justifications in Section V below.

[17] *See* discussion of tying and bundling at Chapter 8, para 8.5.

[18] *See* R. O'Donoghue and A. J. Padilla, *The Law and Economics of Article 82 EC* (Oxford, Hart Publishing, 2006), p. 507.

4. – Predatory Conduct
Robbert Snelders, Andrew Leyden and Andrea Lofaro

remained a constant source of controversy.[19] It is only relatively recently that robust theories explaining why a firm might have an incentive to predate have been formalised by economists using the tools of game theory. Before the emergence of these models, there was no convincing economic theory that explained how a firm could profitably engage in predation.

4.15   Traditional arguments for the prohibition of predatory pricing centred on the idea that the predator might have access to greater financial resources than the prey (which might be a small firm or new entrant) and would therefore be able to sustain losses for a longer time period. By charging a high price after the prey's exit from the market, the dominant firm could then recoup its lost profit. While this "deep-pockets" story has a certain intuitive appeal, it is far from satisfactory as a theory of antitrust harm,[20] since it relies on the questionable assumption that the predator has access to greater financial resources than the prey.[21] No dominant firm would even attempt such a strategy against an equally efficient rival with access to equal financial resources. The Chicago School demonstrated that the traditional view of predation provides no sound reasons why entrants should be assumed to lack access to such resources.[22] In particular, even if an equally efficient producer does not have its own financial resources, capital markets would supply the funds necessary to maintain an efficient producer in business.[23]

4.16   The Chicago School critique and the debates that followed focussed attention on the issues that need to be addressed by any coherent economic theory of predation. Post-Chicago theorists used game theory to show that, in the

---

[19] As Easterbrook observed, it is unclear whether there are so many predation theories because it is *"a common but variegated phenomenon"* or rather *"for the same reason that 600 years ago there were a thousand positions on what dragons looked like"*. F. H. Easterbrook, *supra* note 5, pp. 263–337.

[20] J. S. McGee, "Predatory Price Cutting: The Standard Oil (N.J.) Case" (1985) 1 *Journal of Law and Economics*, pp. 137–69.

[21] Other less damaging elements of the critique included the observation that the costs to the larger firm resulting from predation should be greater than those to the smaller firm because of its larger output base; the observation that the small firm could re-enter once the price rise had taken place; and the observation that the large firm could eliminate its rival in a less costly way simply by acquiring it. These challenges were subsequently largely addressed by those pointing out that the large firm could reduce prices selectively so as not to incur costs over its entire output base; that entry and re-entry might not be possible as a result of sunk costs; and that predation could form part of a strategy to reduce the acquisition price of a rival.

[22] *See* R. H. Bork, *The Antitrust Paradox: A Policy at War with Itself* (New York, Basic Books, 1978), and F. H. Easterbrook, *supra* note 5, pp. 263–337.

[23] Even in the event that the prey leaves the market, predation would still bear no fruit for the dominant company, because once prices are raised following market exit, the prey's plant will be re-opened either by the previously-expelled rival or a new entrant.

4. – Predatory Conduct
Robbert Snelders, Andrew Leyden and Andrea Lofaro

presence of imperfect information, predation might be profitable provided that certain assumptions hold true. The Commission makes explicit reference to the following three types of models in its *Guidance Paper*: (1) financial market models; (2) signalling models; and (3) reputation models.[24]

1. Financial Market Models

Following the Chicago critique, game theorists refined the basic "deep-pockets" model to explain how predatory conduct might indeed impose financial constraints on the dominant company's rivals due to information asymmetries in capital markets.[25] If financial institutions have imperfect information, predatory behaviour might increase the perceived risk of lending money to the prey. In this model it is assumed that financial institutions are unable to observe how a firm uses the funds they make available. To protect themselves, they therefore only provide credit to firms with a certain minimum asset base. By predating, the dominant firm can reduce the prey's profits, erode its assets, and therefore reduce its ability to borrow. Since financial institutions cannot observe the managers' actions, they cannot be sure whether profits are low because management is inefficient or because of predatory conduct. If they knew management were efficient, they could prevent predation by announcing that they will continue to make funds available to the prey despite the predator's attempt to exclude them from the market.[26] In the absence of such knowledge, a dominant firm can use predatory pricing to manipulate the willingness of financial institutions to lend to its equally efficient rivals.

4.17

---

[24] *See Guidance Paper supra* note 3, para. 68.

[25] *See* L.G. Telser, "Cutthroat Competition and the Long Purse" (1966) 9 *Journal of Law and Economics*, pp. 259–77. *See also*, J.P. Benoit, "Financially Constrained Entry in a Game with Incomplete Information" (1984) 15(4) *The RAND Journal of Economics*, pp. 490–99; P. Bolton and D. Scharfstein, "Long-Term Financial Contracts and the Theory of Predation", (1987) *Mimeo, Harvard University. See also* D. Fudenberg and J. Tirole, "A "Signal-Jamming" Theory of Predation" (1986) 17(3) *The RAND Journal of Economics*, pp. 366–76.

[26] A related argument emphasises the "*moral hazard*" inherent in open-ended commitments by financial institutions to finance a firm indefinitely. Banks are unwilling to make such commitments to new entrants (even when they face predation) as it reduces their incentives to compete as hard as possible. *See* M. Motta, *Competition Policy: Theory and Practice* (Cambridge, Cambridge University Press, 2004), p. 421.

4. – Predatory Conduct
Robbert Snelders, Andrew Leyden and Andrea Lofaro

2. Signalling Models

4.18   Signalling models of predation are based on the idea that firms do not have knowledge of each other's costs.[27] A dominant firm might therefore have an incentive to 'signal' its costs to rivals through prices. If the incumbent charges low prices that do not maximise its profits in the short run, potential entrants might interpret this as a signal that the incumbent has low costs. As a result, the potential entrant would conclude that the incumbent is able to compete fiercely in case of entry and would consequently refrain from entering altogether. The incumbent knows this and hence, under certain circumstances, might find it profitable to sacrifice short-run profits in order to deter entry by influencing the entrant's beliefs about the strength of post-entry competition.

4.19   This model assumes that the incumbent could be one of two types: strong (if its costs are low) and weak (if its costs are high). The incumbent knows whether it is a strong type or weak type. The entrant, on the other hand, does not know the incumbent's costs, but can observe prices charged by the incumbent before deciding whether to enter the market. The entrant would prefer to enter if it knew the incumbent were weak, but would rather stay out if it knew the incumbent were strong.

4.20   In the second scenario, predation of a very different nature takes place. The weak incumbent finds it profitable to set a price below its short-run profit maximising level that is equal to the price a strong incumbent would have chosen if it were profit maximising. As such, the weak incumbent mimics a strong incumbent. The price the potential entrant observes in the market conveys no information about the costs of the incumbent, and the entrant must therefore rely on some prior belief about whether the incumbent is strong or weak. If the entrant believes that the incumbent is in fact strong, the incumbent can successfully deter entry that would otherwise have taken place.[28] To the extent that the gains to consumers from the lower initial price (which the

---

[27] P. Milgrom and J. Roberts, "Limit Pricing and Entry Under Incomplete Information: An Equilibrium Analysis" (1982) 50(2) *Econometrica*, pp. 443–59. Robert and Scharfstein later extended the theory to cover post-entry predation. *See* J. Roberts, "A Signalling Model of Predatory Pricing" (1986) 38 *Oxford Economic Papers* (supp), pp. 75–93, and D. Scharfstein, "A Policy to Prevent Rational Test-Market Predation" (184) 2 *The Rand Journal of Economics*, pp. 229–43.

[28] Given that the price charged is that which maximises the profits of a strong incumbent, the strong type would have also chosen a price that deters entry. However, this would not have been predatory pricing since it is the efficiency of the incumbent that makes entry unattractive.

4. – Predatory Conduct
Robbert Snelders, Andrew Leyden and Andrea Lofaro

weak incumbent had to charge to hide its high costs) do not outweigh the losses to consumers from the subsequent elimination of competition, then this type of predation can lead to competitive harm.

3. Reputation Models

Reputation models are based on the notion that firms might decide to predate in order to establish a reputation for being "tough" or aggressive in the face of new entrants.[29] Despite the fact that building such a reputation would be costly in the short term, it might eventually pay off, especially where it deters new entry across a large number of markets.

4.21

Reputation models typically apply in a situation in which the incumbent has to defend a number of similar markets from a series of entries. The classic example is that of an incumbent with a chain of stores in several different cities, with one potential entrant in each.[30] As in the signalling model, entrants must decide whether to enter each of the incumbent's markets in turn. If entry occurs, the incumbent will decide either to "fight" (charge a low price that forces exit) or "accommodate" (charge a higher price that allows the entrant to remain in the market). If an incumbent has low costs, it will always find it profitable to fight entry. However, this is not anticompetitive predation, but rather a case of market entry being unattractive as a result of the incumbent's efficiency. On the other hand, if an incumbent has high costs, in the short run it would be more profitable to accommodate the new entrant. Fighting is a rational strategy only if it would deter future entry.

4.22

The key question is therefore whether a weak incumbent can deter future entry by choosing to fight. If potential entrants know whether the incumbent is strong or weak, any such attempts will be futile. In the simplest case, where there are two markets and two potential entrants, it is clear that regardless of whether the weak incumbent chooses to fight the first attempt at entry, it will not choose to fight the second (as there is no future entry to deter). Knowing that it cannot deter entry in the second market, the weak incumbent will have

4.23

---

[29] D. Kreps and R. Wilson, "Reputation and Imperfect Information" (1982) 27 *Journal of Economic Theory*, pp. 253–79. *See also* P. Milgrom and J. Roberts, "Predation, Reputation and Entry Deterrence" (1982) 27 *Journal of Economic Theory*, pp. 280–312.

[30] This example is originally due to Nobel Prize laureate in economics Reinhard Selten, who called it "*the chain–store paradox*" (R. Selten, "The Chain-Store Paradox" (1987) 9 *Theory and Decision*, pp. 127–59).

4. – Predatory Conduct
Robbert Snelders, Andrew Leyden and Andrea Lofaro

no incentive to fight in the first market. The same logic applies in more complicated cases where there are a large (but finite) number of markets.[31] There will be no incentive to fight in the last market, and so no incentive to fight in the second last, and so on.

4.24 Suppose, however, that potential entrants cannot be sure whether an incumbent is strong or weak. In these circumstances a weak incumbent would find it profitable to fight an initial attempt at entry in order to establish a reputation for being strong, and so deter entry in the remaining markets.[32] Potential entrants decide whether an incumbent is strong or weak on the basis of its reaction to past entry. A weak incumbent must consider the trade-off between sacrificing present profits to invest in its reputation (fighting) and sacrificing its reputation to maintain its present profits (accommodating). The key insight this model brings is that where the incumbent is dominant across a large number of markets, even minor uncertainty as to the incumbent's strength can make an initially costly investment in reputation pay off in the long run. A strong reputation will allow the incumbent to recoup its losses by charging monopoly prices across multiple markets without any threat of entry.

4. Concluding Remarks

4.25 The Chicago School made an important contribution to the economic theory of predation by exposing the weak points in the traditional view. Post-Chicago theorists have contributed three key insights. First, predatory pricing can manipulate financial markets by reducing the willingness to banks to lend to a challenger. Secondly, a significant factor in predation is what the entrant expects the incumbent will do following entry. Where information is incomplete, predation can be used to influence the likelihood of new entry by sending false signals as to the incumbent's cost structures, or creating a reputation for cutthroat behaviour. Finally, where the incumbent is active across a range of markets, an "investment" in predatory conduct in one market can be recovered over time across various markets.

4.26 Provided certain assumptions hold true, these models demonstrate that predation can be a profitable strategy in theory. However, this does not mean

---

[31] The logic cannot be applied if there are infinitely many markets in which entry could take place as there is no "final" market in which accommodation is certain to be preferred.
[32] D. Kreps and R. Wilson, *supra* note 29, pp. 253–79.

4. – Predatory Conduct
Robbert Snelders, Andrew Leyden and Andrea Lofaro

that predation is likely to be a common phenomenon in practice. As the Commission recognises, predation is an inherently risky strategy for a firm (given that its immediate impact is a reduction in short term profits) and is therefore *"to a certain extent self-deterring"*.[33] Any economic framework aimed at assessing allegations of predatory pricing must therefore set a high threshold for intervention or risk chilling legitimate price competition.

III.   Cost Benchmarks

The principles set out in the *Guidance Paper* are based on the premise that, in general, only conduct that would exclude a hypothetical "as efficient" competitor is abusive.[34] By definition, such a competitor has the same costs as the dominant company, and thus can be foreclosed only if the dominant company prices below its own costs. In order to apply this test, it is first necessary to determine an appropriate measure of costs to use as a benchmark. The candidates for the relevant cost measure in predatory pricing cases include:

4.27

- Marginal Cost ("MC");
- Average Variable Costs ("AVC");
- Average Avoidable Costs ("AAC");
- Long-Run Average Incremental Costs ("LRAIC"); and
- Average Total Cost ("ATC").

This section provides a description of each of these cost measures with reference to the example of a hypothetical dominant company, called Domco, which enjoys a market share of 95 per cent. Domco's business comprises a large factory and its costs consist of two elements. First, Domco must make repayments on a loan it took out to finance the construction of the factory. This repayment amounts to €100 per annum for the 20-year life of the loan (which is also the life of the factory) and does not vary according to the level of the factory's output. Secondly, Domco incurs costs for each unit of output it produces. Specifically, it costs Domco €5 to produce each of the first

4.28

---

[33] *See Discussion Paper supra* note 5, para. 97. The *Guidance Paper* is unfortunately not as explicit in emphasising the intrinsically costly nature of predation. *See Guidance Paper supra* note 3.
[34] *Ibid.*, para. 67.

4. – Predatory Conduct

Robbert Snelders, Andrew Leyden and Andrea Lofaro

100 units of output and €7 to produce each unit beyond the first 100 in any given year.[35]

1. Marginal Cost ("MC")

4.29 Marginal cost is the cost of producing the last unit of output. From the point of view of economic theory, a firm's marginal costs play a central role in determining its price and output. A firm that is maximising its profits in the short run will set its output level such that its marginal cost (the change in costs resulting from the production of the last unit of output) equals its marginal revenue (the change in revenues resulting from the sale of the last unit of output). If a firm's marginal revenue is greater than its marginal cost it can increase profits by producing and selling an extra unit of output. Conversely, if a firm's marginal cost is greater than its marginal revenue, it can increase profit by ceasing to produce and sell the last unit of output.

4.30 In the case of Domco, marginal cost depends on the level of output. If Domco's output is between 0 and 100 units, its marginal cost is €5, *i.e.*, as long as Domco is producing fewer than 100 units, the extra cost incurred by producing one extra unit is €5. However, if Domco produces 100 units or more, its marginal cost is €7. The extra cost incurred by producing 101 rather than 100 units (or 102 rather than 101 units) is €7.

2. Average Variable Costs ("AVC")

4.31 Average variable cost is defined as total variable costs (*i.e.*, those costs that would increase if a firm chose to increase its output) divided by the total number of units produced. Typical variable costs include raw materials, fuel, energy and operation.

4.32 In the case of Domco, the first 100 units of output can be produced for €5 each but the next 100 units would cost €7 each. This cost structure means that Domco's average variable cost varies according to the level of output it produces. In particular:

---

[35] This could happen, for instance, if the company would need to pay workers overtime wages to produce more than 100 units.

4. – Predatory Conduct
Robbert Snelders, Andrew Leyden and Andrea Lofaro

- If Domco chooses to produce 100 units then its AVC will be (€5*100 units)/100 units = €5;
- If Domco chooses to produce 150 units then its AVC will be (€5*100 units + €7*50 units)/150 units = €5.67;
- If Domco chooses to produce 200 units then its AVC will be (€5*100 units + €7*100 units)/200 units = €6.

These concepts are illustrated in the chart below. The solid line represents **4.33** Domco's variable cost curve, which illustrates the total variable costs that would be incurred by Domco for each level of output produced. As long as Domco's production does not exceed 100 units, it has a constant AVC of €5 per unit. This is illustrated by the first part of the cost curve, which has a slope of 5. The total variable cost of producing 200 units is €5*100+€7*100=1,200. The AVC for the production of all 200 units is equal to the ratio of total variable costs, *i.e.*, €1,200, to the total number of units produced, *i.e.*, 200. This is represented by the slope of the dashed line, which equals 6. As output increases between 100 and 200 units, AVC would increase from 5 to 6, and would be represented in the graph below by the slope of a line connecting the origin to the variable cost curve.

Figure 4.1: Calculation of Average Variable Costs.

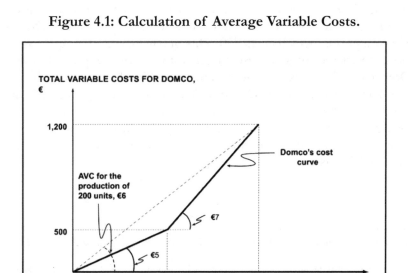

4. – Predatory Conduct
Robbert Snelders, Andrew Leyden and Andrea Lofaro

3. Average Avoidable Costs ("AAC")

4.34 Average avoidable cost is the average cost per unit that could have been avoided if the company had not produced a discrete amount of (extra) output.[36] In other words, it is the total cost that could be saved by foregoing the production of a certain number of units, divided by the number of units. On the basis of the cost assumptions outlined above (*i.e.*, €5 for the first 100 units and €7 for the next 100 units), if Domco originally produces 90 units and then increases its output to 110 units, its avoidable cost would be: (€5*10 units + €7*10 units)= €120. The average avoidable cost for these 20 units is therefore €120/20 units = €6.

4.35 As the Commission notes, for practical purposes, the use of AAC will usually produce the same results as the AVC standard that has previously been used in Article 102 TFEU case law.[37] In Domco's case, AAC would indeed be identical to AVC because the avoidable costs it faces when deciding whether to increase output are all clearly captured by the notion of variable costs. However, there are instances where AAC could also include costs that might be considered fixed. To illustrate this, suppose that Domco currently produces 100 units at a cost of €5 per unit, and it can produce up to another 100 units by using a more expensive technology costing €7 per unit. Assume further that the use of this technology requires Domco to purchase a permit, which costs €50. This outlay may not be captured by the notion of variable costs because it does not vary with output.[38] In this case, if Domco decides to use the more expensive technology in order to increase its production to 120 units, Domco's AAC will be equal to (€7*20 units + €50)/20 units = €9.5. This logic hinges on the fact that Domco could well choose *not* to expand its capacity in this way (*i.e.*, by acquiring an expensive permit). Hence, any increase in fixed costs incurred in doing so is, in principle, avoidable as well.

---

[36] This corresponds to the definition of AAC set out in the *Guidance Paper. See Guidance Paper supra* note 3.

[37] *Ibid.*, para. 26, n. 2.

[38] Some might argue that this product-specific outlay should be considered a variable cost over the output range 100 to 101 units, since the expansion of output from 100 to 101 units requires the €50 expenditure. An advantage of the AAC concept is that it is more explicit than AVC, which is not as well defined, in ensuring that this cost is taken into account.

4. – Predatory Conduct
Robbert Snelders, Andrew Leyden and Andrea Lofaro

The measure of AAC varies depending on the time period over which it is **4.36** assessed. For example, suppose that Domco must incur an additional cost each month that is essential to maintain its equipment in working order. On a day to day basis, that would not change Domco's AAC, but if Domco's pricing were considered over (for example) a six-month period, these monthly instalments should form part of a properly constructed measure of avoidable cost of production. This would reflect the fact that Domco had a choice each month to cease production and avoid incurring its monthly maintenance costs.

These examples illustrate the importance of timing when assessing whether **4.37** to include certain costs in the measure of AAC. The extent to which costs are avoidable tends to increase as the time period over which output decisions are viewed increases. Thus, AAC is typically an increasing function of the time period chosen for the assessment of a firm's behaviour, which may itself depend on the nature of the allegation of predation.

4.   Long-Run Average Incremental Costs ("LRAIC")

Average incremental cost is defined as the increase in cost associated with a **4.38** given increase in output, divided by that increase in output.[39] This includes product-specific outlays that might not be captured by the (more ambiguous) concept of average variable cost. At the outset, all firms can make a decision not to produce or sell a given product at all, *i.e.*, to sell zero output of that product at zero cost. This point forms the benchmark for the increment

---

[39] The concepts of avoidable and incremental cost are similar and are often used interchangeably. Both helpfully dispense with the need to define costs as "fixed" or "variable" and focus the analysis by relating cost concepts to the consequences of firm's decisions. Some authors, for example Bolton et al (2000), have merged the concepts by defining AAC as the cost that a firm could have avoided had it not produced the predatory *increment* of sales (P. Bolton, J. F. Brodley and M. H. Riordan, "Predatory Pricing Strategic Theory and Legal Policy" (2000) 88 *Georgetown Law Journal*, pp. 2239–330). This definition is close to that used in the *Guidance Paper*, which refers to "*the costs that could have been avoided if the company had not produced a discrete amount of (extra) output, in this case the amount allegedly the subject of abusive conduct*". See Guidance Paper *supra* note 3. Other authors, for example Baumol (1996), make an explicit distinction by including in AAC only that part of AIC which concerns outlays that are not sunk (W. J. Baumol, "Predation and the Logic of the Average Variable Cost Test" (1996) 39(1) *Journal of Law and Economics*, pp. 49–72). In other words, AAC is taken to refer to costs that could have been avoided by ceasing an activity, whereas AIC is taken to refer to the costs that must be incurred by engaging in an activity. Applying this distinction to the example above, AAC would be below AIC if the permit could only be resold for less than its full value, say for €25, so that the average cost that could be avoided by producing 100 rather 120 units (once the permit has been purchased) is (€7*20 + €25)/20 = €8.25.

4. – Predatory Conduct
Robbert Snelders, Andrew Leyden and Andrea Lofaro

considered in the concept of long-run average incremental cost (LRAIC). LRAIC is therefore the average of all the costs that a company incurs to produce a particular product, assuming that it starts afresh. To extend the example in the previous section, Domco's LRAIC would be as follows at various levels of output, recalling that Domco must pay €100 per annum in loan repayments:

- If Domco chooses to produce 80 units, its LRAIC equals (€100 + €5*80 units)/80 units = €6.25.

- If Domco chooses to produce 100 units, its LRAIC equals (€100 + €5*100 units)/100 = €6

- If Domco chooses to produce 120 units, requiring the purchase of the permit costing €50 for the use of the more expensive technology, its LRAIC equals (€100 + €50 + €5*100 units + €7*20 units)/120 = €6.6

4.39 Therefore, if Domco produces 100 rather than 80 units, its LRAIC decreases because the higher level of output would allow the fixed cost associated with the loan to be spread over a broader output base. However, if Domco chooses to produce 120 rather than 100 units, its LRAIC increases as it incurs the incremental cost of acquiring the permit necessary to produce above 100 units.

4.40 Note that at each output level LRAIC is higher than a measure of AAC that focuses on the time period over which the loan repayment is unavoidable. This is because LRAIC includes sunk costs, which would normally be excluded from AAC (which is normally concerned with a shorter time period). For example, the AAC associated with the production of 100 units would not include the €100 loan repayment and so would be (€5*100 units)/100 units = €5 as opposed to the LRAIC of €6 in the example above.

5. Average Total Cost ("ATC")

4.41 Average total cost is the average of all variable and fixed costs. If the firm produces only one product, then ATC and LRAIC are identical. For multi-product firms, ATC will be higher than LRAIC because ATC includes costs that are common to the production of all products, whereas LRAIC excludes costs that are not incremental to the production of a particular product.

4. – Predatory Conduct
Robbert Snelders, Andrew Leyden and Andrea Lofaro

Suppose Domco produces two products: widgets at a cost of €5 per unit and gadgets at a cost of €10 per unit (regardless of the quantity produced). Assume further that both widgets and gadgets are produced at the same factory, for which Domco has to repay a loan of €100 per annum. In this case, the LRAIC of producing widgets is simply €5, since the loan costs would be incurred by Domco irrespective of whether it chose to produce widgets as well as gadgets, and is therefore not a cost that is incremental to widget production. On the other hand, measures of ATC attempt to allocate some of these common costs to the production of widgets. If Domco produces 100 widgets and 100 gadgets, the ATC of widgets will be (€5*100 units + a part of €100 loan)/100 units, while the ATC for gadgets will be (€10*100 + remaining part of €100 loan)/100 units. Thus, the ATC for each product depends on how the common loan cost is eventually split between the two products. There is no sound economic logic that would lead one to prefer one allocation of common costs over any other. As a result, any rule for allocating common costs between products is essentially arbitrary. ATC is therefore not an economically meaningful measure whenever the allegedly predating firm produces more than one product (that is, in virtually all cases). This has led Baumol to argue that: *"any conclusion about the predatory character of a price that is based on a calculation of average total cost must be disregarded. The ATC numbers can offer absolutely no substantive economic information, and they are apt to constitute an invitation to anticompetitive action"*.[40]

4.42 Nevertheless, various conventions exist for allocating common costs between products. For example, in its *Discussion Paper*,[41] the Commission stated: *"[w]here necessary to apply a cost benchmark based on ATC, the Commission will allocate common costs in proportion to the turnover achieved by the different products unless other cost allocation methods are for good reasons standard in the sector in question or in case the abuse biases the allocation based on turnover"*.[42]

4.43 The *Guidance Paper* leaves open the possibility of using ATC as a benchmark.[43]

---

[40] *See* W. J. Baumol, *supra* note 39, pp. 49–72.

[41] *See Discussion Paper supra* note 5.

[42] *See Guidance Paper supra* note 3, para. 65.

[43] The *Guidance Paper* states that the Commission is *"likely"* to rely on AAC and LRAIC, but does not explicitly rule out ATC. *Ibid.*, para. 26.

4. – Predatory Conduct
Robbert Snelders, Andrew Leyden and Andrea Lofaro

6. Evaluation of Cost Benchmarks

4.44   As the examples above show, whether pricing behaviour will be considered predatory will depend greatly on the cost benchmark used. AAC may be significantly higher than AVC since the former can include fixed costs associated with the production of a given output, whereas the latter only includes variable costs. LRAIC may be significantly higher than AAC because it includes sunk costs that the firm cannot avoid whereas AAC excludes these costs. ATC may be significantly higher than LRAIC because it includes costs that are not specific to the production of the product in question but are common to multiple products. Finally, MC, which focuses on the additional cost to produce an extra unit of output rather than an average across a set of units, can be lower than or higher than all the other cost benchmarks. In the following sections, the usefulness of each cost benchmark are analysed from both a theoretical and practical perspective.

6.1. *Marginal Cost ("MC")*

4.45   Where a firm's marginal cost of production for a given output exceeds its price, the firm is selling at least a part of that output at a loss. The firm could increase its overall profits by reducing its output by one unit, since the cost saving it would make (equal to its MC) would be greater than the revenues it would forego (which can be no greater than the price at which it sells the last unit). Therefore, a price below MC must imply profit sacrifice.

4.46   However, using the marginal costs to assess predation in practice is fraught with difficulties, as these costs cannot be readily inferred from conventional business accounts. While a firm's MC may be constant in principle, it often differs according to the level of output produced by the firm (as it does for Domco in the example above). Proper identification of marginal costs requires precise knowledge about the changes in the company's costs for all *hypothetically possible* levels of output.[44] In reality, the firm's cost information is likely to be much less detailed than is required for such an assessment. Due to this data limitation, MC is rarely used in reality as a benchmark. In an influential 1975 article, Areeda and Turner concluded that while the marginal cost is the most defensible benchmark for determining whether a price is predatory,

---

[44] Formally, one needs to know the firm's cost function in order to be able to determine marginal costs for all levels of output.

4. – Predatory Conduct
Robbert Snelders, Andrew Leyden and Andrea Lofaro

practical considerations would necessitate relying on an imperfect alternative, based on the concept of average variable cost.[45]

Subsequent authors, however, have rejected the notion that measures based on the concept of average variable cost should be viewed as an imperfect alternative to marginal cost and argue that the AVC test proposed by Areeda and Turner (or some variant of that test) is preferable, even in principle, to a marginal cost test.[46] **4.47**

6.2. *Average Variable Costs ("AVC")*

Areeda and Turner advocated the use of the AVC benchmark to assess predation because pricing below AVC is irrational for a profit-maximising firm. This is because a firm that is pricing below its AVC can reduce its losses by shutting down and producing zero output.[47] The AVC benchmark is based on the notion that predatory pricing rules should only be concerned with preventing the elimination of "as efficient" competitors. Indeed, all of the benchmarks considered below are "in the spirit" of the Areeda-Turner test. Nevertheless, AVC as a cost benchmark has two major drawbacks. **4.48**

First, AVC is a measure of the costs associated with producing the entire output, while typically of greater interest is the cost of producing a particular portion of output (the "predatory increment"). In the context of a predatory pricing analysis, what matters most is to understand whether a firm could have increased its short-term profits by producing x fewer units rather than focusing solely on whether it could have increased its short-run profits by producing nothing at all. **4.49**

Secondly, the concept of variable cost is ambiguous in some circumstances. If a firm needs to expand capacity and thereby incur a one-off lump sum cost in order to predate, there may be some controversy over whether the "fixed" cost associated with this extra capacity should be included in the company's AVC. **4.50**

---

[45] *Supra* note 10, pp. 697–733. *See* discussion of the basic rules on predatory pricing in Section IV below.

[46] *See* W. J. Baumol, *supra* note 39, pp. 49–72.

[47] To see why this is the case, consider that if a firm produces output, it obtains a profit equal to $Q^*(P–AVC)$ – FC, while if it stops production its profit is simply – FC, where FC is the fixed cost. Whenever $P < AVC$, the first term, $Q^*(P–AVC)$, is negative and so losses are lower if the company produces nothing at all and simply incurs the fixed cost.

4. – Predatory Conduct
Robbert Snelders, Andrew Leyden and Andrea Lofaro

6.3. *Average Avoidable Costs ("AAC")*

4.51 The concept of average avoidable cost helpfully shifts attention from the debate over whether costs are "fixed" or "variable" and focuses the analysis by relating the costs in question to the consequences of firm's decisions. AAC is a compelling benchmark for two reasons. First, if a firm is targeting certain customers with below AAC pricing, an "as efficient" competitor could not serve those customers on equally attractive terms without incurring a loss. In other words, below AAC pricing can give rise to the foreclosure of an "as efficient" competitor. Secondly, if a dominant firm is pricing below AAC it is clearly sacrificing profits in the short term. Therefore, it is reasonable to require that a firm pricing below AAC justifies its actions in terms of the procompetitive benefits that it believes its conduct delivers.

4.52 The *Guidance Paper* sets out the logic for using the AAC benchmark as follows: *"Failure to cover AAC indicates that the dominant undertaking is sacrificing profits in the short term and that an equally efficient competitor cannot serve the targeted customers without incurring a loss"*.[48]

4.53 A similar but arguably more general test would compare the revenues generated by a certain pricing or output decision to the avoidable costs associated with that decision. The two tests are identical if all units are sold at the same price, but the latter is more directly related to the issue being investigated, namely whether the firm has engaged in an exclusionary conduct. Moreover, the test based on revenues and avoidable costs is more easily applicable to situations where the price and cost of a single unit are ill defined, for example, because different customers pay different prices but share much of the costs.[49]

4.54 As noted above, the AAC incurred in producing a given output will depend on the relevant time period over which output decisions are viewed to take place. Viewed over a longer time period, a firm may have scope to avoid certain costs associated with production that it cannot avoid over a shorter term. AAC may therefore be a function of the relevant time period as well as of the incremental output produced.

---

[48] *See Guidance Paper supra* note 3, para. 26.
[49] A typical example is airline pricing schemes, also known as "yield management", whereby the price of each ticket depends on a large number of parameters such as seats availability, flexibility, comfort class, and so on. Yet, the majority of costs are common to all passengers of that particular flight.

4. – Predatory Conduct
Robbert Snelders, Andrew Leyden and Andrea Lofaro

This implies that AAC is a sufficiently flexible concept to deal with allegations **4.55** of predation under a wide range of different circumstances. For example, there is no reason why an AAC benchmark would be considered too lenient in the case of a firm that incurs a "fixed" cost by installing new production capacity, which allows it to produce additional units at a very low marginal cost, with the sole intention of producing incremental output to exclude a competitor. Appropriately applied, the AAC benchmark can be constructed to include the "fixed" costs associated with introducing that production capacity, if circumstances suggest it would be reasonable to do so. The concept of avoidable costs also provides sufficient flexibility to assess long-term exclusionary strategies. To the extent that the firm can control (avoid) more costs over a longer timeframe, these costs can be included in the (long term) avoidable cost measure.

6.4. Long-Run Average Incremental Costs ("LRAIC")

The *Guidance Paper* states that the Commission may also consider LRAIC as a **4.56** relevant cost benchmark for assessing predation, but LRAIC has two major drawbacks. The first is that it would at all times require a dominant firm to set prices at a level that would cover costs that the firm cannot control except in the very long term (where all costs are avoidable). In some cases, this may place unreasonable restrictions on the pricing behaviour of a firm.

This can be illustrated as follows. Suppose that Domco produces and sells **4.57** 100 units per year at a price of €6 each with fixed costs equal to €100 per annum (the loan repayment) and variable costs equal to €5 per unit. Domco's LRAIC at this level of output equals (€100 + €5*100 units)/100 units = €6. Now suppose that an entrant comes into Domco's market and steals 33 units from Domco, thus winning a 33 per cent market share. How can Domco respond on price in order to compete with the entrant? First of all, Domco will recalculate its LRAIC, given that now it sells only 67 units. By repeating the calculations above, the new LRAIC corresponding to the production of 67 units will equal (€100 + €5*67 units)/67 units = €6.5.

Thus, if Domco wants to ensure that it does not set prices below LRAIC, it **4.58** has not only to accommodate the entry, but also to increase its prices. This result is driven by the fact that the fixed costs of Domco's loan have to be spread over a smaller number of units (67 versus 100) when the entry occurs. Obviously raising its price in-line with the increase in LRAIC does not make

4. – Predatory Conduct

Robbert Snelders, Andrew Leyden and Andrea Lofaro

any commercial sense. Domco can make sales that contribute to its profits as long as it maintains its price above €5. By increasing its price to match its LRAIC so as to avoid attention from competition authorities, Domco would lose even more customers and profits, and also deny its customers the benefits of price reductions that increased competition may have otherwise brought about.

4.59 The second drawback lies in the fact that prices above LRAIC may only raise competitive concerns in the long term, if an "as efficient" rival is unable to fully recover fixed costs, and is forced to exit the market (or operate ineffi-ciently) as a result of its financial constraints.

4.60 Nevertheless, LRAIC appears to have been accepted as a cost benchmark that may be appropriate under certain circumstances by competition authorities on both sides of the Atlantic. As noted, the *Guidance Paper* implies that it will consider the LRAIC when assessing whether an equally efficient competitor could be foreclosed from the market: "*Failure to cover LRAIC indicates that the dominant undertaking is not recovering all the (attributable) fixed costs of producing the good or service in question and that an equally efficient competitor could be foreclosed from the market*".[50]

4.61 This suggests that in order to guarantee avoidance of being charged with pre-dation, dominant firms are required to price above LRAIC, even though the Commission has endorsed the AAC benchmark as appropriate for assessing whether profit sacrifice has taken place.[51]

6.5. Average Total Cost ("ATC")

4.62 As discussed above, the concept of ATC is only distinct from that of LRAIC when a firm produces multiple products with certain common costs. How-ever, in these circumstances the ATC measure is inevitably arbitrary since there is no economically meaningful way to allocate fixed costs (*e.g.*, admin-istrative overheads) across different products. Unfortunately, however, the *Guidance Paper* does not rule out the possibility that the Commission will take into account common costs, *i.e.*, attempt to calculate an ATC measure, under certain circumstances. Specifically, the Commission states that: "[i]*n situations*

---

[50] *See Guidance Paper supra* note 3, para. 26.
[51] *Ibid.*, para. 64.

4. – Predatory Conduct
Robbert Snelders, Andrew Leyden and Andrea Lofaro

where common costs are significant, they may have to be taken into account when assessing the ability to foreclose as efficient competitors".[52]

Thus, the implication is that if economies of scope are significant, then domi-   **4.63**
nant firms will be required to cover some proportion of the common fixed costs when competing with rivals who do not benefit from such economies, even though that would not form part of a properly calculated LRAIC. But that essentially states that if a dominant firm is much more efficient than a rival because of significant economies of scope, the Commission will oblige it to behave as if any such efficiency advantage does not exist.

7. Measuring Costs in Practice

The cost measures discussed above are economic constructs. Unfortunately,   **4.64**
AVC or LRAIC are unlikely to feature as entries in a firm's accounts. Typically, therefore, it is necessary to recover an approximation of the relevant cost benchmark through a detailed analysis of a firm's management accounts.[53] The difficulty of recovering a good approximation of the relevant cost measure will vary on a case by case basis according to the nature of the industry involved and the nature of the allegedly abusive action. The exercise requires a deep understanding of the firm's cost structure, including the extent to which each cost item would be saved if the firm did not take a given action.

The discussion of the measurement of AAC in the Commission's *Intel* deci-   **4.65**
sion provides a useful illustration of the difficulties involved in measuring costs appropriately.[54] As exemplified in that case, there is scope for significant disagreement over which costs are avoidable over a given timeframe. Intel had submitted an analysis of whether Intel's rebates were capable of foreclosing an "as efficient" competitor. The Commission rejected the measure of cost Intel used in this analysis. In the Commission's view, Intel's analysis underestimated the avoidable cost by excluding certain cost items, such as a marketing subsidy that was directly proportional to the amount of purchases,

---

[52] *See Guidance Paper supra* note 3, para. 25, n. 18.
[53] Statutory accounts will usually be insufficiently disaggregated.
[54] The Commission used AAC as the relevant benchmark to assess the exclusionary effect of Intel's rebate scheme as it saw this as a conservative cost measure (*i.e.,* one that is more favourable to Intel). *See* Case COMP/37.990 *Intel*, Commission Decision of 13 May 2009, not yet published, para. 1037.

4. – Predatory Conduct
Robbert Snelders, Andrew Leyden and Andrea Lofaro

which the Commission considered avoidable over the course of one year.[55] The Commission put forward as a *prima facie* measure the Cost of Goods Sold ("CoGS"), which was directly observable from Intel's accounts. In its statement of objections ("SO") against Intel, the Commission indicated that any arguments by Intel that its accounting CoGS included items that were fixed for the purposes of short-run pricing decisions would have to be evaluated on an item by item basis. Intel duly replied to the SO with a report arguing that the CoGS measure was inappropriate and did indeed include components that were unavoidable over a one-year time horizon.[56]

4.66 Intel argued that its consolidated accounts included products other than the x86 central processing units ("CPUs") that were the focus of the investigation, and that for these products CoGS accounted for a higher proportion of gross revenue than for x86 CPUs. This caused the proportion of gross revenues represented by CoGS for the x86 CPUs to be lower than the company-wide proportion.[57] Secondly, Intel argued that CoGS could be split into two broad categories: Product Cost of Sales ("PCoS") and Other Costs of Sales ("OCoS"). It argued that OCoS was made up of costs that were entirely unavoidable and that even a proportion of PCoS was made up of manufacturing overheads that were unavoidable. Intel did concede, however, that some marketing expenditures were avoidable and included these in its revised measure.[58]

4.67 The Commission embarked on a detailed consideration of the ability to avoid various cost items within PCoS (such as materials costs, payroll costs, period costs and office operations) and within sales and marketing costs. It found contrary to Intel's arguments that:

> "[I]t is manifestly not the case... that a decision by, for instance HP and Dell, to switch a substantial amount of x86 CPU purchases away from Intel (within a one year time horizon) would not have any influence whatsoever on the amount of staff necessary within Intel to service HP and Dell, or on the number of workers needed to produce x86 CPUs, on the need to reduce outsourcing, or on savings in equipment".[59]

---

[55] *See supra* note 54, para. 1042.
[56] *Ibid.*, para. 1044.
[57] *Ibid.*, para. 1046.
[58] *Ibid.*, para. 1050.
[59] *Ibid.*, para. 1052.

4. – Predatory Conduct
Robbert Snelders, Andrew Leyden and Andrea Lofaro

The Commission's decision also points out that a correct measure of AAC **4.68**
should in principle take into account the most profitable alternative use of
the production inputs used to produce the units in question.[60] It stated that if
an employee dedicated to producing x86 CPUs can be redeployed to another
type of production (for instance chipsets or flash memory), it would not be
correct to treat his salary as unavoidable. More generally, it noted that even
if resources cannot be avoided or redeployed to other uses, as long as Intel is
foregoing profitable sales to other customers due to capacity constraints, then
a correct measure of AAC should include the opportunity cost of not selling
the x86 CPUs to another customer (perhaps at a discounted rate).[61]

Intel's submission included a regression analysis that attempted to assess the **4.69**
extent to which changes in output affect changes in cost.[62] Intel's contention
was that if a particular cost item was not positively correlated with output (*i.e.*,
if it did not tend to fall when the level of output falls) then this should lend
support to the view that it is an unavoidable cost. The Commission heavily
criticised this analysis as being susceptible to a number of problems, including "*simultaneity*".[63] The issue of simultaneity arises when attempting to infer
a meaning from the correlation of two variables that are jointly determined
by a common process. In particular, the Commission noted that an increase
in the cost of a raw material could lead to increased spending per chip on
raw materials but a reduction in final output as some of that cost increase
is passed on to customers in the form of higher prices. This would weigh
against finding a positive correlation between raw materials costs and output,
and could therefore wrongfully lead to the view that raw materials represent
an unavoidable cost.

IV. The Basic Rules on Predatory Pricing Under Article 102 TFEU

1. The Areeda-Turner Test

The Areeda-Turner test is based on the notion that a prohibition on preda- **4.70**
tory pricing should only protect those competitors who are as efficient as the

---

[60] *See supra* note 54, para. 1060.
[61] *Ibid.*, para. 1064.
[62] *Ibid.*, para. 1066.
[63] Other problems included omitted variable bias and wrongly specifying the temporal dependence between the
variables. *Ibid.*, paras 1067–81.

4. – Predatory Conduct
Robbert Snelders, Andrew Leyden and Andrea Lofaro

dominant company. In theory, at least, a test based on such cost benchmarks will not afford any protection to less efficient firms whose high costs prevent them from competing effectively. However, the test is approximate, and has been subject to criticism on a number of levels. Importantly, as discussed above, the division between fixed and variable costs is entirely dependent on the industry and the period of time in question.[64]

4.71 Despite its inherent shortcomings, the Areeda-Turner test represents an objective, administrable standard for predatory conduct, and has been widely (although not universally) accepted in the United States,[65] the European Union[66] and individual Member States.[67] The most pronounced legacy of the Areeda-Turner test is the rigour it has brought to predation analysis, and the corresponding reduction in the success rate for predatory pricing cases. As an illustration, in the seven years following the publication of the Areeda-Turner article, the success ratio for predatory pricing plaintiffs in the United States fell from 77 per cent in 1975 to 8 per cent in 1982.[68]

2. The *AKZO* Rules

4.72 The European Union rules on predatory pricing originate in the *AKZO* judgment[69] of the Court of Justice. The case arose from a Commission decision that AKZO abused its dominant position in the organic peroxides market[70] by following a predatory course of action against a competitor. ECS was a small company which sold benzoyl peroxide to the flour sector, whereas AKZO, a large multinational, sold the same product to the plastics sector. ECS expanded to the plastics sector, and captured one of AKZO's largest customers. AKZO retaliated by threatening to attack ECS in the flour sector by offering below-cost prices to their customers. As regards the test for predatory

---

[64] To overcome this problem, Areeda and Turner subsequently proposed that certain costs should always be considered fixed (interest, depreciation, and taxes which do not vary with output). *Supra* note 10, pp. 697–733, para. 715c.

[65] *See US v AMR and American Airlines*, 335 F.3d 1109 (10th Cir. 2003). *See also* H. Hovenkamp, *The Antitrust Enterprise: Principle and Execution* (Harvard University Press, 2005), pp. 165–67.

[66] *See AKZO*.

[67] *See, e.g.*, Case 1009/1/1/02, *Aberdeen Journals Limited and The Office of Fair Trading*, UK Competition Appeal Tribunal Decision of 23 June 2003.

[68] J. Hurwitz and W. E. Kovacic, "Judicial Analysis of Predation: The Emerging Trends" (1982) 35 *Vanderbilt Law Review*, pp. 140–145, quoted in P. Bolton, J. F. Brodley and M. H. Riordan, *supra* note 39, p. 2254, n.90.

[69] *See AKZO*.

[70] AKZO was dominant in the peroxides market as a whole, not a particular market segment.

4. – Predatory Conduct
Robbert Snelders, Andrew Leyden and Andrea Lofaro

pricing, the Commission explicitly rejected not only the Areeda-Turner criteria, but *"any per se test based on marginal or variable cost"*.[71] The Commission focused instead on the *"convincing documentary evidence"* of AKZO's *"detailed plan"* to eliminate ECS as a competitor in the plastics sector.[72]

On appeal, the Court of Justice adopted a compromise between the Commission's intent-based analysis and a cost-based test. The Court of Justice set out two principal rules, which form the basis for all subsequent EU predatory pricing law.[73] **4.73**

- **Pricing below AVC.** The first rule adopts the Areeda-Turner position that pricing below AVC *"must be regarded as abusive"*.[74]
- **Pricing below ATC but above AVC.** The second rule states that prices below ATC but above AVC must be regarded as abusive *"if they are determined to form part of a plan to eliminate a competitor"*.[75]

The first rule creates a (very strong) presumption of predation. This presumption can, however, be rebutted in limited cases.[76] The second rule does not create any presumption of predation. Where prices are above AVC it is for the Commission to prove that the dominant company has eliminatory intent. This rule, therefore, departs substantially from the Areeda-Turner test, which expressly rules out predation where prices are above average variable cost.[77] As noted above, the *Guidance Paper* proposes the use of AAC instead of AVC. In most cases, the use of AAC and AVC will produce the same result, but AAC is arguably a superior benchmark, as it is less ambiguous in its treatment **4.74**

---

[71] *See* Case IV/30.698 *supra* note 2, para. 77.

[72] *Ibid.*, para. 81.

[73] *See AKZO*, paras 70 *et seq*; Case T-83/91 *Tetra Pak International v Commission* (*"Tetra Pak II Judgment 1994"*) [1994] ECR II-755, para. 150, on appeal Case C-333/94 P *Tetra Pak International v Commission* (*"Tetra Pak II Judgment 1996"*) [1996] ECR I-5951; Joined Cases T-24 to 26 and 28/93 *supra* note 2, paras 139–41, on appeal Joined Cases C-395 and 396/96 P *supra* note 2; and Case COMP/38.233 *Wanadoo*, Commission Decision of 16 July 2003, not yet published.

[74] *See AKZO*, paras 70 *et seq.*

[75] *Ibid.*, paras 70 *et seq.*

[76] *See* section on objective justifications in Section V below.

[77] Areeda and Turner conclude, *"prices at or above marginal cost, even though they are not profit-maximizing, should not be considered predatory. If a monopolist produces to a point where price equals marginal cost, only less efficient firms will suffer larger losses per unit of output; more efficient firms will be losing less or even operating profitably"*. *See supra* note 10, pp. 697–733. In contrast, the ECJ held in *AKZO* that prices above AVC might drive from the market undertakings which are *"perhaps as efficient"* as the dominant undertaking but which, because of their smaller financial resources, are incapable of withstanding the competition waged against them. *See AKZO*, para. 72.

of "fixed" costs incurred when producing incremental output, and also allows attention to be focused on the production of a particular portion of output.[78] In *AKZO,* the Court of Justice did not consider the legality of above-cost price cuts, and it was long assumed that they would not be subject to predatory pricing analysis. However, as discussed below, in subsequent cases, strategic above-cost pricing has been held to infringe Article 102 TFEU.[79]

3. Pricing Above AVC/AAC but Below ATC

4.75 The second *AKZO* rule provides that prices above AVC but below ATC are only abusive where they form part of a *"plan for eliminating a competitor"*.[80] This rule constitutes the Court's recognition that companies often have rational reasons to price below ATC, at least in the short term. While such sales do not cover the total cost of production, they allow for the recovery of all variable costs and a portion of fixed costs. As such, pricing between AVC and ATC is a grey area, in which below-cost pricing may or may not be deemed to be predatory. Accordingly, additional elements are required to prove that such pricing forms part of a predatory strategy. Although a narrow construction of the *AKZO* rule would require proof of the intention to eliminate a competitor, it is now clear that the concept is wider than this, and encompasses an intention to drive out competition more generally.[81] In particular, the Court of Justice makes it clear that an intention to foreclose or "pre-empt" a market will satisfy the test, even if no other undertakings compete on that market at the time.[82]

4.76 Two principal categories of evidence can be used to show the existence of a plan to eliminate competition. First, the Commission can rely on "direct" evidence, *i.e.,* documentary evidence to prove the company's intentions. Secondly, the Commission can deduce the existence of an intention to eliminate competitors from "indirect" evidence, *i.e.,* the market structure, the circumstances of the case and other *"convergent factors"*[83] proving that a given price cut

---

[78] *See* discussion of cost benchmarks in Section 0 above.

[79] Joined Cases T-24 to 26 and 28/93 *supra* note 2, paras 139–41, on appeal Joined Cases C-395 and 396/96 P *supra* note 2.

[80] *See AKZO,* para. 41; Case COMP/38.233 *supra* note 73, para. 256.

[81] *See AKZO,* para. 72.

[82] Case C-202/07 P *France Télécom v Commission* [2009] ECR I-2369.

[83] Case T-83/91 *Tetra Pak II Judgment 1994 supra* note 73, para. 151. Confirmed in Case C-333/94 P *Tetra Pak II Judgment 1996 supra* note 73.

4. – Predatory Conduct
Robbert Snelders, Andrew Leyden and Andrea Lofaro

can be explained only as part of a predatory strategy. While there is no clear hierarchy between the two categories of evidence, in practice the Commission has placed greater reliance on documentary evidence, to the detriment of indirect factors, which arguably allow for a more objective determination of intent.

4.77   From the Commission's practice, there appears to be a reasonably high standard of proof in order to establish the existence of a predatory scheme. In sum, evidence of a plan to predate will typically involve some combination of the following direct and indirect factors: (1) detailed documentary evidence of an exclusionary plan; (2) sustained price cuts; (3) specific retaliatory threats to competitors; (4) a strategy of profit sacrifice offset against future recoupment; (5) mounting losses over time; and (6) significant growth in the dominant firm's market share.

3.1.   Direct Evidence of Intent

4.78   So far, the European Union institutions have expressly relied on documentary evidence of the dominant firm's intent in every case in which predatory pricing was established. In *AKZO*, the Commission and the Court of Justice inferred eliminatory intent from documentary evidence of direct threats against ECS, such as internal documents detailing a plan, with figures, to eliminate ECS from the market, as well as statements by employees, and minutes of meetings.[84] Similarly, in *Tetra Pak II*, the Commission relied on a report by the board of directors referring to the need to make "*major financial sacrifices in the area of prices and supply terms in order to fight competition*".[85] In *Wanadoo*,[86] the Commission also referred to intent evidence in order to prove that Wanadoo executed a predatory plan to "*pre-empt the market by stealing the march on competitors*".[87] Although Wanadoo objected to the Commission's reliance on certain documents on the grounds that they represented "*informal*" discussions as part of the company's decision-making process, the Commission attached weight to the fact that certain exclusionary statements came from

---

[84] *See AKZO.*
[85] Case IV/31.043 *Tetra Pak II* ("*Tetra Pak II Decision 1991*"), Commission Decision of 24 July 1991, OJ 1992 L 72/1, para. 51.
[86] Case COMP/38.233 *supra* note 73.
[87] *Ibid.*, para. 111.

4. – Predatory Conduct

Robbert Snelders, Andrew Leyden and Andrea Lofaro

senior managers and that the evidence, taken as a whole, displayed *"unity of purpose"* throughout the organisation.[88]

4.79 In line with its policy of adopting "economics-based" enforcement priorities, the Commission claims to be mindful of the fact that predatory intent is difficult to distinguish from a dominant firm's general and legitimate intent to prevail over the competition. As Elhauge notes, *"even the most competitive firm wants to drive its rivals out of the market"*.[89] Indeed, placing undue reliance on documentary evidence of "intent" risks chilling legitimate price competition. In the hands of a competition authority, low prices combined with *"aggressive and violent metaphors"* can easily be retrospectively characterised as evidence of a predatory scheme.[90] There is the danger that such an approach would simply lead to self-censorship within dominant undertakings in order to escape liability for predatory conduct. This would lead to arbitrary results: conduct that would otherwise be illegal might escape Article 102 TFEU simply by virtue of careful use of language, whereas legitimate pricing behaviour might attract liability if accompanied by an aggressively-worded internal document. As a matter of logic, if the circumstances of the case render a predatory strategy unlikely to succeed, this ought to override otherwise "incriminating" documentary evidence.[91]

3.2. Indirect Evidence of Intent

4.80 The *Discussion Paper* expressly recognises the importance of indirect evidence of intent to carry out a predatory scheme. Although the Commission appears to view such evidence as a subsidiary source of proof,[92] it is arguable that preference should be given to indirect evidence in light of the pitfalls of over-reliance on past statements of intent.[93] In essence, "indirect evidence" of intent refers to factors that show that a given price cut can be explained only

---

[88] Case COMP/38.233 *supra* note 73, para. 122.

[89] E. Elhauge, *"Comments of Professor Elhauge on DG Competition Discussion Paper on Exclusionary Abuses"*, March 2006, p. 5.

[90] D. Crane, *supra* note 5, p. 15. In *Napier Brown*, the Commission looked with disfavour on an internal memo stating that, "[i]f *we are to succeed in seeing off the Whitworths threat, we MUST attack on all fronts. It is time to get nasty!"* (Case IV/30.178 *Napier Brown/British Sugar* ("*Napier Brown*"), Commission Decision of 18 July 1988, OJ 1988 L 284/41, para. 17).

[91] Helpfully, the *Guidance Paper* expressly states that *"it is less likely that the dominant undertaking engages in predatory conduct if the conduct concerns a low price applied generally for a long period of time"*. *Guidance Paper supra* note 3, para. 73.

[92] *Ibid.*, para. 21; *See also Discussion Paper supra* note 5, para. 115.

[93] *See supra* note 18, p. 252.

4. – Predatory Conduct
Robbert Snelders, Andrew Leyden and Andrea Lofaro

as part of a predatory strategy. This includes: (1) the actual or likely exclusion of competitors; (2) whether price cuts are aimed at particular customers;[94] (3) whether the predator incurred specific costs to maintain the predatory strategy (*e.g.*, by expanding capacity); (4) the scale and duration of price cuts; (5) the concurrent use of other exclusionary strategies; (6) the possibility to cross-subsidise losses with profits from other markets; and (7) the likelihood of recoupment.[95]

The Commission and the European Union courts relied on "indirect evi- **4.81** dence" in both *AKZO* and *Tetra Pak II*. In *AKZO*, the Commission and the Court relied on the selectivity of AKZO's price cuts and the fact that AKZO subsidised price cuts in the flour additives sector through below-cost transfer prices from its plastics and elastomers division to infer predatory intent.[96] In *Tetra Pak II*, the European Union courts looked to a number of objective factors to show that the dominant firm's intent was predatory, including (1) the duration of price cuts (and the fact that losses were made over a six-year period); (2) evidence that the dominant firm imported products to Italy in order to sell them at a price 35 per cent lower than their purchase price (and 20–50 per cent lower than in other Member States); (3) evidence that prices continued to fall even though this entailed even greater losses; and (4) an increase in Tetra Pak's sales during a period of market expansion, followed by a reduction in sales once the abusive practices stopped.[97]

Of the so-called "indirect" factors, the targeting of price cuts at specific cus- **4.82** tomers has been particularly important in the Commission's analysis of predatory pricing cases. The Commission's attitude towards targeted price cuts is summed up in the *Guidance Paper*, which states that "*it is less likely that the dominant undertaking engages in predatory conduct if the conduct concerns a low price applied generally for a long period of time*".[98] Conversely, the Commission is more likely to make a finding of predation where price cuts are specifically targeted at marginal customers, as was the case in *AKZO* itself. Such an approach can be justified by the observation that unless price discrimination is possible, a predatory strategy will result in a dominant firm incurring a loss on every

---

[94] *See also Guidance Paper supra* note 3, para. 72 ("*It may be easier for the dominant undertaking to engage in predatory conduct if it selectively targets specific customers with low prices, as this will limit the losses incurred by the dominant undertaking*".).

[95] *Discussion Paper supra* note 5, p. 112. *See also supra* note 82, para. 111.

[96] *See AKZO.*

[97] *Supra* note 85, on appeal Case T-83/91 *Tetra Pak II Judgment 1994 supra* note 73.

[98] *Guidance Paper supra* note 3, para. 73.

4. – Predatory Conduct

Robbert Snelders, Andrew Leyden and Andrea Lofaro

sale it makes. On the other hand, if price cuts can be targeted, a dominant firm can limit its losses. For example, in a market where brand differentiation is possible, a dominant firm might be able to foreclose new entrants with a "fighting brand" which is sufficiently distinct from its main brand not to force an across-the-board price cut.[99]

3.3.   Interplay Between Direct and Indirect Evidence

4.83   Reliance on indirect evidence is arguably more in line with an "economics-based" approach to the enforcement of Article 102 TFEU, as the focus is on market structure and competitive effects as opposed to speculation as to the meaning of internal communications. On the other hand, provided it is not used in an overly formalistic manner, the "prism" of direct intent evidence can also be useful in an effects-based analysis.[100] As Easterbrook put it, "*lawyers [...] know less about the business than the people they represent [...] The judge knows even less about the business than the lawyers*".[101] Thus, direct evidence of a company's decision-making process can be used to "*disambiguate an ambiguous practice*"[102] by explaining the purpose behind a given action and its consequences.[103] It would be difficult to imagine the Commission developing a case on the basis of the economic models described in the *Guidance Paper* (namely the signalling, reputation and financial market theories) without relying on some form of documentary evidence. This approach has been approved by the Court of Justice in *Tomra*,[104] where it reaffirmed that an abuse is an "objective concept", but endorsed the use of internal documents to inform the Commission's "*understanding of the economic rationale of [the undertaking's] behaviour, its strategic aspects and its likely effects*".[105] Similarly, while the existence of an "as-efficient" competitor is an objective question, determining the competitive constraints "felt" by a dominant undertaking will inevitably involve subjective considerations.[106] Finally, as discussed below,[107] evidence of a deliberate plan

---

[99] *See* R. Posner, *Antitrust Law* (2nd Ed., Chicago, University of Chicago Press, 2001), p. 209.

[100] A. Bavasso, "The Role of Intent under Article 82; From 'Flushing the Turkeys' to 'Spotting Lionesses in Regent's Park'" (2005) 26(11) *European Competition Law Review*, pp. 616–23.

[101] F. H. Easterbrook, "The Limits of Antitrust" (1984) 63(1) *Texas Law Review*, pp. 1–40 (cited in *Brooke Group v Brown & Williamson Tobacco*, 509 US 209 (1993), n. 18 (Stevens, J., dissenting), p. 258).

[102] *See supra* note 99, p. 216.

[103] *Ibid.*, p. 216. *See also Guidance Paper supra* note 3, para. 20.

[104] Case C-549/10 P *Tomra Systems and others v Commission ("Tomra Judgment 2012")*, not yet reported.

[105] *Ibid.*

[106] *See Guidance Paper supra* note 3, para. 68.

[107] *See* discussion of growth markets in Section V.3 below.

4. – Predatory Conduct
Robbert Snelders, Andrew Leyden and Andrea Lofaro

to exclude a competitor can be particularly helpful where cost benchmarks are very difficult to apply, or the existence of detrimental effects on consumer welfare is not easy to determine. This applies particularly in growth markets, or high-tech sectors with a tendency to "tip" in favour of one market standard.[108]

4.   Recoupment

The notion of predatory pricing is premised on the idea that a dominant company sacrifices short-term profits with the intention of making future gains. In other words, predatory behaviour is an "investment" which is recovered by maintaining a dominant position in the long run. Economic literature therefore emphasises that it is the ability to recoup that renders predatory pricing a rational strategy.[109] On the other hand, if price-cutting does not lead to recovery at a later stage, rivals may have either been able to offset the effects of below-cost selling, or new entry may have kept prices at the competitive level.[110] In either case, in the absence of recoupment, consumers have arguably not been harmed. In fact consumers may have benefited from lower prices during the supposed period of predation, and are left with prices no higher (or perhaps even lower) than they were initially. Secondly, economists argue that antitrust law ought to err on the side of caution when it comes to intervening in pricing behaviour.[111] Cost rules are notoriously difficult to apply, particularly where multi-product firms have common costs across their lines. Recoupment analysis therefore acts as a useful secondary filter to ensure that antitrust law does not have a chilling effect on low pricing by dominant firms.

4.84

On the other hand, there are reasons to be sceptical towards a strict recoupment requirement. First, a recoupment condition could produce perverse results in certain cases. The deeper the price cuts during the predatory period, the more difficult it will be for the dominant firm to recoup, as a very large price increase will be required following the exit of competitors from the

4.85

---

[108] *See* T. Eilmansberger, "How to Distinguish Good from Bad Competition under Article 82 EC: In Search of Clearer and More Coherent Standards for Anti-competitive Abuses" (2005) 42 *Common Market Law Review*, p. 148. *See also Guidance Paper supra* note 3, para. 20.

[109] *See, e.g.,* S. Bishop and M. Walker, *The Economics of EC Competition Law: Application and Measurement* (2nd Ed., London, Sweet & Maxwell, 2002), p. 229.

[110] P. Bolton, J. F. Brodley and M. H. Riordan, *supra* note 39, pp. 2267–70.

[111] *Ibid.,* pp. 2267–270.

4. – Predatory Conduct
Robbert Snelders, Andrew Leyden and Andrea Lofaro

market.[112] Paradoxically, this means that a recoupment condition is less likely to be fulfilled the greater the cut in the dominant firm's prices, even though intuitively a radical price cut could be a clear indicator of a predatory strategy.[113] Secondly, predatory pricing can have anticompetitive effects even if it does not cause market exit. The reputation theory of predatory pricing is based on the notion that market entry is most likely to be discouraged where the dominant firm maintains prices just slightly above the competitive level, thereby indicating to potential rivals that their profitability on that market would be low.[114] This effect is particularly pronounced where the predator is dominant on a range of markets, as predation on one market can also discourage entry on the others.[115] Thirdly, unless recoupment has in fact already occurred by the time the Commission is examining the case, recoupment analysis is an inherently speculative enterprise. In particular, it would be necessary to show that there would be no new entry, and that customers would be willing to pay supracompetitive prices for the dominant firm's products despite a prolonged period of low pricing.[116]

4.86   Proof of recoupment would involve an analysis of whether "*the predatory scheme alleged would cause a rise in prices above a competitive level that would be sufficient to compensate for the amounts expended on the predation*".[117] In essence, this would entail calculating the losses incurred by the dominant firm through predating, and compare it with the (likely) gains it would realise once the competition has been eliminated.[118] In carrying out such an analysis, a regulator may also examine structural features of the market[119] such as the dominant company's market share, the current market concentration, and relevant capacity constraints or barriers to entry. Market share and concentration indicate the set of sales over which a predator might enjoy pricing power, as well as the likelihood of a competitor undercutting an attempted price increase. If capacity constraints exist, competitors will have

---

[112] *See* C.S. Hemphill, "The Role of Recoupment in Predatory Pricing Analyses" (2001) 53 *Stanford Law Review*, p. 1595.

[113] There are numerous reasons why a firm might wish to engage in such conduct. Even though the strategy may be costly overall, it may be preferable to allowing a particularly efficient competitor to enter the market. A firm might decide that the losses from predatory conduct are outweighed by the risk of potentially losing their entire business. *See* C.S. Hemphill, *ibid.*, p. 1595.

[114] *See* discussion of the reputation theory in Section II.3 above.

[115] P. Bolton, J. F. Brodley and M. H. Riordan, *supra* note 39, pp. 2241–62.

[116] *See supra* note 18, p. 255.

[117] *See Brooke Group v Brown & Williamson Tobacco*, *supra* note 101, p. 226.

[118] *See supra* note 112, p. 1590. For an example of this analysis carried out by a court, *see ibid.*, p. 226.

[119] *See* C.S. Hemphill, *ibid.*, p. 1595.

4. – Predatory Conduct
Robbert Snelders, Andrew Leyden and Andrea Lofaro

less incentive to reduce price to undercut an attempt at recoupment. Barriers to entry reduce the ability of potential competitors to enter the market in response to price increases following the predation period. Conversely, where a market is "highly diffuse and competitive, or where new entry is easy",[120] recoupment is unlikely.

4.1. No Recoupment Condition Under Article 102 TFEU

While most economists argue that a reasonable prospect of recoupment is essential to a predatory strategy, whether proof of recoupment should be required as a matter of law is another question. Many commentators argue that it should be.[121] Indeed, in the United States, a plaintiff must demonstrate that the predator had a "dangerous probability" of recouping the costs of a predatory strategy.[122] As a result, predatory pricing actions very rarely succeed before United States courts.[123] The European Union courts, however, have rejected a recoupment condition. In *Tetra Pak II*, the Court of Justice found that *"in the circumstances of the case"* it would not be appropriate *"to require in addition proof that Tetra Pak had a realistic chance of recouping its losses"*.[124] The "circumstances" alluded to by the Court included various structural features of the market, notably the fact that Tetra Pak had a quasi-monopoly, and that the alleged predation occurred in a market separate from the one in which Tetra Pak was dominant (which opened the possibility of cross-subsidisation). While the language used might suggest that the Court left open the possibility of requiring proof of recoupment in other cases, the judgment goes on to state that it *"must be possible to penalise predatory pricing whenever there is a risk that competitors will be eliminated"*, which would "[rule] *out waiting until such a strategy leads to the actual elimination of competitors"*.[125]

4.87

---

[120] *See Brooke Group v Brown & Williamson Tobacco*, *supra* note 101, p. 226.

[121] *See, e.g.*, P. Bolton, J. F. Brodley and M. H. Riordan, *supra* note 39, pp. 2267–70; *See also* W. J. Baumol, "Principles Relevant to Predatory Pricing", Swedish Competition Authority, *Pros and Cons Series: The Pros and Cons of Low Prices*, October 2003, pp. 19–20.

[122] *See supra* note 6. *See also* J. B. Baker, "Predatory Pricing After Brooke Group: An Economic Perspective", (1994) 62 *Antitrust Law Journal*, pp. 585–603.

[123] The recoupment requirement is seen as having sounded the "death knell" of predatory pricing claims in the US. *See supra* note 112, pp. 1581–612.

[124] Case C-333/94 P *Tetra Pak II Judgment 1996 supra* note 73.

[125] *Ibid.*

4. – Predatory Conduct
Robbert Snelders, Andrew Leyden and Andrea Lofaro

4.88 Although intervening developments offered some support for a recoupment requirement in EU law,[126] the judgment of the Court of Justice in *Wanadoo* has put it beyond doubt that proof of recoupment is not required for a finding of predation under Article 102 TFEU. Wanadoo challenged the Commission's finding that it charged below AVC in order to "pre-empt" competition in the high-speed Internet access market.[127] Both the Court of First Instance[128] and the Court of Justice upheld the Commission decision in its entirety.[129] The Court of Justice held unequivocally that "*demonstrating that it is possible to recoup losses is not a necessary precondition for a finding of predatory pricing*".[130] The Court first referred to *Tetra Pak II*, stating that this case "*dispensed with*" the necessity of showing recoupment where pricing is below AVC.[131] The Court went on to hold that even if recoupment were not possible, this would not prevent the undertaking concerned from reinforcing its dominant position. In the Court's view, once competitors withdraw, "*the degree of competition existing on the market, already weakened precisely because of the presence of the undertaking concerned, is further reduced, and customers suffer loss as a result of the limitation of the choices available to them*".[132] The Court of Justice did, however, recognise the usefulness of a recoupment analysis in assessing an objective justification advanced by defendants, or as indirect evidence of predatory intent where pricing is between AVC and ATC.[133]

4.89 The Court's reasoning was likely heavily influenced by the fact that a finding of predation under EU law presupposes the existence of a dominant position (unlike, *e.g.*, the United States, where the offence of attempted monopolisation

---

[126] In his opinion on *Compagnie Maritime Belge*, Advocate General Fennelly stated that a recoupment requirement was implicit in the *AKZO* judgment, and that "*recoupment should be part of the test for abusively low pricing by dominant undertakings*". *See* Advocate General Fennelly in Joined Cases C-395 and 396/96 P *supra* note 2.

[127] Case COMP/38.233 *supra* note 73.

[128] Case T-340/03 *France Télécom v Commission* [2007] ECR II-107.

[129] *Supra* note 82.

[130] *Ibid.*, para. 113.

[131] *Ibid.*, para. 113.

[132] It is noteworthy that the Court assumes that a predatory strategy will result in market exit. This reasoning would not hold if a predatory strategy were to fail outright, *i.e.*, no market exit occurred. In this connection, the Commission "*does not consider that it is necessary to show that competitors have exited the market in order to show that there has been anticompetitive foreclosure. The possibility cannot be excluded that the dominant undertaking may prefer to prevent the competitor from competing vigorously and have it follow the dominant undertaking's pricing, rather than eliminate it from the market altogether. Such disciplining avoids the risk inherent in eliminating competitors, in particular the risk that the assets of the competitor are sold at a low price and stay in the market, creating a new low cost entrant*". *See* Discussion Paper *supra* note 5, para. 69.

[133] *Supra* note 82, para. 11.

4. – Predatory Conduct
Robbert Snelders, Andrew Leyden and Andrea Lofaro

is recognised).[134] As the Court notes, a finding of dominance implies that competition is "already weakened" on the market, based on an analysis of barriers to entry, capacity constraints, market share and market concentration. In this sense, dominance acts as a "first-stage" filter in a manner similar to a finding of recoupment based on market structure, since the same factors are relevant to both.[135] In many cases, therefore, a recoupment requirement would arguably make no difference to the outcome.[136]

On the other hand, one could object to the Court's reasoning on the grounds **4.90** that proof of dominance is not a complete substitute for a recoupment requirement. First, market conditions can evolve, and dominance during the predation phase does not guarantee that a predator will be successful in recouping its losses later on.[137] Secondly, the Court has recognised the possibility of predation in markets other than that in which the predator is dominant.[138] This issue tends to arise where the dominant company is protected by a legal monopoly or exclusive or special rights.[139] Since the abuse produces effects on a non-dominated market, a finding of dominance is no substitute for a recoupment analysis. Thirdly, in the case of predatory pricing by collectively dominant firms, a finding of recoupment seems particularly necessary, as there must be some way of distinguishing predatory price cuts from the destabilisation of the oligopoly.[140]

4.2. The Commission's Approach

Although the Commission has successfully resisted the imposition of a recoup- **4.91** ment condition under EU law, it has nonetheless analysed the likelihood of

---

[134] Although, as Posner notes, "*to obtain a monopoly through predatory pricing would require building enormous productive capacity in advance of the campaign of predatory pricing in order to be ready to supply the market's entire output*" (emphasis in original). *See supra* note 99, p. 209. As such, predation is even more unlikely to be carried out by non-dominant firms.

[135] *See supra* note 112, p. 1587.

[136] Even in cases in which the Commission did not engage in an express analysis of recoupment, it seemed likely on the facts. In *AKZO* and *Tetra Pak II* the companies were dominant across a broad portfolio of products, and only engaged in price cutting to fend off a competitor.

[137] *See supra* note 18, p. 258.

[138] Case C-333/94 P *Tetra Pak II Judgment 1996 supra* note 73.

[139] *See Discussion Paper supra* note 5, para. 69, para. 101. *See also* Case COMP/35.141 *Deutsche Post*, Commission Decision of 20 March 2001, OJ 2001 L 125/27.

[140] *See supra* note 18, p. 259.

4. – Predatory Conduct
Robbert Snelders, Andrew Leyden and Andrea Lofaro

recoupment in a number of cases.[141] As the Court noted in *Wanadoo*, even if proof of recoupment is not a strict requirement under Article 102 TFEU, it can nevertheless be useful for rebutting an objective justification advanced by defendants, or as indirect evidence of predatory intent where pricing is between AVC/AAC and ATC. The *Guidance Paper* is broadly consistent with this approach. Although it rejects a formal recoupment condition, the Commission states that, generally speaking, consumers are more likely to be harmed "*if the undertaking is likely to benefit from the sacrifice*".[142] On the other hand, the Commission expressly states that it will intervene even if the dominant company is not necessarily in a position to increase its prices above the level persisting in the market before the conduct.[143] Instead, the Commission will look at the possibility of recoupment as one element in its analysis of competitive foreclosure, combined with consideration of other factors, such as entry barriers.

4.92 This is consonant with the Commission's approach in the *Wanadoo* decision, where the foreclosure analysis was based primarily on barriers to entry in the market for high-speed Internet access. The Commission queried whether barriers to entry "*guarantee the dominant undertaking the maintenance in the long-term of a large degree of market concentration in its favour*".[144] On the facts, the Commission identified a number of barriers to entry including (1) high switching costs for subscribers; (2) the high financial cost of entering and reaching a viable scale in the Internet access market (*e.g.*, advertising); (3) the fact that it is not viable for a new entrant to create upstream infrastructure; and (4) the fact that Wanadoo had already attained high shares and profitable margins whereas other competitors had not.[145]

---

[141] Case COMP/38.233 *supra* note 73; Case IV/30.698 *ECS/AKZO*, Commission Decision of 14 December 1985, OJ 1985 L374/1; *Supra* note 85; Case COMP/35.141 *supra* note 139.

[142] *Discussion Paper supra* note 5, para. 71.

[143] *Ibid.*, para. 71: "*This does not mean that the Commission will only intervene if the dominant undertaking would be likely to be able to increase its prices above the level persisting in the market before the conduct. It is sufficient, for instance, that the conduct would be likely to prevent or delay a decline in prices that would otherwise have occurred. Identifying consumer harm is not a mechanical calculation of profits and losses, and proof of overall profits is not required. Likely consumer harm may be demonstrated by assessing the likely foreclosure effect of the conduct, combined with consideration of other factors, such as entry barriers. In this context, the Commission will also consider possibilities of re-entry*".

[144] Case COMP/38.233 *supra* note 73, para. 337.

[145] *Ibid.*, para. 337.

4. – Predatory Conduct

Robbert Snelders, Andrew Leyden and Andrea Lofaro

5.   Market-Specific Issues

5.1.   *Predatory Pricing to Extend a Dominant Position*

In the normal course of events, predatory pricing will only be considered **4.93** abusive where it is used to protect or strengthen an existing dominant position.[146] In most cases, the dominant company will attempt to do so by engaging in predatory pricing in the market in which it is dominant. A dominant company might also try to protect or strengthen that dominant position through predatory pricing in a separate but adjacent market.[147] In *Tetra Pak II*, however, a dominant undertaking was found to have infringed Article 102 TFEU in a situation in which the alleged predation was carried out in order to obtain an advantage on the non-dominated market. The case involved the adjacent aseptic and non-aseptic container markets. Tetra Pak was found to be dominant on the aseptic market, but not the non-aseptic market. The Commission nevertheless held that Tetra Pak abused its dominance on the aseptic market through its pricing conduct on the non-aseptic market, which was designed to produce a competitive advantage on the non-aseptic market.[148]

This determination was upheld by both the Court of First Instance[149] and **4.94** the Court of Justice.[150] The Court of Justice held that the application of Article 102 TFEU presupposes a link between the dominant position and the alleged abusive conduct, and noted that such a link does not generally exist where conduct on a market other than the dominated market produces effects on that distinct market.[151] The Court nevertheless found that Article 102 TFEU could apply in such a scenario, provided that it was justified by "*special circumstances*".[152] The Court of Justice then noted several such

---

[146] *Discussion Paper supra* note 5, para. 101.

[147] *Ibid.*, para. 101. Although the Commission cites *AKZO* as an example of this strategy, it should be noted that the Court held that although organic peroxides had various uses, including both the flour and plastics segments, they all formed part of one market.

[148] *Supra* note 85.

[149] The CFI held that Tetra Pak's practices on the non aseptic were caught by Article 102 TFEU "*without it being necessary to establish the existence of a dominant position on those markets taken in isolation, since that undertaking's leading position on the non-aseptic market, combined with the close associative links between those markets and the aseptic markets, gave Tetra Pak freedom of conduct compared with the other economic operators on the non-aseptic markets, such as to impose on it a special responsibility under Article* [102]". *See* Case T-83/91 *Tetra Pak II Judgment 1994 supra* note 73, para. 122.

[150] Case C-333/94 P *Tetra Pak II Judgment 1996 supra* note 73.

[151] *Ibid.*, para. 27.

[152] *Ibid.*, para. 27.

4. – Predatory Conduct

Robbert Snelders, Andrew Leyden and Andrea Lofaro

"special circumstances", including: (1) the fact that Tetra Pak held 78 per cent of the overall market in both aseptic and non-aseptic cartons; (2) Tetra Pak's "quasi-monopolistic" 90 per cent share of the aseptic market; (3) the fact that Tetra Pak's strength in the aseptic sector made it a "favoured supplier" of non-aseptic systems; and (4) the "close associative links" between the two markets (the materials in question were used to package the same products, approximately 35 per cent of Tetra Pak's customers bought both categories of product, and its most important competitor was also present on all the relevant markets). In light of these factors, the Court of Justice held that the application of Article 102 TFEU was justified.[153]

4.95   *Tetra Pak II* cannot be taken as authority for the proposition that dominance in one market always prohibits below-cost pricing on another, distinct market. The case does, however, open up the possibility of findings of abuse where the two markets are closely related, and "special circumstances" provide the dominant undertaking with the ability to leverage its position. Such circumstances are likely to be rare in practice. Some commentators even view *Tetra Pak II* as an example of the extra responsibilities shouldered by undertakings in a position of *"super-dominance"*.[154] The *Discussion Paper* also downplays the significance of the case, noting that it was wholly exceptional in light of the strong links between the relevant container markets, and Tetra Pak's *"quasi-monopolistic"* position.[155]

5.2.   *Multi-products/Cross Subsidies (Deutsche Post)*

4.96   Predatory cross-subsidies represent another category of cases in which dominance and abuse occur on different markets. Cross-subsidies arise where diversified firms use revenues generated in one area of their activities to fund another. Cross subsidisation is not abusive in itself, and is in fact a normal part of the operation of multi-product companies. Cross-subsidies nevertheless raise a number of competition law issues,[156] particularly in the case of State undertakings, which have the ability to use revenues from their "reserved"

---

[153] Case C-333/94 P *Tetra Pak II Judgment 1996 supra* note 73, para. 28.
[154] *See, e.g.*, A. Jones and B. Sufrin, *EC Competition Law* (3rd Ed., Oxford, Oxford University Press, 2008), p. 455.
[155] *Discussion Paper supra* note 5, para. 101, n. 67.
[156] These arise particularly in the utilities and other heavily regulated markets. *See* L. Hancher and J. Buendia Sierra, "Cross-Subsidization and EC Law" (1998) 35 *Common Market Law Review*, pp. 901–45.

4. – Predatory Conduct
Robbert Snelders, Andrew Leyden and Andrea Lofaro

activities to distort competition on non-regulated markets.[157] Where there is a link between losses on one market and profits on another (*i.e.*, a cross-subsidy) this can be condemned as predatory pricing, provided that prices are below an appropriate measure of cost.[158]

Predation by cross-subsidy only occurs where there the dominant and non-dominant markets are closely related. In *Deutsche Post*,[159] for example, there was a clear link between the letter post market (which was reserved by law to Deutsche Post) and the parcel delivery market (which was open to competition). Deutsche Post allegedly used profits from its letter post business to cross-subsidise losses in its parcel service. As part of its statutory duties, Deutsche Post had an obligation to maintain a letter post infrastructure, but this infrastructure could be used for both letter post and parcels. For over five years, Deutsche Post used this infrastructure to run a loss-making parcel business. The Commission held that in the absence of its common infrastructure and the likelihood of continued funding from its profitable activities,[160] Deutsche Post would long have exited the parcel segment. The Commission therefore imposed a structural remedy separating Deutsche Post's parcel and letter post activities.

4.97

As regards the legal test to verify the existence of a "cross-subsidy", the Commission queried whether the two products covered both (1) their own incremental costs and (2) their combined "total" costs (employing a definition of "total cost" that includes all joint and common costs shared between both activities, but without allocating them to a particular product). The Commission stated the test as follows:

4.98

> "[C]ross-subsidisation occurs where the earnings from a given service do not suffice to cover the incremental costs of providing that service and where there is another

---

[157] *See* Case C-280/00 *Altmark Trans GmbH and Regierungspräsidium Magdeburg v Nahverkehrsgesellschaft Altmark GmbH, and Oberbundesanwalt beim Bundesverwaltungsgericht* [2003] ECR I-7747. *See also* Joined Cases C-83 and 93 to 94/01 *Chronopost SA, La Poste and French Republic v Union française de l'express (Ufex), DHL International, Federal Express International (France) SNC and CRIE SA* [2003] ECR I-6993; Case T-175/99 *UPS Europe v Commission* [2002] ECR II-1915 and Case C-320/91 *Procureur du Roi v Paul Corbeau* [1993] ECR I-2533.

[158] *See* Notice from the Commission on the application of the competition rules to the postal sector and on the assessment of certain State measures relating to postal services, OJ 1998 C 39/2. *See also* Guidelines on the application of EEC competition rules in the telecommunications sector, OJ 1991 C 233/2. *See also* Case T-175/99 *ibid.*, para. 62.

[159] Case COMP/35.141 *supra* note 139.

[160] *Ibid.*, para. 6.

4. – Predatory Conduct
Robbert Snelders, Andrew Leyden and Andrea Lofaro

> *service or bundle of services the earnings from which exceed the stand-alone costs. The service for which revenue exceeds stand-alone cost is the source of the cross subsidy and the service in which revenue does not cover the incremental costs is its destination".*[161]

4.99 Since Deutsche Post's non-reserved parcel business did not even cover its own incremental costs (indeed, *"every sale … represented a loss"*[162]) the Commission held that it did not need to verify whether the other element of the test was satisfied.

4.100 Some commentators argue that it is unclear what difference a cross-subsidy analysis makes to predatory pricing cases.[163] The Commission's cross-subsidy analysis does help to identify the source of funding for a predatory scheme (typically a State-conferred monopoly). But this is unlikely to make any difference to the outcome: Deutsche Post's below-cost pricing could have been regarded as predatory regardless of the source of financing. The *Discussion Paper* states that cross-subsidy analysis is mainly relevant where the source of the subsidy is a legal monopoly.[164] As such, it seems that cross-subsidy analysis is employed by the Commission as a filter to identify cases where State-conferred monopoly power enables predatory conduct. Controversially, however, the *Discussion Paper* goes on to suggest that there is no requirement to prove the existence of a dominant position where a legal monopoly is used to fund predatory pricing on a non-dominated market.[165] The *Guidance Paper* does not discuss this theory (which would potentially amount to a significant extension of the domain of predatory pricing law). If the Commission were to pursue such a case, however, it is submitted that there should at least be proof of "close associative links" between the markets in question (as in *Tetra*

---

[161] Case COMP/35.141 *supra* note 139, para. 6. This definition is reminiscent of the so-called Faulhaber rule, which recognises that when the production of one unit of output entails both product-specific fixed costs and common costs, charging a price equal to the marginal cost of that unit does not suffice to ensure that this output is not subsidised by other activities. The price should also cover some part of the fixed and the common costs, and should therefore be equal or above the average incremental cost to guarantee that the activity in question is not the recipient of a subsidy. *See* G.R. Faulhaber, "Cross-Subsidization: Pricing in Public Enterprises" (1975) 65(5) *The American Economic Review*, pp. 966–77. *See also* E.E. Bailey and A.F. Friedlaender, "Market structure and multiproduct industries" (1982) 20 *The Journal of Economic Literature*, pp. 1024–48; T.J. Brennan, "Cross-Subsidization and Cost Misallocation by Regulated Monopolists" (1990) 2(1) *Journal of Regulatory Economics*, pp. 37–51.
[162] Case COMP/35.141 *supra* note 139, para. 36.
[163] *See supra* note 18, p. 269.
[164] *Discussion Paper supra* note 5, para. 125.
[165] *Ibid.*, para. 125.

4. – Predatory Conduct

Robbert Snelders, Andrew Leyden and Andrea Lofaro

Pak II[166]) and a robust theory of anticompetitive foreclosure on the non-dominant market.

5.3. Start-up Losses

Entry to certain industries requires large up-front investment that is only **4.101** recouped as demand grows over time. In such industries, if the assessment of costs were limited to the start-up phase, the measure of costs would be misleadingly high. Although losses are incurred in the short-run, the company might nevertheless be profitable over time. Such losses therefore merit special treatment under Article 102 TFEU, insofar as they must be corrected for cost amortisation over time and the depreciation of assets. Such considerations do not bear on whether these losses can be recovered in future, which is properly seen as a question of objective justification.[167]

There are a number of possible solutions to this problem. The simplest is **4.102** a variation on the Areeda-Turner analysis and involves a consideration of whether profitability was "reasonably anticipated"[168] by the dominant firm on the basis of the information available at the time.[169] In *Wanadoo*, the Commission applied a similar method, with two specific adjustments, in order to assess the dominant firm's start-up costs. First, the Commission excluded losses incurred over a period of fourteen months on the basis that at that point, the high-speed Internet market had not developed sufficiently for a test of predation to be meaningful.[170] Secondly, the Commission allowed for losses to be depreciated over a period of four years on the basis that they are a long-term investment in customer acquisition.

However, the Commission rejected Wanadoo's proposed discounted cash **4.103** flow ("DCF") method. This type of analysis consists of two steps. First, a forecast is made of future cash flows. These projected net cash flows are then discounted at an adjusted rate and aggregated to yield a net present value ("NPV") figure. So the argument goes, if the NPV of a given project is positive, it is rational to carry it out. If the NPV is negative, then it is rational not to carry the project out, or to abandon it. The Commission rejected this

---

[166] *See* Case C-333/94 P *Tetra Pak II Judgment 1996 supra* note 73, discussed in Section IV.5.1 above.

[167] *See* discussion of objective justification at Section V below.

[168] *See supra* note 10, pp. 697–733.

[169] *Ibid.*, pp. 697–733.

[170] *Ibid.*, para. 71.

4. – Predatory Conduct

Robbert Snelders, Andrew Leyden and Andrea Lofaro

approach on the grounds that: (1) DCF analysis may show that a given strategy was likely to produce positive returns, but it does not explain whether those returns are due to "legitimate" pricing or the ability to charge high prices due to the exclusion of competitors; (2) DCF only takes into account the undertaking's customers during a specific period, to the exclusion of benefits realised by the undertaking due to growth in later periods; and (3) due to imperfect information, it will not always be possible to correctly reconstruct an undertaking's anticipated revenues.[171]

5.4. Free Services

4.104 The application of predatory pricing rules to free services raises distinct considerations. This is notably the case in two-sided markets and in particular online services such as online search, image/video hosting, social networking, *etc.*, where providers rarely charge the end user directly, but rather monetise their services through selling advertising. Since the provision of online services for free implies by definition that the provider is charging a "price" below its AAC, complainants might allege that a provider of such services is engaging in predation. For example, a competitor might allege that an online provider is engaging in "predatory" conduct by making available a free version of an existing service with a view to eliminating competition from paid providers, thereby gaining the ability to charge a fee itself at a later date. This type of allegation is likely to arise repeatedly as online service providers progressively make available free online versions of services that previously had been made available only against a fee.[172]

4.105 Any such theory raises fundamental conceptual problems that render the application of predatory pricing rules difficult, if not impossible. First, such a theory presupposes that a relevant antitrust "market" can exist for the provision of free services, even in the absence of any trading relationship between the service provider and the end user. In cases relating to, *e.g.*, free TV services, the Commission has declined to define a relevant market in such

---

[171] *See supra* note 10, pp. 697–733, para. 96.

[172] So far, only one national case, *Bottin Cartographes v Google,* has endorsed such a theory. Bottin Cartographes alleged that since Google was providing online mapping services for free, Bottin could not compete, since it provided similar against an annual subscription fee. The Paris Commercial Court held that since Google offered its services for free to end users, it did not cover its variable costs (or any costs whatsoever) and concluded on that basis that Google was engaging in "predatory" conduct, without taking into account the fact that Google monetised its free services through advertising. *See Bottin Cartographes v Google Inc. & Google France*, Paris Commercial Court Judgment of 31 January 2012. This judgment could be overturned on appeal.

4. – Predatory Conduct
Robbert Snelders, Andrew Leyden and Andrea Lofaro

circumstances (finding rather that the relevant market relates to the sale of advertising space).[173] Secondly, such a theory disregards the economic rationale behind the provision of free online services. The logic of a predation theory (namely that the dominant company is deliberately incurring losses in the short run with the aim of gaining the ability to raise its own prices later) cannot apply in sectors where technology has rendered the provision of free services economically efficient. The marginal costs for web-based services are typically zero or near zero, since the costs of an additional user availing of the service (by, *e.g.*, entering a query on a search engine) are negligible. Thirdly, in many cases charging for access to an online service would not be rational, since even modest burdens (such as user registration, entry of credit card details, or other payment means) would very likely deter many users. As the Commission has recognised, even if the burden is minimal, users have learned to expect online services to be made available conveniently and for free.[174] Online providers therefore tend to earn revenues through the display of advertising.

In these circumstances, far from constituting predation, it is usually both **4.106** rational and efficient not to charge the end user but to monetise online services through advertising or other means. Condemning such behaviour as predatory would risk chilling innovation, and damaging consumer welfare by hindering the provision of free online services, particularly where such services were previously only available against a fee. Indeed, national authorities investigating allegedly predatory conduct in advertising-funded free markets (*e.g.*, free newspapers) have limited their analysis to the prices charged for advertising, and did not question the provision of consumer-facing goods or services for free.[175]

6.   Above-cost "Predatory Pricing"

Despite the strong suggestion in *AKZO* that pricing above ATC is *per se* **4.107** legal,[176] the Court of Justice has confirmed that abusive price-based conduct

---

[173] *See, e.g.,* Case IV/M.878 *RTL 7*, Commission Decision of 14 February 1997, para. 7.

[174] As the Commission noted in *Microsoft/Skype*, "*Skype is currently offered for free to customers and if prices were charged for this service, the large majority of consumers would switch to alternative providers … as for instance Google, Facebook, Viber, ooVoo or Fring. Commercial bundling is therefore unlikely in this free market*". Case COMP/M.6281 *Microsoft/Skype*, Commission Decision of 7 October 2011, paras 76, 157.

[175] *See, e.g.,* Case 1005/1/1/01 *Aberdeen Journals v Director General of Fair Trading*, UK Competition Appeal Tribunal Decision of 19 March 2002.

[176] *See AKZO.*

4. – Predatory Conduct
Robbert Snelders, Andrew Leyden and Andrea Lofaro

under Article 102 TFEU is not limited to below-cost pricing.[177] Unfortunately, however, the decisional practice of the Commission and the courts in this regard has proceeded on an *ad hoc* basis, without developing clear rules to explain which above-cost price cuts are legitimate and which are not. If above-cost price cuts are to be deemed abusive, it seems particularly urgent to develop a clear standard. Over-deterrence of above-cost price cuts would have a particularly chilling effect on legitimate pricing behaviour.

4.108   The concern with above-cost predatory pricing relates to the ability of incumbent firms to lower their prices or increase capacity to beat new entrants, while keeping prices above their own costs. Because the entrant has higher costs or lower quality, it will exit the market, at which point the incumbent will increase prices. To most economists this is a classic example of the normal competitive process: it is natural that a more efficient incumbent should price a new entrant out of the market. The concern, however, is that such reactive price cuts not only drive out individual entrants, but could have a deterrent effect on subsequent attempts at entry. The incumbent is thereby allowed to perpetuate monopoly profits at a level above that which the next most efficient firm would charge.[178] The classic example of this dynamic is found in the airline sector, where it is alleged that monopolists in "hub" airports abuse their dominance by adding capacity in response to new entry. The added capacity causes prices to fall (but remain above-cost) before returning to monopoly levels once the new entrant retreats from the market.[179]

4.109   A similar argument emphasises the notion that cost-based rules alone are inappropriate to assess predation, since they allow firms to circumvent the law by altering other business parameters, such as their capacity investments. As in the airline example, firms could expand their capacity and increase output in response to entry, but without pricing below AVC. Following the exit of the rival, the firm could restrict output and raise prices to monopoly levels once again. To avoid circumvention of the law it was argued that dominant firms

---

[177] *See* Joined Cases C-395 and 396/96 P *supra* note 2, paras 111–14, as well as the Opinion of the Advocate General Fennelly, para. 133.

[178] *See, e.g.*, M. Armstrong and J. Vickers, "Price Discrimination, Competition and Regulation" (1993) 41(4) *Journal of Industrial Economics*, pp. 335–59. *See* R. Schmalensee, "On the Use of Economic Models in Antitrust: The ReaLemon Case" (1979) 127(4) *University of Pennsylvania Law Review*, pp. 994–1050.

[179] *See, e.g.*, *US v AMR, American Airlines and American Eagle*, 140 F. Supp. 2d 1141 (2001).

4. – Predatory Conduct
Robbert Snelders, Andrew Leyden and Andrea Lofaro

should be restricted from increasing output for a period of 12–18 months following new market entry.[180]

6.1. Critique of a Ban on Above-cost Price Cuts

The bulk of academic opinion, however, argues that above-cost pricing should be presumptively lawful.[181] This conclusion is primarily based on the assumption that equally efficient firms can compete where pricing is above cost, so such a restriction would only facilitate inefficient entry. As Areeda and Turner argued, low prices at or above average cost are competition "*on the merits*" and exclude only less efficient rivals.[182] This argument alone, however, does not address the concerns set out above. The fact that a competitor is less efficient than the incumbent does not necessarily mean that it is preferable to allow such a firm to exit the market, as it could nevertheless exercise some competitive constraint on the incumbent. Every competitive market has firms that are less efficient than the others. In such circumstances, workable competition between the incumbent and a less-efficient firm is still arguably better than no competition at all.[183]   **4.110**

A more systematic critique of a restriction on above-cost price cuts, however, demonstrates that limiting the ability of dominant firms to price above costs confers no long-term welfare gain and can in fact inflict long-term costs on both consumer welfare and productive efficiency.[184] As Elhauge has demonstrated, in a simple model pitting an efficient incumbent against a less-efficient entrant, the following scenarios represent the possible effects of a restriction on above-cost price cuts in response to entry: **4.111**

- If the less efficient entrant would have tried to enter the market even without a restriction on the incumbent's pricing, the welfare effects

---

[180] O.E. Williamson, "Predatory pricing: a strategic and welfare analysis" (1977) 87(2) *Yale Law Journal*, pp. 290–92. A similar proposal is that dominant firms should be prohibited from increasing price when a new entrant ceases operations after being driven from the market. If a dominant firm wished to drive its competitors out of the market through low pricing, it would then be forced to maintain those prices in the longer term, precluding any possibility of recoupment. W.J. Baumol, "Quasi-permanence of price reductions: a policy for prevention of predatory pricing" (1979) 89(1) *Yale Law Journal*, pp. 2–3.

[181] For a survey of the literature *see* E. Elhauge, "Why Above-Cost Price Cuts To Drive Out Entrants Are Not Predatory – And the Implications for Defining Costs and Market Power" (2003) 112(4) *The Yale Law Journal*, pp. 681–827.

[182] *See supra* note 10, p. 706.

[183] *See supra* note 181, p. 699.

[184] *See supra* note 181, p. 802.

4. – Predatory Conduct
Robbert Snelders, Andrew Leyden and Andrea Lofaro

of a restriction would be unambiguously negative. Consumers of both the incumbent and the entrant would pay high prices post-entry. Production would shift to a less-efficient entrant, while the incumbent's operating efficiency would decrease, due to, *e.g.*, lost economies of scale.

- If a less efficient entrant is weakly encouraged to enter, consumers who buy from the entrant might pay less in the short run, but those who buy from the incumbent would likely be forced to pay more than they would otherwise. Production will again shift to the less-efficient entrant, decreasing the incumbent's operating efficiency.

- Where the new entrant is as efficient as the incumbent, the welfare effects of a price restriction are unambiguously negative. Since the incumbent cannot drop prices, consumers of both the incumbent and the new entrant would be forced to pay more. Since there would be no incentive to cut costs, the incumbent's efficiency would decrease.

- In the case of entrants that can become equally efficient only following entry, effects on consumer welfare are likely to be negative, as consumers of both the incumbent and the new entrant will pay higher post-entry prices. As above, production will shift to a less efficient entrant, reducing the efficiency of the incumbent.

4.112 It should be noted that a restriction on above-cost price cuts would also have negative effects on the dynamic incentives of both potential entrants and incumbents. If less efficient entry is to be facilitated, the incentives for potential entrants to innovate and thereby become as efficient as incumbents are reduced.[185] Similarly, although a restriction might encourage incumbents to price slightly lower in order to deter entry in the first place, the restriction would also lessen the incentives for incumbents to innovate to reduce their costs. Even if they reduce their costs, they still run the risk of finding themselves unable to compete for new customers, as the restriction would prevent them from passing on any efficiency gains to consumers in order to win new share.

6.2. *Above-cost Price Cuts as an Abuse under Article 102 TFEU*

4.113 The Commission has found above-cost price cuts to infringe Article 102 TFEU in numerous cases. In *Hilti*,[186] the Commission examined a dominant

---

[185] *See supra* note 181, p. 802.
[186] Cases IV/30.787 and 31.488 *supra* note 2.

4. – Predatory Conduct

Robbert Snelders, Andrew Leyden and Andrea Lofaro

nail gun manufacturer's attempts to discourage purchasers of its nail guns from purchasing compatible nails from other manufacturers. These included a combination of price and non-price measures, such as a refusal to honour guarantees where customers used competing nails, tied sales, an attempt to curb exports, and discriminatory pricing policies. Hilti offered larger discounts and other offers (including in some cases free products) to customers who purchased both nails and guns from Hilti compared to those who purchased Hilti guns but competing nails. In the Commission's view, these discounts were not based on efficiency considerations, but were designed solely to prevent consumers from buying competitors' nails. In finding these measures abusive, the Commission relied exclusively on the selective nature of the discounts, going so far as to state that the abuse in this case did *"not hinge on whether the prices were below costs"* but rather *"the fact that, because of its dominance, Hilti was able to offer special discriminatory prices to its competitors' customers with a view to damaging their business, whilst maintaining higher prices to its own equivalent customers"*.[187] On appeal, the Court of First Instance upheld the Commission decision, on the basis that Hilti's strategy was *"not a legitimate mode of competition,"*[188] because it deterred other undertakings from competing on the market for nails. The Court did not make any attempt to explain how Hilti's above-cost prices excluded rivals or deterred market entry.

In *Compagnie Maritime Belge*[189] the Commission held that various measures adopted by CEWAL, a shipping conference offering services between certain European ports and the Democratic Republic of the Congo (then Zaire), constituted an infringement of Article 102 TFEU. This included CEWAL's practice of employing "fighting ships", whereby the conference set sailing times as close as possible to those of its only competitor, G&C, and set special discounts for those sailings. The Commission found (and CEWAL itself admitted) that these measures were adopted with the express purpose of driving G&C from the market. Both the Court of First Instance and the Court of Justice agreed that this practice constituted an abuse, explicitly rejecting the appellants' argument, based on *AKZO*, that selective low prices

4.114

---

[187] Cases IV/30.787 and 31.488 *supra* note 2, para. 81.

[188] Case T-30/89 *Hilti v Commission ("Hilti")* [1991] ECR II-1439, para. 100.

[189] Cases IV/32.448 and 32.450 *Cewal*, Commission Decision of 23 December 1992, OJ 1993 L 34/20, upheld on appeal in Joined Cases T-24 to 26 and 28/93 and in Joined Cases C-395 and 396/96 P *supra* note 2. *See also* Cases IV/34.621 and 35.059 *Irish Sugar ("Irish Sugar Decision 1997")*, Commission Decision of 14 May 1997, OJ 1997 L 258/1, affirmed on appeal in Case T-228/97 *Irish Sugar v Commission ("Irish Sugar Judgment 1999")* [1999] ECR II-2969 and Case C-497/99 P *Irish Sugar v Commission ("Irish Sugar Judgment 2001")* [2001] ECR I-5333.

4. – Predatory Conduct

Robbert Snelders, Andrew Leyden and Andrea Lofaro

could not be abusive as a matter of law unless they were below an appropriate measure of cost. However, the Court of Justice was careful to limit its ruling to the specific circumstances of the case, which hinged on three features of CEWAL's conduct: (1) CEWAL "admitted" that the purpose of its conduct was to eliminate a rival; (2) the conference apportioned the reduction in revenue among its members; and (3) competition was already weakened since European Union legislation allowed liner conferences to engage in collective price setting. The Court of Justice was at pains to limit its ruling to the specific facts of the case, noting in particular CEWAL's quasi monopoly (over 90 per cent share). Thus, the Court of Justice did not *"rule generally on the circumstances in which a liner conference may legitimately, on a case by case basis, adopt lower prices than those of its advertised tariff in order to compete with a competitor who quotes lower prices"*.[190] The Commission similarly states that *Compagnie Maritime Belge* should be seen as a wholly exceptional case and confined to its own facts.[191]

6.3. Evaluation of the Article 102 TFEU Case Law

4.115   From the case law above it seems that it is open to the Commission to find prices above ATC abusive. But it is not clear what principles are to be used to distinguish between legitimate and illegitimate above-cost price cuts. As noted above, restrictions on price above ATC run a great risk of chilling price competition, and there is a broad consensus among economists that above-cost price cuts rarely, if ever, damage consumer welfare. Even if one accepts that they can, it is questionable whether implementing a rule against such cuts will remedy the situation by causing higher entry levels or lower prices.[192] Whatever the precise contours of the rule under Article 102 TFEU, it is clear that it should be enforced sparingly. The risk of over-enforcement in the case of above-cost predatory pricing is much greater than in the case of below-cost practices. Any future gains realised through a restriction on price cuts are inherently speculative, whereas lower prices, whatever the purpose behind them, at least produce clear consumer benefits in the short-run. As Hovenkamp argues, until there is a rule that can reliably identify anticompetitive above-cost price cuts, a consumer-oriented antitrust policy *"has no choice but*

---

[190] Case C-497/99 P *ibid.*, paras 118 and 119.

[191] *See Discussion Paper supra* note 5, para. 128.

[192] *See supra* note 181, pp. 681–827.

4. – Predatory Conduct
Robbert Snelders, Andrew Leyden and Andrea Lofaro

to adhere to the admittedly under deterrent below cost pricing requirements of the Areeda-Turner or some similar rule".[193]

One explanation of the European Union case law thus far is that price cuts above ATC are unlawful only when combined with other anticompetitive practices, such as loyalty rebates, tying, or exclusive contracts.[194] Under this theory, low pricing could never be abusive in and of itself, but where such pricing makes sense only as part of an overall exclusionary strategy, it can nevertheless form part of an abuse. This approach at least has the virtue of immunising above-cost price cuts from Article 102 TFEU where they are not accompanied by other, potentially abusive, conduct. This does not explain *Compagnie Maritime Belge*, but both the Commission[195] and the Court of Justice itself[196] are of the view that this case was exceptional. In practice, this scenario is very unlikely to arise again. As explained above, the case involved collectively dominant companies with a near-monopoly, who applied a clear strategy to exclude a competitor through selective price cuts, while collectively sharing the loss of revenues. Normally, such conduct would constitute a *per se* violation of Article 101 TFEU, but that provision was rendered inapplicable due to European Union legislation which permitted the setting of shipping rates. **4.116**

Recent developments confirm the "exceptional" nature of *Compagnie Maritime Belge*. In his opinion on *Post Danmark*, Advocate General Mengozzi endorsed this view, holding that the *Compagnie Maritime Belge* judgment is only of "marginal" relevance.[197] As such, he held that its scope should be limited to situations where: (1) an exclusionary intent could be inferred from circumstances unrelated to the price level; (2) the company is "superdominant"; or (3) pricing practices formed part of a general pattern of abusive conduct, none of which was true in the case of *Post Danmark*.[198] In its judgment on *Post Danmark*, the Court of Justice did not address Advocate General Mengozzi's arguments, but held that where a dominant company sets selectively low prices at "*a higher level than ... average total costs ... it cannot be considered that such prices* **4.117**

---

[193] H. Hovenkamp, "Post-Chicago Antitrust: A Review and Critique" (2001) 257 *Columbia Business Law Review*, pp. 259–66.

[194] This was Advocate General Fennelly's approach in *Compagnie Maritime Belge*. *See* Advocate General Fennelly in Joined Cases C-395 and 396/96 P *supra* note 2.

[195] *See Discussion Paper supra* note 5, para. 128.

[196] *See* Joined Cases C-395 and 396/96 P *supra* note 2.

[197] Advocate General Mengozzi in Case C-209/10 *Post Danmark v Konkurrencerådet*, not yet reported.

[198] *Ibid.*, paras 92–96.

4. – Predatory Conduct
Robbert Snelders, Andrew Leyden and Andrea Lofaro

have anticompetitive effects".[199] Thus, while the Court of Justice did not expressly overrule *Compagnie Maritime Belge*, its ruling strongly suggests that price cuts above ATC are presumptively legal. It remains to be seen how this ruling will sit with the Commission's *Guidance Paper*, which leaves open the possibility of condemning above-cost pricing on the basis of its expansive notion of "sacrifice", but unfortunately does not provide clear guidance on when the Commission would take action against such conduct.[200]

V. Objective Justifications

4.118 Since the Areeda-Turner rule was originally proposed, it has become apparent that cost benchmarks are complex to apply and often produce arbitrary results. Competition authorities and courts have therefore refrained from basing their assessments solely on the basis of costs-based tests. It is now generally accepted that even prices below AVC/AAC can have an objective justification.[201] As the Commission states in the *Discussion Paper*, "*in a case where a presumption of predatory pricing is established, the dominant company may rebut that finding by justifying its pricing behaviour even if the price is below the relevant cost benchmark*".[202] Moreover, modern economic theory recognises that strategies that appear predatory at first sight might have a legitimate explanation. Such a "business justification" or "efficiencies defence" serves as a means of filtering out cases where below-cost pricing is more likely to be welfare-enhancing, rather than part of a plan to exclude or discipline rivals. This reasoning is particularly applicable to "high tech" markets, which often involve massive start-up losses in order to achieve the scale necessary for network effects.

4.119 The *Guidance Paper* states that the Commission will examine claims put forward by a dominant undertaking that its conduct is justified either by (1) objective necessity or (2) by demonstrating that it produces substantial efficiencies, which outweigh any anticompetitive effects. It should be noted, however, that the *Guidance Paper* goes on to state that efficiencies are generally unlikely in the

---

[199] *See supra* note 197, para.36.

[200] *See* discussion of the *Guidance Paper* at Section VI.1 below.

[201] *See, e.g.*, Case T-83/91 *Tetra Pak II Judgment 1994 supra* note 73, para. 147 ("[I]*t may be acceptable for an undertaking in a dominant position to sell at a loss in certain circumstances*"); and Case COMP/38.233 *supra* note 73, paras 305 *et seq. See also*, R. Whish, *Competition Law* (5th Ed., London, LexisNexis UK, 2003) p. 706; V. Korah, *An Introductory Guide To EC Competition Law And Practice* (7th Ed., Oxford, Hart Publishing, 2000) p. 127.

[202] *See Discussion Paper supra* note 5, para. 130.

4. – Predatory Conduct
Robbert Snelders, Andrew Leyden and Andrea Lofaro

case of predatory conduct.[203] All defences in the Article 102 TFEU context must meet a proportionality test,[204] and it is incumbent upon the dominant undertaking to provide the evidence necessary to demonstrate that it is met.[205]

1. The "Meeting Competition" Defence

Even dominant firms face strong competition from time to time, forcing **4.120** them to adapt their behaviour to market conditions. Sometimes this will entail temporary below-cost pricing – not with the intention of driving a competitor from the market – but simply to meet the prices offered by competitors. Since *United Brands*,[206] the principle that a dominant firm is *"allowed to take such reasonable steps as it deems appropriate to protect its commercial interest"*[207] has been well established in the jurisprudence of the European Union courts. From the earliest predatory pricing cases, the Commission has also accepted that dominant undertakings have the right to minimise short-run losses in this manner.[208] In *AKZO*, the Commission imposed interim remedies prohibiting AKZO from supplying goods below cost, except where *"it is necessary to do so in good faith to meet (but not to undercut) a lower price shown to be offered by a supplier ready and able to supply to that customer"*.[209] Similarly, in *Hilti*,[210] *British Sugar*,[211] *BPB Industries*,[212]

---

[203] *See Guidance Paper supra* note 3, paras 29, 74.

[204] The dominant undertaking must prove: (1) that the efficiencies have been, or are likely to be, realised as a result of the conduct; (2) that the conduct is indispensable to the realisation of those efficiencies (*i.e.*, there must be no less anticompetitive alternatives to the conduct that are capable of producing the same efficiencies); (3) that the likely efficiencies brought about by the conduct outweigh any negative effects on competition and consumer welfare in the affected markets; and (4) that the conduct does not eliminate effective competition. *Ibid.*, para. 30.

[205] *Ibid.*

[206] Case 27/76 *United Brands and United Brands Continentaal v Commission* ("*United Brands*") [1978] ECR 207.

[207] *Ibid.*, para. 18; *see also* Case T-228/97 *Irish Sugar Judgment 1999 supra* note 189, paras 112 and 189, and Case T-65/89 *BPB Industries and British Gypsum v Commission* ("*BPB Industries*") [1993] ECR II-389, paras 117 and 189. Similarly, under US law, section 2(b) of the Robinson-Patman Act provides a statutory basis for the meeting of competition as a legal defence to an allegation of illegal price discrimination. In order to establish the defence the seller must show that offer in question was made in "good faith" to meet an equally low price of a competitor.

[208] *See Discussion Paper supra* note 5, para. 131.

[209] Case IV/30.698 *supra* note 141, Art. 4.

[210] Cases IV/30.787 and 31.488 *supra* note 2. Although Hilti was prohibited from engaging in price discrimination, the Commission provided for an exception allowing Hilti to lower prices where necessary to meet a competitive offer, make promotions, or to generate sales that Hilti would not otherwise make.

[211] *Napier Brown supra* note 90, para. 31. The Commission held that although undercutting a competitor's prices would be an abuse, matching them would be permissible.

[212] Case *Iberian Trading UK Ltd v BPB Industries Plc and British Gypsum Ltd* [1990] 4 CMLR 464, para. 133. The Commission accepted BPB's price reductions because they were neither predatory nor part of a scheme of "*systematic alignment*".

4. – Predatory Conduct
Robbert Snelders, Andrew Leyden and Andrea Lofaro

Tetra Pak II,[213] *Irish Sugar,*[214] and *Digital,*[215] the Commission accepted the principle that dominant companies have the right to reduce prices where this would be necessary in order to meet a comparable offer made by a competitor. On the other hand, it is clear from the jurisprudence of the European Union courts that in light of the "special responsibility" of dominant undertakings, their right to align their prices with competitors is not absolute.[216]

1.1.   Status of the Defence under European Union Law

4.121   *Wanadoo* is the most recent case in which the "meeting competition" defence was advanced. Wanadoo, a high-speed Internet service provider, was found to have charged predatory prices on the French market for high-speed Internet access for residential customers. The Commission found that the prices charged by Wanadoo failed to cover its variable costs between March and August of 2001, and that full costs were not covered from August 2001 to October 2002.[217] Wanadoo claimed that it was merely meeting the prices charged by its competitors. The Commission held that while a dominant operator is *"not strictly speaking prohibited from aligning its prices on those of competitors"*, this option is not open to it where it *"would result in its not recovering the costs of the service in question"*.[218] This statement might be read as ruling out the possibility of a meeting competition defence below AVC/AAC, but the Commission nevertheless proceeded to examine Wanadoo's argument and rejected it on the facts.[219]

4.122   On appeal to the Court of First Instance, Wanadoo argued that the Commission could not deny a dominant company of its *"right [...] to align its conduct on that of its competitors"*.[220] The Court of First Instance accepted that a dominant undertaking is entitled to take *"reasonable steps"* in order to protect

---

[213] *Supra* note 85, para. 148. The Commission assessed Tetra Pak's argument that it was merely meeting competition, but rejected it on the facts.

[214] Cases IV/34.621 and 35.059 *supra* note 189, para. 134. The Commission found that dominant firms are *"entitled to defend that position by competing with other firms on its market"*.

[215] M. Dolmans and V. Pickering, "*The 1997 Digital Undertaking*" (1998) 19(2) *European Competition Law Review,* pp. 108–15, para. 3.1. The Commission found that dominant companies were allowed to offer proportionate price reductions in individual cases *"to meet comparable service offerings of a competitor"*.

[216] *Supra* note 82.

[217] Case COMP/38.233 *supra* note 73, paras 405–08.

[218] *Ibid.*, paras 405–08.

[219] *Ibid.*, para. 331, where the Commission states that *"the argument based on competitors' prices would have been admissible in principle"*.

[220] *Ibid.* para. 172. Wanadoo was citing the ECJ precedent in the *AKZO* case (*See* Case IV/30.698 *supra* note 2).

4. – Predatory Conduct
Robbert Snelders, Andrew Leyden and Andrea Lofaro

its commercial interests[221] but not where it is *"aimed [...] also at strengthening and abusing"*[222] its dominance. The Court of First Instance implicitly invoked the *"special responsibility"* of dominant undertakings[223] to hold that in certain circumstances they *"may be deprived the right to adopt a course of conduct or take measures which are not in themselves abuses and which would be unobjectionable if adopted or taken by non-dominant undertakings"*.[224] Wanadoo could not, therefore, rely on an "absolute right" to align its prices on those of its competitors where those prices are below its costs.[225] This element of the Court of First Instance's ruling was upheld on appeal to the Court of Justice.[226]

In the wake of the *Wanadoo* appeal, the status of the "meeting competition" defence under EU law remains ambiguous. There is a key distinction between price cuts below AVC/AAC and those between AVC/AAC and ATC. As noted above, where prices are below AVC, each sale makes a loss, while sales merely below ATC can be loss minimising, at least in the short run. Accordingly, prices below ATC but above AVC/AAC should in principle be treated more leniently. **4.123**

1.2. Prices Below AVC/AAC

A strict reading of the *Wanadoo* judgment suggests that "meeting competition" is not a defence below AVC.[227] A better reading of the judgment, however, is that the defence *is* available in principle, provided that the dominant undertaking's response is proportionate to the defence of its legitimate interests (keeping existing customers) and is not in fact designed to exclude competitors. The Court's formulation (*"aimed [...] also at strengthening and abusing"*[228]) **4.124**

---

[221] Case COMP/38.233 *supra* note 73, para. 185. The CFI cited *United Brands supra* note 206, para. 189; *BPB Industries supra* note 207, para. 117; and Joined Cases T-24 to 26 and 28/93 *supra* note 2, para. 146.

[222] *See supra* note 82, para. 18.

[223] The special responsibility of dominant firms was recently noted by the CFI: "*Furthermore, according to the case law, dominant undertakings have a special responsibility not to allow their conduct to impair genuine undistorted competition on the common market*". Joined Cases T-191 and 212 to 214/98 *Atlantic Container Line and others v Commission 2003* [2003] ECR II-3275, para. 1109. *See also*, Case 322/81 *Nederlandsche Banden Industrie Michelin v Commission* ("*Michelin I*") [1983] ECR 3461, para. 57; and Case T-228/97 *Irish Sugar Judgment 1999 supra* note 189, para. 112.

[224] Case T-228/97 *ibid.*, para. 186. The CFI cited Case T-111/96 *ITT Promedia v Commission* ("*ITT Promedia*") [1998] ECR II-2937, para. 139.

[225] *Supra* note 128.

[226] *Supra* note 82.

[227] *See* M. Gal, "Below-Cost Price Alignment: Meeting or Beating Competition? The France Telecom Case" (2007) 28(6) *European Competition Law Review*, pp. 382–91 and *supra* note 128.

[228] *Supra* note 128, para. 187.

4. – Predatory Conduct
Robbert Snelders, Andrew Leyden and Andrea Lofaro

suggests that the defence contains a strong intent element. In other words, as a threshold matter, the defence is never available if the dominant undertaking intends not only to meet an offer from a competitor, but also to "protect its interests" by eliminating that competitor outright. Otherwise the defence is available in principle.

4.125   At first blush, allowing a dominant firm to meet competition below AVC/AAC seems irreconcilable with the basic premise of the Areeda-Turner rules, namely that such sales can only be explained as part of an attempt to eliminate a rival.[229] The *Discussion Paper* therefore states that the defence *"can normally not be applied"* below AVC/AAC.[230] On the other hand, it is possible to imagine cases, such as a price war between relatively close rivals, in which pricing below AVC/AAC could be justified. In *Berlingske Gratisaviser*,[231] for example, the Danish Competition Council held that since a dominant newspaper company's rival was selling its advertising space below AVC, the dominant company was also entitled to price below AVC to meet (but not undercut) that rival. As O'Donoghue notes, this solution has a "pragmatic appeal" since it allows for such a company to defend its interests without granting it the ability to systematically exclude competitors through relying on the meeting competition defence.[232] It is submitted, however, that such cases will be quite rare, as a finding of dominance seems implausible in the presence of a rival with the ability to price below AVC for a sustained period (unless the Commission is relying on a leveraging theory, as in *Tetra Pak II* or *Deutsche Post*).

1.3.   Prices below ATC but above AVC

4.126   Matching or indeed beating a competitor's price is less likely to be exclusionary between ATC and AVC. As noted above, the Court allows the "meeting competition" defence provided that the prices in question are not also "aimed" at "strengthening and abusing" a dominant position. The Court's

---

[229] *See* P. Bolton, J. F. Brodley and M. H. Riordan, *supra* note 39, p. 2275. *See also* P. Areeda and D. F. Turner, *supra* note 10, p. 713 ("[T]*hese justifications are either so rarely applicable or of such dubious merit for a monopolist that the presumption of illegality for prices below both marginal costs and average [variable] cost should be conclusive*").

[230] *See Discussion Paper supra* note 5, para. 83.

[231] *MetroXpress Danmark v Berlingske Gratisaviser,* Danish Competition Authority Decision of 29 May 2002, discussed in the Danish Competition Council's Annual Report (2002), Section 2.5. *See* Danish Competition Council, *"2 Promotion of Competition"*, Annual Report 2002.

[232] *See supra* note 18.

4. – Predatory Conduct
Robbert Snelders, Andrew Leyden and Andrea Lofaro

intent-based formulation implies that, to a large extent, the analysis of the "meeting competition" defence will overlap with the determination of eliminatory intent under the second *AKZO* rule. In most cases, therefore, the success or failure of the plea will turn on whether there is a "plan" to eliminate a rival. The dominant firm's response must, however, also be proportionate and fulfil the other criteria set out below. As with all "objective justifications", the Commission claims that the burden of proof rests with the dominant firm,[233] but this assertion seems particularly questionable with regard to the "meeting competition" defence. Between AVC and ATC, proof of intent to eliminate a competitor is a constitutive element of the abuse, and must therefore be proven by the Commission.

1.4. *Elements of the Defence*

As noted above, in essence, the "meeting competition" defence operates by negating any suggestion that a dominant firm intends to exclude its rivals. From the available case law, it appears that the following factors must be present in order to make out the defence: (1) the price cuts must be designed to defend against attempts to capture regular customers; (2) the dominant company must act in good faith; and (3) the price cuts must not undercut a competitor's lower price. In addition, as with all objective justifications, the company's response must be *"suitable, indispensable and proportionate"*[234] to the competitive challenge posed by competitors. In other words, there must be no other less anticompetitive means to minimise the dominant firm's losses, the price cuts must be limited in time, and the conduct must not significantly delay or hamper entry or expansion by competitors.[235] Finally, the *Discussion Paper* adds that objective justification is not possible if it is established that the conduct involves extra investments in capacity and does not minimise losses directly resulting from the action taken by certain competitors.[236]

4.127

1.4.1. Price Cuts Must Be Defensive

As the name suggests, to avail of the "meeting competition" defence, price cuts must be defensive in nature. In other words, they must be adopted in

---

[233] *See Discussion Paper supra* note 5, para. 82.
[234] *Guidance Paper supra* note 3, para. 30. *See also ibid.*, para. 132.
[235] *Ibid.*, para. 132.
[236] *Ibid.*, para. 82.

4. – Predatory Conduct
Robbert Snelders, Andrew Leyden and Andrea Lofaro

reaction to attempts to capture the dominant firm's share, not used as an offensive tool to gain new customers. A different interpretation would not be compatible with the *United Brands* formulation that a dominant company is entitled to protect its legitimate trade interests *"if they are attacked"*.[237] An "attack" in this sense will usually consist of an actual offer from a competitor to the company's regular customers, but it might be sufficient that the dominant company can reasonably expect a competitor to make such an offer in the near future.[238] On the other hand, the "meeting competition" defence cannot be used to justify below-cost pricing in order to *"prevent, frustrate or slow down entry by a rival"*.[239]

Wanadoo offers a useful illustration of this point. The Commission rejected the argument that Wanadoo was meeting competition, on the basis that the dominant firm's behaviour was not part of a defensive strategy of meeting actual competitive threats, but rather an attempt to pre-empt the market by deterring entry.[240] First, Wanadoo's behaviour was not reactive in nature: many of the allegedly predatory prices were put in place before rivals even entered the market.[241] In fact, subsequent entrants aligned their prices to Wanadoo rather than the other way around. Secondly, Wanadoo did not just meet its competitors' prices, but in fact undercut them significantly.[242] Thirdly, certain key Wanadoo pricing decisions were made well in advance of rivals' announcements,[243] suggesting that Wanadoo was pre-empting rather than responding to competitive threats.

1.4.2. The Dominant Company Must Act in Good Faith

The dominant company must ensure that there is documentation of competing offers, or at least that it is justified in its belief that its regular customers

---

[237] *See United Brands supra* note 206, para. 189 ("[T]*he fact that an undertaking is in a dominant position cannot deprive it of its entitlement to protect its own commercial interests when they are attacked, and…such an undertaking must be allowed the right to take such reasonable steps as it deems appropriate to protect those interests*[…]").

[238] This expectation could be based on, *e.g.*, general marketing material from the competitor indicating which products will be offered, where and at which price. *See supra* note 215, pp. 108–15.

[239] *See Discussion Paper supra* note 5, para. 132.

[240] Case COMP/38.233 *supra* note 73.

[241] *Ibid.*, para. 321.

[242] *Ibid.*, paras 323–25.

[243] *Ibid.*, para. 326.

4. – Predatory Conduct
Robbert Snelders, Andrew Leyden and Andrea Lofaro

are being attacked. In its interim decision in *ECS/AKZO,*[244] for example, the Commission required AKZO to show that a competing supplier had offered a lower price, and that this supplier was *"ready and able"* to supply customers.[245] By definition, a good faith standard does not require absolute certainty, but the dominant firm must at least have some evidence as to the likely existence and pricing of a competing offer.

This requirement is nevertheless problematic for dominant companies because the very act of obtaining information about a competing offer carries antitrust risk. Receiving such information directly from a competitor would constitute a horizontal exchange of price information, contrary to Article 101 TFEU. Even obtaining price information from customers is not risk-free. In *ECS/AKZO,* AKZO obtained details from its customers of offers made by other suppliers of flour additives, for the purpose of later quoting a price just below the lowest competing offer. The Commission considered that this conduct formed part of AKZO's exclusionary commercial policy and was therefore abusive under Article 102 TFEU. The Court of Justice upheld this element of the Commission's assessment, holding that obtaining price information from a customer *"where such a practice forms part of a plan to eliminate a competitor [...] cannot be regarded as a normal means of competition"*.[246] Similarly, in *Hoffman-La Roche,*[247] the Commission held that so-called *"English clauses"* in distribution contacts, designed to encourage customers to disclose competing prices, were *per se* abusive.

Dominant suppliers seeking to meet competition through cutting prices therefore face a dilemma. To avoid liability under Article 101 TFEU, they must obtain the relevant information about competing offers from customers (but even this is not without risk) and under *Hoffmann-La Roche,* they cannot create an incentive for customers to provide it. Thus, suppliers will have to

---

[244] Case IV/30.698 *supra* note 2, Art. 4.

[245] Case IV/30.698 *ECS/AKZO,* Commission Decision of 29 July 1983, OJ 1983 L 252/13, para. 34. Similarly, in *Digital,* the Commission accepted commitments providing that Digital was entitled to meet comparable service offerings of a competitor, but that price cuts could not be offered *"until Digital has completed an internal review process designed to verify that the proposed allowance is offered in good faith as a proportional response to real or (based on information from the customer or other reliable sources) reasonably anticipated competitive offerings"*. *See* Case IV/M.1120 *Compaq/Digital,* Commission Decision of 23 March 1998 and *supra* note 215, pp. 108–15.

[246] *See AKZO,* para. 148.

[247] Case 85/76 *Hoffmann-La Roche v Commission* (*"Hoffmann-La Roche"*) [1979] ECR 461.

4. – Predatory Conduct
Robbert Snelders, Andrew Leyden and Andrea Lofaro

rely on information spontaneously provided by customers.[248] In practice, it appears that the most a dominant supplier can do to prove "good faith" is to document the existence of a competing offer, relying on information voluntarily supplied by reliable customers, along with other factors, *e.g.*, proof that they were threatened with a termination of purchases if the competing offer were not met, and that efforts were made to confirm the offer, either by documentary evidence or by assessing its reasonableness in terms of available market data.[249]

1.4.3. Meeting but not Beating Competition

As a rule, the dominant company may meet but not beat a competitor's offer. Thus, in *AKZO*, the Commission's interim measures prohibited AKZO from engaging in below-cost selling, except "*in respect of a particular customer and only if it is necessary to do so in good faith to meet (but not to undercut) a lower price*".[250] Similarly, in *Wanadoo*, the Commission objected to the fact that Wanadoo undercut its competitors' prices significantly.[251] The Commission has, however, displayed some willingness to allow exceptions to this principle. In *BPB Industries*, for example, the Commission accepted a price reduction to a level which was "*broadly equivalent to or slightly below*" the competitor's prices.[252] Indeed, in practice, whether a given price adjustment meets or undercuts a competitor's offer often gives rise to considerable uncertainty. Most companies regularly fend off attacks for various customers from many competitors, all of whom offer different prices. Dominant companies are therefore often in a situation where meeting the lowest price necessarily implies beating the prices offered by other competitors. Such conduct should not be characterised as an abuse, as this would effectively tie the dominant company's hands. Further, it ought to be permissible to undercut the price of a rival who also competes on non-price terms, *e.g.*, free delivery, after-sales support or other supplementary services, provided that any such price adjustment is proportionate to the competing offer.

---

[248] In *Hoffmann-La Roche*, the ECJ admitted that the customers "*have an obvious commercial interest in not disclosing*" information about competing offers to a dominant supplier. *Ibid.*, para. 107.

[249] *See, e.g.*, *Falls City Industries v Vanco Beverage*, 460 US 428 (1923), p. 2.

[250] *See* Case IV/30.698 *supra* note 2, Art. 4.

[251] Case COMP/38.233 *supra* note 73, paras 323–25.

[252] Case IV/31.900 *BPB Industries*, Commission Decision of 5 December 1988, OJ 1989 L 10/50, paras 131–34.

4. – Predatory Conduct
Robbert Snelders, Andrew Leyden and Andrea Lofaro

2. Short Term Promotions

On occasion, the Commission has permitted dominant undertakings to **4.128** implement short-term price reductions when launching a new product or attempting to enter a new market.[253] The *Discussion Paper* also recognises this defence, stating that a dominant company may wish to show that a low price *"is part of a one-off temporary promotion campaign to introduce a new product and where the duration and extent of the campaign are such that exclusionary effects are excluded"*.[254]

It is unclear, however, in what circumstances this is permissible, and in par- **4.129** ticular whether this defence would be available where prices are below AVC, or only where they are between AVC and ATC. There are strong arguments for allowing such a defence, even below AVC, particularly where a new product requires consumer familiarity before the market is willing to pay an above-cost price. Charging below cost during a promotional period allows customers to become familiar with the product, in the hope that they will be willing to pay the full price once its virtues are proven. Such a strategy is analogous to advertising, and is clearly not "predatory" in the sense that the success of subsequent price increases does not depend on the foreclosure of competitors, but on consumers becoming familiar with the merits of the product. Such a promotional offer would constitute a clear example of normal competition "on the merits" whether prices are below AVC/AAC or ATC. This argument would also apply where the promotional pricing is directed at new customers of an existing product.[255] Nevertheless, for short-term promotions to be permissible under Article 102 TFEU, it is clear that the price reduction should be temporary and limited in scope. Firms cannot use the guise of a short-term promotion to hide systematic below-cost selling intended to eliminate a rival.

---

[253] *See, e.g., supra* note 215, pp. 108–15. In its 1997 undertaking, Digital was allowed to reduce prices for "short-term promotional programs" provided that they were above cost and available on a non-discriminatory basis.

[254] *Discussion Paper supra* note 5, para. 110.

[255] *See supra* note 18, p. 293.

4. – Predatory Conduct

Robbert Snelders, Andrew Leyden and Andrea Lofaro

3. Efficiencies in Growth Markets

4.130 In *Wanadoo*, although the Commission made it clear that "*the fact that a sector is a growth sector does not in itself mean that it is not covered by the competition rules*",[256] below-cost pricing in such markets is much more likely to have a non-exclusionary purpose. This concern arises particularly in high tech markets and network industries, which often require large, risky investments in infrastructure or patents, and therefore necessarily involve losses in the start-up phase. Efficiencies can lead to recovery of initial losses over time, as cost savings are realised through the company's greater scale and scope or enhanced learning experience. This is similar to promotional pricing, but the key difference is that the recovery of initial losses is due to the dominant firm's ability to reduce costs over time, as opposed to a subsequent price increase.[257]

4.131 "Emerging" or "growth" markets are not easily defined in the abstract (and no definition is offered under EU competition law), but the relevant characteristic for the purposes of Article 102 TFEU analysis is uncertainty as to future demand and market developments. For example, the Commission's *Framework Directive* on the regulation of the communications sector refers to "*newly emerging markets, where de facto the market leader is likely to have a substantial market share but should not be subjected to inappropriate obligations*".[258] On this basis, emerging markets are those where: (1) there is a high degree of uncertainty because the sector is new, and (2) intervention should be carefully balanced and justified.[259] This suggests that in such markets there might be a presumption against early intervention, or at least an enhanced burden of proof before remedies are to be imposed. On the other hand, it must be recognised that many growth markets, particularly those with strong network effects or high switching costs, have a propensity to "tip" in a manner that is difficult to reverse. In these markets there may be considerable costs associated with failing to intervene (or intervening too late) in order to prevent abusive conduct.

---

[256] Case COMP/38.233 *supra* note 73, paras 323–25.

[257] *See supra* note 18, p. 294.

[258] Parliament and Council Directive 2002/21/EC of 07 March 2002 on a common regulatory framework for electronic communications networks and services ("*Framework Directive*"), OJ 2002 L 108/33, recital 27.

[259] P. Crocioni, "Leveraging of Market Power in Emerging Markets: A Review of Cases, Literature, and a Suggested Framework" (2008) 4(2) *Journal of Competition Law and Economics*, p. 496.

4. – Predatory Conduct
Robbert Snelders, Andrew Leyden and Andrea Lofaro

The Commission's approach to growth markets is not very consistent. On **4.132** the one hand, the *Guidance Paper* states that in general *"it is considered unlikely that predatory conduct will create efficiencies"*.[260] In the *Discussion Paper*, however, the Commission recognised that in certain cases, pricing below AVC/AAC could be justified by *"strong learning effects"*.[261] Moreover, the Commission has attached great importance to scale and scope economies and network effects in other cases.[262] Despite the *Guidance Paper*'s general scepticism towards efficiencies, it does explicitly recognise the possibility of *"efficiencies related to expanding the market"*,[263] but does not provide any further guidance as to how they might be demonstrated in practice. Unfortunately, the Commission has not issued any guidelines establishing clear economic tests to distinguish legitimate from illegitimate start-up losses. In practice, much turns on the facts of each case, and evidentiary problems are particularly acute in dynamic markets. This is largely because there will be little evidence of the rationale for start-up losses aside from a dominant company's business plan, which for obvious reasons is unlikely to contain express statements of a plan to predate. Further, by its nature, this defence applies in risky, speculative markets, where it is very difficult to predict whether competitors will survive. A strategy which appears predatory in retrospect might in fact reflect a company's best assessment of its legitimate options at the time. Helpfully, the *Guidance Paper* at least recognises that *"undertakings should not be penalised for incurring ex post losses where the ex ante decision to engage in the conduct was taken in good faith"*.[264]

As O'Donoghue argues, in the absence of a clear financial test to distinguish **4.133** legitimate from illegitimate start-up losses, the Commission should fall back on evidence of intent.[265] First, the Commission could produce documentary evidence of exclusionary intent, as in *Wanadoo*, where it showed that there was an express plan to incur whatever losses were necessary to *"pre-empt the*

---

[260] *Discussion Paper supra* note 5, para. 133.

[261] *Ibid.*, para. 131.

[262] In a case involving alleged pricing abuses committed by the stock exchange Euronext in response to new entry by the London Stock Exchange on the Dutch market, the Commission concluded that *"There are good reasons in this case to believe that a digressive fee schedule is welfare enhancing. This is because it stimulates marginal trading, making markets more liquid (with macroeconomic externalities on cost of capital and enhanced return to risk-equivalent investments). This form of pricing existed prior to LSE's entry, and is, furthermore, also used by most other exchanges"*. See DG COMP Competition Policy Newsletter (2005), No. 3, pp. 69–71.

[263] *See Guidance Paper supra* note 3, para. 74.

[264] *Ibid.*, fn 43.

[265] *See supra* note 18, p. 297.

4. – Predatory Conduct
Robbert Snelders, Andrew Leyden and Andrea Lofaro

market".[266] Secondly, in the absence of express intent evidence, the Commission could also rely on "convergent factors" that demonstrate anticompetitive purpose when taken as a whole.[267] Such evidence would need to prove that the business plan or projections a dominant company claims to have relied on are *"unjustified or implausible"*,[268] or in other words have been concocted in order to avoid liability under Article 102 TFEU. The *Wanadoo* Decision's strong reliance on extensive documentary evidence of intent, actual or likely exclusionary effects, and the probability of recoupment through price increases, suggests that a high evidentiary threshold ought to apply before start-up losses can be found to be predatory. This would also be consistent with the Commission's approach to abuses of dominance in specific growth sectors.[269] Nevertheless, as with all defences to predatory pricing, the Commission's position is that it is incumbent upon the dominant undertaking to provide the evidence necessary to demonstrate that a defence has been made out, and that the pricing practice in question was proportionate to a procompetitive objective.[270]

VI. Future Perspectives

4.134   The Commission's *Guidance Paper* sets out a slightly modified framework for the analysis of predatory pricing, stating that a dominant undertaking engages in predatory conduct *"by deliberately incurring losses or foregoing profits in the short term [...] so as to foreclose or be likely to foreclose one or more of its actual or potential*

---

[266] *See* Case COMP/38.233 *supra* note 73. *See also* Cases COMP/37.451, 37.578, 37.579 *Deutsche Telekom* ("*Deutsche Telekom Decision 2003*"), Commission Decision of 21 May 2003, OJ 2003 L 263/9, where the Commission applied the *AKZO* rules to a margin squeeze case in the broadband internet sector, holding that the rules required both below-cost selling and evidence that the prices in question were "*set as part of a plan aimed at eliminating a competitor*" (para. 179). *See also* discussion of *Wanadoo* as a margin squeeze case at Chapter 5, Section VI.4.2.

[267] *See* Case IV/30.698 *supra* note 2, para. 80; Case COMP/38.233 *supra* note 73, para. 271. *See also* P. Lowe, *EU Competition Practice on Predatory Pricing – Introductory address to the Seminar "Pros and Cons of Low Prices"*, speech given at the Seminar "Pros and Cons of Low Prices", Stockholm, December 5, 2003.

[268] *See* Office of Fair Trading, *Competition Act 1998: The application in the telecommunications sector*, OFT 417, February 2004, para. 7.23 ("*It will not always be possible for an undertaking to meet all the targets set out in its business plan. Evidence of an abuse of dominance may be provided, however, where a business case is based on unjustified and implausible assumptions or where there has been a failure by the undertaking to take remedial action once it became apparent that it would not meet the targets*".).

[269] *Framework Directive supra* note 258, recital 27.

[270] *See Guidance Paper supra* note 3, para. 30.

4. – Predatory Conduct
Robbert Snelders, Andrew Leyden and Andrea Lofaro

competitors with a view to strengthening or maintaining its market power, thereby causing consumer harm".[271] Thus, the Commission will in the future conduct a cumulative two-step analysis of: (1) "sacrifice" and (2) "anticompetitive foreclosure". The second of these criteria is the most important addition: the emphasis on proving actual or likely anticompetitive effects is a welcome step away from the formalism of the *AKZO* test. It is important to note, however, that the Commission remains constrained by the case law of the Court. The Commission provides no legal basis for its proposed analytical framework, which is a clear departure from the existing case law. In reality, while the *Guidance Paper* may inform the Commission's internal decision-making as regards which cases to pursue, once formal proceedings are underway, the Commission will almost certainly supplement its reasoning with a finding that the relevant *AKZO* test is fulfilled (or not).

1. The *Guidance Paper:* Sacrifice

The notion of sacrifice covers situations where, either by "charging a lower price for all or a particular part of its output" or "expanding its output", the dominant undertaking incurs losses that could have been avoided.[272] The Commission adopts the AAC benchmark in order to determine when a company is incurring avoidable losses, stating that *"in most cases"*, prices below AAC are a *"clear indication"* of sacrifice.[273] In practice, the Commission is therefore likely to apply a slightly modified version of the first *AKZO* rule in order to determine if there has been a sacrifice of revenues. For the reasons explained above, the use of the AAC benchmark is a welcome evolution. **4.135**

More questionable, however, is the Commission's blanket statement that *"sacrifice [...] does not only include pricing below AAC"*.[274] To determine if there has been above-cost predation, the Commission intends to investigate whether the dominant undertaking is receiving revenues lower than could have expected from *"reasonable alternative conduct"* that is *"economically rational and practicable"*.[275] The formulation used by the Commission appears broad enough to encompass sacrifice of profit where prices remain above ATC (or LRAIC). The **4.136**

---

[271] *See Guidance Paper supra* note 3, para. 63.

[272] *Ibid.*, para. 64.

[273] *Ibid.*, para. 64.

[274] *Ibid.*, para. 65.

[275] *Ibid.*, para. 65.

4. – Predatory Conduct
Robbert Snelders, Andrew Leyden and Andrea Lofaro

Commission does not cite any legal basis for this assertion, and on their face, such restrictions would mark a departure from the "as efficient" competitor test. Indeed, despite the Commission's statement that it will normally only intervene where an alleged pricing abuse is capable of hindering an "*as efficient*" competitor, the *Guidance Paper* goes on to state that in "*certain circumstances*" it will intervene where a less efficient competitor exerts a competitive constraint.[276]

4.137 Unfortunately, the Commission does not explain what type of circumstances it has in mind. The *Discussion Paper* referred to the possibility of above-cost predation in situations where a dominant firm enjoys certain "*non-replicable advantages*" or "*where economies of scale are very important*", meaning that new entrants must operate at a significant cost disadvantage until they attain the "*minimum efficient scale*".[277] Placing restrictions on the pricing conduct of dominant firms in such circumstances, which might be termed the "not-yet-as-efficient" competitor rule, is not ruled out by the *Guidance Paper*. An explicit rejection of this theory would have been welcome: as discussed above, the welfare effects of implementing such a restriction are ambiguous at best, and probably negative in most cases.[278] Nevertheless, the *Guidance Paper* states that the Commission will take a "dynamic view" of any constraints exerted by a less efficient competitor, since "*in the absence of an abusive practice such a competitor may benefit from demand-related advantages, such as network and learning effects, which will tend to enhance its efficiency*".[279]

4.138 The Commission's broad notion of above-cost "sacrifice" could create a new category of abuse. As noted above, the existing cases on above-cost predatory pricing involved situations in which pricing conduct was combined with other abuses, and the wholly exceptional *Compagnie Maritime Belge* scenario.[280] If the Commission does intend to expand the notion of predatory pricing to include other above-cost pricing conduct, it is regrettable that it does not provide detailed reasoning to explain the situations in which it would apply, and elaborate criteria allowing undertakings to clearly distinguish which prices are legitimate and which are not. Moreover, as noted, the Court of Justice held in *Post Danmark* that where a dominant company sets selectively low prices

---

[276] *See Guidance Paper supra* note 3, paras 23-24.
[277] *See Discussion Paper supra* note 5, para. 129.
[278] *See* discussion of above-cost predation in Section IV.6 above.
[279] *See Guidance Paper supra* note 3, para. 24.
[280] *See* discussion of *Compagnie Maritime Belge* in Sections IV.6.2. and IV.6.3. above.

4. – Predatory Conduct
Robbert Snelders, Andrew Leyden and Andrea Lofaro

at *"a higher level than [...] average total costs [...] it cannot be considered that such prices have anticompetitive effects"*.[281] If *Post Danmark* represents a retrenchment by the Court of Justice from *Compagnie Maritime Belge*, it is unclear whether the Commission will have the ability to pursue dominant firms for allegedly abusive above-cost price cuts in future.

In the Commission's defence, it should be noted that according to the two- **4.139** step framework set out in the *Guidance Paper*, a finding of above-cost "sacrifice" does not necessarily mean that there has been an abuse, since there must also be "anticompetitive foreclosure", which constitutes a discrete step in the Commission's analysis. In this context, the Commission at least recognises that only pricing below LRAIC is normally capable of producing foreclosure effects.[282]

2. The *Guidance Paper*: Anticompetitive Foreclosure

The most important element of the *Guidance Paper* is the Commission's com- **4.140** mitment to analyse the foreclosure effects of an allegedly predatory scheme. The keystone of the Commission's analysis is the "equally efficient competitor" test, but, as noted, the Commission considers that it is free to depart from this analysis in certain (unspecified) circumstances.[283] Aside from the general factors relevant to foreclosure analysis in all abuse of dominance cases (such as the degree of dominance, market concentration, barriers to entry, buyer power, evidence of actual foreclosure, *etc.*),[284] the Commission states that in the case of a pricing abuse it will *"generally investigate whether and how the suspected conduct reduces the likelihood that competitors will compete"*.[285] In this connection, the Commission makes reference to the three models of predation described above, namely (1) signalling theories; (2) reputation theories; and (3) financial markets theories.

It is noteworthy that the Commission states that pricing below AAC should **4.141** be regarded as a clear indication of sacrifice, but makes no reference to the *AKZO* presumption of predation below AVC/AAC in its discussion

---

[281] *See supra* note 197, para. 36.
[282] *See Guidance Paper supra* note 3, para. 67.
[283] *Ibid.*, para. 24.
[284] *Ibid.*, para. 20.
[285] *Ibid.*, para. 68.

4. – Predatory Conduct
Robbert Snelders, Andrew Leyden and Andrea Lofaro

of anticompetitive foreclosure.[286] Similarly, in its discussion of its general approach to price-based abuses, the Commission states that even if the data show that the prices charged by a dominant firm have the potential to foreclose equally efficient competitors, the Commission will merely *"integrate this in the general assessment of anticompetitive foreclosure"*.[287] Rather than a presumption that predation has occurred by virtue of below-cost pricing, therefore, the *Guidance Paper* clearly indicates that the Commission also intends to prove in each case that anticompetitive effects have been or are likely to be produced, regardless of the price charged by the dominant company.

3. The Path Forward

4.142 In conclusion, the *Guidance Paper*, while imperfect, constitutes an important recognition that the application of formalistic legal rules to firms that price below certain cost measures often makes no economic sense.[288] That said, it is still unclear how the Commission will apply the new analytical framework in practice, and its impact is limited by the fact that certain key aspects of the Commission's long-standing approach remain unchanged. In particular, it is disappointing that the Commission emphasises that it is not required to show a probability of recoupment, pours cold water on the possibility of making efficiencies claims,[289] and continues to conflate consumer harm with a generalised analysis of market power, stating that generally speaking consumers are *likely* to be harmed if the dominant undertaking can reasonably expect its market power to increase as a result of a predatory scheme.[290]

4.143 Within the framework set out in the *Guidance Paper* there is nonetheless scope for a more balanced approach in several key respects. Five areas merit particular mention. First, although the Commission reaffirms its intention to rely on documentary evidence of the dominant firm's intent,[291] the Commission ought to nonetheless rely primarily on objective evidence of the likelihood

---

[286] *See Guidance Paper supra* note 3, para. 67-73.

[287] *Ibid.*, para. 27.

[288] See Case C-413/06 P Bertelsmann and Sony Corporation of Americav. Impala [2008] ECR II-4951, pp. 124–125. The Court of Justice recognised that in applying competition rules, it is *"necessary to avoid a mechanical approach involving the separate verification of each … criteria taken in isolation, while taking no account of the overall economic mechanism"*.

[289] *Ibid.*, para. 74.

[290] *Ibid.*, para. 72.

[291] *Ibid.*, paras 66, 20.

4. – Predatory Conduct

Robbert Snelders, Andrew Leyden and Andrea Lofaro

of success of a predatory strategy where such evidence is available. Secondly, although the Commission has kept open the possibility of condemning above-cost "predatory" pricing, such determinations are of questionable legality and the Commission's jurisdiction ought to be exercised sparingly, if at all. Thirdly, notwithstanding the *Wanadoo* Decision, the Commission ought to adopt a balanced approach to the "meeting competition" defence and recognise the need for dominant companies to incur losses in order to expand "emerging" markets. Fourthly, although the issue is not explicitly dealt with by the *Guidance Paper*, it would be absurd to apply predatory pricing rules to free services, particularly online services in two-sided markets.[292] Finally, it is to be hoped that the Commission will live up to its commitment to engage in a rigorous analysis of anticompetitive foreclosure in predation cases. In particular, the Commission should not simply assume that the exit of market rivals in response to aggressive pricing indicates that there has in fact been anticompetitive foreclosure. As the Court of Justice recognised in *Post Danmark*:

> *"[N]ot every exclusionary effect is necessarily detrimental to competition. [...] Competition on the merits may, by definition, lead to the departure from the market or the marginalisation of competitors that are less efficient and so less attractive to consumers from the point of view of, among other things, price, choice, quality or innovation".*[293]

---

[292] *See* Section IV.5.4 above.
[293] *See supra* 197, para. 22.

5. – Margin Squeeze
Francisco Enrique González-Díaz and Jorge Padilla

Margin Squeeze

Francisco Enrique González-Díaz and Jorge Padilla*

I.   Introduction

A margin squeeze is a pricing practice, carried out by a vertically integrated **5.1**
firm active in both an upstream and a related downstream market, consisting of selling an input product or service at such a price that leaves
its client-competitors with an insufficient margin to continue to compete
downstream. This practice, in theory, *squeezes* the downstream firm's margin
between the upstream price and the downstream price, because the downstream firm must pay the upstream price in order to sell in the downstream
market.

One of the many difficulties with the notion of margin squeeze, and perhaps **5.2**
one of the main reasons why the European law on margin squeeze remains
unsettled and evolving, is the need to identify a sufficient margin, from a
competition law perspective, for downstream firms. It is fairly settled that
excessive prices can constitute an abuse within the meaning of Article 102 (*see*
Chapter 10). It is also well settled that predatory prices can constitute an abuse
of dominance and can violate Article 102 (*see* Chapter 4). The margin squeeze
abuse is said to constitute yet another form of *unfair pricing* (*see* Section VI.1
below). As addressed in this chapter, the contours of this form of *unfair pricing* are still being defined, though the General Court's decision in *Telefónica* (in
2012), the Court of Justice's preliminary ruling in *TeliaSonera* (2011), the Court
of Justice's decision in *Deutsche Telekom* (in 2010), and the 2009 Commission's

* Jorge Padilla is a senior managing director at Compass Lexecon. The authors wish to thank Jorge Piernas,
José Baño, Farrell Malone and Ben Holles for their valuable contribution to this chapter.

5. – Margin Squeeze
Francisco Enrique González-Díaz and Jorge Padilla

Guidance Paper on Article 102 (the *"Guidance Paper"*) have begun to square the corners of the margin squeeze abuse.[1]

5.3 In the European Union, an abusive margin squeeze has been said to occur when a vertically integrated firm, dominant in an upstream market and supplying *an objectively necessary* input to competitors operating in the downstream market, charges prices (or fails to take action to avoid charging prices) that leave an *insufficient margin* for downstream competitors to continue operations in the downstream market. As discussed *infra*, Article 102 liability for such conduct has been imposed on at least four separate occasions by the European Commission,[2] and many more times by national competition authorities and tribunals.[3]

5.4 The General Court's 2008 judgment in *Deutsche Telekom* was the first clear indication from a European Union court that margin squeeze constituted an independent abuse of Article 102 TFEU.[4] In that case, the General Court held that *"there is an abusive margin squeeze if the <u>difference</u> between the <u>retail prices charged</u> by a <u>dominant undertaking</u> and the <u>wholesale prices it charges</u> to its competitors for <u>comparable services</u> is <u>negative</u>, or <u>insufficient to cover</u> the <u>product-specific costs</u> to the <u>dominant operator</u> of providing <u>its own retail services</u> on the <u>downstream market</u>."*[5] This view was later confirmed by the Court of Justice in *TeliaSonera*.[6]

5.5 This general characterisation of the so-called *abusive* margin squeeze includes several implicit assumptions (underlined above). In each case, the choice of *which prices to consider, what level of production* and *which products or services* to include

---

[1] *See* Case T–336/07 *Telefónica v Commission* (*"Telefónica Judgment 2012"*), not yet reported; Case C–52/09 *Konkurrensverket v TeliaSonera Sverige* (*"TeliaSonera Judgment 2011"*) [2011] ECR I–527; Case C–280/08 P *Deutsche Telekom v Commission* (*"Deutsche Telekom Judgment 2010"*) [2010] ECR I–9555; Guidance on the Commission's enforcement priorities in applying Article 82 of the EC Treaty to abusive exclusionary conduct by dominant undertakings (*"Guidance Paper"*), OJ 2009 C 45/7.

[2] *See* Section III.1.4.

[3] C. Veljanovski, "Margin squeeze and competition law: an overview of EU and national case law". *e-Competitions*, No. 46442, p. 2. Also, *see, e.g.*, in the UK Case CA 98/20/2002 BSkyB Investigation: *Alleged Infringement of the Chapter II Prohibition*, Decision of the Director General of Fair Trading of 17 December 2002.

[4] Case T-271/03 *Deutsche Telekom v Commission* (*"Deutsche Telekom Judgment 2008"*) [2008] ECR II–477. Confirmed on appeal in Case C–280/08 P *Deutsche Telekom v Commission* (*"Deutsche Telekom Judgment 2010"*) [2010] ECR I-9555.

[5] Case T-271/03 *Deutsche Telekom v Commission* (*"Deutsche Telekom Judgment 2008"*) [2008] ECR II-477, para. 92. Confirmed on appeal, *Deutsche Telekom Judgment 2010 supra* note 1.

[6] *TeliaSonera Judgment 2011 supra* note 1, paras 31–34.

5. – Margin Squeeze
Francisco Enrique González-Díaz and Jorge Padilla

in the analysis (and over *what timeframe*), *which costs* to include in the analysis, and *what degree of market power* to require of the undertaking at issue, may be critically important to the result, and are addressed in turn in the following sections.

The remainder of this chapter is organised as follows: Section II describes **5.6** the abuse of margin squeeze and provides an overview of some key aspects of the abuse. Section III reviews the relevant European Union and national precedents, as well as United States law. Section IV addresses the relevance of refusal to supply precedents and the *Oscar Bronner* jurisprudence. Section V addresses a number of recurring issues in margin squeeze cases. Section VI addresses the economics of margin squeeze, including a discussion of whether upstream excessive pricing and/or downstream predatory pricing are, or should be, required for a finding of margin squeeze abuse. Section VII concludes.

II. Margin Squeeze Defined

This Section presents a simple model of margin squeeze, and then addresses **5.7** the characteristics of margin squeeze in practice, including its status as a possible independent abuse of Article 102.

1. A Simple Model of Margin Squeeze

Consider a vertically integrated firm, Firm 1, which is the only firm active **5.8** in the upstream market. It sources from its own upstream operations a key input that is used in the production of a final product in the downstream market. There are several other producers of the downstream product, including Firm 2, which produces the downstream product with inputs purchased from Firm 1 at price w per unit. Firm 1 charges a downstream price (the price to consumers) of p_1. Firm 2, after purchasing the input from Firm 1 at a wholesale price w, produces the finished product for the downstream market and charges price p_2. Depending on the characteristics of the products and the conditions of competition in the downstream market, Firm 2's price, p_2, may be more or less constrained by Firm 1's price. In particular, suppose that Firm 2, to make any sales at all, will have

5. – Margin Squeeze
Francisco Enrique González-Díaz and Jorge Padilla

to price its product at $p_2 \leq p_1$. This situation is depicted in the following graphic:

Figure 5.1: A Simple Model of Margin Squeeze.

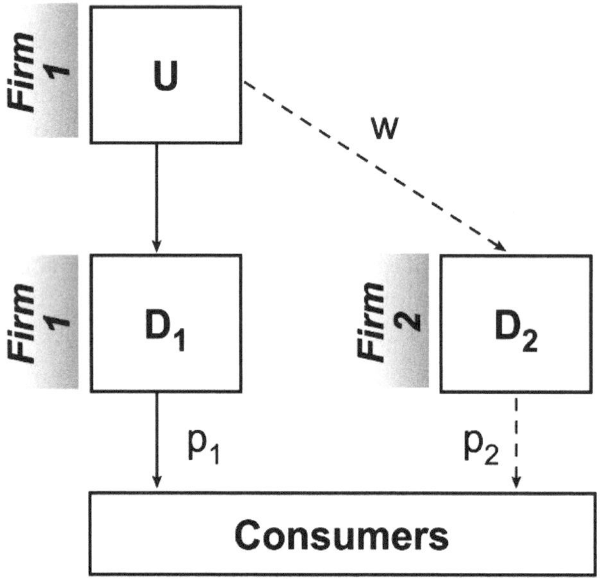

5.9 Firm 1 can engage in a margin squeeze in one of three ways: (1) it can raise the price of the input, w, and thus increase the per-unit costs of Firm 2. If the price of w is high enough, including potentially such that $w > p_2$, Firm 2's margin will be squeezed – in the extreme case its margin will be eliminated (where $w > p_2$); (2) Firm 1 can lower its own downstream price, p_1, thus putting pressure on any existing margin between w and p_2, and in the extreme eliminate any margin whatsoever; or (3) Firm 1 can do both – that is, raise the price of the input, w, and lower its downstream price, p_1, again potentially to the point where $w > p_2$. In each case, Firm 1 would be using its monopoly position in the upstream market (by assumption, it is the only provider of the input needed by Firm 2 and there are no close enough substitutes) in order to reduce Firm 2's margin. If Firm 1 is successful, Firm 2 may not be able to continue operating and will have to exit.

5.10 There are multiple assumptions underlying this example, including that the firm engaged in margin squeeze must be vertically integrated, *i.e.*, active in both *markets*, that it has a significant degree of market power in the input market, and that it must be providing an objectively necessary, essential input, to competitors in the downstream market.

5. – Margin Squeeze
Francisco Enrique González-Díaz and Jorge Padilla

1.1. Vertical Integration and Presence in Two Markets

To engage in a margin squeeze, a firm has to be active in both the upstream and **5.11** downstream market. Without vertical integration, a firm charging too high a price at the wholesale level or too low a price at the retail level may be engaged in excessive pricing or predatory pricing, respectively, but cannot be engaged in a margin squeeze.[7] This follows because if the firm were not vertically integrated it would not stand to benefit, at least not directly, from any harm to competition caused by the margin squeeze at a different level of the market.[8] The firm has to be the upstream provider of certain goods or services, and it must also be active downstream of those upstream activities if it is to take any advantage of its pricing decisions upstream or downstream. For example, in the *Deutsche Telekom* case, the incumbent upstream operator Deutsche Telekom offered network access at two levels – it offered wholesale unbundled local loop access to its competitors in the upstream market, and retail access to the internet to consumer subscribers in the downstream market.[9]

That the dominant firm must be present in two markets should also be con- **5.12** sidered in light of EU precedent relating to tying (*see* Chapter 8) and refusals to deal (*see* Chapter 7). As to the latter, the judgment of the Court of Justice in *IMS Health* confirms that the nature of a firm's presence in each of the relevant markets matters. For example, in the context of the licensing of upstream IP rights, there can only be abuse downstream "*where the undertaking which requested the license does not intend to limit itself essentially to duplicating the goods or services already offered on the secondary market by the owner of the intellectual property right, but intends to produce new goods or services not offered by the owner of the right and for which there is a potential consumer demand.*"[10]

In the case of a margin squeeze, a dominant undertaking may, according to EU **5.13** precedent, be engaged in an abuse even where the downstream rival merely resells the upstream input. This is an important distinguishing feature of the margin squeeze abuse and one which rationale does not become immediately apparent.

---

[7] *See, e.g.*, Case COMP/38.233 *Wanadoo*, Commission Decision of 16 July 2003, not yet published (the upstream operator had a majority interest in the company operating in the relevant downstream market, but the Commission nevertheless analysed the case as a predatory pricing case).

[8] *See, e.g.*, P. Crocioni and C. Veljanovski, "Price Squeezes, Foreclosure and Competition Law" (2003) 4 *Journal of Network Industries*, pp. 39–40.

[9] Given the importance of being active at two levels, had the wave of telecommunications liberalisation and deregulation required the structural separation of the telecommunications firms' upstream and downstream network operations, it is likely that many of the leading margin squeeze cases would never have come about – the firms would not have had the ability to effect a *squeeze* in competitors' margins.

[10] Case C–418/01 *IMS Health v NDC Health* ("*IMS Health*") [2004] ECR I–5039, para. 49.

5. – Margin Squeeze

Francisco Enrique González-Díaz and Jorge Padilla

As to the difficulty associated with requiring that the downstream products sold by competitors be differentiated in a margin squeeze context, it is unclear whether a vertically integrated dominant firm has the incentive to squeeze competitors that sell differentiated products. In fact, standard margin squeeze tests are defined to fit market scenarios where the vertically integrated company and its competitors sell homogeneous products. Moreover, when downstream products are differentiated it is not possible to conclude from a failed margin squeeze test that the vertically integrated upstream and downstream price combination will have exclusionary effects. The reason for this is that competitors who sell higher quality products than the vertically integrated firm need not make losses at wholesale/retail price combinations that are unprofitable for the vertically integrated firm.

1.2. Upstream Dominance

5.14 Because a margin squeeze derives from the margin available to firms in the marketplace (*i.e.*, the difference between the upstream and downstream prices), if a firm does not have enough market power to affect that margin, it will not be possible to bring about an abusive margin squeeze. Issues related to upstream dominance, and whether downstream dominance is also required for a margin squeeze to take place, are addressed in Sections V.1 and V.2 below.

1.3. Objective Necessity of the Upstream Input

5.15 The upstream input provided by the dominant firm must be objectively necessary for the supply of the competing downstream firm's products or services, otherwise a firm attempting to squeeze a downstream competitor would be confronted with substitution to other inputs. Even if there are no other upstream alternatives for the particular type of input provided by the dominant upstream firm, there may be alternatives in the downstream market (possibly involving a shift in production process) that provide a means of avoiding the use of the dominant firm's input.[11] A related question is whether the upstream input, which clearly must be a necessary input to downstream competitors, must also be an essential and/or indispensable input – *i.e.*, one with which downstream competition cannot do without.[12] Whether the upstream input must be essential for a finding of margin squeeze is addressed further in Section V.1 below.

---

[11] *See, e.g., Deutsche Telekom Judgment 2008 supra* note 5, para. 141, *See, e.g., supra* note 8, pp. 40–42.

[12] While in certain cases it is possible to establish that the upstream input is in fact essential, in others, *e.g., Telefónica*, whether the upstream input was technically *essential* has been hotly debated. *See* the appeal in case C–295/12 P, brought on 13 June 2012 by Telefónica S.A. and Telefónica de España S.A.U. against the judgment of the General Court delivered on 29 March 2012, in *Telefónica Judgment 2012 supra* note 1 (grounds of appeal 1 and 4).

5. – Margin Squeeze
Francisco Enrique González-Díaz and Jorge Padilla

2.   Margin Squeeze in Practice

Identifying a margin squeeze in practice has proven particularly difficult, in   **5.16**
part because the facts and circumstances change in each case. A review of
EU precedents and guidance papers demonstrates how varied the characterisation of a margin squeeze can be (the cases are addressed in more detail in
Section III below):

Table 5.1: Margin Squeeze Characterisations at European Union Level.

Precedent/ Authority (Year)	Description of Margin Squeeze
National Carbonising (1975)	"From this general principal the ... Commission deduced that the enterprise in a dominant position may have an obligation to arrange its prices so as to allow a *reasonably efficient manufacturer* of the derivatives a margin sufficient to enable it to survive in the long term."[13]
Napier Brown (1988)	"The maintaining, by a dominant company, which is dominant in the markets for both a raw material and a corresponding derived product, of a margin between the price which it charges for a raw material to the companies which compete with the dominant company in the production of the derived product and the price which it charges for the derived product, which is insufficient to reflect that dominant company's own costs of transformation ... with the result that competition in the derived product is restricted, is an abuse of dominant position."[14]
European Union Access Notice (1998)	"the margin between the price charged to competitors on the downstream market (including the

---

[13] Case *National Carbonizing*, Commission Decision 76/185/ECSC of 29 October 1975, OJ 1976 L 35/6, para. 15.
[14] Case IV/30.178 *Napier Brown/British Sugar* ("*Napier Brown*"), Commission Decision of 18 July 1988, OJ 1988 L 284/41, para. 66.

5. – Margin Squeeze
Francisco Enrique González-Díaz and Jorge Padilla

Precedent/ Authority (Year)	Description of Margin Squeeze
	dominant company's own downstream operations, if any) for access and the price which the network operator charges in the downstream market <u>is insufficient to allow a *reasonably efficient service provider* in the downstream market to obtain a normal profit</u> (unless the dominant company can show that its downstream operation is exceptionally efficient)."[15]
IPS (2000)	"Price squeezing may be said to take place when an undertaking which is in a dominant position on the market for an unprocessed product and itself uses part of its production for the manufacture of a more processed product, while at the same time selling off surplus unprocessed product on the market, sets the price at which it sells the unprocessed product at such a level that those who purchase it do not have a sufficient profit margin on the processing to remain competitive on the market for the processed product."[16] But noting: "[i]n the absence of abusive prices being charged ... for the raw material ... or of predatory pricing for the derived product ..., the fact the applicant cannot, seemingly because of its higher processing costs, remain competitive in the sale of the derived product cannot justify characterising [the] pricing policy as abusive."[17]
Deutsche Telekom (2003)	<u>"the difference between the retail prices charged by a dominant undertaking and the wholesale prices it charges</u> its competitors for comparable services <u>is negative, or insufficient to cover the product-specific costs</u> to the dominant operator

---

[15] Commission Notice on the application of the competition rules to access agreements in the telecommunications sector – framework, relevant markets and principles ("*Telecom Access Notice*"), OJ 1998 C 265/2.

[16] Case T-5/97 *Industrie des poudres sphériques v Commission* ("*IPS*") [2000] ECR II-3755, para. 178.

[17] *Ibid.*, para. 179.

5. – Margin Squeeze
Francisco Enrique González-Díaz and Jorge Padilla

Precedent/ Authority (Year)	Description of Margin Squeeze
	of providing its own retail services on the down-stream market."[18]
Article 82 Discussion Paper (2005)	"the margin between the price for the upstream input charged to competitors on the downstream market and the downstream price charged by the input owner is insufficient to allow a *reasonably efficient competitor* to obtain a normal profit. The typical benchmark for a reasonably efficient competitor is *the integrated input owner*. A margin squeeze could therefore be demonstrated by showing that the input owner's own downstream operations could not trade profitably on the basis of the upstream price charged to its competitors by its upstream operating arm."[19]
Telefónica (2007)	"Telefónica's retail prices and the price for wholesale access at regional level, on the one hand, and the margin between the retail prices and the price for wholesale access at national level, on the other hand, was insufficient to cover the costs that an operator as efficient as Telefónica would have to incur" to provide retail broadband access."[20]
RWE (2009)	"There is evidence that RWE may have intentionally set its transmission tariffs at an artificially high level in order to squeeze RWE's competitors' margins. Such a behaviour has the effect of preventing even an as efficient competitor to compete effectively on the downstream gas supply markets or

---

[18] Cases COMP/37.451, 37.578, 37.579 *Deutsche Telekom* ("*Deutsche Telekom Decision 2003*"), Commission Decision of 21 May 2003, OJ 2003 L 263/9, para. 107.

[19] DG Competition discussion paper on the application of Article 82 of the Treaty to exclusionary abuses ("*Discussion Paper*"), December 2005, para. 220.

[20] Case COMP/38.784 *Telefónica S.S. (broadband)* ("*Telefónica Decision 2007*"), Commission Decision of 4 July 2007, not yet published, para. 7.

5. – Margin Squeeze
Francisco Enrique González-Díaz and Jorge Padilla

Precedent/ Authority (Year)	Description of Margin Squeeze
	limiting competitors' or potential entrants' ability to remain in or enter the market."[21]
Article 102 Guidance Paper (2009)	"Finally, <u>instead of refusing to supply,</u> a dominant undertaking may <u>charge a price for the product on the upstream market which, compared to the price it charges on the downstream market, does not allow even an</u> *equally efficient competitor* <u>to trade profitably</u> in the downstream market on a lasting basis (a so-called "margin squeeze")."[22]

5.17 While not necessarily inconsistent with each other, these different definitions of margin squeeze may give rise to different results depending on the precise meaning given to their constituent elements.[23] This is particularly likely to be the case at the national level, where national competition agencies are required to interpret these precedents. As stated by the UK Court of Appeals Tribunal in the *Albion Waters* case: "*We take as our starting-point the ways in which the test for margin squeeze has been formulated in the guidance and the case-law. The precise formulation seems to be tailored to the context, and the language used on each occasion is open-ended rather than purporting to lay down a definitive test.*"[24]

3. Margin Squeeze as a Distinct and Autonomous Pricing Violation of Article 102

5.18 In its 1998 *Telecom Access Notice*, the European Commission took the view that a margin squeeze constitutes an infringement of Article 102, when "*the dominant company's downstream operations could not trade profitably on the basis of the upstream price charged to its competitors by the upstream operating arm of the dominant company*"[25] or

---

[21] Case COMP/39.402 *RWE Gas Foreclosure* Commission Decision of 18 March 2009, OJ 2009/C 133/06, para. 30 (commitments decision).

[22] *Guidance Paper supra* note 1, para. 80.

[23] *See* Case CA98/20/2002 *supra* note 3, para. 344 ("*The practical application of a test for margin squeeze may be complex. Precedents have not related to multi-product, high technology, expanding distribution businesses with different revenues and costs that are not in a steady state.*").

[24] *Dwr Cymru Cyfyngedig v Albion Water Ltd & Anor* [2008] EWCA Civ 536, para. 87.

[25] *See supra* note 15, para. 117.

5. – Margin Squeeze
Francisco Enrique González-Díaz and Jorge Padilla

when "*the margin between the price charged to competitors on the downstream market (including the dominant company's own downstream operations, if any) for access and the price which the network operator charges in the downstream market is insufficient to allow a reasonably efficient service provider in the downstream market to obtain a normal profit (unless the dominant company can show that its downstream operation is exceptionally efficient).*"[26] In its *Telecom Access* Notice the Commission thus considered the possibility of identifying a margin squeeze by reference either to the costs of the dominant firm itself or to the costs of a reasonably efficient rival (the difference between these two possible tests is addressed in further detail in Section V.3 below).

Two years later, however, in *Industrie des Poudres Sphériques* ("*IPS*"), the General Court addressed whether a margin squeeze could exist absent abusive pricing upstream or predatory pricing downstream – that is, whether a margin squeeze could be considered as an independent abuse. In its judgment, the General Court concluded that "*[i]n the absence of abusive prices being charged ... for the raw material ... or of predatory pricing for the derived product ..., the fact the applicant cannot, seemingly because of its higher processing costs, remain competitive in the sale of the derived product cannot justify characterising* [the] *pricing policy as abusive.*"[27] **5.19**

The General Court, therefore, suggested that absent abusive pricing upstream, or predatory pricing downstream, there could be no separate margin squeeze abuse. **5.20**

However, in its second judgment dealing with margin squeeze, the Deutsche Telekom judgment, the General Court held that "there is an abusive margin squeeze if the difference between the retail prices charged by a dominant undertaking and the wholesale prices it charges to its competitors for comparable services is negative, or insufficient to cover the product-specific costs to the dominant operator of providing its own retail services on the downstream market. ... It is true that, in the contested decision, the Commission establishes only that the applicant has scope to adjust its retail prices. However, the abusive nature of the applicant's conduct is connected with the unfairness of the spread between its prices for wholesale access and its retail prices, which takes the form of a margin squeeze. Therefore, in view of the abuse found in the contested decision, the Commission was not required to demonstrate in that decision that the applicant's retail prices were, as such, abusive."[28] **5.21**

---

[26] *See supra* note 15, para. 118.

[27] *IPS supra* note 16, para. 179.

[28] *Deutsche Telekom Judgment 2008 supra* note 5, paras 166 and 167. Confirmed on appeal, *Deutsche Telekom Judgment 2010 supra* note 1, para. 183.

5. – Margin Squeeze
Francisco Enrique González-Díaz and Jorge Padilla

5.22   This apparent tension between the General Court's judgments in *IPS* and *Deutsche Telekom*, was resolved by the Court of Justice first in *Deutsche Telekom* and more recently in *TeliaSonera*.[29] The question put to the Court of Justice in *TeliaSonera* was whether a margin squeeze can be properly defined as an independent form of pricing abuse – that can occur even where there is no abusive pricing upstream or predatory pricing downstream, or whether, and more in line with the judgment in *IPS*, a margin squeeze can only occur when there is abusive pricing upstream or predation downstream. In *TeliaSonera*, the Court found that "*since the unfairness, within the meaning of Article 102 TFEU, of such a pricing practice is linked to the very existence of the margin squeeze and not to its precise spread, it is in no way necessary to establish that the wholesale prices for ADSL input services to operators or the retail prices for broadband connection services to end users are in themselves abusive on account of their excessive or predatory nature, as the case may be (Deutsche Telekom v Commission, paragraphs 167 and 183).*" However, later on in the judgment, the Court indicated "*[i]n particular, that squeeze may be the result not only of an abnormally low price in the retail market, but also of an abnormally high price in the wholesale market.*"[30] The difference between an abnormally low price and a predatory price and that between an abnormally high price and an abusive price remains to be clarified. The relationship between margin squeeze and refusal to supply is addressed in Section IV below.

III.   Summary of European Union and National Precedents

5.23   Although margin squeeze cases have attracted increasing attention following the liberalisation of, in particular, the energy and telecommunications markets in the late nineties, the earliest cases date back to the 1975 *National Carbonising* case. Since then, the Commission and the European Union courts have had relatively limited opportunities to address the notion and possible specificities of a margin squeeze. The situation has been somehow different at the national level, where there has been a proliferation of cases in recent years. In this Section, these various precedents are summarised, highlighting the change in emphasis and perceived rule of law as the Commission precedent and case law has developed.

---

[29] *TeliaSonera Judgment 2011 supra* note 1, paras 34, 98.
[30] *Ibid.*, paras 34, 98.

5. – Margin Squeeze

Francisco Enrique González-Díaz and Jorge Padilla

1. European Commission and European Courts Decisions

1.1. *National Carbonising (1975)*

National Carbonising was the first European Union decision describing the con- **5.24**
duct of margin squeeze. In this case the Commission adopted an interim
measures decision pending a decision on the merits of the claims.[31] Its prec-
edential value is thus limited.

The National Carbonising Company (NCC), a manufacturer of coke, pur- **5.25**
chased all of its required inputs (coal) from the National Coal Board (NCB),
which was a publicly owned company with a near-monopoly position (95 per
cent share) in the production of coal in the UK. National Coal Board's subsidiary, National Smokeless Fuels (NSF), was active in the downstream market
for the sale of coke and had approximately 84 per cent of the market for
industrial and domestic hard coke and 88 per cent of the market for domestic
hard coke in the UK.[32] National Carbonising Company claimed that it was
unable to compete downstream and thus lodged a complaint against National
Coal Board and National Smokeless Fuels, alleging that National Coal Board's
upstream price, when considered alongside National Smokeless Fuels's downstream price, resulted in a margin that was insufficient for National Carbonising
Company to continue operating economically downstream. That is, National
Carbonising Company alleged that National Coal Board and National Smokeless Fuels were engaged in an unlawful margin squeeze related to the supply
(upstream) and sale (downstream) of coal and coke, respectively.[33]

In its interim measures decision, the Commission held that National Coal **5.26**
Board, because of its near monopoly position in the production of coal as
a raw material in the downstream production of coke, "*may abuse its dominant
position if it acts in such a way as to eliminate the competition from these manufactures in
the market for derivatives. From this general principal the … Commission deduced that
the enterprise in a dominant position may have an obligation to arrange its prices so as to
allow a reasonably efficient manufacturer of the derivatives a margin sufficient to enable it
to survive in the long term.*"[34]

---

[31] *Supra* note 13, para. 22.

[32] *Ibid.*, paras 2–3.

[33] NCC's specific claim was that this constituted a violation of Article 60 of the ECSC Treaty (or the equivalent
of Article 102).

[34] *Supra* note 13, para. 15.

5. – Margin Squeeze
Francisco Enrique González-Díaz and Jorge Padilla

5.27 The Commission provided no real guidance as to what this rather vague formulation – an *"obligation to arrange its prices"* – would mean in this context, although it appears to foreshadow the Court of Justice's formulation in *Michelin v Commission*, a decade later, that a firm in a dominant position *"has a special responsibility not to allow its conduct to impair undistorted competition on the common market."*[35]

5.28 Notwithstanding this, the Commission concluded that *"on the basis of the facts available ... NCB/NSF, while subject to this obligation, appeared not to have acted contrary to it. It is against this conclusion that NCC has sought relief from the Court of Justice of the European Communitie*s".[36] National Carbonising Company's application for interim measures sought the ability to produce domestic coke *on an economic basis* pending the outcome of the case before the Court.

5.29 The Court ruled that: *"it is for the Commission to take the measures of conservation which it considers strictly necessary, and subject to all appropriate guarantees, for the purpose of keeping in operation the two NCC plants threatened with closure and only for the shortest time it considers to be necessary for the completion of the proceedings in the main action."*[37] The Commission granted the interim measures – which were essentially a reduction in the selling price: *"in view of the losses being incurred by NCC this survival can only be ensured by ordering NCB to forego temporarily such part of the price of coking coal supplied to NCC."*[38]

1.2. British Sugar/Napier Brown (1988)

5.30 *Napier Brown* was the first Commission decision actually finding that a firm had engaged in an abusive margin squeeze under Article 102. Napier Brown, a sugar merchant, purchased industrial raw sugar from British Sugar, the largest producer and seller of sugar in the United Kingdom, for repackaging and sale to retailers. British Sugar was the dominant supplier of raw and granulated sugar to industrial and retail customers in the UK, and was thus active – and dominant – in both the upstream and downstream markets for the sale of sugar. Napier Brown alleged, and the Commission concurred, that British

---

[35] Case 322/81 *Nederlandsche Banden Industrie Michelin v Commission* (*"Michelin I"*) [1983] ECR 3461, para. 57.

[36] *Supra* note 13, p. 7.

[37] *Ibid.*, p. 7. As noted by the Commission, the Court order made it clear that the Commission could adopt interim measures even if the services of the Commission did not consider that, on the basis of the facts known to them, a violation of the Treaty had been committed.

[38] *Ibid.*, pp. 7, 8.

5. – Margin Squeeze
Francisco Enrique González-Díaz and Jorge Padilla

Sugar priced its downstream retail sugar at such a level as to leave an *unreasonably low margin* for repackagers (such as Napier Brown) to compete. In deciding that British Sugar's pricing practices were abusive, the Commission considered that "*any company equally efficient in repackaging as BS without a self-produced source of industrial sugar, would have been*" forced to exit.[39]

As for the role played by imports, the Commission described various difficulties with importing sugar (*e.g.*, transport costs, currency fluctuations) and the fact that British Sugar established its prices at such a level that importing sugar was not a viable solution. More accurately, the Commission stated that "*during the period of investigation, BS has set British prices just under that at which it would be consistently profitable to undertake imports. The role of imports has therefore been as a complement to domestic sugar, rather than as a fully competitive alternative.*"[40] **5.31**

Moreover, the Commission found that "*should BS have maintained this margin in the long-term, NB, or any company equally efficient in repacking as BS without a self-produced source of industrial sugar, would have been obliged to leave the United Kingdom retail sugar market.*"[41] Even if the Commission did not explicitly refer to the indispensability of the inputs, it appears that sugar supplied by British Sugar was the only economically viable alternative for Napier Brown. **5.32**

In finding the abuse, the Commission also relied on British Sugar's dominance in both the upstream and the downstream market, and referred to British Sugar's own "*costs of transformation,*"[42] but did not specifically address what this measure of costs entailed. Because it concluded that an equally efficient rival would not have been able to compete in the downstream market, the Commission found that British Sugar had engaged in an abusive margin squeeze. **5.33**

1.3. *Industrie Des Poudres Sphériques (2000)*

Following *Napier Brown*, it took over a decade – twelve years – before a margin squeeze case was tested before the European Courts. In *Industrie des Poudres Sphériques* ("IPS"), IPS sought to purchase primary calcium metal from Péchiney Électrométallurgie ("PEM") in order to produce broken calcium metal for resale to consumers. In the context of a broader commercial **5.34**

---

[39] *Napier Brown supra* note 14, para. 66.
[40] *Ibid.*, para. 54.
[41] *Ibid.*, para. 66.
[42] *Ibid.*, para. 66.

5. – Margin Squeeze

Francisco Enrique González-Díaz and Jorge Padilla

dispute, including anti-dumping proceedings, IPS complained to the Commission, alleging that the price charged by Péchiney Électrométallurgie for primary calcium metal was too high relative to the price charged by Péchiney Électrométallurgie for its own broken calcium metal offering in the downstream market, and that this price made it impossible for IPS to compete in the downstream market for broken calcium metal. The Commission rejected IPS's claims, and found that there was no basis to conclude that competition law had been infringed.[43] IPS appealed.

5.35   Early in its discussion of IPS's appeal, the General Court seemed to consider the margin squeeze claim in the *National Carbonising* context of whether the prices charged by Péchiney Électrométallurgie would provide IPS the *"profit necessary to remain on the market,"* and concluded that, in fact, IPS could remain on the market.[44] However, later in the judgment, in addressing more specifically the alleged margin squeeze, the Court seemed to switch from a direct assessment of the magnitude of the margins, and whether these were sufficient to compete over the long term, to an assessment of whether Péchiney Électrométallurgie had engaged in abusive pricing upstream of predatory pricing downstream. In this first European Union Court case addressing margin squeeze, the General Court thus held, in relevant part: "[i]*n the absence of abusive prices being charged by PEM for the raw material … or of predatory pricing for the derived product …, the fact the applicant cannot, seemingly because of its higher processing costs, remain competitive in the sale of the derived product cannot justify characterising PEM's pricing policy as abusive.*"[45]

5.36   The General Court also noted that IPS had not shown, on the facts, that the price of the upstream product, primary calcium metal, was *"such as to eliminate an efficient competitor from the broken calcium metal market"*.[46] In *IPS* the General Court thus appeared to hold that a margin squeeze can only infringe Article 102 if the dominant firm's: (1) upstream price is "excessive,"[47] or (2) downstream price (for the output/derivative product) is predatory.

---

[43] *IPS supra* note 16, para. 30.

[44] *Ibid.*, para. 172.

[45] *Ibid.*, para. 179.

[46] *Ibid.*, para. 179.

[47] For the case law development of the concept of excessive pricing, *see* Chapter 10. *See also, e.g.,* Case 27/76 *United Brands and United Brands Continentaal v Commission* ("*United Brands*") [1978] ECR 207; Case 26/75 *General Motors Continental v Commission* ("*General Motors*") [1975] ECR 1367; Case COMP 36.570 *Sundbusserne v Port of Helsingborg*, Commission Decision of 23 July 2004, not yet published. In this last Decision, the Commission stated that any conclusion that a company's prices are excessive must be based on sufficient and convincing evidence. *See* para. 194.

5. – Margin Squeeze
Francisco Enrique González-Díaz and Jorge Padilla

1.4. Deutsche Telekom AG (2003 Commission Decision, 2008 General Court, 2010 Court of Justice)

The 2008 judgment in *Deutsche Telekom* (confirmed by the Court of Justice in **5.37** 2010) was the first case in which the General Court had an opportunity to consider margin squeeze in the context of a regulated industry.[48]

Deutsche Telekom is the incumbent telecommunications operator in Ger- **5.38** many. Prior to the liberalisation of telecommunications markets, it held a legal monopoly in the retail provision of fixed-line telecommunications services ("retail access") in Germany, which it offered through fixed-line local loops ("local loops") that physically connected homes to the telephone network (in 2003 Deutsche Telekom was the provider for more than 95 per cent of retail access throughout Germany). Since 1997, and as a result of deregulation of the German telecommunications industry, Deutsche Telekom was required to provide access to its local loops to other telecommunications operators ("local loop wholesale access") at rates that were approved by the relevant tele-communications regulatory authority. Deutsche Telekom could also set down-stream retail access prices, but these prices were subject to a retail price cap.[49]

In 2003, the Commission found that Deutsche Telekom was dominant *"on all* **5.39** *the relevant markets, namely the wholesale market in access services for competitors and the retail markets in narrowband and broadband access services for residential and business cus-tomers"* and that Deutsche Telekom had abused its dominant position because *"the charges to be paid to DT for wholesale access … are so expensive that competitors are forced to charge their end-users prices higher than the prices DT charges its own end-users for similar services."*[50] The General Court upheld the Commission's decision, and in the process addressed several novel issues relevant to margin squeeze.

First, Deutsche Telekom argued that the applicable regulatory framework pre- **5.40** vented it from carrying out any possible margin squeeze as upstream prices were regulated and approved by the German regulatory authority, and down-stream prices were regulated by a retail price cap. The Commission considered that in order to show *"that there is a margin squeeze it is sufficient that there should be a disproportion between the two charges such that competition is restricted. Of course it has*

---

[48] *Deutsche Telekom Judgment 2008 supra* note 5.
[49] *Ibid.*, para. 18.
[50] *Deutsche Telekom Decision 2003 supra* note 18, paras 96, 102.

5. – Margin Squeeze

Francisco Enrique González-Díaz and Jorge Padilla

also to be shown that the undertaking subject to price regulation has the commercial discretion to avoid or end the margin squeeze on its own initiative."[51]

5.41   Deutsche Telekom did not have the possibility to reduce its upstream prices for wholesale access to the local loop. Wholesale access charges were approved in advance by the German Regulatory authority, and were based on the cost of efficient service provision. Once approved, Deutsche Telekom was required to apply the wholesale access charges through the period of validity.

5.42   Despite that, the Commission found that Deutsche Telekom had sufficient margin of manoeuvre to avoid a margin squeeze because it could – even within the downstream retail price cap system – increase its retail prices after obtaining authorisation of the regulatory authority. The General Court agreed.[52] The interplay between regulation and the law of margin squeeze is addressed further in Sections IV and V.7 below.

5.43   Secondly, Deutsche Telekom argued that there could be no margin squeeze if retail access prices were not themselves abusive (in this case, predatory). Because wholesale prices were fixed by regulation, Deutsche Telekom could at most only control retail prices. Nevertheless, the Commission concluded that Deutsche Telekom had engaged in a margin squeeze, because in order "*to show that there is a margin squeeze it is sufficient that there should be a disproportion between the two charges such that competition is restricted.*"[53] The Commission thus considered that in order to establish whether Deutsche Telekom had engaged in a margin squeeze there was no need to show that its retail access prices were abusive.

5.44   The General Court agreed with the Commission's approach, and considered that the "*abusive nature of the applicant's conduct is connected with the unfairness of the spread between its prices for wholesale access and its retail prices, which takes the form of a margin squeeze. Therefore, in view of the abuse found in the contested decision, the Commission was not required to demonstrate in that decision that the applicant's retail prices were, as such, abusive.*"[54] The question of whether upstream and/or downstream prices must be abusive in order for there to be a margin squeeze is addressed in Section VI.1 below.

---

[51] *Deutsche Telekom Decision 2003 supra* note 18, para. 105.

[52] *Deutsche Telekom Judgment 2008 supra* note 5, para. 131. Confirmed on appeal, *Deutsche Telekom Judgment 2010*, para. 85.

[53] *Deutsche Telekom Judgment 2008 supra* note 5, para. 38 (referring to para. 105 of *Deutsche Telekom Decision 2003 supra* note 18).

[54] *Deutsche Telekom Judgment 2008 supra* note 5, para. 167. Confirmed on appeal, *Deutsche Telekom Judgment 2010 supra* note 1, paras 169–83.

5. – Margin Squeeze
Francisco Enrique González-Díaz and Jorge Padilla

Thirdly, Deutsche Telekom argued that the Commission's calculation of the **5.45**
relevant margin for the purpose of establishing a margin squeeze improperly
considered only the revenues stemming from retail access and did not account
for the revenues derived from the many and varied telecommunications services
(including call charges) that could be offered by competitors purchasing wholesale access. Had the Commission done so, the available margin to downstream
competitors would have likely been higher, and a finding of margin squeeze
would thus have been less likely.[55] The Commission rejected this argument, as
it considered that the provision of retail access had to be considered separately
from that of services (such as call charges). The General Court held that the
Commission was indeed entitled to do so.[56] The broader issue raised by Deutsche
Telekom's argument, *i.e.*, that of how to assess margin squeeze in the context of
a multi-product firm, where each product has both product-specific costs and
an element of common costs, is addressed further in Section V.4 below.

Fourthly, in addressing the appropriate test for margin squeeze, the General **5.46**
Court noted that "[A]lthough the Community judicature has not yet explicitly
ruled on the method to be applied in determining the existence of a margin squeeze, it nevertheless follows clearly from the case-law that the abusive nature of a dominant undertaking's pricing practices is determined in
principle on the basis of its own situation, and therefore on the basis of its
own charges and costs, rather than on the basis of the situation of actual or
potential competitors."[57] The General Court thus established that, at least
in principle, the relevant costs to consider for the purposes of establishing
whether or not a particular company has squeezed its competitors' margins
are those of the dominant firm as "any other approach could be contrary to
the general principle of legal certainty."[58]

Finally, the Commission addressed the proof of the effects of the alleged **5.47**
abusive margin squeeze. Deutsche Telekom argued that, in order to find a conduct abusive, there must be some proof of effects in the market. The Commission disagreed with this position: "The concept of abuse is an objective

---

[55] *Deutsche Telekom Judgment 2008 supra* note 5, paras 155–58.

[56] *Ibid.*, para. 200. Confirmed on appeal, *Deutsche Telekom Judgment 2010 supra* note 1, para. 228.

[57] *Deutsche Telekom Judgment 2008 supra* note 5, para. 188. Confirmed on appeal, *Deutsche Telekom Judgment 2010 supra* note 1, paras 201–202.

[58] *Deutsche Telekom Judgment 2008 supra* note 5, para. 192 ("[i]*f the lawfulness of the pricing practices of a dominant undertaking depended on the particular situation of competing undertakings, particularly their cost structure-information which is generally not known to the dominant undertaking-the latter would not be in a position to assess the lawfulness of its own activities*"). *Deutsche Telekom Judgment 2010 supra* note 1, para. 202. The ECJ set the prevalence of the equally efficient competitor in stricter terms in *TeliaSonera Judgment 2011 supra* note 1, paras 41–5.

5. – Margin Squeeze
Francisco Enrique González-Díaz and Jorge Padilla

concept relating to the behaviour of an undertaking in a dominant position which is such as to influence the structure of a market."[59] The Commission cited the judgment of the Court of Justice in *AKZO*, that "there is abuse of a dominant market position where a dominant undertaking uses its pricing policy to eliminate its competitors and hence strengthen its own position."[60] However, in spite of having maintained that "by proving the existence of a margin squeeze, [it] ha[d] …done enough to establish the existence of an abuse of a dominant market position", the Commission went on to examine the anticompetitive effects deriving from the margin squeeze.[61]

5.48 On appeal, the General Court also referred to the notion of abuse as an objective concept,[62] but it confirmed the need to establish anticompetitive effects and indeed stated that "*the anti-competitive effect which the Commission [was] required to demonstrate relate[d] to the possible barriers which the applicant's pricing practices could have created for the growth of competition in [the market for retail access services]*".[63] According to the General Court, the applicant's conduct had given rise to anticompetitive effects not only on the retail access market but also on the telephone calls market, the reason being that the applicant, as the owner of the fixed network, "*unlike its competitors, d[id] not have to try to offset losses suffered on the retail access market [with the profits made on other markets, such as the telephone calls market] on account of the pricing practices of a dominant undertaking*".[64] In order to reach these conclusions, the General Court relied on the small market shares acquired by the applicant's competitors in the retail access market since liberalisation as evidence of the anticompetitive effects caused by the applicant's pricing practices.[65]

5.49 The ECJ upheld the General Court's analysis, stating that "*the General Court correctly rejected the Commission's arguments to the effect that the very existence of a pricing practice of a dominant undertaking which leads to the margin squeeze of its equally efficient competitors constitutes an abuse within the meaning of Article 82 EC, and that it is not necessary for an anti-competitive effect to be demonstrated*".[66] The Court noted that "*in the absence of any effect on the competitive situation of competitors, a pricing practice such as that at issue cannot be classified as exclusionary if it does not make their market*

---

[59] *Deutsche Telekom Decision 2003 supra* note 18, para. 178.
[60] *Ibid.*, para. 179, by reference to Court of Justice in Case C–62/86 *AKZO Chemie v Commission* ("*AKZO*") [1991] ECR I–3359, para. 70.
[61] *Deutsche Telekom Decision 2003 supra* note 18, para. 180, *et seq.*
[62] *Deutsche Telekom Judgment 2008 supra* note 5, para. 233.
[63] *Ibid.*, para. 235.
[64] *Ibid.*, para. 238.
[65] *Ibid.*, para. 239.
[66] *Deutsche Telekom Judgment 2010 supra* note 1, para. 250.

5. – Margin Squeeze
Francisco Enrique González-Díaz and Jorge Padilla

penetration any more difficult".[67] Furthermore, and as regards the proof of effects in the specific case, the ECJ held that the General Court had been correct in holding "*that the Commission had established that the particular pricing practices of the appellant gave rise to actual exclusionary effects on competitors who were at least as efficient as the appellant itself*" in the retail access market.[68]

1.5. *Konkurrensverket v TeliaSonera Sverige AB*

The *TeliaSonera* ruling was issued by the Court in February 2011, after the **5.50** Stockholm District Court made a preliminary reference within the context of a dispute between the Swedish competition authority and TeliaSonera Sverige AB ("TeliaSonera"), the country's historic fixed telephone network operator. In this judgment, the Court clarified the circumstances in which the spread between the wholesale prices for ADSL input services and the retail prices for broadband connection services provided to end users – both fixed by a vertically integrated telecommunications undertaking – could constitute an abuse of a dominant position within the meaning of Article 102 TFEU. The Court held that this would indeed be the case if the spread was negative or if it was insufficient to cover the specific costs of the ADSL input services that the downstream section of *TeliaSonera* had to incur in order to be able to provide its retail services, precluding an as efficient competitor from effectively competing on the downstream market.[69] The Court also stated its position with regard to a number of long-debated legal issues.

First, as regards the prices and costs that must be taken into account when **5.51** applying the margin squeeze test, the Court noted that as a general rule only those of the vertically integrated firm in the retail services market must be considered, but not those of its competitors.[70] This is so unless particular circumstances concur, such as *inter alia* the impossibility to identify the cost structure of the dominant undertaking for objective reasons.[71]

Secondly, with respect to the relevance of the existence of an anticompetitive **5.52** effect to establish that a pricing practice is abusive, the Court held that this constitutes an essential requirement.[72] Such an anticompetitive effect must

---

[67] *Deutsche Telekom Judgment 2010 supra* note 1, para. 254.
[68] *Ibid.*, para. 259.
[69] *TeliaSonera Judgment 2011 supra* note 1, para. 32.
[70] *Ibid.*, para. 41.
[71] *Ibid.*, para. 45.
[72] *Ibid.*, para. 61.

5. – Margin Squeeze
Francisco Enrique González-Díaz and Jorge Padilla

refer to the actual or potential creation or consolidation of barriers to entry or growth on the retail services market.[73]

5.53 Thirdly, the Court referred to a series of factors which are irrelevant when assessing whether a margin squeeze exists or not. First, the fact that *TeliaSonera* was subject to no regulatory obligations to supply the inputs on the wholesale market was deemed not to be a decisive element to determine whether the conduct in question was abusive,[74] since margin squeeze constitutes an independent form of abuse, different from a refusal to supply.[75] Secondly, the degree of market dominance is immaterial as far as the categorisation of a conduct as an abuse is concerned, and may solely be relevant with regard to the extent of the effects of such a conduct.[76] Thirdly, an abusive margin squeeze may exist if the vertically integrated undertaking is dominant on the upstream market, it being irrelevant that it is not also dominant in the retail market.[77] Fourthly, the issue of whether the excluded customers are new or already existing ones is not relevant to the assessment of whether a conduct is abusive, as long as an actual or potential anticompetitive effect exists.[78] Fifthly, it is not necessary that the dominant firm is able to recoup the losses it incurs, as an undertaking engaging in margin squeeze may not necessarily suffer losses and moreover, recoupment has not even been established as a precondition in relation to other autonomous abuses, such as predatory pricing.[79] Finally, the fact that the market affected by the conduct at issue is a rapidly growing one with high levels of technology and investment is also irrelevant, since such factors may only be borne in mind within the context of the analysis of the undertaking's costs, but not when determining the actual nature of the conduct.[80]

1.6. *Telefónica (2007 Commission Decision, 2012 General Court)*

5.54 In the *Telefónica* decision, which was adopted approximately four years after *Deutsche Telekom*, the Commission revisited the concept of margin squeeze in the context of a regulated industry, and again found that an incumbent telecommunications provider had engaged in an abusive margin squeeze.

---

[73] *TeliaSonera Judgment 2011 supra* note 1, para. 62.
[74] *Ibid.*, para. 59.
[75] *Ibid.*, para. 56.
[76] *Ibid.*, para. 81.
[77] *Ibid.*, para. 89.
[78] *Ibid.*, paras 90–95.
[79] *Ibid.*, paras 96–103.
[80] *Ibid.*, paras 110–1.

5. – Margin Squeeze
Francisco Enrique González-Díaz and Jorge Padilla

Telefónica was the incumbent Spanish telecommunications operator and owned **5.55** a nationwide fixed telephone network. Competitors in the downstream market that wish to offer retail broadband services have the possibility under the current Spanish regulatory framework to purchase wholesale broadband access from Telefónica. The Commission distinguished different types of wholesale broadband access and identified three different relevant markets (wholesale broadband access at national level, wholesale access at the regional level, and wholesale access at local loop level). The Commission found that Telefónica had engaged in margin squeeze in both the regional and national level markets but not at local loop level. Specifically, the Commission considered that *"Telefónica's retail prices and the price for wholesale access at regional level, on the one hand, and the margin between the retail prices and the price for wholesale access at national level, on the other hand, was insufficient to cover the costs that an operator as efficient as Telefónica would have to incur to provide retail broadband access."* [81] The case is noteworthy in several respects.

First, in *Telefónica* the Commission alleged, for the first time, that certain conduct **5.56** amounted to a margin squeeze despite the fact that, *inter alia*, Telefónica's national and regional wholesale access services were not necessary (much less essential) to compete in the downstream market for the retail provision of broadband access to the Internet. Telefónica argued that because it had no duty to deal with its rivals under *Oscar Bronner*, it could not violate Article 102 *"simply because [its] products have been offered to competitors as a result of a regulatory obligation imposed under the Spanish telecommunications law."* [82] The Commission disagreed, *"in the light of the specific factual, economic and legal context of the case,"* and found that the *Oscar Bronner* jurisprudence was not applicable. [83] The General Court confirmed this view by indicating that a margin squeeze constitutes an independent abuse and that Telefónica's interpretation of *Oscar Bronner* would diminish the effective application of Art. 102 TFEU. [84] Issues related to margin squeeze, refusals to supply, and the *Oscar Bronner* line of cases are addressed in more detail in below.

Secondly, Telefónica, argued that there could not be an unlawful margin **5.57** squeeze in the absence of excessive pricing upstream or predatory pricing downstream. Deutsche Telekom had argued this unsuccessfully in 2003 with respect to predatory prices downstream but it did not apparently claim that

---

[81] *Telefónica Decision 2007 supra* note 20, para. 7. This decision was appealed before the General Court, by application lodged on October 1, 2007.

[82] *Ibid.*, para. 301.

[83] *Ibid.*, paras 302, 309.

[84] *Telefónica Judgment 2012 supra* note 1, paras 180, 181.

5. – Margin Squeeze

Francisco Enrique González-Díaz and Jorge Padilla

its prices were neither predatory downstream nor abusive upstream. As in *Deutsche Telekom*, both the Commission and the General Court also rejected Telefónica's argument in this regard.[85]

5.58   Thirdly, Telefónica challenged the Commission's reasoning based on the interplay between the regulatory requirements imposed by the State, on the one hand, and the application of the competition laws, on the other. The Commission found that, because competitors in the relevant market developed along an *"investment ladder"* of products and services, they would be unable to compete if there were a margin squeeze on any one rung of the ladder. The General Court took the view that Article 102 of the Treaty provides for a complementary *ex post* control to the *ex ante* control exercised by the regulator.[86] The Court reached this conclusion despite Telefónica's claims that the mandated obligation to provide access at national and regional levels was based on regulatory and not Article 102 related considerations, that this obligation was mandated on pricing terms and conditions geared towards achieving a regulatory objective and that the *ex post* intervention of the Commission on Article 102 grounds in a context where it could not have breached this provision under *Oscar Bronner* would illegally interfere with the regulatory powers of National Regulatory Authorities under European Union law thus placing the goals pursued by the Spanish Regulatory Authorities at risk. Indeed the Spanish Regulatory Authorities were seeking, *inter alia*, to guarantee access to Telefónica's ADSL infrastructure at competitive prices, while avoiding to subsidise access up to a point that could compromise the economic viability of Telefónica's cable competitors and/or eliminate the incentives of all downstream competitors of Telefónica (whether cable or DSL operators) to invest in their own networks.

5.59   Fourthly, Telefónica argued that there were no demonstrable negative effects of its conduct on competition – competitors had developed successful entry strategies, even on particular "rungs" of the investment ladder, and Telefónica's market share had been declining significantly over this period.[87] The General Court found that the Commission had shown the probable effects of the conduct although its analysis relied more on inferences of the likely effects of a margin squeeze itself (this issue is discussed further in Section V.5 below) than on an actually showing of effects.[88]

---

[85] *Telefónica Judgment 2012 supra* note 1, paras 186, 187.
[86] *Ibid.*, para. 293.
[87] *Telefónica Decision 2007 supra* note 20, paras 390–4.
[88] *Telefónica Judgment 2012 supra* note 1, paras 268 *et seq.*

5. – Margin Squeeze
Francisco Enrique González-Díaz and Jorge Padilla

Fifthly, in its decision, confirmed by the General Court, the Commission laid **5.60** out and the General Court accepted the *"methodology used to assess the existence of a margin squeeze,"* which included, in particular: (1) the use of the *"equally efficient competitor"* test (addressed in Section V.3 below), (2) the use long-run average incremental costs as a measure of costs (addressed in Section VI.4 below), (3) the use of both the period-by-period and the discounted cash flow methodology to assess the profitability of Telefónica's pricing behaviour (addressed in Section VI.4 below), and (4) a requirement that Telefónica's prices be replicable by an equally efficient supplier on the basis of each and every one of Telefónica's products in each of the relevant wholesale markets (addressed in Section V.4 below).[89]

2. National Cases on Margin Squeeze

Although there have been several recent margin squeeze cases at the Euro- **5.61** pean level, in general, there are relatively few Commission or European Union courts' precedents. This is in clear contrast with the proliferation of cases decided by national competition authorities in recent years, the vast majority of which concerned liberalised markets that were characterised by the previous granting of exclusive or special rights.

Given the developing nature of the European Union law on margin squeeze **5.62** the developments and trends at national level merit due consideration.[90] The following national authorities have adopted recent decisions in the field of margin squeeze: Belgium,[91] Bulgaria,[92] Cyprus,[93] Czech Republic,[94] Denmark,[95]

---

[89] Confirmed by the General Court, *Ibid.*, paras 198–265.

[90] *See* C. Veljanovski *supra* note 3.

[91] M. Peeters, "The Belgian Competition Council Establishes Abuse of Dominant Position in Termination Rates Case *(Base/BM)*" (May 2009) *e-Competitions*, No. 28404.

[92] *See* A. Svetlicinii, "The Bulgarian Competition Authority fines margin squeeze on the construction services market (International Fair Plovdiv)" (June 2010) *e-Competitions*, No. 31626.

[93] *Areeba/Cyprus Telecommunications Authority*, Cyprus Competition Authority Decision of 20 May 2006; *see also* A. Lykotrafiti, "The Cyprus Competition Authority Fines the Telecommunications Incumbent €3.8 Million for Abusive Conduct in the Mobile Telephony Market *(Areeba/CYTA)*" (January 2006) *e-Competitions*, No. 13610.

[94] *See* T. Čihula and M. Forýtek, "A Czech court holds that a request for information is inadmissible only if clearly excessive in a case concerning an abuse of dominance in the telecom sector *(Telefónica)*" (March 2012) *e-Competitions*, No. 45893.

[95] Case 3/1120–0100–0557/MHA/SEK *Song Networks/TDC– SONOFON*, Danish Competition Council Decision of 28 April 2004.

5. – Margin Squeeze
Francisco Enrique González-Díaz and Jorge Padilla

France,[96] Finland,[97] Greece,[98] Hungary,[99] Italy,[100] Norway,[101] Portugal,[102] Spain,[103] Sweden,[104] and the United Kingdom.[105]

---

[96] Decision n°07–D–43 *EDF/Direct Energie*, French Competition Council Decision of 10 December 2007. *See also* L. Guillet, "The Paris Court of Appeal quashes the decision of the French Competition Authority in a margin squeeze case (*SFR–France Telecom*)" (January 2011) *e-Competitions*, No. 35324. *See also* E. Provost, "A French Appeal Court rejects the applicability of Art. 101 and 102 TEU but upholds the findings that two telecom operators had abused their dominant positions in the telephony markets (*Orange Caraïbe and France Telecom*)" (September 2010) *e-Competitions*, No. 33595. *See also* J. Vogel, "The French Civil Supreme Court invalidates the restrictive interpretation of the concept of the effect on trade between member States (*Orange Caraïbe*)" (January 2012) *e-Competitions*, No. 44140. *See also* European Competition Network Brief, "The French Competition Authority issues a first commitment decision concerning competition concerns in the Internet connectivity market (*France Telecom, Cogent*)" (20 September 2012) *e-Competitions*, No. 50107.

[97] *Lännen Puhelin*, Finnish Competition Authority Decision of 25 October 2004.

[98] *See* Autorité de la Concurrence, "Pratiques de ciseau tarifaire", *Rapport Annuel 2008*, pp. 158 *et seq.* and Decision n° 512/63 *Organismós Tilepikoinonión tis Elládos*, Greek Competition Authority Decision 23 February 2009. A. Papanikolaou, "The Greek Telecommunications Regulator Prohibits the Incumbent's 'Double-Play' Bundled Offering of Unlimited International Call Taking into Account a Risk of a Margin Squeeze of its Competitors (*OTE*)"(May 2009) *e-Competitions*, No. 26136.

[99] Case Vj–100/2002/72 *Magyar Távközlési*, Hungarian Competition Authority Decision of 22 January 2004.

[100] Case No. 13752 A351 *Telecom Italia*, Italian Antitrust Authority Decision of 16 November 2004; *see also* M. Polo, "Price Squeeze: Lessons From the Telecom Italia Case" (2007) 3(3) *Journal of Competition Law and Economics*, pp. 453–70. *See also* S. Lembo, "The Italian Competition Authority initiates a new investigation against the incumbent telecom national operator to assess whether it refused to grant physical access to its telephone and broadband network and whether it applied aggressive pricing policy *vis à vis* business customers based in ULL areas (*Wind Fastweb/Telecom Italia conduct*)" (June 2010) *e-Competitions*, No. 32221.

[101] *See* H. Nordling, "A Norwegian District Court dismisses a counter-claim against a subsidiary of the incumbent railway operator for abusing its dominant position (*CargoNet, CargoLink*)" (June 2011) *e-Competitions*, No. 38518.

[102] M. Mendes Pereira and M. Ouaki, "The Portuguese Competition Authority Fines Two Telecoms Operators €53 M for Abuse of Dominant Position in the Wholesale and Retail Broadband Markets" (September 2009) *e-Competitions*, No. 28306.

[103] P. Ibañez Colomo, "The Spanish Competition Authority Adopts a Prudent Approach on Alleged Price Squeeze and Discriminatory Practices by the Telecommunications Incumbent on Interconnection and Termination Fees (*Uni2–MCI WorldCom/Telefónica Móviles*)" (December 2004) *e-Competitions*, No. 187. *See also* H. Auf'mkolk, "The EU General Court dismisses Spanish telecom incumbent's appeal against a Commission decision that imposed a €151 million fine on the company for a margin squeeze in the regulated national broadband market (*Telefónica/Commission*)"(March 2012) *e-Competitions*, No. 45020.

[104] DNR 1135/2004 *TeliaSonera*, Swedish Competition Authority Decision of 21 December 2004. *See also* Report from hearing in *TeliaSonera Judgment 2011 supra* note 1 (where the District Court referred many of the questions addressed in this chapter to the Court of Justice; the Competition Authority has suggested, for example, that a margin squeeze can exist where the upstream input is not essential, and where there is no showing of anticompetitive effects). *See also* European Competition Network Brief, "The Swedish Competition Authority welcomes the EU Court of Justice preliminary ruling on "margin squeeze" as a stand-alone antitrust abuse in the telecom sector (*TeliaSonera*)" (February 2011) *e-Competitions*, No. 36596. *See also* D. Henry, P. Werner and M. Maier, "The European Court of Justice clarifies the scope of the law in relation to pricing practices of vertically integrated companies in the telecommunications sector (*TeliaSonera*)" (February 2011) *e-Competitions*, No. 45026. *See also* H. Andersson, "The Swedish Market Court finds that national postal operator abused its dominant position in the market for bulk mail deliveries (*Bring CityMail Sweden / Posten Meddelande*)" (June 2011) *e-Competitions*, No. 38529.

[105] Case 1016/1/1/03 *Genzyme v Office of Fair Trading*, UK Competition Appeal Tribunal Decision of 11 March 2004; Case 1046/2/4/04 *Albion Water v Water Services Regulation Authority*, UK Competition Appeal Tribunal Decision of 18 December 2006.

5. – Margin Squeeze
Francisco Enrique González-Díaz and Jorge Padilla

Given the complexity of the cases and lack of clear direction (at least histori- **5.63**
cally) at EU level, it is not surprising that national regulatory and competition
authorities may find it difficult to navigate margin squeeze claims. For example, the competition authority of Cyprus declined to review one price squeeze
claim, in part because the *"omissions, obscurities, and contradictions"* in the diverse
formulas applied to assess margin squeeze prevented it from safely choosing
the most appropriate one for the determination of the price squeeze.[106]

The UK Competition Authority has considered margin squeeze on several **5.64**
occasions, including in its investigation of BSkyB in 2002 (which ultimately
was not pursued)[107] and, of British Telecom (again, ultimately concluding
there was no abuse) pricing policies.[108]

In *Genzyme* the UK Competition Appeal Tribunal upheld the finding of the **5.65**
OFT that there was a margin squeeze, and noted: *"where an undertaking that is
dominant in an upstream market supplies an essential input to its competitors in a downstream market, on which the dominant company is also active, at a price which does not
enable its competitors on the downstream market to remain competitive. Such a practice is
called a margin squeeze"* or *"price squeeze."*[109]

In a more recent case, *Albion Water*, the UK Competition Appeal Tribunal **5.66**
upheld a finding that the incumbent and dominant water provider, Dŵr
Cymru, had engaged in a margin squeeze related to its downstream water
distribution services. The case has a complicated procedural structure, but
the 2008 opinion of the Court Appeals Tribunal upholding the finding of
margin squeeze is interesting in several respects. First, it included an extensive
discussion of European Union margin squeeze precedents, and relied heavily
on those precedents in the decision. Secondly, it explicitly addressed an open
issue in margin squeeze cases – whether abusive pricing upstream, or predatory pricing downstream, are required in a margin squeeze case. It ultimately
decided that such abusive pricing was not required (*see* Section VI.1 below).
Thirdly, it is a good example, post-*Deutsche Telekom* and *Telefónica*, of the difficulties faced by national authorities and national courts when applying the

---

[106] *Areeba/Cyprus Telecommunications Authority supra* note 93.

[107] Case CA98/20/2002 *supra* note 3 (*"The Director considers that the correct test, consistent with these precedents, should
determine whether an undertaking as efficient in distributing as BSkyB can earn a normal profit when paying the wholesale prices
charged by BSkyB to its distributors, and that this should be tested by reference to BSkyB's own costs of transformation."*).

[108] Case CW/00613/04/03 *Freeserve.com – BTOpenworld's Broadband Pricing*, Decision of the Office of Communications (OFCOM) of 20 November 2003.

[109] Case 1016/1/1/03 *supra* note 105, para. 491 (citing *IPS supra* note 16).

5. – Margin Squeeze

Francisco Enrique González-Díaz and Jorge Padilla

Commission and the General Court's margin squeeze precedents. As noted above, the Tribunal described that "[t]*he precise formulation seems to be tailored to the context, and the language used on each occasion is open-ended rather than purporting to lay down a definitive test.*"[110]

5.67 In its most recent guidelines, the OFT characterises margin squeeze in the following way:

> "*Where a vertically integrated undertaking is dominant in an upstream market and supplies a key input to undertaking that compete with it in a downstream market, there is scope for it to abuse its dominance in the upstream market. The vertically integrated undertaking could subject its competitors to a price or margin squeeze by raising the cost of the key input ... and/or by lowering its prices in the downstream market. The integrated undertaking's total revenue may remain unchanged. The effect would be to reduce the gross margin available to its competitors, which might well make them unprofitable.*"[111]

5.68 In case S/0207/09, the Council of the Spanish National Competition Commission ("CNC") found, following an investigation initiated by the Investigations Division of the CNC, that Abertis Telecom S.A. ("Abertis") had engaged in a constructive refusal of access, *inter alia*, by means of a margin squeeze.[112] In order to fully understand this decision, it must be borne in mind that there are two different product markets within the value chain enabling television signals to be transported from their production centres to

---

[110] *Dwr Cymru Cyfyngedig v Albion Water Ltd & Anor supra* note 24, para. 87.

[111] Office of Fair Trading, *Competition Act 1998: The application in the telecommunications sector*, OFT 417, February 2000, para. 7.26; *see also* Office of Fair Trading, *Assessment of Conduct: Draft Competition Law Guideline for Consultation*, OFT 414a, April 2004, p. 24, ("*a margin squeeze may occur in an industry where a vertically integrated undertaking is dominant in the supply of an important input for a downstream market in which it also operates. The vertically integrated undertaking could then harm competition by setting such a low margin between its input price (e.g. wholesale price) and the price it sets in the downstream market (e.g. retail price) that an efficient downstream competitor is forced to exit the market or is unable to compete effectively.*"); *see also* P. Palmigiano, "*The Abuse of 'Margin Squeeze' Under Article 82 of the EC Treaty and its Application to New and Emerging Markets*", May 2005, p.12 (addressing Oftel Analytical Framework regarding margin squeeze, which provide that margin squeeze generally arises where a firm: "*(1) is vertically integrated, i.e., operates in both upstream and downstream markets; (2) is dominant in the upstream market, so that downstream competitors have a degree of reliance upon the firm upstream input; (3) sets a margin between its downstream retail price and upstream wholesale charge (paid by downstream competitors) that is insufficient to cover its downstream costs; (4) on an 'end-to-end' basis, i.e., aggregating across the firm's upstream and downstream activities, the firm maybe profitable; (5) but an equally (or more) efficient downstream competitor could be unable to compete, because, in effect, it is being charged a higher price for the upstream input than its competitor, the vertically integrated firm's own downstream arm.*").

[112] Case S/0207/09 *Transporte Televisión*, Spanish Competition Authority Decision of 8 February 2012, p. 1.

5. – Margin Squeeze
Francisco Enrique González-Díaz and Jorge Padilla

the final viewer: (1) the market for wholesale services of access to the transmission centres for the broadcasting of digital terrestrial television ("DTT") signals (upstream), and (2) the DTT signal transport retail services market (downstream).[113] According to the CNC, Abertis, which is vertically integrated, is in a dominant position on both of these markets.[114] In fact, Abertis' national network of transmission centres cannot be replicated and consequently other undertakings may only provide transport services by gaining access to Abertis' broadcasting network.[115]

In its decision, the CNC concluded that Abertis engaged in a margin squeeze **5.69** between the wholesale prices at which access to transmission centres was granted, and the retail prices at which transport services were provided to national and certain regional televisions.[116] In order to do so, the CNC analysed, compared and estimated the costs, revenues and margins obtained by Abertis in its contracts with different television operators.[117] A number of key issues relating to the methodology adopted by the Investigations Division were particularly disputed.

First, despite Abertis' allegations that the "as efficient competitor" test had **5.70** been misapplied, the Council of the CNC confirmed the validity of the Investigations Division's analysis on the basis of the notion of residual demand.[118] The CNC stated that this test had to be applied taking into account the costs of the dominant undertaking assuming a comparable, although not necessarily identical, level of demand.[119] Secondly, as to the utilisation of the LRAIC, Abertis also criticised its application to the specific facts of the case since it believed that it led to an overestimation of its costs, that some of its estimates had been corrected and that its investments had been wrongly valued. The CNC confirmed the Investigations Division's calculations once again, on technical grounds.[120] A third controversial issue was the time horizon adopted by the Investigations Division. More specifically, the fact that the Investigations Division analysed whether a positive return could be achieved within a five-year period, except in regional scenarios, in which contracts were often

---

[113] *See supra* note 112, p. 115.
[114] *Ibid.*, p. 115.
[115] *Ibid.*, pp. 116–117.
[116] *Ibid.*, p. 142.
[117] *Ibid.*, pp. 119–120.
[118] *Ibid.*, pp. 120–124.
[119] *Ibid.*, p. 122.
[120] *Ibid.*, pp. 124–126.

5. – Margin Squeeze

Francisco Enrique González-Díaz and Jorge Padilla

awarded during even shorter periods.[121] Fourthly, in line with EU case law and taking into account the maturity of the relevant market, the Council applied a period-by-period approach to cost comparisons.[122] Finally, there was also disagreement as to the estimations of revenue,[123] capital expenditure, recurring operating costs[124] and the wholesale costs of access.[125]

5.71   The CNC considered that Abertis' conduct constituted a margin squeeze in breach of Article 2 of the Spanish Competition Act and Article 102 of the TFEU.[126] It was also of the view that Abertis' conduct had an anticompetitive exclusionary effect on the retail market.[127] The CNC noted that entry in the retail market at issue was technically viable and economically possible and that therefore, the lack of effective competitors could only be the result of the pricing policy adopted by Abertis.[128] Furthermore, the conduct could not be considered objectively justifiable, since Abertis was free to set its commercial policy[129] as its retail prices and wholesale prices were not regulated until 2010 and even then they were only maximum prices.[130] Finally, the CNC added that the contested practice weakened the bargaining position of TV broadcasters *vis-à-vis* Abertis even more.[131]

3.   United States Precedents

5.72   Margin squeeze law in the United States has developed in stark contrast to the law of margin squeeze in the EU.[132] In its 2009 *Pacific Bell v Linkline Communications* judgment, the United States Supreme Court unanimously held that, under the United States antitrust laws, there is no independent claim or cause of action for *margin squeeze*. The Court considered that absent a showing of an *antitrust duty to deal* or *predatory pricing*, the fact that a vertically integrated dominant firm

---

[121] *See supra* note 112, pp. 126–127.

[122] *Ibid.*, p. 126.

[123] *Ibid.*, pp. 127–130.

[124] *Ibid.*, pp. 130–134.

[125] *Ibid.*, pp. 134–135.

[126] *Ibid.*, p. 135.

[127] *Ibid.*, p. 136.

[128] *Ibid.*, p. 135.

[129] *Ibid.*, p. 137.

[130] *Ibid.*, p. 137.

[131] *Ibid.*, p. 136.

[132] *See* G.A. Hay and K. McMahon, "The diverging approach to price squeezes in the United States and Europe" 8(2) *Journal of Competition Law & Economics*, pp. 259–96.

5. – Margin Squeeze
Francisco Enrique González-Díaz and Jorge Padilla

or monopolist leaves no margin between the price it charges to competitors for wholesale services and the price it charges to downstream customers does not violate the antitrust laws.[133] Citing the decision in *Verizon v Trinko*, the Court held: *"if a firm has no antitrust duty to deal with its competitors at wholesale, it certainly has no duty to deal under terms and conditions that the rivals find commercially advantageous."*[134]

The *Linkline* judgment is in sharp contrast with European Union precedents, **5.73** at least in two ways. First, as described above, Commission and now the European Union courts do consider that there is an independent pricing claim for margin squeeze.[135] Secondly, both the Commission/European Union courts[136] and national regulatory authorities[137] have recently challenged alleged margin squeeze practices in cases where the company accused of the practice is not subject to an antitrust duty to deal under the relevant European Union precedent, *Oscar Bronner*.[138]

In the United States, the debate about "margin squeeze" has been linked to **5.74** the more general debate about whether the antitrust laws should protect competition (no *margin squeeze* as an independent claim) or competitors ("margin squeeze" as an independent claim). According to some authors *"more than ever before, the United States and Europe appear to be at a fork in the road over whether the law of monopolisation exists to protect consumers or to ensure that a specified number of firms will profitably populate a market."*[139]

4.   Overview of the Relevant Precedents

The following Table provides an overview of the relevant European as well **5.75** as some of the more prominent national precedents in margin squeeze cases.

---

[133] *Pacific Bell Telephone v Linkline Communications* ("*Linkline*"), 555 US 438 (2009).

[134] *Ibid.*

[135] This position is however currently challenged before the European Courts in the *Telefónica* appeal (C-295/12 P *Telefónica de España v Commission*, pending).

[136] *TeliaSonera Judgment 2011 supra* note 1; *Telefónica Decision 2007 supra* note 20.

[137] *See, e.g.,* Case 1016/1/1/03 *supra* note 105; Case 1046/2/4/04 *supra* note 105 and *Dwr Cymru Cyfyngedig v Albion Water Ltd & Anor supra* note 24.

[138] Case C-7/97 *Oscar Bronner v Mediaprint Zeitungs- und Zeitschriftenverlag and others* ("*Oscar Bronner*") [1998] ECR I-7791, paras 43–46. In that case, the Court of Justice held that for a firm to have a duty to deal under Article 102, access to the firm's relevant input must be (1) indispensable (*i.e.,* that no viable alternative exists); and (2) the denial of access thereto should lead to the elimination of all competition on the downstream market.

[139] *Supra* note 132, pp. 259–96, p. 261.

5. – Margin Squeeze

Francisco Enrique González-Díaz and Jorge Padilla

The columns identify some of the more recurring issues raised in margin squeeze cases. These issues are addressed in more detail in the remainder of the Chapter. However, as noted by one national appeals court, "[T]*here is good sense in [the] observation that the fact that the decided cases have shared a common feature does not mean that the feature is an essential ingredient of the test for margin squeeze.*"[140]

Table 5.2: Overview of the Relevant Precedents.

Case (Year)	Margin Squeeze?	Dominance Upstream or Down-stream?	Excessive Up or Predation Down?	Type of Costs Used	Measure of Competitor Efficiency for Margin Squeeze
National Carbonising (1975)	Possible	Both	Not addressed.	Not addressed	Reasonably Efficient (though assessed with respect to dominant firm's costs)
Napier Brown (1988)	Yes	Both	Not addressed.	Not addressed specifically – refers to "transforma-tion costs"	Equally Efficient
IPS (2000)	No	Down-stream	Finding of abusive pri-cing upstream or down-stream required.	Not addressed specifically – refers to "higher processing costs"	Efficient Competitor
Deutsche Telekom (2003/2008/ 2010)	Yes	Both	Not required.	LRAIC	Equally Efficient
Telefónica (2007/2010)	Yes	Upstream	Not Required	LRAIC	Equally Efficient

---

[140] *Dwr Cymru Cyfyngedig v Albion Water Ltd & Anor supra* note 24, para. 95.

5. – Margin Squeeze
Francisco Enrique González-Díaz and Jorge Padilla

Case (Year)	Margin Squeeze?	Dominance Upstream or Down-stream?	Excessive Up or Predation Down?	Type of Costs Used	Measure of Competitor Efficiency for Margin Squeeze
TeliaSonera (2011)	N/A	Upstream	Not required	Not addressed	Equally Efficient and only in limited circumstances reasonably efficient
RWE (2009)	Possible	N/A[141]	Not addressed	Not addressed specifically – refers to "asymmetric cost elements"	Equally Efficient
BSkyB (2002)	No	Upstream	Not Addressed	Costs of trans-formation.	Equally Efficient
BT (2002)	No	No Conclusion	Implies predation not necessary.	LRAIC	Equally Efficient
Genzyme (2004)	Yes	Upstream	Not Addressed	Considered whether costs of distribution were included in wholesale price.	Reasonably Efficient and Equally Efficient[142]
Ablion Water (2008)	Yes	Upstream	Abusive Pricing Not Required	LRAIC; issue of whether the downstream costs had to be "transfor-mative" or avoided[143]	Equally Efficient

[141] Even though the Commission did not address the issue of whether dominance was required both upstream and downstream, it did acknowledge in its description of the markets that RWE may have held a dominant position not only in the gas transmission market (upstream) but also in the downstream supply market, although when assessing the possible margin squeeze it only considered the behaviour of the TSO (the upstream subsidiary of RWE).

[142] The OFT considered whether a reasonably efficient downstream rival could continue to operate, but also assessed Genzyme's actual costs, and thus whether Genzyme itself would make losses on the downstream prices charged. *See, e.g.*, Case 1016/1/1/03 *supra* note 105, para. 381.

[143] *Dŵr Cymru* argued that the margin squeeze test required that the dominant undertaking "*displace (rather than duplicate) the activities of the dominant undertaking on the downstream market.*" *See* Case 1046/2/4/04 *supra* note 105, paras 92 *et seq.*

5. – Margin Squeeze
Francisco Enrique González-Díaz and Jorge Padilla

IV. Oscar Bronner, Constructive Refusals to Supply, the Relevance of Regulation and TeliaSonera

5.76 In *Oscar Bronner*, the Court of Justice established the conditions under which a dominant firm would have a duty to deal with its rivals.[144] In this case the Court held that, to be actionable, a refusal to supply must:

(1) Be likely to eliminate all competition on the downstream market;

(2) Be incapable of being objectively justified; and

(3) Involve an input that is indispensable for the provision of the downstream service.[145]

5.77 With respect to the last criterion, the Court of Justice held that indispensability requires, in particular, that *"there is no actual or potential substitute in existence."*[146]

5.78 From an economic perspective, there is little doubt that a margin squeeze can be conceptualised as a constructive refusal to supply,[147] given that the supplier of an indispensable input may either refuse to supply or simply charge prices that make it impossible for a competitor to operate profitably in the downstream market. In other words, an outright refusal to supply is equivalent to setting an infinitely high wholesale price for a given input. Considered in this light, the rationale behind Telefónica and Telia's argument is straightforward, as one might expect the rationale for the *Oscar Bronner* criteria to apply with equal force in the case of margin squeeze. As acknowledged by Advocate General Jacobs in *Oscar Bronner*:

> *"[T]he justification in terms of competition policy for interfering with a dominant undertaking's freedom to contract often requires a careful balancing of conflicting considerations. In the long term it is generally pro-competitive and in the interest of consumers to allow a company to retain for its own use facilities, which it has developed for the purpose of its business. For example, if access to a production, purchasing or distribution facility were allowed too easily there would be no*

---

[144] *Oscar Bronner supra* note 138.

[145] *Ibid.*

[146] *Ibid.*, para. 41.

[147] *See, e.g., Guidance Paper supra* note 1, paras 75–90 (addressing margin squeeze alongside refusal to supply). *See also* S. C. Salop, "Refusal to deal and price squeezes by an unregulated, vertically integrated monopolist" (2010) 76(3) *Antitrust Law Journal*, pp. 709–40.

5. – Margin Squeeze
Francisco Enrique González-Díaz and Jorge Padilla

incentive for a competitor to develop competing facilities. Thus while competition was increased in the short term it would be reduced in the long term. Moreover, the incentive for a dominant undertaking to invest in efficient facilities would be reduced if its competitors were, upon request, able to share the benefits. Thus the mere fact that by retaining a facility for its own use a dominant undertaking retains an advantage over a competitor cannot justify requiring access to it."[148]

Despite the parallels between the refusals to supply and margin squeezes, in **5.79** *Telefónica*, the Commission formally rejected the view that a margin squeeze should be analysed as a constructive refusal to supply, and thus governed by the *Oscar Bronner* line of cases.[149] The Commission considered that the circumstances in Telefónica's case were different from those in *Oscar Bronner*, because Telefónica had a duty to supply its upstream inputs to competitors, and moreover that duty had been established *"with a view to promoting competition and the consumer interest."*[150] The Commission apparently took the view that the Spanish regulatory framework had struck an appropriate balance between preserving downstream competition (by requiring access upstream) and protecting Telefónica's incentives to invest in upstream infrastructure in the first place.[151] The Commission concluded that *"in light of the specific factual, economic and legal context of the case … the legal test applied by the Court of Justice in Oscar Bronner is not applicable in the present case."*[152]

Although the Commission did not apply the *Oscar Bronner* criteria where there **5.80** was an existing regulatory duty to supply competitors, there remained the question whether the Commission would apply the *Oscar Bronner* criteria in cases where there is, in fact, no duty (regulatory or otherwise) to supply competitors. For some time, there were indications that it would. Indeed, in December 2008, the Commission confirmed the characterisation of margin squeeze as a constructive refusal to supply. The *Guidance Paper* states that the Commission will only pursue refusal to supply cases, including margin squeeze cases, as an administrative priority when:

---

[148] *Oscar Bronner supra* note 138, para. 57. *See also* in similar terms, Advocate General Mazák in *TeliaSonera*, para. 21.

[149] *Oscar Bronner supra* note 138.

[150] *Telefónica Decision 2007 supra* note 20, paras 302–3.

[151] *Ibid.*, para. 303. In any event, the Commission dismissed any notion that Telefónica's incentives were at stake in the case, explaining that it was very likely that Telefónica's investments in infrastructure bore no relation to the products at issue in the case – broadband access.

[152] *Ibid.*, para. 309.

5. – Margin Squeeze
Francisco Enrique González-Díaz and Jorge Padilla

- the refusal/margin squeeze relates to a product or service that is objectively necessary to be able to compete effectively on a downstream market. The Commission refers in this respect to the *Oscar Bronner* judgment;[153]
- the refusal is likely to lead to the elimination of effective competition on the downstream market; and
- the refusal is likely to lead to consumer harm.[154]

5.81 The Commission did seem, therefore, to accept that the *Oscar Bronner* criteria regarding refusals to supply also governed margin squeeze claims. However, consistent with its decision in *Telefónica*, the Commission confirmed that it would not follow this approach in all cases. In paragraph 82 of the *Guidance Paper*, the Commission introduced an exception to the application of the above criteria. This exception would apply to *"certain specific cases,"* where *"it may be clear that imposing an obligation to supply is manifestly not capable of having negative effects on the input owner's and/or other operators' incentives to invest and innovate upstream, whether ex ante or ex post."*[155] The Commission considers this likely to be the case where:

- *"regulation compatible with Community law already imposes an obligation to supply on the dominant undertaking and it is clear, from the considerations underlying such regulation, that the necessary balancing of incentives has already been made by the public authority when imposing such an obligation to supply;"* or

- *"the upstream market position of the dominant undertaking has been developed under the protection of special or exclusive rights or has been financed by state resources."* [156]

5.82 In either of these two scenarios, the Commission is likely to apply, as it did in the *Telefónica* decision, Article 102 to an alleged margin squeeze even if the *Oscar Bronner* conditions are not met, *i.e.*, even where competitors can replicate the input in question or have alternative means of obtaining an input and/or even if competition in the downstream market is unlikely to be eliminated.

---

[153] *See Guidance Paper supra* note 1, para. 83.
[154] *Ibid.*, para. 81.
[155] *Ibid.*, para. 82.
[156] *Ibid.*

5. – Margin Squeeze
Francisco Enrique González-Díaz and Jorge Padilla

In the Commission's view, in these cases, *"there is no reason for the Commission to deviate from its general enforcement standard of showing likely anti-competitive foreclosure, without considering whether the three circumstances* [analogous to the Oscar Bronner criteria] *are present."*[157]

Regarding the first scenario, the Commission considers it "clear" that the **5.83** imposition of an obligation to supply in such cases will not harm the dominant firm's incentives to invest; however, even if this exception were to be acceptable as a matter of law and economics, such an exception would arguably require that the relevant regulation was imposed with competition law in mind, and goes no further than what would be consistent with *Oscar Bronner*. Indeed regulators and competition authorities may pursue different aims. Given these different aims, it cannot be assumed that, when balancing incentives, regulators will come to the same conclusion as a competition authority would. Regulators may impose access duties where a competition authority would not, and the price set by a regulator may be different to that set under competition law criteria. Regulation and competition policy do not necessarily require the same balancing of incentives.[158] Indeed, when considering whether to impose access obligations, national regulatory authorities may take into account factors that go beyond the protection of competition in the relevant markets.[159] For instance they are not required to consider whether or not access is indispensable for companies to compete downstream, or whether the refusal to provide access is likely to lead to the elimination of effective competition downstream, in addition, in setting access prices, they may take into account the need not to discourage investment in alternative infrastructures.

---

[157] *See Guidance Paper supra* note 1, para. 82.

[158] When deciding whether to require access, the aim of a regulator is to encourage the emergence of competition in a market, whereas, the aim of European competition laws is to prevent restrictions on existing or potential competition. In this vein, the Parliament and Council Directive 2002/19/EC of 7 November 2002 on access to, and interconnection of, electronic communications networks and associated facilities ("*Access Directive*"), OJ 2002 L 108/7, Article 12 states that a National Regulatory Authority ("NRA") may *"impose obligations to meet reasonable requests for access to, and use of, specific network elements and associated facilities, inter alia in situations where the NRA considers that denial of access or unreasonable terms and conditions having a similar effect would hinder the emergence of a sustainable competitive market at the retail level …"*.

[159] *See Access Directive*, Article 12 (*"(i) the technical and economic viability of using or installing competing facilities, in the light of the rate of market development, taking into account the nature and type of interconnection and access involved; (ii) the feasibility of providing the access proposed, in relation to the capacity available; (iii) the initial investment by the facility owner, bearing in mind the risks involved in making the assessment; (iv) the need to safeguard competition in the long term; (v) where appropriate, any relevant intellectual property rights; and (vi) the provision of pan-European services"*.

5. – Margin Squeeze
Francisco Enrique González-Díaz and Jorge Padilla

5.84   In any case, even if a national regulatory authority and an antitrust authority were to pursue the same aims, the question arises whether the Commission could pursue a margin squeeze case simply because a regulator has mandated access to a specific upstream product, in particular, where that access has been mandated under terms and conditions that would not be the same as those mandated by competition law if the *Oscar Bronner* conditions were not applied. Indeed, regulators and competition authorities may disagree about the price of access as they did in *Telefónica*. Regulators may set higher access prices than a competition authority would require in a margin squeeze case in order, for example, to encourage investment in alternative infrastructure.[160] This is yet another reason why there is a question as to whether competition authorities can use the existence of access regulation as a valid ground for pursuing a margin squeeze case and second-guess the access price to a non-essential facility decided by the regulator. Indeed, if a competition authority relies on the judgment of a regulator that requiring access will not harm investment incentives, it should also accept, so the argument runs, the judgment of the regulator as to the price at which access has no harmful effects whether this a maximum or a fixed price.

5.85   As to the second scenario, the Commission considers that when a company's market position has been achieved through state financing or state-granted exclusive rights, an obligation to supply (and thus liability for margin squeeze) would not undermine the profitability of the investments in question. However, the investment incentives of a company that gained its market position through state financing would be lower if the investors had known *ex ante* that a margin squeeze case was likely to be brought *ex post*. It is thus questionable to assume that where the investor is a government it will spend money without taking account the impact this will have on its finances in the future. In any case, some of the assets in question may have been paid for by market investors after privatisation, even if the company originally gained its market position through state financing. Similarly, some of the investment in the relevant assets may have been made after a company stopped benefiting from exclusive rights. Also, the fact that a company benefited from exclusive rights for a period does not guarantee that it earned a return on any investments it

---

[160] *See* J. Bouckaert and F. Verboven, "Price Squeezes in a Regulatory Environment" (2004) 26(3) *Journal of Regulatory Economics*, pp. 321–51.

5. – Margin Squeeze
Francisco Enrique González-Díaz and Jorge Padilla

made during that period (*e.g.*, it may have been providing universal services wholly or partly at a loss).[161]

In any event, paragraph 82 of the *Article 102 Guidance Paper* provides examples **5.86** where the Commission considers that an appropriate balancing of incentives may have taken place, such that the *Oscar Bronner* criteria may have less relevance to margin squeeze cases, rather than scenarios where those criteria will not apply.

Setting aside the regulatory context and the *Telefónica* case where the Com- **5.87** mission explicitly declined to apply the *Oscar Bronner* criteria, the Commission's *Guidance Paper* clearly indicated that the Commission would apply the *Oscar Bronner* criteria to all refusals to supply – including margin squeeze cases. That is, the Commission would only be likely to pursue margin squeeze cases where: (1) the refusal/margin squeeze relates to a product or service that is objectively necessary to be able to compete effectively on a downstream market; (2) the refusal is likely to lead to the elimination of effective competition on the downstream market; and (3) the refusal is likely to lead to consumer harm.

This was also the view adopted by Advocate General Mazák[162] in *TeliaSonera* **5.88** when confronted with this issue, "*I consider that it may be inferred from the judgment in Bronner (see points 14 to 16 above), from my Opinion and the General Court's judgment in Deutsche Telekom v Commission (cited in footnote 14), from the Commission's decision-making practice and from the Guidance on the Commission's enforcement priorities that in those cases where there is no regulatory obligation to provide the input, such as here, a dominant undertaking which through its pricing arrangements operates a margin squeeze will abuse its dominant position where that input is indispensable to enabling a competitor to enter into competition with it on the downstream market. Such arrangements constitute in my view a form of refusal to deal.*"

---

[161] The distinction between companies that have, in the past, been granted special or exclusive rights and all the others for Article 102 purposes appears to be at odds with the principles of impartiality *vis à vis* the type of property ownership and the principle of equality between public and private companies laid down by the Treaty. *See, e.g.*, Article 295 EC and, *inter alia*, Case 2005/145/EC Commission Decision of 16 December 2003 on the State aid granted by France to EDF and the electricity and gas industries, OJ 2005 L 49/9, para. 97. *See* F. E. González Díaz and J. Padilla, "The *linkLine* Judgment – A European Perspective" (2009) 1 *CPI Antitrust Chronicle*.

[162] Advocate General Mazák in Case C-52/09 *Konkurrensverket v TeliaSonera Sverige* ("*TelioSonera Judgment 2011*"), [2011] ECR I-527, para. 18. *See also* A. G. Verheyden and S. Clerckx, "The ECJ Advocate General Mazák seeks to affirm judgment in margin squeeze case (*Deutsche Telekom*)" (April 2010) *e-Competitions*, No. 33702.

5. – Margin Squeeze
Francisco Enrique González-Díaz and Jorge Padilla

5.89   However, the Court of Justice followed a different approach in its judgment. The Court, at the behest of the Commission, concluded that a margin squeeze should be considered a distinct infringement of Article 102 in all cases where the dominant company places its products on the market irrespective of whether there is a regulatory obligation to supply or not.

5.90   Indeed, the Court held: "[t]*he Court has stated that notwithstanding such legislation, if a dominant vertically integrated undertaking has scope to adjust even its retail prices alone, the margin squeeze may on that ground alone be attributable to it … It follows from the foregoing that, a fortiori, where an undertaking has complete autonomy in its choice of conduct on the market, Article 102 TFEU is applicable to it … it cannot be inferred from paragraphs 48 and 49 of that judgment [Oscar Bronner] that the conditions to be met in order to establish that a refusal to supply is abusive must necessarily also apply when assessing the abusive nature of conduct which consists in supplying services or selling goods on conditions which are disadvantageous or on which there might be no purchaser … if Bronner were to be interpreted otherwise, in the way advocated by TeliaSonera, that would, as submitted by the European Commission, amount to a requirement that before any conduct of a dominant undertaking in relation to its terms of trade could be regarded as abusive the conditions to be met to establish that there was a refusal to supply would in every case have to be satisfied, and that would unduly reduce the effectiveness of Article 102 TFEU. … It follows that the absence of any regulatory obligation to supply the ADSL input services on the wholesale market has no effect on the question of whether the pricing practice at issue in the main proceedings is abusive.*"[163]

5.91   The Court's reasoning appears to be based on two different arguments. On the one hand, it rests on an interpretation that the Court in *Oscar Bronner* had not provided a specific reply to the question at issue. On the other hand, it is based on the assumption that applying the *Oscar Bronner* criteria to a margin squeeze would reduce the effectiveness of Article 102 TFEU, the implicit concern being that all or most pricing/commercial terms and/or practices could be assimilated to some sort of refusal to supply.

5.92   Independently of whether or not the Court of Justice gave in *Oscar Bronner* an actual response to the question raised in *TeliaSonera*[164] it is far from obvious that assimilating a margin squeeze to a constructive refusal to supply would diminish the effectiveness of Article 102 TFEU.

---

[163] *TeliaSonera Judgment 2011*, para. 58.
[164] *Oscar Bronner supra* note 138, para. 48 *et seq.*

5. – Margin Squeeze
Francisco Enrique González-Díaz and Jorge Padilla

First, this is the position adopted by the Commission in its *Guidance Paper*[165]   **5.93**
and the US Supreme Court. Secondly, whilst exclusive dealing and tying may
be associated with a refusal to supply, this does not imply that those abuses
should be treated as such (outright or constructive) and in fact they are not
treated in this manner either in the Commission's *Guidance Paper* or by the US
Courts. This is because the pattern of a typical exclusive dealing and/or tying
practice is very different from the pattern of an (outright or constructive)
refusal to deal. While the aim of a refusal to supply or of a margin squeeze
is to reserve the use of an input/facility to its producer/owner or to establish its price, exclusive dealing arrangements and tying strategies may margin-
alise or exclude competitors operating in the input market. In fact, exclusive
dealing and tying abuses need not involve vertically integrated undertakings.
Moreover, a dominant firm which enters into exclusive dealing arrangements
covering a substantial portion of the market can foreclose competitors even
if it does not sell an indispensable product or service. Likewise, a dominant
firm may successfully leverage its dominance in a given market onto another
through tying even when its products are not indispensable.

Thirdly, as noted by DG Comp's Economic Advisory Group on Competi-   **5.94**
tion Policy,[166] the effective application of Article 102 TFEU requires ensuring
that companies cannot circumvent competition policy constraints by way of
attempting to achieve the same end results through the use of different commercial practices. This can only be achieved "[b]*y focusing on the effects of company
actions rather than on the form that these actions may take*", so that "*any specific practice
is assessed in terms of its outcome and two practices leading to the same result* [are] *therefore
subject to a comparable treatment.*" Since, as explained above, the outcomes of a
refusal to supply and a margin squeeze are identical, the competitive assessment of these practices should also be identical to ensure that "*anti-competitive
behaviour does not outwit legal provisions*".[167]

---

[165] *See Guidance Paper supra* note 1, recital 76.

[166] P. Rey and others, "An Economic Analysis to Article 82", Report by the Economic Advisory Group on Competition Policy ("*EAGCP Report*"), July 2005, pp.1–53, p. 2

[167] According to the European Union Courts' case-law, a margin squeeze is said to occur, as explained above, when the dominant undertaking's prices would force an *as-efficient competitor* in the retail market to sell at a loss. Nevertheless, while a margin squeeze may exclude an *as-efficient competitor*, there is no evidence that it might hurt a more efficient competitor. This, in turn, means that the anticompetitive impact of an outright refusal to deal may be greater than that of a margin squeeze, because an outright refusal to deal excludes all competitors (including more efficient competitors).

5. – Margin Squeeze
Francisco Enrique González-Díaz and Jorge Padilla

5.95 Fourthly, there appears to be no basis to be concerned that "*if Bronner were to be interpreted otherwise, in the way advocated by TeliaSonera, that would, as submitted by the European Commission, amount to a requirement that before any conduct of a dominant undertaking in relation to its terms of trade could be regarded as abusive the conditions to be met to establish that there was a refusal to supply would in every case have to be satisfied, and that would unduly reduce the effectiveness of Article 102 TFEU.*"[168] Indeed, what *Oscar Bronner* requires is that prior to imposing an obligation to deal ex Article 102 competition authorities and courts check, *inter alia*, whether the input/facility in question is indispensable. This task is not more burdensome than defining a market, proving dominance and/or establishing any of the other conditions of application of Article 102. It is just a proper check to ensure, *inter alia*, that dynamic competition and investment incentives are duly respected. In addition, and as opposed to other terms of trade that may restrict competition such as tying and/or exclusive dealing there is an inherent link between the indispensability of the input/facility and the legality of a refusal to supply and/or a margin squeeze as if the input or facility is not indispensable within the meaning of *Oscar Bronner*, competitors can actually replicate the assets/procure the input and thus compete whereas by definition an exclusive dealing/tying arrangement may actually prevent competitors from supplying/replicating the input/facility in question, even if the input is not indispensable.

5.96 Thus, from the viewpoint of effective enforcement and optimal deterrence there appears to be no justification for not applying the *Oscar Bronner* legal standard to margin squeezes.[169]

V. Recurring Issues In Margin Squeeze Cases

5.97 Despite the fact that the various European court precedents and Commission decisions, including the Commission decisions in *Deutsche Telekom* and *Telefónica*, the European Courts' rulings in those two cases and the Court of Justice ruling in *TeliaSonera*, provide considerable guidance on how margin squeeze practices would be evaluated by the Commission and the European Union courts, there remain, however, a number of significant open issues with respect to its assessment. We address these issues in what follows.

---

[168] *TeliaSonera Judgment 2011 supra* note 1, para. 58.
[169] *See* C. F. Beckner and S. C. Salop, "Decision Theory and Antitrust Rules" (1999) 67 Antitrust Law Journal, pages 41–76.

5. – Margin Squeeze
Francisco Enrique González-Díaz and Jorge Padilla

1. Essentiality of Inputs

Prior to *TeliaSonera* it was settled that a finding of margin squeeze requires, at **5.98** the very least, a showing of dominance. The question arose, however, whether the particular facility or input in question should also be "essential" to competing downstream, and, if so, what "essential" meant.

In *Deutsche Telekom*, the Commission found that "*from the point of view of competi-* **5.99** *tors seeking entry to the German market, the density of Deutsche Telekom's fixed network, together with the technological facilities it offers, make wholesale access to that network the only commercially viable option,*"[170] and the General Court (affirming the Commission's finding in this regard), found that Deutsche Telekom's "*wholesale services are ... indispensable to enabling a competitor to enter into competition with the applicant on the downstream market.*"[171] Although the Commission found that the upstream input was the only commercially viable option, and appeared to rely on this finding in concluding that there was a margin squeeze, it did not formally require that the upstream input be *essential*. And although the Commission considered whether there were alternatives to access the local loop in Germany, it explained that this analysis was conducted for the purposes of market definition (and thus not for an independent finding of essentiality).[172] The other margin squeeze precedents are similar – *i.e.*, while the Commission implicitly concluded that the input in question was essential to downstream competition, it did not establish an explicit requirement of essentiality.[173]

---

[170] *Deutsche Telekom Decision 2003 supra* note 18, para. 65.

[171] *Deutsche Telekom Judgment 2008 supra* note 5, para. 237.

[172] The Commission considered, in some detail, the availability of other options for access, and concluded that these alternatives were not viable ("*Lack of Alternative Infrastructure*"). See *Deutsche Telekom Decision 2003 supra* note 18, paras 83–90.

[173] This is true of older precedents as well. In *National Carbonizing*, although the complainant NCC purchased the relevant input (coking coal) from the dominant firm NCB, which controlled over 85 per cent of the available coking coal inputs, the Commission did not make an independent finding that supply from NCB was essential (though this was likely to be the case) (*see supra* note 13). The same holds true in *Napier Brown*, where the dominant firm British Sugar was the largest producer in the UK and the only processor of sugar beet in the UK. The Commission considered, and dismissed, alternative sources of supply, but did not provide an indication of what level of indispensability, or essentiality, was required. It did find that Napier Brown could not continue to operate in the UK market without supply from British Sugar: "*the role of imports on the British market has been as a complement to domestic sugar, rather than as fully competitive alternative*" and that "*[i]t is clear from the facts as set out above that should British Sugar have maintained this margin in the long term, Napier Brown, or any company equally efficient in repackaging as British Sugar without a self-produced source of industrial sugar, would have been obliged to leave the United Kingdom retail sugar market.*" See *Napier Brown supra* note 14, paras 47, 66.

5. – Margin Squeeze

Francisco Enrique González-Díaz and Jorge Padilla

5.100 In *IPS*, the General Court did recognise the essentiality of the input. In this case, the Commission had rejected a claim of margin squeeze, in part because it found that there were sufficient alternative supplies of the input available to the complainant – including from producers in Canada, Russia, and China. The General Court upheld the Commission's reasoning[174] and suggested that some level of essentiality will be required.[175]

5.101 The issue of essentiality of the dominant firm's input was raised again in *Telefónica*. In that case, Telefónica argued – as part of its argument that the *Oscar Bronner* criteria should apply in the case – that its national and regional access products were not essential or necessary to operate on the downstream market, because (1) these products and their underlying infrastructure could and had been replicated by competitors,[176] (2) there were alternative ADSL access products including Telefónica's wholesale local loop access offerings, and (3) there were a number of competing technologies that provided a significant competitive constraint on Telefónica, including, broadband cable providers, which were not reliant on Telefónica's ADSL network for service.[177] The Commission rejected these arguments,[178] essentially by dismissing the applicability of the *Oscar Bronner* case law and by considering that a finding of indispensability was not required for a finding of margin squeeze. In defending its finding of a margin squeeze, the Commission referred to other cases – including *Deutsche Telekom* and *Napier Brown*, where alternatives may have existed.[179]

5.102 Neither the Commission nor the General Court tackled the issue of the indispensability of Telefónica's inputs expressly.[180] However the Commission considered that *Oscar Bronner* was not relevant because of the "*special circumstance of the case,*" the "*legal and economic context,*" and the "*specific facts of the case,*" which were claimed to differ from those of *Oscar Bronner*. The General Court simply

---

[174] *IPS supra* note 16, paras 43 *et seq.*

[175] The French Court of Cassation, for example, has held in a margin squeeze case that a showing that there is no possible alternative input is not required. Instead, the level of essentiality is but one factor to consider in assessing any anticompetitive effects arising as a result of the pricing practices by the dominant firm. Decision 04–D–48 *SFR–France Telecom*, French Court of Cassation Judgment of 3 March 2009. The Court of Cassation held that the FCC was required to assess whether the implemented practices had as their object or effect to harm or impede competition on the market for calls made by professional clients from landlines to mobile phones.

[176] Regarding Telefónica's wholesale network, it had been fully replicated at the national level (by way of ADSL–IP and ADSL–IP total products) and partially at the regional access level (GigADSL product).

[177] *Telefónica Decision 2007 supra* note 20, para. 268.

[178] *Ibid.*, para. 560.

[179] *Ibid.*, para. 734.

[180] *Ibid.*, paras 301–09 and *Telefónica Judgment 2012 supra* note 1, paras 180–82.

5. – Margin Squeeze
Francisco Enrique González-Díaz and Jorge Padilla

referred to the *TeliaSonera* judgment, reasoning that since a margin squeeze constitutes a distinct infringement of Article 102 and that the *Oscar Bronner* doctrine was not applicable, it was not necessary for the input to be indispensible in order to conclude that there had been a margin squeeze.[181]

According to *Oscar Bronner*, an input is indispensable only when: (1) there **5.103** is no *"real or potential alternative"* (even if they are less advantageous for the downstream market) and (2) the input cannot be duplicated by others (including potentially with the assistance of a third party) or the duplication is not *"economically viable."*[182]

In the *Telefónica* case, neither of the *Oscar Bronner* requirements appeared to **5.104** be met[183] as there were other real or potential alternatives to Telefónica's national/regional wholesale access for the provision of a retail service and the national/regional network could be replicated, at the levels at which the infringement was found.[184]

In its *Guidance Paper*, the Commission provided some additional guidance – **5.105** and confirmation on the degree of essentiality in margin squeeze cases. The Commission explained that, as a matter of enforcement priority, it would focus *"on cases where the upstream product or service concerned is objectively necessary for competitors to be able to compete effectively on the downstream market."*[185]

Regardless of its application in margin squeeze cases, the requirement of **5.106** objective necessity (as described in the *Guidance Paper*) is consistent with at least some level of essentiality of the input and appears to go beyond the establishment of dominance on the part of the upstream provider of the input.

It follows from the judgment in *TeliaSonera*, described above, that the need for **5.107** indispensability may not constitute a *conditio sine qua non*, at least in all cases, to finding a margin squeeze incompatible with Article 102 TFEU.

---

[181] *See Telefónica Judgment 2012 supra* note 1, paras 180–182.

[182] *Oscar Bronner supra* note 138, para. 46.

[183] *See IMS Health supra* note 10, para. 28.

[184] Telefónica's wholesale network had been replicated in its entirety at the wholesale national level and in its fundamental elements, at the wholesale regional level. In this sense, *see, Telefónica Decision 2007 supra* note 20, para. 301.

[185] *Guidance Paper supra* note 1, paras 23 *et seq.*

5. – Margin Squeeze
Francisco Enrique González-Díaz and Jorge Padilla

> *"The possibility cannot be ruled out that, by reason simply of the fact that the wholesale product is not indispensable for the supply of the retail product, a pricing practice which causes margin squeeze may not be able to produce any anti-competitive effect, even potentially. Accordingly, it is again for the referring court to satisfy itself that, even where the wholesale product is not indispensable, the practice may be capable of having anti-competitive effects on the markets concerned."*

5.108 As the Court suggests, the question of indispensability has not necessarily become moot, as, at least, it is likely to play a key role in determining the effects of the conduct in the market and hence the existence of an infringement.[186]

2. Downstream Dominance

5.109 While it is clear that a margin squeeze abuse requires, at least, dominance in the upstream market, the question of whether dominance is also required at the downstream level remained unanswered, or a *"vexed issue"*,[187] until the Commission's decision in *Telefónica* (where the Commission found that downstream dominance was not required).[188] This interpretation has now also been confirmed by the Court of Justice in *TeliaSonera*[189] and the General Court in *Telefónica*.[190] The primary question regarding downstream dominance, is whether in its absence a margin squeeze can give rise to any harm to competition and/or consumer welfare.

5.110 In essentially every margin squeeze case decided prior to *Telefónica*, the Commission found the firm engaged in the margin squeeze to be dominant in both the upstream and downstream market.[191] It has thus not had the opportunity to take a view as to whether a margin squeeze could exist in the absence of

---

[186] *See infra* Section V.5.

[187] D. Geradin and R. O'Donoghue, "The Concurrent Application of Competition Law and Regulation: The Case of Margin Squeeze Abuses in the Telecommunications Sector" (2005) 1(2) *Journal of Competition Law and Economics*, p. 407.

[188] *Telefónica Decision 2007 supra* note 20, para. 243.

[189] *TeliaSonera Judgment 2011 supra* note 1, paras 41 and 45.

[190] *Telefónica Judgment 2012 supra* note 1, para. 146.

[191] In *IPS* the Commission did not need to rule on the issue of dominance since there was no finding of margin squeeze (*see IPS supra* note 16). In the 2004 *Genzyme* case in the United Kingdom, Genzyme was not dominant in the relevant downstream market – the provision of home services for the drug – but Genzyme's pricing practice was expected to *"eliminate any competition"* in that market even though Genzyme was without (at least initially) any market power (*see* Case 1016/1/1/03 *supra* note 105, para. 554).

5. – Margin Squeeze
Francisco Enrique González-Díaz and Jorge Padilla

downstream dominance. However, in its most recent margin squeeze decision, *Telefónica*, the Commission explicitly decided that it is not necessary to find a dominant position in the downstream market in order to establish the existence of an abusive margin squeeze:

> "*It also results from Industrie des Poudres Sphériques that it is not necessary to prove that Telefónica is dominant in the downstream market in order to establish that the company has engaged in an abusive margin squeeze. As held by the Court of Justice in Tetra Pak II, the fact that a dominant Company's abusive conduct has its adverse effects on a market distinct from the dominated one does not detract from the applicability of Article 82 of the Treaty. Margin squeeze is an example of leveraging of market power from one market (in which there is dominance) into another (in which the abusive undertaking is active – but not necessarily dominant – and in which an extension of market power from the market in which there is dominance is sought).*"[192]

The Commission's primary argument with respect to downstream dominance stems from the *Tetra Pak II* judgment,[193] where a dominant company, through a tying practice, was held to abuse its dominant position in one market by leveraging that dominant position in a market in which it was not dominant. The Commission's position in *Telefónica*, that downstream dominance is not required for a finding of an abusive margin squeeze, therefore relies on the possibility that harm to competition can occur in a different market to that in which the firm is held to be dominant.

5.111

While these precedents suggest that there is no need to hold a dominant position at both the upstream and downstream level for a firm to squeeze its rivals, from an economic perspective, some degree of market power downstream would be required if a firm were to profitably engage in this practice. This is so because for a firm to engage profitably in margin squeeze it must capture some of the sales of the firms that are squeezed out of the market. Without (1) a significant degree of market power downstream, or (2) evidence that the vertically integrated firm and its downstream competitor are close competitors, it is unlikely that a margin squeeze strategy would be profitable. Indeed, if the firm engaged in margin squeeze is not dominant downstream, or if the downstream market is in fact competitive, it is not clear how this

5.112

---

[192] *Telefónica Decision 2007 supra* note 20.

[193] Case C-333/94 P *Tetra Pak International v Commission* ("*Tetra Pak II Judgment 1996*") [1996] ECR I-5951, paras 27–31.

5. – Margin Squeeze
Francisco Enrique González-Díaz and Jorge Padilla

particular pricing practice would have any effect on competition at all, let alone on consumers. Indeed, if the vertically integrated upstream dominant firm does not enjoy market power downstream it will not be able to impose a margin squeeze on its downstream competitors, since its rivals may be able to prosper even if their prices are above those of the vertically integrated firm. As a result, an upstream/downstream price configuration that may cause losses to the vertically integrated firm need not be loss-making for its downstream competitors. In other words, when the vertically integrated firm is not dominant downstream, it has no *de facto* control over the margins of its downstream competitors. In these circumstances, the vertically integrated firm's prices would not determine, albeit would influence, the downstream prices of its competitors. In *Tetra Pak* the tying abuse at issue guaranteed that the dominant firm (in the tying market) obtained additional sales in the tied market. In the margin squeeze context, without market power downstream, the upstream dominant provider of the input may not benefit at all from this practice in the downstream market since, as opposed to a tying case, a margin squeeze may lead to a loss of revenues upstream without the offsetting guarantee that, as a result of its pricing practices, consumers will buy its products.[194] On the other hand, if the firm is also dominant in the downstream market, there is a greater probability that the margin squeeze will result in additional sales for the dominant firm and thus be profitable.[195]

5.113 In any event, and in the absence of downstream dominance, it would seem appropriate to require a particularly clear, concrete and strong showing of actual anticompetitive effects in the downstream market.[196] Indeed, without downstream dominance or a clear, concrete and strong showing of how the margin squeeze will result in significant benefits to the dominant firm in the downstream market, it would be difficult to prove that the dominant firm has any incentive to engage in a margin squeeze in the first place.[197]

---

[194] *See, e.g.*, J. Faull and A. Nikpay (Eds.), *The EC Law of Competition* (2nd Ed., Oxford, Oxford University Press, 2007), p. 174; *supra* note 187, p. 408.

[195] J. Kallaugher, *The 'Margin Squeeze' Under Article 82: Searching for Limiting Principles*, Report presented during the GCLC Conference on Margin Squeeze under EC Competition Law with a special focus on the Telecommunications Sector, London, December 10, 2004, available at http://www.coleurope.eu/content/gclc/documents/03%20Kallaugher%20paper.doc, p. 33.

[196] Some authors have also noted that without a requirement of downstream dominance, it would be *curious and anomalous* for a margin squeeze abuse to be easier to prove than price predation, which does require a showing of dominance in the relevant (downstream) market where the pricing practice is taking place. *See, e.g.*, *supra* note 187, pp. 407–08.

[197] *See, e.g.*, the Chicago critique, discussed in Section VI.2.

5. – Margin Squeeze
Francisco Enrique González-Díaz and Jorge Padilla

3. The Reasonably Efficient *Versus* the Equally Efficient Competitor Test

3.1. Precedents

In order to establish, in practice, whether a margin squeeze has taken place, it **5.114** is necessary first to calculate a margin, which itself must be done by reference to some measure of costs. The predominant method to date has consisted of considering whether a firm operating with the same costs as the dominant firm, or an "equally efficient" competitor, could profitably operate on the dominant firm's pricing terms. Under this test, a margin squeeze occurs if a firm as efficient as the dominant firm could not continue to operate given the margin between the dominant firm's upstream and downstream prices.[198] Although the equally efficient competitor test has intuitive appeal, there are alternative cost tests, including considering the costs of a "reasonably efficient" competitor, or the costs of actual downstream competitors. As shown in Table 5.3 below, the European precedents and the more prominent UK margin squeeze cases are essentially unanimous in the use of the equally efficient competitor test:

Table 5.3: Reasonably Efficient versus Equally Efficient Competitor Test.

Precedent/Authority	Reasonably Efficient	Equally Efficient
National Carbonising (1975)[199]	X	X
IPS (2000)[200]	X	X

[198] Under this test, prohibiting a margin squeeze ensures that *the dominant company cannot squeeze itself. See* P. Crocioni, "Price Squeeze and Imputation Test – Recent Developments" (2005) 26(10) *European Competition Law Review*, p. 562.

[199] *Supra* note 13, para. 14. In this case, the Commission explicitly referred to the costs of a reasonably efficient competitor, but then in application considered the case with respect to the costs of the dominant firm.

[200] *IPS supra* note 16. The Court uses the as efficient competitor test, but also conducts an analysis of the actual costs of the downstream competitor. It also makes a final reference to an efficient competitor in general in para. 80. Although it is not specified whether it refers to an as efficient or a reasonably efficient competitor, due to its context, it probably refers to the first.

a. The Court analyses the sufficiency of the margins, on the basis of the costs and revenues of the actual competitor downstream, rather than the dominant firm. For this reason, a priori it would seem that the test applied is more favourable to the operator downstream than the as-efficient competitor test, since it would also protect less efficient competitors in addition to as-efficient ones.

5. – Margin Squeeze
Francisco Enrique González-Díaz and Jorge Padilla

Precedent/Authority	Reasonably Efficient	Equally Efficient
Napier Brown (1988)[201]		X
Deutsche Telekom (2008)[202]		X
Telefónica (2007)[203]		X
TeliaSonera (2010)[204]	Only under limited circumstances	X

"181 The price at which low-oxygen calcium metal was sold to IPS was FRF 37, whereas the price at which broken calcium metal was sold by IPS had to be, in order to remain competitive with that of PEM, FRF 46, the price charged by PEM in 1995, as the file shows (annex 6 to the rejoinder) and since IPS has failed to prove that such a price had dropped to FRF 42. Therefore the difference, for IPS, between the price of low-oxygen calcium metal and the price of broken calcium metal which it had to charge in order to remain competitive on the market is FRF 9. In that context, it must be held that the range of FRF 9 to 11 corresponding to the calculation, put forward by the applicant, of the profit necessary in order to keep itself on the market was observed."

b. However, when this is applied to the facts, the CFI is more restrictive:

"179 ... the applicant's complaints concerning the alleged exclusion effect of the price proposed by PEM must be rejected in view of the fact that the applicant has failed to prove even the very premise on which its argument is predicated, namely, the existence of abusive pricing of the raw material. In the absence of abusive prices being charged by PEM for the raw material, namely low-oxygen primary calcium metal, or of predatory pricing for the derived product, namely broken calcium metal, the fact that the applicant cannot, seemingly because of its higher processing costs, remain competitive in the sale of the derived product cannot justify characterizing PEM's pricing policy as abusive. In that regard, it must be pointed out that a producer, even in a dominant position, is not obliged to sell its products below its manufacturing costs."

"180. Moreover, the applicant has not shown that the price of low-oxygen calcium metal is such as to eliminate an efficient competitor from the broken calcium metal market".

---

[201] *Napier Brown supra* note 14, paras 65–6 ("[t]*he maintaining, by a dominant company, which is dominant in the markets for both a raw material and a corresponding derived product, of a margin between the price which it charges for a raw material to the companies which compete with the dominant company in the production of the derived product (on the one hand) and the price which it charges for the derived product (on the other), which is insufficient to reflect that dominant company's own costs of transformation ... with the result that competition in the derived product is restricted, is an abuse of dominant position*" and "*the margin between industrial and retail prices was reduced to the point where the wholesale purchaser with packaging operations as efficient as those of the wholesale supplier could not profitably serve the retail market*").

[202] *Deutsche Telekom Judgment 2008 supra* note 5, paras 107 and 140.

[203] *Telefónica*, paras 311-2. In the *Telefónica* case the Commission referred to both tests for identifying a margin squeeze: "*A margin squeeze can be demonstrated by showing that the dominant company's own downstream operations could not trade profitably on the basis of the upstream price charged to its competitors by the upstream operating arm of the dominant company ('equally efficient competitor' test). A margin squeeze can also be demonstrated by showing that the margin between the price charged to competitors on the upstream market for access and the price which the downstream arm of the dominant operator charges in the downstream market is insufficient to allow a reasonably efficient service provider in the downstream market to obtain a normal profit ('hypothetical reasonably efficient competitor test')*" but it only used the equally efficient competitor test. *See* para. 311.

[204] *TeliaSonera Judgment 2011 supra* note 1, para. 41–45.

5. – Margin Squeeze
Francisco Enrique González-Díaz and Jorge Padilla

Precedent/Authority	Reasonably Efficient	Equally Efficient
Article 102 Guidance Paper[205]		X
European Union Telecom Access Notice[206]	X	X
Genzyme (2004)	X	X
Albion Waters (2008)[207]		X
UK Office of Fair Trading[208]	X	X

In its Telecom Access Notice, the Commission referred both to the efficient competitor test and the reasonably efficient competitor test, without expressing a preference for one test over the other and without explicitly recognising a distinction between them: **5.115**

- Equally efficient competitor: whether "*the <u>dominant company's downstream operations are able to trade profitably</u> on the basis of the upstream price charged to its competitors by the upstream operating arm of the dominant company.*"[209]
- Reasonably efficient competitor: whether "*the margin between the price charged to competitors on the downstream market (including the dominant company's own downstream operations, if any) for access and the price which the network operator charges in the downstream market is insufficient to allow a <u>reasonably efficient</u> service provider in the downstream market to obtain a normal profit.*"[210]

---

[205] *Guidance Paper supra* note 1, para. 80 ("*the price it charges on the downstream market, does not allow even an equally efficient competitor to trade profitably in the downstream market ...*").

[206] The *Telecom Access Notice* does not express a preference for one test over the other. *See Telecom Access Notice supra* note 15, paras 117–18.

[207] *Dŵr Cymru Cyfyngedig v Albion Water Ltd & Anor supra* note 24, para. 90.

[208] Office of Fair Trading, *Competition Act 1998: The application in the telecommunications sector, supra* note 111, at 7.26 ("*whether the dominant undertaking would be profitable in the relevant downstream market if it had to pay the same input prices as its competitors*").

[209] *Telecom Access Notice supra* note 15, para. 117.

[210] *Ibid.*, para. 118. Later, the Commission expressed its preference for the dominant firm's own costs when assessing a margin squeeze abuse as follows: "*The suspicion of a "margin squeeze" arises when the spread between access and retail prices of the incumbent's corresponding access services is not wide enough to reflect the incumbent's own downstream costs. In such a situation, alternative carriers normally complain that their margins are being squeezed because this spread is too narrow for them to compete with the incumbent. ... Provided access and retail services are strictly comparable, a situation of a margin squeeze occurs where the incumbent's price of access combined with its downstream costs are higher than its corresponding retail price.*" *See* European Commission, *Pricing Issues In Relation To Unbundled Access To The Local Loop*, ONP Committee, ONPCOM 01–17, June 25, 2001, pp. 1–17, at 5.

5. – Margin Squeeze
Francisco Enrique González-Díaz and Jorge Padilla

5.116   In *Industrie des Poudres Sphérique*s, the first European Union court margin squeeze judgment, the General Court seemed to suggest that, in determining whether there is a margin squeeze, it may be appropriate to check its existence both on the basis of the "as efficient competitor" test and on the dominant firm's and the downstream competitor's actual costs.[211] However, in the *Deutsche Telekom* case the General Court confirmed the analysis of the Commission, who had relied "*exclusively on* [Deutsche Telekom's] *charges and costs, instead of on the particular situation of ... actual or potential competitors, in order to assess whether* [Deutsche Telekom's] *pricing practices were abusive.*"[212] In support of this position, the General Court referred to the *AKZO* judgment,[213] as well as to *IPS*[214] and *Napier Brown* cases,[215] where only the costs of the dominant undertaking were considered.[216] According to the General Court,

> "*[a]ny other approach could be contrary to the general principle of legal certainty. If the lawfulness of the pricing practices of a dominant undertaking depended on the particular situation of competing undertakings, particularly their cost struc-ture - information that is generally not known to the dominant undertaking – the latter would not be in a position to assess the lawfulness of its own activities.*"[217]

5.117   The General Court has therefore held that the "equally efficient competitor test" is the legally preferable one. The Commission has endorsed the "equally efficient competitor test" as the most appropriate one in its *Guidance Paper*.[218] As to the Court of Justice, it has also followed the same approach although it has not completely ruled out the possibility to use the reasonably efficient competitor in certain cases.

---

[211] *See supra* note 16.

[212] *Deutsche Telekom Judgment 2008 supra* note 5, para. 186.

[213] *AKZO supra* note 60, para. 74, where the Court of Justice took into consideration exclusively the charges and costs of the dominant undertaking, AKZO, in order to assess whether its pricing practice was abusive.

[214] *IPS supra* note 16, para. 179 (General Court stated that the sole fact that the applicant "*cannot, seemingly because of its higher processing costs, remain competitive in the sale of the derived product cannot justify characterizing* [the dominant undertaking's] *pricing policy*"). *See supra* note 200.

[215] *Deutsche Telekom*, para. 191.

[216] *See* P. Palmigiano *supra* note 111, at 15.

[217] *Deutsche Telekom*, para. 192.

[218] *See Guidance Paper supra* note 1, para. 80. The Commission already proposed it, *see Discussion Paper supra* note 19. Although the *Discussion Paper* refers to the two tests laid down in the *Telecom Access Notice* in that paragraph, it states in other parts that the relevant test for Article 102 is the *as efficient competitor* test, *see Telecom Access Notice supra* note 15, paras 64, 66.

5. – Margin Squeeze
Francisco Enrique González-Díaz and Jorge Padilla

"In order to assess the lawfulness of the pricing policy applied by a dominant undertaking, reference should be made, as a general rule, to pricing criteria based on the costs incurred by the dominant undertaking itself and on its strategy ... That said, it cannot be ruled out that the costs and prices of competitors may be relevant to the examination of the pricing practice at issue in the main proceedings. That might in particular be the case where the cost structure of the dominant undertaking is not precisely identifiable for objective reasons, or where the service supplied to competitors consists in the mere use of an infrastructure the production cost of which has already been written off, so that access to such an infrastructure no longer represents a cost for the dominant undertaking which is economically comparable to the cost which its competitors have to incur to have access to it, or again where the particular market conditions of competition dictate it, by reason, for example, of the fact that the level of the dominant undertaking's costs is specifically attributable to the competitively advantageous situation in which its dominant position places it."[219]

3.2. The Reasonably Efficient Competitor Test

5.118 Some authors have suggested that, while the General Court and the Court of Justice have clearly expressed a preference for the "equally efficient" competitor test, this preference does not require its use in every case going forward.[220] Indeed, they claim that although in *Deutsche Telekom* the General Court held that it was lawful for the Commission to rely on the costs of Deutsche Telekom in its assessment of whether a margin squeeze had taken place, this does not mean that some other test, including the reasonably efficient competitor test, cannot be used in other cases.[221]

5.119 In support of this point, some authors have suggested that the exclusive application of the equally efficient competitor test may be inappropriate. In particular, the use of this test may penalise dominant companies for being less efficient than their competitors, or for having regulatory duties that are exclusive to the dominant firm and result in higher costs.[222]

---

[219] *TeliaSonera Judgment 2011 supra* note 1, paras 41 and 45.

[220] P.-A. Buigues and R. Klotz, "Margin Squeeze in Regulated Industries: The CFI Judgment in the *Deutsche Telekom* Case" (2008) 7(1) *CPI Antitrust Chronicle*.

[221] *Ibid.*, p. 24; B. Amory and A. Verheyden, "Comments on the CFI's Recent Ruling in *Deutsche Telekom v. European Commission*" (2008) 5(1) *CPI Antitrust Chronicle*.

[222] Some authors have even argued that *"an imputation test alone cannot identify whether a price squeeze is anticompetitive. This test should be applied only after it has been determined that the preconditions for an abusive price squeeze exist. Otherwise, cases where margins are low but unrelated to a competitive abuse will erroneously be treated as an abusive price squeeze"*, *see* C. Veljanovski *supra*

5. – Margin Squeeze
Francisco Enrique González-Díaz and Jorge Padilla

5.120   In these instances, even if the dominant entity's competitors, let alone consumers, were not actually harmed as a result of the dominant firm's pricing, a margin squeeze could be found and punished, potentially severely, by the relevant competition authority. Similarly, if downstream competitors offer differentiated products, they will face a less elastic demand, and thus charge, to some extent, higher prices.[223] In these cases, relying exclusively on the dominant firm's costs would fail to take into account whether rivals operate under different cost structures (or even different revenue streams) to those of the dominant company. This suggests that in cases where a margin squeeze has been found on the basis of the "equally efficient competitor test", it may be appropriate, as a double-check, to assess the costs and profitability of the presumed victims of the dominant firm's conduct.

5.121   In sum, there may be situations where the dominant company's competitors or, most importantly, consumers may not be actually harmed as a result of the dominant firm's pricing policy but despite that the use of the as efficient competitor test may lead to a finding of abuse. This possibility, however likely, suggests that the "equally efficient" competitor test may need to be coupled, at least in certain cases, with a "reality check" based on the costs and profitability of the downstream competition.

5.122   Another issue closely related to the application of the "as efficient competitor test" concerns the upstream services taken into account to carry out the profitability or imputation test. The use of the "as efficient competitor test" requires that competitors use the same set of upstream services as those used by the dominant firm. Indeed, if the dominant company and the allegedly squeezed competitor use different upstream services, a comparison of their costs and profitability on a given upstream service may be misleading (this issue is addressed further in Section 5.4, *infra*).

---

note 3, p. 5. According to this author, "*a dominant network operator's pricing may fail a price squeeze test due to high but cost-oriented wholesale prices because regulated-minus percentages are set too high, inefficiency, poor performance, bad product and/or difficult market, rather anti-competitive behavior.*"

[223] It is important to note that competitors may be less efficient for reasons completely unrelated to the dominant firm's behaviour. This was the case in *National Carbonizing* where the Commission acknowledged that the losses of the dominant firm's competitors downstream were due to market specific conditions, *i.e.*, the dominant firm had more long-term supply contracts so it was able to sell more than its competitors (*see supra* note 13). In *IPS*, the complainant generally had larger per-unit processing costs for calcium metal, and these higher costs were independent of the conduct of the firm allegedly engaged in a price squeeze (PEM) (*see IPS supra* note 16, para. 184–5).

5. – Margin Squeeze
Francisco Enrique González-Díaz and Jorge Padilla

For these and other unrelated reasons, such as the goal of promoting competition by correcting the advantages allegedly enjoyed by former monopolies,[224] several national competition and judicial authorities use the reasonably efficient competitor test,[225] or at least use the *"as efficient"* and the *"reasonably efficient"* tests in a complementary fashion.[226] Moreover, in the Commission's *Guidance Paper*, after stating that the Commission will normally only intervene where a conduct has or is capable of hampering competition from competitors who are considered as efficient as the dominant undertaking,[227] it is added that *"the Commission recognises that in certain circumstances a less efficient competitor may also exert a constraint which should be taken into account when considering whether a particular price-based conduct leads to anti-competitive foreclosure."*[228]

5.123

4.   Relevant Products: The Need for Comparable Services

Regardless of whether the applicable margin squeeze test ought to consider the costs of the dominant firm itself and/or the costs of some hypothetical or "reasonably efficient" competitor, it is essential that the cost comparison take account of the specific circumstances of the services and inputs in question. The issue of the comparability of the products and services in question has grown in importance as the complexity of margin squeeze cases has increased when dealing with firms offering bundles of products and/or involving overlapping inputs with both product-specific costs and some costs that are common to all the firm's products.

5.124

The Commission is well aware of this issue, as it has arisen in a number of recent margin squeeze cases in the telecommunications sector. For example, in *Deutsche Telekom*, the Commission took the view that in order to establish an abuse, a comparison should be made between *"the retail prices charged by a dominant undertaking and the wholesale prices it charges its competitors for comparable services."*[229] While easy to state as a general guideline, this principle is not easy

5.125

---

[224] *See* in this regard Decision n° 512/63 *supra* note 98.

[225] Case 1016/1/1/03 *supra* note 105.

[226] *See, e.g.*, Case CW/00760/03/04 *Own-initiative Investigation against BT about potential anticompetitive exclusionary behaviour*, Decision of the Office of Communications (OFCOM) of 12 July 2004. But *see* Case No.19020 A376 *Aeroporti di Roma/Tariffe aeroportuali*, Italian Competition Authority Decision of 23 October 2008, para. 223 (use of equally efficient competitor test).

[227] *Guidance Paper supra* note 1, para. 23.

[228] *Ibid.*, para. 24.

[229] *Deutsche Telekom Decision 2003 supra* note 18, para. 107.

5. – Margin Squeeze
Francisco Enrique González-Díaz and Jorge Padilla

to apply when rivals have the opportunity to, and in fact do, generate multiple streams of revenues from the purchase of an input (such as wholesale access to a network). In this situation the assessment of the price charged by the dominant firm (the wholesale access cost to the downstream competition) and the resulting margins of downstream competitors, are more complicated.[230]

5.126 In the *Deutsche Telekom* case, the Commission assessed a margin squeeze between the upstream wholesale price for access charged by Deutsche Telekom to other downstream operators and the downstream retail price for access charged by Deutsche Telekom to consumers. The Commission excluded from its analysis the prices of call services, even though, as Deutsche Telekom argued, the retail price of access is meaningless unless considered alongside the price of the call (and other) services offered over the network.[231]

5.127 The Commission excluded call charges from its analysis of Deutsche Telekom's retail pricing for two reasons: (1) because it was consistent with European Union directives related to tariff rebalancing (*i.e.*, the requirement that a distinction should be made between the initial connection charge, monthly rental charges, and the prices of various types of calls),[232] and (2) because it was also consistent with the economics of the margin squeeze test in the case at hand – the "*test seeks to compare charges for two particular services at different commercial levels. The comparison would be distorted if revenue from call traffic were to be included, because call services, which are additional to access services, cannot also be included in the calculation on the wholesale side.*"[233] The General Court agreed, finding that "[e]*quality of opportunity as between the incumbent operator and owner of the fixed network, such as the applicant, on the one hand, and its competitors, on the other, therefore means that prices for access services must be set at a level which places competitors on an equal footing with the incumbent operator as regards the provision of call services*" and, as a result, "*it was necessary to consider the existence of a margin squeeze in relation to access services alone, and thus without including telephone call charges in its calculation.*"[234]

---

[230] A. Renda, "Treatment of Exclusionary Abuses Under Article 82 of the EC Treaty: Comments on the European Commission's Guidance Paper", *CEPS Task Force Reports*, September 10, 2009, p. 81 (explaining that the standard model assumes "*a) there is a simple, linear vertical chain of production, i.e. a single, clearly-identifiable upstream product and a single, clearly-defined downstream product in which the upstream product is a high, fixed proportion of total costs, and b) rivals have no opportunity for additional revenues on the retail market.*").

[231] *Deutsche Telekom Decision 2003 supra* note 18, paras 114–19.

[232] *Ibid.*, paras 121–25.

[233] *Ibid.*, paras 126–28.

[234] *Deutsche Telekom Judgment 2008 supra* note 5, paras 199–200.

5. – Margin Squeeze
Francisco Enrique González-Díaz and Jorge Padilla

On appeal, the ECJ confirmed the General Court's appreciations, by stating that "*the General Court ... could lawfully infer ... that the principle of tariff rebalancing does require that retail prices for access services and retail prices for call services be considered separately for the purpose of determining whether the relevant pricing practices of the appellant are abusive*"[235] and by establishing that "*the General Court was ... entitled, in paragraph 199 of the judgment under appeal, not to include [call services] in its analysis for the purpose of ascertaining whether there was equality of opportunity in the relevant market*".[236] It considered that to do otherwise could eventually lead to restrictions of competition in a downstream market different to the relevant market at stake.

In sum, the Commission rejected Deutsche Telekom's argument that it should **5.128** consider revenues from call services as part of the downstream price in an assessment of whether Deutsche Telekom engaged in a margin squeeze. Instead, the Commission compared only the wholesale price of access to a weighted average price for retail access, without having regard to additional revenues from call services.[237]

In *Telefónica* the Commission applied the same approach but also required **5.129** a product-by-product assessment at the upstream level, *i.e.*, an analysis of whether there was a margin squeeze at each individual "step" of the so-called "investment ladder" available to competitors. In other words, the Commission considered whether Telefónica's retail prices were replicable on the basis of each of Telefónica's upstream products rather than on the basis of a mix of these wholesale inputs.[238] Telefónica was thus confronted with the same issue as Deutsche Telekom, but both at the wholesale and at the retail level. The Commission considered that alternative competing network operators "*are likely to follow a step-by-step approach to continuously expanding their infrastructure investments ...[and] ... it is therefore necessary that there should not be any margin squeeze in relation to any "step" of the ladder, i.e., in relation to any wholesale product.*"[239]

---

[235] *Deutsche Telekom Judgment 2010 supra* note 1, para. 226.

[236] *Ibid., 2010*, para. 236.

[237] *Deutsche Telekom Decision 2003 supra* note 18, para. 137.

[238] Telefónica argued that these competitors could either rely on local loop unbundling alone or on a mix of national, regional and local loop access depending on the business case. As Telefónica explained, the optimal input use in the Spanish market would lead operators as efficient as Telefónica to use different services based on their relative merits.

[239] *Telefónica Decision 2007 supra* note 20, para. 392.

5. – Margin Squeeze
Francisco Enrique González-Díaz and Jorge Padilla

5.130 However, it has been argued that only a myopic entrant, unable to foresee the consequences of the future profitability of its retail activity, would need positive margins in all the steps of the ladder to compete aggressively. The "ladder of investment" theory would make no sense in that case, because entry would be dynamic and new entrants would understand that certain products would be more profitable than others. More generally, it must be noted that if the downstream rivals of the vertically integrated upstream dominant firm are thought to pursue an investment ladder strategy, then they should be prepared to suffer some early financial losses in order to build a customer base, which will then be profitably migrated to a new infrastructure in the future. In addition, it would be questionable to apply a period-by-period test[240] when the alleged victims of the margin squeeze are engaged in a dynamic investment ladder strategy. Moreover, it would make no sense to infer/presume anticompetitive effects in such cases when the margin squeeze only takes place during a limited period of time (one or two years). Finally, the incentive to engage in a margin squeeze when that strategy is limited to one of the steps of the ladder is bound to be small. Downstream competitors may in fact avoid that step altogether and jump to the next one, and even if that were not possible, they may accelerate their investments so as to only have to rely on that "squeezed" step for as little time as possible.

5.131 In sum, the Commission required a product-by-product assessment of the margin squeeze in both *Deutsche Telekom* and in *Telefónica*. In *Deutsche Telekom*, the Commission was concerned with competing operators' ability to replicate (in addition to merely selling retail access) the profitability of Deutsche Telekom, for example, as a result of effectively selling call services on top of retail access. In *Telefónica*, the Commission was also concerned with whether competing operators would find it profitable to use each of the available wholesale products independently regardless of the availability of the local loop or of a mix of wholesale products.

5.132 *Deutsche Telekom* and *Telefónica* demonstrate how complicated the assessment of a margin squeeze can be when dealing with multi-product firms both at the upstream and at the downstream levels. These cases also suggest that the Commission will apply the margin squeeze test on the basis of a simplifying product-by-product approach regardless of the actual behaviour of the firms

---

[240] *See infra.*

5. – Margin Squeeze
Francisco Enrique González-Díaz and Jorge Padilla

operating on the market, *i.e.*, regardless of whether these firms compete by offering individual products or bundles of products.

This approach may lead to misleading results. If, in practice, competitors **5.133** use a mix of wholesale inputs in order to offer their retail products and/or services and/or a bundle of retail products, this should be considered in the analysis, as ignoring this reality may have significant consequences for any margin squeeze assessment, given that the alternative operators' costs of supplying retail services may be lower when they use an optimal combination of wholesale products or when they supply a bundle of products instead of just one.

5.   Anticompetitive Effects

In *Deutsche Telekom*, the Commission cited both the *AKZO* judgment (with **5.134** respect to predatory pricing) and the *Napier Brown* decision (with respect to margin squeeze, where the firm in question was dominant in both the upstream and the downstream market), for the proposition that *"by proving the existence of a margin squeeze, the Commission has therefore done enough to establish the existence of an abuse of a dominant market position."*[241] That is, the Commission considered that there was no need to carry out an assessment of anticompetitive effects to establish the existence of an abuse. Nevertheless the Commission did consider the actual effects of Deutsche Telekom's pricing, and on appeal Deutsche Telekom argued (unsuccessfully) that, in fact, its behaviour resulted in no anticompetitive effects.

Although in addressing this issue the General Court did not explicitly hold **5.135** that a finding of anticompetitive effects is actually required, it noted that *"the anti-competitive effect which the Commission is required to demonstrate relates to the possible barriers which the applicant's pricing practices could have created for the growth of competition in that market."*[242] In other terms, while the General Court did not explicitly require a finding of anticompetitive effects, it did assess – and ratify – the Commission's finding of effects in its Decision. The Commission did assess anticompetitive effects even though it took the position that it was not legally required to do so, and the General Court did control this analysis on appeal

---

[241] *Deutsche Telekom Decision 2003 supra* note 18, paras 179-80 (citing *AKZO supra* note 60, para. 70; *Napier Brown supra* note 14).
[242] *Deutsche Telekom Judgment 2008 supra* note 5, para. 235.

5. – Margin Squeeze
Francisco Enrique González-Díaz and Jorge Padilla

as if, in fact, the Commission were required to do it. On appeal, however, the Court of Justice did address this issue specifically and concluded that the General Court had held *"without any error of law, that the anti-competitive effect which the* <u>*Commission is required to demonstrate*</u>*, as regards pricing practices of a dominant undertaking resulting in a margin squeeze of its equally efficient competitors, relates to the possible barriers which the appellant's pricing practices could have created for the growth of products on the retail market in end-user access services and, therefore, on the degree of competition in that market."*[243]

5.136 In *Telefónica*, the Commission reiterated that, in its view, proof of anticompetitive effects is not necessary in Article 102 cases, citing *British Airways* for the proposition that an infringement of Article 102 may be shown simply by demonstrating *"the abusive conduct of the undertaking in a dominant position tends to restrict competition, or in other words, that the conduct is capable of having, or likely to have, such an effect."*[244] Nevertheless, the Commission, as it did in *Deutsche Telekom*, engaged in a description of the likely impact of Telefónica's practices on competition.[245]

5.137 In *TeliaSonera*, the Court of Justice made it clear that a showing of anticompetitive effects is necessary in order for the Commission to demonstrate the existence of an infringement of Article 102.[246] It did note that *"the effect does not necessarily have to be concrete, and it is sufficient to demonstrate that there is an anticompetitive effect which may potentially exclude competitors who are at least as efficient as the dominant undertaking"*.[247] It then provided guidance as to when such effects would take place.

5.138 The Court distinguishes two basic scenarios in which it would be justified to consider that a margin squeeze is reasonably capable of having anticompetitive effects, where the product is indispensable and where the margin is negative.

---

[243] *Deutsche Telekom Judgment 2010 supra* note 1, para. 252.

[244] *Telefónica Decision 2007 supra* note 20, para. 543 (citing Case T-219/99 *British Airways v Commission* ("*British Airways*") [2003] ECR II-5917, para. 293).

[245] *Telefónica Decision 2007 supra* note 20, para. 543 *et seq.*

[246] *TeliaSonera Judgment 2011 supra* note 1, para. 61: "*The Court has ruled out the possibility that the very existence of a pricing practice of a dominant undertaking which leads to the margin squeeze of its equally efficient competitors can constitute an abuse within the meaning of Article 102 TFEU without it being necessary to demonstrate an anti-competitive effect.*"

[247] *Ibid.*, para. 64.

5. – Margin Squeeze
Francisco Enrique González-Díaz and Jorge Padilla

According to the Court of Justice where access to the supply of the whole-   **5.139**
sale product is indispensable for the sale of the retail product, the *"at least
potentially anti-competitive effect of a margin squeeze is probable."* In particular the
Court of Justice stated that: *"Where access to the supply of the wholesale product is
indispensable for the sale of the retail product, competitors who are at least as efficient as
the undertaking which dominates the wholesale market and who are unable to operate on
the retail market other than at a loss or, in any event, with reduced profitability suffer a
competitive disadvantage on that market which is such as to prevent or restrict their access to
it or the growth of their activities on it (see, to that effect, Deutsche Telekom v Commission,
paragraph 234)".*[248] The logic of the Court appears to be that in those cases
where following the application of the imputation test the Commission has
established the existence of a margin squeeze *and* that the product is indispensable there may be a *iuris tantum* presumption of anticompetitive effects.
Thus, the burden of disproving anticompetitive effects would shift to the
dominant company.

Under the second scenario, *i.e.*, if the margin is negative, (*i.e.*, whenever there is   **5.140**
a negative difference between the wholesale price of the product and the retail
price) *"an effect which is at least potentially exclusionary is probable."*[249] In this case,
the Court seems to suggest that when the margin squeeze is in itself apparent
there may also be a *iuris tantum* presumption of anticompetitive effects. The
burden of disproving anticompetitive effects would thus yet again shift to the
dominant company.

While the ECJ is indeed correct in believing that indispensability and/or nega-   **5.141**
tive margins make it "more likely" that a margin squeeze under the as efficient
competitor test would produce anticompetitive effects, it is not true that such
effects may be deemed "likely" (*i.e.,* more likely than not) even when such
conditions are met. When the input is indispensable, an equally efficient competitor may not avoid being harmed by substituting inputs. When the wholesale price exceeds the downstream (or retail) price, downstream competitors
may be forced to endure losses even when they are relatively more efficient
than the vertically integrated upstream dominant firm. However, even where
the input is indispensable, a more efficient downstream competitor and/or

---

[248] *See TeliaSonera Judgment 2011,* paras *70 et seq.*
[249] *Ibid.,* para. 71, *"[i]f the margin is negative, in other words if, in the present case, the wholesale price for the ADSL input
services is higher than the retail price for services to end users, an effect which is at least potentially exclusionary is probable, taking
into account the fact that, in such a situation, the competitors of the dominant undertaking, even if they are as efficient, or even
more efficient, compared with it, would be compelled to sell at a loss."*

5. – Margin Squeeze
Francisco Enrique González-Díaz and Jorge Padilla

a competitor selling (vertically or horizontally) differentiated products will remain an effective competitor even when an as efficient competitor selling the same products than the dominant firm will not. Likewise, a downstream firm selling products of superior quality than the vertically integrated firm will continue to constitute an effective competitive constraint in the downstream market even if the margin charged by the dominant firm is negative. The reason for this is that the downstream price charged by the vertically integrated firm will not constrain the price charged by downstream competitors selling superior products.

5.142 The question thus arises what burden of proof the Commission will have to meet in those cases where the product is not indispensable and the margin (as understood by the Court) is not negative.

5.143 According to the Court of Justice, where the product is not indispensable, the Commission will have to show that the practice may be capable of having anti-competitive effects on the market: "*However, taking into account the dominant position of the undertaking concerned in the wholesale market, the possibility cannot be ruled out that, by reason simply of the fact that the wholesale product is not indispensable for the supply of the retail product, a pricing practice which causes margin squeeze may not be able to produce any anti-competitive effect, even potentially. Accordingly, it is again for the referring court to satisfy itself that, even where the wholesale product is not indispensable, the practice may be capable of having anti-competitive effects on the markets concerned.*"[250] Where the margin remains positive, the Commission ought to demonstrate that the application of the pricing practice was, by reason, for example, of reduced profitability, likely to have the consequence that it would be at least more difficult for the operators concerned to trade on the market concerned.[251]

5.144 It thus appears that in the event that the input is not indispensable and/or the margin is not negative, the Commission will need to satisfy a higher burden of proof and that this would likely require, at the very least, that the Commission check the impact of the margin squeeze on the profitability of competitors and thus, when the data are available, a showing of concrete effects. However, the exact extent of this burden remains unclear.

---

[250] *See TeliaSonera Judgment 2011 supra* note 1, para. 72.
[251] *Ibid.*, para. 74.

5. – Margin Squeeze
Francisco Enrique González-Díaz and Jorge Padilla

In its *Telefónica* judgment, rendered after *TeliaSonera*, the General Court did **5.145** not appear to follow the test set out in *TeliaSonera*. Instead it undertook its own assessment of whether the Commission had established the existence of probable effects. The General Court justified this approach by arguing that *Telefónica*'s arguments regarding the indispensability of the product were made only in support of its allegation that a margin squeeze was a "*de facto*" refusal to supply and not in relation with the effects of the conduct on the market.[252]

The General Court held that the Commission had duly motivated the existence **5.146** of probable effects. In this connection, it took the view that the Commission had correctly inferred that it was probable that the conduct of *Telefónica* limited the ability of DSL operators to grow sustainably in the downstream market and that its conduct probably harmed consumers.

When confronted with Telefónica's arguments that those conclusions were **5.147** not corroborated by any concrete showing of effects, and/or consistent with the actual evolution of the market, the Court simply stated that "*the Commission did not incur in a manifest error of assessment when concluding that it was probable that Telefónica's conduct strengthened the barriers to entry and expansion in the market and if the resulting distortions had not existed, competition would have been more intense in the downstream market, which would have benefit consumers in terms of price, choice and innovation.*"

Although the General Court confirmed the need to establish probable effects, **5.148** it set a very low standard of proof on the Commission to show probable effects and a very high standard of proof on the applicant to refute them. Indeed, the General Court's decision suggests that the mere existence of a margin squeeze may be sufficient to create a presumption of probable effects.[253]

6. Role of Objective Justification, Efficiencies, and Meeting Competition

Although there is no explicit provision in Article 102 providing for an effi- **5.149** ciencies defence or a defence that a particular practice be objectively justified, both the case law of the European Courts and Commission precedent have

---

[252] *Telefónica Judgment 2012 supra* note 1, para. 182.
[253] The judgment is under appeal.

5. – Margin Squeeze
Francisco Enrique González-Díaz and Jorge Padilla

nevertheless established that a firm may present evidence that its actions were objectively justified (*see* generally Section IV above). The objective justification defence has been raised in a number of cases,[254] and, as explained in the *Guidance Paper*, the Commission will consider the defence in the context of refusals to supply and margin squeeze. Specifically:

> "*The Commission will consider claims by the dominant undertaking that a refusal to supply is necessary to allow the dominant undertaking to realise an adequate return on the investments required to develop its input business, thus generating incentives to continue to invest in the future, taking the risk of failed projects into account. The Commission will also consider claims by the dominant undertaking that its own innovation will be negatively affected by the obligation to supply, or by the structural changes in the market conditions that imposing such an obligation will bring about, including the development of follow-on innovation by competitors.*"[255]

5.150 There are indeed several reasons why a dominant firm might, at least temporarily, price in a manner consistent with a margin squeeze. For example, a "*firm may have perfectly legitimate and pro-competitive motives for setting low prices*", including, for example, promoting complementary products, launching a new product, and achieving economies of scale.[256] The objective justifications for pricing practices that amount to margin squeeze may coincide with those for predatory pricing (*see* Section V).

5.151 Prior to the *Telefónica* case, the Commission did not discuss extensively the issue of objective justification or efficiencies in margin squeeze cases. In *Telefónica*, however, it included an extensive assessment of these issues. Telefónica had argued: (1) that its losses were part of an attempt to expand into new markets, with a view to achieving profitability in the future, (2) that its pricing practices were necessary to compete ("meeting competition"), and (3) that its pricing practices benefited consumers through resulting efficiencies in operation.[257]

5.152 Although the Commission recognised that each of these grounds could constitute a potential defence to an abusive margin squeeze claim, it considered

---

[254] Case 311/84 *Centre belge d'études de marché – Télémarketing v CLT and IPB* ("*Télémarketing*") [1985] ECR 3261; Case T-30/89 *Hilti v Commission* ("*Hilti*") [1991] ECR II–1439.

[255] *Guidance Paper supra* note 1, para. 89.

[256] D. Spector, "Some Economics of Margin Squeeze" (2008) 1 *Concurrences*, No. 15302, p. 25.

[257] *Telefónica Decision 2007 supra* note 20, para. 620.

5. – Margin Squeeze
Francisco Enrique González-Díaz and Jorge Padilla

that the burden fell on Telefónica to prove the defence in each case. With respect to the first claim, that Telefónica's losses were made in an attempt to expand the market, the Commission rejected it by reference to its findings that had Telefónica paid the wholesale prices it was charging competitors, it would not have made a profit in any period during the relevant timeframe, and *"Telefónica's initial downstream losses could not be expected by the company to be recovered by future profits over a reasonable period (5 years and 4 months …)"*.[258] In Telefónica's case, the market expansion argument could be made because Telefónica was, by at least some measures, operating at a loss. For margin squeeze more generally, the "market expansion" argument is not likely to apply where the dominant firm does not incur any current losses in order to expand the market or achieve future efficiency gains.[259]

With respect to the meeting competition defence, which the Commission recognised *"may be a legitimate aim"*[260] it held that *"the meeting competition defense may not legitimise a margin squeeze that enables the vertically integrated company to impose losses on its competitors that it does not incur itself. The meeting competition defense may not legitimise behaviour whose effect is to leverage and abuse an upstream dominance"*.[261] This statement appears to effectively preclude the use of the meeting competition defence in margin squeeze cases. Moreover, the Commission would have apparently rejected Telefónica's meeting competition defence in any event, because it concluded that there were *"other economically practicable and less anti-competitive alternatives"* (including lowering wholesale prices). Because Telefónica's pricing activities were not *"suitable, indispensable and proportionate,"* the requirements for the meeting competition defence did not apply.[262]   **5.153**

Finally, the Commission considered Telefónica's argument that its pricing practices generated other efficiencies, including economies of scale and learning effects, which benefited consumers. As with the meeting competition defence, the Commission concluded that Telefónica's pricing practices *"cannot be regarded as temporary or aimed at searching scale economies and learning*   **5.154**

---

[258] *Telefónica Decision 2007 supra* note 20, para. 629.

[259] *See, e.g.*, L. Ferrari Bravo and P. Siciliani, "Exclusionary Pricing and Consumer's Harm: The European Commission's Practice in the DSL Market" (2007) 3(2) *Journal of Competition Law and Economics*, pp. 265–67.

[260] *Telefónica Decision 2007 supra* note 20, para. 638 (citing *United Brands supra* note 47, paras 189–91).

[261] *Telefónica Decision 2007 supra* note 20, para. 638.

[262] *Ibid.*, para. 639.

5. – Margin Squeeze

Francisco Enrique González-Díaz and Jorge Padilla

effects because Telefónica's downstream activity still generates losses more than 5 years after its start.[263]

5.155 In its discussion of economies of scale, the Commission expressed scepticism that this claimed efficiency – which *"may be included among the rational justification for below cost pricing"*[264] – apply in the context of a margin squeeze. In the Commission's view, one of the very purposes of a margin squeeze is for the dominant company to benefit from economies of scale either more quickly, or exclusively, vis-à-vis the other firms in the market. The result, in the Commission's view, is *"a combination of being at a higher point on the learning curve than competitors and having higher output thanks to below-cost pricing may have exclusion effects capable of consolidating the dominant company's hegemony"*.[265] The Commission thus effectively concluded that it is unlikely to accept scale economies and learning effects as an efficiency in the context of margin squeeze: *"it may not serve to legitimise a margin squeeze that enables the vertically integrated company to impose losses upon its competitors that it does not incur itself "*.[266]

5.156 However, the benefits deriving from this efficiency were recognised by the national regulator in *Telefónica*, which considered that the scale economies achieved by Telefónica had benefited all operators as it led to an improvement of the capacity of the wholesaler's products, while the nominal price remained at a stable level.[267] The benefits of efficiencies were passed on to other operators, therefore facilitating new entrants and the expansion of the broadband market.[268]

5.157 Moreover, as explained by Advocate General Jacobs in *Syfait*[269] the incentive to innovate can underpin an efficiencies defence, and the Commission in *Microsoft* acknowledged that preserving incentives to innovate can be

---

[263] *Telefónica Decision 2007 supra* note 20, para. 650.

[264] *Ibid.*, para. 652.

[265] *Ibid.*, para. 651.

[266] *Ibid.*, para. 652.

[267] Case MTZ 2003/1000 *Telefónica de España*, Spanish Telecommunications Regulator (CMT) Decision of 31 March 2004 p. 254.

[268] *"With bitstream access, new entrants participate in the economies of scale (e.g., they use the DSLAM installed by the incumbent) thus levelling off the economies of scale of the incumbent"*. Bitstream Access – ERG Consultation Document (14 July 2003).

[269] Advocate General Jacobs in Case C–53/03 *Synetairismos Farmakopoion Aitolias & Akarnanias and others v GlaxoSmithKline ("Syfait")* [2005] ECR I–4609, para. 100.

5. – Margin Squeeze
Francisco Enrique González-Díaz and Jorge Padilla

considered an objective justification.[270] In *Telefonica*, the company defended that its efforts had produced and would continue to produce efficiencies, that at the lower wholesale prices (contemplated by the Commission) Telefonica could not have justified further investments, and that in such case such efficiencies would have never arisen. In essence, Telefónica claimed that its incentives to further develop and invest in infrastructure are clearly a function of the expected and available return to that investment. Efficiencies from investment and innovation will not arise if this balance is struck incorrectly.

The economic literature confirms that this type of pricing can favour competition and improve consumer welfare when there are efficiencies associated with the expansion of the market (*i.e.*, network effects). For example, Bolton, Brodley and Riordan conclude that when network effects are present, a profit maximising undertaking may initially set prices below cost, and that this will not be anticompetitive if the period in which prices are below costs is only long enough to achieve sufficient scale.[271] **5.158**

In sum, although the Commission theoretically accepted that the meeting competition defence and efficiencies considerations may justify pricing practices that may otherwise be abusive, the *Telefónica* decision appears to leave little room for these defences to play any meaningful role in the context of a margin squeeze. **5.159**

7. The Relevance of Regulation in Margin Squeeze Analysis

Following the *Deutsche Telekom* and *Telefónica* cases, it appears settled that European competition law applies concurrently and/or in addition to sector specific regulation. The *Guidance Paper* takes this principle a step further, and provides, that where sector-specific regulation exists, Article 102 not only apply, but that the *Oscar Bronner* case law, which set the conditions under which an undertaking may have a duty to deal with its competitors, will not apply. **5.160**

---

[270] *See* Case COMP/37.792 *Microsoft*, Commission Decision of 24 March 2004, not yet published, para. 783. Although the Commission rejected the objective justification in the specific circumstances of the case, it indeed acknowledged the possibility to invoke such a justification in order to preserve incentives to innovate.

[271] P. Bolton, J F. Brodley and M. H. Riordan, "Predatory Pricing Strategic Theory and Legal Policy" (2000) 88 *Georgetown Law Journal*, pp. 2281–82.

5. – Margin Squeeze
Francisco Enrique González-Díaz and Jorge Padilla

As stated by the Court of Justice in *Deutsche Telekom*,[272] and acknowledged by the General Court in *Telefónica*:[273]

> "[C]ompetition rules laid down by the EC Treaty supplement in that regard, by an ex post review, the legislative framework adopted by the Union legislature for ex ante regulation of the telecommunications markets."

5.161　This leaves an important unresolved issue as to whether, when, and how a competition authority (including the European Commission) should intervene in the presence of a national regulatory action which may itself have been imposed for the very purpose of fostering competition in the marketplace.

5.162　The Commission's approach in *Deutsche Telekom* and *Telefónica* is in stark contrast to the approach followed in the United States. In *Trinko*, the United States Supreme Court considered the application of the U.S. antitrust laws in the context of sector specific regulation. In refusing to impose an antitrust duty to deal on the incumbent telecommunications operator, the Supreme Court held *"one factor of particular importance is the existence of a regulatory structure designed to deter and remedy competition harm. Where such a structure exists, the additional benefits to competition provided by antitrust enforcement will tend to be small and it will be less plausible that the antitrust laws contemplate such additional scrutiny."*[274]

5.163　In the view of the Supreme Court, when sector specific regulation has been put in place to prevent anticompetitive conduct, the role of the antitrust laws may be more limited. In addition to this general observation, the Supreme Court also noted its concern that the application of the antitrust laws in addition to a specific regulatory framework may generate false positives, because even *"under the best of circumstances,"* applying the antitrust laws *"'can be difficult,' because 'the means of illicit exclusion, like the means of legitimate competition, are myriad.'"*[275] Even ignoring the possibility of false positives, the Supreme Court considered that, at least within the framework of the specific regulatory provisions at issue, it may be beyond the practical ability of the courts to control anticompetitive practices, given that this would likely require continuous supervision and the imposition of highly detailed behavioural conditions.[276]

---

[272] *Deutsche Telekom Judgment 2010 supra* note 1, para. 92.

[273] *Telefónica Judgment 2012 supra* note 1, para. 293.

[274] *Verizon Communications v Law Offices of Curtis v Trinko* ("*Trinko*"), 540 US 398 (2004), p. 412.

[275] *Ibid.*, p. 414 (citing *United States v Microsoft*, 253 F.3d 34 (D.C. Cir. 2001)).

[276] *Trinko supra* note 274, pp. 412, 414–15.

5. – Margin Squeeze
Francisco Enrique González-Díaz and Jorge Padilla

Although the Supreme Court did not explicitly hold that the competition laws do not apply in the context of sector-specific regulation, it did favour deference to any existing regulatory framework over the *ex post* application of the antitrust laws.

The Commission, the General Court and the Court of Justice did not follow **5.164** this approach in *Deutsche Telekom* (which was decided a year before the United States Supreme Court's decision in *Trinko*). The General Court noted that a practice that would otherwise violate Article 102 may not be condemned where the *"anticompetitive conduct* [at issue] *is required of undertakings by national legislation or if the latter creates a legal framework which itself eliminates any possibility of competitive activity on their part."* [277] However, as demonstrated by the Commission's treatment of Deutsche Telekom's conduct, the Commission will hold the dominant firm to the strictures of Article 102 even if it has acted within the bounds of its regulatory obligations and despite the scrutiny of the National Regulatory Authority. [278] As explained by the General Court, in order for this regulatory exception to apply, *"the restrictive effects on competition must originate solely in the national law."* [279]

In *Deutsche Telekom*, both the upstream and the downstream prices were subject **5.165** to regulation and had been approved by the relevant regulatory authority. This was insufficient, however, to shield Deutsche Telekom from liability under Article 102. The General Court held that dominant companies may only rely on regulation as a defence under Article 102 EC where they can show that they have no margin of manoeuvre. Because Deutsche Telekom could have theoretically applied to the national regulatory authority for authorisation to alter its prices (in particular, to raise retail prices), it could have avoided a margin squeeze. [280] This rationale was also applied by the General Court in *Telefónica*. [281]

The Commission thus reserves the right to intervene and even second-guess **5.166** the decisions adopted by national regulatory authorities whenever the practical

---

[277] *Deutsche Telekom Judgment 2008 supra* note 5, para. 85.
[278] *See, e.g.*, S. Genevaz, "Margin Squeeze after *Deutsche Telekom*" (2009) 1(1) *CPI Antitrust Chronicle,* p. 30.
[279] *Deutsche Telekom Judgment 2008 supra* note 5, para. 87; *Ibid.*, paras 77–96.
[280] *Ibid.*, paras 122–124.
[281] *Telefónica Judgment 2012 supra* note 1, paras 327–37. *See also TeliaSonera Judgment 2011 supra* note 1, paras 50–51.

5. – Margin Squeeze
Francisco Enrique González-Díaz and Jorge Padilla

implications of their regulatory action is deemed to result, in its view, in prices that may be inconsistent with European Union competition laws.[282]

5.167 National regulatory authorities may be presumed, in most cases, to be better placed to judge the appropriateness of the degree of regulation required to preserve and develop conditions of effective competition in the regulated market in question, and to balance the necessary degree of regulation and the need to preserve the incentives to invest in the continued growth of the industry. Competition law, when applied in an *ad hoc* fashion, as demonstrated in *Deutsche Telekom* and *Telefónica*, may not necessarily be compatible with the objectives of the national regulatory authorities in any particular case. In this context, it is submitted, European Union law, including the principles of legal certainty,[283] subsidiarity, and proportionality should ultimately guide the inter-play between regulation and Commission intervention as the case law on the liability of undertakings subject to State action cannot provide a sufficient basis to arbitrate this complex interaction.

5.168 In addition the need to avoid contradictory decisions from competition and regulatory authorities and to encourage investment would seem to advocate for competition law intervention either in the absence of *ex ante* regulation, or when the regulatory action itself breaches competition law and NRAs are not willing to modify national regulation to accommodate the Commission's analysis.[284]

5.169 Indeed, when the effects of a course of conduct are mostly limited to one Member State and the conduct has been subject to close regulatory scrutiny by national authorities, it may be more appropriate for the Commission to

---

[282] *See also supra* note 187, p. 415. Another commentator considers that, "*to the extent that the dominant firm has some flexibility to adapt its prices, it is under a positive obligation to adopt a pricing policy that avoids a margin squeeze. This onerous obligation is based on the established principle of 'special responsibility' which a dominant firm owes to the marketplace, and which has played a prominent role in the thinking of the Court in recent cases decided under Article [102]*". P. Alexiadis, "Informative and Interesting: The CFI Rules in *Deutsche Telekom v. European Commission*" (2008) 5(1) *CPI Antitrust Chronicle*, pp. 10–11.

[283] The principle of legal certainty, which requires that "*rules imposing charges on the taxpayer must be clear and precise so that he may know without ambiguity what are his rights and obligations and may take steps accordingly. See* Court of Justice judgment in Joined Cases 92 and 93/87 *Commission v France and United Kingdom and Northern Ireland* [1989] ECR 405, p. 405, para. 22 and Case 169/80 *Administration des douanes v Gondrand Frères and Garancini* [1981] ECR 1931, para. 17.

[284] In the *Trinko* judgment the Supreme Court of the United States concluded that when there is an existing "*regulatory structure designed to deter and remedy competition harm*," competition law would have a very restricted field of application, due to the limited benefits deriving from antitrust legislation in these cases. *See Trinko supra* note 274.

5. – Margin Squeeze
Francisco Enrique González-Díaz and Jorge Padilla

refuse to analyse the case on the basis of "lack of community interest." This would be compatible with the subsidiarity principle, which states that: "*in areas which do not fall within its exclusive competence, the Union shall act only if and in so far as the objectives of the proposed action cannot be sufficiently achieved by the Member States, either at central level or at regional and local level* [...]"[285]

In cases where national authorities have taken a decision in a particular case, **5.170** the Commission should consider very carefully whether to intervene (*e.g.*, by intervening only where there are exceptional circumstances), and even then to intervene only where there are clear benefits from European Union action. Finally, when analysing a particular course of conduct in the presence of national regulations, the Commission has also to comply with the principle of proportionality, which provides that: "*the content and form of Union action shall not exceed what is necessary to achieve the objectives of the Treaties.*"[286] Commission action that runs counter – or is even in tension with – an existing national regulatory framework will need to be carefully justified.

While there remains uncertainty surrounding the extent to which the Com- **5.171** mission will apply the competition laws of the Treaty in the context of sector-specific and/or national regulation, it is clear from the Commission precedents that dominant firms cannot rely on an existing regulatory framework – even if that framework was put in place to foster competition in the relevant market – to shield their commercial practices from Article 102 liability.

VI. Economics of Margin Squeeze

Margin squeeze has been considered an abuse of Article 102 because it may **5.172** result in the exclusion of equally efficient competitors. However, the notion that a margin squeeze is a rational strategy to exclude rivals, or even necessarily harmful to competition or consumer welfare in the first place, is not without detractors. Some economists have argued that, save in exceptional circumstances, absent excessive prices upstream, or predatory pricing downstream, there cannot be harm from margin squeeze. The Chicago School approach is even stronger – and suggests that the carrying out of a margin squeeze in an

---

[285] Consolidated version of the Treaty on the Functioning of the European Union, OJ 2010 C 83/49, Article 5(3).
[286] *Ibid.*, Article 5(4).

5. – Margin Squeeze

Francisco Enrique González-Díaz and Jorge Padilla

attempt to exclude downstream rivals is not a rational strategy on the part of a dominant upstream firm.[287] Other commentators have gone yet even further, suggesting that a margin squeeze may actually increase efficiency in particular markets, for example by eliminating double marginalisation or excluding inefficient competitors.[288] This Section provides an overview of these arguments in the context of the broader treatment of margin squeeze.

1. Need for Excessive Prices Upstream or Predatory Downstream Prices

5.173 According to the Commission, the abuse of margin squeeze arises because the prices charged by the vertically integrated firm leave an insufficient margin for downstream rivals to compete effectively. However, according to industrial organisation economics a margin squeeze is unlikely to exist unless the prices charged by the dominant firm are either excessive upstream or predatory downstream.

1.1. *Margin Squeeze Pricing*

5.174 A simple model of pricing can demonstrate that, in the absence of excessive prices upstream or predatory prices downstream, and under reasonable assumptions, there will generally be a positive margin for downstream rivals:

5.175 Start with the wholesale price, w, and consider that this price is not excessive, *i.e.*, that it is does not exceed the cost of production and marketing upstream, including an appropriate return on capital costs. This implies: w is approximately equal to $c_{wholesale}$, where $c_{wholesale}$ is the upstream long-run incremental cost to the incumbent/dominant input provider.

5.176 Suppose also that the retail price is not predatory – *i.e.*, the retail price is not below the downstream cost, which should include both the cost of the wholesale product and the long-run incremental costs of retailing (*e.g.*, retail marketing costs). This implies: $p \geq c = c_{wholesale} + c_{retail}$.

---

[287] *See* R. H. Bork, *The Antitrust Paradox: A Policy at War with Itself* (New York, The Free Press, 1995); *supra* note 8, p. 35.

[288] D. W. Carlton, "Should 'Price Squeeze' Be A Recognized Form of Anticompetitive Conduct" (2008) *Journal of Competition Law & Economics* 4(2), pp. 271–8.

5. – Margin Squeeze
Francisco Enrique González-Díaz and Jorge Padilla

Since the margin squeeze test is satisfied if $p \geq w + c_{retail}$, it is immediate that **5.177** this test is satisfied when (a) the wholesale price is not excessive (since $w = c_{wholesale}$) and (b) the retail price is not predatory (since $p \geq c_{wholesale} + c_{retail}$).[289]

In sum, if upstream prices are not excessive and downstream prices are not **5.178** predatory, then there will generally be some positive margin for downstream rivals. This only leaves a narrow set of cases where there is a positive margin but, for whatever reason, it is deemed insufficient for a downstream rival to compete. Of course, if the downstream rival is assumed to be equally efficient, this analysis would seem to exhaust the set of cases where there could be a margin squeeze – *i.e.*, only where there is no margin for the downstream rival.

1.2.   European Union and National Precedents

While the line of economic reasoning summarised above would very likely be **5.179** successful under current US law, the Commission and the recent judgments of the General Court and the Court of Justice have so far rejected the notion that a margin squeeze requires a showing of either excessive pricing or predatory pricing.

In the *IPS* case, the General Court stated: *"In the absence of abusive prices being* **5.180** *charged by PEM for the raw material, … , or of predatory pricing for the derived product, … , the fact that the applicant cannot, seemingly because of its higher processing costs, remain competitive in the sale of the derived product cannot justify characterising PEM's pricing policy as abusive."*[290]

---

[289] Note that the key assumption behind this result is that the cost standard used in excessive pricing and predatory pricing is the same, *i.e.*, upstream prices are considered excessive if they are above the long-run incremental upstream costs of production and distribution, including a reasonable return on capital, and downstream prices are predatory if they are below the end-to-end long-run incremental costs (including a reasonable return on capital) of the vertically integrated dominant company. Suppose, instead, that predation was established by comparing prices to short-run costs, or that no reasonable return on capital was accounted for when testing for predation. In that case, a margin squeeze would be possible, even if unlikely, even when w is not excessive or p is predatory. Hence, requiring that the upstream price is excessive or the downstream price is predatory before a margin squeeze is found may lead to a limited number of type II errors. And yet, even in that case, it may be optimal to adopt a legal rule that restricts margin squeeze infringements to situations where either w is excessive or p is predatory from an error-cost perspective. The reason being that those conditions may limit the risk of significant type I errors associated with intervention in emerging/dynamic markets at a reasonable cost in terms of the likelihood of type II errors.

[290] *IPS supra* note 16, para. 179.

5. – Margin Squeeze
Francisco Enrique González-Díaz and Jorge Padilla

5.181 The General Court's reasoning seems to be in line with the *Linkline* judgment, where the U.S. Supreme Court held that in order to give rise to anticompetitive effects, a plaintiff must establish a duty to deal (under *Trinko*) or predatory pricing (under *Brooke Group*).[291] Otherwise, the alleged insufficient margin between the two prices cannot give rise to an abuse where none existed otherwise.

5.182 However, in every case since *IPS*, the Commission has not followed this approach. For example, in *Deutsche Telekom*, the Commission explained that a margin squeeze occurred when *"the difference between the retail prices charged by a dominant undertaking and the wholesale prices it charges its competitors for comparable services is negative, or insufficient to cover the product-specific costs to the dominant operator of providing its own retail services on the downstream market."* [292] The General Court stated in *Deutsche Telekom* that *"the abusive nature of the applicant's conduct is connected with the unfairness of the spread between its prices for wholesale access and its retail prices, which takes the form of a margin squeeze,"* [293] and *"... in view of the abuse found ... the Commission was not required to demonstrate ... that the applicant's retail prices were, as such, abusive."* [294] This conclusion was repeated by the Commission in *Telefónica*, where the Commission explained *"there is no need to demonstrate that either the wholesale price is excessive in itself or that the retail price is predatory in itself."* [295] More recently, the Court of Justice has also adopted the same view in its judgments in *Deutsche Telekom* [296] and *TeliaSonera*: *"[i]t must moreover be made clear that since the unfairness, within the meaning of Article 102 TFEU, of such a pricing practice is linked to the very existence of the margin squeeze and not to its precise spread, it is in no way necessary to establish that the wholesale prices for ADSL input services to operators or the retail prices for broadband connection services to end users are in themselves abusive on account of their excessive or predatory nature, as the case may be."* [297]

5.183 Prior to these judgments, national cases already interpreted *Deutsche Telekom* and *Telefónica* as not requiring any independent showing of excessive upstream prices or predatory downstream prices. In *Albion Water*, for example, the Court of Appeals held, in relevant part:

---

[291] *Linkline.*

[292] *Deutsche Telekom Decision 2003 supra* note 18, para. 107.

[293] *Deutsche Telekom Judgment 2008 supra* note 5, para. 167.

[294] *Ibid.*

[295] *Telefónica Decision 2007 supra* note 20, para. 283.

[296] *Deutsche Telekom Judgment 2010 supra* note 1, paras 167 and 183.

[297] *TeliaSonera Judgment 2011 supra* note 1, para. 34.

5. – Margin Squeeze
Francisco Enrique González-Díaz and Jorge Padilla

"[T]he evidence strongly suggested that the price was excessive. In itself, however, this has no bearing on the central issue concerning the correct test for a margin squeeze. Nor did it play any material part in the reasoning that led the Tribunal to its conclusion …that the margin squeeze amounted to an abuse. In so far as the argument on this point brought in the IPS case, it suffices to state that in our judgment the IPS case is consistent with the other authorities on margin squeeze and, in particular, we reject the contention that it stands as authority for the proposition that a dominant undertaking does not engage in a margin squeeze in the absence of an excessive upstream price or a predatory downstream price. We agree with the Tribunal that the judgment does not introduce a gloss on the margin squeeze test as it appears in the guidance."[298]

Regardless of the above, from an economic perspective there seems to be little doubt that a finding of abuse where upstream prices are not abusive, or where downstream prices are not predatory, could have undesired consequences.[299] Indeed, if, confronted with the current view of the Commission, a dominant firm reduces the upstream price in order to avoid a margin squeeze, in circumstances where there is no duty to deal, this could result in an efficient dominant company having to bear losses in the provision of the upstream product. In this scenario, the dominant company would no longer have the incentive to invest in upstream infrastructure, and in the extreme this could lead to the collapse of the upstream market. By the same token, if the dominant firm were to be obliged to increase price downstream in order to avoid a margin squeeze (which the Commission considered Deutsche Telekom should have done in that case) this would immediately lead to price increases to consumers and would artificially raise the profitability of inefficient players in the market, thus benefiting inefficient competitors to the detriment of consumer welfare. **5.184**

In sum, as explained above, this approach may lead to interventions that negatively affect the dominant firm's incentive to invest in infrastructure (if the remedy involves raising upstream prices) or, alternatively, may lead to higher retail prices and a loss of consumer welfare (if the remedy involves raising downstream prices). **5.185**

---

[298] *Dwr Cymru Cyfyngedig v Albion Water Ltd & Anor supra* note 24, para. 110.
[299] *Supra* note 288.

5. – Margin Squeeze

Francisco Enrique González-Díaz and Jorge Padilla

2. The Chicago Critique

5.186   The Chicago critique considers that it is not possible for an upstream monopolist to increase its profits by leveraging its upstream market power in the downstream market. This follows because any profit from the upstream monopoly can be obtained from the pricing and sale of the monopolist's product upstream, and it is not possible to increase overall profits by affecting the ability of rivals to compete downstream, for example, through a margin squeeze.

5.187   According to this theory, it would be irrational for an upstream monopolist to use its upstream input price as a means to foreclose rivals in the downstream market. If downstream rivals are as least as efficient as the upstream monopolist, the upstream monopolist would benefit more from raising its prices upstream (even above the profit-maximising price in a stand-alone upstream market) in order to extract more of the surplus from the downstream rival's efficiency advantage than by excluding efficient competitors downstream.[300] Excluding the rival could result in significant losses to the upstream monopolist.

5.188   For example, consider the markets depicted in Figure 5.2 below, which shows an integrated Firm 1 operating upstream (U) and downstream (D_1), and a downstream rival operating only downstream (D_2). Firm 1 may engage in margin squeeze by setting a wholesale price $w > p$, and the vertically integrated Firm 1 will not necessarily incur losses. At the same time, however, there is an opportunity cost of setting $w > p$ – the integrated Firm 1 will not benefit from sales of the input (at price w) to Firm 2 because Firm 2 will be squeezed from the marketplace. If w is greater than the integrated Firm 1's marginal cost of producing the input, this opportunity cost could grow very large – especially if the downstream firm's sales are substantial, the downstream firm is more cost efficient, and/or if the downstream firm sells products that are differentiated from those of Firm 1.[301]

---

[300] *See, e.g., supra* note 8, pp. 35–36.
[301] *See supra* note 8, p. 37; *see also supra* note 256, p. 25.

5. – Margin Squeeze
Francisco Enrique González-Díaz and Jorge Padilla

Figure 5.2: Margin Squeeze.

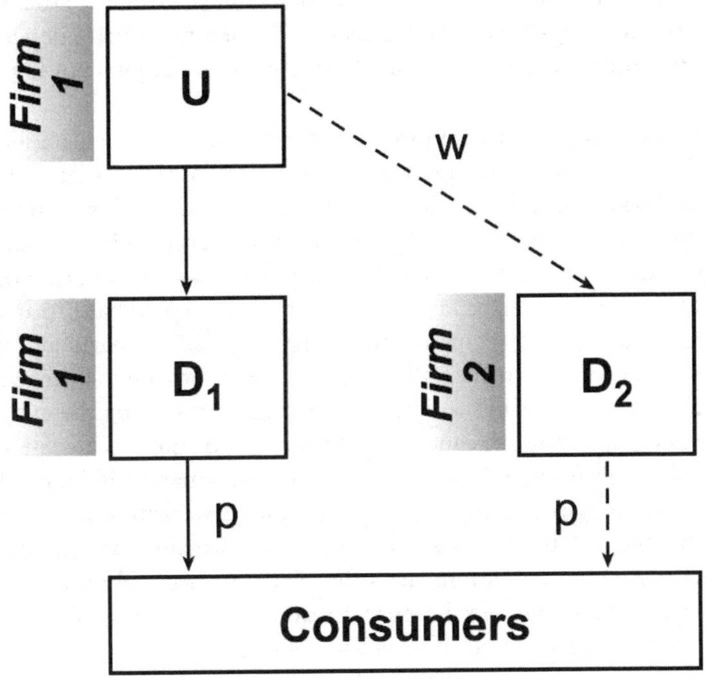

The Chicago critique, however, only holds under very particular assump- **5.189**
tions about, *inter alia*, the nature of the downstream market – including the
assumption that this market is perfectly competitive.[302] Post-Chicago industrial organisation economists have shown that when those assumptions fail to
hold it may be profitable for integrated firms to increase the upstream input
price (contrary to the Chicago critique) – such a price increase may increase
profits either upstream[303] or downstream.[304]

First, an increase in the upstream input price, w in Figure 5.2, will result in **5.190**
higher prices downstream (Firm 2 is takes w as its input cost, and, all else
equal, an increase in marginal cost w will result in a higher price charged by

---

[302] *See, e.g., supra* note 256, p. 23; *see also* M. D. Whinston, "Tying, Foreclosure and Exclusion" (1990) 80(4)
American Economic Review, supra note 8, p. 36.

[303] P. Rey and J. Tirole, "A Primer on Foreclosure", in M. Armstrong and R. H. Porter (Eds.), *Handbook of
Industrial Organization* (Amsterdam, North-Holland, 2007), Vol. III, pp. 2145–220; *supra* note 256, p. 24.

[304] S. C. Salop and D. T. Scheffman, "Cost-Raising Strategies" (1987) 36(1) *Journal of Industrial Economics*, and
supra note 256, p. 24.

5. – Margin Squeeze

Francisco Enrique González-Díaz and Jorge Padilla

Firm 2). By raising its downstream rivals' costs, the integrated firm can effectively increase the downstream price. These higher prices downstream may or may not result in higher overall profits for the integrated firm, depending on which effect dominates (higher prices result in larger margins but fewer sales).

5.191   Secondly, the higher upstream price w will result in an immediate increase in margin from the sale of the input to the downstream rival. Again, this higher margin will come with decreased sales of the input to the downstream rival – with ambiguous results on overall profits for the integrated firm.[305] In general, in order to determine whether the vertically integrated upstream monopolist has the incentive to engage in a margin squeeze, one would have to analyze the profits made under two scenarios: the margin squeeze scenario and the non-exclusionary scenario. Profits will be higher under a margin squeeze scenario if the increase in profits in the downstream market following the exclusion of the non-integrated downstream competitors exceeds the sacrifice in upstream profits. This will occur when (a) the downstream margin is high relative to the upstream margin, and (b) the upstream dominant firm is able to capture a significant share of the business lost by its downstream competitors. It must be noted that these conditions are more likely to hold when the dominant firm enjoys market power in the downstream market because if dominant, its downstream margins will be large and it will be in a position to capture some of the business lost by competitors. They are also more likely to hold when its downstream competitors are not more efficient and do not sell differentiated products or address market niches which are not covered by the dominant player.

3.   Elimination of Inefficient Rivals: Vertical Integration and Double Marginalisation

5.192   As discussed above, the margin squeeze abuse would take place at least in those cases where vertically integrated, dominant firms set a price for the input relative to the downstream price that leaves an insufficient margin for the downstream firm to compete effectively. More specifically, there is no requirement that there be excessive prices upstream or predatory prices downstream in order for a margin squeeze to be an abuse of Article 102.

---

[305] *Supra* note 8, pp. 36–37. *See also* N. Economides, "The Incentive for Non-Price Discrimination by an Input Monopolist" (1998) 16(3) *International Journal of Industrial Organization*.

5. – Margin Squeeze
Francisco Enrique González-Díaz and Jorge Padilla

However, although the Commission has held that a margin squeeze may exclude a rival (and thus harm a competitor) even though there is no excessive pricing upstream or predation downstream, there is considerable debate over whether such exclusion results in harm to competition as a whole. In fact, economists have developed a variety of arguments why a margin squeeze – in the absence of excessive upstream prices or predatory downstream prices – should be viewed as a means to eliminate inefficient rivals rather than as an anticompetitive abuse of market power.

Vertically integrated firms will, all else equal, charge a lower downstream price **5.193** than a firm operating only in the downstream market. That is, vertically integrated firms have strong incentives to avoid the second markup that will result from non-integrated production.[306] Downstream firms have an incentive to set their downstream price at some level above the cost of the input it obtains from the vertically integrated firm. The vertically integrated firm (or any other upstream producer that sells the input to the downstream firm), however, will have already obtained a margin on the sale of the input to the downstream firm. The result is a higher downstream price and lower output downstream. This is known as double marginalisation.[307]

Vertically integrated firms, *i.e.*, firms which source or produce their own **5.194** inputs, will only set one price, corresponding to a single mark up, and in the case of the vertically integrated firm, the downstream price will in general be lower and output will be higher (compared to a firm selling to a downstream retailer, *e.g.*). In sum, vertical integration is efficient – by eliminating double marginalisation the integrated firm is able to earn higher profits at a lower price to consumers and also more consumers are able to acquire the product in question.

Because, under current Commission and European Union Courts precedent, **5.195** a vertically integrated firm can engage in margin squeeze and violate Article 102 even without charging excessive prices upstream or predatory pricing downstream, the law of margin squeeze may discourage efficient vertical integration. As summarised by various commentators, the existence of a margin squeeze abuse "*requires a vertically-integrated firm to set input and final product prices*

---

[306] J. Tirole, *The Theory of Industrial Organization* (Cambridge, MIT Press, 1988), p. 174 (citing J. J. Spengler, "Vertical Integration and Antitrust Policy" (1950) 58(4) *Journal of Political Economy*, pp. 347–52).
[307] *Ibid.*

5. – Margin Squeeze
Francisco Enrique González-Díaz and Jorge Padilla

at a level at which a non-integrated rival can make an adequate profit. Unless the dominant firm is actually discriminating between the prices charged to its downstream business and rivals, the duty not to margin squeeze effectively requires the dominant firm to create a unique set of prices at which non-integrated downstream rivals can survive. And this duty applies even if the dominant firm is not losing money overall." [308]

5.196 While a vertically integrated firm's pricing practices may leave no "living margin" for a non-integrated downstream firm, the exclusion of that non-integrated firm will simply give rise to the elimination of a firm likely to engage in double marginalisation. Competition authorities should thus balance the anticompetitive effects of a margin squeeze with its procompetitive effects in the form of a reduction of double marginalisation.

4. Costs Analysis in Margin Squeeze Cases

5.197 Once it is settled which firm's costs will be considered for the purposes of assessing the margin in margin squeeze cases, it is also necessary to agree on a measure of the relevant costs for purposes of comparison, and over what timeframe (or output level) to consider those costs. In a margin squeeze case, the type of costs considered may dictate whether a particular pricing practice constitutes a margin squeeze. Each firm has fixed and variable costs of production, the question of whether and, if at all, which fixed costs should be included in the measure of costs is particularly relevant to determining the margin in each case (and the question of what method to use in calculating such costs over which periods of time, *e.g.*, period-by-period or discounted cash flows) and may not be straightforward. In recent Commission precedents, including *Deutsche Telekom* and *Telefónica*, the European Commission addressed these issues in some detail.

4.1. Measures of Costs

5.198 The following measures of cost have been considered both by the Commission and by the economic literature:[309]

---

[308] *Supra* note 187, pp. 394–95.
[309] *See supra* note 1.

5. – Margin Squeeze
Francisco Enrique González-Díaz and Jorge Padilla

- Average total cost ("ATC") is the average of all costs of producing the relevant quantity of units, including all fixed and variable costs.

- Average variable cost ("AVC") is the average of the variable costs of production of the relevant quantity of units.

- Long run average incremental cost ("LRAIC") is the long-run average cost of production, including all product-specific fixed costs, regardless of when the costs are incurred and regardless of whether the fixed costs are sunk (and thus not recoverable). Product-specific fixed costs, for purposes of the definition of LRAIC, do not include common costs that are not incremental – *i.e.*, common costs that would not be avoided by not producing the relevant quantity of units.[310]

- Average avoidable cost ("AAC") is the average of all costs, including variable and product-specific fixed costs that could have been avoided by not producing the relevant quantity of units. Because sunk costs cannot be avoided, AAC excludes sunk costs.

5.199 In predation cases, the Commission has generally considered two cost standards: average variable cost (AVC) and average total cost (ATC), where the latter is the sum of average variable and average fixed costs. As set out in *AKZO*, in general a price above ATC is considered lawful, a price below AVC is likely to be abusive, and a price between AVC and ATC is most likely lawful, barring further evidence that the firm's pricing practice is intended to exclude competitors.[311] In the *Guidance Paper* however, the Commission states that AAC will be used as the appropriate starting point for assessing whether a conduct entails a profit sacrifice.[312]

5.200 LRAIC are generally higher than AAC, because LRAIC includes all fixed costs, whether or not sunk, incurred prior to any decision to produce a given quantity. AAC includes only those fixed costs incurred to produce the given quantity. When applied in the context of a margin squeeze case, the use of LRAIC rather than AAC will, all else equal, make it more likely that a given

---

[310] In *Telefónica*, the Commission described LRAIC as "*the product-specific costs associated with the total volume of output of the relevant product. It is the difference between the total costs incurred by the firm when producing all products, including the individual product under analysis, and the total costs of the firm when the output of the individual product is set equal to zero, holding the output of all other products fixed. Such costs include not only all volume sensitive and fixed costs directly attributable to the production of the total volume of output of the product in question but also the increase in the common costs that is attributable to this activity.*" See *Telefónica Decision 2007 supra* note 20, para. 319.

[311] *See, e.g., AKZO supra* note 60, para. 71.

[312] *Guidance Paper supra* note 1, para. 64.

5. – Margin Squeeze
Francisco Enrique González-Díaz and Jorge Padilla

pricing practice will constitute margin squeeze. LRAIC are in general higher than AAC, so a firm whose pricing practices – and resulting margins – are being measured against LRAIC rather than against AAC will be more likely to be engaged in an abusive margin squeeze.

5.201 The reason why AAC is not commonly used in the context of margin squeeze cases while it is recommended for those concerning predation is that a margin squeeze need not involve end-to-end financial losses and hence, can be profitably sustained for a long period of time, *i.e.*, until its full exclusionary potential materialises.

5.202 In *Deutsche Telekom* and *Telefónica*, the Commission used a measure of LRAIC as the appropriate measure of cost against which to measure the incumbent Deutsche Telekom's margin. In *Telefónica*, the Commission explained the reason for this approach as follows:

> "*The idea is that, if the revenues associated with the downstream activity fall below LRAIC, a rational and profit-maximising firm, at least as efficient as Telefónica – in particular enjoying the same economies of scale and scope – 'has no economic interest in offering downstream services in the medium term. It could increase its overall result by either raising downstream prices to cover the additional costs of providing the service or – where there is no demand for this service at a higher price, to discontinue providing the service,' while holding its output of all other products fixed. In the present case, LRAIC is an appropriate measure of Telefónica's downstream costs below which the spread between Telefónica's upstream and downstream prices provides evidence of a margin squeeze.*"[313]

5.203 The use of LRAIC takes account of common costs of production only insofar as they are incremental – that is, only insofar as they are necessary to produce the additional units under consideration. In the regulatory context, another common measure of costs – *fully distributed costs* – allocate all common costs to particular production activities and will in many cases result in a higher cost of production for the given units.[314] While LRAIC constitute an appropriate measure of the incremental costs incurred to produce a given number of additional units, when considering whether to invest in production

---

[313] *Telefónica Decision 2007 supra* note 20, paras 321–2.
[314] Fully distributed costs in some cases may arbitrarily assign common fixed costs.

5. – Margin Squeeze
Francisco Enrique González-Díaz and Jorge Padilla

in the first place it may be more appropriate to consider fully distributed costs. For example, as recognised by the European Regulators Group, "[i]*n the context of an ex ante regulatory tool,* [LRAIC] *may provide too low a threshold for retail prices, constraining the potential for entry by efficient entrants when the avoidable cost standard does not guarantee the recovery of the fixed costs of entry.*"[315] Because LRAIC may not fully account for the fixed costs of entry – in particular for entry into industries involving multiple products with common costs of production (*e.g.,* the telecommunications sector), the use of LRAIC as a measure of costs for the assessment of margin squeeze may deter entry (or prevent existing firms from expanding their product portfolios into related product lines).

In *Deutsche Telekom* and *Telefónica*, the Commission used LRAIC, as "*the relevant cost measure for the assessment of a margin squeeze in the telecommunications sector is the long run average incremental cost (LRAIC).*"[316]   **5.204**

4.2.   Recovery of Cost

Another issue related to the assessment of costs in price squeeze cases is the time horizon over which the costs of production and their recoupment are to be considered. In particular, in growing industries or in the context of recently launched products, the per-unit costs of a given product may be particularly high during its first years of commercialisation and its LRAIC, or any measure of average cost that includes the incremental fixed costs incurred to produce the output in question, will be relatively high. In such cases it may not be appropriate to consider the firm's average cost at its current operating level in calculating the relevant margin in a margin squeeze case.   **5.205**

The Commission addressed this issue in *Wanadoo,*[317] which although it was not formally a margin squeeze case it involved a vertically integrated entity alleged to be engaged in predatory pricing downstream.[318] The Commission had to address how Wanadoo's costs should be considered over time. Wanadoo was   **5.206**

---

[315] European Regulators Group, "*Report on the Discussion on the Application of Margin Squeeze Tests to Bundles*", March 2009.

[316] *Telefónica Decision 2007 supra* note 20, para. 318 (the Commission further explained that this was "*in accordance with the economic theory and with the practice of the Commission* [in Deutsche Telekom]").

[317] Case T–340/03 *France Télécom v Commission* [2007] ECR II–107.

[318] Wanadoo Interactive was part of the France Télécom group. 99.9 per cent of its capital was owned by Wanadoo S.A, which at the same time was 70–72.2 per cent owned by France Télécom, during the period covered by this Decision. Some authors pointed out that the main reason not to undertake a margin squeeze analysis was

5. – Margin Squeeze

Francisco Enrique González-Díaz and Jorge Padilla

found to be dominant in the downstream market for high-speed Internet access for residential customers (its parent, France Telecom, as the incumbent telephone operator in France, also had very high shares – over 80 per cent – in the upstream wholesale market).[319] The Commission found that Wanadoo priced its high-speed Internet access service below its variable costs – that is, the Commission found that Wanadoo had engaged in predatory pricing. The alleged abuse consisted of the setting of retail prices at a level that did not cover average costs, which in the case of Wanadoo were the payments due to France Télécom (its parent) for network access.[320]

5.207 The Commission examined two issues related to the timing of cost recovery:

5.208 First, in calculating Wanadoo's costs, the Commission considered the recovery of both fixed and variable costs, and considered those costs over a four-year period. Wanadoo and the Commission were in agreement that costs (costs of acquiring new customers) should be spread over a period of time, as Wanadoo was likely to incur an immediate loss to acquire and establish the service for a customer, but would expect to generate revenues associated with that customer that would be, over time, sufficient to cover those costs. However, Wanadoo argued that the Commission should have used a discounted cash-flows method, which would attribute only the present discounted value of the (total, and long-term) costs associated with a subscriber (and adjusted to take account of cost reductions over time). The Commission rejected the discounted cash-flows approach, because such an approach would, in its view, not correctly identify whether Wanadoo was actually carrying out a predatory pricing strategy within the short term. The General Court upheld the Commission's methodology.[321]

5.209 Secondly, Wanadoo disagreed with the Commission's methodology in any event, because the Commission considered only the level of costs and revenues at the

---

the difficulty for the Commission to prove the degree of influence France Telecom exerted on Wanadoo, which was a separate legal entity.

[319] Internet access services were defined by the Commission as consisting in *"an Internet service provider (ISP) offering Internet access via a terminal and a wide range of services such as navigation, email, downloading of files and applications, hosting of personal pages, user networking, etc."* at para. 13 of the Decision (*see Telefónica*). The Commission considered that the ADSL technology was the only real alternative for operators to enter into the retail market.

[320] The costs recognised by the Commission were the customer acquisition costs and others such as platform costs, customer services or administration costs.

[321] *Supra* note 317, para. 156.

5. – Margin Squeeze
Francisco Enrique González-Díaz and Jorge Padilla

time of a customer subscription, and did not account for how those costs and revenues changed over the period of the subscription.[322] Wanadoo thus argued that while the Commission was appropriately considering costs and revenues over some period of time, it should have adjusted the levels of those costs and revenues to reflect the reality that costs were going down. In Wanadoo's view, the Commission was required to "*look at all the information at its disposal on the date of the decision*,"[323] including any reductions in costs that may have occurred over time. The Commission, and the General Court, disagreed. The latter actually held that "*the Commission was entitled to consider that the revenue and costs applicable after the infringement cannot be relevant for the purposes of assessing the rate of recovery of costs during the period investigated. According to the case law, Article* [102 TFEU] *refers to the position occupied by the undertaking concerned on the common market at the time when it active in a way which is alleged to amount to an abuse.*"[324]

5.210 The issue of the time horizon for the recovery of costs also arose in *Telefónica*. As in *Wanadoo*, Telefónica argued in favour of a DCF methodology as, by incorporating updated information on costs and revenues associated with particular services, this methodology would demonstrate that Telefónica was, in fact, generating a positive cash flow (or had an expected positive cash flow) over time. For example, Telefónica argued that its unit costs should be calculated on the basis of long-term volumes, comparing Telefónica's unit revenues with the unit costs calculated on the basis of the (higher) volumes that would be achieved in the longer term. According to the Commission: "*in a growing industry characterised by important fixed costs, unit costs may be high in the beginning of the life of the product just because of a low utilisation of the capacity of the network*."[325] However, the Commission rejected this possibility, because Telefónica had surpassed its expectations for break-even volumes and thus its losses could not be explained by the inclusion of the present level of costs in the calculation.[326]

5.211 Regarding the discounted cash flow methodology, the Commission initially recognised that both the Court of Justice[327] and the Commission's practice[328]

---

[322] *Supra* note 317, para. 123.

[323] *Ibid.*, para. 124.

[324] *Ibid.*, para. 152.

[325] *Telefónica Decision 2007 supra* note 20, para. 323.

[326] *Ibid.*, para. 323.

[327] *AKZO supra* note 60, *Tetra Pak II supra* note 193.

[328] *Supra* note 317.

5. – Margin Squeeze
Francisco Enrique González-Díaz and Jorge Padilla

had been to assess the profitability of the dominant undertaking using the "period by period" approach (which compares, by relevant period, *e.g.*, a year, the observed revenues and costs of the undertaking to assess whether there is a gain or a loss) and not the discounted cash flow method (which considers costs and revenues over a longer time horizon, discounting future values). However, the Commission conducted the analysis using both methods, and explained its methodology with respect to the discounted cash flows method in great detail.[329] Ultimately, the Commission did not have to decide which method would govern, as it concluded on the facts that either methodology was sufficient to demonstrate that Telefónica had engaged in a margin squeeze.

5.212   Telefónica's position was that the DCF methodology is the method used most often by companies when launching new investment projects and therefore generated a more realistic picture the investment profitability. Because the analysis is designed to assess the expected revenues and costs of the company over time, the methodology can provide an indication of whether a company's behaviour is part of an exclusionary strategy. For example, DCF can provide information about possible effects. If a company's strategy generates net cash flows that, once discounted and aggregated, involve an overall positive profit, it is less likely that the strategy is exclusionary. An equally efficient competitor can possibly replicate the strategy and generate a positive profit even if it must incur short-run losses.

5.213   Even though the DCF analysis is based on future predictions and is therefore uncertain, future values are, by definition, discounted. The method therefore gives relatively more importance to the cash flows that (1) are produced soon and (2) provide less uncertainty. On the contrary, less weight is put on those cash flows that generated after in time or that are more uncertain to obtain.

5.214   The broad discretion afforded by the General Court to the Commission in its decision in *Wanadoo*, which was cited by the Commission in *Telefónica*,[330] regarding the choice of methodology used to calculate the recovery of cost of dominant firms (which, of course, is an integral and key element in the determination of whether a margin squeeze has taken place) was confirmed by the General Court in *Telefónica* where the Court as it repeatedly subjected

---

[329] *Telefónica Decision 2007 supra* note 20, paras 332–385.
[330] *Ibid.*, para. 331.

5. – Margin Squeeze
Francisco Enrique González-Díaz and Jorge Padilla

the Commission's choices regarding the methodology used (in particular, when calculating the terminal value of the investments) to the manifest error of assessment standard.[331]

Finally, because *"it is for the dominant company to prove that the method used by the* **5.215** *Commission is unlawful,"*[332] it seems that the burden will be on the dominant undertaking to demonstrate why any particular method chosen by the Commission does not accurately account for the firm's costs and revenues in the market.[333]

Another interesting case in this context is the UK Ofcom Pay TV Statement, **5.216** of 31 March 2010, which led to the adoption of three decisions requiring that Sky Sports be offered at prices set by Ofcom, on platforms other than Sky's, permitting Sky to offer its pay TV services on digital terrestrial TV, and agreeing to consult on a proposed decision to refer two related film markets (market for the sale of premium movie rights and premium movie services) to the Competition Commission. This Statement is relevant in the present context due to its reference to the calculation of the margin and resulting wholesale prices and more specifically to the discounted cash flow analysis. In this field Ofcom adopted a methodology different to that used by the Commission, modeling cash flows over a ten-year period and including a terminal value at the end of such a period in order to reflect the ongoing business value.[334] According to Ofcom, this methodology is appropriate insofar as it *"reflect[s] strong growth in subscriber numbers over the first five years of the analysis, followed by a shallow growth between years five and nine, after which a steady state is assumed for the terminal value calculation".*[335] Ofcom considers that the whole lifetime of

---

[331] *Telefónica Judgment 2012 supra* note 1, paras 212–31.

[332] *Supra* note 317, para. 153.

[333] This position may be in tension with holdings of the European courts, which have stated that *"It is accordingly necessary for the Commission to produce sufficiently precise and consistent evidence to support the firm conviction that the alleged infringement took place."* See Case T-38/02 *Groupe Danone v Commission* [2005] ECR II-4407, para 217. It is also necessary that evidences put forward by the Commission are *"capable of demonstrating to the requisite legal standard the existence of the circumstances constituting an infringement."* See Joined Cases T-67, 68, 71 and 78/00 *JFE Engineering and others v Commission* [2004] ECR II-2501, para. 173. The direct consequence steaming from the Commission's obligation to ground its infringing of competition law decisions is that any reasonable doubt as to the existence of such an infringement must benefit the company at stake, according with the principle of *"in dubio pro reo."* See Advocate General Vesterdorf in Joined Cases T-1 to 4 and 6 to 15/89 *Rhône-Poulenc and others v Commission* [1991] ECR II-867, section I.E.2. *See also* Joined Cases T-67, 68, 71 and 78/00 *JFE Engineering and others v Commission*, para. 177, and *United Brands supra* note 47, para 265.

[334] Ofcom, "Pay TV Statement", of 31 March 2010, para. 10.139.

[335] *Ibid.*, para. 10.142.

5. – Margin Squeeze
Francisco Enrique González-Díaz and Jorge Padilla

a hypothetical entrant's businesses must be taken into account since its aim is not to foster short-term entrance of weak competitors, but rather to enable the entrance of efficient competitors who are prepared to invest and generate effective stable competition.[336]

VII.   Conclusion and the Path Forward

5.217   In 2009, the *Guidance Paper* provided the latest indication from the Commission on its likely future approach to margin squeeze enforcement. There, the Commission considered margin squeeze as a type of refusal to supply. Based on the characteristics and economics of margin squeeze, this seemed to be the appropriate approach.

5.218   Three years later, however, the rulings of the European Courts in *Deutsche Telekom*, *TeliaSonera* and *Telefónica* present a very different understanding of margin squeeze. Indeed, under the current jurisprudence, margin squeeze is an autonomous and distinct violation of Article 102 TFEU and as such is subject to its own legal idiosyncrasies.

5.219   Over this period, the European Courts, as opposed to the US Courts, have expanded the meaning and boundaries of the notion of margin squeeze to encompass cases where the input supplied by the dominant undertaking was indispensable, as well as those where there was a regulatory obligation to supply, and ultimately, any case where a vertically integrated dominant company supplies its wholesale products to its competitors.

5.220   In *TeliaSonera* the Court of Justice has provided an answer (although some doubt its correctness) to some of the key issues that surround this infringement. The Court of Justice has made it clear that from a legal perspective margin squeeze is a distinct infringement from refusal to supply, and therefore that, in order to establish and infringement, the Commission does not need to show that the price upstream is abusive or the price downstream is predatory. The Court has also held that a vertically integrated dominant company might engage in margin squeeze even when the wholesale products it sells are not indispensable to its competitors.

---

[336] *Ofcom, "Pay TV Statement", of 31 March 2010,* para. 10.140.

5. – Margin Squeeze
Francisco Enrique González-Díaz and Jorge Padilla

These developments have created a very paradoxical situation in which a ver- **5.221** tically integrated dominant company is, to some extent, incentivised not to supply its competitors since the legal standard for refusal to supply is stricter (*i.e.*, the products must be indispensible, following *Oscar Bronner*) than that applicable to a margin squeeze in particular if the Court of Justice follows the General Court in *Telefonica* with regard to the question whether the Commission has to show actual detrimental effects on competition or just probable effects.

The explanation for such a policy choice, as *TeliaSonera* suggests, would **5.222** appear to be that otherwise most if not all Article 102 infringements would be brought under the refusal to supply analogy and thus the effectiveness of Article 102 would be diminished. However, for the reasons outlined above such an analogy seems questionable both from an economic perspective and arguably, from a legal perspective.

The controversial expansion of the concept of margin squeeze endorsed by **5.223** the Court of Justice in *TeliaSonera* despite the Commission's *Guidance Paper* and the unfavourable opinion of the Advocate General coupled with the position adopted by the Courts with regard to *ex ante* regulation, places companies and regulators in a very difficult situation.

In light of all the above, a careful reconsideration of the economics and pol- **5.224** icy objectives of margin squeeze law would appear to be justified.

6. – Exclusive Dealing: Exclusive Obligations, Quasi-Exclusive Obligations and Rebates
Romano Subiotto QC and Justin Coombs

Exclusive Dealing: Exclusive Obligations, Quasi-Exclusive Obligations and Rebates

Romano Subiotto QC and Justin Coombs*

I.   Introduction

The Commission's *Guidance Paper*[1] describes exclusive dealing as an action   **6.1**
by a dominant undertaking *"to foreclose its competitors by hindering them from selling to customers through use of exclusive purchasing obligations or rebates"*.[2] Exclusive
dealing commonly designates, then, conduct that creates an exclusive, or quasi-
exclusive, relationship between a seller and a purchaser, which a dominant
undertaking uses to foreclose its competitors by hindering access to channels of
distribution,[3] and which can take the form of price or non-price based conduct.

Both Articles 101 and 102 TFEU may apply to exclusive dealing.[4] Historically,   **6.2**
application of these provisions has differed. The enforcement of Article 101
has been more economics-based, while exclusive dealing has traditionally been
treated as a *per se* abuse under Article 102, since the judgment of the Court of
Justice in *Hoffmann-La Roche*,[5] although the judgment of the General Court in

---

* The authors wish to thank Cristina Sjodin for her valuable contribution to this chapter.

[1] Guidance on the Commission's enforcement priorities in applying Article 82 of the EC Treaty to abusive exclusionary conduct by dominant undertakings (*"Guidance Paper"*), OJ 2009 C 45/7.

[2] *Ibid.*, para. 32. According to the Commission's *Guidance Paper*, the notion of exclusive dealing also includes exclusive supply obligations where a dominant undertaking tries to foreclose its competitors by hindering them from purchasing from suppliers or incentives with the same effect.

[3] *Ibid.*, para. 32. For the Commission, such input foreclosure could result in anticompetitive behaviour if the exclusive supply obligation or incentive ties most of the efficient input so that suppliers and customers competing with the dominant undertaking are unable to find alternative efficient sources of input supply.

[4] Concerning the application of Article 101, the Commission's Guidelines on Vertical Restraints explain that "[t]he possible competition risks of single branding are foreclosure of the market to competing suppliers and potential suppliers, softening of competition and facilitation of collusion between suppliers in case of cumulative use and, where the buyer is a retailer selling to final consumers, a loss of in-store inter-brand competition. Such restrictive effects have a direct impact on inter-brand competition" (Guidelines on Vertical Restraints, OJ 2010 C 130/1, para. 130).

[5] *See* Case 85/76 *Hoffmann-La Roche v Commission* (*"Hoffmann-La Roche"*) [1979] ECR 461. The first Commission's decision adopted under Article 102 TFEU concerned, *inter alia*, exactly the problem of exclusive dealing. *See* Case IV/26.760 *GEMA I*, Commission Decision of 2 June 1971, OJ 1971 L 134/15.

6. – Exclusive Dealing: Exclusive Obligations, Quasi-Exclusive Obligations and Rebates
Romano Subiotto QC and Justin Coombs

Van den Bergh Foods[6] partially questioned this approach. Likewise, the *Guidance Paper* proposes using a more economics-based approach in applying Article 102 TFEU, although the European courts appear to have disavowed this approach.

6.3 This chapter describes the various possible forms of exclusivity and the relevant case law in this field. First, it analyses exclusive obligations and quasi-exclusive obligations. It then provides an overview of rebates before finally drawing some conclusions.

II. Exclusivity Obligations

6.4 Exclusivity obligations entered into by undertakings may assume different forms. One may draw a broad distinction between exclusive distribution agreements and exclusive purchasing agreements, depending on the party benefiting from the exclusivity.

6.5 In an exclusive distribution agreement, the supplier agrees to sell his product only to one distributor for resale in a particular territory. At the same time, the distributor is usually limited in his freedom to actively sell in other exclusively allocated territories. In an exclusive purchasing agreement, one party, the reseller, agrees with the other, the supplier, to purchase certain goods specified in the agreement for resale only from the supplier.

6.6 Exclusive distribution primarily endangers "intra-brand" competition (that is, competition between distributors of the same supplier, or "brand"), and only in a subsidiary way affects inter-brand competition (competition between different suppliers or brands). Exclusive-purchasing agreements may make access to the market more difficult for competing manufacturers, and thus mainly affect inter-brand competition.[7]

6.7 Aside from exclusivity obligations, a dominant firm may also impose quasi-exclusive obligations, which have a similar competitive effect.

---

[6] Case T-65/98 *Van den Bergh Foods v Commission* ("*Van den Bergh Foods*") [2003] ECR II-4653.

[7] Exclusive obligations can also be distinguished depending on the way in which competitors' access to the market is affected. First, exclusive obligations can limit a competitor's access to a downstream selling market by binding intermediaries or final retailers of the dominant firm. Secondly, another possibility, albeit less common, is the exclusive obligation whereby a dominant firm restricts a competitor's access to key upstream inputs. *See* R. O'Donoghue and A. J. Padilla, *The Law and Economics of Article 82 EC* (Oxford, Hart Publishing, 2006), p. 361.

6. – Exclusive Dealing: Exclusive Obligations, Quasi-Exclusive Obligations and Rebates
Romano Subiotto QC and Justin Coombs

The next part of this chapter describes the different types of exclusivity obli- **6.8** gations and is structured as follows. Section II.1 analyses exclusive purchasing agreements and Section II.2 analyses exclusive distribution arrangements. Section II.3 examines quasi-exclusive agreements. Section II.4 undertakes an economic analysis of exclusivity practices. Finally, Sections II.5 and II.6 describe the current enforcement priorities of the Commission and the possible future developments that will characterise this area.

1. Exclusive Purchasing

An exclusive purchasing obligation requires a customer to purchase all its **6.9** needs for a specific product exclusively or to a large extent from one supplier.[8] Where a dominant undertaking enters into a supply obligation with a distributor, the clause may lead to foreclosure of the dominant undertaking's competitors and harm to consumers. Indeed, competitors are hindered from having access to the channels of distribution necessary to have a downstream outlet for their products. Anticompetitive foreclosure arises where most of the suppliers competing with the dominant undertaking are unable to find alternative efficient channels through which to distribute their products.

The way in which the Commission and the courts have approached such **6.10** agreements under Article 102 TFEU has changed over time, moving from a *per se* interpretation to a more effects-based approach.

1.1. *Historical Overview*

Historically, the Commission and the courts have applied a *per se* rule to exclu- **6.11** sive purchasing obligations under Article 102 TFEU. In *Hoffman-La Roche*, the Commission concluded that contracts entered into by Roche (the dominant undertaking in the vitamins market), which were conditional upon the purchasers buying all of their annual requirements from it, constituted an abuse of its dominant position.[9] The judgment of the Court of Justice upheld the Commission's conclusion. The Court clearly stated that *"an undertaking which is in a dominant position on a market and ties purchasers – even if it does so at their request – by an obligation or promise on their part to obtain all or most of their requirements exclusively*

---

[8] *See Guidance Paper*, paras 23–33.
[9] Case IV/29.020 *Vitamins* ("*Hoffmann-La Roche Decision 1976*"), Commission Decision of 9 June 1976, OJ 1976 L223/27.

6. – Exclusive Dealing: Exclusive Obligations, Quasi-Exclusive Obligations and Rebates
Romano Subiotto QC and Justin Coombs

from the said undertaking abuses its dominant position within the meaning of Article 86 of the Treaty, whether the obligation in question is stipulated without further qualification or whether it is undertaken in consideration of the grant of a rebate".[10]

6.12 According to the Court of Justice, this kind of agreement, whether the exclusivity is express or implied,[11] is incompatible with the objective of undistorted competition in the common market. Unless there are exceptional circumstances, such agreements constitute an unjustified burden on the purchaser. Indeed, the fact that the dominant undertaking's contracting partner is itself a powerful undertaking and that the contract is clearly not the outcome of pressure imposed by the dominant firm does not preclude the finding of abuse. Interestingly, the Court indirectly justified its approach on the basis of the "special responsibility" of the dominant company. In fact, given that competition in the relevant market is already weakened by the presence of the dominant firm, it is appropriate to conclude that such exclusive purchasing agreements concluded by the firm constitute, *in principle*, an abuse.[12] Economic considerations, be it the purchasing power of the buyer, the real foreclosure effect arising by the agreement or the harm to consumers, are completely irrelevant.

6.13 The *Hoffman-La Roche* principle was readily applied in subsequent cases. For instance, in *BPB Industries*,[13] the Court of First Instance proposed this strict approach again, concluding that various mechanisms used by British Plasterboard to induce buyers to purchase exclusively from the dominant firm were illegal. However, this case also contained indications of a softening in the approach of the Court to exclusive purchasing obligations. The Court of First Instance noted that such obligations must be assessed in light of *"the effects of such commitments on the functioning of the market concerned … and in their specific context"*, but *"cannot be unreservedly accepted in the case of a market where … competition is already restricted".*[14]

6.14 This interpretation seems far from the appreciation of exclusive dealing made under Article 101 TFEU. In addition to softening their approach with regard to cases involving the block exemption regulations, and therefore with regard

---

[10] *See Hoffmann-La Roche*, para. 89.
[11] *See* Section II.3 on Quasi-Exclusive Obligations below.
[12] *See Hoffmann-La Roche*, para. 121.
[13] Case T-65/89 *BPB Industries and British Gypsum v Commission* ("*BPB Industries*") [1993] ECR II-389.
[14] *Ibid.*, paras 65–67.

6. – Exclusive Dealing: Exclusive Obligations, Quasi-Exclusive Obligations and Rebates
Romano Subiotto QC and Justin Coombs

to undertakings with limited or no market power, the courts have also softened their approach in cases involving undertakings enjoying market power. Indeed, in the *Interbrew* case,[15] the Commission seemed not to object to an exclusive supply agreement notified under Regulation 17/62 (and then assessed under Article 101 TFEU), which was concluded between certain pubs and Interbrew, a brewer who held approximately 56 per cent of the relevant market.

Commentators have correctly pointed out that it seems illogical for there to   **6.15** be a material difference in outcome depending on which provision happens to be applied.[16] Given the fact that: one of the parties to the exclusive contract is dominant in the relevant market must have an impact on the assessment, it does not justify concluding that any exclusive purchasing agreement entered into by a dominant firm must be, in itself, unlawful.[17] It is therefore to be welcomed that this strict approach to Article 102 TFEU has been relaxed somewhat.

1.2.   *Existing Rules*

Under Article 101 TFEU, the block exemption on vertical agreements may   **6.16** cover exclusive purchasing agreements,[18] provided that: (1) the supplier has a market share of no more than 30 per cent of the relevant market on which it sells the contract goods or services, and the buyer a market share of no more than 30 per cent of the relevant market on which it purchases the relevant contract goods or services; (2) the exclusive purchasing contract contains no hard-core restrictions[19] (such as resale price maintenance); and, (3) the exclusivity lasts for less than five years.[20]

An exclusive purchasing agreement that falls outside the scope of the block   **6.17** exemption must be assessed under Article 101 TFEU. The Commission initially seemed to suggest that exclusive purchasing agreements could not *in principle* be exempted under Article 101(3) TFEU where the supplier was dominant,[21]

---

[15] Case COMP/37.904 *Interbrew*, Commission Notice of 20 November 2002, OJ 2002 C 283/14.

[16] *Supra* note 7, p. 360.

[17] *Ibid.*, p. 357.

[18] *See* Commission Regulation (EU) 330/2010 of 20 April 2010 on the application of Article 101(3) of the Treaty on the Functioning of the European Union to categories of vertical agreements and concerted practices, OJ 2010 L 102/1.

[19] *Ibid.*, Article 4.

[20] *Ibid.*, Article 5(a).

[21] Commission Notice – Guidelines on Vertical Restraints, OJ 2000 C 291/1, para. 135.

6. – Exclusive Dealing: Exclusive Obligations, Quasi-Exclusive Obligations and Rebates
Romano Subiotto QC and Justin Coombs

but following criticism of this suggestion, the Commission later moved away from this position.[22]

6.18   As for the assessment of exclusive purchasing agreements under Article 102 TFEU, the way to a more economic approach was opened by the judgment in *Van den Bergh Foods*,[23] where, in contrast to the strict approach outlined above, the Court of First Instance moved further towards an effects-based analysis. As will be analysed in more detail below,[24] the Commission and the Court of First Instance found that Van den Bergh Foods, the dominant firm in the impulse ice cream market in Ireland, required its purchasers to purchase *de facto* exclusively from it. It required that only its products be stored in the freezer cabinet it provided to shops for free, and in practice most shops did not have enough space for more than one freezer cabinet. The Court looked beyond the face of the clause at issue and analysed its actual effects. Even though the clause did not impose any formal exclusivity obligations, it *de facto* prevented the retailers concerned from supplying other brands. While they were free in theory to offer competitive products, retailers could only do so provided that they placed these products within a distinct freezer cabinet. Constraints in terms of place and financial investment impeded most retailers from installing an additional freezer and, as a result, from selling other brands. The Court therefore considered that "[t]*he exclusivity clause has the effect of preventing the retailers concerned from selling other brands of ice cream (or of reducing the opportunity for them to do so), even though there is a demand for such brands, and of preventing competing manufacturers from gaining access to the relevant market*".[25] The Court thus appreciated the effect of the arrangement in question, and thereby rejected the *per se* approach.

6.19   Although the judgment in *Van den Bergh Foods* moves away from the interpretation of *Hoffmann-La Roche*,[26] the scope of the effects-based analysis is not clear. In fact, certain factors suggest that the judgment of the Court of First Instance has a more limited scope. First, the case at stake was very specific, since both Articles 101 and 102 TFEU were applicable. Consequently, a *per se* approach would have been in strong contrast with the approach under Article 101

---

[22] Commission Notice – Guidelines on the application of Article 81(3) of the Treaty ("*Notice on Article 101(3) TFEU*"), OJ 2004 C 101/97, para. 106; and *supra* note 4, para. 132.

[23] *See Van den Bergh Foods supra* note 6.

[24] *See* Section II.3 on Quasi-Exclusive Obligations.

[25] *See Van den Bergh Foods supra* note 6, para. 160.

[26] *See Hoffmann-La Roche supra* note 5.

6. – Exclusive Dealing: Exclusive Obligations, Quasi-Exclusive Obligations and Rebates
Romano Subiotto QC and Justin Coombs

TFEU. Secondly, although the Court of First Instance recognises the need for an effects-based analysis, its statement seems to be nothing more than an affirmation of principle. In fact, apart from the reference to the 40 per cent of tied outlets in the relevant market,[27] no real effects-based analysis was conducted by the Court, especially when comparing it to the thorough assessment under Article 101 TFEU to be found in the same judgment.

Nevertheless, the judgment suggests that the current approach of the Commission and of the courts is to look closely at the actual or likely effects of a particular agreement in the relevant market, and at whether it harms consumers rather than just to presume that the exclusive purchasing agreement is *per se* illegal. This conclusion is further reinforced by the position adopted by the Commission before and after *Van den Bergh Foods*. For example, in *Frankfurt Airport*,[28] the Commission objected to the airport's conclusion of long-term exclusive purchasing obligations concerning the provision of ramp-handling services, but allowed the airport to conclude exclusive purchase contracts lasting one year. This Decision clearly highlights a more effects-based approach; had the *Hoffman-La Roche* reasoning been applied, any exclusive purchasing agreement, regardless of its length, would have been considered illegal. Dominant firms will be able to objectively justify the imposition of such obligations where "*the anti-competitive effects are kept to the minimum necessary for the attainment of some economic advantage*".[29] While this demonstrates some softening of the approach, it is noticeable that exclusive purchasing imposed by a dominant firm is assumed to have an anticompetitive effect and can be permitted only if this effect is objectively justified. **6.20**

The Commission's *Discussion Paper*[30] was also oriented towards an effects-based approach. In particular, it recognised that the single-branding obligation may have "*efficiency enhancing effects*" as well as "*anti-competitive effects*".[31] Among the former, reference was made to the relationship-specific investments made by the supplier in order to supply a specific customer. In this case, a single-branding obligation allowing the supplier to earn back the investment would **6.21**

---

[27] *See Van den Bergh Foods supra* note 6, para. 160.

[28] Case IV/34.801 *FAG - Flughafen Frankfurt/Main* ("*Frankfurt Airport*"), Commission Decision of 14 January 1998, OJ 1998 L 72/30.

[29] J. Faull and A. Nikpay (Eds.), *The EC Law of Competition* (2nd Ed., Oxford, Oxford University Press, 2007), para. 4.321.

[30] DG Competition discussion paper on the application of Article 82 of the Treaty to exclusionary abuses ("*Discussion Paper*"), December 2005.

[31] *Ibid.*, para. 138.

6. – Exclusive Dealing: Exclusive Obligations, Quasi-Exclusive Obligations and Rebates
Romano Subiotto QC and Justin Coombs

not have amounted to an infringement of Article 102 TFEU. In line with the *Discussion Paper*, the current Commission *Guidance Paper* focuses on a more effects-based approach to exclusionary abuses by dominant undertakings.

2. Exclusive Distribution

6.22   Exclusive distribution agreements arise when a *"supplier agrees to sell his product only to one distributor for resale in a particular territory. At the same time, the distributor is usually limited in his active selling into other exclusively allocated territories".*[32] One common rationale for exclusive distribution is that, by granting exclusivity over its products, the supplier aims to provide the distributor with incentives to promote those products and provide better services to customers, thus avoiding the *free-riding* phenomenon. Without the protection offered by the exclusivity, the distributor may refrain from marketing the product adequately or may be unwilling to offer additional services, since competitors could take advantage of the distributor's efforts without bearing the relative costs.[33]

6.23   The assessment of exclusive distribution agreements has evolved remarkably. Initially, exclusive distribution agreements fell almost automatically under Article 101(1) TFEU, since they jeopardised the main objective of the Treaty by partitioning the market. The Court then began recognising the potential necessity and positive effects on welfare of exclusivity.[34] The Commission further developed a new approach, by introducing the so-called "first generation" block exemptions, which it later replaced with a more economic-based approach set forth in "new generation" block exemptions. Exclusive distribution agreements are rarely assessed under Article 102 TFEU and are more commonly analysed under Article 101.

---

[32] *Supra* note 4, para. 151. In a broader sense, exclusive distribution concerns agreements whereby a supplier appoints one distributor to be the exclusive outlet for his products, either for a defined territory or for a particular class of customers. *See* P. Roth and V. Rose (Eds.), *Bellamy & Child: European Community Law of Competition* (6th Ed., Oxford, Oxford University Press, 2008), p. 429.

[33] *See generally*, F. Tuytschaever, A. Vanderelst and F. Wijckmans, *Vertical Agreements in EC Competition Law* (Oxford, Oxford University Press, 2006); V. Korah and D. O'Sullivan, *Distribution Agreements under the EC Competition Rules* (Oxford, Hart Publishing, 2002); J. Goyder, *EU Distribution Law* (4th Ed., Oxford, Hart Publishing, 2005), pp. 63 *et seq.*

[34] Case 258/78 *L.C. Nungesser and Kurt Eisele v Commission* ("*Nungesser*") [1982] ECR 2015.

6. – Exclusive Dealing: Exclusive Obligations, Quasi-Exclusive Obligations and Rebates
Romano Subiotto QC and Justin Coombs

Consten and Grundig[35] may be considered the landmark judgment in relation to **6.24** exclusive distribution. The Court of Justice stated that both Articles 101 and 102 TFEU may prohibit exclusive distribution agreements where they have as their effect the restriction of competition within the same brand.[36] In this case, Grundig, a German manufacturer, had conferred upon Consten, a French dealer, the exclusive right to sell its products in France. In parallel, Grundig prohibited its non-French dealers from exporting to France. This effect was achieved by assigning the Grundig French trademark to Consten, thus completely protecting it from intra-brand competition and parallel imports.

The Court of Justice held that the situation results *"in the isolation of the French* **6.25** *market and makes it possible to charge for the products in question prices that are sheltered from all effective competition"*.[37] Therefore, the agreement constituted an infringement of Article 101(1) TFEU and was not justified under Article 101(3) TFEU. This jurisprudence opened the way to the formal enactment of Regulation 67/67,[38] which exempted exclusive distribution agreements in so far as they did not hinder parallel imports, and to the subsequent practice of the Commission.[39]

The current Regulation 330/2010[40] and the Guidelines on Vertical Restraints[41] **6.26** adopt a more economic and flexible approach in that, in order for a vertical agreement to be exempted, the supplier must not possess market power and a substantial degree of competition must remain in the market. According to Article 3 of Regulation 330/2010, the exemption applies only where the supplier has a market share of no more than 30 per cent of the relevant market on which it sells the contract goods or services, and the buyer has a market share of no more than 30 per cent of the relevant market on which it purchases the relevant contract goods or services. Pursuant to Article 6 of Regulation 330/2010, the exemption may be declared inapplicable where a network

---

[35] Joined Cases 56 and 58/64 *Établissements Consten and Grundig-Verkaufs v Commission* ("*Consten and Grundig*") [1966] ECR 299.

[36] *Ibid.*, p. 342. The Court clarified the scope of Article 101, specifying that it applies: (1) to restrictions of competition between undertakings operating in different levels of the markets (*i.e.*, vertical agreements); and, (2) to restrictions of intra-brand competition.

[37] *Ibid.*, p. 343.

[38] Commission Regulation 67/67/EEC of 22 March 1967 on the application of Article 85(3) of the Treaty to certain categories of exclusive dealing agreements ("*Regulation 67/67*"), OJ 1967 57/849.

[39] Cf. Case T-77/92 *Parker Pen v Commission* [1994] ECR II-549.

[40] *Supra* note 18.

[41] *Supra* note 4.

6. – Exclusive Dealing: Exclusive Obligations, Quasi-Exclusive Obligations and Rebates
Romano Subiotto QC and Justin Coombs

of similar agreements cover more than 50 per cent of the relevant market, thereby foreclosing access to the distribution system for new suppliers.

6.27 The above exemption is conditional on the absence of so-called hardcore restrictions. Independent of the market power enjoyed by the supplier, such clauses represent a restriction of competition by object, and may not be deemed to fulfil the four criteria of Article 101(3) TFEU.[42] The hard-core restrictions that are particularly dangerous and are likely to be included in an exclusive distribution agreement are: (1) resale price maintenance (*i.e.*, direct or indirect determination of the resale price of the product or service in the agreement by the supplier); and, (2) the limitation of passive sales by the distributor outside the territory assigned to it.[43]

6.28 However, the question arises as to how the agreement is assessed when the threshold provided by Regulation 330/2010 is exceeded. First, agreements where the relevant party's market share exceeds the threshold provided for by the Regulation are not automatically presumed to be illegal, but require individual examination.[44] Secondly, paragraph 127 of the Guidelines on Vertical Restraints recalls that, "[*a*]*ccording to settled case law, the application of Article 101(3) cannot prevent the application of Article 102. Moreover, since Articles 101 and 102 both pursue the aim of maintaining effective competition on the market, consistency requires that Article 101(3) be interpreted as precluding any application of the exception rule to restrictive agreements that constitute an abuse of a dominant position*". As a result, the conclusion of an exclusive distribution agreement may amount to an abuse of dominance where it produces foreclosure or exploitative effects.

6.29 In contrast to exclusive purchasing agreements, exclusive distribution agreements are rarely assessed under Article 102 TFEU. The *De Beers*[45] Decision provides one example (although it is only a decision pursuant to Article 9 of Regulation 1/2003 which renders enforceable commitments offered by De Beers to the Commission).[46] It only evaluates the competition concerns

---

[42] *See, however*, the judgment of the Court of Justice in Joined Cases C-501, 513, 515 and 519/06 P *Glaxo Smith-Kline Services and others v Commission and others* [2009] ECR I-9291.

[43] *Supra* note 18, Article 4(a) and 4(b).

[44] *Supra* note 18, Recital (9).

[45] Case COMP/38.381 *De Beers*, Commission Decision of 22 February 2006, not yet published. *See also*, Case T-170/06 *Alrosa v Commission* [2007] ECR II-2601.

[46] Council Regulation (EC) 1/2003 of 16 December 2002 on the implementation of the rules on competition laid down in Articles 81 and 82 of the Treaty ("*Regulation 1/2003*"), OJ 2003 L 1/1.

6. – Exclusive Dealing: Exclusive Obligations, Quasi-Exclusive Obligations and Rebates
Romano Subiotto QC and Justin Coombs

arising from the practice without concluding as to the existence of an infringe-ment. The case concerned an agreement by which De Beers undertook to buy from Alrosa a substantial amount of rough diamonds every year – De Beers and Alrosa being two major suppliers of rough diamonds, and De Beers being also vertically integrated while disposing of its own distribution system. The Commission *"took the preliminary view that this agreement would lead to 'de facto' distribution exclusivity to the benefit of De Beers"*.[47] As a result, Alrosa would be prevented *"from acting as an alternative and independent supplier on the rough diamond market outside the CIS Member States"*,[48] thereby foreclosing De Beers' competi-tors on the downstream distribution market by hindering their access to the input supplied by Alrosa.

Purchasing power features prominently in the scheme of Regulation 330/2010 **6.30** because the market share thresholds for the application of the block exemp-tion now also depend on the buyer having no more than a 30 per cent share of the market on which it purchases the contract goods or services.

3.   Quasi-exclusive Obligations

Aside from exclusivity obligations, a dominant firm may also try to impose **6.31** obligations on its purchasers, which – although not requiring outright exclusivity – have a similar competitive effect. These are referred to collectively as quasi-exclusive obligations. Such obligations can be imposed by contractual means (as in Sections II.3.1. and II.3.2. below) or by other incentives (as in Section II.3.3. below). We shall consider each in turn.

3.1.   Requirement Contracts for Less than 100 Per Cent of the Purchaser's Needs

This delineates a situation where the dominant firm refuses to contract with **6.32** the purchaser unless the purchaser agrees to purchase a certain percentage of his total requirements from the dominant firm. The general rule is that, given that a requirement to contract for less than 100 per cent of the purchaser's needs can be no worse than a contract requiring outright exclusivity, if an exclusive deal would be legal, so too would a requirement to contract for less than 100 per cent of the purchaser's needs.[49] The exact percentage required to

---

[47] Case COMP/38.381 *Supra* note 45.
[48] *Ibid.*, paras 31–32.
[49] *Supra* note 7, p. 369.

6. – Exclusive Dealing: Exclusive Obligations, Quasi-Exclusive Obligations and Rebates
Romano Subiotto QC and Justin Coombs

constitute abuse depends on the circumstances of the individual case and, in particular, on the make-up of the market in question.[50] The correct approach is to look at how much of total demand is foreclosed to rivals as a result of the clause rather than just looking at the percentage requirement alone. For example, in *Hoffman-La Roche*, the dominant firm required customers to source "most" (in this case, between 75 per cent and 80 per cent) of their requirements from Roche. The Commission (whose Decision[51] was later upheld by the Court of Justice[52]) considered that, in the circumstances of the case, this amounted to an abuse of Roche's dominant position in the vitamins market.

6.33 Furthermore, the Commission will look at other factors in conjunction with the market share percentage to assess whether there has been an abuse. This was the case in *Michelin II*,[53] which concerned requirements imposed by the dominant firm for membership of the "Michelin Friends Club" that granted preferential terms, including a market share percentage, for dealers who satisfied certain criteria. In relation to its finding as to the existence of an abuse, the Commission (whose Decision[54] was later upheld by the Court of First Instance[55]) considered as relevant the fact that Michelin required dealers to hold extra stock to meet spontaneous demand for Michelin products immediately, in addition to the market share percentage required. It follows from this that, even though the contract might require a relatively low percentage of total requirements to be sourced from the dominant firm, a finding of abuse is likely if other potentially exclusionary behaviour is present.

6.34 In the absence of an outright exclusivity clause or of a specific percentage of total requirements, the Commission will look at whether the contract should nonetheless be characterised as exclusive, based on the wording of contractual clauses and of the circumstances of the case, including evidence of the parties' intentions. For example, in *Prokent/Tomra*, the Commission concluded, based on a number of documents relating to negotiations with customers, that agreements designating Tomra as the *"preferred, main or primary supplier"* were in fact intended to be exclusive in the same way as agreements

---

[50] Although some commentators, including Richard Whish, have argued for a particular market share threshold to apply, Whish argues for an 80 per cent threshold. *See* R. Whish, *Competition Law* (4th Ed., Butterworths LexisNexis, 2001), pp. 642–43.

[51] *Hoffmann-La Roche Decision 1976 supra* note 9.

[52] *See Hoffmann-La Roche v Commission.*

[53] Case T-203/01 *Manufacture française des pneumatiques Michelin v Commission* ("*Michelin II*") [2003] ECR II-4071.

[54] Case COMP/36.041 *Michelin*, Commission Decision of 20 June 2001, OJ 2002 L 143/1.

[55] *See Michelin II supra* note 53.

6. – Exclusive Dealing: Exclusive Obligations, Quasi-Exclusive Obligations and Rebates
Romano Subiotto QC and Justin Coombs

framed in express exclusivity terms.[56] On appeal, the General Court dismissed Tomra's claim that the terms used in these agreements were too vague to give rise to an enforceable obligation under any applicable national contract law and therefore did not prevent customers from purchasing from competitors. The Court pointed out that, consistent with the *Hoffman-La Roche* case law, exclusivity did not require customers to be tied by a formal obligation, it being sufficient that the supplier's practices, as in Tomra's case, gave customers an incentive to source exclusively or almost exclusively from the dominant company.[57] In fact, the Court noted that the agreements at issue also contained individualised quantity commitments and retroactive rebates based on volume targets.[58] Moreover, evidence on file indicated that Tomra itself closely monitored compliance with the agreements and had exercised pressure on individual customers.[59]

3.2. Requirement Contracts Expressed in Terms of Volume

The approach to requirement contracts expressed in terms of volume, where **6.35** the dominant firm requires the purchaser to buy a certain volume of products from it, is very similar to the approach to percentage-based requirements just described. Although requirement contracts expressed in terms of volume have generally been treated less harshly than requirement contracts expressed in terms of a percentage of the purchaser's total needs,[60] the approach is in reality the same as in Section II.3.1. above. It is necessary to examine what proportion of the buyer's total requirements[61] this amount represents and then to apply the same approach as outlined above.

---

[56] Case COMP/38.113 *Prokent/Tomra*, Commission Decision of 29 March 2006 ("*Tomra Decision 2006*"), not yet published, paras 114–18. When reviewing the Commission decision on appeal, the General Court held that the Commission's conclusion was not undermined, but rather, reinforced by the fact that certain customers had sought to include in their "preferred supplier" agreement a clause allowing them to purchase machines from Tomra's competitors for testing purposes. In fact, such a clause suggested that purchasing from competitors was in reality seen as an exception to exclusivity, which was, in particular, limited to the testing of the machines. *See* Case T-155/06 *Tomra Systems and others v Commission* ("*Tomra Judgment 2010*") [2010] ECR II-4361, para. 56, upheld by the Court of Justice in Case C-549/10 P *Tomra Systems and others v Commission* ("*Tomra Judgment 2012*"), not yet reported.

[57] *Tomra Judgment 2010*, para. 59.

[58] *Ibid.*, para. 60.

[59] *Ibid.*, para. 65.

[60] *Supra* note 7, p. 368.

[61] Case C-234/89 *Stergios Delimitis v Henninger Bräu* [1991] ECR I-935, para. 30.

6. – Exclusive Dealing: Exclusive Obligations, Quasi-Exclusive Obligations and Rebates
Romano Subiotto QC and Justin Coombs

3.3. *De Facto Requirement Contracts*

6.36 Even if a purchaser is in principle free to purchase competing products, an abuse may still occur if the overall contractual position is equivalent to an exclusive dealing arrangement. The use of rebates to this end will be fully considered in Section III, but here we will consider some of the other mechanisms used by dominant firms to achieve outright or quasi-exclusivity.

3.3.1. English Clauses

6.37 A dominant firm may also seek to reserve to itself the (quasi-) totality of a customer's demand by including an "English Clause" in the contract (also known as "Meet-or-Release Clause"). Such a clause requires a purchaser who receives an offer at a lower price to give the dominant firm the option of matching that offer, and only if it declines to do so can the purchaser take supplies from the competitor.[62] In *Hoffman-La Roche*,[63] the Commission held that such a clause was only slightly less harmful from an antitrust perspective than an exclusive dealing obligation. The Decision was later upheld on appeal by the Court of Justice,[64] which highlighted the importance of the fact that such a clause allowed Roche itself to decide (by adjusting prices or not) whether it would permit its customers to buy from competitors.

3.3.2. Equipment Placing

6.38 A dominant firm cannot use the incentive of the free provision of equipment to impose *de facto* exclusivity on its purchasers. In *Van den Bergh Foods*, the Commission (whose Decision[65] was later upheld by both the Court of First Instance[66] and the Court of Justice[67]) concluded that the dominant firm's provision of freezer cabinets free of charge to retailers on condition that they were to be used exclusively for the storage of its ice cream products constituted an abuse. While the Commission acknowledged that such agreements may be commercial practice in the ice cream market, it decided that, for a company in a dominant position to impose exclusive storage of its products,

---

[62] *See, for instance, supra* note 32, p. 980.

[63] *Hoffmann-La Roche Decision 1976 supra* note 9, para. 65. *See also* Guidelines on Vertical Restraints, according to which English clauses *"can be expected to have the same effect as a single branding obligation, especially when the buyer has to reveal who makes the better offer"* (*supra* note 4, para. 129).

[64] *See Hoffmann-La Roche supra* note 5, paras 102–08.

[65] Cases IV/34.073, 34.395 and 35.436 *Van den Bergh Foods*, Commission Decision of 11 March 1998, OJ 1998 L 246/1.

[66] *See Van den Bergh Foods supra* note 6.

[67] Case C-552/03 P *Unilever Bestfoods (Ireland) v Commission,* [2006] ECR I-9091.

6. – Exclusive Dealing: Exclusive Obligations, Quasi-Exclusive Obligations and Rebates
Romano Subiotto QC and Justin Coombs

had the practical effect of preventing retailers from dealing with other suppliers over a long period of time and thus constituted an abuse.[68] Although the retailers were not contractually required to purchase ice cream exclusively from Van den Bergh, retailers were, in practice, unlikely to purchase a second freezer for their shops. Thus, the effect on competition of such an equipment-placing clause was the same as that of a requirement contract; namely, Van den Bergh was able to achieve *de facto* exclusivity of supply.[69]

3.3.3. Slotting Allowances

Slotting allowances refer to payments made by a manufacturer to a retailer in consideration of the retailer stocking the manufacturer's product. In certain cases, a manufacturer who is dominant in the relevant market could use such payments to acquire exclusivity.[70] Generally, slotting allowances on their own do not create competition problems. However, should the relevant contract contain a clause that is harmful from an antitrust perspective, the slotting allowance arrangement could constitute abuse of the dominant firm's market position. For example, in *Coca-Cola*,[71] the Commission considered that the dominant firm's action of requiring retailers to devote shelf space exclusively to its products constituted an abuse. **6.39**

3.3.4. Category Management

Category management refers to a range of practices whereby a supplier (who is often a dominant firm in the relevant market) and a retailer work together to maximise the retail performance of a particular product category. Such programmes can often have procompetitive effects, such as increased sales and lower product prices for consumers. Therefore, it is not surprising that a Commission-sponsored study treating the issue supports the view that such practices are only abusive where anticompetitive effects are produced.[72] This would be the case where, for example, the dominant firm uses its role in the category management programme to promote its own products (by way of pricing, product placement or promotions) to the detriment of those of its competitors.[73] **6.40**

---

[68] *See also* the analysis in *supra* note 32, p. 981.

[69] *Supra* note 50, p. 677.

[70] *Supra* note 7, p. 370.

[71] Case COMP/39.116 *Coca-Cola*, Commission Decision of 22 June 2005, not yet published.

[72] Dobson Consulting, *Buyer Power and its Impact on Competition in the Food Retail Distribution Sector of the European Union*, Report prepared for the European Commission – DGIV Study Contract No. IV/98/ETD/078, May 1999, p. 191, App. 3. *See also* Guidelines on Vertical Restraints *supra* note 4, para. 213.

[73] *Supra* note 7, p. 373. *See also* Guidelines on Vertical Restraints *supra* note 4, para. 210.

6. – Exclusive Dealing: Exclusive Obligations, Quasi-Exclusive Obligations and Rebates
Romano Subiotto QC and Justin Coombs

4. Economics

4.1. Introduction

6.41 As explained above, exclusive dealing can be broadly categorised as either exclusive distribution or exclusive purchasing. In both cases, the Commission may be concerned that the conduct will create foreclosure effects.

6.42 In the case of exclusive distribution, the supplier commits that it will distribute only through one distributor, and refuses to deal with any other distributor. Competing distributors are excluded from supplying this product. If the supplier is a dominant firm and its product is popular with end consumers, this conduct may lead to the exclusion of the rival distributors.

6.43 Such exclusion can have a direct impact on competition since it eliminates competition in the downstream market between distributors of the dominant firm's product. This affects "intra-brand" competition, that is to say, competition between distributors of the same upstream supplier. In practice, this restriction on intra-brand competition might not be of much concern if there is strong competition upstream between the dominant firm and its rivals, *i.e.*, strong "inter-brand" competition. As explained below, exclusive distribution may in fact help to increase inter-brand competition.

6.44 Exclusive purchasing occurs when the dominant firm will supply customers only if they agree to purchase all of their requirements from the dominant firm. Exclusive purchasing can directly affect competition in the upstream market. In principle, it can lead to the exclusion of the dominant firm's rivals, or potential rivals, since they are no longer able to supply their customers. In practice, however, the impact will depend on the structure of the market and other factors. For example, upstream rivals are unlikely to be excluded if exclusivity covers only a small proportion of their potential customers. In addition, it may be that these rivals could themselves supply a customer's entire requirements. If they can, there should be no risk of exclusion – the rivals simply compete against the dominant firm for the exclusive right to supply each customer. Competition will be harmed only if rivals are prevented from competing to supply a customer's entire requirements.

6.45 In some situations, exclusive distribution might be combined with exclusive purchasing. For example, the distributor might agree not to distribute rival

6. – Exclusive Dealing: Exclusive Obligations, Quasi-Exclusive Obligations and Rebates
Romano Subiotto QC and Justin Coombs

products in return for the exclusive right to distribute the product. This could potentially lead to a reduction in both intra-brand and inter-brand competition.

The economic effects of these practices were the subject of controversy **6.46** and debate in the late twentieth century. This debate began with the so-called "Chicago Critique", which questioned whether these practices would ever have anticompetitive effects and argued that they were much more likely to be motivated by the pursuit of efficiencies. Subsequent research identified situations where this critique was not valid and anticompetitive effects could arise. The outcome of this debate suggests that each case needs to be assessed based on the specific facts of the market and industry involved.

The rest of this section is structured as follows. First, we explain the Chicago **6.47** Critique and describe some of the efficiencies that might motivate exclusive dealing. We then explain the main post-Chicago theories, which suggest that these practices can create anticompetitive effects. Lastly, we draw some conclusions.

4.2. *The Chicago Critique*

We explained above how exclusive dealing can lead to foreclosure effects. We **6.48** now consider the question: why would the dominant firm want to do that?

At one time, the answer to this question was thought to be obvious: so that it **6.49** can charge higher prices downstream and earn higher profits at the expense of its customers. However, during the 1970s and 1980s, a group of economists and legal commentators associated with the University of Chicago argued that this is unlikely to be the case. They argued that firms do not have incentives to engage in foreclosure and that exclusive dealing and other vertical restraints are likely to benefit consumers. Subsequent work by other economists has shown that, although vertical restraints can benefit consumers, they can also be anticompetitive. Each case requires a detailed examination of its facts before one can say what effects are produced.

Below, we first set out the so-called "Chicago Critique", and explain why firms **6.50** might not have any incentive to engage in foreclosure that might harm consumers. We first consider exclusive distribution, and then exclusive purchasing. We then discuss how exclusive dealing could create efficiencies.

6. – Exclusive Dealing: Exclusive Obligations, Quasi-Exclusive Obligations and Rebates
Romano Subiotto QC and Justin Coombs

4.2.1. Exclusive Distribution

6.51 In the pre-Chicago world, it was expected that an upstream firm would use vertical restraints to monopolise the downstream market.

6.52 Suppose the firm has market power upstream, but there is competition downstream. We know that a monopolist will be able to charge higher prices and supply a lower level of output than firms that face competition. By committing to supply only one distributor, the firm can establish a monopoly in the downstream market. We might expect that this would allow the downstream firm to increase prices, reduce output, and earn higher profits than a firm that faced effective competition in the downstream market. In return for granting exclusivity, the upstream firm would demand a share of these increased profits.

6.53 The weakness of this simple analysis is that it ignores the fact that the upstream firm already has market power in the upstream market. It can already charge monopolistic prices to downstream firms. Does it gain any advantage by monopolising the downstream market or can it already extract all potential monopoly rents through the price it charges to downstream firms?

6.54 This question is at the heart of the arguments put forward by economists and legal commentators associated with the University of Chicago, such as Robert Bork and Richard Posner. The Chicago School argued that the upstream firm would seldom have the incentive to foreclose competition in the downstream market.[74]

6.55 One key insight of the Chicago School was the argument that there is only one monopoly profit to be exploited in any vertically-related production process. This is shown diagrammatically in Annex 1. In summary, providing certain assumptions are met – in particular, that the downstream market is perfectly competitive – then this analysis shows that there is only one monopoly profit to be earned. If the upstream firm already has market power, it can already capture all the available monopoly profits through the price it charges the downstream firm. There is no additional profit that can be earned by monopolising the downstream market.

---

[74] *See* R. H. Bork, *The Antitrust Paradox: A Policy at War with Itself* (New York, Basic Books, 1978) and R. Posner, *Antitrust Law* (Chicago, University of Chicago Press, 1976).

6. – Exclusive Dealing: Exclusive Obligations, Quasi-Exclusive Obligations and Rebates
Romano Subiotto QC and Justin Coombs

This very powerful result led the Chicago School to conclude that, provided cer- **6.56**
tain assumptions hold, an upstream firm has no incentive to attempt to foreclose
and monopolise a downstream market. In fact, the upstream firm might earn
lower profits by doing so. By reducing downstream competition, it is likely to end
up with higher downstream costs. This would reduce its own output and profits.

4.2.2.   Exclusive Purchasing

A similar analysis can be used to argue that exclusive purchasing is unlikely to **6.57**
have an anticompetitive motive.

In the case of exclusive purchasing, it is the customer, rather than the dominant **6.58**
firm, that agrees to exclusivity. The customer agrees that it will purchase only
from the dominant firm. This raises the question of why the customer is willing
to make this commitment. By doing so, it gives up its freedom to purchase from
other suppliers and potentially confers some market power on the upstream
firm – or helps the upstream firm to bolster its existing market power.

Clearly, the customer will only agree to exclusivity if it gains some advantage. **6.59**
Therefore the dominant firm has to compensate the customer for giving up
its freedom to purchase from other suppliers. In other words, it has to offer a
lower price and share its profits with its customer. However, if the dominant
firm has to offer a lower price in order to obtain exclusivity, where is the benefit to the dominant firm?

The implication here is that exclusive purchasing will be used only when it cre- **6.60**
ates efficiencies. Only in that situation would it make sense for the upstream
firm to offer lower prices in return for an exclusive purchasing commitment.
In addition, since upstream suppliers would then be willing to accept lower
prices in return for exclusivity, the exclusivity can in fact lead to more intense
price competition and lower prices for consumers.

4.2.3.   Efficiencies

The implication of the Chicago Critique is that there is no anticompetitive **6.61**
rationale for vertical restraints such as exclusive dealing. Instead, it suggests
that vertical restraints are used only when they increase efficiency. We consider below some of the reasons why exclusive dealing might create efficiencies that benefit firms and consumers.

6. – Exclusive Dealing: Exclusive Obligations, Quasi-Exclusive Obligations and Rebates
Romano Subiotto QC and Justin Coombs

4.2.3.1.   Free-riding between Downstream Firms

6.62   A downstream firm may provide services on which competing downstream firms can free-ride. Downstream firms sometimes provide services that create what economists call a positive "externality"; as well as benefiting the downstream firm providing the service, they also create benefits for other downstream firms. Where externalities exist, the relevant product or service will normally be under-provided.[75]

6.63   Consider, for instance, car dealers that offer test-drives to potential customers. Suppose that there are two dealers, one that offers test-drives and one that does not. The second dealer will incur lower costs by not offering test-drives and will, therefore, be able to undercut the first dealer. Customers would be likely to go for a test-drive at the first car dealer, but then buy the car at the second dealer where prices are lower. The second dealer is free-riding on the services provided by the first dealer.

6.64   In this situation, the first dealer will be left with no customers. It will be forced to stop offering test-drives so that it can lower its prices and compete with the second dealer. This outcome reduces the profits of the car manufacturer. If customers cannot test drive its products, it is likely to lose sales. The car manufacturer might therefore need to prevent this free-riding problem. Exclusive distribution would be one way to achieve this.

6.65   Note that the free-riding problem between downstream firms can harm both the upstream firm and consumers. Consumers might benefit from the services provided by downstream firms. For example, car buyers will generally value the opportunity to test drive cars since it helps them to choose between competing models. They are likely to place a higher value on a car they have tested, so the availability of test-drives will increase consumer welfare.

6.66   If exclusive distribution ensures that downstream firms do not under-provide certain services, it will increase output and consumer welfare.

---

[75] L. G. Telser, "Why Should Manufacturers Want Fair Trade II?" (1990) 33(2) *Journal of Law and Economics*, pp. 409–17.

6. – Exclusive Dealing: Exclusive Obligations, Quasi-Exclusive Obligations and Rebates
Romano Subiotto QC and Justin Coombs

4.2.3.2. Free-riding between Upstream Firms

Free-riding can also occur among upstream firms. A downstream firm might **6.67** invest in services such as technical support, promotion, training, or equipment that helps increase demand for the upstream good as well as the downstream good. Since both the upstream firm and the downstream firm benefit from these investments, they should both contribute to their costs. However, suppose that these investments can also be applied to a rival upstream firm's product. The upstream firm might be worried that one of its upstream rivals can start supplying the downstream firm and free-ride on the investments it has financed. It will not be willing to make investments that can benefit its rivals.

For example, a firm that distributes financial products, such as life insurance **6.68** and pensions, will need to train its staff so that they comply with regulatory requirements. This training will benefit the upstream product providers who might, therefore, be willing to provide financial support for this investment. However, they may be reluctant to provide this support if the training could also benefit competing upstream firms.

Again, a vertical restraint (in this case, an exclusive purchasing arrangement) **6.69** can be used to overcome this problem so that the efficient level of investment takes place. In this situation, exclusive purchasing could therefore increase output and welfare.

4.2.3.3. Hold-up Problems and Specific Investments

In some markets, firms must make specific investments in order to trade with **6.70** each other.[76] For example, a car dealer might have to train its staff and invest in dedicated facilities to service the manufacturer's cars. The resulting knowledge and equipment might not be transferable to a different manufacturer's cars. The dealer will make these investments if the wholesale price at which the manufacturer sells the cars allows the dealer to make a high enough margin to recover these investments. However, once it has made these investments, the dealer is at risk of being "held-up" by the car manufacturer. The car manufacturer can now increase the wholesale price of its cars knowing that the dealer can use its assets only to sell that manufacturer's cars. Knowing this risk, the car dealer will not make the necessary investments in the first place.

---

[76] D. Besanko and M. K. Perry, "Equilibrium Incentives for Exclusive Dealing in a Differentiated Products Oligopoly" (1993) 24(4) *The RAND Journal of Economics*, pp. 646–68.

6. – Exclusive Dealing: Exclusive Obligations, Quasi-Exclusive Obligations and Rebates
Romano Subiotto QC and Justin Coombs

6.71 Exclusive dealing can overcome this problem and lead to higher investment. For example, if the manufacturer agrees not to supply the dealer's competitors, it is in effect giving up some bargaining power – it can no longer threaten to use alternative dealers if the first dealer does not accept the price increase. By giving up some bargaining power, the manufacturer makes the relationship with the dealer more equal and reduces its ability to hold up the dealer. The dealer is then more likely to make manufacturer-specific investments. If consumers value the services that the dealer provides using these investments, this will lead to higher output and welfare.

4.2.3.4. Quality Certification

6.72 In some markets, the quality of service provided by retailers might affect the consumer's decision over whether to buy the good.[77] For example, if a product is sold by an exclusive shop in an expensive shopping area, consumers might assume that the product is of a high quality. If the product is also available at discount retailers, they might conclude that the product is of a lower quality. The manufacturer might therefore decide to supply only "high-quality" retailers in order to signal the high quality of the product to consumers.

4.2.3.5. Double Marginalisation

6.73 Exclusive dealing may also be beneficial to consumers if it helps avoid a problem known as "double marginalisation".[78]

6.74 There may be market power at both the upstream and downstream level in many markets. This may lead to both the upstream and downstream firms charging a price above marginal cost, which is often called a "double mark-up" or "double marginalisation".

6.75 Double marginalisation occurs if the upstream and downstream firms both have market power and set prices independently. Like any firm with market power, the upstream firm restricts supply of the input in order to achieve a higher price. However, if downstream firms also possess market power, they will restrict output further in order to increase their profits given the input

---

[77] H. P. Marvel and S. McCafferty, "Resale Price Maintenance and Quality Certification" (1984) 15(3) *The RAND Journal of Economics*, pp. 346–59.
[78] *See, for example*, D. W. Carlton and J. M. Perloff, *Modern Industrial Organization* (3rd Ed., Addison Wesley, 1999), p. 524.

6. – Exclusive Dealing: Exclusive Obligations, Quasi-Exclusive Obligations and Rebates
Romano Subiotto QC and Justin Coombs

price. This restriction of downstream output benefits the downstream firm because it allows it to charge higher prices and earn higher profits, but it harms the upstream firm, which now earns profits on fewer sales of the input.

The downstream firm's decision to restrict output imposes a negative exter- **6.76** nality on the upstream firm (*i.e.*, when setting its output level, the downstream firm does not take account of the impact of restricting output on the profits of the upstream firm). This effect is shown diagrammatically in Annex 2.

Firms (collectively) and consumers are both worse off under double margin- **6.77** alisation than if price setting was coordinated:

- Consumers are worse off because prices are higher and output lower than with coordinated pricing; and,
- Firms are worse off because profits are lower.

The firms can avoid this outcome by entering into an exclusive dealing **6.78** arrangement and coordinating their pricing decisions. When setting prices for the final good, they can take account of the negative externality of the output restriction in the downstream market and choose the output level that maximises total industry profits. This output level is higher than under double marginalisation, so consumers are also better off. Since joint profits are higher, they should be able to agree on a transfer price that leaves both firms better off than under double marginalisation.

4.2.4.   Conclusion on the Chicago Critique

In summary, the Chicago Critique argues that exclusive dealing is unlikely to **6.79** be motivated by anticompetitive objectives. Instead, we should assume that it is motivated by the pursuit of efficiencies.

4.3.   Post-Chicago Models

4.3.1.   Introduction

The Chicago School provided an important challenge to the accepted view of **6.80** vertical restraints. It had a significant influence on the application of competition law, leading the US authorities to adopt a less interventionist approach towards vertical issues during the 1980s.

6. – Exclusive Dealing: Exclusive Obligations, Quasi-Exclusive Obligations and Rebates
Romano Subiotto QC and Justin Coombs

6.81   However, the Chicago Critique, and in particular the one-monopoly-profit result, are based on a set of assumptions. A number of economists have demonstrated that when these assumptions are relaxed, it can be profitable to use exclusive dealing to foreclose markets.

4.3.2.   Restoring Upstream Market Power

6.82   A key criticism of the one-monopoly-profit result is that it looks at the behaviour of firms and consumers at one point in time. In practice, decisions may be taken over a period of time. Downstream firms may make decisions today on what to purchase and how much to pay that commit them to these obligations for a significant period of time. In the meantime, the dominant firm can change its behaviour. For example, an oil and gas producer may make a long-term commitment to use a pipeline to deliver its product to the market. The pipeline owner can then take decisions about whom else to supply with access to the pipeline. Some economists have argued that, in this situation, an upstream firm will not be able to extract the full monopoly profit from downstream firms if it cannot commit to restrict future output.[79]

6.83   In order to earn monopoly profits, the dominant firm must restrict output to the monopolistic level so that it can charge a downstream firm the monopoly price. However, once it has sold this output level, the dominant firm has an incentive to supply more units of output to new entrants to the downstream market (provided the price paid still exceeds its marginal cost). These sales will lead to an increase in downstream output, reducing the price of the final good. The dominant firm benefits, but the downstream firms that paid the monopoly price for the input are now no longer able to cover their costs because of the fall in the price of the final good. The new entrant can cover its costs at the lower downstream price because it pays less for the input.

6.84   In this situation, the failure of the dominant firm to commit to restrict output will prevent it from earning its full monopoly profit. The initial downstream firms will know that the dominant firm has an incentive to increase sales (by

---

[79] P. Rey and J. Tirole, "A Primer on Foreclosure", in M. Armstrong and R. H. Porter (Eds.), *Handbook of Industrial Organization* (Vol. III, Amsterdam, North-Holland, 2007), pp. 2145–220. *See also*, O. Hart and J. Tirole, "Vertical integration and market foreclosure" (1990) *Brookings Papers on Economic Activity*, pp. 205–76. P. Baake, U. Kamecke and H.-T. Normann, "Vertical Foreclosure versus Downstream Competition with Capital Precommitment" (2004) 22(2) *International Journal of Industrial Organization*, pp. 185–92.

6. – Exclusive Dealing: Exclusive Obligations, Quasi-Exclusive Obligations and Rebates
Romano Subiotto QC and Justin Coombs

supplying new entrants), so they will not be prepared to pay the full monopoly price in the first place.

For example, suppose that an airport has a monopoly over an airport service **6.85** to a particular destination, and supplies landing and take-off slots to a particular airline. Initially, the airport will want to supply the volume of slots that maximises its monopoly profits. Now, the airline will know that once it has bought these slots, the airport has an incentive to sell further slots to other airlines. The airline will therefore not be willing to pay the monopoly price unless it receives some commitment that the airport will not supply its rivals.

The dominant firm can avoid this problem by entering into exclusive supply **6.86** agreements through which it commits not to supply new entrants.

Such arrangements could raise concerns since they involve reducing intra- **6.87** brand competition so that the upstream firm can ensure that it is able to fully exploit its pricing power. This might typically occur in the market for a luxury good, where a supplier commits only to supply a limited number of "high-end" retailers and not to supply retailers who compete vigorously on price.

However, such an arrangement need not necessarily raise competition con- **6.88** cerns. First, as explained above, such an arrangement may have efficiency benefits. Secondly, providing there is sufficient inter-brand competition (which might focus more on quality and innovation than on price), we should not be concerned about the level of intra-brand competition.

It is tempting to assume that if the upstream firm has a dominant position, there **6.89** must by definition be a lack of inter-brand competition, and that we should therefore be concerned by any restriction of intra-brand competition. However, since a dominant position can be found at market shares as low as 40 per cent, the dominant firm may well face some significant competition upstream.

4.3.3.   Defensive Leveraging

A second line of argument sees vertical restraints as a method by which a **6.90** dominant firm can protect or enhance its market power by excluding potential entrants or foreclosing existing upstream competitors.[80]

---

[80] D. W. Carlton and M. Waldman, "The Strategic Use of Tying to Preserve and Create Market Power in Evolving Industries" (2002) 33(2) *The RAND Journal of Economics*, pp. 194–220.

6. – Exclusive Dealing: Exclusive Obligations, Quasi-Exclusive Obligations and Rebates
Romano Subiotto QC and Justin Coombs

6.91   Firms entering the upstream market will either need to be able to supply downstream firms or enter as vertically integrated firms. If the upstream firm signs exclusive purchasing arrangements with all downstream firms, any new entrant will have to enter both the upstream market and the downstream market simultaneously, which can make entry more costly and risky. In particular, a firm that is more efficient than the incumbent in the upstream market might be deterred from entering both markets if it is not sufficiently efficient at the downstream activity. This effect could lead to the exclusion of more efficient entrants upstream.

6.92   The Chicago Critique described above suggested that such a strategy would fail because customers would not be willing to enter into exclusive purchasing arrangements unless they are compensated through lower prices, which therefore makes such arrangements unprofitable for the dominant firm. However, there are situations where the dominant firm might find it profitable to enter into such arrangements.

6.93   First, the dominant firm's customers might be unwilling to switch all of their purchases to rivals. They may have to buy at least some sales from the dominant firm. This might occur if the dominant firm supplies a "must-stock" brand. For example, in markets for branded consumer goods there may be a significant number of consumers who would purchase only the dominant firm's brand. Retailers may then be reluctant to de-stock this brand since they will lose a significant number of consumers. The dominant firm will be in a strong bargaining position so that it can impose exclusivity on its customers without paying "compensation" in the form of lower prices. In addition, in such a situation, it would be difficult for one of the dominant firm's rivals to capture a retailer's entire business. So we would not see rival manufacturers competing to become an exclusive supplier to each customer.

6.94   Secondly, if there are economies of scale upstream, an upstream rival would then need to be able to supply a large proportion of all customers in order to gain sufficient scale to compete effectively. This may be difficult if the dominant firm has exclusive purchasing agreements with a large proportion of customers, particularly if these agreements have a long duration and their termination dates are staggered – so it would take a long time for a rival to secure enough contracts to benefit from economies of scale.

6. – Exclusive Dealing: Exclusive Obligations, Quasi-Exclusive Obligations and Rebates
Romano Subiotto QC and Justin Coombs

4.4. *Quasi-exclusive Obligations*

Quasi-exclusive obligations raise essentially the same economic issues as the **6.95** exclusivity obligations described above. In both cases, there should be no assumption that an obligation will have an anticompetitive effect, even if it is imposed by a dominant firm. It is also important to consider whether the obligation may create efficiencies that might outweigh any impact on competition.

The various obligations described above are all analogous to an exclusive pur- **6.96** chasing requirement. In each case, the Commission's concern would be that the obligation, in effect, requires the customer to purchase all, or at least a significant proportion, of its requirements from the dominant firm. These obligations therefore raise the same economic issues as an exclusive purchasing requirement, discussed in the section above, and many of the same issues as rebates, discussed in Section III below. Indeed, as already mentioned above, rebates are arguably simply one type of quasi-exclusive obligation.

In summary, quasi-exclusive obligations are capable of foreclosing competitors **6.97** only if the dominant firm's competitors cannot replicate the dominant firm's contracts (and this effect will not harm consumers if the only reason why the competitor cannot replicate the dominant firm's offer is because it is not as efficient as the dominant firm). If an equally efficient competitor can simply offer the same contract terms and stand just as much chance of capturing the customer as the dominant firm, then there should be no competition concern. Firms can compete on the merits to become the quasi-exclusive supplier.

However, such competition on the merits might not be possible if competi- **6.98** tors cannot compete to supply the whole of each customer's demand. They might not be able to compete for the whole customer's requirements if the dominant firm supplies a must-stock product, or if competitors lack sufficient capacity that cannot easily be expanded, for example. In this situation, the dominant firm may be able to impose conditions that customers would not accept from competitors of the dominant firm.

If competitors are foreclosed from supplying certain customers, then this **6.99** could foreclose those competitors from the market. This will depend on the proportion of the market from which they are foreclosed and whether the

6. – Exclusive Dealing: Exclusive Obligations, Quasi-Exclusive Obligations and Rebates
Romano Subiotto QC and Justin Coombs

remaining demand allows them sufficient scale to compete effectively – which will depend on the importance of economies of scale.

6.100 Lastly, even if they produce anticompetitive effects, quasi-exclusive obligations may benefit consumers if they bring about significant efficiency benefits. These potential benefits were explained in the section above. Exclusive purchasing (and by extension quasi-exclusive obligations) may be necessary to incentivise manufacturers to make investments that are specific to one distributor, particularly if those investments might otherwise benefit rival manufacturers. Quasi-exclusive obligations may also help overcome the double-marginalisation problem. In addition to those effects, some kinds of quasi-exclusive obligations might provide the dominant firm with more certainty over future demand for its products, which can help it to reduce costs.

4.5. Conclusions

6.101 Unfortunately, economic theory does not provide any easy answers to the question of whether exclusive dealing will or will not benefit consumers. What it tells us is that there are many situations where exclusive dealing can produce efficiency benefits, but also some situations where it can create anticompetitive effects. As in most areas of unilateral conduct, it points towards an assessment of the facts of each case, with a presumption that these arrangements will benefit consumers unless there is a clear and well-supported theory of harm.

6.102 In the case of exclusive distribution, a key factor is likely to be the balance between inter-brand and intra-brand competition. While exclusive distribution can soften intra-brand competition, this should not be of concern provided sufficient inter-brand competition remains.

6.103 In the case of exclusive purchasing the key question is whether there is anything to stop the dominant firm's rivals from replicating its offer and competing to supply its customers on a similar exclusive basis. This is likely to depend on whether customers are free to move their entire purchase requirements away from the dominant firm, which might not be possible if the dominant firm supplies a must-stock brand, for example. An additional issue is whether there are economies of scale upstream and the extent and duration of the dominant firm's exclusive arrangements with the customer base. If rivals face significant economies of scale and a significant proportion of the market is covered by exclusive contracts of long duration, it may be difficult for a

6. – Exclusive Dealing: Exclusive Obligations, Quasi-Exclusive Obligations and Rebates
Romano Subiotto QC and Justin Coombs

competitor to break into the market. Similar issues are also relevant in the assessment of quasi-exclusive obligations and loyalty rebates discussed later in this chapter.

5.   Commission Enforcement Priorities

As part of the Commission's ongoing review of the application of Article **6.104** 102 TFEU, in February 2009, the Commission adopted the *Guidance Paper*. As was the case for the *Discussion Paper*, the purpose of the *Guidance Paper* was to highlight the Commission's increasingly effects-based approach to Article 102 TFEU cases[81] by laying down a framework of priorities that will allow stakeholders to know in what situations the Commission is most likely to intervene. This involves an explanation by the Commission as to how the dominant firm's allegedly abusive conduct is likely to restrict competition and thereby harm consumers. It should be noted that the Commission does not need to establish that the dominant undertaking's conduct actually harmed competition, only that there is convincing evidence that harm is likely.[82]

Regarding the exclusivity obligations, the Commission set forth a two-step **6.105** linear test based on the capacity of suppliers to compete on equal terms for each individual customer's entire demand.[83] Thus, the Commission's approach indirectly recalls the difference between contestable and non-contestable demand explained with regard to rebates.[84] If competitors can compete on equal terms for each individual customer's entire demand, exclusive purchasing obligations are generally unlikely to constitute an abuse of a dominant position, unless switching supplier is impossible because of the long-term duration of the obligation. On the contrary, if competitors cannot compete for the entire demand of a customer, then the exclusive obligation may amount to an abuse.

But when are competitors unable to compete for the entire demand? According **6.106** to the Commission, this happens where: (1) the dominant undertaking is an unavoidable trading partner (*e.g.*, where its product is a so-called "must stock item"

---

[81] As was seen, for example, in Case COMP/37.792 *Microsoft*, Commission Decision of 24 March 2004 ("*Microsoft Decision 2004*") not yet published.

[82] *Guidance Paper supra* note 1, para. 20.

[83] *Ibid.*, para. 36.

[84] *See* Section III on Rebates.

6. – Exclusive Dealing: Exclusive Obligations, Quasi-Exclusive Obligations and Rebates
Romano Subiotto QC and Justin Coombs

preferred by many consumers) or, (2) the competitors' capacity constraints do not allow them to satisfy the entire demand. In our opinion, either condition is almost always met by a dominant undertaking, therefore limiting the number of cases where an exclusivity obligation is *unlikely* to fall within Article 102 TFEU. Anyhow, it is worth noting that, whether those conditions are met or not, they do not provide the dominant undertaking with legal certainty in terms of the lawfulness of its conduct. The Commission leaves the door open to the possibility of finding an abuse, even in such a scenario.[85]

6.107   If the alleged conduct is likely to constitute an abuse, the second step of the Commission's test allows the dominant firm to rebut this finding of a likely negative effect by showing that the conduct creates efficiencies which leave consumers overall better off. This may be the case where the exclusive dealing arrangement is necessary in order to earn back certain relationship-specific investments made in order to supply specific customers.[86] However, and differently from the *Discussion Paper,* the Commission clearly states that compensation accorded to the purchaser in return for accepting the exclusivity obligation may be beneficial to it, but not increase overall consumer welfare.[87] Thus, according to the Commission, *"it would be wrong to conclude automatically from this that all the exclusive purchasing obligations, taken together, are beneficial for customers overall, including those currently not purchasing from the dominant undertaking, and the final consumers"*.[88] In other words, it does not matter how many customers will benefit from the obligation, since as far as the obligation harms other purchasers (not buying from the dominant undertaking) or some consumers, the obligation may infringe Article 102 TFEU.[89]

6.108   The underlying theme of the *Guidance Paper* is the adoption of a more effects-based approach to the application of Article 102 TFEU. This would seem to

---

[85] In addition to what is explicitly stated with regard to exclusive obligations, the Commission will also look at the following general factors, as it does for any form of abuse: the position of the dominant undertaking, the position of the dominant undertaking's competitors, the position of the customers or input suppliers, the extent of the allegedly abusive conduct, possible evidence of actual competitive foreclosure, direct evidence of any exclusionary strategy. *See Guidance Paper,* para. 20.

[86] *Ibid.,* para. 46.

[87] *Ibid.,* para. 34.

[88] *Ibid.*

[89] The Commission's *Guidance Paper* seems to treat quasi-exclusive obligations in a similar way as outright exclusivity obligations. *Ibid.,* para. 33.

6. – Exclusive Dealing: Exclusive Obligations, Quasi-Exclusive Obligations and Rebates
Romano Subiotto QC and Justin Coombs

involve the aligning of its application with that of Article 101 TFEU (with regards to which an effects-based approach has been used for some time).[90]

6. Future Developments

At present, future developments are difficult to foresee. In fact, no significant **6.109** case involving pure exclusivity obligations has been initiated following *Van den Bergh Foods* and the Commission's *Discussion Paper* and *Guidance Paper*. However, two significant points may be inferred from the Commission's *Guidance Paper*. First, the trend to regroup the different forms of abuses under a common umbrella, therefore focusing on the main effects of the abuse; this is, for instance, the case for exclusivity obligations, which are treated together with rebates. Secondly, the Commission's attempt to set objective criteria for determining the abuse. Those criteria are based, where possible, on economic parameters such as the contestable or non-contestable demand of a customer or clear cost benchmarks. However, despite the effort at simplification, it is often difficult to apply these objective criteria in practice. Thus, as far as exclusivity obligations are concerned, it is not easy to distinguish between the contestable and non-contestable demand. As a result, the dominant undertaking cannot be certain as to whether or not its conduct is violating competition rules.

III. Rebates

1. Definition and Types of Rebates

Rebate is the term used to describe a pricing discount generally given by a **6.110** manufacturer of a good to a wholesaler in return for a certain type of behaviour. The Commission defines conditional rebates in the *Guidance Paper* as *"rebates granted to customers to reward them for a particular form of purchasing behaviour. The usual nature of a conditional rebate is that the customer is given a rebate if its purchases over a defined reference period exceed a certain threshold. ..."*[91] Rebates are

---

[90] What has not been established, however, is a percentage threshold above which a requirements contract will automatically be considered as an exclusivity obligation and thus, as a likely consequence, abusive. By way of contrast, under Article 101 TFEU, a requirements contract for more than 80 per cent of the purchaser's total needs is treated as a "non-compete obligation". *See supra* note 18, Article 1(d). It remains to be seen whether a similar approach will be taken under Article 102 TFEU.

[91] *See Guidance Paper supra* note 1, para. 37.

6. – Exclusive Dealing: Exclusive Obligations, Quasi-Exclusive Obligations and Rebates
Romano Subiotto QC and Justin Coombs

a very common part of commercial life and originate from normal business concerns on both sides. A customer will expect a better deal if it brings a large amount of its business to one particular supplier; equally, suppliers will want to avail themselves of mechanisms that entice customers to remain loyal.[92]

6.111 The conditions attached to the rebate determine what type of rebate is at issue. The main distinction in this respect is between "loyalty rebates" and "quantity rebates". A loyalty or "fidelity" rebate involves the giving of a discount to a wholesaler on condition that the wholesaler buys all, or most, of its requirements from the manufacturer granting the discount. Such rebates are individualised in the sense that they depend on the purchasing practice of the particular wholesaler. Loyalty rebates are also generally associated with the notion of exclusivity as they aim to tie most, or all, of a wholesaler's purchases to one manufacturer. The closer they tend towards total exclusivity, the more likely loyalty rebates will be found to be objectionable. "Quantity" or "volume discounts", in contrast, involve giving customers a discount if their purchases exceed a specific amount. The amount in question is decided in advance by the manufacturer and is objective in the sense that it applies to all purchasers meeting the level necessary. Although quantity discounts can lead to exclusivity or quasi-exclusivity, this is not always the case. Courts are aware, however, that a quantity rebate is often used to disguise what is, in reality, a loyalty discount. This happens where the threshold level necessary to obtain the discount is set with the aim of corresponding to all or most of the customer's purchasing requirements.[93] What then appears to be an objective quantity discount is in fact a subjective loyalty discount.[94]

6.112 Another type of rebate is a "sales target scheme". This involves granting a discount to any purchaser whose sales exceed its own sales in the previous

---

[92] Rebate schemes are often used as a means of maintaining a current customer. For example, volume discounts are often applied as an incentive to keep a large customer, while carefully designed target discounts can be used to keep customers who are considered likely to take their business to another supplier.

[93] Obviously, this requires the supplier to be able to estimate accurately its customers' purchasing requirements. However, this requirement is likely to often be fulfilled in practice. For example, in the *Tomra* case, the General Court rejected Tomra's claim that the Commission had not demonstrated Tomra's ability to correctly estimate its customer demand requirements in order to establish individualised quantity commitments and individualised retroactive rebate schemes. Indeed, the Commission had stressed that, in addition to sometimes receiving estimates of future requirements from the customers themselves, Tomra had access to information related to customer purchases in the previous year(s), to other relevant data, such as the number and size of the customers' outlets and, finally, to Tomra's own market research. *See Tomra Judgment 2010 supra* note 56, paras 79–80.

[94] For examples of this practice, *see Hoffmann-La Roche supra* note 5; Case T-228/97 *Irish Sugar v Commission* ("*Irish Sugar*") [1999] ECR II-2969 and Case C-549/10 P *Tomra Systems and others v Commission*, not yet reported.

6. – Exclusive Dealing: Exclusive Obligations, Quasi-Exclusive Obligations and Rebates
Romano Subiotto QC and Justin Coombs

year. This type of scheme is a cross between the objective quantity discount, in that the general rule is fixed in advance and applies to everyone, and the individualised loyalty discount, insofar as the actual fact of receiving the discount is dependent on the customer's specific sales performance in relation to its own record from the previous year. This type of system is potentially anticompetitive as it encourages loyalty and does so where it counts most for the purchaser: at the margin.

The importance of the distinctions between different types of rebates lies in the fact that certain rebates are more susceptible to scrutiny by the Commission and the European courts than are others. For example, loyalty discounts attract more attention than quantity discounts. This is because they induce the customer to be loyal for the wrong reasons. The customer stays with the manufacturer because of the clever business mechanism the rebate represents, and not due to factors related to "competition on the merits". Such factors include the fact that the manufacturer offers a better service or a higher quality product. Similarly, individualised schemes are more likely to raise concern than standardised ones as they are more clearly aimed at achieving exclusivity. **6.113**

This brings us to another important issue in relation to rebates, which is their relationship with exclusivity. For rebate schemes, exclusivity is often, but not always present. In this regard, the *Guidance Paper* may be criticised for classifying conditional rebates as "exclusive dealing". First, rebates do not always imply outright exclusivity and, secondly, even if they do entail exclusive dealing with a customer, rebates should only be illegal if they involve pricing below cost and are conditional on such exclusivity.[95] **6.114**

Rebates are a contentious area of the law and have been the subject of much debate, particularly in recent years. They are highly problematic as it is far from obvious how to regulate them. Rebates do not necessarily involve sacrifice and often lead to lower prices, which in turn is good for consumers, who are supposed to be at the heart of what competition law strives to protect. It is thus hard to take a clear-cut position on the legality of rebates under EU competition law. In addition, many notions necessary to determine whether a given rebate scheme is lawful or not have themselves not been properly defined. Examples include concepts such as "competition on the merits" and **6.115**

---

[95] John Temple Lang makes this point succinctly in his article, J. Temple Lang, "A Question of Priorities – The European Commission New Guidance on Article 82 is Flawed" (2009) 8(2) *Competition Law Insight*, p. 3.

6. – Exclusive Dealing: Exclusive Obligations, Quasi-Exclusive Obligations and Rebates
Romano Subiotto QC and Justin Coombs

"normal competition". If we do not know what "good" competition is, it is difficult to know what it is not. Although perceived as being at the less serious end of the spectrum when compared to outright exclusivity agreements, questions regarding the legal status of rebates are often much more difficult.

1.1. *Historical Overview*

6.116 Decisions of the Commission and judgments of the European courts have evolved in their treatment of rebate schemes. Below is an attempt to trace this evolution and to distill some principles from the cases in order to identify the current law on rebates.

1.1.1. Hoffmann-La Roche, Court of Justice, 1979 (Exclusive Dealing)

6.117 *Hoffmann-La Roche*[96] is a landmark case in the area of rebates. Here, for the first time, the Court clearly elaborated on the distinction between loyalty rebates and quantity rebates. It based this distinction on the fact that loyalty rebates aim to prevent customers from obtaining their supplies from competing producers and the fact that their effect is to apply dissimilar conditions to equivalent transactions.[97] The Court held the rebates at issue to be loyalty inducing, despite the fact that they appeared to be *prima facie* quantity discounts. This was because Roche used to make estimates of the requirements of its customers for the year ahead so as to set the volumes for obtaining the rebate at similar levels. This enabled it to supply all or nearly all of each customer's requirements. The Court of Justice held that such loyalty rebates were prohibited by Article 102 TFEU as Hoffmann-La Roche was already dominant and the rebates resulted in a weakening of competition in the market.

6.118 One questionable aspect of the judgment is the strictness of the Court's approach towards loyalty rebates. There appears to be an absence of analysis of the effects of the rebate scheme in the judgment. A change is evident in later judgments, where effects of rebates are more often discussed, with particular emphasis on consumer harm.

---

[96] *See Hoffmann-La Roche supra* note 5.
[97] *Ibid.*, para. 90.

6. – Exclusive Dealing: Exclusive Obligations, Quasi-Exclusive Obligations and Rebates
Romano Subiotto QC and Justin Coombs

1.1.2. Michelin I, Court of Justice, 1985 (Individualised Volume Targets)

Michelin I[98] concerned target discounts whereby tyre dealers were rewarded for **6.119** achieving their own individual annual sales target in relation to the purchase of replacement tyres for vehicles in France. The scheme was set up to encourage each dealer to sell more Michelin tyres than it had in the previous year.

The Court of Justice began by distinguishing the case at hand from that at issue **6.120** in *Hoffmann-La Roche*. In *Michelin I*, the dealers were not required to enter into an exclusive dealing agreement or to obtain a specific proportion of their supplies from Michelin. The Court therefore considered it necessary to take all of the circumstances into account, particularly the criteria and rules governing the granting of the discount. The Court's inquiry centred on whether the discount tended *"to remove or restrict the buyer's freedom to choose his sources of supply, to bar competitors from access to the market, to apply dissimilar conditions to equivalent transactions with other trading parties or to strengthen the dominant position by distorting competition"*.[99]

Factors affecting the judgment of the Court that the rebates in question con- **6.121** stituted an abuse of Article 102 TFEU included: (1) the long reference period over which the rebate was calculated (one year);[100] (2) the wide divergence between Michelin's market share and those of its main competitors;[101] and, (3) the lack of transparency in the entire discount system of Michelin, whose rules changed over time and whose targets and scale of discounts were never communicated in writing to the dealers. The Court thus concluded that the scheme was designed to prevent dealers from being able to freely choose the most favourable offer on the market at any given time without suffering an appreciable economic disadvantage.[102]

1.1.3. BPB Industries, Court of First Instance, 1993
(Promotional Payments)

BPB Industries[103] involved discounts that were granted to customers in certain **6.122** areas in the United Kingdom if they bought more than a certain quantity of

---

[98] Case 322/81 *Nederlandsche Banden Industrie Michelin v Commission* ("*Michelin I*") [1983] ECR 3461.
[99] *Ibid.*, para. 73.
[100] *Ibid.*, para. 81.
[101] *Ibid.*, para. 82.
[102] *Ibid.*, para. 85.
[103] *See BPB Industries supra* note 13.

6. – Exclusive Dealing: Exclusive Obligations, Quasi-Exclusive Obligations and Rebates
Romano Subiotto QC and Justin Coombs

plasterboard from BPB. BPB argued that the discounts constituted normal competition and that it should have the right to defend its commercial interests.

6.123 Upholding the Commission Decision, which was later confirmed by the Court of Justice, the Court of First Instance acknowledged that promotional payments are a standard practice forming part of normal commercial life. In fact, the Court of First Instance expressly confirmed that "*exclusive purchasing commitments cannot, as a matter of principle, be prohibited*" and therefore are not *per se* abusive. The Court however limited this conclusion to "*normal competitive market situations*", emphasising the "*special responsibility*" of dominant undertakings not to impair genuine competition in the common market.[104] The exclusive purchasing commitments were therefore considered to be abusive. This solution was expressly justified by "*the fact that where … an economic operator holds a strong position in the market, the conclusion of exclusive supply contracts in respect of a substantial proportion of purchases constitutes an unacceptable obstacle to entry to that market*".[105]

6.124 The consideration that a "substantial proportion" of purchases were affected, thereby foreclosing other competitors, appears to be a decisive factor in the finding of an abuse.

1.1.4. Irish Sugar, Court of First Instance, 1999 (Individualised Volume Targets)

6.125 Evidence of the fact that the Court will look behind allegations that a rebate scheme is a quantity discount to see how it operates in practice can also be found in the case of *Irish Sugar*.[106] Here, the Court of First Instance rejected the argument that the rebates in question were quantity discounts because they were too closely related to the customer's total requirements for retail sugar.[107]

1.1.5. Michelin II, Court of First Instance, 2004 (Individualised and Standardised Target Rebates)

6.126 Michelin was again condemned by the European courts in *Michelin II*,[108] but this time in relation to replacement tyres for vehicles in the Netherlands. The

---

[104] *See BPB Industries supra* note 13, para. 67.
[105] *Ibid.*, para. 68.
[106] *See Irish Sugar supra* note 94.
[107] *Ibid.*, para. 213.
[108] *See Michelin II supra* note 53.

6. – Exclusive Dealing: Exclusive Obligations, Quasi-Exclusive Obligations and Rebates
Romano Subiotto QC and Justin Coombs

case concerned many types of loyalty-inducing payments, including both individualised target rebates and standardised target rebates. Unsurprisingly in light of previous cases, the Court of First Instance condemned the individualised target rebates as contrary to Article 102 TFEU. However, for the first time, the Court also condemned the standardised discounts at issue. The Court of First Instance began by posing almost a presumption of legality *vis-à-vis* quantity rebate systems. It emphasised in this regard that such a system will not infringe Article 102 TFEU unless the criteria and rules for granting the rebate reveal that the system is not based on an economically justified countervailing advantage.[109] The Court then went on to examine whether the rebates were justified by the volume of business they brought or by any economies of scale they allowed the supplier to make.[110] As Michelin provided no specific information in that regard,[111] the Court was forced to conclude that Michelin's system infringed Article 102 TFEU.

1.1.6. Prokent/Tomra, European Commission, 2006 (Quantity Commitments and Retroactive Rebates)

Prokent/Tomra[112] is an interesting case, in particular because it was the first **6.127** decision to have been issued after the *Discussion Paper* was published.[113] Commentary anticipating publication of the Decision suggested hope for a detailed analysis of the foreclosure effects of the rebates in question.[114] The Decision certainly attempts to analyse such effects and concludes for their existence in the case at hand. However, whether such analysis is sufficiently thorough and economics-based is open to question. The Commission's analysis was, in any event, upheld by both the General Court and the Court of Justice, which appeared reluctant to depart from the traditional form-based approach in favour of a more economic approach.[115]

---

[109] *See Michelin II supra* note 53, para. 59.

[110] *Ibid.*, para. 100.

[111] *Ibid.*, para. 108.

[112] *Tomra Decision 2006 supra* note 56.

[113] RBB Economics, *Tomra: Rolling Back Form-based Analysis of Rebates?*, RBB Brief 21, February 2007, p. 1.

[114] A. Jones and B. Sufrin, *EC Competition Law* (3rd Ed., Oxford, Oxford University Press, 2008), p. 513.

[115] *See Tomra Judgment 2010 supra* note 56; and *Tomra Judgment 2012 supra* note 56. The General Court found that the Commission had fulfilled its duty to carry out an "*assessment of all the circumstances and, thus, also of the context in which those agreements operate*" in order to determine whether the practices at issue were "*intended to restrict or foreclose competition on the relevant market or* [were] *capable of doing so*" (*see Tomra Judgment 2010 supra* note 56, para. 215). According to the General Court, the Commission even went beyond this requirement by analysing the actual effects of Tomra's practices (*Tomra Judgment 2010 supra* note 56, para. 219).

6. – Exclusive Dealing: Exclusive Obligations, Quasi-Exclusive Obligations and Rebates
Romano Subiotto QC and Justin Coombs

6.128   Tomra, a supplier of reverse vending machines (RVMs) and related products (in particular backroom equipment), was found to be a dominant supplier of such machines, enjoying a market share of 80 per cent or more in
various national markets. The company implemented various anticompetitive
practices, including exclusivity agreements as well as agreements containing
individualised quantity targets or individualised retroactive rebate schemes
(corresponding to the customers' total or almost total demand for RVM solutions). Regarding its examination of possible foreclosure effects, the Commission began by acknowledging that the main possible negative effect of rebates
is foreclosure of the market for competitors and potential competitors.[116] The
Commission's conclusion that the rebates *did* result in a foreclosure effect
involved a number of considerations. First, the Commission noted that Tomra
kept a stable market share in each national market and on the EEA market.
While on individual national markets the position of Tomra has varied in
different countries, its market share has always been on average around 80
per cent and never below 38 per cent.[117] Furthermore, while Tomra's market
position remained more or less unchanged, the market position of its rivals
continued to be weak, despite growth shocks that would normally lead to new
entry or increased market shares of rivals. On the contrary, some of the rivals
left the market either due to insolvency or due to acquisition.[118] The Commission also noted that there was a relation between the tied market demand
and the changes in position of the market players. Usually, Tomra would sell
a higher number of machines during the years when more of the total market
demand was covered by its exclusionary agreements.[119] Finally, the Commission made a few other observations on additional factors, which it considered
to be indicative of the exclusionary effect of Tomra's practices. For example,
notwithstanding occasional surges in demand and the fact that entry into the
relevant market was not exceedingly costly, the market continued to be almost
monopolistic throughout the reference period. The Commission concluded
by noting that some customers started purchasing more of the competing
products after the expiry of their agreements with Tomra.[120]

6.129   The level of economic analysis demonstrated by the Commission is more evident if one looks to its rebuttal of the economic arguments invoked by Tomra

---

[116] *Tomra Decision 2006 supra* note 56, para. 333.
[117] *Ibid.*, paras 335–36.
[118] *Ibid.*, paras 337–39.
[119] *Ibid.*, para. 340.
[120] *Ibid.*, paras 342–46.

6. – Exclusive Dealing: Exclusive Obligations, Quasi-Exclusive Obligations and Rebates
Romano Subiotto QC and Justin Coombs

to justify its rebate schemes. The Commission rejected the line of reasoning put forward in Tomra's economic study, mainly due to the fact that Tomra had made unjustified off-equilibrium assumptions, that is, the assumption that the incumbent as well as the competitor behave irrationally.[121] The Commission also highlighted the need to distinguish between *ex ante* and *ex post* analysis. Here, the Commission explained that when Tomra set the thresholds that a customer should reach in order to benefit from the rebate scheme, it did so based on the expected demand of its customers. To look in retrospect at what that demand actually was and then to attempt to rely on it to argue that the actual demand level did not correspond to the level at which the rebate was set is not meaningful because, according to the Commission, this *ex post* empirical evidence did not play any role when the level at which the rebates were set was being determined. The Commission thus concluded that Tomra's economic study was theoretically ill founded.[122] The Commission also held that Tomra had failed to submit any evidence to support its arguments concerning cost efficiencies.[123]

Though not entering into a detailed and complex economic assessment of **6.130** its own, the Commission responded to the economic arguments raised by Tomra with an arguably equal level of sophistication and rigor. It explained clearly why it believed the economic study put forward by Tomra was ill-founded. The Commission's analysis of a possible foreclosure effect is, however, less impressive. Unfortunately, the Commission did not go quite as far as the novel approach it proposed in its *Discussion Paper*, or the approach advocated in the *Guidance Paper* (which, admittedly, had not yet been written at that time). Instead, it confined itself to employing a reasoning that is, to a great extent, reminiscent of past cases, relying on easily observable factors, such as recent entry and market share. As mentioned, on appeal, the General Court and the Court of Justice declined Tomra's invitation to consider an effects-based approach and aligned themselves with the Commission's conclusions as regards foreclosure. In particular, Tomra claimed that the Commission should have analysed whether a competitor could still profitably remain on the RVM market by serving only the "contestable" part of the market, *i.e.*, the part of the demand not tied by Tomra's practices. For this purpose, according to Tomra, the Commission should have determined the "minimum viability threshold", *i.e.*, the minimum profitability necessary to operate on the RVM market. The Courts, however, rejected this argument by stating that "*foreclosure*

---

[121] *Tomra Decision 2006 supra* note 56, paras 364-69.

[122] *Ibid.*, para. 376.

[123] *Ibid.*, para. 391.

6. – Exclusive Dealing: Exclusive Obligations, Quasi-Exclusive Obligations and Rebates
Romano Subiotto QC and Justin Coombs

by a dominant undertaking of a substantial part of the market cannot be justified showing that the contestable part of the market is still sufficient to accommodate a limited number of competitors".[124] Indeed, first, competitors and customers should be able, respectively, to compete and benefit from competition on the entire market and not just on a portion of it.[125] Secondly, it should not be for the dominant undertaking to determine the number of viable competitors that may compete for the remaining contestable part of the demand.[126]

6.131 In addition, Tomra also criticised the Commission's failure to examine Tomra's costs and argued that a comparison between costs and prices was essential in order to establish that its retroactive rebates scheme restricted competition, as provided by the *Guidance Paper*.[127] However, the Court of Justice found that the invoicing of "negative prices", *i.e.*, prices below costs, was not a prerequisite for considering retroactive rebates to be abusive and that other circumstances were relevant instead, such as the rebates' ability to prevent customers from sourcing from competing producers.[128] Moreover, the Court, as suggested by Advocate General Mazák in his opinion,[129] stated that the *Guidance Paper* "*had no relevance to the legal assessment of … the contested decision, which was adopted in 2006*", *i.e.*, before the *Guidance Paper* was published.[130]

1.1.7. British Airways, Court of Justice, 2007 (Individualised Volume Targets)

6.132 The case of *British Airways*[131] originated from a complaint made by Virgin against British Airways ("BA") in which Virgin alleged that the incentives which BA gave to its agents to sell more BA tickets than they would otherwise have done, produced exclusionary effects and were thus contrary to

---

[124] *See Tomra Judgment 2010 supra* note 56, para. 241; and *Tomra Judgment 2012 supra* note 56, para. 42. In this respect, the General Court found that it would be artificial to determine the non-contestable part of the market without a prior analysis of the circumstances of the case, as carried out by the Commission in its decision (*Tomra Judgment 2010 supra* note 56, para. 242). The General Court found that Tomra's practices had foreclosed two fifths of total demand during the relevant timeframe and in the countries at issue, which was considered sufficient to constitute a "*considerable proportion*" of the market (*Tomra Judgment 2010 supra* note 56, para. 243).
[125] *Ibid.*, para. 241; and *Tomra Judgment 2012 supra* note 56, para. 42.
[126] *Ibid.*, para. 241; and *Ibid. supra* note 56, para. 42.
[127] *Tomra Judgment 2012 supra* note 56, paras 51–52.
[128] *Ibid. supra* note 56, paras 71–73.
[129] Advocate General Mazák in Case C-549/10 P *Tomra Systems and others v Commission*, not yet reported, para. 37.
[130] *Tomra Judgment 2012 supra* note 56, para. 81.
[131] Case T-219/99 *British Airways v Commission* ("*British Airways*") [2003] ECR II-5917.

6. – Exclusive Dealing: Exclusive Obligations, Quasi-Exclusive Obligations and Rebates
Romano Subiotto QC and Justin Coombs

Article 102 TFEU. BA's incentives included payments to agents for meeting or exceeding the amount of sales that they made in the previous year.

The judgment of the Court of First Instance could be said to constitute **6.133** explicit recognition of the fact that even loyalty-inducing rebate schemes are not *per se* abusive under Article 102 TFEU and may be justified on economic grounds. Although BA did not succeed in proving that its rebate scheme was justified in this way, the Court of First Instance, in this judgment at least, left the theoretical possibility open for an undertaking in a dominant position to justify loyalty rebates on economic grounds.[132] The judgment of the Court of Justice also came out after the publication of the *Discussion Paper* and yet did not seem to be influenced very much by the economic effects-based approach adopted therein.[133]

1.1.8. Intel, European Commission, 2009 (Conditional Rebates and Payments)

Intel[134] was decided by the Commission in May 2009. It is the first decision **6.134** issued by the Commission after the Commission published its *Guidance Paper*.[135] Although it did not apply to the Decision as proceedings were initiated before it was published, the Commission stated that its Decision was in line with the orientations set out in the *Guidance Paper*.

One of the practices engaged in by Intel, which was found to be in contraven- **6.135** tion of Article 102 TFEU, was the use of conditional rebates and payments. Intel was found to hold a dominant position in the worldwide x86 CPU market. Intel gave wholly or partially hidden rebates to computer manufacturers on condition that they bought all, or almost all, of their x86 CPUs from Intel. Such rebates were found to effectively prevent customers from choosing alternative products.[136] The percentage purchase requirements in order to benefit from the rebate varied from customer to customer. Some required total exclusivity (100 per cent), while others required less, for example 80 per cent. The

---

[132] Case T-219/99 *British Airways v Commission* ("*British Airways*") [2003] ECR II-5917, para. 271.

[133] Jones criticises the judgment of the Court of Justice for this, noting that, despite the issuance of the *Discussion Paper* in the interim period, the judgment of the Court of First Instance was "*upheld by the Court of Justice, largely on the basis of its previous case law*" (*see supra* note 114, p. 504).

[134] COMP/37.990 *Intel*, Commission Decision of 13 May 2009, not yet published. *See also* Press Release IP/09/745 of 13.05.2009.

[135] *See Guidance Paper supra* note 1.

[136] *Supra* note 134, paras 926–1001.

6. – Exclusive Dealing: Exclusive Obligations, Quasi-Exclusive Obligations and Rebates
Romano Subiotto QC and Justin Coombs

Commission made it clear that it did not object to rebates in themselves, but to the specific conditions attached to the rebate schemes run by Intel.

6.136 The Commission found that the rebates in question constituted fidelity rebates. Referring to the *Hoffmann-La Roche* case law, it concluded that the obligation for customers to obtain all or most of their requirements exclusively from Intel constituted an abuse of dominant position.[137]

6.137 Endorsing the formalistic *per se* approach adopted in this previous case law, the Commission considered that this finding was sufficient to establish a breach of Article 102 TFEU. However, it went on to conduct an economic analysis of the capability of the rebates to foreclose an "as efficient competitor" from the market. The Commission considered that this was required neither by case law nor by the *Guidance Paper* in order to conclude that a breach of Article 102 TFEU had been committed, since the latter did not apply to proceedings initiated before it was published. The Commission nevertheless decided to follow the methodology in the *Guidance Paper*. This was done for the sake of consistency with its intention to move towards an effects-based approach, expressed in numerous policy documents, but it is doubtful whether a negative outcome of the foreclosure test would have changed the Commission's conclusion.[138] The Commission applied this "as efficient competitor" test by relying on three factors: (1) the contestable share (*i.e.*, the amount of a customer's demand that can realistically be switched to a competitor in any given period); (2) a relevant time horizon; and, (3) a relevant measure of viable costs (in that case, average avoidable costs). If the rebate scheme amounts to pricing below average avoidable costs, an as efficient competitor would have to price its products below a viable level in order to gain the contestable share. The foreclosure effect would thereby be established. Applying this test to the case at hand, the Commission concluded that Intel's rebates were capable of having or likely to have anticompetitive foreclosure effects since even a competitor as efficient as Intel would be prevented from satisfying the computer manufacturers' requirements. This capacity to foreclose as efficient competitors was established by the fact that Intel was able to use the non-contestable share of demand of each customer as leverage to decrease the price for the contestable share of demand.[139] The way

---

[137] *Supra* note 134, para. 964.

[138] The Commission presents the economic analysis as an additional but not indispensable line of argumentation, "*on the top of showing that the conditions of the case-law have been fulfilled*" (*see* Case COMP/37.990 *Intel*, Commission Summary Decision of 22 September 2009, OJ 2009 C 227/13, para. 28).

[139] *Supra* note 134, para. 1005.

6. – Exclusive Dealing: Exclusive Obligations, Quasi-Exclusive Obligations and Rebates
Romano Subiotto QC and Justin Coombs

the Commission carried out this "as efficient competitor" analysis has however been criticised in academic literature.[140]

As to consumer harm, the Commission found that consumer choice in terms of price and quality would have been greater had consumers also been offered the product of their preferred OEM and/or retailer with x86 CPUs from Intel's competitors.[141] The Commission rejected arguments put forward by Intel attempting to justify the rebates. The Commission found that Intel had not submitted sufficient evidence to prove that the scheme merely constituted a reaction to price competition. In relation to alleged efficiencies, the Commission found that Intel had failed to establish the existence of such efficiencies and to demonstrate how the exclusivity agreements were necessary (or even suitable) in order to attain them.   **6.138**

Turning to the alleged objective justifications of Intel's practices, the Commission stated that a dominant company had to demonstrate that it had no equally effective alternative in achieving the legitimate goal with a less restrictive or less exclusionary effect and that the conduct is "proportionate", in the sense that the legitimate objectives pursued by Intel should not be outweighed by the exclusionary effects.[142] This appears to be a rather demanding threshold that was, according to the Commission, not met in the circumstances of the case.   **6.139**

The Commission therefore considered Intel's practices to be abusive, despite the fact that in the course of the investigation period, AMD had actually gained market shares and the price of x86 CPUs had decreased. In support of this finding of a *per se* abuse disconnected from the actual effects of the practices, the Commission referred to *Compagnie Maritime Belge:* "*the fact that the result sought is not achieved is not enough to avoid practice being characterised as an abuse of dominant position*".[143] As a result, it imposed a fine on Intel of €1.06 billion.   **6.140**

---

[140] In particular, Geradin challenges the Commission's determination of the "contestable share" of the demand relying on documents that were not available to Intel, contrary to the principle of legal certainty (*see* D. Geradin, "The Decision of the Commission of 13 May 2009 in the Intel Case: Where is the Foreclosure and Consumer Harm?", *TILEC Discussion Papers*, Paper No. 2010–022, October 16, 2009, pp. 17–8).

[141] *Supra* note 134, para. 1603.

[142] *Ibid.*, para. 1624.

[143] Joined Cases T-24-26 and 28/93 *Compagnie Maritime Belge Transports and others v Commission* [1996] ECR II-1201, para. 149.

6. – Exclusive Dealing: Exclusive Obligations, Quasi-Exclusive Obligations and Rebates
Romano Subiotto QC and Justin Coombs

6.141 The Decision is currently under appeal before the General Court. In addition to the alleged violation of its defence rights and the inappropriate level of the fine, Intel reproaches the Commission for having found that the rebates were *per se* abusive without having established their actual foreclosure effect. It argues that, in implementing the "as efficient competitor" test, the Commission failed to take account of the fact that the market was actually highly competitive. Indeed, AMD's share had increased from 8 to 22 per cent and prices had fallen by 36 per cent during the period of investigation. In essence, the appeal contends that the Commission has failed to apply the "effects-based" approach, stepping stone of the "modernisation" of Article 102 TFEU.

1.2. Existing Rules

6.142 The existing rules on rebates focus essentially on the question of foreclosure. There is no need to prove actual effects of the conduct. While consumer harm is the supposed guiding principle, it is examined through the lens of anticompetitive foreclosure, as will be seen from our examination of the *Guidance Paper* below. It may be regrettable, but a case from the Court of Justice is probably needed in order to make a decisive and complete shift away from potential anticompetitive foreclosure and towards proven consumer harm.

6.143 It is possible to look to recent case law of the Community courts to decipher the approach currently adopted when rebate schemes are at issue. *Intel*[144] may provide us with clues about the most up-to-date way that the Commission approaches potentially illegal rebate schemes. The Commission did not object to rebates in themselves but to the conditions Intel attached to those rebates. The "as efficient competitor test" was used to demonstrate the unfairness of the conditions. The Commission did rely on the consumer harm test, but only indirectly by pointing to evidence that Intel's rebates impaired the ability of rival manufacturers to compete and innovate. This way of approaching consumer harm appears consistent with previous case law. A European Commission Memo[145] on the Decision claimed that the case was based on a consistent pattern of court jurisprudence, including *Hoffmann-La Roche*,[146] *British Airways*[147] and *Irish Sugar*.[148] The Memo also pointed out that, while

---

[144] *Supra* note 134. *See also* Press Release IP/09/745 of 13 May 2009.
[145] Press Release MEMO/09/235 of 13 May 2009.
[146] *See Hoffmann-La Roche supra* note 5.
[147] *See British Airways supra* note 131.
[148] *See Irish Sugar supra* note 94.

6. – Exclusive Dealing: Exclusive Obligations, Quasi-Exclusive Obligations and Rebates
Romano Subiotto QC and Justin Coombs

the *Guidance Paper* did not apply to the case, since proceedings were initiated before it was issued, the Decision was nevertheless in line with the effects-based analysis put forward in the *Guidance Paper*.

Although the Commission does not adopt a *per se* approach to rebates, its stance **6.144** is undoubtedly still too rigorous. Arguably, there should be a need to prove actual effects. Furthermore, the possible defences, which may be invoked to justify the use of rebates, are interpreted strictly. Possible defences include the following: the rebate system is necessary in order to obtain cost advantages; the system is necessary in order to encourage customers to purchase greater quantities and so to avoid double marginalisation; and, the system is necessary in order to encourage the supplier to make relationship-specific investments so that it is able to supply a particular customer. While the complainant does not need to prove actual harm to consumers, the dominant undertaking, on the contrary, is required to *"provide all the evidence necessary to demonstrate that the conduct is objectively justified"*.[149] If a firm is relying on the efficiency defence, it must show that: (1) the efficiencies have been or are likely to be realised; (2) the conduct is indispensable to the realisation of those efficiencies; (3) the efficiencies outweigh negative effects; and, (4) the conduct does not eliminate effective competition.[150] The cases of *Prokent/Tomra* and *British Airways*, discussed above, demonstrate how difficult it can be to prove that a rebate scheme is objectively justified on economic grounds.

2.   Economics

2.1.   Introduction

A conditional rebate is a discount or price reduction that firms offer to cus- **6.145** tomers who meet certain conditions, normally when a customer reaches a volume target for their purchases.

Rebates are a form of price competition. They are one of the ways by which **6.146** firms reduce prices in order to win business. While this means that competition law should generally be in favour of firms offering rebates, there are some situations where rebates might have anticompetitive effects. Quantity-based

---

[149] *See Guidance Paper supra* note 1, para. 31.
[150] *Ibid.*, para. 30.

conditional rebates can in some circumstances have similar effects to exclusive purchasing obligations discussed above.

6.147   Given that rebates are a form of price competition, Article 102 TFEU needs to be applied carefully in order to avoid the risk of prohibiting procompetitive and proconsumer business practices. In practice however, as discussed above, the application of Article 102 TFEU to rebates is controversial. Cases such as *Michelin II* and *British Airways* have raised concerns that the law laid down by the courts may in fact have a chilling effect by focusing too much on the form of rebate schemes rather than their actual effects on competition and consumers.[151] At the same time, the European Commission has tried to provide some indication as to when rebates will or will not create anticompetitive effects in its *Guidance Paper*.[152]

6.148   In this section, we identify circumstances where rebates might have anticompetitive effects and compare this analysis with the (very different) approaches set out by the European courts on the one hand and the Commission on the other.

2.2.   Foreclosure Effects

6.149   As explained above, conditional rebates are a form of price reduction. Suppose that a firm charges a price of €100, but offers a €10 rebate on each purchase a customer makes once it has purchased 1,000 units. In effect, the price has been reduced from €100 to €90 once the volume target is met.

6.150   Since rebates are equivalent to a price cut, we should in principle be able to use the tests for predation established in the case law and set out in the Commission's *Guidance Paper* to assess whether a rebate has an anticompetitive effect. If the rebate causes the "effective price" (the price that a competitor must match to win a customer's business) to fall below cost, then there is a risk of an anticompetitive effect. If the effective price remains above cost, there should be no concern.

6.151   However, the effective price will depend on the design of the rebate scheme. It is therefore useful to distinguish between two types of rebates: incremental rebates and retroactive rebates. We will discuss each in turn.

---

[151] *See Michelin II supra* note 53; *British Airways supra* note 131; and Case C-95/04 P *British Airways* [2007] ECR I-02331.

[152] *See Guidance Paper supra* note 1, paras 37–45.

6. – Exclusive Dealing: Exclusive Obligations, Quasi-Exclusive Obligations and Rebates
Romano Subiotto QC and Justin Coombs

2.2.1. Incremental Rebates

An incremental rebate works as follows: using the example above, once the **6.152** customer has purchased 1,000 units, it will pay a reduced price of €90 on all *additional* purchases. In other words, it pays €100 for the first 999 units and €90 for the 1,000th unit onwards.

Using this example, suppose a customer has already purchased 999 units from **6.153** the dominant firm and is now looking to purchase some additional units. Once the threshold has been reached, a competitor offering an identical product will have to offer a price of €90 or less in order to take additional sales away from the dominant firm. So there will be no anticompetitive effect in this case unless €90 is below cost.

In practice, the impact of an incremental rebate will depend on whether the **6.154** competitor can compete for the whole business of the customer or only for some purchases. A rebate is more likely to raise concerns when customers are forced to make at least some purchases from the dominant firm. This situation might arise, for example, if new entrants have limited capacity relative to customers' demands. It might also arise if the dominant firm's product is a "must-stock brand". There may be some end consumers who are interested in purchasing only the dominant firm's product. As a consequence, distributors and retailers must stock some minimum volume of the dominant firm's product.

If the dominant firm has some secure base of assured sales, a concern can **6.155** arise that it might leverage that position to foreclose competitors from the potentially contestable portion of its customers' business. It does that by charging a high price for the assured sales (the volume below the quantity threshold) and a low price for contestable sales (above the threshold).

This leads to two preliminary questions in any analysis of incremental rebates: **6.156** (1) does the dominant firm enjoy some volume of assured sales that cannot be contested by competitors? and (2) does it set a volume threshold such that all contestable sales are sold at the rebated price? If the answer to both questions is yes, then a competitor will have to match the rebated price in order to compete for the contestable sales. The relevant question is whether this price level would foreclose an equally efficient competitor, which we can assess using the tests for predation discussed above.

6. – Exclusive Dealing: Exclusive Obligations, Quasi-Exclusive Obligations and Rebates
Romano Subiotto QC and Justin Coombs

6.157   If, in contrast, some or all of the sales below the threshold are contestable, the effective price the competitor must match is the average price across all contestable sales (which will lie somewhere between the initial price and the rebated price).

6.158   In its *Guidance Paper*, the Commission states that it will apply a predation test to assess whether the effective price has an anticompetitive effect. If the effective price is above long-run average incremental costs, the Commission will normally conclude that there is no anticompetitive effect. If the price is below average avoidable costs, the Commission will normally conclude that it is capable of having an exclusionary effect. If the effective price lies between these two measures of cost, the Commission will investigate further. In particular, it will consider whether rivals can use counter-strategies to compete with the dominant firm.[153]

2.2.2.   Retroactive Rebates

6.159   A retroactive rebate reduces the price of *all* units, including those already purchased to reach the volume threshold. Using the same example as above, if the rebate is retroactive, any customer who purchases up to 999 units will pay €100 per unit, but any customer who purchases 1,000 units or more will pay €90 for *all* units it purchases, including the first 999 units.

6.160   The distinction between incremental and retroactive rebates is important because a retroactive rebate can cause effective prices to be very low, or even negative, for the last units purchased to reach the threshold. In the example above, suppose a customer has already purchased 999 units and is considering whether to buy one additional unit. The effective price the customer pays for this 1,000th unit is not in fact €90, because purchasing this unit means it will receive a rebate worth €9,990 (€10 multiplied by 999 units) on their previous purchases. The effective price of the 1,000th unit is therefore *minus* €9,900.

6.161   Clearly, a negative price will fail any price cost test, but this does not necessarily mean that such a retroactive rebate will have an anticompetitive effect. The effect will depend on (1) how the volume threshold compares to customers' actual purchase requirements and (2) the proportion of sales below the volume threshold that are potentially contestable.

---

[153] *Guidance Paper supra* note 1, para. 44.

6. – Exclusive Dealing: Exclusive Obligations, Quasi-Exclusive Obligations and Rebates
Romano Subiotto QC and Justin Coombs

Figure 6.1 illustrates these relationships. The incumbent dominant firm sells to **6.162** a customer whose total purchase requirements are the quantity A. The quantity B is the dominant firm's captive sales to this customer, and the remaining quantity (A minus B) is the contestable purchases by the customer. The firm sets a price of P_1, but if the customer meets a volume target of X, it receives a retroactive rebate, which reduces prices for all purchases to P_2.

Figure 6.1: Application of Retroactive Rebate by Dominant Firm.

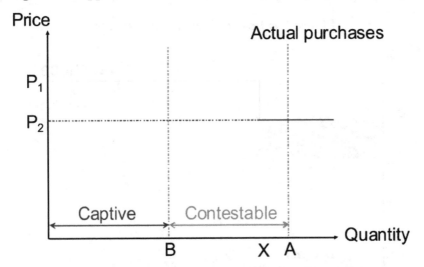

It is worth noting at this point that if, in contrast to the position shown in **6.163** Figure 6.1, the volume threshold was higher than the customer's total requirements (so X was above A), the rebate would have no effect. The customer would pay price P_1 for all purchases, and the only relevant question would be whether P_1 was a predatory price.

However, given the position shown in Figure 6.1, the customer will pay the **6.164** rebated price of P_2 if it purchases all its requirements from the dominant firm. The question we must then ask is: what effective price must a competitor offer in order to capture the customer's contestable sales (the quantity between B and A)?

Suppose that the customer switches all its contestable sales from the domi- **6.165** nant firm to a competitor. Previously, it could have purchased all of its

6. – Exclusive Dealing: Exclusive Obligations, Quasi-Exclusive Obligations and Rebates
Romano Subiotto QC and Justin Coombs

requirements from the dominant firm at a price of P_2, but now, the price it pays the dominant firm for the initial quantity B will increase to P_1. This is because its purchases from the dominant firm will now fall below the volume threshold, so it will lose the benefit of the rebate on the purchases it must make from the dominant firm. This lost rebate is shown by the shaded rectangle in Figure 6.2 (which equals the size of the rebate, P_1 minus P_2, multiplied by the quantity of non-contestable purchases, B).

Figure 6.2: Loss of Retroactive Rebate.

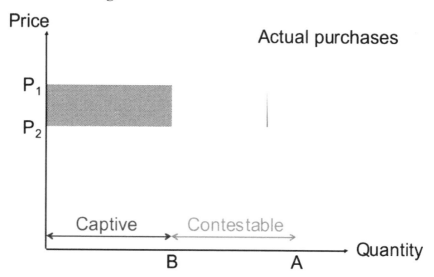

6.166 The competitor therefore has to offer a price below P_2 that compensates the customer for this lost rebate. This lower price is shown as P_3 in Figure 6.3. At a price of P_3, the competitor's price advantage over the dominant firm on the contestable purchases compensates the customer for the rebate lost on its captive purchases from the dominant firm. This is shown by the fact that the two shaded rectangles in Figure 6.3 are of equal size.

6.167 A retroactive rebate will therefore lead to effective prices, which are below the rebated price level. This phenomenon is sometimes called a "suction effect".

6. – Exclusive Dealing: Exclusive Obligations, Quasi-Exclusive Obligations and Rebates
Romano Subiotto QC and Justin Coombs

Figure 6.3: Suction Effect.

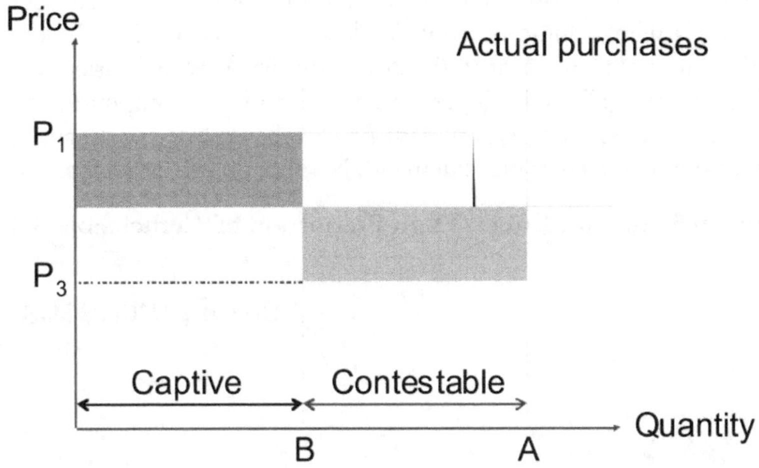

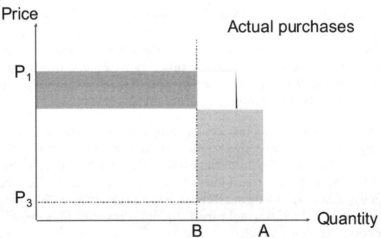

The extent of this suction effect depends on the proportion of sales that **6.168** are contestable. If this proportion is low (so B is high), the competitor must compensate the customer for the rebate lost on a high volume of sales. Moreover, this compensation must be paid by reducing the price across a small volume of contestable sales. Consequently, the competitor must offer a very low price, as shown in Figure 6.4. Over very small volumes, this price could become negative (as in the numerical example above).

Figure 6.4: Suction Effect/Low Proportion of Contestable Sales.

6. – Exclusive Dealing: Exclusive Obligations, Quasi-Exclusive Obligations and Rebates
Romano Subiotto QC and Justin Coombs

6.169 Conversely, if the proportion of contestable sales is high, the volume of sales on which the rebate is lost will be small, and this lower compensation can be spread over a high volume of contestable sales. Consequently, the competitor's price can be much closer to the dominant firm's rebated price, as shown in Figure 6.5. At the limit, if all sales are contestable, the competitor can compete simply by matching the dominant firm's rebated price of P_2 and capturing the whole of the customer's demand. No suction effect occurs.

Figure 6.5: Suction Effect/High Proportion of Contestable Sales.

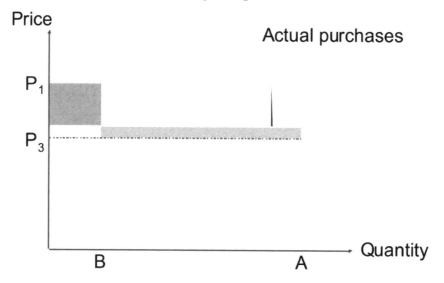

6.170 The analysis above shows that whether a retroactive rebate has a foreclosing effect is a complex question. The effective price a competitor has to match will depend on the relationships between the volume threshold, customers' actual purchase requirements and the proportion of sales, which are potentially contestable. Whether this effective price has an exclusionary effect will then depend on how it compares to the dominant firm's costs.

6.171 Even if this analysis shows that a competitor would be excluded from supplying the particular customer, this would not necessarily show whether the competitor would be excluded from the market. That would depend on whether the customer, or group of customers, where an exclusionary effect occurs, is such a significant part of the market that it would undermine the competitor's ability to enter and remain on the market. Could the competitor simply supply other customers, for example?

6. – Exclusive Dealing: Exclusive Obligations, Quasi-Exclusive Obligations and Rebates
Romano Subiotto QC and Justin Coombs

These complex economic issues have not had a noticeable impact on the case **6.172**
law, as reflected in *Michelin II* and *British Airways*.[154] In both of these cases, the
Commission found that volume-related retroactive rebates infringed Article
102 TFEU and the Court of First Instance upheld the Commission Decisions. In *British Airways* the Court of Justice upheld the judgment of the Court
of First Instance on appeal.

In both cases, the Court of First Instance upheld the Commission's conclu- **6.173**
sions that the retroactive rebate schemes involved infringed Article 102 TFEU
because they were capable of producing loyalty-inducing effects. In *British
Airways*, the Court of Justice stated that the relevant test was whether the
rebates *"are capable, first, of making market entry very difficult or impossible for competitors* [of the dominant firm] *and, secondly, of making it more difficult or impossible for
its* [customers] *to choose between various sources of supply or commercial partners"*.[155]

In principle, this would suggest undertaking the sort of analysis described **6.174**
above, but in practice, the Commission was not required to establish the
effective price faced by competitors or compare prices against any measure
of cost. Instead, the Court noted that the loyalty-inducing effect of a rebate
scheme is *"particularly strong"* when the rebate is retroactive.[156] This seems to
imply that any retroactive rebate will be found by the courts to be capable of
producing anticompetitive effects.

Despite the relatively formalistic approach of the courts, the Commission has **6.175**
shown a willingness to take a more effects-based approach. Its *Guidance Paper*
set out a sophisticated analysis based around four steps: (1) comparing the
volume threshold with the customer's purchase requirements; (2) assessing
the proportion of purchase requirements that are contestable; (3) calculating
the effective price over that volume; and then (4) comparing this price with
the dominant firm's costs.[157]

Whilst this approach is grounded in sound economic principles, it provides lit- **6.176**
tle legal certainty for dominant firms using retroactive rebates. In the case of

---

[154] *See Michelin II supra* note 53; *British Airways supra* note 131; and *supra* note 150.

[155] *See* Case C-95/04 P *supra* note 151, para. 68.

[156] *Ibid.*, para. 73.

[157] *See Guidance Paper supra* note 1, paras 41–4. In its decision in *Prokent/Tomra*, which pre-dates the *Guidance Paper*,
the Commission appears to have partially implemented this approach. It attempted to estimate effective prices
but did not compare them to any measure of costs. *See Tomra Decision 2006 supra* note 56.

6. – Exclusive Dealing: Exclusive Obligations, Quasi-Exclusive Obligations and Rebates
Romano Subiotto QC and Justin Coombs

predation or of an incremental rebate, a dominant firm will know the price that it is charging and must compare this price with its costs.[158] In the case of retro-active rebates, it must calculate the *effective* price that a competitor would need to match. This calculation requires information on customers that the dominant firm is unlikely to know with any certainty, so it is unlikely to be able to assess whether its rebates might be found to infringe Article 102 TFEU. Even if firms have this information, calculating the effective price for each customer is a complex process that firms are unlikely to be able to perform easily.

2.3. Efficiencies

6.177 As with exclusive dealing, there are many legitimate reasons why firms might use conditional rebates. At their simplest, they can be viewed as a form of price competition. They can also reflect the lower costs involved in supplying higher volumes to a customer. More generally, firms use conditional rebates because they provide strong incentives for customers to meet their volume targets, which can reduce the firm's costs and improve efficiency.

6.178 First, rebates can create the same efficiencies as exclusive purchasing, discussed in Section III.1.2 above:

6.179 If the parties negotiate over both price and volume, they will generally agree on higher volumes than they would if they agreed only on prices up front, which will benefit themselves but also final consumers. They will agree on higher volumes because they can eliminate inefficiencies associated with double marginalisation,[159] described in Section III.1.2 above.[160] Rebates can incentivise firms to make investments in their distributors. To the extent that they provide greater certainty over demand from each customer, they can help address problems of free-riding between upstream suppliers discussed in Section II.4.2 above.

6.180 In addition, rebates can create further efficiencies by providing greater certainty over future levels of output.

---

[158] With an incremental rebate the firm might not know the effective price a competitor will have to meet, but it will know that this price can be no lower than the rebated price.

[159] Double marginalisation occurs when the product is an input sold to a downstream firm and both the supplier and the customer have market power in their respective markets. They will then both increase prices to mono-poly levels to maximise their individual profits, but because they ignore the impact this has on the output of the other firm, their combined profits (and output) are lower than they would achieve if they jointly set prices.

[160] S. Kolay, J. A. Ordover and G. Shaffer, "All Units Discounts in Retail Contracts" (2004) 13(3) *Journal of Economics & Management Strategy*, pp. 429–59.

6. – Exclusive Dealing: Exclusive Obligations, Quasi-Exclusive Obligations and Rebates
Romano Subiotto QC and Justin Coombs

The supplier can plan input purchases and production more efficiently if it **6.181** knows more about the volumes it will be selling.[161] Firms incur certain fixed costs, such as the costs of setting up a production line. They may also incur costs that cannot be avoided in the short run, such as hiring staff or entering into long-term contracts with their own suppliers. If firms are uncertain about their future output, these costs may be too high – they may end up hiring more staff than necessary or buying raw materials that they do not need. Firms can minimise these costs if they can more accurately predict the quantities that they will supply and then size their operations accordingly.

Sometimes a supplier needs to invest in order to supply a particular customer. **6.182** It will be more willing to do so if it has an agreement that provides greater certainty about the volumes the customer will buy.[162] A supplier will make these investments if the expected profits exceed the costs involved. The more certainty a supplier has over its future sales to that customer, and therefore its future profits from that customer, the more likely it is to make that investment.

2.4.   Conclusions

In conclusion, conditional rebates are a form of price competition and they **6.183** can also achieve efficiencies that other pricing schemes are unlikely to match. However, they can also have anticompetitive effects very similar to an exclusive purchasing obligation.

As with exclusive purchasing, a key issue is whether the dominant firm has an **6.184** assured base of captive sales. In the absence of these captive sales, rebates will be anticompetitive only if they are predatory. In the case of incremental rebates, the assessment of their effects is in any case almost identical to an analysis of whether a price is predatory. In the case of retroactive rebates, the analysis is more complex and involves calculating the effective price that a competitor would have to match, which depends on the size of the assured base of sales. In practice, this makes it very difficult for dominant firms to assess whether their retroactive rebates may infringe Article 102 TFEU, since this analysis requires information on their customers that they are unlikely to possess.

---

[161] E. Feess and A. Wohlschlegel, *All-Unit Discounts and Competing Entrants*, paper presented at the American Law & Economics Association 18th Annual Meeting, May 16–17, 2008.
[162] *Supra* note 7; R. O'Donoghue and J. Temple Lang, "Defining Legitimate Competition: How to Clarify Pricing Abuses under Article 82 EC" (2002) 26(1) *Fordham International Law Journal*, pp. 83–162.

6. – Exclusive Dealing: Exclusive Obligations, Quasi-Exclusive Obligations and Rebates
Romano Subiotto QC and Justin Coombs

6.185 As with exclusive purchasing, a further question is whether the proportion of the market that might be foreclosed in this way is large enough to exclude those competitors from the market – which will depend both on the size of the remaining contestable demand and the significance of economies of scale.

6.186 Lastly, any anticompetitive effect needs to be balanced against the efficiencies that rebates, which are essentially a form of price competition, can create.

3. Commission Enforcement Priorities

6.187 The Commission initiated a review of its approach to Article 102 TFEU in 2005. Its first significant step in that process came in December 2005, when DG Competition issued the *Discussion Paper*[163] setting out possible principles for the Commission's application of Article 102 TFEU to exclusionary abuses. In the *Discussion Paper*, rebates are treated as a separate kind of exclusionary abuse and are dealt with alongside single branding.[164] The *Discussion Paper* draws a clear distinction between conditional and unconditional rebates,[165] and explains how the Commission's assessment will vary depending on which type of rebate system is at issue.[166]

6.188 The *Discussion Paper* resulted in mixed reactions but, on the whole, received much criticism. For example, Bill Allan[167] criticised the Commission for using a "disarmingly simple" test in order to judge whether or not a conditional rebate is lawful. Not all commentary on the *Discussion Paper* was so harsh, however. For a more nuanced approach, one can look to Victoria Mertikopoulou's article.[168]

---

[163] *See Discussion Paper supra* note 30.

[164] *Ibid.*, paras 134–76.

[165] *Ibid.*, para. 137.

[166] *Ibid.*, paras 151–76.

[167] Allan also criticised the application of principles developed in relation to predatory pricing to unconditional rebates as being *"unduly restrictive"*. Allan claims the Commission was too cautious in its attempt to strike the right balance between prohibiting rebates due to their possible anticompetitive effects and allowing them due to their potential to produce procompetitive effects. Finally, he concludes his comments on rebates by arguing that the Commission restricts unnecessarily the possibility of invoking efficiency defences and advocates the meeting competition defence as constituting an additional possible justification for otherwise unlawful rebate schemes (*see* B. Allan, "A Commentary on DG Competition's Discussion Paper" (2006) 2(1) *Competition Policy International*, pp. 42–82).

[168] V. Mertikopoulou, "DG Competition's Discussion Paper on the Application of Article 82 EC to Exclusionary Abuses: the Proposed Economic Reform from a Legal Point of View" (2007) 28(4) *European Competition Law Review*, pp. 241–51.

6. – Exclusive Dealing: Exclusive Obligations, Quasi-Exclusive Obligations and Rebates
Romano Subiotto QC and Justin Coombs

She comments that the Commission has gone a *"long way in modernizing EC competition rules"* and notes that an *"emphasis on economics"* is evident from the *Discussion Paper*. She too, however, levels some criticism against the *Discussion Paper*, listing problems involved in employing the equally efficient competitor test. She deplores the confusion between the concepts of predation and rebates, which she believes the *Discussion Paper* creates, and regrets the absence of emphasis on the traditional distinction between quantity and loyalty rebates.

Three years on, the long-awaited next step by the Commission came with the publication of the *Guidance Paper*.[169] Although the *Guidance Paper* is not legally binding[170] and is certainly not beyond criticism,[171] it is to be welcomed insofar as it represents a positive step in the right direction and a notable improvement on its predecessor, the *Discussion Paper* of 2005. **6.189**

The general tenor of the literature following publication of the *Guidance Paper* seems to be positive regarding the Commission's attempt to focus on consumer harm and to tend towards a more economics based approach. However, a consistent theme emerging in the aftermath of the *Guidance Paper* is the mix of confusion, ambiguity, and contradiction inherent in the publication, which results in a lack of legal certainty. Such uncertainty is regrettable, particularly as the *Guidance Paper* was essentially aimed at providing more clarity for businesses trying to determine whether their behaviour would be considered unlawful under Article 102 TFEU.[172] This is of particular importance as, in this historically problematic area of the law, there are often important financial interests at stake for the undertakings concerned. **6.190**

Part of the confusion is undoubtedly due to the fact that the Commission attempted, on the one hand, to respect the formality of the old case law, and, on the other, to introduce some novel economic thinking into the approach it proposes for future cases. This inevitably entailed a balancing act, which left some unhappy with the result. One central criticism relating to this confusion **6.191**

---

[169] *See Guidance Paper supra* note 1.

[170] The Commission itself makes this clear from the outset by stating at page 1 of the *Guidance Paper* that the document *"has no enforcement status"*.

[171] *See*, for example, J. Killick and A. Komninos, "Schizophrenia in the Commission's Article 82 Guidance Paper: Formalism Alongside Increased Recourse to Economic Analysis" (2009), 2(1) *CPI Antitrust Chronicle*.

[172] *See Guidance Paper supra* note 1, para. 2.

6. – Exclusive Dealing: Exclusive Obligations, Quasi-Exclusive Obligations and Rebates
Romano Subiotto QC and Justin Coombs

is the way in which the Commission refers to the consumer harm test.[173] The Commission supposedly places it at the heart of the analysis, and yet, phrases coming directly after mention of the test seem to undermine its role in the Commission's assessment. For example, paragraph 5 of the *Guidance Paper* refers to harm to consumers but then immediately after speaks of the importance of protecting the competitive process.[174] Other types of qualifications add to the uncertainty created by the *Guidance Paper*.[175] From now on, rivals that are not currently efficient, but are likely to become efficient in the future, will be taken into account by the Commission. As Derek Ridyard points out, *"this simply begs the question of how the Commission proposes to make this assessment of potential future efficiency, and of how dominant firms should second guess that judgment in evaluating whether they are obliged to accommodate a less efficient rival"*.[176] Furthermore, the Commission plans to examine whether *"realistic and effective counterstrategies are open to rivals"*. Again, it is hard to know what sort of behaviour the Commission would consider here.

6.192 Under section III of the *Guidance Paper*, which deals with the Commission's general approach to exclusionary conduct, the Commission lists the specific factors it will take into account in determining whether there is consumer harm. In fact, the factors only go towards demonstrating whether competitors are being foreclosed. The Commission does not require separate proof of consumer harm but seems ready to assume its existence from the fact that foreclosure is likely. Such an assumption is evident in the statement from the *Guidance Paper* that the Commission's enforcement activity must ensure that *"dominant undertakings do not impair effective competition by foreclosing their rivals in an anti-competitive way <u>and thus having an adverse impact on consumer welfare</u>"* (emphasis added).[177] Looking at the only Commission Decision published since the *Guidance Paper* was issued,[178] it is interesting to note that, although, as seen above, the *Guidance Paper* was not applicable to the Commission's Decision in *Intel*, the Commission linked anticompetitive conduct to consumer harm in a way similar to that in the *Guidance Paper*. The Commission held that foreclosure of

---

[173] J. Killick and A. Komninos *supra* note 171, pp. 5–6.

[174] The very same criticism is also made by Y. Katsoulacos, "Some Critical Comments on the Commission's Guidance Paper on Art. 82 EC" (2009) 2(1) *CPI Antitrust Chronicle*, p. 4.

[175] For a longer discussion of the uncertainties raised by the *Guidance Paper*, *see supra* note 95.

[176] D. Ridyard, "The Commission's Article 82 Guidelines: Some Reflections on the Economic Issues" (2009) 30(5), *European Competition Law Review*, p. 234.

[177] *See Guidance Paper supra* note 1, para.19.

[178] *Supra* note 134.

6. – Exclusive Dealing: Exclusive Obligations, Quasi-Exclusive Obligations and Rebates
Romano Subiotto QC and Justin Coombs

Intel's rivals led to consumer harm in the form of reduced choice in terms of the variety and prices of products available.

Overall, it can be said that the *Guidance Paper* is indispensable but insufficient. **6.193** It is useful in introducing, to some extent, more economics and effects-based thinking and in removing some of the uncertainties, which lingered after the *Discussion Paper* of 2005. It does not, however, answer all questions and it creates some problems of their own. John Temple Lang encourages the Commission to supplement the *Guidance Paper* with a notice on exploitative abuses, discrimination and reprisals. He also calls for the Commission to support its guidance papers on Article 102 TFEU by solid and clear legal reasoning.[179] Others make an implicit suggestion that the hands of the Commission are tied and that it is up to the courts to bring about real change in this area.[180] Whichever course of action is to be followed, it is clear that this is not the end of the story on the desirable treatment of rebate systems under Article 102 TFEU.

4. Future Developments

Any future developments are largely dependent on case law, as the *Discussion* **6.194** *Paper* and the *Guidance Paper* are of persuasive authority only, especially as far as national authorities and national courts are concerned. There is no indication that the case law is likely to take a dramatic turn towards the absolute application of effects-based principles. This is evident from the recent cases of the Commission in *Intel*[181] and of the courts in *Tomra* (September 2010 and April 2012)[182] and *British Airways* (March 2007).[183] While the General Court could decide to move towards a more effects-based approach when reviewing the *Intel* decision (in which the Commission applied the methodology of the *Guidance Paper*), it remains to be seen if it will choose to do so. Since the conclusion reached by the Commission in *Intel* was ultimately independent of the outcome of its economic analysis, the General Court may well decide to adjudicate the *Intel* decision without regard to the Commission's analysis.

---

[179] *Supra* note 95, p. 5.
[180] G. Zohios, "Commission Guidance Paper on the Application of Art. 82: A Step Towards Modernization or a Step Away?" (2009) 2(1) *CPI Antitrust Chronicle*, p. 7.
[181] *Supra* note 134.
[182] *See Tomra Judgment 2010 supra* note 56; and *Tomra Judgment 2012 supra* note 56.
[183] *See Case* C-95/04 *supra* note 151.

6. – Exclusive Dealing: Exclusive Obligations, Quasi-Exclusive Obligations and Rebates
Romano Subiotto QC and Justin Coombs

6.195   In any event, it is hoped that both the Commission and the courts will strike a balance in the future between a formal approach and an effects-based approach when assessing rebate schemes brought to their attention. It is important to distinguish carefully between the cases that justify intervention and those where the natural forces of the market should be allowed to operate without interference.

6.196   In any case, the legal debate surrounding the treatment of rebate schemes is still very much alive. A definitive answer on which liability standard should be applied has yet to be given. Nicholas Economides,[184] examined various possible liability standards in this context and proposed a structured rule of reason approach that focuses more on consumer surplus comparisons than on cost savings. Maybe if the Commission could clearly distinguish between consumer harm on the one hand and anticompetitive foreclosure on the other, we would already be on the way towards a clearer and more sound conceptual basis for assessing the legality of rebate systems from a European law perspective.

IV.   Conclusions

6.197   In conclusion, the *Guidance Paper* is to be welcomed as advancing the Commission's application of Article 102 TFEU to exclusivity and rebate schemes. In particular, it has helped shift the emphasis of the analysis to a focus on economic effects. However, there are still areas where the Commission's approach could benefit from further review.

6.198   First, the Commission still seems very reluctant to acknowledge the potential efficiency benefits of these practices. This contrasts, in particular, with its approach under Article 101 TFEU. More generally, there still appears to be some gap between the more effects-based approach under Article 101 TFEU and continuing remnants of a *per se* approach under Article 102 TFEU, in particular in respect of exclusive purchasing.

6.199   Secondly, the approach to conditional rebates appears to leave a gap between the *Guidance Paper* and actual practice, and also sets out an approach that is too complex to provide useful guidance to firms. Conditional rebates are a form of price competition. They can also achieve efficiencies that other pricing

---

[184] N. Economides, "Loyalty/Requirement Rebates and the Antitrust Modernization Commission: What is the Appropriate Liability Standard?" *New York University Law and Economics Research Papers*, Paper No. 09–15, June 29, 2009.

6. – Exclusive Dealing: Exclusive Obligations, Quasi-Exclusive Obligations and Rebates
Romano Subiotto QC and Justin Coombs

schemes are unlikely to match. However, recent judgments of the European courts seem to have in practice treated retroactive rebates as close to a *per se* prohibition of Article 102 TFEU.

The Commission has tried to redress this problem by setting out in its *Guidance Paper* an approach that would identify whether or not a retroactive rebate will have an anticompetitive effect. The Commission's approach is based on sound economic analysis but it is too complex, with too many uncertain variables, to allow a dominant firm to assess whether or not its pricing scheme will infringe Article 102 TFEU. Dominant firms are increasingly taking the view that any type of retroactive rebate creates too much antitrust risk and are reluctant to use such schemes at all. **6.200**

This is clearly an unsatisfactory outcome. Competition law should not place a blanket prohibition on a business practice, which is often procompetitive and proconsumer. **6.201**

In the United States, courts have often taken the opposite approach to the European Union courts. In many cases (such as *Barry Wright v ITT Grinnel, Concord Boat v Brunswick,* and *Virgin Atlantic Airways v British Airways*), retroactive rebates have been viewed as legal provided that the average price across all units is not predatory.[185] This approach would provide a great deal of legal certainty but is perhaps a step too far. Indeed, the US Department of Justice has declared that it does not rule out the possibility that retroactive rebates could create anticompetitive effects when the average price across all units is above costs.[186] **6.202**

The judgment of the General Court in *Intel* will hopefully help to clarify the law in this area, while giving economic analysis a more central role. **6.203**

---

[185] *Barry Wright v ITT Grinnel,* 724 F.2d 227 (1st Cir. 1983); *Concord Boat v Brunswick,* 207 F.3d 1039 (8th Cir. 2000); *Virgin Atlantic Airways v British Airways,* 257 F.3d 256 (2nd Cir. 2001). The contrast is perhaps best illustrated by the experience of British Airways. Its volume-related discounts to travel agents were prohibited in Europe, but found to be legal in the United States. For a useful summary of these cases, *see* US Department of Justice, *Competition and Monopoly: Single-Firm Conduct Under Section 2 of the Sherman Act,* September 2008, pp. 108–10. It should be noted that the legal position of retroactive rebates in the United States is unclear since no case has been decided by the Supreme Court.

[186] *Ibid.,* pp. 116–17.

6. – Exclusive Dealing: Exclusive Obligations, Quasi-Exclusive Obligations and Rebates
Romano Subiotto QC and Justin Coombs

Annex 1

6.204 The "single-monopoly-profit" result is illustrated in Figure A.1 below and Figures A.2 and A.3 on the following pages.

Figure A.1: Upstream Monopolist.

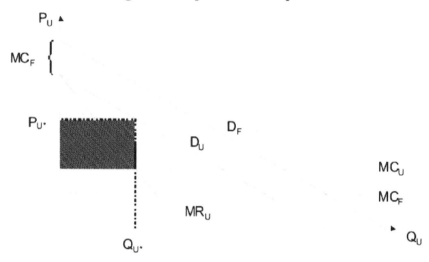

6.205 We make the following assumptions in this analysis:

6.206 There is an upstream monopolist producing a good U, which is used by downstream firms to produce the downstream good F.

6.207 The good U is used only to produce the downstream good F. It has no other uses.

6.208 The input U is used in fixed proportions to produce the downstream good F. In other words, each unit of F always requires the same number of units of U to produce it. This assumption is realistic in some, but not all, industries. For example, cars and engines are used in fixed proportions. Car manufacturers do not sell cars with two engines or half an engine. In contrast, airplanes sometimes use two, three, or four engines. Aircraft and engines are not used in fixed proportions. For simplicity, we assume that each unit of F requires one unit of U.

6. – Exclusive Dealing: Exclusive Obligations, Quasi-Exclusive Obligations and Rebates
Romano Subiotto QC and Justin Coombs

The upstream monopolist has a constant marginal cost. **6.209**

All downstream firms have the same constant marginal costs as each other. **6.210**

Figure A.1 shows the demand curve (D_U) faced by the upstream monopolist. **6.211** The demand curve D_U is called a "derived demand". It is the demand for U by the downstream firms producing F and, therefore, depends on the demand they face for their output of F. In other words, the demand for U is derived from the demand for F.

The derivation of the demand curve D_U is shown in Figure A.1. The demand **6.212** for U is equal to the downstream demand for F (shown as D_F in Figure A.1) less the downstream marginal cost of producing F (MC_F). The maximum that the downstream firms will be willing to pay for any unit of U is the price they receive for F less their own marginal cost. The demand curve D_U therefore sits below the demand curve D_F, and the distance between them is equal to the downstream marginal costs (MC_F) at every quantity.

For example, suppose that the constant downstream marginal cost (MC_F) is **6.213** €10, and that there is demand for 10 units of the final good at a price of €100. At this quantity, the maximum price the upstream monopolist can charge is €90 (€100 minus €10).

The upstream monopolist maximises its profit by supplying the quantity $Q_U{}^*$, **6.214** where its marginal cost, MC_U, equals its marginal revenue, MR_U. The shaded area on Figure A.1 shows the upstream monopolist's profit.

Suppose the monopolist now uses exclusive dealing to create a downstream **6.215** monopoly supplier of F, and in return receives a share of the downstream firm's profits. We want to know whether monopolising the downstream market will increase industry profits. If industry profits do not increase, there is no incentive to monopolise the downstream market. Figure A.2 looks at industry profits if there are monopolies both upstream and downstream.

The industry demand curve is the downstream demand curve D_F, and the **6.216** industry's marginal cost is shown by the curve MC_{U+F}, which equals the sum of the upstream marginal cost MC_U and the downstream marginal cost MC_F. Industry profits are maximised supplying the quantity $Q_F{}^*$, where industry marginal cost, MC_{U+F}, equals industry marginal revenue MR_F. The shaded area in Figure A.2 shows the industry profit.

6. – Exclusive Dealing: Exclusive Obligations, Quasi-Exclusive Obligations and Rebates
Romano Subiotto QC and Justin Coombs

Figure A.2: Industry Profits.

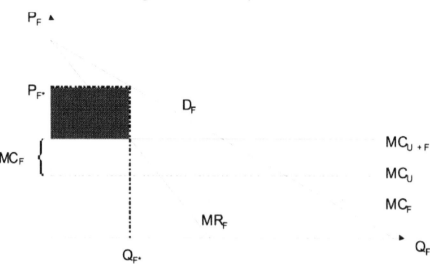

6.217 Figure A.3 superimposes the equilibrium in Figure A.1 over the equilibrium in Figure A.2. We can do this because one unit of F is used to produce one unit of U. We see that the same output is supplied in both cases: Q_U^* equals Q_F^*. We also see that industry profit is the same whether there is a monopoly in both U and F, or only in U.

Figure A.3: Profits of an Upstream Monopoly and an Upstream and Downstream Monopoly.

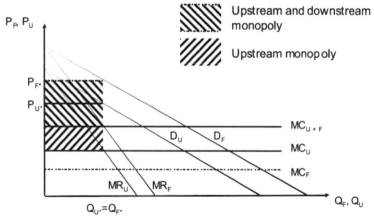

6. – Exclusive Dealing: Exclusive Obligations, Quasi-Exclusive Obligations and Rebates
Romano Subiotto QC and Justin Coombs

In summary, there is only one monopoly profit to be exploited, and the **6.218** monopolist could already capture the whole monopoly profit through the price that it charged for U. It gains nothing from monopolising F as well.

Annex 2

Figure A.4 illustrates the double marginalisation problem. The market demand **6.219** is shown by the demand curve D. We assume that the input is used by the downstream firm in fixed proportions of one unit of the input for every unit of the downstream good produced. For simplicity, we also assume that there is a single downstream monopolist, although the same key result occurs if we have downstream oligopolists engaging in Cournot-style competition. To make the diagram easier to read, we also assume that downstream marginal costs are zero.

The upstream monopolist charges a price P_U^*, equating its marginal cost **6.220** (MC_U) and its marginal revenue (MR_U) at output Q_U^*. However, this price then becomes the marginal cost faced by the downstream firm. Since the downstream firm is also a monopolist it will equate marginal cost with marginal revenue and will purchase only Q_F^*, charging consumers P_F^*.

Figure A.4: Double Marginalisation.

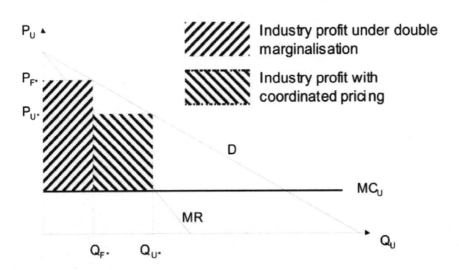

6. – Exclusive Dealing: Exclusive Obligations, Quasi-Exclusive Obligations and Rebates
Romano Subiotto QC and Justin Coombs

6.221 The consequence is that industry profit would be higher if the upstream firm coordinated its pricing with the downstream firm. They would then set a final price of P_U and supply the output Q_U. Industry profits would be higher, so the two firms should be able to agree a set of prices that leaves them both better off than under double marginalisation. Interestingly, though, consumers would also be better off since output would be higher and prices would be lower.

Refusal to Deal

*Maurits Dolmans and Matthew Bennett**

I.   Introduction

The law on refusal to deal is perhaps one of the most controversial topics in   **7.1**
the field of competition law, for various reasons. The cases tend to be public
and hotly debated, arising in areas such as information technology, telecommunications, energy and life sciences that are drivers of economic development. Fines can be very high. The criteria are not always clear. A duty to deal
interferes with two basic principles of the free market system: the freedom
to choose one's contract partner and exclusivity of property rights including
intellectual property. Balancing these principles against freedom to compete
requires a thoughtful analysis of policy objectives that may depend on political
decisions, may change over time, and may lead to different outcomes between
industries. Finally, it is one of the areas where the law differs most between the
two leading jurisdictions with a deep antitrust history, the United States and the
European Union.

To define clear criteria to identify an abusive refusal to deal, it is necessary   **7.2**
first to understand the economic considerations for and against refusals to
deal (Section II on economic analysis), as well as the legal framework in the
TFEU (Section III) that determines to what extent these considerations are
recognised in law and how they should be balanced (Section I.1 on freedom
of contract and property right and Section I.2 on the analytical framework
and concepts for balancing these against the objectives of competition policy). Sections IV and V are more practical, and describe the conditions for an

---

* Maurits dedicates his contribution to this chapter to the memory of Howard S. Weber, 1946–2007, of Hogan &
Hartson, gifted co-counsel in parts of the *Microsoft* case, but also a most interesting, loyal and warm person, imbued
with integrity, humanity, and a passion for justice, music, history, travel, his family, and his cello. He is missed as a
friend.

7. – Refuse to Deal
Maurits Dolmans and Matthew Bennett

abusive refusal to supply, derived from the case law in this area. This chapter will conclude with a discussion of remedies (Section VI).

II. Framework for Economic Analysis

7.3   Like many areas in competition economics, refusal to supply is a practice that may generate both benefits and harm to consumers. There is no reason to presume that refusal to supply by a dominant undertaking is necessarily abusive. Indeed, as we outline below, there are good reasons why competition law generally allows undertakings, including dominant ones, the freedom to choose their trading partners. This section sets out the economic reasoning that lies behind the legal view that refusal to supply should be found abusive only in exceptional circumstances.

7.4   The section starts by setting out the different types of refusal to supply (Section II.1). It then discusses the potential benefits to consumers of allowing firms to refuse to supply their products to competitors (Section II.2) and how refusals to supply might impact dynamic competition and the incentives of firms to invest or innovate (Section II.3). The fourth part describes how refusals to supply might be used to foreclose competition and harm consumers (Section II.4), followed by a conclusion (Section II.5).

1. What is a Refusal to Supply?

7.5   Refusal to supply can occur within a number of different industry structures. First, a vertically integrated firm may have a key input that is required to create a derivative product. This may be because it has the sole right to make the product (for example due to a patent), or simply because it controls access to the input (for example due to sole ownership). In this case, the firm refuses to supply the input to downstream competitors (*see* Figure 7.1). Of course, an integrated firm without a monopoly position upstream may also choose not to supply downstream competitors. However, as will be seen, refusals from vertically integrated companies with significant market power form both the majority of the case law and economic literature. Correspondingly, they also form the majority of the analysis within this section. A firm without upstream market power would normally have incentives to supply downstream rivals in order to gain upstream market share and gain revenues knowing that a rival will supply the input if it does not.

7. – Refuse to Deal
Maurits Dolmans and Matthew Bennett

Figure 7.1: Refusal to Supply by a Vertically Integrated Company.

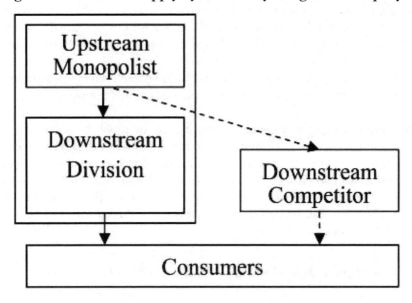

Figure 7.2: Refusal to Supply by an Non-vertically Integrated Company.

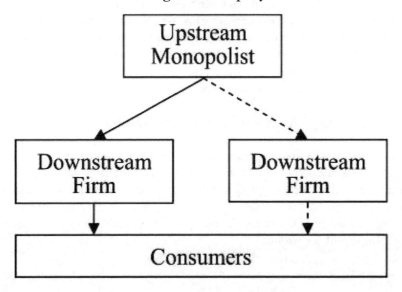

7. – Refuse to Deal
Maurits Dolmans and Matthew Bennett

7.6 Secondly, a non-vertically integrated monopoly upstream supplier of a key input may choose to limit the number of downstream firms with whom it partners to create a final product. For example, the owner of a patent may decide that it only wants to license its patent to selected manufacturers, who invest in further development of complementary technology. Likewise, the owner of a scarce resource may only want to sell this resource to a limited number of downstream firms. This non-integrated refusal to supply is illustrated in Figure 7.2.

7.7 The third setting involves selected distribution or retailing. A manufacturer may choose to retail or distribute its product by itself, or through other retail or distribution partners. In these cases, the manufacturer may refuse to supply its product to certain distributors or retailers. Whilst this chapter discusses some of the economics of such agreements, we refer the interested reader to a fuller discussion of vertical agreements under Article 101 TFEU, a topic outside the scope of this book.

2. Why Might a Refusal to Supply be Beneficial to Consumers?

7.8 Firms normally have an incentive to find the best partners for their products. Finding the best downstream partner for their products allows upstream firms to sell more, and make greater profits. In most cases, this will benefit rather than harm consumers. This section outlines how refusals to supply are often necessary for a manufacturer to provide the correct incentives for downstream firms to incorporate, market, or sell its products. In particular, it looks at each of the main theories regarding why refusal to supply may be efficient and provide consumer benefits. This section does not consider the dynamic benefits to innovation that a refusal to supply may or may not generate. These are discussed separately in Section II.3.

2.1. Refusal to Supply in Order to Minimise Double Marginalisation

7.9 The concept of double marginalisation has been well understood for some time and the intuition behind it is fairly simple.[1] Firms charge margins on their products in order to make profits. However, if the manufacturing and sale of a product involves two stages by two different firms, then each firm tends to charge a margin. This raises the prospect of a double margin – that is, a margin on top of a margin.

---

[1] J. J. Spengler, "Vertical Integration and Antitrust Policy" (1950) 58(4) *Journal of Political Economy*, pp. 347–52.

7. – Refuse to Deal
Maurits Dolmans and Matthew Bennett

The higher the aggregate margin, the lower the quantity demanded downstream and hence the lower the quantity sold upstream. When the upstream and downstream firms are separate, the downstream firm does not take account of the negative effect that doubling the margin has on the upstream firm's profit: it only takes account of the direct effect of the higher margin on its own profit. **7.10**

A single, vertically integrated firm setting a downstream price seeks to maximise the entire system profit rather than only the profit made downstream. This vertically integrated price is lower than the non-vertically integrated price. The vertically integrated firm internalises the fact that raising the downstream price reduces both the quantity supplied and profits made upstream. Thus, relative to a non-vertically integrated structure, vertical integration both reduces consumer prices and increases the aggregate system profit. **7.11**

In a context of double marginalisation, a refusal to supply to less efficient or non-innovative firms may be a rational strategy for vertically integrated firms. Downstream competitors that are equally or less efficient – and even firms that are more efficient downstream – may charge a higher price than the vertically integrated firm. Refusing to supply such competitors may be both beneficial to the vertically integrated firm (by increasing its sales) and to consumers (by removing the double marginalisation). **7.12**

The extent of double marginalisation depends on the degree of competition both upstream and downstream. The greater the degree of competition downstream, the lower the downstream margin. At the limit, under perfect competition, there is no downstream margin and hence no double marginalisation issue. The same applies to the upstream firm. Correspondingly, double marginalisation is only likely to be a significant issue when the upstream and downstream markets are not fully competitive which may be the case, for instance, if there are economies of scale or scope. **7.13**

Vertical integration is not the only way to align the upstream and downstream firms. It may be possible to replicate the vertically integrated structure through the use of contracts. At its simplest, this is achieved by a two-part tariff consisting of a fixed amount, independent of quantity sold, and a variable amount depending upon the quantity. The upstream firm sets the variable portion of its charge equal to the marginal cost of producing the input. This reduces the upstream margin to (close to) zero and allows the downstream firm to capture **7.14**

7. – Refuse to Deal
Maurits Dolmans and Matthew Bennett

the entire vertically integrated system profits by setting the profit-maximising price. The upstream firm can then set a fixed charge, sometimes termed as the "franchise fee", at a level that divides up the system profits appropriately.[2]

7.15 Using such a tariff structure may, however, not be possible, in particular where the upstream supplier attempts to set the franchise fee at the complete system profit level. Where there is considerable uncertainty downstream, or the downstream firm is risk adverse, the downstream firm is unlikely to want to sign such a contract.[3] By paying the upstream firm the full monopoly profit in an upfront franchise fee, the downstream firm holds all the risk of demand not being fulfilled, whilst the upstream firm holds none. Correspondingly, with significant uncertainty and risk adversity, it may not be possible to replicate the benefits of the vertically integrated structure through two-part tariffs.

7.16 Refusals to supply may also play a role in setting the franchise fee and hence internalise the double marginalisation problem. In order for an owner of a patent to maximise the franchise fee, it will only license its product to one downstream firm, as licensing it to a greater number of non-innovative firms may reduce the profits it can make. For this reason, it may choose to refuse to license other downstream rivals. However, as noted in Section II.4, such a refusal to supply may also have detrimental effects.

2.2. Refusal to Supply in Order to Maintain Quality

7.17 A second reason why an upstream firm may refuse to supply a downstream firm is because it does not believe that the downstream firm's quality is sufficiently high. This is pertinent where the upstream firm's brand is noticeable in the end product, or where quality affects volumes of sales. The upstream firm may not want to see its products sold alongside, or as part of, a product that may erode its brand image. For example, a car tyre manufacturer may not want to supply a car manufacturer whose products have a poor reputation. If there are problems with the car, or the car is unsafe, it may not only be the

---

[2] Other contracts that can achieve the equivalence of a vertically integrated structure include minimum sales quantity (where the minimum quantity is set at or above the monopoly level), maximum retail price maintenance (where the maximum price is set at or below the monopoly level) and, as discussed below, territorial protection. *See* G. F. Mathewson and R.A. Winter, "An Economic Theory of Vertical Restraints" (1984) 15(1) *The RAND Journal of Economics*, pp. 27–38.

[3] For a discussion of the equivalence of different types of vertical restraints including two part tariffs, *see* P. Rey and J. Tirole, "The Logic of Vertical Restraints" (1986) 76 *American Economic Review*, pp. 921–39.

7. – Refuse to Deal
Maurits Dolmans and Matthew Bennett

car manufacturer's reputation that is affected, but also the tyre manufacturer's reputation.

This is also relevant when one considers distribution and retail arrangements.[4] **7.18** Upstream manufacturers gain from their distributors and retailers making efforts to sell their products. For example, a more prominent position in supermarkets is more likely to increase the manufacturer's sales. Likewise, retail sales staff with specific knowledge of the manufacturer's product will increase the sales of its product. Thus, manufacturers may refuse to supply retailers who do not meet certain minimum standards of distribution.[5]

In both cases, there is a parallel with the double marginalisation issue previ- **7.19** ously discussed. When the downstream firm picks its level of quality, or sales effort, it looks to maximise the amount of profits it makes downstream. If it is not vertically integrated, it will not internalise the impact of lower sales effort or quality on the upstream firms' sales or reputation. Like double marginalisation, the failure by the downstream firm to take this externality into account results in lower than optimal service/quality levels, and hence lower than optimal system profits.

Vertical integration combined with a refusal to supply other downstream **7.20** firms is one way of solving the problem. Another way may be to refuse to supply downstream firms that do not meet certain quality, or sales effort, criteria. Although beyond the scope of this chapter, this provides much of the underlying rationale for the treatment of exclusive and selective distribution under Article 101 TFEU.

2.3. *Refusal to Supply in Order to Prevent Downstream Free-riding*

A manufacturer's desire to maintain its partners' quality standards creates **7.21** a further potentially beneficial rationale for refusal to supply – to prevent free-riding.[6] If an upstream manufacturer wants to provide incentives for its

---

[4] *See* H. P. Marvel and S. McCafferty, "Resale Price Maintenance and Quality Certification" (1984) 15(3) *The RAND Journal of Economics*, pp. 346–59.

[5] In addition, like the tyre manufacturer, branded product manufacturers may not want to be associated with lower quality retailers due to reputation reasons. For example manufacturers of highly branded perfumes may not want their products to be sold in discount stores alongside air fresheners.

[6] *See* L. G. Telser, "Why Should A Manufacturer Want Fair Trade?" (1960) 3 *Journal of Law and Economics*, pp. 86–105. *See also supra* note 2, G. F. Mathewson and R. A. Winter, pp. 27–38.

7. – Refuse to Deal
Maurits Dolmans and Matthew Bennett

downstream retailers to invest in sales efforts or quality, it needs to ensure that these investments do not also benefit retailers who do not invest. Failure to do this may result in a situation akin to the prisoner dilemma. All the retailers (as well as the manufacturer) would benefit if everyone invested in the effort, but each retailer would have the temptation to free-ride and not invest in the effort. The result may be a situation where no retailer wants to invest for fear of other retailers free-riding on its investment.

7.22   For example, suppose that a retailer, at the behest of the upstream television manufacturer, creates a sales area to display televisions and invests in training assistants in the key features of the manufacturer's televisions. Suppose that the upstream manufacturer is also obliged to sell its televisions to Internet retailers without any conditions. The retailer who has incurred the costs to train its staff wants to recoup those costs by charging a higher price for the television. The Internet retailer, without those costs, can charge a lower price. If the brick-and-mortar retailer tries to charge higher prices, it risks consumers buying the television from the Internet retailers. Worse, if consumers value the investment, the store owner risks consumers coming to the store to view and select their television (thus causing the retailer costs), and then going to the Internet retailer to buy it at the cheaper price.[7]

7.23   The implication is that where investments cannot be fully realised by the distributor or retailer, there is a possibility that no one will make the investment. The result is that the manufacturer is worse off because it sells less. However, consumers may also be worse off if they value the service that the retailer will no longer provide.

7.24   Of course, the upstream firm may be able to mitigate this problem by drawing up contracts specifying minimum quality standards for all its distributors or retailers. However, this may not always be possible. In particular, it is readily acknowledged in the economics literature that complete contracts are difficult

---

[7] A nice example of free-riding was Dixon.co.uk's advertising campaign in September 2009. Dixons placed a series of advertisements that told consumers to go to high end retail stores, talk to the sales staff to find out which is the best television for them, and then go to Dixons.co.uk online and buy it cheaper. The advertisement alluding to John Lewis stated: "*Step into middle England's best loved department store* [John Lewis], *stroll through haberdashery to the audio visual department where an awfully well brought up young man will bend over backwards to find the right TV for you, then go to Dixons.co.uk and buy it.*"

7. – Refuse to Deal
Maurits Dolmans and Matthew Bennett

to write.[8] Moreover, even if such contracts are possible to draft, they may be costly to enforce.

One way of solving this problem is to allocate exclusive geographic territories **7.25** to a single retailer or distributor, thus eliminating free-riding. The ability to allocate exclusive territories will depend upon the manufacturer's ability to refuse to supply other distributors or retailers within that territory, including Internet retailers. An alternative to exclusive geographic territories is selective distribution. Once again, the ability to refuse to supply those firms that do not meet the required standards is integral to such agreements.

2.4. Refusal to Supply to Prevent Upstream Free-riding

A free-riding problem may also exist upstream. Investments that the down- **7.26** stream firm makes in order to improve sales may not be specific to one upstream firm. In this case, other upstream suppliers may also benefit from the investment that the downstream firm makes. This creates a free riding problem upstream: the upstream firm wants to provide the downstream firm with funding in order to make the investments to improve its sales, but it does not want other upstream rivals to benefit as well.[9]

For example, an upstream perfume manufacturer may be willing to supply **7.27** retailers with a cabinet in order to ensure that its perfumes are displayed in a desirable manner. But if the perfume manufacturer cannot guarantee that the retailer will not display rival perfumes in the same cabinet, then the perfume manufacturer may not be willing to provide it. The potential for rival perfume manufacturers to free-ride on the perfume manufacturer's investment deters it from making the investment.

The result is identical to the downstream free-riding result: the upstream firm **7.28** invests a sub-optimal amount into the downstream retail environment. The possibility of upstream free-riding creates negative incentives for the upstream

---

[8] *See, e.g.*, Tirole (1999) who classifies the causes of incomplete contracts into three categories (1) the difficulty in foreseeing unforeseen contingencies, (2) the costs of writing contracts and (3) the costs of enforcing contracts. J. Tirole, "Incomplete Contracts: Where Do We Stand?" (1999) 67(4) *Econometrica*, p. 781.

[9] Depken et al (2002) test the theory of upstream free-riding in the context of US dairy industry. Dairy farmers subsidise generic campaigns to promote milk; however, the authors find that the level of investment is suboptimal with respect to joint profit maximisation. C. A. Depken, D. R. Kamerschen and A. Snow, "Generic Advertising of Intermediate Goods: Theory and Evidence on Free Riding" (2002) 20(3) *Review of Industrial Organization*, pp. 205–20.

7. – Refuse to Deal
Maurits Dolmans and Matthew Bennett

manufacturer. One solution to this problem is for the manufacturer to sign non-compete agreements with the retailer. Another solution may be to sign contracts with the retailer that stipulate what the retailer is allowed to do. However, both solutions require some ability for the manufacturer to refuse to supply those retailers who do not agree to its conditions.

2.5. *Refusal to Supply in Order to Reduce Hold-up Problems*

7.29 Firms may need to make investments that are highly specific to a particular product or manufacturer. The more specific it is to a firm, the less it can be used for other firms.[10] Such firm specific investments may create the risk of being opportunistically "held-up" after they have been sunk.[11]

7.30 Hold-ups can occur either upstream or downstream. In the context of a hold-up originating upstream, an upstream manufacturer may ask a retailer to install a display that can only fit its products. The retailer may ask for some additional margin to fund the additional investment. However, once the downstream firm has sunk the investment, the upstream firm can opportunistically appropriate the benefits from the investment without paying for them. First, the upstream firm may simply try to withhold supplies in an attempt to renegotiate the contract or impose additional conditions. Because the downstream firm has already invested the cost, and it cannot recover that investment or use it for another product, it may be in a weak bargaining position with the manufacturer. Secondly, once the downstream investment has been sunk, the upstream firm may allow other downstream firms to enter and free-ride on the investment. This will benefit the upstream firm, but harm the downstream firm.

7.31 Knowing that such opportunistic possibilities exist for the manufacturer, downstream firms may not make the investment unless the manufacturer can commit, or contract, not to exploit it once the investment has been made.[12]

---

[10] This is the opposite of the upstream free-riding problem discussed above. When investments are completely firm specific there is no possibility of free-riding.

[11] Williamson (1983) lists a number of different contexts in which asset specificity may arise, (1) site location specificity – being located in the same geographic site; (2) physical asset specificity – having products with design characteristics which mean they can't be used elsewhere; (3) human asset specificity – having human capital that is highly trained in a specific product; (4) dedicated assets – assets invested that would not have been made except for prospect of partner sales; and (5) intangible assets – brand assets that cannot easily be transferred. O. Williamson, "Credible Commitments: Using Hostages to Support Exchange" (1983) 73 *American Economic Review*, pp. 519–40.

[12] This was articulated by Williamson (1971) as "On the one hand, it may be prohibitively costly, if not infeasible, to specify contractually the full range of contingencies and stipulate appropriate responses between stages.

7. – Refuse to Deal
Maurits Dolmans and Matthew Bennett

One such commitment device is an exclusive territory. By providing the distributor with an exclusive territory, the manufacturer provides a commitment that it will not expropriate the downstream distributor's investment. First, it increases the downstream firm's relative bargaining power. Secondly, exclusive territories remove the possibility of the upstream firm allowing other distributors (or its own downstream business) to free-ride on the downstream firm's investment. Once again, the use of exclusive territories or selective distribution requires firms having an ability to refuse to supply all downstream firms.

Another example of refusal to supply which may help resolve a hold-up problem arises in patent licensing, especially (but not exclusively) in the context of *de jure* or *de facto* standards. In a situation where the licensee might otherwise hold up the patentee, a patentee may refuse to license its patents to a prospective licensee unless the latter promises to cross-license its patents to the former. Whilst the literature on this is currently scarce, the ability to reciprocate the threat of a refusal to supply and the corresponding mutually assured destruction may result in an efficient outcome if it results in neither of the firms holding each other up. **7.32**

As stated above, hold-ups may also originate from downstream. If an upstream firm invests in research and development in order to create a new product or process, there may be a temptation for the downstream firm to try and appropriate that investment *ex post* by only paying the marginal cost of the product. Such appropriation may be particularly problematic in the case of process innovations, where it may be difficult to prevent expropriation given the lack of a tangible good. The granting of patents and associated rights to enforce the exclusion that patents entail is a key element in solving the potential for hold-up. **7.33**

2.6. *Refusal to Supply in Order to Facilitate Price Discrimination*

Finally, an upstream firm may want to refuse to supply downstream competitors in order to allow it to price discriminate between different sets of consumers **7.34**

On the other hand, if the contract is seriously incomplete in these respects but, once the original negotiations are settled, the contracting parties are locked into a bilateral exchange, the divergent interests between the parties will predictably lead to individually opportunistic behaviour and joint losses." O. Williamson, "The Vertical Integration of Production: Market Failure Considerations" (1971) 61 *American Economic Review*, pp. 112–23. *See also* O. Williamson, *Markets and Hierarchies: Analysis and Antitrust Implications* (New York, The Free Press, 1975).

7. – Refuse to Deal
Maurits Dolmans and Matthew Bennett

downstream. Such price discrimination can either be across different sets of consumers or within the context of add-on services such as aftermarkets.[13]

7.35 For example, within the context of add-on services, a manufacturer may wish to offer maintenance services for its installed base at a price above the marginal cost in order to contribute to the overall fixed cost (including service staff) for providing a service that may cover thinly populated areas. The fact that it is pricing above marginal cost provides incentives for rival maintenance services to enter and undercut the vertically integrated firm. This may reduce the vertically integrated firm's ability to cross-subsidise customers which are supplied below cost.

7.36 Whether refusals to supply spare parts or consumables to rival maintenance suppliers in order to facilitate price discrimination in such a case benefits consumers or not depends upon the specific circumstances. At very simple static analysis, the consumers paying below cost will benefit from the refusal to supply, whilst the consumers paying above cost will be harmed. Overall, it is often very difficult to draw strong predictions regarding how price discrimination will affect static consumer welfare, even leaving aside more complicated issues regarding dynamic competition effects.[14] However, a necessary (but not sufficient) condition of price discrimination to increase aggregate welfare is that price discrimination increases aggregate output.[15] Intuitively, if aggregate output is not increasing after the refusal to supply restores price discrimination, then consumers who benefit will not outweigh the consumers who lose.

3.   Refusal to Supply and the Incentives to Invest and Innovate

7.37 The sections above have thus far concentrated on how refusals to supply may provide benefits to price, quantity and quality in a static setting. However,

---

[13] For a more general discussion of price discrimination literature *see* Armstrong (2006) who concludes that "*The welfare effects of allowing price discrimination are ambiguous, both with monopoly and with oligopoly supply*". M. Armstrong, "Price discrimination" (2006) *MPRA Paper*, ID 4693.

[14] For example price discrimination may also have the dynamic effects of intensifying competition, or may facilitate restricting entry, as is discussed in Section II.4. *See Ibid.*

[15] Schmalensee (1981) showed that, if demand for the products is independent and marginal costs are constant, the total output must increase with price discrimination in order for total welfare to increase. This general result was later extended for competition and non-linear cost functions. R. Schmalensee, "Output and Welfare Implications of Monopolistic Third-Degree Price Discrimination" (1981) 71(1) *American Economic Review*, pp. 242–47. *See also* M. Schwartz, "Third-Degree Price Discrimination and Output: Generalizing a Welfare Result" (1990) 80(5) *American Economic Review*, pp. 1259–62.

7. – Refuse to Deal
Maurits Dolmans and Matthew Bennett

one of the main arguments against general obligations to supply involves the dynamic incentives for innovation and investment.

The impact that a refusal to supply rivals may have on innovation has played a key role in many recent cases. On the one side, defendants in these cases have argued that being forced to supply their product will reduce their incentives to innovate, to the detriment of consumers. On the other side, complainants in these cases have argued that without supply of the product, they will not have the ability to innovate, resulting in a detriment to consumers. **7.38**

This section looks at the potential impact of refusals to supply on the incentives to innovate for both defendants and complainants. The section first sets out why this argument has attracted so much debate. Secondly, it looks at the relationship between competition and innovation, a relationship that is key to understanding the dynamic impact of refusals to supply. It then discusses the possible impact of forcing firms to supply on both their own and their rivals' incentives to innovate. Finally, it summarises the literature and provides some policy implications. **7.39**

3.1. Why are Innovation and Investment Important?

Economic growth is a key driver behind increases in both the quality of life and increases in society's welfare (provided that the true costs of such growth are internalised in the price).[16] Investment and innovation play a key role in driving productivity and growth within the economy.[17] **7.40**

From a consumer's perspective, the direct benefits from innovations can be represented in two ways. First, firms may conduct innovations or investments that result in lower production costs. This reduces both costs and price, thereby increasing welfare. This is shown in Figure 7.3. Reducing production costs from MC to MC' results in a reduction in price from p to p', increasing consumer welfare from A to ABC (a net increase of B and C). Figure 7.3 **7.41**

---

[16] A growth rate of 2.5 per cent per annum leads to a doubling of GDP within 28 years. Increasing growth to 5 per cent reduces the time taken to double GDP to just 14 years. Consequently even small changes to growth rates over time can have huge changes in GDP.

[17] Cameron (2003) looked at the relationship between R&D and Total Factor Productivity (TFP) in UK manufacturing firms during the 1980s. He found that a 1 per cent increase in R&D increased TFP by 0.2 to 0.3 per cent. G. Cameron, "Why Did UK Manufacturing Productivity Growth Slow Down in the 1970s and Speed Up in the 1980s?" (2003) 70(277) *Economica*, pp. 121–41.

7. – Refuse to Deal
Maurits Dolmans and Matthew Bennett

looks at the impact of the cost decrease on only the firm that incurs it. More generally, however, there may be additional welfare effects as rival firms are forced to lower their prices in order to stay competitive, a dynamic which is discussed further below.

Figure 7.3: Process Investment/Innovation.

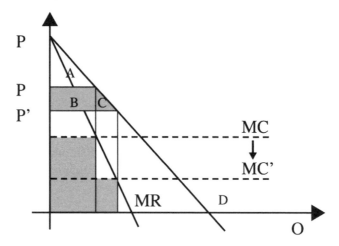

Figure 7.4: Product Innovation.

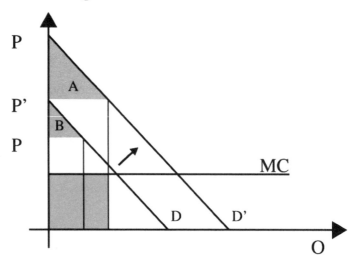

7. – Refuse to Deal
Maurits Dolmans and Matthew Bennett

Secondly, firms may invest in research and development that leads to new **7.42** products. New products that are more desirable to consumers shift the demand curve out to the right. All else equal, consumers have a higher willingness to pay for the product (due to its greater functionality or quality). This is represented in Figure 7.4. The new product shifts consumer demand from D to D'. Even though this results in an increase in price of p to p', this improves consumer welfare because the increase in the usefulness of the product (represented by their willingness to pay) is greater than the increase in price. Total consumer welfare increases from triangle A to triangle B. Similar to process innovation, there may also be an impact on competitors' offerings. In the simple model above, given the choice between the old product at price p and the new product at price p', consumers will pick the new product (as it provides higher consumer surplus). This may mean that competitors reduce the price of the old product (providing a further gain in consumer surplus) or attempt to innovate themselves. These competitor dynamics are looked at in further detail in the next section.

So, how big are these gains? Whilst the diagrams above provide some idea of **7.43** the size of the potential gains, as discussed, they do not take account of the wider impacts on the market. However, economists in quantifying the gains from process and product innovation have found that the gains are remarkably large. Indeed, these gains may be significantly greater than any gains made from increased competition over time. For example, a study in 2003 estimated that the increased variety from the innovation of online bookstores enhanced consumer welfare by between $731 million and $1.03 billion in 2000 – approximately 7–10 times larger than the gains from increased competition and lower prices in the market over the same period.[18]

---

[18] E. Brynjolfsson, Y. Hu and M. D. Smith "Consumer Surplus in the Digital Economy: Estimating the Value of Increased Product Variety at Online Booksellers" (2003) 49(11) *Management Science*, pp. 1580–96. Gentzkow (2008) estimated that the introduction of an online version of the Washington Post newspaper increased consumer welfare by $45 million per year. M. Gentzkow, "Valuing New Goods in a Model with Complementarity: Online Newspapers" (2007) 97(3) *American Economic Review*, pp. 713–44. Hausman (1997) estimated that the creation of a new flavour of Cheerios (a cereal) increased consumer welfare by $78.1 Million. J. A. Hausman, "Valuation of New Goods Under Perfect and Imperfect Competition", in T. F. Bresnahan and R. J. Gordon (Eds.), *The Economics of New Goods* (Chicago, University of Chicago Press, 1997), pp. 207–48. *See also* A. Petrin, "Quantifying the Benefits of New Products: The Case of the Minivan" (2002) 110(4) *Journal of Political Economy*, pp. 705–29.

7. – Refuse to Deal
Maurits Dolmans and Matthew Bennett

7.44   Furthermore, rather than the benefits from innovation only accruing to producers, it appears that the majority of benefits accrue to consumers. For example, a recent study of innovations in post-war US concluded that 98 per cent of the benefits from innovation in US economy accrued to the users of the new technology, whilst only two per cent went to the producers of the innovations.[19]

7.45   These benefits are not guaranteed, however. Many of the innovations and investments that firms make never come to fruition. The pharmaceutical industry is a particularly good example. It is estimated that, within the pharmaceutical industry, between 4,000 and 10,000 molecules are subjected to early screening in order to have a single approved drug.[20] Only one in 10 drugs at the pre-clinical trials ever makes it to the market.[21] This small probability of being able to bring a successful product to the market means that the costs per successful product are extremely high. It has been estimated that, in 2003, it cost $800 million to bring a single successful drug to market.[22] Furthermore, even when it is possible to bring a drug to market, the distribution of revenues amongst the drugs is highly skewed. A study showed that, among 100 drugs introduced into the market, the top 10 realise from 48 to 55 per cent of total revenues. The least lucrative 80 out of 100 barely cover, or less than cover, their average capitalised research and testing costs.[23]

7.46   In summary, innovation is one of the key drivers for consumer welfare. Gains to consumers through static competition between firms may well be significantly outweighed by the gains from innovation. However, these gains are fragile and depend upon the uncertain success of investment and innovation. Therefore policies that influence the rate of innovation and

---

[19] W. D. Nordhaus, "Schumpeterian Profits in the American Economy: Theory and Measurement", *NBER Working Paper Series*, Working Paper No. 10433, April 2004.

[20] *See* Scherer (2007) for a discussion of the pharmaceutical industry. F. M. Scherer, "Pharmaceutical Innovation" in *KSG Working Paper Series*, Paper No. RWP07-004, and in *AEI-Brookings Joint Center Working Series*, Paper No. 07–19, July 2007, available at http://ssrn.com/abstract=902395.

[21] O. Gassmann, G. Reepmeyer and M. von Zedtwitz, *Leading Pharmaceutical Innovation: Trends and Drivers for Growth in the Pharmaceutical Industry* (2nd Ed., Berlin, Springer, 2008).

[22] J. A. DiMasi, R. Hansen and H. Grabowski, "The Price of Innovation: New Estimates of Drug Development Costs" (2003) 22(2) *Journal of Health Economics*, pp. 151–85.

[23] H. Grabowski and J. M. Vernon, "A New Look at the Returns and Risks to Pharmaceutical R&D" (1990) 36(7) *Management Science*, pp. 804–21.

7. – Refuse to Deal
Maurits Dolmans and Matthew Bennett

investment, such as refusal to supply, are likely to have profound effects on consumers.

3.2. The Relationship between Competition and Innovation

The relationship between competition and innovation is complicated and often contested between those who believe that more competition drives innovation, and those who believe that more competition reduces innovation. This contention is compounded by the wealth of theoretical and empirical evidence that supports both sides. However, as will be discussed, academics have most recently found increasing support for the existence of an "inverted U" or "bell curve" shaped relationship between competition and innovation. *See* Figure 7.5 below.　　**7.47**

The belief that concentration drives competition was first put forward by Schumpeter. He proposed that market power was a necessity for innovation due to the need to secure research finance.[24] Accordingly, the Schumpeterian school of thought has argued that high degrees of concentration are by themselves not evidence of lack of effective competition.　　**7.48**

The opposing school of thought, first developed by Arrow, argued that monopolies have lower incentives to innovate than competitive firms, particularly with regard to cost-lowering processes.[25] Monopolies worry about the cannibalisation of existing product's profits through the introduction of new products, the so-called "replacement effect". Firms in a competitive market do not face this constraint to the same degree for two main reasons. First, their products are already facing competition, and hence the loss from cannibalisation is lower than those in a monopoly. Secondly, if they do not innovate, their rival may. Therefore, it is better to cannibalise one's own profits than wait for a rival to do it. The Arrow argument was subsequently built on by literature arguing the additional existence of an "efficiency effect". Competition leads　　**7.49**

---

[24] "*As soon as we go into the details and inquire into the individual items in which progress was most conspicuous, the trail leads not to the doors of those firms that work under conditions of comparatively free competition but precisely to the doors of the large concerns.*" J. Schumpeter, *Capitalism, Socialism and Democracy* (New York, Harper & Brothers, 1950).

[25] K. Arrow, "Economic Welfare and the Allocation of Resources for Invention", in R. R. Nelson (Ed.), *The Rate and Direction of Inventive Activity* (Princeton, Princeton University Press, 1962), pp. 609–25.

7. – Refuse to Deal
Maurits Dolmans and Matthew Bennett

to greater technical progress through entrants' innovative behaviour and their provocation of incumbent firms.[26]

7.50 Many of the empirical studies, like the theoretical literature, also show diverging relationships between competition and innovation.[27] More recently, these two opposing literatures have been somewhat reconciled by papers postulating that the true relationship is a complex, "inverted U-shape" structure.[28] At low levels of competition, where there is a monopoly or very few firms, innovation is low. This is a combination of the replacement effect (a monopolist has little desire to cannibalise itself) and the efficiency effect (without competition, there is little to provoke the incumbent into greater innovative behaviour). As competition increases, the relationship predicts that innovation will increase. Greater competition pushes firms to try to escape it by out-innovating each other. This structure of firms competing to escape by innovation results in the highest level of innovation. However, at high levels of competition, innovation starts to fall because the potential for other firms to imitate the innovation starts to increase, and the prospect of an adequate return on investment in innovation decreases as a result. With more firms, the possibility of being copied shortly after innovating increases. Therefore, at high levels of competition, the potential gains post-innovation are reduced (similar to the Schumpeterian effect). This is illustrated in Figure 7.5.

---

[26] *See, e.g.*, J. Reinganum, "Uncertain Innovation and the Persistence of Monopoly" (1983) 73(4) *American Economic Review*, pp. 741–8.

[27] For example, Dasgupta and Stiglitz (1980) show that concentration is correlated with higher industry-wide and per-firm R&D efforts. P. Dasgupta and J. Stiglitz, "Industrial Structure and the Nature of Innovative Activity" (1980) 90(358) *The Economic Journal*, p. 288. Aghion and Howitt (1992) show that lack of market power to appropriate returns from innovation leads firms to avoid risky, drastic innovation. P. Aghion and P. Howitt, "A Model of Growth through Creative Destruction" (1992) 60(2) *Econometrica*, p. 341. Other empirical investigations have shown a positive relationship between innovation and competition: S. Nickell, "Competition and Corporate Performance" (1996) 104(4) *Journal of Political Economy*, pp. 724–46. Finally recent literature has show a more complicated relationship between innovation and competition. For example, Blundell, Griffith, Van Reenen (1999) find that whilst dominant firms do tend to innovate more, increased industry concentration dampens innovative activity. In markets with growing dominance, however, the increase in industrial concentration outweighs the dominance effect and the overall of aggregate innovation tends to fall. R. Blundell, R. Griffith and J. Van Reenen, "Market Share, Market Value and Innovation in a Panel of British Manufacturing Firms," (1999) 66(3) *Review of Economic Studies*, pp. 529–54.

[28] *See, e.g.*, P. Aghion, C. Harris, P. Howitt and J. Vickers, "Competition, Imitation and Growth with Step-by-Step Innovation" (2001) 68(3) *Review of Economic Studies*, pp. 467–92. This has also been examined empirically, *see* P. Aghion and others, "Competition and Innovation: An Inverted-U Relationship" (2005) 120(2) *Quarterly Journal of Economics*, pp. 701–28.

7. – Refuse to Deal
Maurits Dolmans and Matthew Bennett

Figure 7.5: Inverted U Relationship between Innovation and Competition.

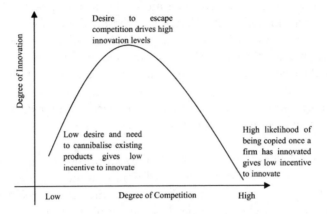

In the inverted U explanation, both the extremes of perfect competition and **7.51** monopoly result in a reduction of innovation relative to moderately competitive markets. Of course, the practical difficulty in using this theory is defining exactly the point at which more competition leads to innovation. This is particularly problematic given that the location of this point is likely to vary by industry.

In summary, it is difficult to come to strong conclusions regarding how one **7.52** might expect the level of innovation to change with an increase in competition, especially when one is not in the situational extremes of monopoly or perfect competition. Whilst a monopolistic market structure (*ex ante*) is unlikely to be optimal for driving innovation, it is widely accepted that introducing obligations to supply wherever one sees concentration (*ex post*) may well have significant detrimental effects on innovation.[29] This is discussed next.

3.3. Refusal to Supply and the Incumbent's Incentives to Invest

The incentive to innovate can be expressed by how much money and effort **7.53** a firm would be willing to spend in order to secure an innovation.[30] When

---

[29] *"If anti-trust agencies tried to eliminate or reduce market power whenever it appeared, this would have the detrimental effect of eliminating firms' incentives to innovate."* M. Motta, *Competition Policy: Theory and Practice* (Cambridge, Cambridge University Press, 2004).

[30] This is a standard analogy in economics, *see, e.g.*, D. W. Carlton and J. M. Perloff, *Modern Industrial Organization* (4th Ed., Pearson, 2005), *"A rational inventor engages in costly research up to the point where the expected marginal return from more research equals its marginal cost."*

7. – Refuse to Deal
Maurits Dolmans and Matthew Bennett

contemplating an investment, a rational firm compares the profits it would obtain if it invests in R&D with the profits it would earn in an otherwise identical world without the investment. This means that it is not just the absolute level of profits after innovation that determines the firm's incentives to invest, but the difference in profits between the two states: innovating and not innovating.[31] Factors that increase the relative level of expected profits in the non-innovation scenario reduce the incentives to innovate. However, factors that increase the relative expected profits in the innovation scenario increase the incentives.[32] With this framework in mind, we turn to the impact that an obligation to license may have on an incumbent's incentive to invest or innovate.

7.54 Consider first the impact of an obligation to supply on the incumbent's profit from innovating. The ability to choose whom to supply to, and on what terms, increases the profits the incumbent can earn after a successful innovation. The incumbent can choose to be the sole supplier of the new product or license it on the terms of its choice. An obligation to supply at terms that it cannot dictate is likely to reduce the profits the incumbent can make from its investment. As discussed above, creation often involves the sinking of fixed costs combined with considerable uncertainty as to success of the innovation. If the incumbent knows that it will be obliged to supply at marginal cost after it has innovated, then it will have no incentive to innovate in the first place. *Ex ante*, the incumbent is faced with two equally unpalatable choices. Either it is successful in its innovation, in which case it attracts rivals imitating its product, free-riding on the incumbent's efforts and fixed costs, or the innovation is a failure, in which case it cannot recover its fixed costs. Either way, sunk costs and efforts would be largely lost with no possibility of reward. In economic terms, this is a market failure that is solved by granting and enforcing rights such as property rights. Consequently, any general obligation to supply has a negative impact on the incentives for innovation.[33]

---

[31] *See, e.g.*, J. Tirole, *The Theory of Industrial Organization* (Cambridge, MIT Press, 1988).

[32] *Ibid.* for a basic model of innovation.

[33] *See, e.g.*, F. M. Scherer, *The Economic Effects of Compulsory Patent Licensing* (New York University, Graduate School of Business Administration, Center for the Study of Financial Institutions, 1977); P. Tandon, "Optimal Patents with Compulsory Licensing" (1982) 90(3) *Journal of Political Economy*, pp. 470–86; and R. Gilbert and C. Shapiro, "Optimal Patent Length and Breadth" (1990) *The RAND Journal of Economics*, pp. 106–12. Mandatory access had a similar effect in other industries. *See* J. Hausman and J. G. Sidak, "A consumer welfare approach to the mandatory unbundling of telecommunications networks" (1999) 109(3) *Yale Law Journal*, pp. 507–39 and J. G. Sidak and D. Spulber, "The Tragedy of the Telecommunications: Government Pricing of Unbundled Network Elements Under the Telecommunications Act of 1996" (1997) *Columbia Law Review*, pp. 1201–81.

7. – Refuse to Deal
Maurits Dolmans and Matthew Bennett

General obligations to supply also have an impact on the incentive to innovate **7.55**
by increasing the incumbent's profit from not investing in the innovation.
Obligations to supply allow the possibility of free-riding.[34] If the incumbent
does not innovate but a rival firm does, then the incumbent can profit from the
rival's innovation through the obligation to supply. The incumbent's expected
profit level when it does not innovate is higher under an obligation to supply.
Furthermore, if every firm had an obligation to supply its innovation to rivals,
no firm would want to be the first to innovate. Each firm would prefer others
to invest and investment and innovation would be reduced.[35]

The net impact of these two effects points to a general obligation to supply **7.56**
having a negative impact on incumbents' and rivals' incentives to innovate.
Indeed the concept of the "essential function" of property rights, which will
be discussed within Section III.2.2, is based on this concept – the need to
ensure an adequate return on owners' past investments.

There is, however, a third effect from an obligation to supply via the resulting **7.57**
increase in the degree of competition in the market. As discussed previously
in the context of the inverted U curve, when markets are highly concentrated,
increases in the degree of competition may increase future innovation by the
incumbent and its rivals. If the incumbent has sole control of an input necessary to compete on the market, an obligation to supply that input may allow
new firms to enter into the market and compete. The increased competition
removes the incumbent's ability to choose a quiet life and not to cannibalise
its existing products profits.

Finally, there may also be further, indirect effects from an obligation to supply. **7.58**
As the incumbent increases its level of innovation to respond to entry, the new
entrants may also respond by increasing their innovation. The direction of
these indirect effects depends on whether competition in innovation between
firms is a strategic substitute or a strategic complement. That is, whether firms
respond to more innovation with less innovation (substitute) or more innovation (complement). Unfortunately, economic theory does not provide a strong

---

[34] "*Early copying of an innovation and free riding on an innovator's efforts undermine the incentive to innovate.*" P. Lowe and
L. Peeperkorn, "Singing in Tune with Competition and Innovation: The New EU Competition Policy towards
Licensing" (2004) 26 *Fordham Corporate Law Institute Thirty-first Annual Conference: Roundtable on Intellectual Property
and Antitrust*, pp. 265–86.

[35] Carlton and Perloff succinctly state this effect as: "*Why would anyone be willing to incur the entire expense of developing
new information, processes, or products if people could benefit from them for free?*", see *supra* note 30, p. 506.

7. – Refuse to Deal
Maurits Dolmans and Matthew Bennett

indication as to whether innovation is generally a strategic complement or substitute. Innovation modelled as a patent race, with two firms racing to secure the patent, generally predicts innovation as a strategic complement.[36] There are, however, also models in which patent races may provide the opposite result. In these models, once a firm gets ahead of its competitor, the competitor perceives it has no ability to catch up, and gives up.[37] If firms' reactions follow these models, there is unlikely to be a further indirect result.

7.59 In summary, there are two potential effects pointing to an obligation to supply reducing innovation. First, there is one potential effect pointing to an obligation to supply increasing innovation (depending upon the level of competition). Secondly, there is an indirect effect that depends on how firms respond to other firms' innovation. Given this, can we say something more generally about the impact of an obligation to supply and the effect on innovation?

7.60 Consider the extreme position where there is a general obligation to supply at marginal cost. This is highly likely to have a negative impact on innovation in society. As discussed above, the first two profit effects are clearly negative. The third, competition specific effect, is also likely to be negative. The inverted U theory predicts that competition will have a negative impact on innovation when competition is so intense that no firm can ever reap the benefits of its innovation. A rule that *always* forces firms to compulsory license has the same impact. Even if there is only one firm in the market, a general rule to compulsory license at cost gives it no incentives to invest. Finally, the indirect effect is likely to be zero: if no firm innovates, then there is no innovation to respond to.

7.61 The implication is that a general obligation to supply reduces innovation. Conversely, an obligation to supply that can be ring fenced to apply only in "exceptional" circumstances may increase the level of innovation. This is the basis for the "exceptional circumstances" criterion discussed in Section III.2.3 below. Obligations to supply have an impact on future incentives to innovate. Any research investments that incumbents have made in order to innovate or produce the product are sunk – it cannot un-produce the innovation.

---

[36] *See, e.g.*, T. Lee and L. L. Wilde, "Market Structure and Innovation: A Reformulation" 1980 94(2) *Quarterly Journal of Economics*, pp. 429–36.

[37] *See, e.g.*, D. Fudenberg, R. Gilbert, J. Stiglitz and J. Tirole, "Preemption, Leapfrogging and Competition in Patent Races" (1983) 22(1) *European Economic Review*, pp. 3–31.

7. – Refuse to Deal

Maurits Dolmans and Matthew Bennett

Therefore, if the obligation to supply only applied to the incumbent's innovation that had already been created, it would have no impact on the incumbent's future innovation for that product. Authorities, however, face a commitment problem. Creating an obligation to supply existing innovative products or technologies leads participants in the markets to expect the authority imposing future obligations to supply for future innovations.[38] The more widely the obligation to supply is phrased and applies, the greater adverse effect it will have on all firms' future incentives to innovate.

The question for the competition authority is therefore how to ring fence an **7.62** obligation to supply to only the specific circumstances in the case in which the net effects are positive, and not create a general precedence. Consequently, an ability to commit to only enforcing an obligation to supply in exceptional circumstances is critical. This desire to commit has similarities with other economic literature regarding institutions and commitment problems. A competition authority may always be tempted to *ex post* change the rules regarding obligations to supply in order to increase static competition within a particular market. However, as previously discussed, this has a detrimental effect on future incentives. Firms will only trust the competition authority if the authority can create a reputation for only applying an obligation to supply in exceptional circumstances. Delegation of final authority to courts that have different objectives than competition authorities may be one way for an authority to provide a credible commitment. Read in this light, the case law on exceptional circumstances discussed in Section III.2.3 below may be interpreted as a clear attempt by courts to ring fence obligations to supply to cover only those situations where the net effects are beneficial to overall innovation.

3.4. Should All Property Rights be Treated Equal?

Should property rights be applied equally across different industries, and **7.63** across different types of property? It has been suggested that rights to intangible assets, such as patents or copyright deserve an even greater deference than property rights to physical assets. Economists have, however, viewed these arguments with some scepticism.

---

[38] *See, e.g.,* the Kok Report: "*companies will only invest in innovation and R&D if they have the certainty that they will be able to reap the rewards of that investment.*" High Level Group, Facing the Challenge – The Lisbon Strategy for Growth and Employment, Report from the High Level Group chaired by Wim Kok, November 2004.

7. – Refuse to Deal

Maurits Dolmans and Matthew Bennett

7.64 First, it has been argued that due to their vulnerability to being copied easily certain assets such as intangible property merit a higher degree of protection than physical property, which is physically in the hands of an owner. That IP may be more easily copied than physical assets may be a strong argument for the allocation of exclusivity for IP, but not necessarily for differences in treatment of different types of property with regards to an obligation of supply.[39] An obligation to supply has the same economic effect on both property rights. In the case of physical property, the owner is forced to share access to a physical asset, whilst in the case of IP, it is forced to share access to the IP. In both cases, the prospect of forced sharing may reduce investment incentives.

7.65 Arguably, industries with high research and development costs and low probabilities of success are more vulnerable to obligations to supply. As previously discussed, the pharmaceutical and medical devices sector may be more vulnerable to interference with property rights because of the large costs required for clinical tests and the dearth of products that become a commercial success. The revenues from these products must be enough to recoup not only the sunk costs of the products in question, but also the costs of many failed projects. The mobile telecommunications sector is another area where investments or research and development play a significant role and there is considerable risk. For example, in 2000, the UK Mobile operators paid £22.5 billion for the spectrum needed to provide 3G services. This investment was made on the expectation of high demand for data services. However, these did not materialise in the time expected and the UK Mobile operators were forced to write down much of their investments.[40]

7.66 It has been argued that there are also situations in which IPRs may not be essential for providing incentives to innovate. For example, the motivation of the open source software development does not appear purely financial. Similarly, internet standards developed by the W3C tend to be IPR-free or royalty-free, and are arguably a highly efficient platform for innovation. Finally, in some cases, R&D and construction of public facilities are funded by government, academic, or charitable institutions. In such instances interference with exclusive rights pursuant to competition law, and the imposition of a compulsory license, may be less controversial. In these cases, however, the

---

[39] *See* R. O'Donoghue and A. J. Padilla, *The Law and Economics of Article 82 EC* (Oxford, Hart Publishing, 2006), pp. 422–3.

[40] For a discussion of the 3G spectrum auctions, *see* K. Binmore and P. Klemperer, "The Biggest Auction Ever: the Sale of the British 3G Telecom Licences" (2002) 112(478) *The Economic Journal*, pp. C74–C96.

7. – Refuse to Deal
Maurits Dolmans and Matthew Bennett

key distinction may be that the institutions are not financially motivated or have made a conscious decision to rely on funding through other sources, like advertising, post-sales services, R&D subsidies, or charging for premium versions while providing basic versions for free ("freemium"). One may want to be careful to differentiate between situations in which a firm makes an unforced decision to provide an open platform, and situations in which the firm is forced to provide its innovations.[41]

A second argument is that certain industries do not use IP as frequently as others as a tool for protecting property or exploiting innovation. For instance, instead of patent protection they might rely on non-disclosure of information, recognition lags, effects of learning curves, or high imitation costs because imitation requires repeating certain research and development efforts and first mover advantages.[42] In such cases, it has been argued that compulsory licensing may have fewer negative effects on innovation. In certain cases, the use of secrecy is more effective than enforcement of IP.[43] Indeed, the fact that firms substitute between patents and secrecy has been demonstrated empirically.[44] A duty to disclose could, however, destroy the very essence of

7.67

---

[41] Guidance on the Commission's enforcement priorities in applying Article 82 of the EC Treaty to abusive exclusionary conduct by dominant undertakings ("*Guidance Paper*"), OJ 2009 C 45/7, para. 82: "*In certain specific cases, it may be clear that imposing an obligation to supply is manifestly not capable of having negative effects on the input owner's and/or other operators' incentives to invest and innovate upstream, whether ex ante or ex post. The Commission considers that this is particularly likely to be the case where regulation compatible with Community law already imposes an obligation to supply on the dominant undertaking and it is clear, from the considerations underlying such regulation, that the necessary balancing of incentives has already been made by the public authority when imposing such an obligation to supply. This could also be the case where the upstream market position of the dominant undertaking has been developed under the protection of special or exclusive rights or has been financed by state resources. In such specific cases there is no reason for the Commission to deviate from its general enforcement standard of showing likely anti-competitive foreclosure, without considering whether the three circumstances referred to in paragraph 81 are present.*"

[42] P. Lowe and L. Peeperkorn, "Intellectual Property: How Special is its Competition Case?" in C-D. Ehlermann and I. Atanasiu (Eds.), *European Competition Law Annual 2005: The Interaction Between Competition Law and Intellectual Property Law* (Oxford, Hart Publishing, 2007), p. 93, F. M. Scherer and D. Ross, *Industrial Market Structure and Economic Performance* (Boston, Houghton Mifflin Company, 1990), pp. 626 *et seq.*

[43] *See, e.g.*, Lowe and Peeperkorn (2004): "[I]*t is clear from studies that in most industries patents do not play a very important role for companies in protecting and exploiting innovation. Natural secrecy, recognition lags, learning curve effects, the imitator's need to duplicate at least a part of the R&D effort to overcome practical production problems [...] and first-mover advantages are all ranked ahead of patents as appropriation mechanisms*". *See* P. Lowe and L. Peeperkorn, "Intellectual Property: How Special is its Competition Case?" in C-D. Ehlermann and I. Atanasiu (Eds.), *European Competition Law Annual 2005: The Interaction Between Competition Law and Intellectual Property Law* (Oxford, Hart Publishing, 2007), p. 93. Lowe and Peeperkorn cite studies of manufacturing industries, which show that for a sample of manufacturing firms in over 100 industries, secrecy was more important than patents for protecting process innovations and product innovations in the late 1990s.

[44] Scherer found that firms subject to compulsory licensing decrees decreased patenting by a statistically and economically significant 15–21 per cent but did not appear to lessen R&D activities. *See* F. M. Scherer *supra* note 33.

the trade secret, and risks creating a precedent requiring an obligation to disclose future trade secrets. Although it may be possible to mitigate some of the immediate risk by requiring confidentiality from the licensee, backed up by strong contractual penalty provisions in case of leaks care should be taken to respect the essence of the owner's rights.

7.68　Thirdly, it has been argued that the fact that IPRs tend to be time limited compared to rights to physical assets, and that conditions and restrictive parameters may apply to IPRs but not physical property rights,[45] means that IPRs deserve a greater protection against applications of Article 102 TFEU than physical property rights. IP law makers have, however, made a conscious choice regarding the length of, and conditions and parameters for, protection for IP based on a trade-off between the loss of competition during the time of protection and the necessity to provide incentives to innovate. A comparable trade-off has been made regarding the nature and scope of protection of physical property. Thus, there appears to be no justification for subjecting IP and physical assets to different rules for an obligation to supply during its protected time period.[46]

4.　Why Might Refusals to Supply be Harmful to Consumers?

7.69　The previous discussion focused on why refusals to supply may generally be beneficial to static and dynamic competition and consumers. However, there are circumstances in which refusals to supply may harm competition, either through allowing a firm to exploit its monopoly power, or by foreclosing

---

[45] Patents, for instance, provide strong protection for ideas and even prohibit innocent infringement, although protection is available only for novel and non-obvious inventions with industrial application, for 20 years, and subject to application procedures and publication of the invention. An idea is "novel" if it does not already form part of the state of the art, and is not obvious to persons skilled in the art. *See* Case COMP/37.792 *Microsoft*, Commission Decision of 27 February 2008 ("*Microsoft Decision 2008*"), not yet published, para. 130 (confirmed on appeal on 27 June 2012 in Case T-167/08 *Microsoft v Commission* ("*Microsoft Judgment 2012*"), not yet reported. Copyright works are protected for much longer (70 years from the death of the author), need not be novel so long as they are original, and require no registration, but protect only the expression of an idea, not the idea itself, and provide no protection against the marketing of independently created works even if they are identical or confusingly similar. A work is original if it is author's own intellectual creation. *See*, for instance, Article 6 of Parliament and Council Directive 2006/116/EC of 12 December 2006 on the term of protection of copyright and certain related rights, OJ 2006 L 372/12; *see also* Article 1(3) of Parliament and Council Directive 2009/24/EC of 23 April 2009 on the legal protection of computer programs, OJ 2009 L 111/16.

[46] Interestingly, it does raise a question of whether exclusivity of physical assets that have been fully recovered over a long period of time, for example, the copper last mile in infrastructure, should be subject to the same time limitations as IP. The Commission's prioritisation guidelines suggest a similar case with regards to physical infrastructure investments made under public ownership rather than private ownership. *See Guidance Paper supra* note 41, para. 82.

7. – Refuse to Deal
Maurits Dolmans and Matthew Bennett

dynamic competition. We now consider these theories. Section II.4.1 sets out the "Chicago Critique" (or "one monopoly profit" theory) and in particular describes in what conditions it makes little economic sense to hold a firm liable under competition law on the basis of a straightforward theory prohibiting the leveraging of upstream monopoly power into the downstream market. We then consider what is sometimes termed as the "post-Chicago" literature regarding the theories of harm associated with refusals to supply (Sections II.4.2 – II.4.4).

4.1. The Leveraging Story and the Chicago Critique

Until the late 1970s, economists and practitioners worried that firms could **7.70** use their monopoly position upstream in order to leverage themselves into a monopoly position downstream. It was hypothesised that if the upstream monopolist refused to supply its product to downstream rivals, the rivals would be unable to produce the derivative product and go out of business. This allowed the monopolist to reserve the downstream market for itself, thus earning profits in both the upstream and downstream markets (*see* Figure 7.1).

In the late 1970s the "Chicago School" led by Robert Bork and Richard Pos- **7.71** ner questioned the validity of this leveraging theory.[47] The Chicago School argued that in a vertically integrated system such as in Figure 7.1 above, there is only one "monopoly" profit that can be extracted from end consumers. The level of this monopoly profit is dictated by the final consumers' willingness to pay, not the point at which it is extracted. Even if the incumbent controls both the upstream and the downstream levels, its profits are fixed by the monopoly price downstream. Following on from this, they argued that an incumbent in a monopoly position upstream can already extract all the downstream rents using a simple two-part tariff (as previously discussed). Controlling the downstream market does not allow the supplier to capture any additional rents, as all the rents are being extracted upstream. The natural corollary of their argument was that because the upstream firm has no anti-competitive incentive to foreclose the downstream market, if it is refusing to supply, this must be because it is efficient to do so (*e.g.*, in order to eliminate multiple margins). This formed the basis of their conclusion that competition law should not impose duties to supply.

---

[47] R. H. Bork, *The Antitrust Paradox: A Policy at War with Itself* (New York, Basic Books, 1978). R. Posner, *Antitrust Law* (Chicago, University of Chicago Press, 1976).

7. – Refuse to Deal
Maurits Dolmans and Matthew Bennett

7.72 This Chicago School argument is more general than the setting described above, and holds in a variety of settings. Downstream markets may be differentiated in the sets of consumers they serve. In this case, an integrated firm still has a strong incentive to supply downstream rivals because they allow it to reach consumers it could not otherwise reach. For example, even though broadband telecom services may have identical inputs, retail suppliers may differentiate themselves downstream with different packages of services or brands. Foreclosing a competitor in a differentiated market does not simply transfer customers from the rival to the incumbent's downstream arm. Some consumers are lost from the market altogether, and hence the incumbent's upstream output is reduced. This implies that a refusal to supply with differentiated markets downstream involves a sacrifice for the incumbent. Because the upstream monopolist can already extract the monopoly profit upstream, a rational monopolist would foreclose (thus sacrificing profits upstream through customers lost from the market), only if the sacrifice was outweighed by an efficiency. This reinforces the Chicago finding that no duty to supply should therefore be imposed.

7.73 Whilst the Chicago critique is very powerful, a 'post-Chicago' literature has identified several theories of harm that are consistent with the one-monopoly profit, and where an order to supply may nevertheless improve consumer welfare. These theories describe situations where firms have an incentive to engage in anticompetitive foreclosure. First, upstream firms may have an incentive to foreclose their competitors because absent the refusal to supply, they may not be able to extract the entire system monopoly rent (Section II.4.2 below). Secondly, upstream firms may have an incentive to foreclose their competitors in order to protect their existing upstream monopoly position from entry or intensified competition (Section II.4.3 below). Finally, upstream firms may have an incentive to soften competition by refusing to supply downstream competitors in order to raise their rivals' costs (Section II.4.4 below).

4.2. Refusal to Supply in order to Restore Monopoly Profit

7.74 The first general class of cases where the "one-monopoly" profit theory may not be a defense against a charge of abusive refusal to supply, concerns situations where the monopolist, absent the refusal to supply, may not be able to extract the entire system monopoly rent. There are several reasons why this may not be possible.

7. – Refuse to Deal
Maurits Dolmans and Matthew Bennett

First, the one-monopoly profit theory relies on the assumption that the **7.75**
incumbent's input is used in fixed proportion for the manufacture of the
end product (for example, every car has only one engine). When different
proportions of the input can be used, for example, using a greater or lower
quantity of raw material to produce a final product, the one-monopoly theory
may break down. If the upstream firm tried to increase the price of the raw
material to the monopoly level, the downstream firm would reduce the quantity it uses. This prevents the upstream firm from capturing the entire system
monopoly rent. The upstream monopolist can only capture the whole system
rent if it vertically integrates and refuses to supply downstream rivals. Without
a refusal to supply, the upstream firm is forced to charge a below-monopoly
price to the downstream firms. By vertically integrating and refusing to supply competing downstream firms, a vertically integrated firm can increase the
downstream price (without the risk of downstream firms substituting away
from the monopolist's product or reducing the volume of input consumed)
and can capture monopoly rents from the entire downstream market that
were previously unattainable.[48]

A similar question of fixed proportion arose in the *Microsoft*[49] interoperabil- **7.76**
ity case. Microsoft argued that client and server operating systems are strict
complements, and that as such, there is no incentive for Microsoft to leverage
from one market to the other. The Commission rejected this argument, however, on the ground that *"the one monopoly profit theory relies on strong assumptions,
which do not hold in this case. In particular, the two products at stake must be perfectly
complementary with fixed ratios. This is not the case for client PC and work group server
operating systems."*[50] In other words, the Commission argued that Microsoft was
not able to extract the one monopoly profit from its position in the client
operating system because customers could choose how many client operating systems they used with a single work group server system and *vice versa*.
If Microsoft attempted to increase its price on the client operating system

---

[48] It should be noted that whilst foreclosure causes price to increase, this increase may or may not be more
socially efficient than non-foreclosure. Schmalensee (1971) looks at the case in which the downstream firm has a
choice between a monopoly input and an inferior competitive input. In equilibrium the downstream firm uses a
suboptimal amount of the monopoly input (as it substitutes to the inferior competitive input). By vertically integrating downstream and refusing to supply other downstream firms, the vertically integrated firm can restore
the socially optimal amount of the monopolised input. R. Schmalensee, "Consumer's Surplus and Producer's
Goods" (1971) 61(4) *American Economic Review*, pp. 682–7.
[49] Case COMP/37.792 *Microsoft*, Commission Decision of 24 March 2004 (*"Microsoft Decision 2004"*) not yet
published.
[50] *Ibid.,* para. 767.

7. – Refuse to Deal
Maurits Dolmans and Matthew Bennett

to extract its profit on a server sale, customers would use a lower number of clients, thus restricting the ability to extract the full monopoly rent.[51] A second reason why the upstream firm may not be able to capture the full system rent is because of a perceived lack of commitment on the part of the upstream firm.[52] As discussed previously, an upstream monopolist can capture the entire monopoly rent by signing a two-part contract with the downstream firm, with a variable fee equal to marginal costs and a franchise fee being set at the monopoly rent level. The downstream firm that signed the contract now has the risk of ensuring that the monopoly quantity is sold on the market. However, the upstream firm now has an incentive to opportunistically sign another contract with another downstream firm, this time at a franchise fee equal to the duopoly profit level. The second downstream firm will have an incentive to sign this, because with two downstream firms, it will make a duopoly profit. However, the first downstream firm will now make a loss. It purchased the franchise at the monopoly level but now competes in a duopoly. Once again, the upstream firm will have an incentive to opportunistically sign a further contract with a third downstream firm, this time at a franchise fee equal to an oligopoly profit. This continues until there is perfect competition and no more rents can be made from selling the franchise fee. The result is that every downstream firm that has signed a contract (except the last) loses money and the upstream monopolist makes more than one monopoly rent.

7.77 If downstream firms are rational, then they will foresee that the upstream firm will have an incentive to opportunistically exploit them. Consequently, no downstream firm will pay more than the perfectly competitive level (knowing this would be the final outcome), and no downstream firm will pay a franchise fee, unless the monopolist can commit not to exploit them. One way to commit is to sign binding exclusive contracts and refuse to supply any other downstream firms. Without such a refusal to supply, none of the downstream firms would be willing to pay the upstream firm an amount close to the monopoly rent.

7.78 One point to note regarding these types of "commitment" models is the interaction with the hold-up problem discussed previously. Signing exclusive

---

[51] This may be partially solved by the use of non-linear tariffs in order to price discriminate across different bundles of servers and clients.

[52] This was first articulated in O. Hart and J. Tirole, "Vertical Integration and Market Foreclosure", in C. Winston and M. N. Baily (Eds.), *Brookings Papers on Economic Activity: Microeconomics* (Brookings Institution Press, 1990), pp. 205–76.

7. – Refuse to Deal
Maurits Dolmans and Matthew Bennett

contracts may not be possible if the upstream firm has a risk of being held up by the downstream firm.[53] By refusing to supply other downstream providers, the monopolist is reducing the number of outside options it has. The lower number of outside options, the more the monopolist is exposed to being held up by the downstream provider it sells to. The result is that, in equilibrium, the two effects may balance. The monopolist may accept that the benefit of having an outside option (and having two downstream firms) is worth the cost of not being able to extract the full monopoly rent.

The conclusion is that the single monopoly rent theory may not hold if the input product is not used in a fixed proportion to the volume of end-products. In these situations, contrary to the Chicago School conclusion, one cannot assume that a refusal to supply is necessarily for efficiency enhancing reasons. **7.79**

4.3. *Refusal to Supply in order to Protect an Upstream Monopoly Position*

The second category of post-Chicago foreclosure theories regards the use of refusals to supply to protect an existing upstream monopoly position from entry or competition. In some cases, the upstream monopolist may face the threat of entry into its monopoly market, by an outside firm or by a downstream firm. To rebut the Chicago School argument, these theories postulate that the monopolist is not trying to gain more than one monopoly rent, but is engaging in the protection of its existing monopoly rent. In this context there are two reasons why a refusal to supply may help the monopolist to protect its monopoly rent. **7.80**

First, in a vertical framework, downstream firms may be the best placed to enter into the upstream monopolist's market. For example, in the *Microsoft* case, the Commission pointed out that "*even when product A and product B are perfectly complementary with fixed ratios, the one monopoly profit theory does not hold when keeping a firm in market B in check reinforces the dominant undertaking's dominant position in market A, erecting barriers against an actual or potential competitive threat in that market.*"[54] The Commission argued that in order to make servers, manufacturers needed to have access to the interoperability specifications from Microsoft necessary to use their servers within a network of Windows computers. The Commission furthermore argued that server manufacturers were well placed **7.81**

---

[53] G. Chemla, "Downstream Competition, Foreclosure, and Vertical Integration" (2003) 12(2) *Journal of Economics and Management Strategy*, pp. 261–89.

[54] *See Microsoft Decision 2004 supra* note 49, paras 768 *et seq.*

7. – Refuse to Deal
Maurits Dolmans and Matthew Bennett

to start providing functionality that competed with Microsoft's client operating system/platform, but could not develop these without the ability to interoperate with Microsoft's platforms.[55] The refusal to supply interoperability specifications therefore protected the Windows platform. Secondly, in a horizontal framework, access to complementary products may be necessary for entrants to compete in a neighbouring market. For example, suppose that there is a single monopolist manufacturer of cars. In order to make a car, any entrant car manufacturer would need to have access to tyres. If the car manufacturer could foreclose all the tyre manufacturers (for example, by refusing to buy their tyres and insourcing tyre production), then it would increase the entry barriers for an entrant coming into car manufacturing. The entrant would not only have to enter into the car manufacturing but it would also have to enter into tyre manufacturing simultaneously, or arrange for the excluded manufacturers to re-enter. In this case, the monopolist would be foreclosing complementary sources so entrants cannot gain access to complementary products, raising the barriers to entry and thus protecting its monopoly position.[56]

7.82 Both of the "protecting a monopoly position" theories of harm involve several important assumptions that must be present for a finding of foreclosure. First, they assume that the two markets are interrelated so that entry into only one market is not possible. Secondly, they assume that entrants cannot coordinate their entry strategies into the market. In the second example, if a car manufacturer and tyre manufacturer coordinated their entry into the market, the incumbent would not be able to prevent them from entering.

7.83 Note that in both of these theories, the incumbent has to sacrifice some of its upstream profits in order to foreclose downstream entry – especially if the downstream firms are differentiated as discussed in Section II.4.1. By not allowing entry, the incumbent is sacrificing some of its monopoly profit today in order to maintain a higher level of monopoly profit in the future.

---

[55] *See Microsoft Decision 2004 supra* note 49, paras 768 *et seq.* ("*Microsoft's internal communication bears witness to anxiety about this possibility: 'Sun, Oracle and Netscape are all pushing a new model of [almost] centralised computing. They all acknowledge that Microsoft holds tremendous sway over the desktop platform, so they all want to quickly strip as much value and spending as possible off the desktop and onto the server where they can charge premium prices and push their own platform offerings.' In view of the close links between the client PC operating system market and the work group server operating system market, Microsoft has an incentive to prevent entry by these identified rivals in the latter.*").

[56] *See, e.g.,* D. W. Carlton and M. Waldman, "The Strategic Use of Tying to Preserve and Create Market Power in Evolving Industries" (2002) 33(2) *The RAND Journal of Economics*, pp. 194–220. *See also* J. P. Choi and C. Stefanadis, "Tying, Investment, and the Dynamic Leverage Theory" (2001) 32(1) *The RAND Journal of Economics*, pp. 52–71.

7. – Refuse to Deal
Maurits Dolmans and Matthew Bennett

Finally, a slightly different theory of foreclosure to maintain a monopoly position **7.84**
focuses on the use of penalty clauses within exclusivity contracts to restrict entry
upstream.[57] In this theory, the refusal to supply is only one stage in a foreclosure
strategy. First, the upstream incumbent refuses to supply any other downstream
firms – thus ensuring there is only one downstream firm. Secondly, the incumbent signs a non-compete contract with the downstream firm with a substantial
penalty clause in case the downstream firm buys from a second source.

Figure 7.6: Exclusive Contracts to Foreclose Entrants.

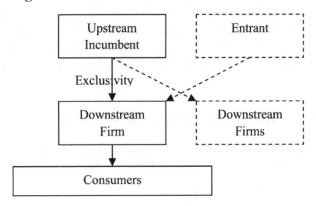

The penalty means an entrant can only enter upstream if it can compensate the **7.85**
downstream firm for the penalty amount. This creates a contractual barrier to
entry for the entrant. This theory differs slightly from the previous two theories
of maintaining a monopoly position because entry may occur – depending on
whether the entrant is sufficiently more efficient than the upstream incumbent
to both charge the same price and compensate the downstream firm for the
penalty. However, because of the penalty, entry occurs less frequently than optimal. Furthermore, when the entrant is foreclosed, it is anti-competitive.[58]

---

[57] The seminal economic paper in this area is P. Aghion and P. Bolton, "Contracts as Barrier to Entry" (1987)
77(3) *American Economic Review*, pp. 388–401.

[58] Note that this theory assumes that a penalty clause is set in an upstream incumbent's contract with the
downstream buyer. Innes and Sexton (1994), however, analyse what will happen if the downstream firm can
contract with the entrant in order to sponsor entry. They show that when the downstream firm can sponsor
more competition, exclusionary contracts (such as penalties for using an entrant) between the incumbent and
the downstream buyer will only foreclose inefficient entrants. R. Innes and R. J. Sexton, "Strategic Buyers and
Exclusionary Contracts" (1994) 84(3) *American Economic Review*, pp. 566–84.

7. – Refuse to Deal
Maurits Dolmans and Matthew Bennett

4.4.   Refusal to Supply in order to Raise Downstream Rival's Costs

7.86   The final strand of literature looks at the possibility of refusing to supply downstream competitors as a way of softening competition by raising down-stream rivals' costs. Here, the object of the refusal to supply is not necessarily to foreclose, but to raise the downstream rival's price by exposing them to a rival's upstream monopoly position.[59] This possibility arises when there are two competing upstream firms. Consider a vertically integrated firm that competes against non-integrated firms upstream and downstream (*see* Figure 7.7 below). If the integrated firm refuses to supply its downstream rival, it exposes the downstream rival to higher prices from the upstream rival's new monopoly position. The upstream rival increases its input price, which effectively raises the downstream price, thus softening downstream competition and increasing the vertically integrated firm's profits. This is the "basic raising rival's cost" mechanism.

Figure 7.7: Raising Rival's Costs by Refusal to Supply.

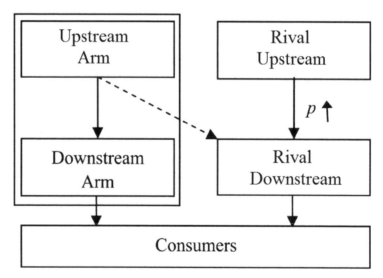

---

[59] *See* J. A. Ordover, G. Saloner and S. C. Salop, "Equilibrium Vertical Foreclosure" (1990) 80 *American Economic Review*, pp. 127–42. In their model both the upstream and downstream firms are separated. The authors look at raising the rival's cost as a motive for vertical integration. Ordover *et al.* assume that competition downstream is in strategic complements (*e.g.*, price). *See also* Salinger (1988) which assumes competition both upstream downstream takes place on strategic substitutes (*e.g.*, quantity). M. A. Salinger, "Vertical mergers and market foreclosure" (1988) 103 *Quarterly Journal of Economics*, pp. 345–56.

7. – Refuse to Deal
Maurits Dolmans and Matthew Bennett

Raising rivals' cost theories are contentious in the economic literature and **7.87** carry several important caveats. We present some of the main ones here. First, the theory is specific to there being only two firms upstream. When there are more than two firms, it becomes more difficult for the integrated firm to profitably refuse to supply. The lost upstream profit from refusing to supply downstream rivals may outweigh any increases in the downstream profits (given the wholesale market only moves from a triopoly to a duopoly).

Secondly, in its simple form, the vertically integrated firm always has an **7.88** incentive to supply to the rival downstream producer once the upstream firm increases its price. This means that the vertically integrated firm must have a commitment to refuse to sell to the rival downstream even at a higher price. This assumption of commitment without specifying where it comes from has been criticised by several economists.[60] However, more recently, other economic theories have looked at relaxing this commitment assumption in the context of vertical mergers.[61]

Thirdly, it assumes that the rival upstream firm does not charge a two-part **7.89** tariff. The rival upstream may be able to charge the rival downstream marginal cost, and take its increased market power in the form of a fixed franchise fee. Because the marginal cost for the downstream rival is not increasing, there is no increase in downstream price, and no increase in profits for the vertically integrated firm. Indeed, by refusing to supply the downstream rival the upstream firm is forgoing upstream profits. Thus, raising rivals costs in the face of two-part tariffs is unlikely to be a profitable strategy unless the downstream rival tries to recoup the sunk costs of the franchise fee by raising prices.

Fourthly, the theory assumes that rivals will not vertically integrate. As previ- **7.90** ously discussed, the result of vertical integration is analogous to that of a

---

[60] *See, e.g.*, D. Reiffen, "Equilibrium Vertical Foreclosure: Comment" (1992) 82(3) *American Economic Review*, pp. 694–7. Gaudet and Long (1996) show that whilst full refusal to supply may not be credible without commitment, it may be credible to reduce downstream supply to increase the downstream price. G. Gaudet and N. Van Long, "Vertical Integration, Foreclosure, and Profits with Double Marginalization" (1996) 5(3) *Journal of Economics and Management Strategy*, pp. 409–32.

[61] For example Choi and Yi (2000) assume that before merger, the upstream firm can supply any downstream firm. However, after the vertical merger the upstream firm specialises in its downstream arm's products creating a degree of asset specificity. This makes it costly to supply rival downstream firms and provides the commitment device needed to raise the rival's costs. J. P. Choi and S. S. Yi, "Vertical Foreclosure with the Choice of Input Specifications" (2000) 31(4) *The RAND Journal of Economics*, pp. 717–43. *See also* E. Avenel and C. Barlet, "Vertical Foreclosure, Technological Choice, and Entry in the Intermediate Market" (2000) 9(2) *Journal of Economics and Management Strategy*, pp. 211–30.

7. – Refuse to Deal
Maurits Dolmans and Matthew Bennett

two-part tariff. If the rival downstream and upstream firm vertically integrate, then it is not possible to raise rival's cost. The newly vertically integrated firm internalises the impact that raising upstream prices will have on downstream profitability. In this case, a refusal means the market simply evolves into two vertically integrated firms competing.[62]

7.91   Finally, it should be noted that, whilst the theory discussed above focuses on raising rivals' costs, there is another strand of relatively recent theory that looks at vertical restraints, such as exclusive territories, as a means to softening competition. When upstream firms use downstream distributors, providing exclusive territories (and hence refusing to supply other distributors) they may reduce interbrand as well as intrabrand competition.[63]

5.   Conclusions of Economic Analysis

7.92   In summary, there is no reason to presume that refusal to supply by an undertaking, even a dominant undertaking, is necessarily abusive. As we have outlined in this section, there are good reasons why competition law generally allows undertakings the freedom to determine their trading partners. Not only are there benefits from refusal to supply in vertical settings, exclusive rights provide a means to recover fixed costs from uncertain innovation or investment. Or, as Abraham Lincoln stated with respect to IP protection, patent law *"secured to the inventor, for a limited time, the exclusive use of his invention; and thereby added the fuel of interest to the fire of genius, in the discovery and production of new and useful things."*[64] However, refusals to supply may also harm consumers. Refusals to supply may

---

[62] Choi and Yi (2000) note that if the upstream rival benefits from its increased market power, it may not have an incentive to vertically integrate with the downstream rival, although downstream firm may have greater incentive to do so. *See* J. P. Choi and S. S. Yi *ibid.*

[63] Without exclusive territories, any increase in price by manufacturers will be passed on fully by distributors (under the assumption that there are many of them and hence perfect competition). By making the distributor a monopoly (through exclusive territories) the manufacturer ensure only a smaller proportion of its price increases are pass through to consumers from the distributor. The manufacturer sees downstream demand as less elastic and so raises price. By delegating price setting to the downstream manufacturers can raise their price elasticity. *See* P. Rey and J. E. Stiglitz, "Vertical Restraints and Producers' Competition" (1988) 32(2–3) *European Economic Review*, pp. 561–8 and P. Rey and J. E. Stiglitz, "The Role of Exclusive Territories" (1995) 26(3) *The RAND Journal of Economics*, pp. 431–51. *See also* P. W. Dobson and M. Waterson, "The Competition Effects of Industry-Wide Vertical Price Fixing in Bilateral Oligopoly" (2007) 25(5) *International Journal of Industrial Organization*, pp. 935–62.

[64] A. Lincoln, "Lecture on Discoveries and Inventions" (1858), in R. P. Basler (Ed.), *Collected Works of Abraham Lincoln* (New Brunswick, Rutgers University Press, 1953).

7. – Refuse to Deal
Maurits Dolmans and Matthew Bennett

be used to foreclose competitors in order to maintain, or restore, a monopoly position. They may also be used to raise rivals' costs and distort competition. So, how does this section suggest policy makers treat a refusal to supply?

First, there is little economic rationale for a general obligation to supply, even **7.93** for dominant companies. Such a policy would reverse the trade off between innovation and competition that property law enshrines, and thus significantly damage incentives to innovate.[65]

Secondly, an obligation of supply should only be imposed where a refusal risks **7.94** harming the dynamic competition process. As the OFT has argued in its 2006 submission to the OECD roundtable on innovation, competition and patents, competition policy should avoid intervention against holders of patent-protected innovation where intervention would pose a significant risk to dynamic efficiency, and competition concerns are solely about static efficiency.[66] Thus, if there is no concern about the extension of market power into related markets or future periods, then there is little justification for intervention.

Finally, in order to minimise the effect of obligations to supply on future **7.95** incentives to innovate, courts and competition authorities need to ring fence their decisions to apply to only highly limited circumstances. This involves a trade-off between the need to deter future, similar, anticompetitive behaviour, and the desire to maintain future incentives to innovate. Courts and competition authorities can achieve this by clearly articulating the theory of harm, and how the specific facts of the case support this theory of harm. This is the subject of the following section.

III. Framework for Legal Analysis

Competition law recognises that policy objectives must be balanced against **7.96** the freedom of competition, freedom of contract and property rights.[67] In the words of Advocate General Jacobs in *Oscar Bronner*, "*the right to choose one's*

---

[65] C. Shapiro, "Competition Policy and Innovation", OECD, *STI Working Papers Series*, Paper 2002/11, 2002, p. 16.
[66] "Policy Roundtables: Competition, Patents and Innovation, 2006", paper submitted by the United Kingdom at OECD's Roundtable discussion, October 2006, pp. 1–371, pp. 178–88.
[67] Case C-418/01 *IMS Health v NDC Health* ("*IMS Health*") [2004] ECR I-5039, para. 48 ("*the balancing of the interest in protection of the intellectual property right and the economic freedom of its owner against the interest in protection of free competition.*"); *see* also Advocate General Tizzano in *IMS Health*; *See Microsoft*

7. – Refuse to Deal
Maurits Dolmans and Matthew Bennett

trading partners and freely to dispose of one's property are generally recognised principles in the laws of the Member States, in some cases with constitutional status. Incursions on those rights require careful justification.[68] Given this constitutional status, it is important to investigate the purpose and scope of these rights and the criteria of allowing exceptions to them. The legal analysis below will show that while these rights enjoy a constitutional status, they are not absolute. They serve various purposes. In part, these are political, such as the desire to preserve individual decisional autonomy and freedom from Government interference in business decisions. In part, they reflect the economic policy discussed previously, such as the desire to foster investment in innovation, creation of wealth, preservation of consumer welfare, and an efficient allocation of resources. These objectives are, and should be, also the objectives of competition policy. Imposition of a duty to supply products and services affects risk/reward calculations of firms, and should therefore be imposed only if they are consistent with these objectives and do not detract from them. Similarly, compulsory licences should not be imposed unless on balance they increase long-term consumer welfare in the form of innovation incentives. Given the degree of speculation inherent in these decisions, they should be the exception rather than the rule, and the burden of proof should be firmly on the competition authority imposing the duty to deal. The *Guidance Paper* appropriately recognises this.[69]

7.97 Sections III.2.1 and III.2.2 below describe the protection of property rights and the right to choose one's trading partner under the Charter of Fundamental Rights. This is followed by a discussion of how these fundamental rights are balanced against the prohibition of abuse of dominance, using the concepts of "existence" and "exercise" of property rights (Section III.2.1), the concepts of "specific subject matter" and "essential function" (Section III.2.2), and the requirement of "exceptional circumstances" (Section III.2.3).

Decision 2004, recital 457; Case T-201/04 *Microsoft v Commission* ("*Microsoft Judgment 2007*") [2007] ECR II-3601, paras 319 and 646 ("*in the balancing of the interest in protection of the intellectual property right and the economic freedom of its owner against the interest in protection of free competition, the latter can prevail only where refusal to grant a licence prevents the development of the secondary market, to the detriment of consumers.*") *See* also R. Whish, *Competition Law* (6th Ed., Oxford, Oxford University Press, 2008), pp. 687–8.

[68] Case C-7/97 *Oscar Bronner v Mediaprint Zeitungs – und Zeitschriftenverlag and others* ("*Oscar Bronner*") [1998] ECR I-7791, Opinion of Advocate General Jacobs, para. 56.

[69] *See Guidance Paper supra* note 41, para. 75.

7. – Refuse to Deal
Maurits Dolmans and Matthew Bennett

1. The Charter of Fundamental Rights

1.1. *Protection of Property Rights*

Article 2 TEU provides that "[t]*he Union is founded on the values of respect for*", **7.98** among other things, "*the rule of law and respect for human rights*".[70] Article 6 TEU refers to the Charter of Fundamental Rights, specifying that it has "*the same legal value as the Treaties*".[71] Moreover, "[f]*undamental rights, as guaranteed by the European Convention for the Protection of Human Rights and Fundamental Freedoms and as they result from the constitutional traditions common to the Member States, shall constitute general principles of the Union's law.*"[72]

Article 17 of the Charter guarantees the right to property: "*Everyone has* **7.99** *the right to own, use, dispose of and bequeath his or her lawfully acquired possessions.*" Paragraph 2 of Article 17 adds that "[i]*ntellectual property shall be protected.*" Article 345 TFEU in turn confirms that "[t]*he Treaties shall in no way prejudice the rules in Member States governing the system of property ownership.*"[73] Property rights in physical objects are exclusive in the sense that the owner can deprive others of enjoyment of the asset, absolute in the sense that they persist even if the asset is not under the physical control or in the possession of the owner, universal in that they can be invoked and enforced against any third party even in the absence of privity of contract, and permanent in that they last for the duration of the asset's existence.[74] The right to property therefore imposes an

---

[70] Consolidated versions of the Treaty on European Union and the Treaty on the Functioning of the European Union, OJ 2008 C 115/1.

[71] The Charter is also consistent with the European Convention on Human Rights. Article 52(3) of the Charter provides that "*In so far as this Charter contains rights which correspond to rights guaranteed by the* [European] *Convention for the Protection of Rights and Fundamental Freedoms, the meaning and scope of those rights shall be the same as those laid down by the said Convention. This provision shall not prevent Union law providing more extensive protection.*" European Convention on Human Rights – as amended by Protocols Nos. 11 and 14, *Council of Europe Treaty Series*, No. 5. *See* Section II.3.3 for an economic analysis.

[72] *See supra* note 70.

[73] Consolidated version of the Treaty on the Functioning of the European Union, OJ 2010 C 83/49.

[74] Rights in intellectual property may be more narrowly circumscribed and subject to exceptions. They tend to be limited in time and subject to conditions (such as patents, copyrights, design rights), they may require specific disclosures, grants or registrations (such as patents, trademarks, and trade names), may not protect against independent development (such as copyright and trade secrets), or may not require owner consent for all forms of exploitation (such as copyrights in software). There was debate in the past whether intellectual property is property, but Article 17(2) of the Charter settles that question. As to trade secrets, the Court of First Instance recognised in *Microsoft Judgment 2007 supra* note 67, para. 289, that it is appropriate to apply a "*presumption that the protocols in question, or the specifications of those protocols, are covered by intellectual property rights or constitute trade secrets and that those secrets must be treated as equivalent to intellectual property rights.*" *See* Section II.3.3. In AstraZeneca v Commission, the

7. – Refuse to Deal
Maurits Dolmans and Matthew Bennett

attendant obligation on Member States and the European Union to refrain from taking property, to protect property against unauthorised taking by others, and to refrain from requiring an owner to supply goods to or suffer the use of property by others without the owner's consent, even if this would lower prices in a market or allow competition to arise. However, this right is not of an absolute nature.[75]

7.100 Paragraph 1 of Article 17 sets out when exceptions can be made: *"No one may be deprived of his or her possessions, except in the public interest and in the cases and under the conditions provided for by law, subject to fair compensation being paid in good time for their loss. The use of property may be regulated by law in so far as is necessary for the general interest."*[76]

7.101 In addition, Article 52(1) of the Charter specifies that "[a]*ny limitation on the exercise of the rights and freedoms recognised by this Charter must be provided for by law and respect the essence of those rights and freedoms. Subject to the principle of proportionality, limitations may be made only if they are necessary and genuinely meet objectives of general interest recognised by the Union or the need to protect the rights and freedoms of others."*[77]

---

appellant company claimed that a registration of a marketing authorisation for a drug is equivalent to a property right. The Court of Justice dismissed an appeal against the General Court ruling, finding that the *"possibility … in Directive 65/65 of deregistering a* [marketing authorisation] *is not equivalent to a property right"*. *See* Case C-457/10 P *Astra Zeneca v Commission*, not yet reported, para. 149.

[75] For instance, the Court of Justice has held that the right to property must be balanced with other fundamental rights. *See, e.g.,* Case C-70/10, concerning SABAM, the Belgian collecting society representing authors, composers and publishers in the field of intellectual property rights, which collects royalties on behalf of their members, and Scarlet, an Internet Service Provider (ISP). SABAM applied to a Belgian court for an injunction ordering Scarlet to install a filtering system to track and block the transmission of copyright-protected files by internet users, which would necessitate Scarlet to monitor communications on its network. In a preliminary ruling, the Court of Justice held that a fair balance had to be struck between, on the one hand, the protection of the intellectual property rights enjoyed by copyright holders, and on the other hand, the freedom to conduct business of ISPs and customers' rights to protection of personal data and to receive or impart information, which are rights safeguarded by the Charter of Fundamental Rights of the EU (Case C-70/10 *Scarlet Extended v Société belge des auteurs, compositeurs et éditeurs SCRL (SABAM)*, not yet reported, paras 49–50). SABAM's request was deemed incapable of meeting this balance. *See also* Case C-360/10 *Belgische Vereniging van Auteurs, Componisten en Uitgevers v Netlog ("SABAM")*, not yet reported, paras 44–50, concerning an online social network. *See also* C-275/06 *Productores de Música de España (Promusicae) v Telefónica de España* [2008] ECR I-271, paras 65–70, in which the right to protection of property was limited by the Court of Justice against the right to respect for private life.

[76] *See* also Protocol No. 1 to the Convention for the Protection of Human Rights and Fundamental, 20 March 1952, Council of Europe Treaty Series, No. 9, Article 1: *"Every natural or legal person is entitled to the peaceful enjoyment of his possessions. No one shall be deprived of his possessions except in the public interest and subject to the conditions provided for by law and by the general principles of international law. The preceding provisions shall not, however, in any way impair the right of a State to enforce such laws as it deems necessary to control the use of property in accordance with the general interest or to secure the payment of taxes or other contributions or penalties."*

[77] Charter of fundamental rights of the European Union, OJ 2007 C 303/17.

7. – Refuse to Deal
Maurits Dolmans and Matthew Bennett

Accordingly, a duty to supply goods, allow access to a facility, or to license an **7.102** intellectual property under competition law requires that the following five cumulative conditions be met:[78]

1.1.1. Conditions Provided by Law

Articles 101 and 102 TFEU, and the equivalent national laws, qualify as "law" **7.103** in the sense of generally applicable and generally known rules adopted by State authorities in the public interest in accordance with a democratic process.[79] As required by the Charter, Article 102 TFEU contains several explicit "cases and conditions" to determine when a duty to deal applies: the owner must be an "undertaking", must have a "dominant position", must engage in "abuse", and this conduct must "affect trade between Member States". Article 102 TFEU and in particular the notion of "abuse" is, however, an open norm. Four specific examples of abusive conduct are listed in paragraphs (a) through (d), but these examples are non-exhaustive.[80] To avoid the arbitrary taking of property even when the basic conditions are met, and to ensure that the rules are sufficiently predictable by firms to allow them to adjust their conduct with sufficient comfort that they comply with the law, further limiting principles must be developed by case law (*see* discussion of "exceptional circumstances" in Section III.2.3.1 below). To remain within the limits of constitutionality, it is important that these limiting principles be applied consistently, and comply with all of the conditions of Article 17(1) and 52(1) of the Charter. Deviation from or extension of the limiting principles developed by case law requires adequate and clear justification.

---

[78] These five conditions are the very foundation of, and circumscribe, the "exceptional circumstances" criterion for compulsory dealing discussed below in Section II.2.3.

[79] This definition is consistent with the meaning of "law" under the European Convention of Human Rights. Although the Convention does not contain any express definition of "law", the Court interpreted it, endorsing a "material" notion of law. The Court requires the law to be accessible, foreseeable and enacted according to its national legal basis (*i.e.*, by the legislative power, by delegation of powers, or created by the case law, especially in common law countries). *See, e.g.*, *Silver and others v United Kingdom*, ECtHR judgment of 25 March 1983, Series A No. 61, para. 86; and *Sunday Times v United Kingdom*, ECtHR judgment of 26 April 1979, Series A. No. 30, paras 47–9. On the absence of a definition of law under the European Charter of Human Rights, *see* D. Triantafyllou, "The European Charter of Fundamental Rights and the "Rule of Law": Restricting Fundamental Rights by Reference" 2002 (39) *Common Market Law Review*, pp. 53–64.

[80] "The list of abusive practices set out in the second paragraph of Article 82 of the Treaty is not exhaustive." (Case C-33/94 *Tetrapak* [1996] ECR I-5951, para. 37).

7. – Refuse to Deal
Maurits Dolmans and Matthew Bennett

1.1.2. Public Interest Objective

7.104 Competition law serves public interest objectives, but it is necessary that each individual instance of the imposition of a duty to deal should itself also be specifically justified by a well-defined public interest objective. Since private interests are not adequate, the convenience of competitors or the short-term benefit of price reduction for a particular customer cannot justify a duty to supply or share property. In addition, competition itself is not a goal of public policy, but a tool.[81] An obligation to deal cannot, therefore, be based merely on the consideration that it will foster (short-term) economic rivalry. It requires a clear link with the ultimate policy objective of competition law. This policy goal of competition law is, of course, a political choice, which may change over time. It is widely accepted that Article 102 TFEU no longer reflects a traditional ordo-liberal approach,[82] but is geared towards maximising long-run consumer welfare.[83] Consumer welfare is principally an

---

[81] *See* discussion below on the elimination of Article 3(1)(g) EC from the TEU.

[82] The ordo-liberal approach relies on the State to ensure a stable environment – based on the rules of a market economy – that allows individuals and firms freedom to act, preserves diversified control of enterprises, reduces the negative effects of a free market economy and protects individuals from the abuse of power. The notions of ordo-liberalism were developed by Walther Eucken (1952). *See* W. Eucken, *Grundsätze der Wirtschaftspolitik* (1st Ed., Mohr, Tübingen, 1952).

[83] *See* Case T-168/01 *GlaxoSmithKline Services v Commission* [2006] ECR II-2969, para. 118: "*In effect, the objective assigned to EC, which constitutes a fundamental provision indispensable for the achievement of the missions entrusted to the Community, in particular for the functioning of the internal market, is to prevent undertakings, by restricting competition between themselves or with third parties, from reducing the welfare of the final consumer of the products in question.*" *See* also Commission Notice – Guidelines on the application of Article 81(3) of the Treaty ("Notice on Article 101(3) TFEU"), OJ 2004 C 101/97, para. 13. "Consumer welfare", as the goal of antitrust law, became the governing standard following *see supra* note 47, p. 66. In the EU framework, an examination to the travaux préparatoires of Article 102 has shown that the drafters intention was to protect customers (*see* R. Whish *supra* note 67, p. 193) and footnote 184 citing P. Akman, "Searching for the Long-Lost Soul of Article 82 EC", CCP Working Paper Series, Paper No. 07–5, March 2007, available at http://competitionpolicy.ac.uk/publications/working-papers-pre-2008. There is some debate whether Microsoft looks back to an ordo-liberal approach (*see* C. Ahlborn and D. S. Evans, "The Microsoft Judgment and its Implications for Competition Policy Towards Dominant Firms in Europe" (2009) 75(3) *Antitrust Law Journal*, pp. 17–20; A. Devlin and M. S. Jacobs, "Microsoft's Five Fatal Flaws" (2009) 67 *Columbia Business Law Review*, pp. 128, 133–4). The Court of First Instance stated in the *Microsoft Judgment 2007 supra* note 67, para. 664: "*Last, it must be borne in mind that it is settled case-law that Article* [102 TFEU] *covers not only practices which may prejudice consumers directly but also those which indirectly prejudice them by impairing an effective competitive structure.*" The Court of First Instance, however, based the abuse on Article 102(b) that prohibits "*limiting innovation to the detriment of consumers*" and analysed the impact of Microsoft's conduct not with respect to competitors' freedom of action or the political implications of the concentration of power in the hands of one firm, but in the light of consumer harm. In that context, the statement that Article 102 TFEU covers "*practices which may prejudice consumers directly but also those which indirectly prejudice them by impairing an effective competitive structure*" should not be controversial. Without effective competition, prices will increase and innovation is affected, to the prejudice of consumers.

7. – Refuse to Deal
Maurits Dolmans and Matthew Bennett

economic notion, but not one that is absolute or uncontroversial.[84] It should be distinguished from overall social welfare and from the interests of other stakeholders such as shareholders and employees in a firm. These, and objectives of income redistribution, are not appropriate goals in the application of competition law unless they coincide with consumer welfare.[85] On the other hand, consumer welfare is not limited to consumers' financial interest. Welfare should take into account consumer benefits from innovation and choice, and arguably may require taking into account price externalities that affect overall consumer interest, such as user safety and environmental sustainability.

1.1.3.   Respect for the Essence of the Rights and Freedoms[86]

As discussed above, as rights *in rem*, property rights in physical assets are in **7.105** principle exclusive, absolute, universal and permanent. These are the characteristics, or "specific subject matter", of property.[87] The "essence" or "essential

---

[84] *See* R. W. Pitman, "Consumer Surplus as the Appropriate Standard for Antitrust Enforcement" (2007) 3(2) *Competition Policy International Journal*, pp. 205–24 and references therein. *See also* A. Edlin and J. Farrell, "Freedom to Trade and the Competitive Process", *NBER Working Paper*, No. 16818, February 2011.

[85] Excessive pricing cases should therefore only rarely lead to obligations to deal absent additional considerations. One area may be where excessive royalties and discriminatory licensing distort competition to the detriment of consumers, as could be the case in certain standards cases. Regarding standards, *see* M. Dolmans, "A Tale of Two Tragedies – A Plea for Open Standards, and Some Comments on the RAND Report" (2010) *Concurrences*, No 1-2012, p. 11 (a refusal or injunction is justified if licensee refuses in turn to license essential IPR on FRAND terms to the licensor, where the licensee cannot pay or refuses to pay a FRAND rate, or where the licensee is unwilling to take a license). But for a broader application, *see* Case T-198/98 *Micro Leader Business v Commission* (*"Micro Leader"*) [1999] ECR II-3989, para. 54 *"Whilst it is true that, under Article 4(c) of Directive 91/250, the marketing by MC of copies of software in Canada does not, in itself, exhaust MC's copyright over its products in the Community (see above, paragraph 34), the factual evidence put forward by the applicant constitutes, at the very least, an indication that, for equivalent transactions, Microsoft applied lower prices on the Canadian market than on the Community market and that the Community prices were excessive." See also* Section V below.

[86] The Explanations Relating to the Charter of Fundamental Rights, OJ 2007 C 303/17 does not clarify what should be meant by "essence of the rights and freedoms". According to the note, "[t]*he purpose of Article 52 is to set the scope of the rights and principles of the Charter, and to lay down rules for their interpretation. Paragraph 1 deals with the arrangements for the limitation of rights. The wording is based on the case-law of the Court of Justice: '... it is well established in the case-law of the Court that restrictions may be imposed on the exercise of fundamental rights, in particular in the context of a common organisation of the market, provided that those restrictions in fact correspond to objectives of general interest pursued by the Community and do not constitute, with regard to the aim pursued, disproportionate and unreasonable interference undermining the very substance of those rights' (judgment of 13 April 2000, Case C-292/97, paragraph 45 of the grounds). The reference to general interests recognised by the Union covers both the objectives mentioned in Article 3 of the Treaty on European Union and other interests protected by specific provisions of the Treaties such as Article 4(1) of the Treaty on European Union and Articles 35(3), 36 and 346 of the Treaty on the Functioning of the European Union".*

[87] *See* case law on "specific subject matter" below, Section III.2.2. and Joined Cases C-241 and 242/91 P *Radio Telefis Eireann (RTE) and Independent Television Publications (ITP) v Commission* (*"Magill"*) [1995] ECR I-743, Opinion of Advocate General Gulmann, paras 36–7.

7. – Refuse to Deal
Maurits Dolmans and Matthew Bennett

function" of the right can be defined by the policy objective the legislature sought to achieve.[88] Protection of property serves the ultimate objective of social welfare, and the freedom and full development of individual potential. Reflecting utilitarian thinking, it recognises that overall welfare of society tends to increase if individuals or firms are allowed exclusive control over assets that they create or develop, provided that the scope and conditions of the rights are clear, and adequate procedures are available for their consistent enforcement.[89] As discussed in the previous section, the right to exclusive enjoyment, and the right to trade assets for other property or services, creates an incentive to invest in production and innovation. It avoids what is called the "tragedy of the commons", the overuse of public goods controlled by no one.[90] Intellectual property laws are an even clearer example of this. If imitators could enter the market without limitation, free-riding on creators' and innovators' investments, a market failure would ensue: the anticipation of being unable to raise price above marginal costs and thus recover sunk R&D expenses and be compensated for risk would discourage market-funded innovation.[91] In sum, the "respect for the essence" of property rights required by the Charter means that any interference with these rights (a) must be exceptional, and

---

[88] *See* case law on "essential function" below in Section III.2.2., and Opinion of Advocate General Gulmann in *Magill supra* note 87, paras 36–7. *See also* Case T-65/98 *Van den Bergh Foods v Commission* ("*Van den Bergh Foods*") [2003] ECR II-4653, para. 170: "*It is settled case-law that, although the right to property forms part of the general principles of Community law, it is not an absolute right but must be viewed in relation to its <u>social function</u>. Consequently, its exercise may be restricted, provided that those restrictions in fact correspond to <u>objectives of general interest pursued</u> by the Community and do not constitute a disproportionate and intolerable interference, impairing the <u>very substance of the rights</u> guaranteed (Hauer, paragraph 23; Case 265/87 Schräder [1989] ECR 2237, para. 15, Case C-280/93 Germany v Commission [1994] ECR I-4973, paragraph 78). … restrictions may be applied on the exercise of the right to property, provided that they are not disproportionate and do not affect the <u>substance</u> of that right.*"

[89] W. R. Cornish and D. Llewelyn, *Intellectual Property: Patents, Copyright, Trade Marks and Allied Rights* (5th Ed., London, Sweet & Maxwell, 2003), pp. 35–6: "[Economists] *argued that only with firm legal recognition of individual ownership would the full value of society's resources come to be realized. Property, with a functioning regime of contract law as its necessary corollary, would maximize exploitation. A synergy of individual transactions would enable the economy to grow and diffuse its riches to an increasing range of its population.*"

[90] G. Hardin, "The Tragedy of the Commons" (1968) 162(3859) Science, pp. 1243–8. Simplified, in the 18th Century, it was found (or argued, by the proponents of enclosure) that common land in Britain was overexploited, because each user had an individual interest in letting the maximum number of cattle freely graze on it, with the result that the fields were exhausted, and everyone suffered. Even today, we exhaust resources and suffer environmental pollution, because we produce goods the price of which does not include the cost imposed on society caused by the pollution of "free" air, soil and water (a "negative externality").

[91] Thus, patent law "*secures to the inventor, for a limited time, the exclusive use of his invention; and thereby adds the fuel of interest to the fire of genius.*" *See* A. Lincoln *supra* note 64. An alternative to using IPRs would be for government, academia, or charitable institutions to fund R&D, or to look for alternative revenue opportunities such as services-funded or advertising-funded R&D.

7. – Refuse to Deal
Maurits Dolmans and Matthew Bennett

(b) serve policy goals that are consistent with the social welfare objectives of property law. Since consumer welfare is a subset of societal welfare, and all members of society are consumers, duty to supply cases under competition law can meet this condition, provided that the objectives of intervention are clearly spelled out and analysed, and the plaintiff or Commission proves that the abusive conduct causes consumer harm or (in compulsory license cases) limits overall innovation.

1.1.4. Proportionality

The fourth condition is that *"limitations may be made only if they are necessary and genuinely meet objectives of general interest recognised by the Union or the need to protect the rights and freedoms of others."*[92] As discussed in greater depth in the sections on "objective justification" and remedies below, this constitutional requirement of proportionality precludes a per se rule prohibiting refusals to supply. Obligations to deal must be limited to exceptional cases,[93] and every such case requires an analysis under a "rule of reason".[94] A duty to supply can be imposed only if it can be shown that (1) the duty to supply serves a defined legitimate public policy objective (consumer welfare) that in the individual case outweighs the private interest invoked by the dominant firm and the public interest in preserving private investment incentives; (2) the duty to deal is effective in achieving that general interest objective (causal link); and, (3) there is no less restrictive alternative than imposing the duty to deal. **7.106**

1.1.5. Fair Compensation Paid in Good Time

This element is, strictly speaking, not one that limits the cases in which a duty to deal is appropriate, but defines the parameters of the remedy. It applies explicitly in cases of expropriation, and in cases of limitation of the exercise of property rights it applies as a consequence of the principle of proportionality. A remedy involving a duty to supply or share assets must not deprive the owner of adequate compensation. This will in most cases involve a payment of money, but there might be exceptional cases, discussed below, where the **7.107**

---

[92] *See supra* note 77, Art. 52(1).
[93] *See also Microsoft Judgment 2007 supra* note 67, para. 331; *Magill supra* note 87, para. 50; Case C-238/87 *Volvo v Erik Veng (UK)* [1988] ECR 6211, para. 9.
[94] *See, e.g., Microsoft Judgment 2007 supra* note 67, paras 688 and 1144–54.

7. – Refuse to Deal

Maurits Dolmans and Matthew Bennett

marginal costs of supply are zero and where the owner has been fairly remunerated already, for instance by increased sales of complementary products, or where the investment costs were borne by a public authority or cross-subsidised from reserved activities. The requirement of fair compensation could also affect non-financial terms and conditions, and may even involve a duty to supply on the claimant's side, such as a cross-license of intellectual property on fair and reasonable terms.[95] This will be discussed further in the context of the remedy, and as shown, calculation of fair compensation is not a simple matter.

1.2.   Right to Choose One's Trading Partner

7.108   Neither the Charter on Fundamental Rights nor the European Convention on Human Rights explicitly protect the freedom to choose one's contract partner. As Advocate General Jacobs stated in *Bronner*, however, "*the right to choose one's trading partner*" is acknowledged as a "*generally recognised principle in the laws of the Member States*".[96] The Commission echoes this in its decisions: "*The system established by Community competition law recognises the principle of free enterprise and the freedom of undertakings to deal with other companies. The right to choose one's trading partners and freely to dispose of one's property are also generally recognised principles in the laws of the Member States.*"[97]

7.109   The Commission confirms in its *Guidance Paper* that "*<u>the Commission starts from the position</u> that, <u>generally speaking</u>, any undertaking, whether dominant or not, <u>should have the right to choose its trading partners and to dispose freely of its property</u>*" (emphasis

---

[95] *See* ETSI, "*ETSI Rules of Procedure, 30 November 2011 – Annex 6: ETSI Intellectual Property Rights Policy*", November 2011, Article 6.1: "*When an ESSENTIAL IPR relating to a particular STANDARD or TECHNICAL SPECIFICATION is brought to the attention of ETSI, the Director-General of ETSI shall immediately request the owner to give within three months an irrevocable undertaking in writing that it is prepared to grant irrevocable licences on fair, reasonable and non-discriminatory terms and conditions under such IPR to at least the following extent: (i) MANUFACTURE, including the right to make or have made customized components and sub-systems to the licensee's own design for use in MANUFACTURE; (ii) sell, lease, or otherwise dispose of EQUIPMENT so MANUFACTURED; (iii) repair, use, or operate EQUIPMENT; and (iv) use METHODS. The above undertaking may be made subject to the condition that those who seek licences agree to reciprocate.*"

[96] *See Oscar Bronner*, Opinion of Advocate General Jacobs, para. 56. The US Supreme Court held in *Verizon Communications v Law Offices of Curtis v Trinko* ("*Trinko*"), 540 US 398 (2004), p. 408 that "*as a general matter, the Sherman Act does not restrict the long recognized right of [a] trader or manufacturer engages in an entirely private business, freely to exercise his own independent discretion as to parties with whom he will deal.*" The same principle was previously stated in *United States v Colgate*, 250 US 300 (1919).

[97] Case COMP/38.096 *Clearstream*, Commission Decision of 2 June 2004, not yet published, para. 217.

7. – Refuse to Deal
Maurits Dolmans and Matthew Bennett

added).[98] The Commission's careful choice of words might be read to suggest that the freedom to choose one's contract partner could be a generally recognised principle in the laws of the Member States, but not one of constitutional status in the European Union. There are, however, a number of provisions in the Charter on Fundamental Rights that indicate that the freedom to choose one's contract partner deserves deference as a true fundamental right.

Specifically, Article 17 of the Charter not only guarantees the right to own and **7.110** use lawfully acquired possessions, but also to "*dispose of and bequeath*" them. Without the freedom to contract, the right to dispose of them or not in accordance with the owner's free will would be emptied of all practical meaning.[99] The free choice of business partners is thus inherent and implicit in the fundamental right to property, and necessary for an efficient society.[100] The same applies to a number of other fundamental rights that encompass the freedom to choose one's contract partner, such as Article 16, the freedom to conduct a business (which, to have useful effect, must include the freedom to decide with whom to do business and whom to select as a supplier or customer).[101]

It is submitted, therefore, that the freedom to choose one's contract partner **7.111** exists as a fundamental right, even in situations that do not involve access to or supply of property.[102] At the very least, the five cumulative conditions discussed above should be applied to any competition law interference with the freedom to choose one's contract partner.

---

[98] *See Guidance Paper supra* note 41, para. 75.

[99] N. Reich, *Understanding EU Law: Objectives, Principles and Methods of Community Law* (Antwerpen – Oxford, Intersentia, 2005), p. 277.

[100] M. Steiner, "Economics in Antitrust Policy: Freedom to Compete vs. Freedom to Contract", Dissertation. com, July 2007: "*The freedom of contact, or the individual autonomy to enter into agreements, has been a key to the foundation of economic development. It ensures, together with private property rights, that assets are transferred to the party, which utilizes the best.*"

[101] In its judgment *Bayer v Commission* the Court of First Instance found that: "*The case-law of the Court of Justice indirectly recognises the importance of safeguarding free enterprise when applying the competition rules of the Treaty*" Case T-41/96 *Bayer v Commission* [2000] ECR II-3383, para. 180. *See* also Article 12, the freedom of assembly and of association (which includes the freedom to pool or share assets in the formation of a business); and Article 15, the right to engage in work and to pursue a freely chosen or accepted occupation, and the right of establishment and to provide services in any Member State (which implies the right to dedicate assets to that end). *See supra* note 77.

[102] In cases involving the supply of services not involving a sale of or sharing of property, there could in certain cases be even greater reticence in imposing a duty to deal, in view of the strict ban on "forced or compulsory labour" in Article 5 of the Charter of fundamental rights, *see supra* note 77.

7. – Refuse to Deal
Maurits Dolmans and Matthew Bennett

2. TFEU Legal Framework Balancing Fundamental Rights Against Freedom to Compete

7.112 This section discusses the manner in which the European courts and Commission have balanced the ban on abuse of dominance under Article 102 TFEU against the fundamental rights to property and freedom of contract. It explains the Court's holdings (explicit in earlier case law and implicit later) with respect to the exercise and existence of property rights, the concepts of specific subject matter and essential function of property rights, and concludes that while in principle a refusal to deal is not an abuse of dominance even if it limits competition, compulsory access can be imposed in "exceptional circumstances." The case law indicates that exceptional circumstances arise where (1) access to the property right is essential for competition in a neighbouring market; (2) all the conditions of an exclusionary or exploitative abuse of dominance are met, including consumer harm; and, (3) the abuse involves an exploitation of a property right in a manner that is inconsistent with or disproportionate to its "essential function".

2.1. *Art 345 TFEU (ex Article 295 EU and ex Article 222 EC) and the "Existence-exercise" Dichotomy*

7.113 As explained above, under Article 52(1) of the Charter, any limitation on the exercise of property rights and the freedom to choose one's contract partner "*must be provided for by law*". A key relevant provision of law, apart from Article 102 TFEU itself, is Article 345 TFEU (ex 295 EU and ex 222 EC). Article 345 TFEU provides that "[t]*he Treaties shall in no way prejudice the rules in Member States governing the system of property ownership*". The Court of Justice has confirmed on various occasions that in accordance with this provision "*the existence of a right conferred by the legislation of a Member State in regard to the protection of … property … cannot be affected by the provisions of the Treaty.*"[103]

7.114 Although the existence of property is untouched, the Court of Justice used to distinguish explicitly the "existence" from the "exercise" of property rights, allowing the Court and competition authorities discretion to curtail property

---

[103] *See, e.g.,* Case 262/81 *Coditel, Compagnie générale pour la diffusion de la télévision, and others v Ciné-Vog Films and others* [1982] ECR 3381, at para. 13. *See also* Case 144/81 *Keurkoop v Nancy Kean Gifts* [1982] ECR 2853, at para. 18; Advocate General Mischo in Case 238/87 *Volvo v Erik Veng (UK)* [1988] ECR 6211; and Case 53/87 *Consorzio italiano della componentistica di ricambio per autoveicoli (CICRA) and Maxicar v Régie nationale des usines Renault* ("*Renault*") [1988] ECR 6039, at para. 10.

7. – Refuse to Deal
Maurits Dolmans and Matthew Bennett

rights where their use could conflict with competition policy.[104] While the difference between "existence" and "exercise" is not clear, it would appear that under Article 345 TFEU, EU law cannot curb the use of a property right so regularly and comprehensively that the right is effectively eliminated and ceases to exist in practice. The Court of Justice differentiated between the existence of a property right conferred by national laws and its exercise, which concerns "*certain aspects of the manner in which the right is exercised*".[105] Other legal systems like US antitrust law similarly recognise that curbing the use of the right is not equivalent to eliminating it.[106]

2.2. The Concepts of "Specific Subject Matter" and "Essential Function"

The distinction between the existence and exercise eliminates a claim of absolute immunity of property rights from the application of competition law, but is not very helpful as a limiting principle. To that end, the Court of Justice defined the concepts of "specific subject matter" and "essential function". According to Attorney General Gulmann in *Magill*, the distinction between specific subject-matter and essential function is that the former is used in EU law to define, in summary fashion, the "core rights" enjoyed by the owner of the intellectual property right in question, whereas the latter defines the legislative purpose for which the right is conferred in the first place.[107] Both concepts are defined by the Court of Justice, based on a review of national law or, where the law has been harmonised, EU directives and regulations. The concepts have been applied to intellectual property, but should apply equally to all property rights and fundamental freedoms. The "specific subject-matter" of a property right normally includes the exclusive right (1) to put the

7.115

---

[104] *See, e.g.*, Case 40/70 *Sirena v Eda and others* ("*Sirena*") [1971] ECR 69, Joined Cases 56 and 58/64 *Établissements Consten and Grundig-Verkaufs v Commission* ("*Consten and Grundig*") [1966] ECR 299 and Case 78/70 *Deutsche Grammophon v Metro-SB-Großmärkte* ("*Deutsche Grammophon*") [1971] ECR 487.

[105] *See* Case 262/81 *supra* note 103, paras 13 *et seq*.

[106] In *United States v Microsoft Corp (Microsoft III)*, the US Court of Appeals for the DC Circuit held that: "*The company claims an absolute and unfettered right to use its intellectual property as it wishes. … That is no more correct than the proposition that use of one's personal property, such as a baseball bat, cannot give rise to tort liability.*" (*United States v Microsoft Corp (Microsoft III)*, 253 F.3d 34 (D.C. Cir. 2001)).

[107] Opinion of Advocate General Gulmann in *Magill*, paras 36–7 "*As the Commission has stated, the concept of the essential function is different from that of the specific subject-matter. The two concepts serve different purposes. In its case-law on Articles 30 and 36 of the Treaty the Court of Justice has used the two concepts at the same time and held that in order to determine the exact scope of the rights conferred on the owner of an intellectual property right, that is in defining the specific subject-matter, regard must be had to the essential function of the right. There is therefore no conflict between finding that the specific subject-matter of copyright includes the exclusive right to reproduce the work and its corollary, the right of first marketing and holding that the essential function of copyright is to protect the moral rights in the work and ensure a reward for creative effort*".

7. – Refuse to Deal
Maurits Dolmans and Matthew Bennett

product into circulation on the EU market for the first time, either directly or through licensees or distributors, and (2) to prevent infringements of the right by third parties unconnected with the proprietor of the right in question.[108] The essential function may differ for different property rights, but generally speaking, it is "*to ensure a reward for the creative effort*".[109] As explained in more detail in Section II above, the essential function of property rights in a market

---

[108] Case C-10/89 *CNL-SUCAL v HAG GF* [1990] ECR I-3711, para.14; *See also Deutsche Grammophon*, para. 11 ("*Article 36 only permits prohibitions or restrictions on the free movement of goods in the Community to the extent that they are justified for the protection of the rights that form the 'specific subject-matter' of the industrial or commercial property.*") Advocate General Jacobs in Case C-10/89 *CNL-SUCAL v HAG GF* [1990] ECR I-3711 ("*The specific subject-matter of an IPR is a fluid concept, which is defined and refined on a case-by-case basis, allowing subtle distinctions, depending on the type of intellectual property issue, as to whether exercise of an IPR is compatible with Arts 28 to 30.*"). For patents, the specific subject-matter is, *inter alia*, to ensure to the holder the exclusive right to utilise an invention regarding the manufacturing and first circulation of industrial products either directly or through licensees. *See* Case 15/74 *Centrafarm and Adriaan de Peijper v Sterling Drug* [1974] ECR 1147; Case 16/74 *Centrafarm and Adriaan de Peijper v Winthrop* [1974] ECR 1183; Case 187/80 *Merck v Stephar and Petrus Stephanus Exler* [1981] ECR 2063; Case 19/84 *Pharmon v Hoechst* [1985] ECR 2281; Case 434/85 *Allen and Hanburys v Generics* (UK) [1988] ECR 1245; Case 35/87 *Thetford and others v Fiamma and others* [1988] ECR 3585; Case C-235/89 *Commission v Italian Republic* [1992] ECR I-777; Case C-30/90 *Commission v United Kingdom of Great Britain and Northern Ireland* [1992] ECR I-829; Case C-191/90 *Generics (UK) and Harris Pharmaceuticals v Smith Kline & French Laboratories* [1992] ECR I-5335; Joined Cases C-267 and 268/95 *Merck and others v Primecrown and others* [1996] ECR I-6285. In relation to design rights, the specific subject-matter comprises the right to prevent third parties from manufacturing, selling or importing without the consent of the design holder products incorporating the design forms or part of it (Case 238/87 *Volvo v Erik Veng (UK)* ("*Volvo*") [1988] ECR 6211; Case C-61/97 *Foreningen af danske Videogramdistributører and others v Laserdisken* [1998] ECR I-5171), but not the right to prevent the transit of a product bearing the design through the territory of a Member State as such involves no use of the appearance of the protected design (Case C-23/99 *Commission v France* [2000] ECR I-7653). For copyright, the specific subject matter is to ensure the protection of the moral and economic rights of their holders. The protection of moral rights enables authors and performers, in particular, to object to any distortion, mutilation or other modification of a work that would be prejudicial to their honor or reputation. Economic rights confer the right to exploit commercially the marketing of the protected work, particularly in the form of licenses granted in return for payment of royalties. *See* Case C-92/92 *Phil Collins v Imtrat Handelsgesellschaft* [1993] ECR I-5145; Joined Cases 55 and 57/80 *Musik-Vertrieb membran and K-tel International v GEMA* [1981] ECR 147. As to trademarks, the specific subject matter is the exclusive right to utilise the trademark for the first circulation of a product and to protect the trademark owner against competitors who would take advantage of the position and reputation of the trademark by selling goods improperly bearing the mark. *See* Case C-10/89 *CNL-SUCAL v HAG GF* [1990] ECR I-371; Case C-9/93 *IHT Internationale Heiztechnik and Uwe Danzinger v Ideal-Standard and Wabco Standard* [1994] ECR I-2789; Case C-349/95 *Frits Loendersloot v George Ballantine & Son and others* [1997] ECR I-6227; Case C-115/02 *Administration des douanes et droits indirects (ADDI) v Rioglass and Transremar* [2003] ECR I-12705.

[109] For copyright, the essential function is "*to protect the moral rights in the work and to ensure a reward for the creative effort*", *see Magill supra* note 87, para. 58; Case 62/79 *Compagnie générale pour la diffusion de la télévision, Coditel, and others v Ciné Vog Films and others* [1980] ECR 881, para. 14; *See* Case 262/81 *supra* note 103. For trademark, the essential function is to "*guarantee the identity of the origin of the trade-marked product to the consumer or ultimate user … by enabling him to distinguish it without any risk of confusion from products of different origin*". *See, ex multis*, Case 102/77 *Hoffmann-La Roche v Centrafarm Vertriebsgesellschaft Pharmazeutischer Erzeugnisse* [1978] ECR 1139, para. 7; Case 3/78 *Centrafarm v American Home Products* [1978] ECR 1823, para. 12; Case C-379/97 *Pharmacia & Upjohn v Paranova* [1999] ECR I-6927, para. 16;

7. – Refuse to Deal
Maurits Dolmans and Matthew Bennett

economy is to provide producers, creators and innovators with the prospect of a return on their investment in production, research and development, and bringing a product to market. It is the policy justification for both intellectual property and property rights in physical assets. The "essential function" thus is the core of the fundamental right to property that competition law must not impinge upon. The *Guidance Paper* reflects the thinking that led the courts to define the notion of "essential function", while not explicitly mentioning the terms, in wording that is worthy of full citation:

> "*any undertaking, whether dominant or not, should have the right to choose its trading partners and to dispose freely of its property. The Commission therefore considers that intervention on competition law grounds requires careful consideration where the application of Article [102] would lead to the imposition of an obligation to supply on the dominant undertaking. The existence of such an obligation – even for a fair remuneration – may undermine undertakings' incentives to invest and innovate and, thereby, possibly harm consumers. The knowledge that they may have a duty to supply against their will may lead dominant undertakings – or undertakings who anticipate that they may become dominant – not to invest, or to invest less, in the activity in question. Also, competitors may be tempted to free ride on investments made by the dominant undertaking instead of investing themselves. Neither of these consequences would, in the long run, be in the interest of consumers.*"[110]

7.116 The concepts of "specific subject matter" and "essential function" are useful as a two-stage litmus test in cases where property rights are invoked as a defence against the application of competition law and free movement rules, and to determine the hard core of property rights that EU law cannot touch in accordance with Article 345 TFEU and the Charter on Fundamental

---

See Case C-349/95 *supra* note 108, para. 24. Cf. also the recent trademark Case C-487/07 *L'Oréal and others v Bellure and others* ("*L'Oréal*") [2009] ECR I-5185. Although not relating to competition law, it is interesting to note the approach of the Court, that the *"functions include not only the essential function of the trade mark, which is to guarantee to consumers the origin of the goods or services, but also its other functions, in particular that of guaranteeing the quality of the goods or services in question and those of communication, investment or advertising"* (para. 58). This should be seen in the context of para. 49, which appears to recognise the need to protect *"its power of attraction, its reputation and its prestige"* and to ensure a reward for *"the marketing effort expended by the proprietor of the mark in order to create and maintain the image of that mark."* Finally, the essential function of patents consists in *"according the inventor an exclusive right of first placing the product on the market so as to allow him to obtain the reward for his creative effort"*, *see* Cases 15/74, 19/84 (para. 26) and Joined Cases C-267 and 268/95 (para. 31) *supra* note 108; Case 187/80 *Merck v Stephar and Petrus Stephanus Exler* [1981] ECR 2063, para. 9.

[110] See *Guidance Paper supra* note 41, para. 75.

7. – Refuse to Deal
Maurits Dolmans and Matthew Bennett

Rights. Properly applied, the test is in two stages. If a firm invokes a property right as a defence against application of competition law or free movement principles, the first step is for the dominant firm to show that its exercise of its rights is within the specific subject matter of the right, as defined by the Court. If it is not, then the property right is no defence. For instance, if a firm attempts to control the resale of a product after it is placed on the market with its consent, it acts outside the scope of the specific subject matter (which is to place the product into circulation on the market in the European Union for the first time), and the property right will be no defence against the full and unrestrained application of EU law. If, on the other hand, the exercise of the right is within the specific subject matter, the Court or Commission must proceed to a second step. The second step is for the complainant or the Commission to show that exceptional circumstances apply (*see* below) including that the exercise of the right – while in accordance with the specific subject matter – is inconsistent with the "essential function" of the right, *i.e.*, not justified by its policy rationale as defined by the European Court.[111] If they fail to show that the firm's exercise of the right is outside the scope of the "essential function", then the exercise is unaffected by EU law and the property right constitutes a defence. If they succeed, the exercise of the right can be prohibited or curbed under competition law of free movement principles. Using an essential facility case comparable to *Commercial Solvents* as an example:[112] a supplier of an indispensable patent terminates a long-standing licence because it wishes to take over the downstream market for a complex product, of which the patented invention is a small but indispensable element. As the owner of the patent, the firm acts within the scope of the specific subject matter of the patent when refusing to license, but this exercise of its right may be beyond the essential function of the right, because it allows the upstream firm to gain exclusive control over production of a downstream product including elements to which the patent right did not extend, and thus reap an excessive reward by excluding all competition and innovation downstream.

---

[111] *See also* G. Tritton, *Intellectual Property in Europe* (London, Sweet & Maxwell, 2008), pp. 648–51.

[112] *See* Joined Cases 6 and 7/73 *Istituto Chemioterapico Italiano and Commercial Solvents Corporation v Commission* ("*Commercial Solvents*") [1974] ECR 223. This example assumes that the patent owner has strategic reasons to monopolise the downstream market, for instance, to pre-empt the downstream supplier from developing its own alternative technology, or to monopolise neighbouring markets for which the product is itself an indispensable input, and that there is significant scope for price increases downstream and reduction of innovation to the prejudice of consumers.

7. – Refuse to Deal
Maurits Dolmans and Matthew Bennett

In sum, while competition law can interfere in exceptional cases with the spe- **7.117**
cific subject matter of an intellectual property right, it must respect and must
not undermine its "essential function" as a driver of innovation, and cannot
be applied in a way that reduces overall net innovation incentives. This is the
effect of Article 345 TFEU and Article 52(1) of the Charter on Fundamental
Rights, which specifies that "[a]*ny limitation on the exercise of the rights and freedoms recognised by this Charter must ... respect the <u>essence</u> of those rights and freedoms*"
(emphasis added).[113]

The Commission does not mention "essential function" or equivalent terms **7.118**
in the *Guidance Paper*. The judgments of the courts are not fully consistent.[114]
While the judgment of the Court of First Instance and the Opinion of Advocate General in *Magill* referred to "essential function" of the design right, the
1988 judgment of the Court of Justice did not. Nor does it in *IMS* or *Ladbroke*. It has been suggested that the Court therefore abandoned the essential
function test as a relevant factor.[115] The term does appear in the 2004 *Microsoft*
Decision,[116] but not in the 2007 judgment of the Court of First Instance in
Microsoft, although the parties referred to the concepts. At the same time, the
notion appears in the 2003 *Van den Bergh Foods* case (a competition case referring to the "very substance" of property rights), in the 2009 *L'Oréal*[117] case
(a trademark case unrelated to competition law, referring to "functions"), and

---

[113] *See supra* note 77.

[114] Recently, the Court seems to refer to "essential function" of the right more rarely, *see* Joined Cases C-236 to 238/08 *Google v Louis Vuitton Malletier and others* ("*Google*") [2010] ECR I-2417; Case T-279/03 *Galileo International Technology and others v Commission* [2006] ECR II-1291; Case C-143/00 *Boehringer Ingelheim and others v Swingward and Dowelhurst* [2002] ECR I-3759; Case T-151/01 *Der Grüne Punkt – Duales System Deutschland v Commission* ("*DSD Judgment 2007*") [2007] ECR II-1607 (abuse of dominant position); *See* Case C-379/97 *supra* note 109 (repackaging).

[115] *See, e.g.*, U. Bath, "Access to Information v. Intellectual Property Rights" (2002) 24(3) *European Intellectual Property Review*, pp. 138–46 and L. Prete, "From Magill to IMS: Dominant Firms' Duty to License Competitors" 2004 15(5) *European Business Law Review*, pp. 1071–086.

[116] *See Microsoft Decision 2004 supra* note 49, para. 711: "*The central function of intellectual property rights is to protect the moral rights in a right-holder's work and ensure a reward for the creative effort. But it is also an essential objective of intellectual property law that creativity should be stimulated for the general public good.*"

[117] *See L'Oréal supra* note 109, para. 58 ("*functions include not only the essential function of the trade mark, which is to guar-antee to consumers the origin of the goods or services, but also its other functions, in particular that of guaranteeing the quality of the goods or services in question and those of communication, investment or advertising*"). This should be seen in the context of para. 49, which recognises the need to protect a trademark's "*power of attraction, its reputation and its prestige*" and the need to ensure a reward for "*the marketing effort expended by the proprietor of the mark in order to create and maintain the image of that mark*".

7. – Refuse to Deal
Maurits Dolmans and Matthew Bennett

in the 2010 *Google v. Louis Vuitton*[118] case (another trademark case unrelated to competition law, referring to the "essential function").

7.119 The failure to mention the term in certain competition cases does not, however, mean that the concepts of specific subject matter and essential function have lost their relevance as analytical tools. The two-stage test is part of the progression of thought that led to the "exceptional circumstances" criterion, and is helpful in defining limiting principles for that criterion. It is inherent in the notion of "abuse" that use of a property right in accordance with its specific subject matter is *prima facie* justified and could not be the basis for liability under Article 102 TFEU without further review.[119] In such a case, Article 102 TFEU can apply only when the property right is exploited for a purpose that is inconsistent with its essential function of fostering innovation or investment in creative activity. This is an important element of the "exceptional circumstances" test and part of the thinking underpinning the "two markets" condition and "new-product" condition in *Magill*, *IMS Health* and *Microsoft*. These conditions can be seen as a restatement and specific application of the essential function and consumer harm tests in cases relating to IPRs.[120] After all, the essential function of IPRs is to foster the development of new products to the benefit of consumers, and if intellectual property rights are instead invoked to suppress innovation, these rights are abused in a fashion that is inconsistent with the policy rationale that led to their creation in the first place. This would be the case, for instance, if an IPR is used to stifle innovation and competition in a neighbouring market for which the property is an essential input but to which the property right in itself does not extend – provided of course that all the remaining elements of an abuse under Article 102

---

[118] *See Google supra* note 114, para. 87, "*Having regard to the essential function of a trade mark, which, in the area of electronic commerce, consists in particular in enabling internet users browsing the ads displayed in response to a search relating to a specific trade mark to distinguish the goods or services of the proprietor of that mark from those which have a different origin, that proprietor must be entitled to prohibit the display of third-party ads which internet users may erroneously perceive as emanating from that proprietor*".

[119] *See also Van den Bergh Foods supra* note 88, para. 170, referring to the "*social function*" of property and that restrictions must not be "*disproportionate*" or "*affect the substance of that right.*"

[120] *See Microsoft Decision 2004 supra* note 49, para. 711 "[t]*he central function of intellectual property rights is to protect the moral rights in a right-holder's work and ensure a reward for the creative effort. But it is also an essential objective of intellectual property law that creativity should be stimulated for the general public good. A refusal by an undertaking to grant a licence may, under exceptional circumstances, be contrary to the general public good by constituting an abuse of a dominant position with harmful effects on innovation and on consumers*".

7. – Refuse to Deal
Maurits Dolmans and Matthew Bennett

TFEU are proven.[121] In such an exceptional circumstance, a compulsory license based on Article 102 TFEU may be justified. It would be regrettable if the terms "specific subject matter" and "essential function" were to fall into disuse in competition cases, but so long as the underlying thinking continues to be used and expressed, and "exceptional circumstances" continue to be limited to cases where property rights are exercised in a manner outside the scope of the "essential function" of the right, compulsory dealing will be limited to cases that are consistent with the fundamental rights in the Charter and the policy rationale of preserving dynamic competition to the benefit of consumers.

2.3. The Requirement of "Exceptional Circumstances"

The principles discussed above (that the existence of property rights cannot be affected and that interference with property and the freedom to chose one's contract partner must respect the essential function of these rights and freedoms) imply that competition law cannot limit the exercise of the rights and freedoms apart from exceptional circumstances. This has become a fundamental principle in all refusal to deal cases from *Magill* onwards. According to the Commission, *"there is no persuasiveness to an approach that would advocate the existence of an exhaustive checklist of exceptional circumstances and would have the Commission disregard a limine other circumstances of exceptional character that may deserve to be taken into account when assessing a refusal to supply"*.[122] Advocate General Jacobs made a very similar statement in *Syfait*, to the effect that *"the factors which go to demonstrate that an undertaking's conduct in refusing to supply is either abusive or otherwise are highly dependent on the specific economic and regulatory context in which the case arises"*.[123] It is necessary, however, to identify limiting principles. Without such principles, dominant firms are not in a

7.120

---

[121] *See Microsoft Decision 2004 supra* note 49, para. 533: *"In summary, there are substantial direct and indirect network effects, not only within each of the two different markets for client PC and work group server operating systems, but also between the two markets. The exploitation of those network effects with a view to leveraging its quasi-monopoly from the client PC operating system market to the work group server operating system market is at the root of the identified abuse of refusal to supply"*. Although the Commission's reasoning does not refer to intellectual property right, the Commission assumed that Microsoft could hold intellectual property rights and proceed accordingly, applying the stricter test laid down for these rights. Therefore, the Commission's conclusion can be applied, mutatis mutandis, to a scenario where an intellectual property right exists. On the lawfulness of the Commission's approach, *see Microsoft Judgment 2007 supra* note 67, paras 284 et seq. *See, e.g.*, Advocate General Gulmann in *Magill*, para. 30. *See also* C-333/94 *Tetra Pak International SA v Commission* (*"Tetra Pak II Judgment 1996"*) [1996] ECR I-5951 qualifying the acquisition of an exclusive license as an abuse, in a situation where the patent in question was the only possible challenge to the dominant acquiror's technology, and the acquiror proceeded to shelve the patent without exploiting it.

[122] *See Microsoft Decision 2004 supra* note 49, recital 555.

[123] *See* Advocate General Jacobs in Case C-53/03 *Synetairismos Farmakopoion Aitolias & Akarnanias and others v GlaxoSmithKline* (*"Syfait"*) [2005] ECR I-4609, para. 68.

7. – Refuse to Deal
Maurits Dolmans and Matthew Bennett

position to decide with sufficient legal certainty when they should respond positively to a request for supply, and when they are entitled to refuse. In a society governed by the rule of law, it is inappropriate to apply Article 102 TFEU in a fashion that is unpredictable by firms making efforts to comply. There is also a risk, that absent limiting principles, firms may feel compelled to supply even if a refusal would have generated dynamic competition, in order to avoid the costs, risk of fines and loss of goodwill associated with antitrust proceedings. This section, therefore, explores the case law concerning exceptional circumstances, and attempts to define limiting principles.

2.3.1.   Case Law

7.121   ***Volvo.*** The initial refusal to deal cases concerned interruption of supplies or discriminatory access, and did not explicitly mention "exceptional circumstances".[124] *Volvo* was the first case that implied the notion of exceptional circumstances, and defined exceptions to the principle that exercise of property rights within the scope of their specific subject matter is *prima facie* legitimate. The Court of Justice held in *Volvo* that:

> *"the right of the proprietor of a protected design to prevent third parties from manufacturing and selling or importing, without its consent, products incorporating the design constitutes the very subject-matter of his exclusive right. It follows that an obligation imposed upon the proprietor of a protected design to grant to third parties, even in return for a reasonable royalty, a licence for the supply of products incorporating the design would lead to the proprietor thereof being deprived of the substance of his exclusive right, and that a refusal to grant such a licence cannot in itself constitute an abuse of a dominant position."*[125]

---

[124] *See Commercial Solvents supra* note 112 (manufacturer of a raw product, nitroprane and aminobutanol, decided to cut off the supplies once it decided to enter the downstream market itself); Case 311/84 *Centre belge d'études de marché - Télémarketing (CBEM) v Compagnie luxembourgeoise de télédiffusion (CLT) and Information publicité Benelux (IPB)* ("*Télémarketing*") [1985] ECR 3261 (dominant television broadcaster company stopped accepting spot advertisements that did not indicate its own subsidiary's telephone number for telesales). *See also* Case IV/29.132 *Hugin/Liptons* ("*Hugin Decision 1977*"), Commission Decision of 8 December 1977, OJ 1978 L 22/23 (refusal to continue to supply a customer with spare parts on the ground that the customer had established a business in servicing and the supply of spare parts in competition with the dominant supplier); Case IV/32.318 *London European/Sabena*, Commission Decision of 4 November 1988, OJ 1988 L 317/47, p. 4 (Sabena created a computerised reservation system that was used by the majority of Belgian travel agents, but refused to grant access to London European, presumably to force it to increase its fares and abandon plans to open a new Brussels-London route).

[125] *See Volvo*, para. 8.

7. – Refuse to Deal
Maurits Dolmans and Matthew Bennett

Volvo was the owner of a UK-registered design right for front wing panels of **7.122**
the Volvo series 200. Veng imported counterfeit copies of these panels into the
United Kingdom from other Member States. Volvo refused to license Veng,
even against a reasonable royalty, and sought injunctive relief. The judgment
represents a careful compromise. On the one hand, the Court acknowledged
that a mere refusal to license could not, in itself, be an abuse. On the other hand,
the Court left the door open for a finding of abuse where the design rights are
used in a manner within the scope of the substance (or specific subject matter)
of Volvo's rights, but inconsistent with the purpose for which the rights were
granted in the first place (the essential function). The Court stated as follows:

> *"It must however be noted that the exercise of an exclusive right by the proprietor
> of a registered design … may[126] be prohibited under Article [102 TFEU] if
> it involves, on the part of an undertaking holding a dominant position, certain
> abusive conduct such as the arbitrary refusal to supply spare parts to independent
> repairers, the fixing of the prices for spare parts at an unfair level or a decision no
> longer to produce spare parts for a particular model even though many cars of that
> model are still in circulation, provided that such conduct is liable to affect trade
> between Member States. In the present case no instance of any such conduct has
> been mentioned by the national court."[127]*

The first and third of the three examples mentioned by the Court involve the **7.123**
use of the design rights in a manner that could (but does not necessarily) go
beyond what is reasonably necessary to fulfil the essential function of Volvo's design right (rewarding its design efforts); namely, refusal to supply spare
parts to independent repairers with the object of reducing competition in the
downstream activity for Volvo car repair, for which the body panels are an
essential input, but as to which Volvo is not entitled to exclusivity, and egre-
gious exploitation of consumers in breach of Article 102(a) TFEU by requiring them to buy a new car when repairs would have been viable. The second
example is unclear and can be criticised, since the essence of an exclusive right
is precisely to ensure that Volvo can charge a price for the body panels above
marginal costs to compensate it for the risks and costs sunk in developing the
model. It may be that the Court had in mind a constructive refusal to supply

---

[126] When citing this paragraph in the *Microsoft Judgment*, the Court of First Instance substituted the word "may" by "[might]". *See Microsoft Judgment 2007 supra* note 67, para. 321. This confirms that while these circumstances could be part of a finding of an abuse, they are not sufficient in themselves to constitute an infringement of Article 102 TFEU.

[127] *See Volvo*, paras 9 and 10.

7. – Refuse to Deal

Maurits Dolmans and Matthew Bennett

to independent repairers through excessive pricing, distorting competition in Volvo car repair.

7.124 It is interesting to note that shortly after the *Volvo* case, when publishing the *Draft Software Directive*, the Commission also published a set of *"Commission conclusions on the occasion of the adoption of the Commission's proposal for a Council Directive on the Legal Protection of Computer Programs"*. These included a statement that Article 102 TFEU could apply *"if a dominant company tries to use its exclusive rights in one product to gain an unfair advantage in relation to one or more products not covered by these rights"*.[128]

7.125 ***Magill.*** The Commission, very soon after *Volvo*, revisited the issue of refusals to supply new customers in the *Magill* case.[129] The Commission found that BBC, ITV and RTE engaged in an abuse by imposing limits on the use of programme information (covered by copyright in the United Kingdom and Ireland) on Magill, preventing it from publishing a comprehensive television programme guide with programme information from all three broadcasters. The broadcasters themselves had no plans to meet the demand for a comprehensive guide. Moreover, it did not cost the broadcasters anything to develop the information; it was a mere "by-product" of the broadcasting activities. In other words, the broadcasters used their copyrights over programme listings, not to foster but to stifle innovation, in a manner inconsistent with the essential function of copyright. The Commission found that the broadcasters' refusal to disclose the copyright-protected listings information was abusive because it enabled the broadcasters to leverage their monopoly in broadcasting activities into the downstream market for TV listings magazines.[130] It ordered the parties to supply the listings to each other and to third parties on demand, on reasonable and non-discriminatory terms.[131]

---

[128] Proposal for a Council Directive on the Legal Protection of Computer Programs (*"Draft Software Directive"*), COM/88/816 final – SYN 183, OJ 1989 C 91/4; Commission conclusions decided on the occasion of the adoption of the Commission's proposal for a Council Directive on the legal protection of computer programs, OJ 1989 C 91/16.

[129] Case IV/31.851 *Magill TV Guide / ITP, BBC and RTE*, Commission Decision of 21 December 1988, OJ 1989 L 78/43, paras 1–2; Case T-69/89 *RTE v Commission* [1991] ECR II-485 and in Case T-76/89 *ITP v Commission* [1991] ECR II-575; and *Magill supra* note 87.

[130] *See* Case IV/31.851 *supra* note 129, para. 23.

[131] It is also important to examine the IPR situation when analysing a duty to deal. It has, for instance, been claimed that U.S. copyright law, by contrast to European copyright laws, contains a stronger internal pro-competitive interest (*e.g.*, "fair use" and "copyright misuse" doctrines), the presence of which lessens the need for strong antitrust scrutiny of copyright holders' behaviour. It has been claimed that had the Magill decision been litigated in the US, a similar result would have been reached as under Article 102 TFEU, but the result would

7. – Refuse to Deal
Maurits Dolmans and Matthew Bennett

On appeal, the Court of Justice sided with the Commission, stating that **7.126** *"the exclusive right of reproduction form[ed] part of the author's rights, so that refusal to grant a licence, even if it is the act of an undertaking holding a dominant position, cannot itself constitute abuse of a dominant position"*[132] but confirmed also that *"the exercise of an exclusive right by the proprietor may, in exceptional circumstances, involve abusive conduct."*[133] The exceptional circumstances in that case were the following:

> *"the [broadcasters] were, by force of circumstance, the only sources of the basic information on programme scheduling which is the indispensable raw material for compiling a weekly television guide.*

> *[V]iewers wishing to obtain information on the choice of programmes for the week ahead [were left] no choice but to buy the weekly guides for each station and draw from each of them the information they needed to make comparisons.*

> *[This] prevented the appearance of a new product, a comprehensive weekly guide to television programmes, which the appellants did not offer and for which there was a potential consumer demand.*

> *[T]here was no justification for such refusal either in the activity of television broadcasting or in that of publishing television magazines ....*

> *[T]he appellants, by their conduct, reserved to themselves the secondary market of weekly television guides by excluding all competition on that market."*[134]

The Court held that *"[s]uch refusal constitutes an abuse under heading (b) of the second* **7.127** *paragraph of Article* [102] *of the Treaty"*. The "new-product" criterion based on Article 102(b) TFEU (which prohibits *"limiting ... technical development to the*

---

likely have been reached on copyright grounds rather than competition law grounds. As a consequence, in Europe, a remedy would only be granted in "exceptional circumstances" and would require the licensee to pay a reasonable royalty for the data, whereas under US copyright law the data would be free for all to take. (A. Katz and P. E. Veel, *"Beyond Refusal to Deal: A Cross-Atlantic View of Copyright, Competition and Innovation Policies"*, 28 July 2011, pp. 24 *et seq.*, 26 *et seq.*).

[132] *See Magill supra* note 87, para. 49.

[133] *Ibid.*, para. 50.

[134] *Ibid.*, paras 53 *et seq.* These mirror the conditions of Article 102(b) TFEU, which prohibits a dominant undertaking from limiting innovation to the prejudice of consumers. *See also* the reference to *Magill* case in *Microsoft Judgment 2007 supra* note 67, para. 322.

7. – Refuse to Deal
Maurits Dolmans and Matthew Bennett

prejudice of consumers") is a restatement and specific application of the thinking underpinning the essential function test in cases relating to IPRs, as described above.

7.128 **Bronner.** The first major case taking up the thread of *Magill* was unrelated to intellectual property, but concerned a demand for the supply of distribution services. Bronner, who published and distributed an Austrian daily newspaper, had asked Mediaprint, which held a very large share of the daily newspaper market in Austria and operated the only nationwide newspaper home-delivery scheme in Austria, for access to Mediaprint's nationwide delivery scheme. Since Mediaprint refused to grant access, in spite of an offer of appropriate compensation, Bronner applied to the Austrian courts, arguing that Mediaprint's refusal amounted to an abuse of dominant position prohibited under Austrian competition law and under Article 102 TFEU. As the issues of this case indirectly involved EU competition law, the Austrian Court referred the matter to the European Court of Justice.

7.129 The Court recited the exceptional circumstances that it had established in *Magill*, and stated:

> "[E]ven if that case-law on the exercise of an intellectual property right were applicable to the exercise of any property right whatever, it would still be necessary, for [that] judgment to be effectively relied upon in order to plead the existence of an abuse within the meaning of Article [102 TFEU] in a situation such as [a demand for a compulsory supply of a service not involving an intellectual property right], not only that the refusal of the service comprised in home delivery be likely to eliminate all competition in the daily newspaper market on the part of the person requesting the service and that such refusal be incapable of being objectively justified, but also that the service in itself be indispensable to carrying on that person's business, inasmuch as there is no actual or potential substitute in existence for that home-delivery scheme."[135]

7.130 This judgment made important refinements to the definition of an "essential facility" and the condition of indispensability, further discussed in Section IV.1 below.

---

[135] *See Oscar Bronner supra* note 68, para. 41.

7. – Refuse to Deal
Maurits Dolmans and Matthew Bennett

IMS Health. The next judgment of the Court of Justice, in *IMS Health*, **7.131**
also confirmed the *Magill* principles.[136] IMS Health developed and marketed
a database for pharmaceutical sales data used, for instance, to calculate the
compensation of pharmaceutical company sales representatives. The data
were organised in accordance with IMS's copyright-protected data structure,
called the "1860 Brick Structure", which divides the German territory into
1,860 local areas. This enabled the grouping of data in a way that is meaningful without infringing German data protection.

Two German companies established by former IMS Health personnel, NDC **7.132**
Health GmbH and Azyx Deutschland GmbH, created their own database
using publicly available pharmacy data, and presented these data in accordance with the 1860 Brick Structure. IMS Health argued that in doing so, they
infringed IMS' copyright in the 1860 Brick Structure, and obtained injunctive
relief. In response, NDC and Azyx raised a competition law defence, and in
parallel complained to the European Commission. They took the position
that IMS should be forced to license the 1860 Brick Structure to its competitors. The Commission adopted an interim decision on 3 July 2001, finding
that customers had contributed to the definition of the 1860 Brick Structure,
which as a result had become a *de facto* industry standard.[137] The Commission
concluded that the 1860 Brick Structure was an essential facility and ordered
IMS Health to license it, on reasonable terms, for use in competing NDC and
Azyx databases. IMS Health appealed.

In the meantime, the German court requested a preliminary ruling from the **7.133**
Court of Justice in the main proceedings on whether IMS Health's conduct
was compatible with the ban on abuse of dominance. The President of the
Court of First Instance accordingly suspended the operation of the Commission's interim measures decision pending review of the preliminary question.[138]

The Court of Justice issued its opinion in IMS Health on 29 April 29 2004, **7.134**
reiterating with reference to Volvo and Magill that "*the exclusive right of reproduc-*
tion forms part of the rights of the owner of an intellectual property right, so that refusal to
grant a licence, even if it is the act of an undertaking holding a dominant position, cannot

---

[136] *IMS Health supra* note 67.
[137] Case COMP/38.044 *NDC Health/IMS Health: Interim measures*, Commission Decision of 13 August 2003,
OJ 2003 L 268/69.
[138] Case T-184/01 R *IMS Health v Commission* [2001] ECR II-3193, confirmed on appeal in *see IMS Health supra*
note 67.

7. – Refuse to Deal
Maurits Dolmans and Matthew Bennett

in itself constitute abuse of a dominant position. Nevertheless, as is clear from that case-law, exercise of an exclusive right by the owner may, in exceptional circumstances, involve abusive conduct."[139]

7.135 It confirmed the *Magill* criteria in holding that apart from having to prove that the property is "indispensable", the plaintiff would have to show that the following conditions were fulfilled: "*The undertaking which requested the licence intends to offer, on the market for the supply of the data in question, new products or services not offered by the owner of the intellectual property right and for which there is a potential consumer demand; the refusal is not justified by objective considerations.*"[140]

7.136 The refusal is such as to reserve to the owner of the intellectual property right the market for the supply of data on sales of pharmaceutical products in the Member State concerned by eliminating all competition on that market.

7.137 In view of the outcome of the preliminary ruling, the Commission withdrew its interim measures decision, in part because questions had arisen as to whether IMS Health could in fact claim to be the owner of the copyright, and reportedly also because NDC and Azyx did not offer a new product, but a direct substitute for the IMS Health database.[141] NDC and Azyx maintained their complaint, which was rejected on 25 June 2009.[142] In the meantime, the German proceedings continued, leading to a judgment of the Landgericht Frankfurt against IMS Health on grounds unrelated to the competition law assessment.[143]

7.138 ***Microsoft.*** The most recent application of the *Magill* and *IMS Health* principles is found in the judgment of the Court of First Instance of 17 September 2007 in *Microsoft*, on appeal against the Commission Decision of March 2004.[144] The Commission and the Court's findings of fact are lengthy and technically complicated, but can be summarised as follows.

---

[139] *See IMS Health supra* note 67, paras 34 *et seq.* (citations omitted).

[140] *Ibid.*, para. 52.

[141] *See* Case COMP/38.044 *supra* note 137, paras 10, 15–6.

[142] The decision is not public.

[143] Case 2-03 O 629/00 *IMS Health v Insight Health*, Frankfurt am Main's Regional Court Judgment of 12 July 2001. The Court found against IMS Health on grounds that IMS Health could not prove it owned the copyrights exclusively. Appeal was lodged on 10 October 2008, and is still pending at the time of writing. Case 11 U 48/08 *IMS Health v Insight Health*, Brandenburg's Higher Regional Court Judgment of 5 December 2006.

[144] *See Microsoft Decision 2004 supra* note 49, p. 23; *See Microsoft Judgment 2007 supra* note 67, not appealed.

7. – Refuse to Deal
Maurits Dolmans and Matthew Bennett

Workgroup servers control networks of personal computers (called "clients") **7.139** and larger computers (called "servers") that provide processing services to clients in the network. Workgroup servers administer access of users to the network and perform tasks, such as filing and printing of electronic documents. To work properly, these servers need to be able to communicate "seamlessly" both with clients and other servers in the network. With a market share of 95 per cent, Microsoft held a near monopoly in operating systems software for personal computers. In contrast, the market for operating systems software for servers was originally characterised by significant competition, with a range of third parties developing and supplying server operating systems. Microsoft was a relatively late entrant in server operating systems. Initially, Microsoft disclosed information for its personal computer operating system and its server operating system to third party developers, in order to facilitate interoperability between Windows-based computers and third-party servers. This changed with Microsoft's Windows 2000 products. Microsoft implemented proprietary protocols in both its Windows operating system and its server operating system (often in the form of extensions to public standards) and refused disclosure of those protocols. The Commission stated that following the change in this policy, Microsoft's market share of workgroup server operating systems *"enjoyed a rapid rise to dominance"*, with shares above 40–60 per cent depending on the market segment.[145]

The Commission found that by denying full interoperability, Microsoft used **7.140** its market power in personal computer operating systems to distort competition in the neighbouring market for workgroup server operating systems. This, in turn, would protect its near-monopoly over personal computer operating systems.[146]

---

[145] *See Microsoft Decision 2004 supra* note 49, para. 590.

[146] *See Microsoft Decision 2004 supra* note 49, paras 769 and 725. *"In this case, it cannot be excluded that in the future there will be companies challenging Microsoft's dominant position in the client PC operating system market. By having achieved a dominant position in the work group server operating system market, Microsoft secures a strategic input important for undertakings wanting to compete in the client PC operating system market, namely interoperability with the Windows work group servers. Indeed, a future competitor in the client PC operating system market will need to provide products interoperable with Microsoft's dominant work group server operating system. As such, by strengthening its dominant position in the work group server operating system market, Microsoft effectively reinforces the barriers to entry in the client PC operating system market"* (emphasis added). This theory is discussed in more detail under Section IV.2. - Refusal to supply in order to protect a monopoly position.

7. – Refuse to Deal

Maurits Dolmans and Matthew Bennett

7.141 The Court of First Instance confirmed the Commission's finding that Microsoft violated Article 102 TFEU by refusing to supply interoperability information for server operating systems, applying the analytical framework developed in *Magill*[147] and *IMS Health*.[148] It reiterated the now familiar mantra that the refusal to license cannot in itself constitute an abuse, and that only in exceptional circumstances could the exercise of an exclusive right give rise to an abuse.[149] The Court of First Instance then held:

"the following circumstances, in particular, must be considered to be exceptional:

    – *in the first place, the refusal relates to a product or service indispensable to the exercise of a particular activity on a neighbouring market;*

    – *in the second place, the refusal is of such a kind as to exclude any effective competition on that neighbouring market;*

    – *in the third place, the refusal prevents the appearance of a new product for which there is potential consumer demand."*[150]

7.142 Once it is established that such circumstances are present, the refusal by the holder of a dominant position to grant a licence may infringe Article 102 TFEU unless the refusal is objectively justified. The Court notes that the circumstance that the refusal prevents the appearance of a new product for which there is potential consumer demand is found only in the case law on the exercise of an intellectual property right. Finally, it is appropriate to add that, in order for a refusal to give access to a product or service indispensable to the exercise of a particular activity to be considered abusive, it is necessary to distinguish two markets; namely, a market constituted by that product or service and on which the undertaking refusing to supply holds a dominant position, and a neighbouring market on which the product or service is used in the manufacture of another product or for the supply of another service.

2.3.2. Analysis of the "Exceptional Circumstances" Requirement

7.143 The case law discussed above indicates that the exceptional circumstances identified in *Magill*, *IMS Health* and *Microsoft* involve the combination of various constant factors, apart from dominance and the refusal itself: (1) a monopoly in an

---

[147] *See Magill supra* note 87.
[148] *See IMS Health supra* note 67.
[149] *See Microsoft Judgment 2007 supra* note 67, para. 331.
[150] *Ibid.*, paras 332–5.

7. – Refuse to Deal
Maurits Dolmans and Matthew Bennett

upstream market for an input product or service that is indispensable for a separate downstream product or service; (2) a finding of consumer harm caused by an abuse other than the mere refusal to license; in other words, a situation where the property right is used as a tool for a purpose other than the essential function (the public policy purpose for which the property right was created in the first place);[151] (3) the exclusion of effective competition on a downstream market; and (4) the absence of an objective justification for the refusal.

2.3.2.1.   No Need to Prove Additional Factual Circumstances?

The statement of the Court of First Instance in *Microsoft* that "*the following circumstances, in particular, must be considered to be exceptional*" (emphasis added)[152] suggests that where the plaintiff or authority has proven the points mentioned above, there is no requirement to prove additional exceptional circumstances.[153] In the *Microsoft* case, the Commission had at some length discussed a number of detailed circumstances that could have been dubbed exceptional, and it is arguable that the finding of "exceptional circumstances" should be seen in the light of these unusual factors. They include (1) an exceptional level and duration of dominance reinforced by network effects, sometimes referred to as "superdominance";[154] (2) that Microsoft's conduct was part of a general pattern

7.144

---

[151] *See Microsoft Decision 2004 supra* note 49, para. 711: "*The central function of intellectual property rights is to protect the moral rights in a right-holder's work and ensure a reward for the creative effort. But it is also an essential objective of intellectual property law that creativity should be stimulated for the general public good. A refusal by an undertaking to grant a licence may, under exceptional circumstances, be contrary to the general public good by constituting an abuse of a dominant position with harmful effects on innovation and on consumers.*"

[152] *See Microsoft Judgment 2007 supra* note 67, para. 332.

[153] *See also Microsoft Decision 2004 supra* note 49, para. 712.

[154] *Ibid.*, para. 471 and paras 459, 470. Firms with substantial – let alone virtual monopoly – market power must be held to the strictest standard of conduct under Article 102 to ensure that their behaviour in the marketplace does not have exclusionary effect. *See* DG Competition discussion paper on the application of Article 82 of the Treaty to exclusionary abuses ("*Discussion Paper*"), December 2005, at 59 ("*In general, the higher the capability of conduct to foreclose and the wider its application and the stronger the dominant position, the higher the likelihood that an anticompetitive foreclosure effect results.*") and Case T-210/01 *General Electric v Commission* [2005] ECR II-5575, para. 550 ("*the greater the dominance of an undertaking, the greater is its special responsibility to refrain from any conduct liable to weaken further, a fortiori to eliminate, competition which still exists on the market.*"). *See also* Advocate General Fenelly in Joined Cases C-395 and 396/96 P *Compagnie maritime belge transports and others v Commission* [2000] ECR I-1365, para. 137, "*To my mind, Article* [102] *cannot be interpreted as permitting monopolists or quasi-monopolists to exploit the very significant market power which their superdominance confers so as to preclude the emergence either of a new or additional competitor. Where an undertaking, or group of undertakings whose conduct must be assessed collectively, enjoys a <u>position of such overwhelming dominance verging on monopoly</u>, ... it would not be consonant with the <u>particularly onerous special obligation affecting such a dominant undertaking not to impair further the structure of the feeble existing competition</u> for them to react, even to aggressive price competition from a new entrant, with a policy ... designed to eliminate that competitor*" (emphasis added).

7. – Refuse to Deal
Maurits Dolmans and Matthew Bennett

of conduct involving a series of past abuses,[155] discrimination,[156] and another ongoing abuse (the tying of the Windows Media Player);[157] (3) that Microsoft disrupted supplies by putting an end to past voluntary disclosures of interoperability information,[158] which was explicitly intended to hamper specifically named rivals[159] and was inconsistent with normal industry practice;[160] (4) not merely distortion of competition in the neighbouring market for workgroup server operating systems, but dominance in that market and a continuing upward trend of Microsoft's market share;[161] and, (5) that the effect of restriction of competition on the server operating system market was to contribute to the maintenance of Microsoft's desktop operating system monopoly.[162] Although the statement of the Court of First Instance implies that there is no requirement to find exceptional circumstances beyond dominance and the three points listed in para. 332ff (quoted above), it is possible that these additional factors – and especially the issue of "superdominance" – nevertheless played a role in the Court's overall assessment of the *Microsoft* case as involving exceptional circumstances.

2.3.2.2. "Exceptional Circumstances" May Involve Various Types of Abuse?

7.145 The *Guidance Paper* specifies that "*[t]he concept of refusal to supply covers a broad range of practices, such as a refusal to supply products to existing or new customers, refusal to*

---

[155] *See Microsoft Decision 2004 supra* note 49, paras 573 *et seq*. The Commission refers to the following behaviours: (1) the refusal to disclose information to other competitors in the work group server operating system market; (2) the discrimination among competitors, by granting more information to certain competitors (*e.g.*, SGI, HP) than to others (*e.g.*, Sun); (3) the policy adopted in licensing certain technologies necessary for interoperability. The Commission also refers to the antitrust proceedings against Microsoft in the United States, concerning the measures taken against Netscape's Web browser and Sun's "Java technologies", *see Microsoft Decision 2004 supra* note 49, paras 14 *et seq*.

[156] *See Microsoft Decision 2004 supra* note 49, para. 574.

[157] *Ibid.*, paras 573 *et seq*.

[158] *Ibid.*, paras 556, 578 et seq. "*The value that* [rivals'] *products brought to the network also augmented the client PC operating system's value in the customers' eyes and therefore Microsoft – as long as it did not have a credible work group server operating system alternative – had incentives to have its client PC operating system interoperate with non-Microsoft work group server operating systems ... Once Microsoft's work group server operating system gained acceptance ... Microsoft's incentives changed and holding back access to information relating to interoperability with the Windows environment started to make sense.*"

[159] *See Microsoft Decision 2004 supra* note 49, paras 774–8 and *Microsoft Judgment 2007 supra* note 67, paras 771 and 1349.

[160] *See Microsoft Decision 2004 supra* note 49, para. 730.

[161] *Ibid.*, para. 590.

[162] *Ibid.*, para. 769.

7. – Refuse to Deal
Maurits Dolmans and Matthew Bennett

license intellectual property rights, including when the licence is necessary to provide interface information, or refusal to grant access to an essential facility or a network."[163]

This suggests that the specific abuse discussed in *Magill*, *IMS Health* and *Micro-* **7.146**
soft, *viz.*, "*limiting … technical development to the prejudice of consumers*" in breach of
Article 102(b) TFEU, is not the only situation where a refusal to supply could
lead to a finding of infringement.

This appears to be borne out by the Court's review of the case law in *Microsoft*. **7.147**
The words "*in particular*" in para. 332 of *Microsoft* (quoted above), suggest that
the circumstances listed in para. 332 of the judgment ("*prevents the appearance
of a new product for which there is potential consumer demand*") are sufficient for
a finding of infringement, but not necessary. The Court of First Instance
notes, for instance, that "*the circumstance that the refusal prevents the appearance of
a new product for which there is potential consumer demand is found only in the case law
on the exercise of an intellectual property right*".[164] The Court did not draw specific
conclusions from this, since the Court agreed with the Commission finding
that Microsoft's refusal was abusive even if it held IPRs in the information at
issue, and the Commission therefore had met the "strictest legal test" for an
abusive refusal to supply.[165] But the combination of these statements indicates
that alternative "exceptional circumstances" might also support a finding of
abuse in a refusal to supply case. The Court of First Instance confirms this
elsewhere, where it explains that even if it had found that one or more of the
circumstances identified in *Magill* and *IMS Health* had been absent in *Microsoft*,
it would have assessed other circumstances invoked by the Commission.[166]
These other circumstances included several elements that, according to the
Commission, allowed it to characterise Microsoft's conduct as abusive:

> "*The first consists in the fact that the information which Microsoft refuses to dis-
> close to its competitors relates to interoperability in the software industry, a matter
> to which the Community legislature attaches particular importance. The second
> characteristic lies in the fact that Microsoft uses its extraordinary power on the
> client PC operating systems market to eliminate competition on the adjacent work*

---

[163] *See Guidance Paper supra* note 41, para. 78.
[164] *See Microsoft Judgment 2007 supra* note 67, para. 334.
[165] *Ibid.*, para. 284.
[166] *Ibid.*, para. 336.

7. – Refuse to Deal
Maurits Dolmans and Matthew Bennett

> *group server operating systems market. The third characteristic is that the conduct in question involves disruption of previous levels of supply.* [167]

7.148 The various forms of abuse that could involve refusals to deal include, therefore, discrimination and interruption of supplies, as discussed below in Section IV.3 provided that all findings of exclusionary abuses must comply with the conditions set out in Article 102(b) TFEU, *viz.*, limiting production, technical development, or outlets of competitors in a downstream market to the prejudice of consumers.

2.3.2.3.   "Exceptional Circumstances" Test Applies in all Compulsory Duty to Deal Cases

7.149 The concept of "exceptional circumstances" is mentioned in many, but not all, cases involving a refusal to deal. All cases where an accusation of abusive refusal to deal was upheld, however, involve the four elements of "exceptional circumstances". [168] This is appropriate. When balancing the interest of free competition against the freedom to choose one's contract partner and the right to property, it is important to keep in mind that the latter two are fundamental rights, whereas the freedom to compete is not. [169] This means that interference with the right of property and freedom to choose one's contract

---

[167] *See Microsoft Judgment 2007 supra* note 67, para. 317. *See also Microsoft Decision 2004 supra* note 49, paras 555–8: "*On a general note, there is no persuasiveness to an approach that would advocate the existence of an exhaustive checklist of exceptional circumstances and would have the Commission disregard a limine other circumstances of exceptional character that may deserve to be taken into account when assessing a refusal to supply. … The case-law of the European Courts therefore suggests that the Commission must analyse the entirety of the circumstances surrounding a specific instance of a refusal to supply and must take its decision based on the results of such a comprehensive examination.*"

[168] *See* Section III.2.3. These are (1) a monopoly in an upstream market for an input product or service that is indispensable for a downstream product or service; (2) a finding of an abuse (with consumer harm) other than the mere refusal to license, in other words, a situation where the property right is used as a tool for a purpose other than the essential function (the public policy purpose for which the property right was created in the first place); (3) exclusion of effective competition on the downstream market; and (4) the absence of an objective justification for the refusal.

[169] Note, however, that Article 16 of the Charter of Fundamental Rights, which recognises the Freedom to conduct a business, could be read to incorporate a freedom to compete. According to the Explanations Relating to the Charter of Fundamental Rights, OJ 2007 C 303/17, p.17, Article 16 "*is based on Court of Justice case-law which has recognised freedom to exercise an economic or commercial activity (see: judgments of 14 May 1974, Case 4/73 Nold KG v Commission [1974] ECR 491, para. 14 of the grounds, and of 27 September 1979, Case 230–78 SpA Eridiana and others [1979] ECR 2749, paras 20 and 31 of the grounds) and freedom of contract (see: inter alia Case 151/78 Sukkerfabriken Nykøbing [1979] ECR 1, para. 19 of the grounds, and judgment of 5 October 1999, C-240/97 Spain v Commission [1999] ECR I-6571, para. 99 of the grounds) and Article 119(1) and (3) of the Treaty on the Functioning of the European Union, which recognises free competition*" (emphasis added).

7. – Refuse to Deal

Maurits Dolmans and Matthew Bennett

partner, even in respect of dominant firms, must not be commonplace, but must remain limited to "exceptional circumstances".[170]

If anything, this is even more so after the entry into force of the TEU than when the Court of Justice rendered its judgment in *Magill* and the Court of First Instance referred to exceptional circumstances in *Microsoft*. Until the entry into force of the TEU, on 1 December 2009, Article 3(1)(g) EU (ex Article 3(g) EC and ex Article 3(f) EC) provided that in order to achieve the aims of the European Union set out in Article 2, its activities were to include "*a system ensuring that competition in the internal market is not distorted*".[171] The Court of Justice relied in various cases on that provision. In *Van den Bergh Foods*, for instance, the Court of First Instance held, when applying competition law to limit the right to property: **7.150**

> "*Article 3(1)(g) EC provides that in order to achieve the aims of the Community, its activities are to include 'a system ensuring that competition in the internal market is not distorted'. It follows that the application of Articles 85 and 86 of the Treaty constitutes one of the aspects of public interest in the Community (see, to that effect, the Opinion of Advocate General Cosmas in Masterfoods and HB, at p. I-11371). Consequently, pursuant to those articles, restrictions may be applied on the exercise of the right to property, provided that they are not disproportionate and do not affect the substance of that right.*"[172]

The Treaty of Lisbon relegated the text of 3(1)(g) to a mere recital to (not an operative provision of) Protocol 27 "*on the Internal Market and* **7.151**

---

[170] *See Microsoft Judgment 2007 supra* note 67, para. 331; Joined Cases C-241 and *see Magill supra* note 87, para. 50; *See Volvo*, para. 9.

[171] In Case 6/72 *Europemballage and Continental Can v Commission* ("*Continental Can*") [1973] ECR 215, the Court of Justice held in para. 24: "*If Article 3[(1)(g)] provides for the institution of a system ensuring that competition in the Common Market is not distorted, then it requires a fortiori that competition must not be eliminated. This requirement is so essential that without it numerous provisions of the Treaty would be pointless.*" *See* also Case C-453/99 *Courage v Bernard Crehan* [2001] ECR I-6297 ("*According to Article 3[(1)(g)] EC), Article [101 TFEU] constitutes a fundamental provision which is essential for the accomplishment of the tasks entrusted to the Community and, in particular, for the functioning of the internal market.*") and Case C-95/04 P *British Airways v Commission* ("*British Airways*") [2007] ECR I-2331, para. 68 ("*Article 82 … forms part of a system designed to protect competition within the internal market from distortions (Article 3(1)(g) EC). Accordingly, Article [102 TFEU], like the other competition rules of the Treaty, is not designed only or primarily to protect the immediate interests of individual competitors or consumers, but to protect the structure of the market and thus competition as such (as an institution), which has already been weakened by the presence of the dominant undertaking on the market. In this way, consumers are also indirectly protected. Because where competition as such is damaged, disadvantages for consumers are also to be feared*" (emphasis added).

[172] *See Van den Bergh Foods supra* note 88, para. 170.

7. – Refuse to Deal
Maurits Dolmans and Matthew Bennett

Competition".[173] While it can be argued that even under the previous Treaties, there was no right to compete,[174] it is now unambiguously clear that Articles 101 and 102 TFEU are mere tools and that the maintenance of free competition is not in itself an objective of the European Union. If anything, therefore, it has become even more difficult for the Commission, antitrust authorities, or the Courts to impose a duty to deal than before. The requirement of "exceptional circumstances" may have become more stringent.

3. Conclusion

7.152   The *Guidance Paper* does not discuss the concept of "exceptional circumstances", but specifies that:

> "[t]*he Commission will consider these practices as an enforcement priority if all the following circumstances are present:*
>
> — *the refusal relates to a product or service that is objectively necessary to be able to compete effectively on a downstream market,*
>
> — *the refusal is likely to lead to the elimination of effective competition on the downstream market, and*
>
> — *the refusal is likely to lead to consumer harm.*"[175]

---

[173] French President Sarkozy said in connection with the debate relating to the elimination of Article 3(1)(g) EU that "*We have obtained a major reorientation on the objectives of the Union. Competition is no longer an objective of the Union or an end in itself, but a means to serve the internal market*", and "*I believe in competition as a means and not an end in itself. This may also give a different legal direction to the Commission.*" B. van Rompuy, "The Impact of the Lisbon Treaty on EU Competition Law: A Review of Recent Case Law of the EU Courts", (2011) 1 *CPI Antitrust Chronicle*, p. 2.

[174] In his letter to the Financial Times Mr. Michel Petite, then-Director General of the European Commission's Legal Service, wrote: "*As a matter of fact, competition is not currently one of the objectives of the European Community set out in Article 2 of the EC Treaty: the reference to 'undistorted competition' appears only in Article 3 on the Community activities to be implemented to attain those objectives. Clearly, an objective that does not exist cannot be lost! The fact that competition is a means and not an objective of the Community has not – over the past 50 years or so – prevented the European institutions, and in particular the European Commission and the European Court of Justice, from taking effective action against any restriction or distortion of competition within the internal market, whether resulting from initiatives taken by undertakings or by member states' public authorities. The text of the 'Constitutional Treaty' provided for a substantial reworking of the above provisions, with an explicit reference to 'free and undistorted competition' linked to the 'internal market' objective. The principal effect of dropping those words from the future 'Reform Treaty' is to bring us back to the present situation.*" (*See* M. Petit, "EU commitment to competition policy is unchanged", *Financial Times*, 27 June 2007).

[175] *See Guidance Paper supra* note 41, para. 81.

7. – Refuse to Deal
Maurits Dolmans and Matthew Bennett

These criteria mirror the three elements in the judgment in *Microsoft*, quoted **7.153** above,[176] which the Court of First Instance said "*must be considered to be exceptional*". Although the *Guidance Paper* is therefore consistent with the "exceptional circumstances" case law, it might cause an inattentive reader to think that convincing the Commission to impose a duty to deal is easier than it is or should be, in two respects.

First, the *Guidance Paper* mentions "exceptional circumstances" only in a foot- **7.154** note, which moreover refers to refusals to license only.[177] This could create an impression *a contrario* that the imposition of a duty to deal could be unexceptional, especially in cases not involving intellectual property. The *Guidance Paper* should be read, however, in the light of the Charter on Fundamental Rights and case law, which makes clear that a duty to deal is not the norm, but the exception, and that as a result, imposition of a duty to deal will not be prevalent, but rare.

Secondly, the third element in *Microsoft* – that "*the refusal prevents the* **7.155** *appearance of a new product for which there is potential consumer demand*" – has been replaced by "*the refusal is likely to lead to consumer harm*". At first sight, this is appropriate, since the suppression of a new product is one (important) example of a situation where an adverse effect on consumer welfare can arise, but there is a concern that this might be read to suggest that a duty to supply can be imposed simply to lower prices. From a static perspective, after all, any case involving conduct that raises prices above a competitive level (the free market equilibrium) causes deadweight loss, and therefore arguably consumer harm. However, the protection of static price competition is already covered by the requirement of elimination of effective competition. Moreover, the very purpose of exclusive rights is to allow a property owner to raise prices or even deny access altogether in order to foster investment in innovation and production. Raising prices above a competitive level in the market for the input (or a product of which the input is a key component) is arguably not, therefore, enough to meet the consumer harm test. The *Guidance Paper* leaves room for this analysis, where it provides that "*the Commission will examine whether, for consumers, the likely negative consequences of the refusal to supply in the relevant market outweigh over time the negative consequences of imposing an obligation to*

---

[176] *See Microsoft Judgment 2007 supra* note 67, paras 332–5.
[177] *See Guidance Paper supra* note 41, and *see* footnote 4 to para. 78, referring to the Magill and IMS Health cases, and stating that "*Those judgments show that in exceptional circumstances a refusal to license intellectual property rights is abusive.*"

7. – Refuse to Deal

Maurits Dolmans and Matthew Bennett

supply."[178] The *Guidance Paper* should not be read to suggest that a refusal to deal is an abuse even where deadweight loss arises in the short term.

7.156 In sum, the legislature has struck a balance by recognising property and freedom to contract as fundamental rights, and endowing property owners with exclusive rights and the freedom to deal with whom it pleases them, to which exceptions can be made only in limited circumstances. The existence of these rights would be undermined if competition authorities or courts were to interfere regularly with their exercise, and interference is therefore allowed only in exceptional circumstances. This means that the normal conditions of Article 102 TFEU must be applied strictly and narrowly. In addition to a finding of a refusal and absence of objective justification:

(1) it is not enough to find dominance in the upstream market. A duty to deal can arise only if the input is truly "indispensable" for entry in a downstream market for a different product, which would require a level closer to monopoly;

(2) it is not enough to find an appreciable restriction of competition in the downstream market. A duty to deal can be imposed only if the conduct "excludes any effective competition", *i.e.*, all effective competition, in the downstream market, which is unlikely if the upstream supplier is not already dominant downstream, with a clear trend towards greater power causally connected to the refusal to deal; and,[179]

(3) it is not enough to find a short-term reduction of consumer welfare. A duty to deal requires evidence that long-term harm arises because the exclusive rights are exercised in a manner that is not in accordance with or disproportionate to their essential function, that is to say, as a tool for an abuse other than the refusal to supply itself, *i.e.*, limiting innovation or the availability to consumers of a new product for which there is clear demand that is not being met otherwise, or restricting competition in neighbouring markets for products dependent on access to, but not covered by, the property rights in question.[180]

---

[178] *See Guidance Paper supra* note 41, para. 81.

[179] *See supra* note 39, p. 444 (the absence of "effective competition" on the market means "dominance on the relevant downstream market, and arguably more").

[180] It could be argued that the consumer welfare condition is also met in cases where business partners have become "locked in" in good faith reliance on actions or statements from the dominant firm to the effect that supplies would be forthcoming or continued on a fair and reasonable price, and where cutting off supplies or

7. – Refuse to Deal
Maurits Dolmans and Matthew Bennett

IV. Conditions for Imposition of a Duty to Deal

When assessing the conditions for exclusionary refusal to deal some basic **7.157** principles must be kept in mind, based on the analysis set out above. First, there cannot be a duty to contract under Article 102 unless there has been a separate identifiable abuse, for which a compulsory licence is the appropriate remedy. The abusive conduct must meet the conditions of Article 102(b), which requires evidence of the following four factors (in addition to dominance and a refusal to supply):

- Limitation of rivals' production, markets or technical development;
- Prejudice to consumers;
- Hindrance of maintenance or growth of competition; and,
- Absence of objective, proportional justification.

A run-of-the-mill violation of Article 102(b) is not enough, however, to jus- **7.158** tify the imposition of a duty to deal. Exceptional circumstances are required. According to the case law of the European courts, exceptional circumstances may arise where the property right is exercised in a manner that is inconsistent with or disproportionate to its "essential function", or where it is used to exclude a product to which the property right does not apply, *i.e.*, where the following conditions are met:

- a property is essential for competition in a neighbouring market and the dominant firm is the only source (Section IV.1 below);
- the property owner refuses to deal with competitors or customers of its competitors (Section IV.2 below);
- this refusal involves consumer harm by reduction of dynamic competition or reduction of quality compared to the product or service that a non-dominant or non-vertically-integrated firm would have the incentive to provide (Section IV.3 below);

---

refusal to supply on FRAND terms reduces competition in a downstream market, raising prices for consumers in that market – directly, if the input is sold at a supra-competitive price, or indirectly, if the refusal or imposition of restrictive terms allow the dominant firm to monopolise the downstream market. *Cf. Broadcom v Qualcomm*, 501 F.3d 297 (3rd Cir. 2007) ("*Deception in a consensus-driven private standard-setting environment harms the competitive process by obscuring the costs of including proprietary technology in a standard and increasing the likelihood that patent rights will confer monopoly power on the patent holder … Deceptive FRAND commitments, no less than deceptive nondisclosure of IPRs, may result in such harm*").

7. – Refuse to Deal
Maurits Dolmans and Matthew Bennett

- the refusal to share the input creates a serious risk of elimination of all effective competition in the downstream market (Section IV.4 below); and,

- The refusal to deal lacks justification, which may be found to be the case if (1) there is proof of exclusionary intent or evidence that a non-dominant or non-vertically-integrated firm would not have refused to supply, and (2) the dominant firm does not prove an objective justification or efficiency defence, or the plaintiff or regulator prove that the justification is not proportionate (Section IV.5 below).[181]

7.159 If these conditions are met, the owner of the essential asset must not unjustifiably discriminate between its own integrated downstream business and third parties competing with it, and a duty to supply on fair and reasonable terms may consequently be imposed.[182] This section discusses each of the above-mentioned elements.[183]

1. Monopoly in Indispensable Input

1.1. "Two Markets" Requirement

7.160 From the very first case imposing a duty to deal, *Commercial Solvents*, it has been clear that a refusal to supply is actionable only if the product or service

---

[181] Para. 81 of the *Guidance Paper* and paras 332 *et seq.* of the *Microsoft* judgment mention items (a), (c) and (d) and imply conditions (b) and e). *See Guidance Paper supra* note 41 and *Microsoft Judgment 2007 supra* note 67.

[182] *See* M. Dolmans, R. O'Donoghue and P.-J. Loewenthal, "Are Article 82 EC and Intellectual Property Interoperable? The State of the Law Pending the Judgment in *Microsoft v. Commission*" (2007) 3(1) *Competition Policy International Journal*, pp. 107–44.

[183] It should be kept in mind, however, that "*there is no persuasiveness to an approach that would advocate the existence of an exhaustive checklist of exceptional circumstances and would have the Commission disregard a limine other circumstances of exceptional character that may deserve to be taken into account when assessing a refusal to supply. … The case-law of the European Courts therefore suggests that the Commission must analyse the entirety of the circumstances surrounding a specific instance of a refusal to supply and must take its decision based on the results of such a comprehensive examination.*" *See Microsoft Decision 2004 supra* note 49, paras 555–8. It is possible, therefore, that other exceptional circumstances may exist that justify a compulsory license, such as in cases where a patent is subject to a promise to license on FRAND terms. *See*, for example, Microsoft's 2008 Interoperability Principles and Microsoft's 2009 Public Undertaking.

7. – Refuse to Deal
Maurits Dolmans and Matthew Bennett

being denied is in a separate market, upstream from the market where the exclusionary effect and consumer harm are felt.[184]

Whether an input for a complex product belongs to a separate market can **7.161** be determined by reference to normal criteria for market definition (reference is made to Chapter 1 on Market Definition). Generally, components are deemed to belong to separate product markets if a small but significant non-transitory increase of the price (SSNIP) of the component is profitable for a hypothetical monopolist supplier of the component, because the profits from the price increase outweigh any losses from reduction in demand for the final product resulting from the price increase. Whether this is the case will depend on a variety of factors, including the price of the withheld component relative to the total price of the complex product and the structure of competition in the market where the integrated product competes.[185] Conversely, it can be argued that they should be treated as belonging

---

[184] *See, e.g.*, Case C-6/73 *Istituto Chemioterapico Italiano and Commercial Solvents Corporation v Commission* [1974] ECR 223; Case *Flughafen Frankfurt v Main*, Commission Decision 98/387/EC of 14 January 1998, OJ 1998 L 173/32; Case 27/76 *United Brands and United Brands Continentaal v Commission* ("*United Brands*") [1978] ECR 207; *See* Télémarketing *supra* note 124; Case C-18/88 *Régie des télégraphes et des téléphones v GB-Inno-BM* [1991] ECR I-5941, para. 18 ("*an abuse … is committed where, without any objective necessity, an undertaking holding a dominant position on a particular market reserves to itself an ancillary activity which might be carried out by another undertaking as part of its activities on a neighbouring but separate market, with the possibility of eliminating all competition from such undertaking.*"); *See Magill supra* note 87; Case IV/34.689 *Sea Containers/Stena Sealink* – Interim measures, Commission Decision of 21 December 1993, OJ 1994 L 15/8; Case T-504/93 *Tiercé Ladbroke v Commission* ("*Ladbroke*") [1997] ECR II-923; *See Oscar Bronner supra* note 68; *See IMS Health supra* note 67, para. 44 ("*it is sufficient that a potential market or even hypothetical market can be identified. Such is the case where the products or services are indispensable in order to carry on a particular business and where there is an actual demand for them on the part of undertakings which seek to carry on the business for which they are indispensable.*"); *See Microsoft Judgment 2007 supra* note 67; Case T-301/04 *Clearstream v Commission* [2009] ECR II-3155. *See* also J. Temple Lang, "European Competition Law and Intellectual Property Rights – A New Analysis" (2010) 11(3) ERA Forum, pp. 411–37, "*It has always been understood that in essential facility cases there must always be two markets. If there were not two markets, the dominant company would be compelled to share a competitive advantage with a direct competitor.*"

[185] *See also* Commission Notice on the definition of relevant market for the purposes of Community competition law ("*Market Definition Notice*"), OJ 1997 C 372/5, para. 56. "*There are certain areas where the application of the principles above has to be undertaken with care. This is the case when considering primary and secondary markets, in particular, when the behaviour of undertakings at a point in time has to be analysed pursuant to Article [102]. The method of defining markets in these cases is the same, i.e., assessing the responses of customers based on their purchasing decisions to relative price changes, but taking into account as well, constraints on substitution imposed by conditions in the connected markets. A narrow definition of market for secondary products, for instance, spare parts, may result when compatibility with the primary product is important. Problems of finding compatible secondary products together with the existence of high prices and a long lifetime of the primary products may render relative price increases of secondary products profitable. A different market definition may result if significant substitution between secondary products is possible or if the characteristics of the primary products make quick and direct consumer responses to relative price increases of the secondary products feasible.*"

7. – Refuse to Deal

Maurits Dolmans and Matthew Bennett

to the same market if a small but significant non-transitory increase of the price of an input leads to a reduction in demand for the final product to such an extent that the price increase would be loss-making for a hypothetical single supplier. The recent *EFIM*[186] case may provide an example. The Commission, however, has a tendency to define separate aftermarkets[187] for secondary products adapted to one specific primary product.[188] It has done so not by applying the SSNIP test, but by relying on the structure of supply and demand.[189] In such cases, however, the Commission may still take the competitive restraint that primary markets may exercise on aftermarkets into account when determining dominance.

7.162 Questions arise in cases where one firm is the sole source of a good and reserves that source for its own activities without ever having supplied third parties. In such a case – where there is demand but no supply and no price for input, and there never has been – is there a separate "market" for the good?

---

[186] Case COMP/39.391 *Printers (EFIM Complaint)* ("*EFIM*"), Commission Decision of 20 May 2009, not yet published. The Commission rejected a complaint alleging that printer manufactures infringed Articles 101 and 102 TFEU by illegally excluding inkjet cartridge (re-) manufacturers from their inkjet cartridges' aftermarkets through patenting strategies, the use of microchips and of recollection programs to shorten the supply of empty cartridges. Insofar as the market definition was concerned, the Commission did not take a clear position, stating, at para. 25, that "*the various markets for cartridges compatible with a certain printer brand may constitute separate relevant aftermarkets, but dominance on the aftermarket can be excluded if competition on the printer market results in effective discipline in the secondary market. Even if each of the various markets for cartridges constitute separate relevant markets,* [i]*t is unlikely that the primary market and the aftermarkets are not closely linked in view of the above-mentioned criteria* [the Pelikan/Kyocera criteria]". The decision was confirmed by the General Court (Case T-296/09 *EFIM v Commission*, not yet reported, but has been appealed to the Court of Justice (Case C-56/12 *EFIM v Commission*, pending). *See also* Case *Pelikan/Kyocera*, in Twenty-fifth Report on Competition Policy (1995), pp. 41–2 and, for the *Info-Lab/Ricoh* case, Case COMP/36.431 *Info-Lab/Ricoh*, in Competition Policy Newsletter (1999), No. 1, pp. 35–7. *See also* J. Temple Lang, "Practical Aspects of Aftermarkets in European Competition Law", (2011) 7(1) *Competition Policy International Journal*, pp. 199–241.

[187] Such markets appear when the purchaser of a primary product will also need to purchase secondary products or services related to the primary product, *e.g.*, toners for photocopiers.

[188] In the Swiss watch manufacturers case, the Commission examined the primary market for luxury and prestige watches, as well as two aftermarkets, namely the market for spare parts and the market for repair and maintenance services in connection with luxury and prestige watches, and reached the prima facie conclusion that those two aftermarkets did not constitute distinct markets and that, therefore, a dominant position did not exist. The General Court found that the Commission made manifest errors of assessment when it concluded that the watch repair and maintenance services market and the market(s) for spare parts did not constitute relevant markets to be examined separately (Case T-427/08 *Confédération européenne des associations d'horlogers-réparateurs v Commission* ("*CEAHR*") [2010] ECR II-05865, paras 10, 25 and 119 *et seq.*). *See also* Case COMP/39.692 *IBM Maintenance Services*, Commission Decision of 13 December 2011, not yet published.

[189] *See, e.g.*, Case T-30/89 *Hilti v Commission* ("*Hilti*") [1991] ECR II-1439, para. 67, confirmed on appeal in Case C-53/92 P *Hilti v Commission* [1994] ECR I-667.

7. – Refuse to Deal
Maurits Dolmans and Matthew Bennett

According to the Commission's *Market Definition Notice*: "*a relevant product market comprises all those products and/or services which are regarded as interchangeable or substitutable by the consumer by reason of the products' characteristics, their prices and their intended use.*"

This definition suggests that the existence of demand is enough for a market to exist even absent supply. This has sometimes also been expressed by economists in the form of the question: "is there a market that is worth monopolising"?[190] The Court of Justice appears to agree. It held as follows in *IMS Health*:

7.163

> "*It is sufficient that a potential market or even a hypothetical market can be identified. Such is the case where the products or services are indispensable in order to carry on a particular business and where there is an actual demand for them on the part of the undertakings which seek to carry on the business for which they are indispensable.*"[191]

The Court of Justice concluded that it was decisive that two different stages of production were identified and that they were interconnected in that the upstream product was indispensable for supply of the downstream product. The *Guidance Paper* confirms this: "*The Commission does not regard it as necessary for the refused product to have been already traded: it is sufficient that there is demand from potential purchasers and that a potential market for the input at stake can be identified.*"[192] The Court did not, however, specify how the national court should assess

7.164

---

[190] *See* National Economic Research Associates, *The Role of Market Definition in Monopoly and Dominance Inquiries,* Office of Fair Trading Economic Discussion Paper 2, OFT 342, July 2001.

[191] *See IMS Health supra* note 67, para. 44. *See also Microsoft Judgment 2007 supra* note 67, para. 335: "*in order that a refusal to give access to a product or service indispensable to the exercise of a particular activity may be considered abusive, it is necessary to distinguish two markets, namely, a market constituted by that product or service and on which the undertaking refusing to supply holds a dominant position and a neighbouring market on which the product or service is used in the manufacture of another product or for the supply of another service. The fact that the indispensable product or service is not marketed separately does not exclude from the outset the possibility of identifying a separate market.*" (*see,* to that effect, *IMS Health*, paragraph 43). Thus, the Court of Justice held at paragraph 44 of IMS Health that it was sufficient that a potential market or even a hypothetical market could be identified and that such was the case where the products or services were indispensable to the conduct of a particular business activity and where there was an actual demand for them on the part of undertakings which sought to carry on that business. The Court of Justice concluded at the following paragraph of the judgment that it was decisive that two different stages of production were identified and that they were interconnected in that the upstream product was indispensable for supply of the downstream product.

[192] *See Guidance Paper supra* note 41, para. 79.

7. – Refuse to Deal
Maurits Dolmans and Matthew Bennett

potential consumer demand (*e.g.*, how many dissatisfied customers would have to be identified).[193]

7.165 Identifying two interconnected different stages of production is easiest in cases of disruption of supplies. In such a case, there is evidence to determine whether there is a separate market.[194] The definition may also be appropriate in cases where it would have made economic sense for a rational non-dominant owner to provide access to or share the facility with third parties, instead of reserving the asset for itself, and especially where other companies in similar situations have done so.[195] In such cases, it can be argued that there would have been an upstream market "but for" the advantage the dominant owner gains by using control over the indispensable facility to monopolise or restrict competition in the downstream market.

7.166 The *Microsoft* case provides an interesting example, without ever explicitly drawing the conclusion that the interoperability information was an upstream market, separate from the client and server operating systems markets. The Commission argued that absent dominance, a platform provider (in that case, a client operating system supplier) has a natural incentive to make its platform compatible with as many complementary products as possible (in that case, server operating systems), and thus to make interoperability information widely available. The availability of a choice of complementary products increases the attractiveness of the desktop operating system. Only when Microsoft had become overwhelmingly dominant in PC operating systems and had a good enough server operating system, could it afford to reduce interoperability of its desktop operating system with impunity – which is equivalent to imposing a

---

[193] *See* D. M. Gitter, "Strong Medicine For Competition Ills: The Judgment of the European Court of Justice in the *IMS Health* Action and its Implications for Microsoft Corporation" (2004) 15(1) *Duke Journal of Comparative & International Law*, pp. 153–92; *See also* M. Dolmans and D. Ilan, "A Health Warning for IP Owners: The Advocate General's Opinion in *IMS* and its Implications for Compulsory Licensing" (2003) 11 *Competition Law Insight*, pp. 12–16.

[194] *See, e.g., Magill supra* note 87 (program listings were previously marketed, although subject to contractual restrictions); *See Microsoft Judgment 2007 supra* note 67 (interoperability information was supplied until Windows 2000); *See* Case C-6/73 *supra* note 184 (aminobutanol was supplied as a raw material for the production of a derivate, ethambutol); Conversely, in *IMS Health*, the existence of two different markets was debatable (database structure was misappropriated by former employees, and never voluntarily licensed).

[195] *See* J. Temple Lang *supra* note 184, p. 7. It is also relevant if the dominant firm itself makes the information available in neighbouring markets. In *Magill*, for instance, the broadcasters made the listings available for daily newspapers and weekly highlights, but excluded comprehensive weekly magazines even though they themselves did not market one. *See supra* note 87.

7. – Refuse to Deal
Maurits Dolmans and Matthew Bennett

"cost" on customers buying desktop operating systems by reducing the choice of complementary products. A non-dominant supplier could not do that without losing market share. Regarding this argument, the Court stated:

> "*In that context, the Court observes that, as the Commission correctly finds at recitals 730 to 734 to the contested decision, it is normal practice for operators in the industry to disclose to third parties the information which will facilitate interoperability with their products and Microsoft itself had followed that practice until it was sufficiently established on the work group server operating systems market. Such disclosure allows the operators concerned to make their own products more attractive and therefore more valuable. In fact, none of the parties has claimed in the present case that such disclosure had had any negative impact on those operators' incentives to innovate.*"[196]

7.167 The implication was that since the interoperability information had been supplied until supply was interrupted, it qualified as an upstream "market" separate from the market for desktop operating systems and server operating systems. By contrast, the mere existence of demand without evidence of past supply arguably cannot suffice for a finding of a hypothetical upstream market in cases where it makes commercial sense for a non-dominant firm to withhold supplies to third parties, and to reserve the raw material, the facility, or the intellectual property for internal use. An innovator may rationally decide, even absent dominance, to recover the investment by selling the innovative product instead of licensing the intellectual property incorporated in it. A firm that has invested in the development of a valuable key component of a complex product may wish to recoup the costs by marketing the system to end-users instead of selling the component to intermediaries for combination with third-party components. As discussed in Section II.2, there are various valid reasons for refusing to supply, and having to supply the component or license the IPR merely because there is demand for it would lead to the counterproductive result that the more innovative or valuable a component or the more brilliant an invention is, the more it would have to be shared. For this reason, upstream goods should not be recognised as a separate market unless the good has been separately marketed before or

---

[196] *See Microsoft Judgment 2007 supra* note 67, para. 702.

7. – Refuse to Deal
Maurits Dolmans and Matthew Bennett

it is commercially rational to market them separately absent upstream and downstream dominance.[197]

7.168 While it is true that there cannot be a general duty to provide an intermediate product precisely when it is most attractive for the complainant to obtain it, the solution need not be to deny the existence of a separate market for the upstream product. In such a case, where it is rational for a non-dominant firm to withhold supplies, the duty to deal could be denied also on grounds of absence of an abuse, exercise within the essential function, or objective justification.

1.2.   Indispensable to Compete

1.2.1.   Introduction

7.169 Where a particular firm's products or services can be duplicated, or where alternative sources of supply are available, the balance of equity and interests militates against imposing a duty to deal. Requiring firms to supply against their will in such cases would discourage investment in creating the asset in the first place and may deprive consumers of the benefits outlined in Sections II.2 and II.3. Accordingly, all cases imposing a *de novo* duty to deal involved indispensable inputs.

7.170 Indispensability implies that the input or information in question is essential for a commercially viable business on the downstream market for which access is sought.[198] The test is whether a substitute is available and, if not, whether a substitute is impossible or extremely difficult to create;[199] in other words, whether there are *"technical, legal or economic obstacles capable of making it impossible or at least unreasonably difficult"*[200] to create alternatives, or to create them within a reasonable timeframe.[201] It must be shown that

---

[197] *See supra* note 39, p. 439.

[198] *See Ladbroke supra* note 184, para. 130 (live pictures of French races not indispensable to compete in the relevant Belgian market).

[199] *See* Advocate General Jacobs in *Oscar Bronner*, at 63–9.

[200] *See IMS Health supra* note 67, para. 28: *"It is clear from paragraphs 43 and 44 of Bronner that, in order to determine whether a product or service is indispensable for enabling an undertaking to carry on business in a particular market, it must be determined whether there are products or services which constitute alternative solutions, even if they are less advantageous, and whether there are technical, legal or economic obstacles capable of making it impossible or at least unreasonably difficult for any undertaking seeking to operate in the market to create, possibly in cooperation with other operators, the alternative products or services"* (emphasis added).

[201] *See* Joined Cases T-374, 375, 384 and 388/94 *European Night Services and others v Commission* (*"European Night Services"*) [1998] ECR II-3141, at para. 209, n. 34.

7. – Refuse to Deal
Maurits Dolmans and Matthew Bennett

the cost of duplicating the allegedly essential facility constitutes a barrier to entry such that there are no viable alternatives to the dominant firm's input,[202] or the cost of such alternatives is *"prohibitively expensive and would not make any commercial sense."*[203] Indispensability is, however, not a binary criterion that is easy to apply. The *Guidance Paper* suggests some leeway, as follows:

> *"In examining whether a refusal to supply deserves its priority attention, the Commission will consider whether the supply of the refused input is objectively necessary for operators to be able to compete effectively on the market. This does not mean that, without the refused input, no competitor could ever enter or survive on the downstream market.[204] Rather, an input is indispensable where there is no actual or potential substitute on which competitors in the downstream market could rely so as to counter – at least in the long-term – the negative consequences of the refusal.[205] In this regard, the Commission will normally make an assessment of whether competitors could effectively duplicate the input produced by the dominant undertaking in the foreseeable future.[206] The notion of duplication means the creation of an alternative source of efficient supply that is capable of allowing competitors to exert a competitive constraint on the dominant undertaking in the downstream market."*[207]

1.2.2.   Case Law Leading to the Indispensability Criterion

To understand the background of the elastic indispensability criterion set out in the *Guidance Paper*, it is useful to review the facts and reasoning in some of the main cases that led to its current definition. The relevant cases are those that involve a duty to deal on an owner of an asset who wishes to reserve

7.171

---

[202] *Ibid.*, para. 209 and *see supra* note 97, para. 227 (Clearstream a *de facto* monopolist and unavoidable trading party for primary clearing and settlement services in Germany).

[203] *See* Case COMP/37.685 *GVG/FS*, Commission Decision of 27 August 2003, OJ 2004 L 11/17, paras 109, 120, and 148.

[204] *See Guidance Paper supra* note 41, para. 83; *See Microsoft Judgment 2007 supra* note 67, paras 428 and 560–63.

[205] *See Guidance Paper supra* note 41, para. 83; *See Magill supra* note 87, paras 52 and 53; *Oscar Bronner supra* note 68, paras 44 and 45; *See Microsoft Judgment 2007 supra* note 67, para. 421.

[206] *See Guidance Paper supra* note 41, para. 83. In general, an input is likely to be impossible to replicate when it involves a natural monopoly due to scale or scope economies, where there are strong network effects or when it concerns so-called "single source" information. However, in all cases account should be taken of the dynamic nature of the industry, and in particular whether or not market power can rapidly dissipate.

[207] *See Oscar Bronner supra* note 68, para. 46, *See IMS Health supra* note 67, para. 29.

7. – Refuse to Deal
Maurits Dolmans and Matthew Bennett

the asset for internal use. Several of the so-called "essential facility" cases are, in fact, discrimination cases,[208] or cases where the owner of the facility already had a contractual relationship with the complainant and the parties merely dispute the conditions of access,[209] or the supplier wishes to cut off supplies.[210] Apart from situations that could be seen as constructive refusal to supply, these are arguably not all true refusal to supply cases, since the owner has itself already made the determination that it wishes to make the asset accessible to outsiders without compulsion, the question being merely on what terms, or whether it wishes to deal only with selected customers, or whether it is no longer convenient. Depending on the specific circumstances, such cases may not raise the same policy concerns to the same degree, and may not to the same extent clash with fundamental rights, as instances where the owner wishes to maintain exclusive use or control of the asset.

---

[208] Compare Case C-18/93 *Corsica Ferries Italia v Corpo dei Piloti del Porto di Genova* (*"Corsica Ferries"*) [1994] ECR I-1783, Commission Decision of 18 July 1988, OJ 1988 L 284/41; *Oscar Bronner supra* note 68, para 30; Case C-18/93 *Corsica Ferries Italia v Corpo dei Piloti del Porto di Genova* (*"Corsica Ferries"*) [1994] ECR I-1783; *European Night Services supra* note 201; Case IV/36.120 La Poste/SWIFT + GUF, Commission Decision of 6 November 1997, OJ 1997 C 335/3, p. 3 (SWIFT settled a complaint by a non-bank regulated financial institution, by allowing access to its communications network previously reserved to banks, even though alternative communications networks were available); Case IV/32.318 *supra* note 124 (discriminatory denial of price-cutting airline's access to computerised reservation system); and Case T-301/04 *supra* note 184 (discriminatory access and pricing concerning primary cleaning and settlement services in relation to registered shares). *See also* J. Temple Lang, "The Principle of Essential Facilities in European Community Competition Law – The Position since Bronner" (2000) 1 *Journal of Network Industries*, pp. 375–405 and J. Temple Lang *supra* note 184, pp. 428–9.

[209] *See* Case IV/34.174 *B&I Line v Sealink Harbours and Stena Sealink*, Commission Decision of 11 June 1992 [1992] 5 C.M.L.R. 255 (B&I, which already had been given access to the facility, complained that Sealink's decision to change its schedule was abusive because it caused the level in the small harbour to raise, thus interrupting B&I's loading and unloading. The Commission ignored indications that Liverpool was an alternative for Holyhead).

[210] *See, e.g., Commercial Solvents supra* note 112 (Commercial Solvents decided to interrupt the supplies of raw material to Zoja, an Italian pharmaceutical company, after that the latter had cancelled some of its purchases and had started obtaining supplies from an alternative distributors at a lower price); *See Hugin Decision 1977 supra* note 124, para. 31; Case 22/78 *Hugin Kassaregister and Hugin Cash Registers v Commission* (*"Hugin Judgment 1979"*) [1979] ECR 1869, para. 1912 (refusal to continue to supply a customer with spare parts on the ground that the customer had established a business in servicing and the supply of spare parts in competition with the dominant supplier); *See United Brands supra* note 184; *See Télémarketing supra* note 124 (Compagnie Luxembourgeoise, the dominant television broadcaster company enjoying a quasi-monopoly in the upstream market for television advertising, *stopped* accepting spot advertisements that did not indicate its own subsidiary's telephone number for telesales); *See* Case C-18/88 *supra* note 184 (RTT, the monopolist telecommunications network operator was granted the exclusive right to approve telephone equipment which was intended to be connected to its network. By using this right, it was reserving to itself the neighbouring market of importing, marketing, connecting, commissioning and maintaining terminal equipment); Case IV/33.544 *British Midland/Aer Lingus*, Commission Decision of 10 April 1992, OJ 1992 L 96/34, p. 34 (Aer Lingus, the dominant airline on the Heathrow-Dublin air-route decided to interrupt the interlining facility with British Midland when the pure latter started to operate a Heathrow-Dublin service in competition with it).

7. – Refuse to Deal
Maurits Dolmans and Matthew Bennett

The issue of indispensability was not discussed in the 1988 *Volvo* case.[211] It **7.172** was clear that Volvo's design right was an exclusive right by law, and it was assumed that the body panels were not replaceable by body panels of any other design. The Court hinted at the possibility that access to the body panels might be essential to independent repairers, but did not elaborate.

Magill. In its 1995 judgment in Magill, the Court of Justice found that the **7.173** broadcasters *"were, by force of circumstance, the only sources of the basic information on programme scheduling which is the indispensable raw material for compiling a weekly television guide"*[212] and that they *"reserved to themselves the secondary market of weekly television guides by excluding all competition on that market … since they denied access to the basic information which is the raw material indispensable for the compilation of such a guide."*[213] This holding introduced a notion taken up in subsequent cases, that indispensability has two aspects: (1) the asset is the only means to enter a downstream market because no substitutes can be found, and no competition is possible in the downstream market without access, and (2) the owner is the sole source of the asset, in the sense that it is not available from any other source.

Ladbroke. In the 1997 *Ladbroke* case,[214] the Court of Justice appeared to **7.174** expand the application of the *Magill* principles, while refraining from imposing a duty to deal in the specific instance. Ladbroke had demanded access to television pictures of French horse races that were available only from PMU, and that were not broadcast in Belgium. Ladbroke wished to show them in its Belgian betting shops. PMU refused to license the pictures. The Court agreed. It confirmed that the refusal could not be qualified as an abuse of dominance *"unless it concerned a product or service which was either essential for the exercise of the activity in question, in that there was no real or potential substitute, or was a new product whose introduction might be prevented, despite specific, constant and regular potential demand on the part of consumers"* (emphasis added).[215] Neither alternative condition was fulfilled. The taking of bets with or without television broadcasts is not a new product, and the fact that televised broadcasts of horse races were not indispensable was proven by the fact that Ladbroke was already present in the betting market in Belgium through its betting shops. Later cases rightly

---

[211] *See Volvo*, para. 8. *See* discussion above, Section III.2.3.1.

[212] *See supra* note 129; *see Magill supra* note 87, para. 53. *See* discussion above, Section III.2.3.1.

[213] *See Magill supra* note 87, para. 56.

[214] *See Ladbroke supra* note 184.

[215] *Ibid.*, para. 131.

did not follow the Court's suggestion that no finding of indispensability is required for a duty to license to arise if the refusal prevents the introduction of a new product, but the *Ladbroke* case illustrates the distinction between what the Court called a "suitable" facility and an "essential" facility.[216]

7.175 **European Night Services.** In *European Night Services*,[217] the Court of First Instance considered "essential facilities" expressly for the first time, albeit in the context of the review of an exemption under Article 101(3) TFEU. In this case, railway transporters had established a joint venture to provide night services from both sides of the English Channel and in the tunnel. The Commission exempted that agreement for a short term and required the transporters to provide not only the joint venture, but also its competitors with access to special locomotives and special crews, which the Commission considered to be essential facilities. The parties appealed. The Court specified that "*a product or service cannot be considered necessary or essential unless there is no real or potential substitute*",[218] and an infrastructure can be considered an essential facility only when such "*infrastructure, product or service is not interchangeable and only, by reason of their special characteristics – in particular the prohibitive costs of/ and time reasonably required for reproducing them – there are no viable alternatives available to potential competitors, which are thereby excluded from the market*".[219]

7.176 The Court considered that the Commission could not validly regard the special locomotives and crews as essential, because: (1) the Commission had not demonstrated why an undertaking having a 5–8 per cent market share could have an influence on the structure of the market in question, and that in any case (2) the Commission had not demonstrated that competitors could not obtain them either directly from manufacturers or indirectly by renting them from other undertakings. The Commission retorted that this possibility was in fact purely theoretical and that only the notifying undertakings actually possessed such locomotives. The Court dismissed this on the ground that "[t]*he fact that the notifying undertakings have been the first to acquire the locomotives in*

---

[216] *See Ladbroke supra* note 184, para. 132: "*the televised broadcasting of horse races, although constituting an additional, and indeed suitable, service for bettors, is not in itself indispensable for the exercise of bookmakers' main activity, namely the taking of bets, as is evidenced by the fact that the applicant is present on the Belgian betting market and occupies a significant position as regards bets on French races. Moreover, transmission is not indispensable, since it takes place after bets are placed, with the result that its absence does not in itself affect the choices made by bettors and, accordingly, cannot prevent bookmakers from pursuing their business.*"

[217] *See European Night Services supra* note 201.

[218] *Ibid.*, para. 208.

[219] *Ibid.*, para. 209.

7. – Refuse to Deal
Maurits Dolmans and Matthew Bennett

question on the market does not mean that they are alone in being able to do so."[220] This laid the foundation for an important consideration, followed by the Court in subsequent cases, that to determine whether a facility is essential, it is necessary to verify not only whether there are actual substitutes in existence, but also whether there are potential substitutes.

Bronner. This principle was also the basis for the Court's judgment in **7.177** *Bronner.*[221] As discussed in more detail above (Section III.2.3.1), Bronner demanded access to a rival's nationwide newspaper delivery network, because Bronner itself was not sufficiently large to set up and operate its own home-delivery scheme in an economically viable way. The Court found that a refusal to grant such an access would violate Article 102 TFEU only if there were evidence "*not only that the refusal of the service comprised in home delivery be likely to eliminate all competition in the daily newspaper market on the part of the person requesting the service and that such refusal be incapable of being objectively justified, but also that the service in itself be indispensable to carrying on that person's business, inasmuch as there is no actual or potential substitute in existence for that home-delivery scheme.*"[222]

The Court recognised that there was in fact only one nationwide home-delivery **7.178** scheme in Austria and that Mediaprint held a dominant position in the market for home delivery services, but observed that other methods of distributing daily newspapers existed, such as by post or through sales in shops and at kiosks, even though they might be less advantageous for the distribution of certain newspapers. The implication is that these alternatives have to be considered substitutes even if they do not belong to the same market as the home delivery network, *i.e.*, even if a significant increase of the home delivery fee (say, by five per cent over a long period of time) would not cause users of the service to switch to these alternatives. The Court was particularly strict with regard to potential substitutes:

> "*it does not appear that there were any technical, legal or even economic obstacles capable of making it impossible, or even unreasonably difficult, for any other publisher of daily newspapers to establish, alone or in cooperation with other publishers, its own nationwide home-delivery scheme and use it to distribute its own daily*

---

[220] *See European Night Services supra* note 201, para. 216.

[221] *See Oscar Bronner supra* note 68, para. 39.

[222] *Ibid.*, para. 41.

7. – Refuse to Deal
Maurits Dolmans and Matthew Bennett

newspapers. It should be emphasised in that respect that, in order to demonstrate that the creation of such a system is not a realistic potential alternative and that access to the existing system is therefore indispensable, it is not enough to argue that it is not economically viable by reason of the small circulation of the daily newspaper or newspapers to be distributed. For such access to be capable of being regarded as indispensable, it would be necessary at the very least to establish ... that it is not economically viable to create a second home-delivery scheme for the distribution of daily newspapers with a circulation comparable to that of the daily newspapers distributed by the existing scheme."[223]

7.179   The expression "alone or in cooperation" established a new test that required that the existence of potential substitutes be assessed not just by reference to the complainant, but to a new entrant as efficient as the incumbent. Thus, Bronner set out that the only way to establish the existence of an essential facility, is to prove that the market *as a whole* is not large enough, and does not generate enough revenues, to allow two distribution systems to exist side-by-side.[224]

7.180   This appropriately analyses the issue from a dynamic rather than a static perspective. A new entrant confronted by a large incumbent cannot merely argue that it is impossible for it to establish a substitute distribution network, even if it teamed up with all other rivals apart from the incumbent. The Court required Bronner to bear the costs of creating a new network, even if it was initially loss-making, and to make due efforts to expand total demand in the market and take market share from Mediaprint (presumably by offering new or more attractive daily newspaper than Mediaprint, and maximising efficiency). Bronner was entitled to use Mediaprint's network only if Bronner could show that even if as a result of these efforts it became as large as Mediaprint, it would still make a loss overall because of the costs of the duplicate distribution network. While demanding, this approach has the benefit of maintaining Mediaprint's incentive to create its own network in the first place without having to take into account the possibility of reduced revenues from having to share its network with its rivals. If Bronner can be an effective

---

[223] *See Oscar Bronner supra* note 68, paras 44–6.

[224] The condition of a market not being big enough to allow two firms to operate together, is analogous to the economic concept of a natural monopoly. The OECD defines natural monopolies as being characterised by *"steeply declining long-run average and marginal-cost curves such that there is room for only one firm to fully exploit available economies of scale and supply the market. In a natural monopoly the average cost curve is below the demand curve for all relevant production points."* R. S. Khemani and D. M. Shapiro, *Glossary of Industrial Organisation Economics and Competition Law*, OECD, Paris, 1993.

7. – Refuse to Deal
Maurits Dolmans and Matthew Bennett

competitor in the newspaper market without access to Mediaprint's network, even with a less efficient distribution, it is not entitled to access. The objective of competition law, after all, is not to assist rivals, but to enable competition that is effective in driving the incumbent's price down and maintain the spur to innovate. The definition of "indispensability" in *Bronner* has become the touchstone of all future duty to deal cases.

IMS Health. In its 2004 judgment in *IMS Health*, discussed above in Section III.2.3.1., the Court of Justice applied the criteria set out in *Bronner*.[225] Pharmaceutical laboratories participated in the definition and improvement of the "1860 brick structure", in meetings regularly organised by IMS Health over a period of years. The Commission argued that it would be difficult for a new entrant to convince the laboratories to duplicate that work, and incur the expense of participating in additional sessions to develop an alternative brick structure for a rival. The Court held that: **7.181**

> "*account must be taken of the fact that a high level of participation by the pharmaceutical laboratories in the improvement of the 1860 brick structure protected by copyright, on the supposition that it is proven, has created a dependency by users in regard to that structure, particularly at a technical level. In such circumstances, it is likely that those laboratories would have to make exceptional organisational and financial efforts in order to acquire the studies on regional sales of pharmaceutical products presented on the basis of a structure other than that protected by the intellectual property right.*"[226]

Applying *Bronner*, the Commission and the plaintiffs would have had to show that NDC and Azyx could not convince sufficient pharmacists, even against payment, to participate in the development of an alternative database structure. The Court considered the possibility that "[t]*he supplier of that alternative structure might therefore be obliged to offer terms which are such as to rule out any economic viability of business on a scale comparable to that of the undertaking which controls the protected structure.*"[227] **7.182**

A further barrier to entry, according to the Commission and the national court, was that IMS Health's database structure had become an industry standard,

---

[225] *See IMS Health supra* note 67, para.28.

[226] *Ibid.*, para. 29.

[227] *Ibid.*, para. 29.

7. – Refuse to Deal

Maurits Dolmans and Matthew Bennett

because IMS Health distributed them free of charge to pharmacies and doctors' surgeries, and clients adapted their information and distribution systems to them. Switching costs were large. The *IMS Health* case thus involves a Stiglerian barrier to entry (and a high one at that): an obstacle created by the incumbent, which the incumbent did not face, but that a new entrant must overcome before it can even begin to build its own business.[228]

7.183 **Microsoft.** These barriers to entry, in the form of network effects giving rise to *de facto* standards, were also at stake in the assessment of indispensability in the most recent case, *Microsoft*. As explained above (Section III.2.3.1.), Sun and others argued that because Microsoft had a near-monopoly in personal computer operating systems that was protected by network effects,[229] and Windows servers communicated with Windows operating system via narrow and technologically privileged links, third-party servers were unable to interoperate with clients running Windows operating systems as effectively as Windows servers could. This meant that third-party servers were unable to compete viably with Windows servers for inclusion in corporate networks connecting and serving Windows clients.[230]

---

[228] G. J. Stigler, *Organization of Industry* (Chicago, The University of Chicago Press, 1968), p. 70 (costs that *"are higher for a new firm than for an existing firm"*).

[229] *See Microsoft Decision 2004 supra* note 49 recitals 448–64 and 515–25; *See Microsoft Judgment 2007 supra* note 67, paras 558–62. Network effects, of positive feedback effects, arise when users value a good higher depending on how many others use it. In this instance, the network effects are indirect, because the perceived value of Windows is derived from the number of other users using applications running on Windows (like Office) and from the volume of applications available on Windows, which is itself derived from the widespread use of Windows.

[230] This was also the basic analysis followed in the case that led to the US Consent Decree, *see United States v Microsoft*, 84 F. Supp. 2d 9 (D.D.Cir. 1999) (Findings of Fact) and *United States v Microsoft*, 87 F. Supp. 2d 30 (D.D.Cir. 2000) (Conclusions of Law) . On appeal, *see United States v Microsoft*, 253 F.3d 34 (D.C. Cir. 2001) *(en banc)*. The Commission concluded, however, that because clients often call on servers not directly but via other servers, and a client-requested task may in fact be performed by a variety of servers working together in a network, it was not longer sufficient to disclose information for client-to-server interoperability, but that server-to-server interoperability was also needed. *See Microsoft Decision 2004 supra* note 49, paras 176–84 and 999. "*The interconnection and interaction ... should not be viewed as intended to enable <u>one</u> Windows work group server to communicate with <u>one</u> Windows client PC. It should rather be described in terms of interoperability within a computer <u>system</u> encompassing several Windows client PCs and several Windows work group servers linked together in a network. Interoperability within this computer system implies both client-to-server and server-to-server interoperability. ... Furthermore, in some circumstances, servers will query other servers <u>on behalf</u> of a client PC. [S]ome client-to-server communications build on the expectation that certain server-to-server communications have taken place. [...] In other words, the proper functioning of a Windows work group network relies on an <u>architecture</u> of client-to-server and server-to-server interconnections and interactions. ... This means that other work group server operating system vendors that want to compete for customers having an existing investment in Windows need access to information relating to interoperability with the Windows domain architecture*" (paras 178–84, emphasis in original). This was upheld by the Court in *Microsoft Judgment 2007 supra* note 67, para. 374. The extension of the disclosure to include also server-to-server interoperability information therefore served to preserve the "useful effect" of the remedy.

7. – Refuse to Deal
Maurits Dolmans and Matthew Bennett

After an exhaustive factual and legal review, the Court of First Instance con- **7.184**
firmed the Commission's finding that *"in order to be able to compete viably with
Windows work group server operating systems, competitors' operating systems must be
able to interoperate with the Windows domain architecture on an equal footing with those
Windows systems."*[231]

The parties hotly debated the two elements of indispensability identified in **7.185**
Magill, namely (1) whether the requested interoperability protocol information is the only means to maintain a viable presence in the market, or whether
substitutes can be found, and (2) whether Microsoft was the sole source.

The first element especially was discussed at great length. Microsoft argued **7.186**
that alternatives were available, including industry standard communication
protocols, and that these were adequate for rivals to survive in the server operating systems market, as demonstrated by the continued existence of competitive servers and the emergence of Linux as a new entrant. In Microsoft's
view, it was sufficient that Windows enabled some degree of interoperability
for third-party products. The Court of First Instance held that the relevant
standard was the degree of interoperability that was necessary for competing
server operating system developers *"to remain viably in the market"*.[232] It drew a
link between the criterion of indispensability and the objective of Article 102
TFEU, which is to preserve effective competition on the relevant market.[233]
The Court therefore investigated in depth what level of interoperability was
needed for effective competition (*i.e.,* competition that drives prices down and
spurs innovation generally, as opposed to niche competition).[234] It found that
Windows represented the "quasi standard" for client operating systems,[235] and
that customers attached great importance to interoperability with Windows
clients and the Windows domain architecture consisting of closely interlinked
client/server and server/server interconnections and interactions.[236] The
Court added that *"in light of the very narrow technological and privileged links that
Microsoft has established between its Windows client PC and work group server operating
systems, and of the fact that Windows is present on virtually all client PCs installed within*

---

[231] *See Microsoft Judgment 2007 supra* note 67, paras 374–421 in combination with paras 228 *et seq.*

[232] *Ibid.,* para. 228.

[233] *Ibid.,* para. 229.

[234] *Ibid.,* paras 337–436 and 207–45.

[235] *Ibid.,* para. 387.

[236] *See, e.g., Microsoft Decision 2004 supra* note 49, paras 383–6, and *see Microsoft Judgment 2007 supra* note 67, paras 381
et seq.

7. – Refuse to Deal

Maurits Dolmans and Matthew Bennett

organisations, ... Microsoft was able to impose the Windows domain architecture as the 'de facto standard for work group computing.' "[237]

7.187 Market studies indicated that while most customers preferred the features and functionality of non-Windows servers, they nevertheless in the majority of cases chose Windows in order to ensure full interoperability in a network including Windows clients and servers.[238] The effect was to gradually eliminate non-Windows servers from the market, with Windows server market share increasing inexorably.[239] The Court added in that regard that,

> *"competitors, with the exception of distributors of Linux products, had been present on the work group server operating systems market for several years before Microsoft began to develop and market such systems. While it is true that on the date of adoption of the contested decision those competitors were still present on the market, the fact remains that their market share fell significantly as Microsoft's share increased rapidly, notwithstanding the fact that some of them, particularly Novell, had a considerable technological advantage over Microsoft. The fact that competition is eliminated gradually and not immediately does not contradict the Commission's argument that the information at issue is indispensable."* [240]

7.188 Linux was found to be several years behind in interoperability also, and although it was growing modestly, that was at the expense of Novell and Unix rather than Windows.

7.189 As to the second element, unavailability from another source, Microsoft argued that reverse engineering allowed rivals to discover the interoperability information. This was dismissed by the Commission and the Court, who concluded that it was flawed and no viable substitute to disclosure,[241] because of the time and expense involved, as well as the fact that Microsoft can simply make a strategic change to its code base to eliminate or substantially weaken

---

[237] *See Microsoft Judgment 2007 supra* note 67, para. 392.

[238] *See, e.g., Microsoft Decision 2004 supra* note 49, paras 637–65, and *Microsoft Judgment 2007 supra* note 67, paras 393 et seq.

[239] *See, e.g., Microsoft Decision 2004 supra* note 49 recitals 590–636, *Microsoft Judgment 2007 supra* note 67, para. 360.

[240] *See Microsoft Judgment 2007 supra* note 67, para. 428.

[241] *See, e.g., Microsoft Decision 2004 supra* note 49 recitals 666–87. The information therefore met the definition of an essential facility given by Advocate General Jacobs in *Bronner* in that independent development *"is impossible or extremely difficult"* (*see* Advocate General Jacobs in *Oscar Bronner* and Advocate General Tizzano in *IMS Health*, para. 28).

Maurits Dolmans and Matthew Bennett

any interoperability achieved.[242] Nor were other solutions adequate, such as the use of industry standard interoperability technology. The Court agreed with the Commission that the "*quasi-monopoly that Microsoft has held on the client PC operating systems market for many years enables it to 'determine to a large extent and independently of its competitors the set of coherent communications rules that will govern the de facto standard for interoperability in work group networks.'*"[243] Microsoft was therefore the sole available source.

TeliaSonera. In the *TeliaSonera* case,[244] which concerned a margin squeeze abuse, the Court of Justice appeared to limit the application of the indispensability requirement.[245] The Court, however, expressly distinguished a margin squeeze from a refusal to supply, stating that the former "*may, in itself, constitute an independent form of abuse distinct from that of refusal to supply.*"[246] *TeliaSonera*, in other words, does not concern a refusal to supply, but the terms and conditions on which a supplier deals with its customers.[247] **7.190**

1.2.3.   Discussion

1.2.3.1.   Defining Indispensability

Microsoft explores the outer limit of the least strict definition of indispensability. It involved a combination of technical and "economic assessment", **7.191**

---

[242] *See Microsoft Decision 2004 supra* note 49, paras 685–7.

[243] *See Microsoft Judgment 2007 supra* note 67, para. 392.

[244] Case C-52/09 *Konkurrensverket v TeliaSonera Sverige* ("*TeliaSonera Judgment 2011*"), not yet reported.

[245] For a further analysis and discussion of the *TeliaSonera* judgment and its implications *see* Chapter 5. *See also* Case T-336/07 *Telefónica v Commission*, not yet reported and Case T-398/07 *Spain v Commission*, not yet reported, subject to appeal.

[246] *See TeliaSonera Judgment 2011 supra* note 244, para. 56.

[247] The Court's statements on the relationship between margin squeeze and refusal to supply deviated from the traditional view that margin squeeze is a type of a constructive refusal to supply. *See Guidance Paper supra* note 41 paras 79 *et seq. See also* Opinion of Advocate General Mazák in *TeliaSonera*, who argued that a margin squeeze is just one particular manifestation of a refusal to supply since the concern in margin squeeze cases is the same as in refusal to supply cases as there is no independent competitive harm caused by the margin squeeze above and beyond the harm which would result from a duty-to-deal violation at the wholesale level. The Advocate General assumed that a margin squeeze is only abusive if the dominant undertaking has a regulatory obligation to supply the input in question or if that input is indispensable: "*[i]f margin squeezes were prohibited purely on the basis of an abstract calculation of the prices and in the absence of any assessment of the indispensability of the input for competition in the market, dominant undertakings' willingness to invest would be reduced and/or they would be likely to raise end-user prices lest they be charged with a margin squeeze*". *See* Advocate General Mazák in Case C-52/09 *Konkurrensverket v TeliaSonera Sverige*, not yet reported, paras 11, 16 and 21. The Court did not provide adequate reasoning to explain its deviation from the traditional view, and it should be relied upon only with caution.

7. – Refuse to Deal
Maurits Dolmans and Matthew Bennett

which gives the Commission a wide margin of appreciation. In most cases, the presence of rivals on the downstream market without access to the facility should be enough to defeat an argument that a facility is essential. However, if a complainant who is in the market wishes to argue that a facility to which it has no access is indispensable, it will have to show that either (1) interruption of access or (2) radical changes in consumer preference lead to its gradual elimination. This in turn requires a detailed market survey, showing the effects of the interruption and proving the causal link with foreclosure, namely clear evidence (of the kind the Court cited in *Microsoft*) that rivals' market share is declining and "but for" the denial of the facility, their market share would have grown because consumers would have preferred the rivals' products or services. This is inherently a heavy burden to prove. *Microsoft* shows that extensive review of market data from a variety of market surveys and technical assessment will be required. The finding in *Microsoft* that its assets are indispensable even though rivals were still in the market who did not have access is arguably due to a unique combination of an overwhelming and long-standing near-monopoly of Windows desktop operating systems and the evolution of related interoperability specifications into a *de facto* industry standard, the interruption of supply of interoperability information, the relatively slow replacement cycle for servers, the clear statement of intent to foreclose,[248] and the great visibility of Windows as a product used by hundreds of millions of consumers. Whether the same arguments may be made in other cases without the *Microsoft*-specific combination of facts remains to be seen.

7.192 *Bronner* arguably imposes a heavier burden of proof on complainants wishing to rely upon the essential facilities doctrine. However, unlike *Microsoft*, *Bronner* involved a refusal to supply where supply had never previously been given. *Bronner* shows that it is not enough for a plaintiff to argue that duplicating the facility be difficult or expensive for the complainant; it should be impossible or unreasonably difficult for all efficient new entrants. The test to be applied is, therefore, an objective one. A particular competitor cannot plead merely that it does not have the wherewithal to duplicate the facility. In the words of Advocate General Jacobs: "*where duplication of the facility is impossible or extremely difficult owing to physical, geographical or legal constraints, this alone might constitute an*

---

[248] The judgment in paras 771 and 1349 referred to a speech given by Mr Gates, President of *Microsoft*, in February 1997 to members of Microsoft's sales force, which "*confirms the existence of a pattern of general conduct designed to restrict the communication of interoperability information, containing as it does, the following declaration: 'What we are trying to do is use our server control to do new protocols and lock out Sun and Oracle specifically … Now, I don't know if we'll get to that or not, but that's what we are trying to do.*" See Microsoft Judgment 2007 supra note 67.

7. – Refuse to Deal
Maurits Dolmans and Matthew Bennett

insuperable barrier to entry, particularly in cases in which the creation of the facility took place under non-competitive conditions, for example through public funding."[249]

Recent cases suggest that in spite of *Bronner*, the Commission is tempted to interpret the indispensability requirement less strictly. In the *ENI* case, for instance, the Commission investigated whether ENI had engaged in a constructive refusal to supply regarding access to its gas pipelines infrastructures used to import natural gas into Italy.[250] The Commission identified ENI's entire gas transport infrastructures as an essential facility, suggesting that access to ENI's infrastructures was objectively necessary for third-party shippers to import gas and compete in the gas supply markets in Italy.[251] In reality, however, it was possible to "duplicate" parts of ENI's transportation infrastructures.[252] Nor was access to, or duplication of, all of ENI's import infrastructures necessary for third parties to either operate on the Italian gas markets, or to compete effectively with ENI on such markets. Moreover, despite having established that the whole pipeline system was essential, the Commission did not ascertain whether the alleged abuse was carried out by ENI on all of its import infrastructures, but focused only on three ENI pipelines. The case was settled with an Article 9 Commitment Decision, and cannot therefore be regarded as precedent.[253] **7.193**

Given the *Bronner* judgment and the significant interference of a direct duty to supply with a company's property rights and fundamental freedoms, indispensability should remain a necessary condition for a finding of a direct refusal to supply under Article 102. *Microsoft* indicates that this should be so **7.194**

---

[249] Advocate General Jacobs in *Oscar Bronner* para. 66.

[250] Case COMP/39.315 *ENI*, Commission Decision of 29 September 2010, not yet published, paras 41–2.

[251] *Ibid.*

[252] Duplication had already occurred: For instance, in 2009, the off-shore LNG terminal Rovigo, built and operated by third parties entered into operation; several other projects had been initiated, and some were well under way.

[253] *See also* other Article 9 Decisions in the energy sector, and in Case COMP/39.692 *IBM Maintenance Services supra* note 188, not yet published. In that decision, the Commission referred to the *TeliaSonera* judgment, stating that "*the Court of Justice recently held that the conditions to be met under the Bronner line of case-law do not necessarily apply when assessing the nature of conduct which consists in supplying services or selling goods on conditions which are disadvantageous or on which there might be no purchaser*" (para. 38). The Commission appeared to rely on *TeliaSonera* in order to argue that it need not show that IBM's inputs were indispensable for third-party activities in the downstream market for mainframe maintenance services for finding an abusive constructive refusal to supply. However, the Commission also stated that it would have been able to prove that IBM's inputs were indispensable in order to provide maintenance services for IBM mainframes. The *IBM Maintenance Services* case ended with commitments, and therefore does not qualify as precedent.

7. – Refuse to Deal
Maurits Dolmans and Matthew Bennett

even in cases of supply interruption. Regarding the scope of the indispensability criterion beyond a direct refusal to supply, *i.e.*, in the case of a constructive refusal to supply, or other broad demands to assist competitors, these are matters that also concern supplies directly and therefore, arguably, should only be caught by the prohibition of Article 102 if the input at issue were indispensable.[254]

1.2.3.2. Barriers to Entry

7.195 An incumbent's economies of scale are often mentioned as a barrier to entry, but the Court in Bronner specified clearly that "*it is not enough to argue that it is not economically viable by reason of the small circulation of the ... newspapers to be distributed*".[255] The analysis should be based on the assumption that the new entrant would achieve alone or together with others "*a circulation comparable to that of the daily newspapers distributed by the existing scheme.*"[256] Only if in such a case entry would still not be "economically viable", would the Court consider intervention. This is logical: the incumbent had to invest time and money into growing to its current size to achieve its current economies, and there is no reason why the new entrant should not have to do the same, so long as the costs and time frame associated with that are comparable.[257]

7.196 This might not be the case if demand is stagnant and there is a minimum efficient scale of operation that does not allow room for more than one market player. It might also not be the case if entry involves enormous sunk costs, and the incumbent has economies of scale and resources that allow it to – and lead to the expectation that it will – engage in long-term price-cutting. If so, the entrant faces large risks that the incumbent did not have to face (assuming the incumbent was the first entrant), and which may qualify as a long-run barrier to entry.

---

[254] T. Graf, "*How Indispensable Is Indispensability?*", Kluwer Competition Law Blog, April 18, 2011.

[255] *See Oscar Bronner supra* note 68, para. 45.

[256] *See Oscar Bronner supra* note 68, para. 46.

[257] A possible exception might apply in cases in which the investment was funded by public sources (*e.g.*, the utilities), and the market has not subsequently paid for this financing in the process of privatisation. *See Guidance Paper supra* note 41, para. 82 and *Discussion Paper supra* note 154, para. 236.

7. – Refuse to Deal
Maurits Dolmans and Matthew Bennett

The wording of the Court shows that it is concerned only with absolute and **7.197**
long-term barriers to entry. The term "barrier to entry" is often used loosely.
It refers to any cost, time or other factor that prevents an entrepreneur from
creating a new firm in a market even though an existing firm earns long-run
profits. If cost curves and prices are identical for different firms, no firm can
earn a long-term margin over and above cost (with cost including a reasonable return on investment and reward for risk). Incumbents can earn a long-
term profit only if new entrants face costs or barriers that incumbents do
not or have not had to deal with, and that are so high as to prevent entry.[258]
While the Commission has not defined barriers to entry in the *Guidance Paper*,
it stated in the *Discussion Paper* that *"barriers to expansion and entry are factors
that make entry impossible or unprofitable while permitting established undertakings to
charge prices above the competitive level"*.[259] In the Commission's *Horizontal Merger
Guidelines*, barriers to entry are described as *"specific features of the market, which
give incumbent firms advantages over potential competitors"*.[260] Examples can be the
network effects protecting an incumbent, exclusive rights or franchises for
the first mover, subsidies to early investors that later entrants do not receive,
new regulation imposing special burdens on new entrants or limiting possibilities for the creation of alternative infrastructures, absolute cost advantages
of incumbents, consumer unwillingness to duplicate efforts or on-premises
equipment, blocking patents, etc.[261]

In *Bronner*, it was made clear by Advocate General Jacobs that even a nar- **7.198**
row interpretation of barriers to entry could be insufficient for a finding of
indispensability. There has to be, in the words of Advocate General Jacobs,
"a genuine stranglehold" on the downstream or related market, or an absolute
barrier. A mere patent is not enough, if it is possible to design around it, or
if market entry (even with a less attractive product) is possible without implementing it. Examples would include mandatory *de jure* standards, successful *de
facto* standards, a true blocking patent,[262] or *"a natural monopoly due to scale or scope*

---

[258] For this definition of long-run barrier to entry, *see* D. W. Carlton and J. M. Perloff, *Modern Industrial Organization* (2nd Ed., New York, Harper Collins College Publishers, 1994), p. 110.

[259] *Discussion Paper supra* note 154, para. 38.

[260] Guidelines on the assessment of horizontal mergers under the Council Regulation on the control of concentrations between undertakings (*"Horizontal Merger Guidelines"*), OJ 2004 C 31/5, para. 70.

[261] *Ibid.*, para. 71.

[262] A blocking patent would have to be both technically and commercially essential. That is to say, it should
be recognised as an essential facility only if (1) it is impossible to implement the technology or specification
without infringing the patent (*i.e.*, the patent cannot be "designed around") and (2) it is impossible to enter the
market viably or remain an effective competitors with implementing the technology or specification.

economies, where there are strong network effects or when it concerns so-called 'single source' information. However, in all cases account should be taken of the dynamic nature of the industry and, in particular whether or not market power can rapidly dissipate."[263] If assets were deemed indispensable based on the past situation, without consideration whether the state of technology or other circumstances have advanced such that finding an alternative becomes feasible, that would dampen the incentive to innovate. As discussed in Sections II.2.3. and II.2.4., entrants in existing markets would attempt to ride on the incumbent's facilities rather than innovating, and creators of new markets could be discouraged by the prospect of having to share their platform or facility with rivals if and when they succeed.

7.199 Incumbents may argue in defence that they in fact incurred costs that subsequent entrants do not have, such as stranded costs related to investments that have been overtaken by new, more cost-efficient technologies, or the cost of developing demand for a new product or service with which consumers were unacquainted and which they initially resisted. There may also be higher maintenance costs for older facilities. These costs should arguably be netted out when determining whether duplicating the asset is economically viable. What matters, after all, is whether the new entrant can duplicate it upon entry, and if it does not have to incur costs that the incumbent had to bear, it cannot use these to invoke a duty to deal.

1.2.3.3. Indispensability in Case of a *de novo* Refusal to Supply and of Disruption

7.200 Finally, the *Commercial Solvents* and *Microsoft* cases suggest that in case of termination of an existing supply arrangement, an input is more likely to be found to be essential than in the case of a refusal to supply a new customer. The *Guidance Paper* confirms that: "*For example, if the dominant undertaking had previously been supplying the requesting undertaking, and the latter had made relationship-specific investments in order to use the subsequently refused input, the Commission may be more likely to regard the input in question as indispensable.*"[264] An interruption of supplies is not, however, enough in itself to prove indispensability. If the customer is able to find another source, even a more expensive one, or to create an alternative facility, alone or together with others in the industry, *Bronner* indicates that the asset is not indispensable. The existence of a previous relationship of supplies

---

[263] *See Guidance Paper supra* note 41, para. 83.
[264] *Ibid.*, para. 84.

7. – Refuse to Deal
Maurits Dolmans and Matthew Bennett

is a relevant factor that may colour the assessment of objective justification, but indispensability is an objective concept unrelated to past supply policies.

2. Refusal to Deal

The *Guidance Paper* indicates that a refusal to supply may arise in many dif-   **7.201**
ferent circumstances, exceptional or not, such as: "*a refusal to supply products to existing or new customers,*[265] *refusal to license intellectual property rights,*[266] *including when the licence is necessary to use interface information,*[267] *or refusal to grant access to an essential facility or a network*".[268]

In assessing whether there is a refusal to supply or not, the Commission and   **7.202**
courts will favour substance over form. Of course, the complainant will have to show evidence that a request was made, that it reached the potential supplier, and that the latter did or should reasonably have understood the request as in fact seeking the access to the specific facility or information that the Commission requires the dominant firm to supply. This last issue gave rise to debate in the *Microsoft* case, where Microsoft, *inter alia*, claimed that Sun did not request access to interoperability information within the meaning of the Commission Decision.[269] The Court held that a dominant firm cannot hide behind a strict or formalistic construction of a supply request, and that a request will be interpreted to include everything that is reasonably necessary to make the request effective. The Court reviewed the correspondence closely and indicated that it would consider a request sufficient if it identifies the nature of the asset to which access is sought, as well as the purpose of the request, and its conditions. Because Sun clearly identified that its goal was to "'*seamlessly communicate*' with the *Windows environment*",[270] the request was interpreted to include everything that was needed to that end (and by implication excluding everything that was not needed). The Court examined the wording of the request "*in the light of the context in which it was written, the identity of its author, the extent of his knowledge of the technologies concerned and the approach adopted by Microsoft up to the time of the adoption*

---

[265] *See Guidance Paper supra* note 41, para. 78 and case law quoted in footnote 3: *See Commercial Solvents supra* note 112.

[266] *Ibid.*, para. 78 and case law quoted in footnote 4: *See Magill supra* note 87; *See IMS Health supra* note 67. Those judgments show that in exceptional circumstances a refusal to license intellectual property rights is abusive.

[267] *Ibid.*, para. 78 and *Microsoft Judgment 2007 supra* note 67.

[268] *Ibid.*, paras 78–9 and case law quoted in footnote 6: *See* Case IV/34.689 *supra* note 184 and *see* Case IV/33.544 *supra* note 210.

[269] See *Microsoft Judgment 2007 supra* note 67, para. 713–776.

[270] *Ibid.*, para. 744.

7. – Refuse to Deal
Maurits Dolmans and Matthew Bennett

of the contested decision".[271] Finally, the Court considered evidence of Microsoft's real intentions, including statements that Microsoft wished to restrict the communication of interoperability information,[272] and accepted the request as sufficiently clear to be understood by the addressee.

7.203 A refusal may come in many forms, ranging from a straightforward negative answer, to a failure to communicate combined with a *de facto* failure to supply, and delay tactics designed to avoid an outright refusal by engaging the prospective customer in interminable exchanges. In this respect too, substance prevails over form. With respect to constructive refusals to supply, the *Guidance Paper* provides that *"it is not necessary for there to be actual refusal on the part of a dominant undertaking; 'constructive refusal' is sufficient. Constructive refusal could, for example, take the form of unduly delaying or otherwise degrading the supply of the product or involve the imposition of unreasonable conditions in return for the supply."*[273] A response by a dominant firm that was *"entirely negative and consisted of raising difficulties"*[274] was found tantamount to a refusal to deal, as was undue delay in answering combined with a claim that the request was unclear when all other addressees of the same request understood it properly,[275] and a dilatory attitude towards a request by one customer in circumstances where the dominant firm adopts a cooperative attitude towards another.[276]

7.204 Even an ostensibly positive answer may be a refusal, if combined with failure to supply, the supply of inadequate material or goods, the imposition of objectively unreasonable conditions, or the imposition of subjectively unreasonable conditions that the dominant firm knows its counterpart will not accept.[277] In

---

[271] *See Microsoft Judgment 2007 supra* note 67, para. 751. The Court also took into account the *"general pattern of conduct on Microsoft's part"* (judgment, para. 767).

[272] *Ibid.*, para. 771, referring to an extract from a speech given by Mr. Gates, President of Microsoft, in February 1997 to members of Microsoft's sales force: *"What we are trying to do is use our server control to do new protocols and lock out Sun and Oracle specifically … Now, I don't know if we'll get to that or not, but that's what we are trying to do."*

[273] *See Guidance Paper supra* note 41, para. 79.

[274] *See* Case IV/34.689 *supra* note 184, para. 71.

[275] *See* Case COMP/37.685 *supra* note 204, para. 123: *"An undue, inexplicable or unjustified delay in responding to a request for access to an essential infrastructure may also constitute an abuse."*

[276] *See supra* note 97, paras 293 *et seq.* (Summary publication, OJ 2004 C 165/11); on appeal, *see* Case T-301/04 *supra* note 184.

[277] Joined Cases C-147 and 148/97 *Deutsche Post v GZS and Citicorp Kartenservice* [2000] ECR I-825, paras 50–60. Of course, there may be a refusal in such a case, but one that may be perfectly legitimate if the conditions are not proven to be objectively unreasonable or unjustified. *See also* Case IV/30.178 *Napier Brown/British Sugar,* Commission Decision of 18 July 1988, OJ 1988 L 284/41 (the Commission qualified as a constructive refusal to supply the behaviour of British Sugar, which responded to a request for industrial sugar by offering only 'special grain' sugar, and at a high price).

7. – Refuse to Deal

Maurits Dolmans and Matthew Bennett

Deutsche Post, the Commission stated that *"the concept of refusal to supply covers not only outright refusal but also situations where dominant firms make supply subject to objectively unreasonable terms."*[278]

The objectively unreasonable terms may be in the form of excessive pricing (Chapter 10), a margin squeeze (Chapter 5),[279] or tying (a refusal to deal unless the customer also accepts to pay for another good or service that it does not want or prefers to obtain from another source; Chapter 8).[280] **7.205**

Supplying quantities that are less than the requested volumes may also qualify as a refusal to supply. In *GlaxoSmithKline (Greece)*,[281] GlaxoSmithKline ("GSK"), in reaction to parallel trade, first suspended supplies to its wholesalers and then supplied them only in quantities sufficient to cover domestic Greek demand. The Court recognised, however, that dominant pharmaceutical companies are entitled to protect their commercial interests in *"a reasonable and proportionate way"* against orders of *"significant quantities of products that are essentially destined for parallel export."*[282] **7.206**

3. Consumer Harm and Exclusionary Conduct Beyond the Mere Refusal to Deal

The third condition for possible imposition of a duty to deal, according to Article 102(b) TFEU and the *Guidance Paper*, is a finding that *"the refusal is likely to lead to consumer harm."*[283] Furthermore, in its *Guidance Paper*, the Commission adds that it will not limit itself to a short-term analysis, but *"will examine whether, for consumers, the likely negative consequences of the refusal to supply in the relevant market outweigh over time the negative consequences of imposing an obligation to* **7.207**

---

[278] Case COMP/36.915 *Deutsche Post – Interception of cross-border mail* ("*Deutsche Post*"), Commission Decision of 25 July 2001, OJ 2001 L 331/40, para. 141.

[279] The Court of Justice clarified that a margin squeeze is an independent form of abuse distinct from a refusal to supply (*see TeliaSonera Judgment 2011 supra* note 244, paras 56–8).

[280] *See Napier Brown supra* note 277 (British Sugar responded to a request for industrial sugar by offering only 'special grain' sugar at a high price); *See Deutsche Post supra* note 278 (Deutsche Post imposed an excessive surcharge for certain cross-border mail); *See Télémarketing supra* note 124 (television telemarketing advertising made conditional on use of the television company's own telesales agency).

[281] Joined Cases C-468 to 478/06 *Sot. Lélos kai Sia and others v GlaxoSmithKline* ("*GlaxoSmithKline*") [2008] ECR I-7139.

[282] *Ibid.*, para. 71.

[283] *See Guidance Paper supra* note 41, para. 81.

supply" (emphasis added).[284] The Commission gives some indication of what consumer harm is:

> "*The Commission considers that consumer harm may, for instance, arise where the competitors that the dominant undertaking forecloses are, as a result of the refusal, prevented from bringing innovative goods or services to market and/or where follow-on innovation is likely to be stifled. This may be particularly the case if the undertaking which requests supply does not intend to limit itself essentially to duplicating the goods or services already offered by the dominant undertaking on the downstream market, but intends to produce new or improved goods or services for which there is a potential consumer demand or is likely to contribute to technical development.*"[285]

7.208 Elsewhere in the *Guidance Paper*, the Commission refers to a broader concept, including "*higher price levels than would have otherwise prevailed or in some other form such as limiting quality or reducing consumer choice.*"[286] Indeed, non-dominant or non-vertically integrated firms would normally have every incentive to supply an input if the addition of value by the buyer or licensee expands demand for the input and thus the supplier's profits.[287] The *Guidance Paper* adds that this reference to increased prices is shorthand for influencing parameters of competition: "*the expression 'increase prices' includes the power to maintain prices above the competitive level and is used as shorthand for the various ways in which the parameters of competition – such as prices, output, innovation, the variety or quality of goods or services – can be influenced to the advantage of the dominant undertaking and to the detriment of consumers.*"[288]

7.209 Especially in the case of a request for a compulsory license to IP, these sections of the *Guidance Paper* must be applied with restraint. As discussed above,

---

[284] *See Guidance Paper supra* note 41, para. 86. This text suggests a balancing test where the Commission on an *ad hoc* basis weighs the benefits of maintaining the dominant firm's innovation incentives against the benefits of enabling innovation by rivals. But the Court of First Instance in *Microsoft* suggested that such a balancing exercise is appropriately done in the context of the assessment of the dominant firm's claim of objective justification, and that the initial test should focus on the competitors' incentives to innovate. "*Last, Microsoft's argument that it will have less incentive to develop a given technology if it is required to make that technology available to its competitors (see paragraph 627) is of no relevance to the examination of the circumstance relating to the new product, where the issue to be decided is the impact of the refusal to supply on the incentive for Microsoft's competitors to innovate and not on Microsoft's incentives to innovate. That is an issue which will be decided when the Court examines the circumstance relating to the absence of objective justification.*" *See Microsoft Judgment 2007 supra* note 67, para. 659.

[285] *Guidance Paper supra* note 41, para. 87.

[286] *Ibid.*, para. 19.

[287] *See* Case COMP/39.315 *supra* note 250, para. 90.

[288] *See Guidance Paper supra* note 41, para. 11.

7. – Refuse to Deal
Maurits Dolmans and Matthew Bennett

every exclusive property right (including intellectual property) allows the owner to raise access prices above the competitive level, in order to allow recovery of past investments and encourage future ones. Moreover, a refusal to supply is not an abuse in itself, even if it has the effect of allowing the owner to increase prices. A finding of consumer harm therefore requires a finding of an abusive element other than the mere refusal to license or the imposition of supra competitive prices. This arises if the exclusive rights are used in a manner that is not in accordance with or disproportionate to their essential function, as a tool for another abuse, such as the limitation of innovation in violation of Article 102(b) TFEU.

3.1. *Consumer Harm – The "New Product" and "Reduction of Innovation" Tests*

Consumer harm arises, for instance, where the competitors that the dominant **7.210** undertaking forecloses are, as a result of the refusal, prevented from bringing innovative goods or services to market and/or where follow-on innovation is likely to be stifled. Using a property right – and especially an intellectual property right – to stifle innovation rather than spurring it, is opposite to the essential function of the right. The "new-product" test applied in *Magill*, *IMS Health* and *Microsoft* must be understood as a proxy to identify conduct that stifles innovation "to the prejudice of consumers" within the meaning of Article 102(b).[289]

3.1.1. "New Product" Need not be an Existing Product

In both the *Magill* and *IMS Health* cases, the Court referred to what it called in **7.211** *IMS Health* "*new products or services not offered by the owner of the intellectual property right and for which there is a potential consumer demand*".[290] In *Magill*, a new product already existed, at least in concept. This does not, however, require that the complainant must always show that the new product already exists – and that it had already infringed the dominant firm's IPRs without a licence. Restriction of innovation and lack of interoperability can prejudice consumers even if there are no new products yet, and if incentives and opportunity to innovate

---

[289] *See Microsoft Judgment 2007 supra* note 67, paras 643–8. *See also* F. Lévêque, "Innovation, Leveraging and Essential Facilities: Interoperability Licensing in the EU Microsoft Case" (2005) 28(1) *World Competition*, pp. 71–91; M. Leistner, "Intellectual Property and Competition Law: The European Development from Magill to IMS Health Compared to Recent German and U.S. Case Law" (2005) 2 *Zeitschrift für Wettbewerbsrecht*, p. 138, paras 150–2; M. Stopper, "Der Microsoft-Beschluss des EuG" (2005) 1 *Zeitschrift für Wettbewerbsrecht*, p. 87, para. 102.
[290] *See IMS Health supra* note 67, para. 52.

7. – Refuse to Deal
Maurits Dolmans and Matthew Bennett

are stifled to such an extent that rivals who in the past have shown a propensity to innovate are being cut out of the market.[291] In *Microsoft*, the complainants showed a history of past innovations (indeed the very concept of workgroup servers was invented by Novell[292]), capacity to continue R&D, ongoing incentives to innovate,[293] and that consumers preferred the features and functionality of the rivals' products "but for" the lack of adequate interoperability.[294] The Court of First Instance agreed and held that:

> *"The circumstance relating to the appearance of a new product, as envisaged in Magill and IMS Health … cannot be the only parameter which determines whether a refusal to license an intellectual property right is capable of causing prejudice to consumers within the meaning of Article 82(b) EC. As that provision states, such prejudice may arise where there is a limitation not only of production or markets, but also of technical development."*[295]

7.212 Microsoft argued that the new-product requirement means that the complainant must prove it will satisfy potential demand by meeting the needs of consumers in ways that existing products do not. That is, a new product must exist that will expand output significantly by bringing in consumers who were not satisfied before, and who would not have purchased a server at all (or a lower volume).[296] This is clearly relevant, but too limited. Microsoft's argument implied that if the downstream or complementary products are so important

---

[291] *See* M. Dolmans, R. O'Donoghue and P.-J. Loewenthal *supra* note 182.

[292] *See* other examples in *Microsoft Judgment 2007 supra* note 67, para. 654.

[293] *See Microsoft Judgment 2007 supra* note 67, para. 658: "*Nor would Microsoft's competitors have any interest in merely reproducing Windows work group server operating systems. Once they are able to use the information communicated to them to develop systems that are sufficiently interoperable with the Windows domain architecture, they will have no other choice, if they wish to take advantage of a competitive advantage over Microsoft and maintain a profitable presence on the market, than to differentiate their products from Microsoft's.*"

[294] "*Due to the lack of interoperability that competing work group server operating system products can achieve with the Windows domain architecture, an increasing number of consumers are locked into a homogeneous Windows solution at the level of work group server operating systems. This impairs the ability of such customers to benefit from innovative work group server operating system features brought to the market by Microsoft's competitors. In addition, this limits the prospect for such competitors to successfully market their innovation and thereby discourages them from developing new products.*" *See Microsoft Decision 2004 supra* note 49, para. 694. For the discussion before the Court, *see Microsoft Judgment 2007 supra* note 67, paras 621–65: "*The limitation thus placed on consumer choice is all the more damaging to consumers because, as already observed at paragraphs 407 to 412 above, they consider that non-Microsoft work group server operating systems are better than Windows work group server operating systems with respect to a series of features to which they attach great importance, such as 'reliability/availability of the … system' and 'security included with the server operating system'.*"

[295] *See Microsoft Judgment 2007 supra* note 67, para. 647.

[296] *See* C. Alhborn, D. S. Evans and A. J. Padilla, "The Logic and Limits of the 'Exceptional Circumstances Test' in *Magill* and *IMS Health*" (2005) 28(4) *Fordham International Law Journal*, pp. 1109–56, pp. 1147–9.

7. – Refuse to Deal
Maurits Dolmans and Matthew Bennett

that all relevant consumers effectively require them, consumer harm could not be found even if significant improvements are smothered. To meet the "new product" test, it may be sufficient to show that quality increased enough to increase users' "willingness to pay" even if output quantity is not increased.

Consumer prejudice is substantial in particular where the rivals' activities could directly or indirectly foster innovation that challenges the dominant firm's monopoly. In *Microsoft*, for instance, it was argued that Microsoft's attempt to take over the server market was not merely inspired by a desire to monopolise that product, but also as a defensive move in the overall "platform war", designed to protect Microsoft's client platform dominance.[297] **7.213**

3.1.2. Consumer Harm Must Arise in a Neighbouring or Downstream Market

While a compulsory licence may be appropriate to enable follow-on innovation, that should not be read to suggest that an IP owner, even a dominant one, must permit follow-on innovation for the same product to which the intellectual property applies or of which it is a key component. It is inherent in an exclusive right that its owner should be entitled to decide whether to license, or itself to exploit the right by selling a product in that market. *See* also Section III.2.2. **7.214**

Thus, in *Microsoft*, while granting Sun's request for a compulsory licence of interoperability information for communications between Windows client platforms and third-party servers, the Commission rejected Sun's request to require Microsoft to license COM Objects and Active Directory technologies to *"run in fully compatible fashion on Solaris"*, and to allow Sun to port the Windows API set to Sun's Solaris operating system. The Commission described this second request as a plan *"to engineer an abstraction layer between applications programmed to the Windows platform and the underlying Solaris operating system, so that Solaris servers … would offer … the same consistent set of APIs as Windows servers"*.[298] Imposing such a licence would have taken away from Microsoft its principal or only legitimate means to distinguish its platform from others on the basis of the merits. The Commission categorically rejected this request at an early stage of the proceedings, and confirmed it in its final Decision.[299] **7.215**

---

[297] *See Microsoft Decision 2004 supra* note 49, para. 769. For a discussion of the economic theories pertaining to protecting monopoly positions, *see* Section II.4.3.
[298] *See Microsoft Decision 2004 supra* note 49, para. 189.
[299] *Ibid.*, para. 189.

7. – Refuse to Deal
Maurits Dolmans and Matthew Bennett

It stressed that the compulsory licence of interoperability information was intended to enable only *"the development of compatible products"*, not the *"copying of Windows"*.[300] Both the Commission and the Court of First Instance noted that third-party server operating systems that sought to interoperate with Windows had developed, and needed to continue to develop, their own substantive functionality rather than just imitate the Windows platform.[301]

7.216 For the same reason, the Commission rejected a request by IBM mainframe emulator vendors to impose on IBM a compulsory licence to patents covering the IBM Mainframe architecture and to the IBM zOS mainframe operating system.[302] In sum, the Commission struck a careful balance in *Microsoft* and in *IBM Mainframe Emulators* to maintain competition on the basis of innovation: neither Microsoft nor IBM were not required to license their *platform* technology to enable rivals to make a directly competing substitute, but Microsoft was required to license its *interoperability* technology to allow Sun and others to innovate within the neighbouring market for server systems communicating with Windows in a corporate network.[303] In other words, the licence allowed

---

[300] *See Microsoft Decision 2004 supra* note 49, para. 572. The Court of First Instance similarly emphasised that the Commission Decision *"does not, and is not designed to, allow Microsoft's competitors to copy its products"*. *See Microsoft Judgment 2007 supra* note 67, para. 700.

[301] *See Microsoft Decision 2004 supra* note 49, *Microsoft Judgment 2007 supra* note 67, paras 654–8. But *see* Microsoft, *"Public Undertaking by Microsoft"*, 16 December 2009 (*"The 2009 Microsoft Undertaking"*). Microsoft issued a voluntary interoperability undertaking requiring it to make interoperability information available (and license associated patents) to allow third-party software and servers to communicate with Office, Windows PC, Windows Server, Share Point/Exchange, Microsoft Office, and Microsoft.NET. The undertaking is interesting in that it extended the holding of the 2007 judgment in *Microsoft* in that the disclosures relating to Office are designed to facilitate the marking of a directly competitive rather the complementary product. The background for this extension, which cannot be seen as a precedent outside its very specific context, is that the near-monopoly of Microsoft's Office Suite of personal productivity applications is a substantial part of the applications barrier to entry protecting the rents from the near-monopoly of Microsoft Windows in the desktop operating systems market. *See Novell v Microsoft,* No. JFM-05-1087, 2005 US Dist. LEXIS 11520 (D. Md. 10 June 2005) (quoting email from Jeff Raikes at Microsoft to Warren Buffet at Berkshire Hathaway (17 August 1997)), quoted in European Committee for Interoperable Systems, *"Microsoft – A History of Anticompetitive Behavior and Consumer Harm"*, 31 March 2009. *See also* M. Dolmans, T. Graf and D. R. Little, "Microsoft's Browser-choice Commitments and Public Interoperability Undertaking" (2010) 31(7) *European Competition Law Review*, pp. 268–75.

[302] In *IBM Mainframe Emulators*, providers of emulator software, *inter alia*, wanted a compulsory license to IBM's zOS software based on the allegation that IBM's refusal to license prevented competition for IBM-compatible mainframe computers. The Commission decided, following an in-depth investigation, to close proceedings in September 2011, and complaints were withdrawn. *See* Press Release IP/11/1044 of 20 September 2011.

[303] In non-technical terms, Microsoft was required to give rivals its vocabulary and grammar book to allow non-Windows Server to speak "Windows" (*i.e.*, understand and respond to requests, but solving tasks and problems in their own way) so that they could compete with Windows servers, but Microsoft was not required to license its APIs and COM objects for porting, so that non-Windows server would become Windows (*i.e.*, present the same platform and solve problems in the same way as Windows).

7. – Refuse to Deal
Maurits Dolmans and Matthew Bennett

the development of innovative complementary products, but not a substitute product (not even an innovative one).

3.1.3. The "New Products" Test Applies in all Compulsory License Cases

Magill and most other compulsory licensing cases require evidence of the **7.217** suppression of a new product or the stifling of innovation. This is appropriate, since it means that both the dominant company and its competitors continue to be under competitive pressure to develop better products, which maximises dynamic competition. But the Court's reasoning in *Ladbroke* was ambiguous, and the examples cited in *Volvo* do not, by definition, involve new products.[304] One explanation might be that at the time the judgment in *Volvo* was rendered, it was not yet widely accepted that competition policy should focus on consumer welfare rather than the protection of competitors. Another explanation could be that the abuses discussed in *Volvo* concern not so much a refusal to license, as an interruption of supplies of body panels. A compulsory licence may be an appropriate remedy in a situation where Volvo has ceased production and supplies of body panels, and has closed down the production lines.

Magill, *IMS Health*, and *Microsoft*, however, are firm in requiring a negative **7.218** impact on innovation. The Court in *IMS Health* stated that a licence would be only justified where the *"undertaking which requested the licence* [does not] *intend to limit itself essentially to duplicating the goods or services already offered on the secondary market by the owner of the copyright, but intends to produce new goods or services not offered by the owner of the right and for which there is a potential consumer demand."*[305]

Similarly, in Microsoft, the Court of First Instance noted with approval that **7.219** *"the Commission ... took particular care to ascertain that Microsoft's refusal was a 'refusal to allow follow-on innovation', that is to say, the development of new products, and not a mere refusal to allow copying."*[306]

Ex-President Vesterdorf of the Court of First Instance pointed out that the **7.220** new product criterion no longer covers only new products in the strict sense of a new product market but also a technical development relating to an

---

[304] *See Volvo*, para. 9.
[305] *See* Case C-481/01 *supra* note 136, para. 49.
[306] *See Microsoft Judgment 2007 supra* note 67, para. 632.

7. – Refuse to Deal
Maurits Dolmans and Matthew Bennett

existing product.[307] This reflects a broadening of the "new product" criterion. He presented an important caveat, that "[s]*ince the conditions under which a refusal to license a product must remain exceptional, this definition or broadening of the, 'new product' criterion must, like any other exception, be interpreted restrictively.*"[308] *A fortiori*, this means that a finding of suppression of innovation is a prerequisite for every compulsory licence case. Any further stretching of the criteria under *Microsoft* would endanger dynamic competition and the essential function of IPRs.

3.1.4. Consumer Harm in Cases not Involving Intellectual Property

7.221 The requirement of consumer harm is not explicitly stated in all cases, but cannot be ignored as a condition, since Article 102(b) TFEU requires it, and it is often implied in the case law. The requirement is important because it is in foreclosure cases that the mistake is most likely to be made of protecting competitors rather than competition. A low price or a better bargain from the dominant company may make it very difficult for its competitors to compete, but low prices and good bargains are what competition law is intended to encourage, and they cannot harm consumers unless the latter are overcharged later or choice or innovation are reduced.

7.222 In cases not involving intellectual property, consumer harm resulting from a refusal to deal creating barriers to entry for a rival may consist not only of limitation of innovation, but also a broader range of effects on consumer welfare such as higher prices, reduced output, elimination of consumer choice, restriction of product variety, or reduction of the quality of goods or services.[309] Some limiting principles are needed, however, since one might argue the Commission and Court in *Microsoft* have already stretched the "two market", "indispensability" and "exclusion of effective competition" criteria to the limits, and accepting in addition that, a mere price reduction could justify a duty to deal which would undermine the principle that a refusal to supply in itself is not an abuse. The case law provides some, but not extensive, guidance. However, under Article 102(b) harm to consumers is an essential element in exclusionary abuse, and the *Guidance Paper* confirms this, although without reference to Article 102(b).

---

[307] B. Vesterdorf, "Article 82 EC: Where Do We Stand After the *Microsoft* Judgement?" (2008) 1(1) *Global Antitrust Review*, pp. 1, 10.

[308] *Ibid.*, pp. 1, 9.

[309] *See Guidance Paper supra* note 41, para. 11.

7. – Refuse to Deal
Maurits Dolmans and Matthew Bennett

In *Sea Containers/Stena Sealink*, it was stated that there was a new kind of service – **7.223** a new fast ferry service to the Holyhead-Dun Laoghaire route, using a wave-piercing catamaran – for which it was inferred that there was a clear and unsatisfied demand, which could be met only if the proposed supplier was given access to the harbour.[310] In *Port of Rødby*, the Commission stated that even in a saturated market, an improvement in the quality of products or services offered as a result of competition is a definite advantage for consumers.[311] In *British Midland/Aer Lingus*, the Commission noted that a duty for dominant airlines to interline (*i.e.*, sell tickets comprising segments performed by different airlines) exists in particular when the refusal or withdrawal of interline facilities is likely to impact the ability of other airlines, not only to sustain existing services, but also to start new ones.[312] This confirms that evidence of frustrating innovation or consumer demand for new products is a key requirement for the imposition of a duty to deal, even in cases not involving intellectual property.

3.1.4.1. Categorisation of the Case Law

Most of the non-IPR cases do not expressly mention consumer harm or **7.224** suppression of innovation. Perhaps this is because most of these cases as a matter of fact concerned discrimination rather than a *de novo* refusal to supply.[313] These may not be true refusal to supply cases, to the extent the supplier has already decided that entering into agreements with rivals allowing them to use the facility is an efficient way of exploiting it and does not prejudice a fair return on investment, and a rational supplier would normally wish to maximise the efficiency of the downstream players in order to expand demand for the upstream supplies. Reference is made to Chapter 9 on Abusive Discrimination.

---

[310] *See* Case IV/34.689 *supra* note 184, paras 68 *et seq*. The case could be regarded as a discrimination case, as access was already being given to a third company, which moreover reduced the scope to argue that the refusal was objectively justified.

[311] Case 94/119/EC *Port of Rødby*, Commission Decision of 21 December 1993, OJ 1994 L 55/52, para. 16

[312] *See* Case IV/33.544 *supra* note 210, para. 26

[313] *See Napier Brown supra* note 277; *See Corsica Ferries supra* note 208; *See European Night Services supra* note 201; *See* Case IV/32.318 *supra* note 124; *See* Case IV/36.120 *supra* note 208.

7. – Refuse to Deal
Maurits Dolmans and Matthew Bennett

7.225 Other cases, such as *Commercial Solvents*,[314] *Hugin*,[315] *United Brands*[316] and *Telemarketing*,[317] involve the disruption of supplies. Irrespective of the fact that they do not concern IPR-protected input, these cases, too, are not true refusal to supply cases, because the supplier deemed it efficient to enter into agreements to supply third parties, and was not concerned about inability to obtain a fair return on investment. The abuse is arguably twofold: (1) frustrating the intermediate customers' legitimate expectations, created by the dominant firm's past statements and agreements to supply, on which the customers relied in good faith when investing in downstream production and distribution; and, (2) leveraging upstream dominance in order to monopolise a downstream market with the object or effect of extracting additional monopoly rents from consumers of the final product. Consumer harm also arises at various levels in these cases. First, intermediate customers are deprived of supplies or condemned to finding alternative sources at appreciably higher prices. Although the *Guidance Paper* recognises this as consumer harm,[318] protecting these customers appears to be the same as protecting competitors. The *Guidance Paper* therefore makes clear that "[w]*here intermediate users are actual or potential competitors of the dominant undertaking, the assessment focuses on the effects of the conduct on users further downstream.*"[319] Secondly, further downstream or at the level of the

---

[314] *See Commercial Solvents supra* note 112. Commercial Solvents, which hitherto had produced the basic products nitropropane and aminobutanol, decided to enter the market for ethambutol, a downstream product. To maximise its chances of success, it decided to cut off supplies to its existing customer who made competing ethambutol. It thus limited horizontal competition. The Court of Justice held that: "*an undertaking which has a dominant position in the market in raw materials and which, with the object of reserving such raw materials for manufacturing its own derivatives, refuses to supply a customer, which is itself a manufacturer of such derivatives, and therefore risks eliminating all competition on the part of this customer, is abusing its dominant position*".

[315] *See Hugin Judgment 1979 supra* note 210, para. 1912.

[316] *See United Brands supra* note 184. The Court did not require proof that all competition from the former distributor was eliminated as a result of the termination of supplies.

[317] *See Télémarketing supra* note 124. *Télémarketing* concerned a television broadcasting company which had jealously watched the profits made by telemarketers using its channels, and after some time proceeded to deny further access and going into telemarketing itself. The Court's recital in *Telemarketing* has become a classic that is often quoted by plaintiffs: "*an abuse within the meaning of Article 86 is committed where, without objective necessity, an undertaking holding a dominant position on a particular market reserves to itself ... an ancillary activity which might be carried out by another undertaking as part of its activities on a neighboring but separate market, with the possibility of eliminating all competition from such undertaking.*" Although the facts of the case still concerned cutting off an existing customer, the wording "*ancillary activity which might be carried out by another undertaking ... on a neighboring but separate market*" appear to be broader.

[318] *See Guidance Paper supra* note 41, para. 19: "*The Commission will address such anti-competitive foreclosure either at the intermediate level or at the level of final consumers, or at both levels.*" A footnote to this paragraphs adds: "*The concept of 'consumers' encompasses all direct or indirect users of the products affected by the conduct, including intermediate producers that use the products as an input, as well as distributors and final consumers both of the immediate product and of products provided by intermediate producers.*"

[319] *See Guidance Paper supra* note 41, para. 19.

7. – Refuse to Deal
Maurits Dolmans and Matthew Bennett

end-users, the consumer harm presumably consists of price increases, or of a reduction of investment incentives. If the downstream product is used in fixed proportion to the upstream product – in which case the supplier would presumably already have raised the price of the input product (*see* discussion of the "single monopoly rent" theory of the Chicago School in Section II.4.2 above) – the dominant firm might try to rebut an accusation of consumer harm by showing that no additional monopoly rent can be reaped from the downstream market, and that its objective can therefore only be to seek downstream efficiencies.

Other cases concerning *de novo* refusals to supply were settled without final decisions and judicial review and therefore have limited value as precedent. Examples are the *1984 IBM Undertaking*,[320] the *1997 Digital Undertaking*,[321] the *1997 SWIFT Undertaking*,[322] and the 2012 *Thomson Reuters Commitments*.[323]   **7.226**

3.1.4.2. Limiting Principles for Imposing a Duty to Supply

In the absence of clear indications from case law, the following proposed limiting principles may be relevant.[324]   **7.227**

First, it can be argued that the "new product" criterion is equally appropriate for all cases involving a refusal to provide access to physical property and intellectual property, since physical and intellectual property are equivalent from a general economic point of view. Absent evidence of the suppression of innovation, the benefits of forced sharing are far from obvious, both for   **7.228**

---

[320] IBM, Undertaking given by IBM, EC Bulletin 10-1984, point. 3.4.1 *et seq*. For its continued application, *see* Press Release IP/88/814 of 15 December 1988.

[321] *See* Press Release IP/98/141 of 10 February 1998; M. Dolmans and V. Pickering, "The 1997 Digital Undertaking" (1998) 19(2) *European Competition Law Review*, pp. 108–15.

[322] *See* Case IV/36.120 *supra* note 208. Apart from the consideration that SWIFT was not a real essential facility, SWIFT argued that access to SWIFT's network was not required to compete in the downstream market: the complainant already competed in the French banking and fund transfer market, which was moreover highly competitive with thin margins, and direct access of La Poste to the SWIFT network did not appreciably improve the structure of competition. SWIFT decided, however, for commercial reasons to settle the case by undertaking to broaden access to its network beyond banks to all financial institutions admitted to European Central Bank-supervised payment systems.

[323] *See* Press Release IP/12/777 of 12 July 2012, Case COMP/39.654 *Reuters Instrument Codes* ("*RICs*"), Proposed Commitments of 12 July 2012, not yet published.

[324] *See also* P. Areeda, "Essential Facilities: An Epithet in Need of Limiting Principles" (1989) 58(3) *Antitrust Law Journal*, pp. 841–53.

7. – Refuse to Deal
Maurits Dolmans and Matthew Bennett

IPR and physical property,[325] and deviate from the general principle that there is no duty to deal, and that compulsory dealing should occur only in "exceptional circumstances". Arguments from complainants that an order to supply will lower prices or increase output downstream, without further investment in innovation and appreciable product differentiation, should be regarded with great caution. A duty to supply is only conceivable, as will be shown below, if it adds real value or significantly improves efficiency.

7.229   For instance, it would be inefficient to require a dominant firm to supply a final or semifinal upstream product that had never been supplied to intermediaries before (but belonging to a hypothetical separate market), in order to create downstream competition where there was none before unless it facilitated a new product or improved innovation. Such an order would in many cases not lower prices without price regulation and, worse, would discourage dynamic competition and would likely add costs due to double marginalisation, as explained above. There should be no duty to supply merely to allow the complainant to distribute the dominant firm's final product, if it does not add real value or significantly improves efficiency in some way. This suggests that a duty to supply should apply to raw material, IP and components only. Moreover, it requires evidence of scope for added-value competition in the downstream market, in the form of new functionality or appreciable increase of efficiency that the dominant firm does not provide and does not plan to offer, and for which there is substantial frustrated demand. Demand from a small subset of customers should not suffice.

7.230   No duty to deal should be imposed on a dominant firm that adequately anticipated switches in consumer demand or created a new product, and where the supply obligation serves to preserve the viability of rivals in a downstream market whose products no longer respond to changed consumer preferences. Imposing an order to supply in such a case would shield rivals from the effects of market forces, protect competitors at the expense of dynamic competition, and creates a moral hazard that competition policy should avoid.

7.231   In cases where the dominant firm continually innovates and improves its input product, no amount of improved price competition can justify an order to supply absent clear evidence of suppression of substantial rival innovation. There should thus be no duty to supply if (1) there is evidence that the

---

[325] *See supra* note 39, pp. 449–50.

7. – Refuse to Deal
Maurits Dolmans and Matthew Bennett

dominant firm made and continues to make very substantial investments in creating and improving its product, and (2) a duty to supply would require it to share its competitive advantage with a rival wishing to market a product competing directly with the dominant firm's product of which the input good is a significant component. An order to share the input would reduce the dominant firm's incentive to invest.

Since a refusal to deal in itself is not an abuse, and every refusal inherently **7.232** reduces the number of competitors downstream, merely adding another competitor in the downstream market should not in itself justify a duty to deal unless it facilitates dynamic competition. The harm to consumers must be something more than the mere static absence of competitors.[326] This point applies *a fortiori* where there is already significant downstream competition without the supply, in which case an order to supply is unjustified on various grounds including not only that the input is not indispensable, but also that interference with the freedom to select one's contract partners, absent the prospect of a new product or real innovation, would have no appreciable positive effect on the effectiveness of downstream competition and on consumer welfare. In the words of Areeda, no duty can be imposed unless *"the plaintiff is essential for competition in the marketplace"*.[327]

3.2. Conclusion

It is interesting to note that while the *Guidance Paper* mentions different kinds **7.233** of consumer harm in the section on anticompetitive foreclosure generally, it provides a restrictive list in the context of refusals to supply. The *Guidance Paper* discusses suppression of "innovative goods or services" and the stifling of "follow-on innovation" where the undertaking which requests supply *"does not intend to limit itself essentially to duplicating the goods or services already offered by the dominant undertaking on the downstream market, but intends to produce new or improved goods or services for which there is a potential consumer demand or is likely to contribute to technical development."*[328] After all, it is implied, a non-dominant or non-vertically-integrated firm would normally not refuse to supply in such circumstances (absent some

---

[326] *See* J. Temple Lang, "Refusal to Contract under Article 82" forthcoming in *Europaraettslig Tidskrift*.

[327] *See* P. Areeda *supra* note 324. *See also* J. Temple-Lang, "Defining Legitimate Competition: Companies' Duties to Supply Competitors and Access to Essential Facilities", in B. E. Hawk (Ed.), *Fordham Competition Law Institute: International Antitrust Law and Policy 1994* (New York, Juris Publishing, 1995), p. 310 ("*If there are a number of competitors in the downstream market and it is competitive, the refusal to supply one more competitor will not have a significant effect on competition.*").

[328] *See Guidance Paper supra* note 41, para. 87.

7. – Refuse to Deal
Maurits Dolmans and Matthew Bennett

efficiency justification). The *Guidance Paper* mentions charging inflated prices, but only in the very specific context of sector-specific price regulation in the upstream market: "*where the price in the upstream input market is regulated, the price in the downstream market is not regulated and the dominant undertaking, by excluding competitors on the downstream market through a refusal to supply, is able to extract more profits in the unregulated downstream market than it would otherwise do.*"[329]

7.234 This may, and hopefully does, signal a desire to limit compulsory dealing to these two very exceptional circumstances.

4. Exclusion of all Effective Downstream Competition

7.235 Article 102(b) TFEU prohibits conduct creating barriers to entry or expansion, or limiting the production, outlets or technical development of competitors of the dominant company.[330] It applies to all forms of exclusion, raising rivals' costs, and other conduct that forecloses equally efficient firms by means other than competition on the merits,[331] including exclusive arrangements with

---

[329] *See Guidance Paper supra* note 41, para. 88.

[330] *See* J. Temple Lang, "European Competition Law and Refusals to Licence Intellectual Property Rights", in Hansen (Ed.), *Intellectual Property Law and Policy*, (Hart Publishing, 2008) Vol.10, p. 282, and cases cited there; J. Temple Lang, "Abuse of Dominant Positions in European Community Law, Present and Future: Some Aspects", in B. E. Hawk (Ed.), *Fifth Annual Fordham Corporate Law Institute, Law & Business* (1979), pp. 25–83, pp. 52 and 60. This point is not mentioned in J. Faull and A. Nikpay (Eds.), *The EC Law of Competition* (2nd Ed., Oxford, Oxford University Press, 2007), p. 403 , but is correctly stated in, *e.g.*, P. Roth and V. Rose (Eds.), *Bellamy & Child: European Community Law of Competition* (6th Ed., Oxford, Oxford University Press, 2008), pp. 1023–6 and in W. D. Braun and L. Ritter, *EC Competition Law – A Practitioner's Guide* (3rd Ed., The Hague, Kluwer Law International, 2004), pp. 434–43; and in A. Frignani and M. Waelbroeck, *European Competition Law* (Ardsley, Transnational Publishers, 1999), pp. 551 *et.seq.* and S. Affolter and others, *Grands principes du droit de la concurrence* (Bâle/Genève/Munich, Bruylant, 1999), pp. 260–5. In *Arkin v Borchard Lines & Others* [2003] EWHC 687 (Comm), para. 293 Colman J. said "*quite simply, an undertaking in a dominant position must not reduce or attempt to reduce the ability of other participants in the market or of the would-be entrants into the market to compete. This principle palpably underlies the reasoning of the European Courts in all the authorities … .*" *See also* L. Gyselen, "Abuse of Monopoly Power Within the Meaning of Article 86 of the EEC Treaty: Recent Developments", in B. E. Hawk (Ed.), *Fordham Competition Law Institute: International Antitrust Law and Policy 1989* (New York, Juris Publishing, 1990), pp. 613–7, 635–6; T. E. Kauper, "Whither Article 86? Observations on Excessive Prices and Refusals to Deal", in B. E. Hawk (Ed.), *Fordham Competition Law Institute: International Antitrust Law and Policy 1989* (New York, Juris Publishing, 1990), pp. 668–85; R. O'Donoghue and J. Temple Lang, "The Concept of an Exclusionary Abuse under Article 82 EC", *GCLC Research Papers on Article 82*, July 2005, available at http://www.coleurop.be/content/gclc/documents/GCLC%20Research%20 Papers%20on%20Article%2082%20EC.pdf. Article 102(b) TFEU can also apply to a dominant firm limiting its own production, in order to raise prices, in which case the principles of exploitative abuse apply.

[331] "*An undertaking in a dominant position cannot have recourse to means other than those within the scope of* competition on the merits" *See* Case T-203/01 *Manufacture française des pneumatiques Michelin v Commission* ("*Michelin II*") [2003] ECR II-4071. *See also Guidance Paper supra* note 41, para. 1, indicating that a dominant firm must only "compete on the merits."

7. – Refuse to Deal
Maurits Dolmans and Matthew Bennett

customers limiting rivals' access to outlets, discounts and rebates conditional on exclusivity, pricing below cost with a view to denying rivals economies of scale or scope, bundling with the object or effect of excluding rivals from the market of the tied product, and "leveraging" of power in one market to exclude competition in a neighboring market.

The concept of "limitation" of rivals' possibilities provides a useful test for **7.236** distinguishing between desirable competition and undesirable exclusion: only conduct creating a barrier to entry for rivals, or "impairing rivals' efficiency"[332] is prohibited. Such barriers allow dominant firms in the long run to raise prices without necessarily attracting entry, and possibly actively deterring it.

Magill and *Microsoft* are examples. In *Magill*, the barrier to entry was the unavail- **7.237** ability of the program listings, whereas in *Microsoft*, the barrier to expansion and continued market presence was the unavailability of up-to-date interoperability information. The key point in both cases was that this impaired the efficiency of rivals in a market that was neighbouring the market for the product to which the intellectual property applied. The broadcasters in *Magill* had exclusive rights to programs listings, and licensed them for weekly highlights and daily newspapers, but not for weekly comprehensive magazines, which constituted a market that was separate from the listings themselves and the broadcasters' magazines, and of which the listings were only one of several elements.[333] Similarly, by denying interoperability information, Microsoft leveraged the near-monopoly in the desktop operating systems market to the neighbouring market of workgroup server operating systems that was separate from the first market and from the market for the Windows interoperability information itself. Moreover, the software modules implementing the interoperability information were not the core of the server operating system. This pattern is found in all cases that led to a finding of infringement.[334]

The *Guidance Paper* confirms that a refusal to supply can only be abusive if **7.238** *"the refusal is likely to lead to the elimination of effective competition on the downstream market."*[335] This applies to both intellectual property and non-IP cases. The Commission assumes that this condition is met if an input is objectively

---

[332] E. Elhauge, "Defining Better Monopolization Standards" (2003) 56 *Stanford Law Review*, pp. 253–344.

[333] *See* Case IV/31.851 *supra* note 129.

[334] *See also Volvo* (body panels to which the design rights apply are separate from the market for independent car maintenance); and *IMS Health supra* note 67 (the development of a brick structure for collecting sales data for pharmaceutical products was separate from the market for supplying this sales data).

[335] *See Guidance Paper supra* note 41, para. 85.

7. – Refuse to Deal

Maurits Dolmans and Matthew Bennett

necessary: "[i]*f the requirements set out in paragraphs 83 and 84* [on objective necessity of the input] *are fulfilled, the Commission considers that a dominant undertaking's refusal to supply is generally liable to eliminate, immediately or over time, effective competition in the downstream market.*"[336]

7.239 Earlier case law was more stringent, and required proof of elimination of all competition,[337] or at least that the refusal "*risks eliminating all competition on the part of this customer*".[338] *Microsoft* lowered the standard to some extent, probably to the limit.[339]

7.240 First, *Microsoft* confirmed that an infringement can be found while the rivals are still present on the downstream market. As argued previously, this is explained by the specific circumstances of the case, which concerned a situation where rivals used to be supplied, and where the disruption of supplies caused gradual but inexorable elimination, as customers switched to Windows 2000 and follow-on products that no longer allowed interoperability with third-party servers on an equal footing. In such a case, as opposed to a case of a request by a new entrant for *de novo* supplies, requiring proof that the rival requesting access is actually excluded from the market before the refusal can be found to eliminate competition, would deprive the remedy of its useful effect. In the words of the Court of First Instance:

> "*The expressions 'risk of elimination of competition' and 'likely to eliminate competition' are used without distinction by the Community judicature to reflect the same idea, namely that Article [102 TFEU] does not apply only from the time when there is no more, or practically no more, competition on the market. If the Commission were required to wait until competitors were eliminated from the market, or until their elimination was sufficiently imminent, before being able to take action under Article [102 TFEU], that would clearly run counter to the objective of that provision, which is to maintain undistorted competition in the common market and, in particular, to safeguard the competition that still exists on the relevant market.*"[340]

---

[336] *See Guidance Paper supra* note 41, para. 85.

[337] *See Magill supra* note 87, *Ladbroke supra* note 184, *Oscar Bronner supra* note 68; *Microsoft Judgment 2007 supra* note 67, paras 585–692. *See* Case T-184/01 *supra* note 138, para. 47.

[338] *See Commercial Solvents supra* note 112, para. 25 and *Télémarketing supra* note 124, paras 25 and 26.

[339] *See Microsoft Judgment 2007 supra* note 67, paras 479 to 620.

[340] *See Microsoft Judgment 2007 supra* note 67, para. 561. This reflects the EU Courts' view that Article 82 is not only concerned with actual anticompetitive effects, but also potential or likely anticompetitive effects. *See* Case T-219/99 *British Airways v Commission* ("*British Airways*") [2003] ECR II-5917 and *see Michelin II supra* note 331.

7. – Refuse to Deal
Maurits Dolmans and Matthew Bennett

Any other approach would have competition authorities and courts stand by **7.241** idly and wait for actual exclusion to materialise before they could act, even where the long-term harm caused by exclusion would be serious, or even irreversible, due to barriers to re-entry.[341] Network effects and economies of scale can result in positive feedback and tipping effects that may lead to a winner-take-all-market.[342] In markets with these characteristics, early intervention may be necessary for an effective enforcement of Article 102. This is even more of a concern in monopoly maintenance cases – which the Commission found that the *Microsoft* case was, because the denial of interoperability raised interoperability barriers to entry and thus reinforced Microsoft's PC operating systems near-monopoly.[343]

Secondly, the Court of First Instance referred to likely elimination of "all **7.242** effective competition" rather than of "all competition". The objective of this nuance is to avoid the situation where a dominant firm would allow one or two small rivals to remain on the market (or in specific niches) as marginalised competitors. The mere presence of a "bonsai" competitor may not appreciably constrain the dominant firm's power over price, and may not provide an adequate spur to innovation.[344] Judge Vesterdorf, who presided over the Court of First Instance in *Microsoft*, explained afterwards that:

> *"what is necessary is that the refusal is likely to eliminate all effective competition. In IMS Health as well as in Magill, it was stressed that the conduct was abusive as it would lead to elimination of all competition on the secondary market. After*

---

[341] *See Microsoft Judgment 2007 supra* note 67, para. 562.

[342] D. L. Rubinfeld, "Antitrust Enforcement in Dynamic Network Industries" (1998) 43 (3/4) *The Antitrust Bulletin*, pp. 859, 865.

[343] *See Microsoft Judgment 2007 supra* note 67, para. 769.

[344] *See Microsoft Judgment 2007 supra* note 67, para. 563. Even before the Microsoft judgment, the Court of Appeal in England held: "*Magill and IMS indicate the circumstances which the Court of Justice and the President of the Court of First Instance respectively regarded as exceptional in the case before them. It does not follow that other circumstances in other cases will not be regarded as exceptional ... there could be a breach of Article 82 without the exclusion of a wholly new product or all competition. This approach seems to me to be warranted by the width of the descriptions of abuse contained in Article 82 itself. I would, in any event, reject the submission of Counsel for Intel that the IMS test requires the exclusion of all competition from all sources. This was not a requirement in Oscar Bronner which referred ... only to all competition from the person requesting the service. Accordingly to the Summary in IMS ... must be read in that light. Were it otherwise liability under Article 82 could be simply avoided by a grant of a licence to an unenergetic rival.*" (Cases A3/2002/1380; A3/2002/1381 Intel Corporation v Via Technologies and Elitegroup Computer Systems (UK), UK Competition Appeal Tribunal Decision of 20 December 2002, para. 48). *See* also T. G. Krattenmaker and S. C. Salop, "Anticompetitive Exclusion: Raising Rivals' Costs to Achieve Power Over Price" (1986) 96(2) *Yale Law Journal*, pp. 209–93 and S. C. Salop and D. T. Scheffman, "Cost-Raising Strategies" (1987) 36(1) *Journal of Industrial Economics*, pp. 19–34.

7. – Refuse to Deal
Maurits Dolmans and Matthew Bennett

> *Microsoft, it is elimination of all effective competition, namely competition which might present a real constraint or a real competitive challenge to the dominant undertaking. This shift from elimination of all to elimination of effective competition appears to have at the same time rendered the conditions for finding an infringement of Article [102 TFEU] less strict by loosening the conditions for finding an abuse in these situations. To most people this shift is probably well-founded, as what is necessary is that there is room for some effective and not just some, however toothless, competition."*[345]

7.243 Nevertheless, even with the nuances added in *Microsoft*, refusal to supply cases still impose a significantly higher standard than the distortion of competition that must be proven for abusive tying, discrimination, or imposing unfair terms and conditions. A finding of downstream dominance is required.[346] This is natural, since the likely elimination of all effective competition is the corollary of the indispensability of the input product: if the input is not indispensable, the refusal to share might restrict supply and raise prices, but would not in itself exclude all effective competition. This in turn reflects the basic rule that a refusal to deal is not abuse in itself and circumstances must be exceptional to merit compulsory dealing, and the basic balancing act between the need to provide incentives to innovate and the need to ensure that all competition (and hence future incentives to innovate) is not removed.

7.244 The *Guidance Paper* indicates that a finding of exclusion of effective competition is not based on a *per se* analysis. The Commission will review the effects based on available evidence on the nature of the product and the structure of and conditions in the market:

> *"The likelihood of effective competition being eliminated is generally greater the higher the market share of the dominant undertaking in the downstream market. The less capacity-constrained the dominant undertaking is relative to competitors in the downstream market, the closer the substitutability between the dominant undertaking's output and that of its competitors in the downstream market, the greater the proportion of competitors in the downstream market that are affected, and the more likely it is that the demand that could be served by the foreclosed*

---

[345] *See supra* note 307, pp. 1–14

[346] O'Donoghue/Padilla state that the absence of *"effective competition"* on the market means *"dominance on the relevant downstream market, and arguably more"* see *supra* note 39, p. 444.

7. – Refuse to Deal
Maurits Dolmans and Matthew Bennett

competitors would be diverted away from them to the advantage of the dominant undertaking."[347]

Other relevant factors will be whether the firm seeking access is efficient or innovative enough to be viable in the long run, and whether even with the supplies it is destined to remain a mere niche player because of the nature of the product it offers. If so, an order to supply is probably not warranted. The same conclusion may be reached even if the firm requesting access is the only competitor, if the market is narrowly defined (for instance, an aftermarket, which might be defined separately even though primary market competition constrains price increases in the aftermarket), and where competitive pressure and potential entry from dynamic neighbouring markets are enough to drive prices down and innovation up.[348]   **7.245**

If there are other firms active on the downstream market, the question arises whether all other firms are equally dependent on the supply and being refused access. If they are not equally dependent but have apparently found or themselves developed alternative sources of supply, a refusal to supply may not exclude "all effective competition" (and would not be indispensable either). In such a case, an order to supply would merely serve to protect a competitor, which is not a justification for imposing a duty to deal.   **7.246**

Finally, intent to exclude rivals is not required for a finding of abuse, although it can be relevant.[349] The notion of abuse is an objective concept.[350] Evidence of intent can be relevant to show a causal connection between the refusal and the exclusion of competition, which a dominant firm cannot easily deny if it anticipated or planned it.[351] It is, moreover, relevant to show absence of   **7.247**

---

[347] *See Guidance Paper supra* note 41, para. 85. *See also Guidance Paper*, para. 20–22.

[348] In *Microsoft*, an argument along these lines was rejected on fact-specific ground including that Microsoft was able to identify *ex ante* and discriminate between servers purchased as workgroup servers and servers bought for other workloads, and that its servers were optimised to meet specific user demand. *See Microsoft Judgment 2007 supra* note 67, paras 480 *et seq.*

[349] M. E. Stucke, "Is Intent Relevant?" (2012) *Journal of Law, Economics and Policy* (forthcoming 2012).

[350] Case 85/76 *Hoffmann-La Roche v Commission* ("*Hoffmann-La Roche*") [1979] ECR 461, para. 91. *See also* Case IV/30.698 *ECS/AKZO*, Commission Decision of 14 December 1985, OJ 1985 L374/1, para. 81: "*The Commission emphasizes that it does not consider an intention even by a dominant firm to prevail over its rivals as unlawful. A dominant firm is entitled to compete on the merits. Nor does the Commission suggest that large producers should be under an obligation to refrain from competing vigorously with smaller competitors or new entrants.*"

[351] *See* Cases IV/30.787 and 31.488 Eurofix-Bauco/Hilti, Commission Decision of 22 December 1987, OJ 1988 L 65/19, para. 81 and *see Michelin II supra* note 331: "*If it is shown that the object pursued by the conduct of an undertaking in a dominant position is to limit competition, that conduct will also be liable to have such an effect [and thus pass the test that the conduct must "tend to restrict competition or,… [be] capable of having that effect"].*"

7. – Refuse to Deal
Maurits Dolmans and Matthew Bennett

objective justification, since it the presence of evidence of exclusionary intent, the dominant firm will find it difficult to convince a regulator or court that the conduct can be justified by non-exclusionary efficiency motivations.[352] But intent without effect is not enough – certainly not for imposition of a duty to supply – while effect without intent may suffice.

5. Absence of Objective Justification, and the Efficiency Defence

5.1. Rule of Reason

7.248   An early Commission Decision on essential facilities held that a "*dominant company may improve its service, but if that improvement will necessarily harm its competitor then its own commercial interests are not enough*".[353] This was far-reaching. The possibility of a justification defence is inherent in the very notion of an "abuse", which does not cover justified use.[354] The *Guidance Paper* confirms this, generally,[355] and specifically in the context of a refusal to deal.[356] The approach in the *Guidance Paper* is based on the statement by the Court of First Instance in *Microsoft*,[357] applying what is generally called the "rule of reason" or "proportionality test":[358]

---

[352] Defendants can only invoke efficiencies that they actually pursue or efficiencies associated with legitimate objectives sought: *See United Brands supra* note 184, paras 189–90: "*an undertaking must be conceded the right to take such reasonable steps as it deems appropriate to protect its said interests* [although] *such behaviour cannot be countenanced if its actual purpose is to strengthen this dominant position and abuse it.*"

[353] *See* Case IV/34.174 *supra* note 209; *See* Case IV/34.689 *supra* note 184, p. 8. These cases should probably be interpreted to mean that the dominant firm's commercial interests cannot justify an abuse of the improvements of the service do not meet the proportionality test.

[354] *See also Magill supra* note 87; *See Oscar Bronner supra* note 68 ("*incapable of being objectively justified*"); *See Télémarketing supra* note 124 ("*without objective necessity*"); *See Syfait supra* note 123, para. 67; *Microsoft Judgment 2007 supra* note 67. *See also United Brands supra* note 184, paras 189–90, 184 ("*an undertaking must be conceded the right to take such reasonable steps as it deems appropriate to protect its said interests [although] such behaviour cannot be countenanced if its actual purpose is to strengthen this dominant position and abuse it*"); *See Hoffmann-La Roche supra* note 350, para. 90; and Case 322/81 *Nederlandsche Banden Industrie Michelin v Commission* ("*Michelin I*") [1983] ECR 3461, paras 73 and 85.

[355] *See Guidance Paper supra* note 41, paras 28–31.

[356] *Ibid.*, paras 89–90.

[357] *See Microsoft Judgment 2007 supra* note 67, para. 688 (and generally, paras 666–711).

[358] Cf. Case United Brands *supra* note 184, paras 189–90: "*The fact that an undertaking is in a dominant position cannot disentitle it from protecting its own commercial interests ..., and ... such an undertaking must be conceded the right to take such reasonable steps as it deems appropriate to protect its said interests. ... Even if the possibility of a counterattack is acceptable that attack must still be proportionate to the threat taking into account the economic strength of the undertakings confronting each other.*"

7. – Refuse to Deal

Maurits Dolmans and Matthew Bennett

> *"although the burden of proof of the existence of the circumstances that constitute an infringement of Article [102 TFEU] is borne by the Commission, it is for the dominant undertaking concerned, and not for the Commission, before the end of the administrative procedure, to raise any plea of objective justification and to support it with arguments and evidence. It then falls to the Commission, where it proposes to make a finding of an abuse of a dominant position, to show that the arguments and evidence relied on by the undertaking cannot prevail and, accordingly, that the justification put forward cannot be accepted."*[359]

Based on this "rule of reason", the *Guidance Paper* identifies several conditions to be completed for a justification or efficiency defence to be accepted:[360] (1) legitimate objective, (2) effectiveness and causal link, (3) necessity, and (4) proportionality. **7.249**

5.1.1. Legitimate Objectives

First, of course, the dominant firm must show that it sought efficiencies or had other objective justifications. The Court of First Instance stated *"it is for the dominant undertaking concerned, and not for the Commission, before the end of the administrative procedure, to raise any plea of objective justification and to support it with arguments and evidence."*[361] The legitimate objective or efficiency must be actually pursued and not a subterfuge or after-the-fact rationalisation. As the Court of Justice indicated in *United Brands*, *"an undertaking must be conceded the right to take such reasonable steps as it deems appropriate to protect its said interests [although] such behaviour cannot be countenanced if its actual purpose is to strengthen this dominant* **7.250**

---

[359] The US Court of Appeals applied the same rule in the US Microsoft case (2001): *"The company claims an absolute and unfettered right to use its intellectual property as it wishes: … That is no more correct than the proposition that use of one's personal property, such as a baseball bat, cannot give rise to tort liability. … Intellectual property rights do not confer a privilege to violate the antitrust laws. … If the monopolist asserts a procompetitive justification - a nonpretextual claim that its conduct is indeed a form of competition on the merits because it involves, for example, greater efficiency or enhanced consumer appeal - then the burden shifts back to the plaintiff to rebut that claim. … If the monopolist's procompetitive justification stands unrebutted, then the plaintiff must demonstrate that the anticompetitive harm of the conduct outweighs the procompetitive benefit." United States v Microsoft*, 253 F.3d 34 (D.C. Cir. 2001).

[360] *See Guidance Paper supra* note 41, para. 90 (*"the Commission will ensure that the conditions set out in Section III D [para. 28–31] are fulfilled."*) These are a parallel to the conditions for exceptions under Article 101(3) TFEU. *See* Notice on Article 101(3) TFEU *supra* note 83. The third condition for an exception under Article 101(3) TFEU ("fair share for consumers") should be covered by the analysis of consumer harm.

[361] *See Microsoft Judgment 2007 supra* note 67, para. 688; *see also* para. 1144.

7. – Refuse to Deal
Maurits Dolmans and Matthew Bennett

position and abuse it."[362] Evidence that the actual intent was not to achieve the efficiency but to foreclose rivals will therefore make it very difficult for an efficiency defence to succeed.

7.251   To qualify as a justification, the benefit sought must be objective and realistic.[363] There is a range of acceptable justifications that will vary from case to case, depending on the facts. The *Guidance Paper* mentions "*technical improvements in the quality of goods, or a reduction in the cost of production or distribution*".[364] Examples related to the facility to which access is sought include capacity limitations for physical facilities and networks,[365] a shortage of inventory, disruption of production, degradation of the quality of a network resulting from attachment of inadequate terminal equipment, and security risks.[366] Other examples, all of which would have to meet the remaining conditions of the rule of reason test, include:[367] if access to the applicant would reduce the efficiency of the downstream users, or have substantial negative impact on the value of the facility; if it would cause the facility to be used uneconomically or affect the owner's revenues from the facility; interference with the quality, improvement, expansion or development of the facility; if the privileged position of the dominant company is due to the fact that it has special or exclusive rights granted to enable the dominant firm to provide a universal service obligation;[368] significant costs or disadvantages to the dominant firm or consumers; or, that the owner of the asset proves actual plans to produce and sell a new product meeting the unsatisfied demand that the complainant claims it wants to meet.[369] Justifications associated with the specific firm requesting access could be: lack of creditworthiness or a history of bad debt; refusal or inability to pay appropriate access fees; refusal to accept appropriate terms and conditions; a relevant history of IPR infringements or breaches of contract that

---

[362] *See United Brands supra* note 184, paras 189–90.

[363] Cf. Notice on Article 101(3) TFEU *supra* note 83, paras 49 et seq.

[364] *See Guidance Paper supra* note 41, para. 30.

[365] If the owner provides access on a non-discriminatory basis to up to an objectively fixed optimum or maximum number of users, it can refuse access to a user who would be 'one too many', unless a rational non-dominant or non-vertically-integrated firm would in that situation expand capacity (*see* below).

[366] *See, e.g.,* Commission Notice on the application of the competition rules to access agreements in the telecommunications sector – framework, relevant markets and principles ("*Telecom Access Notice*"), OJ 1998 C 265/2, para. 91.

[367] *See supra* note 327. *See Notice on Article 101(3) TFEU supra* note 83, paras 64 *et seq.*

[368] J. Temple Lang, "State Measures Restricting Competition Under European Union Law", in W. D. Collins (Ed.), *Issues in Antitrust Law and Policy* (American Bar Association Section on Antitrust Law, 2008), Vol. 1, Chap. 9, pp. 221–48.

[369] *See supra* note 307, p. 1, 10.

7. – Refuse to Deal
Maurits Dolmans and Matthew Bennett

could jeopardise the confidentiality of trade secrets that the firm requests; the requesting party's inability to use the facility; inadequate quality of its offering (especially if there is a demand to access to distribution or consumer-facing facilities); or, lack of adequate professional and technical skills needed to share and benefit from the facility.

In *Microsoft*, the question arose whether a dominant firm may invoke the desire **7.252** to maintain its incentive to innovate. In general terms, this aspect is already reflected in the requirement of exceptional circumstances. The Court of First Instance dismissed the argument on the ground that "[i]*f the mere fact of holding intellectual property rights could in itself constitute objective justification for the refusal to grant a licence, the exception established by the case law could never apply*."[370] It is for this reason not enough to make general allegations that "[d]*isclosure would ... eliminate future incentives to invest in the creation of more intellectual property, without specifying the technologies or products to which it thus referred*."[371] The wording suggests, however, that the Court will assess the situation differently if the dominant company is able to sufficiently demonstrate or quantify the reduction of its innovation incentives. In other words, for a justification based on the need to maintain innovation incentives to succeed, a dominant firm would need to invoke and prove specific factual considerations beyond general policy arguments, for instance, that (1) the anticipated loss of downstream revenues by granting compulsory access in the specific instance is not compensated by payment of the fee that the downstream rival can and is willing to pay, and (2) the loss by granting compulsory access jeopardises recovery of proven non-depreciated investments in the facility, the funding of necessary maintenance or improvements of the facility, or (especially in dynamic markets) the funding of ongoing development work to keep up with changing market demands.[372] The existence of a loss, or reduction of innovation incentives, thus depends on the level of the access fee that can be charged. Microsoft expressed a concern that its products would be cloned. This would have been a justification, but the Commission and the Court found that

---

[370] *See Microsoft Judgment 2007 supra* note 67, para. 690.

[371] *Ibid.*, para. 698. Nevertheless, the Commission and the Court of First Instance took the trouble to verify whether there was a disincentive, and found that there was none, as demonstrated by the consideration that Microsoft itself had stated that the disclosure requirements under the MCPP (the US Consent Decree) had not diminished its innovation, and that generally speaking, improved interoperability increases the value of a platform because of the availability of a greater range of complementary products.

[372] *See supra* note 307, p. 1, 10: "*Another objective justification might be that the IPR concerned is the only and fundamental basis for its production and that, if a licence were to be given to create competition vis-à-vis the dominant undertaking – because it follows from the judgment that the product need not be a new one but just a technical development – that might deprive the undertaking of its very economic basis.*"

7. – Refuse to Deal

Maurits Dolmans and Matthew Bennett

in the specific circumstances and conditions of the remedy, rivals could not and had no incentive to copy its products.[373] The *Guidance Paper* confirms that the Commission will consider specific – as opposed to general – claims:

> *"The Commission will consider claims by the dominant undertaking that a refusal to supply is necessary to allow the dominant undertaking to realise an adequate return on the investments required to develop its input business, thus generating incentives to continue to invest in the future, taking the risk of failed projects into account. The Commission will also consider claims by the dominant undertaking that its own innovation will be negatively affected by the obligation to supply, or by the structural changes in the market conditions that imposing such an obligation will bring about, including the development of follow-on innovation by competitors. ... In particular, it falls on the dominant undertaking to demonstrate any negative impact which an obligation to supply is likely to have on its own level of innovation."*[374]

7.253 This means that the Commission, as well as the General Court, demands that the dominant company sufficiently substantiate the reduction of its innovation incentives. A difficult question is that of the compensation. As stated above, a refusal or inability to pay appropriate access fees and to accept appropriate terms and conditions can justify a refusal to deal. This point will be discussed in the remedy section (Section VI), considering that the fee payable pursuant to a remedy should presumably be no more or less than the fee that the facility owner is entitled to ask in the first place.

7.254 There are indications that a refusal to supply cannot be justified by lack of capacity if a non-dominant or non-vertically-integrated firm in the circumstances would have invested in expansion of capacity. In various cases in the energy sector, the Commission concluded that capacity hoarding, capacity degradation and strategic underinvestment to protect a dominant position in retail gas sales constituted an abusive refusal to supply.[375] This is a departure from

---

[373] *See Microsoft Judgment 2007 supra* note 67, paras 198–206, 240–2 and 656–8. But *see* the *IBM Mainframe Emulators* investigation, above, where this argument was accepted in the specific circumstances of the case.

[374] *See Guidance Paper supra* note 41, paras 89–90. The Commission adds: *"If a dominant undertaking has previously supplied the input in question, this can be relevant for the assessment of any claim that the refusal to supply is justified on efficiency grounds."*

[375] *See* Case COMP/39.402 *RWE Gas Foreclosure* Commission Decision of 18 March 2009, OJ 2009/C 133/06; Case COMP/39.316 *GDF Foreclosure*, Commission Decision of 3 December 2009, not yet published, paras 23–8; Case COMP/39.317 *E.ON Gas Foreclosure*, Commission Decision of 4 May 2010, not yet published, paras 36–41; *See* Case COMP/39.315 *supra* note 250.

past practice. Traditionally, the Commission had regarded capacity constraints as an objective justification for a refusal to supply.[376] Since the cases were settled with commitments under Article 9 of Regulation 1/2003, under threat of a very large fine and structural remedies, they do not constitute precedent.

5.1.2. Effectiveness and Causal Link

The second condition is whether *"the efficiencies have been, or are likely to be, realised* **7.255** *as a result of the conduct."*[377] This means that the conduct must be effective, or reasonably capable of achieving the legitimate goal. The dominant firm will wish to explain the causal link between the refusal to deal and the legitimate objective it seeks, to show that its argument is not theoretical, nor a sham or subterfuge for exclusionary intent. Nevertheless, the Court of First Instance in *Microsoft* specified that it *"falls to the Commission … to show that the* [justification] *relied on by the undertaking cannot prevail".*[378]

The Notice on Article 101(3) TFEU contains a clarification that may be rel- **7.256** evant also for the assessment of causal connections between refusal to deal and claimed efficiencies:[379]

> *"The causal link between the agreement and the claimed efficiencies must normally also be direct. Claims based on indirect effects are as a general rule too uncertain and too remote to be taken into account. An example of indirect effect would be a case where it is claimed that a restrictive agreement allows the undertakings concerned to increase their profits, enabling them to invest more in research and development to the ultimate benefit of consumers. While there may be a link between profitability and research and development, this link is generally not sufficiently direct to be taken into account."*[380]

---

[376] *See, inter alia, Discussion Paper supra* note 154, para. 234: *"It may be an objective justification for a refusal to start supplying that an undertaking seeking access is not able to provide the appropriate commercial assurances that it will fulfil its obligations. In the case of an essential facility, access may be denied if the facility is capacity constrained or if granting access would lead to a substantial increase in cost that would jeopardize the economic viability of the facility holder."*

[377] *See Guidance Paper supra* note 41, para. 30.

[378] *See Microsoft Judgment 2007 supra* note 67, paras 688, 1144.

[379] Even though the Notice on Article 101(3) TFEU addresses coordinated behaviour, its principles might also be applicable to a refusal to supply under Article 102(b) TFEU, *see supra* note 83. One reason for this is that the efficiency defence under Article 102 TFEU (*see Guidance Paper supra* note 41, paras 28 *et seq.*) is in some ways comparable with the exception of Article 101(3) TFEU.

[380] *See* Notice on Article 101(3) TFEU *supra* note 83, para. 54.

7. – Refuse to Deal

Maurits Dolmans and Matthew Bennett

7.257 This is consistent with the position of the Court of First Instance in *Microsoft* that general claims of the need to preserve innovation incentives are taken into account by requiring "special circumstances", but cannot constitute objective justification for the refusal to deal.

5.1.3. Necessity

7.258 The third condition under the rule of reason test is that "*the conduct is indispensable to the realisation of those efficiencies: there must be no less anticompetitive alternatives to the conduct that are capable of producing the same efficiencies, the likely efficiencies brought about by the conduct outweigh any likely negative effects on competition and consumer welfare in the affected markets.*"[381] If a legitimate objective and a causal link are convincingly alleged, the plaintiff or competition authority must show there are less restrictive and effective alternatives.[382]

7.259 The Notice on Article 101(3) TFEU contains relevant considerations. For instance, it explains that the efficiencies should be "specific" to the conduct in question

> "*in the sense that there are no other economically practicable and less restrictive means of achieving the efficiencies. … Undertakings … are not required to consider hypothetical or theoretical alternatives. The Commission will not second-guess the business judgment of the parties. It will only intervene where it is reasonably clear that there are realistic and attainable alternatives. The parties must only explain and demonstrate why such seemingly realistic and significantly less restrictive alternatives to the agreement would be significantly less efficient. … A restriction is indispensable if its absence would eliminate or significantly reduce the efficiencies … or make it significantly less likely that they will materialise. The assessment of alternative solutions must take into account the actual and potential improvement in the field of competition by the elimination of a particular restriction or the application of a less restrictive alternative. The more restrictive the restraint the stricter the test under the third condition.*"[383]

---

[381] *See Guidance Paper supra* note 41, para. 30.

[382] For an example of the application of this principle, *see Microsoft Judgment 2007 supra* note 67, para. 1155.

[383] *See* Notice on Article 101(3) TFEU *supra* note 83, paras 75 *et seq.*

7. – Refuse to Deal
Maurits Dolmans and Matthew Bennett

Consistency suggests that the same approach should apply to the necessity criterion under the rule of reason test for purposes of Article 102 TFEU. **7.260**

5.1.4.   Proportionality

The most controversial element of the rule of reason analysis is the proportionality test. As discussed within the economics section (Section II), it may indeed be difficult to balance various parties' innovation incentives and draw conclusions, without quantitative data that are very difficult to obtain. The 2004 *Microsoft* Decision provides an example of the how a balancing test could work. **7.261**

As explained, Microsoft did not invoke a specific efficiency objective that it claimed to pursue, and instead relied on general arguments on efficiencies and innovation incentives associated with the freedom to contract and protection of intellectual property. The Commission nevertheless considered Microsoft's position that a compulsory licence would chill its innovation incentive. It distinguished between interoperability technology on the one hand, and general operating system technology on the other, and concluded that the disclosure of interoperability information (externals) does not affect Microsoft's incentives to innovate the operating system itself.[384] Since no source code or internal code is disclosed, the Commission found that there is no risk of cloning.[385] In fact, because of the difficulty of implementing specifications designed for another system, rivals will have to be more efficient and add real value to benefit from the disclosure obligation.[386] Nor is Microsoft's incentive to innovate foreclosed since, according to the Commission, *"there is ample scope for differentiation and innovation [by Microsoft] beyond the design of interface specifications."*[387] The Commission also noted that the US remedies (the Microsoft Communications Protocol Program) did not reduce incentives to innovate either.[388] Conversely, the prospect of exclusion would reduce third parties' incentives to innovate, as well as Microsoft's incentives to innovate operating systems, while **7.262**

---

[384] *See Microsoft Decision 2004 supra* note 49, para. 698.

[385] *Ibid.*, paras 713–22. Because of time lag and disadvantages, *"Microsoft's competitors will have to provide additional value to the customer, beyond the mere interoperability of their products … if such products are to be commercially viable"* (*see* para. 722). In fact, because of the difficulty of implementing specifications designed for another system, rivals will have to be more efficient to benefit from the disclosure obligation (*see* paras 721–33.).

[386] *Ibid.*, paras 721–33.

[387] *Ibid.*, para. 698.

[388] *Ibid.*, para. 728.

7. – Refuse to Deal

Maurits Dolmans and Matthew Bennett

"competitive pressure would increase Microsoft's own incentives to innovate."[389] Ultimately, application of a balance-of-interest test led the Commission to the following conclusion: "[O]*n balance, the possible negative impact of an order to supply on Microsoft's incentive to innovate is outweighed by its positive impact on the level of innovation of the whole industry (including Microsoft). As such, the need to protect Microsoft's incentives to innovate cannot constitute an objective justification that would offset the exceptional circumstances identified.*"[390]

7.263 Microsoft criticised this as a new test, which was vague and unforeseeable, legally defective and marking a radical departure from the tests defined in the case law.[391] The Court of First Instance concluded that this was a misreading, and that while the Commission had taken the trouble to rebut Microsoft's arguments, the Court somewhat surprisingly concluded that this should not be seen as applying a balancing test. *"The Commission came to a negative conclusion but not by balancing the negative impact which the imposition of a requirement to supply the information at issue might have on Microsoft's incentives to innovate against the positive impact of that obligation on innovation in the industry as a whole, but after refuting Microsoft's arguments"*[392] that Microsoft's innovation incentives would be negatively affected.

7.264 Perhaps for this reason, the *Guidance Paper* does not refer to a balancing test. Instead, the *Guidance Paper* in its section on the "General Approach to Exclusionary Conduct" introduces a principle akin to the condition for exception under Article 101(3) that efficiencies cannot justify elimination of all competition in respect of a substantial part of the products in question. The *Guidance Paper* suggests that regardless of the benefits, the conduct must:

> *"not eliminate effective competition, by removing all or most existing sources of actual or potential competition. Rivalry between undertakings is an essential driver of economic efficiency, including dynamic efficiencies in the form of innovation. In its absence the dominant undertaking will lack adequate incentives to continue to create and pass on efficiency gains. Where there is no residual competition and no foreseeable threat of entry, the protection of rivalry and the competitive process outweighs possible efficiency gains. In the Commission's view,*

---

[389] *See Microsoft Decision 2004 supra* note 49, para. 725.

[390] *Ibid.*, para. 783

[391] *Ibid.*, paras 669–71. Note that a balancing test appears to apply in US antitrust law: *"If the monopolist's procompetitive justification stands unrebutted, then the plaintiff must demonstrate that the anticompetitive harm of the conduct outweighs the procompetitive benefit."* See *United States v Microsoft*, 253 F.3d 34 (D.C. Cir. 2001).

[392] *See Microsoft Judgment 2007 supra* note 67, para. 710.

7. – Refuse to Deal

Maurits Dolmans and Matthew Bennett

exclusionary conduct which maintains, creates or strengthens a market position approaching that of a monopoly can normally not be justified on the grounds that it also creates efficiency gains."[393]

These statements should be applied with caution. On a narrow reading they **7.265** appear to significantly restrict the scope for an efficiency defence. Especially for dynamic markets,[394] where successful market players may have strong but temporary market positions (approaching that of a monopoly), these statements might be read to exclude certain efficiency defences based on a reduction of incentives to innovate. This would be contrary to the explicit acknowledgment of such an efficiency defence in the refusal to supply sections of the *Guidance Paper* (quoted above).[395] Moreover, it is not based on a statement by the Court, and if applied too readily, could be distorted into a *per se* rule. Under the case law of the Court, dominant firms should be allowed a chance to justify a refusal to supply by reference to their specific circumstances – even if "exceptional circumstances" are found, *i.e.*, even if input is indispensable, the plaintiff's innovation is reduced, and effective competition downstream is excluded. A *per se* rule in such a case is inconsistent also with the Commission's own desire to assess all cases in the light of their actual economic effect, which is one of the cornerstones of the "more economic approach".

5.2. Burden of Proof

The *Guidance Paper* leaves open some questions on the allocation of the bur- **7.266** den of proof of the various steps of the rule of reason analysis. It is incumbent on the dominant undertaking to demonstrate any negative impact which an obligation to supply is likely to have on its own level of innovation, and to prove efficiencies and objective justifications it sought.[396] It is not unreasonable to require the dominant firm also to provide whatever evidence it has on the causal link between the conduct and the efficiencies, but the burden of proof for the remainder of the test is firmly on the Commission. The general discussion of the efficiency defence in the *Guidance Paper* suggests that "[i] *t then falls to the Commission to make the ultimate assessment of whether the conduct concerned is not objectively necessary and, based on a weighing-up of any apparent anti-competitive effects against any advanced and substantiated efficiencies, is likely to result in*

---

[393] *See Guidance Paper supra* note 41, para. 30.

[394] On dynamic markets, *see* Chapter 1 on Market Definition.

[395] *See Guidance Paper supra* note 41, paras 89–90.

[396] *See Microsoft Judgment 2007 supra* note 67, para. 688 and *see Guidance Paper*, paras 31 and 90.

7. – Refuse to Deal

Maurits Dolmans and Matthew Bennett

consumer harm."[397] The Court in *Microsoft* was more general, stating: "*It then falls to the Commission, where it proposes to make a finding of an abuse of a dominant position, to show that the arguments and evidence relied on by the undertaking cannot prevail and, accordingly, that the justification put forward cannot be accepted.*"[398] The *Guidance Paper* should be read and applied in this light.

V. Exploitative Refusal to Deal

7.267   The imposition of excessive fees or exploitative terms could constitute a constructive refusal to supply, and the *Guidance Paper* (although dealing only with exclusionary abuse) includes pricing above the competitive level as an example of consumer harm.[399] But can the imposition of "unfair terms" in breach of Article 102(a) TFEU qualify as an additional abusive element justifying an order to supply absent any evidence of exclusionary abuse?

7.268   The Court of Justice mentioned in *Volvo* that "*the exercise of an exclusive right by the proprietor of a registered design … may*[400] *be prohibited under Article* [102 TFEU] *if it involves, on the part of an undertaking holding a dominant position, certain abusive conduct such as … the fixing of the prices for spare parts at an unfair level.*"[401] It is doubtful whether this was intended to refer to exploitative abuses, since the fixing of prices for spare parts at an unfair level has an exclusionary effect, to the extent that it constitutes a constructive refusal to sell indispensable spare parts to independent car repair shops. A duty to license may be a way to redress a situation where Volvo raises barriers to entry to independent repairers, although a duty to supply the body panels themselves on non-abusive terms may be more appropriate, and pursuant to the principle of proportionality, the IP owner should at least be given the choice.

7.269   The Court touched upon this issue again in *Micro Leader Business*.[402] Micro Leader imported French language versions of the Microsoft Office suite from

---

[397] *See Guidance Paper supra* note 41, para. 31.

[398] *See Microsoft Judgment 2007 supra* note 67, paras 688 and 1144.

[399] *See Guidance Paper supra* note 41, para. 11.

[400] When citing this paragraph in the *Microsoft* judgment, the Court of First Instance substituted the word "*may*" with "*might*". *See Microsoft Judgment 2007 supra* note 67, para. 321. This confirms that while these circumstances could be part of a finding of an abuse, they are not sufficient in themselves to constitute an infringement of Article 102 TFEU.

[401] *See Volvo*, paras 9–10.

[402] *See Micro Leader supra* note 85, paras 51–7.

7. – Refuse to Deal
Maurits Dolmans and Matthew Bennett

Canada into France, at prices below those prevailing in Europe. Microsoft invoked its trademarks and copyrights to stop the grey imports, arguing that its rights had not been exhausted. Micro Leader complained, but the Commission sided with Microsoft and rejected the complaint. The Court agreed that Microsoft's rights had not been exhausted, but annulled the Commission Decision, holding that the Commission had made a manifest error in not ascertaining whether there was evidence of price differentiation suggesting excessive pricing: "[w]*hilst, as a rule, the enforcement of copyright by its holder, as in the case of the prohibition on importing certain products from outside the [European Union] into a Member State of the* [European Union], *is not in itself a breach of Article* [102 TFEU] … *such enforcement may in exceptional circumstances, involve abusive conduct*".[403] This case did not involve a refusal to deal, but suggests that invoking an intellectual property right to bolster an excessive pricing policy could be found in breach of Article 102 TFEU if there is also evidence of discrimination, and that a compulsory licence (or an order to permit grey imports) could be an appropriate remedy for excessive pricing. Microsoft eventually reached a settlement with Micro Leader, which led to the closure of the case without a final decision. The Court of First Instance in *Microsoft* states that "*a reading of the judgment in Micro Leader Business indicates that the factual situations where the exercise of an exclusive right by an intellectual property right-holder may constitute an abuse of a dominant position cannot be restricted to one particular set of circumstances.*"[404]

It is highly questionable, however, whether excessive pricing by a dominant **7.270** firm should give rise to a duty to allow intra-brand competition in product covered by intellectual property, especially when the grey importer adds no value or innovative element whatsoever to the product, or in the absence of a FRAND promise by the licensor. Every exclusive property right allows the owner to raise access prices above the competitive level, in order to allow recovery of past investments and encourage future innovation. In the words of the US Supreme Court in *Trinko*,

> "*[t]he mere possession of monopoly power, and the concomitant charging of monopoly prices, is not only not unlawful; it is an important element of the free-market system. The opportunity to charge monopoly prices—at least for a short period—is what attracts 'business acumen' in the first place; it induces risk taking that produces innovation and economic growth. To safeguard the incentive to*

---

[403] *See Micro Leader supra* note 85, paras 56.
[404] *See Microsoft Decision 2004 supra* note 49, para. 557.

7. – Refuse to Deal
Maurits Dolmans and Matthew Bennett

innovate, the possession of monopoly power will not be found unlawful unless it is accompanied by an element of anticompetitive conduct." [405]

7.271 It may be that the Court in *Micro Leader Business* had in mind an exceptional situation where indirect network effects and *de facto* standards associated with the Office suite create an insuperable barrier to entry, inhibiting the self-correcting mechanism of the free market and where discrimination undermined the argument that the high price was reasonably necessary to fund innovation. There is, however, no indication in the judgment, and in the absence of a final judgment, great caution should be exercised in relying on this case.

VI.   Remedies

7.272 Once a facility is found to be essential and an obligation to supply exists, the Commission has the power under Article 7 of Regulation 1/2003[406] to require the undertaking concerned to bring the infringement to an end. A remedy normally reflects the abuse and, if the abuse is a refusal to deal, the remedy would be an order to deal. The Commission's powers include, moreover, the authority to do anything that is necessary to ensure that the remedy has a useful effect (*"effet utile"*) in restoring conditions of effective competition, including the imposition of interim measures pending an in-depth review of the case.[407] Similarly, the Commission may set a reasonable deadline for full implementation of the remedy with appropriate speed to minimise ongoing negative effects of the abuse.[408] For a detailed discussion on remedies in a refusal to deal case see Section IV.3 of Chapter 12.

---

[405] *See Trinko supra* note 96, para. 407.

[406] Council Regulation (EC) 1/2003 of 16 December 2002 on the implementation of the rules on competition laid down in Articles 81 and 82 of the Treaty (*"Regulation 1/2003"*), OJ 2003 L 1/1.

[407] *See* Article 7(1) of *Regulation 1/2003* (*"it may impose on them any behavioural or structural remedies which are proportionate to the infringement committed and necessary to bring the infringement effectively to an end."*). Case 792/79 R *Camera Care v Commission* [1980] ECR 119.

[408] If the undertaking does not fully implement the remedy before the time limit set by the Commission's Decision, periodic penalty payments may be imposed. *See* Case COMP/37.792 *Microsoft*, Commission Decision of 12 July 2006, not yet published, fixing the definitive amount of the periodic penalty payment imposed on Microsoft (confirmed on appeal in *Microsoft Judgment 2007 supra* note 67).

Tying and Bundling

Thomas Graf and David R. Little*

I. Introduction

A supplier of two distinct products or services can offer these products or services separately or combined as part of a "package". This chapter considers the different forms of packaged sales that suppliers offer and when these packages of products and services may raise antitrust issues. **8.1**

The bundling together of separate products and services is a widespread commercial activity. It is often beneficial for companies and consumers, enabling companies to differentiate their offerings and consumers to benefit from better or more cost-effective solutions. Absent market power, only useful and attractive packages are likely to succeed. If the packaged whole is in some way inferior to the sum of its parts, consumers will choose to source their components elsewhere on a stand-alone basis (or will purchase a competing bundle). If a company is not dominant its bundling practices should therefore not raise competition law concerns. **8.2**

However, if a company holds a position of dominance it may be able to use packaged sales to exclude competitors and harm consumers. A company may use its market power in the supply of one product to create packaged offerings capable of excluding competition from superior rival solutions. This strategy can be used to deter rivals from entering a market segment or to extend market power into adjacent markets. For this reason, Article 102(d) TFEU prohibits "*making the conclusion of contracts subject to acceptance by the other parties of supplementary obligations which, by their nature or according to commercial usage, have no connection with the subject of such contracts*". **8.3**

The challenge for competition authorities is how to distinguish tying and bundling practices liable to harm competition and consumers from those that will likely generate countervailing consumer benefits. Given the ubiquity of **8.4**

---

* The authors are grateful for the assistance of Shin-Shin Hua.

8. – Tying and Bundling
Thomas Graf and David R. Little

packaged sales, and their sometimes ambiguous implications for consumer and/or total welfare, an effects-based approach is critical.

8.5   In discussing packaged sales, the terms "tying" and "bundling" are frequently used interchangeably in the literature. This is potentially a source of confusion. We ascribe the following meaning to these terms:

- "Tying" occurs when a supplier sells one product, the "tying product", only together with another product, the "tied product". As a result, customers who want the tying product must also acquire the tied product. The defining characteristic of a tie is therefore the inability to obtain the tying product separately, while the tied product may or may not be available individually.

- "Mixed bundling", or bundling for short, arises when a supplier offers both products separately, but offers a package of the two products at a discount.[1] If the discount is set at a level that renders it economically unrealistic for a customer to obtain the two products separately, mixed bundling is equivalent to a tie.[2]

II.   Economic Theory of Tying and Bundling

8.6   Before discussing the legal analysis of tying and bundling under EU competition law it is useful to review the economic theory in this area. The economic analysis of tying and bundling practices has generated a rich and varied literature ranging from propositions that such practices are almost never anti-competitive to propositions that tying and bundling practices by dominant firms are almost always harmful.

---

[1] *See* Guidance on the Commission's enforcement priorities in applying Article 82 of the EC Treaty to abusive exclusionary conduct by dominant undertakings ("*Guidance Paper*"), OJ 2009 C 45/7, para. 48.

[2] The approach to mixed bundling adopted by the Commission in the *Guidance Paper* is in line with its guidance on predatory pricing by dominant companies. The Commission will assess the price of the tied component based on the long run incremental costs associated with the tied product. That is, the mixed bundling strategy is not unlawful where the incremental price paid by a customer for each of the dominant undertaking's products in the mixed bundle covers the dominant undertaking's long run incremental costs of including the product in the bundle. *Ibid.*, para. 60. *See also*, DG Competition Discussion paper on the application of Article 82 of the treaty to exclusionary abuses ("*Discussion Paper*"), paras 189–90. Commentators have argued against the extension of a predatory pricing analysis to tying cases generally. *See* D. W. Carlton and M. Waldman, "How economics can improve antitrust doctrine towards tie-in sales" (2005) 1(1) *Competition Policy International*, pp. 27–40.

8. – Tying and Bundling
Thomas Graf and David R. Little

1. The Chicago School Theory

Prior to the late 1970s, the US courts had developed an increasingly strict **8.7** stance *vis-a-vis* tying arrangements (the Commission and EU courts did not issue a prohibition decision in a tying case until *Hilti* in 1988).[3] Some authors questioned the analysis of the courts as lacking evidential rigour; one well-respected commentator went so far as to denounce the state of the law on tying as being "*completely irrational*".[4] In a number of cases, the evidence against the impugned company was criticised as equivocal at best.[5]

Disaffected with the state of the law and the questionable economic analy- **8.8** sis underpinning certain decisions, economists of the Chicago School (in particular, Director, Levi, Bowman, Posner, Telser, McGee, and Bork) postulated that a firm would only ever tie or bundle products for procompetitive reasons. Their conclusions were based on what became known as "the "single monopoly profit theory", *i.e.*, that a monopolist can extract only one monopoly rent.[6]

The Chicago School maintained that if the tying product A is already sold **8.9** at a price which extracts the full monopoly profit from customers, the effect of tying product A with a separate product B is to raise the effective price of product A beyond consumers' maximum willingness to pay for A. The tying strategy is therefore unprofitable, since it sacrifices sales of the tying product. The Chicago School concluded that a monopolist could only earn a

---

[3] *See* Cases IV/30.787 and 31.488 *Eurofix-Bauco/Hilti* ("*Hilti Decision 1987*"), Commission Decision of 22 December 1987, OJ 1988 L 65/19; Case T-30/89 *Hilti v Commission* ("*Hilti Judgment 1991*") [1991] ECR II-1439; Case C-53/92 P *Hilti v Commission* ("*Hilti Judgment 1994*") [1994] ECR I-667; and Case IV/30.178 *Napier Brown/British Sugar* ("*Napier Brown*"), Commission Decision of 18 July 1988, OJ 1988 L 284/41.

[4] R. H. Bork, *The Antitrust Paradox: A Policy at War with Itself* (2nd Ed., New York, The Free Press, 1993), page 368. Bork dismissed objections to tying arrangements in frank terms: "*The law's theory of tying arrangements is merely another example of the discredited transfer-of-power theory, and perhaps no other variety of that theory has been so thoroughly and repeatedly demolished in the legal and economic literature. That the law's course remained utterly undeflected for so long casts an illuminating and, if you are of a sardonic turn of mind, amusing sidelight upon the relation of scholarship to judicial law making.*"

[5] For example, because the evidence did not show conclusively that the entity engaged in the tying practice was dominant (*International Salt Co. v United States*, 332 U.S. 392 (1947)), or because the second product that would have been "monopolised" was a commodity product (*Carbice Corp. of America v America Patents Development Corp.*, 283 US 27, 32 (1931)), or because the tie had been shown to be only partially effective (*Northern Pacific R. v United States*, 356 US 1 (1958)).

[6] R. H. Bork, *supra* note 4, p. 372.

8. – Tying and Bundling
Thomas Graf and David R. Little

single monopoly profit and it was not possible for the monopolist to leverage monopoly power across markets. [7]

2. Critique of the Chicago School Theory

8.10 The principal contribution of the Chicago School was to challenge the erroneous assumption that market power is automatically extended from one product to another simply by selling them together. As such, it highlighted the need for more analytical rigour in the review of tying practices.[8] However, the Chicago School's single monopoly profit theory has since been shown to be subject to important limitations. Just as it would be wrong to assume that every bundling practice by a firm with market power is anticompetitive, it cannot be assumed, as the Chicago School does, that such bundling practices are always benign. On the contrary, the single monopoly profit theory holds only in the presence of several important assumptions:

- Buyers do not use varying amounts of the tied product with the tying product;
- Buyer demand for the two products has a strong positive correlation;
- Buyers do not use varying amounts of the tying product; and
- The competitiveness of the tied and tying markets is fixed.[9]

8.11 The single monopoly profit theory fails where any of these assumptions do not hold. Thus where, for example, there are economies of scale rather than constant returns to scale, and where competition is imperfect in the tied market, the Chicago School theory cannot exclude the possibility that tying may increase monopoly rents.

---

[7] *See* A. Director and H. Levi, "Law and the Future: Trade Regulation", (1956) 51 (281) *Northwestern University Law Review*, p. 281 and 286; R. Schmalenese "Commodity Bundling by Single-Product Monopolies" (1982) 25 *Journal of Law and Economics,* pp. 67–71.

[8] RBB Economics, "Tying and bundling – cause for complaint?" RBB Brief 16, January 2005, available at http://www.rbbecon.com/publications/downloads/rbb_brief16.pdf, p. 2.

[9] E. Elhauge, "Tying, bundled discounts, and the death of the single monopoly profit theory" (2009), 123(2) *Harvard Law Review*, p. 400. *See also*, M. D. Whinston, "Tying, Foreclosure and Exclusion" (1990) 80(4) *American Economic Review*, pp. 837–59. Whinston's paper was the first to authoritatively rebut the single monopoly profit theory, demonstrating that where the tying product is not essential, and the tied product can be used in non-fixed proportions with the tying product or without the tying product at all, tying allows the supplier to extract additional monopoly profit.

8. – Tying and Bundling
Thomas Graf and David R. Little

Even where the assumptions of the Chicago School theory hold, the Chicago **8.12**
School theory remains a static model of competition. The theory does not
take into account that a company may have dynamic, strategic incentives to
engage in tying and bundling.[10] Furthermore, the Chicago School theory
fails to consider the incentives of a multi-product firm with market power
in several markets to combine these together in order to enhance its market
power.

3. Reasons for Tying and Bundling Explored in the Economic Literature

The economic literature has confirmed that a dominant company may engage **8.13**
in tying or bundling for reasons that are procompetitive or perhaps neutral.
But the post-Chicago School literature has also identified several anticompetitive reasons why a company may engage in a tying or bundling strategy.[11]
While the application of Article 102 TFEU is based on an objective concept
of abuse for which the motives of a firm are not determinative, understanding the reasons and incentives for engaging in tying and bundling practices is
important to frame the analysis of such practices.

3.1. Cost Savings

Tying and bundling may be used to achieve cost savings. This may be the case **8.14**
where the cost to the supplier of selling multiple goods separately (for example, production, packaging, and stocking costs) are significant. For example,
it is likely more costly for a software supplier to produce three discs each
containing one programme than to produce a single disc (capacity constraints
permitting) containing all three programmes.

3.2. System Assembly and System Quality Issues

Bundling can be an important "value-added" service that makes available **8.15**
more and better products to a wider audience. This may be the case, in particular, where the bundled whole is greater than the sum of its individual
parts, and where the integration of these separate parts requires considerable
technical expertise. An oft-cited example is a car, which *"comprises a bundle of*

---

[10] B. Nalebuff and D. Majerus, "Bundling, Tying, and Portfolio Effects" (2003) No. 1, *DTI Economics Paper,* p. 19.
[11] *See ibid.* for a detailed discussion of reasons for a company to tie or bundle.

8. – Tying and Bundling
Thomas Graf and David R. Little

an engine, wheels, and many other components ranging from satellite navigation systems to cup-holders". Self-assembly by consumers or intermediaries of these different components would be prohibitively expensive – "*scale and scope economies make a centralised production process by the car manufacturer more efficient*".[12]

8.16   A further reason for bundling is the preservation of system quality. A company may combine sales of product A with its own complementary product B in order to preserve the quality of A and in order to reduce the risk of malfunction or degradation. This is an issue of brand protection and blame attribution. A supplier may be more confident that its product A will continue to work well only if paired with its own product B. If the customer instead uses a third party's B product, the supplier may not be able to guarantee that A, or the system as a whole, will work as intended. The supplier may therefore worry that, absent the tie, customers may incorrectly attribute blame to the supplier's product A rather than the third-party's product B. However, where product A is designed to support complementary products from different suppliers, as would be the case, for example, with many platform products, or where there is significant customer demand for mixing and matching products from different suppliers, such arguments may not necessarily hold.[13]

3.3.   Pricing Strategies

8.17   Bundling and tying may also be used to implement more effective pricing. Such practices can for example be used to achieve a Cournot pricing effect (*i.e.*, charging a lower price for product A results in more sales of complementary product B). As in the case of vertical integration, which can be used to eliminate "double marginalisation", a supplier may bundle complementary A and B products together in order to retain for itself the benefits of lowering the price of product A. In the absence of a tie or bundled offering, a rival supplier of complementary product B might be able to appropriate a portion of these gains to itself.

8.18   A company with market power may also use tying or bundling to support differential pricing strategies that increase sales and returns. A monopolist will generally prefer not to set one price for all customers because a sole price

---

[12] S. Bishop and M. Walker, *The Economics of EC Competition Law: Concepts, Application and Measurement* (3rd Ed., London, Sweet & Maxwell, 2010), p. 277.
[13] *Ibid.*, p. 281.

8. – Tying and Bundling
Thomas Graf and David R. Little

excludes those customers not willing to pay the monopoly price and concedes profits to those customers that would have been prepared to pay more. Tying or bundling is an effective response to customers that value the bundled products differently. The supplier can serve supra-marginal customers who would not have bought at the single monopoly price, while gaining a greater portion of the value that infra-marginal customers attribute to the product.

An example of tying used as a form of price discrimination is metering. **8.19** Metering is a form of pricing under which the customer pays a "per-use" fee. The per-use fee is levied through tied sales (for example, charges for toner cartridges for photocopiers). Customers who use the main product A with greater intensity (and therefore likely value product A more highly) will pay a higher price for this benefit in the form of greater purchases of the consumable complement, product B. The supplier engaging in the tying strategy can price discriminate more effectively between consumers who value the non-consumable product A differently (as reflected in their different usage intensities). To understand the effectiveness of this strategy, consider an alternative scenario, in which the supplier instead seeks to exploit heavy users' higher valuation of product A by charging a higher price for A. In this scenario, infra-marginal, low intensity users might not buy product A at all. By seeking to charge a price for product A that corresponds to the heavy users' maximum willingness to pay, the supplier risks sacrificing revenues from low-intensity users that would have purchased product A at a lower price.

More generally, tying and bundling can be used to compensate for differ- **8.20** ent valuations of the products by different customers, especially if demand for the bundled goods is *negatively* correlated.[14] Economic literature suggests that such a strategy becomes more effective as the monopolist includes more products in the bundle. This is because customer price heterogeneity typically decreases as the number of components in a bundle increases.[15] When estimating the value of products, customers and consumers tend to think in terms of price "ranges" rather than single prices. A bundled price for two products in effect represents a series of different prices, with each customer

---

[14] G Stigler, *Organization of Industry* (Chicago, The University of Chicago Press, 1968), Chapter 15 "A note on block booking".

[15] *See, e.g.*, A. Brandenburger and V. Krishna, "Bundling", *HBS Premier Case Collection* (1991). The authors illustrate this effect using bundled sale of classic music concert tickets. The authors find that while there is a wide spread of customer valuations for any one concert, there is much less variation in customer valuation of a "series ticket" that bundles several concerts into one package.

8. – Tying and Bundling
Thomas Graf and David R. Little

allocating portions of the bundled price to the two products depending on their subjective "acceptable price range" for the individual products. As the number of products in the bundle increases, the aggregate "range" of acceptable prices increases. (It may also become more challenging for the customer to value the bundled components individually, and this price obscurity may encourage a customer to purchase the bundle.)

8.21 The welfare implications of differential pricing strategies depend largely on the particular factual and economic conditions of the case and may be hard to determine with certainty in practice.[16] In some circumstances such conduct may be welfare-enhancing. Even if customers that value one product highly may pay higher prices under a bundled pricing system, this does not necessarily reduce total welfare (rather, it will redistribute surplus between supplier and buyer). Moreover, customers for whom the product has less value or who would not otherwise buy the product may pay lower prices,[17] with positive consequences for *ex post* total welfare, *i.e.,* the sum of consumer welfare and seller's welfare.[18] But in other circumstances, price discrimination may reduce both consumer and *ex post* total welfare, especially if price discrimination is and fails to match prices with buyers' valuations (unless the reallocation of output is compensated by an output-increasing efficiency).[19] Moreover where tying and bundling practices by a dominant firm foreclose competition and restrict innovation, such adverse effects must be balanced against possible efficiency gains from price discrimination effects.[20] The question therefore ultimately is not so much whether the use of tying and bundling strategies as a

---

[16] *See* K. Kühn, R. Stillman and C. Caffarra, "Economic theories of bundling and their policy implications in abuse cases: an assessment in light of the Microsoft case" (2005) 1(1) *European Competition Journal*, pp. 85 and 91. D. W. Carlton and M. Waldman, *supra* note 2, pp. 27–40. Motta has argued that if all consumers were to transition away from purchasing separate products to purchasing the bundle, the combined effect of deadweight loss and customer-to-producer transfer of surplus means that total welfare will decrease. *See* M. Motta, *Competition Policy: Theory and Practice* (Cambridge, Cambridge University Press, 2004).

[17] *See, e.g.,* Office of Fair Trading, *Assessment of Individual Agreements and Conduct,* OFT 414, September 1999, para. 3.3.8.

[18] *See, e.g.,* P. Papandropoulos, "Article 82: Tying and bundling" (2006) *Competition Law Insight,* p. 5; E. Elhauge, *supra* note 9; D. W. Carlton and M. Waldman, *supra* note 2.

[19] *See, e.g.,* E. Elhauge, *supra* note 9; H. R. Varian, "Price Discrimination", in R. Schmalensee and R. Willig (Eds.), *Handbook of Industrial Organization* (Vol I, Amsterdam, North-Holland, 1989), Ch. 10, pp. 597, 600 and 617. It has also been argued that if all consumers were to transition away from purchasing separate products to purchasing the bundle, the combined effect of deadweight loss and customer-to-producer transfer of surplus means that total welfare will decrease, *see* M. Motta, *supra* note 16.

[20] Nalebuff argues that although price discrimination provides a reason to bundle, the gains from using bundling to price discriminate are generally small as compared with the gains from using bundling as an entry deterrent, *see* B. Nalebuff, "Bundling as an Entry Barrier" (2004) 119(1) *The Quarterly Journal of Economics,* p. 160.

8. – Tying and Bundling
Thomas Graf and David R. Little

means of price discrimination produces benefits or not, but whether any such benefits outweigh possible restrictive effects on competition and innovation.

3.4. *Tying and Bundling as an Exclusionary Strategy*

So far, we have considered explanations for tying and bundling that are either procompetitive or at least ambiguous in their effects on welfare. However, post-Chicago School economic theory has also shown that tying and bundling practices can be used to increase market power and exclude competitors, to the ultimate detriment of consumers. In order to understand how this is possible, it is necessary to incorporate a dynamic element into the economic analysis. Specifically, one must consider how bundling and tying can affect incentives to enter and expand within the tying market, the tied market, and other adjacent product markets.[21]   **8.22**

We illustrate these theories using a simple set of examples. We assume three separate product markets. Product market A is the tying product market; product market B is the tied product market; product market C is adjacent to A and B. A dominant company may have a strategic incentive to use tying or bundling practices to exclude competition in any of these markets.   **8.23**

Figure 8.1: Tying and Bundling in Adjacent Markets.

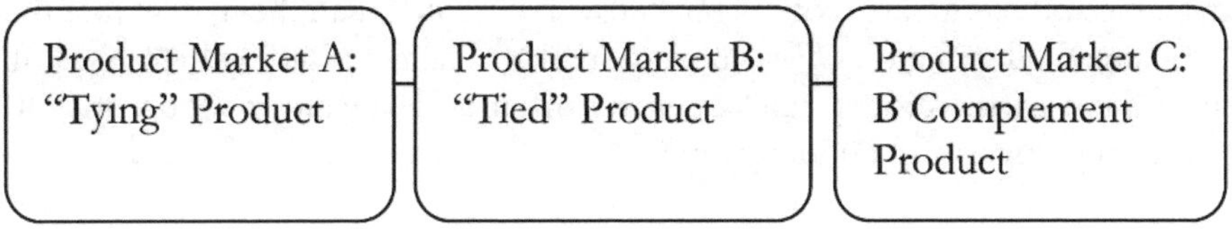

Product Market A: "Tying" Product	Product Market B: "Tied" Product	Product Market C: B Complement Product

3.4.1. Tying to Extend a Monopoly into the Tied Product Market

The classic exclusionary tying theory of harm involves the dominant supplier in market A tying its A product with its B market product to foreclose competition in the market for B. The *Guidance Paper* focuses on this theory of harm.[22] The dominant company uses the tie to link a dominant product with a large customer base to a weaker product. The consumers' high valuation of A stimulates sales   **8.24**

---

[21] D. W. Carlton and M. Waldman, *supra* note 2. E. Elhauge, *supra* note 9, pp. 400, 417–8.

[22] "An undertaking which is dominant in one product market (or more) of a tie or bundle (referred to as the tying market) can harm consumers through tying or bundling by foreclosing the market for the other products that are part of the tie or bundle (referred to as the "tied market" and, indirectly, the "tying market"). *Guidance Paper*, para. 48.

8. – Tying and Bundling
Thomas Graf and David R. Little

of the weaker product . Even if, absent the tie, customers would not otherwise have purchased the second product, they now have an incentive to use it because it has been included in the bundle with a highly-used product. Provided that the total price of the tied offering does not exceed an individual customer's valuation of the package, the customer will also acquire product B from the dominant company. This may be the case even if the customer attributes a low value to the dominant company's B product (or to the B product more generally).

8.25 The strategy may be particularly successful where the tied product market is subject to economies of scale or network effects.[23] Tying may increase scale economies or network effects in favour of the tied product. As the number of users of that second product grows, its costs per user decrease and its utility for users may increase, generating positive network externalities to the benefit of the dominant company. Concurrently, the tie may increase the costs and degrade the relative quality of rival products by diminishing or limiting the size of their networks.

8.26 The dominant company may have an incentive to foreclose competition in the market for tied product B, if tying and tied product are not consumed in fixed proportions. In that case, the dominant company can generate additional rents by expanding its market power to the B market.[24] Economic literature also recognises that dominant firms may have an interest to expand their market power through strategic tying where the target product market is dynamic and has greater commercial growth potential than the market that the firm already dominates.[25] Fast-moving markets characterised by high rates of innovation are therefore prime targets for offensive leveraging conduct, including through tying and bundling practices.

3.4.2. Tying to Protect a Dominant Position in the Tying Market

8.27 A tie can also serve to protect the dominant company's monopoly position in A by creating barriers to entry or expansion in that market. This is conceivable for example in the following circumstances:

---

[23] B. Nalebuff and D. Majerus, *supra* note 10, p. 55.

[24] In *Microsoft*, the Commission rejected Microsoft's claim that it had no incentive to leverage its market power into work group servers *inter alia* by noting that PC and work group server operating systems were not consumed in fixed proportions, Case COMP/37.792 Microsoft ("*Microsoft Decision 2004*"), Commission Decision of 24 March 2004, not yet published, para. 767.

[25] *See, e.g.*, D. W. Carlton & M. Waldman, "The Strategic Use of Tying to Preserve and Create Market Power in Evolving Industries", (2002) 33(2) *The RAND Journal of Economics*, pp. 194–220.

8. – Tying and Bundling
Thomas Graf and David R. Little

- Excluding competition in B may protect the dominant company's position in A where rivals need to establish a position in the B market in order to enter the A market successfully. This may be because customer demand for A depends on the availability of compatible B products or rivals need the additional revenues, or economies of scale or scope achieved through increased sales in the B market in order to finance entry or expansion in the A market.[26] By foreclosing competition in B, the incumbent may be able to exclude entry also in the A market. In Microsoft, the Commission noted that foreclosing competition in media players allowed Microsoft *"to reduce the prospects of successful entry into the client PC operating system market"*.[27] This was because it would deprive rival operating systems of support from compatible cross-platform media players that could play popular content and would therefore make entry in PC operating systems *"harder and less likely to be successful"*.[28]

- This strategy is likely to be most effective where the goods are complementary and therefore demand is positively correlated and where entry into A is costly. As Carlton and Waldman explain, where quick entry into the primary market is easy (*e.g.,* because there are low costs of entry or because it is simple to imitate the incumbent's primary product), the foreclosure strategy is less likely to be successful. Rather, the entrant can quickly release its own primary product A in order to stimulate demand for the B product and defeat the incumbent's foreclosure strategy.

- Another scenario where the tie may protect the dominant company's position in the A market is where rivals need to generate network effects in the B market in order to drive sales of their A product. Again, in this scenario, by tying A and B, the dominant company can protect its position in the A market. In Microsoft, the Commission considered media players to *"have the potential to contribute strategic applications"* because of their *"technological and commercial potential, as well as their attendant indirect network effects"*.[29]

- Excluding competition in product market B can also serve to protect the dominant company's position in product market A where the B product has the potential to evolve into a substitute for A (that is, the A and B product markets could merge) or otherwise erode demand for

---

[26] *See, e.g.,* D. W. Carlton & M. Waldman, "The Strategic Use of Tying to Preserve and Create Market Power in Evolving Industries", (2002) 33(2) *The RAND Journal of Economics,* pp. 194–220.

[27] *Microsoft Decision 2004,* para 974.

[28] *Ibid.,* para. 973.

[29] *Microsoft Decision 2004,* para 973.

8. – Tying and Bundling
Thomas Graf and David R. Little

the dominant company's A product. This was the theory of harm that was developed in the US Microsoft case[30] and also featured in the EU browser tying case. The Commission described this theory in the following terms:

"The large-scale deployment of modern web applications poses a potential threat to the business of vendors of client PC operating systems … Web browsers have the potential to partly replace the underlying client PC operating system(s) as the main tool for accessing and running such web applications. Many existing web applications can be accessed on various web browsers regardless of the underlying client PC operating system. The use of web applications therefore can reduce the dependency of customers on specific operating system platforms for running the applications they require … the Commission took the preliminary view that, through the tying of Internet Explorer to Windows, Microsoft countered the perceived "platform threat" from other web browsers because no application written specifically for Microsoft's web browser Internet Explorer, which is only available on Windows, would give its users an option to switch web browsers or even the underlying operating system."[31]

8.28 Finally, tying and bundling can serve as a means to constrain rivals that have already entered. The strategy can help a dominant company to mitigate losses as compared with a counterfactual in which the dominant company, upon entry of a rival, reverted to an independent sale of the stand-alone products.[32] This is because only some of the entrant's customers will be acquired from the dominant company. The entrant's other customers do not represent lost demand for the dominant company. Rather, they are customers that previously did not purchase at all from the dominant company, such as customers interested in acquiring the B good but with a lower or no demand for the A good, or customers who were not prepared to pay the bundled price. Carbajo, De Meza and Seidman characterised this competition between bundled and unbundled offerings as a form of product differentiation, through which the dominant company wins high-value customers and the entrant picks up

---

[30] *United States v. Microsoft Corp.*, 84 F. Supp. 2d 9 (D.D.C 1999) (Findings of Fact), para. 409, *"To the detriment of consumers, however, Microsoft has done much more than develop innovative browsing software of commendable quality and offer it bundled with Windows at no additional charge. As has been shown, Microsoft also engaged in a concerted series of actions designed to protect the applications barrier to entry, and hence its monopoly power, from a variety of middleware threats, including Netscape's Web browser and Sun's implementation of Java. Many of these actions have harmed consumers in ways that are immediate and easily discernible. They have also caused less direct, but nevertheless serious and far-reaching, consumer harm by distorting competition."*

[31] Case COMP/39.530 *Microsoft (Tying)* (*"Browser Commitment Decision"*) Commission Decision of 16 December 2009, not yet published, paras 57–8.

[32] B. Nalebuff, *supra* note 20, p. 173

8. – Tying and Bundling
Thomas Graf and David R. Little

low-value customers not well-served by the dominant company's bundling strategy.[33]

3.4.3. Tying to Extend a Monopoly into a Third Market

Tying can also be used to extend a monopoly into a market adjacent to the tied product market, where demand for the B and C goods is complementary. By using a tie between dominant product A and product B to increase consumption of B, the dominant company can also stimulate demand for consumption of the complementary product C. This leveraging strategy is therefore most likely to be effective where increased consumption of B will stimulate demand for the dominant company's C product. This could be the case, for example, if the dominant company's B product could only interoperate with its version of the C product. As noted above, a dominant firm may have an interest in engaging in strategic tying conduct where the target product market is dynamic and has greater commercial and growth potential than the market in which the firm currently has market power.[34] Thus, in *Microsoft*, the Commission noted that the media player market was "*a strategic gateway to a range of related markets*", including encoding to software, formal licensing, digital rights management, and content distribution.[35]

8.29

3.5. Concluding Thoughts on Economic Theory

The discussion above illustrates the complexities associated with the economic analysis of tying and bundling cases, which makes antitrust enforcement in this area challenging. Faced with such complexity and ambiguity, some authors have advocated a bright-line approach, with some arguing that tying by firms with market power should be outlawed even where there is no foreclosure of competition[36] and others arguing for a *per se* (or modified *per se*) legality rule in tying cases.[37] The better view is that there cannot be a presumption for or against the harmful nature of tying and bundling practices.[38]

8.30

---

[33] J. Carbajo, D. De Meza, D. Seidman, "A Strategic Motivation for Commodity Bundling" (1990) 38 *Journal of Industrial Economics*, pp. 283–98. *See also* Y. Chen, "Equilibrium Product Bundling," (1997) 70 *The Journal of Business*, pp. 85–103.

[34] *See, e.g.*, D. W. Carlton & M. Waldman (2002), *supra* note 25, 194–220.

[35] *Microsoft Decision 2004*, paras 975–6.

[36] E. Elhauge, *supra* note 9, pp. 397–481.

[37] C. Ahlborn, D. S. Evans and A. J. Padilla, "The Antitrust Economics of Tying: A Farewell to Per Se Illegality" (2004) 49 *Antitrust Bulletin*, pp. 287–341.

[38] *See* K. Kühn, R. Stillman and C. Caffarra, *supra* note 16, p. 106: "[t]*he [one] view essentially relies on a blanket assertion of efficiencies while downplaying the applicability of anti-competitive theories of bundling. The second downplays efficiencies and relies simply on the theoretical possibility of anticompetitive effects in some models to claim anticompetitive effects in specific cases. Both approaches cannot be a basis for sound competition policy towards bundling*".

8. – Tying and Bundling
Thomas Graf and David R. Little

8.31 What can be concluded with some certainty from the economic literature is that tying and bundling are unlikely to result in adverse effects on competition, unless: (1) the firm has market power, (2) the tied or bundled goods are complementary, and (3) there is asymmetry in the product lines of the dominant firm and its rivals that impairs competition between bundled packages.[39] Beyond these initial filters, there is no substitute for a careful and rigorous review of the facts of a particular case to determine benefits or adverse effects of a tying or bundling practice.

III. Legal Analysis of Tying and Bundling Conduct under Article 102

8.32 There have been relatively few Commission decisions prohibiting tying and bundling practices.[40] Prior to the seminal *Microsoft* decision, the Commission

---

[39] *See* K. Kühn, R. Stillman and C. Caffarra, *supra* note 16, p. 106.

[40] There are, however, a much larger number of cases under the EU Merger Regulation in which bundling and tying theory have been discussed. These include: Case COMP/M.3304 *GE/Amersham*, Commission Decision of 21 January 2004; Case COMP/M.2416 *Tetra Laval/Sidel*, Commission Decision of 13 January 2003 (*see also* Case T-502 *Tetra Laval v Commission* [2002] ECR II-4381 and Case C-12/03 P *Commission v Tetra Laval BV* [2005] ECR I-987); Case COMP/M.2220 *General Electric/Honeywell*, Commission Decision of 1 March 2001 (*see also* Case T-210/01 *General Electric v Commission* [2005] ECR II-5575); Case COMP/M.4561 *GE/Smiths Aerospace*, Commission Decision of 23 April 2007; Case COMP/M.4747 *IBM/Telelogic*, Commission Decision of 5 March 2008; Case COMP/M.5125 *Marel/SFS*, Commission Decision of 21 April 2008; Case COMP/M.5264, *Invitrogen/Applied Biosystems*, Commission Decision of 11 November 2008; Case COMP/M.5152 *Posten AB/Post Danmark A/S*, Commission Decision of 21 April 2009; Case COMP/M.5547 *Koninklijke Philips Electronics/Saeco International Group*, Commission Decision of 17 July 2009; Case COMP/M.5529 *Oracle/Sun* Microsystems, Commission Decision of 21 January 2010; Case COMP/M.5732 *Hewlett-Packard/3COM*, Commission Decision of 12 February 2010; Case COMP/M.5771 *CSN/Cimpor*, Commission Decision of 15 February 2010; Case COMP/M.6025 *Ardagh/Impress*, Commission Decision of 29 November 2010; Case COMP/M.5932 *News Corp/BskyB*, Commission Decision of 21 December 2010; Case COMP/M.5999 *Sanofi-Aventis/Genzyme*, Commission Decision of 12 January 2011; Case COMP/M.5984 *Intel/McAfee*, Commission Decision of 26 January 2011; Case COMP/M.6117 *Assa Abloy/Cardo*, Commission Decision of 9 March 2011; Case COMP/M.6128 *Blackstone/Mivisa*, Commission Decision of 25 March 2011; Case COMP/M.6126 *Thermo Fisher/Dionex Corporation*, Commission Decision of 13 May 2011; Case COMP/M.6189 *Imerys/Rio Tinto Talc Business*, Commission Decision of 7 July 2011; Case COMP/M.6292 *Securitas/Niscayah Group*, Commission Decision of 2 August 2011; Case COMP/M.6267 *Volkswagen/MAN*, Commission Decision of 26 September 2011; Case COMP/M.6281 *Microsoft/Skype*, Commission Decision of 7 October 2011; Case COMP/M.6388 *Ecolab/Nalco Holding Company*, Commission Decision of 8 November 2011; Case COMP/M.6393 *Astrium Holding/Vizada Group*, Commission Decision of 30 November 2011; Case COMP/M.6380 *Bridgepoint/Infront Sports and Media*, Commission Decision of 20 December 2011; Case COMP/M.6490 *EADS/Israel Aerospace Industries/JV*, Commission Decision of 16 July 2012.

8. – Tying and Bundling
Thomas Graf and David R. Little

adopted prohibition decisions in six cases involving tying allegations.[41] The Commission brought proceedings to a close informally in four other investigations.[42] Since *Microsoft*, the Commission has considered anticompetitive tying and bundling in a further six investigations. None has resulted in a prohibition decision to date.[43]

While the case law is not extensive, the Commission decisions and Court rulings in this area have clarified the legal framework for analysing tying and   **8.33**

---

[41] Case IV/26.760 *GEMA I,* Commission Decision, Commission Decision of 2 June 1971, OJ 1971 L 134/15; *Hilti Decision 1987 supra* note 3; Case IV/32.318 *London European/Sabena,* Commission Decision of 4 November 1988, OJ 1988 L 317/47; Case IV/31.043 *Tetra Pak II,* Commission Decision of 24 July 1991, OJ 1992 L 72/1; Case IV/34.801 *FAG – Flughafen Frankfurt/Main ('Frankfurt Airport'),* Commission Decision of 14 January 1998, OJ 1998 L 72/30; Case COMP/37.859 *De Post-La Poste,* Commission Decision of 5 December 2001, OJ 2002 L 61/32. We do not include in this total decisions in which the Commission referred variously to "tying" or "tied" sales but where the conduct is more accurately described as a different form of abuse (*e.g.,* loyalty rebates). For example in Case IV/26.918 *European Sugar Industry,* Commission Decision of 2 January 1973, OJ 1973 L 140/17, the Commission concluded Südzucker Verkaufs GmbH had been *"tying its clients through granting fidelity rebates"*. In Case IV.29.491 *Bandengroothandel Frieschebrug BV/NV Nederlandsche Banden-Industrie Michelin,* Commission Decision of 7 October 1981, OJ 1982 L 11/28, the Commission analysed a complex discounting system that had the *"effect of tying, with respect to organizational and commercial matters, independent dealers closely to the undertaking"* (para. 40). In Case COMP/36.041 *Michelin,* the Commission investigated Michelin's use of loyalty-inducing rebates that had the *"object and effect* [of] … *tying* … *dealers to Michelin"* (*see* Commission Decision of 20 June 2001, OJ 2002 L 143/1 para. 227).

[42] IBM entered into informal undertakings in order to address initial Commission concerns relating to "memory bundling" (*see* Fourteenth Report on Competition Policy, pp. 77–79). In *Oliofiat,* the Commission took the view that Fiat Auto *"had been imposing an obligation on its dealers and authorized repairers to use in car servicing, and to sell over the counter, only lubricants and complementary products sold and manufactured by Fiat under the brand name Oliofiat* [which may have] … *impeded access by competing lubricant suppliers to a significant part of the Italian market"* (Seventeenth Report on Competition Policy (1987), pp. 77–78). In *Novo Nordisk,* the Commission resolved through "discussions" allegations that Europe's leading insulin producer had refused to guarantee its "insulin pen" products where customers used third-party compatible components (a form of technical tie). Case *Novo Nordisk,* Twenty-first Report on Competition Policy (1996), para. 62. Bundling concerns also appear to have been raised in relation to AC Nielsen's provision of retail tracking services. The Commission closed its investigation on the strength of informal undertakings entered into by AC Nielsen. *See* Twenty-sixth Report on Competition Policy (1996), para. 64.

[43] Tying was considered in Case COMP/37.761 *Euromax/Imax,* Commission Decision of 25 March 2004, not yet published; Case COMP/39.116 *Coca-Cola,* Commission Decision of 22 June 2005, not yet published; Case COMP/39.511 *IBM Corporation; Microsoft supra* note 31, Browser Commitment Decision; Case COMP/39.230 *Rio Tinto Alcan,* Commission Decision of 20 December 2012, not yet published and Case COMP/39.523 *Slovak Telekom,* Commission Decision of 3 September 2009, not yet published. The Commission settled the cases involving Coca-Cola and Microsoft with commitments (*see Browser Commitment Decision* and Case COMP/39.116 *Coca-Cola*). The complaints against IBM were withdrawn. At the time of writing, commitments had been offered in the Alcan case but the Commission had not yet adopted a final decision. In the Slovak Telekom case tying concerns do not feature in a press release accompanying the publication of the Commission's SO, which suggests that the Commission may have dropped this theory of harm. Tying issues were also considered in three Article 17 sector inquiries: *Retail Banking and Business Insurance, Gas and Electricity,* and *Sale of Sports Rights to Internet and 3G Mobile Operators.*

8. – Tying and Bundling
Thomas Graf and David R. Little

bundling practices.[44] In *Microsoft*, the Commission identified five cumulative conditions for an abusive tie under Article 102 TFEU:[45]

- Dominance of the seller in the market for the tying product;
- Existence of a tied product that is separate from the tying product;
- Coercion to take both the tying and the tied product, *i.e.*, customers are denied a realistic choice of buying the tying product without the tied product;
- Foreclosure of competition that harms consumers; and
- Absence of an objective and proportionate justification for the tie.

8.34 The Court of First Instance confirmed that the five conditions were "*consistent both with Article 82 EC and with the case law*" and followed from "*the very concept of bundling*".[46]

8.35 The five-pronged test establishes an effects-based analysis for tying conduct. Tying by a dominant company is not *per se* illegal under European Union competition law. The *Guidance Paper* acknowledges that tying and bundling practices are commonplace and can provide customers with "*better products or offerings in most cost effective ways.*"[47] It is therefore necessary to show that tying has anticompetitive effects and that there are no objective benefits outweighing these anticompetitive effects. In this analysis, the criteria of dominance, separate products, and coercion serve as initial filters to exclude conduct that is by its nature unlikely to raise competition concerns. If these elements are satisfied, it is necessary to review the competitive effects of the tie and balance any restrictive effects against possible pro-competitive effects.

---

[44] *Hilti Decision of 1987, supra* note 3, Judgment of 1991 and Judgment of 1994; Case IV/31.043 *Tetra Pak I (BTG Licence)* ("*Tetra Pak I Decision 1988*"), Commission Decision of 26 July 1988, OJ 1988 L 272/27; Case IV/31.043 *Tetra Pak II* ("*Tetra Pak II Decision 1991*"), Commission Decision of 24 July 1991, OJ 1992 L 72/1; Case T-83/91 *Tetra Pak International v Commission* ("*Tetra Pak II Judgment 1994*") [1994] ECR II-755; Case C-333/94 P *Tetra Pak International v Commission* ("*Tetra Pak II Judgment 1996*") [1996] ECR I-5951; *Microsoft Decision 2004 supra* note 24; Case T-201/04 Microsoft v Commission ("*Microsoft Judgment 2007*") [2007] ECR II-3601.

[45] *Microsoft Decision 2004, ibid.*, para. 794.

[46] *Microsoft Judgment 2007, supra* note 44, para. 859.

[47] *Guidance Paper supra* note 1, para. 49.

8. – Tying and Bundling
Thomas Graf and David R. Little

1. Dominance of the Seller in the Market for the Tying Product

Dominance is a pre-requisite for any finding of abuse under Article 102 **8.36** TFEU. In the case of a tying infringement, the supplier must hold a dominant position in the market for the tying product.[48] Dominance in the tied market is not required. If there is effective competition in the tying product, customers will have realistic alternatives to the tied offer and no competition law concerns should arise.

There are no special considerations that apply to dominance as such in the **8.37** context of tying compared to other forms of abuse under Article 102 TFEU. We therefore refer generally to the discussion of dominance in Chapter 2 above. That said, the extent of market power over the tying product can be relevant for an assessment of restrictive effects. The greater the dominance, the more likely restrictive effects will be, keeping everything else equal. In addition, the size and importance of the dominant tying market relative to the tied market may also be relevant. If the tying market is small compared to the tied market or a large portion of demand in the tied market is independent of the tying market, then restrictive effects may be less likely. Thus, in *Microsoft*, the theory of harm advanced against Microsoft's tying of Windows Media Player to Windows rested to an important extent on the "ubiquity" of the Windows operating system that Microsoft was leveraging in favour of Windows Media Player.[49]

2. Existence of a Separate Tied Product

A crucial distinction within a tying analysis is between those components that **8.38** form part of an indivisible whole and those that may be used together but which are nevertheless distinct and separate. This "distinct product" or "two product" test acts as a screen for unproblematic cases.[50] Unless the dominant company's conduct involves two distinct products, no tying or bundling claim

---

[48] *Hilti Decision 1987 supra* note 3 para. 74, "*The ability to carry out its illegal [tying] policies stems from its power on the markets for Hilti-compatible cartridge strips and nail guns (where its market position is strongest and the barriers to entry are highest) and aims at reinforcing its dominance on the Hilti-compatible nail market (where it is potentially more vulnerable to new competition).*"

[49] *Microsoft Decision 2004 supra* note 24, paras 833, 843–48.

[50] A. Renda, "Treatment of Exclusionary Abuses Under Article 82 of the EC Treaty: Comments on the European Commission's Guidance Paper", *CEPS Task Force Reports*, September 10, 2009, pp. 58–9.

8. – Tying and Bundling
Thomas Graf and David R. Little

can arise.[51] Where two components in fact form a single, integrated product, a tying claim must fail.[52]

2.1.   Approach of the Commission and the Courts to Separate Product Analysis

8.39   In *Microsoft*, the General Court made clear that "*the distinctness of products for the purpose of an analysis under Article 82 EC has to be assessed by reference to customer demand*".[53] Accordingly, the *Guidance Paper* states that two products are distinct for the purpose of a tying analysis if, "*in the absence of tying or bundling, a substantial number of customers would purchase or would have purchased the tying product without also buying the tied product from the same supplier, thereby allowing stand-alone production for both the tying and the tied product*".[54] The *Guidance Paper* however does not explain how the existence (or absence) of such separate demand is to be established. The Commission and the Courts have considered different factors in this regard.

2.1.1.   Presence of Independent Suppliers

8.40   In older cases, such as *Hilti* and *Tetra Pak II*, the Commission and the Courts focused on the existence of independent suppliers for the tied product as evidence for the distinctiveness of the two products.[55] However, this criterion cannot in itself be determinative. The absence of independent suppliers may in fact be the consequence of the tying's foreclosure. Conversely, the existence of independent suppliers does not necessarily imply that tied and tying product are separate, notably if the independent suppliers serve a different market. For example, the existence of independent suppliers of car spare parts does not imply that cars are tied products. In *Microsoft*, the Commission and the General Court therefore relied on a combination of different factors to establish the distinctiveness of the products at issue.

---

[51] *Microsoft Decision 2004 supra* note 24, para. 800 ("*The existence of distinct products is the second precondition for tying. Products that are not distinct cannot be tied in a way that is contrary to Article 82*").

[52] Case T-86/95 *Compagnie générale maritime and others v Commission* [2002] ECR II-1011, para. 159.

[53] *Microsoft Judgment 2007 supra* note 44, para. 917.

[54] *Guidance Paper supra* note 1, para. 51. Virtually the same formulation is also used in the Commission's Guidelines on Vertical Restraints, Commission Guidelines on Vertical Restraints OJ 2010 C 130/1, para. 215. In *Microsoft*, the Commission formulated the test as to whether there is separate demand for the tied product, *Microsoft Decision 2004*, para. 803. The difference is in our view largely semantic. What matters is ultimately whether there is demand to acquire tying and tied product from separate sources.

[55] *Hilti Judgment 1991 supra* note 3, para. 67; *Tetra Pak II Judgment 1994 supra* note 44, para. 82; *Tetra Pak II Judgment 1996 supra* note 44, paras 36–7.

8. – Tying and Bundling
Thomas Graf and David R. Little

2.1.2. Functionality of Products

One element that both the Commission and the General Court emphasised in **8.41**
Microsoft was the significant difference in functionality between tying and tied
product, with the the General court noting that *"it is clear from the description of
those products [...] that client PC operating systems and streaming media players clearly
differ in terms of functionalities"*.[56]

2.1.3. Customer Conduct

Another important indicator is the conduct of customers prior to the tie, **8.42**
notably whether customers bought the tying product alone or in combination
with alternatives to the tied product before the tying started. In *Microsoft*, the
Commission showed that Microsoft's Windows Media Player prior to the tie
was generally considered to be of inferior quality and *"unpopular with customers
because it did not work very well"*.[57] The Commission also pointed to users that
sought to remove Windows Media Player from their systems.[58]

2.1.4. The Dominant Company's Conduct

The dominant company's own commercial conduct may also provide an **8.43**
indication for the nature of the products at issue. In *Microsoft*, the Court
and the Commission noted that Microsoft treated Windows Media Player
as a separate product from Windows, including through distinct promotion,
distinct licensing conditions, and the offer of standalone versions of Windows
Media Player for other operating systems.[59]

2.1.5. Rationale for the Tie

The Court and the Commission in *Microsoft* also considered Microsoft's **8.44**
rationale for tying Windows Media Player. The Court noted that Microsoft
had conceded that there were no technical reasons for its tying and pointed to
internal Microsoft documents that showed that the tie *"was primarily designed*

---

[56] *Microsoft Judgment 2007 supra* note 44, para. 926.
[57] *Microsoft Decision 2004 supra* note 24, para. 819.
[58] *Ibid.*, para. 807.
[59] *Microsoft Judgment 2007 supra* note 44, paras 928–30.

8. – Tying and Bundling
Thomas Graf and David R. Little

to make Windows Media Player more competitive with RealPlayer", Windows Media Player's principal rival.[60]

2.1.6. Commercial Usage

8.45 While Article 102(d) TFEU refers to the imposition of obligations that "*by their nature or according to commercial usage, have no connection*", the Courts in past cases have dismissed arguments based on "natural links" or "commercial usage". In *Tetra Pak II*, the Court of Justice noted that the list of abusive practices under Article 102 TFEU is not exhaustive and that therefore a tie of two products may constitute an abuse absent an objective justification, even if the two products are linked by nature or commercial usage.[61] In *Microsoft*, the General Court reiterated that natural links or commercial usage do not necessarily exclude a finding of separate products.[62] It also pointed out that "*it is difficult to speak of commercial usage in an industry that is 95% controlled by Microsoft*".[63]

2.1.7. Complementarity of Product

8.46 The case law also makes clear that complementarity of two products does not necessarily indicate that they form a single whole. Two products are complementary if their demand is positively correlated such that customers that buy product A may also want a complementary product B. It does not follow, however, that customers will always want to buy the two complementary products from the same supplier. In fact, as seen economic theory indicates that foreclosure effects are more likely where products are complementary. In *Hilti*, the General Court dismissed an argument that Hilti nail gun cartridges were useless without compatible nails and that therefore the two products were not separate. The Court noted that to accept Hilti's argument would have been "*tantamount to permitting producers of nail guns to exclude the use of consumables other than their own branded products in their tools*".[64] Similarly, in *Microsoft*, the General Court dismissed Microsoft's argument that customers wanted operating systems with streaming media players because it "*amounts to contending that*

---

[60] *Microsoft Judgment 2007 supra* note 44, paras 936-7.
[61] *Tetra Pak II Judgment 1996 supra* note 44, para. 37.
[62] *Microsoft Judgment 2007 supra* note 44, paras 938–42.
[63] *Ibid.*, para. 921.
[64] *Hilti Judgment 1991 supra* note 3, para. 68. *See also Microsoft Judgment 2007 supra* note 44, para. 921.

8. – Tying and Bundling
Thomas Graf and David R. Little

complementary products cannot constitute separate products".[65] What matters for separate product analysis is therefore not whether customers that buy one product will also want to buy a complementary product (*e.g.*, tennis rackets and tennis balls) but whether there is demand to acquire the two complementary products from separate sources.

It follows from a review of the case law on tying, that there is no single determinative criterion for establishing whether two products are separate for the purpose of a tying analysis. As the General Court summarised in *Microsoft*, "*a series of factors*" are relevant, including "*the nature and technical features of the products concerned, the facts observed on the market, the history of the development of the products concerned and also [the dominant firm's] commercial practice.*"[66]   **8.47**

2.2. *Separate Products Test and Market Definition*

Past case law shows that the two products test is distinct from market definition. Thus, in *Microsoft*, the Commission engaged in an independent review of the two product criterion that was separate from its finding that PC operating systems and media players constituted two separate relevant markets. Indeed, the question of whether two components constitute separate products for the purpose of tying analysis cannot be conflated with market definition. The existence of separate relevant markets for two components does not necessarily imply that an integrated product consisting of the two components constitutes a tie of two separate products. This is because the two components may be supplied at the same time in several relevant markets, in some of which the components may qualify as separate products, while on others they may be part of an integrated whole. Such asymmetries can arise in a number of scenarios, include the following: **8.48**

2.2.1. Different Manufacturing or Distribution Levels

The manufacturing and distribution of an integrated product can take place over several steps in a chain. In such circumstances, the outcome of the two products test may be different for different levels in the chain. For example, a car wheel and a motor will be components of a single integrated product at the level of car sales to end-consumers. But at the level of components   **8.49**

---

[65] *Hilti Judgment 1991 supra* note 3, para. 68. *See also Microsoft Judgment 2007 supra* note 44, para. 921.
[66] *Ibid.*, para. 925.

8. – Tying and Bundling
Thomas Graf and David R. Little

supplies to car manufacturers the two would likely be viewed as separate products. Thus, the existence of a separate market for components (or independent suppliers) at one level is not determinative for the separate products test at the other. In *Microsoft*, the focus was on supply of operating systems and media players to PC OEMs. The Commission and the Court therefore rejected Microsoft's argument that end-users wanted an "*out-of-the-box*" experience of an integrated systems. This was because PC OEMs could act as "*intermediaries*" to create an "*out-of-the-box*" experience for users through the combination of operating system and third-party media players.[67] It follows, that the separate products test must take place with reference to the correct level of production and distribution that is at issue in a given case.

2.2.2. Generalists v Specialists

8.50 In many industries, both generalists and specialists may offer their products or services (for example daily newspapers and specialised magazines). Such specialists may be found to form part of the same market as the generalists or to constitute separate relevant markets. But a finding that specialists form distinct markets does not in itself imply that the generalist that covers services or products of different specialists is engaging in tying of separate products, as opposed to offering a single integrated product. For example, specialised sports magazines may be in a separate market from daily newspapers, but that does not make the sports section of the newspaper a separate product. The definition of separate markets for specialists answers the question whether specialists are a substitute for the generalist services. But it does not answer the question whether a generalist service should be subdivided for the purpose of tying analysis into separate products. In fact, if generalist services are considered to form a separate relevant market, that may be indicative that such services offer a genuine integration function that customers value.

2.2.3. Aftermarkets

8.51 Secondary markets, or "aftermarkets", such as markets for consumables or after sales maintenance services, raise complex issues of both market definition and application of the separate products test. The definition of a separate aftermarket for individual components or the presence of independent component suppliers on such an aftermarket does not imply that the supply

---

[67] *Hilti Judgment 1991 supra* note 3, para. 68. *See also Microsoft Judgment 2007 supra* note 44, para. 964 and 1155.

8. – Tying and Bundling
Thomas Graf and David R. Little

of the original integrated equipment in the primary market constitutes tying of separate products.

Another question that arises in connection with aftermarkets is whether the **8.52** supply of original equipment and sale of aftermarket products should be viewed as forming part of a single whole or two distinct activities. Both the Commission and the Courts recognise that to address this question it is necessary to consider the interaction between primary market and secondary aftermarket.[68] The key question in this respect is whether competition in the primary market constrains the actions of the original equipment supplier in the aftermarket.

The principles governing this issue have been developed mainly in connection **8.53** with the supply of printers and printer cartridges.[69] The Commission and the General Court have confirmed that printer and cartridges should be treated as a single whole, based on four main factors (i) customers have information on total lifecycle costs; (ii) it is likely that customers make informed choices based on total costs; (iii) it is likely that a sufficient number of customers would switch primary products if there were price increases on the secondary market; and (iv) such an adjustment would take place within a reasonable period of time.[70]

In the *Luxury Watches* case, the Commission held that luxury watches and spare **8.54** parts for such watches constituted a single market because (i) existing customers could switch to other watches and (ii) new customers might not chose the watch in question in the event of an increase in repair prices.[71] The General Court annulled the decision on the facts, but it confirmed the analytical principles applied by the Commission. In particular, the Court's review suggests that it considered the threat from switching of existing customers and the loss of new customers to be alternative reasons to exclude the existence of two distinct

---

[68] Commission Notice on the definition of relevant market for the purposes of Community competition law ("*Market Definition Notice*"), OJ 1997 C 372/5; Case *Pelikan/Kyocera*, in Twenty-fifth Report on Competition Policy (1995) pp. 41–2, and 140; , pp. 41–2, and 140; Commission decision in *Info-Lab/Ricoh*, DG COMP Competition Policy Newsletter (1999), No. 1, pp. 35–7; Case T-427/08 *Confédération européenne des associations d'horlogers-réparateurs v Commission* ("*CEAHR*") [2010] ECR II-05865; Case T-296/09 *EFIM*, not yet reported. The Commission and the Courts address this issue sometimes under the heading of market definition and sometimes as part of dominance analysis. As a matter of substance, it should not matter at what point in the analysis the question is considered, as long as it is in fact properly reviewed.

[69] And more recently in the *Luxury Watches* case, Case T-427/08 *supra* note 68.

[70] Case *Info-Lab/Ricoh supra* note 68, and *EFIM*, *supra* note 68.

[71] *See* Case T-427/08, *supra* note 68.

8. – Tying and Bundling
Thomas Graf and David R. Little

markets. Even if existing customers may not be able to switch, the threat from losing new customers in the primary market may be sufficient on its own to constrain the behaviour of the original equipment supplier in the aftermarket.

2.3.   Relevant Moment in Time

8.55   Supply and demand may evolve over time as a result for example of changes in customer habits or technical developments. This may affect the qualification of whether two products are distinct or form part of an integrated whole. But it is equally possible that demand for sourcing the two products separately would remain stable over time, absent the tying by a dominant company, because for example there are benefits in selecting best-of-breed components. The General Court in *Microsoft* therefore noted that the separate products test must be conducted by reference "*to the factual and technical situation that existed at the time when [...] the impugned conduct became harmful*".[72] The intuition behind their conclusion is that the dominant company should not pre-empt how demand and markets evolve through a restrictive tying practice.

2.4.   Overlap between the "Separate Products" Test and the Review of "Objective Justifications"

8.56   There is some overlap between the two product criterion and the review of objective justifications for a tie. Thus, in *Tetra Pak II*, the Commission seems to have considered the distinct products question as part of its review of objective justifications,[73] while the General Court in *Microsoft* discussed possible technical reasons for the tie as part of the separate products test. The stage at which questions pertaining to the separate products test are considered is not purely academic because the dominant company bears the burden of establishing objective justifications.

8.57   In this hierarchy of analytical steps, the separate product criterion should serve as an initial, but important filter, to exclude practices that are unlikely to harm competition. If the combination of two components creates sufficiently substantial integration value, such that acquiring the components separately from different sources is not a good substitute for obtaining the integrated product, then the two complements should be considered to form

---

[72] *Microsoft Judgment 2007, supra* note 44, para. 914.
[73] *Tetra Pak II Judgment 1996 supra* note 44, para. 119.

8. – Tying and Bundling
Thomas Graf and David R. Little

part of a single whole and the analysis should end. If, on the other hand, the integration value is not sufficiently high to exclude demand for acquiring the components from separate sources then the two components qualify as separate products. But this does not preclude the possibility to establish objective justifications for the tie, although the dominant company will bear the burden of proving such efficiencies.

3. Coercion

Coercion defines the nature of the anticompetitive conduct that characterises tying and bundling practices.[74] If customers are not forced or pressured to take the two products together then there cannot be a tie and there should be no adverse impact on competition.[75] The essence of the coercion inherent in a tie consists in denying choice: Customers wishing to acquire the dominant tying product are refused a realistic choice of obtaining the tying product without also taking the tied product.[76] In *Microsoft*, the General Court noted that the notion of denying choice expressed *"in different words the concept that bundling assumes that consumers are compelled, directly or indirectly, to accept supplementary obligations such as those referred to in Article [102(d)]"*.[77] Coercion can take different forms.

8.58

---

[74] For the US *see, e.g., Suburban Propane v Proctor Gas*, 953 F.2d 780,788 (2d Cir. 1992); *Stephen Jay Photography v Olan Mills*, 903 F. 2d 988,991 (4th Cir. 1990); *Unijax v Champion Intl.*, 683 F.2d 678, 685 ('2nd Cir. 1982); *Bob Maxfield v American Motors*, 637 F.2d 1033, 1037 (5th Cir.), cert. denied, 454 U.S. 860 (1981); *Ungar v Dunkin Donuts*,531 F.2d 1211, 1219, (3rd cir), cert. denied, 429 U.S 823 (1976); *Belliston v Texaco*, 455 F.2d 175, 184 (10th Cir.) cert denied, 408 U.S 928 (1972); *Montvale Management Group v The Snowshoe Co.*, 1984 -1 Trade Cas. ¶ 65,990 at 68, 375 (N.D.W.V. 1984).

[75] Some authors have argued that there is no need for a coercion criterion, *see* H. Schmidt, *Competition Law, Innovation and Antitrust: An Analysis of Tying and Technological Integration* (Edward Elgar 2009). The author argues that *"it is misleading to call coercion a requirement for tying: rather, coercion is what tying does – it is the abuse"*. See also, N. Economides and I. Lianos, "The Elusive Antitrust Standard on Bundling in Europe and in the United States in the Aftermath of the Microsoft Cases" (2009) 76 *Antitrust Law Journal*, p. 519: *"We argue that the coercion criterion should be abandoned because it offers little information in terms of anti-competitive effects and consumer harm"*. But such arguments do not explain how tying conduct should be identified or why it would raise competition law concerns absent an element of coercion.

[76] *Hilti Decision 1987, supra* note 3, para. 75 the Commission found that *"these [tying] policies leave the consumer with no choice over the source of his nails and as such abusively exploit him"*. In *Tetra Pak II Judgment 1994*, the General Court noted that: *"where an undertaking in a dominant position directly or indirectly ties its customers by an exclusive supply obligation, that constitutes an abuse since it deprives the customer of the ability to choose his sources of supply and denies other producers access to the market"*.

[77] *Microsoft Judgment 2007, supra* note 44, para. 864.

8. – Tying and Bundling
Thomas Graf and David R. Little

3.1. *Refusal to Supply the Tying Product without the Tied Product*

8.59   A dominant company can engage in a tie by refusing to make the dominant tying product available without the tied product. This can take the form of technical commingling as in the *Microsoft* case or a *de facto* refusal to supply the tying product without the tied product. The difference between a tie and a refusal to supply case is that the refusal in the case of a tie is directed at customers for which the dominant company and its rivals compete. It is not a case of a request from the rival for supply by the dominant company. Tying is therefore an instance of customer foreclosure, while an abusive refusal to supply represents a special form of input foreclosure.

3.2. *Contractual Obligations*

8.60   Contractual coercion occurs where the terms of the contract or license under which the dominant company supplies the tying product also require the customer to acquire the tied product from the dominant company,[78] or where the dominant company will not guarantee the tying product unless the customer also takes the tied product.[79] In *Tetra Pak II*, the Commission suggested that contractual tying may be particularly difficult to justify.[80]

3.3. *Financial Coercion*

8.61   Financial coercion takes place where the dominant company prices a stand-alone version of the tying product at such a high level compared to the bundle of tying and tied product that it becomes commercially unrealistic for customers to purchase the standalone version. The *Discussion Paper* noted that *"mixed bundling (commercial tying) is an indirect measure to achieve the same result as through contractual tying by inducing customers to purchase the tied product through granting bonuses, rebates, discounts or any other commercial advantage"*.[81] The question of the level at which a pricing practice becomes equivalent to a tie is discussed further below. The dividing line between mixed bundling and other forms of

---

[78] *Tetra Pak II Judgment 1994 supra* note 44, para. 137.

[79] Case *Novo Nordisk*, *supra* note 42, para. 62. *See also Hilti Decision 1987*, *supra* note 44, para. 79.

[80] *Tetra Pak II Decision 1991*, *supra* note 44, para. 119: *"If there is genuinely no technical alternative, such an obligation is unnecessary. However, if such an alternative does exist, the choice should be left to the user."*

[81] *Discussion Paper*, *supra* note 2, para. 182. Tirole has advocated applying a unified test to all tying, pure bundling, and mixed bundling practices. *See* J. Tirole, "The Analysis of Tying Cases: A Primer" (2005) 1(1) *Competition Policy International Journal*, pp. 1–25. Whereas Tirole advocates a unified predation test, Economides and Lianos advocate a unified foreclosure test. *See* N. Economides and I. Lianos, *supra* note 75, pp. 41 *et seq.*

8. – Tying and Bundling
Thomas Graf and David R. Little

packaged sales is somewhat blurred. For example, while *Hilti* is thought of as a classic "tying" case, the tying was achieved not only through technical means but also through a system of inducive discounts to customers. The rebates offered in *Tetra Pak II* and *Michelin II* also had a tying effect.[82] Similar conceptual difficulties arise in respect of the decisions in *Napier Brown-British Sugar*,[83] and *DePoste-La Poste*.[84]

3.4. *No Requirement that Customers use the Tied Good*

The General Court explained in *Microsoft* that the concept of coercion does **8.62** not require that customers are compelled to use the tied product. The only relevant question at this stage of the analysis is whether they are compelled to acquire the product. The question whether such coercion results in customers using the tied product at the expense of rival third-party products is a question of the effects of the tie.[85]

3.5. *No Requirement that Customers Pay a Separate Price for the Tied Good*

The *Microsoft* decision makes clear that it is not necessary for a tie to show **8.63** that the customer is forced to pay for the tied product. In *Microsoft*, Microsoft argued that end users were not required to pay anything extra for the media player functionality in Windows and therefore there was no "coercion".[86] The argument did not persuade the Court of First Instance, which held that: "*it does not follow from either Article 82(d) EC or the case law on bundling that consumers must necessarily pay a certain price for the tied product in order for it to be concluded that they are subject to supplementary obligations within the meaning of that provision*"[87] The Court of First Instance cautioned further that simply because there is no separate price indicated for the tied good, this does not mean it is free. The price of the tied good may have been internalised in the price of the tying good.[88]

---

[82] R. Whish, *Competition Law* (7th Ed., Oxford, Oxford University Press, 2012), p. 737.

[83] *Napier Brown, supra* note 3.

[84] *De Post-La Poste, supra* note 41.

[85] *Microsoft Judgment 2007, supra* note 44, paras 951, 953, and 970–71.

[86] J-F. Bellis, *The Commission's Microsoft Tying Case – Implications for Innovation Throughout the High-Technology Sector,* Van Bael & Bellis, 2007, pp. 10.

[87] *Microsoft Judgment 2007, supra* note 44, para. 969.

[88] *Microsoft Judgment 2007, supra* note 44, para. 968.

8. – Tying and Bundling
Thomas Graf and David R. Little

4. Restrictive Effect on Competition for the Tied Product

8.64 A tie is only abusive if it results in anticompetitive foreclosure. That is the tie must be capable and likely to foreclose equally efficient rivals and harm consumers. [89] The concept of anticompetitive foreclosure, the evidence used to demonstrate foreclosure, and the degree of foreclosure required have all been considered in earlier Chapters of this book. This section focuses instead on foreclosure effects in tying and bundling cases. We consider, in particular, the extent to which the *Guidance Paper's* discussion of anticompetitive foreclosure in the context of tying practices reflects the economic theory and the prevailing case law.

8.65 The *Guidance Paper* deals with mixed bundling practices separately from tying practices. This implies that the discussion of tying and "bundling" refers to pure bundling, *i.e.,* where the packaged goods are not available separately.[90] In keeping with the economics-grounded, effects-based approach of the *Guidance Paper*, the discussion of possible anti-competitive foreclosure effects recalls many of the theories of harm identified in the economic literature (described above):

- Tying may lead to anticompetitive effects in either the tied market or the tying market, or both at the same time. The *Guidance Paper* notes that even when the aim of the tying practice is to protect the dominant undertaking's position in the tying market, this is done indirectly through foreclosing the tied market.

- The *Guidance Paper* observes that tying may be used to prevent a substitution effect towards the tied product in circumstances where the two products are inputs to a production process and the dominant company seeks to increase the price of the tying product.

- The *Guidance Paper* notes that if the prices the dominant undertaking can charge in the tying market are regulated, tying may allow the dominant undertaking to raise prices in the tied market in order to

---

[89] Specifically, "*a situation where effective access of actual or potential competitors to supplies or markets is hampered or eliminated as a result of the conduct of the dominant undertaking whereby the dominant undertaking is likely to be in a position to profitably increase prices to the detriment of consumers*". See *Guidance Paper, supra* note 1, para. 19. As paragraph 11 of the *Guidance Paper* clarifies: "*the power to maintain prices above the competitive level and is used as shorthand for the various ways in which the parameters of competition – such as prices, output, innovation, the variety or quality of goods or services – can be influenced to the advantage of the dominant undertaking and to the detriment of consumers*".

[90] A. Renda, *supra* note 50, p. 61.

8. – Tying and Bundling
Thomas Graf and David R. Little

compensate for the loss of revenue caused by the regulation in the tying market. The ability of companies in regulated markets to exploit their privileged position in order to cross-subsidise competition in a second market remains a major concern under EU law. The theory of cross-subsidisation from regulated markets has been explored recently, *inter alia*, in *Post Danmark*[91] and *Telefonica*,[92] albeit in the context of margin squeeze rather than tying.

- The *Guidance Paper* identifies the economic theory that tying can be used to stifle competition in the tied market and thereby deprive (potential or actual) rival suppliers of the tying product of alternative complements to their product.

- The *Guidance Paper* also identifies factors that are relevant in assessing whether foreclosure is likely. In addition to general factors that are relevant for any foreclosure analysis, such as (1) the extent of the company's dominant position, (2) presence of economies of scale, network effects or other barriers to entry, (3) the position of competitors and customers, (4) data on market development, and (5) internal documents,[93] the *Guidance Paper* also discusses factors that are more specific to a review of tying practices.

- The Guidance Paper notes that foreclosure may be greater if the tying practice is established on a lasting basis, for example, through technical tying.[94] That said, there is a serious question whether there should be a *priori* a higher presumption of anticompetitive foreclosure effects in the case of technical integration, compared to other forms of packaging, such as contractual tie-ins or *de facto* ties. To the contrary, some authors have argued that in the case of technical integration and product design measures competition law intervention should be subject to a higher threshold. For example, Bo Vesterdorf, the former president of the General Court, has suggested that intervention in product design measures is only warranted if these measures produce no value at all and only serve to harm competitors.[95] This is consistent

---

[91] Case C-209/10 *Post Danmark v Konkurrencerådet*, not yet reported.

[92] Case T-336/07 *Telefónica v Commission*, not yet reported.

[93] *Guidance Paper*, para. 20

[94] *Ibid.*, para. 53.

[95] Bo Vesterdorf, *"Article 82 EC: Where do we stand after the Microsoft judgement?"*, (2008) Global Antitrust Review, 1: *"as long as the dominant undertaking limits itself to improving the quality of its products – and therefore enhance their competitiveness – and as long as it does not use action – without any value to their own products or productivity – simply and only to interfere with the competitors' development opportunities on the market, a technical development or improvement of their products is to the advantage of competition and thus to the advantage of consumers"*.

8. – Tying and Bundling
Thomas Graf and David R. Little

with the findings in *Microsoft* where the General Court concluded that there were no technical reasons for Microsoft's tying and that Microsoft had tied Windows Media Player as a strategic measure directed against RealNetworks, the main competitor of Windows Media Player.[96] Irrespective of the legal standard that should apply to product design measures, a competitive analysis of such measures will at least have to take into account that technical integration may produce pro-competitive benefits that are not available through other forms of packaging and will need to accord some discretion and flexibility to the company under investigation on how to develop its products. Otherwise, there is a risk that competition law intervention may chill product development and innovation.

8.66 Other relevant factors that the *Guidance Paper* cites for foreclosure analysis in tying cases, include the number of different products that are included in a bundle[97] and whether the tie leaves insufficient customers to sustain competitors of the tied product.[98] The Guidance Paper's list is not exhaustive. An assessment of possible foreclosure effects will have to take into account all relevant circumstances of an individual case. As noted above, elements that may also be significant in such an assessment include the importance of sales of the tying product relative to the tied product and the degree of complementarity between the tying and the tied product. A further relevant consideration is whether (equally efficient) competitors have viable counter-strategies to react to the tie. Thus, in *Microsoft*, an important question was whether downloading offered a viable alternative to competing media players. The Commission and the General Court concluded that downloading could not compensate for the foreclosure of the PC OEM channel that resulted from Microsoft's tying.[99]

5. Coercion and Foreclosure in Mixed Bundling

8.67 In the case of mixed bundling practices, the dominant company ostensibly offers the dominant tying product on a stand-alone basis. But it offers a package of the tying product and tied product at a discount compared to

---

[96] Case T-201/04 *Microsoft* [2007] ECR II-3601, paras 936–937.
[97] *Guidance Paper*, para. 54.
[98] *Ibid.*, para. 55.
[99] Case T-201/04 *Microsoft* [2007] ECR II-3601, paras 1049–52.

8. – Tying and Bundling
Thomas Graf and David R. Little

the sum of their stand-alone prices. The key question in such a case is at what level a package discount is equivalent to a tie that is liable to foreclose competition.

Older cases suggest that the Commission and the EU Courts in the past con- **8.68** sidered any discount or at least any "significant" discount for packages including dominant products to amount to a *per se* abuse:

- In *Hoffmann-La Roche*, the Court of Justice considered that bundled rebates applied by Roche across a range of vitamins were abusive because they created "*a strong incentive to purchasers to let Roche alone supply the whole or part of their requirements of vitamins or of certain groups of vitamins*".[100]

- In *Digital*, the Commission took the view that a significant financial "incentive" to buy the package could suffice for a tying case. In its settlement with Digital, the Commission accepted a maximum package discount of no more than 10 per cent of the sum of the price for each component in the package.[101]

- In *Coca-Cola*, the Commission raised concerns with regard to discounts offered only to retailers that purchased non-cola soft drinks together with cola-flavoured soft drinks. The Commission explained that "*rebates linked to the purchase of several products belonging to separate markets were [...] contrary to Article [102]*".[102] As a result, Coca-Cola agreed not to condition its discounts on the purchase of both cola-flavoured soft drinks and other soft drinks.

- In *Tetra Pak II*, the Commission decision upheld by the Courts required that "*[...] no customer may enjoy, in any form whatever, and whether for equipment or for cartons, discounts or more favourable payment terms not justified by an objective reciprocal concession. Thus, discounts on cartons should be granted solely according to the quantity of each order, and orders for different types of carton may not be aggregated for that purpose*".[103]

- In *De Post-La Poste*, the Commission held that making a preferential tariff for general postal services conditional upon customers

---

[100] Case 85/76 *Hoffmann-La Roche v Commission* ("*Hoffmann-La Roche*") [1979] ECR 461, paras 110–111.
[101] Case *Digital Undertaking*, Twenty-seventh Report on Competition Policy (1997), p. 153. *See also* M. Dolmans and V. Pickering, "*The 1997 Digital Undertaking*" (1998) 19(2) *European Competition Law Review*, pp. 108–15.
[102] *Coca-Cola Italia Undertaking*, Nineteenth Report on Competition Policy (1989), para. 50
[103] *Tetra Pak II Decision 1991*, *supra* note 44, para. 174.

8. – Tying and Bundling
Thomas Graf and David R. Little

subscribing to business-to-business postal services constituted an abuse of a dominant position.[104]

8.69 More recently, the Commission suggested in the *Guidance Paper* that it would assess bundled discount systems based on an "incremental price" analysis. According to the *Guidance Paper*, a multi-product rebate is anticompetitive if it is so large that equally efficient competitors offering only some of the components cannot viably compete against the discounted bundle. The nature of the equally efficient competitor test differs according to whether the dominant company's rivals are capable of replicating the dominant company's bundle or not:

- Where rivals are incapable of replicating the bundle, the Commission will test whether the incremental price of the tied product in the bundle covers the dominant company's long-run average incremental costs ("LRAIC") from including the product in the bundle. This is done by fully allocating the discount to the list price of the tied product. In the case of a multi-product bundle, the full discount is allocated to each of the tied products. If the resulting net price is above the LRAIC of the tied product, the Commission considers that an equally efficient competitor selling the stand-alone product would be able to compete with the dominant undertaking.[105] Where the incremental price is below the LRAIC, however, this may prevent expansion or entry by an equally efficient rival.[106]

- Where the evidence suggests that rivals are capable of replicating the bundle, the *Guidance Paper* indicates that the Commission will apply a different test. The Commission views this as bundle-to-bundle competition and will therefore assess whether the price of the bundle as a whole is predatory – *i.e.,* below average variable costs of the bundle – rather than limiting the analysis to the costs of the tied product.[107]

8.70 The approach proposed in the *Guidance Paper* has been referred to as a "modified predatory pricing rule", similar to that applied by the Ninth Circuit in *Cascade Health Solutions v. PeaceHealth* and by the UK Office of Fair Trading in

---

[104] *De Post-La Poste, supra* note 41.
[105] *Guidance Paper, supra* note 1, para. 60.
[106] *Ibid.*
[107] *Ibidem,* para. 61.

8. – Tying and Bundling
Thomas Graf and David R. Little

BSkyB.[108] This approach had been advocated by a number of authors[109] and represents a more differentiated form of analysis compared to past case law. It remains to be seen however whether and to what extent it can and will be applied in practice.

6. Objective Justification

As noted above, combining the sale of several products may generate a num-   **8.71**
ber of procompetitive effects, creating economies of scope, and generating efficiencies in distribution or production.[110] Reflecting this consideration, the review of tying and bundling practices under Article 102 TFEU considers whether such practices generate countervailing benefits that outweigh the purported harms to the competitive process. The dominant company bears in principle the burden of proving the existence of possible justifications for its conduct. Once the company has established such proof it is for the Commission to show that the justification does not outweigh the identified restrictions.[111]

The *Guidance Paper* identifies two broad forms of conduct that may be open   **8.72**
to justification, which it describes as conduct that is "*objectively necessary*" and conduct that produces "*substantial efficiencies*".[112] "Objective necessity" in the terminology of the Guidance Paper refers to external benefits that arise outside the dominant company, such as health and safety benefits.[113] "Efficiencies" refers to internal benefits that arise within the company's business and that are passed-on to consumers, such as cost savings or improvements in product quality.[114]

---

[108] *Cascade Health Solutions v PeaceHealth*, 515 F.3d 883 (9th Cir. 2008); Case CA98/20/2002 *BSkyB Investigation: Alleged Infringement of the Chapter II Prohibition*, Decision of the Director General of Fair Trading of 17 December 2002. *See also*, R. O'Donoghue and A. J. Padilla, *The Law and Economics of Article 82 EC* (Oxford, Hart Publishing, 2006), pp. 506–507.

[109] J. Tirole, *supra* note 81, p. 2. ("*This paper argues that tying is likely to be systematically harmful to consumers when it is a tool of predatory action, and should not be treated as a separate offense*"); J. Langer, Tying and Bundling as a Leveraging Concern Under EC Competition Law (Kluwer Law International, 2007), pp. 170–71; *See also* R. O'Donoghue and A. J. Padilla, *supra* note 108, pp. 505–07.

[110] K. Kühn, R. Stillman and C. Caffarra, *supra* note 16, pp. 103.

[111] Case T-201/04 *Microsoft* [2007] ECR II-3601, para. 1144; Case C-95/04 *British Airways* [2007] ECR I-2331, para. 69; Case T-321/05 *AstraZeneca* [2010] ECR II-2805, para. 686; *Guidance Paper*, para. 31.

[112] *Guidance Paper*, para. 28.

[113] *Ibid.*, para 29.

[114] *Guidance Paper*, para. 30.

8. – Tying and Bundling
Thomas Graf and David R. Little

8.73 In addition to external benefits and internal efficiencies, the Courts have recognized more generally that a dominant company has in principle the right to protect its *"own commercial interests"*.[115] This implies that the dominant company may not necessarily have to show that its conduct generates direct tangible benefits that accrue to others. It may be sufficient to demonstrate that preventing the company from engaging in the conduct at issue would represent a disproportionate interference with the company's own legitimate interests. In the context of tying practices, this may be relevant in particular in the case of objections against product integration and product design. Because product design is an aspect of competition on the merits, an observation that design measures foreclose competitors cannot necessarily suffice for a finding of abuse. This does not imply that product design decisions are always immune from competition law intervention. But a company's legitimate interest in retaining discretion and flexibility in developing its products should be taken into account in a balance of all relevant interests involved.

8.74 In the following sections, we discuss in more detail the type of justifications that have been discussed in past case law in connection with tying practices.

6.1. External Benefits

8.75 The *Guidance Paper*'s reference to "objective necessity" to describe external benefits seems somewhat inaccurate, because "objective necessity" is one of the legal criteria for assessing any possible justification, regardless of whether it is based on "external" or "internal" benefits. As discussed further below, the dominant company must show that its conduct is necessary to achieve the claimed benefits. The distinction between "external" and "internal" benefits is also not that clear cut. For example, a combined sale of two products to ensure their proper operation may have both "external" benefits by making the product safer for users and at the same time "internal" benefits by enhancing the quality of the product and protecting the company's brand. That said, the Commission and the Courts have traditionally been more skeptical as a matter of principle about attempts to invoke public interest grounds, such as health and safety, as justifications.

8.76 In *Hilti*, the dominant undertaking claimed that the use of third-party nails with its nail guns raised safety concerns. Hilti argued that improper operator

---

[115] Case 27/76 *United Brands* [1978] ECR 207, para 69; Case T-65/89 *BPB Industries* [1993] ECR II-389, para. 69; Case T-321/05 *AstraZeneca* [2010] ECR II-2805, para. 672.

8. – Tying and Bundling
Thomas Graf and David R. Little

training, substandard cartridges and substandard nails could all raise safety concerns, and that adequate safety could only be assured through production and quality control of a whole system comprising guns, cartridges and nails. Producers of any of the component parts could not *"through the production of an individual item of the system guarantee its integrity"*.[116] However, the Commission was not persuaded, noting that Hilti had not raised the safety concerns until after the Commission had received a complaint from a competitor, and had failed to write to customers or competitors expressing its safety concerns.[117] The Commission's reasoning was endorsed by the Court of First Instance. The Court held that if Hilti had genuine safety concerns, the company could have taken alternative measures, for example, by asking the relevant national authorities to declare that using third party nails and strips with Hilti tools was dangerous. The Court of First Instance emphasised that it was *"not the task of an undertaking in a dominant position to take steps on its own initiative to eliminate products which, rightly or wrongly, it regards as dangerous or at least as inferior in quality to its own products"*.[118] Ultimately, neither the Commission nor the Court accepted that Hilti's actions were rooted in genuine safety concerns. Rather, they viewed them as a means for Hilti to perpetuate its dominant position faced with competitive substitutes.[119]

The same logic underpinned the Commission's decision and the judgment of **8.77** the Court of First Instance in *Tetra Pak II*. In that case, the dominant company had invoked public health concerns, in order to justify the marketing of complete carton-packaging systems under which the customer was required to use only Tetra Pak cartons with Tetra Pak machines. Tetra Pak's objective justification case conflated the public health ground of justification with the "legitimate commercial interest" ground that had been accepted in principle in *United Brands*.[120] Tetra Pak thus argued that the marketing of complete packaging systems through the use of tied sales was objectively justified *"by the concern to protect public health __and thus its reputation__ through exclusive control of the*

---

[116] *Hilti Decision 1987, supra* note 3.

[117] Nalebuff notes that the facts of Hilti are consistent with the Chicago School theory. Specifically, the nail market was competitive, while Hilti held a legal monopoly by virtue of its patent protected explosive cartridge technology. Chicago School theory would dictate that Hilti could have raised the same profits that it raised through its tying strategy by selling the nail guns at the monopoly price and selling its nails at marginal cost. *See* B. Nalebuff and D. Majerus, *supra* note 10, p. 21.

[118] *See Hilti Judgment 1991, supra* note 3, para. 118, recalled at para. 138 of *Tetra Pak II Judgment 1994, supra* note 44.

[119] *See also* A. Albors-Llorens, pp. 1727, 1740 and 1743.

[120] Case 27/76 *United Brands and United Brands Continentaal v Commission ("United Brands")* [1978] ECR 207; Case IV/32.279 *BBI/Boosey and Hawkes*, Commission Decision of 29 July 1987, OJ 1987 L 286/36; and Case T-65/89 *BPB Industries and British Gypsum v Commission ("BPB Industries")* [1993] ECR II-389.

8. – Tying and Bundling
Thomas Graf and David R. Little

entire packaging process" (emphasis added). The dominant company argued that cartons were more sophisticated than traditional containers such as bottles and that this "*entail[ed] a significant risk of technical errors liable to cause serious problems in vulnerable sectors of the population*".[121] The Court rejected Tetra Pak's arguments. The tied-sale clauses (and other clauses analysed in the Commission's prohibition decision) "*went beyond their ostensible purpose*". The Court considered them unreasonable in the context of protecting public health and exceeding the recognised rights of an undertaking to protect its commercial interests.

8.78 Other grounds of justification that relate to external factors include the lawful exercise of property rights. The argument in such cases is that the tie is justified by property rights of the dominant company in the tied product.[122] If the dominant company has intellectual property over the tied product, this is not only an issue of justification but also effect, because exclusive rights over the complement may rule out restrictive effects from the tie. Thus, in *Hilti* and *Tetra Pak II*, the Court noted that a third party should be free to sell complements for a dominant product, "*unless in doing so it infringes a competitor's intellectual property*".[123] In *Windsurfing*, the Commission confirmed by the Court, considered whether third-party surfboards infringed Windsurfing's patents, but concluded that this was not the case.[124]

6.2. Internal Efficiencies

8.79 The *Guidance Paper* requires that, in order to serve as a defence to a tying infringement, efficiencies must satisfy the following cumulative conditions:[125]

- The efficiencies are certain or likely: the tying has already or is likely to generate the alleged efficiencies.
- The tie must be necessary to achieve the efficiencies: there must be no less restrictive means to achieve the efficiencies. This is

---

[121] *Tetra Pak II Judgment 1994*, *supra* note 44, paras 125–26.

[122] *See Van den Bergh Foods*, in which the dominant undertaking argued that the exclusive dealing conditions were necessary to protect its property (*i.e.*, the ice-cream freezers) from being used by competing ice-cream suppliers. Cases IV/34.073, IV/34.395 and IV/35.436 *Van den Bergh Foods*, Commission Decision of 11 March 1998, OJ 1998 L 246/1, paras 269–70; Case T-65/98 *Van den Bergh Foods v Commission* ("*Van den Bergh Foods*") [2003] ECR II-4653, paras 164–66.

[123] *Hilti Judgment 1991*, para. 68, *Hilti Judgment 1992*, paras 11–16, *Tetra Pak II Judgment 1991*, para. 83, *Tetra Pak II Judgment 1994*, para. 36.

[124] Case 193/83 *Windsurfing v Commission* [1978] ECR 611.

[125] *Guidance Paper*, *supra* note 1, para. 30.

8. – Tying and Bundling
Thomas Graf and David R. Little

a well-established limiting principle, referred to in the *Microsoft* decision.[126]

- The efficiencies offset the anticipated foreclosure effects: likely efficiencies brought about by the tying outweigh any likely negative effects on competition and consumer welfare in the affected markets.

- No absolute elimination of competition: tying should not eliminate all or most sources of actual or potential competition.

The *Guidance Paper*'s general discussion of the efficiencies defence identifies **8.80** technical improvements in the quality of goods, or a reduction in the cost of production or distribution as examples of possible efficiencies.[127] In its specific discussion of efficiencies in the context of tying, the *Guidance Paper* indicates that it will consider:[128]

- Whether the tying generates savings in production or distribution to the benefit of customers.

- Whether the tying reduces transaction costs for customers that would otherwise be forced to buy the components separately.

- Whether the tying produces "*substantial savings*" on packaging and distribution costs for suppliers.

- Whether combining two independent products into a new, single product might enhance a supplier's ability to bring that product to market to the benefit of consumers.

- Whether the tying allows the supplier to pass on efficiencies arising from producing the bundle or purchasing "*large quantities of the tied product*".

The *Guidance Paper*'s discussion of tying does not expressly mention quality **8.81** improvements, but its general discussion of justifications identifies quality improvements as a justification.[129] More generally, the list of possible justifications is not exhaustive. It remains open to the dominant company to invoke other legitimate considerations that may justify a tie.

---

[126] *See Microsoft Decision 2004, supra* note 24, paras 963–67.

[127] *Guidance Paper, supra* note 1, para. 30(1).

[128] *Guidance Paper, supra* note 1, para. 62.

[129] The Commission's Vertical Restraints Guidelines expressly recognize that in the case of tying and bundling arrangements an "*efficiency may exist where tying helps to ensure a certain uniformity and quality standardisation*", Commission Notice – Guidelines on Vertical Restraints, OJ 2000 C 291/1, para. 222.

8. – Tying and Bundling
Thomas Graf and David R. Little

8.82 No new tying prohibition decisions have been adopted since the introduction of the *Guidance Paper*. Accordingly, there has not yet been an opportunity for applying the efficiencies test as set out in the *Guidance Paper*. However, although prior to the publication of the *Guidance Paper*, there had been no explicit provision for an Article 102 efficiencies defence akin to that available under Article 101,[130] the case law that precedes the *Guidance Paper* may nevertheless provide some interpretative assistance:

- Even if the dominant undertaking is able to show that a combination of two products generates efficiencies, it may have to explain why that combination must come from the dominant company.[131] Thus in *Microsoft*, while the Commission acknowledged that pre-installation of a media player lowered customers' transaction costs by providing an "out of the box" software solution, the Commission noted that this function was provided by PC OEMs. There was therefore no reason why Microsoft should reserve to itself the role of providing the packaged solution.[132]

- The claimed efficiencies must relate specifically to the conduct that is at issue. Thus, in *Microsoft*, the Commission and the General Court dismissed arguments of Microsoft based on product integration, because the Commission was not challenging the ability of Microsoft to sell an integrated version of its products that combined a media player with Windows. The Commission objected that Microsoft did not offer an unbundled version of Windows alongside the integrated version. Microsoft was unable to provide a valid justification for its failure to provide such an option.[133]

---

[130] J. Modrall, C. Schaberg and J. Soloway, "*Article 82 Exclusionary Conduct Discussion Paper: An Interview with Michael Albers and Luc Peeperkorn*", 2006.

[131] *See, e.g., Microsoft Judgment 2007, supra* note 44, para. 1150.

[132] *Microsoft Decision 2004, supra* note 24, paras 956–58. The Commission also rejected the justification that tying the media player to the operating system reduced transaction costs that would result from the need to maintain a separate distribution system for the tied media player, and that these savings were then passed on to customers who in turn saved transaction costs related to the second purchasing act of selecting and installing a separate media player. However, the argument failed, since the cost of software distribution for the undertaking is insignificant, and it was highly important that consumers were able to choose their preferred software applications.

[133] Case T-201/04 *Microsoft* [2007] ECR II-3601, paras 1146–1149. *See* also United States v. Microsoft, in which Microsoft attempted to argue that the tying of Internet Explorer with Windows provided Windows customers with the benefit of browser functionality. The argument was rejected because it failed to explain why it was necessary for Microsoft to deny customers (OEMs or consumers) the choice combining operating system and browser if they so wished. As the District Court surmised, "*if consumers genuinely prefer a version of Windows bundled with Internet Explorer, they do not have to be forced to take it; they can choose it in the market*". United States v. Microsoft Corp., 84 F. Supp. 2d 9 (D.D.C 1999) (Findings of Fact), para. 191.

8. – Tying and Bundling
Thomas Graf and David R. Little

6.3. Indispensability and Proportionality

With respect to both external benefits and internal efficiencies, the Commission will assess whether the conduct in question is necessary and proportionate to the aims pursued. The tying practice must be the least restrictive means to achieve the substantiated benefits.[134] The proportionality test is the final and central filter in the application of Article 102 TFEU to the conduct of dominant undertakings.[135] It allows the Commission and Courts to look at the company's tying conduct in the round and weigh up the competing legitimate interests in allowing or prohibiting the tie. The proportionality test comprises three limbs:

8.83

- *Effectiveness.* First, the dominant undertaking must show that the tie effectively allows the firm to achieve the claimed benefits.

- *Necessity.* Secondly, the dominant company must show that the tie is necessary to achieve the claimed benefits, *i.e.*, it must show that the denial of customer choice through a tying practice is the only way for the demonstrated benefits to be achieved. Thus, in *Hilti*, while the Commission did not exclude that Hilti might hold genuine concerns about the safety of using competitors' products with its own, the Commission did not consider that this necessitated recourse to a tying practice coupled with a selective distribution system.[136] Hilti had failed to take expected, less restrictive steps that a company with such safety concerns could be expected to take, such as the notification of national authorities responsible for product safety.[137]

- *The balance of interests.* The final limb of the proportionality test requires the dominant company to demonstrate that the balance of interest militates in favour of the tie. There is a presumption that the interests of preserving undistorted competition outweigh the interests of

---

[134] Advocate General Kirschner in Case T-51/89 *Tetra Pak Rausing v Commission* ("*Tetra Pak I*") [1990] ECR II-309, para. 68 (*"the undertaking in a dominant position may act in a profit-oriented way, strive through its efforts to improve its market position and pursue its legitimate interests: but in so doing it may employ only such methods as are necessary to pursue those legitimate aims. In particular it may not act in a way which, foreseeable, will limit competition more than necessary."*).

[135] M. Dolmans and T. Graf, "Analysis of Tying Under Article 82 EC: The European Commission's Microsoft Decision in Perspective" (2004) 27(2) *World Competition*, p. 236.

[136] Before the Commission, Hilti conceded that its overall conduct was not the least restrictive means to address the safety concerns it had expressed, but argued that the selective distribution system facilitated by its tying practice was the least restrictive mechanism. *See Hilti Decision 1987, supra* note 3, para. 88.

[137] *Ibid.*, paras 89–93. *Hilti Judgment 1991, supra* note 3, paras 115–8.

8. – Tying and Bundling
Thomas Graf and David R. Little

the dominant company.[138] The dominant company must therefore demonstrate that it does not reserve for itself the benefits realised from the tying practice, but passes on these benefits to consumers. The balance of interests is likely to be most exhaustive in borderline cases, possibly involving technical ties, where demonstrable efficiencies must be balanced against the detrimental impact on innovation and consumer choice.

IV.   Concluding Remarks

8.84   Despite the relatively limited number of tying cases under EU competition law, the development of decisional practice and case law from early tying cases in *Hilti* and *Tetra Pak II* to the *Microsoft* case suggests that the Commission and the EU Courts have embraced an effects-based approach to tying analysis that requires a detailed and careful review of the specific facts and economic conditions of a particular case. In such an assessment, the five legal conditions that case law has identified as requirements for a finding of a tying abuse (dominance, separate products, coercion, foreclosure, and absence of objective justification) serve as successive filters to exclude practices that are unlikely to harm competition and consumers.

---

[138] Advocate General Cosmas in Case C-344/98 *Masterfoods Ltd v HB Ice Cream Ltd* [2000] ECR I-11369, para. 101.

9. – Abusive Discrimination
Anne Layne-Farrar, Alice Setari and Paul Stuart

Abusive Discrimination

Anne Layne-Farrar, Alice Setari and Paul Stuart

I. Introduction

The notion of "abusive discrimination" encompasses a wide range of con- **9.1**
duct that may be enacted by a company holding a dominant position. Broadly
speaking, abusive discrimination may be distinguished between exclusionary
and non-exclusionary discrimination.[1]

---

[1] For an overview of articles, *see* P. Akman, "To Abuse, or Not to Abuse: Discrimination Between Consumers"
(2007) 32 *European Law Review*, pp. 499–502; J. B. Baker, "Competitive Price Discrimination: The Exercise of Market
Power Without Anticompetitive Effects (Comment on Klein and Wiley)" (2003) 70(3) *Antitrust Law Journal*,
pp. 643–54; W. Bishop, "Price Discrimination Under Article 86: Political Economy in the European Court" (1981)
44(3) *Modern Law Review*, pp. 282–95; S. Carbonneau and others, "Price Discrimination and Market Power" (2004)
Emory Economics, p. 413; N. Economides, "The Incentive for Non-Price Discrimination by an Input Monopolist"
(1998) 16(3) *International Journal of Industrial Organization*, pp. 271–84; A. S. Edlin, M. Epelbaum and W. P. Heller,
"Is Perfect Price Discrimination Really Efficient: Welfare and Existence in General Equilibrium" (1988) 66 *Econometrica*,
pp. 897–922; T. P. Gehrig and R. Stenbacka, "Price Discrimination, Competition and Antitrust", Swedish
Competition Authority, *Pros and Cons Series: The Pros and Cons of Price Discrimination*, November 2005, D. Geradin, *Pricing
Abuses by Essential Patent Holders in a Standard-Setting Context: A View from Europe*, paper prepared for the Conference at
University of Virginia on Remedies for Dominant Firm Misconduct, June 4–5, 2008, D. Geradin and N. Petit, "Price
Discrimination Under EC Competition Law: Another Antitrust Doctrine in Search of Limiting Principles?" (2006)
2(3) *Journal of Competition Law and Economics*, pp. 479–531; D. Geradin and N. Petit, "Price Discrimination under
EC Competition Law: The Need for a case-by-case Approach", *GCLC Working Paper Series*, Working Paper 07/05,
2007, p. 7; D. Gerard, "Price Discrimination Under Article 82(c) EC: Clearing up the Ambiguities", *GCLC Research
Papers on Article 82*, July 2005, p. 122; B. Klein and J. S. Wiley, "Competitive Price Discrimination as an Antitrust
Justification for Intellectual Property Refusals to Deal" (2003) 70(29) *Antitrust Law Journal*, pp. 599–613;
S. Martinez Lage and R. Allendesalazar, "Community Policy on Discriminatory Pricing: A Practitioner's Perspective",
in C-D. Ehlermann and I. Atanasiu (Eds.), *European Competition Law Annual 2003: What Is Abuse of Dominant Position?*
(Oxford, Hart Publishing, 2006), p. 341; R. O'Donoghue and J. Temple Lang, "Defining Legitimate Competition:
How to Clarify Pricing Abuses under Article 82 EC" (2002) 26(1) *Fordham International Law Journal*, pp. 83–162;
J. Temple Lang, "Anticompetitive Non-Pricing Abuses Under European and National Antitrust Law", in
B. E. Hawk (Ed.), *Fordham Competition Law Institute: International Antitrust Law and Policy 2003* (New York, Juris
Publishing, 2004), pp. 235–340; J. Temple Lang, "*Article 82 EC – The Problems and The Solution*", FEEM Working
Paper No. 65.2009 presented at the Conference "Ten years of Mercato Concorrenza Regole", Milan, June 30,
2009, J. Temple Lang, "Rebates, Price Discrimination and Refusal to Contract – The Commission's Guidance
Paper on Article 82" (2010) *Europaraettslig Tidskrift*, pp. 47–78; J. Temple Lang, "The Requirement for a
Commission Notice on the Concept of Abuse Under Article 82 EC", *CEPS Special Reports*, December 10, 2008;
M. E. Levine, "Price Discrimination Without Market Power" (2002) 19(1) *Yale Journal of Regulation*, pp. 1–36;

9. – Abusive Discrimination
Anne Layne-Farrar, Alice Setari and Paul Stuart

9.2 Exclusionary discrimination refers to conduct enacted by the dominant company to protect its market position in the market where it holds a dominant position (*e.g.*, by granting discounts and/or rebates resulting in "discriminatory" prices being charged to its customers with a view to foreclosing competitors, so-called "primary line discrimination"), or to favour its own integrated activities in a related market (*e.g.*, by applying to its subsidiaries active in a downstream market more favourable terms and conditions for the input supplied than those applied to third party downstream competitors, so-called "secondary line discrimination"). Non-exclusionary discrimination is also a form of secondary line discrimination between third party customers or suppliers of the dominant company, resulting in these customers/suppliers being put at a competitive disadvantage with one another.

9.3 A specific instance of abusive discrimination is contemplated by Article 102(c) TFEU, according to which: "[a]*ny abuse by one or more undertakings of a dominant position within the internal market or in a substantial part of it shall be prohibited as incompatible with the internal market in so far as it may affect trade between Member States. Such abuse may, in particular, consist in: … (c) applying dissimilar conditions to equivalent transactions with other trading parties, thereby placing them at a competitive disadvantage.*"[2] The vast majority of commentators are in agreement that Article 102(c) TFEU deals with secondary line discrimination between the dominant company's customers or suppliers, while conduct consisting of exclusionary discrimination should fall within the scope of Article 102(b) TFEU, which prohibits abuses aimed at "*limiting production, markets or technical development to the prejudice of consumers.*"[3]

R. O'Donoghue and A. J. Padilla, *The Law and Economics of Article 82 EC* (Oxford, Hart Publishing, 2006); D. Ridyard, "Exclusionary Pricing and Price Discrimination Abuses Under Article 82 – An Economic Analysis" (2002) 23(6) *European Competition Law Review*, pp. 286–303; R. Schmalensee, "Output and Welfare Implications of Monopolistic Third-Degree Price Discrimination" (1981) 71(1) *American Economic Review*, pp. 242–47; G. J. Stigler, *A Theory of Price* (4th Ed., New York, MacMillan, 1987); Swedish Competition Authority, "The Pros and Cons of Price Discrimination", Swedish Competition Authority, *Pros and Cons Series*, November 2005; H. R. Varian, "Price Discrimination and Social Welfare" (1985) 75(4) *American Economic Review*, pp. 870–75; H. R. Varian, "Price Discrimination", in R. Schmalensee and R. Willig (Eds.), *Handbook of Industrial Organization* (Amsterdam, North-Holland, 1989), Vol. I, Ch. 10, pp. 597–654; M. Waelbroeck, "Price Discrimination and Rebate Policies Under EU Competition Law", in B. E. Hawk (Ed.), *Fordham Competition Law Institute: International Antitrust Law and Policy 1995 & Policy* (New York, Juris Publishing, 1996), Ch. 10, pp. 147–60; L. Zanon di Valgiurata, "Price Discrimination Under Article 86 of the E. E. C. Treaty: The United Brands Case" (1982) 31(1) *International and Comparative Law Quarterly*, pp. 36–58; and S. Evrard and others, "Recent Developments in the United States, EU and Asia at the Intersection of Antitrust and Patent Law" (2009) 3(2) *CPI Antitrust Chronicle*.

[2] Consolidated version of the Treaty on the Functioning of the European Union, OJ 2010 C 83/49.

[3] *Ibid.*

9. – Abusive Discrimination
Anne Layne-Farrar, Alice Setari and Paul Stuart

The difference is not merely formalistic, but one of substance.[4] This reflects **9.4** the fact that, as discussed in more detail in Section III below, the test to be applied to determine whether conduct is abusive because it constitutes exclusionary or non-exclusionary discrimination is (or at least should be) different. Arguably, and in line with the principles enshrined in the *Guidance Paper*,[5] exclusionary discrimination should be considered as abusive, *inter alia*, if it is likely to foreclose the dominant company's competitors, while non-exclusionary discrimination should be considered in breach of Article 102(c) TFEU if it puts the dominant company's customers or trading partners at a competitive disadvantage. However, the Commission's decisional practice and the European courts' case law are far from clear on this key distinction. Both the Commission and the European courts have been inconsistent in the legal test applied to assess the legality of discriminatory conduct by dominant companies.

The remainder of this chapter delves into the details of these issues. **9.5** Section II discusses the constituent element common to all types of abusive discrimination (whether exclusionary or not) potentially falling within the scope of Article 102 TFEU, namely the existence of an unjustified discrimination. Section III discusses the additional constituent elements of the abuse of exclusionary and non-exclusionary discrimination in light of the Commission's decisional practice and the European courts' case law, as well as specific issues that are likely to arise when dealing with this type of conduct. Section IV provides an overview of the economics of discrimination, discussing, in particular, the various forms of price discrimination from an economic viewpoint, the conditions for price discrimination to occur, and the welfare effects of price discrimination. Section V outlines certain considerations *de jure condendo* on the future of abusive discrimination under EU law.

II. Unjustified Discrimination

The first constituent element of any discrimination abuse, whether exclusion- **9.6** ary or not, is not surprisingly the existence of an unjustified discrimination.

---

[4] *See* D. Geradin and N. Petit, "Price Discrimination Under EC Competition Law: Another Antitrust Doctrine in Search of Limiting Principles?", (2006) 2(3) *Journal of Competition Law and Economics*, pp. 479–531.

[5] Guidance on the Commission's enforcement priorities in applying Article 82 of the EC Treaty to abusive exclusionary conduct by dominant undertakings ("*Guidance Paper*"), OJ 2009 C 45/7.

9. – Abusive Discrimination
Anne Layne-Farrar, Alice Setari and Paul Stuart

An unlawful discrimination, in turn, arises in the following two scenarios: (1) when a dominant company applies dissimilar conditions to equivalent transactions without any objective justification; or (2) when a dominant company applies equivalent conditions to different transactions without any objective justification.[6]

9.7 In either scenario, the following (mainly factual) questions must be answered to determine whether an unlawful discrimination actually occurred: (1) are the transactions at hand equivalent; (2) are the conditions applied to these transactions equivalent; and (3) if different conditions are applied to similar transactions (or similar conditions are applied to different transactions), is the differential treatment objectively justified?

9.8 It must be noted from the outset that, while conceptually different in practice, as will emerge from the discussion in the remainder of this Section, the factual analysis to be carried out to answer the question whether two or more transactions are comparable and whether any differential treatment is objectively justified is essentially the same. This reflects the fact that the determination whether, on the facts, two transactions are equivalent is carried out by reference to essentially the same factors (*e.g.*, products involved, costs, commercial context, customer-related factors, timing) that come into consideration when determining whether the differential treatment between two transactions is objectively justified. Conversely, the determination of whether equal or different conditions are applied to the relevant transactions by and large constitutes a separate question of fact, the answer to which typically depends on the applicable terms and conditions to the relevant transactions.

9.9 We next discuss how the Commission and the European courts have addressed each of the above questions when assessing the existence of an unjustified discrimination in previous cases.

1. Equivalent Transactions

9.10 The starting point of any unjustified discrimination assessment is whether the transactions at stake are to be considered as "equivalent". When carrying

---

[6] The Court of Justice extended the notion of price discrimination to situations in which similar conditions are applied to different transactions. *See* Case 13/63 *Italian Republic v Commission* [1963] ECR 165.

9. – Abusive Discrimination
Anne Layne-Farrar, Alice Setari and Paul Stuart

out this analysis, both the Commission and the European courts have taken into account a number of factors such as product characteristics, costs, commercial context, customer related factors, and timing, each of which may play a different role in the final determination of the equivalence between transactions, depending on the circumstances of the case.

1.1. Same or Similar Products

The fact that transactions involve the same or similar products (and/or services) is a strong indicator of their equivalence. **9.11**

By way of example, in *Chiquita*,[7] the Commission found that United Brands, **9.12** the dominant company in the sale of bananas in a substantial part of the European Union, violated Article 102 TFEU by charging a different price for the sale of its branded "Chiquita" bananas depending on the Member State where the customers were established and carried out their business as ripeners and/or distributors. The Court of Justice upheld the Commission's decision in *United Brands*[8] and found that the transactions with various customers located in different Member States were "equivalent" given that the products supplied to each such customer were essentially the same. The fact that the products sold, Chiquita bananas, had the same geographic origin, belonged to the same variety, had been brought to the same degree of ripening, and were of similar quality led the Commission and the Court of Justice to conclude that the transactions under examination were equivalent.[9]

In *Aéroports de Paris*,[10] the Commission found that the fees charged to ground- **9.13** handling companies by Aéroports de Paris (airport manager at the Orly and Roissy-Charles-de-Gaulle airports) as consideration for its airport management services provided and for the licence to carry out ground-handling services, differed depending on whether these companies provided the relevant services for third parties or were air carriers providing these services to their own operations (so-called "self-handling").[11] Since the services provided by Aéroports de Paris to all ground-handlers were essentially the same, the

---

[7] Case IV/26.699 *Chiquita*, Commission Decision of 17 December 1975, OJ 1976 L 95/1.
[8] Case 27/76 *United Brands and United Brands Continentaal v Commission* ("*United Brands*") [1978] ECR 207.
[9] *Ibid.*, paras 204 and 225.
[10] Case IV/35.613 *Alpha Flight Services/Aéroports de Paris* ("*Aéroports de Paris Decision 1998*"), Commission Decision of 11 June 1998, OJ 1998 L 230/10.
[11] *Ibid.*

9. – Abusive Discrimination
Anne Layne-Farrar, Alice Setari and Paul Stuart

Commission concluded that the two sets of transactions at stake (*i.e.*, the transactions between Aéroports de Paris and ground-handlers for third parties, on the one hand, and the transactions between Aéroports de Paris and self-handlers, on the other), were equivalent. To reach this conclusion, the Commission also relied on the fact that there were no factual or legal differences between providers of ground-handling services for third parties and providers of self-handling services and/or the activities that these providers carried out. The Commission ultimately took the view that the different fees charged by Aéroports de Paris to ground-handlers for third parties and to self-handlers were not objectively justified.[12]

9.14 The equivalence of the services provided by the dominant company also played an important role in the assessment of the equivalence of the transactions at hand in *Clearstream*.[13] The case concerned an alleged discrimination by Clearstream, the central security depositary in Germany, which provided clearing, settlement, and custody services for securities, and which held a dominant position in the market for primary clearing and settlement services for securities issued according to German law. The Commission and the Court of First Instance found that Clearstream engaged, *inter alia*, in discriminatory pricing by charging its customer Euroclear Bank SA higher prices than those charged to other similarly situated customers for primary clearing and settlement services that were in essence the same as those provided to such customers. As discussed in more detail in this Subsection, when assessing the equivalence of the transactions at stake, the Commission and the Court of First Instance also took other factors into account, including whether providing the relevant services to Euroclear Bank SA entailed higher costs for Clearstream than providing these services to the other customers.[14]

9.15 *Scandlines*[15] is a case in which the Commission took the view that the services the complainant claimed to be equivalent were in fact different, and that the discrimination allegation was therefore unfounded. The Commission

---

[12] The Commission Decision was upheld by the European courts in Cases T-128/98 *Aéroports de Paris v Commission* ("*Aéroports de Paris Judgment 2000*") [2000] ECR II-3929 and C-82/01 P *Aéroports de Paris v Commission* ("*Aéroports de Paris Judgment 2002*") [2002] ECR I-9297.

[13] Case COMP/38.096 *Clearstream* ("*Clearstream Decision 2004*"), Commission Decision of 2 June 2004, not yet published; Case T-301/04 *Clearstream v Commission* ("*Clearstream Judgment 2009*") [2009] ECR II-3155.

[14] *Clearstream Decision 2004, supra* note 13, para. 311; *Clearstream Judgment 2009, supra* note 13, para. 190, *supra* note 13.

[15] Case COMP/36.568 *Scandlines Sverige v Port of Helsingborg* ("*Scandlines Decision 2004*"), Commission Decision of 23 July 2004, not yet published.

9. – Abusive Discrimination
Anne Layne-Farrar, Alice Setari and Paul Stuart

examined the complaint lodged by ferry operator Scandlines Sverige AB alleging that Helsingborgs Hamn AB, the company responsible for running the port of Helsingborg in Sweden, infringed Article 102 TFEU by levying excessive and discriminatory charges for services provided to ferry operators.[16] According to Scandlines Sverige AB, *inter alia*, the prices charged by Helsingborgs Hamn AB to ferry operators were discriminatory when compared to the charges applied to certain cargo operators. The Commission rejected Scandlines Sverige AB's complaint on the ground that, while the seaside facilities provided by the port to both ferries and cargo vessels were the same, the landside facilities provided to each of them differed considerably. Cargo vessels used cranes and other equipment for loading/unloading cargo, while ferries used ramps and gangways for embarking/disembarking vehicles and passengers. It was therefore not possible to compare the level of the total port charges charged respectively to the ferry operators and the cargo operators meaningfully due to the differences in the underlying service provided, which resulted in the non-equivalence of the relevant transactions.[17]

It is, however, possible that transactions involving equivalent or similar products, at least in terms of characteristics, appearance, and functionality, may not be considered as equivalent due to other factors, including the different consumer perception of these products. The typical example is that of branded versus non-branded products, which are often similar when applying the above parameters, but which the customers do not perceive as equivalent due to the presence or not of the brand. Transactions involving branded goods may therefore not be considered as equivalent to transactions involving similar/substitutable non-branded goods (even regardless of the fact that branded goods may be of a higher quality than non-branded goods, which would constitute an additional differentiating factor). **9.16**

Similarly, the fact that a product constitutes a new product that the dominant company is in the process of launching on the market should arguably constitute a sufficient ground to justify the dominant company charging a different price to its customers for this new product from the price that it used to charge to its customers for its existing products. **9.17**

---

[16] Case COMP/36.568 *Scandlines Sverige v Port of Helsingborg* ("*Scandlines Decision 2004*"), Commission Decision of 23 July 2004, not yet published.

[17] *Ibid.*, paras 251–53.

9. – Abusive Discrimination
Anne Layne-Farrar, Alice Setari and Paul Stuart

1.2.   Similar Costs

9.18 Establishing that two or more transactions involve substitutable, similar, or
even the same, products or services may not be sufficient to conclude that
these transactions are equivalent (while the fact that they involve different
or not substitutable products or services may be enough to conclude that
these transactions are not equivalent). Other factors may have to be taken into
account, including the costs incurred by the dominant company to perform
the transactions.

9.19 As mentioned, in *Clearstream*, after establishing that the services provided by
Clearstream to each of Euroclear Bank SA and some of its other customers
were comparable, the Commission and the Court of First Instance went on to
analyse whether the relevant transactions could nonetheless be distinguished
(or, which is the same, whether the differential treatment could be justified)
based on the different costs possibly incurred by Clearstream when providing
its services to Euroclear Bank SA and to other customers. These differences
in cost might be due, in turn, to the volume of the services provided and/or
to the time of the day (day-time, as opposed to night-time) when they were
provided. On the facts, however, the Commission concluded that Clearstream
did not put forward sufficient evidence to justify that transaction costs for
Euroclear Bank SA's transactions were higher than the costs to process the
other customers' transactions.

9.20 Another example is *Brussels National Airport*,[18] in which the system of discounts on landing fees at Brussels airport granted to carriers by the airport
operator was under examination by the Commission. Brussels National Airport was found to hold a dominant position on the market for aircraft landing
and take-off services at Brussels airport.[19] The system of discounts in place
operated by reference to the monthly amount of fees due by carriers, which,
in turn, depended on the number of movements in a month and on the
weight of the aircrafts used. The Commission found that the minimum number of daily frequencies needed to reach the required monthly fee amount to
qualify for a discount was so high that only a carrier based in the airport could
reach it. The Commission therefore concluded that the discount system was
discriminatory since it had the effect of applying dissimilar conditions (*i.e.*,

---

[18] Case 95/364/EC *Brussels National Airport*, Commission Decision of 28 June 1995, OJ 1995 L 216/8.
[19] *Ibid.*

9. – Abusive Discrimination
Anne Layne-Farrar, Alice Setari and Paul Stuart

different fees) to carriers for equivalent transactions (*i.e.*, the same landing and take-off services provided by the airport operator to all airlines). The fact that the discount system was non-linear (as the fee reductions increased more than proportionally to the number of landings/take-offs) further accentuated the differences between the carriers benefiting from the discount and the other airlines.[20] The airport operator argued that the transactions involving the various airlines were not equivalent and that the differential treatment was justified due to the different costs involved. According to the airport operator, the costs of supplying landing and take-off services to carriers with large volumes of traffic were lower than the costs of supplying the same services to carriers with smaller volumes. The Commission, however, rejected this argument as unfounded. The Commission took the view that, with respect to the specific type of services at stake (*i.e.*, the services required for handling the take-off or landing of an aircraft), the only economies of scale that might have been achieved (*e.g.*, at the invoicing level) were too insignificant to justify the difference in fees deriving from the application of the discount system under examination.[21]

9.21   Finally, the Commission and the European courts will also not allow a dominant company to rely on the existence of different costs in carrying out two transactions involving similar products to escape a finding of unjustified discrimination when it has been the very behaviour of the dominant undertaking that has created the cost difference. For example, in *Deutsche Bahn*,[22] the Commission Decision, upheld by the Court of First Instance, found that Deutsche Bahn abused its dominant position on the rail transport market in Germany

---

[20] Case 95/364/EC *Brussels National Airport*, Commission Decision of 28 June 1995, OJ 1995 L 216/8, para. 13.

[21] *See* Case IV/35.703 *Portuguese Airports*, Commission Decision of 10 February 1999, OJ 1999 L 69/31, confirmed in Case C-163/99 *Portuguese Republic v Commission* [2001] ECR I-2613, para. 52 – also involving the system of take-off and landing charges applied by ANA-EP, the public undertaking that enjoyed the exclusive right to manage several airports in Portugal, which, according to the Commission, resulted in favouring airlines operating domestic flights over airlines favouring intra-European flights – where the Court of Justice held that "*where as a result of the thresholds of the various discount bands, and the levels of discount offered, discounts (or additional discounts) are enjoyed by only some trading parties, giving them an economic advantage which is not justified by the volume of business they bring or by any economies of scale they allow the supplier to make compared with their competitors, a system of quantity discounts leads to the application of dissimilar conditions to equivalent transactions.*" *See also* Case IV/35.767 *Ilmailulaitos/Luftfartsverket* ("*Finnish Airports*"), Commission Decision of 10 February 1999, OJ 1999 L 69/24, paras 44–56, which features a rather detailed discussion of the claimed higher costs for the airport operators generated by international flights as opposed to domestic flights, and at the end of which the Commission rejected all arguments put forward by the airport operator and concluded that none of the arguments advanced justified the discriminatory take-off and landing fee system at hand.

[22] Case IV/33.941 *HOV SVZ/MCN*, Commission Decision of 29 March 1994, OJ 1994 L 104/34 and Case T-229/94 *Deutsche Bahn v Commission* [1997] ECR II-1689.

9. – Abusive Discrimination
Anne Layne-Farrar, Alice Setari and Paul Stuart

by charging higher per-kilometre rates for railway transport of containers on the routes between a Belgian or a Dutch port (so-called "western ports") and Germany than for railway transport on the routes between various locations within Germany and the German ports (so-called "northern ports"), where Deutsche Bahn's subsidiary Transfracht was active.[23] Since it was not contested that Deutsche Bahn provided essentially the same transport services both to/from the western ports and to/from the northern ports, and that the per-kilometre rates it applied were different on the two routes, to show that the transactions were not equivalent (and/or to justify the differential treatment), Deutsche Bahn argued, *inter alia*, that the costs associated with the provision of transport services over the two routes were different. The Commission and the Court of First Instance acknowledged the existence of the cost difference claimed by Deutsche Bahn, however, they also took the view that this cost difference did not justify the difference in rates, given that it had been Deutsche Bahn's own behaviour that had created it. Deutsche Bahn had voluntarily adopted rationalisation measures that had reduced costs, but only for traffic to and from the northern ports, without giving valid reasons for why the journeys to and from the western ports had been excluded from these measures.[24]

1.3. *Commercial Context*

9.22 The Court of First Instance has accepted, at least as a matter of principle, that the different commercial context of two transactions (*e.g.*, different competitive conditions on the relevant markets) may be invoked to distinguish two transactions or to justify their differential treatment. In *Deutsche Bahn*, Deutsche Bahn argued that the stronger inter-modal competition on the western journeys could explain the higher rates on these routes compared to the northern routes. The Court of First Instance took the view that this factor could in principle be invoked to distinguish two transactions or justify their differential treatment, but also held that it could not be usefully relied upon by Deutsche Bahn in the case at hand. The Court of First Instance noted that the greater intensity of competition on the western journeys could not justify the higher tariffs applied on those journeys. According to the Court of First Instance, more intense inter-modal competition, if anything, should

---

[23] Case T-229/94, *ibid*.
[24] *Ibid*, paras 88–89.

9. – Abusive Discrimination
Anne Layne-Farrar, Alice Setari and Paul Stuart

have given rise to lower fares on the western journeys compared to the northern journeys.[25]

Similarly, the fact that a product is sold into a new market, where the dominant company was not active before, appears to constitute sufficient ground to justify, at least for a certain period, that the dominant company charges a different price for the products sold into the new market from the price charged for the products sold into the markets where it is already present.

9.23

1.4. Timing of Transactions

When assessing whether two or more transactions are equivalent, it is equally important to determine the timing of their occurrence. Transactions that occur at the same time or, at least, over the same time period, can be compared. Conversely, transactions that take place at different points in time or, in any event, in different time periods ought not to be considered as equivalent.

9.24

In *ABG/Oil Companies*,[26] the Commission stated that in order to determine whether cuts made by the dominant company in the petrol supply to certain customers and not to others constitute an abuse of a dominant position, the same reference period ought to be chosen for all buyers. Moreover, this reference period ought to be long enough to reflect seasonal variations in the market, and take into account the latest changes in dealings between buyers and sellers in the market.[27]

9.25

The moment in which contracts are concluded may also be relevant in deciding whether or not two transactions are equivalent. The typical example is that of IP licenses, where the value of a license will change depending on whether other licenses having the same object have already been granted. In these cases, the object of the contract may be the same, but the value attached to the transaction will necessarily differ, therefore potentially allowing for a differential treatment.

9.26

---

[25] Case IV/33.941 *HOV SVZ/MCN*, Commission Decision of 29 March 1994, OJ 1994 L 104/34 and Case T-229/94 *Deutsche Bahn v Commission* [1997] ECR II-1689, para. 91.

[26] Case IV/28.841 *ABG/Oil Companies*, Commission Decision of 19 April 1977, OJ 1977 L 117/1.

[27] *Ibid.* In this Decision, the Commission accused British Petroleum and one of its subsidiaries of abusing their dominant position during the 1973 oil crisis with regard to ABG, which acted as a purchasing cooperative of oil on behalf of the 19 members of the AVIA group. The Commission decided that British Petroleum had abused its dominant position by reducing its supplies to ABG proportionally to a much greater extent than in relation to its other customers.

9. – Abusive Discrimination
Anne Layne-Farrar, Alice Setari and Paul Stuart

1.5. Customer-related Factors

9.27 Certain customer-related factors can equally be relied upon to distinguish otherwise equivalent transactions or to justify a differential treatment between equivalent transactions.

9.28 The *Benzine* judgment clarified that, in times of shortage of supply, a dominant supplier is entitled to favour its long-standing traditional customers to the possible detriment of its occasional customers.[28] Moreover, at least according to some commentators, the fact that a customer is a new market entrant or a start up company should also justify the dominant company granting this customer more favourable conditions than to other well-established market players.[29] The *Kanal 5* judgment[30] also confirms that certain customer-specific factors (in the case at hand, the fact that one customer was a public television broadcaster, whereas other customers were commercial television broadcasters, and thus did not have either advertising revenues or revenues deriving from subscription fees) should be taken into account when assessing the equivalence between two transactions.

9.29 In *Clearstream*, the Commission rejected Clearstream's claim that the transactions at hand ought to be distinguished due to the different activities carried out by Euroclear Bank SA and by the customers which the Commission claimed had been discriminated against by Clearstream, but did not exclude as a matter of principle that this factor may be relevant when assessing the equivalence between two transactions (or the objective justification of a differential treatment).[31]

9.30 There are, however, a number of customer-related factors that cannot be relied upon to justify a discriminatory treatment by a dominant company.

---

[28] Case 77/77 *Benzine en Petroleum Handelsmaatschappij and others v Commission* ("*Benzine*") [1978] ECR 1513, para. 32.

[29] See J. Temple Lang, "*Article 82 EC – The Problems and The Solution*", FEEM Working Paper No. 65.2009 presented at the Conference "Ten years of Mercato Concorrenza Regole", Milan, June 30, 2009, and, by the same author, "Rebates, Price Discrimination and Refusal to Contract – The Commission's Guidance Paper on Article 82" (2010) *Europaraettslig Tidskrift*.

[30] Case C-52/07 *Kanal 5 and TV 4 v Föreningen Svenska Tonsättares Internationella Musikbyrå* ("*STIM*") [2008] ECR I-9275.

[31] *Clearstream Judgment 2009, supra* note 13, para. 311.

9. – Abusive Discrimination
Anne Layne-Farrar, Alice Setari and Paul Stuart

For example, a dominant undertaking cannot rely on the customer-related **9.31** factor that the quantities purchased from it constitute the totality of the customer's requirement to justify the granting of exclusivity rebates resulting in the application of different prices to different customers for the same type and quantity of product.[32]

United Brands also appears to establish that a dominant company is not entitled **9.32** to price discriminate between its customers depending on their geographic location (unless, of course, these differences reflect differences in cost for the dominant company in supplying these customers) and, in particular, based on the local market conditions of the territories where these customers operate. United Brands argued before the Court of Justice that it applied different prices to its customers for the same products because they carried out their activities in different countries with different marketing conditions and different retail selling price levels that depended on differences in wages, currencies, and density of competition. The Court of Justice, however, took the view that, when setting the price of its products, United Brands was entitled to take into account market conditions, but not to determine the price of its products based solely or mainly on the competitive conditions prevailing in the market where its customers re-sold the bananas. According to the Court, United Brands could have based its prices on the interplay between supply and demand on the market where it sold its products directly, but not on the downstream national markets. The Court therefore concluded that United Brands could not rely on price differences at the retail level between the various Member States to charge a different price for the same product to the various ripeners/distributors, given that it is they alone, not the dominant company, which operate on, and have to bear the risks of, the consumer market.[33]

Similarly, in *Irish Sugar*,[34] the Commission found that Irish Sugar abused its **9.33** dominant position on the markets for sugar retail and industrial sale in Ireland, *inter alia*, by enacting a discriminatory scheme of sugar export rebates in breach of Article 102 TFEU. The scheme was found to discriminate between exporting customers, as well as between exporting customers and customers

---

[32] Case 85/76 *Hoffmann-La Roche v Commission* ("*Hoffmann-La Roche*") [1979] ECR 461, para. 90.
[33] *United Brands*, para. 228, *supra* note 8.
[34] Cases IV/34.621 and 35.059 *Irish Sugar* ("*Irish Sugar Decision 1997*"), Commission Decision of 14 May 1997, OJ 1997 L 258/1.

9. – Abusive Discrimination
Anne Layne-Farrar, Alice Setari and Paul Stuart

who sold to the Irish market, since the rebates were granted to customers intending to export the sugar to other Member States and not to customers supplying the domestic Irish market.[35] Irish Sugar tried to justify charging different prices to exporting and non-exporting customers on the basis of an alleged difference in these customers' respective competitive positions. The Court of First Instance rejected Irish Sugar's argument and took the view that Irish Sugar was not entitled to price its sugar *"by reference to current and potential buyers from its customers according to their location"*[36] instead of by reference to supply and demand on the market where it sold the sugar to its customers.

9.34   Based on these judgments, it is equally doubtful whether a dominant company is allowed to price discriminate between its customers based on each such customer's valuation of the product or price elasticity, by charging – all other things being equal – higher prices to those customers for which the product has a higher value, and lower prices to those customers for which the product has a lower value. However, this outcome is to some extent counter-intuitive, particularly from an economic perspective, as it is generally understood that pricing according to a customer's own price elasticity is efficiency enhancing.[37]

9.35   The Commission and the European courts further rejected arguments according to which the different effects that the various customers' conduct might have on the dominant company's business should justify a finding that the transactions with these various customers are not equivalent, and/or that the differential treatment is objectively justified.

---

[35] Case T-228/97 *Irish Sugar v Commission ("Irish Sugar Judgment 1999")* [1999] ECR II-2969, para. 125. The Commission had also found there to be price discrimination by Irish Sugar against competing sugar packers in Ireland, which were sourcing their industrial sugar from Irish Sugar. Only those customers, which were also rival sugar packers, did not enjoy any rebate on the price of industrial sugar for their business in Ireland. Irish Sugar claimed that such discrimination was justified by the fundamental difference between sugar packers on the one hand and the processing industry on the other, in their capacity as buyers of industrial sugar. Irish Sugar argued that only the latter's consumption reduced the applicant's structural over-supply, thus rendering it a service not rendered by the packers. The Court of First Instance dismissed this argument since Irish Sugar did not submit any evidence showing why the purchases from customers, which were not sugar packers were more capable of reducing its structural overcapacity (the Court also hinted at the fact that the reason for this might be that purchases from competing sugar packers may prevent Irish Sugar from itself discharging more sugar on the retail market therefore confirming the abusive nature of the conduct).

[36] *Ibid.*, para. 141.

[37] J. Temple Lang, *"Article 82 EC – The Problems and The Solution"*, *supra* note 29; D. Gerard, "Price Discrimination Under Article 82(c) EC: Clearing up the Ambiguities", *GCLC Research Papers on Article 82*, July 2005.

9. – Abusive Discrimination
Anne Layne-Farrar, Alice Setari and Paul Stuart

In the *Virgin/British Airways*[38] case, British Airways' practice of applying different commission rates to travel agents operating in the United Kingdom according to whether or not they had achieved their sales objectives by comparison to a certain reference period was the crucial issue. In order to decide whether the different commission rates applied to agents were discriminatory and therefore contrary to Article 102 TFEU, it was necessary to establish in the first place whether the services rendered by them could be considered as equivalent. The Commission and the courts took the view that, to the extent that two travel agents achieve the same amount of revenue from the sale of British Airways tickets, the transactions involving British Airways and each of these agents are equivalent. They also held that the fact that one of these agents increased its sales compared to a previous reference period, thereby benefiting British Airways' business, does not make the two transactions different, and does not justify a differential treatment of the two agents through different commission rates.[39] In other words, according to the Commission and the courts, it was irrelevant that, from British Airways' point of view, the agent who increased its turnover in sales of British Airways tickets had been particularly useful by bringing additional passengers, thereby meriting a reward.[40] **9.36**

2. Dissimilar Conditions

Once it is established that two transactions are equivalent (or different) based on one or more of the elements discussed (as well as, potentially, on additional factors that may be relevant in the case), the next step in assessing whether an unjustified discrimination occurred is to determine whether the dominant company applied dissimilar (or similar) conditions to the relevant transactions. **9.37**

The determination of whether the conditions applied to two transactions are "similar" is again a fact-specific exercise involving a detailed analysis not only of the price charged by the dominant company (including any applicable discount and/or rebate), but also of the other commercial conditions applied to the relevant transactions, including payment terms and conditions. **9.38**

---

[38] Case IV/34.780 *Virgin/British Airways*, Commission Decision of 14 July 1999, OJ 2000 L 30/1.
[39] Case T-219/99 *British Airways v Commission* ("*British Airways Judgment 2003*") [2003] ECR II-5917 and Case C-95/04 P *British Airways v Commission* ("*British Airways Judgment 2007*") [2007] ECR I-2331.
[40] *British Airways Judgment 2003, supra* note 39, paras 127 *et seq.*

9. – Abusive Discrimination
Anne Layne-Farrar, Alice Setari and Paul Stuart

3. Objective Justification

9.39 Assuming discrimination, *i.e.*, the application of dissimilar conditions to equivalent transactions or of similar conditions to different transactions, is established, the third step in an unjustified discrimination assessment is to determine whether the discrimination is objectively justified.

9.40 As discussed, while conceptually separate from the determination of equivalence between two transactions, in practice, this assessment is generally carried out in the context of the assessment of the equivalence between transactions and by reference to the same parameters. This approach reflects the fact that the factors that are generally invoked by a dominant company and taken into account by the Commission and the European courts to determine whether two transactions are equivalent (*e.g.*, product-related, cost-related, customer-related, market-related, and time-related factors) are the same factors that are generally used to determine whether a differential treatment is objectively justified.

9.41 In other words, when two transactions are found to be equivalent (or different) not only based on a *prima facie* review of the products and prices involved, but after a careful assessment of those factors identified above that are relevant for the transactions at hand, it is hard to see what considerations would objectively justify a differential (or similar) treatment between these transactions. Where two transactions are found to be equivalent (or different) simply based on a *prima facie* review of the products and prices involved, however, a differential (or similar) treatment can still be objectively justified based on a careful assessment of one or more additional factors.

III. Exclusionary versus Non-exclusionary Discrimination

9.42 Once it is established that an unjustified discrimination by a dominant company has occurred, the possible effects of any such discrimination ought to be analysed. If the discrimination may result in the foreclosure of the dominant company's competitors, then, provided certain conditions are met, the conduct could give rise to an exclusionary discrimination abuse. If the discrimination may have an impact on competition between the dominant

9. – Abusive Discrimination
Anne Layne-Farrar, Alice Setari and Paul Stuart

company's customers (or suppliers),[41] then, provided certain conditions are met, the conduct could give rise to a non-exclusionary discrimination abuse.[42] As discussed in more detail in the remainder of this Section, the same conduct may give rise in some instances to both exclusionary and non-exclusionary discrimination.

The distinction between exclusionary and non-exclusionary discrimination **9.43** matters not only from a theoretical viewpoint, but also in practice. This reflects the fact that a dominant company would likely have a greater incentive to engage in abusive discrimination when the conduct is likely to favour directly or indirectly its own activities by excluding competitors, than when this discrimination is likely to result only in placing its customers/suppliers at a competitive disadvantage. This, in turn, strongly suggests that a dominant company engaging in secondary line non-exclusionary discrimination is more likely to engage in this conduct for legitimate business reasons than when it engages in exclusionary discrimination, and that the Commission and the

---

[41] The notion of discrimination equally applies to a dominant supplier of products or services who engages in unjustified discrimination between its customers and to a dominant buyer who engages in unjustified discrimination between its suppliers. This is well illustrated by the *BdKEP* decision (Case COMP/38.745 *BdKEP/ Deutsche Post AG and Bundesrepublik Deutschland* ("*BdKEP*"), Commission Decision of 20 October 2004, not yet published), where the Commission took the view that applicable German law induced Deutsche Post to discriminate unlawfully against commercial providers of mail preparation services in breach of Article 102 TFEU read in conjunction with Article 106 TFEU. The Commission considered that the market for mail preparation services (including one or more of the following: collecting mail, placing mail in mailbags complying with certain standards, bundling and sorting mail, and delivering mail to the access point of Deutsche Post's network) was upstream of Deutsche Post's reserved mail delivery activities. The Commission noted that German law allowed Deutsche Post to grant discounts on the postal tariffs to those senders carrying out in-house the above mail preparation services and delivering the pre-sorted mail to Deutsche Post's sorting centres, but not to commercial providers of these types of services, which were obliged by law to deliver the mail to the nearest access points to Deutsche Post's network, and therefore could not qualify for any discount (which was only available for mail delivered to Deutsche Post's sorting centres, not to the local access point). According to the Commission, German law resulted in extending Deutsche Post's market power to the market for the provision of mail preparation services to the detriment of third-party providers, which did not have access to the relevant discounts while still providing pre-sorting and delivery services to Deutsche Post, as well as in discriminating between major senders, which had access to Deutsche Post's sorting centres and applicable discounts, and self-provision intermediaries (as well as their customers) with comparable volumes of mail, which did not have access to these discounts. *See also British Airways*, where the Commission and the Courts sanctioned British Airways' abusive behaviour on the purchase of air travel agency services in the United Kingdom: *supra* note 39, *British Airways Judgment 2003* and *British Airways Judgment 2007*.

[42] *See* J. Temple Lang, "Rebates, Price Discrimination and Refusal to Contract – The Commission's Guidance Paper on Article 82" (2010) *Europaraettslig Tidskrift*.

9. – Abusive Discrimination
Anne Layne-Farrar, Alice Setari and Paul Stuart

courts should take this fundamental difference into account when applying Article 102 TFEU.[43]

1. Exclusionary Discrimination

9.44 Unjustified discrimination may result in foreclosure of the dominant company's competitors. To the extent that any such conduct would give rise to an exclusionary abuse of the kind that forms the subject matter of the *Guidance Paper*, the possible abusive nature of any such discrimination would have to be analysed in light of the principles enshrined therein.[44] In other words, generally speaking, when assessing whether unjustified discrimination gives rise to an exclusionary abuse in breach of Article 102 TFEU, it would need to be assessed whether effective access of actual or potential competitors to supplies or markets would be hampered or eliminated as a result of the conduct of the dominant undertaking, whereby the dominant undertaking would likely be in a position profitably to increase prices to the detriment of consumers.[45]

9.45 A review of the Commission's decisional practice and of the European courts' case law confirms that unjustified discrimination may give rise to an exclusionary discrimination abuse in two main instances: (1) when the unjustified discrimination consists of the dominant company applying different contractual terms and conditions (including, but not limited to, pricing) to its customers, which may result in the foreclosure of the dominant company's competitors on the market where it holds such dominant position (so-called "primary line discrimination"); and (2) when the unjustified discrimination consists of the dominant company applying more favourable contractual terms and conditions to its downstream operations than to third party downstream competitors thereby potentially foreclosing such competitors from the downstream market (so-called "exclusionary secondary line discrimination").

---

[43] R. O'Donoghue and A. J. Padilla, *The Law and Economics of Article 82 EC* (Oxford, Hart Publishing, 2006), p. 554.

[44] According to the *Guidance Paper*, "*the aim of the Commission's enforcement activity in relation to exclusionary conduct is to ensure that dominant undertakings do not impair effective competition by foreclosing their competitors in an anti-competitive way, thus having an adverse impact on consumer welfare, whether in the form of higher price levels than would have otherwise prevailed or in some other form such as limiting quality or reducing consumer choice.*" See Guidance Paper, para. 19, *supra* note 5.

[45] For a more detailed discussion, *see* Chapter 2.

9. – Abusive Discrimination
Anne Layne-Farrar, Alice Setari and Paul Stuart

1.1. Primary Line Discrimination

9.46 Unjustified discrimination may have exclusionary effects *vis-à-vis* the dominant company's competitors on the market where the dominant position exists. The potentially abusive nature of this type of exclusionary discrimination ought to be assessed solely in light of the principles enshrined in the *Guidance Paper*, which specifically discusses the most common types of conduct falling within this category, *i.e.*, rebates and discounts, predatory pricing, and/or tying and bundling.[46] The fact that the relevant conduct may also be discriminatory in nature should not have any impact on its assessment as a possible exclusionary abuse. The assessment should rather focus on the relevant conduct's possible foreclosure effects. However, this does not mean that if the relevant conditions are met, such conduct should not also be scrutinised under Article 102(c) TFEU as possible non-exclusionary secondary line discrimination. Instead, this assessment ought to be separate and independent from the analysis of the conduct as possible exclusionary discrimination, and ought to be based on the different legal test applicable to non-exclusionary secondary line discrimination abuses enshrined in Article 102(c) TFEU.

9.47 The case law provides numerous examples of primary line exclusionary discrimination stemming from the contractual terms and conditions applied to customers by the dominant company.[47] Primary line discrimination may result from the discounts and/or rebates granted by the dominant company to its customers. This was the case, for example, in *Suiker Unie*,[48] *Hoffman La-Roche*,[49] and *Michelin I*,[50] where the Court of Justice concluded that the exclusionary conduct at issue consisted of the dominant company granting loyalty-inducing rebates to its customers thereby foreclosing competitors' access to the

---

[46] Predatory pricing is discussed in Chapter 4. Exclusive dealing, including discounts and rebates is discussed in Chapter 6. Tying and bundling is discussed in Chapter 8.

[47] *See supra* note 4.

[48] Joined Cases 40 to 48, 50, 54 to 56, 111, 113 and 114/73 *Coöperatieve Vereniging "Suiker Unie" and others v Commission ("Suiker Unie")* [1975] ECR 1663.

[49] *Hoffmann-La Roche, supra* note 32.

[50] Case 322/81 *Nederlandsche Banden Industrie Michelin v Commission ("Michelin I")* [1983] ECR 3461, para. 90. The Commission's finding of abusive discrimination was, however, annulled by the Court of Justice on the ground that the Commission did not put forward sufficient evidence to demonstrate that the differences in treatment between the various Michelin dealers were due to unequal criteria, and that there was no legitimate commercial reason capable of justifying them.

market, but also resulted in charging different prices to customers purchasing the same quantities of the relevant products.[51]

9.48   *British Airways*[52] is a good example of the same discriminatory conduct being scrutinised both as exclusionary primary line discrimination and as non-exclusionary secondary line discrimination. British Airways granted to its travel agents financial incentives conditional upon the agent increasing its sales of British Airways tickets compared to an earlier reference period. These incentives were assessed both as exclusionary primary line discrimination, due to their fidelity-enhancing nature (which, according to the Commission and the European courts, was capable of having an exclusionary effect *vis-à-vis* British Airways' competitors on the market for travel agency services in the United Kingdom), and as non-exclusionary secondary line discrimination under Article 102(c) TFEU, due to their alleged effects on competition between travel agents. In other words, in *British Airways*, the Commission and the courts correctly carried out two separate assessments based on different legal tests of whether British Airways' conduct constituted exclusionary and non-exclusionary discrimination (albeit, as discussed in more detail below, the way the Commission and the courts applied the "competitive disadvantage" requirement provided for by Article 102(c) TFEU does give rise to some interpretation questions).[53]

9.49   In *Post Danmark*,[54] the Danish Competition Council (Konkurrencerådet) had held that Post Danmark abused its dominant position on the market for the distribution of unaddressed mail in Denmark by granting selective discounts to customers of its principal rival, Forbruger-Kontakt.[55] The Konkurrencerådet

---

[51] *See also* Case T-65/89 *BPB Industries and British Gypsum v Commission* ("*BPB Industries*") [1993] ECR II-389, where the Court of First Instance found that BPB, the dominant supplier of plasterboard in Ireland and Northern Ireland, discriminated against those among its customers (by not granting them a rebate that was available to other customers) that agreed to purchase and import into Northern Ireland third party plasterboard, with a view to dissuading such customers from dealing with foreign importers and protecting its dominant position; *Irish Sugar*, where Irish Sugar, *inter alia*, granted so-called "border" rebates to certain retail customers situated at the border with Northern Ireland to restrict low price sugar imports and protect its dominant position, as well as various types of target rebates to other customers to restrict competition from other sugar packers.

[52] *Supra* note 38 and *British Airways Judgment 2003, supra* note 39.

[53] *See also BPB Industries, supra* note 51, where the Court of First Instance, while assessing the primary line discrimination aspect of the conduct at stake, also hinted at BPB's intent to penalise those merchants that intended to import plasterboard into Northern Ireland and therefore to the non-exclusionary secondary line discrimination aspect of BPB's conduct.

[54] Case C-209/10 *Post Danmark v Konkurrencerådet*, not yet reported.

[55] A press release is available in Danish at http://www.kfst.dk/index.php?id=28653; *ibid*.

9. – Abusive Discrimination
Anne Layne-Farrar, Alice Setari and Paul Stuart

considered that this constituted both primary line discrimination, by charging Forbruger-Kontakt's former customers cheaper rates than Post Danmark's own pre-existing customers without being able to justify those differences by reference to costs, and secondary line discrimination, in that it put Post Danmark's existing customers on an unequal footing in terms of rates and rebates relative to Forbruger-Kontakt's former customers. On a preliminary reference from Post Danmark's appeal, the Court of Justice held that a policy by which a dominant undertaking charges low prices to certain major customers of a competitor does not amount to an exclusionary abuse under Article 102 TFEU merely because the price that the dominant undertaking charges is lower than the average total cost, but higher than the average incremental cost, pertaining to that activity. The Court of Justice considered that if a dominant company sets its prices at a level covering most of the costs attributable to the supply of the goods or services in question, it will, as a general rule, be possible for an equally-efficient competitor to compete with those prices without suffering losses that are unsustainable in the long term. Rather, to assess the existence of anticompetitive effects, the Court of Justice held that it is necessary to consider whether that pricing policy, without objective justification, produces an actual or likely exclusionary effect, to the detriment of competition and, thereby, of consumers' interests.

Cewal[56] is an example of primary line discrimination consisting of the dominant company applying selective (predatory) price cuts to its customers with a view to protecting its dominant position. The "fighting ships" strategy enacted by Compagnie Maritime Belge consisted of offering liner services at the closest possible dates to those in which its main competitor G&C was offering its services, and of charging different (lower) prices for these services compared to those normally charged, so as for these prices to be at the same level as, or at lower level than, G&C's prices. The Commission and the courts concluded that the above practice, which also resulted in discriminatory prices being charged to Compagnie Maritime Belge's customers for the same services essentially depending on whether G&C was offering a competing service at the relevant time, was enacted with a view of removing Compagnie Maritime Belge's only competitor from the relevant market, and was therefore anticompetitive.[57]

9.50

---

[56] *See* Cases IV/32.448 and 32.450 *Cewal*, Commission Decision of 23 December 1992, OJ 1993 L 34/20.

[57] While the Commission Decision specifically addressed the secondary line discrimination aspect of Cewal's conduct (*see ibid.*, para. 83: "[m]*oreover, Cewal's establishment of fighting rates different from those of the conference tariff, by which the conference is bound in order to benefit from the block exemption, has a discriminatory effect against shippers who, having*

9. – Abusive Discrimination
Anne Layne-Farrar, Alice Setari and Paul Stuart

9.51   Finally, primary line discrimination may arise from a dominant company's tying and bundling practices. In *Van den Bergh Foods*,[58] the Commission found that Van den Bergh, which held a dominant position on the market for the supply of impulse ice cream in Ireland, supplied its ice cream products and freezer cabinets at an "inclusive" price that included the capital costs of the cabinet, its maintenance costs, and the value of the ice-cream products. All retailers were charged the same price, irrespective of the ownership of the cabinets in which the products are stocked. Thus, a retailer with its own freezer cabinet paid the same price for the ice cream as a retailer accepting the offer of a freezer. In its Statement of Objections, the Commission took the view that Van den Bergh discriminated against retailers who had not taken its freezer cabinet, but who nonetheless purchased ice cream from it. The Commission provisionally concluded that the inclusive pricing policy not only served as an inducement to grant exclusivity to the detriment of competing suppliers of impulse ice cream, but also gave rise to discrimination between trading partners by treating dissimilar situations in a similar fashion. Retailers with their own freezer cabinets effectively paid for a service which they did not receive and, in so doing, were forced to subsidise cabinet provision to those taking the cabinets; the former retailers thereby placed themselves at a competitive disadvantage *vis-à-vis* the latter ones. Following the Commission's objections, Van den Bergh Foods agreed to abandon the policy of "inclusive pricing" in 1995, and introduced a differential or dual pricing scheme.

1.2.   Exclusionary Secondary Line Discrimination

9.52   Unjustified discrimination may equally have exclusionary effects *vis-à-vis* the dominant company's competitors on a downstream market where the dominant company is also active. This is the case when the dominant company applies more favourable contractual terms and conditions to its downstream

---

to load on dates some time from the sailing dates of G&C ships, must therefore pay the higher regular conference tariff for the carriage of the same goods, and thus also constitutes a clear abuse of a dominant position in breach of Article 86(c)). This is because shippers have dissimilar conditions imposed on them for equivalent transactions, which places those who are forced to pay higher rates at a competitive disadvantage"). On appeal, the Courts did not comment on this issue (*see* Joined Cases C-395 and 396/96 P *Compagnie Maritime Belge Transports and others v Commission* [2000] ECR I-1365). *See also* Cases IV/30.787 and 31.488 *Eurofix-Bauco/Hilti*, Commission Decision of 22 December 1987, OJ 1988 L 65/19, where the Commission found that Hilti engaged in selective or discriminatory policies directed against the businesses of both competitors and competitors' customers in the form of selective price cuts or other advantageous terms, which the Commission and the courts, however, only considered as exclusionary conduct, without paying specific attention to the secondary line discrimination angle.

[58] Cases IV/34.073, 34.395 and 35.436 *Van den Bergh Foods*, Commission Decision of 11 March 1998, OJ 1998 L 246/1.

9. – Abusive Discrimination
Anne Layne-Farrar, Alice Setari and Paul Stuart

operations than to third party downstream competitors, thereby potentially foreclosing such competitors from the downstream market (so-called "exclusionary secondary line discrimination").

The *Guidance Paper* specifically addresses conduct akin to this type of exclu-   **9.53**
sionary discrimination. Refusal to deal (discussed in detail in Chapter 7), for example, could be viewed as the most extreme form of exclusionary secondary line discrimination, as it entails a dominant company which supplies a key input to operate on the downstream activities reserving this input to itself, while refusing to provide it to its downstream competitors. Following the same approach, instances of exclusionary secondary line discrimination could be viewed as a form of constructive refusal to deal. Similarly, margin squeeze (discussed in detail in Chapter 5) could also be viewed as a form of exclusionary secondary line discrimination, to the extent that it involves the dominant company providing a key input to downstream competitors at less favourable terms and conditions than those applied to its integrated downstream operations.

More generally, and regardless of whether the relevant behaviour is specifi-   **9.54**
cally discussed in the *Guidance Paper*, to the extent that it constitutes potentially exclusionary conduct, any unjustified discrimination that may result in the foreclosure of the dominant company's downstream competitors to the advantage of the dominant company's own integrated activities ought to be assessed in light of the principles enshrined therein. In other words, when assessing this type of conduct, the relevant test to apply ought to be whether effective access of actual or potential competitors to supplies or markets would be hampered or eliminated as a result of the conduct of the dominant undertaking, whereby the dominant undertaking would likely be in a position profitably to increase prices to the detriment of consumers.

The case law features few examples of exclusionary secondary line   **9.55**
discrimination.

In *Deutsche Post*,[59] the Commission found that Deutsche Post abused its domi-   **9.56**
nant position on the market for the forwarding and delivery of incoming cross-border letter mail in Germany from the United Kingdom by charging

---

[59] Case COMP/36.915 *Deutsche Post AG – Interception of cross-border mail* ("*Deutsche Post*"), Commission Decision of 23 July 2001, not yet published.

9. – Abusive Discrimination
Anne Layne-Farrar, Alice Setari and Paul Stuart

to the British Post Office (the complainant in the case at hand) a fee sur-charge to those mailings originating in the United Kingdom, but containing a reference to an entity residing in Germany, which Deutsche Post considered as so-called "ABA remailing", *i.e.*, letters originating from Germany (A), but posted in the United Kingdom (B) for delivery in Germany (A). The Commis-sion considered that this conduct gave rise to an exclusionary abuse against the British Post Office on the market for outgoing cross-border letter mail from the United Kingdom to Germany, since the additional costs incurred by the British Post Office as a result of Deutsche Post's surcharge, in combi-nation with the frequent disruption of the mail traffic routed by the British Post Office to Germany, could induce UK customers to use Deutsche Post's services in the United Kingdom to ensure a speedy and uninterrupted con-veyance of their mail to Germany. In other words, in the Commission's view, Deutsche Post's conduct amounted to exclusionary secondary line discrimina-tion on the market for outgoing cross-border mail in the United Kingdom.

9.57 In *Clearstream*, the Commission and the Court of First Instance concluded that Clearstream engaged in unjustified discrimination against Euroclear Bank SA by delaying the latter's access to Clearstream's primary clearing and settlement services in Germany, while, at the same time, granting access to these services within a much shorter time period to other customers, including Clearstream's own subsidiary CBL, which competed with Euroclear Bank SA on the down-stream market for secondary clearing and settlement of cross-border security transactions. In *BdKEP*,[60] the Commission found that the applicable German postal law prevented Deutsche Post's upstream competitors in the provision of mail preparation services from obtaining discounts on the postal tariff for their clients. This resulted in extending Deutsche Post's dominant position from the postal services reserved to it by law to the upstream mail preparation service market, where it operated in competition with third party providers. Since only Deutsche Post could offer these discounts, it had a competitive advantage *vis-à-vis* independent mail preparation service providers

9.58 Also in the case of exclusionary secondary line discrimination, the same unjustified discrimination may form the subject matter of a separate and inde-pendent inquiry based on the different legal test provided for by Article 102(c) TFEU to assess whether it constitutes non-exclusionary secondary line dis-crimination. In *Deutsche Post*, for example, the Commission not only found an

---

[60] *BdKEP, supra* note 41.

9. – Abusive Discrimination
Anne Layne-Farrar, Alice Setari and Paul Stuart

abuse of exclusionary secondary line discrimination, but also took the view that Deutsche Post, by charging a surcharge fee and by substantially delaying the delivery of suspected ABA remailing, applied dissimilar conditions to equivalent transactions (the forwarding and delivery of incoming cross-border mail) thereby placing some of its customers that are in direct competition with each other at a competitive disadvantage[61] – "non-exclusionary secondary line discrimination".

More generally, if it were to be concluded that an unjustified discrimination **9.59** is likely to lead to the foreclosure of the dominant company's downstream competitors and therefore constitutes abusive exclusionary secondary line discrimination, in all likelihood, the same conduct would also be considered in breach of Article 102(c) TFEU, as it would likely result in placing the third-party downstream operator at a competitive disadvantage *vis-à-vis* the dominant company's own integrated activities. The opposite, however, is not necessarily true. This reflects the fact that unjustified discrimination that does not constitute exclusionary discrimination may still constitute non-exclusionary secondary line discrimination. As discussed in more detail in the next Subsection, the "competitive disadvantage" test provided for by Article 102(c) TFEU, which is applicable to secondary line discrimination, is different from the foreclosure test enshrined in the *Guidance Paper*, which is applicable to instances of exclusionary discrimination. By way of example, in *Deutsche Bahn*, the Commission and the Court of First Instance concluded that Deutsche Bahn's discriminatory tariffs resulted in placing competitors active in the so-called "western journeys" at a competitive disadvantage *vis-à-vis* Deutsche Bahn's subsidiary Transfracht, active on the so-called "northern journeys", and therefore violated Article 102 TFEU; but, neither made any finding concerning the possible exclusionary effect of the conduct at hand.

2. **Non-exclusionary Discrimination**

Other than potentially affecting competition between the dominant company **9.60** and its competitors (whether these competitors operate on the same market where the dominant position exists or in a downstream market where the dominant company is also present), unjustified discrimination between the

---

[61] In the case at hand, mail order companies based in the United Kingdom, which in their correspondence indicated a reference to an entity located in Germany as opposed to mail order companies which did not indicate any such reference.

9. – Abusive Discrimination
Anne Layne-Farrar, Alice Setari and Paul Stuart

dominant firms' customers or suppliers (so-called "secondary line discrimination") may also affect competition between these trading parties. This is the type of non-exclusionary discrimination that is contemplated by Article 102(c) TFEU, according to which "[a]*ny abuse by one or more undertakings of a dominant position within the internal market or in a substantial part of it shall be prohibited as incompatible with the internal market in so far as it may affect trade between Member States. Such abuse may, in particular, consist in: … (c) applying dissimilar conditions to equivalent transactions with other trading parties, thereby placing them at a competitive disadvantage*".[62]

9.61 The text of Article 102(c) TFEU makes it clear that the notions of "other trading parties" and of "competitive disadvantage" are the key elements (other than the existence of an unjustified discrimination) of the abuse of non-exclusionary secondary line discrimination.

2.1. Other Trading Parties

9.62 Article 102(c) TFEU provides that the dominant company's abusive discrimination is carried out *vis-à-vis* "other trading parties", which should be put at a competitive disadvantage as a result of the unjustified discrimination. The vast majority of commentators[63] maintain that the reference to "other trading parties", read in conjunction with the additional requirement that these parties should be put at a competitive disadvantage following the unjustified discrimination, contributes to limiting the scope of application of this provision to discrimination taking place between traders, as opposed to final consumers. There are, however, commentators who have taken the opposite stance and argued that Article 102(c) TFEU also applies to discrimination between final consumers.[64] This very question was left open by the Commission in *BdKEP*.[65]

---

[62] *Supra* note 2.

[63] *Supra* note 43, p. 553.

[64] *See* P. Akman, "To Abuse, or Not to Abuse: Discrimination Between Consumers" (2007) 32 *European Law Review*, pp. 499–502. According to P. Akman, the ban on discrimination under Article 102(c) also covers discrimination in business-to-consumer transactions and the late decisional practice of the Commission supports this conclusion. By way of example, in Case IV/36.888 *1998 Football World Cup*, Commission Decision of 20 July 1999, OJ 2000 L 5/55, the Commission found that the requirement imposed by the organising committee that the public provided an address in France to be able to order on-line entry tickets for the football matches was found to discriminate between different groups of consumers and to be an abuse of a dominant position under Article 102(c) TFEU. As to the argument that consumers do not compete with one another, and thus cannot be put at a competitive disadvantage, according to this author, the Commission's decisional practice evolved in such a way as effectively to remove the "competitive disadvantage" requirement from the constituent elements of this abuse.

[65] *BdKEP*, para. 92, *supra* note 41.

9. – Abusive Discrimination
Anne Layne-Farrar, Alice Setari and Paul Stuart

In *Deutsche Post*, the Commission took the view that the notion of "trading **9.63** party" may also encompass entities without a direct commercial relationship with the dominant company (in the case at hand, UK mail senders), while acknowledging that the term "trading partner" normally refers to a voluntary commercial relationship between two undertakings.[66] In *BdKEP*, the Commission confirmed that for an undertaking to be a dominant company's trading party, the undertaking does not need to have a contractual relationship with the dominant company, but that mere business contacts are generally considered to be sufficient.[67]

Article 102(c) TFEU would equally apply to unjustified discrimination between **9.64** the dominant company's own integrated activities on a separate market and third-party customers or suppliers. Article 102(c) TFEU would apply to the possible secondary line non-exclusionary effects of the discrimination, while the primary line exclusionary effects would have to be assessed under Article 102(b) TFEU based on the principles applicable to exclusionary abuses. As emerges from the text of Article 102(c) TFEU, the type of discrimination contemplated by this provision does not focus on the possible foreclosure effects of the unjustified discrimination *vis-à-vis* the dominant company's competitors, but rather on the possible distortions of competition between third-party customers or suppliers of the dominant company (or between the dominant company's own integrated activities and third parties).

2.2. *Competitive Disadvantage*

The "competitive disadvantage" requirement therefore emerges as the key **9.65** distinguishing feature between exclusionary discrimination abuses (whether primary or secondary line) and the non-exclusionary (secondary line) discrimination abuses contemplated by Article 102(c) TFEU.

The European courts' case law confirms that placing the dominant com- **9.66** pany's trading parties at a competitive disadvantage constitutes an element of any secondary line non-exclusionary discrimination abuse in breach of Article 102(c) TFEU. As clarified by Advocate General Kokott in her opinion in the *British Airways* case,[68] Article 102(c) TFEU lays down a two-stage test to find an abuse of a dominant position: the existence of an unjustified

---

[66] *Deutsche Post*, para. 130, *supra* note 59.
[67] *BdKEP*, para. 92, *supra* note 41.
[68] Advocate General Kokott in *Brtish Airways Judgment 2007*, *supra* note 39.

9. – Abusive Discrimination
Anne Layne-Farrar, Alice Setari and Paul Stuart

discrimination enacted by a dominant company and this discrimination resulting in a competitive disadvantage for the dominant company's customers or suppliers. In the Advocate General's words: "*the expression thereby placing them at a competitive disadvantage included in the provision at hand is 'more than just an explanatory addition with declaratory effect'* ".[69]

9.67 Article 102(c) TFEU therefore dictates that a dominant company's business practice should not distort competition on an upstream or downstream market, *i.e.*, between its suppliers or customers, and the business partners of the dominant undertaking should not be unjustifiably advantaged or disadvantaged in their competition with one another as a result of the dominant company's discriminatory conduct. Accordingly, for Article 102(c) TFEU to apply, it ought first to be determined that a relationship of competition exists between the relevant trading partners of the dominant undertaking, and secondly that the conduct of the dominant undertaking is likely in the particular case to distort that competition, *i.e.*, to prejudice the competitive position of some of the dominant undertaking's trading partners in relation to the others. This interpretation of Article 102(c) TFEU was confirmed by the Court of Justice, in its judgment in *British Airways*. The Court followed Advocate General Kokott's opinion on this point and held that, in order for Article 102(c) TFEU to apply, there must be a finding not only that the behaviour of an undertaking in a dominant market position is discriminatory, but also that it tends to hinder the competitive position of some of the business partners of that undertaking in relation to the others.[70]

9.68 In principle, establishing the "competitive disadvantage" requirement involves a two-step analysis. First, the existence of a competitive relationship between the dominant company's customers (or suppliers) should be established, and secondly, a negative impact on these customers' (or suppliers') competitive position deriving from the discriminatory conduct should be determined.

9.69 However, the Commission and the courts have generally assessed the existence of the competitive disadvantage requirement by following a less rigorous approach. In practice, what the Commission and the courts have generally done is to skip – or in any event address very superficially – the issue of whether the dominant company's customers affected by the unlawful

---

[69] Advocate General Kokott in *Brtish Airways Judgment 2007, supra* note 39, para. 124.
[70] *British Airways Judgment 2007, supra* note 39.

9. – Abusive Discrimination
Anne Layne-Farrar, Alice Setari and Paul Stuart

discrimination are actual or potential competitors, and instead focus their assessment on whether the unlawful discrimination is likely to have an impact on these customers' market position. Moreover, the Commission's and the courts' assessment of the impact of the unlawful discrimination has also traditionally not been very detailed. The Commission and the courts often limited themselves to assuming the existence of a competitive disadvantage from the existence of an unlawful discrimination, without even carrying out an *ad hoc* assessment.[71]

The following analysis briefly discusses the Commission's and the courts' **9.70** assessment of the "competitive disadvantage" requirement in a number of secondary line non-exclusionary discrimination cases. Other cases, in which the Commission and/or the courts (wrongly) relied on the notion of competitive disadvantage to support a finding of exclusionary discrimination are not discussed, given the view that Article 102(c) TFEU should not apply to these cases, which therefore should not be considered as relevant to the present analysis.[72]

In *United Brands*, the Commission discussed to some limited extent the com- **9.71** petitive disadvantage requirement.[73] The Commission found that United Brands' business practice of charging different prices to its ripeners/distributors depending on the country of destination of the product, and of preventing these ripeners/distributors from reselling green bananas outside their territory, had the effect of tending to maintain substantially differing price levels in each of the Member States in question. Thus the Commission found

---

[71] A rigorous assessment of the competitive disadvantage requirement would entail, *inter alia*, defining the relevant product and geographic markets in which the dominant company's customers or suppliers are active to determine whether they are actual (or potential) competitors. By way of example, in *Ladbroke* (Case T-504/93 *Tiercé Ladbroke v Commission* ("*Ladbroke*") [1997] ECR II-923, para. 124), the Court of First Instance took the view that the market of "*televised pictures and news of French horse-races*" was ancillary to the betting market, which was national in scope. This entailed that PMI's refusal to license the performing rights of French horse races to Ladbroke in Belgium, while, at the same time, licensing the same rights to other players in other Member States, could not be considered to put Ladbroke at a competitive disadvantage *vis-à-vis* its competitors, as no other license had been granted in Belgium. If the Court of First Instance had considered the downstream market where the licensees operated as EEA-wide in scope, it would have necessarily reached the opposite conclusion, as it could no longer have found that "*the refusal to supply Ladbroke was not discriminatory just because no one had been licensed in Belgium*". This example shows how complex the assessment of the competitive disadvantage requirement would be if this requirement were to be interpreted more strictly by the Commission or by the courts. *See* D. Gerard, *supra* note 37.

[72] *See, e.g., Suiker Unie, Hoffmann-La Roche,* and *Michelin I, supra* notes 48, 32 and 50.

[73] *United Brands*, para. 233, *supra* note 8.

9. – Abusive Discrimination
Anne Layne-Farrar, Alice Setari and Paul Stuart

that United Brands' practices placed certain of these ripeners/distributors on an unequal competitive footing if they wanted to sell United Brands' bananas in Member States other than those where they were established (which would be relatively easy for them to do, provided that they were allowed to sell green United Brands bananas, since most of them bought the bananas in Rotterdam or Bremerhaven and used their own means of transport) and therefore at a competitive disadvantage.

9.72 The Commission and the courts equally paid little attention to the competitive disadvantage requirement in cases mainly dealing with discrimination on the ground of nationality (*e.g.*, *Corsica Ferries*[74]) and/or with the legality of national monopolies, (*e.g.*, *Merci Convenzionali*[75]), as well as in most of the airport cases (*Brussels National Airport*,[76] *Portuguese Airports*,[77] *Spanish Airports*,[78] and *Finnish Airports*[79]). In his opinion in *Corsica Ferries*, Advocate General Van Gerven even went as far as stating that it is not necessary that the trading partners of the undertaking responsible for the abuse should suffer a competitive disadvantage against each other or against the undertaking in the dominant position for Article 102(c) TFEU to apply.[80]

9.73 The one case in which the Commission engaged in at least a slightly more detailed assessment of the competitive disadvantage requirement was in *Aéroports de Paris*.[81] There, the Commission carefully scrutinised the impact of the discriminatory fees paid to Aéroports de Paris by ground-handling service providers to third parties, as well as by airlines also engaged in self-handling, and concluded that the different level of fees resulted in a distortion

---

[74] Case C-18/93 *Corsica Ferries Italia v Corpo dei Piloti del Porto di Genova* ("*Corsica Ferries*") [1994] ECR I-1783.

[75] Case C-179/90 *Merci convenzionali porto di Genova v Siderurgica Gabrielli* ("*Merci Convenzionali*") [1991] ECR I-5889.

[76] *Supra* note 18, para. 13. In its Decision, the Commission limits itself to pointing out by way of example that under the system of discounts on landing fees established by Belgian law, Sabena, the only company based at Brussels airport, was the only airline qualifying for the above discounts. In particular, Sabena achieved an 18 per cent discount on its take-off and landing fees on the Brussels–London route while BM, one of Sabena's competitors on this route, did not receive any discount. The Commission concluded that BM was placed at a competitive disadvantage *vis-à-vis* Sabena.

[77] Case IV/35.703, *supra* note 21, para. 35. On the competitive disadvantage issue, the Commission limited itself to noting that "*it is obvious that such a system* [the differentiated landing charges system at hand] *has the direct effect of placing intra-Community services at a disadvantage by artificially altering the cost to the undertakings, depending on whether they operate domestic or intra-Community services*".

[78] Case 2000/521/EC *Spanish Airports*, Commission Decision of 26 July 2000, OJ 2000 L 208/36.

[79] *See Finnish Airports*, *supra* note 21 para. 43, which mirrors almost *verbatim Portuguese Airports*, *supra* note 21, para. 35.

[80] Advocate General Van Gerven in *Corsica Ferries*, para. 34, *supra* note 74.

[81] *Aéroports de Paris Decision 1998*, paras 125–26, *supra* note 10.

9. – Abusive Discrimination
Anne Layne-Farrar, Alice Setari and Paul Stuart

of competition between service providers since the differential tariffs had an impact on the price of the handlers' services (as well as, indirectly, between airlines using these services).

Many decisions, however, may be characterised by a fairly concise discussion **9.74** of the "competitive disadvantage" requirement. In *Soda-ash – Solvay*,[82] the Commission looked at the costs of the dominant company's customers and found that, in the glass sector, which accounted for the majority of soda-ash consumption, soda ash accounted for 70 per cent of the customers' raw materials cost. On this basis, the Commission concluded that Solvay's discriminatory pricing had an impact on customers' profitability and competitive position.[83] In *Deutsche Post*, the Commission found that Deutsche Post's surcharge procedure placed UK senders, which may be in competition with each other, at a competitive disadvantage, without going into the detail of how that disadvantage might manifest itself in practice.[84] In *Scandlines*, the Commission at least addressed the issue whether these parties operated on the same product market and provided substitutable services, finally concluding that the complainant did not bring forward sufficient evidence on the degree of substitutability between these services.[85]

BdKEP is a good example of the possible confusion that a loose or unclear **9.75** definition of the competitive disadvantage requirement and, more generally, the lack of a clear analytical framework may generate.[86] In this Decision, the Commission took the view that Article 102(c) TFEU ought to be interpreted as also applying to primary line exclusionary abuses since the notion of "competitive disadvantage" provided for therein encompasses the scenario of the dominant company's customers being impaired in their ability to compete with the dominant company. As regards the application of Article 102 TFEU to secondary line non-exclusionary discrimination situations, the Commission further noted that a broad interpretation of the "competitive disadvantage" requirement also covering unjustified discrimination between customers who do not compete on the same market should be warranted, particularly when the discrimination is also prohibited by other principles of EU law (*e.g.*, discrimination based on nationality or aimed at market partitioning).

---

[82] Case IV/33.133 *Soda-ash – Solvay, ICI*, Commission Decision of 19 December 1990, OJ 1991 L 152/21.
[83] *Ibid.*, para. 185.
[84] *Deutsche Post*, para. 131, *supra* note 59.
[85] *Scandlines*, para. 284, *supra* note 15.
[86] *BdKEP*, paras 93–95, *supra* note 41.

9. – Abusive Discrimination
Anne Layne-Farrar, Alice Setari and Paul Stuart

9.76 As previously discussed, the judgment of the Court of Justice in *British Airways* should have finally shed some light on the applicable analytical framework to secondary line non-exclusionary discrimination cases and on the interpretation of the competitive disadvantage requirement. The same judgment also ruled on the evidentiary standard to be met for the competitive disadvantage requirement provided for by Article 102(c) TFEU to be established. The Court of Justice held that, for the competitive disadvantage requirement to be established to the requisite legal standard, it is sufficient to demonstrate that the unjustified discrimination tends, having regard to all the circumstances of the case, to lead to a competitive distortion between the dominant company's trading partners. In the case at hand, the Court found that the Commission could legitimately infer from the fact that British Airways' discriminatory remuneration system materially impacted travel agents' revenue that agents competed intensely with each other, that their ability to compete depended on their financial resources, and that British Airways' remuneration schemes therefore gave rise to discriminatory effects within the meaning of Article 102 TFEU.

9.77 To conclude, particularly following the *British Airways* case, it can be expected that the Commission and the courts will pay greater attention than they have done in the past to the "competitive disadvantage" requirement enshrined in Article 102(c) TFEU. This renewed attention to the "competitive disadvantage" requirement is confirmed by the *Kanal 5* judgment. In that case, the Court of Justice stated that, in order to determine whether the conduct of a national copyright management organisation consisting of charging different royalties for the television broadcast of musical works protected by copyright to commercial or public networks constitutes an abuse of a dominant position in breach of Article 102(c) TFEU, the national court ought to determine, *inter alia*, whether the commercial broadcasters compete on the same market as the public broadcasters.

9.78 On the other hand, the relatively low evidentiary standard set by the Court in *British Airways* to show the existence of a competitive disadvantage should, in all likelihood, make it relatively easy for the Commission to "recycle" essentially the same facts that it uses to demonstrate the existence of an unjustified discrimination also to prove that the conduct at hand "tends to" place the dominant company's customers at a competitive disadvantage. The *Clearstream* judgment appears to confirm this.[87] In *Clearstream*, even though the Court

---

[87] *Clearstream Judgment 2009, supra* note 13, paras 192–94, *supra* note 13.

9. – Abusive Discrimination
Anne Layne-Farrar, Alice Setari and Paul Stuart

acknowledged that, in order to establish a violation of Article 102 TFEU, it is necessary to demonstrate that unjustified discrimination tends to lead to a distortion of competition between the dominant company's trading partners, it also contented itself with relying on the fact that the discrimination lasted for a period of five years and was enacted by a company with a *de facto* monopoly on the relevant market to conclude that the discrimination *"could not fail to cause"*[88] a competitive disadvantage.

While the competitive disadvantage requirement could have evolved into a **9.79** major constituent element of any secondary line non-exclusionary discrimination abuse, it is unlikely to become a central additional element of this specific abusive conduct following the *British Airways* judgment. This development is regrettable, as a stricter interpretation of the competitive disadvantage requirement would likely have contributed to focus the Commission's and the courts' attention on the differences between exclusionary and non-exclusionary discrimination and the legal tests applicable to each of these abuses.

3. Specific Issues

Before concluding the overview of the status of EU law on abusive discrimi- **9.80** nation, it is worth analysing briefly some discrete issues that may arise in abusive discrimination cases.

3.1. *Knowledge of Discrimination*

For there to be abusive discrimination in breach of Article 102 TFEU, there **9.81** is no requirement that dominant firms adopt anticompetitive behaviour intentionally or that they have knowledge of the harm caused by their conduct. As the European courts have often reiterated, the concept of abuse is an objective one that relates to the behaviour of an undertaking in a dominant position that is capable of influencing the structure of a market;[89] it does not imply any intention to harm. The fact that the undertaking had no intent or aim of distorting competition or the fact that it had struggled to maintain competition is irrelevant for a finding under Article 102 TFEU. This may be problematic for undertakings in situations where they were truly unaware

---

[88] *Clearstream Judgment 2009, supra* note 13, paras 194, *supra* note 13.
[89] *Aéroports de Paris Judgment 2000*, paras 170–73, *supra* note 12.

9. – Abusive Discrimination
Anne Layne-Farrar, Alice Setari and Paul Stuart

of discriminating, *i.e.*, for example, when they charge different prices to a customer that initially was not a competitor but that then started competing with them. This distinction is very important in practice and requires particular attention and constant monitoring on the part of undertakings.

3.2. *Discrimination on Grounds of Nationality*

9.82 A review of the Commission's decisional practice and of the European courts' case law shows that many cases labelled as "abusive discrimination" cases are actually instances of discrimination on the ground of nationality enacted by a dominant company (often as a result of the provisions of a national law or regulation). In these cases, the Commission and the courts essentially limit themselves to establishing the existence of a discrimination on the ground of nationality, while dedicating very little attention, if any, to the other constituent elements of an abuse of a dominant position, whether exclusionary or non-exclusionary.

9.83 In *GVL*,[90] the Commission sanctioned as an abuse of a dominant position in breach of Article 102(c) TFEU the discriminatory conduct enacted by GVL, the German copyright royalty collecting society. GVL required foreign artists seeking its management services to be German residents. In the Commission's view, this conduct placed non-German or non-German resident artists, whose work was broadcast or publicly reproduced in Germany, at a competitive disadvantage compared to German or German resident artists, as the former category of artists could receive no royalty payments. As regards the impact of the discrimination, the Commission limited itself to pointing out that, as a result of GVL's conduct, German or German resident artists had an economic advantage over foreign artists, which could affect competition between them as, in the case of artists, *"even slight financial disadvantages have a considerable impact on their trading position on the market"*.[91]

9.84 In *Corsica Ferries*,[92] an Italian court made a preliminary reference to the Court of Justice asking whether EU law precluded an undertaking in a dominant position with the exclusive right to provide compulsory piloting services in the port of Genoa from applying different conditions for identical services depending on whether the undertakings operated transport services with

---

[90] Case IV/29.839 *GVL*, Commission Decision of 29 October 1981, OJ 1981 L 370/49.
[91] *Ibid.*, para. 55.
[92] *Corsica Ferries*, *supra* note 74.

9. – Abusive Discrimination
Anne Layne-Farrar, Alice Setari and Paul Stuart

vessels authorised to carry on maritime cabotage, *i.e.*, flying the Italian flag (at the relevant time, only vessels flying the Italian flag could provide cabotage services in Italy). When assessing the compatibility of this conduct with Articles 102 TFEU read in conjunction with Article 106 TFEU (since the relevant conduct was mandated by the Italian authorities, which approved the discriminatory tariffs), the Court limited itself to referring to the discriminatory nature of the practice without any assessment of its impact on competition between transport service providers. However, the Court did make a cursory reference to the effects of the discrimination when assessing the compatibility of the conduct with the principles of the Treaty on freedom to provide services. The Court noted that differences in tariffs had an effect on the cost of the piloting services and therefore placed the transport service providers discriminated against at a disadvantage in comparison with economic operators who benefited from the preferential tariffs.[93]

The abovementioned airport cases (namely *Brussels National Airport, Portuguese Airports, Spanish Airports,* and *Finnish Airports*) are also good examples of the Commission's action under Article 102(c) TFEU against unjustified discrimination based on nationality. In each of these cases, the Commission and the courts limited themselves to establishing that the take-off and landing fee system enacted by the airport operator gave rise to unjustified discrimination on the ground of nationality in favour of local airlines, which used the relevant airport(s) as a hub, without, however, engaging in any meaningful discussion of the impact of the discrimination on competition between airlines. The *1998 Football World Cup* Decision[94] (discrimination on grounds of nationality due to the requirement for customers to provide a French postal address to be able to purchase tickets for the 1998 football World Cup games in France) illustrates the same point. There, the Commission even went as far as taking the position that, while the application of Article 102 TFEU often requires an assessment of the effect of an undertaking's behaviour on the structure of competition in a given market, its application in the absence of such an effect cannot be excluded. Accordingly, the Commission continued, Article 102 TFEU can properly be applied, where appropriate, to situations in which a dominant undertaking's behaviour directly prejudices the interests of consumers, notwithstanding the absence of any effect on the structure of competition.[95]

9.85

---

[93] *Corsica Ferries, supra* note 74, para. 21.

[94] Case IV/36.888, *supra* note 64.

[95] *Ibid.*, para. 100.

9. – Abusive Discrimination
Anne Layne-Farrar, Alice Setari and Paul Stuart

3.3. *Discrimination Aimed at Partitioning the Common Market*

9.86 There is also a line of "abusive discrimination" cases in which the Commission and the courts seem to have taken issue with discriminatory conduct due to it leading to an artificial partitioning of the common market, rather than because of its likely exclusionary impact on the dominant company's rivals and/or of its placing the dominant company's customers or suppliers at a competitive disadvantage.

9.87 *United Brands* is a good example. The Commission and the Court of Justice found that United Brands' conduct – consisting of charging different prices to ripeners/distributors active in different Member States, while also making sure that these customers were contractually prohibited from engaging in arbitrage to eliminate the price discrimination by means of parallel trade (by preventing them from reselling green bananas) – violated Article 102(c) TFEU because this conduct resulted in a compartmentalisation of the common market. The existence of a competitive disadvantage for ripeners/distributors was in essence deduced from the conduct's market partitioning effects.

9.88 Similarly, Irish Sugar's discriminatory border rebates – consisting of charging lower prices to customers established along the border between Ireland and Northern Ireland with a view to reducing the imports of cheaper sugar from Northern Ireland – were viewed by the Commission and the Court of First Instance as, *inter alia*, an attempt to disrupt the very essence of a common market. These practices were held to be a violation of Article 102(c) TFEU, without any discussion of their likely market impact.[96]

9.89 *Tetra Pak II*[97] is another good example. In the Commission's and the Court of Justice's view, one of the (many) abusive aspects of Tetra Pak's conduct in that case consisted of applying different prices for the same products in different Member States, thereby creating an artificial partitioning of the common market. The Court found that Tetra Pak's discriminatory pricing could not be justified based on objective market conditions and concluded that this conduct was in breach of Article 102(c) TFEU, again, however, without carrying out any analysis of the competitive disadvantage requirement.

---

[96] *Irish Sugar, supra* note 34.
[97] Case IV/31.043 *Tetra Pak II ("Tetra Pak II Decision 1991")*, Commission Decision of 24 July 1991, OJ 1992 L 72/1; Case T-83/91 *Tetra Pak International v Commission ("Tetra Pak II Judgment 1994")* [1994] ECR II-755; and Case C-333/94 P *Tetra Pak International v Commission ("Tetra Pak II Judgment 1996")* [1996] ECR I-5951.

9. – Abusive Discrimination
Anne Layne-Farrar, Alice Setari and Paul Stuart

If, in the future, the Commission were to take issue with conduct by an abusive **9.90** company that may result in an artificial partitioning of the common market as an abusive discrimination in breach of Article 102(c) TFEU,[98] the Commission ought not to limit itself to establishing the existence of an unjustified discrimination and the fact that this discrimination may lead to an artificial partitioning of the common market, as it did in the cases discussed above. In order to establish a violation of Article 102(c) TFEU, the Commission ought also to establish that the unjustified discrimination places the dominant company's trading parties at a competitive disadvantage. In the absence of such finding, the Commission should not be allowed to rely on Article 102(c) TFEU as the legal basis to condemn conduct that may potentially lead to partitioning of the common market. As advocated by a number of authors,[99] the Commission should use Article 102(c) TFEU to intervene against this type of conduct only as a last resort, where the other tools available to it, such as, *e.g.*, Article 106 TFEU in combination with the TFEU provisions concerning freedom to provide services (to the extent that the conduct is mandated or encouraged by a State act), did not prove effective to address the conduct's market partitioning effects.

3.4. *Discrimination by Patent Pool Members*

Patent pools consist of multiple patent owners centralising their IP rights to **9.91** a certain organisation so that the members of the pool may agree to cross-license patents relating to a particular technology and thus obtain necessary licenses from the organisation. Members of a patent pool are free to negotiate and determine royalties for the technology package and each technology's share of the royalties, either before or after the standard is set.[100] However, if

---

[98] Conduct aimed at partitioning the internal market such as that aimed at preventing parallel trade may also fall within the scope of Article 102 TFEU, although not necessarily within the scope of Article 102(c) TFEU, as it does not presuppose a finding of discrimination between different transactions. *See, e.g.*, Advocate General Jacobs in Case C-53/03 *Synetairismos Farmakopoion Aitolias & Akarnanias and others v GlaxoSmithKline* ("*Syfait*") [2005] ECR I-4609 and Joined Cases C-468 to 478/06 *Sot. Lélos kai Sia and others v GlaxoSmithKline* ("*GlaxoSmithKline Judgment 2008*") [2008] ECR I-7139.

[99] *See* D. Gerard, *supra* note 37, and Geradin and Petit, *supra* note 4.

[100] *See* Commission Notice – Guidelines on the application of Article 81 of the EC Treaty to technology transfer agreements ("*2004 Technology Transfer Guidelines*"), OJ 2004 C 101/2, para. 225. A technical standard is an established norm or requirement that may be developed unilaterally, by a corporation or regulatory body, or by groups such as trade unions and associations. It is usually a formal document that establishes uniform engineering or technical criteria, methods, processes and practices.

9. – Abusive Discrimination
Anne Layne-Farrar, Alice Setari and Paul Stuart

the pool has a dominant market position, royalties and licensing terms should be fair, non-discriminatory, and non-exclusive.[101]

9.92 As to possible forms of price discrimination by patent pool members, it must be preliminarily remarked that, in technology licensing, a number of factors are taken into account when setting royalties, including the size and value of the portfolios held by potential licensees. This entails that setting uniform and identical royalties will not always favour innovation and technology transfer, as the holders of larger patent portfolios would not be able to negotiate better terms and conditions with licensors.[102]

9.93 As regards exclusionary discrimination in the context of patent pools, there has been some discussion of vertically integrated pool members discriminating against non-integrated manufacturing-only licensees.[103] The issue in this context is that without patents of its own to trade in cross licensing, the manufacturing-only firm *should* pay higher royalties. The question then becomes whether the difference in royalties is justified by the absence of a cross license. There are empirical methods to make that determination, but they require data that may not always be available.

9.94 It also ought to be noted that secondary line non-exclusionary discrimination cases involving patent pools are very rare, if not unheard of, as a dominant non-vertically integrated licensor or pool of licensors does not typically have any incentive to price discriminate between licensees. Since royalties are generally calculated on the basis of the number of products manufactured and/or sold by the licensee, a non-vertically integrated licensor typically benefits from downstream competition that leads to expanded output. The only possible exception to the above general rule would appear to be the case in which strong competition on the downstream market would depress the price

---

[101] *See* S. Evrard and others, "Recent Developments in the United States, EU and Asia at the Intersection of Antitrust and Patent Law" (2009) 3(2) *CPI Antitrust Chronicle*. *See also*, A. S. Layne-Farrar, A. J. Padilla and R. Schmalensee, "Pricing Patents for Licensing in Standard Setting Organizations: Making Sense of FRAND Commitments" (2007) 74(3) *Antitrust Law Journal*, pp. 671–706.

[102] D. Geradin, *Pricing Abuses by Essential Patent Holders in a Standard-Setting Context: A View from Europe*, paper prepared for the Conference at University of Virginia on Remedies for Dominant Firm Misconduct, June 4–5, 2008, p. 9.

[103] *See* V. Denicolò and others, "Revisiting Injunctive Relief: Interpreting eBay in High-Tech Industries with Non-Practicing Patent Holders" (2008) 4(3) *Journal of Competition Law and Economics*, pp. 571–608.

9. – Abusive Discrimination
Anne Layne-Farrar, Alice Setari and Paul Stuart

of the products and therefore reduce the licensor's royalties.[104] In this scenario, the dominant licensor may have an incentive to disfavour one or more downstream competitors to reduce competition and keep prices high. Even in this scenario, however, it may not be in the dominant licensor's interest to reduce the number of competitors downstream as this would likely result in an increase of the few remaining players' bargaining power.

In any event, if any secondary line non-exclusionary discrimination case **9.95** involving patent pools were to arise, any such case should be tackled by applying the same principles that would apply had the case arisen in any other context. In other words, the fact that a patent pool is involved ought not to constitute a reason to deviate from the general principles according to which a violation of Article 102(c) TFEU can be established in the presence of an abusive discrimination by a dominant company, and of the dominant company's trading parties being placed at a competitive disadvantage as a result of this conduct.[105]

3.5. Consumer Harm in Secondary Line Non-exclusionary Discrimination

Based on the *Guidance Paper*, consumer harm in the form of anticompetitive **9.96** foreclosure or, at least, the likelihood thereof, is a constituent element of any exclusionary abuse and therefore should also be considered as such for the abuse of both primary line and secondary line exclusionary discrimination. However, this does not appear to be the case with the abuse of non-exclusionary secondary line discrimination enshrined in Article 102(c) TFEU, in light of the interpretation of this provision emerging from the Commission's decisional practice and the European courts' case law. As discussed, the mere existence of discriminatory practices is often enough for the Commission and the courts to assume consumer harm. At its most rigorous, a finding that the conduct at hand tends to put some of the dominant company's trading parties at a competitive disadvantage seems to suffice to qualify an unjustified discrimination by a dominant company as abusive conduct.

Certain commentators have argued that consumer harm should be a pre- **9.97** requisite for a secondary line non-exclusionary discrimination to be found

---

[104] *Supra* note 102.
[105] *See* A. Layne-Farrar, "Non-Discriminatory Pricing: What is Different (and What is Not) about IP Licensing in Standard Setting", June 29, 2009.

9. – Abusive Discrimination
Anne Layne-Farrar, Alice Setari and Paul Stuart

abusive.[106] The lack of any consumer harm requirement, coupled with the relatively loose interpretation by the Commission and the courts of the "competitive disadvantage" requirement, risks condemning as abusive conduct that has no direct negative effect on consumer welfare, nor even any material effect on the competitive conditions on the market where the discriminated players operate. Moreover, as discussed in more detail in Section IV below, economic theory tells us that secondary line non-exclusionary discrimination generally leads to higher output levels (and therefore is generally welfare-enhancing), and does not typically have a negative impact on consumer welfare.

9.98 A solution to avoid possible "Type 1" errors in this context, while remaining within the boundaries of the European courts' case law, may consist of interpreting the competitive disadvantage requirement more strictly. This stricter interpretation would require the Commission to show that the unjustified discrimination would tend to damage the structure of competition (or, in the words of the *Guidance Paper*, harm the *"effective competitive process"*[107]) in the market where the discriminated trading parties are active, thereby also likely negatively impacting final consumers. Another possible alternative to avoid over-enforcement of Article 102 TFEU would be to allow the dominant company to invoke the lack of consumer harm as an objective justification for its conduct, as a last resort defence once all constituent elements of the abuse have been established. While not easy to rely upon in practice (as it would entail the dominant company proving a negative), this objective justification would at least provide the dominant company with the opportunity to demonstrate, based on economic or other types of evidence depending on the specific circumstances of the case, that its conduct could not likely result (or, alternatively, did not result) in consumer harm.

3.6. Objective Justification

9.99 Another issue that may arise in abusive discrimination cases is the possibility for the dominant company to escape liability by showing that the discrimination is necessary or efficiency enhancing.

---

[106] *See* J. Temple Lang, *"Article 82 EC – The Problems and The Solution"*, *supra* note 1; and J. Temple Lang, "The Requirement for a Commission Notice on the Concept of Abuse Under Article 82 EC", *CEPS Special Reports*, December 10, 2008.

[107] *See Guidance Paper*, para. 6, *supra* note 5.

9. – Abusive Discrimination
Anne Layne-Farrar, Alice Setari and Paul Stuart

As regards exclusionary discrimination, the principles embodied in the *Guidance Paper* should apply.[108] A dominant company should therefore be able to escape liability if it is able to demonstrate that the discrimination is objectively necessary (*e.g.*, for health or safety reasons related to the nature of the product)[109] or is efficiency enhancing, *i.e.*, the likely and substantiated efficiencies stemming from it would outweigh any possible foreclosure effect, and the conduct in question is indispensable and proportionate to attain these efficiencies.[110] As regards non-exclusionary discrimination, the above-discussed "lack of consumer harm" justification could arguably be invoked by a dominant company to escape a finding of non-exclusionary secondary line discrimination.   **9.100**

3.7. Meeting Competition

The question also arises as to whether a dominant company that lawfully meets its competitors' prices, but, by so doing, also engages in price discrimination, should be liable for abusive discrimination.   **9.101**

If the dominant company's conduct constitutes lawful meeting competition, then such conduct, even if discriminatory, should not constitute unlawful exclusionary discrimination in breach of Article 102 TFEU because it would not have any foreclosure effect *vis-à-vis* the dominant company's competitors.   **9.102**

It is, however, conceivable that conduct meeting competition may give rise to non-exclusionary secondary line discrimination by placing the dominant company's trading parties at a competitive disadvantage. This outcome is not necessarily welcome as it may give rise to even greater legal uncertainty in an area of the law that already lacks clear rules for companies to abide by. Such ambiguity can create disincentives for potentially procompetitive pricing conduct by the dominant company. As previously discussed, a possible solution may consist in the Commission and the Courts applying a higher evidentiary standard when assessing the existence of a competitive disadvantage and/or in allowing the dominant company to put forward a "lack of consumer harm" defence in Article 102(c) TFEU cases.   **9.103**

---

[108] *See Guidance Paper*, paras 28-31, *supra* note 5.

[109] *See ibid.*, para. 29.

[110] *See ibid.*, para. 30.

9. – Abusive Discrimination
Anne Layne-Farrar, Alice Setari and Paul Stuart

3.8. *MFN Clauses*

9.104 Another issue consists of the interrelation between abusive discrimination and so-called "Most Favored Nation" or "MFN" clauses, *i.e.*, those clauses pursuant to which one party commits to offer to the other party the best contractual terms that it offers to any of its counterparts for the same products or services. If entered into by a dominant supplier/buyer, MFN clauses prohibit a supplier from giving more favourable terms to any other buyer/supplier without also giving them to the buyer/supplier in question. As such, these clauses would seem, at least *prima facie*, to be in line with the objectives pursued by Article 102 TFEU, *i.e.*, to prohibit unjustified discrimination.[111]

9.105 It is undeniable that, under certain conditions, MFN clauses can generate important procompetitive effects, *e.g.*, by facilitating price adjustments in long-term contracts. The impact of MFN clauses is also positive on transaction and information costs. All these advantages should enable the beneficiary of the clause to lower its prices. When the beneficiary of the MFN clause is the seller, the buyer has no incentive to pay a high price to any seller, which tends to intensify the bargaining and to lower prices.

9.106 However, MFN clauses are not always procompetitive. Competition authorities are often suspicious towards MFN clauses, especially (but not only) when the buyer benefits from the clause. This reflects the fact that, by making the actual price levels in the market more easily detectable, MFN clauses facilitate coordination between sellers and monitoring of pricing behaviour. More generally, the Commission considers that contractual clauses requiring a trading party to disclose rivals' prices might be contrary to Article 101 TFEU[112] and/or to Article 102 TFEU.[113] Moreover, MFN clauses can reduce the seller's incentive to lower prices. If the beneficiary of the clause is the buyer, the clause can be considered a penalty on price cuts: since the seller is obliged to grant the same discount to all MFN beneficiaries, the seller has no incentive to offer lower prices to any one buyer. Finally, MFN clauses can act as a barrier to entry. This is obvious for other buyers when the beneficiary of

---

[111] For example, in its Decision concerning Hoffman La Roche's acquisition of Cornage (Case IV/M.950 *Hoffman-La Roche/Boehringer Mannheim*, Commission Decision of 3 May 2011), the Commission accepted Roche's commitment to granting each licensee a "most-favoured-customer" clause to ensure non-discriminatory terms in granting a licence.

[112] *See Hoffmann-La Roche* on such clauses, also called "English clauses", *supra* note 32.

[113] *See* Case IV/29.021 *BP Kemi/DDSF*, Commission Decision of 5 September 1979, OJ 1979 L 286/32.

9. – Abusive Discrimination
Anne Layne-Farrar, Alice Setari and Paul Stuart

the clause is a dominant buyer. In this case, MFN clauses clearly raise rivals' costs and the sellers are deterred from offering better contractual conditions to other buyers, since those conditions would have to be extended to their main purchaser. Potential new entrants are therefore sharply disadvantaged, MFN clauses making them more unlikely to be competitive and thus to enter the market.

Although there is no formal European case law on MFN clauses, two cases **9.107** illustrate the Commission's suspicion, at least when the beneficiary of the MFN clause is dominant in a downstream market. In a case settled in 1996, the Commission objected to a MFN clause in a contract between AC Nielsen and retail stores for the supply of sales data, while AC Nielsen was dominant in the market for retail tracking services for certain goods. The Commission opened formal proceedings and argued that such contracts created barriers to entry, and that AC Nielsen might have abused its dominant position.[114] In a more recent case, after an investigation of the Commission about the territorial restrictions in the gas sector, Gazprom and E.On Ruhrgas committed themselves to delete the "most-favoured customer" clauses that obliged Gazprom to offer similar conditions to Ruhrgas as it would have offered to Ruhrgas' competitors in Germany. Although the Commission does not mention Rurhgas' dominant position,[115] this case makes clear that the MFN clauses were considered barriers to entry in the German gas market and led to a compartmentalisation of the European gas market and to territorial restrictions.[116]

To summarise, while MFN clauses are *prima facie* compliant with the prohi- **9.108** bition of abusive discrimination, they may still have anticompetitive effects. Some may be caught by Article 101 TFEU to the extent that these clauses favour horizontal coordination between market players. Some may fall within the scope of application of Article 102 TFEU to the extent that they may contribute to strengthen a dominant position, as when MFN clauses are accompanied by clauses obliging purchasers to obtain their requirements exclusively from one undertaking or by fidelity rebates granted in a market where the structure of competition has already been weakened by the presence of an

---

[114] *See* Twenty-sixth Report on Competition Policy (1996), para. 64.

[115] Dominant position found by the German Bundeskartellamt in Case B8–113/03-1 *E.ON Ruhrgas AG*, Bundeskartellamt Decision of 13 January 2006.

[116] *See* Press Release IP/05/710 of 10 June 2005 in relation to Case COMP/38.307 *PO/Territorial restrictions Germany ("Gazprom")*, not yet published.

9. – Abusive Discrimination
Anne Layne-Farrar, Alice Setari and Paul Stuart

undertaking operating in a dominant position.[117] Given the above, a dominant company should be allowed to include MFN clauses in its supply/purchase agreements provided it is also able to show that their operation in practice is not likely to give rise to the above anticompetitive effects.[118]

IV. Economics of Discrimination

9.109 Given the history of the Commission's and European courts' reasoning, one might suppose that economics has clearly established that the mere existence of price discrimination leads to consumer harm and/or reduced social welfare. That is not the case. Indeed, as an initial matter, it is important to note that the word "discrimination" is not pejorative from an economics perspective; it simply means that prices differ across purchasers when the costs of serving those purchasers do not (or, alternatively, that prices are the same across purchasers when costs do differ). In fact, as explained below, price discrimination can improve economic efficiency and can even make consumers better off as compared to uniform pricing.[119] The economics of price discrimination therefore do not necessarily justify the decisions reached in the majority of the Commission and court cases covered above, as we discuss below. We begin with the basics, describing the forms that price discrimination can take, the necessary conditions for a firm to be able to implement differential pricing, and then close the economics discussion with welfare effects.

1. The Forms of Price Discrimination

9.110 Distinct from the two legal forms of discrimination delineated above (primary line and secondary line), economics makes additional categorisations of its own. Specifically, the form that price discrimination takes depends importantly on the structure of the market, the nature of market power,

---

[117] *Hoffmann-La Roche*, *supra* note 32, para. 107.

[118] For a more detailed discussion, *see supra* note 43, pp. 585–591.

[119] Price discrimination is, unfortunately, a rather technical field within economics, and the market outcomes and predictions are highly dependent on the model specified and the assumptions made. For a discussion of price discrimination in monopoly settings, *see* H. R. Varian, "Price Discrimination", in R. Schmalensee and R. Willig (Eds.), *Handbook of Industrial Organization* (Amsterdam, North-Holland, 1989), Vol. I, Ch. 10, pp. 597–654. For a thorough survey of the literature on price discrimination in oligopolistic markets, *see* L. A. Stole, "Price Discrimination and Competition", in M. Armstrong and R. H. Porter (Eds.), *Handbook of Industrial Organization* (Amsterdam, North-Holland, 2007), Vol. III, Ch. 34, p. 2223.

9. – Abusive Discrimination
Anne Layne-Farrar, Alice Setari and Paul Stuart

heterogeneity among consumers, and the availability of various segmenting mechanisms. Generally, price discrimination can take one of three forms, which were assigned the imaginative monikers of first, second, and third degree price discrimination.[120] Overlapping with these three categories, price discrimination is either "direct" – to the extent that prices depend upon differences among purchasers that are observable by the supplier – or "indirect" – if purchasers instead self-select into different pricing levels.

First degree price discrimination, sometimes referred to as "perfect" price discrimination, is a *direct* price discrimination method. It occurs when the seller is able to capture the entire surplus from a transaction by pricing each and every unit sold at exactly the customer's willingness to pay for the good. A classic example here is the small town doctor that charges each patient according to his or her ability to pay. This is accomplished by setting prices inversely proportional to the customer's elasticity of demand (*i.e.*, inverse to the customer's price sensitivity). In other words, the seller is able to perfectly discern the value that each customer places on its good and charge a price exactly equal to that value. One cent more and the customer will not conclude the transaction because the price will exceed his or her perceived value; one cent less and the seller will leave some surplus value to the customer, thus falling short of perfect discrimination. **9.111**

As is obvious from the description, first degree price discrimination demands that the seller have tremendous knowledge about each and every potential customer. Not surprisingly, this is quite difficult to achieve in practice – even for a monopolist. As a result, none of the cases discussed above involve first degree, perfect price discrimination. Nonetheless, some sellers are able to approach perfect price discrimination, especially when prices are individually negotiated, such as, for example, in the sale of certain inputs for manufacturing, or in the sale of automobiles to end consumers. **9.112**

Second degree price discrimination is far easier for sellers to accomplish because it is *indirect*. In this case, the seller simply sets prices to vary by the total quantity purchased, which is why second degree price discrimination is sometimes referred to as non-linear pricing or volume discounting. Thus, **9.113**

---

[120] Within these three categories, there are different variations of price discrimination, such as price discrimination based on the customer's purchase history, product bundling (similar to volume discounts, but where different products rather than larger quantities trigger the discount), price rigidities (where prices rise under certain circumstances but do not fall), and so forth.

9. – Abusive Discrimination
Anne Layne-Farrar, Alice Setari and Paul Stuart

customers pay a different price per unit based on the number of units they purchase.

9.114   This form of price discrimination is quite familiar: groceries frequently offer "buy one, get one free" deals; retailers may offer one shirt for €20 but offer two shirts for the sale price of €30; and, mobile service providers often set the price-per-minute for calls at a lower rate when customers commit to talking for some threshold number of minutes in a given month. As these examples illustrate, this widespread form of price discrimination is seen throughout the economy, often in fairly competitive markets.

9.115   From among the cases discussed above, the pricing scheme in *Brussels National Airport* is the clearest example of second degree price discrimination. In that case, the landing fees at issue were based on the volume of landings and take-offs at the airport. The Commission found that the threshold number of landings required to qualify for the lower fee was set so that only those airlines based in Brussels would ever qualify. Moreover, the Commission found that any economies of scale were so insignificant that they could not be used to justify the discounts given.

9.116   Third degree price discrimination occurs when sellers use observable, objective factors to set prices. For example, prices can vary by time of day (an *indirect* form of price discrimination): movie theatres and performance arts events typically offer cheaper tickets for matinées as compared to evening showings, and newspapers sometimes offer their main edition paper for a lower price in the evening as compared to when it is first sold in the morning, thus reflecting the lower value of "old news". Another version of third degree price discrimination relies on the observable characteristics of the customer (a *direct* form of price discrimination). So, prices may vary by age – small children may enter a museum for free and students often may ride public transportation for a discounted price compared to the adult fare. Or, prices may vary by gender, such as when nightclubs offer free admission to women on "ladies' night". The notion behind all of these examples is that the group receiving the discounted price is thought to be more price sensitive (more price elastic) than the group paying the relatively higher price. For example, children are not likely to value a visit to an art museum to the same extent as the adults bringing them; offering free admission for children can increase attendance among parents. Like second degree price discrimination, then, third degree price discrimination is also prevalent throughout the economy.

9. – Abusive Discrimination
Anne Layne-Farrar, Alice Setari and Paul Stuart

Most of the cases discussed above fall under third degree price discrimina- **9.117** tion. For example, in *Aéroports de Paris*, prices were set according to whether ground handling was provided by a third party or was instead self-supplied. Similarly, in *Scandlines*, port fees differed according to whether the entity was a ferry or a cargo ship. Both of these instances involved prices based on objectively observable traits.

2. How Price Discrimination is Accomplished

It takes more than simply setting differential prices for a seller to accomplish **9.118** price discrimination. Instead, price discrimination is only feasible if the following three conditions are met.

First, firms must have some degree of *short-run market power*. Markets charac- **9.119** terised by perfect competition – a rare phenomenon in practice – are comprised of firms with no market power at all and hence are always characterised by a single price (set equal to marginal cost). In non-perfectly competitive markets, while entry may lead to zero economic profits in the long run, firms must have some degree of pricing power in order to maintain price discrimination, at least in the short run. Note that some of the Article 102 TFEU cases discussed above have often involved a monopolist (such as a single port authority, for instance), but monopoly power is not required, as the relatively competitive oligopoly examples of price discrimination among clothing retailers, grocers, and night clubs make clear.

Secondly, it must be *possible to segment consumers* either directly or indirectly. That **9.120** is, sellers must be able to identify directly customers with different preferences or at least observe traits that tend to be associated with different preferences (such as age, gender, etc.). The cases discussed provide clear examples: it is easy to distinguish between a ferry and a cargo ship, or rail transport that runs between Germany and a "western port" or a "northern port".

Thirdly, arbitrage across differently priced goods *must be infeasible*. This last **9.121** condition means that customers must not be able to undo the price differences set by the seller. If a customer qualifying to purchase the good at a relatively low price can promptly resell it to another customer who does not qualify for the relatively low price, then price discrimination is untenable. When arbitrage is possible, the seller will be unable to sell any of its goods at the higher price

9. – Abusive Discrimination
Anne Layne-Farrar, Alice Setari and Paul Stuart

regardless of whether the other two conditions are met, so discrimination is unwound and all goods are *de facto* sold at the lowest price level (or at that level plus the transaction costs of arbitrage).

9.122 As noted above, United Brands prevented arbitrage by imposing a contractual provision on its customers. It prohibited its ripener/distributor customers from reselling green bananas across geographic areas. Had United Brands not imposed this contractual restriction, any price differences that it attempted to impose on the sale of ripe bananas across geographic regions would have been undone by ripeners/distributors based in lower price regions reselling green bananas to ripeners/distributors based in higher price regions, eventually leading to equalised banana prices (less the additional transport and transaction costs).

3. The Welfare Effects

9.123 In an ideal world, competition policy would be directed only at those firm behaviours that harm competition and ultimately harm consumer welfare. The key question, then, is: does price discrimination result in either of these problems? In order to answer that question, we must ask another question: compared to what? Thus, a benchmark is typically needed.

9.124 Let us start with the most straightforward case: the welfare implications of perfect price discrimination practiced by a monopolist. In this scenario, the seller sets prices to perfectly mimic each customer's private valuation and hence extracts every cent of surplus. This has two key effects. First, the deadweight loss associated with monopolies (the surplus that goes neither to the producer nor to consumers) is eliminated. Secondly, total welfare (consumer plus producer surplus) is increased as compared to uniform pricing and, as a result, the outcome is entirely efficient. Of course, consumers would have zero surplus in this case, with the monopolist appropriating all gains from the transaction. The obvious counterfactual here is uniform pricing practiced by the same monopolist, which is well known to result in a deadweight loss. The deadweight loss derives from the fact that the monopolist sets prices (sometimes well) above marginal costs, which leads to *too few* goods sold as compared to the most efficient (perfectly competitive) market outcome. To the extent that, in this scenario, allowing price discrimination enhances total welfare and has no impact (whether positive or negative) on consumer welfare, there is no economic justification for a prohibition of price discrimination.

9. – Abusive Discrimination
Anne Layne-Farrar, Alice Setari and Paul Stuart

The welfare analysis becomes more complex in the more common scenarios **9.125** of markets characterised by imperfect competition or by a monopolist with imperfect price discrimination. In these scenarios, the analysis of the welfare effects of price discrimination needs to consider the welfare changes from allowing firms to price discriminate as opposed to mandating uniform prices.

Unfortunately, there are no crisp theoretical rules for determining the welfare **9.126** implications deriving from price discrimination in these more complex but common circumstances. The general rule is that if output increases under price discrimination as compared to uniform pricing, then discrimination is likely to be beneficial. In turn, the output effect depends on the structure of the market, the nature of competition between firms within that market, customer preferences, and any differences between those preferences. As a result, the question of welfare effects is case specific and must be empirically determined. Nonetheless, some general statements can be made.

First, there is one particular market structure that is viewed as generally **9.127** problematic for price discrimination: when the seller is vertically integrated. Whereas firms that are upstream suppliers only have little if any incentive to disadvantage one of their customers over another, vertically integrated firms compete with their downstream customers. For example, not only was Irish Sugar the sole beet sugar processor in Ireland and Northern Ireland, it was also Ireland's largest supplier, with a market share over the relevant time period of around 90 per cent. Hence, Irish Sugar competed with its customers that purchased sugar with an intent to sell at least some of their purchases into Ireland. By granting discounts only to those customers that sold sugar strictly outside of Ireland, Irish Sugar would have been able to maintain relatively higher prices for domestic Irish sales, which in turn would soften the competition that its distribution arm faced. Irish consumers would therefore likely pay higher prices than they would have in the absence of price discrimination. Of course, an assessment of the conduct's likely impact on competition would still need to be conducted, but in such instances of vertically integrated firms practicing discrimination, there is a clear motive to distort competition.

Secondly, and more generally, output is the key factor in any price discrimina- **9.128** tion welfare inquiry: an increase in aggregate output is a necessary (but not sufficient) condition for price discrimination to increase welfare.[121] To a large

---

[121] *See* R. Schmalensee, "Output and Welfare Implications of Monopolistic Third-Degree Price Discrimination" (1981) 71(1) *American Economic Review*, pp. 242–7.

9. – Abusive Discrimination
Anne Layne-Farrar, Alice Setari and Paul Stuart

extent, the welfare impact of price discrimination depends on whether this practice results in broadening the market, increasing output by enabling sales that would not otherwise occur. That is an empirical question, whose answer must be ascertained on a case-by-case basis.

9.129   In most settings, the ability to price discriminate benefits sellers. Most obviously, if a firm can charge a higher price for some subset of sales than would otherwise be the case under uniform pricing, the seller's profits will rise. This is not always the case though. In markets where sellers have the ability to coordinate, they might prefer uniform prices because price discrimination can trigger vigorous competition between the sellers, which, in turn, can lead to lower overall prices and lower profits than the relatively higher uniform price enables. In this case, uniform prices act as a price floor commitment for sellers, enabling them to keep overall prices higher. Certainly where prices are set through bilateral negotiations, customers are likely to pay higher prices if all sellers can commit to uniform prices – buyers have little incentive to negotiate for their best deal if the seller is unable to offer customer specific discounts. This dynamic is the reason that cartels often mandate uniform prices among their members – allowing for price discrimination can open the door to individually profitable "cheating", which can cause the cartel to collapse.[122]

9.130   Another benefit for sellers derives from the nature of some production investments. Specifically, when sellers offer products or services that require large upfront investments, the use of price discrimination can spread those investments over a larger revenue base than may be possible with uniform pricing. One example would be firms that make sizeable, and often risky, R&D expenditures in order to develop innovative products. These firms need to be able to recover those investments and make a return on the risk incurred, otherwise the investments will not be made in the first instance. Because price discrimination can enable firms to broaden the market and increase their revenues, it can also assist with the recoupment of such risky investments.

9.131   The pharmaceutical industry offers a good vehicle for considering the welfare effects of price discrimination in a scenario featuring a monopolist and imperfect price discrimination. If we think only of the short term, lower drug

---

[122] Indeed, one screen for identifying cartels is the "variance screen", which looks at price levels and variance before and during an alleged cartel. *See* R. M. Abrantes-Metz and others, "A Variance Screen for Collusion" (2005) 24(3) *Journal of Industrial Organization*, pp. 467–86.

9. – Abusive Discrimination
Anne Layne-Farrar, Alice Setari and Paul Stuart

prices are clearly better for consumers than higher ones. However, uniform prices for consumers do not typically imply low prices. Instead, the uniform price that enables a pharmaceutical firm to adequately recoup its fixed costs (upfront R&D, clinical trials, etc.) could easily exceed the lowest price offered under price discrimination, meaning that uniform prices imply a price increase for at least some consumers and may therefore reduce the aggregate quantity of the drugs sold. In fact, it may be the case that certain geographic markets or customer segments with high price elasticities (highly responsive to price changes) would be foreclosed from buying the drug altogether under uniform pricing if the uniform price set by the drug company to cover its fixed costs exceeded the reservation price that the particular consumer group was willing to pay. When we consider the factors involved in pharmaceutical drug production and pricing, then, even with a short-term view, it is clear that price discrimination can expand output and may be welfare enhancing. As a result, the evidentiary bar should be set relatively high for establishing abusive price discrimination as practiced by a dominant firm with large upfront costs (such as in pharmaceuticals), to ensure that uniform prices are not imposed in those instances where they would be harmful to consumers in the aggregate.

Adding in the longer-term dynamics of pharmaceutical product development **9.132** only reinforces this point. Since the pharmaceutical industry is decidedly influenced by the long term, through R&D investments and stringent government drug approval processes, a longer term view recognises that upfront efforts are not only expensive, but are also risky and thus require prices to exceed the (relatively nominal) marginal costs of producing an approved drug. Generally, in industries where risky upfront investments are required to bring new products to market, those products which are ultimately successful in the market must not only earn an adequate return on their own sunk costs, but must also compensate for the inevitable failures. When expected profits are not anticipated to cover adequately risky fixed investments, those risky upfront investments will not be made.[123]

---

[123] This is a fundamental concept in financial economics, but risk-adjusted rewards are often overlooked in other areas. For a discussion of risk and reward in a financial context, see J. Jaffe, S. A. Ross and R. W. Westerfield, *Corporate Finance* (7th Ed., McGraw-Hill Irwin, 2005), pp. 255–337. Note that the pharmaceutical example is a complicated one because it is not simply a matter of adjusting *ex post* payoffs to account for failed R&D efforts. Instead, expected returns can affect firms' risk preferences, meaning that reduced rewards can lead to greater risk aversion. How increased risk aversion ultimately affects consumer welfare is an open question, but it may actually reduce consumer welfare by relatively increasing investment in "small" incremental projects as opposed to more pioneering ones. See, e.g., J. J. Ganuza, G. Llobet, and B. Domínguez, "R&D in the Pharmaceutical Industry: A World of Small Innovations" (2009) 55(4) *Management Science*, pp. 539–51.

9. – Abusive Discrimination

Anne Layne-Farrar, Alice Setari and Paul Stuart

9.133   The same rationale also applies in markets characterised by imperfect competition: even with some competition in the marketplace, uniform prices do not necessarily equate to "low" prices, due to fixed costs and/or risky investments. Consider, for example, office equipment, such as photocopier machines. This durable equipment involves a sizeable upfront purchase price plus follow-on service payments to maintain the equipment in working order. In a market with several copy machine suppliers and no price discrimination, sellers compete on the purchase price and on the aftermarket to provide machine service, and aftermarket competition can be even more intense than that for the sale of original equipment as independent service operators (or "ISOs", *i.e.*, entities focusing on aftermarket service but not selling their own copier) may enter as well.

9.134   One application of price discrimination in durable good markets involves lowering the upfront purchase price of the copier while raising the aftermarket price of service, which is maintained via restrictive service agreements that prevent the ISOs from servicing the equipment.[124] On its face, this arrangement might appear to be an anticompetitive foreclosure on the aftermarket for copier service, along the lines of *United Brands* and the restrictions on the resale of green bananas. There is, however, another explanation. This pricing structure in effect lowers the cost of owning a copier for less-intensive users, as they will pay less for the machine but have few service calls, while it raises the total ownership cost for more-intensive users, who will pay less for the machine, but more for their greater number of service calls. In this case, price discrimination may increase the overall market for copiers since marginal users can now afford to purchase a copier, whereas with lower service costs without restrictions but higher equipment prices, those customers were priced out of the market.

9.135   On the other hand, aggregate output may fall in the presence of imperfect price discrimination by either a monopolist or an oligopolist. This can occur when the quantity sold to the group of purchasers facing the relatively higher discriminatory price falls by more than the increase in quantity sold for the group facing the relatively lower discriminatory price. The possibility for lower output is the reason an empirical assessment is needed to determine consumer welfare effects.

---

[124] *See* B. Klein and J. S. Wiley, "Competitive Price Discrimination as an Antitrust Justification for Intellectual Property Refusals to Deal" (2003) 70(29) *Antitrust Law Journal*, pp. 599–613.

9. – Abusive Discrimination
Anne Layne-Farrar, Alice Setari and Paul Stuart

When considering imperfect price discrimination, however, we need to look **9.136** beyond market-level output in the assessment of the total welfare effects and also consider the allocation of any given output across customers. With a uniform price, inter-consumer misallocations are not possible. Under price discrimination, however, aggregate output may not be efficiently distributed to the highest-value users. For example, under the third degree price discrimination example of public transport, suppose that some students are not at all budget constrained, but in fact hold substantial savings. Other prime age adults, in contrast, may face serious budget constraints. Sellers, however, cannot identify these individuals that run counter to the generalisation on which their price discrimination is premised. In this case, price discrimination will lead to relatively greater purchases by the wealthy student than without the discount and fewer purchases by the constrained adult as compared to the relatively lower uniform price adults would otherwise pay, even if the adult actually values the good more than the student does. This prospect emphasises the shortcomings of third degree price discrimination, based on observable, but fallible, population characteristics.

There also may be so-called "cross-segment" inefficiencies associated with **9.137** second and third degree price discrimination in oligopoly markets if a given consumer is served by an inefficient firm. For instance, a customer may choose to purchase from a more distant or higher-cost firm simply to obtain a price discount, when a closer or more efficient firm (offering higher, presumably uniform, prices) would be better from a social perspective. This example highlights the discrepancy between privately beneficial decisions (purchasing from the distant supplier to keep own costs low) versus socially beneficial decisions (purchasing from a closer supplier to keep overall industry costs low).

As a result of these two possible inefficiencies – misallocation and cross- **9.138** segment – if output levels are the same under both price discrimination and uniform pricing, then price discrimination will generally be deemed to be welfare reducing. When output falls under price discrimination as compared to uniform prices, we need not even look at allocation issues as it is clear that the discriminatory pricing is harmful. Unfortunately, the converse does not automatically hold. As mentioned above, increased output is a strong signal of increased welfare, but for a complete assessment, we should consider allocation effects as well. For practical purposes, however, and especially in light of perennially constrained budgets, since increased output is a strong signal of increased welfare, the Commission would be better served by devoting its

9. – Abusive Discrimination
Anne Layne-Farrar, Alice Setari and Paul Stuart

limited resources to other cases and ignoring those where there is evidence of increased output.[125]

9.139 In light of the broad view that many forms of price discrimination are pro-competitive, and since separating the procompetitive from the anticompetitive requires case-specific analysis, it is surprising that the Commission and the European courts have made so little effort to investigate and assess the consumer harm effects in the Article 102 TFEU cases brought to date. Without a record of investigation in these cases, we can draw no conclusions on welfare *ex post*. It is likely, however, that, firms have been penalised for anticompetitive discrimination when no harmful effects for consumers resulted from that discrimination, at least in some of the abusive discrimination cases condemned by the Commission and the European courts.

V. The Future of Abusive Discrimination under EU Law

9.140 Before concluding the analysis of abusive discrimination under EU law, a number of remarks can be put forward on the possible future developments of this complex area of competition law.

9.141 As a starting point, to ensure consistency in how abusive discrimination cases are dealt with, it is important that in the future the Commission and the courts clearly distinguish between exclusionary (whether primary or secondary line) and (secondary line) non-exclusionary abusive discrimination cases and apply the appropriate legal test to each type of conduct. As discussed, unjustified discrimination may have exclusionary effects *vis-à-vis* the dominant company's competitors, whether on the market where the company holds the dominant position or on a downstream market. In this case, after establishing the existence of an unjustified discrimination, in line with the principles enshrined in the *Guidance Paper*, it ought to be determined whether the conduct is likely to result in anticompetitive foreclosure. Conversely, if the unjustified discrimination is not liable to affect the dominant company's competitors, but rather its trading parties, *i.e.*, customers or suppliers, after establishing an unjustified discrimination, it ought to be assessed whether this conduct tends to put these trading parties at a competitive disadvantage.

---

[125] L. A. Stole, *supra* note 119, pp. 2221–99.

9. – Abusive Discrimination
Anne Layne-Farrar, Alice Setari and Paul Stuart

In this respect, the judgment of the General Court on the issue of abusive discrimination in the *Soda-ash – Solvay* case is a good example of how not to carry out an abusive discrimination assessment.[126] In the judgment, the General Court confirmed the Commission's decision that Solvay's rebate and discount practices were in breach of Article 102 TFEU because of their exclusionary and discriminatory nature. When assessing the compatibility of Solvay's conduct with Article 102(c) TFEU, the Court limited itself to establishing the existence of an unjustified discrimination, without analysing whether the conduct was likely to result in placing Solvay's trading parties at a competitive disadvantage (since Solvay was not vertically integrated downstream, the secondary line discrimination could not be exclusionary in nature). The fact that the Court completely ignored the competitive disadvantage requirement of this type of abuse is already rather worrying. Even more worrying, however, is the Court's reasoning in rebutting Solvay's arguments. To Solvay's claim that the customers between which the discrimination took place were active in separate downstream glass markets, and therefore were not in competition with each other, the Court replied that the relevant market is the market for soda ash, not the market for glass, and that it was therefore not necessary to distinguish between different types of glass producers among soda ash customers.[127] Similarly, to Solvay's argument that soda ash costs represented a low proportion of the glass price (and therefore that the discrimination would likely have had a limited impact on competition downstream), the Court replied that this factor is not such to put into question the discriminatory nature of the conduct at hand.[128] One could reasonably have hoped for a more thorough and systematic assessment of abusive discrimination practices than that followed by the General Court in *Soda-ash – Solvay*.

9.142

More recently, however, in *Post Danmark*, the Court of Justice did accept that in order to conclude that a discriminatory pricing policy gives rise to anticompetitive effects, one could not simply rely upon the fact that the lower price charged by the dominant undertaking to a competitor's major customers was at a particular level relative to the costs attributed to the activity concerned. Rather, the Court of Justice held that it is necessary to consider whether that

9.143

---

[126] Case T-57/01 *Solvay v Commission* ("*Solvay Judgment 2009*") [2009] ECR II-4621. The judgment of the General Court was set aside, and the decision of the Commission quashed by the Court of Justice for infringement of Solvay's rights of defence. It was thus not necessary for the Court of Justice to examine the grounds of appeal as regards the existence of discrimination (*see* Case C-109/10 P *Solvay v Commission*, not yet reported).

[127] *Solvay Judgment 2009, supra* note 126, para. 400.

[128] *Ibid.*, para. 401.

9. – Abusive Discrimination
Anne Layne-Farrar, Alice Setari and Paul Stuart

pricing policy, without objective justification, produces actual or likely exclusionary effects.[129] In that regard, the Court of Justice appears to have endorsed the view that after establishing the existence of an unjustified discrimination, one must still determine whether the conduct is likely to result in anticompetitive foreclosure in order to find an infringement of Article 102 TFEU.

9.144 Absent a finding of anticompetitive foreclosure and/or of competitive disadvantage, any unjustified discrimination ought not to be considered in breach of Article 102 TFEU. The Commission ought therefore to refrain from bringing abusive discrimination cases in instances where the unjustified discrimination, even if based on nationality, has no exclusionary effect and/or does not place any of the dominant company's trading parties at a competitive disadvantage, or where the only possible effect that may derive from the unjustified discrimination is the artificial partitioning of the common market. If the relevant conduct constitutes a violation of Article 102 TFEU and/or of other provisions of the TFEU because of its likely effects on the market (other than foreclosing third-party competitors and/or placing the dominant company's trading parties at a competitive disadvantage), it should be dealt with by the Commission and the courts as such, and not as instance of abusive discrimination.

9.145 In secondary line non-exclusionary discrimination cases, the Commission and the courts ought not lose sight of the fact that, as stated by Advocate General Kokott's opinion and by the judgment of the Court of Justice in the *British Airways* case, competitive disadvantage constitutes a separate and additional constituent element of the specific abusive conduct contemplated by Article 102(c) TFEU, which should be proved by the Commission. Moreover, as discussed, to avoid Type I errors in the enforcement of this provision, a welcome development of the Commission's decisional practice and of the European courts' case law in the interpretation of the "competitive disadvantage" requirement would consist of exploring in more detail than it has been done so far whether and how the unjustified discrimination is likely to negatively affect the competitive process on the market where the dominant company's customers or suppliers operate and result in consumer harm. Alternatively (or in addition), the dominant company ought to be entitled to escape liability by proving that the unjustified discrimination is not likely to result in consumer harm.

---

[129] *Supra* note 54.

9. – Abusive Discrimination
Anne Layne-Farrar, Alice Setari and Paul Stuart

A more cautious approach to the application of Article 102 TFEU to second- **9.146** ary line non-exclusionary discrimination cases is also supported by economic theory, which shows that, to the extent that its net effect is to increase total output, this type of price discrimination is generally welfare enhancing and tends not to be detrimental to consumer welfare. In particular, this form of discrimination can lead to additional markets being served that would otherwise be excluded if uniform pricing were mandated.[130]

Recent developments in this area of law in the United States lend further sup- **9.147** port to the conclusion that secondary line non-exclusionary discrimination cases should not, and do not, constitute an enforcement priority for competition agencies around the globe, and only account for a limited portion of the total antitrust civil claims brought by private plaintiffs. They have not, however, completely disappeared.

In the United States, there exists a long-standing statutory prohibition of **9.148** (price) discrimination, which applies regardless of whether the firm engaging in price discrimination has monopoly power. Pursuant to the Robinson-Patman Act enacted in 1936, sellers are prohibited from offering different prices to different purchasers of *"commodities of like grade and quality"*[131] where the difference injures competition. According to the law, different discount levels, or lower prices, can be offered only where: (1) the same discount is practically available to all purchasers; (2) a lower price is justified by a lower per-unit cost of selling to the "favoured" buyer; (3) a lower price is offered in good faith to meet (but not beat) the price of a competitor; or (4) a lower price is justified by changing conditions affecting the market or marketability of the goods, such as where goods are perishable or seasonal or the business is closing or in bankruptcy.

Over the last few decades, the doctrinal debate in the United States on **9.149** price discrimination has focused on the economic soundness of the non-discrimination rule enshrined in the Robinson-Patman Act.[132] As confirmed

---

[130] As Professor Richard Schmalensee observed several decades ago, "[i]*f discrimination makes possible a large volume of such new sales, it can lead to an increase in welfare even if total sales to previously served markets fail to expand."* See supra note 121.

[131] Robinson-Patman Act of 1936, 15 U.S.C. § 13.

[132] See Antitrust Modernization Commission, *Report and Recommendations*, April 2007. In addition, the US law literature is replete with articles that argue the Robinson-Patman Act is bad law. See, e.g., H. Hovenkamp, "Antitrust at the Millennium (Part I): The Robinson-Patman Act and Competition: Unfinished Business"

9. – Abusive Discrimination
Anne Layne-Farrar, Alice Setari and Paul Stuart

by the US Supreme Court, the purpose of the Robinson-Patman Act was historically to protect small businesses from larger businesses: "[t]*he legislative history of the RPA makes it abundantly clear that Congress considered it to be an evil that a large buyer could secure a competitive advantage over a small buyer solely because of the large buyer's quantity purchasing ability. The RPA was passed to deprive a large buyer of such advantage*".[133] To the extent that it is aimed at protecting competitors, not effective competition, contrary to the ultimate aim of antitrust provisions, the economic soundness from an antitrust viewpoint of the Robinson-Patman Act rules has been repeatedly questioned.[134] In April 2007, a Report by the Antitrust Modernization Commission heavily criticised the Robinson-Patman Act, and even recommended repealing it. According to the Report, the Robinson-Patman Act "*does not promote competition …. Instead, the Act protects competitors, often at the expense of competition that otherwise would benefit consumers, thereby producing anticompetitive outcomes*".[135] The Report also noted that the Robinson-Patman Act is not even an adequate way to achieve the original objective behind its adoption, *i.e.*, protecting small businesses. In particular, the Report observes that the Robinson-Patman Act has "*the unintended effect of limiting the extent of discounting generally and therefore has likely caused consumers to pay higher prices than they otherwise would*".[136] Indeed, the Report observed that "[w]*ide agreement exists that many forms of price discrimination are procompetitive and beneficial to consumers.*"[137] The Report therefore concluded that the Robinson Patman Act is "*fundamentally inconsistent with the antitrust laws, which protect price and other types of competition that benefit consumers*",[138] and recommended that Congress should repeal the Act in its entirety.

9.150 In terms of administrative and judicial enforcement, it is noteworthy that the Federal Trade Commission has issued only one Robinson-Patman Act complaint since 1992.[139] As a result, while it has not been officially repealed, the Robinson-Patman Act is largely ignored by the US agencies. Similarly, private

---

(2000) 68 *Antitrust Law Journal*, pp. 125–44; W. J. Liebeler, "Let's Repeal it" (1976) 45 *Antitrust Law Journal*, pp. 18–43; and F. M. Rowe, "Price Discrimination, Competition, and Confusion: Another Look at Robinson-Patman" (1951) 60(6) *Yale Law Journal*, p. 929.

[133] *Federal Trade Commission v Morton Salt*, 334 US 37 (1948).

[134] *See* Antitrust Modernization Commission, Report and Recommendations, *supra* note 132.

[135] *Ibid.*, p. 317.

[136] *Ibid.*

[137] *Ibid.*

[138] *Ibid.*

[139] *Ibid.*

9. – Abusive Discrimination
Anne Layne-Farrar, Alice Setari and Paul Stuart

litigation has also significantly decreased in the recent years,[140] in particular following the 1993 judgment of the Supreme Court in *Brooke Group*.[141] By raising the evidentiary burden for Robinson-Patman Act cases to the level required under Section 2 of the Sherman Act (*"primary line injury is of the same general character as the injury inflicted by predatory pricing schemes actionable under § 2 of the Sherman Act"*[142]), the Supreme Court essentially eliminated any pre-existing advantage for plaintiffs deriving from relying on a violation of the Robinson Patman Act. *Brooke Group* thus means that plaintiffs making primary line civil claims under the Robinson-Patman Act, *i.e.*, damage claims brought by the direct customers of the company accused of price discrimination asking for compensation for the damage suffered as a result of the unlawful discrimination, ought to show that the damage they suffered resulted from a predatory-like conduct. Following the judgment of the Supreme Court in *Brooke Group*, primary line damage claims for violation of the Robinson-Patman Act essentially stopped.

Even for secondary line (non-exclusionary) Robinson-Patman Act damage claims a strong uncertainty remains. The main issue at stake is how to make the defence of competitors compatible with the defence of competition. As noted, the Robinson-Patman Act prohibits price discrimination *"where the effect of such discrimination may be substantially to lessen competition or tend to create a monopoly in any line of commerce, or to injure, destroy, or prevent competition with any person who either grants or knowingly receives the benefit of such discrimination, or with customers of either of them"*.[143] In its opinion in *Volvo Trucks North America v Reeder-Simco GMC*,[144] the Supreme Court reaffirmed that the Robinson-Patman Act should be construed *"consistently with broader policies of the antitrust laws"*[145] and that it *"would resist interpretation geared more to the protection of existing competitors than to the stimulation of competition"*.[146] This statement appears to support the conclusion that, even in the context of secondary line non-exclusionary discrimination cases, plaintiffs would have to show some type of harm to competition stemming from the discrimination. However, the final part of the opinion of the

9.151

---

[140] According to the Antitrust Modernization Commission, between 1997 and 2007, of 200 reported cases with Robinson-Patman Act claims filed in federal court, only three jury verdicts in favour of plaintiffs were affirmed on appeal. One of these three was reversed by the Supreme Court. *Ibid.*, p. 316.

[141] *Brooke Group v Brown & Williamson Tobacco*, 509 US 209 (1993).

[142] *Ibid.*, pp. 221–22.

[143] *Supra* note 131, Section 2(a).

[144] *Volvo Trucks North America v Reeder-Simco GMC*, 126 S. Ct. 860 (2006).

[145] *Ibid.*, p. 870.

[146] *Ibid.*, p. 872.

9. – Abusive Discrimination
Anne Layne-Farrar, Alice Setari and Paul Stuart

Supreme Court in the same case states that a *"hallmark of the requisite competitive injury … is the diversion of sales or profits form a disfavoured purchaser to a favoured purchaser,"* and *"a permissible inference of competitive injury may arise from evidence that a favoured competitor received a significant price reduction over a substantial period of time."*[147] Thus, the decision seems to allow the Court to infer the existence of harm to competition from the very fact that an unjustified discrimination took place. Robinson-Patman Act secondary line (non-exclusionary) discrimination claims are therefore still current in the United States – at least for the time being.

9.152 Abusive discrimination cases revolve around two key issues, one of which is factual and one of which is legal. The factual question to address in every abusive discrimination case is whether an unjustified discrimination actually occurred, *i.e.*, whether two transactions are equivalent and were treated differently (or are different and were treated equally) and, which in essence is the same, whether the differential treatment was objectively justified. Once it is established that an unjustified discrimination occurred, the legal question to address is whether the appropriate test to apply is that provided for by the *Guidance Paper* for exclusionary discrimination (anticompetitive foreclosure) or by the case law for non-exclusionary discrimination (competitive disadvantage). The application of the appropriate legal test to the established discrimination would answer the question whether the conduct at hand constitutes a violation of Article 102 TFEU.

---

[147] *Ibid.*, p. 860.

10. – Excessive Pricing
Marcus Glader and Ioannis Kokkoris

Excessive Pricing

*Marcus Glader and Ioannis Kokkoris**

"A strong argument can be made that, although the result may expose the public to the evils of monopoly, the Act does not mean to condemn the resultant of those very forces which it is its prime object to foster: finis opus coronat. The successful competitor, having been urged to compete, must not be turned upon when he wins."[1]

I. Introduction

There is a direct link between the question of dominance and the effects of its exploitation in the market. An economic definition of dominance would coincide with a plausible definition of excessive pricing, *i.e.*, that a company can persistently sustain profits above the competitive level without inducing customer switching or attracting new entry. Assessing profits in this way can be a powerful tool to determine dominance.[2] Nevertheless, dominance is not itself illegal under EU competition law. Article 102(a) TFEU provides that an abuse may particularly consist of *"directly or indirectly imposing unfair purchase or selling prices or other unfair trading conditions"*. The Court of Justice has held that *"charging a price which is excessive because it has no reasonable relation to the economic value of the product supplied would be … an abuse"*.[3] This puts the enforcer in a difficult conundrum – where should the line be drawn between the legal operation of a dominant enterprise and the illegal imposition of unfair prices and other terms?

10.1

There has been an intense debate on the interpretation and potential enforcement of the prohibition under Article 102(a) TFEU. For neoclassical

10.2

---

* Marcus Glader is a partner at Advokatfirman Vinge, LLD and visiting lecturer at Lund University, Sweden. Ioannis Kokkoris is Professor of Law and Economics at the University of Reading and Executive Director of the Centre for Commercial Law and Financial Regulation (CCLFR). The views expressed are strictly personal and do not necessarily reflect the views of any affiliated firm, institution or client.

[1] Judge Learned Hand in *United States v Aluminum of America*, 148 F.2d 416 (2nd Cir. 1945).
[2] *See* Oxera, *Assessing Profitability in Competition Policy Analysis*, Office of Fair Trading Economic Discussion Paper 6, OFT 657, July 2003.
[3] Case 27/76 *United Brands and United Brands Continentaal v Commission* ("*United Brands*") [1978] ECR 207, para. 250.

10. – Excessive Pricing
Marcus Glader and Ioannis Kokkoris

economists, the fair value of a good or service is given by its competitive market price. The latter is determined by the price that would result from the equilibrium of demand and supply in a competitive market.[4] However, the theoretical benchmark that neoclassical economists suggest is impractical and disproportionate as a measure for unfair pricing and would render the pricing of every profit-maximising firm with market power abusive. It is fair to say that, according to the majority view,[5] excessive pricing may raise concerns when there are significant barriers to entry, in which case new players will be deterred from entering the market and competing away monopoly rents.[6]

10.3 This is also an area where the European Union has taken a different approach compared to the United States. Whereas exclusionary conduct is an offence against antitrust law in both the European Union and the United States, exploitative conduct is only prohibited under EU law.[7] Section 2 of the Sherman Act prohibits "monopolisation" – *i.e.*, the anticompetitive attainment and maintenance of monopoly power. One of the most important assumptions underlying the US regime is the belief that a free marketplace will generally self-correct and yield the best allocation of economic resources. The US approach therefore includes strong remedies against anticompetitive agreements and monopolisation (including criminal charges and treble damages), but no prohibition of the exploitation of a monopoly as such.[8]

---

[4] *See* A. Marshall, *Principles of Economics* (1st Ed., London, Macmillan, 1890) and D. S. Evans and A. J. Padilla, "Excessive Prices: Using Economics to Define Administrable Legal Rules" (2005) 1(1) *Journal of Competition Law and Economics*, pp. 97–122.

[5] *See* indicatively M. Motta and A. de Streel, "Exploitative and Exclusionary Excessive Prices in EU Law", in C-D. Ehlermann and I. Atanasiu (Eds.), *European Competition Law Annual 2003: What Is Abuse of Dominant Position?* (Oxford, Hart Publishing, 2006), pp. 91–126; R. O'Donoghue and A. J. Padilla, *The Law and Economics of Article 82 EC* (Oxford, Hart Publishing, 2006), p. 617; B. Lyons, "The Paradox of the Exclusion of Exploitative Abuse", *CCP Working Paper Series*, Paper No. 08-1, December 2007.

[6] Some authors have argued that excessive prices may not attract new entry of viable competitors, irrespective of entry barriers. *See, e.g.,* A. Ezrachi and D. Gilo, "Are Excessive Prices Really Self-Correcting?" (2008) 5(2) *Journal of Competition Law & Economics*, pp. 249–68. Ezrachi and Gilo argue that if the entrant regards the dominant undertaking as more efficient than it is, it is unlikely to enter, even if the dominant firm is charging an excessive price.

[7] M. Gal, "Monopoly Pricing as an Antitrust Offense in the U.S. and the EC: Two Systems of Belief About Monopoly?" (2004) 49 *Antitrust Bulletin*, pp. 343–84.

[8] The US approach is clearly illustrated in *Standard Oil of New Jersey v United States*, 221 US 1 (1911), p. 62: "*by the omission of any direct prohibition against monopoly in the concrete, [the Sherman Act] indicates a consciousness that the freedom of the individual right to contract, when not unduly or improperly exercised, was the most efficient means for the prevention of monopoly, since the operation of the centrifugal and centripetal forces resulting from the right to freely contract was the means by which monopoly would be inevitably prevented if no extraneous or sovereign power imposed it and no right to make unlawful contracts having a monopolistic tendency were permitted.*" *See also* M. Gal, *supra* note 7, pp. 343–84.

10. – Excessive Pricing
Marcus Glader and Ioannis Kokkoris

Given the difficulties in establishing when a price is excessive and the fact **10.4**
that price control may have an adverse impact on investment and innovation, the Commission has been wisely restrictive in its enforcement of
Article 102(a) TFEU. Since excessive prices typically induce entry and expansion by competitors, markets can often be assumed to self-correct artificially
high prices. Moreover, where the market involves natural monopolies, sector-
specific regulation (possibly supervised by a designated agency) is often a
more appropriate tool than price control by competition authorities under
the antitrust laws. The Commission itself has explained reluctance to engage
in price regulation:

> *"The existence of a dominant position is not itself against the rules of competi-*
> *tion. Consumers can suffer from a dominant company exploiting this position, the*
> *most likely way being through prices higher than would be found if the market were*
> *subject to effective competition. However, the Commission in its decision-making*
> *practice does not normally control or condemn the high level of prices as such.*
> *Rather it examines the behaviour of the dominant company designed to preserve its*
> *dominance, usually directly against competitors or new entrants who would normally*
> *bring about effective competition and the price level associated with it."*[9]

There are thus strong policy reasons to suggest that the enforcement of **10.5**
Article 102 TFEU generally should focus on anticompetitive foreclosure.
Against this background, it is not surprising that the number of excessive
pricing cases in the European Union is rather limited.[10] The Commission

---

[9] Twenty-fourth Report on Competition Policy (1994), para. 207. *See also* the Fifth Report on Competition Policy (1975), and the Twenty-seventh Report on Competition Policy (1997).

[10] Some national competition authorities such as the Dutch NMa and the UK Office of Fair Trading have been fairly active. There have been a small number of excessive pricing cases that have been decided by the national competition authorities. Some of these cases involved other abuses as well, and some of them (mainly Central and Eastern European Countries) involved excessive pricing in previously state owned monopolies. In Denmark, *see Elsam*, (Danish Competition Council Decision of 30 November 2005; Danish Competition Appeal Tribunal Decision of 14 November 2006 and Danish Competition Authority Decision of 20 June 2007); in Belgium, *see* Case 99-RPR-1 *Importers of Motorcycles*, Competition Council Decision of 21 January 1999, appealed in Cases 2005/MR/3 and 2005/MR/4 *Importers of Motorcycles*, Brussels' Court of Appeal Decision of 2 February 2009, Case 2004-VM-30 *Source Belgium v Febelco*, Competition Council Decision of 25 March 2004 and Case 2006-I/O-12 *FNUCM and Unizo v Banksys*, Competition Council Decision of 31 August 2006; in Estonia, *see* Case 3-3-1-66-02 *AS Eesti Telefon*, Supreme Court Judgment of December 2002; in Hungary, *see* Case Vj-116/2005/84 *TIGÁZ Tiszántúli Gázszolgáltató*, Hungarian Competition Council Decision of 20 June 2006, Case Vj-156/2005/42 *E.ON Észak-dunántúli Áramszolgáltató*, Hungarian Competition Council Decision of 26 April 2007, and Case Vj-93/2003 *Excessive price increase in the cable TV sector*, Estonian Competition Council Decision of 9 December 2003; in Italy, *see* Case No. 10115 A306 *Veraldi/Alitalia*, Italian Competition Authority Decision of 14 November 2001; in Latvia, *see* Case No.765/03/05/12k *Olaines kudra*, Latvian Competition

10. – Excessive Pricing
Marcus Glader and Ioannis Kokkoris

has been reluctant to act as price regulator and has focused primarily on exclusionary abuses and facilitating market entry.[11] Moreover, in several of the cases the Commission has brought, the excessive pricing claim was part of a larger conduct involving other abuses.[12] Nevertheless, it is clear that the TFEU includes a prohibition against unfair exploitation of dominance and that this may be an effective provision, both for competition authorities and private parties in disputes before national courts. Although the Treaty provision is quite broad and leaves room for interpretation, and economic theory is struggling to define what would constitute an excessive price, certain important tests and limiting principles have been developed through judgments and decisions over time.

10.6   This chapter first describes the rule of law regarding excessive pricing as developed by the Commission and the courts. The legal tests and "comparators" to assess excessive pricing will be presented and evaluated. We then discuss the application of the excessive pricing prohibition to products and services covered by intellectual property rights ("IPR"). This is an area where the debate has been particularly intense, given that limitations on pricing could prevent IPR owners from fully recovering their investment in research and development ("R&D") and realising the value of their exclusive property right. Intervention could thus discourage risk taking and investment in innovation. Nevertheless, as indicated by case law and research, it is relevant to distinguish

---

Council Decision of 7 June 2004; in the Netherlands, *see* Case 2910/700 *Interpay*, Dutch Competition Authority Decision of 28 April 2004, Case 3528/199 *Kabeltarieven UPC*, Dutch Competition Authority Decision of 27 September 2005, and Case 3588/201 *Kabeltarieven Casema*, Dutch Competition Authority Decision of 27 September 2005; in Poland, *see* Case DDI-63/2002 *OPCC President v Polskie Koleje Państwowe Intercity* ("*PKP Intercity*"), Polish Office for Protection of Competition and Consumers ("OPCC") Decision of 7 August 2002; in the United Kingdom, *see* Case 1001/1/1/01 *Napp Pharmaceutical Holdings*, UK Competition Appeal Tribunal Decision of 15 January 2002, *Attheraces v British Horseracing Board* [2005] EWHC 1553 (ch) and [2007] EWCA Civ 38), and Case 1046/2/4/04 *Albion Water v Water Services Regulation Authority*, UK Competition Appeal Tribunal Decision of 18 December 2006. *See further:* I. Kokkoris (Ed.), *Competition Cases from the European Union. The Ultimate Guide to Leading Cases of the EU and All 27 Member States* (London, Sweet and Maxwell, 2007).

[11] *See* M. Gal, *supra* note 7, pp. 343–84; also *supra* note 5. The Commission has responded to complaints on excessive pricing but has closed several investigations, *e.g.*, Case COMP/37.761 *Euromax/Imax*, Commission Decision of 25 March 2004, not yet published, Case *Sterling Airway*, in Tenth Report on Competition Policy (1980), paras 136–38, Case IV/37.770 *Electricity transmission tariffs in the Netherlands*, Twenty-ninth Report on Competition Policy (1999), p. 165.

[12] *See, e.g.*, *United Brands*, *supra* note 3; Case 26/75 *General Motors Continental v Commission* ("*General Motors*") [1975] ECR 1367; Case IV/30.615 *British Leyland*, Commission Decision of 2 July 1984, OJ 1984 L 207/11; as well as national cases such as Case 1001/1/1/01 *Napp Pharmaceutical Holdings*, UK Competition Appeal Tribunal Decision of 15 January 2002.

10. – Excessive Pricing
Marcus Glader and Ioannis Kokkoris

cases where market power is derived from an underlying collaborative arrangement from cases where the IPR owner's pricing of its stand-alone technology simply reflects the demand for the underlying property right. Finally, we conclude by discussing certain public policy aspects related to the enforcement of Article 102(a) TFEU.

II. Excessive Pricing Treatment under Article 102 TFEU

1. Interpretation of Article 102(a) TFEU in European Union Case Law

1.1. Early Cases

In its first finding of excessive pricing, the Commission found that General Motors had charged an excessive price for inspections of foreign cars imported into the Belgian market.[13] The inspection procedure was mandated by public law and exclusively reserved to the car manufacturer. The price charged by General Motors for the relevant services was twice as high as those charged by other firms carrying out similar inspections for other car brands. Since there was an *"extraordinary disparity between actual costs incurred and prices actually charged"*, the Commission found the price to be contrary to Article 102(a) TFEU.[14] On appeal, the Court of Justice confirmed that an abuse might lie, *inter alia, "in the imposition of a price which is excessive in relation to the economic value of the service provided, and which has the effect of curbing parallel imports by neutralizing the possibly more favourable level of prices applying in other sales areas in the European Union, or by leading to unfair trade in the sense of Article* [now 102(a) TFEU]".[15] While the Court did not uphold the Commission Decision,

10.7

---

[13] Case IV/28.851 *General Motors Continental*, Commission Decision of 19 December 1974, OJ 1975 L 29/14; prior to this case, there had been indications that excessive pricing could constitute an abuse: *see* Case 40/70 *Sirena v Eda and others ("Sirena")* [1971] ECR 69 and Case 78/70 *Deutsche Grammophon v Metro-SB-Großmärkte ("Deutsche Grammophon")* [1971] ECR 487.

[14] Case IV/28.851 *supra* note 13, para. 8. The Commission also found an infringement of Article 102 TFEU on the additional ground that the pricing structure was discriminatory and restricted parallel trade (*see* para. 9).

[15] *See General Motors, supra* note 12, para. 12. The Court nevertheless annulled the Commission Decision on the ground that (1) the inspections only constituted an occasional activity on the part of General Motors (which had just taken over the responsibility for them from the state testing-stations) and were of very limited importance in relation to the inspections that it normally carried out (the Commission's case was based on the price charged for five individual inspections), and (2) that, before the Commission started its investigations, General Motors had very quickly reduced the charge to a level that was more in line with the real costs of operation.

10. – Excessive Pricing
Marcus Glader and Ioannis Kokkoris

it nevertheless introduced the notion that the price should be assessed in the light of the "economic value" of the product or service provided. This has remained the basic definition for assessing unfair pricing.

1.2.   The United Brands Case

10.8   In *United Brands*,[16] the Commission found that the marketing of bananas grown and imported by United Brands infringed Article 102 TFEU by, among other abuses, imposing excessive prices.[17] Also in this case, however, the Court of Justice later annulled the excessive pricing charge.

10.9   The Court noted that it should be assessed whether a dominant undertaking has used its dominant position *"in such a way as to reap trading benefits which it would not have reaped if there had been normal and sufficiently effective competition"*.[18] The Court repeated the notion previously stated in *General Motors*,[19] that a price which has *"no reasonable relation to the economic value of the product supplied"* is excessive.[20] According to the Court, one possible way to calculate the excessive nature of a price for a given product is by comparing the product's sales price and its costs of production, which would allow one to determine the amount of the seller's profit margin.[21] For this purpose, the Court provided a two-prong test:[22]

- whether the difference between the costs actually incurred and the price actually charged is excessive, and,

---

[16] *See United Brands, supra* note 3.

[17] The case related to a number of alleged abuses: (1) requiring its distributor/ripeners in the Belgo-Luxembourg economic union, Denmark, Germany, Ireland and the Netherlands to refrain from reselling its bananas while still green; (2) in respect of its sales of Chiquita bananas, by charging other trading parties (distributor/ripeners other than the Scipio group), dissimilar prices for equivalent transactions; (3) imposing unfair prices for the sale of Chiquita bananas on its customers in the Belgo-Luxembourg economic union, Denmark, the Netherlands and Germany; and (4) refusing from 10 October 1973 to 11 February 1975 to supply Chiquita bananas.

[18] *See United Brands, supra* note 3, para. 249.

[19] *See General Motors, supra* note 12.

[20] *See United Brands, supra* note 3, para. 250.

[21] *See United Brands, supra* note 3, para. 251.

[22] *Ibid.*, para. 252.

10. – Excessive Pricing
Marcus Glader and Ioannis Kokkoris

- if the answer to this question is affirmative, whether the price imposed is either <u>unfair in itself</u> or <u>when compared to competing products</u> (emphasis added).

The first part of the test (investigating the margin) considers whether the price **10.10** is "excessive". The second part of the test is necessary in order to determine if the excessive price is "unfair" and thus illegal under Article 102 TFEU, either "in itself" or by way of comparison to competing products. The Court added that other methods may be devised to determine whether the price of a product is unfair.[23]

In *United Brands*, the Commission's allegation of excessive pricing was **10.11** essentially based on the difference between the prices charged to banana ripeners in Ireland and those charged in other Member States, which was considerable, sometimes as much as 100 per cent. From this difference, the Commission deduced that United Brands was making a very substantial and excessive profit in some Member States.[24] The Court nevertheless quashed the Decision as far as the excessive pricing allegation was concerned. The Court held that the Commission had not calculated the production costs of the United Brands bananas, and was therefore not able to determine whether the selling price to ripeners/distributors was excessive.[25] While noting that cost calculation can be associated with sometimes insuperable difficulties, the Court found that calculating United Brands' costs would have been possible in this case.[26]

The Commission also analysed the existence of price discrepancies between **10.12** branded and unbranded bananas, finding that Chiquita bananas were sold at a premium of 30–40 per cent when compared to United Brands unbranded bananas, but the Court did not address this comparison. The Court considered, however, the price differential between United Brands and its competitors. While United Brands may have held a high margin for its products in certain countries, the price differential with United Brands' competitors was

---

[23] *Ibid.*, para. 253.
[24] *Ibid.*, para. 260.
[25] *Ibid.*, paras 251, 261–2 and 267.
[26] *Ibid.*, paras 254–6.

10. – Excessive Pricing
Marcus Glader and Ioannis Kokkoris

only seven per cent, which, according to the Court, could not "*automatically be regarded as excessive and consequently unfair.*"[27]

10.13   The Court's test in *United Brands* has been criticised for lack of objectivity, legal uncertainty, and lack of functionality. The first prong of the test is difficult to apply in practice. The test does not provide any guidance on what costs should be taken into account in making the price/cost analysis, and it does not clarify where to draw the line between high and excessive price. The second prong of the United Brands test does not specify what profit margin a dominant firm should be allowed or how to draw conclusions from comparisons with other firms. Generally speaking the Commission's intervention in instances of excessive pricing involved margins around 100 per cent and, even following the Commission's intervention, considerable margins were still allowed to exist.[28]

1.3.   Post United Brands Developments

10.14   Following *United Brands*, there have been a number of cases in which the concept of excessive pricing has been further developed.

1.3.1.   British Leyland

10.15   In *British Leyland*,[29] the Commission argued that British Leyland was charging an excessive price for certificates of conformity for imported vehicles and was thus impeding parallel trade. The Court of Justice[30] upheld the Decision, noting that fees that are disproportionate to the economic value of the service provided can be excessive. The Court of Justice found that British Leyland was charging for certificates for left-hand drive cars more than six times the price for equivalent certificates for right-hand drive cars. According to the Court, both services consisted of a simple administrative check, which did not entail significant costs. Furthermore, providing certificates for left-hand cars was not significantly more costly for the supplier than providing

---

[27] *See United Brands, supra* note 3, para. 266.

[28] *See* E. Pijnacker Hordijk, "Excessive Pricing Under EC Competition Law: An Update in the Light of 'Dutch Developments'" in B. E. Hawk (Ed.), *Fordham Competition Law Institute: International Antitrust Law and Policy 2001* (New York, Juris Publishing, 2002), pp. 463–95, and M. Gal, *supra* note 7, pp. 343–84.

[29] Case IV/30.615 *supra* note 12.

[30] Case 226/84 *British Leyland v Commission* ("*British Leyland*") [1986] ECR 3263.

10. – Excessive Pricing
Marcus Glader and Ioannis Kokkoris

right-hand car certificates.[31] The discriminatory nature of the price, indicating that it was set to make re-importation of left-hand drive less attractive, was accepted by the Court as additional proof that the price for left hand drive certificates was not set in relation to cost.

1.3.2.   SACEM II and III

The *SACEM II* and *SACEM III* cases[32] concerned the prices (royalties)   **10.16** charged by the French collecting society SACEM to discotheque owners for the use of their music repertoire to be played in discotheques. The question was whether the imposition of a royalty based on 8.5 per cent of a discotheque's turnover was unfairly high.[33] The Court noted that, on each domestic market, one collecting society holds a monopoly, representing all authors of musical works. Each national collecting society in turn has reciprocal representation contracts with copyright-management societies in other countries, intended to make all protected musical works, whatever their origin, subject to the same conditions for all users in the same Member State. This also enables copyright-management societies to rely on the arrangement for the protection of their repertoires in other countries.[34] Considering the nature of the service, it was recognised that a cost-price comparison would be impossible. For the underlying copyright, no extra cost is incurred that has a direct relationship to each licence of the work. In fact, there is no production cost of music licensing other than administrative costs for the collecting society. The *SACEM* cases were the first occasions where the Court of Justice made a comparison between the allegedly excessively priced products of a dominant firm with the prices of other firms offering equivalent products/services in other geographic markets. The Court of Justice held that where the dominant undertaking charges prices at a level appreciably higher than those charged in other Member States, and where a comparison of the price levels can be made on a consistent basis, this is indicative of an abuse. In such a case, it is for the undertaking in question to justify the difference by reference to objective and

---

[31] *See British Leyland, supra* note 30, para. 28.

[32] Joined Cases 110, 241 and 242/88 *François Lucazeau and others v Société des Auteurs, Compositeurs et Editeurs de Musique and others ("SACEM II")* [1989] ECR 2811 and Case 395/87 *Ministère Public v Jean-Louis Tournier ("SACEM III")* [1989] ECR 2521.

[33] *See SACEM II,* para. 21; and *SACEM III,* paras 4–5.

[34] *See SACEM III,* para. 19.

10. – Excessive Pricing
Marcus Glader and Ioannis Kokkoris

relevant dissimilarities between the situation in the Member State concerned and the situation prevailing in all the other Member States.[35]

10.17   SACEM challenged the appropriateness of the comparison. According to SACEM, royalties calculated on the basis of the turnover of a discotheque, as in France, were not comparable to those determined by reference to the floor area of the establishment in question, as in other Member States.[36] SACEM also claimed that the difference in pricing was justified due to the high prices charged by discotheques in France, the traditionally high level of protection provided by copyright in France, and a supplementary mechanical reproduction fee applicable to the use of recorded music.[37] SACEM further pointed to different collection methods in the different Member States.[38] These arguments were dismissed by the Court. The Court instead found that one of the most marked differences between the copyright-management societies in the various Member States was the level of operating expenses.[39] The Court noted that costs that are due to the inefficient operation and lack of competition cannot be used to justify a high price level, and stated that the possibility cannot be ruled out *"that it is precisely the lack of competition on the market in question that accounts for the heavy burden of administration and hence the high level of royalties"*.[40]

1.3.3.   Deutsche Post

10.18   In *Deutsche Post*,[41] the Commission alleged that Deutsche Post infringed Article 102 TFEU on four different grounds: (1) discrimination; (2) refusal to supply; (3) imposition of unfair selling prices; and (4) the limitation of production, markets and technical development. The abusive behaviour consisted of Deutsche Post intercepting, surcharging, and delaying letter mail coming from abroad, but originating from a sender in Germany. By shipping mail to the United Kingdom and having them re-mailed to Germany, the German companies escaped Deutsche Post's monopoly prices in the market for domestic mail and benefited from the significantly lower tariffs applicable

---

[35] *See SACEM II,* paras 25 and 33; and *SACEM III,* paras 38 and 46.
[36] *See Ibid. SACEM II,* paras 23–24 and 31; and *SACEM III,* paras 36–37.
[37] *See Ibid. SACEM II,* para. 26; and *SACEM III,* para. 39.
[38] *See Ibid. SACEM II,* para. 28; and *SACEM III,* para. 41.
[39] *See Ibid. SACEM II,* para. 29; and *SACEM III,* para. 42.
[40] *See Ibid. SACEM II,* para. 27; and *SACEM III,* para. 29.
[41] Case COMP/36.915 *Deutsche Post AG – Interception of cross-border mail* (*"Deutsche Post"*), Commission Decision of 25 July 2001, OJ 2001 L 331/40.

10. – Excessive Pricing
Marcus Glader and Ioannis Kokkoris

to post sent from the United Kingdom.[42] The excessive pricing charge was based on the surcharge – terminal due – applied to the forwarding of such incoming cross-border mail,[43] the aim of which was allegedly to make this type of circumvention less attractive, thus hindering commercial remailing companies from competing with Deutsche Post's monopoly services on the domestic market.

In this case, Deutsche Post's monopoly prevented a comparison between the prices charged by the dominant company and its competitors. Moreover, no reliable cost data existed for the relevant time period. An alternative benchmark had to be used. In these circumstances, it was considered appropriate to compare the terminal dues to the domestic tariffs as a yardstick for assessing the cost of delivery. This cost of delivery was then compared to the cost of delivery for a similar service in another Member State.[44]   **10.19**

Incoming cross-border mail was found to be charged the full domestic tariff, although the cost of delivering such mail (including a reasonable profit margin) only represented, at the very most, 80 per cent of the costs of distributing domestic mail.[45] The fact that Sweden Post set terminal dues at 70 per cent of the domestic tariff to cover the delivery costs of incoming cross-border mail, despite conditions which should indicate that the delivery costs ought to be higher (a large but sparsely populated country) as compared to those in Germany, convinced the Commission that Deutsche Post's unsubstantiated claim that its costs of delivery for incoming cross-border letter mail should exceed 80 per cent of the domestic tariff was not credible.[46] The tariff charged by Deutsche Post was found to have no sufficient or reasonable relationship to real costs or to the real value of the service provided and the imposition of this tariff could not be objectively justified.[47]   **10.20**

---

[42] Case COMP/36.915 *Deutsche Post AG – Interception of cross-border mail* (*"Deutsche Post"*), Commission Decision of 25 July 2001, OJ 2001 L 331/40, paras 8-12.

[43] *Ibid.*, para. 134.

[44] *Ibid.*, para. 160.

[45] *Ibid.*, paras 160–66.

[46] *Ibid.*, paras 166–67.

[47] Based on the Commissions benchmark, it was held that the price was 25 per cent above the estimated average cost and the estimated economic value for that service. In this context, it was stressed by the Commission that postal services and in particular the bulk mailings examined here involve the processing and mailing of large volumes in respect of which the profit margin per item is low (around 3 per cent). *See Deutsche Post, supra* note 42, paras 162 and 167.

10. – Excessive Pricing
Marcus Glader and Ioannis Kokkoris

1.3.4. Scandlines

10.21   In *Scandlines*,[48] the Commission evaluated whether the port fees charged to ferry operators by the Port of Helsingborg were excessive. In doing so, the Commission closely followed the *United Brands* test. Accordingly, the Commission first attempted to make a comparison between the costs actually incurred and the price charged. In the absence of a realistic breakdown of Port of Helsingborg's costs allocated to ferry operations, the Court sought to make an approximate calculation and allocation of the costs, based mainly on audited financial reports provided by Port of Helsingborg.[49] This was made difficult by the fact that most of the costs were both fixed and indirect (overhead, maintenance costs of the fixed assets leased from the City of Helsingborg, and the leasehold paid by Port of Helsingborg to the City of Helsingborg).[50] In practice, the Commission found it impossible to segregate out of the approximate total costs (all costs incurred by Port of Helsingborg to be attributed to all services provided to the ferry operators active on the Helsingborg-Elsinore route) attributable to services covered by the port charges.[51]

10.22   Based on the Commission's approximate cost/price analysis,[52] however, it appeared that the ferry operations generated profits whereas, in general, the other operations of the port generated losses.[53] Because the costs to be covered by the port charges are necessarily lower than the total costs, it was concluded that if the port charges were to be found excessive in relation to the total costs, they would, *a fortiori*, be excessive in relation to the costs of

---

[48] Case COMP/36.568 *Scandlines Sverige v Port of Helsingborg* ("*Scandlines Decision 2004*"), Commission Decision of 23 July 2004, not yet published.

[49] *Ibid.*, paras 115–16.

[50] *Ibid.*, para. 118.

[51] *Ibid.*, paras 118–19.

[52] The cost/price analysis took into account, on the one hand, the Port's total revenues derived from the ferry operations (the aggregated port charges invoices by the Port to Scandlines, Sundbusserne and HH-ferries, plus the amounts charged to them pursuant to the specific agreements), and on the other hand, all costs incurred by the Port which can be reasonably attributed to services provided to the ferry operators active on the HH route. *See* the Commission's amended approximate cost/price analysis in *Scandlines Decision 2004, supra* note 48, Appendix 3.1, para. 29.

[53] In the period 1994–2000, operating income/turnover varied between [40 per cent–60 per cent] and [50 per cent–70 per cent] for the ferry operations and between [−30 per cent; −17 per cent] and [2 per cent–15 per cent] for the other operations. *See Scandlines Decision 2004, supra* note 48, para. 122.

10. – Excessive Pricing
Marcus Glader and Ioannis Kokkoris

the service charged within the port charges.[54] The Commission's finding that the revenues from the service were higher than the costs did not, however, alone sustain an abusive conduct.[55] As previously stated in *United Brands*, the Commission found that a high profit margin does not necessarily lead to the conclusion that the price is unfair. The Commission emphasised that a distinction must be made between the assessment of the difference between the price and the production costs – the profit margin – and the assessment of whether the price is unfair.[56]

When assessing whether the price imposed was unfair, according to the **10.23** second part of the *United Brands* test, either in itself or when compared to other ports, the Commission first addressed the conditions for a valid comparison between prices charged by other ports. The Commission found that each port applies its own specific charging system (*e.g.*, as regards the repartition between ship fees and goods fees), that most ship owners who frequently use a certain port often have individual agreements and pay less than the official tariff, and that ports differ substantially from each other in terms of services provided, overall activities, assets, investments, and level of revenues.[57] This made valid and meaningful comparisons difficult. Similarly, comparing prices charged to different classes of customers was also difficult since the services provided were partly different and some of the activities were loss making. After evaluating possible comparisons between the port fees charged to the ferry operators and those charged to cargo vessels,[58] the fees charged by the port of Elsinore (located at the opposite side of the Helsingborg-Elsinore route),[59] and fees in other ports, the Commission found insuperable difficulties in establishing a valid benchmark.

Turning to the question of whether the prices charged were excessive in **10.24** themselves, the Commission stated that the previous case law offered little guidance on how to make such a determination, other than the fact that

---

[54] *See Scandlines Decision 2004, supra* note 48, paras 141 and 160. *See* the Commission's amended approximate cost/price analysis in Appendix 3.1, para. 30.

[55] *Ibid.*, paras 102, 142 and 216.

[56] *Ibid.*, paras 146–51 and 158.

[57] *Ibid.*, para. 162.

[58] *Ibid.*, para. 176.

[59] *Ibid.*, para. 181.

10. – Excessive Pricing
Marcus Glader and Ioannis Kokkoris

what should be assessed is whether there is a *"reasonable relation to the economic value of the product"*.[60] The Commission did not exclude that the question of whether a price is unfair may be assessed within a cost-plus framework, evaluating the production costs, the price (or the profit margin), and the economic value of the product or service. However, the Commission added that in such an assessment, the economic value cannot simply be determined by adding to the costs incurred in the provision of this product or service a profit margin that would be a predetermined percentage of the production costs.[61] In the case at hand, the Commission found, first of all, uncertainties as to the precise determination of the incurred costs and, secondly, no information regarding what a "reasonable" profit margin should be.[62] The Commission also considered that the assessment of the reasonable relation between the price and the economic value of the product or service must also take into account the relative weight of non-cost related factors such as demand-side aspects.[63] It was noted that customers are willing to pay more for something specific attached to the product or service that they consider more valuable. In this case, the unique port location was in itself valuable as it created and sustained demand on the market for transport services on ferries, and on the market for the provision of port services to ferry operators without necessarily implying higher production costs for the provider of the port services. The fact that it is valuable for the customer as well as for the provider increases the economic value.[64] Taking into account all these factors, the Commission concluded that there was insufficient evidence to conclude that the port charges had no reasonable relation to the economic value of the services and facilities provided to the ferry operators.

10.25   The following table illustrates the comparators that have been used in excessive pricing cases.[65]

---

[60] *See Scandlines, supra* note 48, paras 217-18. *See* the Commission's amended approximate cost/price analysis in Appendix 3.1, para. 30.
[61] *Ibid.,* paras 219–21.
[62] *Ibid.,* paras 221–25.
[63] *Ibid.,* paras 228–32.
[64] *Ibid.,* para. 234.
[65] The table is based on the illustration provided in M. Motta and A. de Streel, *supra* note 5, pp. 91–126.

10. – Excessive Pricing
Marcus Glader and Ioannis Kokkoris

Table 10.1: Comparators in Excessive Pricing Cases.

	Cost of dominant firm	Other prices of the dominant firm (discrimination)	Price of other firms offering similar products
Same relevant market (product and geographic)	*United Brands (1978)*[66] *CICCE (1985)*[67] *SACEM II (1989)*[68] *Ahmed Saeed (1989)*[69] *Scandlines (2004)*[70]		**Competitor comparison** *United Brands (1978)* *Parke Davis (1968)*[71] *Renault (1988)*[72]
Other relevant market in the same Member State		*General Motors (1975)*[73] *British Leyland (1986)*[74]	*General Motors (1975)* *Bodson (1988)*[75]
Other relevant market in another Member State	*Deutsche Post (2001)*[76]	*United Brands (1978)*	**Benchmarking** *Sirena (1971)*[77] *Deutsche Grammophon (1971)*[78] *SACEM II (1989)* *SACEM III (1989)*[79] *Deutsche Post (2001)* *Scandlines (2004)*

---

[66] Case IV/26.699 *Chiquita*, Commission Decision of 17 December 1975, OJ 1976 L 95/1, appealed in *United Brands, supra* note 3.

[67] Case 298/83 CICCE v *Commission ("CICCE")* [1985] ECR 1105.

[68] See *SACEM II, supra* note 32.

[69] Case 66/86 *Ahmed Saeed Flugreisen and Silver Line Reisebüro v Zentrale zur Bekämpfung unlauteren Wettbewerbs ("Ahmed Saeed")* [1989] ECR 803.

[70] See *Scandlines Decision 2004, supra* note 48.

[71] Case 24/67 *Parke, Davis and Co. v Probel and others ("Parke Davis")* [1968] ECR 55.

[72] Case 53/87 *Consorzio italiano della componentistica di ricambio per autoveicoli (CICRA) and Maxicar v Régie nationale des usines Renault ("Renault")* [1988] ECR 6039.

[73] Case IV/28.851 *supra* note 13, appealed in *General Motors, supra* note 12.

[74] Case IV/30.615 *supra* note 12, appealed in *British Leyland, supra* note 30.

[75] Case 30/87 *Corinne Bodson v Pompes funèbres des régions libérées ("Bodson")* [1988] ECR 2479.

[76] See *Deutsche Post, supra* note 42.

[77] See *Sirena, supra* note 13.

[78] See *Deutsche Grammophon, supra* note 13.

[79] See *SACEM III, supra* note 32.

10. – Excessive Pricing
Marcus Glader and Ioannis Kokkoris

2. Comparators to Assess Excessive Prices

10.26   As illustrated by the case law, there are a number of different comparative methods that can be employed to assess whether prices are excessive and unfair under Article 102 TFEU.

10.27   Economic theory suggests two determinants of economic value. One is based on the cost of production and the other is based on the competitive price. Both of these are vague concepts. The economic value of a product cannot simply be determined by adding a given profit margin to the production costs. The economic value must be determined with regard to the particular circumstances of the case and may take into account also non-cost related factors.[80] In addition, the competitive price is difficult to determine and it is challenging to draw clear conclusions from price differentials between firms or markets.

2.1. *Price/Cost Comparison*

10.28   The price/cost comparison remains the most fundamental screening tool for excessive pricing cases, at least as long as costs can realistically be estimated. Comparing the price charged by the dominant undertaking with the production cost of the product provides an indication of the profit margin. Unless this is positive and substantial, no claim of excessiveness can reasonably be made. However, making such a comparison presents two difficulties. First, it is often difficult to calculate the production costs for a specific product. Secondly, even when there is a substantial margin, assessing whether that margin is excessive and unfair (*i.e.*, out of proportion to the economic value of the product or service) is probably even more difficult.

10.29   It is evident that costs cannot always be accurately estimated in the presence of significant shared fixed costs including long-term investments, complex corporate structures, multiple products, cost-saving innovations, as well as IPR.[81]

---

[80] For example, in certain cases, the "economic value" may exceed the cost of supply where there are additional benefits not reflected in the costs of supply.

[81] *See CICCE, supra* note 67. The case concerned whether television companies had acted improperly by fixing *unfair licence fees* for films in the form of too low license fees. Whether the price was unfair was held to depend on the relationship between the price paid and the economic value of the service provided. In that regard, the Commission stated that the economic value of a film was very variable, depending on (1) the artistic quality of the film, (2) the film's success in the cinemas, (3) the size of the potential television audience, (4) whether the

10. – Excessive Pricing
Marcus Glader and Ioannis Kokkoris

The Court of Justice recognised in *United Brands* the: **10.30**

> *"considerable and at times very great difficulties in working out production costs which may sometimes include discretionary apportionment of indirect costs and general expenditure and which may vary significantly according to the size of the undertaking, its object, the complex nature of its set up, its territorial area of operations, whether it manufactures one or several products, the number of its subsidiaries and their relationship with each other".*[82]

As previously discussed, in *Scandlines*[83] the Commission evaluated whether the **10.31**
port fees charged to ferry operators by the Port of Helsingborg were excessive
by comparing these fees to the costs actually incurred, most of which were both
fixed and indirect.[84] Due to the lack of precise data and to the intricacy between
the services and facilities provided within the port charges and those provided
within specific agreements, a segregation of the costs incurred attributable to
services covered by the port charges from the total costs was not possible.[85]

As O'Donoghue and Padilla point out, economic theory suggests that an **10.32**
appropriate cost benchmark could be the Long-Run Average Incremental
Cost ("LRAIC").[86] The LRAIC takes into account the total value of the costs
that are needed to enter a market and begin supplying a product, as an average

---

film was being shown for the first time, (5) the time for which broadcasting rights were granted, etc. The Commission argued that in view of the many different criteria of assessment, the abuse had to be established not in relation to all films for which broadcasting rights had been purchased but in relation to each film. The Commission also pointed out that no comparison could be made between the production cost of a film and the licence fee paid by a television company to broadcast that film since the amortisation of a film was based not only on the sale of broadcasting rights to television companies but also on showings in cinemas, exports and the exploitation of new technologies. By the same token, the Commission considered that the film licence fees paid by television companies could not be compared with the cost of a television film produced by one of those companies, since the television film remained the property of the television company which produced it, whereas in the case of cinematographic films, the television company merely purchased the right to show them once or on a number of occasions. As a result, they could continue to be exploited commercially at cinemas, on television, through exportation and on video cassette and video disk. For all those reasons, the Commission considered that CICCE's application failed to substantiate the alleged abuse. It therefore stated that it intended to proceed no further with the matter. This case shows the difficulties of assessing the value of intellectual property rights.

[82] *See United Brands, supra* note 3, para. 254.

[83] *See Scandlines Decision 2004, supra* note 48.

[84] *Ibid.,* para. 118.

[85] *Ibid.,* paras 118–19.

[86] *See* R. O'Donoghue and A. J. Padilla, *supra* note 5, p. 614.

10. – Excessive Pricing
Marcus Glader and Ioannis Kokkoris

over total output. Only the costs that are causally related to the activity at issue are included, other common costs are not.[87]

10.33   Reckon argues that the relevant cost measure is the "forward-looking avoidable cost", which indicates the costs that a hypothetical new entrant (taking into account the efficiency of the entrant, as well as economies of scale/scope) would avoid by not entering.[88] The time period over which costs are estimated should be the life of the relevant hypothetical investment and the cost of capital should reflect the avoidable cost to the new entrant of raising the necessary capital and bearing the relevant risk. Too low a profit margin may reduce *ex ante* investment and be a disincentive for efficiency, harming consumers in the long run.

10.34   In *Ahmed Saeed*,[89] the Court of Justice used *Directive 87/601*[90] to solve the problem of calculating the "incremental" cost of production. *Directive 87/601*, which lays down the criteria to be followed by the aeronautical authorities for approving tariffs, was used to construct an appropriate cost measure to determine whether prices were excessive in the airline sector. Certain interpretative criteria for assessing whether the rate employed was excessive were inferred from Article 3 of *Directive 87/601*:

> *"tariffs must be reasonably related to the long-term fully allocated costs of the air carrier, while taking into account the needs of consumers, the need for a satisfactory return on capital, the competitive market situation, including the fares of the other air carriers operating on the route, and the need to prevent dumping."*

10.35   Neoclassical economic theory suggests that a competitive price is equal to the marginal cost/incremental cost. However, the marginal cost cannot be

---

[87] *See* Guidance on the Commission's enforcement priorities in applying Article 82 of the EC Treaty to abusive exclusionary conduct by dominant undertakings ("*Guidance Paper*"), OJ 2009 C 45/7, para. 26, n. 2: *"Average avoidable cost is the average of the costs that could have been avoided if the company had not produced a discrete amount of (extra) output, in this case the amount allegedly the subject of abusive conduct. In most cases, AAC and the average variable cost (AVC) will be the same, as it is often only variable costs that can be avoided. Long-run average incremental cost is the average of all the (variable and fixed) costs that a company incurs to produce a particular product. LRAIC and average total cost (ATC) are good proxies for each other, and are the same in the case of single product undertakings. If multi-product undertakings have economies of scope, LRAIC would be below ATC for each individual product, as true common costs are not taken into account in LRAIC. In the case of multiple products, any costs that could have been avoided by not producing a particular product or range are not considered to be common costs. In situations where common costs are significant, they may have to be taken into account when assessing the ability to foreclose equally efficient competitors."*

[88] P. Fernandes, *On Exploitative Excessive Pricing Under EC Law*, Reckon Working Paper prepared for a presentation at the Autoridade da Concorrência, Lisbon, January 9, 2006.

[89] *See Ahmed Saeed, supra* note 69.

[90] Council Directive 87/601/EEC of 14 December 1987 on fares for scheduled air services between Member States ("*Directive 87/601*"), OJ 1987 L 374/12.

10. – Excessive Pricing
Marcus Glader and Ioannis Kokkoris

the benchmark against which one compares the price, as in most industries (including very competitive ones) prices are higher than marginal cost/incremental cost.

Even when an appropriate cost calculation can be undertaken, making the **10.36** judgment of what is a "fair" profit margin remains problematic. Prices above the competitive level in the neoclassical sense are the norm rather than the exception, and cannot be used as a guideline. It would render the pricing of every profit-maximising dominant firm abusive. What could constitute an abuse would be pricing that is well above what can be considered to be fair compensation for achieving a dominant position (the attainment of which is not illegal pursuant to Article 102 TFEU). In certain industries, profits may be high due to economies of scale/scope or other efficiencies and profitability analyses misleading. The use of profitability analysis can be justified where there are other companies with similar capabilities as the dominant undertaking, to which a comparison can be made.[91] In dynamic industries where innovation constitutes a key competitive variable, prices will need to be set significantly over marginal costs to fund initial capital investments and compensate for associated risk.[92] In the context of IPR, it should be noted that, as established in the *Parke Davis*[93] and *Renault*[94] cases, a higher sale price for IP protected products as compared with that of the unprotected product produced by independent suppliers does not necessarily constitute an abuse of a dominant position.

2.2. Comparison with Competitors or Competitive Markets

A comparison with competitors' prices was one of the comparators used in **10.37** *United Brands*. The difference in price amounted to seven per cent, which was not deemed to be significant enough to establish that United Brands' prices were excessive. The Court, however, did not state what an excessive difference would have been. In *General Motors*, the Commission looked at other car manufacturers' prices of conformity inspections, which were necessary for

---

[91] What constitutes a fair margin may also depend on the specific firm. Thus, a firm's profit margin may be lower/higher than the representative industry profit margin, depending on the cost structure of the firm. However, to assess the fairness of the profit margin, account should be taken of the representative industry profit margin.

[92] *See* R. O'Donoghue and A. J. Padilla, *supra* note 5, p. 608.

[93] *See Parke Davis, supra* note 71.

[94] *See Renault, supra* note 72.

10. – Excessive Pricing
Marcus Glader and Ioannis Kokkoris

permission to import their cars into Belgium. The Commission found a 200 per cent price difference abusive.[95]

10.38 Another method used for making the assessment of unfairness, is based on a comparison between the profits earned in the dominated market and the profits that would be earned in a competitive market. In *Bodson*,[96] the Court of Justice held that prices for funeral services were excessive based on a comparison of the prices charged in a legal monopoly market with those in a competitive market. The concession to provide "external services" for funerals were in some French communes granted to one undertaking, while in other communes the same service was left unregulated or operated by the State. The Court concluded that it must be possible to make a comparison between the prices charged by the group of undertakings that hold concessions and those charged elsewhere. Such a comparison could provide a basis for assessing whether or not the prices charged by the concession holders are fair. The difficulty with this approach lies in finding appropriate comparators. In some cases, using econometric analysis can assist in isolating the effects of differences between the different comparison variables.[97]

10.39 For an argument that prices are excessive, it should in any event be demonstrated that the lower prices are profitable, and that the prices are different without justification. Such an assessment must take into consideration any differences in quality among the products of competitors as well as differences in production, supply and transport costs, which may reasonably induce differences in the prices charged.

2.3. Comparison with Other Geographic Markets

10.40 Alternatively, a comparison of the prices charged in different geographic areas can be used as a benchmark. An analysis of the dominant company's prices

---

[95] *General Motors, supra* note 12, was later overturned by the Court of Justice on account of the inspections only constituting an occasional activity on the part of General Motors and one of minute importance in relation to the inspections that it normally carried out, notably since, following complaints, and before the Commission began its investigations, General Motors had very quickly reduced the charge to a level that was more in line with the real costs of operation.

[96] *See Bodson, supra* note 75.

[97] It might be possible in some cases to correct for this by excluding the effects of differences between comparators that cannot be considered to represent abnormal restrictions on competition in the market under investigation. However, the level of uncertainty introduced in the analysis by a series of adjustments for differences between comparators may mean that evidence obtained by such a process is insufficient to prove an infringement. *Supra* note 88.

10. – Excessive Pricing
Marcus Glader and Ioannis Kokkoris

in different geographical areas must illustrate that prices are both profitable and discriminatory in order for the Commission to allege that one of them is excessive. The comparison must be done on a consistent basis, involving the same quality and volumes of products and similar market (*e.g.*, presence of maverick competitor or a strong buyer)[98] and demand conditions. Differences in direct costs (such as taxes), local marketing and sales efforts, employment costs, local overhead expenses, and local differences in product offering or quality must also be taken into account.[99]

In *United Brands*, the Court looked at the different pricing of the dominant firm **10.41** in other Member States. However, different levels of consumers' affluence, as well as different price charging structures and presence of local taxes,[100] are only a few of the complications that cross-Member State comparisons entail. As the Court of Justice stated in *United Brands*, prices may differ across regions for a multiple of reasons, thus expecting a dominant firm to adopt a harmonised price across Member States is unrealistic.

The *SACEM* cases[101] were the first cases where a comparison was made **10.42** between the alleged excessive prices of the products of the dominant firm with the prices of other firms operating in other geographic markets. The Court of Justice established that

> *"[w]hen an undertaking holding a dominant position imposes scales of fees for its services which are <u>appreciably higher than those charged in other Member States</u> and where a <u>comparison of the fee levels has been made on a consistent basis</u>, that difference must be regarded as indicative of an abuse of dominant position. In such a case it is for the undertaking in question to justify the difference by reference to objective dissimilarities between the situation in the Member State concerned and the situation prevailing in all the other Member States"* (emphasis added).[102]

In the *SACEM* cases, the Court of Justice focused on a price comparison with **10.43** other geographic markets, irrespective of the level of profits. The Court of

---

[98] For example, the presence of a strong buyer may affect the level of the prices that the dominant firm can set in a market where it is not dominant, and thus induce erroneous comparisons.
[99] *See, e.g.*, M. Dolmans, *The Concept of Abuse Under Article 82 EC – Profit Sacrifice or Proportionality Test?*, Global Competition Law Centre, Second Annual Conference held in Brussels on 16–17 June 2005.
[100] *See* R. O'Donoghue and A. J. Padilla, *supra* note 5.
[101] *See SACEM II* and *SACEM III*, *supra* note 32.
[102] *See SACEM II*, para. 25 ; and *SACEM III*, para. 38.

10. – Excessive Pricing
Marcus Glader and Ioannis Kokkoris

Justice noted that excessive or disproportionate costs of a monopoly under-taking (*i.e.*, operating inefficiently due to the lack of competition) should not be taken into account.[103]

2.4. Comparison Over Time

10.44   Additionally, comparison over time can be made as a means to assess the excessiveness of prices. In *British Leyland*, the Court of Justice examined the development of prices over time in order to assess whether the dominant undertaking had increased its prices to excessive levels. The Court found that British Leyland had increased its prices by 600 per cent.

2.5. Comparison with "Ex ante" Benchmarks

10.45   In cases where the dominant position is created or reinforced by a collab-orative arrangement, it may be appropriate to compare the prices charged *ex post* to the price level that would have applied *ex ante*, before the coordina-tion occurred. This may be the case in particular in connection with industry standards or the pooling of property rights, such as in collecting societies or patent pools. The aim is to analyse to what extent the dominant firm is exploiting the market power added from the restriction of competition, rather than charging a price that reflects the value of the underlying property right. This type of comparison will be analysed in more detail in Section III below.

2.6. Combination of Comparators

10.46   In order to prove the excessive pricing in *Napp*,[104] the UK Office of Fair Trading[105] ("OFT") compared Napp's prices with (1) its own prices and costs; (2) the costs of its next most profitable competitor; (3) its competitors' prices; and (4) the prices charged by Napp in other markets. The UK Competition Appeal Tribunal[106] ("CAT") added that Napp's pricing to the community segment had remained unchanged for 20 years (10 of which after the expiry of the patent). Since Napp was in a near monopolistic position, the comparisons

---

[103] *See further, SACEM II*, paras 29–30.

[104] Case 1001/1/1/01 *Napp Pharmaceutical Holdings*, UK Competition Appeal Tribunal Decision of 15 January 2002.

[105] The OFT reports on competition concern not only existing laws but also draft legislation to the UK Govern-ment, typically in the form of market studies. OFT's website: http://www.oft.gov.uk.

[106] The CAT is a specialist judicial body with cross-disciplinary expertise in law, economics, business and accoun-tancy whose function is to hear and decide cases involving competition or economic regulatory issues. CAT's website: http://www.catribunal.org.uk.

10. – Excessive Pricing
Marcus Glader and Ioannis Kokkoris

that the OFT conducted indicated some discrepancies. The CAT confirmed that the OFT decision did not elaborate on the degree of similarity of the outcomes of the comparisons that is needed in order to prove an excessive pricing allegation.

Similarly, in *Scandlines*, the Commission effectively applied all the tests to the extent they were relevant. The Commission looked into several possible comparators (comparison between the port fees charged by Port of Helsingborg to ferry operators and cargo vessels;[107] comparison with the port of Elsinore;[108] comparison to other ports[109]) before concluding that none of them were suitable in this particular case. Implicit in the approach of using several cost, price and profitability benchmarks simultaneously to assess the pricing policy is the notion that no single benchmark is capable of producing reliable results.[110] Finding excessive pricing only where a consistent result can be found seems a rather sound approach from a policy perspective.

10.47

As Roberts correctly notes, the value of the comparator depends on its ability to assess the extent of the differences in prices, and to what extent the differences derive from differences in competitive rivalry as opposed to other factors (such as differences in the cost of supply).[111] A successful and objective comparison shall be provided by a method that represents not only the actual prices charged by the dominant firm, but also the prices that would result in a competitive market. In addition, the effectively competitive prices should be prices that are sustainable for an efficient firm under the specific market conditions.

10.48

Gal provides a helpful illustration of the degree of price excessiveness that has been considered excessive.[112]

10.49

---

[107] *See Scandlines Decision 2004, supra* note 48, paras 176–80.
[108] *Ibid.*, paras 181–85.
[109] *Ibid.*, paras 202–07.
[110] *See* R. O'Donoghue and A. J. Padilla, *supra* note 5, p. 632.
[111] S. Roberts, "Assessing Excessive Pricing: the Case of Flat Steel in South Africa" (2008) 4(3) *Journal of Competition Law and Economics*, p. 875.
[112] The table is based on the illustration provided by M. Gal, *supra* note 7, pp. 343–84.

10. – Excessive Pricing

Marcus Glader and Ioannis Kokkoris

Table 10.2: Degree of Price Excessiveness.

Case	Alleged price differentials that constitute an abuse	Price allowed	Test for excessiveness
Sirena (Court of Justice)[113]	"particularly high"	Not determined	Not determined
Deutsche Grammophon (Court of Justice)[114]	"particularly marked difference"	Not determined	Price comparisons
General Motors (Commission and Court of Justice)[115]	40 times actual costs	Commission: eight times actual costs Court of Justice: not determined	Court of Justice: price/ cost in light of all circumstances
United Brands (Commission and Court of Justice)[116]	Up to and over 100 per cent price margins	Commission: price decrease of 15 per cent; Court of Justice: not determined	Commission: price comparison; Court of Justice: price/cost
British Leyland (Commission and Court of Justice)[117]	Over 500 per cent price differences	Price decrease of 66 per cent	Price of comparable service
Ahmed Saeed (Court of Justice)[118]	"excessively high" interpretative criteria: "long-term fully allocated cost … the need for satisfactory return on capital"	Not determined	Interpretative criteria inferred from European Union Direc- tive in the same sector
SACEM (Court of Justice)[119]	Several times higher	Not determined	Price comparison
Bodson (Court of Justice)[120]	Prices of others "markedly lower"	Not determined	Price comparison

---

[113] *See Sirena, supra* note 13, para. 17.

[114] *See Deutsche Grammophon, supra* note 13.

[115] Case IV/28.851 *supra* note 13, appealed in *General Motors, supra* note 12.

[116] Case IV/26.699 *supra* note 66, appealed in *United Brands, supra* note 3.

[117] Case IV/30.615 *supra* note 12, appealed in *British Leyland, supra* note 30.

[118] *See Ahmed Saeed, supra* note 69.

[119] *See SACEM II and SACEM III, supra* note 32.

[120] *See Bodson, supra* note 75.

10. – Excessive Pricing
Marcus Glader and Ioannis Kokkoris

Case	Alleged price differentials that constitute an abuse	Price allowed	Test for excessiveness
ITT Promedia (Commission)[121]	Margins over 900 per cent	Price decrease of 90 per cent	
Deutsche Telekom (Commission)[122]	100 per cent differences	Price decrease of 38 per cent and 78 per cent	International price comparisons and cost/ price differences

III. Excessive Pricing of Intellectual Property Rights – Collaborative Arrangements and the *ex ante* Approach

1. Introduction

Excessive pricing cases are difficult to get right. Moreover, the risk of Type II **10.50** errors (over-enforcement) could have significant negative effects on consumer welfare, particularly in innovative industries where (short-term) monopoly profits are the fuel of the market machinery.

Against this background, it is often argued that modern antitrust enforcement **10.51** should stay away from any price control in markets where IPRs are important. As a general rule, that must be correct. Such markets are often characterised by high sunk costs and up-front risks, where the incentives to invest and innovate lie in the prospect of high profits ("monopoly profits" in the neoclassical microeconomic sense) that may await the successful innovator. Moreover, high-technology markets are often characterised by rapid technical development, which may allow newcomers to overthrow incumbent companies by offering products and services of superior quality and performance. Antitrust enforcement is usually better equipped to identify and remedy anticompetitive conduct that forecloses access to markets and raises entry barriers, and should focus on preventing artificially high price-levels by targeting the cause of the problem rather than the symptom.

---

[121] Case IV/35.268 *ITT Promedia NV/Belgacom* ("*ITT Promedia Decision 1997*"), in Twenty-seventh Report on Competition Policy (1997), para. 67.
[122] Case T-271/03 *Deutsche Telekom v Commission* ("*Deutsche Telekom Judgment 2008*") [2008] ECR II-477.

10. – Excessive Pricing
Marcus Glader and Ioannis Kokkoris

10.52 There are, however, a number of cases where the authorities and courts have, directly or indirectly, analysed the pricing of IPRs. As seen from the previous sections, some landmark excessive pricing cases concern the royalties charged by *collecting societies*, where important elements of the comparator tests were developed.[123] In addition, recent disputes and cases in the area of the licensing of intellectual property ("IP") in the context of *industry standards* have increasingly attracted attention and significant legal and economic research to this type of situation, both in the European Union and the United States. Similarly, the authorities on both sides of the Atlantic have reviewed important *patent-pools* (including the terms under which the pooled IP is licensed) and issued guidance on the legal standards that apply to such arrangements.

10.53 Common in these cases is that there is an *underlying collaborative horizontal arrangement* concerning the IPR. Such arrangements are of increasing importance as in many industries there is a growing need to pool or select complementary technologies or property rights. It is also a situation where the underlying arrangements, while allowing for significant efficiencies, can (1) eliminate competition between competing technologies or other IP-protected assets; (2) lead to lock-in of customers; and (3) result in insurmountable barriers to entry for rivals. These factors tend to restrict the ability of the market to "self-correct" within a reasonable period of time. As a consequence, it is generally accepted that these types of horizontal arrangements are subject to competition law scrutiny.

10.54 In the area of industry standards, significant legal and economic thinking has been presented and published in the wake of highly publicised cases and investigations. Various contradicting views regarding the determination of "fair and reasonable" royalties for patents that are essential[124] to an industry standard have been expressed.[125] Interestingly, it appears that a common ground is forming between economists, lawyers, and antitrust enforcers on both sides of the Atlantic regarding the basic conceptual framework. This is based on an *ex ante* approach that distinguishes pricing that reflects the value of the underlying IP from a price charged as a result of market power gained by horizontal coordination. Such a development is noteworthy, particularly since it relates to such a contentious subject as the pricing of IPR. At the same

---

[123] *See SACEM II* and *SACEM III*, *supra* note 32.

[124] A patent is technically essential if, in the absence of a licence, the standard could not be implemented without infringing the patent.

[125] *See, e.g.,* A Layne-Farrar, "Be my FRAND: Standard Setting and Fair, Reasonable and Non-discriminatory Terms" (March 2010), with references.

10. – Excessive Pricing
Marcus Glader and Ioannis Kokkoris

time, this does not mean that controversies are in any way over. Significant challenges remain in its practical implementation. But the debate on when antitrust intervention may be justified and what the legal standards should be for proving a violation becomes significantly more productive if some level of agreement can be reached at the conceptual level.

In the following, we will analyse the background and potential application of **10.55** the *ex ante* approach, both from a legal and economic perspective.

2. Collaborative Arrangements Involving IPRs – Efficiencies and Market Power

All antitrust cases that put limits on the free use of property rights, and in **10.56** particular IPRs, receive much attention and criticism. The main concern is that such restrictions will reduce innovation and investment incentives and inhibit dynamic competition. The welfare effects of innovation are clear, and the legal standards ought to promote technical development and competition through innovation, rather than maximising static price competition.[126]

It is therefore important to distinguish the cases that involve exploitation of **10.57** market power that is derived from a collaborative arrangement as opposed to market power that may result from the underlying property right as such. Restricting the rights of property holders to enjoy and reap the benefits of the value of this right is something different from placing limitations on the exploitation of market power that results from arrangements whereby competition from rival property owners is reduced.

Even if the collaborative arrangement may create market power and be sub- **10.58** ject to antitrust scrutiny, it should be emphasised that it often serves a pro-competitive and consumer welfare-enhancing purpose. As a result, in the era of modern antitrust policy, these arrangements are analysed under the rule of reason in the United States and under a similar balancing test in Europe. Provided they are set up to pursue a procompetitive objective, properly structured and executed, they are usually permitted under the antitrust standards. Therefore, antitrust intervention under Article 102 TFEU should be limited to prevent abuses that undermine these institutions and their procompetitive and welfare-enhancing characteristics.

---

[126] *See, e.g.*, M. Glader, *Innovation Markets and Competition Analysis – EU Competition Law and US Antitrust Law* (Cheltenham, Edward Elgar, 2006).

10. – Excessive Pricing
Marcus Glader and Ioannis Kokkoris

2.1. Welfare and Efficiency Enhancing Properties

10.59 Standardisation, if properly executed, generally leads to economic efficiency and substantial consumer benefits.[127] Industry standards create compatibility and interoperability among products, which is increasingly essential to many industries, not least in the IT, telecom, and other network industries. This allows customers and consumers around the world to connect, interact, and to enjoy the benefits and convenience of new and improved products and services. Frequently, network effects mean that the customer value increases the more people use the same product or service.[128]

10.60 Agreement on certain technological formats and trajectories also reduces risks. Manufacturers might otherwise have to choose one out of several potential standards to support, and consumers might hesitate to purchase a certain product until a *de facto* standard has emerged and alternative technical formats have become obsolete. This also means that the standardisation process leads to rationalisation of production, economies of scale, network effects for introduction of new technologies, unified platforms for the development of new products, R&D efficiencies, etc. It also stimulates competition and lowers prices in the markets for the standardised products and components by increasing the substitutability among different manufacturers' products.

10.61 Patent pools typically reduce transaction costs, *i.e.*, through one-stop licensing of complementary inputs. Patent pools often also lead to lower prices (licensing fees) and increased efficiency due to avoided double-marginalisation, hold-up, and litigation costs.

10.62 Similarly, collecting societies achieve *"substantial economies of scale in the administration, licensing and enforcement and as a result* [collecting societies] *are often regarded as an indispensable mechanism for the licensing, administration and enforcement of the public*

---

[127] *See, e.g.*, M. A. Lemley, "Intellectual Property and Standard-Setting Organizations" (2002) 90(6) *California Law Review*, pp. 1889–980; *Broadcom v Qualcomm*, 501 F.3d 297 (3rd Cir. 2007): *"Private standard setting advances* [the goal of maximizing consumer welfare] *on several levels. In the end-consumer market, standards that ensure interoperability of products facilitate the sharing of information among purchasers of products from competing manufacturers, thereby enhancing the utility of all products and enlarging the overall consumer market. … This, in turn, permits firms to spread the costs of research and development across a greater number of consumers, resulting in lower per-unit prices. … Industry-wide standards may also lower the cost to consumers of switching between competing products and services, thereby enhancing competition among suppliers."*
[128] D. Geradin and M. Rato, "Can Standard-Setting Lead to Exploitative Abuse? A Dissonant View on Patent Hold-Up, Royalty Stacking and the Meaning of FRAND" (2007) 3(1) *European Competition Journal*, pp. 103 *et seq.* According to the network effect theory, a good or service is valuable to a customer depending on the number of customers already owning that good or using that service. Each new user of the product derives private benefits, but also confers external benefits on existing users.

10. – Excessive Pricing
Marcus Glader and Ioannis Kokkoris

performance right".[129] It would be associated with prohibitive transaction costs if every copyright holder had to transact with every user (be that a TV or radio station, bar, disco, etc.), and monitor that the contracts are honoured and that non-contracting entities are not using the protected works. By representing all (or at least a large number of) copyright holders in a country, collecting societies may be essential to create markets for copyright works by significantly lowering transaction costs through economies of scale in the administration and licensing of copyright materials.[130] Their existence also reduces the risk for users, such as a TV station, of inadvertently infringing any particular work.

Moreover, by having reciprocal arrangements by which the national collecting societies represent their foreign equivalents and also license their repertoires, each collecting society can provide for a blanket licence that allows the licensee to publicly perform any works from the entire worldwide repertoire.[131]   **10.63**

---

[129] A. Katz, "The Potential Demise of Another Natural Monopoly: Rethinking the Collective Administration of Performing Rights" (2005) 1(3) *Journal of Competition Law and Economics*, p. 545. In most countries, copyright protected music cannot lawfully be performed publicly without the prior approval of the copyright holder. In the case of public performance or broadcast of sound recordings, authorisation, normally combined with a payment or royalties, may be needed not only from both the composer and the author of the lyrics, but also from the producer of the sound recording and the performing artists.

[130] Technical developments may however solve the problem transaction and monitoring costs. The US Department of Justice early flagged for the possibility that collecting societies in the traditional sense may lose its *raison d'être* with time. "[A]s *'conditions change' – such as if 'developments in computer technology' solves 'the difficult problem of accounting for millions of separate performances each year', which 'might warrant a completely new approach'* " S. Calkins, "Broadcast Music Inc. v. Columbia Broadcasting System, Inc., 441 U.S. 1 (1979)", *Wayne State University Law School Research Paper Series*, Paper No. 07-24, July 30, 2007, para. 1617 citing the Memorandum for the United States as Amicus Curiae, *K-91 v Gershwin Publishing* (filed Dec. 1967), included as appendix to Brief for the United States as Amicus Curiae, BMI, *K-91 v Gershwin Publishing*, 389 US 1045 (1968). Indeed, the European Commission recently found that CISAC had violated Article 101 TFEU in so far as concerned digital distribution: *"Although the markets for the licensing and administration of public performance rights for satellite, cable and internet use display distinct characteristics, the practices of the collecting societies in terms of licensing, administration and reciprocal representation remain almost identical to the traditional ways of operating in the commercial premises licensing market (such as discos, bars) where local monitoring is necessary."* See Case COMP/38.698 *CISAC Agreement* ("*CISAC*"), Commission Decision of 16 July 2008, not yet published, para. 45. For a critical analysis of the need for collecting societies as currently organised, *see supra* note 129, pp. 541–93. Among other things, Katz points to the fact that in 1979, only 13 per cent of all ASCAP and BMI publishers received any royalties from television broadcasts and less than 0.8 per cent received more than 75 per cent of all television performance royalties. This would suggest that the market is much less dispersed than one might think.

[131] These economic properties have been acknowledged by competition authorities and courts. The European Commission recently noted: *"The licensing of copyright can be ensured by individual or collective management. However, individual management is in many instances not feasible; as either the applicable national law provides for compulsory collective management, sometimes even pursuant to Community law, or the market features render any individual management inefficient or impossible. Indeed, for many small or medium-sized right holders, it seems that individual management does not represent a viable option for the management of public performance rights. It is, therefore, often necessary to have recourse to collective management, and direct management of the rights by the author is wholly exceptional."* See *CISAC, supra* note 130, para. 42. Similarly, the US Supreme Court in its landmark judgment in 1979 provided the following economic rationale: *"ASCAP and*

10. – Excessive Pricing
Marcus Glader and Ioannis Kokkoris

2.2. Market Power and Dominance

10.64 The crux of the matter is that these benefits regularly come with a price. Similar for these arrangements is that they tend to reduce competition in one dimension in order to achieve important efficiencies and stimulate competition in another. They may therefore create market power that did not exist before, beyond the potential market power of the underlying IP.

10.65 Choosing an industry standard means agreeing on technological formats at various levels. The selection process often ranges from broad technical concepts down to detailed attributes or features. When making these choices, there are often different alternatives to choose from. In other words, an industry standard is likely to "lock out" technical alternatives. As modern standards frequently include technologies that are subject to patent claims (granted or pending), "*standardisation may also confer market power on an essential patent holder which he may not otherwise have possessed*".[132]

10.66 The significance of the market power that the IPR owner may realise as a result of having its IP included in the standard is *inter alia* dependent on the following factors:

> 1. The level of competition that existed *ex ante*, before the technology selection was made. The closer the substitutes were, the more inter-technology competition has been eliminated;[133]

---

the blanket license developed together out of the practical situation in the marketplace: thousands of users, thousands of copyright owners, and millions of compositions. Most users want unplanned, rapid, and indemnified access to any and all of the repertory of compositions and the owners want a reliable method of collecting for the use of their copyrights. Individual sales transactions in this industry are quite expensive, as would be individual monitoring and enforcement, especially in light of the resources of single composers." See Broadcast Music v Columbia Broadcasting System, 441 US 1 (1979), para. 20.

[132] N. Banasevic and C. Madero Villarejo, "Standards and Market Power" (2008) 5(1) *CPI Antitrust Chronicle*, M. A. Lemley and C. Shapiro, "Patent Hold Up and Royalty Stacking" (2005) 85 *Texas Law Review*, pp. 1991–2049; W. J. Baumol and D. G. Swanson, "Reasonable and Non-discriminatory (RAND) Royalties, Standards Selection, and Control of Market Power" (2005) 73 *Antitrust law Journal*, pp. 1–58: "*On the one hand, while there is no presumption that control of such IP rights automatically or necessarily bestows market or monopoly power on their owners, adopting standards that depend on private IP rights carries the risk of creating a degree of market power that distorts competition and generates returns in excess of those contemplated by the IP laws.*"

[133] Even if there *ex ante* would be few alternatives presented to the SSO, the market power of a patent holder may be limited before the standard has been adopted. For example, if faced with too high royalty demands *ex ante*, the industry may consider that the value added by the new technology is limited (compared to the technology in current generation products), and may prefer to defer standardisation to await further technical development or to allow SSO participants to develop competing alternatives.

10. – Excessive Pricing
Marcus Glader and Ioannis Kokkoris

2. The level of competition that exists between alternative standards *ex post*. In some industries, rival standards and proprietary solutions coexist and compete effectively, making it less likely that an essential patent holder for one of those alternatives would possess market power.[134] If the IP holder were to raise the price of its input, the downstream implementer of the standard would be unable to compete. However, for important standards this is not always true; and

3. The level of "lock-in" that occurs in the selection process, or thereafter. If standardisation is quick and unproblematic, and the standardised products uncomplicated, there may be little to prevent the industry from simply inventing around or redefining a standard in the event that one or several IP holders were to raise prices. However, standardisation may be a complicated and on-going process, where new iterations of technical specifications are developed over time, but where the technical trajectories are determined or limited by the earlier technical choices. This makes it practically and economically very difficult to undo or change the standard in the event of unforeseen price increases. Technologies and patents soon become unavoidable. Moreover, industry makes specific investments in the techniques involved, developing infrastructure and products that implement the standard. Since downstream manufacturers can count on competitors' products being closely substitutable (complying with the same standard), time is often of the essence in these investments. This would mean that implementers of the standard are soon locked-in to the selected technological format and that it becomes commercially indispensable to comply with the standard. Investments like these *"can give rise to substantial obstacles to the use of alternative technologies and lead to 'lock-in'"*.[135]

A finding of dominance would nevertheless have to be based on an assessment of the individual IP holder's position. This includes, for example,   **10.67**

---

[134] *See* N. Banasevic and C. Madero Villarejo, *supra* note 132, p. 2.

[135] *See* W. J. Baumol and D. J. Swanson, *supra* note 132, p. 9; J. Farrell and others, "Standard Setting, Patents, and Hold-up" (2007) 74 *Antitrust Law Journal*, pp. 603–70. Elements relating to the individual IP holder's position are obviously also relevant to the question of market power and dominance, such as the extent to which the IP holder is vertically integrated and depend on cross-licences from other IP holders/licensees to enable its own downstream operations.

10. – Excessive Pricing
Marcus Glader and Ioannis Kokkoris

the extent to which the IP holder is vertically integrated and dependent on cross-licences from other IP holders/licensees to enable its downstream operations.

10.68 Patent pools are very likely to eliminate inter-technology competition if they include predominantly substitutable technologies. Such patent pools are likely to run afoul of Article 101 TFEU since they lead to few efficiencies, if any, rather akin to a cartel. This is different if the pool only comprises technologies that are essential to comply with a certain standard or to produce a certain product (for which there are, by definition, no substitutes). However, the pool may create market power and give rise to a standard. It is easy to imagine, for example, that holders of such patents could create a pool that increases rates to the outside world and cross-license internally at lower rates. The terms and conditions of the licence may therefore be caught by Article 101(1) TFEU. If non-essential but complementary technologies are included, exclusionary effects can arise if the pool has a significant market presence.

10.69 In order to do the job, collecting societies represent and license the protected works of a large number of right holders, and in most countries, there is only one society. This means that a single monopolistic entity becomes the sole seller in the market. Price competition between copyright holders is eliminated. The collecting society could have an interest in maximising revenues by being an unavoidable business partner for anyone who needs access to the repertoire – prices could be set at a monopolistic level. In other words, when a collecting society holds a significant repertoire, it will normally have significant market power, which is derived from the pooling arrangement and which is stronger than that of individual copyright holders.[136]

---

[136] *"When copyright holders compete among themselves their ability to price discriminate and extract greater portions of the consumers' surplus is restricted. Every song is unique and its copyright holder faces a downward sloping demand curve, and consequently competition between songs does not usually result in their prices converging to marginal cost. Competition between songs, however, prevents their copyright holders from attempting to extract the whole surplus from consumers because such an attempt might cause the user to choose another song (perhaps of another artist in the same genre), whose copyright holder is willing to charge a slightly lower price. However, when all sellers of the differentiated products collude or merge, they can collectively set the price of their products at the monopoly level."* See *supra* note 129, p. 551.

10. – Excessive Pricing
Marcus Glader and Ioannis Kokkoris

3. Antitrust Regulation

As seen, these horizontal agreements are similar from an economic perspec- **10.70**
tive. If properly devised, they create significant efficiencies, but may also confer significant market power on IP holders, individually or collectively. It is
therefore generally accepted that antitrust law is relevant to the conditions
under which these arrangements are formed and operated.

Agreements on standard-setting and technology pools must comply with the **10.71**
requirements of Article 101 TFEU. In the absence of hard-core restrictions, it
is necessary to consider whether the agreement leads to a restriction of competition on a relevant market. Where the agreement on an industry standard
restricts competition between alternative technological formats or substitutable technologies and/or creates barriers to entry for products that do not
comply with the standard in question, the standard setting agreement risks
creating market power. Apart from the conditions for access to the standard
setting process as such, the terms under which access to the resulting standard
is made available may be key to the conditions for competition in downstream
markets. This is particularly likely to be the case where a substantive part
of the industry is involved in the standard development and is committed
to implementation of the resulting standard. The Commission's prescription
for important industry standards is therefore IPR policies that require participants to commit to licensing on Fair, Reasonable and Non-Discriminatory
("FRAND") terms.[137]

Similarly, the *2003 Technology Transfer Guidelines* draw the connection between **10.72**
standards and patent pools:

> *"A technology pool, for instance, can result in an industry standard, leading to a
> situation in which there is little competition in terms of the technological format.
> Once the main players in the market adopt a certain format, network effects may
> make it very difficult for alternative formats to survive. This does not imply,
> however, that the creation of a de facto industry standard always eliminates com-
> petition within the meaning of the last condition of Article [101(3) TFEU].
> Within the standard, suppliers may compete on price, quality and product features.*

---

[137] Guidelines on the applicability of Article 101 of the Treaty on the Functioning of the European Union to
horizontal co-operation agreements, OJ 2011 C 11/1, paras 283, 285, 287–291, 324.

10. – Excessive Pricing
Marcus Glader and Ioannis Kokkoris

However, in order for the agreement to comply with Article [101(3) TFEU], it must be ensured that the agreement does not unduly restrict competition and does not unduly restrict future innovation. "[138]

10.73 The same may apply to patent pools more generally: "[w]*here the pool has a dominant position on the market, royalties and other licensing terms should be fair and non-discriminatory and licences should be non-exclusive*".[139] Both the sets of guidelines thus prescribe under some circumstances FRAND licensing obligations under Article 101 TFEU.[140]

10.74 While the Commission has addressed industry standards and patent pools predominantly under Article 101 TFEU, recent cases have highlighted the potential application of Article 102 TFEU to abuses of individual IP holders in the standards context.

10.75 In July 2007, the Commission issued a Statement of Objections against Rambus.[141] The Commission believed that Rambus had infringed Article 102 TFEU "*by claiming unreasonable royalties for the use of certain patents*" for Dynamic Random Access Memory ("DRAM") chips. According to the Commission, Rambus engaged in intentional deceptive conduct in the context of the standard-setting process, *i.e.*, by not disclosing the existence of patents and patent applications, which it later claimed were relevant to the adopted standard. This type of behaviour is known as a "patent ambush" (and will be discussed in more detail in Chapter 11). The Commission considered that, without its patent ambush, Rambus would not have been able to charge the royalty rates it did. In other words, either the Standard Setting Organisation ("SSO") would have excluded the technology in question had it known about Rambus patent claims, or it would at least have required Rambus to make a commitment to license any essential patents on FRAND terms. Rambus abused its dominant

---

[138] Commission Notice – Guidelines on the application of Article 81 of the EC Treaty to technology transfer agreements ("*2004 Technology Transfer Guidelines*"), OJ 2004 C 101/2, para. 152.

[139] *Ibid.*, para. 226.

[140] One could express this as a general legal duty to license or otherwise allow access to essential prerequisites for participation in the market on non-discriminatory and reasonable terms where patent pool, joint venture or other group of companies, in order to achieve important efficiencies, reach an agreement, such as an industry standard, that otherwise would involve a substantial restriction of competition. This is also the principle that emanates from the Commission's practice such as in Case *Salora-IGR Stereo Television*, in Eleventh Competition Policy Report (1981), para. 94, and Case IV/36.539 *British Interactive Broadcasting/Open*, Commission Decision of 15 September 1999, OJ 1999 L 312/1.

[141] *See* Press Release MEMO/07/330 of 23 August 2007.

10. – Excessive Pricing
Marcus Glader and Ioannis Kokkoris

market position created by having its technology included in the standard *"by subsequently claiming unreasonable royalties for the use of those relevant patents."*[142] According to the Commission's Statement of Objections, the appropriate remedy to such an abuse would be that Rambus charge *"a reasonable and non-discriminatory royalty rate … the precise amount of which should be determined having regard to all the circumstances of the case"*.[143] Rambus ultimately committed to cap its royalty rates for products compliant with the JEDEC standards for five years. As part of the overall remedy package, Rambus agreed to charge zero royalties for chip standards that were adopted when Rambus was a JEDEC member, in combination with a maximum royalty rate of 1.5 per cent for the later generations of JEDEC DRAM standards.[144] The Commission decided that these commitments were adequate to meet the concerns expressed in its Statement of Objections and adopted a Decision that rendered them legally binding.

In October 2007, the Commission announced that it had opened formal **10.76** antitrust proceedings against Qualcomm, following complaints lodged in October 2005 by mobile phone and chipsets manufacturers. The alleged infringement under Article 102 TFEU concerned the terms under which Qualcomm licensed its patents essential to the WCDMA (or UMTS) standard for 3G mobile communications. The Commission's investigation focused on Qualcomm's dominance and licensing terms and royalties. *"In a context of standardisation, a finding of exploitative practices by Qualcomm in the WCDMA licensing market contrary to Article 102 TFEU may depend on whether the licensing terms imposed by Qualcomm are in breach of its FRAND commitment."*[145] In other words, the issue was not whether Qualcomm had failed to disclose the fact that it claimed to have essential patents, but whether it had failed to license on FRAND terms. The complaints were based on the understanding that *"the economic principle underlying FRAND commitments is that essential patent holders should not be able to exploit the extra power they have gained as a result of having technology based on their patent incorporated in the standard"*.[146] In July 2008, Nokia and Qualcomm announced that the companies had agreed to settle all litigation between the companies, including the withdrawal by Nokia of its complaint to the Com-mission, entering into a 15-year licensing agreement. In April 2009, Broadcom

---

[142] *See* Press Release MEMO/07/330 of 23 August 2007.
[143] *Ibid.*
[144] Press Release IP/09/1897 of 9 December 2009.
[145] Press Release MEMO/07/389 of 1 October 2007.
[146] *Ibid.*

10. – Excessive Pricing
Marcus Glader and Ioannis Kokkoris

and Qualcomm announced a similar settlement and patent agreement. In November 2009, the Commission closed the formal proceedings, referring to the withdrawn complaints and noting that the case *"raised important issues about the pricing of technology included in an industry standard"* and that such assessments may be very complex.[147]

10.77 Whereas the Commission predominantly has addressed competition issues of standards and patent pools under Article 101 TFEU, and, more recently, under Article 102 TFEU, the reverse is true for collecting societies. Although case law from the Commission and the courts enforcement shows that agreements and concerted practices between different national collecting societies in the European Union, as well as contracts with their respective members (the copyright owners), can be found restrictive of Article 101 TFEU,[148] the formation of the collecting societies as such have generally been presumed to be acceptable under Article 101 TFEU.[149] The terms and conditions that collecting societies impose on licensees have typically been addressed under Article 102 TFEU.[150]

10.78 In *SACEM II*, the Court of Justice was asked whether a rate charged by the French musical copyright management society SACEM, that was manifestly higher than those applied by identical societies in other Member States, was excessive under Article 102 TFEU. SACEM was charging a rate of 8.25 per cent of the turnover of the discotheques, which, according to a study by the Commission, was more than four times the European average. The Court of Justice replied that:

> *"When an undertaking holding a dominant position imposes scales of fees for its services which are appreciably higher than those charged in other Member States and where a comparison of the fee levels has been made on a consistent basis, that*

---

[147] Press Release MEMO/09/516 of 24 November 2009.

[148] *See SACEM II* and *SACEM III, supra* note 32, and *CISAC supra* note 130, appealed in Case T-442/08 *CISAC v Commission*, not yet reported.

[149] At the national level, certain collecting societies have been considered organised in a manner that does not bring about the efficiencies typically associated with these arrangements. *See, e.g.,* Cases FT 2875-06 and FT 27829-06 *Administration av litterära rättigheter i Sverige* ("*ALIS*"), Stockholm City Court Judgments of 26 August 2008.

[150] The same applies to conditions imposed on rights holders: *see, e.g.,* Case 127/73 *Belgische Radio en Televisie and société belge des auteurs, compositeurs et éditeurs v SABAM and Fonior* ("*BRT-II*") [1974] ECR 313; Case IV/26.760 *GEMA I*, Commission Decision of 2 June 1971, OJ 1971 L 134/15; Case 7/82 *Gesellschaft zur Verwertung von Leistungsschutzrechten (GVL) v Commission* [1983] ECR 483.

10. – Excessive Pricing
Marcus Glader and Ioannis Kokkoris

difference must be regarded as indicative of an abuse of a dominant position. In such a case, it is for the undertaking in question to justify the difference by reference to objective dissimilarities between the situation in the Member State concerned and the situation prevailing in all the other Member States."[151]

Since a price-cost analysis would say very little, if anything, about the excessiveness of royalty in these situations, the Court of Justice thus found it appropriate to benchmark the price of one colleting society with that of equivalents in other Member States. In doing so, the Court skipped the first part of the *United Brands* test. If the comparison shows substantial price differences between Member States, the burden of proof shifts to the dominant firm to show that its price is not excessive. This may be appropriate if the concern is potential x-inefficiencies associated with the creation of a national monopoly.[152] However, comparison between national monopolies appears less appropriate for assessing the pricing of the underlying, pooled, property rights.[153] Arguably, collecting societies representing significant repertoires would be subject to a similar FRAND requirement that applies to certain standards and patent pools. In fact, in the United States, the antitrust authorities have particularly

10.79

---

[151] *See SACEM II, supra* note 32, para. 38. SACEM subsequently reduced its royalty, first to 7.18 per cent and following an opinion by the French Conseil de la Concurrence to 4.39 per cent. *See* M. Motta and A. de Streel, *supra* note 5, pp. 91–126.

[152] These inefficiencies were the focus of the Court of Justice, which stated that: "*It is apparent from the documents before the Court that one of the most marked differences between the copyright-management societies in the various Member States lies in the level of operating expenses. Where – as appears to be the case here, according to the record of the proceedings before the national court – the staff of a management society is much larger than that of its counterparts in other Member States and, moreover, the proportion of receipts taken up by collection, administration and distribution expenses rather than by payments to copyright holders is considerably higher, the possibility cannot be ruled out that it is precisely the lack of competition on the market in question that accounts for the heavy burden of administration and hence the high level of royalties.*" *See SACEM II, supra* note 32, para. 29.

[153] Most recently, in Case C-52/07 *Kanal 5 and TV 4 v Föreningen Svenska Tonsättares Internationella Musikbyrå* ("*STIM*") [2008] ECR I-9275 regarding the Swedish collecting society STIM, the Court of Justice repeated that it would be appropriate under Article 102 TFEU to ascertain whether the royalties levied by STIM "*are reasonable in relation to the economic value of the service provided by that organisation*", referring to Case IV/28.851 *supra* note 13 and *United Brands, supra* note 3, para. 28. The *STIM* case did not however concern an allegation of excessive pricing as such, and the Court of Justice did not further elaborate on relevant legal standards or tests in this respect. Interestingly, however, the Court of Justice ruled that a certain remuneration model, which involved royalties levied on the revenue of the broadcasting company, would not be abusive provided that: (1) the charge is proportionate to the amount of music works protected by copyright actually broadcast or likely to be broadcast; (2) there is no other more accurate method that permits the audience to be identified; and (3) the level of use of the works does not result in a disproportionate increase in the administrative and supervision costs. The Court of Justice also held that differences of approach between the royalties charged to public and commercial television companies might amount to a discriminatory practice under Article 102(c) TFEU.

10. – Excessive Pricing
Marcus Glader and Ioannis Kokkoris

clearly laid out Reasonable and Non-Discriminatory ("RAND") obligations *vis-à-vis* the two major US collecting societies.[154]

4. Benchmarking Excessive Royalty Claims

4.1. *Traditional Benchmarks, FRAND and IP Licensing*

10.80 Article 102 TFEU is applicable also for the licensing of IP. Nevertheless, if the analyses set out in the *United Brands* test are difficult to apply in regular circumstances, these are generally even more difficult to apply in the context of IP licensing. First of all, it would be very difficult to work out the actual costs of providing the licence. The marginal cost of licensing is generally very low. An appropriate cost benchmark must deal with difficult issues of R&D, other fixed costs, risks, and similar parameters. As acknowledged by the Commission, "[i]*n principle, cost-based methods are not well adapted to this context because of the difficulty in assessing the costs attributable to the development of a particular patent or groups of patents*".[155] Moreover, determining what "in itself" would be an unfairly high margin would be a subjective exercise, and comparisons with other licensors' terms and the conditions under which other technologies are licensed may tell us little about economic value and fairness.[156] To second-guess royalty rates under Article 102(a) TFEU in such circumstances runs the risk of putting regulatory hamstrings on successful innovators and dynamic industries.

10.81 In this context, it is relevant to distinguish the categories of cases where value and market power is derived from collaborative arrangements, such as an industry standard.

---

[154] In the US, collecting societies have been at the core of antitrust litigation for much of the last century. It took until 1979 and *Broadcast Music v Columbia Broadcasting System*, 441 US 1 (1979), before the Supreme Court decided that the American Society of Composers, Authors and Publishers' ("ASCAP") blanket licences to copyrighted musical compositions at negotiated fees should be assessed under the rule of reason rather than as a price-fixing arrangement that would be *per se* illegal under the antitrust laws. Since 1941, the licences issued by ASCAP and the other major US collecting society, Broadcast Music, Inc. ("BMI"), have been subject to consent decrees agreed with the DoJ. These decrees include various conditions that have been revised a number of times, but from early on and still today, these decrees require, *inter alia*, non-exclusivity in licensing and non-discrimination between "similarly situated" licensees. The ASCAP decree provides for a fee-setting Rate Court to be established in the District Court in Southern New York for hearing license disputes. Moreover, it provides that the burden of proof falls upon ASCAP to show that its royalties are "reasonable". Similarly, the DoJ and BMI modified their respective decrees and instituted a Rate Court provision in 1994.

[155] Guidelines *supra* note 137, para. 289.

[156] *See* D. S. Evans and A. J. Padilla, *supra* note 4, pp. 108 *et seq.*

10. – Excessive Pricing
Marcus Glader and Ioannis Kokkoris

The rationale for requiring that participants in the standard setting process **10.82** make an irrevocable commitment to license essential IPR on FRAND terms, in particular is to *"prevent IPR holders from making the implementation of the standard difficult by refusing to license or by requesting unfair or unreasonable fees (in other words excessive fees) after the industry has been locked-in or by charging discriminatory royalty rates".*[157] For important industry standards, the standardised technology should be available on FRAND terms in order to safeguard competition in the downstream markets and to secure that a fair share of the benefits from standardisation accrue to consumers. This connects the requirements under Articles 101 and 102 TFEU. In cases that involve terms and conditions that allegedly are discriminatory and/or unfair and excessive, there appears to be good reasons to apply Article 102 TFEU in a manner that is consistent with Article 101 TFEU. This would not only be attractive from a legal dogmatic point of view, it would also mean that individual IP holders can be held accountable under Article 102 TFEU for unilateral practices that threaten to render the underlying arrangement anticompetitive. While SSOs are free to define the contractual meaning of FRAND, and may choose to clarify what FRAND means for the purpose of their standards, in which case, contractual obligations may not necessarily mean the same as the competition law obligations under Articles 101 and 102 TFEU, the economic rationale behind the FRAND concept appears to be the same – a fair remuneration for IPR owners, based on the value of the underlying property right, coupled with protection from abuse of *ex post* power.

It is therefore appropriate to consider what FRAND means and how it may **10.83** be made operational to assess royalty terms.

4.2. The Economic Meaning of Fair and Reasonable

There is a growing agreement in the economic literature that the economic **10.84** meaning of RAND or FRAND must be that the holders of patents that are essential to the implementation of the industry standard should not charge royalties that are disproportionate to what they could have charged under the competitive conditions that applied *ex ante*, prior to the adoption of the standard. According to Swanson and Baumol:

---

[157] Guidelines *supra* note 137, para. 287. Firms can make FRAND commitments or similar undertakings also outside of collaborative SSOs, for example as a means to promote the adoption of proprietary technologies, which can lead to a *de facto* standard.

10. – Excessive Pricing
Marcus Glader and Ioannis Kokkoris

> *"If the primary goal of obtaining RAND licensing commitments is to prevent IP holders from setting royalties that exercise market power created by standardisation, then a concept of a 'reasonable' royalty for purposes of RAND licensing must be defined and implemented by reference to ex ante competition, i.e., competition in advance of standard selection."*[158]

10.85   In their view, a "reasonable" royalty for RAND purposes *"is or approximates the outcome of an auction-like process appropriately designed to take lawful advantage of the state of competition ex ante … between and among available IP options".*[159]

10.86   According to the economic theory described, the owners of essential IP should not be allowed to exploit the power gained (and reap the benefits resulting) from the horizontal standard-setting agreement. They should, however, be allowed to charge royalties that correspond to the underlying, competitive, value of their patents.

10.87   Commission officials have stated that *"the obvious benchmark for what is a 'reasonable' price is what would have been the hypothetical ex ante situation".*[160]

10.88   The recognition of the *ex ante* approach has spurred various developments and refinements. Even if consensus is emerging on the broad contours of a relevant framework, challenges remain in practical modelling and potential implementation.

4.3.   Potential Applications of the ex ante Approach

4.3.1.   Preventive Use

10.89   Swanson and Baumol argue that while the formal auction models they present *"provide only limited guidance in applying the RAND concept in the messy circumstances of concrete disputes … the analysis presented [in their paper] is quite powerful as a roadmap to a method both for defining and determining the level of a reasonable RAND royalty".*[161] In this respect, they encourage SSOs to elicit up-front competition

---

[158] *See* W. J. Baumol and D. J. Swanson, *supra* note 132, pp. 1–58.
[159] *See* W. J. Baumol and D. J. Swanson, *supra* note 132, p. 57.
[160] *See* N. Banasevic and C. Madero Villarejo, *supra* note 132.
[161] *See* W. J. Baumol and D. J. Swanson, *supra* note 132, p. 24.

10. – Excessive Pricing
Marcus Glader and Ioannis Kokkoris

in the submission of particularised licensing terms to enable a comparison with the IP holders' licensing terms *ex post*.

Various proposals have been made to encourage SSOs to deal with licensing issues *ex ante*, before the standard is set and the industry has become locked in. These include actual *ex ante* auctions, bilateral licensing negotiations, and disclosure by the patent holders of the most restrictive terms they might apply in the future. *Ex ante* auctions or negotiations would thus allow SSO members to collectively discuss – before lock-in – a royalty rate, or at least a maximum rate for incorporated technology. Such a regime could foster inter-technology competition based on quality and price before the standard is agreed on and lock-in occurs. If offered licensing terms and conditions are unattractive, the standard can still be adjusted to avoid IPR that are considered too expensive. At the *ex ante* stage, the terms offered by the IPR owners and acceptable to the other SSO members thus provide an indication of "power" achieved through superior technology compared to the available alternatives. **10.90**

Then FTC-chair, Deborah Platt Majoras, gave a publicised address, in which she pointed out the procompetitive benefits of standardisation and the fact that the US antitrust agencies had not seen frequent instances of naked collusion in the standard-setting context. However, "[w]*hat has become more common, though, is the potential for an intellectual property rights owner to 'hold up' other members of a standard-setting organization after a standard has been set.*"[162] According to Majoras, if, at the start of the process, any one of a number of competing formats could win the standards battle, then no single format will command more than a competitive price. However, when agreements on (F)RAND rates are vague, they may not fully protect industry participants from the risk of hold up. **10.91**

Such proposals have raised antitrust concerns – in particular that it could be seen as collective price-fixing that would be *per se* prohibited – which have dissuaded SSOs from developing *ex ante* mechanisms.[163] According to Majoras, joint *ex ante* royalty discussions that are reasonably necessary to avoid hold up **10.92**

---

[162] D. Platt Majoras, "Recognizing the Procompetitive Potential of Royalty Discussions in Standard Setting", Remarks of FTC Chairman Deborah Platt Majoras, prepared for the conference on Standardization and the Law: Developing the Golden Mean for Global Trade, Stanford, California, September 23, 2005.

[163] *See, e.g., Sony Electronics v Soundview Technologies*, 157 F. Supp. 2d 180 (D. Conn. 2001), p. 185.

10. – Excessive Pricing
Marcus Glader and Ioannis Kokkoris

do not however warrant *per se* condemnation. Rather, they merit the balancing undertaken in a rule of reason review:

> *"They may allow the 'buyers' (the potential licensees in the standard-setting group) to get a competitive price from the 'sellers' (the rival patentees vying to be incorporated into the standard that the group is adopting) before lock in ends the competition for the standard and potentially confers market power on the holder of the chosen technology. ... If joint ex ante royalty discussions succeed in staving off hold up, we can generally expect lower royalty rates to lead to lower marginal costs for the standardised product and lower consumer prices."*[164]

10.93   Similar to the statements by the FTC and the DoJ, Commission officials have expressed their support for *ex ante* schemes. Cecilio Madero and Nicholas Banasevic express their support for *ex ante* schemes that allow for competition between rival technologies on both quality and price, whereby "[t]*he price is auctioned down to the competitive level before the standard is selected, and the problem of artificially inflated ex post pricing as a result of the standard is avoided*".[165] According to these officials, antitrust concerns "*should not be used as a smokescreen to hinder the uptake of ex ante type schemes*".[166] The *2004 Technology Transfer Guidelines* convey a similar message.[167] In the *2011 Horizontal Guidelines,* the Commission took limited steps in this direction, explaining that, as long as it does not involve a price-fixing scheme, agreements providing for unilateral *ex ante* disclosures of most restrictive licensing terms, will not, in principle, restrict competition within the meaning of Article 101(1).[168]

10.94   While it appears that SSOs in most cases would not have to fear antitrust condemnation, practical problems in the development of actual *ex ante* licensing models may prove more difficult to overcome. The adoption of such procedures can be difficult due to the nature of the standardisation process. Complex standards may involve very large numbers of patents, develop over a significant period of time during which new features are added (but where selection is confined by previous technology choices) and unknown applications mature into issued patents. In such circumstances, effective *ex ante* measures (whether auctions, bilateral royalty negotiations, or unilateral

---

[164] *See supra* note 162.
[165] *See* N. Banasevic and C. Madero Villarejo, *supra* note 132.
[166] *See* N. Banasevic and C. Madero Villarejo, *supra* note 132.
[167] *See 2004 Technology Transfer Guidelines, supra* note 138.
[168] Guidelines *supra* note 137, paras 274 and 299.

10. – Excessive Pricing
Marcus Glader and Ioannis Kokkoris

declarations of licensing terms) seem difficult to make operational. For other standards, the opportunities for *ex ante* pricing may be better. Both the US and the EU authorities have been careful to stress that they do not prescribe specific schemes to SSOs. It is up to the SSOs to develop the policies that are most appropriate to their needs.

Against this backdrop, it seems unlikely that a policy promoting *ex ante* measures within SSOs would be a panacea. As the Commission puts it,   **10.95**

> *"an effective standard setting process should take place in a non-discriminatory, open and transparent way to ensure competition on the merits and to allow consumers to benefit from technical development and innovation. Standards bodies should be encouraged to design clear rules respecting these principles. However, in a specific case where there appear to be competition concerns, the Commission will investigate and intervene as appropriate."*[169]

4.3.2.   *Ex post* Application of *ex ante* Benchmarks

Under the *ex ante* approach, a "reasonable" royalty should be determined based on an assessment of the competitive environment before the creation of the standard.[170] It is when *ex post* disputes occur that some commentators see the merits of the *ex ante* model to be employed to assess the royalty rates that parties have set through bilateral negotiations.[171]   **10.96**

The *2011 Horizontal Guidelines* state that *"it may be possible to compare the licensing fees charged by the undertaking in question for the relevant patents in a competitive environment before the industry has been locked into the standard (ex ante) with those charged after the industry has been locked in (ex post)."*[172] In the same way higher prices charged or other onerous terms imposed for the licensing of a technology after, as compared to before, a standard was set or lock-in occurred could indicate an abuse, evidence of consistent pricing can show there is no exercise   **10.97**

---

[169] Press Release IP/09/1897 of 9 December 2009.

[170] G. S. Cary and others, "Antitrust Implications of Abuse of Standard-Setting" (2008) 15(5) *George Mason Law Review*, p. 1260.

[171] A. S. Layne-Farrar, A. J. Padilla and R. Schmalensee, "Pricing Patents for Licensing in Standard Setting Organizations: Making Sense of FRAND Commitments" (2007) 74(3) *Antitrust Law Journal*, pp. 671–706.

[172] Guidelines *supra* note 137, para. 289. *See also* Press Release MEMO/09/544 of 9 December 2009: *"How do you assess what a reasonable royalty is in general? Obviously, it depends on the specifics of every case. The ex ante price that was being charged for a technology before a standard was set could be good benchmark."*

10. – Excessive Pricing
Marcus Glader and Ioannis Kokkoris

of hold-up. Similarly, where a technology is chosen from existing alternative technologies and the licensing terms actually applied by the IP holder are known to the SSO participants at the time of standardisation, this may be evidence of a "revealed preference".

10.98 When considering *ex post* intervention against alleged excessive pricing, other case-specific evidence may also shed light on royalty expectations when the technology was included in the standard at hand. This may include statements by the IP holder about reasonable cumulative rates for the anticipated standard and the individual IP portfolio, as well as more specific commitments.

10.99 The *ex ante* benchmark may also work where there were *ex ante* substitute technologies and data are available on their price and relative quality. In such a situation, the *ex ante* price of a given technology is likely to correspond to the value compared to the next best alternative (the price of the next best alternative plus the opportunity cost of not using the best technology).[173] Also, in the absence of clear *ex ante* pricing data, the SSO may, for example, have evaluated the qualities and merits of different technologies. The closer the *ex ante* alternatives, the more competitive the *ex ante* technology market would have been and the lower the expected royalties would have been. The result of such an analysis may not be an exact figure, but a benchmark range with which to compare prices actually charged.

10.100 Moreover, the *ex ante* benchmark analysis could be supplemented by more traditional benchmarks. "Consistent comparisons" with prices of similar products (as laid out in *United Brands* and *SACEM*) could be used as proxies, for example considering:

- Royalties charged by the same IP holder for the same or comparable technologies under competitive market conditions; and
- Royalties charged by other licensors for complementary essential patents for the same standard.

---

[173] *See* J. Farrell and others, *supra* note 135, pp. 611 *et seq.* Nevertheless, also in the absence of *ex ante* alternatives, the IP holder may have committed to not exploiting the *ex post* hold-up power created by standardisation. In *Broadcom v Qualcomm, supra* note 127, p. 316, the court noted that ETSI's rules were such that "*even if Qualcomm's WCDMA technology was the only candidate for inclusion in the standard, it still would not have been selected by the relevant [SSOs] absent a FRAND commitment*".

10. – Excessive Pricing
Marcus Glader and Ioannis Kokkoris

In this respect, an *ex ante* analysis could also be invoked by the licensor to justify the royalty rates charged. An IP holder may point to evidence of the relative superiority of its technology compared to available alternatives as a justification for higher royalties compared to other IP holders.[174]   **10.101**

In the FTC's investigation of Rambus, no *direct* evidence was found as to what royalty rates would have resulted from *ex ante* negotiations in the absence of Rambus' patent ambush. Moreover, although there were alternative technologies available *ex ante*, the record did not permit the FTC to precisely quantify the closeness of substitution between Rambus' technologies and the alternatives, and the degree to which those alternatives would have entailed higher costs to the implementer to achieve the same performance. To determine an *ex post* FRAND royalty, the FTC looked to real-world examples of negotiations involving similar technologies.[175]   **10.102**

Given the uncertainties that may prevail in the benchmark analysis, intervention may be restricted to non-marginal cases (*i.e.*, where the *ex post* royalty is clearly higher than the *ex ante* benchmark(s) indicate(s)). In such circumstances, the exploitation of the *ex post* hold-up power would not only mean that the IP holder "*made use of the opportunities arising out of its dominant position in such a way as to reap trading benefits which it would not have reaped if there had been normal and sufficiently effective competition*",[176] in a manner potentially disallowing customers and consumers a fair share of the benefits resulting from the collaborative effort. Such behaviour could also undermine the integrity and procompetitive nature of the standard-setting activities.   **10.103**

Normally, parties are able to come to reasonable outcomes through negotiations, but it is relevant to recognise that such negotiations are conducted "in the shadow of the law". Although competition authorities should (continue to) take a restrictive approach to excessive pricing claims, in particular when they involve IPR, there is a role for antitrust as an ultimate remedy when abuses occur. That would enable parties to solve most of these issues without the involvement of the authorities.   **10.104**

---

[174] It has been suggested that the *ex ante* rate should be treated as a safe harbour for licensors rather than as a benchmark for determining if a rate is reasonable. *See supra* note 128, pp. 103 *et seq.*

[175] Opinion of the Commission on Remedy of February 5, 2007 in the matter of Rambus Inc., FTC Docket No. 9302. According to the FTC, Rambus agreed that "*the best way to determine these* [RAND] *rates is by examining rates for other comparable licenses in the industry.*"

[176] *See United Brands, supra* note 3, para. 279.

10. – Excessive Pricing
Marcus Glader and Ioannis Kokkoris

4.3.3. Extensions to other Situations

10.105 A similar model can be applied to other equivalent situations – such as collecting societies and patent pools – with appropriate adaptation. For patent pools, in particular where they can be expected to give rise to *de facto* industry standards, the *ex ante* concept as discussed and developed in the context of standards would work without significant changes.

10.106 For collecting societies with monopoly power, it seems appropriate to follow the same rationale and apply an *"ex ante* like" approach, assessing the price that individual copyright owners could have charged "in absence of the horizontal agreement". Since economies of scale and reduction of transaction costs constitute the rationale for the pooling of these rights in the first place, it would be appropriate to consider the price that the right holders could individually have charged, if transaction costs did not make direct licensing uneconomical or impossible. That would be a relevant benchmark for the price of the copyright. It is plausible that evidence about the competitive price that right holders are charging in competitive situations (absent horizontal coordination) will be more frequently available given the modern technological advancements that facilitate direct distribution and digital monitoring.

10.107 The courts have never analysed collecting societies' royalty claims in this way. In recent cases, the Court of Justice has reiterated the opaque concept of "economic value".[177] Even if the suggested approach comes with evidentiary challenges, it is a theoretically and economically sound basis for addressing excessive pricing allegations, allowing the court or authority to appraise appropriate benchmarks.

10.108 Apart from the value of the underlying property right, the collecting society could legitimately charge the licensees for the costs and services of efficient management and licensing. X-inefficiencies have been the concern of the courts in the past and the administrative fees could also be subject to scrutiny. Whether the level of such fees is reasonable could potentially be addressed by comparison to the administration fees charged by other collecting societies, as indicated by the case law.

---

[177] *See STIM, supra* note 153.

10. – Excessive Pricing
Marcus Glader and Ioannis Kokkoris

IV. Conclusions

There appear to be good arguments for a restrictive interpretation and appli-   **10.109**
cation of the prohibition of excessive pricing. The OFT, in its guidelines on
Chapter II prohibition (equivalent to Article 102 TFEU), states that:

> *"There may … be many objective justifications for prices that are apparently*
> *excessively high. First, in competitive markets prices and costs vary over time and*
> *there are likely to be periods when high profits can be earned. This is an important*
> *part of the competitive process since it can encourage increased output or entry to*
> *a market. Secondly, undertakings in competitive markets might be able to sustain*
> *high profits for a period of time if they are more efficient than their competitors.*
> *This might occur if an undertaking has developed lower-cost techniques of pro-*
> *duction, supplies higher quality products or is more effective at identifying market*
> *opportunities. To be an abuse, prices would have to be persistently excessive with-*
> *out stimulating new entry or innovation."*[178]

This suggests that several considerations should be taken into account, which   **10.110**
would limit the scope for intervention under Article 102(a) TFEU.

1. Incentives to Innovate and Invest

Significant profits may be the result of innovation and efficiency as well as of   **10.111**
excess demand and constrained capacity. High profits in innovative markets
are procompetitive since they induce innovation from actual and potential
market players. The opportunity to charge high prices and earn monopoly
profits, at least for a short period, is desirable in that it attracts investment and
business talent, and yields innovation and growth.

Evans and Padilla[179] argue that the cost of a Type I error[180] in excessive pricing   **10.112**
cases is given by a reduction in the incentives for R&D where firms operate,
not only in the sectors where intervention takes place but in all the sectors of
the economy. Type I errors are likely to be large, *inter alia*, in dynamic industries

---

[178] Office of Fair Trading, *Abuse of a dominant Position*, OFT 402, December 2004.

[179] *See* D. S. Evans and A. J. Padilla, *supra* note 4, pp. 116 *et seq.*

[180] "Type I error" occurs when a conduct that is not anticompetitive is prohibited.

10. – Excessive Pricing
Marcus Glader and Ioannis Kokkoris

where firms compete for the market launching new products and services. Type II errors[181] are likely to be costly when the price-cost margin is large and the elasticity of demand is high. The costs of Type II errors are necessarily small in industries where there are no barriers to entry and in which short-term profits are competed away over time as new firms enter. The authors believe that the weight of the evidence favours a *per se* legal approach, since competition authorities and courts (or indeed any economist) generally will not be able to distinguish between efficient (fair) and inefficient (unfair) prices. They add, however, that when the firm enjoys a (near) monopoly position that is not the result of past investments or innovations, barriers to entry are insurmountable, prices charged by the firm widely exceed its average total costs, and there is a risk that those prices may prevent the emergence of new goods and services in adjacent markets, then enforcement against excessive prices may be justified.

10.113   When authorities and courts are considering excessive pricing, and in particular relating to the pricing of IP, there is a legitimate concern about interference with the investment and innovation incentives created by the property rights. It is therefore relevant to (1) distinguish cases where excessive pricing results from the exploitation of persistent market power resulting from a collaborative agreement, as opposed to the general exploitation of a property right; and (2) apply a model (or "benchmark") that does not interfere with IPR owners' legitimate exploitation of their underlying property rights.

10.114   By distinguishing these two categories of cases the risk of applying precedents in contexts for which they are not appropriate will be reduced.

10.115   As regards appropriate benchmarks, the merits of the *ex ante* approach has already been described. *Ex post* pricing (and/or the imposition of other terms and conditions) that is clearly disproportionate compared to *ex ante* (and other relevant) benchmarks and involves the exploitation of *ex post* hold-up power could be exploitative and potentially anticompetitive, since it tends to: (1) disallow customers and consumers a fair share of the benefits resulting from the collaboration; (2) reduce expansion and competitiveness in downstream markets; and (3) undermine the integrity of the standardisation process (or similar arrangements) that normally bring great efficiencies, stimulate innovation, and disseminate technology.

---

[181] "Type II error" occurs when a conduct that is anticompetitive is not prohibited.

10. – Excessive Pricing
Marcus Glader and Ioannis Kokkoris

2. Regulatory Role

Enforcement of Article 102 TFEU against high prices risks rendering the **10.116** competition authority a quasi-regulator.[182] The authority would then have to conduct ongoing monitoring and reconsider its decision in light of market developments. Ongoing price regulation of a dominant firm can inhibit natural market processes. Actual and potential competitors are less likely to enter or expand in the market if they find it hard to compete against the low prices of the regulated firm (especially in the presence of incumbency advantages). Due to the possible deficiencies in accurately intervening against excessive pricing, authorities may be well advised to avoid imposing fines for excessive pricing or encouraging private damages actions.[183]

Blumenthal[184] adds that an effective remedy will address a particular restraint **10.117** that can be excised through a prohibitory injunction. He adds that a remedy that entails ongoing regulation of prices and profits by courts or competition authorities is almost certain to fail. If price regulation is the only means to achieve improved competition in a monopolised market, it should be done by a sectoral regulator with expertise and specialised knowledge of the market.[185] Motta and de Streel also argue in favour of sector-specific regulators who will have better sectoral knowledge and expertise compared to a competition authority and be better placed to impose and monitor behavioural remedies. When excessive pricing is observed in cases that involve natural monopolies, entry barriers, economies of scale, as well as low R&D potential, they should be dealt with by regulatory bodies.

In *Deutsche Telekom*,[186] the Commission performed a cost-profit analysis and **10.118** an international price comparison, which demonstrated that price levels were

---

[182] *See further* E. Paulis, "Article 82 EC and Exploitative Conduct" in C-D. Ehlermann and M. Marquis (Eds.), *European Competition Law Annual 2007: A Reformed Approach to Article 82 EC* (Oxford, Hart Publishing, 2008), pp. 515–24.

[183] A. Fletcher and A. Jardine, *"Towards an Appropriate Policy for Excessive Pricing"*, paper prepared for the 12th Annual EUI Competition Law and Policy Workshop, Florence, June 8–9, 2007.

[184] W. Blumenthal, *"Discussant Comments on Exploitative Abuses Under Article 82 EC"*, paper prepared for the 12th Annual EUI Competition Law and Policy Workshop, Florence, June 8–9, 2007.

[185] *Supra* note 99.

[186] *See Deutsche Telekom Judgment 2008, supra* note 122.

10. – Excessive Pricing
Marcus Glader and Ioannis Kokkoris

100 per cent higher than in comparable competitive markets.[187] The Commission nevertheless closed the file after the introduction of a full-scale tariff regulation for wholesale and retail roaming charges.[188] Similarly, the regulation on international roaming imposed caps on wholesale and retail prices for international roaming and price transparency measures. Due to these regulatory developments, the DG Competition closed its investigations. Vranakis argues[189] that the Commission instead experienced difficulties in seeking to establish excessive pricing under Article 102 TFEU.

10.119 Motta and de Streel argue that two types of excessive pricing cases may be distinguished. In some of the excessive pricing cases, the dominant undertaking enjoyed a legal monopoly (*General Motors*,[190] *British Leyland*[191]) and the abuse created a serious impediment to the internal market. The second type of excessive pricing cases include cases where the dominant undertaking was active in markets recently being opened to competition (*Deutsche Post*,[192] *O2*,[193] *Vodafone*[194]) and any pricing abuse may have weakened the political momentum for the liberalisation programme.[195] The authors add that the Commission relied on national regulators limiting its intervention when the sectoral regulator had no legal power to intervene (mobile termination rates, roaming charges, or international leased lines tariffs), or was not intervening

---

[187] In January 2000, the Commission instigated a sector inquiry in order to examine competition in mobile roaming. The sector inquiry indicated potential exploitative abuse of dominance and the Commission launched two competition investigations in the wholesale roaming markets issuing a statement of objections to O2 and Vodafone in the UK. In February 2005, the Commission issued a statement of objections to T-Mobile and Vodafone in Germany. These cases did not lead to formal decisions, but resulted in price decreases initiated by the parties (by 30 to 40 per cent on average). In *O2*, the Commission concluded in the statement of objections that O2 had a monopoly position on the market for the provision of wholesale roaming services on its network. O2 charged tariffs that were significantly higher than its costs or tariffs charged for comparable services. However, the Commission closed its file without any finding of infringement against O2.

[188] *See* B. Amory and Y. Desmedt, "The European Ombudsman's First Scrutiny of the EC Commission in Antitrust Matters," (2009) 30(5) *European Competition Law Review*, pp. 205–11.

[189] E. Vranakis, "Guilty as charged? The verdict on the Commission's decision to regulate international roaming prices on the basis of Article 95 EC" (2008) 13(1) *Tottels Communications Law*, pp.12–16.

[190] Case IV/28.851 *supra* note 13, appealed in *General Motors*, *supra* note 12.

[191] Case IV/30.615 *supra* note 12, appealed in *British Leyland*, *supra* note 30.

[192] *See Deutsche Post*, *supra* note 42.

[193] Case COMP/38.369 *T-Mobile Deutschland/O2 Germany – Network Sharing Rahmenvertrag* ("*O2*"), Commission Decision of 16 July 2003, OJ 2004 L 75/32.

[194] Case COMP/38.074 *Vodafone + 10* ("*Vodafone*"), Commission Decision of 8 February 2001, OJ 2001 C 42/13.

[195] *See* M. Motta and A. de Streel, *supra* note 5, pp. 91–126.

10. – Excessive Pricing
Marcus Glader and Ioannis Kokkoris

appropriately (international accounting rates, fixed retention or termination charges, national leased lines tariffs).[196]

3. Structural Conditions

Motta and de Streel articulate a set of conditions that must hold simultane- **10.120** ously for an excessive pricing abuse to be established.[197] The first necessary but not sufficient condition concerns high and non-transitory barriers to entry. In the presence of such barriers, market forces and entry cannot constrain the dominant undertaking so that excessive pricing is not self-correcting. If the competition authority can achieve elimination of entry barriers, then such elimination will induce the same correcting results on excessive prices that entry itself would induce without the intervention of the authority.[198]

4. Synthesis

Emil Paulis, Director of Policy and Strategic Support at DG Competition, **10.121** argued as follows:

> *"I consider these practical difficulties* [of determining an excessive price] *so convincing and the risk of competition authorities arriving at the wrong result so great that <u>enforcement actions against exploitative conduct in my view should only be taken as a last resort</u>. In many markets, prices may temporarily be high but once market forces have had the time to play out the prices will come back to more normal levels. In such cases it would be unwise to run the risk of taking a wrong decision, and furthermore to spend enforcement resources, on solving a problem that would solve itself over time anyway." (emphasis added)*[199]

---

[196] *See* M. Motta and A. de Streel, *supra* note 5, pp. 91–126.

[197] *See Ibid.*

[198] Katsoulacos argues that based on the "as efficient competitor test" exclusion of less efficient rivals may not be deemed abusive, even though these firms can impose some competitive constraints on the dominant under-taking. In these cases, a prohibition against excessive pricing may lead to improvement in consumer welfare. According to Katsoulacos intervention should require evidence of long-term excessive profits, absence of new entry, and innovation in the presence of high profits. Y. Katsoulacos, "Exploitative Practices in Article 82" (2006) *European Enterprise Journal.*

[199] *See supra* note 182, pp. 516–17.

10. – Excessive Pricing
Marcus Glader and Ioannis Kokkoris

10.122　One of the most significant arguments against intervention is that inefficiently high price levels will normally attract new entrants to the market. In the absence of very substantial barriers to entry, intervention against excessive pricing may enhance the dominant position since the intervention is making entry less attractive. It is thus more efficient to focus on and remedy exclusionary practices that limit competition, impede entry, and prevent markets from self-correcting.

10.123　Intervention against excessive prices can have a range of negative implications such as, *inter alia*, reduced innovation and investment incentives when successful firms are made subject to price regulation. This can cause significant welfare losses in the market. If dominance is acquired through innovation and growth, enforcement against perceived excessive pricing should be avoided.

10.124　Enforcement against excessive prices could be endorsed if market forces have limited power to constrain a position of dominance, and sector-specific regulation does not exist and is not a realistic alternative. Intervention should be conducted with great caution and the burden of proof placed upon the competition authorities or other claimants, bearing in mind that in most circumstances there will be no objective or generally accepted method to estimate an excessive price or profit margin. Intervention should be limited to cases in which the inefficiency created by the pricing can be expected to have adverse consequences on consumer welfare.

10.125　In order to constitute an abuse, prices would have to be persistently excessive without stimulating new entry or innovation. The analysis could include all the relevant comparison methods applicable in the particular situation. The strength of the case will depend on the quality and consistency of the various comparators applied.

Other Abuses

Frédéric de Bure*

I.   Introduction

The list of practices contained in Article 102 TFEU is not an exhaustive enu-   **11.1**
meration of the abuses of a dominant position prohibited by the Treaty.[1] The
Court of Justice has held that the practices there mentioned are merely examples of abuses of a dominant position and does not exhaust the methods of
abusing a dominant position.[2] The Court has further held that the strengthening of an undertaking's position may constitute an abuse prohibited under
Article 102 TFEU, regardless of the means by which it is achieved, and even
irrespective of any fault by the dominant company.[3] It follows, therefore, that
an infinite variety of actions carried out by dominant companies could fall
within the scope of Article 102 TFEU. In addition to the traditional categories of abuses discussed in the previous Chapters, the Commission has
sanctioned, or at least investigated, several other practices that may constitute
abuses of a dominant position.

These "other" abuses cannot be grouped together under a single category.   **11.2**
This Chapter discusses several examples of abuses that may each constitute
a unique sub-category. They do, however, have the following common characteristics: first, although they include both exclusionary and exploitative
practices, they are non-pricing abuses. Secondly, none of them is covered
by the Commission's Guidance Paper on enforcement priorities in applying
Article 102 of the EC Treaty to abusive exclusionary conduct by dominant

---

* The author gratefully acknowledges the contribution of colleague Laurence Bary of the Paris office of Cleary
Gottlieb Steen & Hamilton LLP and Flora Pitti-Ferrandi.

[1] Joined Cases C-395 and 396/96 P *Compagnie Maritime Belge Transports and others v Commission* [2000] ECR I–1365,
para. 112.
[2] Case C-280/08 P *Deutsche Telekom v Commission* ("*Deutsche Telekom Judgment 2010*") [2010] ECR I–9555, para. 173.
[3] Case 6/72 *Europemballage and Continental Can v Commission* ("*Continental Can*") [1973] ECR 215, paras 27 and 29;
Case T-128/98 *Aéroports de Paris v Commission* ("*Aéroports de Paris Judgment 2000*") [2000] ECR II–3929, para. 170.

11. – Other Abuses
Frédéric de Bure

undertakings ("*Guidance Paper*"), and therefore they do not appear to be part of the Commission's enforcement priorities in relation to Article 102 TFEU.[4] Thirdly, they are not necessarily listed in the text of Article 102 TFEU, but are instead the result of a broad, and sometimes controversial, interpretation of this Article. Finally, they are often at the outer boundaries of the notion of abuse within the meaning of Article 102 TFEU and tend to overlap with the scope of application of other competition and non-competition rules, such as rules regarding anticompetitive agreements, merger control law, but also consumer protection, intellectual property and/or contract law.

11.3 The "other" abuses raise the question of the limits of Article 102 TFEU. Indeed, it may be argued that there are circumstances in which specific *ex ante* rules may be more efficient than the indefinite extension of antitrust remedies. Moreover, dominant companies need a certain level of legal certainty to be able to operate on the market. It is unclear whether dominant companies should bear a "special responsibility" for practices that are not clearly defined as falling within the scope of Article 102 TFEU and that remain subject to the changing interpretation of the regulators and of the courts. Although the *Guidance Paper* should provide additional certainty, the Commission acknowledged that its scope is limited to certain specific types of exclusionary conduct, which, based on its experience, appear to be the most common. The *Guidance Paper* therefore does not provide any guidance with respect to "other" abusive conduct that may fall within the scope of Article 102 TFEU.[5]

11.4 On the other hand, regulators must be able to adapt to a constantly evolving economic and business environment. Dominant companies continuously elaborate new strategies and practices to further their commercial interests. The "other" abuses category is evidence that the concept of abuse under Article 102 TFEU is flexible enough to capture these anticompetitive strategies and practices.

11.5 These "other" abuses can be broken down into four sub-categories: (1) procedural abuses; (2) contractual abuses; (3) structural abuses; and (4) abuses relating to the limitation of production, market, or technical equipment.

---

[4] Guidance on the Commission's enforcement priorities in applying Article 82 of the EC Treaty to abusive exclusionary conduct by dominant undertakings ("*Guidance Paper*"), OJ 2009 C 45/7.
[5] *Ibid.*, para. 7.

11. – Other Abuses
Frédéric de Bure

II. Procedural Abuses

1. Definition

Both the Commission and the Courts have recognised that, under certain cir-   **11.6**
cumstances, the misuse of public procedures or regulations (*e.g.*, judicial procedures or administrative authorisation processes) by a dominant undertaking
may constitute an infringement of Article 102 TFEU. This may be the case in
particular where procedures and regulation are used in order to exclude competitors from the market, or to prevent them from entering the market. Until
now, although the Commission has examined this type of abuses in several
cases, it has only imposed a fine in relation to an abuse falling within this category on one occasion. Nevertheless, the general statement contained in the
AstraZeneca Decision clearly shows that the Commission considers procedural
abuses as a separate (and novel) category of abuses. In its Decision, the Commission stated that:

> *"[t]he use of public procedures and regulations, including administrative and*
> *judicial processes, may also, in specific circumstances, constitute an abuse, as the*
> *concept of abuse is not limited to behaviour in the market only[6] and misuse of*
> *public procedures and regulations may result in serious anticompetitive effects on*
> *the market."[7]*

It is generally understood that dominant undertakings have a special respon-   **11.7**
sibility with regard to the common market, *i.e.*, they must refrain from taking measures that might impair genuine undistorted competition, and that,
as a result, they may not be able to behave on the market in the same way as
non-dominant undertakings.[8] However, even dominant undertakings should
be free to have full recourse to public procedures and regulations; if not,

---

[6] Case C-395 and 396/96 P *Compagnie Maritime Belge Transports and others v Commission* [2000] ECR I–1365, paras
82–88; Case T-111/96 *ITT Promedia v Commission* ("*ITT Promedia*") [1998] ECR II–2937; Case IV/32.450 *French-
West African shipowners' committees*, Commission Decision of 1 April 1992, OJ 1992 L 134/1.
[7] Case COMP/37.507 *Generics/AstraZeneca*, ("*AstraZeneca Decision 2005*") Commission Decision of 15 June 2005,
not yet published, para. 328. Confirmed by the General Court, Case T-321/05 *AstraZeneca v Commission* ("*Astra-
Zeneca Judgment 2010*") [2010] ECR II-2805 and by the Court of Justice, Case C-457/10 P *AstraZeneca v Commission*
("*AstraZeneca Judgment 2012*"), not yet reported..
[8] *See* Case 322/81 *Nederlandsche Banden Industrie Michelin v Commission* ("*Michelin I*") [1983] ECR 3461, para. 57;
supra note 1, para. 85; and Case T-83/91 *Tetra Pak International v Commission* ("*Tetra Pak II Judgment 1994*") [1994]
ECR II-755, para. 114.

11. – Other Abuses
Frédéric de Bure

they would be deprived of the right to avail themselves of the legal remedies at their disposal. This raises the question of whether the application of Article 102 TFEU should extend to practices, such as the use of a right. The current position of the Commission and of the European courts is that the *abuse*, rather than the mere *use*, of a right may infringe Article 102 TFEU. This position is consistent with the classic concept of the "abuse of rights" that exists in the legal systems of most Member States as well as in the European Union's legal order.[9]

11.8   In *Volvo*, the Court clearly stated that the application of Article 102 TFEU could not result in an undertaking being deprived of the substance of a right (*e.g.*, a dominant undertaking cannot be deprived of an IP right and should in principle be allowed to refuse to license this right).[10] However, the Court also found that the exercise of such right may be prohibited under Article 102 TFEU if it involves certain abusive conduct that may affect competition by an undertaking holding a dominant position. Furthermore, in *Tetra Pak I*, the General Court found that, although the substance of a right could not constitute an abuse in itself, both the acquisition and the exercise of a right could constitute an abuse under certain circumstances.[11] Accordingly, although Article 102 TFEU cannot affect the substance of a right, it may restrict the behaviour of dominant undertakings upstream during the process leading to the acquisition of a right or downstream during the exercise of that right.

11.9   More specifically, the analysis of the case law reveals that the misuse of such procedures and regulations are likely to be held abusive where three cumulative conditions are met: (1) there is a clear intentional strategy on the part of a dominant company to foreclose competition; (2) there is no objective justification for the behaviour in question; and (3) the authorities or bodies applying such procedures have little or no discretion. Each of these criteria is discussed in greater detail below.

---

[9] Case C-441/93 *Panagis Pafitis and others v Trapeza Kentrikis Ellados and others* [1996] ECR I–1347, paras 67–70; Case C-367/96 *Alexandros Kefalas and others v Elliniko Dimosio and Organismos Oikonomikis Anasygkrotisis Epicheiriseon* [1998] ECR I–2843. Whether a right by its very nature can be abused may be questionable. *See, e.g.*, F. Schauer, "Can Rights Be Abused?" (1981) 31 *The Philosophical Quarterly*, pp. 225–30.
[10] Case 238/87 *Volvo v Erik Veng (UK)* ("*Volvo*") [1988] ECR 6211, para. 8.
[11] Case T-51/89 *Tetra Pak Rausing v Commission* ("*Tetra Pak I Judgment 1990*") [1990] ECR II–309, paras 23–24. *See also ITT Promedia supra* note 6, para. 123.

11. – Other Abuses
Frédéric de Bure

1.1. Exclusionary Strategy

11.10 The mere use or misuse of a public procedure or regulation is not enough in and by itself to give rise to a violation of Article 102 TFEU. Even dominant companies can legitimately use, and even misuse, public procedures without violating any competition laws. As the Commission emphasised, *"the objective of competition enforcement is not to penalise such misconduct per se, but rather to prevent the anticompetitive effects of such misconduct in the marketplace"*.[12] In order to be found abusive, the use of public procedure or regulation must have an anticompetitive objective. This follows from the fact that conduct that would otherwise be permissible, even on the part of a dominant undertaking, may be deemed to be abusive if its purpose is anticompetitive, in particular if it is part of a larger plan to eliminate competition.[13] Although abuse is traditionally an objective concept that does not necessarily require the existence of intent, it appears that procedural abuses may essentially arise as a result of a deliberate exclusionary strategy. In that respect, the General Court found in *AstraZeneca* that intention *"constitutes a relevant factor which may, should the case arise, be taken into consideration by the Commission"*.[14] In fact, in every precedent, the qualification of behaviour as abusive resulted from strong evidence that public procedures or regulations were used with a clear exclusionary intent.[15] In *AstraZeneca*, the Commission did not consider the misuse of the patent system or the deregistration of the market authorisation for certain drugs to be abusive by themselves. It was only because such practices were part of a deliberate exclusionary strategy that they constituted an infringement of Article 102 TFEU. Similarly, in *ITT Promedia*, the Commission clarified that court access was a fundamental right and that vexatious litigation may only constitute an abuse of a dominant position if *"the action is conceived in the framework of a plan whose goal is to eliminate competition"*.[16] The *Rambus* case also concerned an allegedly "intentional deceptive conduct" of Rambus in the context of a standard-setting process.[17] Based on the available precedents, it is difficult to conceive an abuse of public procedures or regulations not involving an exclusionary intent.

---

[12] *See* Case COMP/37.507 *supra* note 7, para. 744.

[13] *Ibid.*, para. 327.

[14] *See* Case T–321/05 *supra* note 7, para. 359.

[15] *See* Case COMP/37.507 *supra* note 7, para. 818.

[16] *See* ITT *Promedia supra* note 6, para. 30.

[17] Case COMP/38.636 *Rambus*, Commission Decision of 9 December 2009, not yet published.

11. – Other Abuses
Frédéric de Bure

1.2. No Objective Justification

11.11   The second condition that should be satisfied in order for the misuse of a public procedure or regulation to be deemed abusive is that there be no objective justification for the dominant undertaking's behaviour. In order to determine whether a practice is objectively justified, the Commission takes several elements into account. First, if the dominant undertaking had recourse to methods other than those that prevail under normal competitive conditions and that are not standard practice in the industry in question, the practice is unlikely to be objectively justified. In addition, the Commission will consider whether the dominant undertaking had a legitimate reason to adopt such behaviour, other than to eliminate competition. In *ITT Promedia*, the Commission and the Court held that the dominant undertaking's behaviour was objectively justified since litigation constituted an attempt to establish what it could legitimately consider to be its rights. Therefore, the legal action undertaken by the dominant company could not constitute a violation of Article 102 TFEU. On the other hand, in *AstraZeneca*, the Commission noted that the dominant company did not sufficiently establish that its practices could be justified on the grounds of public health or therapeutic concerns. Moreover, the Commission found that the uncertainties of the applicable legal framework were not an objective justification for the dominant company's conduct.

1.3. No or Little Discretion of the Public Authorities

11.12   The third condition that should be met in order for the misuse of a public procedure or regulation to be deemed abusive is that the relevant authorities or bodies must have little or no discretion in their application of the procedures or regulations in question. The particularity of procedural abuses is that they involve public or regulatory authorities, and therefore the behaviour of the dominant company does not necessarily have a direct impact on the market. In that respect, the European courts distinguish between (1) requests that the public authorities are bound to accept or comply with and (2) a simple attempt to influence the authorities in the exercise of their discretion.[18] In the latter case, the act, which ultimately has an impact on the market, is the result of the public authorities exercising their discretion. The fact that the dominant company may have prompted or advocated for the course of action ultimately enacted by the public authorities cannot be sufficient to hold the dominant

---

[18] *See supra* note 1, para. 82.

11. – Other Abuses
Frédéric de Bure

company liable for such an action. However, when the authorities act further to a request by a dominant company and have no margin of discretion, such request could be found abusive under Article 102 TFEU. In *AstraZeneca*, the Commission emphasised the fact that the authorities had little discretion to verify the information provided by AstraZeneca in the requests for extended patent protection, or to act on the company's request to withdraw a marketing authorisation. In *ITT Promedia*, the issue was not raised, but it is clear that courts have little discretion to accept or refuse a legal action on face value. Conversely, it is doubtful whether an attempt by a dominant undertaking to influence, for example, the Commission's and Council's decision in antidumping proceedings would be found to be abusive given these authorities' wide margin of discretion in the conduct of their investigation.

2.   Precedents

2.1.   *Vexatious Litigation*

To date, *ITT Promedia* is the only case in which the Commission analysed an allegation of vexatious litigation under Article 102 TFEU.[19]   **11.13**

In *ITT Promedia*, the Commission found that the initiation of legal proceedings   **11.14** by a dominant undertaking could be considered to be an abuse under Article 102 TFEU. ITT Promedia, the exclusive publisher of commercial telephone directories in Belgium since 1969, claimed that the incumbent telephony operator Belgacom had abused its dominant position in several ways, including by initiating vexatious litigation against it before the Belgian courts. The complainant referred to a series of lawsuits and counterclaims regarding the renewal of ITT Promedia's exclusive right to publish directories using Belgacom's subscriber data.

In this case, the Commission considered that bringing an action before a court   **11.15** does not constitute an abuse unless two cumulative conditions are met.[20] First, the action cannot reasonably be considered to be an attempt by the dominant undertaking to establish its rights and can therefore only seek to harass the opposite party. Secondly, the action must be conceived in the framework of

---

[19] *See* S. Preece, "ITT Promedia v. E.C. Commission: Establishing and Abuse of Predatory Litigation?" (1999) 20(2) *European Competition Law Review*, pp. 118–22.

[20] Case IV/35.268 *ITT Promedia/Belgacom*, in Twenty-seventh Report on Competition Policy (1997), para. 11.

11. – Other Abuses
Frédéric de Bure

a plan whose goal is to eliminate competition. In order to establish an abuse, the action must therefore be manifestly groundless and intended to eliminate competition. It follows that a dominant undertaking can legitimately attempt to eliminate competition based on an action with proper grounds, or, at least theoretically, file a series of groundless claims in courts provided that they are not part of a larger strategy to eliminate competition. In this case, the Commission concluded that the above two conditions were not met and therefore decided to reject the complaint. First, Belgacom's actions against ITT Promedia were not groundless and could reasonably be construed as attempts to establish the legal rights under Belgian law arising from its monopoly position. Secondly, they could not be viewed as being part of a deliberate strategy to eliminate competition, since two of the actions were actually counterclaims within the framework of legal proceedings initiated by ITT Promedia.

11.16   On appeal, the General Court dismissed ITT Promedia's application, thus affirming the Commission's Decision.[21] The Court found that the first of the two cumulative criteria was not met since Belgacom's actions were intended to assert what Belgacom could reasonably consider to be its rights at the time it brought the action, and therefore it was not necessary to examine whether the second criteria was satisfied. More generally, the Court emphasised that it is only in "wholly exceptional circumstances" that the bringing of legal proceedings by a dominant undertaking will constitute an abuse of a dominant position.[22] Given that access to the court is a fundamental right under Articles 6 and 13 of the European Convention for the Protection of Human Rights, as well as a general principle in the constitutional traditions of all of the Member States, the cumulative criteria defined by the Commission must be applied strictly.[23]

2.2. Misuse of Patent Registration Procedures

11.17   *AstraZeneca*[24] was the first (and only) case in which the Commission sanctioned a misuse of patent registration procedures under Article 102 TFEU.

---

[21] *See ITT Promedia supra* note 6. The Court did not rule on the correctness of the Commission's cumulative criteria, but only assessed whether the Commission had correctly applied those criteria.

[22] *Ibid.*, paras 60–61.

[23] Case 222/84 *Marguerite Johnston v Chief Constable of the Royal Ulster Constabulary* [1986] ECR 1651. *See also* Charter of fundamental rights of the European Union, OJ 2000 C 364/1, Art. 47: "*Everyone whose rights and freedoms guaranteed by the law of the Union are violated has the right to an effective remedy before a tribunal in compliance with the conditions laid down in this Article.*".

[24] *See* Case COMP/37.507 *supra* note 7. The decision followed a complaint by Generics Limited and Scandinavian Pharmaceuticals Generics AB. *See* in particular C. Breuvart and J.-P. Gunther, "Misuse of Patent and

11. – Other Abuses
Frédéric de Bure

AstraZeneca, a pharmaceutical company, was fined €60 million for abuse of a dominant position on several national markets in relation to its anti-ulcer drugs. The Commission identified two distinct infringements of Article 102 TFEU that were both aimed at preventing or delaying the entry of generics into the relevant markets: 1) AstraZeneca made deliberate misleading representations to the patent offices of certain Member States and 2) AstraZeneca submitted request to the relevant authorities for deregistration of the market authorisation of its anti-ulcer drug.

The infringements took place in the particular regulatory framework of the pharmaceutical sector in the European Union. In the pharmaceutical industry, the objective of encouraging innovation is to be weighed against the preservation of competition. Innovation is rewarded through special patent protection for a limited period of time. After patent registration, and, before being launched on the market, a new drug must obtain a market authorisation confirming that the drug can be safely sold to consumers. This involves a series of tests and trials (either through a centralised procedure covering all Member States at once,[25] or through a mutual recognition procedure)[26] that may take several years to complete. In order to "compensate" for this gap between the time of the patent registration and the actual marketing of the product, Regulation 1768/92[27] provides for a Supplementary Protection Certificate ("SPC") that extends patent protection for up to five years. Once patent protection has expired, European Union law favours the market entry of generic producers in order to foster competition. Accordingly, applicable regulations provide a

11.18

Drug Regulatory Approval Systems in the Pharmaceutical Industry: an Analysis of US and EU Converging Approaches" (2005) 26(12) *European Competition Law Review*, pp. 669–84; M. P. Negrinotti, "The Abuse of Regulatory Procedures in the Intellectual Property Context: The AstraZeneca Case" (2008) 29(8) *European Competition Law Review*, pp. 446–59; F. Liberatore and F. Murphy, "Abuse of Regulatory Procedures - The AstraZeneca Case" (2009) 30(5, 6 and 7) European Competition Law Review (Issue 5, pp. 223–29; Issue 6, pp. 289–300; Issue 7, pp. 314–23).

[25] *See* Council Regulation (EEC) 2309/93 of 22.07.1993 laying down Community procedures for the authorization and supervision of medicinal products for human and veterinary use and establishing a European Agency for the Evaluation of Medicinal Products, OJ 1993 L 214/1, subsequently repealed by Parliament and Council Regulation (EC) 726/2004 of 31.03.2004 laying down Community procedures for the authorisation and supervision of medicinal products for human and veterinary use and establishing a European Medicines Agency, OJ 2004 L 136/1.

[26] Council Directive 65/65/EEC of 26.01.1965 on the approximation of provisions laid down by Law, Regulation or Administrative Action relating to proprietary medicinal products, OJ 1965 22/369, subsequently repealed by Parliament and Council Directive 2001/83/EC of 6 November 2001 on the Community code relating to medicinal products for human use, OJ 2001 L 311/67.

[27] Council Regulation (EEC)1768/92 of 18.06.1992 concerning the creation of a supplementary protection certificate for medicinal products ("*Regulation 1768/92*"), OJ 1992 L 182/1.

11. – Other Abuses
Frédéric de Bure

simplified market authorisation procedure for generic drugs that avoids the burden of extensive tests and trials. The Commission found that AstraZeneca had implemented a twofold strategy to (1) procure unfair benefit from SPC protection and (2) prevent generic manufacturers and parallel importers from obtaining a simplified market authorisation.

11.19 AstraZeneca's first abuse involved the misuse of the patent system in several Member States. AstraZeneca was found to have voluntarily provided misleading information to patent authorities in order to obtain extended patent protection for its bestselling anti-ulcer drug, Losec. SCP protection was only available for drugs that had obtained a first market authorisation prior to a certain cut-off date, this deadline being sometimes different depending on the Member State.[28] In order to ensure that extra-patent protection would be granted in each country, AstraZeneca interpreted the term "first market authorisation" in different ways (*e.g.*, date of publication of the authorisation versus date of grant of the authorisation). Furthermore, when questioned by the patent authorities and within the framework of proceedings brought before certain national courts by generic manufacturers, AstraZeneca deliberately concealed material information. The Commission found that these practices formed part of a "*highly centralised and coordinated strategy*"[29] to unduly obtain extra patent protection in several Member States. The Commission did not consider AstraZeneca's actions to constitute "*normal business behaviour*"[30] and took the view that these actions could not be justified by the alleged lack of clarity of applicable regulations. Moreover, patent authorities only exercised a "*limited degree of discretion*"[31] when granting the SPC. Finally, the Commission analysed the effects of the infringement and concluded that it had delayed the entry of less expensive generic versions of Losec to the detriment of national health systems and consumers.

11.20 AstraZeneca's second abuse concerned misuses of procedures relating to the market authorisation for generic manufacturers of the Losec drug. AstraZeneca submitted a request to deregister the market authorisation for the Losec capsule in several Member States, and launched the Losec tablet instead under a new market authorisation. The withdrawal of capsule Losec from the market had

---

[28] *See Regulation 1768/92 supra* note 27, Art. 19(1). The deadline was 1 January 1982 for Belgium and Italy; 1 January 1988 for Denmark and Germany; and 1 January 1985 for most other countries.
[29] *See* Case COMP/37.507 *supra* note 7, para. 626.
[30] *Ibid.*, para. 626.
[31] *Ibid.*

11. – Other Abuses
Frédéric de Bure

the effect of preventing generic manufacturers and parallel importers from obtaining a simplified market authorisation for generic capsule drugs, since the reference product was no longer marketed.[32] Competitors could not apply for authorisations to market generics of the Losec tablet either, since under applicable regulations a reference drug benefits from a 10-year protection from the date on which it obtains its first market authorisation. Therefore, by replacing the Losec capsule with a slightly different version presented in the form of a tablet, AstraZeneca increased the costs of its rivals who had no other option than to apply for market authorisation through the normal procedure, which required extensive clinical tests and trials. On a practical level, this resulted in extended protection for Losec against competition from generic products.

AstraZeneca argued that there were no legal provisions preventing it from deregistering its market authorisation, and that it was a reasonable thing to do since maintaining a marketing authorisation for a product imposes substantial obligations on the holder. AstraZeneca further argued that the switch from capsule to tablet form could be objectively justified, since the tablet form has real qualitative advantages, especially for elderly people who have difficulties in swallowing. The Commission acknowledged that the withdrawal of Losec capsules or the launch of a new formulation was not an abuse in and by itself.[33] However, based on the documents seized during the investigation, the Commission found that AstraZeneca's behaviour did not *"constitute standard industry practice"* and demonstrated clear *"exclusionary intent"*.[34] One key consideration to establish exclusionary intent was that AstraZeneca deregistered its market authorisation for Losec capsules selectively, *i.e.*, only in those Member States where this strategy was more likely to succeed because generic firms and parallel traders were unlikely to obtain a market authorisation through the normal procedure.[35] Moreover, in the Commission's view, the switch from capsule to tablet had "no objective justification" — and in particular, no therapeutic justification — other than to delay the entry into the market of generic producers and parallel importers. The Commission also emphasised that the public

11.21

---

[32] *See supra* note 26, Art. 4, paras 3 and 8(a)(iii). The simplified procedure provided for the following cumulative conditions: the generic product is similar to the reference product; the patent protection has expired; and the referenced product has obtained market authorisation – and is actually marketed – in the relevant Member State.

[33] *See* Case COMP/37.507 *supra* note 7, para. 793.

[34] *Ibid.*, paras 788–94.

[35] Standards to obtain market authorisation have not been harmonised by EU law. Some Members States therefore apply stricter rules than others.

11. – Other Abuses
Frédéric de Bure

authorities had little or no discretion with respect to the decision to deregister the drug. The Commission concluded that AstraZeneca's strategy was aimed at securing a *de facto* extension of the duration of the patent protection in several countries until a newly patented and improved version of Losec could be launched. As a result, national health systems and consumers were deprived access to less expensive generic drugs.

11.22 When determining the amount of the fine, the Commission considered that both abuses were serious infringements, but took into account the fact that similar abuses were unlikely to occur again following the subsequent changes to the regulatory framework and that some aspects of the abuses were new.

11.23 The Commission Decision was appealed before the General Court.[36] The General Court upheld the Commission's reasoning regarding the characterisation of both abuses although it reduced the fine imposed on AstraZeneca in relation to the second abuse. As regards the first abuse, AstraZeneca held in particular that acquiring or extending an intellectual property right could not be considered abusive, except possibly in very specific circumstances where the fraudulently obtained patent would be enforced and that enforcement would meet the conditions set out in the *ITT Promedia* case set forth above. In contradiction to this, the Court ruled that (1) giving misleading information to public authorities in order to be unduly granted an exclusive right is not compatible with the special responsibility of an undertaking in a dominant position not to impair, by conduct falling outside the scope of competition on the merits, undistorted competition in the common market – even though the authorities did not let themselves be misled or competitors obtained, subsequent to the unlawful grant of the exclusive rights, the revocation of those rights; (2) it is not necessary, to characterise an abuse, that the exclusive right obtained as a result of misleading representations has been enforced, since public regulations normally require competitors to respect that exclusive right; and (3) the existence of specific remedies which make it possible to rectify, or even annul, patents and SPCs granted unlawfully is not capable of altering the

---

[36] *See* Case T–321/05 *supra* note 7. AstraZeneca brought an action before the Court for annulment of the Commission's decision or for a reduction of the fines imposed. AstraZeneca challenged the decision on three main grounds. First, the company alleged that the Commission mistakenly defined the relevant market. Secondly, the applicant claimed that the alleged infringements had no effects on the market since the dishonestly obtained rights could not be enforced. Thirdly, the Commission had no right to impose an obligation to maintain a marketing authorisation for a product that was no longer marketed only because it would make it easier for generics and parallel traders to enter the market.

11. – Other Abuses
Frédéric de Bure

conditions of application of the prohibitions laid down in competition law.[37] AstraZeneca's claims were therefore rejected.

As regards the second abuse, the General Court held that a dominant under- **11.24** taking *"cannot use regulatory procedures in such a way as to prevent or make more difficult the entry of competitors on the market, in the absence of grounds relating to the defence of the legitimate interests of an undertaking engaged in competition on the merits or in the absence of objective justification."*[38] In the present case, AstraZeneca's behaviour therefore fell outside the scope of competition on the merits and constituted an abuse, even though its decision to deregister the capsules was compliant with other legal rules – in particular public health legislation.[39] However, the Court decided to reduce the fine in view of the fact that the Commission failed to provide evidence that the deregistration of the marketing authorisations were capable of preventing parallel imports of Losec in some of the countries at stake (Denmark and Norway), and, *a fortiori,* that the cessation, or the sharp decline, of parallel imports of Losec in those two countries was caused by AstraZeneca's conduct. In accordance with the principle that doubt must operate to the advantage of the addressee of the infringement decision, the Court decided to reduce the fine by €17.5 million. The judgment has been confirmed by the Court of Justice.[40]

More recently, the Commission investigated allegations by Spanish pharma- **11.25** ceutical company Almirall that its German competitor Boehringer Ingelheim had abusively filed for unmeritorious patents regarding new treatments of chronic obstructive pulmonary disease (COPD). Although the Commission suggested that such practices could fall within the scope of Article 102 TFEU, it decided to close its investigation in 2011 after Boehringer agreed to withdraw the litigious patent applications.[41] In this case, Boehringer had filed patent applications for new treatments of CODP combining three broad categories of active substances treating COPD with a new active substance that had been discovered by Almirall. Almirall objected to these filings, alleging that the patents were unmeritous, but once granted could nonetheless block, or considerably delay, the market entry of its own innovative combination medicines. The patent applications allegedly also had a negative impact on

---

[37] *See* Case T–321/05 *supra* note 7, paras 352–68.
[38] *Ibid.,* para. 672.
[39] *Ibid.,* para. 677.
[40] *See* Case C-457/10 P *supra* note 7.
[41] *See* Press Release IP/11/842 of 6 July 2011.

11. – Other Abuses
Frédéric de Bure

Almirall's efforts to bring to market the product based on the active substance discovered by Almirall (so called "mono-product"). The requested patents were first granted to Boehringer but later revoked by the UK High Court of Justice and the European Patent Office. The Commission suggested that filing for patents in order to prevent a competitor from obtaining a marketing authorisation for a new product could be considered abusive under Article 102 TFEU if the patent applications were filed and the patents obtained based on misleading information.[42]

2.3. Misuse of Trademark Registration Procedures

11.26 In *Osram/Airam*, the Commission commented on the possibility that the misuse of trademark registration procedures could constitute an abuse of a dominant position. The case, however, was closed without the Commission reaching a final decision on the merits.[43] The Commission suggested that "*a firm in a dominant position in a substantial part of the common market that registers a trade mark when it knows or ought to have known that that mark is already used by a competitor in other Member States may infringe Article* [102 TFEU]" since this registration restricts the competitor's opportunities to penetrate the market dominated by the relevant firm. In that case, Airam, a small Finnish lamp manufacturer, filed a complaint against Osram claiming that Osram had abused its dominant position on the German market by registering the "Airam" trademark in Germany. Osram claimed it had done so to avoid potential confusion with its trademark "Osram", but it is possible that Osram's action had an exclusionary objective, therefore potentially constituting an exclusionary abuse of procedure.

2.4. Misuse of Antidumping Procedures

11.27 On two occasions, the Commission analysed cases involving an alleged abuse of antidumping procedures. Although it has never concluded that an infringement has occurred, the Commission did not exclude the possibility that the

---

[42] *See* Press Release IP/11/842 of 6 July 2011.

[43] Case *Osram/Airam*, in Eleventh Report on Competition Policy (1981), p. 66. *See also* Case *Bayer/Tanabe agreement*, in Eighth Report on Competition Policy (1978), paras 125–27: Bayer (Germany) and Tanabe (Japan), two competing manufacturers of pharmaceuticals and chemicals, had look-alike trademarks (the Bayer cross versus the five-rings of Tanabe). Tanabe was able to use and register its trademark in all EU Member States except Germany where the German courts had found that it could be confused with the Bayer cross. Tanabe then filed a complaint with the Commission alleging that Bayer's exercise of its rights of action for trademark infringement before the German courts was an abuse of a dominant position under Article 102 TFEU. However, the case was settled before the Commission could take a decision.

11. – Other Abuses
Frédéric de Bure

misuse of antidumping proceedings could in some cases constitute an abuse of a dominant position.

In *Soda-ash – Solvay*, the Commission pointed out that the existing antidump- **11.28** ing measures against Soda-ash low cost imports from outside the European Union had provided Solvay with a substantial degree of protection within the European Union.[44] The Commission also noted that Solvay was pushing for the renewal and extension of antidumping duties against imports from the US and Eastern Europe. The Commission, however, did not find that Solvay's actions, even if they were to be characterised as an abuse of antidumping procedures, constituted an abuse of Article 102 TFEU.[45]

In *Industries des poudres sphériques*, a complainant claimed that Péchiney had **11.29** used the antidumping proceedings in order to strengthen its dominant position on the calcium metal market.[46] The Commission rejected the complaint, but the complainant filed an appeal before the General Court. The Court pointed out that seeking a legal remedy and, in particular, the participation by an undertaking in an investigation conducted by the EU institutions, could not be deemed, in and of itself, to infringe Article 102 TFEU. Moreover, the Court found that the applicant had not established Péchiney's intent to use the antidumping procedure in order to exclude it from the market. The appeal was therefore dismissed.

From the Court's reasoning in *Industries des poudres sphériques* it may be inferred, **11.30** *a contrario*, that, if the applicant had adequately established the exclusionary intent of the dominant company, the misuse of the antidumping procedure could constitute an abuse under Article 102 TFEU. This conclusion would, however, fail to take into account the fact that the competent authorities in antidumping proceedings enjoy a significant margin of discretion in their decision-making, which seems incompatible with a finding of abuse on the part of the dominant company.

---

[44] Case IV/33.133 *Soda-ash – Solvay, ICI*, Commission Decision of 19 December 1990, OJ 1991 L 152/21 (the decision was subsequently annulled on procedural grounds; *see* Case T–32/91 *Solvay v Commission* [1995] ECR II–1825 and Joined Cases C-287 and 288/95 P *Commission v Solvay* [2000] ECR I–2391.

[45] The condemned behaviours related to exclusivity agreements and loyalty rebates, not to any misuse of antidumping proceedings.

[46] Case T-5/97 *Industrie des poudres sphériques v Commission* ("*IPS*") [2000] ECR II–3755, paras 211–9.

11. – Other Abuses
Frédéric de Bure

2.5. *Abuse of Standardisation Procedures*

11.31 With the development of technology markets, standard setting has become an increasingly important means of obtaining the advantages of interoperability between the equipment used and combining complementary technologies. The standardisation process may give rise to several antitrust issues and lead to new forms of procedural abuses.

11.32 *Rambus* was the first case in which the Commission investigated a so-called "patent ambush".[47] A patent ambush occurs when, during a standard-setting process, a member of the standard-setting organisation hides the fact that it holds essential intellectual property rights over the standard being developed. Once the proposed standard has been adopted, companies wishing to implement the standard are "locked in" and can be forced to pay substantial royalties to the patent holder.

11.33 Rambus is a US company active in the market for memory chips, a type of electronic memory processor that provides temporary storage of data in electronic devices. During the 1990s, Rambus participated in the elaboration of industry standards within a standard-setting organisation. During this period, it intentionally omitted to disclose the fact that it controlled patents and patent applications that were later claimed by Rambus to be relevant to the adopted standards. By hiding the existence of its patents, Rambus breached the standard-setting organisation's policy, according to which all members were required, or at least expected, to disclose their intellectual property rights. With respect to the alleged anticompetitive effects of the practice, the Commission noted that if it had been aware of the existence of Rambus' intellectual property rights, the standard-setting body would probably have chosen a different technology since a number of patent-free alternatives were available and costs appeared to be a central issue in the industry.[48] The Commission issued a Statement of Objection in July 2007, reaching the preliminary conclusion that Rambus had infringed Article 102 TFEU by intentionally engaging in deceptive conduct and, as a result, claiming unreasonable royalties for the use of its patents.[49] However, the investigation was closed in December 2009 following a commitment decision, based on

---

[47] *See supra* note 17.

[48] E. G. Petristsi, "The Case of Unilateral Patent Ambush Under EC Competition Rules" (2005) 28(1) *World Competition*, pp. 25–42.

[49] *See* Press Release MEMO/07/330 of 23 August 2007.

11. – Other Abuses
Frédéric de Bure

Article 9 of Regulation 1/2003.[50] In its commitment, Rambus agreed to charge no royalties in relation to the standards that were adopted when Rambus was a member of the standard-setting body.[51]

It is not clear whether the "patent ambush" may be considered by the Commission to be an abuse in and of itself, the excessive royalties being only one of the possible consequences of that initial abuse, or if it constitutes only the background for a pricing abuse (*i.e.*, imposing excessive royalties).[52] In the latter case, "patent ambush" would just be another form of excessive pricing (*see* Chapter 10). In the *Rambus* case, it seems that Rambus became dominant only after the patent ambush occurred, hence it could be argued that Article 102 TFEU did not apply to the "ambush" practice.[53] However, the commitment to charge zero royalties for the standards that were adopted when Rambus was a member of the standard-setting body seems to be tailored to remedy the patent ambush in itself more than the pricing abuse (for which a commitment to license the technology under FRAND terms would have sufficed). Although the commitment decision in *Rambus* does not qualify as a real precedent, it is a strong sign that "patent ambush" may fall in itself within the scope of Article 102 TFEU.

11.34

In January and April 2012, respectively, the Commission opened two different proceedings against Samsung and Motorola for possible violations of Article 102 TFEU within the framework of standard-setting procedures, consisting again in mixed practices involving both pricing and procedural aspects.[54] The Commission's investigations focus *inter alia* on whether the undertakings abused their dominant positions by seeking and – in Motorola's case – enforcing injunctions obtained in court against their competitors for IP rights violations on the basis of patents that Samsung and Motorola had

11.35

---

[50] *See supra* note 17; Council Regulation (EC) 1/2003 of 16.12.2002 on the implementation of the rules on competition laid down in Articles 81 and 82 of the Treaty ("*Regulation 1/2003*"), OJ 2003 L 1/1.

[51] In the US, the Federal Trade Commission ("FTC") found that Rambus had violated Section 2 of the Sherman Act, and imposed a remedy applying to all relevant products imported into or exported from the US (*See* FTC Final Order of 5 February 2007 in the matter of FTC Final Order of February 5, 2007 in the matter of Rambus Inc., FTC Docket No. 9302. Subsequently, in April 2008, the DC Court of Appeals overturned the FTC's order against Rambus, holding that the FTC failed to demonstrate that Rambus inflicted any harm on competition (*Rambus v F.T.C.*, 522 F.3d 456, 469 (DC Cir. 2008)).

[52] I. Govaere, "In Pursuit of an Innovation Policy Rationale: Stakes and Limits under Article 82 TEC" (2008) 31(4) *World Competition*, pp. 541–56.

[53] *See* M. Dolmans, "Standards for Standards" (2002) 26(1) *Fordham International Law Journal*, pp. 163–208.

[54] *See* Press Releases IP/12/89 of 31 January 2012 and IP/12/345 of 3 April 2012.

11. – Other Abuses
Frédéric de Bure

declared essential to produce standard-compliant products, therefore failing to honour their irrevocable licensing commitments made to standard-setting organisations.[55]

11.36 Unlike Rambus, Samsung and Motorola disclosed their essential patents to the relevant standard-setting organisations during the standardisation process, as was required from them, and subsequently committed themselves to license these patents under FRAND terms to third parties. However, once the standards adopted, several competitors – including Apple and Microsoft – started using the patents without entering into a FRAND licensing agreement with Samsung and Motorola, either because they considered the patents to be void or because they disagreed on the terms proposed by the licensors. Each Samsung and Motorola therefore initiated legal actions to seek injunctions preventing Apple and Microsoft to market products incorporating their patented technologies. On 9 December 2011, Motorola obtained such an injunction against Apple from the Mannheim Regional Court in Germany, in spite of Apple's claim that Motorola was in fact refusing to license the patents under FRAND terms, in violation of their commitments to the standard-setting organisations. Motorola enforced the injunction until it was cancelled by the Higher Regional Court of Karlsruhe in February 2012. All other requests by Motorola and Samsung have so far been rejected by the courts.

11.37 The Commission sent a Statement of Objections to Motorola in May 2013,[56] and is actively investigating Samsung's practices. The Commission has reached the preliminary conclusion that recourse by Motorola to injunctions on the basis of its mobile phone standard-essential patents distorted the negotiation process for a FRAND licence with Apple and therefore amounted to an abuse of a dominant position prohibited by EU antitrust rules. Although the Commission accepts that recourse to injunctive relief is generally a legitimate remedy for patent-holders in case of patent infringements, it considers that such conduct may be abusive in exceptional circumstances where standard-essential patents are concerned and the company against which an injunction is sought has shown to be willing to enter into a FRAND licence. According to the Commission, such practices can lead to less consumer choice with regard to interoperable products and less innovation. Although both investigations are still at a preliminary stage, the Commission appears to consider that the mere fact of seeking an injunction – even if the claim is denied or

---

[55] *See* Press Releases IP/12/89 of 31 January 2012 and IP/12/345 of 3 April 2012.
[56] *See* Press Release IP/13/406 and MEMO/13/403 of 6 May 2013.

11. – Other Abuses
Frédéric de Bure

if the injunction is not enforced – may be considered abusive under Article 102 TFEU.[57] In *Motorola*, the Commission seems generally concerned that the threat of injunctions can distort licensing negotiations and lead to licensing terms that the licensee of the standard-essential patents would not have accepted absent this threat. The fact that an injunction was enforced constitutes an aggravating factor. This implies that beyond the discussion about the right level of royalties under FRAND terms, patent litigation may be considered abusive in itself in the specific standardisation context. Therefore, the abuse would consist in a procedural abuse by misuse of legal proceedings based on intellectual property law. Although it is not possible to foresee the outcome of both investigations, they constitute a strong indication that the Commission is watchful of the new potentially anticompetitive conducts that may arise in the field of standard-setting procedures.

3. Discussions and Outlook

3.1. *Article 102 TFEU versus Specific Regulations: Where are the Limits?*

A frequent criticism relating to abuses of procedure is that they unduly extend the scope of Article 102 TFEU to situations that are normally governed by other bodies of rules.[58] In *AstraZeneca*, the company claimed that the alleged abuse was essentially an intellectual property law matter, the rules of which provide specific remedies in cases of fraud, and that it therefore should not fall within the scope of antitrust laws. The same argument could be made in *Boehringer*, *Rambus*, or the more recent *Samsung* and *Motorola* cases. In *GlaxoSmithKline*, although the case related to a vertical agreement under Article 101 TFEU, the General Court made it clear that, in the pharmaceutical sector, where prices are regulated, anticompetitive effects deriving from an allegedly anticompetitive agreement should not be inferred from the terms of the agreement.[59] The United States Supreme Court followed a similar reasoning in the *Trinko* case where it ruled that in regulated sectors competition law should not apply when the regulatory rules constitute an alternative means of ensuring competitive conduct.[60] The Commission takes the view, which was later reinforced by the General Court, that Article 102 TFEU applies

11.38

---

[57] *See* Press Release IP/13/406 and MEMO/13/403 of 6 May 2013.

[58] *See, e.g.,* F. Liberatore and F. Murphy, *supra* note 24.

[59] Case T-168/01 *GlaxoSmithKline Services v Commission* ("*GlaxoSmithKline Judgment 2006*") [2006] ECR II–2969, para.147.

[60] *Verizon Communications v Law Offices of Curtis v Trinko* ("*Trinko*"), 540 US 398 (2004).

11. – Other Abuses
Frédéric de Bure

even in the presence of specific regulations. Competition law is designed to control anticompetitive conduct, while other laws are intended to control certain behaviours regardless of their effect on competition. Conduct that is a breach of applicable regulations may be fully compliant with competition law because it does not have any anticompetitive effects.[61] Conversely, conduct that is compliant with the applicable regulatory framework may be in violation of Article 102 TFEU. In the *AstraZeneca* case, the Court stated clearly that *"where behaviour falls within the scope of the competition rules, those rules apply irrespective of whether that behaviour may also be caught by other rules, of national origin or otherwise, which pursue separate objectives"*.[62] A regulatory procedure may therefore be used in full compliance with the specific rules that apply and nevertheless constitute an abuse of a dominant position.

3.2.   *Are Procedural Abuses Compatible with the Effects-based Doctrine?*

11.39   Another frequent question is whether procedural abuses should only be prohibited where authorities can actually prove the (likely) resulting anti-competitive foreclosure effects in the market. For example, one of the main arguments submitted by AstraZeneca to the Court is that the first abuse, which concerned intentions and preparatory acts (applying for an SPC and briefing patent agents), did not have any material effect since in most Member States, SPCs were ultimately not granted or subsequently cancelled by national courts following judicial review. Similarly, the Commission decided to open proceedings against Samsung merely for seeking to get injunctions from the courts, even though no injunction was ever actually granted. More generally, one may wonder if procedural abuses may fit within the effects-based doctrine favoured in the *Guidance Paper*.[63] The question of whether the use or misuse of a procedure has actual anticompetitive effect in the market has little relevance to the qualification of the conduct as an abuse. In fact, procedural abuses are typically intentional abuses that generally form part of a deliberate exclusionary strategy. Therefore, evidence of actual effects is not required. It is settled case law that, a violation of Article 102 TFEU may result from the anticompetitive object of the practice in question.[64] Since procedural abuses

---

[61] *See* Case COMP/37.507 *supra* note 7, para. 744.

[62] *See* Case T–321/05 *supra* note 7, para. 366.

[63] *See Guidance Paper supra* note 4.

[64] Case T–203/01 *Manufacture française des pneumatiques Michelin v Commission* ("*Michelin II*") [2003] ECR II–4071, para. 241; Joined Cases T–24 to 26 and 28/93 *Compagnie Maritime Belge Transports and others v Commission* [1996] ECR II–1201, para. 149, confirmed by Joined Cases C–395 and 396/96 P *supra* note 1, paras 118–20. *See also*

11. – Other Abuses
Frédéric de Bure

typically have an intentional dimension, they could be treated as anticompetitive conduct by object. The fact that the exclusionary strategy was not fully implemented and/or did not produce the desired effects may therefore be relevant when determining the amount of the fine, as exemplified by the General Court's decision in the AstraZeneca case,[65] but not when assessing the existence of a violation of Article 102 TFEU.

3.3. *A Convergence between the European Union and the US?*

An analysis of the US case law with respect to abuses of procedures shows increasing convergence between the European Union and the United States.[66] **11.40**

US antitrust authorities have analysed the issue of abuses of procedure. The US Federal Trade Commission ("FTC") and the US courts have addressed the exclusionary use of intellectual property rights in the pharmaceutical sector for some years now. In the *Biovail* and *Bristol-Myers Squibb* cases, the FTC found that practices very similar to those enacted by *AstraZeneca* – namely, improper listing of patents and misrepresentative statements with the Federal Drug Administration ("FDA") in order to obtain longer protection from competition for their branded drugs — amounted to unlawful monopolisation in breach of Section 2 of the Sherman Act.[67] **11.41**

In both cases, the anticompetitive practice related to improper listing of patents in the so-called "Orange Book". Like in the European Union, brand name manufacturers seeking to market a new drug in the United States must first obtain a marketing authorisation from the FDA. The application submitted to the FDA must provide information regarding (1) the safety and efficiency of the drug and (2) any patents protecting the drug. The patents are listed in the "Orange Book". As the FDA has neither the expertise nor the resources to resolve complex patent coverage issues, it does not scrutinise the manufacturers' bases for listing patents in the Orange Book. When entering the market, a generic drug manufacturer must certify that, to the best of its knowledge, the drug does not infringe any patent listed in the Orange Book or that the patent is not valid. In turn, if the brand drug manufacturer considers **11.42**

Case C-202/07 P *France Télécom v Commission* [2009] ECR I–2369, paras 107–13. *See also* Case COMP/37.990 *Intel*, Commission Decision of 13 May 2009, not yet published, para. 923.

[65] *See* Case T-321/05 *supra* note 7.

[66] *See* C. Breuvart and J.-P. Gunther, *supra* note 24.

[67] *Biovail* ("*Biovail*"), 134 F.T.C. 407 (2002) and *Bristol-Myers Squibb* ("*Bristol-Myers Squibb*"), 135 F.T.C. 444 (2003).

11. – Other Abuses
Frédéric de Bure

that the generic drug would in fact infringe one of its patents, it can file a patent infringement suit that automatically freezes the generic drug application for a period of 30 months. In *Biovail*, the FTC found that Biovail, a Canadian manufacturer of branded drugs, had engaged in unlawful monopolisation by wrongfully listing a patent in the Orange Book in relation to its Tiazac drug. When the listing of the patent was challenged by generic drug manufacturers seeking to enter the market, Biovail filed a patent infringement application based on misleading information in order to trigger the 30-month stay process and therefore delay the market entry of generic versions of Tiazac. In *Bristol-Myers Squibb* ("BMS"), BMS used the same tactic to protect its BuSpar, Taxol, and Platinol drugs. It provided misleading information to the FDA in order to have its patent listed in the Orange Book and initiated groundless lawsuits against generic competitors in order delay their entry into the market. The FTC found that both Biovail and BMS had engaged in unlawful monopolisation practices and ended the cases by entering into Consent Agreements.

11.43   Interestingly, the second abuse identified by the Commission in the *AstraZeneca* Decision (the de-listing of authorised drugs) is also similar to the practices sanctioned by US courts in the *Abbott Laboratories v Teva Pharmaceuticals USA* judgment.[68] A federal court found that the fact that Abbott stopped marketing a former version of its TriCor drug and changed its code in the National Drug Data File to "obsolete" prevented generic drug manufacturers from entering the market, and therefore constituted an infringement of Section 2 of the Sherman Act.

11.44   As regards vexatious litigation, the findings of the Court of Justice in *ITT Promedia* are in line with the US case law on "sham" litigation. In its 1993 landmark case, *Professional Real Estate*, the US Supreme Court found that a company could infringe antitrust law by bringing "sham" litigation to court, but only insofar as two cumulative conditions are met.[69] First, the lawsuit should be objectively baseless in the sense that no reasonable litigant could realistically expect success on the merits. Secondly, the action should constitute an attempt to interfere directly with a competitor's business relationship through the *use,* rather than the *outcome,* of the litigation process as an anticompetitive weapon. These two conditions are applied strictly, and although litigants often raise sham litigation as a defence against competitors' claims, the argument is rarely successful.

---

[68] *Abbott Laboratories v Teva Pharmaceuticals USA*, 432 F.Supp.2d 408 (D. Del. 2006).
[69] *Professional Real Estate Investors v Columbia Pictures Industries* ("*Professional Real Estate*"), 508 US 49 (1993).

11. – Other Abuses
Frédéric de Bure

Other cases were investigated on both sides of the Atlantic. Rambus was **11.45** found in violation of Article 2 of the Shearman Act by the FTC, although the decision was subsequently annulled based on the fact that the agency had not provided sufficient evidence.[70] Both Samsung and Motorola are currently facing an antitrust investigation of the US authorities for the same facts as in the European Union.

3.4. *Isolated Cases or a New Category of Abuses?*

It is still unclear whether the above line of cases forms a new category of **11.46** abuses or should just be treated as very fact-specific isolated cases.

Certain factors militate in favour of the latter conclusion, including the fact **11.47** that procedural abuses are particularly difficult to detect since evidence of an exclusionary intent is required, the exact same abuse is unlikely to occur twice since the legislation is often modified after the first case is detected (in that respect, changing the legislation is often an easier and quicker remedy than to start an antitrust investigation against a given practice), and that competition authorities may be reluctant to intervene in areas that are at the boundaries between competition law and other regulations.

There are also, however, reasons to believe that procedural abuses are fre- **11.48** quent and particularly harmful. In recent years, the Commission indicated its willingness to treat non-price exclusionary abuses as a priority, and a significant proportion of the new Article 102 TFEU cases include a form of procedural abuse. For example, the report by the Commission on its inquiry in the pharmaceutical sector identified the possible misuse of the patent system by pharmaceutical companies as an area of concern that may give rise to Article 102 TFEU cases in the future.[71] The Commission's findings indicate that originator companies use a variety of strategies to extend the breadth and duration of their patent protection and affect the ability of generic competitors to enter the market. The Commission also noted that systematic litigation could also be an efficient means of deterring generic companies or potential competitors, in particular for smaller ones.

---

[70] *Rambus v F.T.C., supra* note 51.
[71] Pharmaceutical Sector Inquiry – Final Report, Commission Staff Working Document of 08.07.09.

11. – Other Abuses
Frédéric de Bure

11.49   Moreover, with respect to standard-setting processes, former Commissioner Neelie Kroes clearly stated that the Commission would encourage "open standards" whenever possible.[72] She also expressed concerns that *"patents are now often used strategically and no longer primarily to protect innovation".*[73] Commissioner Almunia has taken the same path. In a recent speech, he insisted in particular on the importance of FRAND access and the need to prevent consumers from being *"held hostage to litigation"*[74] such as the actions initiated by Samsung and Motorola. The Commission considers that proprietary technology should only be used in standards when there are no clear and demonstrable benefits over non-proprietary alternatives, and subject to *ex ante* disclosure of the existence of essential patents. Given that standardisation will remain a key issue in the coming years, the Commission will likely scrutinise dominant companies' behaviour carefully, in particular in the information technology sector, which may give rise to new Article 102 TFEU cases in the future.

11.50   Finally, the procedural abuse category remains unexplored to a significant extent. Although IP rights are certainly a privileged area for these types of abuses, the category could be extended to a number of other procedures, *e.g.*, where the State or a regulator gives access to a scarce resource (*e.g.*, radio frequencies, telephony licence, satellite slots). Moreover, competition authorities could identify new forms of abuses. For example, the accumulation of patents in relation to a single technology or product has never been investigated, but it may raise significant competition issues. A common strategy is the creation of "patent clusters" or "patent thicket" by filing numerous patents applications in order to make it more difficult for competitors to see whether they can enter the market without infringing one of the many patents and/or initiate systematic litigation in order to delay market entry. Another strategy is to file voluntary "divisional patent" applications, *i.e.*, a patent application that relates to a previously filed application (the "parent" application) in order to ensure protection on certain aspects that have not been tackled in the parent patent application. Although in principle they cannot extend the content of the original application nor the protection period, multiple "divisional patent" applications sometimes adopt an overly broad appreciation of the original content of the application. They also extend the examination period of the patent office, as the examination of divisional applications continues even if the parent application is withdrawn or revoked. This can add to the legal

---

[72] Press Release SPEECH/08/317 of 10 June 2008.
[73] *Ibid.*
[74] Press Release SPEECH/12/453 of 15 June 2012.

uncertainty for competitors. Such strategies appear to be particularly common in highly innovative industries and may in the future raise major issues under Article 102 TFEU.

III. Contractual Abuses

Besides unfair prices (analysed in Chapter 10), Article 102(a) TFEU also **11.51** prohibits the direct or indirect imposition of unfair trading conditions. This applies to situations where a dominant company imposes abusive non-price contractual terms on its trading partner that could not be obtained under normal competitive conditions. Applicable jurisprudence has also established that merely entering into a contractual relationship with a trading partner may constitute an abuse under certain circumstances. Finally, the performance of a contract may be found to infringe Article 102 TFEU.

The "special responsibility" of dominant undertakings not to hinder compe- **11.52** tition therefore imposes upon them the obligation to be fair in their contractual relationships with their trading partners, which can also be interpreted as the obligation not to take advantage of their dominant position. Although contractual abuses are traditionally defined as exploitative abuses, an analysis of the Commission's decision-making practice and of the European courts' case law reveals that contractual abuses may nonetheless have exclusionary effects.

1. Abusive Contracting

The General Court has held that in certain circumstances "*the conclusion of a* **11.53** *contract or the acquisition of a right may amount to abuse for the purposes of Article* [102 TFEU] *if that contract is concluded or that right is acquired by an undertaking in a dominant position*".[75] This follows from established case law according to which, in specific circumstances, undertakings in a dominant position may be deprived of the right to adopt a course of conduct or take measures which are not in and of themselves abusive, and which would not be objectionable if adopted or implemented by non-dominant undertakings.[76] Of course, the mere fact

---

[75] See *ITT Promedia supra* note 6, para. 139. *See also Tetra Pak I Judgment 1990 supra* note 11, para. 23.
[76] See *Michelin I supra* note 8, para. 57.

11. – Other Abuses
Frédéric de Bure

that a dominant undertaking concludes a contract or acquires a right does not constitute an abuse *per se*. However, the General Court has held in *Tetra Pak* that there is no need for a "*supplementary element, external to the agreement*",[77] in order to characterise abusive contracting. The decisive factors in the finding of a violation of Article 102 TFEU are the "*specific circumstances of the case*" and in particular the effects of the contract, or of the acquisition of the right, on the structure of competition in the relevant market.[78] In practice, precedents are extremely rare and case-specific. In *Ahmed Saeed*, for example, the Court of Justice held that the application of tariffs that were the result of a concerted action falling under the scope of the prohibition in Article 101 TFEU could be qualified as an abuse within the meaning of Article 102 TFEU if the agreement simply reflected the fact that the dominant undertaking had convinced the other undertakings to apply the tariffs in question.[79]

11.54   In most cases, an abuse is found to exist based on a detailed analysis of the provisions of a given contract entered into by a dominant undertaking.

2.   Abusive Contract Terms

11.55   Although there are very few precedents, the prohibition of unfair trading conditions could cover a wide variety of circumstances. The tests applied by the Commission and the Court of Justice weigh the anticompetitive effects of a clause against the potentially legitimate reasons for the restriction.

2.1.   The Applicable Test

11.56   The limited number of cases relating to unfair trading under Article 102 TFEU makes it difficult to define the applicable tests. The objective is to prevent dominant companies from imposing unjustified clauses that they would not be able to impose under normal market conditions and that would result in the restriction of competition and/or the exploitation of their trading partners in the "specific circumstances of the case".

11.57   In earlier decisions, the question of the existence of an unfair trading provision depended on whether there was an "absolute necessity" for the clause

---

[77] *See Tetra Pak I Judgment 1990 supra* note 11, para. 24.

[78] *Ibid.*, paras 23–24.

[79] Case 66/86 *Ahmed Saeed Flugreisen and Silver Line Reisebüro v Zentrale zur Bekämpfung unlauteren Wettbewerbs* ("*Ahmed Saeed*") [1989] ECR 803, paras 34 *et seq.*

11. – Other Abuses
Frédéric de Bure

to exist in order to fulfil the purpose of the contract.[80] In *Tetra Pak II Decision 1991*, the Commission verified whether the clauses at stake (*see* below) were reasonably necessary in light of the object of the contract.[81] In *TACA*, the Court recalled that, unlike Article 101, Article 102 TFEU does not provide for any exemptions, and that abusive practices are prohibited regardless of the advantages that they may generate.[82] Therefore, the mere fact that restrictions to competition contained in a contract are necessary to achieve certain benefits sought by the contract, cannot justify an abuse of Article 102 TFEU.[83] Since there is no exemption from the application of Article 102 TFEU, the only acceptable justification is where the dominant company can show that the *"purpose of* [the] *practices is reasonably to protect its commercial interests in the face of action taken by certain third parties and that they do not therefore in fact constitute an abuse"*.[84] Moreover, in light of their special responsibility not to impair competition, the practices of dominant undertakings must be *"proportionate to the objective they seek to achieve"*.[85] In *DSD*, the Commission and the Court confirmed that the test included an assessment of the proportionality of the clause to the objective of the contract.[86]

As a result, case law suggests that an unfair contractual term imposed by **11.58** a dominant company may fall within the scope of Article 102 TFEU if it has a negative effect on the structure of competition, unless two cumulative conditions are met. First, the object of the contract and the clause must be legitimate and reasonable in light of the commercial interests of the dominant undertaking. Secondly, the restriction must be strictly necessary for the attainment of the object of the contract. This assessment requires balancing the interests of both parties to the contract and ensuring that the measure is proportionate to the objective it seeks to achieve (*i.e.*, that it could not be achieved in a less restrictive way). Because the test is cumulative, if it appears that the sole object of the clause is to restrict competition or to exploit the

---

[80] Case 127/73 *Belgische Radio en Televisie and société belge des auteurs, compositeurs et éditeurs v SABAM and Fonior* ("*BRT-II*") [1974] ECR 313, para. 11.

[81] Case IV/31.043 Tetra Pak II ("*Tetra Pak II Decision 1991*"), Commission Decision of 24 July 1991, OJ 1992 L 72/1, upheld on appeal in *Tetra Pak II Judgment 1994 supra* note 8, paras 105–7.

[82] Joined Cases T-191 and 212 to 214/98 *Atlantic Container Line and others v Commission* ("*TACA Judgment 2003*") [2003] ECR II–3275, para. 1112.

[83] *Ibid.*, paras 1112–6.

[84] *Ibid.*, para. 1114.

[85] *Ibid.*, para. 1120.

[86] Case COMP/34.493 *DSD* ("*DSD Decision 2001*"), Commission Decision of 20 April 2001, OJ 2001 L 166/1, para. 112.

trading partner (as was the case in *Tetra Pak* and *AAMS* — *see* Section III.2.2 below), it is not necessary to evaluate the proportionality of the restriction.

2.2. Precedents

11.59   Even if the definition of "unfair trading conditions" remains unclear, a few precedents from the Commission and the Court of Justice provide some examples of prohibited clauses. In general, unfair contractual terms constitute only one aspect of a more complex abuse.

11.60   In *BRT-II*, the Court evaluated allegedly unfair contractual terms in relation to the assignment of copyrights to copyright collection societies.[87] SABAM enjoyed a *de facto* monopoly on the management of copyrights in Belgium. The contracts between SABAM and its members included a clause whereby the authors assigned all of their present and future copyrights to SABAM. In the event that a member wanted to leave the society, this clause remained valid for five years after such member's withdrawal. One of the questions referred to the Court for a preliminary ruling was whether SABAM was imposing unfair contractual terms on its members within the meaning of Article 102 TFEU. The Court stated that all of the relevant interests should be taken into account for the purpose of ensuring a balance between providing maximum freedom for authors, composers, and publishers to dispose of their works, and allowing for the effective management of their rights by SABAM (which is an unavoidable partner). The Court further noted that the object of the copyright management society was the protection of the rights and interests of its members and that the assignment of the authors' copyrights was necessary for the fulfilment of that objective. However, the assessment of the legality of the contested clause under Article 102 TFEU depended on whether the clause exceeded "*the limit absolutely necessary for the attainment of* [its] *object*".[88] In that case, the Court concluded that the compulsory assignment of both present and future copyrights constituted an unfair contractual condition, especially if such assignment was required for an extended period after the member's withdrawal. SABAM had unnecessarily restricted its members' freedom to exercise their copyrights and therefore had abused its dominant position. The Commission and the Court adopted a similar line of reasoning

---

[87] *See BRT-II supra* note 80.
[88] *Ibid.*, para. 11.

11. – Other Abuses
Frédéric de Bure

in several subsequent cases regarding the conditions for the assignment of copyrights.[89]

In *Tetra Pak II*, the Commission held to be illegal a wide variety of clauses **11.61** introduced by Tetra Pak, a company specialised in the carton packaging of liquid and semi-liquid food products (mainly milk), in its customer contracts.[90] The case involved a wide array of both exclusionary (*e.g.*, predatory pricing) and exploitative abuses, and the unfair contractual terms constituted only a small portion of the infringement. It is nevertheless a good example of the types of unfair contractual terms that may be prohibited under Article 102 TFEU. The contracts concerned the lease, purchase, and use of packaging machines and carton packaging by Tetra Pak's customers. The following provisions were found to be abusive:

- **First, the restrictions preventing a customer from adding accessories to or modifying the machine without Tetra Pak's consent.** According to the Commission, the obligations *"deprived the purchaser of certain aspects of his property rights"* and had the *"effect of making the customer totally dependent on Tetra Pak's equipment and services"*.[91] It also foreclosed potential competitors from entering the repair and maintenance market.

- **Secondly, the clauses granting an exclusive right to maintain and repair its equipment and an exclusive right to supply spare parts.** This provision had the same effect as an exclusive supply provision and gave Tetra Pak the status of exclusive provider with respect to the supply of repair and maintenance services and spare parts for its products. The Commission found that these clauses effectively bound the customer to Tetra Pak and precluded them from procuring any maintenance and repair services and spare parts from the user's own technical staff or from another competitor.[92]

- **Thirdly, the requirement that Tetra Pak's consent be obtained for the resale or transfer of use of the equipment, reserving to Tetra Pak the right to repurchase the equipment at a pre-arranged fixed**

---

[89] Case IV/26.760 *GEMA I*, Commission Decision of 2 June 1971, OJ 1971 L 134/15; and Case 125/78 *GEMA, Gesellschaft für musikalische Aufführungs- und mechanische Vervielfältigungsrechte v Commission* [1979] ECR 3173.
[90] *Tetra Pak II Decision 1991 supra* note 81, upheld on appeal in *Tetra Pak II Judgment 1994 supra* note 8, paras 105–7.
[91] *See Tetra Pak II Decision 1991 supra* note 81, para. 107.
[92] *Ibid.*, para. 108.

11. – Other Abuses
Frédéric de Bure

price, and the requirement that any subsequent vendor assume the same obligations. These clauses, which are close to a bundling agreement, were found by the Commission to infringe competition rules by their very nature, granting Tetra Pak sole ownership of the rights to any improvements on the equipment made by the user.[93]

- **Fourthly, the duration of lease agreements.** The Commission found that a nine-year duration was excessive and abusive, as it limited the entry of new competitors in the packaging markets.[94]

- **Fifthly, the stipulation that honouring the guarantee was subject to compliance with all of the terms of the contract, including but not limited to those terms affecting the operation of equipment.** This clause reinforced the anticompetitive effects of the other clauses by ensuring that these clauses be enforced throughout the term of the guarantee.[95]

11.62   The Commission concluded that Tetra Pak had abused its dominant position on the relevant markets by *"the imposition on users of Tetra Pak products in all Member States of numerous contractual clauses [...] having the essential object of unduly binding them to Tetra Pak and of artificially eliminating potential competition"*.[96] Further, the Commission found that the disputed clauses had no relation to the purpose of the contracts. Both the General Court and the Court of Justice upheld the Decision.[97]

11.63   In *TACA,* the Commission analysed the terms of various service contracts entered into between TACA, a liner conference offering transatlantic liner services, and shippers.[98] Service contracts are contracts by which the shipper undertakes to provide a minimum quantity of cargo to be transported by the conference. Among other infringements of Articles 101 and 102 TFEU, the Commission found that some of the clauses had important exclusionary effects and constituted an abuse of a collective dominant position by TACA's members. In particular, the following terms of the contract were found to be

---

[93] *See Tetra Pak II Decision 1991 supra* note 81, para. 115.

[94] *Ibid.,* paras 144–46.

[95] *Ibid.,* paras 129–30.

[96] *Ibid.,* para. 170.

[97] *See Tetra Pak II Judgment 1994 supra* note 8, upheld on appeal in Case C–333/94 P *Tetra Pak International v Commission* ("*Tetra Pak II Judgment 1996*") [1996] ECR I–5951.

[98] Case IV/35.134 *Trans-Atlantic Conference Agreement* ("*TACA Decision 1998*"), Commission Decision of 16 September 1998, OJ 1999 L 95/1, upheld on appeal in *TACA Judgment 2003 supra* note 82.

11. – Other Abuses
Frédéric de Bure

contrary to Article 102 TFEU: (1) The restriction on TACA members entering into individual service contracts with shippers; and (2) once that restriction was lifted, the application in any individual service contract of certain terms and conditions agreed upon collectively by the conference, such as the prohibition of contingency clauses;[99] the minimum duration of the service contracts; the ban on multiple contracts; and the penalty levels imposed on shippers who had breached the service contract.

11.64 The Commission and the General Court found these practices unfair since their purpose was to reduce competition by restricting the availability and content of service contracts.[100] They also found that TACA's members had failed to demonstrate that the practices were objectively justified.[101]

11.65 In *AAMS*, the Commission found that the Amministrazione Autonoma dei Monopoli di Stato ("AAMS"), a public body attached to the Italian Ministry of Finance, which, *inter alia*, was engaged in the production, import, export, and wholesale distribution of manufactured tobaccos, held a dominant position on the market for the wholesale distribution of cigarettes in Italy and had abused its position through the conclusion of standard distribution agreements with certain cigarette manufacturers.[102] In *AAMS*, the Commission condemned multiple unfair clauses included in these agreements, such as: (1) a time limit for the introduction of new cigarette brands in the Italian market (*i.e.*, a bi-annual limitation); (2) a limit on the number of new brands allowed on the Italian market; and (3) a monthly quota on the number of cigarettes allowed on the Italian market.

11.66 These clauses were found to be unfair since they had an exclusionary effect *vis-à-vis* actual and potential AAMS competitors on the market for the wholesale distribution of cigarettes and on the downstream retail market.[103]

---

[99] Contingency clauses typically provide that if the tariff rate drops below the shipper's service contract rate, or if the conference enters into another service contract with a smaller volume commitment and a lower rate, the shipper who signed the first contract is automatically entitled to the lower rate.

[100] *See TACA Decision 1998 supra* note 98, upheld on appeal in *TACA Judgment 2003 supra* note 82.

[101] *Ibid.*

[102] Case IV/36.010 *Amministrazione Autonoma dei Monopoli di Stato* ("*AAMS Decision 1998*"), Commission Decision of 17 June 1998, OJ 1998 L 252/47, upheld on appeal in Case T-139/98 *Amministrazione Autonoma dei Monopoli di Stato v Commission* ("*AAMS Judgment 2001*") [2001] ECR II-3413.

[103] *Ibid.*

11.67 In *DSD*, the Commission found that the contractual terms concerning the use of the dominant firm's "green dot" logo on the sales packaging of its custom-ers were abusive.[104] Der Grüne Punkt – Duales System Deutschland ("DSD"), the only undertaking in Germany that operated a nation-wide system for the collection and recovery of sales packaging, had entered into standard agree-ments with the packaging manufacturers and distributors participating in the system. The agreement governed, *inter alia*, the use of DSD's "green dot" logo. It provided in particular that contractual partners had to (1) use the logo on all registered packaging for domestic consumption in Germany, and (2) pay DSD a licence fee for all packaging bearing the "green dot" logo which it sells on German territory. It follows that partners had to pay a fee for the entire quantity of their packaging, even if they made no use of the service offered by DSD or if they used it for only some of their packaging.[105] As a result, packaging manufacturers and distributors had little interest in using competing systems. The Commission claimed that the fee should have been based, not on the intensity of use of the logo, but the costs incurred by DSD, which, in turn, depended on partner's use of the DSD's services. The Com-mission found that *"DSD* [did] *not appear to have any reasonable interest in linking the fee payable by its contractual partners not to the exemption service actually used but to the extent to which the mark is used"*.[106] The Commission concluded that DSD's clauses were unfair contractual terms because DSD had failed *"to comply with the principle of proportionality"* since the price that was being charged for the service was not proportional to the cost of supplying it.[107] Such practices had the effect of both exploiting DSD's customers and preventing entry of com-petitors in violation of Article 102 TFEU.

3. Abuse of the Exercise of Contractual Obligations

11.68 Even if a contractual provision does not constitute an abuse at the time a contract is concluded, the abuse may result from the abusive enforcement of the clause. In that respect, the European courts have established that *"[a]* claim *for performance of a contractual obligation may also constitute an abuse for the purposes of Article* [102 TFEU] *if, in particular, that claim exceeds what the parties could reasonably*

---

[104] *See DSD Decision 2001 supra* note 86, upheld in Case T-151/01 *Der Grüne Punkt – Duales System Deutschland v Commission* (*"DSD Judgment 2007"*) [2007] ECR II-1607.

[105] *See DSD Decision 2001 supra* note 86, paras 100–02.

[106] *Ibid.*, paras 111–13.

[107] *Ibid.*, para. 112.

11. – Other Abuses
Frédéric de Bure

expect under the contract or if the circumstances applicable at the time of the conclusion of the contract have changed in the meantime".[108] Similarly, an undertaking in a dominant position which enjoys an exclusive right with an entitlement to agree to waive that right has a duty to make reasonable use of the veto right conferred upon it by the agreement with respect of third parties' access to the market.[109]

The *ITT Promedia* case concerned the renewal of a contract entered into on **11.69** 9 May 1984 between Belgacom, the Belgian incumbent telephony operator, and ITT Promedia, a Belgian company whose main business was the publication of commercial telephone directories in Belgium. The contract granted ITT Promedia with an exclusive right to publish and distribute telephone directories in Belgium for a period of ten years starting on 1 January 1985 and ending upon the publication of the complete tenth edition of the official telephone directories. ITT Promedia challenged the application of one of the provisions of the 1984 agreement, which provided that "*to enable* [Belgacom] *to ensure continuity of the publication*" after the end of the exclusivity, ITT was to transfer to it free of charge "*the licences resulting from patents or similar forms of legal protection granted in relation to works performed or carried out in connection with this agreement*".[110] The applicant claimed that the performance of this clause by Belgacom was abusive, in particular Belgacom's demand that ITT transferred its Pages d'Or trademark. Although the General Court stated that, in theory, a claim for the performance of a contractual obligation may also constitute an abuse for purposes of Article 102 TFEU, it also decided that ITT had not submitted any evidence to show that the application of the agreement by Belgacom had exceeded what the parties could have reasonably expected at the time the contract was concluded. In particular, the Court held that, based on the wording of the clause, it could not be ruled out that trademarks were intended to be covered by the clause.[111]

Thus, even if a provision does not constitute an abuse at the time the agree- **11.70** ment was entered into, it can nevertheless be considered to be an abuse of a dominant position if, in the future, its application exceeds the parties expectations or the conditions changed. This rule is derived from classic contract laws ("*imprévision*" in French administrative law[112] or "*frustration*" in English

---

[108] *See ITT Promedia supra* note 6, para. 140.

[109] *See* joined Cases T-24 to 26 and 28/93 *supra* note 64, para. 108. Upheld on appeal, *see supra* note 1.

[110] *See ITT Promedia supra* note 6, para. 143.

[111] *Ibid.*, paras 143–46.

[112] Case n°59928 *Gaz de Bordeaux*, French Conseil d'Etat Judgment of 30 March 1916.

11. – Other Abuses
Frédéric de Bure

common law[113]). It confirms that the assessment under Article 102 TFEU is not only an *in abstracto* analysis of the contractual terms, but should also consider the dominant company's conduct throughout the life of the agreement.

4. Discussions and Outlook

4.1. *Limited Case Law*

11.71 There are very few Article 102 TFEU cases relating to unfair contractual terms. This scarcity of case law may be the result of the facts that: (1) even absent a dominant position, abusive clauses are already prohibited under European Union and national legislations (2) other areas of antitrust law also address the issue of unfair clauses that have a detrimental effect on competition; and/or (3) the fight against unfair non-price contractual terms is not a competition policy priority.

4.2. *Consumer and Commerce Laws*

11.72 Besides Article 102 TFEU, other legislations aim at protecting both consumers and undertakings against unfair contract terms and do not require demonstrating the existence of a dominant position of one of the parties. The protection of consumers against unfair contractual terms has traditionally been organised directly by Member States. In most countries, specific laws are designed to protect consumers, setting standards in terms of pre-contractual information, repairs and warranties, product quality and safety, consumer privacy, and abusive clauses. A number of specific rules have also been enacted at the European Union level in order to define the basic consumer rights that apply to consumer contracts across the European Union, in particular in order to prevent unfair terms for consumers. These include, *inter alia*, European Union legislation governing unfair terms.[114] Moreover, certain national laws prohibit contractual provisions that result in a substantial imbalance of the rights and obligations of the parties to a contract. This prohibition does not require the existence of a dominant position (or the demonstration of

---

[113] *Taylor v Caldwell* [1863] EWHC QB J1 122 ER 309; 3 B. & S. 826.
[114] *See* Council Directive 93/13/EEC of 05 April 1993 on unfair terms in consumer contracts, OJ 1993 L 95/29. *See also* Proposal for a Directive of the European Parliament and of the Council on consumer rights, October 8, 2008, which contains both (1) a new black list of unfair contract terms prohibited across the EU in all cases and (2) an EU-wide grey list of contract terms deemed to be unfair if the trader does not prove the contrary.

11. – Other Abuses
Frédéric de Bure

an effect on intra-Community trade).[115] The possibility for the parties to rely upon *ad hoc* national law provisions that do not require establishing the existence of a dominant position to challenge alleged unfair terms included in their contracts makes it less common that Article 102 TFEU be invoked in these circumstances.

4.3.   Antitrust Laws

Antitrust legislation outside Article 102 TFEU specifically prohibits certain unfair **11.73** contractual terms, which also explains the scarcity of contractual abuses. For example, distribution agreements fall within the scope of Article 101 TFEU. The Vertical Agreement Block Exemption Regulation and the related guidelines define the types of restrictions that a supplier may impose on its distributors.[116] Another example is the Technology Transfer Block Exemption Regulation that defines the types of restrictions that a licensor may impose on a licensee under Article 101 TFEU.[117] In addition, the broad application of Article 101 TFEU further limits the scope of Article 102 TFEU (although Articles 101 and 102 TFEU may be applied simultaneously).[118] A good example is the distinction between unilateral conduct and agreements. Although Article 101 TFEU does not apply in principle to unilateral conduct, it follows from the relevant case law that the unilateral policy of one party may nonetheless fall within the scope of Article 101 TFEU if the other party has tacitly acquiesced to such policy.[119] If the supplier held a dominant

---

[115] For instance, Article L.442–6–I–2 of the French *Code de Commerce* strictly prohibits a provision that imposes or attempts to impose a commercial partner to accept certain obligations creating a substantial imbalance in the rights or obligations of the parties. Such prohibition does not require the existence of a dominant position, even if some commentators ask that economic dependence situation is reckoned as a condition of application of this Article. The existence of a violation under Article L.442–6–I–2 of the French *Code de Commerce* is therefore easier to demonstrate than a violation of Article 102(a) TFEU. Moreover, under Article L.132–1 of the French *Code de la Consommation*: "*In agreements concluded between a professional business and a non-professional body or a consumer, provisions that have as their object or effect to create a significant imbalance between the rights or obligations of the parties, to the detriment of the non-professional body or consumer, are deemed abusive.*" The regulatory part of the French *Code de la Consommation* gives examples of some clauses that are always considered as abusive, such as: "*Suppressing or reducing the right of the non-professional body or consumer to claim damages in case of a failure by the professional business to fulfil any of its obligations.*"

[116] *See* Commission Regulation (EU) 330/2010 of 20 April 2010 on the application of Article 101(3) of the Treaty on the Functioning of the European Union to categories of vertical agreements and concerted practices, OJ 2010 L 102/1, and Guidelines on Vertical Restraints, OJ 2010 C 130/1.

[117] *See* Commission Regulation (EC) 772/2004 of 27 April 2004 on the application of Article 81(3) of the Treaty to categories of technology transfer agreements ("*Technology Transfer Block Exemption Regulation*"), OJ 2004 L 123/11, and Commission Notice – Guidelines on the application of Article 81 of the EC Treaty to technology transfer agreements ("*2004 Technology Transfer Guidelines*"), OJ 2004 C 101/2.

[118] *See supra* note 1, para. 33.

[119] Case T-41/96 *Bayer v Commission* [2000] ECR II-3383.

11. – Other Abuses
Frédéric de Bure

position, this conduct could arguably also fall within the scope of Article 102 TFEU.

4.4. Competition Policy

11.74 In recent years, competition authorities – in particular the Commission – have clearly focused their efforts on exclusionary abuses as evidenced by the publication of the *Guidance Paper*.[120] Moreover, price abuses have been scrutinised more closely than non-price abuses, which, at present, do not appear to constitute a priority in terms of competition policy enforcement.

4.5. An Obsolete Category of Abuses?

11.75 Another question relates to the relevance of non-price contractual abuses in the context of modern antitrust law. Most of the cases are relatively old, at least according to common standards in competition law, *i.e.*, more than 10 years old. Moreover, non-price contractual abuses have generally been addressed in a subsidiary manner in the context of a broader infringement. Given the current enforcement priorities, it is unclear whether new cases are likely to be investigated by the Commission, at least individually (*i.e.*, not within the context of a broader infringement). However, some national competition authorities continue to penalise unfair contractual clauses under Article 102 TFEU. For instance, the French Competition Authority imposed interim measures on Google because it found that some contractual dispositions were not clear enough and had been applied to customers in a discriminatory way.[121] Such example shows that the broad category of unfair contractual terms offers competition authorities considerable flexibility to deal with new forms of abuse. The precedent described above could thus be useful in finding legal solutions to unique situations and assessing complex contracts.

IV. Structural Abuses

11.76 Actions by dominant undertakings can be considered to be abusive under Article 102 TFEU when they negatively impact the competitive structure of the market. The Court of Justice has established that Article 102 TFEU *"is not only aimed at practices which may cause damage to consumers directly, but also at those*

---

[120] *See Guidance Paper supra* note 4.
[121] Case no 10-MC-01 *Relative à la demande de mesures conservatoires présentée par la société Navx*, French Autorité de la concurrence Decision of 30 June 2010.

11. – Other Abuses
Frédéric de Bure

which are detrimental to them through their impact on an effective competition structure".[122]
Since every exclusionary abuse could be called a structural abuse, this Section focuses on the direct alterations of the market structure through mergers and acquisitions. Although merger control has become the main competition law instrument to preserve the competitive structure of the market, the rules on abuses of a dominant position could still be relevant in a number of situations.

1. Article 102 TFEU and Merger Control

1.1. *Before the Merger Regulation*

Before the entry into force of the Merger Regulation in 1989,[123] the Commission and the Court of Justice used Article 102 TFEU to exert a form of control over concentrations between undertakings. In *Continental Can*, the Court of Justice established that Article 102 TFEU could be applied to concentrations that strengthened a pre-existing dominant position by altering the structure of competition. The Court found that "*[an a]buse may therefore occur if an undertaking in a dominant position strengthens such position in such a way that the degree of dominance reached substantially fetters competition, i.e., that only undertakings remain in the market whose behaviour depends on the dominant one*".[124] Following this landmark case, the Commission used Article 102 TFEU as an informal means of *ex post* merger control in a number of cases, including *Pilkington/BSN-Gervais-Danone*,[125] *Amicon Corp./Fortia AB/Wright Scientific Ltd*,[126] *British Airways/British Caledonian*[127] and *Consolidated Goldfields/Minorco*.[128]   **11.77**

In *Tetra Pak I*, the Commission analysed the impact of the acquisition by Tetra Pak of Liquipak.[129] Before the transaction, Tetra Pak was already dominant on the markets for the supply of carton packaging equipment and   **11.78**

---

[122] *See Continental Can supra* note 3, para. 26.
[123] Council Regulation (EEC) 4064/89 of 21 December 1989 on the control of concentrations between undertakings ("*Merger Regulation*"), OJ 1989 L 395/1; now replaced by Council Regulation (EC) 139/2004 of 20 January 2004 on the control of concentrations between undertakings ("*EC Merger Regulation*"), OJ 2004 L 24/1.
[124] *See Continental Can supra* note 3, para. 26.
[125] Case *Pilkington/BSN-Gervais-Danone*, in Tenth Report on Competition Policy (1980), paras 152–55.
[126] Case *Amicon/Fortia/Wright Scientific*, in Eleventh Report on Competition Policy (1981), para. 112.
[127] Case *British Airways/British Caledonian*, in Eighteenth Report on Competition Policy (1988), para. 81.
[128] Case *Consolidated Goldfields/Minorco*, in Nineteenth Report on Competition Policy (1989), para. 68.
[129] Case IV/31.043 *Tetra Pak I (BTG Licence)* ("*Tetra Pak I Decision 1988*"), Commission Decision of 26 July 1988, OJ 1988 L 272/27, upheld on appeal in *Tetra Pak I Judgment 1990 supra* note 11.

11. – Other Abuses
Frédéric de Bure

related cartons. Liquipak had an exclusive licence from the British Technology Group ("BGT") relating to a new milk-packaging process. As a result of the transaction, Tetra Pak acquired the exclusive licence and thus obtained a decisive advantage over its competitors. Specifically, the Commission found that the acquisition of the exclusive licence prevented, or delayed, the entry of a new competitor into the market. Based on the *Continental Can* precedent, the Commission concluded that *"Tetra abused its dominant position by the acquisition of* [the BGT] *exclusive licence which had the effect of strengthening its already dominant position, further weakening existing competition and rendering even more difficult the entry of any new competition"*.[130] Had the transaction been assessed under merger control rules, Tetra Pak might have addressed the competition concerns identified by the Commission by, for example, lifting the exclusivity of the licence.

11.79   The Council adopted the Merger Regulation in 1989, ending the Commission's innovative use of Article 102 TFEU for *ex post* review of mergers.

1.2.   After the Merger Regulation

11.80   Even after the entry into force of the Merger Regulation, Article 102 TFEU remains theoretically applicable to concentrations between undertakings. The Merger Regulation is secondary legislation and cannot exclude the application of the provisions of the Treaty. In practice, however, the Commission has not applied Article 102 TFEU to a concentration since the Merger Regulation was adopted. This can be explained by the following reasons. First, Article 21 of the Merger Regulation expressly provides that Regulation 1/2003 concerning the implementation of Articles 101 and 102 TFEU shall not apply to concentrations regardless of whether they have a Community dimension.[131] Therefore, even if the Commission decided to apply Article 102 TFEU to a concentration, it would lack the power to carry out investigations, adopt a final decision, or impose fines. Secondly, if the Merger Regulation or national merger rules provide for an *ex ante* system of control, there is little need for an *ex post* review of concentrations under Article 102 TFEU.

11.81   On one occasion, in *UPS Europe*, the General Court expressed views on the possible application of Article 102 TFEU in the context of merger control.[132]

---

[130] *See Tetra Pak I Decision 1988 supra* note 129, para. 60.
[131] *See Regulation 1/2003 supra* note 50.
[132] Case T-175/99 *UPS Europe v Commission* ("*UPS Europe*") [2002] ECR II-1915.

11. – Other Abuses
Frédéric de Bure

When Deutsche Post acquired joint control of DHL by purchasing 22 per cent of its shares, the Commission cleared the transaction subject to certain commitments under merger control rules. Following the Commission's Decision, UPS filed a complaint under Article 102 TFEU. UPS claimed that Deutsche Post had abused its dominant position by using profits derived from activities for which it enjoyed a legal monopoly (*i.e.*, reserved postal services) to finance the acquisition of control in a company that is active on a non-reserved market. The Court found that the mere fact of financing the acquisition through funds derived from the reserved market was not an abuse in itself. However, it did not exclude the possibility of applying Article 102 TFEU if the funds used for the acquisition originated from abusive practices by the dominant undertaking in the reserved market. The Court concluded that

> *"in the absence of any evidence to show that the funds used by Deutsche Post for the acquisition in question derived from abusive practices on its part in the reserved letter market, the mere fact that it used those funds to acquire joint control of an undertaking active in a neighbouring market open to competition does not in itself, even if the source of those funds was the reserved market, raise any problem from the standpoint of the competition rules and cannot therefore constitute an infringement of Article [102 TFEU]".[133]*

The Court therefore dismissed the application. Although competition author-   **11.82**
ities are unlikely to apply merger control rules and Article 102 TFEU concomitantly, this case shows that this may nonetheless happen in particular circumstances.

In addition, Article 102 TFEU can still be a useful instrument to fill in the   **11.83**
gaps of merger control, in particular in relation to concentrations that do not have Community dimension and that also fall short of national merger rules. Merger control jurisdiction generally depends on the application of turnover thresholds (this is the case at the European Union level, as well as in most European Union Member States). Turnover thresholds have the advantage of clarity, but they do not reflect the market power of the parties or the likely impact of the transaction on competition. It follows that merger control rules do not apply to transaction of a small dimension regardless of whether they affect competition. For example, a dominant company that would take advantage of its "deep pockets" to systematically acquire small innovative

---

[133] Case T-175/99 *UPS Europe v Commission* ("*UPS Europe*") [2002] ECR II-1915, para. 61.

11. – Other Abuses
Frédéric de Bure

competitors could escape merger control rules. To deal with these situations, some Member States have adopted an extensive interpretation of Article 22 of the Merger Regulation to refer to the Commission concentrations that lacked a Community dimension, but which raised substantive concerns (but this presupposes that at least the national turnover thresholds are met).[134] Another solution, which may be workable regardless of whether a proposed concentration is reportable at the European Union or at the national level) would be to use Article 102 TFEU based on the Commission's general competence of Article 105 TFEU.[135] This could be appropriate, in particular with respect to series of small transactions having a cumulative anticompetitive effect. Article 102 TFEU could also be applied to situations where a dominant company acquires an essential asset (*e.g.*, an IP right, a trademark, a technology, a facility), as it was the case in the *Tetra Pak* precedent.[136] On 27 July 2012, the Commission issued a Statement of Objection to Servier, a French drug manufacturer, taking the view that the acquisition by Servier, which appeared to be dominant in the market for perindopril, of the scarce competing technologies available to produce perindopril rendered generic market entry more difficult or delayed, and may therefore be considered abusive.[137] The procedure is ongoing.

2. Article 102 TFEU and Minority Shareholdings

11.84 Other structural abuses could be envisaged in the case of minority shareholdings. The acquisition of minority shareholdings may only be assessed directly under the merger control rules to the extent that it confers effective (sole or joint) control of the target company. Control is defined by Article 3(2) of the Merger Regulation as the possibility of exercising decisive influence on an undertaking. Non-controlling minority shareholdings are not concentrations and do not fall within the scope of the Merger Regulation.

11.85 However, even in the absence of control, the incentives of competing firms to compete vigorously may be reduced if one holds a significant stake in the other. A dominant company holding a minority shareholding in a competitor

---

[134] *See* Case COMP/M.4980 *ABF/GBI Business*, Commission Decision of 23 September 2008.

[135] The Commission declared at the time of the adoption of the Merger Regulation that it reserved the right to take action in accordance with Article 105 TFEU (*See Merger Regulation supra* note 123).

[136] *See Tetra Pak I Decision 1988 supra* note 129, upheld on appeal in *Tetra Pak I Judgment 1990 supra* note 11.

[137] *See* Press Release IP/12/835 of 30 July 2012.

11. – Other Abuses
Frédéric de Bure

could interfere with its competitor's business strategy or weaken the position of its competitor. Minority shareholdings may also provide the dominant company with an opportunity to access strategic commercial information and/or with an incentive to raise its prices if the competitor in which it holds a minority stake were to capture a sufficient quantity of the dominant company's lost sales to make the price increase profitable for the dominant company (which would capture part of the competitors' increased profits via its minority stake). Finally, the acquisition of minority shareholdings by a dominant company may deter the target company from adopting a given strategy or entering a given market.

11.86 In exceptional circumstances, Article 102 TFEU has been found to apply to acquisitions of minority shareholdings that do not confer control over the target company. In *Philip Morris*, the Court of Justice found that an abuse of a dominant position could arise where a minority shareholding does not confer control, but nevertheless gives the dominant company "*at least … some influence on* [the] *commercial policy*" of the participated competitor.[138] In *Gillette*, the Commission concluded that Gillette's acquisition of "*some influence*" over the Wilkinson Sword wet-razor business had infringed Article 102 TFEU by weakening Wilkinson's competitive position and strengthening Gillette's dominant position.[139] In practice, the extent to which it may be concluded that a non-controlling minority shareholding is capable of having an anticompetitive impact must be analysed on a case-by-case basis. The frontier between "some influence" and a "decisive influence" is sometimes difficult to determine precisely *ex ante*.

11.87 More recently, in *Ryanair/Aer Lingus*, the General Court confirmed the limits of the application of merger control rules to the acquisition of minority shareholdings and the relevance of Article 102 TFEU. The *Ryanair/Aer Lingus* transaction involved a merger of two Irish airlines. Ryanair had first acquired a 25 per cent non-controlling minority shareholding in Aer Lingus before launching a public bid for the entire share capital. This latter transaction was notified to the Commission and prohibited under merger control

---

[138] Joined Cases 142 and 156/84 *British-American Tobacco Company and R. J. Reynolds Industries v Commission* ("*Philip Morris*") [1987] ECR 4487, para. 65.

[139] Cases IV/33.440 *Warner-Lambert/Gillette and others* and IV/33.486 *BIC/Gillette and others* ("*Gillette*"), Commission Decision of 10 November 1992, OJ 1993 L 116/21. Please note that the facts of these decisions occurred before the entry into force of the Merger Regulation.

11. – Other Abuses
Frédéric de Bure

rules.[140] However, the Commission refused Aer Lingus' request that it order Ryanair to divest its 25 per cent minority shareholding in Aer Lingus.[141] The Court confirmed that the Commission was not empowered to order Ryanair to divest a minority shareholding that did not confer control and was not therefore reportable under the Merger Regulation.[142] Indeed, the acquisition of a shareholding which does not confer control of a company – that is to say the possibility of exercising decisive influence over the activity of the undertaking – does not constitute a merger which is deemed to have arisen for the purposes of that regulation. Instead, the President of the Court recommended using Article 102 TFEU:

> *"[w]hilst Article [101 TFEU] might, prima facie, be difficult to apply in cases, such as the present, in which the infringement in question arises from the acquisition of shares on the market and, therefore, the necessary meeting of minds might be difficult to establish, the applicant may ask the Commission to initiate a procedure under Article [102 TFEU] if it believes that Ryanair enjoys a dominant position on one or more markets and is abusing that dominant position by interfering with a direct competitor's business strategy and/or by exploiting its minority shareholding in a direct competitor to weaken its position."*[143]

11.88 It follows that a dominant undertaking that would acquire a minority shareholding that may confer upon it the ability to interfere with a competitor's business strategy, or to weaken the position of that competitor, may violate Article 102 TFEU. However, this could potentially raise the question of the parallel application of Article 102 TFEU on the one hand and national merger control rules on the other hand to minority shareholdings, when national merger legislations allow for such review. In *Ryanair/Aer Lingus*, for instance, the British Office of Fair Trading (OFT) decided to investigate the acquisition of Ryanair's 25 per cent minority shareholding in Aer Lingus based on UK merger control law.[144]

---

[140] Case COMP/M.4439 *Ryanair/Aer Lingus*, Commission Decision of 27 June 2007.

[141] Case COMP/M.4439 *Ryanair/Aer Lingus*, Commission Decision of 11 October 2007.

[142] Case T-411/07 *Aer Lingus Group v Commission* [2010] ECR II-3691.

[143] Case T-411/07 R, *Aer Lingus Group v Commission* [2008] ECR II-411, para. 104.

[144] *See* Office of Fair Trading, "OFT refers Ryanair's minority stake in Aer Lingus to Competition Commission", Press Release of 15 June 2012.

11. – Other Abuses
Frédéric de Bure

3. Other Relevant Cases

In *TACA*, the Commission found that the members of the TACA liner con- **11.89**
ference held a collective dominant position on the relevant market and that
they had abused that collective dominant position "*by altering the competitive
structure of the market so as to reinforce the TACA's dominant position*"[145] (in addition
to the finding of abusive contractual terms discussed in Section III above).
The Commission found that the TACA had taken measures to restrict the
ability of potential competitors to enter the market independently (*i.e.*, without being a party to the conference agreement). The condemned practice was
not the creation of a barrier to entry on potential competitors, but rather consisted of inducing competitors to enter the market as TACA members instead
of independently. The General Court acknowledged that a measure inducing competitors to join a conference agreement could constitute an abuse
of a dominant position.[146] However, it also found that the Commission had
not established a sufficient degree of inducement by TACA members *vis-à-vis*
competitors to join the conference to find an abuse of dominant position and
annulled the Decision with respect to this specific finding.

V. Abuses Relating to Limitation of Production, Market or Technical Developments

Cases falling within the "other abuses" category based on Article 102(b) **11.90**
TFEU, which prohibits "*limiting production, markets or technical developments to the
prejudice of consumers*", relate to: (1) the limitation of the normal development
of competition; (2) failure to satisfy demand; and (3) abusive inefficiency.

1. Limitation of the Normal Development of Competition

Practices of dominant undertakings aimed at restricting the "normal devel- **11.91**
opment of competition" may constitute an infringement of Article 102(b)
TFEU.[147]

---

[145] *TACA Decision 1998 supra* note 98, paras 550–76.
[146] *TACA Judgment 2003 supra* note 82, paras 1338–348.
[147] *See supra* note 119.

11. – Other Abuses
Frédéric de Bure

11.92 In *British Telecommunications*, the Commission found that British Telecommunications, a UK company enjoying a statutory monopoly for the management of telecommunications networks and postal services in the United Kingdom, had infringed Article 102 TFEU by prohibiting the activities of private-message forwarding agencies handling international telecommunication traffic (*i.e.*, telex messages originating in or destined for locations abroad).[148] The Court of Justice upheld the Commission's Decision confirming that British Telecommunications had abused its dominant position by limiting the development of a new market and a new technology to the prejudice of its customers.

11.93 Some of the abuses found by the Commission in the *Microsoft* case could also be analysed as limitations of the normal development of competition.[149] Lack or absence of interoperability could indeed be viewed as means to prevent competing offers from being developed, although it is still unclear whether such practices could be considered abusive without any refusal to deal/supply. In *Microsoft*, the interoperability issue was analysed in the framework of a refusal to supply (*i.e.,* what was found abusive was Microsoft's refusal to give access to interoperability information). However, one could wonder whether, in particular in the area of new technologies, the lack of interoperability by a dominant company could in itself constitute an abuse that would not necessarily have to meet the strict criteria of refusal to deal/supply. On 1 March 2012, the Commission announced that it has opened proceedings against MathWorks Inc., a US-based software company, for allegedly distorting competition in the market for the design of commercial control systems by preventing competitors from achieving interoperability with its products. The Commission not only criticises MathWorks' refusal to provide a competitor with end-user software licences, but also the fact that MathWorks failed to provide interoperability information – even though it is doubtful whether such failure could constitute a separate abuse.[150]

---

[148] Case IV/29.877 *British Telecommunications*, Commission Decision of 10 December 1982, OJ 1982 L 360/36, upheld in Case 41/83 *Italian Republic v Commission* [1985] ECR 873.

[149] Case COMP/37.792 *Microsoft* ("*Microsoft Decision 2004*"), Commission Decision of 24 March 2004, not yet published, upheld by General Court in Case T-201/04 *Microsoft v Commission* ("*Microsoft Judgment 2007*") [2007] ECR II-3601.

[150] *See* Press Release IP/12/208 of 1 March 2012.

11. – Other Abuses
Frédéric de Bure

2. Failure to Satisfy Demand

In *Höfner,* the Court of Justice reviewed in a preliminary ruling the effects of **11.94**
national legislation giving exclusivity over job brokerage services to a German
State employment agency.[151] According to German law, measures taken by
the agency were intended, within the economic and social policy of the
government, to: achieve and maintain a high level of employment, constantly
improve job distribution, and promote economic growth. However, the State
employment agency failed to ensure that it was able to adequately meet the
demand for its services. The Court held that granting an exclusive right was
not incompatible with Article 102 TFEU as such, but that it may violate
competition law if the undertaking in that position could not avoid abusing
its dominant position merely by exercising the exclusive rights granted to it.
The Court found that there is an abuse of a dominant position in a situation
where (1) the company holding the exclusive right is *"manifestly not in a position
to satisfy the demand prevailing on the market"* and (2) *"the effective pursuit of such
activities by private companies is rendered impossible by the maintenance in force of a
statutory provision"*.[152]

Until now, the Commission has never sanctioned an abusive failure to satisfy **11.95**
demand under Article 102 TFEU. The only decision where a similar issue
was discussed is the *P&I Clubs* Decision.[153] In that case, the Commission
assessed the compatibility with competition rules of two agreements between
the members of the International Group of Protection & Indemnity Clubs
("P&I Clubs"). P&I Clubs are mutual non-profit-making associations that
provide marine insurance services (*i.e.,* P&I insurance service) to their members, the ship-owners. The two agreements were (1) a claim-sharing agreement between mutual associations and (2) an agreement between the clubs
to establish some rules on the methods for offering services to a ship-owner
who already was a member of another club. The Commission investigation
followed a complaint by an association of ship-owners, alleging that the agreements created a single insurance product that limited the range of insurance
cover available in the market to the prejudice of consumers. This restriction
allegedly left a very substantial share of demand unsatisfied. The Commission found that the P&I Clubs had a collective dominant position in the

---

[151] Case C-41/90 *Klaus Höfner and Fritz Elser v Macrotron ("Höfner")* [1991] ECR I-1979.
[152] *Ibid.,* para. 31.
[153] Cases IV/30.373 *P&I Clubs, IGA* and IV/37.143 *P&I Clubs, Pooling Agreement ("P&I Clubs")*, Commission
Decision of 12 April 1999, OJ 1999 L 125/12.

11. – Other Abuses
Frédéric de Bure

market of P&I insurance and analysed whether the agreements gave rise to an abuse under Article 102(b) TFEU. It held that it could only intervene if there was *"clear and uncontroversial evidence that a very substantial share of demand is being deprived of a service that it manifestly needs, and that, therefore, the International Group is really exploiting its dominant position in an abusive way"*[154] and concluded that the test was not met in that case.

11.96 After *Höfner*, this Decision confirms that failure to satisfy demand is another kind of exploitative abuse. Moreover, it shows that this abuse is not necessarily limited to situations where a legal monopoly exist, although this latter scenario is certainly the most common situation in which such an abuse may be found. Absent a legal monopoly, the fact that "a very substantial share of demand is being deprived of a service that it manifestly needs" cannot in itself be sufficient to establish the existence of an abuse of dominant position. At the very least, the costs that the dominant company would have to incur to meet the additional demand ought to be analysed, as well as whether the limitation of supply is part of an abusive exploitative strategy by the dominant company, or is it rather just the expression of its freedom to decide how best to run its business. It is therefore difficult to imagine that this kind of infringement could be extended outside the scope of legal monopolies, absent exceptional circumstances.

3. Inefficiency

11.97 In *Merci Convenzionali*, the Court of Justice gave a preliminary ruling in which it held that the refusal by an undertaking enjoying a legal monopoly to use modern technology could constitute an abuse of its dominant position under Article 102 TFEU.[155] Merci Convenzionali Porto di Genova SpA ("Merci") had been granted by the Italian State an exclusive concession for the handling of loading operations in the harbour of Genoa. Among other practices, Merci refused to have recourse to modern technology for loading operations arguing that modern technologies would be detrimental to employment. This resulted in an increase in costs for customers and prolonged delays in performance. The Court found, *inter alia*, that Merci's refusal to use modern technologies

---

[154] *See supra* note 153, para. 128.
[155] Case C-179/90 *Merci convenzionali porto di Genova v Siderurgica Gabrielli ("Merci Convenzionali")* [1991] ECR I-5889.

11. – Other Abuses
Frédéric de Bure

could have the effect of limiting technical development, to the prejudice of consumers in violation of Article 102(b) TFEU.

Interestingly, the Court decided not to apply the exact same solution as in **11.98** *Höfner*. It could have concluded that Merci had abused its dominant position because it was manifestly incapable of satisfying the demand present on the market for loading operations and the effective exercise of these activities by other undertaking was made impossible by the legal monopoly granted to Merci. In any event, although the qualification of the abuse is different, both cases concern an abusive failure to effectively ensure the development of a market that fall within the scope of Article 102 TFEU.

12. – Remedies
Thomas Graf and David R. Little

Remedies

Thomas Graf and David R. Little*

I.   Introduction

This Chapter discusses the remedies and penalties that may be applied in   **12.1**
respect of infringements of Article 102 TFEU. The discussion in this chapter focuses on public enforcement by the Commission and the EU courts.
While this is the core of EU antitrust enforcement, actions brought by private claimants before national courts are an increasingly important complement to public enforcement activity.[1] Private enforcement is a fast developing
area of EU competition law, with a raft of recent national law decisions
advancing practitioners' understanding of the relationship between EU and
Member State law. We refer the reader to the growing, body of doctrine in
this area.[2]

A 2006 OECD report summarised the importance of remedies in abuse of   **12.2**
dominance cases:

> *"It is often difficult to determine whether a firm is dominant, and it can be exceed-*
> *ingly hard to distinguish conduct that enhances competition from conduct that*
> *harms it. Correctly concluding that a firm is dominant and that it abused its*

---

* The authors are grateful for the assistance of current and former colleagues, including: Maurits Dolmans,
Alice Setari, Sofie de Nil, Andrea de Vos, Shin-Shin Hua, Jon Zimmerman and Lea Zuber.

[1] Private enforcement is facilitated and encouraged by Recital 7, Article 6, and Article 15 of Council Regulation
(EC) 1/2003 of 16 December 2002 on the implementation of the rules on competition laid down in Articles 81
and 82 of the Treaty ("*Regulation 1/2003*"), OJ 2003 L 1/1.
[2] *See, e.g.* C. Cook, "Private Enforcement of Competition Law in Member State Courts: Experience to Date and
the Path Ahead" (2008) 4(2) *Competition Policy International*; M Siragusa, *EU Competition Law – Cartels and Horizontal Agreements* (Leuven Claeys & Casteels 2007), paras 4.226 *et seq.*; J. Temple Lang, "Commitment Decisions and
Settlements with Antitrust Authorities and Private Parties Under European Antitrust Law", *Fordham Antitrust
Conference*, September (2005).

12. – Remedies
Thomas Graf and David R. Little

dominance, however, may do little good for competition if the ensuing remedy or sanction is too lenient, too severe, too late, not administrable, or otherwise poorly conceived or implemented. Flawed remedies not only may allow continuing harm to competition by not properly addressing the competition problem, but also may themselves harm competition by preventing conduct by the dominant firm that would benefit consumers."[3]

1. The Legal Basis for Remedies for Abuse of Article 102 TFEU

12.3 Although Article 102 TFEU sets out the broad parameters of an abuse of a dominant position, the Article makes no reference to the remedies that should be imposed once an abuse has been established. The legal basis for remedies for breach of Article 102 TFEU is instead found in the secondary law, specifically Regulation 1/2003. Article 7 of Regulation 1/2003 provides:

> *"Where the Commission, acting on a complaint or on its own initiative, finds that there is an infringement of Article 81 or of Article 82 of the Treaty, it may by decision require the undertakings and associations of undertakings concerned to bring such infringement to an end. For this purpose, it may impose on them any behavioural or structural remedies which are proportionate to the infringement committed and necessary to bring the infringement effectively to an end. Structural remedies can only be imposed either where there is no equally effective behavioural remedy or where any equally effective behavioural remedy would be more burdensome for the undertaking concerned than the structural remedy. If the Commission has a legitimate interest in doing so, it may also find that an infringement has been committed in the past."*

12.4 Article 7 of Regulation 1/2003 empowers the Commission to adopt binding Decisions that impose behavioural or structural remedies proportionate to the infringement committed. Recital 12 of the Regulation clarifies that structural measures will only be proportionate where *"there is a substantial*

---

[3] OECD Policy Roundtable, *"Remedies and Sanctions in Abuse of Dominance Cases"*, DAF/COMP (2006) 19, para. 2.

12. – Remedies
Thomas Graf and David R. Little

risk of a lasting or repeated infringement that derives from the very structure of the undertaking".[4]

2.   Mandatory and Voluntary Remedies

Broadly speaking, there are two remedy "tracks" in Article 102 infringement   **12.5**
cases: the "voluntary track" and the "mandatory track". The main features of each are summarised in Table 12.1, below. Faced with an infringement or possible infringement of Article 102, the Commission may pursue the following options.

- The Commission may limit itself to finding and punishing an infringement by way of an Article 7 prohibition decision, without further requirements. This may, for example, be appropriate where the undertaking concerned has already corrected its behaviour, such that a cease-and-desist order or other remedial measures would be redundant, but there is nevertheless value in establishing a precedent.[5]

- Alternatively, the Commission may issue an Article 7 decision with the intention of requiring a change in the company's conduct, through (1) a cease-and-desist order, and (2) if needed, more far reaching remedies. In either case, the decision may include a fine, to punish the infringement and deter future anticompetitive conduct.

- Finally, the Commission may pursue the voluntary track in order to secure remedies, formalising the agreed commitments in an Article 9 decision.[6] In this case, no fine will be imposed and there will be no formal infringement finding.

---

[4] *See* Cases IV/30.787 and 31.488 *Eurofix-Bauco/Hilti*, Commission Decision of 22 December 1987, OJ 1988 L 65/19. Note that the Commission may also adopt infringement decisions in respect of conduct that has already been terminated by the dominant undertaking. *See, e.g.*, Case 7/82 *Gesellschaft zur Verwertung von Leistungsschutzrechten (GVL) v Commission* [1983] ECR 483, paras 16–28. *See also* Case C-119/97 P *Union française de l'express (Ufex), formerly Syndicat français de l'express international (SFEI), DHL International and Service CRIE v Commission and May Courier* [1999] ECR I-1341, paras 93 and 94 ("*The Commission is required to assess in each case how serious the alleged interferences with competition are and how persistent their consequences are.* [...] *If anticompetitive effects continue after the practices which caused them to have ceased, the Commission thus remains competent under Articles 2,3(g) and 86 of the Treaty to act with a view to eliminating or neutralizing them.*").

[5] *See supra* note 3.

[6] *Ibid.*, pp. 183–5.

12. – Remedies
Thomas Graf and David R. Little

Table 12.1: Overview of Mandatory and Voluntary Remedy Tracks.

	Mandatory Remedies Track	**Voluntary Remedies Track**
Description	Commission imposes remedies on undertaking following formal finding of Article 102 infringement.	Undertaking subject of Article 102 investigation proposes measures to address initial Commission concerns, with measures subsequently formalised in written document.
Legal Basis	Article 7(1), Regulation 1/2003 Recital 12, Regulation 1/2003	Article 9(1), Regulation 1/2003 Recital 13, Regulation 1/2003
Statement of objections	Yes	Not necessarily
Finding of infringement	Yes	No
Available Features of Remedy	Cease and desist order Behavioural measures Structural measures (exceptionally: *see* Recital 12, Regulation 1/2003) Fines	Cease and desist order Behavioural measures Structural measures No fines (*see* Recital 13, Regulation 1/2003)
Related Measures	**Interim measures.** Commission may impose interim measures under Article 8(1) of Regulation 1/2003 on the basis of a prima facie finding of infringement "*in cases of urgency due to the risk of serious and irreparable damage to competition*".	**Informal undertakings.** The precursor to the Regulation 1/2003 commitments procedure. The legal basis was Regulation 17/62.[7]

12.6   The Commission does not need to choose between voluntary and mandatory tracks at the start of the investigation. The Commission has indicated that "*investigations that are eventually closed with a commitments decision start much like prohibition procedures*" and that the choice between these routes "*will [...] depend on the degree of cooperation shown by the undertakings under investigation.*"[8]

---

[7] Council Regulation (EEC) 17 of 6 February 1962 first regulation implementing Articles 85 and 86 of the Treaty ("*Regulation 17/62*"), OJ 1962 13/204.
[8] Note by the European Commission for the OECD Policy Roundtable, *supra* note 3, pp. 181–86, para. 26.

12. – Remedies
Thomas Graf and David R. Little

The Commission has made increasing use of the "voluntary track". Explaining **12.7** when the voluntary track may be appropriate, the Commission has commented: *"if the company under investigation is willing to propose sufficient remedies, a decision under Article 9 may be chosen for reasons of expediency and efficient use of resources, since proceedings are faster and less burdensome".*[9] Thus, commitment decisions have in recent years been used in cases concerning the liberalization of former monopoly sectors (which can be complex),[10] and in fast-moving technology markets, where speed of intervention may be critical (*Rambus*,[11] *Microsoft (Tying)*[12], *IBM Mainframe Maintenance Services*).[13] Most recently, the Commission indicated its preference to resolve the ongoing Google investigation through Article 9 commitments. In June 2012, Commissioner Almunia invited Google to submit commitments under Article 9, stating publicly: *"I want to give the company the opportunity to offer remedy proposals that would avoid lengthy proceedings. By early July, I expect to receive from Google concrete signs of their willingness to explore this route. In case we engage in negotiations to address our concerns and the proposals we receive turn out to be unsatisfactory, formal proceedings will continue through the adoption of a Statement of Objections."*[14]

The threat of lengthy formal proceedings may thus serve as a means to extract **12.8** concessions in commitment proceedings under Article 9 of Regulation 1/2003.

---

[9] Note by the European Commission for the OECD Policy Roundtable, *supra* note 3, pp. 181–86, para. 26.

[10] *See, e.g.,* Case COMP/39.402 *RWE Gas Foreclosure* Commission Decision of 18 March 2009, OJ 2009/C 133/06, Case COMP/39.316 *GDF Foreclosure*, Commission Decision of 3 December 2009, not yet published; Case COMP/37.966 *Distrigaz*, Commission Decision of 11 October 2007, not yet published; Case COMP/39.315 *ENI*, Commission Decision of 29 September 2010, not yet published; Case COMP/39.317 *E.ON Gas Foreclosure*, Commission Decision of 4 May 2010, not yet published; Case COMP/39.351 *Swedish Interconnectors*, Commission Decision of 14 April 2010, not yet published; Case COMP/39.386 *Long Term Electricity Contracts France*, Commission Decision of 17 March 2010, not yet published; Cases COMP/39.388 *German Electricity Wholesale Market* and COMP/39.389 *German Electricity Balancing Market*, Commission Decision of 26 November 2008, not yet published.

[11] Case COMP/38.636 *Rambus*, Commission Decision of 9 December 2009, not yet published.

[12] Case COMP/39.530 *Microsoft (Tying)* (*"Browser Commitment Decision"*) Commission Decision of 16 December 2009, not yet published.

[13] Case COMP/39.692 *IBM Maintenance Services*, Commission Decision of 13 December 2011, not yet published.

[14] Press Release SPEECH/12/428 of 8 June 2012.

12. – Remedies
Thomas Graf and David R. Little

II.   Key Objectives

12.9   The following key objectives for effective remedies can be distilled from the case law and applicable legislation:

- **The remedy must bring the infringement to an end.** Regulation 1/2003 states that the purpose of a remedy is to bring the infringement effectively to an end. Above all else, therefore, the remedy must ensure that the impugned conduct is terminated (if that has not already happened).

- **The remedy may address competitive distortions resulting from the abuse.** Regulation 1/2003 specifies that the infringement should be brought *"effectively"* to an end. This provides a basis for the Commission to design a remedy that addresses competitive distortions resulting from the infringement, although such remedies require special justification.

- **The discretion of the Commission in developing remedies is limited by general principles of EU law.** Given the discretion of the Commission to design remedies all limiting principles are required. Article 7(1) of Regulation 1/2003 therefore requires that remedies imposed in Article 102 TFEU cases must be *"proportionate to the infringement committed"*. The same principle is set out in Article 5 of the TFEU, which states that *"any action by the European Union should not go beyond what is necessary to achieve the objective of this Treaty"*.

- **The remedy must have useful effect (anti-circumvention).** The Commission is competent to implement remedial measures required *"to prohibit conduct that may have an equivalent effect to the identified abuse"*.

- **Structural or behavioural remedies may be adopted but there is a legislative preference in favour of the latter.** While the Commission may choose between structural or behavioural remedies, Regulation 1/2003 emphasises that the former should be imposed only by way of last resort.

- **Commission decisions may also provide for fines.** Fines are primarily punitive in nature. However since they are also intended to serve as a deterrent to future infringements by the undertaking and others, they may be considered to contain a prospective, market-affecting element. We therefore include them in our discussion of remedies.

12.10   Below, we offer some reflections on each of these principles.

12. – Remedies
Thomas Graf and David R. Little

1. The Remedy Must Bring the Infringement to an End

First and foremost, remedies must bring to an end the infringement that has **12.11** been committed. Thus, in most cases, the remedy comprises a "cease and desist" order, *i.e.,* a statement in the Commission's decision requiring that the dominant undertaking put an end to the conduct at issue. The Commission has elected not to impose a cease and desist order in cases where the dominant company has already put an end to the conduct at issue at the time of the Commission's decision.[15] While a cease and desist order may be redundant in such cases, an infringement decision may nevertheless be useful. First, it increases legal certainty by establishing an unambiguous precedent that the conduct concerned is unlawful. Secondly, it enables the Commission to impose a fine sanctioning the behaviour, if deemed necessary and proportionate.[16]

The requirement to bring an infringement to an end may be a negative require- **12.12** ment to refrain from committing some abusive act, or a positive obligation to do something that the undertaking had unlawfully refrained from doing.[17] Thus, for example, where the abusive conduct consists in the exclusionary refusal to supply a customer with access to a particular input, the undertaking can be compelled to supply that input to the customer.

2. The Remedy Must Address All Competitive Distortions Resulting from the Infringement

Regulation 1/2003 does not simply state that the remedy must bring the infringe- **12.13** ment to an end, but that it must bring the infringement *"effectively"* to an end. Accordingly, remedies need not merely mirror the infringements that they are

---

[15] *See, e.g.,* Case COMP/38.096 *Clearstream* (*"Clearstream Decision 2004"*), Commission Decision of 2 June 2004, not yet published. *See also,* Case COMP/36.915 *Deutsche Post – Interception of cross-border mail* (*"Deutsche Post"*), Commission Decision of 25 July 2001, OJ 2001 L 331/40; Case COMP/34.493 *DSD* (*"DSD Decision 2001"*), Commission Decision of 20 April 2001, OJ 2001 L 166/1; Case COMP/37.685 *GVG/FS*, Commission Decision of 27 August 2003, OJ 2004 L 11/17; Case IV/36.888 *1998 Football World Cup*, Commission Decision of 20 July 1999, OJ 2000 L 5/55; and Cases IV/34.073, 34.395 and 35.436 *Van den Bergh Foods*, Commission Decision of 11 March 1998, OJ 1998 L 246/1.

[16] *See supra* note 3, p. 183.

[17] *See* Joined Cases 6 and 7/73 *Istituto Chemioterapico Italiano and Commercial Solvents Corporation v Commission* (*"Commercial Solvents"*)[1974] ECR 223.

12. – Remedies
Thomas Graf and David R. Little

intended to address. The inclusion of the word "*effectively*" in Article 23 of Regulation 1/2003 provides a legal basis for the Commission to impose requirements that not only put a stop to the infringement committed, but are apt to address the wider anticompetitive distortions caused by the infringement.[18] This was confirmed by the Court of Justice in *Ufex*.[19] Citing *Continental Can*,[20] the Court held that if anticompetitive effects persist beyond the cessation of the conduct which caused them, the Commission remains competent to take action to "eliminate or neutralise" such effects. However, such actions require the Commission to identify special justifications. Thus, in *Atlantic Container Line*, the General Court annulled an order of the Commission, requiring the defendants to give customers an option to renegotiate service contracts because the Commission had not provided sufficient reasons for such an order.[21] The Court's discussion in *Atlantic Container Line* suggests that the Court considers measures that rectify competitive effects beyond halting the infringement to be the exception rather than the rule. The Court emphasised with reference to past case law holding that remedies "*must not exceed what is appropriate and necessary to attain the objective sought, namely re-establishing of compliance with the rules infringed*".[22]

2.1.   Are there Particular Markets Susceptible to Additional Competitive Distortions?

12.14   Some markets may be more susceptible to persistent restrictive effect than others. Network industries are a good example.[23] In economics literature, a product market is considered to be characterised by direct network effects where demand for the good depends on how many other consumers purchase it (*e.g.*, fax machines).[24] A product market exhibits indirect network effects where the value of the products increases as the number, quality, and range of complementary products available increases. As the Commission observed in *Microsoft*: "*In*

---

[18] Lianos refers to this as an "outcome oriented" approach. *See* I. Lianos, "Competition Law Remedies: In Search of a Theory", *CLGE Working Paper*, Law and Governance in Europe Working Paper Series No. 14/2011, April 2011. The broad discretion of the Commission to design remedies in Article 102 TFEU cases contrasts with the codified practice of the Commission in merger control. *See* Commission Notice on remedies acceptable under Council Regulation (EEC) 4064/89 and under Commission Regulation 447/98, 2001 OJ C 68/3.

[19] *See* Case C-119/97 P, *supra* note 4, paras 94 and 95.

[20] Case 6/72 *Europemballage and Continental Can Company v Commission* ("*Continental Can*") [1973] ECR 215, paras 24 and 25.

[21] Case T-395/94 *Atlantic Container Line and others v Commission* ("*TACA Judgment 2003*") [2002] ECR II-875, paras 410–20.

[22] *Ibid.*, para. 410.

[23] P. Hellstrom, F. P. Maier-Rigaud, F. Wenzel Bulst, "The Remedies in European Antitrust Law" (2009) 76 *Antitrust Law Journal*, pp. 43–63, p. 48.

[24] H. Varian, J. Farrell, and C. Shapiro, "The Economics of Information Technology" (Cambridge University Press 2004), p. 33.

12. – Remedies
Thomas Graf and David R. Little

industries exhibiting strong network effects, consumer demand depends critically on expectations about future purchases. If consumers expect a firm with a strong reputation in the current (product) generation to su-cceed in the next generation, this will tend to be self-fulfilling as the consumers direct their purchases to the product that they believe will yield the greatest network gains."[25]

Essentially, in network industries, a dominant company (through illegal prac-   **12.15**
tices) may procure a self-reinforcing advantage. If the undertaking were merely
fined and ordered to cease the anticompetitive conduct in question, the network effects advantage may continue to propagate. Additional measures may
be required to reverse this trend and re-create the level playing field that existed
prior to the dominant company's abusive conduct. It follows that a remedy
imposed for the purpose of neutralising ill-gotten network effects should not
return the market to a phase that precedes the point in time immediately prior
to inception of the anticompetitive conduct. Otherwise, the remedy would
expropriate benefits won by the dominant company through fair competition.

Indirect network effects (where they exist) may also entrench further the   **12.16**
dominant product through a similar vicious circle in respect of complementary products. This creates an ecosystem around the dominant product that
enhances its value and makes it more difficult for a competing product (that
does not benefit from a comparable ecosystem) to penetrate the market. This
is the "applications barrier to entry" theory accepted by Judge Jackson in the
US *Microsoft* proceedings.[26]

While network industries may be susceptible to additional competitive distor-   **12.17**
tions, such distortions can also arise in other markets where supplier, customer or consumer conduct and perceptions or usage become entrenched in
favour of the dominant product.

2.2.   How Can these Additional Competitive Distortions be Addressed?

How these additional competitive distortions are addressed in order to rem-   **12.18**
edy the abuse "effectively" will vary on a case-by-case basis. Regulation 1/2003
affords the Commission a certain discretion to develop remedies that are tailored
to the specifics of the infringement concerned. That discretion however is more
constrained under Article 7 of Regulation 1/2003, compared to Article 9 of Regulation 1/2003, given the stricter application of the proportionality principle

---

[25] Case COMP/37.792 *Microsoft* ("*Microsoft Decision 2004*"), Commission Decision of 24 March 2004, para. 438.
[26] *See United States v Microsoft*, 84 F. Supp. 2d 9 (D.D.Cir. 1999) (Findings of Fact), paras 36–52.

12. – Remedies
Thomas Graf and David R. Little

and the need to leave the defendant choice between different forms of resolving the identified concern.[27] Generally speaking, the essence of most remedies in Article 102 matters, especially in infringement cases, has therefore been a kind of "mirror image" of the infringement committed.

12.19 However, in a small number of cases, mostly under Article 9 of Regulation 1/2003, the Commission has developed novel solutions to address possible wider competitive distortions, resulting from an Article 102 infringement. Chief among these are the measures negotiated between Microsoft and the Commission in *Microsoft (Tying)*. In that case, the Commission took the initial view that *"as long as Microsoft only ships and licenses Windows together with Internet Explorer, OEMs face negative incentives to bundle an additional web browser"*.[28] The Commission also preliminarily concluded that content providers and software developers operating under resource constraints look at installation and usage shares of web browsers when deciding the basis of which technology to develop web applications or to create web content. Developers therefore had an incentive *"to primarily target Internet Explorer, or at least not to develop only for other web browsers"*.[29] Rather than merely requiring the elimination of the technical and commercial distribution tie between Internet Explorer and Windows, the Commission developed with Microsoft additional measures intended to address the potential foreclosure effects identified in its preliminary assessment. These included a "browser Choice Screen" – a menu showing alternative browsers to Internet Explorer, with links to download the required software. The Commission noted that the browser choice screen remedy agreed in that case not only:

> *"Enhanced competition in the web browser market which could result from the implementation of the Commitments"* but *"would also substantially weaken the network effects that the Commission preliminarily identified in the Statement of Objections as currently favouring Internet Explorer. More competition should also lead to a more widespread use of web browsers which run on multiple operating system platforms."*[30]

2.3. Structural Measures

12.20 While structural remedies, as noted, are generally a last resort, the Commission has used such measures in a number of abuse of dominance cases in the energy

---

[27] Case T-24/90 *Automec v Commission* [1992] ECR II-2223.
[28] *See Browser Commitment Decision, supra* note 12, para 44.
[29] *Ibid.,* para. 56.
[30] *Ibid.,* paras 104, 106–7.

12. – Remedies
Thomas Graf and David R. Little

sector. Thus, in *ENI*,[31] the Commission investigated possible foreclosure in Italian gas supply markets. The theory of harm developed in the Commission's preliminary analysis was that ENI had refused to supply transport capacity to third party shippers that would have enabled them to import gas into Italy. The Commission found that ENI's anticompetitive efforts and incentives to limit supply to competitors derived from structural features, *i.e.*, the vertical integration of the company. According to the Commission, merely supplying access to competitors would not have addressed the structural source of ENI's incentives to foreclose rivals.[32] Accordingly, the Commission and ENI developed a solution whereby ENI committed to the structural divestment of its international transport activities for the import of gas into Italy from Russia and from Northern Europe. Third party requests for access to the relevant pipelines would be reviewed by an independent entity unconnected to ENI.[33] Similar structural commitments have been entered into in E.ON and in RWE Gas Foreclosure.

These structural measures are probably explained by the special legal right, that **12.21** incumbent national energy companies traditionally held and reflect case law on undertakings benefitting from such special or exclusive rights, such as the judgment in RTT. In that case, the Court of Justice considered the legality of rules that conferred on the dominant telephony operator, which also sold telephone equipment, the right to approve the telephone installations of its competitors. The Court held that entrusting an undertaking which markets terminal equipment with the task of drawing up the specifications and granting type-approval conferred upon that undertaking a power to determine at will which terminal equipment would be connected to the public network. The undertaking benefiting from this position was thereby placed at an advantage *vis-á-vis* its competitors. This was liable to distort competition by undermining equality of opportunities as between the various economic operators. Accordingly, the Court held that the maintenance of effective competition required that the drawing up of technical specifications and the granting of type-approval be

---

[31] *See* Case COMP/39.315, *supra* note 10.

[32] In this respect *see also* Case IV/30.698 *ECS/AKZO*, Commission Decision of 14 December 1985, OJ 1985 L 374/1; on appeal Case C 62/86 *AKZOChemie v Commission ("AKZO")* [1991] ECR I-3359. The Commission found that AKZO had abused its dominant position in the supply of organic peroxides through a series of predatory pricing infringements. The Commission required AKZO to put an end to the pricing infringements and also to extend its discounting practices to cover both customers for whom it competed against ECS and its other customers. The Court of Justice noted that the extension of the discounting practice to the remaining AKZO customers could *"prevent the repetition of the infringement and [...] eliminate its consequences"*.

[33] *See* Case COMP/39.315, *supra* note 10. *See also*, DG COMP Competition Policy Newsletter (2011), No. 1, pp. 18–23.

12. – Remedies
Thomas Graf and David R. Little

carried out by an independent body.[34] The principles developed in *RTT* were applied in *Raso*,[35] in which the Commission analysed the undertaking's exercise of its exclusive right to supply temporary workers for stevedoring and other port services. The Court held that rules granting the former dock-work company the exclusive right to supply temporary labour to terminal concessionaires and to other undertakings authorised to operate in the port and to compete with the same operators on the market in dock services, created a conflict of interest because "*merely exercising* [this] *monopoly will enable the undertaking to distort in its favour the equal conditions of competition between the various operators on the market in dock-work services*".[36] The company was thereby led to abuse its monopoly by imposing on its competitors in the dock-work market unduly high costs for the supply of labour or by supplying them with labour less suited to the work to be done.

2.4. Information Remedies and Renegotiation Options

12.22 In another set of cases, the Commission has imposed information and renegotiation requirements on dominant undertakings. These remedies require the undertaking to inform its customers of the infringement decision and of the consequent nullity of certain contractual provisions. *Mastercard* offers a good example. In that case, Mastercard was required within six months of the decision to communicate all changes of the association's network rules and the repeal of decisions to (1) all financial institutions holding a license for issuing and/or acquiring in the MasterCard payment organisation in the EEA, and (2) to all clearing houses and settlement banks which clear and/or settle POS payment card transactions in the MasterCard payment organisation in the European Economic Area.[37] In *Astra Satellite*,[38] the Commission required defendant companies to inform those with whom they had contracted that they were entitled to renegotiate the terms of their contracts or terminate them with reasonable notice. Similarly, in *ECS/AKZO*, the Commission required AKZO to inform customers that had been the subject of exclusivity agreements that the infringement had been brought to an end. In *Coca-Cola*, undertakings entered into by the company included a provision requiring that certain Coca-Cola entities include

---

[34] Case C-18/88 *Régie des télégraphes et des téléphones v GB-Inno-BM* [1991] ECR I-5941. *See*, in particular, paras 25 and 26.

[35] Case C-163/96 *Criminal proceedings against Silvano Raso and Others* [1998] ECR I-533.

[36] Case C-163/96 *Criminal proceedings against Silvano Raso and Others* [1998] ECR I-533, para. 29.

[37] Cases COMP/34.579 *MasterCard*, COMP/36.518 *EuroCommerce*, COMP/38.580 *Commercial Cards*, Commission Decision of 19 December 2007, not yet reported, para. 33. The UK Competition Commission has used international remedies in market investigations.

[38] Case IV/32.745 *Astra*, Commission Decision of 23 December 1992, OJ 1993 L 20/23.

12. – Remedies
Thomas Graf and David R. Little

in their general conditions of sale a statement that the customer was free to list, buy, and sell any carbonated soft drink of any third party.[39]

2.5. Pre-empting Future Abuses

In *Tetra Pak II*,[40] the Commission included supplementary requirements in the **12.23** remedy intended to pre-empt possible future abuses by the dominant undertaking. The Commission not only issued a cease and desist order but also required Tetra Pak to take a series of measures to open up markets on which it was active, including: (1) amending machine purchase/lease contracts and carton supply contracts to eliminate clauses identified as abusive, (2) ensuring that the differences in price of Tetra Pak's products across Member States resulted solely from local market conditions; (3) ensuring that customers within the European Union had access to prices charged in other Member States and could be supplied by any Tetra Pak subsidiary; (4) refraining from practicing predatory or discriminatory pricing and/or from granting discriminatory discounts; and (5) refraining from refusing orders from customers that were not end users of Tetra Pak products.

3. The Commission's Discretion in Designing Remedies is Limited by the Principle of Proportionality

The primary limit upon the Commission's discretion in defining remedies is **12.24** the general EU principle of proportionality.

3.1. Re-establishing Compliance with the Rules Infringed

The principle of proportionality comprises two limbs. First, measures must be **12.25** no more restrictive than necessary to achieve a legitimate objective. Second, where there are several equally appropriate and necessary alternative remedial options, the least onerous alternative must be chosen.[41] In practice, the two limbs of the proportionality test are examined in the round by the Commission and the Courts, since where less onerous but equally effective measures can be identified, it will be evident that the measures ultimately chosen are more restrictive than was necessary to achieve the objective pursued. Considerations

---

[39] *See* Case COMP/39.116 *Coca-Cola*, Commission Decision of 22 June 2005, not yet published.

[40] Case IV/31.043 *Tetra Pak II ("Tetra Pak II Decision 1991")*, Commission Decision of 24 July 1991, OJ 1992 L 72/1.

[41] The least onerous measures will usually be a behavioural rather than structural remedy. The latter is only likely to be proportionate *"where there is a substantial risk of a lasting or repeated infringement that derives from the very structure of the undertaking"*. *See* Recital 12, *Regulation 1/2003*.

12. – Remedies
Thomas Graf and David R. Little

of proportionality determine the choice between structural and behavioural undertakings,[42] as well as the choice among remedies belonging to either category.

12.26   The same principle has been reiterated in a number of subsequent cases.[43]

12.27   In *Magill*, the Court of Justice held that: "*the burdens imposed on undertakings in order to bring an infringement of competition law to an end must not exceed what is appropriate and necessary to attain the objective sought, namely re-establishment of compliance with the rules infringed.*"[44] The same principle has been reiterated in a number of subsequent cases.[45]

12.28   In *Automec*, the Court of First Instance held that "*the Commission undoubtedly has the power to find that an infringement exists and to order the parties concerned to bring it to an end, but it is not for the Commission to impose upon the parties its own choice from among all the various potential courses of action which are in conformity with the Treaty*".[46] While the observations of the Court of First Instance in *Automec* concerned a distribution system that infringed Article 101, the same principles apply also for remedies under Article 102 since they are an expression of the general principle of proportionality.

12.29   In *Alrosa*,[47] the Court of Justice placed limits on the extent to which the principle of proportionality can be invoked to challenge a commitment decision under Article 9 of Regulation 1/2003. In that case, the Court of Justice considered the application of the proportionality principle in the context of Article 9 commitments proceedings. The Commission had examined a supply arrangement under which De Beers, the world's largest rough diamond producer, agreed to purchase quantities of rough diamonds from Alrosa, the second largest producer globally.[48] Following negative feedback in response to joint commitments proposed by De Beers and Alrosa, the Commission accepted revised commitments proposed unilaterally by De Beers. The commitments offered by De Beers envisaged a progressive reduction and eventual

---

[42] Recital 12 of *Regulation 1/2003* provides that: "[c]*hanges to the structure of an undertaking as it existed before the infringement was committed would only be proportionate where there is a substantial risk of a lasting or repeated infringement that derives from the very structure of the undertaking.*"

[43] Case T-395/94 *Atlantic Container Line and others v Commission* ("*TACA Judgment 2003*") [2002] ECR II-875, para. 410; Case T-201/04 *Microsoft v Commission* ("*Microsoft Judgment 2007*") [2007] ECR II-3601, para. 1276.

[44] Joined Cases C-241 and 242/91 P *Radio TelefisEireann (RTE) and Independent Television Publications (ITP) v Commission* ("*Magill*") [1995] ECR I-743, para. 93.

[45] *Supra* note 23, p. 49.

[46] Case T-24/90 *Automec v Commission* [1992] ECR II-2223 para. 52.

[47] Case C-441/07 P *European Commission v Alrosa Company Ltd.*, 29 June 2010.

[48] *See, e.g.*, DG COMP Competition Policy Newsletter (2010), No. 3, pp. 17–22.

12. – Remedies
Thomas Graf and David R. Little

cessation of all rough diamond trading between the companies. Despite not consenting to the De Beers commitments, Alrosa would have been prevented from selling to De Beers. Alrosa challenged the legality, in particular the proportionality, of the commitments.

At first instance, the General Court held that the Commission was required in **12.30** the context of Article 9 proceedings to conduct a full proportionality assessment. The General Court's findings appeared to place an active duty on the Commission to identify less restrictive measures in the context of commitment discussions, and to propose these as alternatives. The Court of Justice annulled the judgment of the General Court and restored the Commission's decision. In doing so, the Court explained that the *"extent and content"* of the principle of proportionality were different in the context of Article 9 and Article 7 proceedings.[49] In an Article 9 proceeding, the Commission need ensure only that the commitments adopted are not more onerous than any other set of equally effective commitments offered by the company. The rationale for imposing a lower standard of review is unclear. The Court may, like the Advocate General, have taken the view that necessity could be presumed as a matter of course in what were ostensibly voluntary proceedings.[50] The findings of the Court of Justice in *Alrosa* seem questionable, particularly in circumstances where the Commission uses the threat of Article 7 proceedings in order to encourage a company to agree to Article 9 commitments. The Court's ruling may set a dangerous precedent: Given the Commission's increasing recourse to the Article 9 mechanism, its overall effect may be to lower the standard of protection afforded to undertakings and third parties in Article 102 proceedings.

4. The Remedy Must Have Useful Effect (Anti-circumvention)

The principle of useful effect (which results from the combination of Articles 3(1)(g), Article 10, Article 101 TFEU, and Article 102 TFEU), provides **12.31** that undertakings, like Member States, shall abstain from measures that could jeopardise the attainment of the objectives of the Treaty.[51] Read together with Article 7(1) of Regulation 1/2003, which requires that the remedy *"effectively"* bring the infringement to an end, this principle provides a basis for

---

[49] *See* Case C-441/07 P, *supra* note 47, para. 38.

[50] F. Wagner-von Papp, "Best and Even Better Practices in Commitment Procedures After Alrosa: The Dangers of Abandoning the 'Struggle for Competition Law'" (2012) 49 *Common Market Law Review*, pp. 929–70. Advocate General Kokott in Case C-441/07 P *Commission v Alrosa* [2010] ECR I-5949.

[51] Case 136/86 *Bureau national interprofessionnel du cognac v Yves Aubert* [1987] ECR 4789, para. 23.

12. – Remedies
Thomas Graf and David R. Little

the Commission to require a company to abstain from conduct that has an equivalent effect to the abuse.

12.32 There are numerous examples of remedies that preclude the undertaking from engaging in conduct through alternative means, that would have the effect of maintaining or restarting the abuse. The decisions have varied in the level of detail they have contained in this respect:

- ***Hilti.***[52] The Commission found that Hilti had committed a series of abuses to hinder the entry of independent suppliers of nails for Hilti nail guns. Article 3 of the Commission's Decision required Hilti to *"bring to an end the infringements referred to [...] to the extent that it has not already done so"* and to *"refrain from repeating or continuing any of the acts or behaviour specified [...] and [...] refrain from adopting any measures having an equivalent effect."*

- ***Tetra Pak.*** The Commission found that Tetra Pak had engaged in a variety of practices aimed at eliminating competition to the detriment of users. Tetra Pak was prohibited from repeating or maintaining such conduct and adopting any measure having equivalent effect.[53]

- ***Michelin.*** Michelin was found to have engaged in a system of loyalty-inducing rebates to dealers in new replacement tyres and retreaded tyres for trucks and buses in France. Article 3 of the Commission's prohibition Decision required Michelin to *"refrain from repeating any such conduct and from adopting any measure having equivalent effect"*.[54]

- ***Microsoft (WMP).***[55] The Commission's remedy required Microsoft to *"refrain from using any technological, commercial, contractual or any other means which would have the equivalent effect of tying Windows Media Player to Windows"*. The Commission's remedy included an indicative list of means by which Microsoft could recreate the effects of the tie, including, *inter alia*, hindering the performance of rival media players by limiting the disclosure of interoperability information required by these rival players to benefit from the same level of interoperability with Windows as Windows Media Player, or punishing or threatening OEMS or users who obtain Windows without Windows Media

---

[52] *See, e.g.,* Cases IV/30.787 and 31.488, *supra* note 4.

[53] *Tetra Pak II Decision 1991 supra* note 40, para. 218.

[54] Case COMP/36.041 *Michelin*, Commission Decision of 20 June 2001, OJ 2002 L 143/1. Upheld in Case T-203/01 *Manufacture française des pneumatiques Michelin v Commission* (*"Michelin II"*) [2003] ECR II-4071.

[55] *See Microsoft Decision 2004 supra* note 25, para. 1012.

12. – Remedies
Thomas Graf and David R. Little

Player.[56] These anti-circumvention examples were*"enumerative and without prejudice as to what other conduct would amount to a measure equivalent in its harmful effects to tying"*.[57]

Paraphrasing Justice Potter Stewart in *Jacobellis v. Ohio*,[58] it would be difficult **12.33** to enumerate in advance all the possible ways in which a remedy could be circumvented by a dominant company. Therefore, while circumvention strategies that are obvious *ex ante* may be expressly identified and prohibited in the Decision, it may still be necessary to include a general anti-circumvention statement in the Decision.

5. Structural Remedies are Measures of Last Resort

Remedies for breach of Article 102 TFEU may be behavioural or structural. **12.34** Behavioural remedies require the undertaking to *"do certain acts or provide certain advantages which have been wrongfully withheld, as prohibiting the continuation of certain actions, practices or situations which are contrary to the TFEU"*.[59] They are intended to alter a dominant undertaking's conduct *"in a context where incentives remain essentially unchanged"*.[60] Structural remedies are intended to effect permanent changes in the corporate governance or structure of the dominant undertaking, where those governance or structural elements are found to be the source of the conduct at issue (or the incentives to pursue that conduct).

Article 7 of Regulation 1/2003 establishes a preference for behavioural rem- **12.35** edies. Structural remedies *"can only be imposed either where there is no equally effective behavioural remedy or where an equally effective behavioural remedy would be more burdensome for the undertaking concerned than the structural remedy"*.[61] Recital 12 of Regulation 1/2003 provides that changes to the structure of an undertaking will only be proportionate *"where there is a substantial risk of a lasting or repeated infringement that derives from the very structure of the undertaking."*[62]

---

[56] *See Ibid.,* para. 1013. *See also Browser Commitment Decision, supra* note 12, para. 100 (*"Microsoft will also not retaliate against OEMs for installing competing web browsers."*).

[57] *See Microsoft Decision 2004 supra* note 25, para. 1014.

[58] *See Jacobellis v Ohio,* 378 US 184 (1964).

[59] *See Commercial Solvents, supra* note 17, para. 45.

[60] *Supra* note 23, p. 47.

[61] *Regulation 1/2003,* Art.7.

[62] Recital 12 of *Regulation* 1/2003.

12. – Remedies
Thomas Graf and David R. Little

12.36 It has been suggested that, in any event, one would expect behavioural remedies to be the norm in Article 102 TFEU cases, given that these cases relate to positive acts or omissions of undertakings.[63] However, this seems true of all Commission competition enforcement tools (with the possible exception of Commission market studies, which will consider companies' conduct but at least initially are intended to look at market structure and dynamics more generally). The stated preference for behavioural remedies may reflect concerns regarding the cost and speed of intervention. Behavioural remedies will in almost all cases be less costly and quicker for the dominant company to implement and, if the Commission can effectively outsource monitoring to third parties, may not be (substantially) more resource intensive for the Commission to oversee. These considerations are consistent with the proportionality principle.

12.37 Behavioural remedies may require the dominant undertaking to either abstain from a particular course of conduct, or to take affirmative action to bring the infringement to an end.[64] Positive obligations have included: the requirement for prices to be raised to a non-exclusionary level,[65] for a compulsory licence to be granted[66] and other forms of compulsory dealing.[67] It has been suggested that "*an order to adopt a certain course of action will be more likely in cases of refusal to deal. It may require a resumption of supply when this has been interrupted by the dominant undertaking… or the provision of access to any facility or information for which this access has been denied.*"[68] Negative obligations have included: the requirement to cease

---

[63] *See, e.g.,* R. O'Donoghue and A. J. Padilla, *The Law and Economics of Article 82 EC* (Oxford, Hart Publishing, 2006), p. 676.

[64] *See Commercial Solvents, supra* note 17, para. 45 ("[Article 3 of *Regulation 17/62*] *must be applied in relation to the infringement which has been established and may include an order to do certain acts or provide certain advantages which have been wrongfully withheld as well as prohibiting the continuation of certain action*[s], *practices or situations which are contrary to the Treaty*").

[65] *See* Case COMP/38.233 *Wanadoo*, Commission Decision of 16 July 2003, not yet published; and Cases COMP/37.451, 37.578, 37.579 *Deutsche Telekom* ("*Deutsche Telekom Decision 2003*"), Commission Decision of 21 May 2003, OJ 2003 L 263/9.

[66] *See* Case 238/87 *Volvo v Erik Veng (UK)* ("*Volvo*") [1988] ECR 6211.

[67] *See* Case IV/31.851 *Magill TV Guide / ITP, BBC and RTE*, Commission Decision of 21 December 1988, OJ 1989 L 78/43 (where certain broadcasting companies to make available their TV listings and to permit their reproduction subject to payment of reasonable royalties). *Cf. supra* note 46, where the Commission refrained from obliging BMW to supply the applicant with vehicles. The Court of First Instance upheld the Commission's decision on this point, and stated that the principle of freedom of contract meant that the Commission could not order a party to enter into a contractual relationship "*where as a general rule the Commission has suitable means at its disposal for compelling an enterprise to end an infringement*".

[68] J. Faull and A. Nikpay (Eds.), *The EC Law of Competition* (2nd Ed., Oxford, Oxford University Press, 2007), para. 4.429.

12. – Remedies

Thomas Graf and David R. Little

and desist from a certain course of abusive conduct, strike offending contractual clauses,[69] unbundle products[70] and ensure non-discriminatory treatment.[71]

Structural remedies may be used to address the effects of abuses that have **12.38** produced a change in the market structure[72] or to tackle behavioural issues the root of which is some aspect of the dominant company's structure.[73] Such structural remedies have also been applied to address dominance concerns in the context of merger control. Thus, in *Continental Can*,[74] the Commission required the dominant undertaking to dispose of a rival that it had purchased (the Decision was subsequently annulled on procedural grounds), and in *Gillette*,[75] the Commission required Gillette to dispose of the 22% equity stake it had acquired in an undertaking that controlled Gillette's principal rival, Wilkinson Sword. Note that the distinction between behavioural and structural remedies may not always be entirely clear. Since the occupation of a dominant position (or the existence of monopoly rights, for example in recently liberalised markets) may deter market entry by rivals, it may in practice be possible to identify structural implications resulting from a behavioural abuse of dominance infringement.

---

[69] The duty to deal may be imposed in a negative manner, by requiring the dominant undertaking to eliminate clauses in distribution agreements that amounted to a refusal to supply / veto right. Thus, in Case IV/36.010 *Amministrazione Autonomadei Monopoli di Stato* ("*AAMS Decision 1998*"), Commission Decision of 17 June 1998, OJ 1998 L 252/47, the Italian State granted AAMS the exclusive right to engage in the production, import, export and wholesale distribution of manufactured tobaccos. After liberalisation of the sector in 1975, AAMS retained a de facto monopoly position in the wholesale distribution of cigarettes. Customers' past practice of using AAMS, the financial difficulties faced by foreign companies wishing to establish an independent distribution network, and the challenging financial climate all reduced incentives for competitors to enter and compete with AAMS. AAMS had developed a model contract for the wholesale distribution in Italy of cigarettes manufactured in any other Member State by another producer, the terms of which were imposed on these foreign firms. Article 2 of that distribution agreement provided that if the foreign firm intended to introduce extra supplies of products in excess of those defined above but not exceeding 30 per cent of the monthly order allowed for each brand, then the amount of such extra supplies had to be agreed with AAMS, taking account of the latter's actual handling capacity and foreseeable demand. The refusal to supply in that case consisted in AAMS's refusal to authorize foreign firms to increase quantities of imported cigarettes. AAMS had refused to grant increases of up to 30 per cent in quantities in respect of two competitors. The Commission required that the offending clause be modified to eliminate this abusive element. *See* Case 118/85 *Commission v Italian Republic* [1987] ECR 2599.

[70] *See* Cases IV/30.787 and 31.48, *supra* note 4, articles 1 and 3; *See also* Cases COMP/34.579 MasterCard, COMP/36.518 EuroCommerce, COMP/38.580 Commercial Cards, *supra* note 37.

[71] *See* Section IV.4 "Remedies in Discrimination Cases" below.

[72] *Supra* note 68, para. 4.435.

[73] *See, e.g.,* Case COMP/39.315, *supra* note 10.

[74] Case IV/26.811 *Continental Can Company* Commission Decision of 9 December 1971, OJ 1972 L 7/25.

[75] Cases IV/33.440 *Warner-Lambert/Gillette and others* and IV/33.486BIC/*Gillette and others* ("*Gillette*"), Commission Decision of 10 November 1992, OJ 1993 L 116/21, p. 21.

12. – Remedies
Thomas Graf and David R. Little

12.39 Although the Commission has a preference for behavioural remedies, the Commission appears to have tended towards adopting structural remedies in certain types of cases. Phillip Lowe has described ownership unbundling – *i.e.*, the structural separation of previously common ownership structure between network and supply activities – as the most effective remedy for foreclosure problems that arise from vertical integration.[76] Remedies of a behavioural nature were considered inadequate to address the concerns identified by the Commission. As noted above, structural remedies have therefore been required in cases concerning vertically integrated companies benefitting from special or exclusive rights.[77]

12.40 Although the preference for behavioural over structural remedies is easily understood in theory, it may not always be clear whether a remedy is structural or behavioural in nature. Take for example, a remedy requiring the license of intellectual property. Intellectual property is an information good. Compelling the licensing of intellectual property is therefore similar to a forced divestiture of assets previously retained for the vertically integrated player's own use. Whereas asset divestitures have traditionally been viewed as structural in nature, IP licensing remedies have been viewed as principally behavioural,[78] since they do not require a structural reorganisation of the dominant undertaking but rather a duty to respond positively to access requests on an ongoing basis.[79] In theory, the categorisation of the remedy as structural or behavioural could affect how often licensing remedies are used. In practice, the distinction is probably theoretical, since licensing will be an appropriate remedy only in exceptional cases and, where this is the case, is likely to be the most appropriate measure available (as well as the least onerous).

---

[76] DG COMP Competition Policy Newsletter (2007), No. 1, pp. 23–34. *See*, more generally, P. Willis & P. Hughes, "Structural Remedies in Article 82 Energy Cases" (2008) 4(2) *Competition Law Review*, pp. 147–74.

[77] *See*, Case COMP/39.315, *supra* note 10. *See* in particular paras 25 and 26; *See* Case IV/30.698, *supra* note 32.

[78] *See, e.g.*, J. Kwoka and D. Moss, citing T. Hoehn, Structure Versus Conduct – a Comparison of the National Merger Remedies Practice in Seven European Countries, 17 INT. J. ECON. BUS. 9 (2010): "*Analysis of European mergers shows that there may be a preference for behavioral remedies in network and infrastructure industries, with access remedies common in information and telecommunications.*" J. Kwoka and D. Moss, "Behavioral Merger Remedies: Evaluation and Implications for Antitrust Enforcement" (November 2011) *The American Antitrust Institute*, p. 7.

[79] *See* UK Competition Commission, "Guidelines for Market Investigations – Their role, assessment, remedies and procedures", June 2012, Annex B, para 31.

12. – Remedies
Thomas Graf and David R. Little

6. Commission Decisions May also Provide for Fines

As described above, Commission prohibition decisions typically also provide **12.41**
for a fine (the Commission cannot impose a fine if the Article 9 commitments
mechanism is used in place of the Article 7 route). Only few abuse cases that
end with an infringement finding avoid a fine. The Commission may choose
not to impose a fine, or to impose only a small fine, where the undertaking
could reasonably have considered that its conduct was lawful. In most cases,
this has been because there was no relevant case law enabling the undertaking
to determine in advance whether its conduct was likely to be abusive.[80] This
was, for example, the case in *1998 Football World Cup*,[81] in which it was also
noted that the ticketing arrangements put in place were similar to those that
had been used in previous tournaments. In *Clearstream*, the Court noted that,
in addition to there being little relevant case law, the area of clearing and settlement services was particularly complex.[82] However, such lenient treatment
remains exceptional. In *Astra Zeneca*, the Court of Justice acknowledged that
the Commission and the EU Courts had not yet ruled on the specific conduct
in which Astra Zeneca had engaged. The Court nevertheless found that the
company *"was aware of the highly anti-competitive nature of its conduct and should have
expected it to be incompatible with competition rules under European Union law."*[83] The
Court of Justice therefore affirmed the General Court's conclusion that the
novelty of the abuses *"did not justify... a finding that there were mitigating circumstances and therefore a reduction in the fine for those reasons"*.[84]

Fines are not, strictly speaking, remedies under Community law since they are **12.42**
not designed to bring a competition law infringement effectively to an end,
although they may deter future infringements.[85] Fines, moreover, have a
different legal basis altogether, namely Article 23 of Regulation 1/2003.

That said, a more holistic view of the relationship between fines and rem- **12.43**
edied measures may better protect undertakings' rights. The fine and the remedied measures imposed under Regulation 1/2003 are, separately, limited by
the principle of proportionality. But the package as a whole (i.e., fines plus

---

[80] *See, e.g., Deutsche Post, DSD Decision 2001* and Case COMP/37.685, *supra* note 15.
[81] *See* Case IV/36.888, *supra* note 15.
[82] *Clearstream Decision 2004*, *supra* note 15.
[83] Case C-457/10 P *Astra Zeneca v Commission* ("*AstraZeneca Judgment 2012*"), not yet reported, para. 164.
[84] *Ibid.*, para. 166.
[85] *Supra* note 23, p. 44.

12. – Remedies
Thomas Graf and David R. Little

remedied measures) is not tested for proportionality. Conceivably, the aggregation of individually proportionate fines and remedies could result in a disproportionate package of measures.[86] Considering fines and remedies in the round might mitigate this risk.

12.44   Irrespective of whether one considers fines to be "remedies" or not, they are capable of reinforcing the rationales pursued by the Commission through the enforcement of Article 102. In *Chemiefarma*, the Court of Justice held that fines have as their objective to suppress illegal conduct and to prevent its recurrence.[87] The Commission's XIIIth report on Competition Policy stated that fines are intended to "*prevent a repetition of the offence, and to make the prohibition in the Treaty more effective*".[88] Fines contribute to enforcement of the competition rules by creating a credible threat of prosecution and punishment that is capable of deterring the undertaking in question and other undertakings from committing antitrust infringements.[89]

III.   Typology of Article 102 Remedies

12.45   This Section provides a typology of the remedial measures that may be adopted to address breaches of Article 102, guided by the principles described above.

1.   Interim Measures

12.46   The Commission may issue an order for interim remedies. Interim remedies are in principle the same as those that may be applied pursuant to a prohibition decision. They are based on a *prima facie* finding that the dominant undertaking has infringed Article 102 TFEU.

12.47   The Commission's power to impose interim measures to enforce competition rules was established in *Camera Care*. Although Regulation 17 made no

---

[86] D. R. Little, "Case for a Primary Punishment Rationale in EC Anti-Cartel Enforcement" (2009) 5(1) *European Competition Journal*, pp. 37–64.

[87] Case 41/69, *ACF Chemiefarma NV v Commission* [1970] ECR 661, para. 10 of the summary.

[88] Thirteenth Report on Competition Policy (1983), para. 62.

[89] W. Wils, "The European Commission's 2006 Guidelines on Antitrust Fines: A Legal and Economic Analysis" *World Competition* (2007), 30(2).

12. – Remedies
Thomas Graf and David R. Little

provision in this respect, the Court of Justice held that the Commission was competent under Article 3 of Regulation 17 to grant interim relief:

> *"[T]he Commission must ... be able ... to take protective measures to the extent to which they might appear indispensable in order to avoid the exercise of the power to make Decisions given by Article 3 from becoming ineffectual or even illusory because of the action of certain undertakings ...[the Commission therefore has] the power to take interim measures which are indispensable for the effective exercise of its functions, and, in particular, for ensuring the effectiveness of any Decisions requiring undertakings to bring to an end infringements which it has found to exist."*[90]

Today, the Commission's power to adopt interim measures to remedy a breach of Article 102 TFEU is based on explicit wording in Article 8(1) of Regulation 1/2003. The Commission may impose interim measures on its own initiative *"in cases of urgency due to the risk of serious and irreparable damage to competition"*. The following elements must be established in order for the Commission to impose interim measures: **12.48**

- **Prima facie infringement of Article 102 TFEU.** There must be *prima facie* evidence that the dominant undertaking has infringed Article 102 TFEU. Irrespective of the procedural safeguards that may be put in place to ensure a full review on the merits, there is necessarily some risk (through confirmation bias) that the outcome of the interim measures review may influence the merits investigation. The Court has therefore scrutinised carefully the various formulations of the *prima facie* standard offered by the Commission with the aim of ensuring that the threshold is not set too high or too low. Despite this conscious effort, the meaning of "prima facie" remains somewhat unclear. In *La Cinq*, the Court of First Instance concluded that *prima facie* was something less than *"clear and flagrant."*[91] Other interpretations offered by the Commission and courts are more opaque. In *Johnson & Firth Brown v Commission*, the President of the Court of Justice found that the application was *"on first examination not manifestly without foundation"*.[92] In *Agricola commerciale olio*, the President of the Court referred to *"serious considerations such as to make the legality of measures doubtful to say the least"*.[93] In *Peugeot*, the Court

---

[90] Case 792/79 R *Camera Care v Commission* [1980] ECR 119, para. 18.
[91] Case T-44/90 *La Cinq v Commission* [1992] ECR II-1, para. 61.
[92] Case 3/75 R *Johnson & Firth Brown v Commission* [1975] ECR 7, para. 1.
[93] Case 232/81 R *Agricola Commerciale Olio and others v Commission* [1981] ECR 2193, para. 5.

12. – Remedies
Thomas Graf and David R. Little

of First Instance followed an evidentiary standard of *"at first sight…* *serious doubts as to the legality"* of the defendant's conduct.[94] Interestingly, in *IMS Health*, the President of the Court of First Instance held that the standard for obtaining interim relief from the Court against Commission interim measures was not higher (as the Commission had argued) but the same as for a final Commission decision.[95]

- **Urgency due to the risk of serious and irreparable damage to competition.** Article 8(1) of Regulation 1/2003 refers to *"urgency due to the risk of serious and irreparable damage to competition"*. As the wording of this provision makes clear, the complainant need show that the conduct presents a risk of serious and irreparable damage to competition, damage to the complainant is not sufficient.[96] The requirement in Regulation 1/2003 to focus on damage to the competitive process is consistent with the principle that competition rules exist to protect competition and not individual competitors.[97] Past case law has noted in this regard that it is necessary to demonstrate an *"intolerable damage to the public interest"*.[98]

- **Damage is considered "irreparable".** Damage is considered irreparable where it could no longer be remedied by the Commission at the term of a full Article 102 TFEU investigation. The threshold is high, which reflects the fact that interim measures are adopted without comprehensive competitive analysis. Interim measures may well distort, rather than promote, competition if they turn out to have been unfounded. For this reason, the President of the Court of First Instance in *IMS Health*, annulled the Commission's interim measures, noting that *"many of the market developments to which immediate execution of the decision is likely to give rise would be very difficult, if not impossible, later to reverse."*[99]

---

[94] Case T-23/90 *Peugeot v Commission* [1991] ECR II-653, paras 62 and 63.

[95] Case T-184/01 R *IMS Health v Commission* [2001] ECR II-3193, paras 60–74, 121.

[96] *Ibid.*, para. 54.

[97] Some commentators have argued that whereas the US antitrust laws and agencies seek to protect the competitive process, the Commission has on occasion sought to protect individual competitors. US commentators' criticism of the Commission was particularly vocal at the time of the decisions in *Aerospatiale-Alenia/de Havilland* and *GE/Honeywell* (Case IV/M.053 *Aerospatiale-Alenia/de Havilland*, Commission Decision of 2 October 1991 and Case COMP/M.2220 *General Electric/Honeywell*, Commission Decision of 1 March 2001. *See, e.g.,* W. J. Kolasky, "Conglomerate Mergers and Range Effects: It's a Long Way from Chicago to Brussels" (2002) 10(3) *George Mason Law Review*, pp. 533–50; D. Patterson and C. Shapiro, "Transatlantic Divergence in GE/Honeywell: Causes and Lessons" (2001) 16(1) *Antitrust Magazine*, pp. 18–26.

[98] *See supra* note 95, para. 53, referring to Case T-44/90, *supra* note 91, para. 28.

[99] *Ibid.*, para. 129.

12. – Remedies
Thomas Graf and David R. Little

- **Balancing exercise.** While Regulation 1/2003 does not expressly provide for the conduct of a balancing exercise between the harm alleged by the applicant and the harm that the defendant alleges would result from granting the interim measures, the Decision in *IMS Health* appears to have introduced such a balancing exercise. In *IMS Health*, the President of the Court indicated that it was necessary to weigh the "*public interest invoked by the Commission*" against the harm that would be caused to *IMS Health* by the forced disclosure of its IPR.[100]

1.1. Characteristics of Interim Measures

Like commitment Decisions or informal undertakings, interim measures place **12.49** restrictions on a dominant undertaking's commercial activities without the foundation of a formal infringement Decision. Unlike a commitment Decision or informal undertaking, however, interim measures are imposed without the consent of the undertaking concerned. Interim measures must be limited in time and the decision ordering interim measures must identify the period of time during which the measures will apply. The measures can be renewed continually for so long as is deemed necessary and appropriate.[101] Remedies imposed pursuant to an interim ruling cannot be more restrictive than the remedies that would be available to the Commission in the event that the complainant ultimately prevailed on the merits,[102] and cannot prejudice the outcome in the main proceedings. Depending on the facts and the nature of the complaint, interim measures orders may impose positive or negative obligations on the defendant. Thus, the interim measures sought or ordered in *Boosey & Hawkes*,[103] *IMS Health*,[104] *Ford*,[105] and *Ecosystem/Peugot*[106] related to positive obligations, whereas *ECS/AKZO*[107] and *Hilti*[108] involved negative obligations.

---

[100] Case T-23/90 *Peugeot v Commission* [1991] ECR II-653, paras 134–49.

[101] *Regulation 1/2003*, Article 8(1)(2).

[102] *See, e.g.,* Cases 228 and 229/82 *Ford of Europe and Ford-Werke v Commission* [1984] ECR 1129; Case C-149/95 P(R) *Commission v Atlantic Container Line and others* [1995] ECR I-2165.

[103] Case IV/32.279 *BBI/Boosey and Hawkes*, Commission Decision of 29 July 1987, OJ 1987 L 286/36.

[104] Case COMP/38.044 *NDC Health/IMS Health: Interim measures*, Commission Decision of 13 August 2003, OJ 2003 L 268/69.

[105] Case IV/30.696, *Distribution system of Ford Werke: Interim measures*, Commission Decision of 18 August 1982, OJ 1982 L 256/20.

[106] Case IV/33.157 *Ecosystem/Peugeot: Provisional measures*, Commission Decision of 4 December 1991, OJ 1992 L 66/1.

[107] Case IV/30.698, *supra* note 32.

[108] Cases IV/30.787 and 31.488, *supra* note 4.

12. – Remedies
Thomas Graf and David R. Little

1.2.   Procedure for Interim Measures

12.50   Article 8 of Regulation 1/2003 provides that *"the Commission, acting on its own initiative may by decision ... order interim measures"*. Because of the reference to the Commission acting on its own initiative, the Commission has stated that *"Article 8 of Regulation 1/2003 makes it clear that interim measures cannot be applied for by complainants under Article 7(2) of Regulation 1/2003"*.[109] Undertakings can however, apply for interim measures before Member State courts. Notwithstanding Article 8 it is commonly accepted that parties can request interim measures within the context of a complaint under Article 102, and that the Commission can, acting on this request, order such measures. That said, to the extent that complainants have no right to interim measures they may not be able to appeal a refusal of such measures, although this has remained untested.

12.51   While interim measures are, in theory, sought and granted only in urgent cases,[110] the process may take several months to process. The addressee enjoys procedural rights, including the right to a hearing and access to file,[111] the oversight of the Commission's Advisory Committee on Restrictive Practices and Dominant Positions,[112] and the requirement that the Commission issue a reasoned decision.[113] In *ECS/AKZO*,[114] interim measures appear to have been obtained within around eleven weeks, but in other cases the process was

---

[109] Commission Notice on the handling of complaints by the Commission under Articles 81 and 82 of the EC Treaty, OJ 2004 C101/65.

[110] The Commission must provide the defendant of an application for interim measures with at least one week to respond to the application. *See* Commission Regulation (EC) No 773/2004 relating to the conduct of proceedings by the Commission pursuant to Articles 81 and 82 of the EC Treaty (*"Regulation 773/2004"*) OJ L 123/18, Article 17(2).

[111] Case 792/79 R, *supra* note 90, para. 20.

[112] Article 14(1) of *Regulation 1/2003*.

[113] Case 792/79 R, *supra* note 90, para. 19, where the Court emphasized that *"when adopting* [interim measures] *the Commission is bound to maintain the essential safeguards guaranteed to the parties concerned by regulation no 17, in particular by article 19* [… And] *the decisions must be made in such a form that an action may be brought upon them before the court of justice by any party who considers he has been injured."* Articles 19(1) and 19(2) of *Regulation 17/62* provide that: *"Before taking decisions* […] *the Commission shall give the undertakings or associations of undertakings concerned the opportunity of being heard on the matters to which the Commission has taken objection* […] *[i]f the Commission or the competent authorities of the Member States consider it necessary, they may also hear other natural or legal persons. Applications to be heard on the part of such persons shall, where they show a sufficient interest, be granted"*.

[114] Case IV/30.698, *supra* note 32. The application for interim measures was lodged on May 13, 1983. The Commission acceded to the request by way of a Decision dated July 29, 1983. *See* discussion in Case 62/86, *supra* note 32, para. 10.

12. – Remedies
Thomas Graf and David R. Little

considerably longer, lasting up to twelve months from the date of application.[115] More generally, interim measures decisions are rare and the Commission has not issued any such measures since the *IMS Health* case.

1.3. Enforcement and Review

Interim measures orders are enforced through the threat of fines or periodic penalty payments in case of non-compliance.[116] The General Court is competent to hear appeals of decisions granting interim measures.[117] Where interim measures have been awarded, the President of the General Court has the power to suspend their application pending the outcome of such appeal, as was the case in *IMS Health*.[118]

12.52

2. Remedies Volunteered by the Undertaking

As described above, broadly speaking there are two "tracks" for complainants and defendants before the Commission. The "voluntary" track refers to the possibility for an undertaking to propose and enter into commitments governing its future conduct. We consider two voluntary routes below. First, commitment decisions under Article 9 of Regulation 1/2003, and, second, informal undertakings.

12.53

2.1. Commitment Decisions

One of the principal innovations introduced by Regulation 1/2003 was Article 9, which empowers the Commission to close an investigation by way of a legally binding commitment decision. Similar to decisions under Article 7 of Regulation 1/2003, commitment decisions are enforcement instruments designed to restore effective competition. Unlike an Article 7 decision,

12.54

---

[115] Case IV/32.279, *supra* note 103 (interim measures granted after around three months); Case IV/30.696, *supra* note 105 (decision granting interim measures issued around six months following application); Case COMP/38.044, *supra* note 104 (interim measures granted after approximately eight months); *supra* note 106 (request for interim measures submitted by applicant in April 1989, Commission Decision adopting interim measures issued in late March 1990).

[116] *See* Articles 23(2)(b) and 24(1)(b) of *Regulation 1/2003*.

[117] Case 792/79 R, *supra* note 90.

[118] *Supra* note 95. Case C-481/01 P(R) *NDC Health v Commission and IMS Health* [2002] ECR I-3401.

12. – Remedies
Thomas Graf and David R. Little

however, Article 9 decisions conclude that there are no longer grounds for action by the Commission, without a finding of infringement.

2.1.1. *Procedural Steps in Commitments Proceedings*

12.55 Based on past practice and in line with the Commission's Best Practices in Proceedings Concerning Articles 101 and 102 TFEU, the Article 9 mechanism will involve the following steps:[119]

- The Commission will open a formal investigation, which is a prerequisite for a subsequent Article 9 commitment procedure.

- The dominant company under investigation can approach the Commission informally at any time during proceedings in order to indicate its willingness to discuss commitments. This may take place after the companies have attempted to resolve the matter through other methods, including informal undertakings. In practice, the Commission is likely to have provided the undertaking with some indication as to its willingness to discuss commitments.

- After this initial approach, the undertaking is entitled to a state-of-play meeting where the Commission will set out its preliminary competition concerns and an indicative timeframe for concluding the discussion of potential commitments. The Commission and the dominant company remain free to withdraw from these discussions at any point. The Commission may decide subsequently to continue formal proceedings under the Article 7 route.

- Based on the preliminary concern identified at the state of play meeting the company may submit an informed offer of commitments that outlines the main elements of the proposed remedy, typically in the form of a term sheet. Once the Commission is satisfied that the company propose commitments address the identified concerns, the Commission, will issue a Preliminary Assessment. This assessment will summarise the main facts of the case and the competition concerns that might justify a prohibition decision. Where the undertaking has submitted commitments after receiving an SO, the Commission

---

[119] *See* Commission Notice on best practices for the conduct of proceedings concerning Articles 101 and 102 TFEU, 2011 OJ C 308/06, p. 6; Antitrust Manual of Procedures, Internal DG Competition working documents on procedures for the application of Articles 101 and 102 TFEU ("*Manual of Procedures*"), March 2012; Press Release MEMO/04/217 of 17 September 2004.

12. – Remedies
Thomas Graf and David R. Little

will not issue a separate Preliminary Assessment. The Preliminary Assessment is not published and third parties have no right of access to it.

- The dominant company will typically be given around one month to respond to the Preliminary Assessment and to propose formally a set of commitments. The response is an opportunity for the dominant undertaking to highlight any factual or legal errors in the Commission's analysis and to influence the text of the final Article 9 decision. Past cases confirm that ongoing discussions with the Commission are possible after the Preliminary Assessment is issued.[120]

- Before the Commission can adopt the commitments and make them legally binding, it must carry out a market test.[121] At this time the Commission will publish three documents: (1) a notice in the Official Journal of the European Union containing a concise summary of the Commission's concerns and outlining the main contents of the commitments; (2) the full text of the proposed commitments (in their non-confidential version), which will be available on the Commission's website; and (3) a press release summarising the Commission's concerns and the proposed commitments in a few paragraphs. Interested third parties will be given a period of at least one month in which to submit observations. The Commission may also, but does not have to, engage in informal market testing prior to the formal market test. After the market test has taken place, the Commission will disclose orally or in writing the main points of the responses from third parties to the undertaking concerned. If the market test is unfavourable, the Commission may require the interested party to submit an amended commitments text.

- If the Commission is satisfied with the outcome of the market test, it will prepare a draft Article 9 decision. This must be submitted for a non-binding opinion to the Advisory Committee on Restrictive Practices and Dominant Positions and the Hearing Officer (the latter will focus on procedural aspects). Their reports will be published in the

---

[120] Cases COMP/39.388 and COMP/39.389, *supra* note 10, Final Report of the Hearing Officer, 2009 OJ C 036/07, where it is noted that the Commission "*adopted a preliminary assessment as referred to in Article 9(1) of Regulation (EC) No. 1/2003 on 7 May 2008. Ensuing discussions with the Commission services led E.ON to submit commitments on 27 May 2008*". *See also*, Case COMP/39.401 E.ON/GDF, Final Report of the Hearing Officer, 2009 OJ C 248/04, where the preliminary assessment was published on 15 October 2008 and the Commitments were submitted on 26 November 2008 as a result of ensuring discussions with the Commission.

[121] This requirement is imposed by Article 27(4) of *Regulation 1/2003*.

12. – Remedies
Thomas Graf and David R. Little

Official Journal. The formal Article 9 decision must then be adopted by the College of Commissioners. A press release is issued on the date of adoption. Once adopted, the decision becomes effective upon notification to the interested undertaking and a redacted version of the Decision and the commitments will be published on the Commission's website.

12.56 The Commission will use a commitment decision to close a case when the commitments offered address the competition concerns it has identified. Commitments which are not related to the concerns or do not meet them will not be accepted by the Commission. Regulation 1/2003 provides that a commitment decision is not appropriate where, in the Commission's view, the nature of the infringement calls for the imposition of a fine.[122]

12.57 The commitment decision will likely be adopted for a specified period. In *Alrosa*, the CFI observed that while the Commission is not obliged to limit in time the effects of decisions adopted pursuant to Article 9, if it fails to do so, the subsequent commitments decision may go beyond what is necessary in order to achieve its objectives.

12.58 An Article 9 decision accepting commitments has legal consequences, bringing an end to proceedings opened in order to establish and punish a potential infringement of competition rules. As for any decision of a European institution creating legal effects, the Commission when adopting an Article 9 decision must comply with general principles of EU law such as the principle of proportionality[123] and the right to be heard. The Commission must, accordingly, substantiate its concerns in its Article 9 decision in such a way as to enable the parties, and subsequently the European courts, to assess the scope of the remedies necessary to address them.

12.59 While discussions between the Commission and the undertaking may ostensibly resemble settlement negotiations, the status of the Commission as both

---

[122] *See Regulation 1/2003*, recital 13. Consequently, the Commission does not apply the Article 9 procedure to secret cartels that fall under the Commission notice on immunity from fines and reduction of fines in cartel cases. *See* Commission's *Manual of Procedures supra* note 119, p. 178.

[123] In *Alrosa*, the Court of Justice held that although Article 9, unlike Article 7 of Regulation No. 1/2003, makes no express reference to proportionality, the principle of proportionality, as a general principle of European Union law, is nonetheless a requirement for any act of the Commission as competition authority; *See* Case C-441/07 P, *supra* note 47, para. 36.

12. – Remedies
Thomas Graf and David R. Little

plaintiff and regulator makes these negotiations somewhat unusual. The Commission and the dominant undertaking are in opposition, in effect bargaining in an attempt to devise a settlement that is satisfactory to both. There is therefore incentive for both sides to argue their corner. But there is not an equality of arms: the Commission is also the ultimate arbiter of the negotiations, competent at first instance to determine whether the undertaking's commitments are adequate and with the legal authority to make the commitments binding. However, at the same time, the Commission must remain objective in its role. Accordingly, where the undertaking proposes several solutions and these include broader concessions than the Commission would have expected, the Commission must exercise self-restraint. The *Alrosa* case demonstrates that, while the Commission need not develop its own more moderate solutions, the Commission must, prior to confirmation, ensure that the commitments agreed are the least restrictive among any equally-efficient solutions proposed by the undertaking.[124] If the Commission fails to do so, or does so incorrectly and overlooks a less restrictive measure with equivalent effect that had been offered, this may constitute a manifest error of assessment.[125]

2.1.2. Content of Commitment Decisions

Commitments adopted under Article 9 may be structural or behavioural. The **12.60** preference expressed by the Commission for behavioural rather than structural remedies in Article 7(1) would appear to apply to all Commission decisions envisaged under Chapter III of Regulation 1/2003, including commitment decisions. This contrasts with commitment decisions in the context of European Union merger control, where structural remedies are preferred.[126] This can be explained by the differing focus of Article 102 TFEU and merger cases. Merger control serves to address transactions that may impact market structure before that structure has been altered by the proposed transaction.[127] Conversely, the application in Article 102 TFEU involves *ex post* control of

---

[124] *See supra* note 47, para. 41 ("[a]*pplication of the principle of proportionality by the Commission in the context of Article 9 of Regulation No 1/2003 is confined to verifying that the commitments in question address the concerns it expressed to the undertakings concerned and that they have not offered less onerous commitments that also address those concerns adequately. When carrying out that assessment, the Commission must, however, take into consideration the interests of third parties.*").

[125] *Ibid.*, para. 42.

[126] Case T-102/96 *Gencor v Commission* [1999] ECR II-753, para. 316; Commission Notice, *supra* note 18, para. 9. *See* E. Wind, "Remedies and Sanctions in Article 82 of the EC Treaty" (2005) 26(12) *European Competition Law Review*, pp. 659–69.

[127] N. Levy, *European Merger Control Law – A Guide to the Merger Regulation* (8th Ed., Lexis Nexis, 2011), p. 14.

12. – Remedies
Thomas Graf and David R. Little

specific <u>conduct</u> by an undertaking that has already taken place. The theory of harm in an Article 102 TFEU case is in principle less speculative than in the case of merger control. The impugned conduct can be remedied more effectively by the implementation of measures designed to address the specific infringement and its effects.

2.1.3. *Application of the Principle of Proportionality in Commitments Cases*

12.61 As mentioned, the Commission's power to impose remedies must have regard to the principle of proportionality.[128] The Commission verifies that the commitments offered address the identified competition concerns and do not manifestly go beyond what is necessary to address them.[129] In verifying whether the commitments are sufficient and that the undertakings have not offered less onerous commitments that also address the concerns adequately, the Commission will also take into consideration the interests of third parties. Below is a selection of Article 9 decisions that provide an overview of the interplay between the Commission's exercise of the power to impose remedies in Article 102 TFEU commitments cases and the principle of proportionality:

- **German Electricity Wholesale and Balancing Market (E.ON).**[130] In the *E.ON* cases the alleged infringements concerned the wholesale and balancing markets for electricity in Germany. While the alleged infringement in the wholesale market consisted of E.ON withholding capacity in order to drive prices up, in the balancing market it consisted of a deliberate preference of E.ON in its function as Transmission System Operator.[131] In the wholesale market, the structural remedies proposed by E.ON and made binding by the Commission consisted in the divestiture of about one quarter of E.ON's generation capacity; while in the balancing market, the structural remedy consisted of the full ownership unbundling of the Transmission System Operator and the network. In both cases, the behavioural alternatives to the structural commitments were considered unlikely to be equally effective in meeting the concerns expressed by the Commission in its Preliminary Assessment.

---

[128] C-441/07 P, *supra* note 47, para. 36.
[129] *See* Commission Notice, *supra* note 119, para. 115.
[130] Cases COMP/39.388 and COMP/39.389, *supra* note 10.
[131] *Supra* note 23, pp. 54–6.

12. – Remedies
Thomas Graf and David R. Little

- **RWE Gas Foreclosure.**[132] In *RWE*'s case, the Commission in its Preliminary Assessment took the view that RWE's gas transmission network could be considered an essential facility and RWE may have pursued a strategy according to which it tried to systematically keep the transport capacities on its own network for itself. The final commitments were considered suitable to remove the Commission's competition concerns expressed in the Preliminary Assessment as the sale of RWE's transmission business would have ensured that RWE would no longer have control over the gas transmission network and could no longer engage in anticompetitive practices relating to access to the network. The Commission also took the view that the structural remedy was necessary as obliging RWE to certain behaviour was considered not equally effective.

- **Gaz de France.**[133] In *Gaz de France* the competition problems identified by the Commission in its Preliminary Assessment concerned the alleged foreclosure by GDF Suez of long period access to gas import capacities in France, mainly because of the long-term reservation by GDF Suez of most of the import capacities in the GRTgaz balancing zones. The Commission considered the final commitments proposed by GDF Suez – consisting in limiting the capacity reserved by GDF Suez – to be a proportionate and necessary solution to the competition problems identified. Moreover, the Commission specified that the proceedings related only to certain alleged practices of GDF Suez in respect of capacities for the import of natural gas into France and that, accordingly, third parties' comments underlining the need for additional commitments concerning, for example, access to storage capacities were unrelated to the subject matter of the proceedings and were disregarded.

- **Rambus.**[134] In *Rambus*, the competition concerns arose from the fact that Rambus may have been claiming abusive royalties for the use of its patents for technologies needed to produce Dynamic Random Access Memory chips. The Commission took the view that the commitments offered relating to the royalty rates, among which a worldwide cap for a five-year period, were sufficient and necessary to address the concerns it had identified. As to the circumstance

---

[132] *See* Case COMP/39.402, *supra* note 10.
[133] *See* Case COMP/39.316, *supra* note 10.
[134] Case COMP/38.636, *supra* note 11.

12. – Remedies
Thomas Graf and David R. Little

that a number of respondents complained, among other things, that the royalty caps set in the commitments were too high, the commission clarified that it must evaluate the whole package of the Commitments and not its individual elements. Thus, even if the possible, minor shortcomings of certain aspects of the remedies were considered to be substantiated, the whole package of commitments (clarification on the scope, package licence, basis for calculating the royalty, removal of the most-favoured-licensee clause and the clarification that future patents were covered by the Commitments) substantially addressed the concerns expressed in the Preliminary Assessment.

- **Microsoft (Tying).**[135] In the *Microsoft (tying)* case, the commitments offered by Microsoft were considered appropriate as they addressed the Commission's competition concerns expressed in the Statement of Objections regarding potential foreclosure effects, the limitation of innovation in web development through the tying of Internet Explorer to Windows, and the potential reinforcement of Microsoft's position on the client PC operating system market. With respect to the coercion of OEMs, pursuant to the commitments, Microsoft would no longer contractually oblige OEMs to ship Internet Explorer with Windows PCs and would also not retaliate against OEMs for installing competing web browsers. Moreover, Microsoft would allow OEMs to turn off Internet Explorer in Windows 7 and subsequent versions of Windows and provide the technical means to do so. The commitments were also considered suitable for providing rival web browsers with an effective opportunity to compete on the merits with Internet Explorer and for enhancing competition on the web browser market by removing Microsoft's artificial distribution advantage brought about by the tying of Internet Explorer to Windows and by informing users about available web browser choices.

- **ENI.**[136] In the *ENI* case, the Commission's main concerns were certain features of the management and operation by ENI of its natural gas transmission pipelines which could have limited third-party access to available and new capacity (*i.e.,* namely the way access to capacity was provided by ENI, for example by hoarding some capacity,

---

[135] *Browser Commitment Decision, supra* note 12.
[136] Case COMP/39.315, *supra* note 10.

12. – Remedies
Thomas Graf and David R. Little

by offering it in a degraded manner or by not investing despite the demand), and could constitute an abuse of a dominant position infringing Article 102 TFEU. The Commission held that the commitment by ENI to divest its share in the companies that own, operate and manage the transport capacity of three international pipelines that bring gas into northern Italy from Russia (the TAG pipeline) and the north of Europe (the TENP/Transitgas system) would address these concerns in a sufficient and proportionate manner. In addition, the Commission held that certain concerns raised by respondents to the market test could not be considered as valid arguments against the effectiveness of the remedies as they were outside the scope of the procedure. By way of example, a number of respondents complained that the commitments did not foresee a capacity release as had been the case in other antitrust proceedings against gas undertakings; nor did the Commission require that ENI divest its Italian national gas transmission grid as a supplementary measure. The Commission, however, took the view that any measure regarding the national network would be out of the scope of the procedure, given its concerns related only to ENI's management of its international import pipelines. As to a possible capacity release, the Commission considered that the theory of harm in ENI's case differed substantially from the other antitrust cases mentioned by the respondents where the main concerns were the long-term reservations by dominant shippers.

2.1.4. *Enforcement of Commitment Decisions*

The Commission may reopen proceedings closed by way of an Article 9 **12.62** decision, upon request or on its own initiative, where: (1) there has been a material change in any of the facts on which the decision was based, (2) the undertaking concerned has acted contrary to the commitments, or (3) it transpires that the commitments decision was based on incomplete, incorrect or misleading information provided by the undertaking concerned.[137] The Commission may also impose a fine on an undertaking that fails to comply with a commitment made binding by an Article 9 decision.[138] The same ceiling for fines is applied as in the case of a fresh infringement of Article 102, *i.e.*, 10% of the undertaking's turnover in the year preceding

---

[137] Article 9(2) of *Regulation 1/2003*.
[138] Article 23(2) of *Regulation 1/2003*.

12. – Remedies
Thomas Graf and David R. Little

the infringement.[139] The Commission may also have recourse to periodic penalty payments in order to enforce a term or terms of an Article 9 decision.[140]

12.63   In October 2012, the Commission issued its first-ever Statement of Objections in relation to an alleged breach of an Article 9 decision.[141] The Statement of Objections set out formal charges against Microsoft in relation to the 2009 commitments decision in the Internet Explorer tying case. As described above, pursuant to that decision, Microsoft was required to display a browser "Choice Screen" on Windows-based PCs sold in Europe running Internet Explorer as the default browser, for a period of five years. The Commission found that during the period February 2011 to July 2012, many Windows users were not shown the Choice Screen. In a July 2012 statement, Microsoft admitted that due to a *"technical error"* it failed to deliver the browser choice screen to PCs running the service pack 1 update to Windows 7. Microsoft estimated that around 28 million PCs were affected, or approximately 10% of PCs falling within the scope of the commitments decision.[142] In addition to a number of technical and compliance undertakings, Microsoft offered to extend the duration of the commitments for fifteen months in order to compensate for the period of non-compliance. In March 2013, Vice-President Almunia announced that the Commission would impose a €561 million fine on Microsoft (representing around 1% of the company's 2012 turnover). Vice-President Almunia stated that Microsoft's conduct amounted to a very serious infringement of EU competition rules, *"irrespective of whether it was intentional or not"*.[143] He emphasised that: *"if companies enter into commitments, they must do what they have committed to do or face the consequences…companies should be deterred from any temptation to renege on their promises or even to neglect their duties"*.[144] We note that fines for breaches of a commitment decision are imposed pursuant to 23(2)(c) of *Regulation 1/2003*, whereas the *2006 Fining Guidelines*[145] are adopted on the

---

[139] *Ibid.*

[140] Article 24(1)(c) of *Regulation 1/2003.*

[141] It has been reported that the Commission is separately reviewing compliance with commitments in a further two cases, involving Standard & Poor's and EDF. *See* M. Newman, "EC May Set New Precedent When Fixing Fine Against Microsoft in Compliance Cases," *MLex*, October 25, 2012.

[142] *See* Microsoft, "Statement of Microsoft Corporation on EU Browser Choice Screen Compliance", Press Release of 17 July 2012.

[143] Press Release SPEECH/13/192 of 6 March, 2013.

[144] Press Release SPEECH/12/760 of 24 October 2012.

[145] Guidelines on the method of setting fines imposed pursuant to Article 23(2)(a) of Regulation No 1/2003 (*"2006 Fining Guidelines"*), OJ 2006 C 210/2.

12. – Remedies
Thomas Graf and David R. Little

basis of article 23(2)(a) of *Regulation 1/2003*. Although the *2006 Fining Guidelines* are not directly applicable, consistent with the guidelines' methodology, the Commission took into account the gravity and duration of Microsoft's infringement and the need to deter, in addition to mitigating circumstances such as Microsoft's cooperation with the investigation.[146]

2.1.5. Efficiencies Resulting from Commitment Decisions

The Commission's Communication to the Parliament and the Council on Regulation 1/2003 notes that the power to issue commitment decisions was intended to: *"pursue the objective of enhancing administrative efficiency and effectiveness in dealing with competition concerns … [and] ensures rapid change in the marketplace".*[147] The two major benefits that were intended to result from the provision for commitment decisions were therefore an increase in administrative efficiency resulting from a reduction in administrative workload, and an increase in the speed of remedial action. With respect to administrative workload, commitment decisions obviate the need for the Commission to prepare and issue an infringement decision, or even a Statement of Objections. Since under an Article 9 commitment decision the dominant undertaking need not acknowledge that it has committed an infringement, it will not appeal a commitment decision, as it might a prohibition decision.[148] These efficiencies can be expected to lower overall enforcement costs.

12.64

Given the Commission's second aim of more timely intervention, one would expect commitment decisions to be used most frequently either in fast moving markets, such as hi-tech markets[149], or where there are other urgent reasons for intervention.

12.65

---

[146] *See supra* note 143.

[147] Communication from the Commission to the European Parliament and the Council, Report on the functioning of Regulation 1/2003 (2009), point 17.

[148] *See, e.g.*, the recent commitments decision issued in *Microsoft*, in which the formalised commitments explicitly state that: *"Nothing in these Commitments may be construed as implying that Microsoft agrees with the Commission's preliminary assessment in the Statement of Objections of 14 January 2009 in Case No. COMP/C-3/39.530. Microsoft has, nevertheless, offered these Commitments pursuant to Article 9 of Regulation 1/2003 to address the Commission's competition concerns. These Commitments are given without any admission by Microsoft that it has engaged in abusive conduct contrary to Article 102 TFEU or any other aspect of EU competition law."* *Browser Commitment Decision*, *supra* note 12.

[149] *See, e.g.*, H. First, "Netscape is Dead: Remedy Lessons from the Microsoft Litigation", New York University Law and Economics Working Papers, Paper 166, December 12, 2008, p. 32.

12. – Remedies
Thomas Graf and David R. Little

2.2. *Informal Undertakings*

12.66   Regulation 17/62 made no provision for the resolution of Commission investigations without any formal infringement finding. However, the Commission developed a practice of accepting informal undertakings from companies prior to and in place of such a finding. Through these informal promises, undertakings agreed to behave in certain ways in exchange for an exemption, a letter of comfort, or the termination or suspension of investigative proceedings.[150] Unlike Article 9 commitment decisions, these informal undertakings were not legally enforceable. But breach would expose the settling company to re-opening of the investigation on the substance. Not all such commitments were publicly acknowledged by the Commission, but it is clear that they were a prominent feature of the Regulation 17/62 regime. Some authors have estimated that the proportion of cases under Regulation 17/62 that were settled without an infringement finding may have been as high as 90%.[151] High-profile or precedent-setting cases settled through informal means were described in the Commission's competition policy reports.[152] This was the case, for example, with respect to the 1984 *IBM* undertakings relating to mainframe interface disclosure and memory bundling,[153] and *Digital Equipment's* undertakings to alter its commercial and pricing policy with respect to certain software maintenance and hardware services.[154]

12.67   As described above, Article 9 of Regulation 1/2003 introduced a formal commitments procedure. As the Commission has made greater use of the Article 9 mechanism, it has settled fewer cases through informal undertakings. Nevertheless, informal undertakings are still sometimes used. Thus, undertakings were made in *OMV/Gazprom*, and *E.ON Ruhrgas/Gazprom*.[155] MasterCard undertook to reduce various multilateral intra-EEA fallback interchange fees for cross-border payment card transactions.[156] Microsoft

---

[150] G. S. Georgiev, "Contagious Efficiency: The Growing Reliance on U.S.-Style Antitrust Settlements in EU Law" (2007) 4 *Utah Law Review*, pp. 971–1037.

[151] Van Bael & Bellis, *Competition law of the European Community* (5th Ed. The Hague: Kluwer Law International, 2010), p. 1156.

[152] A resume of a number of these cases is provided in R. O'Donoghue and A. J. Padilla, *supra* note 63, pp. 706–07.

[153] *See* DG COMP Competition Policy Newsletter (1998) No. 3, pp. 7–11. A comprehensive discussion of the IBM cases on both sides of the Atlantic and the EU undertakings is provided in J. Vickers, "A Tale of Two EC Cases: *IBM* and *Microsoft*" (2009) 1(1) *CPI Antitrust Chronicle*.

[154] Case *Digital Undertaking*, Twenty-seventh Report on Competition Policy (1997), para. 69.

[155] European Commission Report on Competition Policy (2005), paras 48 and 49.

[156] *See* Press Release MEMO/09/143 of 1 April, 2009.

12. – Remedies
Thomas Graf and David R. Little

gave a "public interoperability undertaking", under which it promised to make interoperability information available (and license associated patents) for a range of server products including email and collaboration servers, Microsoft Office, and Microsoft.NET, as well as to comply with certain obligations with respect to Open Standards.[157] Informal undertakings therefore remain a plausible enforcement option for the Commission, even in complex cases.[158]

3. Infringement Decisions

As described above, the Commission is empowered under Article 7 of Regulation 1/2003 to issue a decision finding that there has been an infringement of Article 102 (and requiring that the infringement be brought to an end). The Commission may issue a declaratory decision where the infringement has since been terminated, provided that the Commission has a legitimate interest in doing so. According to the Court of Justice, there is a legitimate interest where it is necessary to clarify the legal position because there is a *"real danger of a resumption of* [the abusive] *practice if* [the company's] *obligation to terminate it were not expressly confirmed"*.[159] In addition to a prohibition decision declaring that an infringement has been committed, the Commission may issue an order requiring the undertaking to refrain from engaging in particular conduct, or where the infringement relates to a failure to act, to take positive steps to address this failure. As explained above, such requirement may extend to conduct having similar effect.

12.68

Infringement decisions in Article 102 cases are almost always accompanied by a fine, as discussed above. The sections that follow discuss the fines and remedies that may accompany a prohibition decision.

12.69

---

[157] Microsoft, *"Public Undertaking by Microsoft"*("*The 2009 Microsoft Undertaking*"), December 16, 2009 ("*The second measure is a "public undertaking" that covers interoperability with Microsoft's products – the way our high-share products work with non-Microsoft technologies. This applies to an important set of Microsoft's products – our Windows, Windows Server, Office, Exchange, and SharePoint products [...] Microsoft will ensure that developers throughout the industry, including in the open source community, will have access to technical documentation to assist them in building products that work well with Microsoft products. Microsoft will also support certain industry standards in its products and fully document how these standards are supported. Microsoft will make available legally-binding warranties that will be offered to third parties.*")

[158] *See* M. Dolmans, T. Graf and D. R. Little, "Microsoft's browser-choice Commitments and Public Interoperability Undertaking" (2010) *European Competition Law Review*, paras 268–75.

[159] *See* Case 7/82, *supra* note 4, para. 27.

12. – Remedies
Thomas Graf and David R. Little

4. Fines

4.1. The Regulatory Framework

12.70   The legal basis for imposing fines on undertakings for breach of Article 102 is found in Recital 29 and Article 23(2) of Regulation 1/2003:

> *"Compliance with Articles 81 and 82 of the Treaty and the fulfilment of the obligations imposed on undertakings and associations of undertakings under this Regulation should be enforceable by means of fines and periodic penalty payments. To that end, appropriate levels of fine should also be laid down for infringements of the procedural rules." (Regulation 1/2003, Recital (29))*

> *"The Commission may by decision impose fines on undertakings and associations of undertakings where, either intentionally or negligently: (a) they infringe Article [101] of Article [102] of the Treaty; [...] or (c) they fail to comply with a commitment made binding by a decision pursuant to Article 9."*[160]

12.71   Article 23(2) establishes an upper boundary for the fines that the Commission is empowered to impose, namely *"10%* [of the undertaking's] *turnover in the preceding business year"* (or, in the case of infringements of an association relating to the activities of its members, 10% of the sum of the total turnover of each member active on the market affected by the infringement of the association). Article 102 cases are typically considered as "very serious" infringements of competition law and fines have, accordingly, in some cases reached the top end of this range.[161]

12.72   Regulation 1/2003 also provides for the use of fines as a tool for ensuring undertakings' compliance during an investigation with the investigative process (and after an investigation):

- Regulation 1/2003 empowers the Commission to impose fines not exceeding 1% of the undertaking's total turnover in the preceding business year where the undertaking, intentionally or negligently, supplies incorrect, misleading, incomplete, or tardy information in

---

[160] Article 23(2) of *Regulation 1/2003.*

[161] Different formulations have been used by the Commission and the Courts, with the conduct variously characterised as "serious" or "very serious" or as infringements of "extreme" or "particular" gravity. *See* F. Dethmers and H. Engelen, "Fines under Article 102 of the Treaty of the Functioning of the European Union" (2011) 2, *European Competition Law Review*, pp. 86–98.

12. – Remedies
Thomas Graf and David R. Little

response to requests for information under Articles 17, 18, or 20 (the specific failures punishable by fine vary slightly depending on the form of information request concerned).

• Fines may also be imposed for obstruction of Commission investigations. In *E.ON Energie*, the Commission fined the company for having, tampered with a seal put in place during a Commission dawn raid at the company's premises. E.ON Energie was fined €38 million, approximately 0.14% of its previous year's turnover. Appeals by the company were dismissed by both the General Court and the Court of Justice. The Court of Justice's ruling clarifies that where the Commission has determined on the basis of evidence, including the breach of seal report, that a seal has been breached, the burden of proof shifts to the undertaking concerned to adduce evidence challenging that finding. In seeking to discharge this burden, the undertaking cannot merely allege that the seal was defective or incorrectly affixed but must adduce cogent evidence in support of its defence and demonstrate a causal link between the defect and the apparent breach of the seal.[162]

Regulation 1/2003 also provides for the imposition of penalty payments in the event that undertakings fail to comply with the terms of a prohibition, interim measures, or commitments decision. (The penalty payments provision may also be applied in order to compel an undertaking to supply complete and correct information requested under Articles 17 or 18(3) of Regulation 1/2003, or where the undertaking has resisted an inspection ordered under Article 20(4) of the Regulation).   **12.73**

---

[162] Case C-89/11 P *E.ON Energie v Commission*, not yet reported, paras 71–80, 84–7. E.ON's sixth ground of appeal alleged that the General Court erred in law and breached the principle of proportionality by failing to take into account various evidential factors when assessing the gravity of infringement and the amount of the fine. These factors included the possibility that the seal had been broken negligently, rather than intentionally, and the size and turnover of E.ON. Advocate General Bot expressed concern that the General Court *"did not form its own opinion"* as regards the proportionality of the fine instead *"relying on the amount fixed in a rather general way by the Commission"* and recommended that the judgment be set aside on this ground (Advocate General Bot, para. 120). The Court of Justice did not follow the Advocate General's recommendation. Recalling its more limited jurisdiction of review, the Court of Justice stated that it could not review the General Court's assessment of the evidence and could only find an error in law by the General Court where the level of the penalty was *"not merely inappropriate, but also excessive to the point of being disproportionate"* (para. 126). The Court of Justice held that the General Court had taken into account relevant factors in determining the amount of the fine, including: (1) the particularly serious nature of a breach of seal; (2) the size of E.ON Energie; and (3) the need to ensure that the fine has a sufficient deterrent effect. In the light of these factors, a fine amounting to 0.14% of E.ON's annual turnover in the year preceding the infringement was not disproportionate. (paras 123–38).

12. – Remedies
Thomas Graf and David R. Little

12.74   Fig. 12.1 and Fig. 12.2 illustrate the fines imposed in Article 102 TFEU cases since the introduction of the euro.[163]

Figure 12.1: Commission Fines in Article 102 Cases Since 1999.

Year of Decision	Parties	Fine (€)
1999	Virgin / British Airways	6,800,000
2000	Soda Ash (Solvay)	20,000,000
2000	Soda Ash (ICI)	10,000,000
2001	Deutsche Post	24,000,000
2001	Michelin	19,760,000
2001	De Post/La Poste	2,500,000
2003	Deutsche Telekom	12,600,000
2003	Wanadoo	10,350,000
2004	Microsoft	497,196,304
2004	Compagnie Maritime Belge	3,400,000
2005	Astra Zeneca	60,000,000
2006	Tomra	24,000,000
2007	Telefónica (WanadooEspana)	151,875,000
2009	Intel	1,060,000,000
2011	TelekomunikacjaPolska	127,554,194

---

[163] The euro was introduced on January 1, 1999, which allows for an easy comparison of fine levels across cases. Fines of €6 million and €273 million were imposed, respectively, on AAMS and TACA, although the latter was annulled on various substantive and procedural grounds. Procedural violations *(E.ON Energie)*, breaches of commitment decisions *(Microsoft-tying)* and periodic penalties for non-implementation *(Microsoft)* have not been reflected in the chart.

12. – Remedies
Thomas Graf and David R. Little

Figure 12.2: Fines in Article 102 Cases (Adjusted for Reductions by Courts).

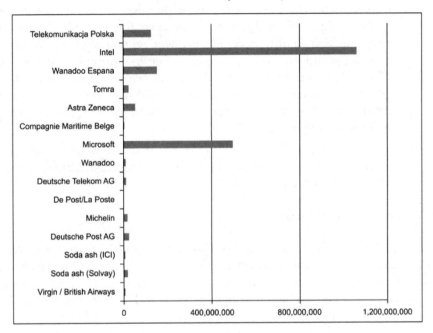

The following trends may be observed:

12.75

- The level of fines imposed for abuse of a dominant position has increased over time, even allowing for inflation. This progression is non-linear. This is unsurprising given that in the intervening period, the Commission revised its *1998 Fining Guidelines* so as to facilitate more severe penalties, and there has been a general hardening of attitude towards violations of competition law.

- The highest fine in the absolute was that imposed on Intel (1.06 billion euros). The lowest was that imposed on De Post/La Poste (2.5 million euros). As a proportion of turnover, the heaviest fines imposed have been against ProkentTomra (around 7%) and Intel (around 4%). In all other cases, fines have been below 2% of the company's turnover and in most cases below 1%.[164]

---

[164] F. Dethmers and H. Engelen, *supra* note 161, p. 88.

12. – Remedies
Thomas Graf and David R. Little

- There are large variations in fine levels over time. These variations cannot be readily explained by differences in the severity of the infringements. However, since the Commission has discretion (up to the statutory fining limit) to adjust fines for, *inter alia*, deterrence purposes,[165] such differences in treatment are unlikely to prove a successful ground on which to appeal a fine for infringing Article 102 TFEU. This is consistent with the Commission's case law on Article 101 TFEU, where fines have been adjusted on grounds of unequal treatment only rarely and with respect to undertakings participating in the same infringement.[166]

- Fines were reduced on appeal in the two *Soda Ash* cases, and in *Astra Zeneca*. In other cases, appeals have been unsuccessful (there was no appeal in *Deutsche Post* or *De Post/La Poste*).

4.2. The 2006 Fining Guidelines

12.76   On June 28, 2006, the Commission published new guidelines for the calculation of fines for European Union competition law infringements, replacing the *1998 Fining Guidelines* (which continued to apply to cases in which a Statement of Objections was issued before September 1, 2006. The *2006 Fining Guidelines* were intended to facilitate higher fines in antitrust cases, including abuse of dominance cases.[167] The *2006 Fining Guidelines* left in place the statutory maximum fine for infringements of the competition rules, which remained 10 per cent of the relevant group's total worldwide turnover in the preceding business year consistent with Article 23(2) of Regulation 1/2003, but made it easier for the Commission to impose higher fines within that upper bound.

4.2.1. The Basic Amount

12.77   Article 23(3), Regulation 1/2003 provides that: "*in fixing the amount of the fine, regard shall be had both to the gravity and to the duration of the infringement*". Under the

---

[165] *Michelin II*, *supra* note 54, para. 254. *See also* Case T-228/97 *Irish Sugar v Commission* ("*Irish Sugar Judgment 1999*") [1999] ECR II-2969, para. 54.

[166] *See, e.g.*, Case T-410/03 *Hoechst v Commission* [2008] ECR II-881, in which the General Court held that the Commission had erred in attributing the role of leader of the cartel on the sorbates market to Hoechst, thereby infringing the principles of equal treatment and sound administration. The General Court reduced the fine from €99 million to €74.25 million.

[167] The Commission stating in an accompanying press release that: "*companies involved in a long lasting infringement in a large market should be prepared to receive significantly higher fines than in the past*." Press Release IP/06/857 of 28 June 2006, and Press Release MEMO/06/256 of 28 June 2006.

12. – Remedies
Thomas Graf and David R. Little

1998 Fining Guidelines, the Commission calculated the starting level for a fine as a lump sum by reference to the nature and the gravity of the infringement. A "deterrence multiplier" could then be applied, and the product of that exercise could then be increased by a further 10 per cent for each year of the undertaking's participation in the infringement. The basic amount could then be modified upwards or downwards to reflect aggravating or attenuating circumstances.

4.2.2.   The 2006 Fining Guidelines

The *2006 Fining Guidelines* adopt a different approach to taking account of gravity and deflation.[168] The *2006 Fining Guidelines* set the starting level by reference to a proportion of the defendant's value of sales in the relevant market affected by the infringement. This is a percentage figure, up to a maximum of 30 per cent of a defendant's affected turnover in the relevant geographic market within the EEA for the last business year of the company's participation in the infringement. The percentage level reflects a range of factors, including the nature of the infringement and its geographic scope. The defendant's worldwide market share may be used as the basis for calculating EEA-wide value of sales. Thus, a defendant with the majority of its activities outside the EEA, with, for example, a 50 per cent share worldwide but only a 20 per cent market share in the EEA, might be attributed a starting amount based on an EEA-wide turnover of 50 per cent of its total relevant market sales in the EEA.

12.78

4.2.3.   Duration of the Infringement

As noted above, Regulation 1/2003 explicitly envisages that the duration of the infringement should be considered when setting the fine. Whereas under the *1998 Fining Guidelines*, a 10 per cent increment was added for each year of participation in the infringement, under the *2006 Fining Guidelines*, a 100 per cent increment is preferred. The basic amount is multiplied by the number of years that the infringement lasted, with any period of more than six months being accounted for as a full year.

12.79

4.2.4.   Recidivism

The *2006 Fining Guidelines* provide for stringent treatment of recidivists. Whereas the Commission's practice under the *1998 Fining Guidelines* had been

12.80

---

[168] *2006 Fining Guidelines, supra* note 145.

12. – Remedies
Thomas Graf and David R. Little

to increase the basic amount by 50 per cent for defendants previously the subject of one or more infringement decisions, the *2006 Fining Guidelines* provide for an increase of up to 100 per cent for each previously established infringement, including infringements punished by national competition authorities. No limitation periods apply.[169]

4.2.5. Deterrence Multipliers

12.81   The *2006 Fining Guidelines* codify the Commission's practice of applying so-called "deterrence multipliers" to increase the basic amount of the fine paid by large multi-product companies with significant operations outside the product market(s) specifically affected by the infringement at issue. The *2006 Fining Guidelines*, however, moved this deterrence uplift stage to the end of the fining calculation. A provision was also included enabling the Commission, in its implementation of the deterrence multiplier, to take account of the gains improperly made by the company as a result of the infringement, where it is able to estimate them, so as to ensure that the fine exceeds the unlawful gain.

4.2.6. Inability to Pay

12.82   The *2006 Fining Guidelines* expressly limit any defence based on a defendant's alleged inability to pay to situations where, based on objective evidence, it appears that the fine otherwise imposed under the *2006 Fining Guidelines* would *"irretrievably jeopardise the economic viability"* of the defendant and *"cause its assets to lose all their value."*[170]

5.   Enforcement of Remedial Measures

12.83   The Commission (and the national competition authorities) disposes of various means of enforcing remedies imposed in Article 102 TFEU cases. Below, we consider (1) periodic penalty payments and (2) monitoring mechanisms.

---

[169] In *Belgian Beer Market*, the Commission increased the basic amount of the fine for recidivism on the basis of infringements that occurred more than 17 years before (Case IV/37.614 *Interbrew and Alken-Maes* ("*Belgian Beer market*"), Commission Decision of 5 December 2001, OJ 2003 L 200/1). On appeal (Case C-3/06 P *Groupe Danone v Commission* [2007] ECR I-1331), the Court of Justice upheld the fine imposed by the Court of First Instance, rejecting the challenge of the lawfulness of increasing the fine for such an old infringement. The Court confirmed that repeat offences by companies, even when many years in the past, should be taken into account when setting fines.

[170] *2006 Fining Guidelines, supra* note 145, para. 35.

12. – Remedies
Thomas Graf and David R. Little

5.1. Periodic Penalty Payments

The Commission's power to impose penalty payments for failure to comply **12.84** with a Commission decision derives from Article 24 of Regulation 1/2003. Article 24 provides that the Commission may, by decision, impose on an undertaking periodic penalty payments not exceeding five per cent of the undertaking's average daily turnover in the preceding business year, in order to compel the undertaking to put an end to an Article 102 TFEU infringement identified according to an Article 7 infringement or Article 9 commitments decision or an Article 8 interim measures order.[171] The Commission's impact assessment on Regulation 1/2003[172] concluded on the basis of the Commission's experience in *Microsoft*, that the Article 24 procedure could be relatively lengthy and cumbersome and suggested that ways to improve its operation be examined.[173]

5.2. Monitoring Mechanisms

As a general matter, the Commission can rely on the dominant company's **12.85** competitors and customers to monitor its compliance with the terms of the commitments. In addition, in many instances, Article 102 TFEU remedies provide for a system of self-reporting by the undertaking on the implementation of the remedy. In some cases, the Commission has required that an independent third party be appointed to act as a Monitoring Trustee, although the remit of such arrangements has been limited by the *Microsoft* judgment.

In *Microsoft*, a Monitoring Trustee was instructed to issue technical opinions **12.86** assessing Microsoft's compliance with the order of the Commission's infringement decisions. The Monitoring Trustee also had *ex officio* powers of investigation, which were couched in broad terms. Upon appeal, the Court of First Instance, annulled the monitoring provisions of the Commission's decision. The Court criticized that the monitoring trustee *"in the performance of his tasks"* was *"independent not only of Microsoft but also of the Commission itself"* because he was *"required to act on his own initiative and upon application by third parties"*.[174]

---

[171] *Regulation 1/2003* also provides for the imposition of daily periodic payments in respect of an undertaking's failure to supply complete and correct information subsequent to a Commission request, or to submit to an inspection which the Commission has order by decision under Article 20(4).

[172] *Supra* note 147.

[173] In June 2012, the General Court largely upheld the periodic penalty fines imposed on Microsoft, commuting the amount by 3.5%, to €860 million.

[174] *Microsoft Judgment 2007 supra* note 43, para. 1269.

12. – Remedies
Thomas Graf and David R. Little

The Court also objected that "*the role envisaged for the monitoring trustee*" was "*not limited to putting questions to Microsoft and reporting the answers to the Commission, or to advice concerning the implementation of the remedies*", but allowed him "*independently of the Commission, access to information, documents, premises and employees and also to the source code*" of Microsoft.[175] The Court therefore concluded that the Commission through the envisaged monitoring mechanism had improperly delegated part of its investigational powers to the monitoring trustee. At the same, time the Court made clear that the Commission is not precluded from appointing technical experts for assistance in the monitoring of remedies, provided that such experts remain under the supervision of the Commission and retain an auxiliary role.

IV. Substance: Article 102 TFEU Abuses and Effective Remedies

12.87 This Section considers how the Commission has sought to remedy specific Article 102 TFEU abuses.

1. Pricing Abuse Remedies

12.88 As discussed in greater detail in Chapters 4 (Predatory Conduct) and 10 (Excessive Pricing) above, a variety of pricing abuses have been considered by the Commission and courts. These include exclusionary pricing abuses, such as: (1) predatory pricing (setting prices below production costs with the aim of driving competitors out of the market);[176] (2) margin squeezing;[177] (3) exclusionary discounting, such as: fidelity or exclusivity rebates, and targeted, retroactive volume rebates, and (4) excessive prices.

---

[175] *Ibid.*, para. 1270.

[176] J. Swift QC, "Selective Price Cuts, Discounts and Rebates ~ EU Competition Law at a Crossroads ~ Form or Effects", in Monckton Chambers *Competition Law ~ Recent Developments before the CAT and the European Courts*, October 27, 2005, p. 2.

[177] Guidance on the Commission's enforcement priorities in applying Article 82 of the EC Treaty to abusive exclusionary conduct by dominant undertakings ("*Guidance Paper*"), OJ 2009 C 45/7, para. 180.

12. – Remedies
Thomas Graf and David R. Little

There is an obvious tension between the Commission's express statement that **12.89** it *"does not wish to set itself up as a price-control authority"*[178] and the appropriate resolution of pricing abuse cases, where such price controls may be required. With the exception of margin squeeze, which we discuss below, the infringement results from a price that is either too high or too low. For some forms of pricing abuse, the remedy may require to abstain from certain pricing forms (*e.g.*, rebates conditioned on exclusivity), without need for the Commission to determine the "proper" price. But for others an appropriate remedy would typically be to increase or lower the price charged by the dominant company to the identified "competitive level".

The received wisdom is that it is not the Commission's role to act as a price **12.90** regulator.[179] The reasons most commonly advanced are the difficulty of determining the competitive price level and the costs required for extensive monitoring. Clearly, there are differences between the role of competition authorities and the role of (sectorial) regulators (that may have price regulation duties).[180] It also seems likely that enforcement costs would increase if the Commission took upon itself price regulation responsibilities. However, the general principle should not call into question the ability of the Commission to impose price controls in the context of Article 102 TFEU pricing abuse cases, where they are the most effective means of addressing the infringement. The difficulties encountered by the Commission in establishing the competitive price level are probably not markedly greater than those of a sectorial regulator. Indeed, the Commission may have acquired considerable insight into the relevant market(s) over the course of the Article 102 TFEU proceedings.

---

[178] Fifth Report on Competition Policy (1975), para. 76; *see also*, DG COMP Competition Policy Newsletter (1998), No. 2, pp. 35–8 (*"The Commission itself never aspired to use Article 86 EC Treaty* [current Article 102 TFEU] *in order to act as a price setting authority"*).

[179] *See* P. Rey and others, "An Economic Approach to Article 82", Report by the Economic Advisory Group on Competition Policy (*"EAGCP Report"*), July 2005, pp. 11–2 ("[C]*onsider the problem of monopoly pricing. One response to the problem might be for the competition authority to intervene, citing excessive pricing by a monopolist as an infraction of the abuse-of-dominance prohibition* [...] *However, a policy intervention on such grounds requires the competition authority to actually determine what price it considers appropriate, as well as how it should evolve over time; for this it is not really qualified. Moreover, such a policy intervention drastically reduces, and may even forego the chance to protect consumers in the future by competition rather than policy intervention. A regime in which consumer protection from monopoly abuses is based on competition is greatly to be preferred to one in which consumer protection is due to political or administrative control of prices"*).

[180] *See*, generally, International Competition Network, *Antitrust Enforcement in Regulated Sectors Working Group – Subgroup 2: Interrelations between antitrust and regulatory authorities*, Report to the Fourth ICN Annual Conference, Bonne, June 2004.

12. – Remedies
Thomas Graf and David R. Little

12.91　While the Commission has a principled aversion to acting as a price regulator, it has nevertheless in several cases ordered that price levels be increased to competitive, non-exclusionary levels.[181] In a number of these cases, the Commission imposed additional reinforcing and/or monitoring measures. Thus, in *ECS/AKZO,* the Commission imposed a suite of remedies linked to price controls, *inter alia,* prohibiting AKZO from granting any terms of credit or conditions of supply that might bring its effective prices below those indicated in the Commission's price schedule.[182] In *Deutsche Post,*[183] the Commission required the company to submit (1) annual itemised statements of transfer prices paid by the company's stand-alone parcel service business for all goods or services procured from Deutsche Post and (2) any agreements concluded by the parcel service business with its six largest mail-order customers that envisaged the granting of rebates.[184]

12.92　In excessive pricing cases including *British Leyland* and *Deutsche Post,*[185] the Commission has imposed remedies requiring the dominant company to lower its prices. As a general rule, however, the Commission is reluctant to take on (let alone craft price control remedies in) excessive pricing cases. This difficulty relates as much to the identification of the abuse as to the potential difficulties in designing a suitable remedy. In predatory pricing cases, the Commission can refer itself to clear cost-based benchmarks for when prices may be abusively low (notwithstanding the difficulties of analysing companies' average variable and/or long-run average incremental costs). Conversely, in excessive pricing cases, *"it is difficult to tell whether in any given case an abusive price has been set for there is no objective way of establishing exactly what price covers costs plus*

---

[181] *See, e.g.,* Case IV/30.698, *supra* note 32, Articles 2 and 3; *Tetra Pak II Decision 1991, supra* note 40, Articles 2 and 3; Case COMP/38.233, *supra* note 65, Article 2.

[182] Case IV/30.698, *supra* note 32, Articles 1 and 3.

[183] Case COMP/35.141 *Deutsche Post,* Commission Decision of 20 March 2001, OJ 2001 L 125/27.

[184] *Ibid.,* Article 2. *See also* the price control and complementary measures imposed in *Austrian Airlines/Lufthansa* (Press Release IP/01/1832 of 14 December 2001; Press Release IP/02/1008 of 5 July 2002 and Notice pursuant to Article 16(3) of Council Regulation (EEC) No 3975/87 of 14 December 1987 concerning case IV/37.730 – Austrian Airlines Österreichische Luftverkehrs AG/Deutsche Lufthansa AG, OJ 2001 C 356/5). The Commission required that where Austrian Airlines and Lufthansa wished to reduce a published fare on a route in response to new entry, the merged entity would be required to apply an equivalent fare reduction (in per cent) on three other Austria-Germany city pairs where no competition existed. O'Donoghue and Padilla question the legality of these measures, since the parties were effectively required to reduce their prices in markets where no abusive conduct had been identified. *See* R. O'Donoghue and A. J. Padilla, *supra* note 63, p. 719. Similar undertakings were made by the merging parties in *Air France/KLM,* with respect to the Lyon-Paris and Paris-Amsterdam routes. Case COMP/M.3280 *Air France/KLM,* Commission Decision of 11 February 2004, para. 166.

[185] Case IV/30.615 *British Leyland,* Commission Decision of 2 July 1984, OJ 1984 L 207/11; Case COMP/35.141, *supra* note 183.

12. – Remedies
Thomas Graf and David R. Little

a reasonable profit margin."[186] The difficulties in assessing the economic value of goods and services, and the difficulties in determining what constitutes a reasonable profit on costs of production, are explored in Chapter 10 (Excessive Pricing) of this book.[187]

The approach of the Commission to margin squeeze cases is a hybrid of the approaches taken in predatory pricing and excessive pricing cases. In margin squeeze cases, it is the spread between the price on the upstream market and the price on the downstream market that determines whether the conduct is abusive – there is no need for either the price of the input to be excessive or the price of the second product to be predatory.[188] In the case of a margin squeeze, the appropriate remedy will be to raise either or both prices to reflect the "competitive spread". The company concerned therefore has some flexibility in addressing the concerns though adjustment of the input or the output price, or both, bearing in mind however that *"reducing the wholesale price may be ineffective if the reductions in wholesale charges are simply competed away in the retail market... increasing the dominant firm's retail price is likely to be pointless if it is already higher than rivals' retail prices."* [189]

12.93

2. Tying Abuse Remedies

Tying abuse remedies typically seek to prohibit the undertaking from requiring customers to acquire both tied and tying products. The expression of this prohibition has varied depending on the nature of the tie. Thus, in cases where the dominant undertaking's contract terms have required the customer to purchase both the tied and tying products, the Commission has ordered the undertaking to eliminate the offending provisions and to commit not to

12.94

---

[186] Fifth Report on Competition Policy (1975), para. 3.

[187] *See*, in particular, Section II.2.1.

[188] *See* Case T-271/03 *Deutsche Telekom v Commission* ("*Deutsche Telekom Judgment 2008*") [2008] ECR II-477, para. 167 ("*the abusive nature of the applicant's conduct is connected with the unfairness of the spread between its prices for wholesale access and its retail prices, which takes the form of a margin squeeze. Therefore, in view of the abuse found in the contested decision, the Commission was not required to demonstrate in that decision that the applicant's retail prices were, as such, abusive*"). Confirmed by the ECJ in Case C-543/09 *Deutsche Telekom v Bundesrepublik Deutschland* ("*Deutsche Telekom Judgment 2011*"), not yet reported. *See also* Case T-398/07 *Spain v Commission*, not yet reported ("*In particular, a pricing practice adopted by a vertically integrated dominant undertaking which is unfair because it effectively squeezes the margins of its competitors on the retail market, because of the spread between the prices of its wholesale products and the prices of its retail products, may constitute an abuse of a dominant position contrary to Article* [102 TFEU].").

[189] *Supra* note 63, p. 720.

12. – Remedies
Thomas Graf and David R. Little

implement similar restrictions in the future.[190] In cases where the dominant undertaking has tied separate products through technical integration, the Commission has required the technical separation of the two products. This was the case in *Microsoft*,[191] in which the Commission required Microsoft to offer in Europe a version of Windows without Windows Media Player preloaded onto the operating system.

12.95 *Microsoft* was the first time that the Commission had adopted a formal infringement decision in a case of technological tying.[192] The case therefore provided the first opportunity to assess the Commission's approach to designing remedies in such complex, technical cases. A number of criticisms have been made of the Commission's approach:

- In a statement released shortly after publication of the Commission's Decision, the DOJ's Assistant Attorney General for Antitrust criticised the proposed unbundling remedy:

  "The European Union has today pursued a different enforcement approach [to that of the US Courts] by imposing a 'code removal' remedy to resolve its media player concerns. The U.S. experience tells us that the best antitrust remedies eliminate impediments to the healthy functioning of competitive markets without hindering successful competitors or imposing burdens on third parties, which may result from the European Union's remedy... imposing 'code removal' remedies may produce unintended consequences. Sound antitrust policy must avoid chilling innovation and competition even by 'dominant' companies. A contrary approach risks protecting competitors, not

---

[190] *Tetra Pak II Decision 1991, supra* note 40; *supra* note 53. *See also* the Commission's commitments decision in Coca-Cola. The commitments enshrined Coca-Cola's commitment not to require purchasers of its best-selling beverage brands (*e.g.*, regular Coke or Fanta Orange) to also purchase less popular brands, conduct that the Commission concluded had *"reduced the variety for final consumers"* and alleviated *"downward pressure on price."* Case COMP/39.116, *supra* note 39, paras 34 and 42.

[191] *Microsoft Decision 2004 supra* note 25.

[192] A technological tie was identified in the IBM case in the 1980s. No formal decision was taken, although IBM committed to supply its CPUs for its mainframes without integrated memory devices (or, in any event, with only the minimum memory necessary for testing integrated). *See* Case IV/30.849 *IBM Personal Computer*, Commission Decision of 18 April 1984, OJ 1984 L 118/24. By contrast, the US competition authorities closed parallel proceedings against IBM without any infringement finding or commitments. Fisher has observed laconically: *"Simply put, IBM had no monopoly to protect, and its bundling actions could not have produced one. By contrast, Microsoft had monopoly power, and its bundling and related actions 'made no business sense' save for the protection of that power"*. *See* F. M. Fisher, "The IBM and Microsoft Cases: What's the Difference?" (2000) 90(2) *American Economic Review*, pp. 180–83.

12. – Remedies
Thomas Graf and David R. Little

competition, in ways that may ultimately harm innovation and the consumers that benefit from it."[193]

- As Apon notes, the observations of the Assistant Attorney General reflect underlying differences in the approach of the European Union and US antitrust authorities, specifically that (unlike the US authorities), the Commission seeks to protect rivalry as an end in itself. Notwithstanding these considerations, the Assistant Attorney General's statement overlooks two factors that we consider important. First, Microsoft was permitted to continue supplying a bundled version of Windows, such that there would be no burden on third parties. Second, the Commission aimed to stimulate dynamic competition in media player technology and, ultimately, greater competition in operating systems by creating incentives for the development of media player technology by third parties.[194]

- Although the Commission defined the relevant market as being worldwide in scope, the Commission imposed a remedy that was merely European Union-wide. The rationale for this territorial limitation was not explained in the Commission's infringement decision.

- The remedy did not include provisions on the pricing of the unbundled Windows version which impaired its effectiveness. In the absence of such provisions, Microsoft did not price Windows', "Edition N" at a lower price compared to the bundled version of Windows. Consumers and OEMs faced with a choice between the bundled and unbundled versions of Windows sold for the same price naturally plumped for the former. By requiring unbundling without

---

[193] *See* US Department of Justice, "Assistant Attorney General for Antitrust, R. Hewitt Pate, Issues Statement on the EC's Decision in its Microsoft Investigation" Press Release of March 24, 2004, available at http://www.justice.gov/opa/pr/2004/March/04_at_184.htm. The wording of the Assistant Attorney-General's statement echoed the prior ruling of the US Court of Appeals in the US Microsoft case. The Court of Appeals had rejected a *"code removal"* remedy in relation to the anticompetitive tying of Internet Explorer with Windows. It was felt that the remedy might be potentially disruptive to the industry, reduce incentives to innovate, and therefore harm consumers. *Massachusetts v Microsoft*, 373 F.3d 1199 (DC Cir. 2004), paras 1210 and 1211. *See* J. Apon, "Cases Against Microsoft: Similar Cases, Different Remedies" (2007) 28(6) *European Competition Law Review*, p. 334.

[194] *See* J. Apon, *supra* note 193, (*"The accusation that the remedy chosen* [in Europe] *would lead to less innovation is also debatable. Microsoft was not the inventor of either media players or browsers, it only made non-drastic derivative innovations to these products. Even if this kind of innovation by Microsoft would be chilled by the decision, the decision may well lead to 'a revival of innovation by competitors, leading to more relevant drastic new innovations.'"*).

12. – Remedies
Thomas Graf and David R. Little

differentiated pricing, the Commission may have hoped to avoid the need to regulate product prices. Vickers concludes that *"the Commission risked less and gained less* [with respect to the tying remedy] *than on interoperability."*[195]

12.96   Certain of these deficiencies were addressed in the 2009 Article 9 decision[196] that closed the Commission's second investigation into anticompetitive tying by Microsoft. Faced with a tie that had been in place for almost fifteen years, entrenching purchasing patterns of OEMs and volume licensees, the Commission developed an innovative solution. The commitments introduced a browser "Choice Screen" from which users and OEMs could select without incurring material research or technical costs from a range of Internet browsers (including Internet Explorer). The remedy therefore addressed some of the circumvention problems seen in the Edition N solution. Microsoft was permitted to ship Windows with Internet Explorer installed as the default browser and no differentiated pricing was required. However, Microsoft was obliged to present consumers and OEMs with an obligatory post-purchase customisation option, effectively a deferred, low-cost choice between three different versions of Windows: (1) a bundled version (if the OEM/consumer chose not to install an additional browser); (2) a "bundled plus" version (if the OEM/consumer chose to install an additional browser(s)); and (3) a *de facto* unbundled version (if the OEM/consumer opted for (2) and also "turned off" Internet Explorer using the simplified mechanism that Microsoft was required to introduce).[197] The remedy therefore addressed a number of the weaknesses identified above with respect to the remedy in the first *Microsoft* case. The browser remedy appears to have been more successful than the remedy in the first *Microsoft* case. Browser market shares in Europe have changed substantially since the Commission's remedy was introduced although not all of this development is necessarily attributable to the Commission's remedy.[198]

---

[195] *See* J. Vickers, *supra* note 153, p. 20.

[196] The Commission also considered the geographic scope of the remedy during market testing, again considering that it was not necessary to impose a world-wide remedy. The EEA was *"a large enough market for the Commitments to be implemented effectively"*. *Browser Commitment Decision, supra* note 12, para. 88.

[197] *See supra* note 196, Annex, clause 1.

[198] *See, e.g.*, B. Rooney, *"Europe Falls Out of Love With IE"*, The Wall Street Journal, January 4, 2011, available at http://blogs.wsj.com/tech-europe/2011/01/04/europe-falls-out-of-love-with-internet-explorer/. The article reports that, for the first time, Internet Explorer was not the most widely used browser in Europe, attributed by one industry analyst to the *"impact of the agreement between European Commission competition authorities and Microsoft"*.

12. – Remedies
Thomas Graf and David R. Little

3.   Refusal to Deal

As described in Chapter 7 (Refusal to Deal), the Commission does not take   **12.97**
lightly the decision to take action in refusal to supply cases.[199] The assessment
of whether intervention is required *"requires careful consideration where the appli-*
cation of Article [102] TFEU would lead to the imposition of an obligation to supply
on a dominant undertaking. Such a finding can only be based on a rigorous case by case
investigation and a careful balancing of conflicting considerations".[200] The Commission
recognises that forcing a competitor to deal with another impinges upon a
company's property rights and contractual autonomy, *i.e.*, the *"right to choose*
one's trading partners and freely to dispose of one's property".[201] Chapter 7[202] provides
a comprehensive discussion of how to balance the competing objectives of
policy enforcement, preserving incentives to innovate and protecting property rights. As the Commission summarised in its *DiscussionPaper*, *"the dominant*
firm must not be unduly restricted in the exploitation of valuable results of the invest-
ment" and that it should *"normally be free to seek compensation for successful projects*
that is sufficient to maintain investment incentives, taking the risk of failed projects into
account".[203] The difficulty of achieving this balance explains why intervention
in refusal to supply cases remains exceptional.[204]

---

[199] *See*, in particular, Section III.

[200] The Unilateral Conduct Working Group, *"Report on the Analysis of Refusal to Deal with a Rival Under Unilateral Conduct Laws"*, presented at the 9th Annual Conference of the ICN, Istanbul, April 2010. Report based on responses to a questionnaire submitted by competition agencies and non-governmental advisors from 43 jurisdictions, p. 34.

[201] Advocate General Jacobs in Case C-7/97 *Oscar Bronner v MediaprintZeitungs- und Zeitschriftenverlag and others* (*"Oscar Bronner"*) [1998] ECR I-7791. *See also Guidance Paper, supra* note 177, para. 75 (*"When setting its enforce-ment priorities, the Commission starts from the position that, generally speaking, any undertaking, whether dominant or not, should have the right to choose its trading partners and to dispose freely of its property. The Commission therefore considers that intervention on competition law grounds requires careful consideration where the application of Article 82 would lead to the imposition of an obligation to supply on the dominant undertaking."*). *See also* B. Ong, "Building Brick Barricades and Other Barriers to Entry: Abusing a Dominant Position by Refusing to Licence Intellectual Property Rights" (2005) 26 *European Competition Law Review,* pp. 213–22 (*"Imposing such duties to supply customers who may compete with the dominant firm is contrary to the basic freedom, of a firm operating in a market economy to choose who it deals with, if at all, and on what terms."*)

[202] *See*, in particular, Section III.2.

[203] DG Competition discussion paper on the application of Article 82 of the Treaty to exclusionary abuses (*"Discussion Paper"*), December 2005, para. 235.

[204] Case COMP/37.792 *Microsoft* (*"Microsoft Decision 2008"*), Commission Decision of 27 February 2008, not yet published, subject to appeal, paras 319, 330–32 and 336. *See Guidance Paper, supra* note 177, para. 75 (*"The existence of such an obligation – even for a fair remuneration – may undermine undertakings' incentives to invest and innovate and, thereby, possibly harm consumers. The knowledge that they may have a duty to supply against their will may lead dominant undertakings – or undertakings who anticipate that they may become dominant – not to invest, or to invest less, in the activity in question. Also,*

12. – Remedies
Thomas Graf and David R. Little

12.98 Once a facility is found to be essential and an obligation to supply exists, the Commission has the power under Article 7 of Regulation 1/2003[205] to require the undertaking concerned to bring the infringement to an end. A remedy normally reflects the abuse and, if the abuse is a refusal to deal, the remedy would be an order to deal. The Commission may set a reasonable deadline for full implementation of the remedy with appropriate speed to minimise ongoing negative effects of the abuse.[206]

12.99 As the Commission noted in *Microsoft*, "*the natural remedy to* [an] *abusive refusal to supply is an order to supply what has been refused*."[207] The refusal might be a new refusal of an input from which the party seeking access has never before benefited, or it might be an input that the dominant undertaking has refused to continue supplying (*e.g.*, *Commercial Solvents*). The input refused could be a physical facility (*e.g.*, *British Midland/Aer Lingus, Port of Rodby, Sea Containers*), information (*Microsoft, IMS Health*), or something else. Although in most cases an order to supply what has been refused will be appropriate, the principle of proportionality requires that the remedy in a refusal to supply case "*not exceed what is appropriate and necessary to attain* [...] *the establishment of compliance with the rules infringed*".[208] As such, where the infringement could be remedied by measures that stop short of compulsory supply of the input, this less burdensome alternative should be used. For example, in *Volvo v Veng*, the undertaking was given a choice between exploiting the technology itself and licensing rivals, or exploiting the technology while committing to supply rivals with spare parts based on that technology at non-excessive prices.

12.100 While the basic principle of ordering the supply of a withheld input is simple, the devil is in the detail. The terms on which supply is mandated raises considerable difficulties and again requires a careful balancing of competing rights and incentives.

---

competitors may be tempted to free ride on investments made by the dominant undertaking instead of investing themselves. Neither of these consequences would, in the long run, be in the interest of consumers.")

[205] *Regulation 1/2003.*

[206] If the undertaking does not fully implement the remedy before the time limit set by the Commission's Decision, periodic penalty payments may be imposed. *See* Case COMP/37.792 *Microsoft* ("*Microsoft Decision 2006*"), Commission Decision of 12 July 2006, not yet published, fixing the definitive amount of the periodic penalty payment imposed on Microsoft (confirmed on appeal in *Microsoft Judgment 2007 supra* note 43).

[207] *See Microsoft Decision 2004 supra* note 25, para. 998.

[208] *See Magill, supra* note 44, para. 93.

12. – Remedies
Thomas Graf and David R. Little

Remedies for abusive conduct should be proportionate. The Court of Jus- **12.101**
tice held in Magill that *"the burdens imposed on undertakings in order to bring an
infringement of competition law to an end must not exceed what is appropriate and necessary to attain the objective sought, namely re-establishment of compliance with the rules
infringed."*[209] This means that the remedy must be effective in eliminating the
abuse, and at the same time the remedy should limit the dominant firm's
freedom of action as little as possible. For instance, if a less-burdensome
remedy can be found that effectively addresses the competition concerns
of a refusal to license, the Commission should not resort to an order for
compulsory licensing, and if there are several effective ways to eliminate an
abuse, the owner of the IPR should be allowed the choice. The scenarios
mentioned in the *Volvo* case can be used to provide a hypothetical example.
The Court held that the exercise of the design right could be an abuse in a
context where Volvo also refused to supply spare parts or fixed the prices
for body panels at an unfair level.[210] In such a case, if a finding of abuse
were made, Volvo should be allowed the choice to either license its design
rights at a reasonable fee or refuse a licence but supply the spare part to
independent repairers at a price that is not excessive and cannot be seen as
a constructive refusal to supply.

The question arises whether antitrust authorities or courts can demand that **12.102**
dominant firms expand capacity, and thus dictate the allocation of their private capital. In a few cases, the Commission considered that the inefficient
use of existing capacity gave rise to a situation of artificial congestion, but
concluded that such a situation could be resolved through (not particularly
costly) organisational measures,[211] by expanding the essential infrastructure
at the expense of the complainant.[212] In other cases, the defendant agreed to

---

[209] *See Magill*, para. 93.

[210] *See Volvo*, paras 9–10.

[211] *See* Case IV/34.801 *FAG – Flughafen Frankfurt/Main ("Frankfurt Airport")*, Commission Decision of
14 January 1998, OJ 1998 L 72/30, paras 86–8; *See* Case 94/119/EC *Port of Rødby*, Commission Decision of
21 December 1993, OJ 1994 L 55/52, para. 15.

[212] *Ibid. See also* Case IV/34.689 *Sea Containers/Stena Sealink – Interim measures*, Commission Decision of
21 December 1993, OJ 1994 L 15/8 Case IV/34.689, paras 70–1.

12. – Remedies

Thomas Graf and David R. Little

release reserved capacity,[213] to manage congestion differently,[214] or to divest its infrastructure.[215]

12.103 Article 102 TFEU should probably not be read as – or used for – creating an obligation on dominant companies to build or expand infrastructures at their own expense to foster competitors' entry, unless there is clear and convincing evidence that a rational non-dominant or non-vertically integrated supplier would have done so. To force dominant companies to make onerous investments could amplify the negative effects that are traditionally associated with the application of the essential facilities doctrine. The possibility for competitors to take advantage of dominant undertakings' productive assets, even when available capacity is lacking, could reduce the incentives to develop new infrastructures or alternative resources[216] and could foster the entry of inefficient competitors. Furthermore, an antitrust obligation to invest in infrastructures

---

[213] In Case COMP/39.316, *supra* note 10, the Commission found that GDF Suez's long-term reservations for most of France's gas import capacity and its behaviour relating to investment and capacity allocation at two liquefied natural gas import terminals in France closed off access to the French gas market to competitors. GDF offered commitments to release a large share of its long-term reservations of gas import capacity into France. In Case COMP/39.317, *supra* note 10, the Commission raised concerns that E.ON's booking on a long-term basis the largest part of the available transport capacity at the entry points into its gas transmission networks prevented other gas suppliers from accessing the German gas market. E.ON committed to release large capacity volumes at the entry points to its gas networks.

[214] *See, e.g.,* Case COMP/39.351, *supra* note 10, the Commission raised concerns that SvenskaKraftnät was limiting the amount of export transmission capacity available on electricity interconnectors situated along Sweden's borders, with the objective of relieving internal congestion on its electricity network. The Commission assumed that this would favour consumers in Sweden over consumers in neighbouring EU and EEA Member States by reserving domestically produced electricity for domestic consumption. To alleviate these concerns, SvenskaKraftnät in particular committed to subdivide the Swedish transmission system into two or more bidding zones and to manage congestion in the Swedish transmission system without limiting trading capacity on interconnectors.

[215] *See, e.g.,* Cases COMP/39.388, *supra* note 10 (The Commission had concerns that E.ON had withdrawn available generation capacity from the German wholesale electricity markets, and had deterred new investors in generation. Additionally, the Commission had concerns that E.ON favoured its production affiliate for providing balancing services and had prevented other power producers from exporting balancing energy into its transmission zone. E.ON committed to divest part of its generation capacity to address the concerns regarding the generation market and to divest its extra-high voltage network.). In Case COMP/39.402, *supra* note 10, the Commission had concerns that RWE had abused the dominant position on its gas transmission network to restrict its competitors' access to the network. The Commission's concerns related to a possible refusal to supply gas transmission services to other companies and to a margin squeeze aimed at RWE's downstream competitors in gas supply. To address the Commission's competition concerns, RWE committed to divest its Western German high-pressure gas transmission network; *See* Case COMP/39.315, *supra* note 10, paras 41–2, (*see* below, leading to divestment).

[216] The reduction of incentives to develop alternative resources would, in the long term, produce the result of consolidating the dominance of the infrastructure holder, as no alternatives would be created. *See also* J. Temple-Lang, "Defining Legitimate Competition: Companies' Duties to Supply Competitors and Access to Essential Facilities", in B. E. Hawk (Ed.), *Fordham Competition Law Institute: International Antitrust Law and Policy 1994* (New York, Juris Publishing, 1995), p. 245.

12. – Remedies
Thomas Graf and David R. Little

is difficult to reconcile with Article 345 TFEU as it would affect infrastructure holders' freedom to invest.[217] Investments in new or existing network infrastructures should rather be encouraged by *ad hoc* regulatory measures. This approach could allow for a more efficient and proportionate approach than using Article 102 TFEU, and would also have the advantage of being designed on the basis of the specific needs of the sector at issue without distorting the incentives of firms active in other product or geographic areas.[218]

The earlier case law on refusal to supply suggests that the Commission has sought   **12.104**
to avoid becoming embroiled in detailed discussions of the terms of access and has instead preferred to leave this to negotiation by the parties.[219] This approach is shown, for example, in *British Midland/Aer Lingus*, where the Commission required Aer Lingus within two months to grant British Midland (through making the necessary changes to its transportation documents) the possibility of interlining on the London-Dublin route and to refrain from any conduct that might jeopardize *"the normal implementation of that arrangement"*.[220] The access requirement would remain in place for two years.[221] In *Sea Containers*, the Commission gave its imprimatur to interim terms of access negotiated and agreed between the two parties.[222] In *Port of Rødby*, the Commission required the Danish Government to inform it within two months of the measures it had taken to enable the development by Euro-Port and Scan-Port of port facilities in Rødby.[223]

3.1. Structural Remedies

In exceptional situations, the Commission may impose structural remedies to   **12.105**
address refusal to supply-type concerns.[224] In *ENI*, the Commission expressed concern about ENI's constructive refusal to supply access to certain pipeline

---

[217] S. Purps and U. Scholz, "The Application of EC Competition Law in the Energy Sector" 2010 1(1) *Journal of European Competition Law & Practice*, pp. 37–51.

[218] G. Faella and P. Merlino, *"L'obbligo d'investire nello sviluppo di infrastrutture: note a margine di due storie parallele"*, Società Italiana di Diritto ed Economia, Seventh Annual Conference, 17 December 2011.

[219] This preference has found some support in the doctrine. *See supra* note 63, p. 723.

[220] Case IV/33.544 *British Midland/Aer Lingus*, Commission Decision of 26 February 1992, OJ 1992 L 96/34, para. 43.

[221] *Ibid.,* paras 43 and 44.

[222] Case IV/34.689 *Sea Containers/Stena Sealink – Interim measures*, Commission Decision of 21 December 1993, OJ 1994 L 15/8, para. 79.

[223] Case 94/119/EC, *supra* note 211.

[224] Article 7 of Regulation 1/2003 provides that: "[s]*tructural remedies can only be imposed either where there is no equally effective behavioural remedy or where any equally effective behavioural remedy would be more burdensome for the undertaking concerned than the structural remedy"*. *See Regulation 1/2003.*

12. – Remedies
Thomas Graf and David R. Little

infrastructures used to import natural gas into Italy.[225] The Commission rejected capacity limitations as a justification, and argued that ENI had engaged in capacity hoarding, capacity degradation and strategic underinvestment, all ultimately aimed at reducing the amount of gas flowing into Italy. The Commission took the view that ENI's strategy derived from the inherent conflict of interest a vertically integrated company faces if it is dominant on downstream sales markets. That conflict was said to have prompted ENI to forgo profitable investments in the upstream market in order to protect the larger profits it obtained in the downstream markets.[226] Under threat of a large fine and structural remedies, ENI committed to divest all of its participation in the companies owning the TAG, TENP and Transitgas pipelines and/or acting as TSOs on such infrastructures. This effectively amounted to ownership unbundling of ENI's gas network infrastructure.

12.106 The Commission's approach in the *ENI* case, as well as in other similar recent cases in the energy sector,[227] suggest that the Commission used its antitrust powers to obtain what is ultimately a regulatory goal, *i.e.*, ownership unbundling of transmission activities, which it has been unable to push through the Council and the Parliament in the context of the adoption of the Third Energy Package.[228]

3.2. Treatment of Physical Inputs as Compared with IPR

12.107 The case law does not suggest any clear difference of approach taken by the Commission in remedying refusals to supply access to physical assets as compared with refusals to supply access to valuable IPR. There may be theoretical arguments in favour of a difference of approach. For example, unlike use of a physical input that is exhaustible or limited by capacity constraints, use of IPR is not necessarily rivalrous. In the case of a physical asset, it may therefore be easier to identify a point at which another company's exploitation of

---

[225] *See* Case COMP/39.315, *supra* note 10, paras 41–42.

[226] *Ibid.*, para. 90.

[227] *See also*, for instance, *supra* note 215 Cases COMP/39.388 and COMP/39.389; *see* COMP/39.402, *supra* note 10.

[228] Full ownership unbundling, though present in Directive 2009/73, is not mandatory as the Directive provides for two alternative unbundling models (Parliament and Council Directive 2009/73/EC of 13 July 2009 concerning common rules for the internal market in natural gas and repealing Directive 2003/55/EC, OJ 2009 L 211/94). That the Commission's ultimate goal was ownership unbundling of transmission activities is also indirectly confirmed by the circumstance that ENI's divestiture commitments accepted by the Commission are unable to address the allegedly abusive hoarding and degradation of secondary capacity, *i.e.*, activities carried out by ENI as a shipper, rather than as a TSO.

12. – Remedies
Thomas Graf and David R. Little

the asset becomes impossible or economically inefficient, which may in turn call into question the imposition of an access remedy. On the other hand (as discussed in Chapter 7), IPR are generally limited in time. However, as a practical matter these theoretical distinctions are not clearly reflected in a difference of approach in the case law. This may be accident rather than design: more recent case law relating to refusals to supply has tended to focus on the licensing of IPR, while the Commission's older case law – in which access to physical assets has been at issue – has typically said very little about remedies.

For both IPR licensing cases and physical input access cases, FRAND principles may provide a useful framework for determining terms and conditions of access that do not simply replace an absolute refusal to deal with a constructive refusal to deal.[229] Although FRAND can be a difficult concept, the case law offers some instruction: **12.108**

If a duty to deal is imposed, the question arises what the terms and conditions should be, and what methodology could be used to determine the access fees, if any. A dominant firm that is found to have illegally refused to deal, may have incentives to deprive the remedy of useful effect by claiming high access fees that are equivalent to a constructive refusal to deal.[230] The Commission must therefore monitor the implementation of the remedy, and if necessary, intervene to ensure its useful effect. The US Supreme Court suggested in *Trinko* that imposing a duty to deal for this reason risks turning antitrust authorities into "*central planners*".[231] That said, it is possible to derive a number of minimum standards from the general principles that govern remedies, abusive pricing, and telecommunications regulation.[232] At the very least, the general principles of on-abusive pricing should apply: the price for the input product should not set in a manner that would in itself be abusive.   **12.109**

---

[229] See *supra* note 25, Article. 5, and the detailed discussion in paras 1005–09.

[230] For example, the Commission imposed a fine on Microsoft in connection with its initial demand for significant royalties for the Workgroup Server Protocol Program that, according to the Commission, were prohibitive and even exceeded the price for the end-product (the royalties charged to server manufacturers for entry-level server operating systems), causing price-squeeze concerns. See Commission Decision imposing fines for excessive royalties *Microsoft Decision 2008 supra* note 204, confirmed on appeal in Case T-167/08 *Microsoft v Commission*, ("*Microsoft Judgment 2012*") not yet reported.

[231] See *Trinko*, where it held that a duty to deal risks turning antitrust authorities in "*central planners*" (*Verizon Communications v Law Offices of Curtis v Trinko* ("*Trinko*"), 540 US 398 (2004), p. 408.).

[232] For a comprehensive view on remedies and pricing in the communication sector, see European Regulators Group, "*Revised ERG Common Position on the approach to Appropriate remedies in the ECNS regulatory framework*", May 2006.

12. – Remedies
Thomas Graf and David R. Little

- Terms are not FRAND if they would introduce new distortions of competition.[233] Thus: (1) the price charged for the input should not be set so high as to constitute a *de facto* refusal to supply (refusal to supply rules) or bear no reasonable relationship to the economic value of the input (excessive pricing rules); (2) nor should the price be discriminatory, *i.e.,* impose a direct or indirect competitive disadvantage on the rivals of the dominant firm in the downstream market; (3) there should be no loyalty discounts, exclusivity discounts, financial tying, or other element in the pricing for the upstream product that could result in the distortion of competition in the downstream market; (4) the price of the downstream product supplied by the dominant firm must not be predatory; (5) the dominant firm must not engage in margin squeeze abuses; and (6) the non-price terms and conditions must not include unfair provisions within the meaning of Article 102 TFEU or restrict competition in breach of Article 101 TFEU.

- As stated in *Microsoft*, "*restrictions should not create disincentives to compete with* [the dominant firm], *or unnecessarily restrain the ability of the beneficiaries to innovate.*"[234]

- For a further discussion of these elements, reference is made to the Chapters on excessive pricing (Chapter 10), abusive discrimination (Chapter 9), other abuses (Chapter 11), tying and bundling (Chapter 8), predatory conduct (Chapter 4), and margin squeeze (Chapter 5). In view of the similarity between essential inputs and *de facto* industry standards, reference is also made to the discussion of FRAND conditions in the Chapter on excessive pricing (Chapter 10).

- Where the refusal to supply is discriminatory or relates to an interruption of supplies, there will be a rebuttable presumption that the fee charged to other customers, or the price imposed before the supplies were interrupted, is a good indication of a fair and reasonable price.[235] This may be countered, for example, if it is shown that comparator markets or agreements are not competitive.

---

[233] *See Microsoft Decision 2004 supra* note 25, para. 1006.

[234] *See Microsoft Decision 2004 supra* note 25, para. 1008.

[235] A remedy should allow differential treatment only if it is justified by proportional objective justifications. This requires that the differential treatment (1) attain a legitimate procompetitive and non-pretextual objective, (2) is effective in attaining that objective, (3) necessary to obtain the objective (there is no less restrictive alternative), and (4) a weighing of the interests of the parties involved (balance-of-interest test) confirms that the benefit to consumers outweighs the consumer harm. For example, a cross-licence may justify a royalty readjustment if it is agreed to at arms' length and fair value is paid on both sides. Ultimately, the royalty system should ensure a level playing field between all participants in the market when dealing with the licensor.

12. – Remedies
Thomas Graf and David R. Little

- In all cases, including *de novo* refusals to deal, a fair and reasonable price is a proportionate one, bearing some rational relation to objective assessment of the innovative value added by the technology protected by the IPR or the costs and risk of creating the input. This is a price equivalent to the inherent value of the property, rather than a price derived from any anticompetitive behaviour.

- As explained in the Commission's *Microsoft* Decision, the royalties and terms and conditions should not reflect the "*strategic value*" stemming from the dominant firm's market power in the upstream market that is being leveraged or in the downstream or neighbouring market where as a result of the refusal to deal, the leveraging had resulted in a dominant position as well.[236] A dominant firm can charge, at most, for the value of innovation or creation of the upstream asset, but cannot charge a fee that would appropriate profits in the downstream market, *i.e.*, cannot request compensation for the opportunity cost of allowing competition in the downstream or neighbouring market. Secondly, the Commission held that in order for a dominant firm to be able to charge a non-nominal remuneration, three conditions must be met: the asset must be the dominant firm's own creation, it must be innovative, and the remuneration must be in line with a market valuation for comparable technologies.[237] In its Microsoft judgment, the General Court held that the "*distinction between the strategic value and the intrinsic value [...] is a basic premise of the assessment of the reasonableness of any remuneration charged by Microsoft*"[238] The Court noted that "*allowing Microsoft to charge remuneration rates reflecting [...] strategic value [...] would in effect allow it to transform the benefits of the abuse into remuneration for the grant of licences*".[239]

Even with these criteria, absent a competitive market, the "innovative value" **12.110** or the "fair market value" of an input product may be difficult to determine. The *Microsoft* case is an interesting example where it was possible, albeit probably an unusual one. The Trustee and the Commission reviewed extensive evidence that the non-patented basic ideas incorporated in the interoperability specifications were generally known in the industry and not novel, and that at the time the interoperability specifications for Windows were developed,

---

[236] *See Microsoft Decision 2004 supra* note 25, para. 1008. Confirmed in *Microsoft Judgment 2012 supra* note 230.

[237] *See Microsoft Decision 2008 supra* note 204, para. 280, paras 116 *et seq* and 165 (appealed in *Microsoft Judgment 2012 supra* note 230).

[238] *Microsoft Judgment 2012 supra* note 230, para. 138.

[239] *Ibid.*, para. 142.

12. – Remedies
Thomas Graf and David R. Little

alternative technologies of equal quality were available that could have been used by third parties "but for" the fact that Microsoft did not use them and they therefore did not allow interoperability with Windows on an "equal footing" with other Windows systems.[240] Moreover, the Trustee and the Commission determined that the information was not of a kind for which – absent a monopoly – licensors would expect to be paid or licensees would be prepared to pay.[241] Indeed, absent a monopoly, it is rational for an operating system developer to disclose interoperability information for free since the availability of fully-interoperable complementary products increases the attractiveness and value of its system, and both Microsoft itself and its rivals made comparable information freely available in situations of non-dominance.[242] The Commission concluded that the non-patented interoperability information had no intrinsic value beyond allowing licensees to interoperate with Microsoft's monopoly products – *i.e.*, no value other than the strategic value of controlling access to the neighbouring market. In its 2012 *Microsoft* judgment, the General Court confirmed the Commission's assessment.[243] The Court agreed that a review of the innovative character of the technologies at issue served as a suitable "*filter for strategic value*".[244]

12.111   The economic theory underpinning this approach seems relatively clear: in competitive conditions and absent strategic considerations, if the technology to be licensed is equivalent to alternative freely available technology, there is no reason to believe that the IPR owner, absent its monopoly, would find a buyer or be able to charge a monopoly price for it.[245] In a competitive and

---

[240] *Ibid.*, para. 280 (appealed in *Microsoft Judgment 2012 supra* note 230). The decision contained a detailed analysis and findings with regard to the absence of innovation (paras 169–219) and a detailed market evaluation of comparable technologies (paras 222–72).

[241] *Ibid.*, paras 223–37 (subject to appeal).

[242] As the Court of First instance found in the *Microsoft Judgment 2007 supra* note 43, para. 307, *"Microsoft's initial policy was to disclose interoperability information, not to retain it, which, among other things, helped Microsoft to introduce its own work group server operating systems on the market"*. In *Microsoft Decision 2004 supra* note 25, paras 223–30, the Commission found that Microsoft itself provided and continued to provide interoperability information of the kind at issue for free in areas where it suits its strategic needs (paras 223–30), and that other developers routinely provide interoperability information without charging royalties (paras 231–37). Absent its monopoly position, the Commission argued that Microsoft would have an inherent interest in making the information at issue available for free since this would drive sales of its software products, in particular its desktop operating systems. Finally, it argued that Microsoft is fully remunerated for the creation of the licensed information through the sale of client and server operating systems.

[243] *Microsoft Judgment 2012 supra* note 230.

[244] *Ibid.*, para. 149.

[245] *See also*, in a standards context, J. Posner in *Apple v Motorola*, No. 1:11-cv-08540, slip op. (N.D. Ill. Jun. 22, 2012), available at https://www.eff.org/sites/default/files/Posner_Apple_v_Motorola_0.pdf, *"The proper method of computing a FRAND royalty starts with what the cost to the licensee would have been of obtaining, just before the patented invention*

12. – Remedies
Thomas Graf and David R. Little

non-collusive environment, royalties for equivalent and competitive techni-cal solutions would tend towards marginal costs. Where technologies are not equivalent, the owner of the better solution is able to charge no more than the incremental value that the licensee expects from the use of the better solution (for instance, because it saves costs, leads to expansion of demand, or allows the licensee to charge higher prices to end users). The fee for the best solution is no higher than the opportunity cost that the licensee would incur if it used the next best alternative.

Apart perhaps from situations comparable to *Microsoft*, it is however generally not easy in practice to determine FRAND prices. That said, several proxies may be available, some of which have been used in past cases under Article 102(a).[246] First, it might be possible to compare the price charged with the his-torical or long-run average incremental cost ("*LRAIC*") of R&D, plus a profit comparable to the normal return on investment in competitive conditions in the industry in question. However, using past R&D expenses as a basis for FRAND pricing is imperfect, especially in dynamic markets such as IT where success is uncertain. It is difficult to determine a fair reward for risk, and future R&D may be very different from, and more or less costly than, past innovation costs. More generally, in some cases the inherent values of the input may be signifi-cantly higher than its LRAIC for example, if there are high development risks. In other cases, the inherent value may be significantly lower than its LRAIC, if alternatives are available. **12.112**

A fallback would be a consistent comparison with the prices of similar products charged by the supplier to third parties for access in competitive markets, fees charged by the supplier to its own downstream business, or the price imposed by rivals for similar technology in competitive environments. Information of **12.113**

---

was declared essential to compliance with the industry standard, a license for the function performed by the patent. That cost would be a measure of the value of the patent qua patent. But once a patent becomes essential to a standard, the patentee's bargaining power surges because a prospective licensee has no alternative to licensing the patent; he is at the patentee's mercy. The purpose of the FRAND requirements, the validity of which Motorola doesn't question, is to confine the patentee's royalty demand to the value conferred by the patent itself as distinct from the additional value – the hold-up value – conferred by the patent's being designated as standard-essential."

[246] See e.g., Case 26/75 *General Motors Continental v Commission* ("*General Motors*") [1975] ECR 1367; Case 27/76 *United Brands and United Brands Continentaal v Commission* ("*United Brands*")[1978] ECR 207; Case 30/87 *Corinne Bodson v Pompesfunèbres des régionslibérées* ("*Bodson*") [1988] ECR 2479; Case 395/87 *Ministère Public v Jean-Louis Tournier* ("*Tournier*") [1989] ECR 2521, para. 38; and *Deutsche Post, supra* note 15.

12. – Remedies
Thomas Graf and David R. Little

this kind played an important role in the *Microsoft* case as well.[247] Two comments should be kept in mind:

- First, even if comparable facilities are made available for a fee, it does not necessarily follow that the dominant owner should be allowed to charge an equivalent fee. It may be that the owner of the comparable facility is able to charge a fee only because the market in which it is active is not competitive. Comparables should be reviewed, but only on a "consistent basis", ensuring that adjustments are made for differences in the relative situations, different volumes, or quality difference. General practices in the industry may provide guidance also.[248]

- Secondly, for a remedy involving a compulsory licensing scheme to work, access must be set at a price low enough for an equally or more efficient licensee to compete viably. In order for a remedy to have a useful effect and achieve its goal (elimination of the abuse as well as restoration of competitive conditions), in some cases, it may require the dominant firm to lower its fees to a sustainable level – or at least the level that would have prevailed absent the exclusionary conduct – until competitive conditions have been restored, and further pricing can be left to the market.

---

[247] The FTC remedy decision in *Rambus* is an interesting example. *See* FTC Final Order of February 5, 2007 in the matter of Rambus Inc., FTC Docket No. 9302, § III.B, and Opinion of the Commission on Remedy of February 5, 2007 in the matter of Rambus Inc., FTC Docket No. 9302, § III.B (overturned on other grounds). *See also* Dissenting Opinion of Commissioner Pamela Jones Harbour of February 5, 2007 in the matter of Rambus, Inc., FTC Docket No. 9302, and Dissenting Opinion of Commissioner J. Thomas Rosch of Feburary 5, 2007 in the matter of Rambus, Inc. FTC Docket No. 9302, available at http://www.ftc.gov/os/adjpro/d9302/070205roschstmnt.pdf. (remedy should be royalty-free). When the FTC found that Rambus set a "patent ambush", it set a royalty of 0.5 per cent for the patents in question (going to zero after three years), where Rambus had asked for a permanent royalty of 2.5 per cent. In determining the terms of such a RAND license, the FTC noted the inherent difficulties attendant to reconstructing marketplace conditions that would have prevailed in the absence of anticompetitive conduct. The FTC held, however, that antitrust defendants should not be allowed to avoid appropriate remedies because determining the but-for world is challenging in practice. Opinion of the Commission on Remedy, pp. 16–19. The FTC found that a RAND license requires a royalty rate no higher than the *ex ante* value of the technology, which "*is the amount that the industry participants would have been willing to pay to use a technology over its next best alternative prior to the incorporation of the technology into a standard.*" Opinion of the Commission on Remedy, p. 17. To determine the specific royalty rate, the FTC turned to "*real-world examples of negotiations involving similar technologies.*" Opinion of the Commission on Remedy, p. 18.

[248] For licensing, for instance, *see, e.g.,* R. Goldscheider, *New Companion to Licensing Negotiations: Licensing Law Handbook* (4th Ed., St. Paul, West Group, 2003), para. 7.02 [8][b].

12. – Remedies
Thomas Graf and David R. Little

In the context of standard-setting, the question has arisen to what extent an **12.114**
IPR owner subject to a FRAND obligation is nonetheless entitled to seek
injunctive relief against infringers of the IPR.[249] Certain patent holders argue
that exclusion of the right to seek injunctions would contravene the Charter
on Fundamental Rights.[250] The same issue arises in the context of remedies for
unlawful refusal to license. The answer is controversial, but even if a FRAND
license obligation is imposed as a remedy, it is likely that a license may be
refused, and consequently the employment of an injunction to prevent the
use of the relevant patent might be justified, in three scenarios.[251] First, where
the licensee controls essential patents reading on the product in question and
refuses to cross-license these to the licensor, or license these to the licensor's
customers, on FRAND terms. Secondly, where a licensee is unable or unwilling to pay a FRAND royalty or commits an actual or anticipatory material
breach of the license that cannot be remedied otherwise. Thirdly, where a
licensee refuses to negotiate in good faith to reach a FRAND licensing agreement and is unwilling to submit the determination of the royalty to a court or
arbitral tribunal.[252]

An appropriate statement to conclude this section is the Commission's con- **12.115**
sideration in the *Discussion Paper* on Abuse of Dominance, a section that does
not appear in the *Guidance Paper*, but that is nevertheless still relevant:

> *"In the assessment of a refusal to supply it must also be kept in mind that the
> indispensable input, be it a raw material, an essential facility or an intellectual*

---

[249] *See* Reference for Preliminary Ruling in *Huawei v ZTE*, Case 4b O 104/12, Decision of Landgericht Duesseldorf,
21 March 2013. *See also* Press Release IP/20/89 of 31 January 2012, and IP/12/1448 of 21 December 2012. *See also*
in a standards context, J. Posner in *Apple v Motorola, supra* note 245,"*I don't see how, given FRAND, I would be justified in
enjoining Apple from infringing the '898 unless Apple refuses to pay a royalty that meets the FRAND requirement. By committing to
license its patents on FRAND terms, Motorola committed to license the '898 to anyone willing to pay a FRAND royalty and thus
implicitly acknowledged that a royalty is adequate compensation for a license to use that patent. How could it do otherwise?*" *See also
Microsoft v Motorola*, 696 F.3d 872, 876 (9th Cir. 2012), "*Implicit in such a sweeping promise [to license a patent on FRAND
terms] is, at least arguably, a guarantee that the patent-holder will not take steps to keep would-be users from using the patented material, such as seeking an injunction, but will instead proffer licenses consistent with the commitment made.*" *See also* K.-U. Kuehn,
F. Scott Morton and H. Shelanski "Standard Setting Organizations Can Help Solve the Standards Essential Patents
Licensing Problem", (March 2013) *CPI Antitrust Chronicle*.
[250] *See* B. Vesterdorf (former President of the European Court of First instance), "IP Rights and Competition
Law Enforcement Questions" (2013) *Journal of European Competition Law and Practice*, p. 1.
[251] *Cf.* Decision and Order, of January 3, 2013 in the matter of *Motorola Mobility and Google*, FTC File No. 121
0120 *See also* M. Dolmans and D. Ilan, "European Antitrust and Patent Acquisitions; Trolls in the Patent" (2012)
8(2) *Competition Law International*.
[252] *See* B. Crabb, denying Apple's request in *Apple v Motorola*, No. 11-cv-178-bbc, slip op. (W.D. Wis. Nov. 2,
2012).

12. – Remedies
Thomas Graf and David R. Little

property right, often is the result of substantial investments entailing significant risks. In order to maintain incentives to invest and innovate, the dominant firm must not be unduly restricted in the exploitation of valuable results of the investment. For these reasons the dominant firm should normally be free to seek compensation for successful projects that is sufficient to maintain investment incentives, taking the risk of failed projects into account. To achieve such compensation, it may be necessary for the dominant firm to exclude others from access to the input for a certain period of time. The risks facing the parties and the sunk investment that must be committed may thus mean that an dominant firm should be allowed to exclude others for a certain period of time in order to ensure an adequate return on such investment,[253] even when this entails eliminating effective competition during this period."[254]

4. Remedies in Discrimination Cases

12.116 Non-discrimination obligations have been employed in a variety of Article 102 cases, including those involving refusals to supply[255] excessive pricing,[256] and essential facility type cases framed in the formal discrimination concerns.[257]

12.117 Two principal issues arise in developing non-discrimination remedies. First, the content of the non-discrimination obligation and, secondly, the way in which the non-discrimination obligation is monitored and enforced.

4.1. The Content of the Non-discrimination Obligation

12.118 The meaning of "non-discriminatory" appears initially to be quite straightforward. The dominant undertaking should afford treatment to a particular

---

[253] *See also* Commission Notice – Guidelines on the application of Article 81(3) of the Treaty ("*Notice on Article 101(3) TFEU*"), OJ 2004 C 101/97, and *see* Joined Cases T-374, 375, 384 and 388/94 *European Night Services and others v Commission* ("*European Night Services*") [1998] ECR II-3141, para. 230.

[254] *Discussion Paper supra* note 203, para. 235.

[255] *See, e.g.,* Case IV/31.851, *supra* note 67; and Case IV/34.600 *Night Services*, Commission Decision of 21 September 1994, OJ 1994 L 259/20.

[256] *See, e.g.,* Case IV/30.615, *supra* note 185; and *Deutsche Post, supra* note 15.

[257] *See, e.g.,* Case 95/364/EC *Brussels National Airport*, Commission Decision of 28 June 1995, OJ 1995 L 216/8; *Tetra Pak II Decision 1991, supra* note 40; Case T-83/91 *Tetra Pak International v Commission* ("*Tetra Pak II Judgment 1994*") [1994] ECR II-755; and Case C-333/94 P *Tetra Pak International v Commission* ("*Tetra Pak II Judgment 1996*") [1996] ECR I-5951.

12. – Remedies
Thomas Graf and David R. Little

customer (which may be a rival or may have no competitive relationship with the dominant company) no less favourable than the treatment accorded to other customers.

However, not all customers are in identical positions – the costs, scale, and bargaining strength of customers will all vary. The question therefore arises whether a non-discrimination obligation does, or indeed, should, require that the dominant undertaking treat its customers identically, or whether on the contrary some difference in treatment is permissible. The former would create an inflexible straitjacket that would preclude the company from reasonably adjusting its practices to the specific circumstances of individual cases. It would also be irreconcilable with the concept of discrimination, which holds that discriminatory treatment only arises where similar situations are treated differently. On the other hand, it seems difficult if not impossible to fix *ex ante* the criteria and conditions that allow differentiation without discrimination.

12.119

The case law offers little guidance. In *United Brands*, no allowance was made for non-material discrimination. In that case, the company was required "*to eliminate differences in the prices charged to its distributor/ripeners in the various Member States concerned, in so far as the transactions are equivalent and as there is no objective justification for those differences*"[258] (emphasis added). In *Irish Sugar*[259], an illustrative list was given of the types of discriminatory discounting practices that fell within the scope of the non-discrimination obligation but it is not clear whether there was any materiality threshold applicable to the requirement that the company "*refrain from applying dissimilar conditions to equivalent transactions with its industrial sugar customers*".[260] In *Tetra Pak II*, having found that the dominant undertaking's conduct included discriminatory pricing,[261] the Commission required that Tetra Pak: (1) "*ensure that any differences between the prices charged for its products in the various Member States result solely from the specific market conditions*" and (2) "*not practise [...] discriminatory prices and [...] not grant to any customer any form of discount on its products or more favourable payment terms not justified by an objective*

12.120

---

[258] Case IV/26.699 *Chiquita*, Commission Decision of 17 December 1975, OJ 1976 L 95/1, section C.

[259] Cases IV/34.621 and 35.059 *Irish Sugar ("Irish Sugar Decision 1997")*, Commission Decision of 14 May 1997, OJ 1997 L 258/1, pp. 1–34.

[260] *Ibid.*, Article 3.

[261] *See Tetra Pak II Decision 1991*, *supra* note 40, para. 220.

12. – Remedies
Thomas Graf and David R. Little

consideration."[262] This suggests that the only circumstance in which differences between similarly placed customers might be authorised is where there was some applicable "objective consideration".

12.121 In the majority of decisions, however, little or no detail is provided on the content of the non-discrimination obligation. Only a simple cease and desist order is made. Thus, in *Aéroports de Paris*, the Commission required that AdP, the airport manager at the Orly and Roissy-Charles-de Gaulle airports, "*apply*[...] *to the suppliers of groundhandling services concerned a non-discriminatory scheme of commercial fees*",[263] providing no further elaboration as to what form of scheme might be deemed "non-discriminatory". In *Brussels National Airport* and *Deutsche Bahn*, the Commission ordered that the infringement be brought to an end but provided no further guidance as to the appropriate formulation of the non-discriminatory terms.[264]

4.2. Monitoring Implementation of the Non-discrimination Obligation

12.122 Remedies for many Article 102 abuses rely on self-policing by the parties concerned (*e.g.*, refusal to supply cases). By contrast, self-policing in the case of non-discrimination obligations is difficult. It is not always easy for an undertaking to prove its suspicion that it is being discriminated against, since the terms on which the dominant company deals with its competitors or subsidiaries are usually confidential. Moreover, even if some information on, *e.g.*, transfer pricing, is available, it may be difficult to judge whether these differences result instead from differences in the customers' positions (*i.e.*, that there is in fact no discrimination as between similarly placed undertakings). The case law has developed two solutions to this difficulty. The first is that the Commission can require the dominant company to report to the Commission on a regular basis, demonstrating its compliance with the non-discrimination obligation. This was the approach followed in *United Brands*.[265] The second is

---

[262] *See* Case IV/31.043 *Tetra Pak I (BTG Licence)* ("*Tetra Pak I Decision 1988*"), Commission Decision of 26 July 1988, OJ 1988 L 272/27, Art. 3. Following an appeal, the General Court elaborated on the remedy imposed in para. 221: "*Although an obligation to communicate price lists follows from Article 3(2) of the Decision, requiring Tetra Pak to give each customer the possibility of obtaining supplies from any Tetra Pak subsidiary it chooses and at the prices charged by that subsidiary, Article 3(3) of the Decision nonetheless does not require discount schedules. It is sufficient if the discount rate is objectively justified which involves its being neither discriminatory nor predatory*".

[263] Case IV/35.613 *Alpha Flight Services/Aéroports de Paris* ("*Aéroports de Paris Decision 1998*"), Commission Decision of 11 June 1998, OJ 1998 L 230/10, Article 2.

[264] In *Clearstream*, the dominant undertaking had already corrected its conduct by the time the Commission's decision was issued, so no non-discrimination requirement was imposed (*Clearstream Decision 2004, supra* note 15).

[265] *See United Brands supra* note 246.

12. – Remedies
Thomas Graf and David R. Little

that, in particularly complex cases, the Commission has relied on the services of a monitoring trustee.[266] A third approach, somewhere between these two alternatives, is to require the dominant undertaking to engage an auditor to review the company's agreements and activities that relate to the infringement in question and certify that in respect of those activities and agreements, no discriminatory conduct has occurred.[267]

---

[266] *Hoffmann-La Roche,* ("*In addition, Roche agrees to the appointment of a trustee, who will be approved by the Commission, and who will be informed of every executed licence agreement and can be contacted by every licensee for reviewing compliance with the principle of non-discrimination. Such trustee will report his conclusions to the Commission.*")
[267] *See supra* note 63, p. 722.

BIBLIOGRAPHY

A.   Books

S. Affolter and others, *Grands principes du droit de la concurrence* (Bâle/Genève/ Munich, Bruylant, 1999).

P. Areeda and H. Hovenkamp, *Antitrust Law* (2nd Ed., Vol. 3, New York, Aspen Publishers, 2002).

R. J. van den Bergh and P. D. Camesasca, *European Competition Law and Economics: A Comparative Perspective* (2nd Ed., London, Sweet & Maxwell, 2006).

S. Bishop and M. Walker, *The Economics of EC Competition Law: Application and Measurement* (2nd Ed., London, Sweet & Maxwell, 2002).

S. Bishop and M. Walker, *The Economics of EC Competition Law: Concepts, Application and Measurement* (3rd Ed., London, Sweet & Maxwell, 2010).

O. Blanco and B. Van Houtte, *EC Competition Law in the Transport Sector* (Oxford, Oxford University Press, 1996).

R. H. Bork, "Legislative Intent and the Policy of the Sherman Act" (1966) 9 *Journal of Law & Economics*, pp. 7–48.

R. H. Bork, *The Antitrust Paradox: A Policy at War with Itself* (New York, Basic Books, 1978).

R. H. Bork, *The Antitrust Paradox: A Policy at War with Itself* (2nd Ed., New York, The Free Press, 1993).

W. D. Braun and L. Ritter, *EC Competition Law – A Practitioner's Guide* (3rd Ed., The Hague, Kluwer Law International, 2004).

D. W. Carlton and J. M. Perloff, *Modern Industrial Organization* (2nd Ed., New York, Harper Collins College Publishers, 1994).

D. W. Carlton and J. M. Perloff, *Modern Industrial Organization* (3rd Ed., Addison Wesley, 1999).

D. W. Carlton and J. M. Perloff, *Modern Industrial Organization* (4th Ed., Pearson, 2005).

W. R. Cornish and D. Llewelyn, *Intellectual Property: Patents, Copyright, Trade Marks and Allied Rights* (5th Ed., London, Sweet & Maxwell, 2003).

W. Eucken, *Grundsätze der Wirtschaftspolitik* (1st Ed., Mohr, Tübingen, 1952).

A. Ezrachi, "The Commission's Guidance on Article 82", in A. Ezrachi (Ed.) *Article 82, Reflection on its Recent Evolution* (Oxford, Hart Publishing, 2009), p. 59.

J. Faull and A. Nikpay (Eds.), *The EC Law of Competition* (2nd Ed., Oxford, Oxford University Press, 2007).

A. Frignani and M. Waelbroeck, *European Competition Law* (Ardsley, Transnational Publishers, 1999).

J. K. Galbraith, *American capitalism: The concept of countervailing power* (Boston, Houghton Mifflin, 1952).

O. Gassmann, G. Reepmeyer and M. von Zedtwitz, *Leading Pharmaceutical Innovation: Trends and Drivers for Growth in the Pharmaceutical Industry* (2nd Ed., Berlin, Springer, 2008).

N. Gauss, *Die Anwendung des kartellrechtlichen Missbrauchsverbots nach Art. 82 EG (Art. 102 AEUV) in innovativen Märkten* (Baden-Baden, Nomos, 2010).

M. Glader, *Innovation Markets and Competition Analysis – EU Competition Law and US Antitrust Law* (Cheltenham, Edward Elgar, 2006).

R. Goldscheider, *New Companion to Licensing Negotiations: Licensing Law Handbook* (4th Ed., St. Paul, West Group, 2003).

J. Goyder, *EU Distribution Law* (4th Ed., Oxford, Hart Publishing, 2005).

H. Hovenkamp, *The Antitrust Enterprise: Principle and Execution* (Harvard University Press, 2005).

J. Jaffe, S. A. Ross and R. W. Westerfield, *Corporate Finance* (7th Ed., McGraw-Hill Irwin, 2005).

R. Joliet, *Monopolization and Abuse of Dominant Position: A Comparative Study of American and European Approaches to the Control of Economic Power* (Liège, Faculté de Droit, 1970).

A. Jones and B. Sufrin, *EC Competition Law* (3rd Ed., Oxford, Oxford University Press, 2008).

I. Kokkoris (Ed.), *Competition Cases from the European Union. The Ultimate Guide to Leading Cases of the EU and All 27 Member States* (London, Sweet and Maxwell, 2007).

V. Korah, *An Introductory Guide To EC Competition Law And Practice* (7th Ed., Oxford, Hart Publishing, 2000).

V. Korah, *An Introductory Guide to EC Competition Law and Practice* (9th Ed., Oxford, Hart Publishing, 2007).

V. Korah and D. O'Sullivan, *Distribution Agreements under the EC Competition Rules* (Oxford, Hart Publishing, 2002).

J. Langer, *Tying and Bundling as a leveraging Concern Under EC Competition Law* (Kluwer Law International, 2007).

N. Levy, *European Merger Control Law – A Guide to the Merger Regulation* (8th Ed., Lexis Nexis, 2011).

N. Levy, *European Merger Control Law: A Guide to the Merger Regulation* (Lexis-Nexis Matthew Bender, 2003).

K. McMahon, "A Reformed Approach to Article 82 and the Special Responsibility not to Distort Competition", in: A. Ezrachi, *Article 82 EC: Reflections on its Recent Evolution* (Oxford, Hart Publishing, 2009), pp. 121–145.

A. Marshall, *Principles of Economics* (1st Ed., London, Macmillan, 1890).

E.-J. Mestmäcker and H. Schweitzer, *Europäisches Wettbewerbsrecht* (2nd Ed., Munich, C. H. Beck, 2004).

M. Motta, *Competition Policy: Theory and Practice* (Cambridge, Cambridge University Press, 2004).

R. Nazzini, *"The Foundations of European Union Competition Law" The Objective and Principles of Article 102* (Oxford, Oxford University Press, 2011), p. 175.

R. O'Donoghue and A. J. Padilla, *The Law and Economics of Article 82 EC* (Oxford, Hart Publishing, 2006).

E. Osterud, *Identifying Exclusionary Abuses by Dominant Undertakings Under EU Competition Law: The Spectrum of Tests* (Kluwer Law International 2010).

R. Posner, *Antitrust Law* (Chicago, University of Chicago Press, 1976).

R. Posner, *Antitrust Law* (2nd Ed., Chicago, University of Chicago Press, 2001).

N. Reich, *Understanding EU Law: Objectives, Principles and Methods of Community Law* (Antwerpen – Oxford, Intersentia, 2005).

P. Roth and V. Rose (Eds.), *Bellamy & Child, European Community Law of Competition* (5th Ed., Oxford, Oxford University Press, 2001), pp. 754–55.

P. Roth and V. Rose (Eds.), *Bellamy & Child: European Community Law of Competition* (6th Ed., Oxford, Oxford University Press, 2008).

F. Russo and others, *European Commission Decisions on Competition, Economic Perspectives on Landmark Antitrust and Merger Cases* (Cambridge, Cambridge University Press, 2010).

F. M. Scherer, *The Economic Effects of Compulsory Patent Licensing* (New York University, Graduate School of Business Administration, Center for the Study of Financial Institutions, 1977).

F. M. Scherer and D. Ross, *Industrial Market Structure and Economic Performance* (Boston, Houghton Mifflin Company, 1990).

H. Schmidt, *Competition Law, Innovation and Antitrust: An Analysis of Tying and Technological Integration* (Edward Elgar 2009).

J. Schumpeter, *Capitalism, Socialism and Democracy* (New York, Harper & Brothers, 1950).

M. Siragusa, *Application of Art. 86: Tying Arrangements, Refusal to Deal, Discrimination and Other Cases of Abuse* (Bruges, 1974).

G. J. Stigler, *A Theory of Price* (4th Ed., New York, MacMillan, 1987).

G. J. Stigler, *Organization of Industry* (Chicago, The University of Chicago Press, 1968).

J. Tirole, *The Theory of Industrial Organization* (Cambridge, MIT Press, 1988).

G. Tritton, *Intellectual Property in Europe* (London, Sweet & Maxwell, 2008).

F. Tuytschaever, A. Vanderelst and F. Wijckmans, *Vertical Agreements in EC Competition Law* (Oxford, Oxford University Press, 2006).

Van Bael & Bellis, *Competition law of the European Community* (5th Ed. The Hague: Kluwer Law International, 2010).

H. Varian, J. Farrell, and C. Shapiro, *The Economics of Information Technology* (Cambridge University Press 2004).

R. Whish, *Competition Law* (4th Ed., Butterworths LexisNexis, 2001).

R. Whish, *Competition Law* (5th Ed., London, LexisNexis UK, 2003).

R. Whish, *Competition Law* (6th Ed., Oxford, Oxford University Press, 2008).

R. Whish, *Competition Law* (7th Ed., Oxford, Oxford University Press, 2012).

O. Williamson, *Markets and Hierarchies: Analysis and Antitrust Implications* (New York, The Free Press, 1975).

B.   Articles Published in Books

C. Ahlborn and A.J. Padilla, "From Faireness to Welfare: Implications for the Assessment of Unilateral Conduct under EC Competition Law), in C. -D. Ehlermann and M. Marquis (Eds.), *A Reformed Approach to Article 82 EC* (Oxford, Hart Publishing, 2008), pp. 55–101.

R. Allendesalazar, "Can We Finally Say Farewell to the "Special Responsibility" of Dominant Companies?", in: C. D. Ehlermann and M. Marquis, European Competition Law Annual 2007: A Reformed Approach to Article 82 EC (Oxford, Hart Publishing, 2008), p. 319.

K. Arrow, "Economic Welfare and the Allocation of Resources for Invention", in R. R. Nelson (Ed.), *The Rate and Direction of Inventive Activity* (Princeton, Princeton University Press, 1962), pp. 609–25.

F. W. Bulst, in E. Langen and H.-J. Bunte (Eds.), *Kommentar zum deutschen und europäischen Kartellrecht* (11th Ed., Luchterhand), Art. 82 EG.

K. Dekeyser and C. Gauer, "The New Enforcement System for Articles 81 and 82 and the Rights of Defense", in B. E. Hawk (Ed.) *Fordham Competition Law Institute: International Antitrust Law and Policy 2004* (New York, Juris Publishing, 2005), pp. 549–86, p. 581.

H. W. Friederiszick, in J. Schwarze (Ed.), *Recht und Ökonomie im Europäischen Wettbewerbsrecht* (Baden-Baden, Nomos, 2006), pp. 29–40.

J. J. Ganuza, G. Llobet, and B. Domínguez, "R&D in the Pharmaceutical Industry: A World of Small Innovations" (2009) 55(4) *Management Science*, pp. 539–51.

D. Gerard, "Private Enforcement in the Area of Cartels", in M. Siragusa, *EU Competition Law – Cartels and Horizontal Agreements*, (Leuven Claeys & Casteels 2007).

L. Gyselen, "Abuse of Monopoly Power Within the Meaning of Article 86 of the EEC Treaty: Recent Developments", in B. E. Hawk (Ed.), *Fordham Competition Law Institute: International Antitrust Law and Policy 1989* (New York, Juris Publishing, 1990), pp. 597–650.

O. Hart and J. Tirole, "Vertical Integration and Market Foreclosure", in C. Winston and M. N. Baily (Eds.), *Brookings Papers on Economic Activity: Micro-economics* (Brookings Institution Press, 1990), pp. 205–76.

J. A. Hausman, "Valuation of New Goods Under Perfect and Imperfect Competition", in T. F. Bresnahan and R. J. Gordon (Eds.), *The Economics of New Goods* (Chicago, University of Chicago Press, 1997), pp. 207–48.

H. Hovenkamp, "Signposts of Anticompetitive Exclusion: Restraints on Innovation and Economies of Scale", in B. E. Hawk (Ed.), *Fordham Competition Law Institute: International Antitrust Law and Policy 2006* (New York, Juris Publishing, 2007), pp. 409–31.

K. H. Hylton "The Law and Economics of Monopolization Standards" in K. H. Hylton (Eds.) *Antitrust Law And Economics* (Cheltenham Edward Elgar Publishing, 2009), pp. 82–115.

T. E. Kauper, "Whither Article 86? Observations on Excessive Prices and Refusals to Deal", in B. E. Hawk (Ed.), *Fordham Competition Law Institute: International Antitrust Law and Policy 1989* (New York, Juris Publishing, 1990), pp. 651–86.

M. Lao, "Defining Exclusionary Conduct under Section 2: The Case for Non-Universal Standards", in B. E. Hawk (Ed.), *Fordham Competition Law Institute: International Antitrust Law & Policy 2006* (New York, Juris Publishing, 2007), pp. 433–68.

A. Lincoln, "Lecture on Discoveries and Inventions" (1858), in R. P. Basler (Ed.), *Collected Works of Abraham Lincoln* (New Brunswick, Rutgers University Press, 1953).

P. Lowe and L. Peeperkorn, "Intellectual Property: How Special is its Competition Case?" in C-D. Ehlermann and I. Atanasiu (Eds.), *European Competition Law Annual 2005: The Interaction Between Competition Law and Intellectual Property Law* (Oxford, Hart Publishing, 2007), pp. 91–104.

P. Lowe and F. Maier-Rigaud, "Quo vadis antitrust remedies", in B. E. Hawk (Ed.), *Fordham Competition Law Institute: International Antitrust Law & Policy 2006* (New York, Juris Publishing, 2007), pp. 597–611, p. 603.

S. Martinez Lage and R. Allendesalazar, "Community Policy on Discriminatory Pricing: A Practitioner's Perspective", in C-D. Ehlermann and I. Atanasiu (Eds.), *European Competition Law Annual 2003: What Is Abuse of Dominant Position?* (Oxford, Hart Publishing, 2006), pp. 325–54.

M. Motta and A. de Streel, "Exploitative and Exclusionary Excessive Prices in EU Law", in C-D. Ehlermann and I. Atanasiu (Eds.), *European Competition Law Annual 2003: What Is Abuse of Dominant Position?* (Oxford, Hart Publishing, 2006), pp. 91–126.

R. O'Donoghue, "Verbalizing a General Test for Exclusionary Conduct under Article 82 EC", in Ehlermann and Marquis (Eds.), *European Competition Law Annual 2007: A Reformed Approach to Article 82* (Oxford, Hart Publishing, 2008).

E. Paulis, "Article 82 EC and Exploitative Conduct" in C-D. Ehlermann and M. Marquis (Eds.), *European Competition Law Annual 2007: A Reformed Approach to Article 82 EC* (Oxford, Hart Publishing, 2008), pp. 515–24.

E. Paulis, "The Burden of Proof in Article 82 Cases", in B. E. Hawk (Ed.), *Fordham Competition Law Institute: International Antitrust Law and Policy 2006* (New York, Juris Publishing, 2007).

L. Peeperkorn and V. Verouden, in J. Faull and A. Nikpay (Eds.), *The EC Law of Competition* (2nd Ed., Oxford, Oxford University Press, 2007).

E. Pijnacker Hordijk, "Excessive Pricing Under EC Competition Law: An Update in the Light of 'Dutch Developments'" in B. E. Hawk (Ed.), *Fordham Competition Law Institute: International Antitrust Law and Policy 2001* (New York, Juris Publishing, 2002), pp. 463–95.

P. Rey and J. Tirole, "A Primer on Foreclosure", in M. Armstrong and R. H. Porter (Eds.), *Handbook of Industrial Organization* (Amsterdam, North-Holland, 2007), Vol. III, pp. 2145–220.

E. Rousseva, "Abuse of Dominant Position Defenses – Objective Justification and Article 82 EC in the Era of Modernization," in G. Amato & C. Ehlermann (Eds.), *EC Competition Law – A Critical Assessment* (Hart Publishing 2007), pp. 377–431.

S. C. Salop, "The Controversy over the Proper Antitrust Standard for Anticompetitive Exclusionary Conduct", in B. E. Hawk (Ed.), *Fordham Competition Law Institute: International Antitrust Law and Policy 2006* (New York, Juris Publishing, 2007), pp. 477–508.

H. Schweitzer, "The History, Interpretation and Underlying Principles of Section 2 Sherman Act and Article 82 EC", in C.-D. Ehlermann and M. Marquis (Eds.), *A Reformed Approach to Article 82 EC* (Oxford, Hart Publishing, 2008), pp. 119–64.

L. A. Stole, "Price Discrimination and Competition", in M. Armstrong and R. H. Porter (Eds.), *Handbook of Industrial Organization* (Amsterdam, North-Holland, 2007), Vol. III, Ch. 34, pp. 2221–299, p. 2223.

J. Temple Lang, "Abuse of Dominant Positions in European Community Law, Present and Future: Some Aspects", in B. E. Hawk (Ed.), *Fifth Annual Fordham Corporate Law Institute, Law & Business* (1979), pp. 25–83.

J. Temple-Lang, "Defining Legitimate Competition: Companies' Duties to Supply Competitors and Access to Essential Facilities", in B. E. Hawk (Ed.), *Fordham Competition Law Institute: International Antitrust Law and Policy1994* (New York, Juris Publishing, 1995), p. 245.

J. Temple Lang, "Anticompetitive Non-Pricing Abuses Under European and National Antitrust Law", in B. E. Hawk (Ed.), *Fordham Competition Law Institute: International Antitrust Law and Policy 2003* (New York, Juris Publishing, 2004), pp. 235–340.

J. Temple Lang, "State Measures Restricting Competition Under European Union Law", in W. D. Collins (Ed.), *Issues in Antitrust Law and Policy* (American Bar Association Section on Antitrust Law, 2008), Vol. 1, Chap. 9, pp. 221–48.

J. Temple Lang, "Anticompetitive Abuses under Article 82 Involving Intellectual Property Rights", in C-D. Ehlermann and I. Atanasiu (Eds.), *European Competition Law Annual 2003: What Is Abuse of Dominant Position?* (Oxford, Hart Publishing, 2006), pp. 589–658.

J. Temple Lang, "Abuse under Article 82 EC: Fundamental Issues and Standard Cases", in Baudenbacher (Ed.), *Neueste Entwicklungen im europäischen und internationalen Kartellrecht, 13 St. Galler Internationales Kartellrechtsforum 2006* (Helbing Lichtenhahn Verlag, Basel 2007), pp. 95–168.

J. Temple Lang, "European Competition Law and Refusals to Licence Intellectual Property Rights", in Hansen (Ed.), *Intellectual Property Law and Policy*, (Hart Publishing, 2008) Vol.10, pp. 282–95.

H. R. Varian, "Price Discrimination", in R. Schmalensee and R. Willig (Eds.), *Handbook of Industrial Organization* (Amsterdam, North-Holland, 1989), Vol. I, Ch. 10, pp. 597–654.

M. Waelbroeck, "Price Discrimination and Rebate Policies Under EU Competition Law", in B. E. Hawk (Ed.), *Fordham Competition Law Institute: International Antitrust Law and Policy1995 & Policy* (New York, Juris Publishing, 1996), Ch. 10, pp. 147–60.

Articles Published in Journals

R. M. Abrantes-Metz and others, "A Variance Screen for Collusion" (2005) 24(3) *Journal of Industrial Organization*, pp. 467–86.

P. Aghion and others, "Competition and Innovation: An Inverted-U Relationship" (2005) 120(2) *Quarterly Journal of Economics*, pp. 701–28.

P. Aghion and P. Bolton, "Contracts as Barrier to Entry" (1987) 77(3) *American Economic Review*, pp. 388–401.

P. Aghion, C. Harris, P. Howitt and J. Vickers, "Competition, Imitation and Growth with Step-by-Step Innovation" (2001) 68(3) *Review of Economic Studies*, pp. 467–92.

C. Ahlborn and D. S. Evans, 'The Microsoft Judgment and its Implications for Competition Policy Towards Dominant Firms in Europe" (2009) 75(3) *Antitrust Law Journal*, pp. 17–20.

C. Ahlborn, D. S. Evans and A. J. Padilla, "The Antitrust Economics of Tying: A Farewell to Per Se Illegality" (2004) 49 *Antitrust Bulletin*, pp. 287–341.

C. Ahlborn, D. S. Evans and A. J. Padilla, "The Logic and Limits of the 'Exceptional Circumstances Test' in *Magill* and *IMS Health*", (2005) 28(4) *Fordham International Law Journal*, pp. 1109–156.

P. Akman, "To Abuse, or Not to Abuse: Discrimination Between Consumers" (2007) 32 *European Law Review*, pp. 499–502.

P. Akman, "Consumer Welfare and Article 82 EC: Practice and Rethoric", (2009) 32(1) *World Competition*, pp. 71–90.

A. Albors-Llorens, "The Role of Objective Justifications, and Efficiencies in the Application of Article 82 EC," (2007) 44 *Common Market Law Review*, pp. 1727–61.

B. Allan, "A Commentary on DG Competition's Discussion Paper" (2006) 2(1) *Competition Policy International*, pp. 42–82.

B. Amory and Y. Desmedt, "The European Ombudsman's First Scrutiny of the EC Commission in Antitrust Matters," (2009) 30(5) *European Competition Law Review*, pp. 205–11.

J. Apon, "Cases Against Microsoft: Similar Cases, Different Remedies" (2007) 28(6) *European Competition Law Review*, pp. 327–36.

P. Areeda, "Essential Facilities: An Epithet in Need of Limiting Principles" (1989) 58(3) *Antitrust Law Journal*, pp. 841–53.

P. Areeda and D. F. Turner, "Predatory Pricing and Related Practices Under Section 2 of the Sherman Act" 88(4) *The Harvard Law Review Association*, pp. 697–733.

M. Armstrong and J. Vickers "Price Discrimination, Competition and Regulation" (1993) 41(4) *Journal of Industrial Economics*, pp. 335–59.

E. Avenel and C. Barlet, "Vertical Foreclosure, Technological Choice, and Entry in the Intermediate Market" (2000) 9(2) *Journal of Economics and Management Strategy*, pp. 211–30.

J. P. de Azevedo and M. Walker, "Dominance: Meaning and Measurement" (2002) *European Competition Law Review*, pp. 363–67.

P. Baake, U. Kamecke and H.-T. Normann, "Vertical Foreclosure versus Downstream Competition with Capital Precommitment" (2004) 22(2) *International Journal of Industrial Organization*, pp. 185–92.

E. E. Bailey and A. F. Friedlaender, "Market structure and multiproduct industries" (1982) 20 *The Journal of Economic Literature*, pp. 1024–48.

J. B. Baker, "Competitive Price Discrimination: The Exercise of Market Power Without Anticompetitive Effects (Comment on Klein and Wiley)" (2003) 70(3) *Antitrust Law Journal*, pp. 643–54.

J. B. Baker, "Predatory Pricing After Brooke Group: An Economic Perspective", (1994) 62 *Antitrust Law Journal*, pp. 585–603.

S. Baker, "The Treatment of Captive Sales in Market Definition: Rules or Reason?" (2003) 4 *European Competition Law Review*, pp. 161–4.

U. Bath, "Access to Information v. Intellectual Property Rights" (2002) 24(3) *European Intellectual Property Review*, pp. 138–46.

W. J. Baumol, "Predation and the Logic of the Average Variable Cost Test" (1996) 39(1) *Journal of Law and Economics*, pp. 49–72.

W. J. Baumol, "Quasi-permanence of price reductions: a policy for prevention of predatory pricing" (1979) 89(1) *Yale Law Journal*, pp. 1–26.

W. J. Baumol and D. G. Swanson, "Reasonable and Non-discriminatory (RAND) Royalties, Standards Selection, and Control of Market Power" (2005) 73 *Antitrust law Journal*, pp. 1–58.

A. Bavasso, "The Role of Intent under Article 82; From 'Flushing the Turkeys' to 'Spotting Lionesses in Regent's Park'" (2005) 26(11) *European Competition Law Review*, pp. 616–23.

C. F. Beckner and S. C. Salop, "Decision Theory and Antitrust Rules" (1999) 67 *Antitrust Law Journal*, pp. 41–76.

J. P. Benoit, "Financially Constrained Entry in a Game with Incomplete Information" (1984) 15(4) *The RAND Journal of Economics*, pp. 490–99.

D. Besanko and M. K. Perry, "Equilibrium Incentives for Exclusive Dealing in a Differentiated Products Oligopoly" (1993) 24(4) *The RAND Journal of Economics*, pp. 646–68.

K. Binmore and P. Klemperer, "The Biggest Auction Ever: the Sale of the British 3G Telecom Licences" (2002) 112(478) *The Economic Journal*, pp. C74–C96.

W. Bishop, "Price Discrimination Under Article 86: Political Economy in the European Court" (1981) 44(3) *Modern Law Review*, pp. 282–95.

R. D. Blair, J. E. Lopatka and J. B. Herndon, "Evaluating Market Power" (1997) 27 *Journal of Reprints for Antitrust Law & Economics*, p. 457–70.

R. Blundell, R. Griffith and J. Van Reenen, "Market Share, Market Value and Innovation in a Panel of British Manufacturing Firms," (1999) 66(3) *Review of Economic Studies*, pp. 529–54.

P. Bolton, J. F. Brodley and M. H. Riordan, "Predatory Pricing: Strategic Theory and Legal Policy" (2000) 88 *Georgetown Law Journal*, pp. 2239–330.

P. Bolton and D. Scharfstein, "Long-Term Financial Contracts and the Theory of Predation", (1987) *Mimeo, Harvard University*.

L. Borlini, "Methodological Issues of the 'More Economic Approach' to Unilateral Exclusionary Conduct. Proposal of Analysis Starting from the Treatment of Retroactive Rebates" (2009) 5 *European Competition Journal*, pp. 409–50.

J. Bouckaert and F. Verboven, "Price Squeezes in a Regulatory Environment" (2004) 26(3) *Journal of Regulatory Economics*, pp. 321–51.

T. J. Brennan, "Cross-Subsidization and Cost Misallocation by Regulated Monopolists" (1990) 2(1) *Journal of Regulatory Economics* pp. 37–51.

C. Breuvart and J.-P. Gunther, "Misuse of Patent and Drug Regulatory Approval Systems in the Pharmaceutical Industry: an Analysis of US and EU Converging Approaches" (2005) 26(12) *European Competition Law Review*, pp. 669–84.

J. F. Brodley, "The Economic Goals of Antitrust: Efficiency, Consumer Welfare and Technological Progress" (1987) 62 *New York University Law Review*, p. 1020.

E. Brynjolfsson, Y. Hu and M. D. Smith "Consumer Surplus in the Digital Economy: Estimating the Value of Increased Product Variety at Online Booksellers" (2003) 49(11) *Management Science*, pp. 1580–96.

G. Cameron, "Why Did UK Manufacturing Productivity Growth Slow Down in the 1970s and Speed Up in the 1980s?" (2003) 70(277) *Economica*, pp. 121–41.

J. Carbajo, D. De Meza, D. Seidman, "A strategic Motivation for Commodity Bundling" (1990) 38 *Journal of Industrial Economics*, pp. 283–298.

S. Carbonneau and others, "Price Discrimination and Market Power" (2004) *Emory Economics*, p. 413.

D. W. Carlton and M. Waldman, "How economics can improve antitrust doctrine towards tie-in sales" (2005) 1(1) *Competition Policy International Journal*, pp. 27–40.

D. W. Carlton and M. Waldman, "The Strategic Use of Tying to Preserve and Create Market Power in Evolving Industries" (2002) 33(2) *The RAND Journal of Economics*, pp. 194–220.

D. W. Carlton, "Should 'Price Squeeze' Be A Recognized Form of Anticompetitive Conduct" (2008) *Journal of Competition Law & Economics* 4(2), pp. 271–8.

G. S. Cary and others, "Antitrust Implications of Abuse of Standard-Setting" (2008) 15(5) *George Mason Law Review*, pp. 1241–63.

R. A. Cass and K. N. Hylton, "Antitrust Intent" (2001) 74(3) *Southern California Law Review*, pp. 657–745.

G. Chemla, "Downstream Competition, Foreclosure, and Vertical Integration" (2003) 12(2) *Journal of Economics and Management Strategy*, pp. 261–89.

Y. Chen, "Equilibrium Product Bundling," (1997) 70 The Journal of Business, pp. 85–103.

J. P. Choi and C. Stefanadis, "Tying, Investment, and the Dynamic Leverage Theory" (2001) 32(1) *The RAND Journal of Economics*, pp. 52–71.

J. P. Choi and S. S. Yi, "Vertical Foreclosure with the Choice of Input Specifications" (2000) 31(4) *The RAND Journal of Economics*, pp. 717–43.

C. Cook, "Commitment Decisions: The Law and Practice Under Article 9" (2006) 29(2) *World Competition*, pp. 209–28.

C. Cook, "Private Enforcement of Competition Law in Member State Courts: Experience to Date and the Path Ahead" (2008) 4(2) *Competition Policy International*.

D. Crane, "The Paradox of Predatory Pricing" (2005) 91(1) *Cornell Law Review*, pp. 1–66.

P. Crocioni, "Leveraging of Market Power in Emerging Markets: A Review of Cases, Literature, and a Suggested Framework" (2008) 4(2) *Journal of Competition Law and Economics*, pp. 449–534.

P. Crocioni, "Price Squeeze and Imputation Test – Recent Developments" (2005) 26(10) *European Competition Law Review*, pp. 558–71.

P. Crocioni and C. Veljanovski, "Price Squeezes, Foreclosure and Competition Law" (2003) 4 *Journal of Network Industries*, pp. 28–60.

K. J. Cseres, "The Controversies of the Consumer Welfare Standard", (2007) 3(2) *Competition Law Review*, pp. 121–173.

P. Dasgupta and J. Stiglitz, "Industrial Structure and the Nature of Innovative Activity" (1980) 90(358) *The Economic Journal*, pp. 266–93.

V. Denicolò and others, "Revisiting Injunctive Relief: Interpreting eBay in High-Tech Industries with Non-Practicing Patent Holders" (2008) 4(3) *Journal of Competition Law and Economics*, pp. 571–608.

C. A. Depken, D. R. Kamerschen and A. Snow, "Generic Advertising of Intermediate Goods: Theory and Evidence on Free Riding" (2002) 20(3) *Review of Industrial Organization*, pp. 205–20.

F. Dethmers and H. Engelen, "Fines under Article 102 of the Treaty of the Functioning of the European Union," (2011) 2 *European Competition Law Review*, pp. 86–98.

A. Devlin and M. S. Jacobs, "Microsoft's Five Fatal Flaws" (2009) *Columbia Business Law Review*, pp. 100–142.

J. A. DiMasi, R. Hansen and H. Grabowski, "The Price of Innovation: New Estimates of Drug Development Costs" (2003) 22(2) *Journal of Health Economics*, pp. 151–85.

A. Director and H. Levi, "Law and the Future: Trade Regulation", (1956) 51(281) *Northwestern University Law Review*.

A. Dixit, "A Model of Duopoly Suggesting a Theory of Entry Barriers" (1979) 399 *Antitrust Law & Economics*, pp. 20–32.

A. Dixit, "The Role of Investment in Entry-Deterrence (1980) 90 *The Economic Journal*, pp. 95–106.

P. W. Dobson and M. Waterson, "The Competition Effects of Industry-Wide Vertical Price Fixing in Bilateral Oligopoly" (2007) 25(5) *International Journal of Industrial Organization*, pp. 935–62.

M. Dolmans, "A Tale of Two Tragedies – A Plea for Open Standards, and Some Comments on the RAND Report" (2010) *Concurrences*, No 1–2012, pp. 7–17.

M. Dolmans and T. Graf, "Analysis of Tying Under Article 82 EC: The European Commission's Microsoft Decision in Perspective" (2004) 27(2) *World Competition*, pp. 225–44.

M. Dolmans, "Standards for Standards" (2002) 26(1) *Fordham International Law Journal*, pp. 163–208.

M. Dolmans, T. Graf and D.R. Little, "Microsoft's browser-choice Commitments and Public Interoperability Undertaking" (2010) 31(7) *European Competition Law Review*, pp. 268–75.

M. Dolmans and D. Ilan, "A Health Warning for IP Owners: The Advocate General's Opinion in *IMS* and its Implications for Compulsory Licensing" (2003) 11 *Competition Law Insight*, pp. 12–6.

M. Dolmans, R. O'Donoghue and P.-J. Loewenthal, "Are Article 82 EC and Intellectual Property Interoperable? The State of the Law Pending the Judgment in Microsoft v. Commission" (2007) 3(1) *Competition Policy International Journal*, pp. 107–44.

M. Dolmans and V. Pickering, "*The 1997 Digital Undertaking*" (1998) 19(2) *European Competition Law Review*, pp. 108–15.

M. Dolmans and D. Ilan, "European Antitrust and Patent Acquisitions; Trolls in the Patent Thickets" (2012) 8(2) *Competition law International*.

M. Dreher, "Die Kontrolle des Wettbewerbs in Innovationsmärkten – Marktabgrenzung und Marktbeherrschung in dynamischen Märkten" (2009) *Zeitschrift für Wettbewerbsrecht*, p. 149.

F. H. Easterbrook, "Predatory Strategies and Counterstrategies" (1981) 48 *University of Chicago Law Review*, pp. 263–337.

F. H. Easterbrook, "The Limits of Antitrust" (1984) 63(1) *Texas Law Review*, pp. 1–40.

N. Economides, "The Incentive for Non-Price Discrimination by an Input Monopolist" (1998) 16(3) *International Journal of Industrial Organization*, pp. 271–84.

N. Economides and I. Lianos, "The Elusive Antitrust Standard on Bundling in Europe and in the United States in the Aftermath of the *Microsoft* Cases" (2009) 76(2) *Antitrust Law Journal*, pp. 483–567.

A. S. Edlin, M. Epelbaum and W. P. Heller, "Is Perfect Price Discrimination Really Efficient: Welfare and Existence in General Equilibrium" (1988) 66 *Econometrica*, pp. 897–922.

T. Eilmansberger, "How to Distinguish Good from Bad Competition under Article 82 EC: In Search of Clearer and More Coherent Standards for Anti-competitive Abuses" (2005) 42 *Common Market Law Review*, pp. 129–77.

E. Elhauge, "Why Above-Cost Price Cuts To Drive Out Entrants Are Not Predatory – And the Implications for Defining Costs and Market Power" (2003) 112(4) *The Yale Law Journal*, pp. 681–827.

E. Elhauge, "Defining Better Monopolization Standards" (2003) 56 *Stanford Law Review*, pp. 253–344.

E. Elhauge, "Tying, bundled discounts, and the death of the single monopoly profit theory" (2009) 123(2) *Harvard Law Review*, pp. 397–481.

D. S. Evans, "Antitrust Issues Raised by the Emerging Global Internet Economy" (2008) 102(4) *Northwestern University Law Review*, pp. 285–306.

D. S. Evans and A. J. Padilla, "Excessive Prices: Using Economics to Define Administrable Legal Rules" (2005) 1(1) *Journal of Competition Law and Economics*, pp. 97–122.

A. Ezrachi and D. Gilo, "Are Excessive Prices Really Self-Correcting?" (2008) 5(2) *Journal of Competition Law & Economics*, pp. 249–68.

J. Farrell and others, "Standard Setting, Patents, and Hold-up" (2007) 74 *Antitrust Law Journal*, pp. 603–70.

G. R. Faulhaber, "Cross-Subsidization: Pricing in Public Enterprises" (1975) 65(5) *The American Economic Review*, pp. 966–77.

L. Ferrari Bravo and P. Siciliani, "Exclusionary Pricing and Consumer's Harm: The European Commission's Practice in the DSL Market" (2007) 3(2) *Journal of Competition Law and Economics*, pp. 243–79.

F. M. Fisher, "Detecting Market Power" (2008) 1 *Issues in Competition Law and Policy*, pp. 353–72.

F. M. Fisher, "The IBM and Microsoft Cases: What's the Difference?" (2000) 90(2) *American Economic Review*, pp. 180–83.

K. Fjell and L. Søgard, "How to test for abuse of dominance", (2006) 2 (Special issue) *European Competition Journal*, pp. 69–83.

D. Fudenberg, R. Gilbert, J. Stiglitz and J. Tirole, "Preemption, Leapfrogging and Competition in Patent Races" (1983) 22(1) *European Economic Review*, pp. 3–31.

D. Fudenberg and J. Tirole, "A "Signal-Jamming" Theory of Predation" (1986) 17(3) *The RAND Journal of Economics*, pp. 366–76.

M. Gal, "Monopoly Pricing as an Antitrust Offense in the U.S. and the EC: Two Systems of Belief About Monopoly?" (2004) 49 *Antitrust Bulletin*, pp. 343–84.

M. Gal, "Below-Cost Price Alignment: Meeting or Beating Competition? The France Telecom Case" (2007) 28(6) *European Competition Law Review*, pp. 382–91.

G. Gaudet and N. Van Long, "Vertical Integration, Foreclosure, and Profits with Double Marginalization" (1996) 5(3) *Journal of Economics and Management Strategy*, pp. 409–32.

A. Gavil, "Exclusionary Distribution Strategies by Dominant Firms: Striking a Better Balance", (2004) 72(1) *Antitrust Law Journal*, pp. 3–82.

M. Gentzkow, "Valuing New Goods in a Model with Complementarity: Online Newspapers" (2007) 97(3) *American Economic Review*, pp. 713–44.

G. S. Georgiev, "Contagious Efficiency: The Growing Reliance on U.S.-Style Antitrust Settlements in EU Law" (2007) 4 *Utah Law Review*, pp. 971–1037.

D. Geradin, P. Hofer, F. Louis, N. Petit and M. Walker, "The Concept of Dominance" (2005), *Global Competition Law Centre*, pp. 6–37.

D. Geradin and R. O'Donoghue, "The Concurrent Application of Competition Law and Regulation: The Case of Margin Squeeze Abuses in the Telecommunications Sector" (2005) 1(2) *Journal of Competition Law and Economics*, pp. 355–425.

D. Geradin and N. Petit, "Price Discrimination Under EC Competition Law: Another Antitrust Doctrine in Search of Limiting Principles?"(2006) 2(3) *Journal of Competition Law and Economics*, pp. 479–531.

D. Geradin and M. Rato, "Can Standard-Setting Lead to Exploitative Abuse? A Dissonant View on Patent Hold-Up, Royalty Stacking and the Meaning of FRAND" (2007) 3(1) *European Competition Journal*, pp. 101–61.

R. Gilbert and C. Shapiro, "Optimal Patent Length and Breadth" (1990) *The RAND Journal of Economics*, pp. 106–12.

D. M. Gitter, "Strong Medicine For Competition Ills: The Judgment of the European Court of Justice in the *IMS Health* Action and its Implications for Microsoft Corporation" (2004) 15(1) *Duke Journal of Comparative & International Law*, pp. 153–92.

I. Govaere, "In Pursuit of an Innovation Policy Rationale: Stakes and Limits under Article 82 TEC" (2008) 31(4) *World Competition*, pp. 541–56.

H. Grabowski and J. M. Vernon, "A New Look at the Returns and Risks to Pharmaceutical R&D" (1990) 36(7) *Management Science*, pp. 804–21.

L. Hancher and J. Buendia Sierra, "Cross-Subsidization and EC Law" (1998) 35 *Common Market Law Review*, pp. 901–45.

G. Hardin, "The Tragedy of the Commons" (1968) 162(3859) *Science*, pp. 1243–8.

O. Hart and J. Tirole, "Vertical integration and market foreclosure" (1990) *Brookings Papers on Economic Activity*, pp. 205–76.

V. Hatzopoulos, "Case C-418/01, IMS Health GmbH v. NDC Health GmbH" (2004) 41(6) *Common Market Law Review*, pp. 1613–38.

J. Hausman and J. G. Sidak, "A consumer welfare approach to the mandatory unbundling of telecommunications networks" (1999) *Yale Law Journal*, pp. 507–39.

B. E. Hawk, "Article 82 and Section 2: Abuse and Monopolizing Conduct" (2008) 2 *Issues of Competition Law and Policy*, pp. 871–93.

G. A. Hay and K. McMahon, "The diverging approach to price squeezes in the United States and Europe" 8(2) *Journal of Competition Law & Economics*, pp. 259–96.

P. Hellstrom, F. P. Maier-Rigaud, F. Wenzel Bulst, "The Remedies in European Antitrust Law" (2009) 76 *Antitrust Law Journal*, pp. 46–63.

C. S. Hemphill, "The Role of Recoupment in Predatory Pricing Analyses" (2001) 53 *Stanford Law Review*, pp. 1581–612.

P. Hofer, M. Williams and L. Wu, "The Economics of Market Definition Analysis in Theory and in Practice" (2007) *Asia-Pacific Antitrust Review*, pp. 10–3.

L. Hou, "Excessive prices within EU competition law" (2011) 7(1) *European Competition Journal*, pp. 47–70.

H. Hovenkamp, "Antitrust at the Millennium (Part I): The Robinson-Patman Act and Competition: Unfinished Business" (2000) 68 *Antitrust Law Journal*, pp. 125–44.

H. Hovenkamp, "Post-Chicago Antitrust: A Review and Critique" (2001) 257 *Columbia Business Law Review*, pp. 259–66.

P. Hughes and P. Willis, "Structural Remedies in Article 82 Energy Cases" (2008) 4(2) *Competition Law Review*, pp. 147–74.

J. Hurwitz and W. E. Kovacic, "Judicial Analysis of Predation: The Emerging Trends" (1982) 35 *Vanderbilt Law Review*, pp. 63–157.

R. Innes and R. J. Sexton, "Strategic Buyers and Exclusionary Contracts" (1994) 84(3) *American Economic Review*, pp. 566–84.

A. E. Kahn, "Standards for Antitrust Policy", (1953) 67(1) *Harvard Law Review*, pp. 28–54.

A. ten Kate and G. Niels, "The Relevant Market: A Concept Still in Search of a Definition" (2008) 5(2) *Journal of Competition Law & Economics*, pp. 297–333.

A. Katz, "The Potential Demise of Another Natural Monopoly: Rethinking the Collective Administration of Performing Rights" (2005) 1(3) *Journal of Competition Law and Economics*, pp. 541–93.

B. Klein and J. S. Wiley, "Competitive Price Discrimination as an Antitrust Justification for Intellectual Property Refusals to Deal" (2003) 70(29) *Antitrust Law Journal*, pp. 599–613.

T. Klein, "SSNIP-Test oder Bedarfsmarktdonzept?" (2010) 2 *Wirtschaft und Wettbewerb*, pp. 169–77.

W. J. Kolasky, "Conglomerate Mergers and Range Effects: It's a Long Way from Chicago to Brussels" (2002) 10(3) *George Mason Law Review*, pp. 533–50.

W. J. Kolasky, "What is competition? A comparison of U.S. and European perspectives" (2004) *The Antitrust Bulletin*, p. 2953.

S. Kolay, J. A. Ordover and G. Shaffer, "All Units Discounts in Retail Contracts" (2004) 13(3) *Journal of Economics & Management Strategy*, pp. 429–59.

T. G. Krattenmaker and S. C. Salop, "Anticompetitive Exclusion: Raising Rivals' Costs to Achieve Power Over Price" (1986) 96(2) *Yale Law Journal*, pp. 209–93.

D. Kreps and R. Wilson, "Reputation and Imperfect Information" (1982) 27 *Journal of Economic Theory*, pp. 253–79.

K. Kühn, R. Stillman and C. Caffarra, "Economic theories of bundling and their policy implications in abuse cases: an assessment in light of the Microsoft case" (2005) 1(1) *European Competition Journal*, pp. 85–121.

J. Temple Lang, "How can the Problems of Exclusionary Abuses under Article 102 TFEU be resolved?" (2012) 37 *European Law Review* pp. 136–55.

M. A. Lemley, "Intellectual Property and Standard-Setting Organizations" (2002) 90(6) *California Law Review*, pp. 1889–980.

M. A. Lemley and C. Shapiro, "Patent Hold Up and Royalty Stacking" (2005) 85 *Texas Law Review*, pp. 1991–2049.

A. S. Layne-Farrar, A. J. Padilla and R. Schmalensee, "Pricing Patents for Licensing in Standard Setting Organizations: Making Sense of FRAND Commitments" (2007) 74(3) *Antitrust Law Journal*, pp. 671–706.

T. Lee and L. L. Wilde, "Market Structure and Innovation: A Reformulation" 1980 94(2) *Quarterly Journal of Economics*, pp. 429–36.

M. Leistner, "Intellectual Property and Competition Law: The European Development from Magill to IMS Health Compared to Recent German and U.S. Case Law" (2005) 2 *Zeitschrift für Wettbewerbsrecht*, p. 138.

A. Lemer, "The Concept of Monopoly and the Measurement of Monopoly Power" (1934) 1(3) *Review of Economic Studies*, pp. 157–75.

F. Lévêque, "Innovation, Leveraging and Essential Facilities: Interoperability Licensing in the EU Microsoft Case" (2005) 28(1) World Competition, pp. 71–91.

M. E. Levine, "Price Discrimination Without Market Power" (2002) 19(1) *Yale Journal of Regulation*, pp. 1–36.

F. Liberatore and F. Murphy, "Abuse of Regulatory Procedures – The Astra-Zeneca Case" (2009) 30(5, 6 and 7) *European Competition Law Review* (Issue 5, pp. 223–29; Issue 6, pp. 289–300; Issue 7, pp. 314–23).

W. J. Liebeler, "Let's Repeal it" (1976) 45 *Antitrust Law Journal*, pp. 18–43.

D. R. Little, "Case for a Primary Punishment Rationale in EC Anti-Cartel Enforcement" (2009) 5(1) *European Competition Journal*, pp. 37–64.

L. Lovdahl Gormsen, "Article 82 EC: Where are we coming from and where are we going to?" (2006) 2(2) *Competition Law Review*, pp. 5–25.

P. Lowe and L. Peeperkorn, "Singing in Tune with Competition and Innovation: The New EU Competition Policy towards Licensing" (2004) 26 *Fordham Corporate Law Institute Thirty-first Annual Conference: Roundtable on Intellectual Property and Antitrust,* pp. 265–86.

P. Marsden, "Microsoft vs. Commission: With Great Power Comes Great Responsibility" (2007) 6(1) *Competition Law Insight*, pp. 3–5.

H. P. Marvel and S. McCafferty, "Resale Price Maintenance and Quality Certification" (1984) 15(3) *The RAND Journal of Economics*, pp. 346–59.

G. F. Mathewson and R. A. Winter, "An Economic Theory of Vertical Restraints" (1984) 15(1) *The RAND Journal of Economics*, pp. 27–38.

P. Milgrom and J. Roberts, "Limit Pricing and Entry Under Incomplete Information: An Equilibrium Analysis" (1982) 50(2) *Econometrica*, pp. 443–59.

J. S. McGee, "Predatory Price Cutting: The Standard Oil (N.J.) Case" (1985) 1 *Journal of Law and Economics*, pp. 137–169.

A. D. Melamed, "Exclusionary Conduct Under the Antitrust Laws: Balancing, Sacrifice, and Refusals to Deal" (2005) 20 *Berkeley Technology Law Journal*, pp. 1247–67.

A. D. Melamed, "Exclusive Dealing Agreements and other Exclusionary Conduct – Are there Unifying Principles" (2006) 73(2) *Antitrust Law Journal*, pp. 375–412.

V. Mertikopoulou, "DG Competition's Discussion Paper on the Application of Article 82 EC to Exclusionary Abuses: the Proposed Economic Reform from a Legal Point of View" (2007) 28(4) *European Competition Law Review*, pp. 241–51.

P. Milgrom and J. Roberts, "Limit Pricing and Entry Under Incomplete Information: An Equilibrium Analysis" (1982) 50(2) *Econometrica*, pp. 443–59.

P. Milgrom and J. Roberts, "Predation, Reputation and Entry Deterrence" (1982) 27 *Journal of Economic Theory*, pp. 280–312.

G. Monti, "The Concept of Dominance in Article 82" (2006) 2(Specia) *European Competition Journal*, pp. 31–52.

G. Monti, "Article 82 EC: What Future for the Effects-Based Approach?" (2010) 1(1) *Journal of European Competition Law & Practice*, pp. 2–11.

B. Nalebuff, "Bundling as an Entry Barrier" (2004) 119(1) *The Quarterly Journal of Economics*, pp. 159–88.

M. P. Negrinotti, "The Abuse of Regulatory Procedures in the Intellectual Property Context: The AstraZeneca Case" (2008) 29(8) *European Competition Law Review*, pp. 446–59.

S. Nickell, "Competition and Corporate Performance" (1996) 104(4) *Journal of Political Economy*, pp. 724–46.

R. O'Donoghue and J. Temple Lang, "Defining Legitimate Competition: How to Clarify Pricing Abuses under Article 82 EC" (2002) 26(1) *Fordham International Law Journal*, pp. 83–162.

B. Ong, "Building Brick Barricades and Other Barriers to Entry: Abusing a Dominant Position by Refusing to Licence Intellectual Property Rights" (2005) 26 *European Competition Law Review*, pp. 213–22.

J. A. Ordover, G. Saloner and S. C. Salop, "Equilibrium Vertical Foreclosure" (1990) 80 *American Economic Review*, pp. 127–42.

P. Papandropoulos, "Article 82: Tying and bundling" (2006) 5(6) *Competition Law Insight*, pp. 3–5.

S. Park, "Market Power in Competition for the Market" (2009) 5(3) *Journal of Competition Law & Economics*, 571–9.

D. Patterson and C. Shapiro, "Transatlantic Divergence in GE/Honeywell: Causes and Lessons" (2001) 16(1) *Antitrust Magazine*, pp. 18–26.

M. Patterson, "The Sacrifice of Profits in Non-Price Predation", *Antitrust* (2003) 18, p. 37.

N. Petit, "Excessive pricing: the flaws of "tea party" competition policy" (2011) 2(6) *Journal of European Competition Law & Practice*, pp. 519–20.

A. Petrin, "Quantifying the Benefits of New Products: The Case of the Minivan" (2002) 110(4) *Journal of Political Economy*, pp. 705–29.

E. G. Petristsi, "The Case of Unilateral Patent Ambush Under EC Competition Rules" (2005) 28(1) *World Competition*, pp. 25–42.

R. W. Pitman, "Consumer Surplus as the Appropriate Standard for Antitrust Enforcement" (2007) 3(2) *Competition Policy International Journal*, pp. 205–24.

M. Polo, "Price Squeeze: Lessons From the Telecom Italia Case" (2007) 3(3) *Journal of Competition Law and Economics*, pp. 453–70.

L. Prete, "From Magill to IMS: Dominant Firms' Duty to License Competitors" 2004 15(5) *European Business Law* Review, pp. 1071–86.

S. Preece, "ITT Promedia v. E.C. Commission: Establishing and Abuse of Predatory Litigation?" (1999) 20(2) *European Competition Law Review*, pp. 118–22.

S. Purps and U. Scholz, "The Application of EC Competition Law in the Energy Sector" 2010 1(1) *Journal of European Competition Law & Practice*, pp. 37–51.

A.-S. Pype, "Dominance in peak-term electricity markets" (2011 32(2) *European Competition Law Review*, pp. 99–105.

R. Rapp, "Predatory Pricing and Entry Deterring Strategies: the Economics of AKZO" (1986) 7 *European Competition law Review*, pp. 233–40.

D. Reiffen, "Equilibrium Vertical Foreclosure: Comment" (1992) 82(3) *American Economic Review*, pp. 694–97.

J. Reinganum, "Uncertain Innovation and the Persistence of Monopoly" (1983) 73(4) *American Economic Review*, pp. 741–48.

P. Rey and J. Tirole, "The Logic of Vertical Restraints" (1986) 76 *American Economic Review*, pp. 921–39.

P. Rey and J. E. Stiglitz, "The Role of Exclusive Territories" (1995) 26(3) *The RAND Journal of Economics*, pp. 431–51.

P. Rey and J. E. Stiglitz, "Vertical Restraints and Producers' Competition" (1988) 32(2–3) *European Economic Review*, pp. 561–68.

D. Ridyard, "Exclusionary Pricing and Price Discrimination Abuses Under Article 82 – An Economic Analysis" (2002) 23(6) *European Competition Law Review*, pp. 286–303.

D. Ridyard, "The Commission's Article 82 Guidelines: Some Reflections on the Economic Issues" (2009) 30(5) *European Competition Law Review*, pp. 230–36.

J. Roberts, "A Signalling Model of Predatory Pricing" (1986) 38 *Oxford Economic Papers* (supp), pp. 75–93.

S. Roberts, "Assessing Excessive Pricing: the Case of Flat Steel in South Africa" (2008) 4(3) *Journal of Competition Law and Economics*, pp. 871–91.

R. C. Romaine and S. C. Salop, "Preserving Monopoly: Economic Analysis, Legal Standards and Microsoft", (1999) 7 *George Mason Law Review*, pp. 617–72.

E. Rousseva, "Modernizing by Eradicating: How the Commission's New Approach to Article 81 EC Dispenses with the Need to Apply Article 82 EC to Vertical Restraints" (2005) 42(3) *Common Market Law Review*, pp. 587–638.

F. M. Rowe, "Price Discrimination, Competition, and Confusion: Another Look at Robinson-Patman" (1951) 60(6) *Yale Law Journal*, pp. 929–75.

D. L. Rubinfeld, "Antitrust Enforcement in Dynamic Network Industries" (1998) 43 (3/4) *The Antitrust Bulletin*, pp. 859–82.

M. Sadowska, "Energy Liberalisation: Excessive Pricing Actions Dusted Off?" (2011) 32(9) *European Competition Law Review*, pp. 471–7.

M. A. Salinger, "Vertical mergers and market foreclosure" (1988) 103 *Quarterly Journal of Economics*, pp. 345–56.

S. C. Salop and D. T. Scheffman, "Cost-Raising Strategies" (1987) 36(1) *Journal of Industrial Economics*, pp. 19–34.

S. C. Salop, "Exclusionary Conduct, Effect on Consumers, and the Flawed Profit-Sacrifice Standard" (2006) 73(2) *Antitrust Law Journal*, pp. 311–74.

S. C. Salop, "Refusal to deal and price squeezes by an unregulated, vertically integrated monopolist" (2010) 76(3) *Antitrust Law Journal*, pp. 709–40.

D. Scharfstein, "A Policy to Prevent Rational Test-Market Predation" (184) 2 *The Rand Journal of Economics*, pp. 229–43.

F. Schauer, "Can Rights Be Abused?" (1981) 31 *The Philosophical Quarterly*, pp. 225–30.

R. Schmalensee, "Consumer's Surplus and Producer's Goods" (1971) 61(4) *American Economic Review*, pp. 682–87.

R. Schmalensee, "Economies of Scale and Barrieers to Entry" (1981) 89(6) *The Journal of Political Economy*, pp. 1228–38.

R. Schmalensee, "On the Use of Economic Models in Antitrust: The ReaLemon Case" (1979) 127(4) *University of Pennsylvania Law Review*, pp. 994–1050.

R. Schmalensee, "Output and Welfare Implications of Monopolistic Third-Degree Price Discrimination" (1981) 71(1) *American Economic Review*, pp. 242–7.

R. Schmalensee, "Commodity Bundling by Single-Product Monopolies" (1982) 25 *Journal of Law and Economics*, pp. 67–71.

M. Schwartz, "Third-Degree Price Discrimination and Output: Generalizing a Welfare Result" (1990) 80(5) *American Economic Review*, pp. 1259–62.

R. Selten, "The Chain-Store Paradox" (1987) 9 *Theory and Decision*, pp. 127–59.

J. G. Sidak and D. Spulber, "The Tragedy of the Telecommunications: Government Pricing of Unbundled Network Elements Under the Telecommunications Act of 1996" (1997) *Columbia Law Review*, pp. 1201–281.

J. G. Sidak and D. J. Teece, "Dynamic Competition in Antitrust Law"(2009) 5(4) *Journal of Competition Law & Economics*, pp. 581–631.

M. Siragusa, "The Application of Article 86 to the Pricing Policy of Dominant Companies: Discriminatory and Unfair Prices" (1976) 16 *Common Market Law Review*, pp. 179–94.

D. Spector, "Some Economics of Margin Squeeze" (2008) 1 *Concurrences*, No. 15302, pp. 21–26.

J. J. Spengler, "Vertical Integration and Antitrust Policy" (1950) 58(4) *Journal of Political Economy*, pp. 347–52.

M. Stopper, "Der Microsoft-Beschluss des EuG" (2005) 1 *Zeitschrift für Wettbewerbsrecht*, p. 87.

M. E. Stucke, "Is Intent Relevant?" (2012) *Journal of Law, Economics and Policy* (forthcoming 2012).

R. Subiotto, "The Special Responsibility of Dominant Undertakings Not to Impair Genuine Undistorted Competition" (1995) 18(3) *World Competition*, p. 30.

P. Tandon, "Optimal Patents with Compulsory Licensing" (1982) 90(3) *Journal of Political Economy*, pp. 470–86.

L. G. Telser, "Cutthroat Competition and the Long Purse" (1966) 9 *Journal of Law and Economics*, pp. 259–77.

L. G. Telser, "Why Should A Manufacturer Want Fair Trade?" (1960) 3 *Journal of Law and Economics*, pp. 86–105.

L. G. Telser, "Why Should Manufacturers Want Fair Trade II?" (1990) 33(2) *Journal of Law and Economics*, pp. 409–17.

J. Temple Lang, "The Principle of Essential Facilities in European Community Competition Law – The Position since *Bronner*" (2000) 1 *Journal of Network Industries*, pp. 375–405.

J. Temple Lang, "A Question of Priorities – The European Commission New Guidance on Article 82 is Flawed" (2009) 8(2) *Competition Law Insight*.

J. Temple Lang, "Refusal to Contract under Article 82" forthcoming in *Europaraettslig Tidskrift*.

J. Temple Lang, "European Competition Law and Intellectual Property Rights – A New Analysis" (2010) 11(3) *ERA Forum*, pp. 411–37.

J. Temple Lang, "Practical Aspects of Aftermarkets in European Competition Law", (2011) 7(1) *Competition Policy International Journal*, pp. 199–241.

J. Temple Lang, "Rebates, Price Discrimination and Refusal to Contract – The Commission's Guidance Paper on Article 82" (2010) *Europaraettslig Tidskrift*, pp. 47–78.

J. Tirole, "Incomplete Contracts: Where Do We Stand?" (1999) 67(4) *Econometrica*, pp. 741–81.

J. Tirole, "The Analysis of Tying Cases: A Primer" (2005) 1(1) *Competition Policy International Journal*, pp. 1–25.

D. Triantafyllou, "The European Charter of Fundamental Rights and the "Rule of Law": Restricting Fundamental Rights by Reference" 2002 (39) *Common Market Law Review*, pp. 53–64.

H. R. Varian, "Price Discrimination and Social Welfare" (1985) 75(4) *American Economic Review*, pp. 870–75.

B. Vesterdorf, "Article 82 EC: Where Do We Stand After the *Microsoft* Judgement?" (2008) 1(1) *Global Antitrust Review*, pp. 1–14.

B. Vesterdorf, "IP Rights and Competition Law Enforcement Questions" (2013) *Journal of European Competition Law and Practice*.

J. Vickers, "Abuse of Market Power" (2005) 115 (6) *The Economic Journal*, pp. F244–61.

E. Vranakis, "Guilty as charged? The verdict on the Commission's decision to regulate international roaming prices on the basis of Article 95 EC" (2008) 13(1) *Tottels Communications Law*, pp. 12–16.

F. Wagner-von Papp, "Best and Even Better Practices in Commitment Procedures After Alrosa: The Dangers of Abandoning the 'Struggle for Competition Law" (2012) 49 *Common Market Law Review*, pp. 929–70.

D. Waelbroeck, "Tough Competition – What is the relevance of intention in article 82 cases?" (2006) 5(6) *Competition Law Insight*.

G. J. Werden, "The *'No Economic Sense'* test for Exclusionary Conduct" (2006) 31 *Journal of Corporation Law*, pp. 293–306.

G. J. Werden, "Competition Policy on Exclusionary Conduct: Towards an Effect-Based Analysis?", (2006) 2 (Special issue) *European Competition Journal*, pp. 53–67.

G. J. Werden, "Identifying Single Firm Exclusionary Conduct: From Vague Concepts to Administrable Rules" (2007) *International Antitrust Law & Policy: Fordham Competition Law 2006*, pp. 509–40.

M. D. Whinston, "Tying, Foreclosure and Exclusion" (1990) 80(4) *American Economic Review*, pp. 837–59.

O. Williamson, "Credible Commitments: Using Hostages to Support Exchange" (1983) 73 *American Economic Review*, pp. 519–40.

O. Williamson, "The Vertical Integration of Production: Market Failure Considerations" (1971) 61 *American Economic Review*, pp. 112–23.

O. E. Williamson, "Predatory pricing: a strategic and welfare analysis" (1977) 87(2) *Yale Law Journal*, pp. 284–340.

W. Wils, "The European Commission's 2006 Guidelines on Antitrust Fines: A Legal and Economic Analysis," *World Competition*, (2007) 30(2).

E. Wind, "Remedies and Sanctions in Article 82 of the EC Treaty" (2005) 26(12) *European Competition Law Review*, pp. 659–69.

L. Zanon di Valgiurata, "Price Discrimination Under Article 86 of the E. E. C. Treaty: The United Brands Case" (1982) 31(1) *International and Comparative Law Quarterly*, pp. 36–58.

Articles Published in Newspapers, Chronicles, Working Papers and Online

C. Ahlborn and others, "*DG Comp's Discussion Paper on Article 82: Implications of the Proposed Framework and Antitrust Rules for Dynamically Competitive Industries*", March 2006, p. 22.

P. Akman, "Searching for the Long-Lost Soul of Article 82 EC", *CCP Working Paper Series*, Paper No. 07–5, March 2007.

P. Alexiadis, "Informative and Interesting: The CFI Rules in *Deutsche Telekom v. European Commission*" (2008) 5(1) *CPI Antitrust Chronicle*.

A. Amelio and D. Donath, "Market Definition in Recent EC Merger Investigations: The Role of Empirical Analysis" (2009) *Concurrences*, No. 3–2009.

B. Amory and A. Verheyden, "Comments on the CFI's Recent Ruling in *Deutsche Telekom v. European Commission*" (2008) 5(1) *CPI Antitrust Chronicle*.

H. Andersson, "The Swedish Market Court finds that national postal operator abused its dominant position in the market for bulk mail deliveries (*Bring CityMail Sweden/Posten Meddelande*)" (June 2011) *e-Competitions*, No. 38529.

Antitrust Modernization Commission, *Report and Recommendations*, April 2007.

M. Armstrong, "Price discrimination" (2006) *MPRA Paper*, ID 4693.

H. Auf'mkolk, "The EU General Court dismisses Spanish telecom incumbent's appeal against a Commission decision that imposed a €151 million fine on the company for a margin squeeze in the regulated national broadband market (*Telefónica/Commission*)"(March 2012) *e-Competitions*, No. 45020.

N. Banasevic and C. Madero Villarejo, "Standards and Market Power" (2008) 5(1) *CPI Antitrust Chronicle*.

W. J. Baumol, "Principles Relevant to Predatory Pricing", Swedish Competition Authority, *Pros and Cons Series: The Pros and Cons of Low Prices*, October 2003, pp. 15–37.

J-F. Bellis, *The Commission's Microsoft Tying Case – Implications for Innovation Throughout the High-Technology Sector*, Van Bael & Bellis, 2007, pp. 1–18.

Bitstream Access – ERG Consultation Document (14 July 2003).

W. Blumenthal, *"Discussant Comments on Exploitative Abuses Under Article 82 EC"*, paper prepared for the 12th Annual EUI Competition Law and Policy Workshop, Florence, June 8–9, 2007.

A. Brandenburger and V. Krishna, "Bundling", *HBS Premier Case Collection* (1991).

P.-A. Buigues and R. Klotz, "Margin Squeeze in Regulated Industries: The CFI Judgment in the *Deutsche Telekom* Case" (2008) 7(1) *CPI Antitrust Chronicle*.

S. Calkins, "Broadcast Music Inc. v. Columbia Broadcasting System, Inc., 441 U.S. 1 (1979)", *Wayne State University Law School Research Paper Series*, Paper No. 07–24, July 30, 2007.

Charles River Associates, *Innovation and Competition Policy: Part 1 – Conceptual Issues*, Office of Fair Trading Economic Discussion Paper 3, OFT 377, March 2002.

T. Čihula and M. Forýtek, "A Czech court holds that a request for information is inadmissible only if clearly excessive in a case concerning an abuse of dominance in the telecom sector (*Telefonica*)" (March 2012) *e-Competitions*, No. 45893.

Copenhagen Economics, *The Internal Market and the Relevant Geographical Market: The Impact of the Completion of the Single Market Programme on the Definition of the Relevant Geographic Market*, Enterprise Directorate-General, Enterprise Papers No. 15, 2004, available at http://ec.europa.eu/enterprise/newsroom/cf/itemlongdetail.cfm?tpa_id=121&item_id=2429.

Dobson Consulting, *Buyer Power and its Impact on Competition in the Food Retail Distribution Sector of the European Union*, Report prepared for the European Commission – DGIV Study Contract No. IV/98/ETD/078, May 1999.

M. Dolmans, *The Concept of Abuse Under Article 82 EC – Profit Sacrifice or Proportionality Test?*, GCLC Second Annual Conference, Brussels, June 16–17, 2005.

N. Economides, "Loyalty/Requirement Rebates and the Antitrust Modernization Commission: What is the Appropriate Liability Standard?" *New York University Law and Economics Research Papers*, Paper No. 09–15, June 29, 2009.

A. Edlin and J. Farrell, "Freedom to Trade and the Competitive Process", *NBER Working Paper*, No. 16818, February 2011.

E. Elhauge, "*Comments of Professor Elhauge on DG Competition Discussion Paper on Exclusionary Abuses*", March 2006.

ETSI, "*ETSI Rules of Procedure, 30 November 2011 – Annex 6: ETSI Intellectual Property Rights Policy*", November 2011.

European Commission, *Pricing Issues In Relation To Unbundled Access To The Local Loop*, ONP Committee, ONPCOM 01–17, June 25, 2001, pp. 1–17.

European Regulators Group, "*Report on the Discussion on the Application of Margin Squeeze Tests to Bundles*", March 2009.

European Regulators Group, "*Revised ERG Common Position on the approach to Appropriate remedies in the ECNS regulatory framework*", May 2006.

European Committee for Interoperable Systems, *"Microsoft – A History of Anticompetitive Behavior and Consumer Harm"*, March 31, 2009.

European Competition Network Brief, "The Swedish Competition Authority welcomes the EU Court of Justice preliminary ruling on "margin squeeze" as a stand alone antitrust abuse in the telecom sector *(TeliaSonera)*" (February 2011) *e-Competitions*, No. 36596.

European Competition Network Brief, "The French Competition Authority issues a first commitment decision concerning competition concerns in the Internet connectivity market *(France Telecom, Cogent)*" (20 September 2012) *e-Competitions*, No. 50107.

D. S. Evans and R. Schmalensee, "Some Economic Aspects of Antitrust Analysis in Dynamically Competitive Industries", *NBER Working Paper Series*, Working Paper No. 8268, May 2001, available at http://ssrn.com/abstract=268877.

D. S. Evans, *Two-Sided Market Definition*, in ABA Section of Antitrust Law, Market Definition in Antitrust: Theory and case studies (forthcoming), November 11, 2009, Chapter XII.

S. Evrard and others, "Recent Developments in the United States, EU and Asia at the Intersection of Antitrust and Patent Law" (2009) 3(2) *CPI Antitrust Chronicle*.

G. Faella and P. Merlino, *"L'obbligo d'investire nello sviluppo di infrastrutture: note a margine di due storie parallele"*, Società Italiana di Diritto ed Economia, Seventh Annual Conference, December 17, 2011.

E. Feess and A. Wohlschlegel, *All-Unit Discounts and Competing Entrants*, paper presented at the American Law & Economics Association 18th Annual Meeting, May 16–17, 2008.

P. Fernandes, *On Exploitative Excessive Pricing Under EC Law*, Reckon Working Paper prepared for a presentation at the Autoridade da Concorrência, Lisbon, January 9, 2006.

H. First, "Netscape is Dead: Remedy Lessons from the Microsoft Litigation", New York University Law and Economics Working Papers, Paper 166, December 12, 2008.

A. Fletcher and A. Jardine, "*Towards an Appropriate Policy for Excessive Pricing*", paper prepared for the 12th Annual EUI Competition Law and Policy Workshop, Florence, June 8–9, 2007.

T. P. Gehrig and R. Stenbacka, "Price Discrimination, Competition and Antitrust", Swedish Competition Authority, *Pros and Cons Series: The Pros and Cons of Price Discrimination*, November 2005.

S. Genevaz, "Margin Squeeze after *Deutsche Telekom*" (2009) 1(1) *CPI Antitrust Chronicl*.

D. Geradin & N. Petit, "Price Discrimination under EC Competition Law: The Need for a Case-by-Case Approach", Global Competition Law Centre Working Paper Series, *GCLC Working Paper Series*, Working Paper 07/05, 2007.

D. Geradin, *Pricing Abuses by Essential Patent Holders in a Standard-Setting Context: A View from Europe*, paper prepared for the Conference at University of Virginia on Remedies for Dominant Firm Misconduct, June 4–5, 2008.

D. Geradin, "The Decision of the Commission of 13 May 2009 in the Intel Case: Where is the Foreclosure and Consumer Harm?", *TILEC Discussion Papers*, Paper No. 2010–022, October 16, 2009.

D. Gerard, "Price Discrimination Under Article 82(c) EC: Clearing up the Ambiguities", *GCLC Research Papers on Article 82*, July 2005.

F.-E. González Díaz and J. Padilla, "The *linkLine* Judgment – A European Perspective" (2009) 1 *CPI Antitrust Chronicle*.

T. Graf, "The General Court of the European Union addresses the competitive analysis of aftermarkets in the luxury watches and spare parts markets (*CEAHR*)" (December 2010) *e-Competitions*, No. 35223.

T. Graf, "*How Indispensable Is Indispensability?*", Kluwer Competition Law Blog, April 18, 2011.

L. Guillet, "The Paris Court of Appeal quashes the decision of the French Competition Authority in a margin squeeze case (*SFR-France Telecom*)" (January 2011) *e-Competitions*, No. 35324.

D. Henry, P. Werner and M. Maier, "The European Court of Justice clarifies the scope of the law in relation to pricing practices of vertically integrated companies in the telecommunications sector (*TeliaSonera*)" (February 2011) *e-Competitions*, No. 45026.

High Level Group, *Facing the Challenge – The Lisbon Strategy for Growth and Employment*, Report from the High Level Group chaired by Wim Kok, November 2004.

P. Ibañez Colomo, "The Spanish Competition Authority Adopts a Prudent Approach on Alleged Price Squeeze and Discriminatory Practices by the Telecommunications Incumbent on Interconnection and Termination Fees (*Uni2-MCI WorldCom/Telefónica Móviles*)" (December 2004) *e-Competitions*, No. 187.

IBM, *Undertaking given by IBM*, EC Bulletin 10–1984, point. 3.4.1 *et seq.*

International Competition Network, *Antitrust Enforcement in Regulated Sectors Working Group – Subgroup 2: Interrelations between antitrust and regulatory authorities*, Report to the Fourth ICN Annual Conference, Bonne, June 2004.

J. Kallaugher, *The 'Margin Squeeze' Under Article 82: Searching for Limiting Principles*, Report presented during the GCLC Conference on Margin Squeeze under EC Competition Law with a special focus on the Telecommunications Sector, London, December 10, 2004, available at http://www.coleurope.eu/content/gclc/documents/03%20Kallaugher%20paper.doc.

Y. Katsoulacos, "Exploitative Practices in Article 82" (2006) *European Enterprise Journal*.

Y. Katsoulacos, "Some Critical Comments on the Commission's Guidance Paper on Art. 82 EC" (2009) 2(1) *CPI Antitrust Chronicle*.

A. Katz and P. E. Veel, "*Beyond Refusal to Deal: A Cross-atlantic View of Copyright, Competition and Innovation Policies*", July 28, 2011.

R. S. Khemani and D. M. Shapiro, *Glossary of Industrial Organisation Economics and Competition Law*, OECD, Paris, 1993.

J. Killick and A. Komninos, "Schizophrenia in the Commission's Article 82 Guidance Paper: Formalism Alongside Increased Recourse to Economic Analysis" (2009) 2(1) *CPI Antitrust Chronicle*.

P. Klemperer, *Bidding Markets*, UK Competition Commission Occasional Paper No. 1, June 2005.

K.-U. Kuehn, F. Scott Morton and H. Shelanski, "Standard Setting Organizations Can Help Solve the Standards Essential Patents Licensing Problem", (March 2013) *CPI Antitrust Chronicle*.

J. Kwoka and D. Moss, "Behavioral Merger Remedies: Evaluation and Implications for Antitrust Enforcement" (November 2011) *The American Antitrust Institute*.

A. Layne-Farrar, "Non-Discriminatory Pricing: What is Different (and What is Not) about IP Licensing in Standard Setting", June 29, 2009.

A Layne-Farrar, "Be my FRAND: Standard Setting and Fair, Reasonable and Non-discriminatory Terms" (March 2010).

S. Lembo, "The Italian Competition Authority initiates a new investigation against the incumbent telecom national operator to assess whether it refused to grant physical access to its telephone and broadband network and whether it applied aggressive pricing policy *vis à vis* business customers based in ULL areas (*Wind Fastweb/Telecom Italia conduct*)" (June 2010) *e-Competitions*, No. 32221.

I. Lianos, "Competition Law Remedies: In Search of a Theory", *CLGE Working Paper,* Law and Governance in Europe Working Paper Series No. 14/2011, April 2011.

P. Lowe, *EU Competition Practice on Predatory Pricing – Introductory address to the Seminar "Pros and Cons of Low Prices"*, speech given at the Seminar "Pros and Cons of Low Prices", Stockholm, December 5, 2003.

A. Lykotrafiti, "The Cyprus Competition Authority Fines the Telecommunications Incumbent €3.8 Million for Abusive Conduct in the Mobile Telephony Market (*Areeba/CYTA*)" (January 2006) *e-Competitions*, No. 13610.

B. Lyons, "The Paradox of the Exclusion of Exploitative Abuse", *CCP Working Paper Series*, Paper No. 08–1, December 2007.

M. Mendes Pereira and M. Ouaki, "The Portuguese Competition Authority Fines Two Telecoms Operators €53 M for Abuse of Dominant Position in the Wholesale and Retail Broadband Markets" (September 2009) *e-Competitions*, No. 28306.

Microsoft, *"Public Undertaking by Microsoft"*("The 2009 Microsoft Undertaking"), December 16, 2009.

Microsoft, "Statement of Microsoft Corporation on EU Browser Choice Screen Compliance", Press Release of 17 July 2012.

J. Modrall, C. Schaberg and J. Soloway, *"Article 82 Exclusionary Conduct Discussion Paper: An Interview with Michael Albers and Luc Peeperkorn"*, 2006.

B. Nalebuff and D. Majerus, "Bundling, Tying, and Portfolio Effects" (2003) No. 1, *DTI Economics Paper*.

National Economic Research Associates, *The Role of Market Definition in Monopoly and Dominance Inquiries,* Office of Fair Trading Economic Discussion Paper 2, OFT 342, July 2001.

M. Newman, "EC May Set New Precedent When Fixing Fine Against Microsoft in Compliance Cases," *MLex*, October 25, 2012.

W. D. Nordhaus, "Schumpeterian Profits in the American Economy: Theory and Measurement", *NBER Working Paper Series*, Working Paper No. 10433, April 2004, available at http://www.nber.org/papers/w10433.pdf?new_window=1.

H. Nordling, "A Norwegian District Court dismisses a counter-claim against a subsidiary of the incumbent railway operator for abusing its dominant position (*CargoNet, CargoLink*)" (June 2011) *e-Competitions*, No. 38518.

R. O'Donoghue and J. Temple Lang, "The Concept of an Exclusionary Abuse under Article 82 EC", *GCLC Research Papers on Article 82*, July 2005, p. 38.

OECD Policy Roundtable, "Remedies and Sanctions in Abuse of Dominance Cases", DAF/COMP (2006) 19.

OECD Competition Committe, *"Policy Roundtables: Monopsony and Buyer Power, 2008"* OECD roundtable discussion.

"Policy Roundtables: Competition, Patents and Innovation, 2006", paper submitted by the United Kingdom at OECD's Roundtable discussion, October 2006.

Office of Fair trading, "OFT refers Ryanair's minority stake in Aer Lingus to Competition Commission", Press Release of June 15, 2012.

Oxera, *Assessing Profitability in Competition Policy Analysis*, Office of Fair Trading Economic Discussion Paper 6, OFT 657, July 2003.

P. Palmigiano, *"The Abuse of 'Margin Squeeze' Under Article 82 of the EC Treaty and its Application to New and Emerging Markets"*, May 2005.

A. Papanikolaou, "The Greek Telecommunications Regulator Prohibits the Incumbent's 'Double-Play' Bundled Offering of Unlimited International Call Taking into Account a Risk of a Margin Squeeze of its Competitors *(OTE)*"(May 2009) *e-Competitions*, No. 26136.

M. Peeters, "The Belgian Competition Council Establishes Abuse of Dominant Position in Termination Rates Case *(Base/BM)*" (May 2009) *e-Competitions*, No. 28404.

M. Petit, "EU commitment to competition policy is unchanged", *Financial Times*, 27 June 2007.

D. Platt Majoras, "Recognizing the Procompetitive Potential of Royalty Discussions in Standard Setting", Remarks of FTC Chairman Deborah Platt Majoras, prepared for the conference on Standardization and the Law: Developing the Golden Mean for Global Trade, Stanford, California, September 23, 2005.

E. Provost, "A French Appeal Court rejects the applicability of Art. 101 and 102 TEU but upholds the findings that two telecom operators had abused their dominant positions in the telephony markets *(Orange Caraïbe and France Telecom)*" (September 2010) *e-Competitions*, No. 33595.

RBB Economics, *Tomra: Rolling Back Form-based Analysis of Rebates?*, RBB Brief 21, February 2007.

RBB Economics, *Tying and bundling – cause for complaint?*, RBB Brief 16, January 2005, available at http://www.rbbecon.com/publications/downloads/rbb_brief16.pdf.

A. Renda, "Treatment of Exclusionary Abuses Under Article 82 of the EC Treaty: Comments on the European Commission's Guidance Paper", *CEPS Task Force Reports*, September 10, 2009, para.81.

A. Renda, "Treatment of Exclusionary Abuses Under Article 82 of the EC Treaty: Comments on the European Commission's Guidance Paper", *CEPS Task Force Reports*, September 10, 2009.

P. Rey and others, "An Economic Approach to Article 82", Report by the Economic Advisory Group on Competition Policy ("*EAGCP Report*"), July 2005, pp. 1–53.

B. Rooney, "Europe Falls Out of Love With IE", *The Wall Street Journal*, January 4, 2011, available at http://blogs.wsj.com/tech-europe/2011/01/04/europe-falls-out-of-love-with-internet-explorer/.

F. M. Scherer, "Pharmaceutical Innovation" in *KSG Working Paper Series*, Paper No. RWP07–004, and in *AEI-Brookings Joint Center Working Series*, Paper No. 07–19, July 2007.

C. Shapiro, "Competition Policy and Innovation", OECD, *STI Working Papers Series*, Paper 2002/11, 2002, p. 16.

M. Steiner, "*Economics in Antitrust Policy: Freedom to Compete vs. Freedom to Contract*", Dissertation.com, July 2007.

M. Stenborg, "Are there biases in the market definition procedure?", ETLA, *Keskusteluaiheita – Discussion Papers*, Paper No. 903, March 2004.

A. Svetlicinii, "The Bulgarian Competition Authority fines margin squeeze on the construction services market (International Fair Plovdiv)" (June 2010) *e-Competitions*, No. 31626.

Swedish Competition Authority, "The Pros and Cons of Price Discrimination", Swedish Competition Authority, *Pros and Cons Series*, November 2005.

J. Swift QC, "Selective Price Cuts, Discounts and Rebates ~ EU Competition Law at a Crossroads ~ Form or Effects", in Monckton Chambers *Competition Law ~ Recent Developments before the CAT and the European Courts*, October 27, 2005, available at http://www.monckton.com/docs/library/CompSeminarOct05JAS.pdf.

J. Temple Lang, "Commitment Decisions and Settlements with Antitrust Authorities and Private Parties Under European Antitrust Law", *Fordham Antitrust Conference*, September (2005).

J. Temple Lang, "The Requirements for a Commission Notice on the Concept of Abuse under Article 82 EC", in *Finnish Competition Law Yearbook 2007*, pp. 271–306, and in *CEPS Special Reports* of December 10, 2008.

J. Temple Lang, "The Requirement for a Commission Notice on the Concept of Abuse Under Article 82 EC", *CEPS Special Reports*, December 10, 2008.

J. Temple Lang, "*Article 82 EC – The Problems and The Solution*", FEEM Working Paper No. 65.2009 presented at the Conference "Ten years of Mercato Concorrenza Regole", Milan, June 30, 2009.

The Unilateral Conduct Working Group, "*Report on the Analysis of Refusal to Deal with a Rival Under Unilateral Conduct Laws*", presented at the 9th Annual Conference of the ICN, Istanbul, April 2010.

US Department of Justice, "Assistant Attorney General for Antitrust, R. Hewitt Pate, Issues Statement on the EC's Decision in its Microsoft Investigation" Press Release of March 24, 2004, available at http://www.justice.gov/opa/pr/2004/March/04_at_184.htm.

US Dep't of Justice & Fed. Trade Comm'n, *Antitrust Enforcement and Intellectual Property Rights: Promoting Innovation and Competition*, April 2007, p. 36.

US Department of Justice, *Competition and Monopoly: Single-Firm Conduct Under Section 2 of the Sherman Act*, September 2008.

B. van Rompuy, "The Impact of the Lisbon Treaty on EU Competition Law: A Review of Recent Case Law of the EU Courts", (2011) 1 *CPI Antitrust Chronicle*.

C. Veljanovski, "Margin squeeze and competition law: An overview of EU and national case law" (June 2012) *e-Competitions*, No. 46442.

A. G. Verheyden and S. Clerckx, "The ECJ Advocate General Mazák seeks to affirm judgment in margin squeeze case (*Deutsche Telekom*)" (April 2010) *e-Competitions*, No. 33702.

J. Vickers, "A Tale of Two EC Cases: *IBM* and *Microsoft*" (2009) 1(1) *CPI Antitrust Chronicle*.

J. Vogel, "The French Civil Supreme Court invalidates the restrictive interpretation of the concept of the effect on trade between member States (*Orange Caraïbe*)" (January 2012) *e-Competitions*, No. 44140.

G. J. Werden, "Essays on Consumer Welfare and Competition Policy" (2009).

G. Zohios, "Commission Guidance Paper on the Application of Art. 82: a Step Towards Modernization or a Step Away?" (2009) 2(1) *CPI Antitrust Chronicle*.

Index